The Yankee Encyclopedia

by
Mark Gallagher

www.SportsPublishingLLC.com

Interior design: Michelle R. Dressen, Kenneth J. O'Brien,
Jeff Higgerson, Emily Washburn, Jim Henehan
Editor: Susan M. McKinney
Statistics and facts editor: Russ Lake
Cover design: Scot Muncaster, Emily Washburn and Kenneth J. O'Brien
Front cover photo: Frank D. Smith
Proofreader: Julie Herman and Cindy McNew

ISBN: 1-58261-683-3

Printed in Canada.

Sports Publishing, L.L.C.
www.SportsPublishingLLC.com

Bernie Williams hoists the coveted World Series trophy after the Game 5 win in the 2000 World Series. (Amy Sancetta, AP/Wide World Photos)

Yankee owner George Steinbrenner (right) and manager Joe Torre have built a baseball dynasty that has been equaled only by the great Yankee teams of the past. (Mark Lennihan, AP/Wide World Photos)

CONTENTS

DEDICATION

I wish to dedicate this work to ALL of the Yankee players, managers, and executives and all those working behind the scenes throughout the storied history of the New York Yankees who have contributed in making this franchise, **THE TEAM OF THE CENTURY!**

ACKNOWLEDGMENTS

There are many elements that go into the completion of a work such as *The Yankee Encyclopedia* and I would like to give my thanks to the many folks without whom this work would not have been possible. To Rick Cerrone and his staff with the New York Yankees Media Relations Department, thank you for your assistance in many aspects of this work. To Walter LeConte, who's exhaustive attention to detail and his love of the Yankees brought this work through the close of the century–the most successful century of any sports franchise in the world. To Phil Sperenza for his special efforts in covering the Yankees' 2000 World Series Championship. To Russ, for his tireless efforts to bring *The Yankee Encyclopedia* up to date for the 21st century. And finally, to the staff at Sports Publishing, thanks for assisting me along the way with the completion of this edition of *The Yankee Encyclopedia.*

M.G.

1

THE RECORD

Babe Ruth, the Yankees' big bludgeon man, pulled up with a strained muscle in his left leg in the game at Cleveland July 19, 1929, and Miller Huggins, boss of the World's Champions, said Ruth would have to warm the bench indefinitely. (AP/WIDE WORLD PHOTOS)

They came to New York from Baltimore in 1903, they stayed to become the Yankees and did they ever conquer! Thirty-eight American League pennants. Twenty-six World Championships. And that's not all.

They captured America's imagination and stirred profound passions. They spawned diehard Yankee fans not only in the New York area but across the nation, and they gave birth to an army of Yankee haters as well. They gained an unequaled identity.

And they built a lasting identification with New York. It would be less than earthshaking if the A's, who have already moved from Philadelphia to Kansas City and then to Oakland, or the Braves, who have shifted from Boston to Milwaukee to Atlanta, were to once again strike out for greener pastures. But if the Yankees were to do the unthinkable, to leave New York...ah, so sorry and misshapen a thought is beyond contemplation.

WHAT WE'RE TALKING ABOUT HERE

New York's legions of National League fans have understandable difficulty deciphering the history of NL baseball in the Big Apple. There have been four NL franchises: the Mutuals (1876), Giants (1883-1957), Brooklyn Dodgers (1890-1957) and Mets (1962 to present) in addition to franchises in the National Association, Players League, American Association and Federal League. But New Yorkers have little trouble with the straightforward—and sterling—history of their one and only AL club, the Yankees.

It is a history that began in the 20th century and is thus uncomplicated by asterisks and explanations of the rules pertaining to pre-1900 baseball, when the game was different in many ways from that played today. The modern game (dating to 1900) and the Yanks are contemporaries—by the Yankees' birth in 1903, professional baseball had most of its growing pains behind it and was fast becoming a widely appreciated institution.

The birth of the Yankees came at an important juncture in baseball history. The year 1903 was the year of the first modern World Series, an event that engendered tremendous fan interest, not to mention the shock created when the AL upstarts from Boston beat the senior circuit's Pittsburgh club, five games to three.

The American League was founded in 1900 and declared itself a major league in 1901. Chicago, Boston, Detroit, Philadelphia, Baltimore, Washington, Cleveland and Milwaukee were the original AL franchises. The league's first franchise change came in 1902 when Milwaukee was dropped in favor of St. Louis. The next change, the one that brought the Baltimore franchise to New York for the 1903 season, was the last one until the St. Louis Browns became the Baltimore Orioles in 1954—delayed repayment to Baltimore for what happened a half century earlier.

Ban Johnson—founder, president and supreme ruler of the AL—needed a New York team and induced two colorful New Yorkers, Frank Farrell and Bill Devery, to plunk down $18,000 for a Baltimore club he saved from ruination during the 1902 season. More than any other man, Ban Johnson was responsible for creating the New York Yankees.

Officially the team was called the New York Highlanders but the press preferred the nickname, Yankees. And sometimes the Highlanders were called Hilltoppers—after Hilltop Park, their ballpark on the old Hill Top, highest elevation of Manhattan.

But the important names were those of the players. Johnson made sure Farrell and Devery had some meal tickets and salted the team with Wee Willie Keeler, Jack Chesbro and Jesse Tannehill. Clark Griffith was named manager. Yet the early years gave little hint of the Yankee power and glory that was to come.

The Highlanders were serious contenders at times, but they fielded some terrible clubs, too, the worst being the editions of 1908 (51-103) and 1912 (50-102). Highlander fans contented themselves by focusing on the performances of Keeler, who had a few good years although past his prime, and "Happy Jack" Chesbro, who in 1904 won 41 games, an AL record that could stand forever.

The first AL superstar to begin his big-league career in New York was Hal Chase. Extolled by many as the greatest fielding first baseman ever, "Prince Hal" was also good with the bat, compiling a .291 batting average over 15 big-league seasons.

But Hal Chase was as controversial as he was skilled. He had gambling connections and was alleged to be a game thrower, and in the end was squeezed out of organized baseball. In his New York career (1905-1913), nevertheless, he brought much needed excitement to Hilltop Park. Knowing fans watched and waited for Chase to commit an error at a critical point in a game. But when he made the tough play, he was the object of everyone's admiration.

The excitement Chase or anyone else brought was welcomed by Farrell, Devery and Johnson, all of whom were negligent both for not punishing Chase for his countless club infractions and for not investigating his suspicious play. Cast in the shadows of the exciting and popular Giants of John J.

McGraw, the market was such that the Highlanders couldn't be too hard on themselves. They had little status and even the legitimacy of their very presence was questioned, the Giants arguing that they had been "invaded" by the AL club. (They had still another nickname, one used by the Giants and other Highlander detractors—the Invaders.)

But the Giants needn't have worried about the leanings of the New York fans; to them belonged a large and loyal following. The tensions between the two clubs seemed unnecessary. And they were on occasion relaxed, as when a spectacular fire in 1911 nearly destroyed the Polo Grounds. Farrell offered the Giants the use of Hilltop Park. The Giants were so grateful that they returned the favor two years later, allowing the Highlanders to share the rebuilt Polo Grounds, which was far superior to Hilltop Park.

So the AL club was now the tenant of an old enemy and tenuous friend. The club's name in this year of 1913 was changed from Highlanders to Yankees.

The Yankees in January of 1915 came under the ownership of two wealthy men, Jacob Ruppert and Tillinghast L'Hommedieu Huston, who acquired the club from a disgruntled Farrell-Devery partnership. Ruppert and Huston promised sweeping changes and hired popular and respected Wild Bill Donovan to manage the club. But it was two player acquisitions that demonstrated the new ownership's resolve to build a winning team.

The contract of Bob Shawkey, who was to be a 20-game Yankee winner for four seasons, was purchased from Connie Mack's Philadelphia A's early in the 1915 season. The following February the Yankees bought the contract of Frank "Home Run" Baker, the game's best third baseman, in another transaction with Mack. Obviously, big-spenders Ruppert and Huston meant business.

Three disappointing years followed, and Donovan was replaced by Miller Huggins. "The Mighty Mite" brought the Yankees home in fourth place in 1918, a season shortened by World War I. But the disruption the war brought to baseball had nowhere near the impact of the revelations of 1920: several Chicago White Sox players had conspired to throw the 1919 World Series for gambling gains. Baseball was terribly sick; baseball fans were terribly hurt. Just in time, two men came along to save the game.

One was Judge Kenesaw Mountain Landis, baseball's first commissioner, who used the sweeping powers given him to restore public confidence in major league baseball. The other was George Herman Ruth who used his power to sweep baseballs over the fence and in the process to draw fans by the thousands through Yankee turnstiles and fans by the millions throughout America to quicken to his exploits.

Babe Ruth was a big, strong youngster who spent a good deal of his youth undergoing "correction" in Baltimore's St. Mary's Industrial School. In the winter of 1919-20 a financially hurting Red Sox owner, Harry Frazee, sold Ruth to the Ruppert-Huston Yankees. Ruth had joined the Red Sox late in the 1914 season as a pitcher but it was his slugging that stirred the baseball world. The excitement did not go unnoticed by the lords of baseball who decided on a juicier ball for 1920 (the ball was further enlivened in 1930). The Babe in 1920 took advantage of both the lively sphere and the reachable right field fence of his new Polo Grounds home, blasting 54 home runs. This broke the previous big-league record that Babe established the previous year—by a mere 25 homers!

Ruth loved New York and New York loved the Babe. His bigger-than-life feats and personality were part of a marvelous time for sports in America. The 1920s—the Golden Age of Sports—had such legendary figures as Red Grange and Knute Rockne in football, Bill Tilden in tennis, Bobby Jones in golf and Jack Dempsey in boxing, to name some of the decade's great heroes. But Babe Ruth was the biggest hero of all, and the sports-minded Roaring Twenties was not only an era he helped to make but an era made for him.

Ruth attracted growing crowds to the Polo Grounds. The Giants and McGraw seethed. Finally the Yankees were asked to pull stakes, and Ruppert and Huston bought land in the Bronx where they built a stadium that was ready for occupancy in 1923. New York's enthusiasm for one man, Ruth, had completely changed the complexion of the city's baseball market. And the game of baseball would never be quite the same, either.

The Yankees won their first AL pennant in 1921. They repeated in 1922 and 1923 and were easily baseball's hottest team. Ruth was a national hero and the Yankees became a team of national popularity, the rivals of the Notre Dame football team in national appeal. But with the glow of affection came the glare of resentment. Pioneer Yankee haters were spawned and they would become legion.

In 1922, with the Yankees and St. Louis Browns embroiled in a bitter struggle for league supremacy, Yankee centerfielder Whitey Witt was knocked unconscious when hit by a bottle that sailed from the midst of a jeering St. Louis crowd.

The fiercest matchup in baseball, the Yankees-Red Sox rivalry, came to full flower in 1921-23. Many of the other Yankee stars besides Ruth had come from Boston and they included pitchers Carl Mays, Waite Hoyt, Bullet Joe Bush, Herb Pennock and Sad Sam Jones. New Englanders still refer to this happy transfer of personnel as "the rape of the Red Sox."

Ruppert's money and astute trading kept a steady stream of talent flowing from Boston during the 1920s. Most of the deals were engineered by a conservative baseball genius, Ed Barrow, whose 1868 origins were in a covered wagon headed west. Barrow had been part of the Red Sox mini-dynasty but left Boston in 1920 to join the Yankees and run the club in an iron-fisted and efficient manner until 1945.

The Yankee-Red Sox feud never really cooled off and later found expression in arguments over the comparative merits of DiMaggio-Williams and Munson-Fisk. Some of the most exciting pennant races in the story of baseball have been between the Yankees and Red Sox.

But every AL team has enjoyed a spirited rivalry with New York. The Philadelphia A's were bitter Yankee rivals in the early glory years, and recently the Baltimore Orioles have become intense Yankee foes. New York has also fought St. Louis, Cleveland, Washington, Detroit, Chicago and the Kansas City Royals in classic struggles for the AL flag.

The Yankees of 1921-23 were diametrically distinguished from the plain-Jane teams of the club's first two decades. They were a carefree, colorful Ruth-led bunch who during one season (1922) fought with each other as much as they battled the opposition. Little Miller Huggins, a man besieged by both his front office and his rowdy players, once admitted that those first years of Yankee success were for him a time of turmoil.

While the Yankees in 1921 and 1922 were the cream of the AL, they were not top dogs at home in New York. In the World Series of both years they were beaten by McGraw's Giants, with all games at the Polo Grounds.

"The House That Ruth Built" soon after its 1923 opening became THE ballpark—and indeed THE sports center. Fittingly, it was the year of the Yankees' first World Championship. They had beaten the hated Giants in the World Series. They owned the World Title, and they were led by the game's greatest-ever player in Ruth. They had a new ballpark that was the envy of baseball, and of New York's three teams, they now had the largest following. The heyday had arrived!

But field domination was not assured. Washington and the Yanks had a neck-and-neck race in 1924 and the Senators finished two games ahead of the Hugmen. The real disaster was 1925, starting in the spring with Ruth's "belly ache heard 'round the world," continuing through a suspension and $5000 fine Huggins imposed on Babe, and ending with the disgruntled Yankees in seventh place.

The Yankee collapse of 1925 was probably the worst in club history (worse than the disappointments of 1929, 1940, 1959, 1965 and 1979). Two of the few jewels in this dung heap of a season were youngster Lou Gehrig and Earle Combs, both of whom showed signs of the greatness that would mark their future play.

Gehrig, who would become the "Pride of the Yankees," replaced Wally Pipp at first base during the 1925 campaign. Unlike Ruth, Lou was a private man. He was surrounded by a loving family and was in the lap of a community long familiar with his athletic greatness, first displayed at Manhattan's Commerce High School and later at Columbia University, and which regarded him as one of its own.

Gehrig was overshadowed in publicity terms by Ruth and later by Joe DiMaggio. But he was admired as a straightforward and steady performer who played day after day—for 2,130 straight games—and thus became known as "The Iron Horse." He swung a bat as powerful as any the game has ever seen. He had 1,995 RBIs and 493 home runs when he retired in 1939, and a lifetime batting average of .340.

Led by Ruth and Gehrig, the Yankees won three consecutive AL pennants in 1926-28. They bowed to the St. Louis Cardinals in the 1926 World Series, best remembered for Grover Cleveland Alexander's strikeout of Tony Lazzeri with two outs and the bases loaded in the seventh inning of Game 7 at Yankee Stadium.

Miller Huggins' 1927 crew is generally regarded as the greatest baseball team in history. The "Murderers' Row" lineup included Ruth, Gehrig, Lazzeri, Combs, Bob Meusel, Joe Dugan and Mark Koenig. Ruth hit his record 60 home runs this year and Gehrig was the league's MVP. Pitching stars were Waite Hoyt, Herb Pennock, Urban Shocker, Dutch Ruether and George Pipgras.

Wilcy Moore in 1927 was the first of a long line of outstanding Yankee relief pitchers who through the years would include Johnny Murphy, Joe Page, Johnny Sain, Ryne Duren, Luis Arroyo, Lindy McDaniel, Sparky Lyle, Rich Gossage, Dave Righetti and Mariano Rivera.

Ruppert, Barrow, Huggins and scout Paul Krichell built the 1927 Yankees who compiled a 110-44 record. So imposing were the Yankees that in pre-World Series batting practice at Forbes Field they psyched out a Pirate team that meekly capitulated in four games. What often has been referred to as "Yankee Class" was now plainly showing.

Their greatness aside, the Yankees were due for a touch of class. They were, after all, representatives of the great city of New York. They wore the distinctive pinstripes the fashionable Ruppert had put them in. They played in a great stadium fast acquiring a storied aura. And they counted among their number the celebrated Babe Ruth.

The Yankees of 1928 were basically the same team as the fabulous 1927 Yankees, but this year the A's gave them a dogfight. The Yankees prevailed, however, and went on to romp over the Cardinals in the Fall Classic, with Ruth hitting .625 and Gehrig .545. They needed only three pitchers in the Series: Hoyt, who won two complete games, Pipgras and Tom Zachary.

FIRST TO CLAIM FLAG—The 1921 Yankee team was the first to win an AL pennant in the franchise's history. Front row (left to right): Johnny Mitchell, Eddie Bennett (mascot), Miller Huggins (manager), Charley O'Leary (coach), and Frank Roth (coach). Second row (left to right): Aaron Ward, Chick Fewster, Wally Pipp, Bob Shawkey, Wally Schang, Babe Ruth, Carl Mays, Waite Hoyt and Chicken Hawks. Back row (left to right): Jack Quinn, Tom Rogers, Alex Ferguson, Elmer Miller, Mike McNally, Rip Collins, Bill Piercy, Frank Baker, Harry Harper, Al De Vormer, Fred Hofmann, Bob Meusel, Bobby Roth, and Roger Peckinpaugh. (New York Yankees Archives)

Urban Shocker, who bravely battled a heart condition while pitching outstandingly during the 1927 season, died in September of 1928. The popular Shocker's death stunned and saddened New York. As time would demonstrate, it was but the first of several tragedies that would deeply hurt the Yankees.

The club was similarly saddened a year later by the unexpected death of Manager Miller Huggins. Ten years later, on July 4, 1939, Lou Gehrig would tell a packed Yankee Stadium: "I may have been given a bad break, but I have an awful lot to live for. All in all, I can say on this day that I consider myself the luckiest man on the face of the earth." The

bad break: a fatal disease that took his life in 1941. And in August of 1979, an outpouring of grief was released in the Stadium over the death of Yankee catcher Thurman Munson who was killed in a flying accident.

Philadelphia's three-year (1929-31) grip on the AL pennant was ended in 1932 with Joe McCarthy, who became Yankee manager in 1931, as skipper. The 1932 World Series was history's most intense; it was enlivened by a series of disputes triggered by the Chicago Cubs' failure to vote a full Series share to fellow Cub and former Yankee Mark Koenig. Babe Ruth led the taunting and the Series acquired an incredibly electric atmosphere. The Yankees pushed aside the Cubs in four straight in a Series that included Ruth's famous "called shot" home run and gave sweet revenge to Joe McCarthy whom the Cubs fired two years earlier.

McCarthy would serve at the Yankee helm longer than any other man—a total of 16 years. But a shortstop from San Francisco who broke in with the club in 1932 was to become the real longevity story in the Yankee chronicle. He was Frank "The Crow" Crosetti, a player or coach for nearly 40 Yankee seasons, 23 of them pennant-winning seasons.

RUTH AND HIS FANS—No one ever drew a crowd the way Babe Ruth did. In this scene, captured in the early 1920s, the Babe is swamped amid a sea of young admirers. That is Ruth in the middle of the throng, wearing a straw hat. (UPI)

TWENTIES GREATS: *The Babe in football garb with Notre Dame's famous football coach, Knute Rockne.*
(New York Yankees Archives)

The year 1932 is significant in the Yankee record for one final reason. It was the year that Jacob Ruppert, impressed with how the St. Louis Cardinals' Branch Rickey was developing talent in the minor leagues, decided to build a Yankee farm system. A baseball-smart Yalie from New Haven, Conn., George Weiss, was named farm director. Weiss, who held the post for 16 years before becoming general manager in 1948, worked closely and well with Ruppert and Barrow in running a farm system that became a pillar of the Yankee dynasty.

McCarthy's men finished second the next three seasons (1933-35). The team suffered a jolt in the off-season of 1934-35 when Ruppert sold Ruth's contract to the Boston Braves, leaving a large void in the 1935 Yankees. The hole was filled the following year when the club acquired a kid whom Weiss and Yankee scouts Bill Essick and Joe Devine urged Ruppert to obtain from the Pacific Coast League, a youngster who hit in 61 consecutive games for the San Francisco Seals—Joe DiMaggio.

DiMaggio quickly established himself as one of the game's great hitters, and his graceful work in center field was the marvel of baseball. He was an intelligent player, never making a mental error. In short, he may have been the most complete player in the history of the game. And there was something electric about him—he was baseball glamor.

But off the field DiMag was as quiet and shy as he was exciting on the field. Another Yankee from the San Francisco Bay area, pitcher Lefty Gomez, kept DiMag loose. Joe and the clever, fun-loving Lefty were perfect opposites—and perfect friends.

DiMaggio was not exactly conspicuous by his silence. None of the Yankees had much to say. McCarthy liked his players on the quiet side. He stressed decorum, favoring athletes in the reserved, noncontroversial—and talented—mold of Lou Gehrig. Besides, it was not a carefree, voluble time; it was not the flamboyant 1920s. The Great Depression had the nation in a miserable grip and anyone with a ticket to a Yankee game had a valuable possession. The ticketholder came to the Stadium expecting to get his hard-earned money's worth, and the Yankees, reliable and themselves hard-working, accommodated. From 1931 until the end of World War II the Yankees, for all their greatness, failed to have a single million-draw season. To some the Yankees seemed aloof, and this was only natural. The Yankees comported themselves well, and having so much for which to be proud, were suspect of considering themselves a team apart from the rest of the major leagues.

Through four seasons (1936-39), the Yankees were never seriously threatened in their relentless claim on the AL pennant which they took by margins of 19½, 13½, 9 and 17 games. They were the most potent of all Bronx Bomber editions.

The Gehrig-Lazzeri-Rolfe-Crosetti infield was sensational, and when in 1938 age caught up with second baseman Lazzeri, Joe Gordon came over from the Newark Bears, the Yanks' outstanding farm club. Outfielders George Selkirk, Tommy Henrich, Jake Powell, Myril Hoag and Charlie Keller lent more than enough power and defense on either side of DiMaggio. Bill Dickey was in his prime and was the best all-around catcher the game had known. The pitching staff was led by Gomez and Red Ruffing, one of the great left-right combinations, and included Monte Pearson, Spud Chandler, Bump Hadley and Johnny Murphy, baseball's best reliever.

The 1936-39 Yankees won four World Championships. Twice they beat the Giants, losing a total of three games in the two Series, and then successfully swept the Cubs and Reds. These Yankees could take the field with any team in history. They were baseball's first four-in-a-row World Champions.

Jacob Ruppert, to whom so much of this success was owed, died in January of 1939 and the club was left to his heirs. Barrow continued to run operations.

After stumbling in 1940 and finishing third, the Yankees in 1941 regained their perch atop the AL. It was a season best remembered for DiMaggio's 56-game hitting streak. It was also the year of the first Yankee-Dodger confrontation in the Fall

WHAT A VIEW!—Here is an amazing aerial view of Yankee Stadium (foreground), the Harlem River and the Polo Grounds (across river) as seen in the 1950s. This photo points out the "long" distance the Yankees were forced to travel when the club was booted out of the Polo Grounds! (New York Yankees Archives)

Classic. This one was won by the Bronx Bombers in five games, helped by a Hugh Casey spitball that eluded catcher Mickey Owen in the ninth inning of Game 4, allowing New York to rally and capture an unbelievable game victory.

The Yankees in 1941 started a little, acrobatic shortstop from Brooklyn named Phil Rizzuto. Rizzuto would win the AL MVP in 1950 and become the greatest all-round shortstop in Yankee history. He was a typical product of the flourishing and successful Yankee farm system.

Rizzuto was carefully seasoned in the minors. In spite of his small stature, he showed potential to Paul Krichell and McCarthy and in the farm network developed into a great fielder, a good contact hitter, one of the game's best bunters, a sensational base runner and a heads-up ballplayer. In his rookie 1941 season in the bigs, Rizzuto was good enough to hit .307.

The World War II years of 1942-45 saw baseball—and in a profound sense, liberty and life itself—hanging by a string. By 1943 most of the best Yankee players were in the military, but the team remained strong enough to win AL pennants in 1942 and 1943. New York fell victim to a St. Louis upset in the 1942 World Series, ending a string of eight consecutive Yankee World Series triumphs. But the avenging Yankees defeated the Cardinals in five games in the 1943 World Series.

In 1945 Larry MacPhail, Dan Topping and Del Webb bought the Yankees from the Ruppert heirs. MacPhail ran the club for three years and in his tenure took a number of initiatives.

He installed lights and brought night baseball to the Stadium. He promoted season ticket sales to the country club set, many of whom were less than life-and-death baseball addicts. He sold blocks of season tickets to corporations which gave them to clients or employees. The market and the crowds grew, and so did the Yankees' corporate image, something the club would later try to shed.

In New York, Mel Allen and Red Barber were baseball's leading voices. Allen began announcing for the Yankees before World War II and was joined by Barber, who came over from the Dodgers, in the mid-1950s. They were as much a part of New York baseball as any player. Allen was unceremoniously released after the 1964 season. Barber in 1966 had the TV cameras trained on the loneliest place in New York—the Stadium stands—and was let go after the season's close. Both Southerners, the mellifluent Allen and the twangy, downhomey Barber captured New York with their easy styles.

MacPhail went through three managers in 1946 (McCarthy, Bill Dickey and Johnny Neun), and for the 1947 season settled on Bucky Harris. The selection immediately paid dividends, Harris leading the Yankees to the 1947 World Championship.

A Yankee addition in 1947 was 38-year-old first baseman George McQuinn, the epitome of what could happen to good players in the Yankee farm system. McQuinn had no chance of cracking the Yankee lineup in the 1930s, not with Lou Gehrig at first, and eventually played for the Reds, Browns and A's. Other good players had the same problem at other positions. Ironically, the Yankees had difficulty finding Gehrig's replacement in 1939. A steady succession of able first basemen followed: Babe Dahlgren (1939-40), Johnny Sturm (1941), Buddy Hassett (1942) and Nick Etten (1943-46) led the Yankees back to McQuinn who hit .304 in 1947.

New York defeated Brooklyn in the 1947 World Series which included Yankee Bill Bevens' near no-hitter and Dodger Al Gionfriddo's great catch of a DiMaggio drive.

Larry MacPhail left the Yankees after the Series and George Weiss became general manager.

Weiss and Bucky Harris did not work well together, and after a disappointing 1948 season, Harris was released. Weiss then unveiled his surprise: Casey Stengel would manage the Yanks in 1949. Stengel had the experience, having been in baseball for nearly 40 years. But he was considered something of a clown.

The press and public came to love the colorful Casey whose confusing language was distinctive enough to attract a label: Stengelese. His pliable face and its many comical expressions were known as Casey's "change of faces." But Casey was as amazing as he was amusing.

He led the Yankees to 10 pennants in 12 years. His Yankee clubs won five straight World Championships (1949-53) his first five years as manager!

One of the most appealing teams in Yankee history was the injury-riddled 1949 club that had to beat Boston in the season's final two games to win the pennant. DiMaggio, battling injuries and illness all season, was the inspiration, and Stengel was the patch-working genius of these scrappy Yankees, who went on to beat the Dodgers for the World Championship.

For Stengel, the next four pennants and World Championships were a little easier, the Bronx Bombers finishing three games ahead of Detroit in 1950 and sweeping Philadelphia in the World Series; five games ahead of Cleveland in 1951 and trimming the Giants in the World Series; two games ahead of Cleveland in 1952 and beating the Dodgers in the World Series; and finishing 8½ games ahead of Cleveland in 1953 and again defeating the Dodgers in the World Series.

The leading pitchers during the successive championship years were Allie Reynolds, who in 1951 hurled two no-hitters; Vic Raschi, who owned a blazing fastball; and Eddie Lopat, a crafty southpaw who dazzled batters with a variety of off-speed pitches. Other important pitchers were Joe Page, Tommy Byrne, Whitey Ford, Tom Morgan, Bob Kuzava and Johnny Sain, and they had behind them the solid likes of Rizzuto, Tommy Henrich, Jerry Coleman, Hank Bauer, Gene Woodling, Joe Collins, Cliff Mapes, Johnny Mize, Bobby Brown, Gil McDougald and Billy Johnson.

Age and injuries forced Joe DiMaggio's retirement following the 1951 season. Finding a team leader to replace him was not easy but a young catcher who joined the club in 1946 seemed to fit the bill. Lawrence Peter Berra, better known as Yogi, by 1948 was a dangerous hitter and one of the big leagues' greatest clutch hitters, and by 1950, having overcome a degree of awkwardness behind the plate, was an excellent defensive catcher. Yogi, along with saying funny things that came to be called "Yogisms," took up the leadership slack.

Whitey Ford as a 21-year-old rookie compiled a 9-1 pitching record for the Yankees in 1950 and saved the pennant. Not blessed with an overpowering fastball, he couldn't just throw; he had to learn how to pitch. The "Chairman of the Board" until his retirement in 1967 was one of the game's great competitors, but he would never abuse a teammate whose poor play may have cost him a victory. Whitey, instead, would relax with a beer. He was probably the classiest pitcher to ever wear pinstripes and may have been the most likable of all the Yankee superstars.

Joining the Yanks in 1951, a year after Ford, was another great ballplayer who would continue the tradition of outstand-

Barnstorming buddies, Babe Ruth and Lou Gehrig, October 12, 1927 (AP/WIDE WORLD PHOTOS)

ing centerfield play that was begun by Earle Combs and continued by DiMaggio. Mickey Mantle was a big, raw-boned 19-year-old with incredible speed and power from both sides of the plate. It was not long before the shy youngster lived up to expectations.

But Mantle, subject of an amazing press buildup, disappointed some people who expected him to make Babe Ruth look like a Little Leaguer. As a matter of fact, were it not for a steady stream of injuries, Mantle could have broken some of Ruth's records. Mickey was still good enough to place among a handful of baseball's greatest players. He roamed center field with skill, belted prodigious homers and ran like a deer on the bases. He was a premier performer and a great draw through the 1968 season.

Stengel had a favorite player, skinny Billy Martin, who happened to be a chum of Mantle and Ford and who was like a son to Casey. No one ever played harder or had more Yankee Pride than Martin. Billy drove himself to win for Stengel, the Yankees, his family and himself. He rose to the occasion when it mattered most: He saved Game 7 of the 1952 World Series with a running, lunging catch of a bases-loaded infield pop-up that nobody else seemed to want. He personally destroyed Brooklyn in the 1953 World Series, hitting .500.

The 1954 Yankees were probably the most frustrated team in history. They had a 103-51 record, winning the most games in Stengel's reign, yet finished eight games behind Cleveland. But the Yankee clubs of the next four years were not to be denied.

Reeling off four AL pennants in a row, Stengel's 1955-58 Yankees consisted of the familiar Ford, Mantle, Berra, Martin, Rizzuto, Gil McDougald, Hank Bauer, Joe Collins, Jerry Coleman, Irv Noren, Tom Morgan and Tommy Byrne plus newcomers Bill Skowron, Andy Carey, Enos Slaughter, Tony Kubek, Bobby Richardson, Norm Siebern, and Elston Howard. Howard in 1955 became the first black ballplayer on the Yankees.

Stengel was a master at using the entire 25-man roster and got the most out of new pitchers Bob Turley, Johnny Kucks, Don Larsen, Bob Grim, Jim Konstanty, Tom Sturdivant, Bobby Shantz, Art Ditmar, Duke Maas and Ryne Duren.

Blanked by Johnny Podres, 2-0, in Game 7, the Yankees lost to the Dodgers in the 1955 World Series. It was the only time the Bums prevailed in the Bronx-Brooklyn rivalry. But, as usually happens when the Yankees get a second chance, they reclaimed the World Championship from Brooklyn in a 1956 World Series highlighted by Yankee pitcher Don Larsen's perfect game, perhaps the single most thrilling game in baseball's long story. Mantle in 1956 showed that he was the game's best player by winning the Triple Crown.

New York won relatively easy AL pennants in 1957 and 1958 and both years met Milwaukee in the World Series. The Braves won in 1957.

It was at the close of the 1957 season that the Giants and Dodgers deserted their Polo Grounds and Ebbets Field homes and headed for the sunnier skies and bigger bucks of California. Thousands of the Big Apple's loyal baseball fans were embittered and New York's baseball climate dampened considerably, hurting Yankee Stadium attendance.

The Yankees of 1958, once again given a second chance, took back the crown from Milwaukee in what was probably Stengel's finest hour. After being down three games to one, the Yankees fought back to win the Series and the grudging admiration of not a few Yankee haters. Bob Turley won Game 5, saved Game 6 and won Game 7.

The Yankees followed their stirring conquest of 1958 with a disastrous 1959 season. But behind this sorry 79-75 campaign, five successive AL pennants (1960-64) were in store.

The 1960 World Series outcome was hard to swallow. The Bronx Bombers set numerous batting records and in three games were especially dominant, bombing Pittsburgh, 16-3, 10-0 and 12-0. No matter. Bill Mazeroski's ninth-inning, Forbes Field homer in Game 7 made World Champions of the Pirates.

The Yankees thereupon fired Stengel and Weiss. The press and public were outraged over Stengel's dismissal. Ironically, Stengel was probably well past his prime as a manager, while Weiss was still very much on top of things. But Weiss was considered a cold man and few tears were shed over his axing.

Weiss had foolishly yielded to racial prejudice and the Yankees would have a price to pay. While teams that had opened their rosters to blacks would be winning, the Yankees because of their late start in signing blacks would in a few years be hurting. Few blacks were signed in the years following the 1955 recruitment of Elston Howard.

Weiss' bigotry will always mar his record, but apart from this stain, his is a record of an astute baseball operator. He milked a farm system of his own design, and if Stengel needed a proven major leaguer, Weiss acquired the likes of such outstanding veterans as Enos Slaughter, Johnny Mize, Jim Konstanty and Johnny Sain. To the dismay of the rest of the AL, he had a sweetheart trading relationship with the Kansas City A's, always giving the A's quantity for quality. In his last A's trade, he plucked Roger Maris, who won league MVP honors in 1960 and 1961, his first two Yankee campaigns.

The 1961 Yankees were 109-53 under rookie Manager Ralph Houk. Power was the hallmark of this team, one of history's greatest. The Bronx Bombers hit a then big league record 240 home runs. (In the 1990s, several clubs eclipsed the Yankee 240 homer total.) Maris hit 61 homers and Mantle 54.

At the Stadium on the final day of the season, Maris dramatically broke Ruth's single-season record, the commissioner's asterisk notwithstanding. But a strange thing was happening: For all his heroics, Maris for some reason was denied popular adulation. Mantle, who so often in the past was treated horribly, at the same time emerged as a fan idol. Until the end of his career, Mantle was one of the most popular athletes in New York sports history.

On top of 1961's Maris-Mantle total of 115 homers, Skowron, Berra, Howard and John Blanchard each hit more than 20. The infield of Skowron-Richardson-Boyer-Kubek was superb, as were outfielders Mantle, Maris, Berra, Hector Lopez and Bob Cerv. The Howard-Blanchard-Berra catching corps had to be the greatest ever seen. Luis Arroyo was outstanding out of the bullpen and the starters included Ralph Terry, Bill Stafford, Rollie Sheldon and Jim Coates, all young pitchers with exceptionally lively arms. But the ace was the veteran of the staff, the 1961 Cy Young Award winner for his 25 victories, Whitey Ford.

The Yankees rolled over Cincinnati in a five-game World Series even though Berra, Maris and Mantle were a combined 6 for 36 at-bat—emphatic testimony to the 1961 club's depth and balance. The great Yankee aggregation would win the AL pennant the next three years.

Major league baseball underwent dramatic change in the 1960s. In 1961, for the first time in AL history, the league expanded to 10 teams. The NL expanded in 1962, and New York was awarded a franchise, the Mets, who rapidly developed a hard-core following. Old Dodger and Giant fans, and youngsters known as "The New Breed," attached themselves to the Mets, and the Yankees were damaged in the New York market.

A few years later the amateur free-agent draft was begun and its purpose of apportioning the talent among the clubs had the effect of building a fence around the Yankee scouting capability.

The game itself had become dominated by pitching; hitting had gone longball and batting averages were depressed. Great old ballparks—Griffith Stadium in Washington, Shibe Park in Philadelphia, Sportsman's Park in St. Louis and League Park in Cleveland—had faded from the scene, and new stadiums were built on waves of renewal and expansion. Both leagues split into divisions in 1969 and again expanded, the AL going from 10 teams to 12.

To return to the front of the '60s and the Yanks' five successive pennants—they won in 1960 and 1961, and in the latter season also won the World Championship, you'll recall. In 1962 they faced San Francisco in the World Series, winning in Game 7, 1-0, behind Ralph Terry. It was an especially delectable victory for Terry; it was Terry who served up the Mazeroski home run that sank the New Yorkers in Pittsburgh in 1960. The game ended when mighty Willie McCovey, with runners on second and third, smashed a wicked liner that second sacker Bobby Richardson speared.

The Los Angeles Dodgers shocked the Yankees in the 1963 World Series, sweeping New York in four games behind fantastic pitching. Ralph Houk then stepped upstairs and was replaced by Yogi Berra.

After early sputtering, Yogi led his 1964 team to a pennant in spite of fierce opposition by Chicago and Baltimore. The club battled St. Louis in the World Series but bowed in seven games. One great moment was Mantle's ninth-inning homer that gave the Yankees a loud and stirring victory in Game 3. But the team's age was showing; the dynasty was beginning to creak.

The 1964 World Series was barely cold when the Yankees blundered; they released the popular Berra as manager. The dynasty fell in 1965, the Yankees dropping out of the first division for the first time since 1925. The CBS ownership that had a year earlier purchased the club from Topping and Webb was dumbfounded.

CBS had expected to reap Yankee glory. It was unprepared to deal with the sagging club now managed by Johnny Keane, a good baseball man but a terrible choice to manage New York. The Yankees sank lower in 1966, falling to the cellar and looking on in disbelief one day as only 413 spectators gathered in the Bronx to witness a game with the White Sox.

For better or worse, the Yankees underwent an image change in the 1960s True, Kubek and Richardson were the mild-mannered, polite Yankees the farm system had always produced. They were in the mold of the "conservative" Yankees the public held for some 30 years. But the changing times wafted in such free spirits as Joe Pepitone, Phil Linz and Jim Bouton. Pepitone, especially, loved fun and found it as a Yankee. With his stylish long hair, Joe reflected the Woodstock generation and gave the Yankees color as well as talent, and both in generous measure.

The 1965 collapse was followed by years of rebuilding under President Mike Burke, General Manager Lee MacPhail and Manager Houk who returned to the dugout early in 1966. In 1966, the declining Yankees suffered through their worst season since 1925, when they finished seventh in an eight-club league. Also, their last-place finish (tenth) was their first as tailender since 1912 when the then-Highlanders posted a 50-102 record. Meanwhile, the Yankees finished ninth in 1967, fifth in 1968, and fifth in 1969.

It was prior to the 1969 spring training camp that near-crippling injuries forced the retirement of Mickey Mantle. Pepitone was now the club's top drawing card. But the Yankees were all but forgotten. They were down, and the Mets were the Miracle Mets—the winners of a dramatic 1969 World Championship.

Houk's 1970 team (93-69) was a surprise second-place club that was built around veterans Roy White, Mel Stottlemyre and Fritz Peterson and budding stars Bobby Murcer and Thurman Munson. Slowly but surely, the winning attitude was coming home to the Bronx but was finding the place in disrepair. Yankee Stadium and its proud old neighborhood were deteriorating. Speculation had it that the Yankees would move to New Jersey.

Thanks to Burke and New York City Mayor John Lindsey, a plan was devised to save the Stadium. (The neighborhood problem, unfortunately, was less soluble.) The Yankees remained at the Stadium through 1973 and then, as the plan dictated, moved to Shea Stadium for the 1974 and 1975 seasons as Yankee Stadium underwent a top-to-bottom, pillar-removing renovation.

CBS in 1973 sold the Yankees to a group headed by George Steinbrenner. A wealthy Clevelander, Steinbrenner's chief interest, besides shipbuilding, was to reestablish the Yankees' winning tradition. More than anyone else, he would be responsible for the Yankees' climb back to the top of baseball.

Steinbrenner reached his objective largely by adapting to the free-agent era that began in the autumn of 1976. He signed the cream of the first crop, pitcher Don Gullett and slugger Reggie Jackson, and in the following years plucked stars like Goose Gossage, Tommy John and Dave Winfield. The Steinbrenner method of spending big money would draw the resentment of those enmeshed in a different kind of baseball economics.

The 1974 Yankees fought out a tight race with Baltimore and Boston and finished two games behind the Eastern Division winning Orioles. New York boasted old favorites Munson, Murcer and White and showcased attractive additions—Graig Nettles, Lou Piniella, Chris Chambliss, Elliott Maddox, Sparky Lyle, Dick Tidrow, Pat Dobson and Rudy May—all acquired in trades.

An artistic 20-game winner for the champion Oakland A's, Catfish Hunter was declared a free agent and following the 1974 season signed a phenomenal Yankee contract. While Catfish enjoyed a great 1975, the Yankees finished a distant third.

Yankee Stadium reopened in 1976 and the Yankees, as they had when it opened in 1923, celebrated by winning the AL flag. Now managed by Billy Martin, who joined them late in 1975, the Yankees ran away with the AL East title, then beat the Kansas City Royals on a dramatic ninth-inning Game 5 homer by Chris Chambliss to win the Championship Series and send the Stadium throng into a frenzy of joy and unleashed frustration. After all, it had been an even dozen years since the Yankees last

1960s INFIELD—Another outstanding Yankee infield was this foursome of the 1960s. Left to right: Clete Boyer (3B), Tony Kubek (SS), Bobby Richardson (2B) and Joe Pepitone (1B). Never has the game seen a finer defensive infield. (New York Yankees Archives)

won a pennant. Cincinnati beat the Yankees in four World Series games despite a Munson bat that hit .529. Still, the Yankees at long last had a pennant under their belt.

Munson was drafted out of Kent State and was signed by former Yankee Gene Woodling. After a brief stint in the minors, the stocky Thurman joined the Yankees late in 1969 and in 1970 was AL Rookie of the Year. The mobile Munson was spectacular defensively and tenacious as a clutch hitter. Following Wally Schang, Bill Dickey, Yogi Berra and Elston Howard, he extended the Yanks' long line of outstanding catchers. The Yankees lost more than a great catcher when Thurman, the AL's MVP in 1976, died in an Aug. 2, 1979 airplane crash; they lost their leader, heart and soul.

The Yankees in 1977 won a sizzling AL East race, finishing 2½ games ahead of Baltimore and Boston. The club was in a fish bowl this season. The sports world looked in as flare-ups involving such stars as Munson and Reggie Jackson broke out from time to time. Many equated the Yankee troubles with the typical trials and tribulations of a soap opera.

In spite of its cohesion deficiency, the club was up to a tremendous stretch run. They were probably the strongest Yankees since 1961, enjoying six solid starters, 26 saves from Sparky Lyle and three 100-RBI hitters in Jackson, Nettles and Munson. New York defeated Kansas City in the Championship Series and Los Angeles in the World Series, Game 6 of which was settled when Jackson hit three consecutive first-pitch homers. It was Reggie's greatest moment.

Reggie Jackson played baseball and football at Arizona State University and broke into major league baseball in 1967 with Charley Finley's Kansas City A's. The club moved to Oakland in 1968 and Reggie, born 22 years earlier in a Philadelphia suburb, became a proponent of the West Coast lifestyle and a star of Oakland teams that won five straight (1971-75) AL West titles. He had a certain presence and he pulled in fans. New York was the proper stage for Reggie, Steinbrenner reasoned.

Incredibly, 1978 was even more topsy-turvy than 1977. Jackson, Martin and Steinbrenner became a stormy triangle, and in July, shortly after the Yankees fell 14 games behind the Red Sox, Martin was replaced by Bob Lemon. The Yankees then embarked on an amazing drive to finish the season tied with Boston. New York prevailed, 5-4, in a thrilling playoff game at Fenway Park and went on to again defeat both the Royals in the AL Championship Series and the Dodgers in the World Series. It was the reborn Yankees' second straight World Championship.

The 1976-78 pennant-winning teams rank with the best in Yankee history. Lyle was great out of the bullpen and in 1978 was joined by the imposing Goose Gossage. Catfish Hunter, Ed Figueroa and Dick Tidrow were mound stars all three years, but most credit for the championships of 1977 and 1978 has to go to pitcher Ron Guidry.

The thin lefty with his smoking fastball and darting slider came into his own in 1977. And his 25-3 1978 season will be remembered as long as baseball is played. New York had Chambliss-Randolph-Nettles-Dent around the diamond (Fred Stanley played shortstop in 1976), the best all-around infield in baseball, and slugging outfielders Jackson, Piniella, White and swift Mickey Rivers. Thurman Munson was the league's best catcher.

New York fell to fourth place in 1979, all hopes of another come-from-behind pennant drive vanishing with Munson's death. The 1980 Yankees regrouped behind Jackson's 41 homers and Gossage's 33 saves to win the AL East. But they lost three in a row to the Royals in the Championship Series.

The 1981 season is best remembered for a mid-season players' strike lasting two months, and an expanded playoff format. After defeating the Brewers and A's in the playoffs, the Yankees fell to the Dodgers in the World Series. There was also a changing of the guard, as Reggie Jackson finished his Yankee career and Dave Winfield joined the club.

Winfield in December 1980 signed a big-money ten-year contract with the Yankees. The deal was so lucrative that even

The M & M boys, Roger Maris (left), and Mickey Mantle (right), pose for the cameras. (AP/WIDE WORLD PHOTOS)

George Steinbrenner was astounded when he discovered how much he might have to pay Winfield when the escalating cost-of-living clause kicked in. George asked Dave to rewrite the deal; Winfield refused. Not very sporting, felt George, and for the next ten years he locked horns with Winfield whenever there was an opportunity.

Jackson, a forgotten and spurned man in 1981, never looked back, signing with the California Angels in 1982. He led the league with 39 homers—including five against the Yankees—and led the Angels to a division title. Meanwhile, the Yankees, attempting to rebuild with speed, used three managers on their way to a lackluster 79-83 season. Adding Ken Griffey and Dave Collins began a pattern in the 1980s of grabbing up proven players without having a viable plan. The Yankees didn't even have an everyday position set aside for Collins. Griffey never quite fit in the picture either.

The Yankees had good enough teams in the 1980s to realistically believe they were just a player or two away from winning a pennant. So long-range planning was ignored in the interest of short-range gains. The Yankees became notorious for trading away their prospects, especially pitchers. It started in 1976 when the Yankees dealt Scott McGregor and Tippy Martinez to Baltimore, and they were stars on pennant-winning Oriole teams in 1979 and 1983. Jose Rijo was traded in 1984; twice he would win 15 games for the Reds, and he was the World Series MVP in 1990. Jim Deshaies was traded for Joe Niekro in 1985; Deshaies won 15 games for the Astros in 1989. Doug Drabek was traded for Rick Rhoden in 1986; Drabek won 22 games and the Cy Young Award in 1990. Bob Tewksbury was traded for Steve Trout in 1987; Tewksbury emerged in the 1990s as a star for the Cardinals.

As the Yankees' pitching deteriorated in the 1980s, they desperately needed these young arms, but instead they were stuck with the washed-up pitchers they got in return. The Yankees weren't immune to giving away position players either; among those that got away were Willie McGee, Fred McGriff and Hal Morris.

Billy Martin returned for Billy III in 1983, a year in which Ron Guidry won 21 games and Dave Righetti pitched a July 4th no-hitter. The Pine Tar Game was played at Yankee Stadium on July 24. A ninth-inning George Brett homer seemingly had put Kansas City ahead of the Yankees, but Martin convinced the umpires that a rule had been broken because pine tar had been applied too high on Brett's bat. The homer was taken away, the Yanks held on to win, and Martin looked brilliant. But only momentarily, because a few days later, American League President Lee MacPhail, reversing his umpires, ruled the homer counted and ordered the game resumed from the point of the Brett homer. The Yankees would lose when the game was finished several weeks later. "If the Yankees lose the pennant by one game, I wouldn't want to be Lee MacPhail living in New York," said Steinbrenner. "Maybe he should go house hunting in Kansas City." The Yankees finished seven games out.

Winfield was the Big Guy, and he played like one, hitting 37 homers with 106 RBIs in 1982 and 32 homers with 116 RBIs in 1983. In 1984, he was challenged by first baseman Don Mattingly, who in his first year as a regular hit 23 homers with 110 RBIs and was sensational around the bag. And Mattingly battled Winfield for the batting title right down to the final day, with Mattingly winning, .343 to .340.

The Yankees signed Mattingly out of Indiana in 1979, and on the strength of hard work and a sweet stroke, Don progressed through the Yankee farm system. He was all baseball—Donnie Baseball, they would call him. He became the darling of the fans, a blue-collar hero in a Rolls Royce decade. Over the next four seasons, he topped himself over and over again in baseball achievements.

"Every year," said Graig Nettles in the spring of 1983, "staying here is like getting traded." Nettles, the greatest third baseman in Yankee history, in March 1984 was traded to San Diego. This was bad news for New York but great for San Diego, as Graig and ex-Yankee Goose Gossage led the Padres to the NL West title.

Yogi Berra managed the Yankees in 1984. He developed a great team atmosphere and won 87 games, but he was canned early in the 1985 season, and the curtain opened for Martin and Billy IV. Mattingly, Winfield and Rickey Henderson, obtained in the off-season, formed a trio of greatness seldom seen in an everyday lineup. Mattingly, the league's MVP, had 145 RBIs. Winfield had 114 RBIs. Henderson scored 146 runs. Additionally, Guidry was nearly as amazing as he had been in 1978, posting a 22-6 record. The Yankees went to Toronto for a season-ending three-game series, needing to sweep the Blue Jays in order to tie them for first place. The Yanks, however, won only two of the games, finishing two games back with a wonderful 97-64 record.

But Martin was fired again, the consequence of an ugly September barroom brawl with Yankee pitcher Ed Whitson, who was another poorly inspired free-agent acquisition. Lou Piniella, the new manager, guided the Yankees to 90 wins in 1986 and 89 wins in 1987. Mattingly, Winfield and Henderson continued to excel, but except for Dave Righetti, who moved to the bullpen in 1984 and set a major-league record with 46 saves in 1986, the pitching was bad. Across the river in Queens, the Mets in 1986 won the World Series, and the Yankees faded into secondary status in New York City.

The 1988 season opened with Billy V, and it would be Martin's final act as Yankee manager. The club had a fine 40-28 record when Billy was fired, but his alcoholism and out-of-control behavior were worse than ever, and he was cut loose in favor of Piniella. Billy, drunk, was killed on Christmas 1989, when he wrecked his truck.

Piniella was saddled with a pitching staff that in 1988 had a miserable 4.26 ERA. Yet, the Yankees remained in the race until losing five of seven games to first-place Boston in September. And, in 1988, the Yankees said good-bye to two old pros from their glory days, Ron Guidry and Willie Randolph. Guidry retired. Randolph signed with the Dodgers.

The Yankees paid dearly for unwise decisions in 1989 and nose-dived to 74-87. Dallas Green, the new manager, blustered and bullied, but the only person to take his bait was Steinbrenner, who replaced Green with Bucky Dent in August. Winfield was sidelined all year after back surgery. Henderson, unhappy, was practically given away. The Yankees could have used pitchers other than the free-agent flops they did sign—Andy Hawkins and Dave LaPoint. New York's ERA ballooned to 4.50.

It got much worse in 1990. Managers were becoming footnotes, but for the record, Dent and Stump Merrill were the managers of the last-place Yankees. Their pathetic 67-95 record represented the most losses by a Yankee team since

1912. Mattingly, suffering from a bad back, had his worst year. Winfield escaped by trade in May. Shortly thereafter, the commissioner's office completed an investigation of Steinbrenner and his association with an admitted gambler, Howard Spira, who had once worked indirectly for Winfield.

On July 30, 1990, Commissioner Fay Vincent permanently banned Steinbrenner from running the Yankees. Vincent, connecting Steinbrenner's admission that he paid Spira $40,000 with the fact that Steinbrenner had inside information on Winfield, ruled that George had acted against the best interests of baseball. Vincent put the emphasis on Steinbrenner's "undisclosed working relationship" with a known gambler.

While superficially the 1991 season was dismal (71-91), a few rays of hope broke through the dark clouds hanging over Yankee Stadium. Rookies were getting legitimate chances, and although eventually some wouldn't measure up, others, including Pat Kelly, Bernie Williams, and perhaps Scott Kamieniecki, seemed to have a future in the Bronx. Buck Showalter was named manager in October, and Mattingly would later say that this was the turning point in the club's fortunes.

Showalter, signed as a player by the Yankees in 1977, had never made the majors as a player. But he had an excellent record managing in the Yankee minors, and in 1990 he joined the big club as a coach. He was extremely low key and a tireless worker, and he expected the same from his players. The Yankees settled down in 1992 and improved their record by five games over 1991.

Actually, General Manager Gene Michael had the best year in 1992. Making a series of tremendous acquisitions, Michael reversed a decade-long negative pattern in this department. In January, Michael signed free agents Danny Tartabull and Mike Gallego; traded Steve Sax to the White Sox for three good arms, Melido Perez, Bob Wickman, and Domingo Jean; and signed reserve catcher Mike Stanley. In November, Michael obtained Paul O'Neill from the Reds for Roberto Kelly. In December, he signed free agents Jimmy Key and Wade Boggs, and obtained Jim Abbott from the Angels for J.T. Snow. In practically no time, Michael had assembled a contender.

On July 24, 1992, Fay Vincent reduced Steinbrenner's lifetime ban to 30 months, and when George returned to the Yankees on March 1, 1993, he found the team in good hands. The Yankees in 1993 were tied for first place with Toronto as late as September 9. Sadly, the only losing month for the Yankees was September (11-15), and they couldn't keep pace with the torrid Blue Jays.

Tinkering with the good chemistry just a little, the Yankees in 1994 roared to a 70-43 record and led the AL East by 6½ games when the season ended in August because of a players' strike. Mattingly hit .304 and was enthusiastic again. O'Neill hit .359 with 21 homers and 83 RBIs. Stanley hit .300 with 17 homers. Boggs hit .342. Tartabull had 19 homers and 67 RBIs. Luis Polonia hit .311 and Bernie Williams .289. Jim Leyritz had 17 homers. Key had a 17-4 record. Steve Howe had 15 saves.

But the discord between the owners and players wiped out the 1994 season. The owners were claiming that their industry was being destroyed by high salaries, and demanded that the players accept a salary cap. The players argued for a free market, and saw a late-inning strike as their only alternative. The owners, who in past power struggles had always been the first to blink, didn't budge this time, and through the winter the deadlock continued with the approaching 1995 season in jeopardy. The future of baseball, in fact, was in jeopardy, as the owners and players wrestled over how to carve up millions and millions of dollars.

Fortunately, there would be—there was—a 1995 season. And there was also, as expected, a considerable loss of fan support. The average attendance at Yankee Stadium was 24,361, down from nearly 30,000 in the last normal season of 1993.

But what a 1995 season it was—and what a year it might have been for the Yanks had it not been for Jimmy Key's rotator cuff problems and mid-season surgery. The loss of Key was critical to both the regular campaign and postseason play.

A court ruling forcing the club owners to reinstate elements of the old collective bargaining agreement led the Major League Baseball Players' Association on April 2 to end its 234-day strike. The owners set a 144-game schedule that began April 24, and the players went back to work. The problems associated with the labor dispute, however, remained unresolved, and negotiations did not resume until November 15, 1995.

The Yankees, having played lackluster baseball most of the season, finished strong, winning 26 of their last 33 games (including 11 of their final 12) for a record of 79-65. While their final-day 6-1 win over Toronto left them seven games behind Boston, that victory did win them a ticket as the American League's first wildcard passenger to the playoffs.

Easily the best of the four first-round series turned out to be that pitting the Yankees against Lou Piniella's Seattle Mariners. In the fifth and final game, the Yankees went up by one run in the 11th inning, but Seattle came back to score twice in the bottom of the inning and advance in the new playoff format.

An earlier extra-inning game had a happier outcome. Jim Leyritz's 15th-inning homer in Game 2, at 1:22 in the morning, gave New York a 7-5 win in a game that required the Yankees to come from behind no less than four times. The dramatic swat triggered recollections of the heroics of Mickey Mantle, who died August 13 at the age of 63.

Some old Yankee institutions faded or teetered in 1995. There was the loss of Mantle. Retirement as a Yankee broadcaster seemed a prospect for Phil Rizzuto after 55 seasons of association with the club. Lou Gehrig's great record of 2,130 consecutive games was broken by Cal Ripken. The Yankees seemed closer to actually leaving Yankee Stadium, the only questions remaining being where and when, most likely as soon as a deal is worked out for a Manhattan or New Jersey site. And General Manager Gene Michael and Manager Buck Showalter, the duo most responsible for the Yanks becoming proficient again, were out of their jobs. Michael was moved to the post of director of major league scouting and Showalter was found on the street, either through nudging or by his won volition, depending on which of two versions is accepted.

In October, 1995, Bob Watson was selected as the new Yankee general manager, replacing Gene Michael. As one of his first moves as GM, Watson hired Joe Torre as the 31st Yankee manager in December, 1995. Watson proved instrumental, along with Michael's contributions, in the development of the club, which would win the World Series title in 1996.

After being eliminated by the Cleveland Indians in the 1997 Division series, the Yankees would come back with a vengeance in 1998 to have a season for the ages. Prior to the start of the '98 season, GM Bob Watson resigned and was replaced by his assistant, 30-year-old Brian Cashman. The 1998 campaign saw the Yankees establish a new American League record by winning 114 games. The season was culminated by a four-game sweep of the San Diego Padres in the World Series for title number 24.

In 1999, amid personal challenges by Joe Torre and Darryl Strawberry and losses of three fathers of Yankee players (Scott Brosius, Luis Sojo and Paul O'Neill), this team demonstrated incredible character, a sense of family unity and resilience throughout the season that is uncommon in modern sports. These traits were those that were passed down from manager Joe Torre to his team-family. The Yankees would go on to defeat the best teams in baseball in the playoffs, making it look easy! The season ended with another four-game sweep (they had swept the Padres a year earlier) of the formidable Atlanta Braves (tomahawk chop and all) in the 1999 World Series. The Yankees won their 37th AL pennant in 2000 and started the new century the same way they had ended the 1900's with another World Championship. This world title (number 26)

came against the New York Mets in five games. It was the first Subway Series since the 1956 Fall Classic against the Brooklyn Dodgers.

In 2001, the Yankees mourned with the world in the aftermath of the September 11th attack on America. Another AL pennant was secured after a tense round of playoff games that were delayed due to 9-11. It was the 38th flag to fly proudly in the Bronx, but the Arizona Diamondbacks kept the Yankees from the World Series title by winning in their last at bat in Game seven.

The 2002 season was highlighted by the free agent acquisition of Jason Giambi, and the 16th 100-win season (another MLB record) for the Yankees. High hopes were in place for another appearance in the ALCS and perhaps another World Series appearance. But the Anaheim Angels quickly dashed all Yankee dreams during the division playoffs. It was the earliest exit by the Yanks in the post season since 1997.

Since 1996, the Yankees have won four World Series titles and manager, Joe Torre, concluding his seventh season ends 2002 with 685 wins, an average of nearly 98 regular season victories during his tenure! The prospects for the Yankees' continued success look very bright, indeed, as the 21st Century continues!

TRADITION OF GREATNESS—From 1928 through 1979, these gentlemen—(left to right) Bill Dickey, Yogi Berra, Elston Howard, and Thurman Munson—provided the Yankees with the best catching in baseball history. (New York Yankees Archives)

YANKEE MANAGERS WINNING PENNANT
(AND WORLD SERIES) IN 1ST YANKEE SEASON*

Year	Manager	AL	WS
1947	Bucky Harris	Won	Won
1949	Casey Stengel	Won	Won
1961	Ralph Houk	Won	Won
1964	Yogi Berra	Won	Lost
1996	Joe Torre	Won	Won

Full seasons only.
Note: Billy Martin won AL Pennant in first full Yankee season in 1976, lost World Series.
Bob Lemon won AL pennant and World Series in incomplete season in 1978, he never managed Yankees for a full season.

YANKEE CLUB RECORD

Year	Standing	Won	Lost	Pct	Manager	Games Won By or Lost By
1903	Fourth	72	62	.537	C. Griffith	17 out
1904	Second	92	59	.609	C. Griffith	1½ out
1905	Sixth	71	78	.477	C. Griffith	21½ out
1906	Second	90	61	.596	C. Griffith	3 out
1907	Fifth	70	78	.473	C. Griffith	21 out
1908	Eighth	51	103	.331	Griffith/Elberfeld	39½ out
1909	Fifth	74	77	.490	G. Stallings	23½ out
1910	Second	88	63	.583	Stallings/Chase	14½ out
1911	Sixth	76	76	.500	H. Chase	25½ out
1912	Eighth	50	102	.329	H. Wolverton	55 out
1913	Seventh	57	94	.377	F. Chance	38 out
1914	Sixth	70	84	.455	Chance/Peckinpaugh	30 out
1915	Fifth	69	83	.454	W. B. Donovan	32½ out
1916	Fourth	80	74	.519	W. B. Donovan	11 out
1917	Sixth	71	82	.464	W. B. Donovan	28½ out
1918	Fourth	60	63	.488	M. Huggins	13½ out
1919	Third	80	59	.576	M. Huggins	7½ out
1920	Third	95	59	.617	M. Huggins	3 out
1921	First	98	55	.641	M. Huggins	by 4½
1922	First	94	60	.610	M. Huggins	by 1
1923*	First	98	54	.645	M. Huggins	by 16
1924	Second	89	63	.586	M. Huggins	2 out
1925	Seventh	69	85	.448	M. Huggins	28½ out
1926	First	91	63	.591	M. Huggins	by 3
1927*	First	110	44	.714	M. Huggins	by 19
1928*	First	101	53	.656	M. Huggins	by 2½
1929	Second	88	66	.571	Huggins/Fletcher	18 out
1930	Third	86	68	.558	B. Shawkey	16 out
1931	Second	94	59	.614	J. McCarthy	13½ out
1932*	First	107	47	.695	J. McCarthy	by 13
1933	Second	91	59	.607	J. McCarthy	7 out
1934	Second	94	60	.610	J. McCarthy	7 out
1935	Second	89	60	.597	J. McCarthy	3 out
1936*	First	102	51	.667	J. McCarthy	by 19½
1937*	First	102	52	.662	J. McCarthy	by 13
1938*	First	99	53	.651	J. McCarthy	by 9½
1939*	First	106	45	.702	J. McCarthy	by 17
1940	Third	88	66	.571	J. McCarthy	2 out
1941*	First	101	53	.656	J. McCarthy	by 17
1942	First	103	51	.669	J. McCarthy	by 9
1943*	First	98	56	.636	J. McCarthy	by 13½
1944	Third	83	71	.539	J. McCarthy	6 out
1945	Fourth	81	71	.553	J. McCarthy	6½ out
1946	Third	87	67	.565	McCarthy/Dickey/Neun	17 out
1947*	First	97	57	.630	B. Harris	by 12
1948	Third	94	60	.610	B. Harris	2½ out
1949*	First	97	57	.630	C. Stengel	by 1
1950*	First	98	56	.636	C. Stengel	by 3
1951*	First	98	56	.636	C. Stengel	by 5
1952*	First	95	59	.617	C. Stengel	by 2
1953*	First	99	52	.656	C. Stengel	by 8½
1954	Second	103	51	.669	C. Stengel	8 out

*Won the World Series

Year	Standing	Won	Lost	Pct.	Manager	Games Won By or Lost By
1955	First	96	58	.623	C. Stengel	by 3
1956*	First	97	57	.630	C. Stengel	by 9
1957	First	98	56	.636	C. Stengel	by 8
1958*	First	92	62	.597	C. Stengel	by 10
1959	Third	79	75	.513	C. Stengel	15 out
1960	First	97	57	.630	C. Stengel	by 8
1961*	First	109	53	.673	R. Houk	by 8
1962*	First	96	66	.593	R. Houk	by 5
1963	First	104	57	.646	R. Houk	by 10½
1964	First	99	63	.611	Y. Berra	by 1
1965	Sixth	77	85	.475	J. Keane	25 out
1966	Tenth	70	89	.440	Keane/Houk	26½ out
1967	Ninth	72	90	.444	R. Houk	20 out
1968	Fifth	83	79	.512	R. Houk	20 out

EAST DIVISION OF AMERICAN LEAGUE

Year	Standing	Won	Lost	Pct.	Manager	Games Won By or Lost By
1969	Fifth	80	81	.497	R. Houk	28½ out
1970	Second	93	69	.574	R. Houk	15 out
1971	Fourth	82	80	.506	R. Houk	21 out
1972	Fourth	79	76	.510	R. Houk	6½ 2 out
1973	Fourth	80	82	.494	R. Houk	17 out
1974	Second	89	73	.549	B. Virdon	2 out
1975	Third	83	77	.519	Virdon/Martin	12 out
1976	First	97	62	.610	B. Martin	by 10½
1977*	First	100	62	.617	B. Martin	by 2½
1978*	First	100	63	.613	Martin/Lemon	by 1
1979	Fourth	89	71	.556	Lemon/Martin	13½ out
1980	First	103	59	.636	D. Howser	by 3
1981**	First/Sixth	59	48	.551	Michael/Lemon	——
1982	Fifth	79	83	.488	Lemon/Michael/King	16 out
1983	Third	91	71	.562	B. Martin	7 out
1984	Third	87	75	.537	Y. Berra	17 out
1985	Second	97	64	.602	Berra/Martin	2 out
1986	Second	90	72	.556	L. Piniella	5½ out
1987	Fourth	89	73	.549	L. Piniella	9 out
1988	Fifth	85	76	.528	Martin/Piniella	5 out
1989	Fifth	74	87	.460	Green/Dent	14½ out
1990	Seventh	67	95	.414	Dent/Merrill	21 out
1991	Fifth	71	91	.438	S. Merrill	21 out
1992	Fourth	76	86	.469	B. Showalter	20 out
1993	Second	88	74	.543	B. Showalter	7 out
1994	First	70	43	.619	B. Showalter	by 6½
1995***	Second	79	65	.549	B. Showalter	7 out
1996*	First	92	70	.568	J. Torre	by 4
1997***	Second	96	66	593	J. Torre	2 out
1998*	First	114	48	704	J. Torre	by 22
1999*	First	98	54	.605	J. Torre	by 4
2000*	First	87	74	.540	J. Torre	by 2½
2001	First	95	65	.594	J. Torre	by 13½
2002	First	103	58	.640	J. Torre	by 10½

| **TOTALS:** | | **8777** | **6548** | **.5727** | | |

*Won the World Series
**Split season due to a strike. Yankees won the First Half
division title (34-22) (.607) and defeated Milwaukee, 3 games to 2,
in Division Series.
***Qualified for playoffs as the wildcard entrant.

AMERICAN LEAGUE PLAYOFFS

Year	Opponent	Won	Lost	Result
1976	Kansas City Royals-ALCS	3	2	Won
1977	Kansas City Royals-ALCS	3	2	Won
1978	Kansas City Royals-ALCS	3	1	Won
1980	Kansas City Royals-ALCS	0	3	Lost
1981	Milwaukee Brewers-Division	3	2	Won
1981	Oakland A's-ALCS	3	0	Won
1995	Seattle Mariners-Division	2	3	Lost
1996	Texas Rangers-Division	3	1	Won
1996	Baltimore Orioles-ALCS	4	1	Won
1997	Cleveland Indians-Division	2	3	Lost
1998	Texas Rangers-Division	3	0	Won
1998	Cleveland Indians-ALCS	4	2	Won
1999	Texas Rangers-Division	3	0	Won
1999	Boston Red Sox-ALCS	4	1	Won
2000	Oakland A's-Division	3	2	Won
2000	Seattle Mariners-ALCS	4	2	Won
2001	Oakland A's-Division	3	2	Won
2001	Seattle Mariners-ALCS	4	1	Won
2002	Anaheim Angels-Division	1	3	Lost

Division Series Record: 6-3
Games Won: 23
Games Lost: 16
Division Series Win Percentage: .589 (39 games)

Championship Series Record: 9-1
Games Won: 32
Games Lost: 15
Championship Series Win Percentage: .680 (47 games)

WORLD SERIES RECORD

Year	Opponent	Won	Lost	Tie	Result
1921	New York Giants	3	5		Lost
1922	New York Giants	0	4	1	Lost
1923	New York Giants	4	2		Won
1926	St. Louis Cardinals	3	4		Lost
1927	Pittsburgh Pirates	4	0		Won
1928	St. Louis Cardinals	4	0		Won
1932	Chicago Cubs	4	0		Won
1936	New York Giants	4	2		Won
1937	New York Giants	4	1		Won
1938	Chicago Cubs	4	0		Won
1939	Cincinnati Reds	4	0		Won
1941	Brooklyn Dodgers	4	1		Won
1942	St. Louis Cardinals	1	4		Lost
1943	St. Louis Cardinals	4	1		Won
1947	Brooklyn Dodgers	4	3		Won
1949	Brooklyn Dodgers	4	1		Won
1950	Philadelphia Phillies	4	0		Won
1951	New York Giants	4	2		Won
1952	Brooklyn Dodgers	4	3		Won
1953	Brooklyn Dodgers	4	2		Won
1955	Brooklyn Dodgers	3	4		Lost
1956	Brooklyn Dodgers	4	3		Won
1957	Milwaukee Braves	3	4		Lost
1958	Milwaukee Braves	4	3		Won
1960	Pittsburgh Pirates	3	4		Lost
1961	Cincinnati Reds	4	1		Won
1962	San Francisco Giants	4	3		Won
1963	Los Angeles Dodgers	0	4		Lost
1964	St. Louis Cardinals	3	4		Lost
1976	Cincinnati Reds	0	4		Lost
1977	Los Angeles Dodgers	4	2		Won
1978	Los Angeles Dodgers	4	2		Won
1981	Los Angeles Dodgers	2	4		Lost
1996	Atlanta Braves	4	2		Won
1998	San Diego Padres	4	0		Won
1999	Atlanta Braves	4	0		Won
2000	New York Mets	4	1		Won
2001	Arizona Diamondbacks	3	4		Lost

World Series Record: 26-12
Games Won: 128
Games Lost: 84
World Series Winning Percentage: .6037 (212 games)*
* Excludes one tie game in 1922

TOTAL CHAMPIONSHIPS

CHAPTER 2

PLAYER BIOGRAPHIES

Babe Ruth watches one of his 714 career home runs travel out of Yankee Stadium during his 60-homer season in 1927. (AP/WIDE WORLD PHOTOS)

LIST OF PLAYERS

The 198 Yankee Selectees
(*entire playing career with Yankees)
Boldface - Active with Yanks through 2002

Aker, Jack
Allen, Johnny
Arroyo, Luis
Bahnsen, Stan
Baker, Frank
Bauer, Hank
Baylor, Don
Berra, Yogi
*Bevens, Bill
Boggs, Wade
Bonham, Ernie
Borowy, Hank
Bouton, Jim
Boyer, Clete
Broaca, Johnny
*Brown, Bobby
Bush, Joe
Byrne, Tommy
Caldwell, Ray
Carey, Andy
Cerone, Rick
Chambliss, Chris
*Chandler, Spud
Chapman, Ben
Chase, Hal
Chesbro, Jack
Clarke, Horace
Coates, Jim
*Coleman, Jerry
*Collins, Joe
Collins, Pat
*Combs, Earle
Cone, David
Conroy, Wid
*Cree, Birdie
*Crosetti, Frank
Daniels, Bert
Davis, Ron
Dent, Bucky
*Dickey, Bill
*DiMaggio, Joe
Ditmar, Art
Dobson, Pat
*Donald, Atley
Downing, Al
Dugan, Joe
Duren, Ryne
Elberfeld, Kid
Espinoza, Alvaro

Etten, Nick
Farr, Steve
Figueroa, Ed
Fisher, Ray
Ford, Russ
*Ford, Whitey
Gamble, Oscar
*Gehrig, Lou
*Gibbs, Jake
Gomez, Lefty
Gordon, Joe
Gossage, Goose
Griffey, Ken Sr.
Griffith, Clark
Grim, Bob
Guetterman, Lee
*Guidry, Ron
Hadley, Bump
Hall, Mel
Hamilton, Steve
Hartzell, Roy
Henderson, Rickey
*Henrich, Tommy
*Hogg, Bill
Howard, Elston
Howe, Steve
Hoyt, Waite
Hunter, Catfish
Jackson, Reggie
Jeter, Derek
John, Tommy
Johnson, Billy
Johnson, Hank
Jones, Sad Sam
Kamieniecki, Scott
Keating, Ray
Keeler, Willie
Kekich, Mike
Keller, Charlie
Kelly, Pat
Kelly, Roberto
Key, Jimmy
Kleinow, Red
Kline, Steve
Knight, Jack
Koenig, Mark
*Kubek, Tony
Kucks, Johnny
Kuzava, Bob
Lake, Joe

LaPorte, Frank
Larsen, Don
Lary, Lyn
Lazzeri, Tony
Leyritz, Jim
Lindell, Johnny
Lopat, Ed
Lopez, Hector
Lyle, Sparky
Maisel, Fritz
*Manning, Rube
*Mantle, Mickey
Maris, Roger
Martin, Billy
Martinez, Tino
*Mattingly, Don
May, Rudy
Mays, Carl
McDaniel, Lindy
*McDougald, Gil
Medich, Doc
Meusel, Bob
Michael, Gene
Mogridge, George
Moore, Wilcy
Morgan, Tom
*Munson, Thurman
Murcer, Bobby
Murphy, Johnny
Nettles, Graig
Noren, Irv
O'Neill, Paul
Orth, Al
Page, Joe
Pagliarulo, Mike
Pearson, Monte
Peckinpaugh, Roger
Pennock, Herb
Pepitone, Joe
Perez, Melido
Peterson, Fritz
Pettitte, Andy
Piniella, Lou
Pipgras, George
Pipp, Wally
Powell, Jack
Pratt, Del
Quinn, Jack
Ramos, Pedro
Randolph, Willie

Raschi, Vic
Rasmussen, Dennis
Rawley, Shane
Reniff, Hal
Reynolds, Allie
*Richardson, Bobby
Righetti, Dave
Rivera, Mariano
Rivers, Mickey
*Rizzuto, Phil
*Rolfe, Red
Ruffing, Red
Russell, Allan
*Russo, Marius
Ruth, Babe
Sain, Johnny
Sax, Steve
Schang, Wally
Scott, Everett
*Selkirk, George
Sewell, Joe
Shantz, Bobby
Shawkey, Bob
Shocker, Urban
Skowron, Bill
Stafford, Bill
Stirnweiss, Snuffy
*Stottlemyre, Mel
Sturdivant, Tom
Sweeney, Jeff
Tartabull, Danny
Terry, Ralph
Tidrow, Dick
Tresh, Tom
Turley, Bob
Velarde, Randy
Ward, Aaron
*Warhop, Jack
Wells, Ed
Wetteland, John
*White, Roy
Wickman, Bob
Williams, Bernie
Williams, Jimmy
Winfield, Dave
Witt, Whitey
Womack, Dooley
Woodling, Gene
Wynegar, Butch

*W*hile every New York Yankee has contributed to the club's successes, 198 of the more than 1,200 ballplayers who have toiled for their noble cause have contributed significantly. Some, to be sure— Ruth, Gehrig, DiMaggio, Mantle, Berra, Hoyt, Ruffing, Munson, Mattingly and Jeter to name several—performed with particular distinction and will remain alive in memory for decades to come. A look at the famed and the less celebrated, the 198—from Jack Aker to Butch Wynegar.

SIGNIFICANT YANKEE PLAYERS

INTRODUCTION

Criteria was necessary for selecting the most significant—not necessarily the best—former Yankees for inclusion in this chapter. These decisions in the original *Yankee Encyclopedia* were mostly subjective, but this time the author drew the lines using statistics. The 198 players are former and current Yankees who played for the club between 1903 and 2002. The 100 nonpitchers were selected based on a minimum of 1400 at-bats. The 98 pitchers had a minimum of 55 decisions plus saves.

Admittedly, some important Yankees were lost by using such an arbitrary system, but it seemed the fairest route. Besides the perfect split between pitchers and nonpitchers, there is a desired balance at other positions, as follows: 12 catchers, ten first basemen, 15 second basemen, 13 third basemen, 14 shortstops, 34 outfielders (averaging 10.67 for each outfield position) and two designated hitters.

Most of what appears in the biographies needs no explanation, but the reader may have a question or two about some editorial decisions. For example, not all nicknames are treated as such, and this is because nicknames such as Yogi, Lefty, and Catfish became so associated with Berra, Gomez, and Hunter, respectively, that to call them by their given names would be unaccommodating to the reader.

[In prior editions, author Mark Gallagher noted: "Baseball records are inadequate to the task of computing some ERAs for pitching careers spent entirely with the Yankees." In this edition, ERAs are given for ALL pitchers included in this biography section. The ERAs are given with the Yanks as well as lifetime ERAs.]
—Editor's Note

AKER, JACK

Nickname: "Chief"
Yankee: 1969-72
Pitcher
Born: July 13, 1940
Birthplace: Tulare, CA
Bat: R; Throw: R
Ht: 6'2"; Wt: 190

CAME TO YANKS: In May, 1969, the Yanks obtained Jack from the expansion Seattle Pilots for pitcher Fred Talbot.

RELIEF SPECIALIST: Jack was one of the best relief specialists in baseball in the late 1960s and early 1970s. (In 1966 he saved 32 games for the Kansas City A's.) He was a member of an outstanding Yankee bullpen that included Lindy McDaniel and Steve Hamilton. In 1969 he led Yankee pitchers in saves (11), and he tied for the club leadership in saves in 1971 (4). Jack's 123 lifetime saves ranks among baseball's top 50 and 31 with the Yanks places him 16th overall. Jack had a 1969 streak of 33 consecutive scoreless innings pitched.

TRADED: The Yanks dealt Jack to the Cubs early in the 1972 season. Later he joined the Mets organization, managing in the Mets' farm system. From 1985-87, Jack was a coach with the Cleveland Indians.

AKER, JACK

Yr.	W-L	Pct.	SA	G	GS	CG	IP	H	BB	SO	SH	ERA
1969	8-4	.667	11	38	0	0	66	51	22	40	0	2.05
1970	4-2	.667	16	41	0	0	70	57	20	36	0	2.06
1971	4-4	.500	4	41	0	0	56	48	26	24	0	2.57
1972	0-0	.000	0	4	0	0	6	5	3	1	0	3.00
4 Yrs.	16-10	.615	31	124	0	0	198	161	71	101	0	2.23
Life.	47-45	.511	123	495	0	0	746	679	274	404	0	3.28

ALLEN, JOHNNY

Yankee: 1932-35
Pitcher
Born: September 30, 1905
Birthplace: Lenoir, NC
Died: March 29, 1959
Bat: R; Throw: R
Ht: 6' Wt: 180

HONORS: In 1977, Johnny was inducted into the North Carolina Sports Hall of Fame.

ROOKIE SENSATION: Johnny was acquired by the Yanks because of the advice given by one of their best scouts, Johnny Nee. He did not reach the ML's until he was 27 years old, but in his rookie season of 1932, Johnny led AL pitchers in winning percentage (.810, 17-4).

WINNING PITCHER: Over his four Yankee seasons, Johnny compiled a tremendous .725 winning percentage. His ML lifetime winning percentage (.654) is the 11th highest in baseball history. Johnny was a great competitor and a man who dreaded losing a game. (Once, while pitching for the Indians, Johnny tore up his room at the Wardman Park Hotel in Washington after a tough loss and the club was asked to leave.)

BAD TEMPER: Johnny was a hotheaded person. On the mound he was a mean, rough and tough character and hitters seldom dug in against him. Off the mound he was sometimes a wild character, especially when he was not sober. Although he was both a great pitcher and competitor, Johnny's terrible temper occasionally got him into trouble. In his early childhood, Johnny grew up in a North Carolina orphanage as a fighter. Later, he fought the other team, his teammates, the umpires and himself. Johnny's great "stuff" as a pitcher allowed him to stay in the ML's when teams would not have stood for his conduct. (Joe McCarthy traded Johnny for just such a reason.)

GREATEST GAME: In a contest played on June 4, 1933, Johnny allowed a first-inning hit against the Philadelphia Athletics. But the A's failed to make another safety in the entire game and Johnny had a nifty 6-0 win on a one-hitter.

TRADED: In December of 1935, the Yanks traded Johnny to Cleveland for pitchers Monte Pearson and Steve Sundra. For the Indians, Johnny pitched exceptional baseball, including the seasons of 1936 (20-10) and 1937 (15-1).

ALLEN, JOHNNY

Yr.	W-L	Pct.	SA	G	GS	CG	IP	H	BB	SO	SH	ERA
1932	17-4	.810	4	33	21	13	192	162	76	109	3	3.70
1933	15-7	.682	1	25	24	10	185	171	87	119	1	4.39
1934	5-2	.714	0	13	10	4	72	62	32	54	0	2.89
1935	13-6	.684	0	23	23	12	167	149	58	113	2	3.61
4 Yrs.	50-19	.725	5	94	78	49	615	544	253	395	6	3.79
Life.	142-75	.654	18	352	241	109	1950	1849	738	1070	17	3.75

World Series

Yr.	G	IP	BB	SO	H	W-L	SA
1932	1	⅔	0	0	5	0-0	0
1 Yr.	1	⅔	0	0	5	0-0	0
Life.	4	1⅓	3	0	6	0-0	0

ARROYO, LUIS

Nicknames: "Yo-Yo" "Little Roundie"
Yankee: 1960-63
Pitcher
Born: February 18, 1927
Birthplace: Penuelas, Puerto Rico
Bat: L; Throw: L
Ht: 5'8"; Wt: 178

CAME TO YANKS: Luis began his professional career in 1948 and played with sporadic success on three different NL teams. He was having a successful 1960 season with the Cincinnati Reds' International League farm team at Jersey City (the team had just relocated from Havana, Cuba due to the unrest caused by the Castro regime) when Yankee scouts saw him pitch against the Yanks' Richmond club in that league. They were impressed with Luis and the trade was made to bring Luis to the Yanks. (By the way, Luis was 9-7 with a 2.27 ERA at Jersey City).

HONORS: *The Sporting News* named Luis AL Fireman of the Year in 1961. He was selected to the AL All-Star team for the 1961 All-Star Games.

1961 SEASON: This was a sensational year for the cigar-smoking little relief pitcher. He led AL pitchers in games pitched (65), saves (29) and games won in relief (15). Only once has a Yankee pitcher saved more games in a season than Luis did in 1961. Many of his saves benefited Whitey Ford who also had a great year. Luis' total of saves plus wins (44) is the fourth highest in baseball history. From July 1 through September 9, 1961, he won 12 consecutive games in relief, an AL record. His

LUIS ARROYO (New York Yankees Archives)

screwball was almost unhittable in 1961. In Game 3 of the 1961 World Series, Luis was the winning pitcher, hurling the last two innings of a 3-2 victory against Cincinnati.

ALL-TIME YANKEE LEADER: Luis is tied for tenth, with Ryne Duren, on the all-time Yankee save list (43).

LATE YANKEE CAREER: In May of 1962, Luis came up with a bad arm and went on the Disabled List. He was never again the same.

RETIREMENT: Luis retired as a player following the 1963 season. He continues to scout for the Yankees in Puerto Rico, a position he has held for the club for many years.

ARROYO, LUIS

Yr.	W-L	Pct.	SA	G	GS	CG	IP	H	BB	SO	SH	ERA
1960	5-1	.833	7	29	0	0	41	30	22	29	0	2.88
1961	15-5	.750	29	65	0	0	119	83	49	87	0	2.19
1962	1-3	.250	7	27	0	0	34	33	17	21	0	4.81
1963	1-1	.500	0	6	0	0	6	12	3	5	0	13.50
4 Yrs.	22-10	.688	43	127	0	0	199	158	91	142	0	3.12
Life.	40-32	.556	44	244	36	10	531	524	208	336	1	3.93

World Series

Yr.	G	IP	BB	SO	H	W-L	SA
1960	1	⅔	0	1	2	0-0	0
1961	2	4	2	3	4	1-0	0
2 Yrs.	3	4⅔	2	4	6	1-0	0
Life. Same.							

BAHNSEN, STAN

Yankee: 1966,'68-71
Pitcher
Born: December 15, 1944
Birthplace: Council Bluffs, IA
Bat: R; Throw: R
Ht: 6'2"; Wt: 185

HONORS: Stan won a number of awards after his great rookie season in 1968. He was selected AL Rookie of the Year by the Baseball Writers, named AL Rookie Pitcher of the Year by *The Sporting News* and picked as the right-handed pitcher on the ML Rookie All-Star team selected by Topps Chewing Gum.

YOUNG PROSPECT: Stan was a hot prospect as a college ballplayer at the University of Nebraska. In 1965 he received an estimated $30,000 bonus to sign with the Yanks. (The Yanks had selected Stan in the third round of the June 1965 amateur draft.)

MINOR LEAGUER: In 1965 Stan was 2-2 for the Yanks' Columbus (GA) club in the Southern League. In 1966 he was 10-7 for Toledo of the International League and pitched a seven-inning no-hitter against Richmond, winning 1-0. He ended the 1966 season pitching in four games for the Yanks (1-1). Pitching for Syracuse of the I.L. in 1967, Stan was 9-11 and pitched a seven-inning perfect game against Buffalo, winning 8-0.

STAR PITCHER: In 1968, Stan immediately became a Yankee star. He pitched more than 200 innings in four straight seasons (1968-71) for the Yanks. Along with Mel Stottlemyre

and Fritz Peterson, Stan formed the Yanks' "big three" from 1968-71. In the 1971 Yankee Stadium home opener, Stan beat Detroit, 5-2. Stan's ranks 12th in ERA (3.10) in Yankee history.

CLUB LEADERSHIP: In 1968 Stan led Yankee pitchers in strikeouts (162) and ERA (2.05).

TRADED: The Yanks traded Stan to the White Sox for infielder Rich McKinney in December 1971. This was a lousy trade for the Yankees, as Stan won 21 games for Chicago in 1972 and continued pitching through 1982.

BAHNSEN, STAN

Yr.	W-L	Pct.	SA	G	GS	CG	IP	H	BB	SO	SH	ERA
1966	1-1	.500	1	4	3	1	23	15	7	16	0	3.52
1968	17-12	.586	0	37	34	10	267	216	68	162	1	2.05
1969	9-16	.360	1	40	33	5	221	222	90	130	2	3.83
1970	14-11	.560	0	36	35	6	233	227	75	116	2	3.33
1971	14-12	.538	0	36	34	14	242	221	72	110	3	3.35
5 Yrs.	55-52	.514	2	153	139	36	986	901	312	534	8	3.10
Life.	146-149	.495	20	574	327	73	2529	2440	924	1359	16	3.60

BAKER, FRANK
(BORN JOHN FRANKLIN BAKER)

Nickname: "Home Run"
Yankee: 1916-19 (retired) '21-22
Third Baseman
Born: March 13, 1886
Birthplace: Trappe, MD
Died: June 28, 1963
Bat: L; Throw: R
Ht: 5'11"; Wt: 173

HONORS: In 1955, Frank was inducted into the Baseball Hall of Fame.

CAME TO YANKS: Frank, the best third baseman in the AL, sat out the entire 1915 season while bound to the Philadelphia A's. In February of 1916, the Yanks bought Frank's contract from the A's for $35,000-40,000.

YANKEE THIRD BASEMAN: From 1916-19 Frank was the Yanks' regular third baseman. He retired after the 1919 season to return to his farm, missing the entire 1920 season. Frank rejoined the Yanks in 1921 and played more games at third base than any other Yankee, helping the club win its first AL pennant. Injured much of the 1922 season, Frank was a reserve third sacker. For a third baseman, Frank ran well. In 1922 his Yankee salary was $16,000, the second highest on the club behind Babe Ruth. Connie Mack picked Frank as his third baseman on Mack's all-time All-Star team, a real tribute.

DEFENSIVE ABILITIES: Frank was one of the best fielders of his era. He was awkward-looking and bowlegged but he made the tough plays look easy and had a great arm. In 1917 he led AL third basemen in putouts (202) and assists (317). In 1918 Frank paced AL third basemen in fielding (.972) and putouts (175). In 1919 he led the AL at his position in putouts (176) and double plays (28). Frank made 11 assists in a 19-inning game played on May 24, 1918, an AL record for third basemen in extra-inning games. Frank is seventh on the all-time third basemen's putout list (2154) and 12th on the total chance list (5631).

CLUB LEADERSHIP: Twice Frank led the Yanks in games played (1918-19), at-bats (1918-19), doubles (1916, 1918), HRs (1918-19), RBIs (1917-18) and slugging (1916, 1918). Three years in a row, Frank led the Yanks in hits (1917-19) and batting (1916-18). His 65 runs scored in 1918 tied for club leadership.

RETIREMENT: Following the 1922 season, Frank retired from baseball, this time for good.

THE LEGEND: Today Frank is thought of as one of the true legends of the game, and his name is always quickly mentioned whenever great third basemen are discussed. And rightfully so. However, Yankee fans should realize that Frank's best playing days were in Philadelphia. Frank was a member of Connie Mack's famous $100,000 infield. He was tagged "Home Run" after hitting game-winning HRs against the Giants in two games of the 1911 World Series, playing for the A's. But the pride Frank developed in Philadelphia playing on four AL champion teams was brought with him to New York and proved invaluable.

Hank Bauer (New York Yankees Archives)

BAKER FRANK

Yr.	G	AB	R	H	2B	3B	HR	RBI	BB	SB	BA	SA
1916	100	360	46	97	23	2	10	52	36	15	.269	.428
1917	146	553	57	156	24	2	6	71	48	18	.282	.365
1918	126	504	65	154	24	5	6	62	38	8	.306	.409
1919	141	567	70	166	22	1	10	83	44	13	.293	.388
1921	94	330	46	97	16	2	9	71	26	8	.294	.436
1922	69	234	30	65	12	3	7	36	15	1	.278	.444
6 Yrs.	676	2548	314	735	121	15	48	375	207	63	.288	.404
Life.	1575	5984	887	1838	315	103	96	987	473	235	.307	.442

World Series

Yr.	G	AB	R	H	2B	3B	HR	RBI	BA
1921	4	8	0	2	0	0	0	0	.250
1922	1	1	0	0	0	0	0	0	.000
2 Yrs.	5	9	0	2	0	0	0	0	.222
Life.	25	91	15	33	7	0	3	18	.363

BAUER, HANK
(BORN HENRY ALBERT BAUER)

Nickname: "Bruiser"
Yankee: 1948-59
Outfielder
Born: July 31, 1922
Birthplace: East St. Louis, IL
Bat: R; Throw: R
Ht: 6'; Wt: 192

HONORS: In 1959, the New York Baseball Writers gave Hank their Ben Epstein "Good Guy" Award. Hank was selected to the AL team for All-Star Games in three consecutive years (1952-54).

PROSPECT AND MILITARY SERVICE: Hank in 1941 signed with the Yanks and played in the minors at Grand Forks, N.D. In January of 1942, he enlisted in the Marines. He was wounded

in some of World War II's most fierce fighting (on Okinawa). When Hank was discharged from the Marines in January of 1946, he went to work as an iron worker and played baseball for a semi-pro team in his hometown of East St. Louis, IL.

MINOR LEAGUER: On the recommendation of Yankee scout Tom Greenwade, Frank Lane gave Hank a $200 bonus to resume his minor league career in 1946 at Quincy, IL. Lane, the club's general manager, converted Hank from a catcher into an outfielder. (Hank also pitched and played the infield in the minors.) After a good year at Quincy, Hank was promoted to the Yanks' Class-AAA club at Kansas City where he enjoyed two more productive years.

FIRST YANKEE GAME: On the day before Labor Day in 1948, the Yanks called Hank up to the big club. Before some 60,000 fans in Yankee Stadium, Hank stroked three singles in his first three ML at-bats!

GOOD POWER: Hank hit with good power, blasting 158 HRs as a Yankee player, the fifth most ever hit by a Yankee right-handed batter. So many of his long hits (and long outs) would have been HRs in other parks, but Yankee Stadium's "Death Valley" (left center field power alley) is tough on right-handed hitters. Hank was placed throughout the Yankee lineup by Casey Stengel, but early in his prime he often batted third and late in his prime he often batted first. (Stengel was fond of lead-off HRs.)

HEART AND SOUL: Hank gave 100% every time he stepped onto a baseball field. He was a tough performer, but he played the game cleanly. No one ever barreled into second base to break up a double play any harder. His burning desire to win made Hank a clutch performer, and Hank believed winning is what made baseball fun. As a result, he played on nine AL champions in his 12 Yankee seasons, and he was pivotal to the Yanks' success. As Casey Stengel liked to point out, Hank was not a player who would make a run, then give one back. Hank was the complete player—he was consistently reliable in the field and ran well. Hank's statistical record proves he played much more than his reputation as a "platooned player" suggests.

NATURAL LEADER: The former Marine was a natural leader on the great Yankee teams of the 1950s. If a Yankee loafed on the field, Hank was the first one to straighten him out. (Hank's economic fortunes depended on his teammates also giving 100% effort, and he forcefully reminded some of this fact from time to time.) Hank's manly face was often described as resembling a "clenched fist" (first used by sportswriter Jim Murray). He was a great influence on young Mickey Mantle, taking the country lad under his wing. Early in Mantle's career, he shared a Manhattan apartment with Hank and Johnny Hopp, and Hank helped Mickey become accustomed to being a ML player. On the field, Mantle admired Hank's desire, hustle and complete unwillingness to quit regardless of the score or situation. In 1955 Hank got behind the plate and caught a game for the Yanks.

CLUB LEADERSHIP: Three times Hank led the Yanks in triples, and in 1957 he tied for the AL high in triples (nine). In 1956 he led the Yanks in at-bats (539). In 1958 he tied for club leadership in doubles (22).

WORLD SERIES: From Game 1 of the 1956 Series through Game 3 of the 1958 Series, Hank hit in 17 consecutive Series games. That is an incredible World Series record, especially considering Series pressure, and one that is given too little attention. He got a key three-run triple and made a game-saving catch in Game 6, the final game of the 1951 Series. Hank knocked in all four Yankee runs in a 4-0 victory over the Milwaukee Braves in Game 3 of the 1958 Series. In that 1958 Series, Hank hit four HRs! He is among the leaders in most lifetime offensive categories in Series play, including being fourth in games played (53); fifth in hits (46); and sixth in at-bats (188).

ALL-TIME YANKEE LEADER: On the top 20 All-Time Yankee list, Hank places 18th with runs scored (792), 20th in both games played (1406) and triples (56).

TRADED: In December, 1959, Hank and Norm Siebern, Don Larsen and Marv Throneberry were traded to the Kansas City A's for Roger Maris, Joe DeMaestri and Kent Hadley.

RESPECTED MANAGER: After his playing days were over, Hank was an AL manager at Kansas City, Baltimore and Oakland. He won the 1966 World Championship as the Oriole manager and was named Major League Manager of the Year by *The Sporting News.* He was also Minor League Manager of the Year at Tidewater in 1972.

BAUER, HANK

Yr.	G	AB	R	H	2B	3B	HR	RBI	BB	SB	BA	SA
1948	19	50	9	9	1	1	1	9	6	1	.180	.300
1949	103	301	56	82	6	6	10	45	37	2	.272	.432
1950	113	415	72	133	16	2	13	70	35	2	.320	.463
1951	118	348	53	103	19	3	10	54	42	5	.296	.454
1952	141	553	86	162	31	6	17	74	50	6	.293	.463
1953	133	437	77	133	20	6	10	57	59	2	.304	.446
1954	114	377	73	111	16	5	12	54	40	4	.294	.459
1955	139	492	97	137	20	5	20	53	56	8	.278	.461
1956	147	539	96	130	18	7	26	84	59	4	.241	.445
1957	137	479	70	124	22	9	18	65	42	7	.259	.455
1958	128	452	62	121	22	6	12	50	32	3	.268	.423
1959	114	341	44	81	20	0	9	39	33	4	.238	.375
12 Yrs.	1406	4784	792	1326	211	56	158	654	491	48	.277	.444
Life.	1544	5145	833	1424	229	57	164	703	521	50	.277	.439

World Series

Yr.	G	AB	R	H	2B	3B	HR	RBI	BA
1949	3	6	0	1	0	0	0	0	.167
1950	4	15	0	2	0	0	0	1	.133
1951	6	18	0	3	0	1	0	3	.167
1952	7	18	2	1	0	0	0	1	.056
1953	6	23	6	6	0	1	0	1	.261
1955	6	14	1	6	0	0	0	1	.429
1956	7	32	3	9	0	0	1	3	.281
1957	7	31	3	8	2	1	2	6	.258
1958	7	31	6	10	0	0	4	8	.323
9 Yrs.	53	188	21	46	2	3	7	24	.245
Life.	Same.								

BAYLOR, DON

Yankee: 1983-85
Designated Hitter, 1B, OF
Born: June 28, 1949
Birthplace: Austin, TX
Bat: R; Throw: R
Ht: 6'11"; Wt: 190

EARLY ML CAREER: Don was one of the great prospects in the Orioles' organization; he broke in with Baltimore in 1970 but didn't start hitting HRs until 1975. He was traded to Oakland in a trade that brought Reggie Jackson to Baltimore in 1976. He reached his potential with the Angels (1977-82), and in his MVP season in 1979, he hit 36 HRs and led the AL in RBIs (139) and runs (120).

FREE AGENT: As a free agent, Don signed with the Yankees, December 1982. The Yanks had lacked power in 1981; Don gave them a powerful DH bat, and speed, and he brought a reputation as a fierce competitor and leader. He broke up double plays with hard slides into second base. He was also a good citizen and in 1985 won the Roberto Clemente Award for humanitarian service.

HIT BY PITCH: Don led the Yankees in most hit by pitched balls in 1983 (13), 1984 (23) and 1985 (24). In 1984, he broke the Yankee record with 18 hit by pitches (HBP), set by Bert Daniels in 1912 and 1913. In 1986, he broke the AL record for HBPs when he was with the Red Sox. Don on August 29, 1985, set the career AL record with his 190th HBP, breaking the record held by Minnie Minoso. Don would finish his career with the ML career record for HBP (267). Pitchers often tried to pitch tight and drive Don off the plate, but he wouldn't budge, and he rarely showed any pain after a HBP.

OFFENSIVE STAR: In 1983, Don led the Yankees in doubles (33), stolen bases (17), and batting (.303); he batted .323 in the second half to reach .300 for the first time in his career. Won Silver Bat Award as DH in AL in 1983. In 1984, Don led the Yanks in HRs (27).

UNHAPPY 1985 SEASON: Don was the regular DH, April through July, and then platooned with Dan Pasqua in August and September; through July 31, Don was hitting .246 with 18 HRs and 67 RBIs, but the rest of the year he hit only .203 with five HRs and 24 RBIs. Don in 1985 was selected to *The Sporting News* AL All-Star team as the DH, but he hit only .216 vs. right-handers, .216 at Yankee Stadium and .206 vs. first-place Toronto. Don was particularly unhappy on April 28 when Yogi Berra was replaced by Billy Martin as manager; Don was so angry he kicked a trash can across the clubhouse. Don was also angry in September when George Steinbrenner said "my big guys aren't coming through."

TRADED: In March of 1986, the Yankees traded Don to the Red Sox for Mike Easler in an even exchange of DHs. After coaching stops in Milwaukee and St. Louis from 1990-92, he was named as the first manager of the 1993 NL expansion team in Colorado. He led the Rockies to a playoff berth in just three seasons, and was named NL Manager of the Year in 1995. After another coaching stop in Atlanta, Don managed the Chicago Cubs from 2000 through the mid-2002 seasons.

BAYLOR, DON

Yr.	G	AB	R	H	2B	3B	HR	RBI	BB	SB	BA	SA
1983	144	534	82	162	33	3	21	85	40	17	.303	.494
1984	134	493	84	129	29	1	27	89	38	1	.262	.489
1985	142	477	70	110	24	1	23	91	52	0	.231	.430
3 Yrs.	420	1504	236	401	86	5	71	265	130	18	.267	.472
Life.	2292	8198	1236	2135	366	28	338	1276	805	285	.260	.436

BERRA, YOGI
(BORN LAWRENCE PETER BERRA)

Yankee: 1946-63
Catcher, OF
Born: May 12, 1925
Birthplace: St. Louis, MO
Bat: L; Throw: R
Ht: 5'8"; Wt: 195

HONORS: Yogi was inducted into the Baseball Hall of Fame in 1972. The Baseball Writers named Yogi the MVP of the AL in three seasons (1951, 1954, 1955). *The Sporting News* selected him to the publication's ML All-Star team in 1950, 1952, 1954, 1956 and 1957, recognizing Yogi as the best catcher in baseball. In January of 1954, the New York Athletic Club named Yogi "The Top Professional Athlete" in New Jersey, the state Yogi elected to make his home. In 1954 Yogi was named "The Top Professional Athlete" of the New York Metropolitan area by the New York Chapter of the B'nai B'rith. In 1959 Yogi was voted the "Most Popular Yankee Player" for the second time by the Catholic Youth Organization of the New York area. Although Yogi was not with the Yanks at the time, in 1967 the New York Chapter of the Baseball Writers gave Yogi the William J. Slocum Award. After Yogi's Yankee playing days were over, his number "8" uniform (also worn by Bill Dickey) was retired. Yogi is honored as a member of the Italian-American Sports Hall of Fame

located in Elmwood Park, Ill.

ST. LOUIS KID: Larry Berra grew up as a poor kid in an Italian section of St. Louis known as "The Hill," playing baseball as often as possible with his buddies, including Joe Garagiola. The neighborhood kids saw a movie in which a character named "Yogi" reminded them of Larry whom they began to call Yogi. To the kids a "Yogi" was considered an unusual character, but to Yankee fans in later years, the word "Yogi" meant a great baseball player. (During his early Yankee days, Berra was known to the public as both Larry and Yogi.) When Yogi became of professional baseball age, both hometown St. Louis clubs, the Browns and Cardinals, made mistakes concerning Yogi. The Browns felt he lacked ability and the Cardinals' Branch Rickey, who gave Garagiola a $500 signing bonus, refused to give Yogi the same bonus. Rickey felt Yogi was too slow and awkward to invest much money in him and told Yogi, "You'll never be a ballplayer. Take my advice, son, and forget about baseball. Get into some other kind of business." (There are some who believe that Rickey gambled and lost; that he knew he was about to join the Dodgers and wanted Yogi for Brooklyn. But most baseball people feel Rickey had too much integrity for such a maneuver. As great a baseball man as Rickey was, he just made a mistake on Yogi.)

YANKEE SIGNING: After being snubbed by the St. Louis teams, a frustrated Yogi went to work pulling tacks at a shoe factory. But Leo Browne, the head of the American Legion baseball program in St. Louis, was convinced of Yogi's ability and contacted George Weiss, then the Yanks' farm director. Weiss sent Yankee coach Johnny Schulte to check Yogi and without seeing Yogi play, Schulte signed Yogi to a salary of $90 a month and gave Yogi the same $500 signing bonus that the Cardinals had given to Garagiola. Schulte was willing to sign Yogi after receiving great scouting reports from all he asked about the youngster. Just before leaving for his first minor league spring training camp in 1943, Yogi received a telegram from Brooklyn GM Branch Rickey asking Yogi to report to the Dodger camp where he would receive a contract and bonus. But Mr. Rickey learned it was too late!

YOUNG PROSPECT: After playing for the Yanks' Norfolk farm club of the Piedmont League in 1943 (seven HRs, 56 RBIs, .253 in 111 games), Yogi enlisted in the Navy in 1944 and saw D-Day action. Thereafter, he returned to base at New London, CT, and played baseball against good competition. Yogi was discharged from the Navy in 1946 and reported to the Yanks' Newark club of the International League. He had a great season (.314,15 HRs, 59 RBIs in only 277 at-bats). The Yanks called up the 21-year-old prospect late in the 1946 season and Yogi hit .364 in the season's final days. Yogi hit a HR at Yankee Stadium in his first ML at-bat. It came off the A's Jesse Flores and from his box Larry MacPhail was heard to shout, "And Mel Ott wanted me to sell him for $50,000!" (The Giants had made an attempt to purchase Yogi when he was playing in the Yankee minors.)

YANKEE CATCHER: Yogi got into only seven Yankee games in 1946. In 1947 Yogi shared Yankee catching chores with Aaron Robinson. Yogi caught 51 games and played 24 games in the outfield. In 1948 he split catching duties with Gus Niarhos. Yogi caught 71 games and played 50 games as an outfielder. From

From left to right: Roy Campanella, Yogi Berra, George "Birdie" Tebbetts, and Andy Seminick. All pose for the photographers prior to the 1949 All-Star Game played at Ebbets Field, Brooklyn on July 12. All four catchers played in the game.

1949-59 he was the regular Yankee catcher. From 1960-62, Yogi played catcher and left field. In 1963 he was a catcher and pinch-hitter. Yogi played his entire ML career with the Yanks except for four games he played with the Mets in 1965.

BILL DICKEY'S PUPIL: In Yogi's first two complete Yankee seasons (1947-48), he was not a good defensive catcher. When Casey Stengel became Yankee manager in 1949, he hired Bill Dickey to teach Yogi the art of catching. Yogi worked hard to make himself a great defensive catcher, with a lot of help from Dickey. The two worked hard for many hours.

DEFENSIVE ABILITIES AS CATCHER: Yogi made himself a great catcher by learning all aspects of the position. In Yogi's first few years, Stengel or Jim Turner called pitches for Yogi. But by 1952, Yogi was calling signals and outsmarting hitters. No one ever called signals better than did Yogi. He caught three no-hitters, a pair by Allie Reynolds in 1951 and the perfect game tossed by Don Larsen in the 1956 World Series. Both Reynolds and Larsen credited Yogi for calling the no-hitters. In 1951 Yogi made 25 double plays as a catcher, the most in Yankee history by a catcher and the fourth highest total in baseball history. From July 28,1957 - May 10, 1959, Yogi set a ML record by catching 148 consecutive games without making

an error. He accepted 950 chances during that streak, also a ML record. Eight times Yogi led AL catchers in games caught (1950-57) and chances accepted (1950-52, '54-57, '59), both AL records. Six times he led AL catchers in double plays (1949-52, '54, '56), an AL record. Yogi is third on the all-time double play list for catchers (175). His 8738 putouts and 9629 chances behind the plate rank 12th for all the catchers in baseball history. The 1699 games he caught ranks 14th in baseball history. Yogi is one of only four catchers to ever field 1.000 for a season (1958). He made two unassisted double plays as a catcher, another AL record. On June 15, 1947 he pulled it against the Browns and did it again against the A's on August 17, 1962.

DEFENSIVE ABILITIES AS LEFTFIELDER: Yogi, a great athlete, was a surprisingly good defensive outfielder, especially late in his career. He played a fine left field. In September of 1961, the Yanks and the second-place Tigers played a crucial series that Detroit needed to win to remain in the pennant race. When Yogi made a miraculous catch to rob Al Kaline of an extra-base hit to left field, a Yankee win was saved and the Tigers' hopes died.

RESPECTED STAR: Many baseball experts and fans felt Yogi was the best player of the 1950s. Famous manager Paul Richards once said, "Berra is the toughest man in baseball, when the game is up for grabs. He is by far the toughest man in the league in the last three innings." Before the start of the 1960 World Series, Pirate Manager Danny Murtaugh observed, "Sure, the Yankees have some big bats in Mantle, Skowron and Howard. But the man we'll worry about most is Yogi Berra."

TIRELESS PERFORMER: Early in his Yankee career, Yogi ducked out of an occasional game when he was tired and was scolded once by Yankee veterans who let Yogi know that the team needed him. From then on Yogi was a tireless player. During the 1950s he caught more than 115 games in every season except 1958 and it was almost impossible to get him to take a day off. He knew the team needed him behind the plate, and being the heart of the team, Yogi was dependable. Even late in his career, Yogi worked long, hard hours. Although he caught only 31 games in 1962 at the age of 37, he caught the entire 22 innings of the famous June 24 marathon game against the Tigers that took seven hours to complete, an AL record. Until that contest, Yogi had not played a game behind the plate all season! In 1949 Yogi played part of the season with a broken thumb. He was a ballplayer's player and an innovative one, too. Yogi was the first catcher to leave a finger outside his catcher's mitt and most catchers followed his example.

RESPONSIBLE CATCHER: As unofficial captain of the Yanks during the 1950s, Yogi took much of the responsibility of Yankee pitching success upon his shoulders. He treated each pitcher differently—some he goaded, some he babied. And Yogi was very protective of young pitchers. After his passed ball in Game 3 of the 1952 World Series, allowing two runs to score in a tough Yankee loss, Yogi protected his young pitcher, Tom Gorman, who had appeared to throw a pitch that was not signaled for. Yogi told the press, "Gorman didn't do nothing wrong. He didn't cross me up, and don't none of you guys believe him if he says he did. I messed up the play. Blame me, not him." The following spring Gorman said of Yogi's support, "It was the most generous thing anyone ever did for me. Up until now, no one would believe me—including Casey. Yogi told him not to listen to me. But I knew what he was doing. He was trying to protect a young kid like me from being branded a goat, as unselfish an act as I've ever experienced. I crossed him up. The blame was mine, not Yogi's."

GREAT HITTER: Yogi hit 30 HRs in 1952 and 1956, the most ever hit by a catcher in the AL at that time. With the Yanks trailing the Indians by a half game on September 16, 1955, the Yanks beat the Red Sox, 5-4, on Yogi's ninth-inning HR. The Indians lost and the Yanks went into first place for good. In seven consecutive years Yogi led the Yanks in RBIs (1949-55). Three times he led the club in at-bats, doubles, and HRs. Twice he led the team in games played, runs, hits and slugging. The 313 HRs Yogi hit as a catcher was the AL record for catchers until broken by Carlton Fisk in the 1990s. Yogi was one of the greatest clutch hitters of all time. He was probably the best bad-ball hitter (along with Roberto Clemente) in history. He swung at anything that looked good to him because he was aggressive at the plate. Fred Hutchinson once overheard someone calling Yogi a bad-ball hitter and remarked, "Yogi's a bad-ball hitter, all right. But don't ever throw him a good one." In 1950 Yogi struck out only 12 times in 597 at-bats!

Yogi Berra served the Yanks as a player, as a coach and manager. (New York Yankees Archives)

SEPTEMBER-OCTOBER STAR: Yogi played his best baseball when it counted the most, down the pennant stretch and in the World Series. He was a leader, a clutch hitter and a source of strength when things got sticky in the heat of a big game. Yogi was recognized around baseball during his era as the man most likely to respond favorably in a pressure situation, and he was involved in many. Yogi played on 10 World Championship teams. No one else in baseball history can say as much.

FUNNY GUY: There is no question that Yogi was one of the most popular people ever to wear a baseball uniform and has been a national celebrity for almost 35 years. Yogi says things that naturally come out funny, and Yankee fans and all of America have enjoyed his remarks, known as "Yogi-isms," for years. However, when Yogi first reached the Yanks, he had to overcome a barrage of ugly remarks from opposing players, fans and the press concerning his features, habits and manner of speaking. When Yogi talked, he did so good-naturedly. But his adversaries were cruel. Yogi's remarks are considered humorous, yet all somehow make sense. When asked about Bill Dickey's tutoring, Yogi replied, "Dickey is learning me his experiences." In 1947 the people of St. Louis held a "Yogi Berra Night" before the Brown-Yankee game and Yogi told the crowd, "I want to thank everyone for making this night necessary." Yogi overcame the unkind reaction to some of his remarks by going along with the joke. Soon a nation loved him. Casey Stengel put it best when he said of Yogi, "They say he's funny.

Well, he has a lovely wife and family, a beautiful home, money in the bank, and he plays golf with millionaires. What's funny about that?" Stengel greatly respected Yogi, often saying he felt only Joe DiMaggio was a better player of all those he ever managed. Casey once said of Yogi, "To me he is a great man. I am lucky to have him and so are my pitchers. He springs on a bunt like it was another dollar." Yogi is a shrewd and successful businessman. Among his many profitable enterprises was the bowling alley he owned in Clifton, NJ, with Phil Rizzuto.

ALL-TIME YANKEE LEADER: Yogi is among the Top 10 in most Yankee All-Time categories through 2002. Yogi places third in both games played (2116) and at-bats (7546), fifth in homers (358) and RBI (1430), sixth in runs (1174) and hits (2148) and tenth in doubles (321). Yogi's nine pinch-hit homers put him in first place for most ever hit by a Yankee.

ALL-STAR GAME: In every season between 1948-62, Yogi was selected to the AL team for the All-Star Game. He hit a HR in the second 1959 All-Star Game.

WORLD SERIES: Yogi has played in more World Series (14) than anyone else in history. He is first on the World Series games played (75), at-bat (259), hit (71) and double (10) lists and he is among the leaders in many other categories. In Game 3 of the 1947 Series Yogi hit the first pinch-hit HR in Series history. He hit a big HR in Game 4, the final game of the 1950 Series. In Game 2 of the 1956 Series Yogi hit the fifth grand slam HR in Series history in a 13-8 Yankee loss to the Dodgers. He hit two clutch HRs to help the Yanks beat the Dodgers in Game 7 of the 1956 Series, 9-0. In Game 5 of the 1956 Series Yogi caught Don Larsen's perfect game. In a losing cause Yogi hit a three-run HR in Game 7 of the 1960 Series. Yogi hit at least one HR in nine World Series, a record he holds with Mickey Mantle. He knocked in at least one run in 11 Series, a Series record. He scored at least one run in 12 Series, also a Series record. He walked at least once in 13 Series, another Series record. Yogi threw out 36 attempted base-stealers in Series play, another Series record.

MANAGER AND COACH: Yogi was a player-coach on the Yanks in 1963. He was the Yanks' manager in 1964 and won the AL pennant, but he was fired after losing the World Series. Yogi in 1965 joined the Mets as a coach under Casey Stengel, and even played in four games. Yogi continued as a Mets coach until he was promoted to manager in 1972; he won the NL pennant in 1973 and was fired in 1975. In 1976, Yogi returned to the Yanks as a coach for Billy Martin, and he remained as coach until managing the Yanks in 1984 and the first few weeks of 1985. When Yogi was fired in 1985, he left the club bitterly. He finished his career in baseball as a coach for the Houston Astros, from 1986-89.

YOGI RETURNS TO YANKEE STADIUM: Shunning all activities at Yankee Stadium for 14 long years due to a bitter disagreement between Yogi and Yankee Principal Owner, George Steinbrenner, Berra was willing to put the past behind him when asked to throw out the first pitch of the April 9,1999 game. (Remember, that it was Steinbrenner's original idea to have DiMaggio throw out this first pitch, but Joe's death opened the door for Yogi to do it.) In a truly emotional moment,

Yogi and George shared many embraces and, indeed, Berra's physical presence on the Yankee mound put a closure to a situation that could finally be healed, thus promoting an even greater closeness within the Yankee family. The contest, witnessed by a sellout crowd of 56,583, was eventually called after 6½ innings due to rain, but the weather surely could not dampen the feelings that were evident that day between Berra and Steinbrenner. Thank you Yogi and George for extending your hearts to one another! Forgiveness is wonderful!

BERRA, YOGI

Yr.	G	AB	R	H	2B	3B	HR	RBI	BB	SB	BA	SA
1946	7	22	3	8	1	0	2	4	1	0	.364	.682
1947	83	293	41	82	15	3	11	54	13	0	.280	.464
1948	125	469	70	143	24	10	14	98	25	3	.305	.488
1949	116	415	59	115	20	2	20	91	22	2	.277	.480
1950	151	597	116	192	30	6	28	124	55	4	.322	.533
1951	141	547	92	161	19	4	27	88	44	5	.294	.492
1952	142	534	97	146	17	1	30	98	66	2	.273	.478
1953	137	503	80	149	23	5	27	108	50	0	.296	.523
1954	151	584	88	179	28	6	22	125	56	0	.307	.488
1955	147	541	84	147	20	3	27	108	60	1	.272	.470
1956	140	521	93	155	29	2	30	105	65	3	.298	.534
1957	134	482	74	121	14	2	24	82	57	1	.251	.438
1958	122	433	60	115	17	3	22	90	35	3	.266	.471
1959	131	472	64	134	25	1	19	69	43	1	.284	.462
1960	120	359	46	99	14	1	15	62	38	2	.276	.446
1961	119	395	62	107	11	0	22	61	35	2	.271	.466
1962	86	232	25	52	8	0	10	35	24	0	.224	.388
1963	64	147	20	43	6	0	8	28	15	1	.293	.497
18 Yrs.	2116	7546	1174	2148	321	49	358	1430	704	30	.285	.483
Life.	2120	7555	1175	2150	321	49	358	1430	704	30	.285	.482

(4 games as a Met in 1965)

World Series

YR.	G	AB	R	H	2B	3B	HR	RBI	BA
1947	6	19	2	3	0	0	1	2	.158
1949	4	16	2	1	0	0	0	1	.063
1950	4	15	2	3	0	0	1	2	.200
1951	6	23	4	6	1	0	0	0	.261
1952	7	28	2	6	1	0	2	3	.214
1953	6	21	3	9	1	0	1	4	.429
1955	7	24	5	10	1	0	1	2	.417
1956	7	25	5	9	2	0	3	10	.360
1957	7	25	5	8	1	0	1	2	.320
1958	7	27	3	6	3	0	0	2	.222
1960	7	22	6	7	0	0	1	8	.318
1961	4	11	2	3	0	0	1	3	.273
1962	2	2	0	0	0	0	0	0	.000
1963	1	1	0	0	0	0	0	0	.000
14 Yrs.	75	259	41	71	10	0	12	39	.274

BEVENS, BILL
(BORN FLOYD CLIFFORD BEVENS)

Yankee: 1944-47
Pitcher
Born: October 21, 1916
Birthplace: Hubbard, OR
Died: October 26, 1991
Bat: R; Throw: R
Ht: 6'3"; Wt: 210

YANKEE STARTER: Bill pitched his entire ML career with the Yanks. He was the ace of the 1945 Yankee pitching staff when he led the club in wins (13), games started (25), complete games (14), innings pitched (184), strikeouts (76), and shut-outs (2). Bill was the Yanks' No. 2 starter and the second most effective hurler (16-13) on the 1946 staff, behind Spud Chandler. He was the No. 3 starter on the 1947 Yanks.

1947 WORLD SERIES: Bill played the lead role in one of the most dramatic scenes in baseball history—Game 4 of the 1947 Series. He had a no-hitter for 8⅔ innings, although he led only 2-1. Then with two runners on base in the bottom of the 9th inning, Brooklyn's Cookie Lavagetto doubled home both men and the Dodgers won, 3-2. Bill had come within one out of pitching the first no-hitter in World Series history, yet he lost the game! It was the last game that Bill ever pitched in the ML's.

END OF ML CAREER: Bill did not pitch in 1948 because of a sore shoulder. His career was finished.

BEVENS, BILL

YR.	W-L	Pct.	SA	G	GS	CG	IP	H	BB	SO	SH	ERA
1944	4-1	.800	0	8	5	3	44	44	13	16	0	2.68
1945	13-9	.591	0	29	25	14	184	174	68	76	2	3.67
1946	16-13	.552	0	31	31	18	250	213	78	120	3	2.23
1947	7-13	.350	0	28	23	11	165	167	77	77	1	3.82
4 Yrs.	40-36	.526	0	96	84	46	642	598	236	289	6	3.08
Life.	Same.											

World Series

Yr.	G	IP	BB	SO	H	W-L	SA
1947	2	11⅓	11	7	3	0-1	0
1 Yr.	2	11⅓	11	7	3	0-1	0
Life.	Same.						

BOGGS, WADE

Yankee: 1993-97
Third Baseman, 1B, P
Born: June 15, 1958
Birthplace; Omaha, NE
Bat: L; Throw: R
Ht: 6'2"; Wt: 197

FROM THE RED SOX TO THE YANKEES: Third base was a problem position the Yankees solved when Wade signed a three-year contract in December, 1992. A .338 hitter in 11 seasons with the Red Sox, Boggs fell out of grace in 1992 when he hit .257. He proved the Red Sox wrong for unloading him in his first game as a Yankee in Fenway Park, going 4 for 4 with a walk. He finished the year hitting .302 and leading third basemen in fielding, .970, for the first time in his career.

THE HITTING MACHINE RETURNS: Boggs in 1994 resembled the old Boggs hitting machine, batting .342. He hit .352 with runners in scoring position; .353 against right-handers; and .359 at Yankee Stadium. Amazingly, Boggs hit .333 when he was in the hole with two strikes. As bonuses, he added 11 homers with 55 RBIs and won his first Gold Glove. Boggs is peerless in terms of batting eye and patience at the plate. He draws walks, and, as a result, his on-base average was .433 in 1994 and .412 in 1995. As he turned 38 in 1996, his only

Wade Boggs watches one of his 3,010 career hits.

drawback was his slow running that clogged up the base paths. Boggs was one of the few Yankee hitters to meet expectations in 1995. He hit .324, fourth best in the league, and he made his 11th straight trip to the All-Star Game. He was also awarded his second Gold Glove.

NOW ON THE HILL FOR THE YANKEES: At Anaheim on August 19, 1997, Wade made his major-league pitching debut in the eighth inning. In a game that was soon to be a 12-4 Yankee loss, Boggs took the mound for New York. He pitched the final inning of the game, faced four Angel batters, walked one, struck out one and allowed no runs.

FINAL TWO SEASONS WITH THE YANKS: In 1996, Wade hit .311 on 156 hits and appeared in his fourth All-Star Game since joining the Yankees and 12th appearance overall. In the 1997 season, his final year with New York, Wade's average sagged off (!?) to .292, a most respectable mark for most players, but not for Boggs, a .331 career-hitter. Wade was granted free agency in November, 1997 and was signed by the expansion Tampa Ray Devil Rays for the '98 season. Wade would eventually clinch his place in the Hall of Fame by notching his 3,000th hit in the latter part of the 1999 season. Through 2002, Boggs is tied with Bill Dickey for sixth place with the highest B.A. (.313) in Yankee History. Wade retired at the conclusion of the 1999 season. In a 18-year MLB career, Boggs surpassed the .300 mark 15 times!

BOGGS, WADE

Yr.	G	AB	R	H	2B	3B	HR	RBI	BB	SB	BA	SA
1993	143	560	83	169	26	1	2	59	74	0	.302	.363
1994	97	366	61	125	19	1	11	55	61	2	.342	.489
1995	126	460	76	149	22	4	5	63	74	1	.324	.422
1996	132	501	80	156	29	2	2	41	67	1	.311	.389
1997	104	353	55	103	23	1	4	28	48	0	.292	.397
5 Yrs.	602	2240	355	702	119	9	24	246	324	4	.313	.407
Life	2440	9180	1513	3010	578	61	118	1014	1412	24	.328	.443

Division Series

YR.	G	AB	R	H	2B	3B	HR	RBI	BB	SB	BA	SA
1995	4	19	4	5	2	0	1	3	3	0	.263	.526
1996	3	12	0	1	1	0	0	0	0	0	.083	.167
1997	3	7	1	3	0	0	0	2	0	0	.429	.429
3 Yrs.	10	38	5	9	3	0	1	5	3	0	.237	.395
Life. Same.												

Championship Series

YR.	G	AB	R	H	2B	3B	HR	RBI	BB	SB	BA	SA
1996	3	15	1	2	0	0	0	0	1	0	.133	.133
1 Yr.	3	15	1	2	0	0	0	0	1	0	.133	.133
Life.	18	74	7	21	2	1	1	8	8	0	.284	.378

World Series

YR.	G	AB	R	H	2B	3B	HR	RBI	BB	SB	BA	SA
1996	4	11	0	3	1	0	0	2	1	0	.273	.364
1 Yr.	4	11	0	3	1	0	0	2	1	0	.273	.364
Life.	11	42	3	12	4	0	0	5	5	0	.286	.381

BOGGS, WADE
(Pitcher)

Yr.	W-L	Pct.	SA	G	GS	CG	IP	H	BB	SO	SH	ERA
1997	0-0	---	0	1	0	0	1	0	1	1	0	0.00
1 Yr.	0-0	---	0	1	0	0	1	0	1	1	0	0.00
Life. Same.												

BONHAM, ERNIE

Nickname: "Tiny"
Yankee: 1940-46
Pitcher
Born: August 16, 1913
Birthplace: Ione, CA
Died: September 15, 1949
Bat: R; Throw: R
Ht: 6'2"; Wt: 215

HONORS: Ernie was selected as one of three pitchers on *The Sporting News'* ML All-Star team in 1942. He was picked to be on the AL team for the 1942 and 1943 All-Star Games.

GREAT PROSPECT: Ernie was a star pitcher for the Yanks' Kansas City farm club in 1940, the year the Yankee pitching staff was struggling. The Yankee front office debated long and hard about whether Ernie should be called up to the big club, realizing the damage to the club's image if the Yanks had to admit their savior was a bush leaguer. In early August, 1940, the Yanks called Ernie up and he was spectacular (9-3). In fact, his ERA was the lowest in the AL (1.90), although he did not pitch enough innings to qualify for the league's ERA championship. There are many who feel that if the Yanks had brought Ernie to the team earlier in the season, the club would have won another pennant. That would have made eight straight Yankee pennants between 1936-43!

1942 SEASON: Ernie was sensational in 1942 (21-5), leading AL pitchers in winning percentage (.808), complete games (22) and shutouts (6). He also led the Yanks in games started (27) and innings pitched (226). Incredibly, "Tiny" completed 81% of his starts and won 21 games in only 28 pitching appearances!

CLUB LEADERSHIP: In two different seasons Ernie led Yankee pitchers in winning percentage, shutouts and ERA.

ALL-TIME YANKEE LEADER: Ernie's ERA as a Yankee pitcher (2.73) is the fourth lowest in Yankee history for those men who have pitched at least 800 innings in a Yankee uniform. He also places 15th in shutouts (17) and 17th in winning percentage (.612). He is 17th in complete games (91).

SOLID STARTER: Besides being the rookie sensation of 1940 and the star pitcher of 1942, Ernie was a solid member of the starting pitching corps for the Yanks in his other seasons with the club. He was the Yanks' seventh starter in 1941 in between his best two years. He was the Yanks' fourth starter in 1943, third starter in 1944, second starter in 1945, and fourth starter in 1946. In his ML career, Ernie walked 1.67 batters per nine innings, ranking among the top 25 in control.

WORLD SERIES: Ernie started one game in each of the 1941, 1942 and 1943 World Series. In Game 5, the final game of the 1941 Series, "Tiny" pitched a brilliant four-hitter against Brooklyn to wrap up the World Championship for the Bronx Bombers, winning 3-1. In the seventh inning of that game he retired the side on three pitches. (Only two others have done that in Series history.)

TRADED: In October, 1946, the Yanks traded Ernie to the Pirates for pitcher Art Cuccurullo.

TRAGIC DEATH: In 1949 Ernie had a 7-4 record with the Pirates when he entered a Pittsburgh hospital for an appendectomy and other abdominal surgery. He died of complications following surgery on September 15, 1949.

BONHAM, ERNIE

Yr.	W-L	Pct.	SA	G	GS	CG	IP	H	BB	SO	SH	ERA
1940	9-3	.750	0	12	12	10	99	83	13	37	3	1.90
1941	9-6	.600	2	23	14	7	127	118	31	43	1	2.98
1942	21-5	.808	0	28	27	22	226	199	24	71	6	2.27
1943	15-8	.652	1	28	26	17	226	197	52	71	4	2.27
1944	12-9	.571	0	26	25	17	214	228	41	54	1	2.99
1945	8-11	.421	0	23	23	12	181	186	22	42	0	3.29
1946	5-8	.385	3	18	14	6	105	97	23	30	2	3.70
7 Yrs.	79-50	.612	6	158	141	91	1177	1108	206	348	17	2.73
Life.	103-72	.589	9	231	193	110	1551	1501	287	478	21	3.06

World Series

Yr.	G	IP	BB	SO	H	W-L	SA
1941	1	9	2	2	4	1-0	0
1942	2	11	3	3	9	0-1	0
1943	1	8	3	9	6	0-1	0
3 Yrs.	4	28	8	14	19	1-2	0
Life. Same.							

BOROWY, HANK

Yankee: 1942-45
Pitcher
Born: May 12, 1916
Birthplace: Bloomfield, NJ
Bat: R; Throw: R
Ht: 6'; Wt: 175

BOROWY, HANK

Yr.	W-L	Pct.	SA	G	GS	CG	IP	H	BB	SO	SH	ERA
1942	15-4	.789	1	25	21	13	178	157	66	85	4	2.52
1943	14-9	.609	0	29	27	14	217	195	72	113	3	2.82
1944	17-12	.586	2	35	30	19	253	224	88	107	3	2.64
1945	10-5	.667	0	18	18	7	132	107	58	35	1	3.13
4 Yrs.	56-30	.651	3	107	96	53	780	683	284	340	11	2.74
Life.	108-82	.568	7	314	214	94	1717	1660	623	690	17	3.50

World Series

Yr.	G	IP	BB	SO	H	W-L	SA
1942	1	3	3	1	6	0-0	0
1943	1	8	3	4	6	1-0	0
2 Yrs.	2	11	6	5	12	1-0	0
Life.	6	29	12	13	33	3-2	0

DEPENDABLE YANKEE STARTER: Hank, a local boy born in New Jersey, was the pride of Fordham University in the Bronx. He began his ML career with the Yankees as a 26-year-old rookie sensation in 1942 (15-4, 2.52 ERA). After such an impressive career start, Hank remained a dependable pitcher of fine quality for the Yanks, averaging 14 wins a season for his four Yankee seasons. Hank was the fourth starter on the 1942 Yanks, the AL champs. He was the second starter on the 1943 Yanks, the World Champions. During World War II, Hank visited Alaska's Aleutian Islands on a tour of servicemen along with other big leaguers.

1944 SEASON: Hank was the ace of the Yankee pitching staff in 1944, leading the club in wins (17), winning percentage (.586), games pitched (35), games started (30), complete games (19), innings pitched (253), strikeouts (107), shutouts (3) and ERA (2.64)! He did it all in 1944. In honor of his efforts, Hank was given the starting assignment for the AL in the 1944 All-Star Game. Hank almost single-handedly kept the Yankee pitching staff together and allowed the Yanks to stay in the 1944 pennant race until late in the year.

WORLD SERIES: In Game 4 of the 1942 Series, the Cardinals hit Hank hard and won a crucial contest. Hank redeemed himself in the 1943 Series when the Yanks avenged their loss of the previous year to St. Louis. After the Yanks and Cards had split the first couple games, Hank pitched eight solid innings at Yankee Stadium to beat the Cards, 6-2, in critical Game 3.

LEFT YANKS IN CONTROVERSY: At the start of the 1945 season Hank was rated the Yanks' best pitcher, and he performed splendidly in the season's first half. But the Yanks created a stir in July of 1945 when they slyly sold Hank's contract to the Cubs for a little less than $100,000. NL clubs were outraged, although it is difficult to document whether any actual waiver rules were violated. (But more strict waiver rules were established as a result of this deal.) Hank's 1945 season was most unusual and successful. He was 10-5 with the Yanks and 11-2 with Chicago, giving him an impressive 21-7 record for the season and making him one of three 20-game winners in modern baseball history to spread one season's successes over both leagues. Hank led the Cubs to the NL pennant, then was 2-2 in the 1945 World Series. It is difficult to understand why the Yanks unloaded Hank, unless it was simply for the money.

BOUTON, JIM

Nickname: "Bulldog"
Yankee: 1962-68
Pitcher
Born: March 8, 1939
Birthplace: Newark, NJ
Bat: R; Throw: R
Ht: 6'; Wt: 170

YOUNG PROSPECT: The Yanks signed Jim to a contract in November, 1958, while Jim was a student at Western Michigan University. From 1959-61 Jim pitched in Yankee farm towns, including Auburn, Kearney, Greensboro, and Amarillo. He was 13-7 for Amarillo in 1961. Jim, one of the many talented pitchers who came through the Yankee farm system during the early 1960s, made the Yanks in 1962.

EARLY ML CAREER: Jim's early Yankee career was a complete success story. He won his first ML start on May 6, 1962, shutting out the Washington Senators, 8-0, on seven hits. Jim was a star of the 1963-64 Yankee teams, winning a combined 39 games over those two seasons. In 1963, Jim's best ML season, he led Yankee hurlers in ERA (2.53) and shutouts (six). In 1964 he led the Yanks in wins (18) and innings pitched (271), besides leading the entire AL in games started (37). After his two great seasons, Jim developed arm trouble and was never the same pitcher again.

ALL-STAR GAME: Jim pitched for the AL in the 1963 All-Star Game.

WORLD SERIES: Jim lost a 1-0 heartbreaker in Game 3 of the 1963 Series. He pitched great ball in the 1964 Series, winning Game 3, 2-1, and Game 6, 8-3.

COLORFUL: Jim constantly knocked off his cap while on the mound to the delight of the Yankee Stadium fans. His development of a knuckleball kept him in MLB after his arm trouble. Jim is known for his keen wit and intellect, qualities he exhibited while on the Yanks. His books and articles on baseball sought to bring sunshine to the game, to contest the secret society of the clubhouse.

LEFT YANKS: In October, 1968, the Yanks sold Jim's contract to the Seattle Pilots.

BOUTON, JIM

Yr.	W-L	Pct.	SA	G	GS	CG	IP	H	BB	SO	SH	ERA
1962	7-7	.500	2	36	16	3	133	124	59	71	1	3.99
1963	21-7	.750	1	40	30	12	249	191	87	148	6	2.53
1964	18-13	.581	0	38	37	11	271	227	60	125	4	3.02
1965	4-15	.211	0	30	25	2	151	158	60	97	0	4.82
1966	3-8	.273	1	24	19	3	120	117	38	65	0	2.69
1967	1-0	1.000	0	17	1	0	44	47	18	31	0	4.67
1968	1-1	.500	0	12	3	1	44	49	9	24	0	3.68
7 Yrs.	55-51	.519	4	197	131	32	1012	913	331	561	11	3.36
Life.	62-63	.496	6	304	144	34	1239	1131	435	720	11	3.57

World Series

Yr.	G	IP	BB	SO	H	W-L	SA
1963	1	7	5	4	4	0-1	0
1964	2	17 ⅓	5	7	15	2-0	0
2 Yrs.	3	24 ⅓	10	11	19	2-1	0
Life. Same.							

BOYER, CLETE

Yankee: 1959-66
Third Baseman, SS
Born: February 8, 1937
Birthplace: Cassville, MO
Bat: R; Throw: R
Ht: 6'; Wt: 165

CAME TO YANKS: In February, 1957, the Yanks obtained Clete, pitchers Art Ditmar and Bobby Shantz, and two others from the Kansas City A's for outfielder Irv Noren, pitcher Tom Morgan, and four others.

YOUNG PROSPECT: In 1955 Clete was one of the most sought-after high school prospects in the country. The Yanks badly wanted Clete at that time but the club had already signed other bonus babies who, because of the rules at the time, were forced to take up room on the Yankee roster. Thus, while it came to be that Clete was signed by the A's, the Yanks kept a close eye on him. When the Yanks obtained Clete in 1957, he was sent to the minors. Clete played for the Yanks' Binghampton club in 1957 and then he starred for Richmond of the International League in 1958 and 1959. (He batted .284 and hit 22 HRs in 1958.) Clete was called up to the Yanks during the 1959 season.

BASEBALL FAMILY: Clete is one of 13 children, including seven boys. All of his brothers played professional baseball, and two of them played ML baseball. His brother Ken was a NL All-Star third baseman, and in the 1964 World Series Clete and Ken played against each other.

DEFENSIVE ABILITIES: Clete was one of the greatest defensive third basemen of all time. He had unbelievable reactions, a sure glove, a keen knowledge of opposing hitters, a rifle arm and tremendous range. He blocked hot smashes with his chest like a hockey goalie. Three times Clete led AL third basemen in assists (1961, '62, '65). In 1962 he led AL third basemen in putouts (187) and in 1965 he led the AL's third sackers in double plays (46). His 46 DPs in 1965 is the Yankee club record for third basemen and the fifth most in baseball history. The 396 assists Clete made in 1962 ranks him tied for eighth on the all-time single season list for third basemen. (Somehow, as usual, Brooks Robinson won the Gold Glove Award in that season, also.) His lifetime fielding average at third base (.965) ranks tenth all-time. Clete also played a fine defensive short-stop. In 1959, 1960, and 1966 Clete did considerable shortstop duty.

BATTING THREAT: Although he did not hit much for average, Clete blasted 13.57 HRs per season for his seven complete Yankee campaigns. He tied for club leadership in triples three times. As a Yankee, 1962 was Clete's best year at the plate (18 HRs, 68 RBIs, .272).

WORLD SERIES: Clete was not very fond of Casey Stengel and he had at least one good reason. In the second inning of Game 1 of the 1960 Series, Stengel cruelly had a pinch-hitter for Clete, who was thrilled to be playing in his first Series game. In the 1961 Series against Cincinnati, Clete made several sensational fielding plays and was the defensive star of the Series. In Game 1 of the 1962 Series he hit a key HR to lead the Yanks to a 6-2 victory over San Francisco. He hit .318 in the 1962 Series, the second highest average on the Yanks. Clete hit a HR in Game 7 of the 1964 Series, although it came in a losing cause.

TRADED: In November, 1966, the Yanks traded Clete to the Atlanta Braves for outfielder Bill Robinson.

YANKEE RETURN: After coaching for Atlanta (1977-79) and Oakland (1980-85), Clete returned to the Yankees in 1987, serving as a roving instructor, a minor-league coach, minor-league manager, and as a base and bench coach in New York.

BOYER, CLETE

Yr.	G	AB	R	H	2B	3B	HR	RBI	BB	SB	BA	SA
1959	47	114	4	20	2	0	0	3	6	1	.175	.193
1960	124	393	54	95	20	1	14	46	23	2	.242	.405
1961	148	504	61	113	19	5	11	55	63	1	.224	.347
1962	158	566	85	154	24	1	18	68	51	3	.272	.413
1963	152	557	59	140	20	3	12	54	33	4	.251	.363
1964	147	510	43	111	10	5	8	52	36	6	.218	.304
1965	148	514	69	129	23	6	18	58	39	4	.251	.424
1966	144	500	59	120	22	4	14	57	46	6	.240	.384
8 Yrs.	1068	3658	434	882	140	25	95	393	297	27	.241	.371
Life.	1725	5780	645	1396	200	33	162	654	470	41	.242	.372

World Series

Yr.	G	AB	R	H	2B	3B	HR	RBI	BA
1960	4	12	1	3	2	1	0	1	.250
1961	5	15	0	4	2	0	0	3	.267
1962	7	22	2	7	1	0	1	4	.318
1963	4	13	0	1	0	0	0	0	.077
1964	7	24	2	5	1	0	1	3	.208
5 Yrs.	27	86	5	20	6	1	2	11	.233
Life. Same.									

BROACA, JOHNNY

Yankee: 1934-37
Pitcher
Born: October 3, 1909
Birthplace: Lawrence, MA
Died: May 16, 1985
Bat: R; Throw: R
Ht: 5'11"; Wt: 190

GREAT PROSPECT: Johnny was a star pitcher for Yale University when Yankee superscout Paul Krichell discovered him. The Yanks later signed this kid pitcher who was given the "unlimited potential" label. As a Yankee rookie in 1934, Johnny hurled a one-hitter.

STARTING PITCHER: In 1934 Johnny was the Yanks' third starter. He was the third starter and second biggest winner (15-7) on the 1935 Yankee pitching staff. Johnny was the fourth starter on the 1936 World Championship Yankee team and he led the club in games pitched (37). This was an excellent pitcher, possessing a great fastball, a good curve and fine control.

DIFFERENT: Johnny was unusual. When he was at Yale he told his coach that he would pitch only once a week because he was saving himself for the big leagues. In September, 1936, Johnny astounded his Yankee teammates when he quit the Yanks, on the eve of a $6000 World Series paycheck, to become a professional boxer. He declared that some day he would fight Joe Louis for the Heavyweight Championship, and the Yankee players followed his "career" closely. But Johnny never won a fight, although he did once lock his wife out of the house because she served stew for dinner. No one ever understood why Johnny threw away that hard-earned World Series check, but there is no denying that Johnny was one of the most colorful Yankees.

LATE ML CAREER: Johnny returned to the Yanks in 1937, pitched in only seven games and had a 1-4 record. The Indians gave Johnny a chance in 1939 and he was 4-2 in 22 games. That was his last ML experience.

BROACA, JOHNNY

Yr.	W-L	Pct.	SA	G	GS	CG	IP	H	BB	SO	SH	ERA
1934	12-9	.571	0	26	24	13	177	203	65	74	1	4.16
1935	15-7	.682	0	29	27	14	201	199	79	78	2	3.58
1936	12-7	.632	3	37	27	12	206	235	66	84	1	4.24
1937	1-4	.200	0	7	6	3	44	58	17	9	0	4.70
4 Yrs.	40-27	.597	3	99	84	42	628	695	227	245	4	4.04
Life.	44-29	.603	3	121	86	42	674	748	255	258	4	4.08

BROWN, BOBBY

Nicknames: "Doc" "Brownie" "Golden Boy"
Yankee: 1946-52 (military) '54
Third Baseman, SS, 2B, OF
Born: October 25, 1924
Birthplace: Seattle, WA
Bat: L; Throw: R
Ht: 6'1"; Wt: 180

YOUNG PROSPECT: Larry MacPhail and George Weiss paid Bobby a bonus estimated to be in the vicinity of $55,000 to sign with the Yanks. That is one of the largest bonuses that the club ever gave. After playing for Newark, the Yanks' top farm club, Bobby reached the Yanks in 1946.

YANKEE THIRD BASEMAN: Bobby played his entire ML career with the Yanks. In 1947 and 1948 he was a utility player. From 1949-51 he was a fixture at third base. (He platooned with Billy Johnson in 1949 and 1950.)

SOLID PERSON: Bobby missed most of the 1952 and 1954 baseball seasons, and all of the 1953 season, while serving in the military. He attended Tulane Medical School in New Orleans during his years with the Yankees and practiced medicine after retiring as a player. Asked in 1978 how he managed juggling two careers, Dr. Brown answered: "I was able to manage a baseball career and attend medical school and later intern because the Yankees allowed me to report either late for spring training or on the first day of the season, and I was able to adjust my medical school and interning schedules to begin in mid-October and extend to the first two weeks in April."

GREAT HITTER: Bobby could handle a bat like few others. His bat was known as the "Magic Wand." Over his combined first three Yankee seasons, Bobby hit .302. In 1947 he hit .333 as a pinch-hitter, making nine pinch-hits for the season to lead the AL. Casey Stengel once said, "Bobby reminds me of a fella who's been hitting for 12 years and fielding one."

DR. BOBBY BROWN (New York Yankees Archives)

WORLD SERIES: Bobby was an excellent player under Series pressure, hitting .439 for four Series! In the 1947 Series Bobby delivered three pinch-hits in three official pinch-hit at-bats, setting a Series record, and in another pinch-hit effort, he walked! Bobby got the key hits in Game 1 and Game 4 of the 1950 Series to help the Yanks sweep the Phillies. Bobby is tied for fourth on the all-time Series triple list (3).

POST YANKEE CAREER: On July 1, 1954, Bobby retired as a ballplayer to devote himself to his medical career. He became a cardiologist in Fort Worth, Texas. He also served as AL president, January 1, 1984 to July 31, 1994.

BROWN, BOBBY

Yr.	G	AB	R	H	2B	3B	HR	RBI	BB	SB	BA	SA
1946	7	24	1	8	1	0	0	1	4	0	.333	.375
1947	69	150	21	45	6	1	1	18	21	0	.300	.373
1948	113	363	62	109	19	5	3	48	48	0	.300	.405
1949	104	343	61	97	14	4	6	61	38	4	.283	.399
1950	95	277	33	74	4	2	4	37	39	3	.267	.339
1951	103	313	44	84	15	2	6	51	47	1	.268	.387
1952	29	89	6	22	2	0	1	14	9	1	.247	.303
1954	28	60	5	13	1	0	1	7	8	0	.217	.283
7 Yrs.	548	1619	233	452	62	14	22	237	214	9	.279	.376
Life.	Same.											

World Series

Yr.	G	AB	R	H	2B	3B	HR	RBI	BA
1947	4	3	2	3	2	0	0	3	1.000
1949	4	12	4	6	1	2	0	5	.500
1950	4	12	2	4	1	1	0	1	.333
1951	5	14	1	5	1	0	0	0	.357
4 Yrs.	17	41	9	18	5	3	0	9	.439
Life.	Same.								

BUSH, JOE
(BORN LESLIE AMBROSE BUSH)

Nickname: "Bullet Joe"
Yankee: 1922-24
Pitcher
Born: November 27, 1892
Birthplace: Brainerd, MN
Died: November 1, 1974
Bat: R; Throw: R
Ht: 5'9"; Wt: 173

CAME TO YANKS: "Bullet Joe" was another of a long line of Red Sox pitchers who made the trip from Boston down to New York in the early 1920s. In December, 1921, the Yanks obtained "Bullet Joe," Sam Jones and Everett Scott from the Red Sox for Roger Peckinpaugh, Jack Quinn, Rip Collins and Bill Piercy.

1922 SEASON: Joe's 1922 season ranks as one of the best in Yankee history. He led the Yanks in wins (26) despite a finger injury. Only three times in Yankee history has a Yankee pitcher won more games in a season than Joe's 26. Joe also led AL pitchers in winning percentage (.788). In this season Joe fielded 77 chances without making an error, tying the Yankee fielding record for pitchers. He started Game 1 and Game 5 of the 1922 World Series.

1923 SEASON: Joe led Yankee pitchers in complete games (23) and innings pitched (276) and he tied for club leadership in

strikeouts (125) and shutouts (3). On July 3 "Bullet Joe" had an amazing performance against the Washington Senators. He pitched 15 innings, allowing only eight hits, to win, 2-1. His HR had sent the game into extra innings! In Game 5 of the 1923 World Series, perhaps the most critical game of the Series, Joe pitched a three-hitter to down the New York Giants, 8-1, helping the Yanks to the club's first World Championship. In that game, played on October 14, Joe became the first Yankee pitcher to win a Series game at Yankee Stadium.

1924 SEASON: Joe was the Yanks' third starter in a somewhat disappointing season (17-16). He had control problems, leading the AL in walks (109), and set a then AL record by leading the AL in wild pitches for the second consecutive season.

COMPETITOR: Joe was a hard thrower and a hard worker on the mound. With each pitch he would let loose a loud grunt that could be heard in the cheap seats. Joe was known to get hot on the mound. He had a few loud arguments with his manager, Miller Huggins, while pitching. Huggins never forgave Joe for one argument during a World Series game.

GREAT HITTER: Joe was an outstanding hitting pitcher. As a Yankee, he hit .326 (1922), .274 (1923) and .339 (1924). Joe hit a combined .313 (104 for 332) for his three Yankee seasons. He hit a pinch-hit HR on Sept. 18, 1924.

TRADED: Although Joe had averaged 20.66 wins per season as a Yankee, the Yanks traded him and two other pitchers to the St. Louis Browns for pitcher Urban Shocker in December, 1924.

BUSH, JOE

Yr.	W-L	Pct.	SA	G	GS	CG	IP	H	BB	SO	SH	ERA
1922	26-7	.788	3	39	30	20	255	240	85	92	0	3.31
1923	19-15	.559	0	37	30	23	276	263	117	125	3	3.43
1924	17-16	.515	1	39	31	19	252	262	109	80	3	3.57
3 Yrs.	62-38	.620	4	115	91	62	783	765	311	297	6	3.44
Life.	196-184	.516	19	489	370	225	3087	2992	1263	1319	35	3.51

World Series

Yr.	G	IP	BB	SO	H	W-L	SA
1922	2	15	5	6	21	0-2	0
1923	3	16⅔	4	5	7	1-1	0
2 Yrs.	5	31⅔	9	11	28	1-3	0
Life.	9	60⅔	20	18	49	2-5	1

BYRNE, TOMMY

Yankee: 1943 (military) '46-51, '54-57
Pitcher
Born: December 31, 1919
Birthplace: Baltimore, MD
Bat: L; Throw: L
Ht: 6'11"; Wt: 182

HONORS: In 1976 Tommy was inducted into the North Carolina Sports Hall of Fame. (He is a graduate of Wake Forest University.)

YOUNG PROSPECT: Tommy was a great prospect in 1940 when the Yanks signed him for a bonus of about $10,000, one of the largest in baseball history up to then. He pitched in the Yankee farm system until he got his chance with the Yanks in 1943. Tommy missed the entire 1944 and 1945 baseball seasons while in the military. He pitched little for the Yanks in 1946 and 1947. In fact, he spent most of the 1947 season back in the minors.

COMING AND GOING: In June of 1951, the Yanks sent Tommy and $25,000 to the St. Louis Browns for pitcher Stubby Overmire. In September of 1954, the Yanks purchased Tommy's contract from Seattle of the Pacific Coast League. Tommy had been a 20-game winner for Seattle, and as Casey Stengel said, "He played first base and the outfield, pinch-hit, and did everything but collect tickets."

BEST SEASONS: Tommy's best years were 1949, 1950 and 1955, although it was in 1948 that he led Yankee pitchers in ERA (3.30). Tommy finished the 1949 season with a 9-1 record and started the 1950 season at 8-1 for an incredible 17-2 combined record over that period. In 1949 he led Yankee pitchers in strikeouts (129) and allowed only 5.74 hits per nine innings for the year, the seventh best single season ratio in ML history. Tommy was selected to the AL team for the 1950 All-Star Game. In 1955 Tommy enjoyed a great comeback season, leading AL pitchers in winning percentage (.762, 16-5), and many polls named him "Comeback Player of the Year." In Tommy's 11 Yankee seasons, he had only two losing campaigns.

GOOD HITTER: Tommy's .378 lifetime slugging average is the ninth highest by a pitcher in ML history. In his lifetime, Tommy hit 14 HRs and 98 RBIs in 601 ML at-bats, hitting .238. On September 15, 1957, he hit a pinch-hit HR.

DELIBERATE AND WILD: Tommy was a notoriously slow worker on the mound, a trait that often upset batters and worked to Tommy's advantage. It occasionally unnerved Casey Stengel, the fielders and the fans, too. Tommy often had control problems, which also contributed to the length of his games. His 179 walks in 1949 is a Yankee record for most walks in a season. Tommy led the MLs in walks three years in a row (1949-51) and in hit batsmen five years straight (1948-52).

ALL-TIME YANKEE LEADER: Tommy is tied for 11th on the all-time Yankee winning percentage list for those pitchers with at least 100 Yankee decisions (.643, 72-40).

WORLD SERIES: In Game 2 of the 1955 Series Tommy pitched a five-hitter to beat the Dodgers, 4-2, and thus became the first lefthander to pitch a complete game against Brooklyn all year. Tommy also got the big hit of the game. (He was an excellent hitting pitcher.) Unfortunately, Tommy lost Game 7 of the 1955 Series, 2-0, to Brooklyn's Johnny Podres. Tommy started Game 3 of the 1949 Series.

RETIREMENT: Tommy pitched for the Yanks until he was 37 years old. He retired as a player after the 1957 season. Since hanging up the spikes, Tommy has been involved in civic affairs in Wake Forest, N.C., rising to the post of mayor.

BYRNE, TOMMY

Yr.	W-L	Pct.	SA	G	GS	CG	IP	H	BB	SO	SH	ERA
1943	2-1	.667	0	11	2	0	32	28	35	22	0	6.54
1946	0-1	.000	0	4	1	0	9	7	8	5	0	5.79
1947	0-0	.000	0	4	1	0	4	5	6	2	0	4.15
1948	8-5	.615	2	31	11	5	134	79	101	93	1	3.30
1949	15-7	.682	0	32	30	12	196	125	179	129	3	3.72
1950	15-9	.625	0	31	31	10	203	188	160	118	2	4.74
1951	2-1	.667	0	9	3	0	21	16	36	14	0	6.86
1954	3-2	.600	0	5	5	4	40	36	19	24	1	2.70
1955	16-5	.762	2	27	22	9	160	137	87	76	3	3.15
1956	7-3	.700	6	37	8	1	110	108	72	52	0	3.36
1957	4-6	.400	2	30	4	1	85	70	60	57	0	4.36
11 Yrs.	72-40	.643	12	221	118	42	994	799	763	592	10	3.93
Life.	85-69	.552	12	281	170	65	1362	1138	1037	766	12	4.11

World Series

Yr.	G	IP	BB	SO	H	W-L	SA
1949	1	3⅓	2	1	2	0-0	0
1955	2	14⅓	8	8	8	1-1	0
1956	1	⅓	0	1	1	0-0	0
1957	2	3⅓	2	1	1	0-0	0
4 Yrs.	6	21⅓	12	11	12	1-1	0
Life. Same.							

CALDWELL, RAY

Nickname: "Slim"
Yankee: 1910-18
Pitcher
Born: April 26, 1888
Birthplace: Corydon, PA
Died: August 17, 1967
Bat: L; Throw: R
Ht: 6'2"; Wt: 190

STAR YANKEE HURLER: In 1910 Ray began his ML career with the Yanks (Highlanders). He was the Yanks' second starter in 1911-12, the sixth starter in 1913 and the undisputed ace of the Yanks' 1914-15 pitching staffs. He had a poor season in 1916, but was once again the Yankee ace in 1917. In the club's early days at the Polo Grounds (beginning in 1913), Ray and Russ Ford were the Yankee pitching stars.

SPITBALL PITCHER: Ray had the spitball in his assortment of pitches. In 1920 the spitball was made illegal, but the 17 ML pitchers who already were pitching the spitter were allowed to continue its use. Ray threw the legalized spitter until the day he retired.

GREAT OFFENSIVE THREAT: Ray was one of the best hitting pitchers of his, or any, era. For ML pitchers, Ray on the all-time lists ranks third in stolen bases (20) and fourth in pinchhits (36). Ray scored 27 runs in 1915, the second most ever scored by a ML pitcher, and he pinch-hit 33 times (nine for 33, .273) to lead the AL. Also, his four HRs tied for the lead among ML pitchers in 1915. Ray was a great base runner.

PINCH-HIT RECORD: In 1915 Ray had three great hitting days in a row. In games played on June 10 and 11 against Chicago, he hit pinch-hit HRs in consecutive games, the only occasion in AL history that a pitcher has accomplished that feat. The next day on June 12, Ray pitched against St. Louis, won the game and hit another HR!

CAREY, ANDY

DEFENSIVE STANDOUT: Ray was a fine fielder and in 1915 led AL pitchers in fielding (.988). He was so sparkling with the glove that he occasionally played center field for the Yanks. In Ray's Yankee career, he played 44 games in the outfield and six games at first base. (It was hard not to have Ray's bat in the lineup.)

GREATEST YANKEE GAME: On July 10, 1917, Ray pitched 9⅔ innings of no-hit ball in relief, defeating the St. Louis Browns, 7-5, in a game that went 17 innings.

DEDICATED BALLPLAYER: Ray was a great competitor. He played hard and aggressively. He is one of two pitchers on whom Ty Cobb twice stole home. The second time it happened, on June 4, 1915, Ray was so mad at Umpire Silk O'Loughlin's safe call that he hurled his glove into the air and was ejected.

CLUB LEADERSHIP: Ray led Yankee pitchers in complete games four times. In consecutive years (1914-15) he led the Yanks in wins. Twice he led the team in ERA, shutouts, strikeouts, innings pitched, games started, and games pitched.

ALL-TIME YANKEE LEADER: Ray is ninth on the all-time Yankee ERA list (3.00) for those former pitchers with at least 800 innings pitched in a Yankee uniform. He is also ninth on the all-time Yankee complete game list (151). He is 11th on the Yanks innings-pitched list (1718). Caldwell also places 16th in strikeouts (803), wins (96), and shutouts (13).

TRADED: In December of 1918, the Yanks traded Ray, Slim Love, Frank Gilhooley, and Al Walters to the Red Sox for Duffy Lewis, Ernie Shore, and Dutch Leonard. (The Yanks then traded Leonard to Washington.) Ray suffered from a sore arm in 1919 and Boston traded him in mid-season to Cleveland.

HAUNTING THE YANKS: Pitching for Cleveland on August 24, 1919, Ray was hit by lightning. After taking a few minutes to get himself together, Ray recorded the final out for a complete-game victory! A few weeks after the lightning incident, Ray on September 10, 1919, pitched a no-hitter against his former teammates, the Yankees. In 1920 Ray's 20 wins for the Indians was a critical factor in depriving the Yanks of an AL pennant. The champion Indians finished three games ahead of the third-place Yanks.

Yankee: 1952-60
Third Baseman
Born: October 18, 1931
Birthplace: Oakland, CA
Bat: R; Throw: R
Ht: 6'1"; Wt: 190

BONUS BABY: Yankee scout Joe Devine discovered Andy on the campus of St. Mary's College and signed him to a Yankee contract in 1951, reportedly giving him a bonus of $60,000-$65,000, one of the largest bonuses that the Yanks ever dished out. Andy played two seasons at Kansas City, before becoming a backup third baseman for the Yanks in 1953. (He also had a short stint with the Yanks in 1952.) The experience at Kansas City, the Yanks' AAA American Association team, was a good one for Andy, because his manager was former Yankee great George Selkirk, one of the shrewdest men in the Yankee organization.

YANKEE THIRD BASEMAN: When Bobby Brown retired as a baseball player in July, 1954, Andy became the regular Yankee third baseman. He held that job through the 1958 season. His 1959 season was ruined by a back ailment and mononucleosis.

ANDY CAREY (New York Yankees Archives)

CALDWELL, RAY

Yr.	W-L	Pct.	SA	G	GS	CG	IP	H	BB	SO	SH	ERA
1910	1-0	1.000	1	6	2	1	19	19	9	17	0	3.72
1911	16-14	.533	1	41	27	19	255	240	79	145	1	3.35
1912	7-16	.304	0	30	26	14	183	196	67	95	3	4.47
1913	9-8	.529	1	27	16	15	164	131	60	87	2	2.41
1914	18-9	.667	1	31	23	22	213	153	51	92	5	1.94
1915	19-16	.543	0	36	35	31	305	266	107	130	3	2.89
1916	5-12	.294	0	21	18	14	166	142	65	76	1	2.99
1917	12-16	.429	0	32	29	21	236	199	76	102	1	2.86
1918	8-8	.500	1	24	21	14	177	173	62	59	1	3.06
9 Yrs.	95-99	.490	5	248	197	151	1718	1519	576	803	17	3.00
Life.	133-120	.526	9	343	261	185	2242	2085	737	1005	20	3.22

INTERESTING, CLEVER: When Andy joined the Yanks he was known for his ability, his eating capacity and his confidence. He was clever, witty and well-liked. Andy's "verbal battles" with Casey Stengel were considered good dugout humor, especially their "discussions" concerning Andy's batting style. Casey wanted him to chop down at the ball and was always yelling at Andy to "butcher boy."

BATTING THREAT: Andy's best season at the plate was 1954 when he hit .302 with 65 RBIs. He was especially hot in the spring when he first became a regular. In 1955 Andy tied Mickey Mantle for the AL triple leadership (11).

DEFENSIVE ABILITIES: In 1955 Andy led AL third basemen in putouts (154), assists (301) and double plays (37). On July 31, 1955, he helped turn four double plays in one game, an AL record for third basemen.

WORLD SERIES: In Game 3 of the 1955 Series Andy pinch-hit an RBI triple, although in a losing cause. His run-scoring single was the deciding run in a 3-1 Yankee victory over the Milwaukee Braves in Game 1 of the 1957 Series. Andy's hit knocked out the great Brave pitcher, Warren Spahn.

TRADED: In May, 1960, the Yanks traded Andy to the Kansas City A's for outfielder Bob Cerv.

CAREY, ANDY

Yr.	G	AB	R	H	2B	3B	HR	RBI	BB	SB	BA	SA
1952	16	40	6	6	0	0	0	1	3	0	.150	.150
1953	51	81	14	26	5	0	4	8	9	2	.321	.531
1954	122	411	60	124	14	6	8	65	43	5	.302	.423
1955	135	510	73	131	19	11	7	47	44	3	.257	.378
1956	132	422	54	100	18	2	7	50	45	9	.237	.339
1957	85	247	30	63	6	5	6	33	15	2	.255	.393
1958	102	315	39	90	19	4	12	45	34	1	.286	.486
1959	41	101	11	26	1	0	3	9	7	1	.257	.356
1960	4	3	0	1	0	0	0	0	0	0	.333	.333
9 Yrs.	688	2130	287	567	82	28	47	258	200	23	.266	.397
Life.	938	2850	371	741	119	38	64	350	268	23	.260	.396

World Series

Yr.	G	AB	R	H	2B	3B	HR	RBI	BA
1955	2	2	0	1	0	1	0	1	.500
1956	7	19	2	3	0	0	0	0	.158
1957	2	7	0	2	1	0	0	1	.286
1958	5	12	1	1	0	0	0	0	.083
4 Yrs.	16	40	3	7	1	1	0	2	.175
Life.	Same.								

CERONE, RICK

Yankee: 1980-84, 1987, 1990
Catcher, P
Born: May 19, 1954
Birthplace: Newark, NJ
Bat: R; Throw: R
Ht: 5'11"; Wt: 190

TRADE TO YANKEES: In November of 1979, the Yankees traded Chris Chambliss (1B), Damaso Garcia (INF) and Paul Mirabella (P) to Toronto for Rick, Tom Underwood (P) and Ted Wilborn (OF). Rick, who graduated from Seton Hall University, was returning to his home area as the successor to the deceased Thurman Munson. Rick had broken into the ML's in 1975, and in 1979 he had finally shown some ability with the bat. Rick had always been considered a good defensive catcher.

SENSATIONAL 1980 SEASON: When Rick reported to spring training, coach Elston Howard told him: "Rick, you're not taking Thurman Munson's place. Nobody can. Just be Rick Cerone." Rick responded with his greatest year and set career highs in batting (.277), HRs (14) and RBIs (85). Led Yankees in games (147), at-bats (519) and doubles (30)—most doubles by a Yankee catcher since 30 by Yogi Berra in 1950. Hit .315 with runners in scoring position. Gained respect on May 26, 1980, when Detroit Manager Sparky Anderson intentionally walked Graig Nettles three times to pitch to Cerone, and each time Rick delivered; he had six RBIs in the game. Led AL catchers by throwing out 47% of potential base stealers (47 for 99). Named to *The Sporting News* and UPI AL All-Star teams. Finished seventh in MVP voting. Phil Rizzuto kept things interesting by comparing Rick to the Mets' Lee Mazzilli for "Italian Stallion" honors in the city.

FRUSTRATIONS: Several weeks before the start of 1981 spring training, Rick infuriated George Steinbrenner by taking his salary dispute to arbitration and winning a salary of $425,000. On April 18, 1981, Rick broke his right thumb on a foul tip and didn't come off the Disabled List until May 24, a large factor in his disappointing season. He broke his left thumb on a tag play at home plate on May 11, 1982, and didn't come off the Disabled List until July 15; meanwhile, on May 12, New York obtained catcher Butch Wynegar, and thereafter Rick was faced with competition for regular catcher. Rick platooned most of 1983 with Wynegar and felt he didn't know where he stood with the club. More platooning and injuries in 1984; on Disabled List, May 7 through July 5, with strained right elbow.

POST-SEASON PLAY: In the 1980 ALCS, Rick became the fifth AL player to hit a HR in his first ALCS at-bat. In the 1981 Division Series vs. Milwaukee, Rick led the Yankees in RBIs (5). Highlights included two doubles in Game 1; a leaping catch up the back screen for final out in Game 2; a locker-room shouting match with Steinbrenner after Game 4; and a long HR to assure victory in the Game 5 clincher. Rick in 1981 hit only .100 in the ALCS and .190 in the World Series, but he did have success vs. Fernando Valenzuela with a double and two-run HR in Game 3 of the World Series.

GOING AND COMING: In December of 1984, the Yankees traded Rick to Atlanta for Brian Fisher (P). In February of 1987, the Yanks signed Rick as a free agent. Rick did the bulk of the catching in 1987 and led AL catchers in fielding (.998), making only one error in 577 chances; he also pitched in two blowouts and retired six of seven batters faced. Rick played for the Red Sox in 1988-89. In December of 1989, the Yanks signed Rick as a free agent, and he was a back-up catcher, hitting .302 in 1990. Played for Mets in 1991.

CERONE, RICK

Yr.	G	AB	R	H	2B	3B	HR	RBI	BB	SB	BA	SA
1980	147	519	70	144	30	4	14	85	32	1	.277	.432
1981	71	234	23	57	13	2	2	21	12	0	.244	.342
1982	89	300	29	68	10	0	5	28	19	0	.227	.310
1983	80	246	18	54	7	0	2	22	15	0	.220	.272
1984	38	120	8	25	3	0	2	13	9	1	.208	.283
1987	113	284	28	69	12	1	4	23	30	0	.243	.335
1990	49	139	12	42	6	0	2	11	5	0	.302	.388
7 Yrs.	587	1842	188	459	81	7	31	203	122	2	.249	.351
Life.	1329	4069	393	998	190	15	59	436	320	6	.245	.343

Divisional Playoff

Yr.	G	AB	R	H	2B	3B	HR	RBI	BB	SB	BA	SA
1981	5	18	1	6	2	0	1	5	0	0	.333	.611
1 Yr.	5	18	1	6	2	0	1	5	0	0	.333	.611
Life. Same.												

Championship Series

Yr.	G	AB	R	H	2B	3B	HR	RBI	BB	SB	BA	SA
1980	3	12	1	4	0	0	1	2	0	0	.333	.583
1981	3	10	1	1	0	0	0	0	0	0	.100	.100
2 Yrs.	6	22	2	5	0	0	1	2	0	0	.227	.364
Life. Same.												

World Series

Yr.	G	AB	R	H	2B	3B	HR	RBI	BB	SB	BA	SA
1981	6	21	2	4	1	0	1	3	4	0	.190	.381
1 Yr.	6	21	2	4	1	0	1	3	4	0	.190	.381
Life. Same.												

CERONE, RICK (Pitcher)

Yr.	W-L	Pct.	SA	G	GS	CG	IP	H	BB	SO	SH	ERA
1987	0-0	---	0	2	0	0	2	0	1	1	0	0.00
1 Yr.	0-0	---	0	2	0	0	2	0	1	1	0	0.00
Life. Same.												

CHAMBLISS, CHRIS

Yankee: 1974-79
First Baseman
Born: December 26, 1948
Birthplace: Dayton, OH
Bat: L; Throw: R
Ht: 6'1"; Wt: 195

HONORS: *The Sporting News* selected Chris as the first baseman on the publication's 1976 AL All-Star team. Chris was picked to be on the AL team for the 1976 All-Star Game.

CAME TO YANKS: In April, 1974, the Yanks obtained Chris and pitchers Dick Tidrow and Cecil Upshaw from the Indians for pitchers Fritz Peterson, Steve Kline, Tom Buskey, and Fred Beene.

YANKEE FIRST BASEMAN: From the time he joined the Yanks until the day he was traded, Chris was the Yanks' regular first baseman, holding the job for six seasons. Chris was a consistent and durable performer, playing in more than 150 games in four consecutive seasons (1975-78).

GREAT HITTER: Chris gave the Yankees a beautiful, classic swing. He used the entire baseball field, hitting the ball where it was pitched. He could hit for either average or power. When

Chris got into one of his torrid hot streaks, he was impossible to get out. Over the three consecutive seasons that the Yanks won the AL pennant (1976-78), Chris was an important run producer, knocking in at least 90 runs in each season. (He totaled 276 RBIs over the three years.)

DEFENSIVE ABILITIES: When Chris joined the Yanks he was a poor defensive first baseman. However, through hard work and constant practice, he made himself the best defensive first baseman in the AL. In 1978 he led AL first basemen in fielding (.997), a mark that also tied the Yankee club record at the position. Chris won the Gold Glove Award for his fielding excellence in 1978. He made all the plays a first baseman must make and he was markedly adept at handling bad throws.

QUIET, CLASS GUY: On a turbulent club with many explosive personalities, Chris was the quiet, steady guy on the Yanks. He always conducted himself in a dignified manner. Never one to squawk, Chris would accept any position in the batting order and these ran from second to eighth. He would quietly take the field and do his job.

CLUB LEADERSHIP: Chris led the Yanks in at-bats three years in a row (1976-78). Twice he led the Yanks in doubles (1975-76). In 1976 he led the club in hits (188), and he tied for club leadership in hits (155) in 1979.

AL CHAMPIONSHIP SERIES: In Game 5 of the 1976 AL playoffs Chris hit one of the most dramatic HRs in baseball history. With the Yanks and Royals locked in a 6-6 tie, Chris led off the bottom of the ninth inning by ripping a HR to win the AL pennant for the Yanks. The Yankee Stadium fans went wild! Chris was also a hero of Game 3 of the 1976 playoffs, driving in three runs, including a two-run HR, to lead the Yanks to a 5-3 victory. From those 1976 playoffs, Chris still has 5-game ALCS batting records for Total Bases (20) and Hits (11). In Game 2 of the 1978 playoffs he tied a Championship Series record by getting four singles. In that Series he also tied records for most consecutive hits (five); most hits in two consecutive games (six); and most singles in a four-game Series (six). Chris also holds many Championship Series fielding records.

WORLD SERIES: In Game 6, the final game, of the 1977 Series, Chris hit an important two-run HR, helping the Yanks defeat the Dodgers, 8-4, to capture the club's first World Championship in 15 years. Chris missed much of the 1978 Series due to a wrist injury.

TRADED: In November, 1979, the Yanks traded Chris, infielder Damaso Garcia and pitcher Paul Mirabella to the Toronto Blue Jays for catcher Rick Cerone, pitcher Tom Underwood and minor league outfielder Ted Wilborn. A month later he was dealt by the Blue Jays to the Braves. Chris played for Atlanta through 1986, with his best season coming in 1982 (20 HRs, 86 RBIs, .270). He finished his ML career with one at-bat with the Yanks in 1988. He also coached for the Yanks in 1988 and was the batting coach from 1996 through the 2000 seasons.

CHAMBLISS, CHRIS

Yr.	G	AB	R	H	2B	3B	HR	RBI	BB	SB	BA	SA
1974	110	400	38	97	16	3	6	43	23	0	.243	.343
1975	150	562	66	171	38	4	9	72	29	0	.304	.434
1976	156	641	79	188	32	6	17	96	27	1	.293	.441
1977	157	600	90	172	32	6	17	90	45	4	.287	.445
1978	162	625	81	171	26	3	12	90	41	2	.274	.382
1979	149	554	61	155	27	3	18	63	34	3	.280	.437
1988	1	1	0	0	0	0	0	0	0	0	.000	.000
7 Yrs.	885	3383	415	954	171	25	79	454	199	10	.282	.417
Life.	2175	7571	912	2109	392	42	185	972	632	40	.279	.415

Championship Series

Yr.	G	AB	R	H	2B	3B	HR	RBI	BA
1976	5	21	5	11	1	1	2	8	.524
1977	5	17	0	1	0	0	0	0	.059
1978	4	15	1	6	0	0	0	2	.400
3 Yrs.	14	53	6	18	1	1	2	10	.340
Life.	17	63	6	18	1	1	2	10	.286

World Series

Yr.	G	AB	R	H	2B	3B	HR	RBI	BA
1976	4	16	1	5	1	0	0	1	.313
1977	6	24	4	7	2	0	1	4	.292
1978	3	11	1	2	0	0	0	0	.182
3 Yrs.	13	51	6	14	3	0	1	5	.275
Life. Same.									

CHANDLER, SPUD
(BORN SPURGEON FERDINAND CHANDLER)

Yankee: 1937-47
Pitcher
Born: September 12, 1907
Birthplace: Commerce, GA
Died: January 9, 1990
Bat: R; Throw: R
Ht: 6'; Wt: 180

HONORS: Spud was named the MVP of the AL in 1943 by both the Baseball Writers and *The Sporting News*. Also in 1943, Spud was named the ML Player of the Year and was picked as one of three pitchers on that season's ML All-Star team, both honors bestowed on him by *The Sporting News*.

COLLEGE STAR: After graduating from high school in Georgia in 1928, Spud attended the University of Georgia and played baseball, football and track. Before a Georgia football game against N.Y.U. at Yankee Stadium, Spud stood on the pitcher's mound holding a football and declared, "Right here is where I'm going to be." Both the Cardinals and Cubs tried to sign Spud while he was in college, but after graduating he signed with the Yanks.

ROUGH ROAD: It took Spud some 4½ years of training in the Yankee farm system before he made the Yanks. Spud made his first ML start in the spring of 1937, pitching a four-hitter but losing a heartbreaking 1-0 decision to the White Sox. He had a 7-4 Yankee record in 1937, but as he approached his 30th birthday, Spud hurt his arm and the Yanks sent him down to Newark for the remainder of the season. Besides helping the Yanks win the 1937 AL pennant, Spud was a star pitcher for the Newark Bears, the great Yankee farm club that won the International League title by 25½ games.

YANKEE STAR: Following a fine 1938 season as the Yanks' fourth starter (14-5), Spud missed most of the 1939 season because of a broken leg. He was one of the top four Yankee starters in the early 1940s, becoming a complete pitcher in 1941 after developing a slider. By 1943 he was about the best pitcher in baseball (20-4). Spud missed most of the 1944-45 seasons while serving in the military. He returned from service in 1946 to win 20 games at the age of 39! At the age of 40 in 1947, Spud led the AL in ERA (2.46) in his final ML season.

DETERMINED AND SMART: Milton Gross once wrote a cover story about Spud in the *Saturday Evening Post* titled "The Yankees' Angry Ace," contributing to Spud's reputation for building anger in himself before starting a game. But Spud felt it was his fierce determination to win that was mistaken for anger. Spud loosened up away from the strictly business atmosphere of the diamond and liked to play practical jokes, along with his roommate Atley Donald. On the mound Spud used his brain. He was successful pitching to Ted Williams, working the ball around and showing the fastball (but offering no fat ones). Spud challenged other hitters.

UNUSUAL FACTS: His unusual name, Spud, was simply an abbreviation of his real first name, Spurgeon. In a 1940 game against Chicago, Spud had six RBIs, two HRs and a grand slam (a rarity for a pitcher), and won, 10-2. Although respected for his pitching control, Spud, in 1940, tied for AL leadership in hit batsmen (six).

1943 SEASON: Spud had one of the greatest pitching years in Yankee history. He started the campaign with a 19-2 record. Then he lost two games; an extra-inning game to the Indians and a 3-2 extra-inning decision to the Senators. In his final start, Spud beat Detroit, 2-1, in 14 innings. He led AL pitchers in wins (20), winning percentage (.833), complete games (20), shutouts (five) and ERA (1.64). His ERA is the lowest ever compiled in a season by a Yankee pitcher. Then in the World Series, Spud won a pair of games and was the Series hero. He won Game 1 by a 4-2 score, then blanked the Cardinals in the final game, 2-0, to regain for the Yanks the World Championship.

CLUB LEADERSHIP: Spud led Yankee pitchers in ERA and shutouts three times. Twice he led the Yanks in wins, innings pitched, strikeouts, complete games and games started. In 1946 Spud led the club in games pitched (34), an unusual accomplishment for a starter.

RELIEF APPEARANCES: Spud started 184 of his ML career 211 appearances (completing better than 50% of his starts). Of his 27 ML relief appearances, 11 came in 1939 when he was used strictly as a relief pitcher. He saved four games in only eight relief games in 1941 and saved both games in a pair of relief appearances in 1946. Spud got the final out and a save in Game 1 of the 1942 World Series to protect Red Ruffing's win. Spud's two-inning relief appearance in Game 3 of the 1947 World Series was his final ML effort.

ALL-STAR GAMES: In 1942, 1943, 1946 and 1947, Spud was selected to the AL team for the All-Star Game. He started and was the winning pitcher of the 1942 All-Star Game, pitching four shutout innings.

GREATEST GAME: Before 69,107 fans at Yankee Stadium on July 1, 1946, Spud entered the ninth inning of a game against the Red Sox with a no-hitter intact. But with one out Boston's Bobby Doerr singled to spoil the potential no-hitter. Spud won the game, 2-1.

BASEBALL'S ALL-TIME LEADER: Including all ML pitchers with at least 100 lifetime ML victories, Spud is second highest in winning percentage in ML history (.717) on the basis of a 109-43 record.

ALL-TIME YANKEE LEADER LIST: Spud is sixth on the all-time Yankee shutout list (26). His career ERA (2.84) is the sixth lowest in Yankee history. Spud is tenth on the all-time Yankee complete game list (109). Chandler also ranks 15th in wins (109) and 16th in innings pitched (1485).

RETIREMENT: Although Spud won the 1947 ERA title, he was bothered during the season by arm miseries that limited his pitching to 128 innings. Spud retired as a pitcher in April of 1948. Without doubt he was one of the greatest pitchers in Yankee history. Spud was a coach for the Kansas City A's from 1957-58.

YANKEE SCOUT: Following his retirement as a player, Spud was a Yankee scout; he wanted to sign Herb Score and Frank Lary, but the Yanks' front office failed to approve the necessary bonus money, and the Yanks lost both pitchers. Scouting for Cleveland in 1962, Spud signed Lou Piniella.

CHANDLER, SPUD

Yr.	W-L	Pct.	SA	G	GS	CG	IP	H	BB	SO	SH	ERA
1937	7-4	.636	0	12	10	6	82	79	20	31	2	2.84
1938	14-5	.737	0	23	23	14	172	183	47	36	2	4.03
1939	3-0	1.000	0	11	0	0	19	26	9	4	0	2.84
1940	8-7	.533	0	27	24	6	172	184	60	56	1	4.60
1941	10-4	.714	4	28	20	11	164	146	60	60	4	3.19
1942	16-5	.762	0	24	24	17	201	176	74	74	3	2.38
1943	20-4	.833	0	30	30	20	253	197	54	134	5	1.64
1944	0-0	.000	0	1	1	0	6	6	1	1	0	4.50
1945	2-1	.667	0	4	4	2	31	30	7	12	1	4.65
1946	20-8	.714	2	34	32	20	257	200	90	138	6	2.10
1947	9-5	.643	0	17	16	13	128	100	41	68	2	2.46
11 Yrs.	109-43	.717	6	211	184	109	1485	1327	463	614	26	2.84
Life. Same.												

World Series

Yr.	G	IP	BB	SO	H	W-L	SA
1941	1	5	2	2	4	0-1	0
1942	2	8⅓	1	3	5	0-1	1
1943	2	18	3	10	17	2-0	0
1947	1	2	3	1	2	0-0	0
4 Yrs.	6	33⅓	9	16	28	2-2	1
Life. Same.							

CHAPMAN, BEN

Yankee: 1930-36
Outfielder
Born: December 25, 1908
Birthplace: Nashville, TN
Died: July 7, 1993
Bat: R; Throw: R
Ht: 6'; Wt: 190

MINOR LEAGUE STAR: Ben's brief minor league career made a favorable impression on scouts. With Asheville of the Sally League in 1928, he hit .336, and he had an outstanding year with St. Paul of the American Association in 1929 (31 HRs, 137 RBIs, .336). The Yanks were happy to obtain him.

POSITION CHANGE: Ben in 1930 began his Yankee career as an infielder, playing third and second base. He quickly proved he was a fine hitter, going .316 in his rookie season, but he was *not* a fine infielder. Joe McCarthy switched him to the outfield in 1931 and there Ben found a home and an opportunity to excel as an all-around player.

EXCITING BALLPLAYER: Ben was exciting. He could hit both for average and with some power, run the bases with speed and daring, and field and throw with the best of them. He led the AL in triples (13) in 1934. On July 9, 1932, he hit a pair of inside-the-park HRs (to go with one over-the-fence shot) at Yankee Stadium and is one of only two ballplayers to achieve that feat in an AL game. On May 24, 1936, he reached base seven times in as many at-bats (two doubles, five walks), an AL record for a nine-inning game.

BASE STEALER: Ben was the speediest Yankee since Fritz Maisel. He led the AL in stolen bases three consecutive seasons (1931-33). The 61 bases he stole in 1931 were the most in the ML's between Ty Cobb's 96 in 1915 and Maury Wills' 104 in 1962. Ben averaged 30.5 stolen bases over his six complete Yankee seasons. He led the AL in times caught stealing four years in a row (1931-34), an AL record. In 1931 he was thrown out 23 times, most in Yankee history.

CLUB LEADERSHIP: In five consecutive seasons (1931-35), Ben led the Yanks in stolen bases. In 1934 he led the Yanks in at-bats (588), and in 1935 he paced the club in doubles (38).

ALL-TIME YANKEE LEADER: Ben is tied for fifth place on the Yanks' all-time stolen base list (184) and his Yankee career-batting mark (.305) is 11th highest among those with at least 1500 Yankee at-bats. He places 15th in triples (64).

DEFENSIVE ABILITIES: Ben was an accomplished outfielder and had a great throwing arm. He was the Yanks' starting leftfielder from 1931-33 and the regular centerfielder in 1934-35. His 24 assists in 1933 led all AL outfielders and set a Yankee assist record for leftfielders. In 1935 he led all AL outfielders in double plays (7) and assists (25), the latter the Yankee record for centerfielders.

QUICK TEMPER: Ben was as well known for his quick temper as for his quick bat. In his early days as a Yank he had some loud arguments with Babe Ruth, but Ben and Babe became good friends. Joe McCarthy was not so understanding; he disliked Ben and his temper and was prepared to trade him when given the chance.

WASHINGTON BRAWL: In a1933 game at Griffith Stadium, Ben slid hard into second base, crushing the Senators' Buddy Myer who reacted by kicking Ben. Both teams charged onto the field and fights broke out everywhere. Following the ejection of Myer, Ben and Yankee Dixie Walker (Ben's roommate), Ben punched out Senator pitcher Earl Whitehill as he walked to the locker room. The entire Washington team then pounced on Ben and Dixie. Meanwhile, on the diamond the Yanks battled Senator fans who were roaming the field and swinging at anyone wearing a Yankee uniform. The upshot was that AL President Will Harridge suspended Chapman, Myer and Whitehill for five days and fined each $100.

ALL-STAR GAMES: As a Yankee player, Ben was selected to the AL team in the first three years that the All-Star Game was staged (1933-35). He led off for the AL in the 1933 game, thus becoming the first AL batter in All-Star Game history.

1932 WORLD SERIES: Ben stroked an important two-run single to lead the Yanks to a 5-2 victory over the Cubs in Game 2. He accounted for six RBIs, second only to Lou Gehrig, in the Yanks' four-game sweep of Chicago. The 1932 Series was the only Series of Ben's career.

TRADED: The Yanks in June of 1936 traded Ben to the Washington Senators for outfielder Jake Powell.

BASEBALL MANAGER: His playing days behind him, Ben managed in the minors and majors for many years. His temper remained alive and occasionally got him into trouble. He was barred from managing in the minors for an entire season for attacking an umpire. As the Phillies' manager in 1947, he was probably the roughest man in the NL in his attacks on rookie Jackie Robinson. He directed brutal slurs toward Robinson, the insults having the unwanted effect of bringing the Dodger team closer together.

CHAPMAN, BEN

Yr.	G	AB	R	H	2B	3B	HR	RBI	BB	SB	BA	SA
1930	138	513	74	162	31	10	10	81	43	14	.316	.474
1931	149	600	120	189	28	11	17	122	75	61	.315	.483
1932	150	581	101	174	41	15	10	107	71	38	.299	.473
1933	147	565	112	176	36	4	9	98	72	27	.312	.437
1934	149	588	82	181	21	13	5	86	67	26	.308	.413
1935	140	553	118	160	38	8	8	74	61	17	.289	.430
1936	36	139	19	37	14	3	1	21	15	1	.266	.432
7 Yrs.	909	3539	626	1079	209	64	60	589	404	184	.305	.445
Life.	1717	6478	1144	1958	407	107	90	977	824	287	.302	.440

World Series

Yr.	G	AB	R	H	2B	3B	HR	RBI	BA
1932	4	17	1	5	2	0	0	6	.294
1 Yr.	4	17	1	5	2	0	0	6	.294
Life. Same.									

CHASE, HAL
(BORN HAROLD HARRIS CHASE)

Nickname: "Prince Hal"
Yankee: 1905-13
First Baseman, OF, 2B, SS, 3B, P
Born: February 13, 1883
Birthplace: Los Gatos, CA
Died: May 18, 1947
Bat: R; Throw: L
Ht: 6'; Wt: 175

YOUNG PROSPECT: From 1902-04, Hal played first base and second base at Santa Clara University where his coach was Joe Corbett, brother of Gentleman Jim Corbett, the boxer. After a game in Los Angeles in 1904, Hal was signed by the Los Angeles franchise of the Pacific Coast League. He quickly became a fan favorite and was recognized as a brilliant defensive first baseman. The Yankees (Highlanders) in October of 1904 drafted Hal in violation of the peace agreement between the PCL and ML baseball, a move that created some contention.

YANKEE STAR: Hal was the Yanks' first baseman from 1905 through May of 1913. He was the club's biggest star during his entire nine-season Yankee tenure and was one of the biggest drawing cards in the MLs. New York fans recognized Hal as a smart player, a reliable hitter and a defensive genius. Grantland Rice put Hal on his all-time "Smart Players" team; Clark Griffith called him the most graceful player he had ever seen. He was picked as the first baseman on the all-time all-star teams of both Babe Ruth and Ed Barrow even while Lou Gehrig was in his prime! Ruth made his selection in 1934 and time did not change his mind. Barrow's team was selected in 1939; however, Ed later made Gehrig his first baseman.

GOOD HITTER: Although Hal is not remembered for his hitting, his .291 lifetime BA proves that he could hit. (He hit .339 to win a NL batting title in 1916, playing for Cincinnati.) Hal led the Yanks in batting, hits and at-bats four times. Twice he led the Yanks in doubles. In an August 30,1906, ten-inning game, he rapped three triples and a double. Hal threw lefthanded and batted right-handed, a real rarity.

CHASE THE PITCHER: In 1908, Hal took the mound for one game for the Highlanders. He pitched one-third of an inning in relief with no walks or strikeouts.

ALL-TIME YANKEE LEADER: Hal ranks third on the all-time Yankee list for stolen bases (248) although he never led the Yanks in stolen bases over a single season! His 40 SBs in 1910 set the single-season record for a Yankee first baseman.

DEFENSIVE WIZARD: Hal was one of the flashiest first basemen in baseball history. He played far off the base line, covering ground throughout the right side of the infield. It is said that he was capable of handling bunts on the THIRD BASE SIDE of the plate and throwing runners out at any base! Although Hal threw lefthanded, in his ML career he played 36 games at second base, two games at shortstop and one game at third base, an unheard of display of versatility. In 1911 he led AL first basemen in putouts (1255) and double plays (62). Ironically, it was the only

Yankee season in which he led the AL in positive fielding statistics. (In 1905, 1909, 1911 and 1912, he led AL first basemen in errors, a seeming contradiction to his fielding reputation.)

DEFENSIVE RECORDS: Hal is 13th on baseball's all-time first basemen's total chances list (19,627). In a nine-inning game played on September 21, 1906, Hal made 22 putouts, an AL record for first basemen which was later tied by Don Mattingly in 1987. In a doubleheader played on August 5, 1905, Hal cleanly accepted 38 chances, an AL consecutive-game record for first basemen.

SUSPICIOUS CHARACTER: At least two Yankee managers, George Stallings (1909-10) and Frank Chance (1913), were convinced that "Prince Hal" threw games for gamblers. He committed this treachery on defense, they believed, because though Hal was rated as a fielder beyond comparison, he had an unfortunate habit of making errors at critical moments. This, sadly, is the real legacy of Hal Chase. Hal was a free spirit, a strange and complex man, a known gambler (and flashy card player) and a ballplayer known for his gambling connections. He was a devout Westerner who was especially happy when in the San Jose, Calif. area. He did not like the East and often said so. Many people felt that Hal's misplays did not add up, not for a defensive wizard. Some hated him and regarded him as a cancer on baseball. There were others, however, who saw Hal as easy-going, likable and generous. To some he was a bad apple, willing to sell himself and teammates to gambling interests; to others he was a talented man who was as disdainful of hard work and responsibility as he was of the East. Sportswriter Jim Price said Hal had "a corkscrew brain."

BASEBALL'S GUILT: This was said of Hal in a June 1913 issue of *The Sporting News:* "That he can play first as it never was and perhaps never will be played is a well-known truth. That he *will* is a different matter." It was generally felt in baseball circles long before 1913 that Hal might have been betting on games, but neither the AL office nor Yankee management ever made a substantive investigation. In fact, authorities mostly ignored reports of corruption among players (especially the drawing cards) and at the time there was plenty of gambling, fixing and game-throwing going on. Players knew of player corruption; they noticed that no one was ever disciplined and thus were encouraged to join it. Also, long before Hal Chase was ever accused of throwing games he continually broke other ML rules, but the National Commission (baseball's governing body) and Yankee management never adequately disciplined him. ML baseball's permissiveness invited the game-rocking scandals that culminated in the Black Sox scandal of 1919.

EARLY CONTROVERSIES: Following the 1905 and 1906 Yankee campaigns, Hal played for San Jose of the outlaw California League each year through November. He said before the 1907 season that he would again play in California unless the Yanks paid him $4000. The Yanks satisfied Hal, but when the 1907 season ended he turned up with San Jose and was hitting .300 late in October when the National Commission ruled that anyone playing in the outlaw league would be suspended from organized baseball. Hal changed his name and kept on playing. He fooled no one. He was suspended but then was reinstated for the 1908 season.

MORE CONTROVERSIES: On September 3, 1908, Hal jumped the Yanks. Kid Elberfeld was made manager on June 24 and Hal may have been angry because the job didn't go to him. He left a statement objecting to a newspaper story questioning his character and honesty. Frank Farrell, the Yanks' owner, called the note an excuse to jump the Yanks and sign in the California League. Now with Stockton, Hal said he was through playing ball in the East. Early in 1909, Hal paid a $200 fine, was reinstated by the National Commission and signed a Yankee contract for $4500. But smallpox kept him from reporting until early May. In 1910 Manager Stallings and Hal had problems and nearly fought in mid-season after Stallings accused Hal of trying to throw a game. Hal stayed in the manager's doghouse; his part-time play was called an "unavoidable absence." *The New York Times* reported on September 20 that Stallings planned to quit if Hal remained on the Yanks. But Farrell and AL President Ban Johnson cleared Hal of throwing games, and on September 23 Farrell forced Stallings' resignation. The next day Hal Chase became the new Yankee manager!

YANKEE MANAGER: During the final 11 games of 1910, Hal managed the Yanks to a 9-2 record. In 1911 the Yanks paid him $6000 to be player-manager, probably making him the highest paid player in the AL, but the Yanks were a mediocre sixth-place team (76-76). Reportedly, Hal had wanted the Yankee managing job for several years. But on November 21, 1911, he was forced to give it up. He agreed to remain with the Yankees as a player only.

YANKEE EXIT: In the spring of 1913 Hal was hitting in the low 200s and was struggling. Yankee Manager Frank Chance told sportswriter Heywood Broun he suspected Hal of throwing games, and Broun printed in the *New York Tribune* a brief, watered-down version of Chance's remarks, stating only that Chance had said that Hal was not playing up to his ability and was "laying down." Nevertheless, a tremendous commotion was kicked off by the story, and two days later, on May 31, the Yanks traded Hal to the White Sox for Babe Borton and Rollie Zeider. A week later as a White Sox player, Hal went two for four at the Polo Grounds. He drew mixed greetings from Yankee fans —a crescendo of boos and cheers.

TURBULENT TIMES: Strange occurrences followed Hal everywhere he went; he was surrounded by suspicion the rest of his baseball career. He was involved in a web of complicated controversies, including more club jumping and league jumping resulting in court injunctions and overruled injunctions, good and bad years, and an apparent blacklisting by AL clubs. On August 9, 1918, Hal was suspended for "indifferent playing" by Cincinnati Manager Christy Mathewson. Mathewson charged Hal with throwing games, but when hearings were held in early 1919, Matty was in Europe with the Army. And although damaging evidence of gambling on games was presented from three Cincinnati teammates, a Giant pitcher and John McGraw, NL President John Heydler ruled that Hal had acted in a "careless manner" but was acquitted because the charges could not be proved. (Privately, Heydler believed Hal was guilty.) Surprisingly, before the 1919 season, Hal signed a Giant contract to play for Manager McGraw (and Mathewson who became a Giant coach).

BANNED FROM BASEBALL: Reports surfaced late in the 1919 season that Giant teammates Hal Chase and Heinie Zimmerman had sold out their team. Meanwhile, NL President Heydler apparently found the proof he needed to nail Hal (Hal's canceled $500 check from a gambler). Hal and Zimmerman were very quietly "indefinitely suspended" from the Giants on orders from Heydler. (The matter was hush-hush and not fully revealed until 1920.) In effect, Hal was banished from ML baseball. In a June 1920 trial, Lee Magee testified that he and Hal, as Cincinnati teammates, on July 25, 1918 bet $500 against the Reds in a game the Reds won. In August 1920, Hal was banned from the Pacific Coast League and two other West Coast circuits for allegedly trying to bribe a Salt Lake City pitcher. Hal denied the charges, blaming his "enemies in baseball."

BLACK SOX SCANDAL: In September of 1920, Hal was linked to the Black Sox scandal in testimony by Rube Benton. Benton said Hal had alerted him to the upcoming 1919 World Series fix, that Hal had received several telegrams from a Bill Burns, a fixer, and that he had won more than $40,000 betting on the Series. Benton testified that Chase and Zimmerman offered him $800 to throw a game in 1919 when all three were Giants. Hal's name continued to be bandied about concerning the Black Sox scandal and other bribes. In October 1920, Hal was indicted by the Cook County Grand Jury, but California refused to allow extradition, so Hal never stood trial. Years later, Hal stated he would have testified in Chicago if he had been given $500 for traveling expenses.

FINAL LIVING YEARS: In the years prior to his death in 1947, Hal made some admissions concerning Rube Benton's testimony. But he claimed that although he had prior knowledge of the 1919 World Series fix, he had not profited from it. Hal never officially tried to clear himself. (In a 1931 letter to Commissioner Landis, he admitted to "past mistakes." Landis indicated he would listen to Hal's story—Benton was a player who had been allowed to continue in baseball—but Hal's lawyer advised him not to pursue the matter.) Hal made no deathbed confessions. That he was involved in the Black Sox scandal, or any other scandal for that matter, is not a certainty. Even several of Hal's former Yankee teammates had trouble sorting fact from fiction and innuendo. Yet Hal was involved in so many controversies on and off the diamond (his second divorce was on grounds of "dissipation and gambling") that it is difficult to view the circumstances of his baseball life without developing an unfavorable impression.

Much of the foregoing was compiled from two invaluable sources: Robert C. Hoie's article, "The Hal Chase Case," which appeared in the 1981 Baseball Historical Review of the Society for American Baseball Research, and the chapter, "Hal Chase: He Had a Corkscrew Brain," in Fred Lieb's book of personal memoirs, Baseball As I Have Known It. Each of these excellent works provides an even-handed view of a complex man. The author is indebted to the late Mr. Lieb and to Mr. Hoie.

CHASE, HAL

Yr.	G	AB	R	H	2B	3B	HR	RBI	BB	SB	BA	SA
1905	126	465	60	116	16	6	3	49	15	22	.249	.329
1906	151	597	84	193	23	10	0	76	13	28	.323	.395
1907	125	498	72	143	23	3	2	68	19	32	.287	.357
1908	106	405	50	104	11	3	1	36	15	27	.257	.306
1909	118	474	60	134	17	3	4	63	20	25	.283	.357
1910	130	524	67	152	20	5	3	73	16	40	.290	.365
1911	133	527	82	166	32	7	3	62	21	36	.315	.419
1912	131	522	61	143	21	9	4	58	17	33	.274	.372
1913	39	146	15	31	2	4	0	9	11	5	.212	.281
9 Yrs.	1059	4158	551	1182	165	50	20	494	147	248	.284	.362
Life.	1917	7417	980	2158	322	124	57	941	276	363	.291	.391

CHASE, HAL (Pitcher)

Yr.	W-L	Pct.	SA	G	GS	CG	IP	H	BB	SO	SH	ERA
1908	0-0	---	0	1	0	0	1/3	0	0	0	0	0.00
1 Yr.	0-0	---	0	1	0	0	1/3	0	0	0	0	0.00
Life. Same.												

CHESBRO, JACK
(BORN JOHN DWIGHT CHESBRO)

Nickname: "Happy Jack"
Yankee: 1903-09
Pitcher
Born: June 5, 1874
Birthplace: North Adams, MA
Died: November 6, 1931
Bat: R; Throw: R
Ht: 5'9"; Wt: 180

HONORS: In 1946 Jack was inducted into the Baseball Hall of Fame, the first Yankee pitcher to be so honored (along with Clark Griffith, another Yankee pitcher who also was inducted in 1946).

YANKEE GREAT: Jack joined the Yanks (Highlanders) in 1903, the first season of the franchise, after having posted a 28-6 record for the NL Pittsburgh Pirates in 1902. Having raided the Pirates of Jack, AL President Ban Johnson arranged for his transfer to New York. Jack was the Yanks' first great pitcher and the ace of the pitching staff between 1903-08, except for 1907 when he missed much of the season because of an ankle injury.

SPITBALL PITCHER: Jack had a fine fastball and a good curveball, but it was the spitball that made him an extraordinary pitcher. He threw the wettest spitter in baseball and it served him well; he won at least 21 games five times in his ML career (1901-04, 1906), and four times in a row. Jack in his lifetime hit 109 batters, placing him 14th on the 20th Century's all-time list, indication that the spitter sometimes got away from him. As a Yankee, Jack hit four HRs.

1904 SEASON: Jack's season may have been the greatest one for any pitcher in baseball history! In his first game in late April, he permitted a leadoff Washington single, then pitched no-hit ball the remainder of the contest, defeating the Senators, 2-0. He completed his first 30 starts and 48 of 51 in all. Jack did not leave a game he started until an August 10 game with Chicago. Down the pennant stretch, Jack was a terror, going 9-2 in September. He won his 41st game on

October 7, beating Boston, 3-2 and putting New York in first place. He lost in Boston on October 8. Two days later, on the last day of the campaign, Jack lost a game and AL pennant to Boston when he let a spitball get away for a wild pitch, allowing the winning run to score. It was an unfitting ending to a spectacular season!

1904 NUMBERS: The numbers were staggering. Jack set AL records for most wins (41), most games started (51) and most complete games (48). He also led AL pitchers in winning percentage (.774, 41-12), games pitched (55), innings pitched (455) and games won in relief (3). Jack holds the Yankee club record for most innings pitched in a season. His 239 strikeout total was the Yanks' record until Ron Guidry broke it in 1978, 74 years later. During the season, Jack won 14 consecutive games, establishing a Yankee club record. (It was also the AL record until Walter Johnson won 16 in a row in 1912.) Jack also allowed 338 hits, the most for a pitcher in one season in Yankee history. Jack won three of four games he was called into as a relief pitcher.

MILESTONES: On April 22, 1903, Jack started and lost to the Senators in the first game in Yankee history, won by Washington, 3-1. In the Yanks' first home opener, played on April 30, 1903, Jack defeated the Senators, 6-2. On May 8, 1903, he six-hit Boston, becoming the first Yankee pitcher to beat the Red Sox in baseball's most intense rivalry. On August 30, 1905, Jack gave up Ty Cobb's first ML hit, a double. Jack won his final game as a Yankee on October 1, 1908, defeating Walter Johnson and Washington, 2-1, on a five-hitter.

UNIQUE RECORD: Jack is the only ML pitcher to ever officially lead the pitchers of both big leagues in winning percentage. With the Pirates in 1902 he led NL pitchers (.824) and as a Yankee in 1904 he led the AL (.774).

LEAGUE LEADER: In 1904 Jack led AL pitchers in just about everything. In 1906, he led the AL in games started (42) and games pitched (49). In 1903 Jack's two HRs led ML pitchers.

CLUB LEADERSHIP: Five times Jack led Yankee pitchers in strikeouts, games started and games pitched. He led the club in victories four times. In three different seasons, Jack led the Yanks in ERA, innings pitched, shutouts and complete games.

ALL-TIME YANKEE LEADER: Jack is third on the all-time Yankee complete game list (168) and ninth on the Yanks' all-time inning pitched list (1953). He is tied for tenth on the Yanks' win (128) list, and he is 11th on the strikeout list (913). Jack's ERA of 2.58 is second best in Yankee history and is the best overall for right-handed pitchers. Chesbro is tied for 13th in shutouts (18), and is 20th in games pitched (269).

LEFT YANKS: A no-longer-effective 35-year-old Jack Chesbro was obtained by the Red Sox in a cash deal made with the Yanks during the 1909 season. Jack finished his ML pitching career that year with a 0-4 record. But in his prime he was one of the game's greatest pitchers.

CHESBRO'S 1904 SEASON COMPARED WITH AL PITCHING RECORDS:

Chesbro—1904		AL Record	
Wins	41	41	— Chesbro, 1904
Winning Percentage	.774	.938	— Allen, 1937
Strikeouts	239	383	— Ryan, 1973
ERA	1.82	1.01	— Leonard, 1914
Games Pitched	55	90	— Marshall, 1979
Games Started	51	51	— Chesbro, 1904
Complete Games	48	48	— Chesbro, 1904
Innings Pitched	455	464	— Walsh, 1908
Shutouts	6	13	— Coombs, 1910

CHESBRO, JACK

Yr.	W-L	Pct.	SA	G	GS	CG	IP	H	BB	SO	SH	ERA
1903	21-15	.583	0	40	36	33	325	300	74	147	1	2.77
1904	41-12	.774	0	55	51	48	455	338	88	239	6	1.82
1905	19-15	.559	0	41	38	24	303	262	71	156	3	2.20
1906	23-17	.575	1	49	42	24	325	314	75	152	4	2.96
1907	10-10	.500	0	30	25	17	206	192	46	78	1	2.53
1908	14-20	.412	2	45	31	20	289	271	67	124	3	2.93
1909	0-4	.000	0	9	4	2	50	70	13	17	0	6.30
7 Yrs.	128-93	.579	4	269	227	168	1953	1747	434	913	18	2.58
Life.	198-132	.600	5	392	332	260	2897	2647	690	1265	35	2.68

CLARKE, HORACE

Nickname: "Hoss"
Yankee: 1965-74
Second Baseman, SS, 3B
Born: June 2, 1940
Birthplace: Fredericksted, St. Croix, Virgin Islands
Bat: Both; Throw: R
Ht: 5'9"; Wt: 170

YOUNG PROSPECT: Yankee scout Jose Seda signed Horace to a contract when Horace was only 17. Horace began in the Yankee organization in 1958, playing at Kearney. From 1959-65 he played at St. Petersburg, Fargo, Binghamton, Amarillo, Richmond, and Toledo. He batted .301 in each of his final two AAA seasons in the International League at Richmond, then Toledo. Horace was called up to the Yanks late in the 1965 season and it soon was apparent that he was the heir to Bobby Richardson's second-base job.

YANKEE SECOND BASEMAN: Horace was the Yanks' utility infielder in 1966, playing mostly shortstop. When Richardson retired after the 1966 season, Horace became the regular Yankee second baseman, holding the job for seven seasons (1967-73). He was the Yankee leadoff man and he was a switch-hitter, one of four Yankee starters who switch-hit in 1968. While playing for the Yanks, Horace lived in the Bronx near Yankee Stadium. On the club he was a nice, quiet guy, but the press often found him to be an easy target for criticism.

DEFENSIVE ABILITIES: Horace was a sure-fielding second baseman. For six consecutive seasons (1967-72) he led AL second basemen in assists, an AL record. His lifetime ML fielding average at second base (.983) is within the top 15 of all time.

CLUB LEADERSHIP: Five times Horace led the Yanks in at-bats. Four times he led the club in stolen bases. He paced the team in runs scored and hits twice in each category.

ALL-TIME YANKEE LEADER: Horace is tied for ninth on the all-time Yankee stolen base list (151). Willie Randolph is the only Yankee second baseman to steal more bases than Horace.

SPOILER OF NO-HITTERS: During the summer of 1970, Horace put on an incredible display of spoiling no-hitters. Within a period of four weeks, Horace made a hit in the ninth inning to end no-hit bids by Kansas City's Jim Rooker, Boston's Sonny Siebert and Detroit's Joe Niekro. No one could remember anything like it. Earlier in the 1970 season, Horace in the ninth inning broke up a potential Jim Palmer bid for a no-hitter!

LEFT YANKS: During the 1974 season, Horace was dealt to the San Diego Padres. His ML career ended in 1974.

CLARKE, HORACE

Yr.	G	AB	R	H	2B	3B	HR	RBI	BB	SB	BA	SA
1965	51	108	13	28	1	0	1	9	6	2	.259	.296
1966	96	312	37	83	10	4	6	28	27	5	.266	.381
1967	143	588	74	160	17	0	3	29	42	21	.272	.316
1968	148	579	52	133	6	1	2	26	23	20	.230	.254
1969	156	641	82	183	26	7	4	48	53	33	.285	.367
1970	158	686	81	172	24	2	4	46	35	23	.251	.309
1971	159	625	76	156	23	7	2	41	64	17	.250	.318
1972	147	547	65	132	20	2	3	37	56	18	.241	.302
1973	148	590	60	155	21	0	2	35	47	11	.263	.308
1974	24	47	3	11	1	0	0	1	4	1	.234	.255
10 Yrs.	1230	4723	543	1213	149	23	27	300	357	151	.257	.315
Life.	1272	4813	548	1230	150	23	27	304	365	151	.256	.313

COATES, JIM

Yankee: 1956, '59-62
Pitcher
Born: August 4, 1932
Birthplace: Farnham, VA
Bat: R; Throw: R
Ht: 6'4"; Wt: 192

YOUNG PROSPECT: The Yanks signed Jim in 1952. From 1952-58 Jim worked his way through the Yankee farm system, stopping for a cup of coffee in New York in 1956. He was 14-11 at Richmond in the AAA International League in 1957. A sore arm caused him to miss almost the entire 1958 season. In 1959 Jim made the Yanks.

VERSATILE PITCHER: Jim held the difficult job of being the short reliever, long reliever and spot starter on the Yankee pitching staff. He was selected to the AL All-Star team for the 1960 All-Star Game. In 1960 Jim led the Yanks in winning percentage (.813, 13-3). In fact, he had a great Yankee career win percentage (.712, 37-15) for his five seasons with the club.

WORLD SERIES: In Game 4 of the 1961 Series Jim combined with Whitey Ford to blank Cincinnati, 7-0. Jim pitched the final four innings of that game to record a save.

TRADED: The Yanks traded Jim to the Washington Senators for pitcher Steve Hamilton in April, 1963.

COATES, JIM

Yr.	W-L	Pct.	SA	G	GS	CG	IP	H	BB	SO	SH	ERA
1956	0-0	.000	0	2	0	0	2	1	4	0	0	13.50
1959	6-1	.857	3	37	4	2	100	89	36	64	0	2.87
1960	13-3	.813	1	35	18	6	149	139	66	73	2	4.28
1961	11-5	.688	5	43	11	4	141	128	53	80	1	3.44
1962	7-6	.538	6	50	6	0	118	119	50	67	0	4.44
5 Yrs.	37-15	.712	15	167	39	12	511	476	209	284	3	3.84
Life.	43-22	.662	18	247	46	13	683	650	286	396	4	4.00

World Series

Yr.	G	IP	BB	SO	H	W-L	SA
1960	3	6⅓	1	3	6	0-0	0
1961	1	4	1	2	1	0-0	1
1962	2	2⅔	1	3	1	0-1	0
3 Yrs.	6	13	3	8	8	0-1	1
Life. Same.							

COLEMAN, JERRY

Yankee: 1949-57
Second Baseman, SS, 3B
Born: September 14, 1924
Birthplace: San Jose, CA
Bat: R; Throw: R
Ht: 6'; Wt: 165

YOUNG PROSPECT: The Yanks signed Jerry in 1942. He was a shortstop in the Yankee farm system, advancing all the way up to the Yanks' top club at Newark. Jerry was a fighter pilot during World War II. He was one of many excellent prospects who came through the Yankee farm system during the late 1940s. He was also one of a long line of Yankee players who came from the San Francisco Bay area (Meusel, Lazzeri, Crosetti, Gomez, DiMaggio, Martin, etc.) In spring training of 1949, Casey Stengel switched Jerry to second base and there Jerry found a home.

YANKEE SECOND BASEMAN: Jerry played his entire ML career with the Yanks. He was a starter in his rookie season and was the regular Yankee second baseman from 1949-51. He missed almost all of the 1952-53 baseball seasons while serving in the military. Jerry was the Yanks' utility infielder in his final four years on the club (1954-57). His best season at the plate was 1950 (.287, 69 RBIs).

DEFENSIVE ABILITIES: Jerry was a slick-fielding second baseman, remembered for his acrobatic maneuvering around second base. He turned the double play beautifully with shortstop Phil Rizzuto. His 137 double plays in 1950, the Yankee record for second basemen, also ranks ninth in baseball's single season top 10. In 1949, Jerry's rookie season, he led AL second basemen in fielding (.981). He was called "Fancy Dan" because of his slick fielding.

ALL-STAR GAME: Jerry was picked to the All-Star team for the 1950 All-Star Game. He batted twice in that game.

WORLD SERIES: Jerry was the hero of the 1950 Series, winning the Babe Ruth Award as the Series MVP. In Game 1 of that Series he produced the game's only run with a sacrifice fly to beat the Phillies, 1-0. Then in the bottom of the ninth inning of Game 3, his single drove in the winning run to break the Phillies' back. He also handled 23 chances without making an error in the

Jerry Coleman

SAN DIEGO MAN: During the 1970s, Jerry worked for the San Diego Padres in a number of capacities. He broadcast Padres games for a long time and then, in October of 1979, Jerry was named Padres' manager. Following the 1980 season, Jerry returned to the Padres' broadcast booth.

COLEMAN, JERRY

Yr.	G	AB	R	H	2B	3B	HR	RBI	BB	SB	BA	SA
1949	128	447	54	123	21	5	2	42	63	8	.275	.358
1950	153	522	69	150	19	6	6	69	67	3	.287	.381
1951	121	362	48	90	11	2	3	43	31	6	.249	.315
1952	11	42	6	17	2	1	0	4	5	0	.405	.500
1953	8	10	1	2	0	0	0	0	0	0	.200	.200
1954	107	300	39	65	7	1	3	21	26	3	.217	.277
1955	43	96	12	22	5	0	0	8	11	0	.229	.281
1956	80	183	15	47	5	1	0	18	12	1	.257	.295
1957	72	157	23	42	7	2	2	12	20	1	.268	.376
9 Yrs.	723	2119	267	558	77	18	16	217	235	22	.263	.339

Life. Same.

World Series

Yr.	G	AB	R	H	2B	3B	HR	RBI	BA
1949	5	20	0	5	3	0	0	4	.250
1950	4	14	2	4	1	0	0	3	.286
1951	5	8	2	2	0	0	0	0	.250
1955	3	3	0	0	0	0	0	0	.000
1956	2	2	0	0	0	0	0	0	.000
1957	7	22	2	8	2	0	0	2	.364
6 Yrs.	26	69	6	19	6	0	0	9	.275

Life. Same.

COLLINS, JOE
(BORN JOSEPH EDWARD KOLLONIGE)

Yankee: 1948-57
First Baseman, OF
Born: December 3, 1922
Birthplace: Scranton, PA
Died: August 30, 1989
Bat: L; Throw: L
Ht: 6'; Wt: 185

1950 Series. Jerry's .364 batting average led all Yankee regulars in the 1957 Series.

BIGGEST HIT: On October 2, 1949, the final day of the season, the Yanks and Red Sox met at the Stadium. They were tied for first place and the winner would be the AL champion. The Yanks held a slim 1-0 lead until exploding for four runs in the eighth inning. The key hit of the rally (the key hit of the game and season) was Jerry's bases-loaded single to right field that scored three runs. The Yanks held on to win, 5-3.

FINE GENTLEMAN: Jerry was one of the game's real gentlemen and always conducted himself with dignity. Good-looking, intelligent and neat, Jerry was the kind of high-class person the Yanks always searched for in that era. When Bobby Richardson joined the Yanks, Jerry went out of his way to share the techniques of playing second base, a rather unselfish act since Richardson was destined to replace Jerry as Yankee second baseman.

RETIREMENT: Jerry left baseball as a player in style after a terrific 1957 World Series. When he hung up the spikes, Jerry joined the Yankee front office as assistant to GM George Weiss. A few years later, he had a pre-game show on television before becoming a regular Yankee TV-radio announcer for many years.

YANKEE SIGNING: As a 16-year-old in 1939, Joe was invited to a workout with the Indians' Wilkes-Barre farm club, but instead practiced that day with the visiting Binghamton team, a Yankee farm club. Binghamton signed Joe to a Class-D contract and he began his career in the Yankee farm system.

MINOR LEAGUER: Between 1939-48 Joe played for Yankee farm teams at Butler, Easton, Akron, Norfolk, Amsterdam, Springfield, Newark, Beaumont and Birmingham. Joe entered the Naval Air Corps in 1942 and returned to baseball in 1946. For Newark in 1946, Joe played in the outfield besides first base, making him a more versatile player. (He finished the year with Beaumont of the Texas League.) In 1947 Joe concentrated on playing first base at Birmingham. He was called up to the Newark Bears in mid-season. In 1948 Joe spent another year with Newark, then moved up to the Yanks at season's end. He endured another year of minor-league seasoning in 1949 and again finished the season in New York.

YANKEE FIRST BASEMAN: Joe played his entire ML career with the Yanks. Between 1952-54 he was the Yanks' regular first baseman. In most of his other Yankee seasons, Casey Stengel platooned Joe, playing him mostly against right-handed pitching. Up to that time, Joe held the first base job on the Yanks longer than anyone since Lou Gehrig. Joe also played 114 games in the outfield during his ML career.

OFFENSIVE THREAT: Joe hit 12 or more HRs in four consecutive seasons (1952-55). He was a good clutch hitter, a noted pull hitter and a fantastic low-ball hitter. He used a variety of batting stances. In his ML career, Joe hit the Indians and White Sox especially well. In a 1952 game in Cleveland, Joe hit a tremendous 475-foot HR into the upper deck. When Allie Reynolds pitched his second no-hitter of 1951, Joe helped his pitcher by blasting a HR. Joe was a fast runner, especially for a first baseman.

TEAM PLAYER: A winner, Joe played on 8 AL champions, 6 World Champions and 5 World Series winners in a row (1949-53). He was a positive influence on the club. He was every player's comrade and Joe enjoyed seeing the guys at each year's Old Timers' Day. When Bill Skowron, a potential job rival, joined the Yanks in 1954, Joe welcomed Bill to the club. He told Skowron that the two of them would work as a first-base team, and a productive team they proved to be. Casey Stengel called Joe "my meal ticket." Unfortunately, a number of injuries damaged Joe's career.

WORLD SERIES: Game 2 of the 1951 Series was a "must win" situation for the Yanks after losing Game 1. With the Yanks ahead, 1-0, in the second, Joe hit a low, inside curveball from the Giants' Larry Jansen for a solo HR. The Yanks won, 3-1. Joe stepped to the plate in the bottom of the seventh in Game 1 of the 1953 Series and with two outs and the score tied, 5-5, pulled a low pitch for a solo HR. The Yanks went on to beat the Dodgers, 9-5. In Game 1 of the 1955 Series, Joe hit 2 HRs—a solo shot and a deep two-run blast—to lead the Yanks to a 6-5 victory over Brooklyn. All four of Joe's career World Series HRs were hit in Yankee Stadium.

RETIREMENT: In spring training of 1958, the Yanks sold Joe's contract to the Phillies. He immediately announced his retirement from baseball because he wanted to be remembered as a Yankee and nothing else. Joe never reported to the Phillies and began a career in public relations in Newark, N.J.

COLLINS, PAT
(BORN THARON PATRICK COLLINS)

Yankee: 1926-28
Catcher
Born: September 13, 1896
Birthplace: Sweet Springs, MO
Died: May 20, 1960
Bat: R; Throw: R
Ht: 5'11"; Wt: 178

EARLY ML CAREER: Pat was a member of the St. Louis Browns for six seasons (1919-24) as a second-string catcher. He joined the Yanks in 1926.

BRONX CATCHING CHORES: During his Yankee career, Pat shared the catching chores with Benny Bengough and John Grabowski. In 1926 Pat led AL catchers in double plays (14). He was an excellent defensive catcher and a fine spray hitter.

1927 YANKEE CATCHER: As long as baseball is played, Pat will be known as the catcher on the legendary 1927 Yanks. Prior to the season's opening, he was expected to be the Yanks' regular catcher because of Bengough's injured arm, but Pat also hurt his throwing arm and was unable to play full-time. The majority of Yankee games in 1927, on the team many consider the greatest of all time, were caught by Pat (89), followed by Grabowski (68) and Bengough (30). Pat hit a respectable .275.

WINNING BALLPLAYER: In each of Pat's three Yankee seasons, the club won the AL pennant and twice the Yanks won the World Championship (1927-28), and a team does not accomplish those feats without solid catching. Pat hit a combined 4-for-8 (.500) in three World Series.

FINAL ML DAYS: The 1928 season was Pat's last as a Yankee player. The great Bill Dickey was groomed to become the Yankee catcher for 1929. The Yanks sold Pat's contract to the Boston Braves and Pat played in seven Boston games in 1929, going 0 for 5 at the plate, his final stint in ML baseball.

COLLINS, JOE

Yr.	G	AB	R	H	2B	3B	HR	RBI	BB	SB	BA	SA
1948	5	5	0	1	1	0	0	2	0	0	.200	.400
1949	7	10	2	1	0	0	0	4	6	0	.100	.100
1950	108	205	47	48	8	3	8	28	31	5	.234	.420
1951	125	262	52	75	8	5	9	48	34	9	.286	.458
1952	122	428	69	120	16	8	18	59	55	4	.280	.481
1953	127	387	72	104	11	2	17	44	59	2	.269	.439
1954	130	343	67	93	20	2	12	46	51	2	.271	.446
1955	105	278	40	65	9	1	13	45	44	0	.234	.414
1956	100	262	38	59	5	3	7	43	34	3	.225	.347
1957	79	149	17	30	1	0	2	10	24	2	.201	.248
10 Yrs.	908	2329	404	596	79	24	86	329	338	27	.256	.421
Life. Same.												

World Series

Yr.	G	AB	R	H	2B	3B	HR	RBI	BA
1950	1	0	0	0	0	0	0	0	.000
1951	6	18	2	4	0	0	1	3	.222
1952	6	12	1	0	0	0	0	0	.000
1953	6	24	4	4	1	0	1	2	.167
1955	5	12	6	2	0	0	2	3	.167
1956	6	21	2	5	2	0	0	2	.238
1957	6	5	0	0	0	0	0	0	.000
7 Yrs.	36	92	15	15	3	0	4	10	.163
Life. Same.									

COLLINS, PAT

Yr.	G	AB	R	H	2B	3B	HR	RBI	BB	SB	BA	SA
1926	102	290	41	83	11	3	7	35	73	3	.286	.417
1927	92	251	38	69	9	3	7	36	54	0	.275	.418
1928	70	136	18	30	5	0	6	14	35	0	.221	.390
3 Yrs.	264	677	97	182	25	6	20	85	162	3	.269	.412
Life.	543	1204	146	306	46	6	33	168	235	4	.254	.385

World Series

Yr.	G	AB	R	H	2B	3B	HR	RBI	BA
1926	3	2	0	0	0	0	0	0	.000
1927	2	5	0	3	1	0	0	0	.600
1928	1	1	0	1	1	0	0	0	1.000
3 Yrs.	6	8	0	4	2	0	0	0	.500
Life. Same.									

COMBS, EARLE

Nicknames: "The Kentucky Colonel," "The Southern
    Gentleman," "The Mail Carrier"
Yankee: 1924-35
Outfielder
Born: May 4, 1899
Birthplace: Pebworth, KY
Died: July 21, 1976
Bat: L; Throw: R
Ht: 6'; Wt: 185

HONORS: Earle was inducted into the Baseball Hall of Fame in 1970. One of his more personal and unusual honors was bestowed in 1928 when the Yankee Stadium bleacher fans presented Earle with an engraved watch.

MINOR LEAGUE STAR: Earle broke into professional baseball in 1922, hitting .344 for Louisville of the tough American Association. In 1923 he was sensational at Louisville, batting .380 with 14 HRs, 145 RBIs, and 241 hits. He was major league material.

CAME TO YANKS: In January of 1924 the Yanks bought Earle's contract from the Louisville minor league club.

YANKEE CENTERFIELDER: Earle played his entire ML career with the Yanks. His rookie season of 1924 ended very early because of an injury, and Babe Ruth maintained Earle's absence cost the Yanks the 1924 pennant. Earle was the regular Yankee centerfielder for nine seasons (1925-33). Blessed with outstanding speed, Earle could really go get fly balls in Yankee Stadium's vast center field. He led all AL outfielders in putouts in 1927 (411) and 1928 (424). He had an accurate arm and made loads of great catches.

LEADOFF MAN: Earle was probably the greatest leadoff batter in Yankee history and he was the leadoff man on "Murderers' Row" in 1927. His offensive responsibility was to get on base so that the big Yankee bats (Ruth, Gehrig, etc.) could knock him in. Earle was often on base: he scored over 100 runs in eight consecutive seasons (1925-32). Earle's lifetime On Base Average (.397) ties him with Richie Ashburn for the eighth highest by a centerfielder.

GREAT CONTACT HITTER: In three seasons (1925, 1927, 1929) Earle made more than 200 hits. In 1927 "The Kentucky Colonel" set Yankee club records for most hits (231), singles (166) and triples (23). During his sensational 1927 season, Earle was third in the AL in total bases (331), following Gehrig and Ruth. Against Detroit on September 22, 1927, Earle rapped three consecutive triples in one game. Earle once hit safely in 29 straight games, the Yankee club record until Joe DiMaggio's 56-game hitting streak. Driving balls hard to all fields, he hit some especially wicked shots up the middle. Primarily because of his great hitting ability, Earle was one of the higher paid regulars on the 1927 Yanks, although he made just $10,000 for the season!

LEAGUE LEADER: In 1927 Earle led the AL in at-bats (648), hits (231) and triples (23). He also led the AL in triples in 1921 (21) and 1930 (22).

CLUB LEADERSHIP: In six seasons Earle led the Yanks in triples. He led the Yanks in hits three times. Twice he led the team in runs scored and stolen bases.

"FIVE O'CLOCK LIGHTNING": During the 1920s, it was Earle who first used the expression "five o'clock lightning" to describe the patented late-inning rallies staged by the Ruth-Gehrig teams. (Sportswriter Frank Graham often used the phrase also.)

ALL-TIME YANKEE LEADER: Earle is second on the all-time Yankee triple list (154). His lifetime .325 batting average is third highest in Yankee history for those players with at least 1500 Yankee at-bats. He is fifth on the all-time Yankee runs scored list (1186). He is 11th on the Yankee double list (309). In addition, Earle is eighth in hits (1866), 14th in at-bats (5748), and 17th in games played (1455).

RELIGIOUS MAN: Earle was an extremely religious man who read the Bible daily. He did not smoke, drink or use profanity, and he was proud of his religious beliefs. His teammates and the fans respected Earle's church-going ways. Earle was a Kentucky schoolmaster. He had an unusually warm personality. He treated everyone the same; like the gentleman that he was. Handling Earle was an easy job for Yankee managers Miller Huggins and Joe McCarthy, and Earle got along splendidly with both of them. (Earle was a pallbearer at Huggins' funeral.) Earle was prematurely gray and looked older than his years.

WORLD SERIES: In the 1926 Series Earle led all Yankee batters in hitting (.357). He scored the winning run in Game 4 of the 1927 Series when Johnny Miljus uncorked a wild pitch in the bottom of the ninth; it was the Series' final game as the Yankees swept the Pirates. A sprained wrist that Earle suffered late in the 1928 season forced him to miss virtually all of that year's Series. He had a HR in Game 4 of the 1932 Series and scored four runs to help the Yanks sweep the Cubs in four games. His lifetime World Series batting average (.350) is the 14th highest in Series history for players with at least 50 Series at-bats.

INJURIES: The sprained wrist Earle suffered after running into the wall at Detroit on the next-to-last day of the 1928 season was the least of the many injuries that plagued his career. He had missed much of 1924 with a broken ankle. It was on July 24, 1934, however, that Earle suffered his most serious injury. Still in his playing prime, and hustling after a fly ball hit deep in St. Louis' Sportsman's Park, Earle crashed into the center field wall. He suffered multiple injuries, including a fractured skull.

RETIREMENT: On July 28, 1935, Earle Combs, one of baseball's greatest centerfielders, retired. He never really regained his form after the 1934 skull fracture.

YANKEE COACH: Following his retirement as a player, Earle remained with the Yanks as a coach. He was a Yankee coach from 1935-44. Earle wore the Yankee uniform continually from 1924-44. As a player and coach, "The Kentucky Colonel" was a member of 11 AL pennant-winning Yankee teams and nine World Champions. In later years Earle was a coach for the Browns (1947), Red Sox (1948-52) and Phillies (1954). Managers loved to have Earle as a coach; not only did he know tons of baseball, but he brought added class to a team as well.

COMBS, EARLE

Yr.	G	AB	R	H	2B	3B	HR	RBI	BB	SB	BA	SA
1924	24	35	10	14	5	0	0	2	4	0	.400	.543
1925	150	593	117	203	36	13	3	61	65	12	.342	.462
1926	145	606	113	181	31	12	8	55	47	8	.299	.429
1927	152	648	137	231	36	23	6	64	62	15	.356	.511
1928	149	626	118	194	33	21	7	56	77	10	.310	.463
1929	142	586	119	202	33	15	3	65	69	11	.345	.468
1930	137	532	129	183	30	22	7	82	74	16	.344	.523
1931	138	563	120	179	31	13	5	58	68	11	.318	.446
1932	144	591	143	190	32	10	9	65	81	3	.321	.455
1933	122	419	86	125	22	16	5	64	47	6	.298	.463
1934	63	251	47	80	13	5	2	25	40	3	.319	.434
1935	89	298	47	84	7	4	3	35	36	1	.282	.362
12 Yrs.	1455	5748	1186	1866	309	154	58	632	670	96	.325	.462

Life. Same.

World Series

Yr.	G	AB	R	H	2B	3B	HR	RBI	BA
1926	7	28	3	10	2	0	0	2	.357
1927	4	16	6	5	0	0	0	2	.313
1928	1	0	0	0	0	0	0	1	.000
1932	4	16	8	6	1	0	1	4	.375
4 Yrs.	16	60	17	21	3	0	1	9	.350

Life. Same.

CONE, DAVID

Yankee: 1995-99
Pitcher
Born: January 2, 1963
Birthplace: Kansas City, MO
Bat: L; Throw: R
Ht: 6'1"; Wt: 190

RETURNS TO NEW YORK: The Yankees on July 28, 1995 obtained David from Toronto for pitching prospects Marty Janzen, Jason Jarvis and Mike Gordon. Cone fit in with New York immediately. "I've never seen a guy who is as much in his element as he is here," observed Yankee Manager Buck Showalter. Cone had experienced New York City with the Mets (1987-92), which included a 20-3 record in 1988. He had become the hired gun, helping Toronto win the 1992 World Series and winning the Cy Young Award with Kansas City, his hometown team, in 1994. But he made friends easily because of his thoughtful personality. In his abbreviated season with the Yanks, David finished the 1995 season with a 9-2 record and 18-8 overall. As a Yankee pitcher, his opponents hit a feeble .223 against him. He won Game 1 of the Division Series versus Seattle and was on his way to winning Game 5 when he ran out of gas.

HEROIC COMEBACK AFTER SURGERY: After starting 1996 at 3-1, David was placed on the 60-day disabled list after it was discovered that he had an aneurysm in his right arm. He underwent surgery on May 10 and it proved to be a success. David made two rehab starts in the minors before returning in grand style to the Yankees. He pitched his first game since May

2 on September 2 at Oakland and turned in a simply heroic performance, holding the A's hitless on 85 pitches for seven innings before giving way to Mariano Rivera, who allowed one hit in the final innings and preserved the Yankee win, 5-0. In the 96 regular season, Cone appeared in just 11 games but came through like a charm in the postseason. He started three games and helped to turn the World Series around, winning Game 3 and allowing Atlanta but one run on six hits in six innings.

ANOTHER SURGERY: In 1997, David went 12-6 with a 2.82 ERA in 29 starts and opponents batted a measly .218 off him. His 222 strikeouts (third in the league) was the third highest total in Yankee history. Ron Guidry, the Cajun lefty, is first all-time with 248 in his phenomenal 25-3 season of 1978 and Jack Chesbro places second in whiffs with 239 way back in 1904, when the Yankees were known as the Highlanders. He appeared in one postseason game versus Cleveland, losing the contest after allowing six runs and seven hits in 3 $\frac{1}{3}$ innings. On October 17, Cone underwent successful arthroscopic surgery on his right shoulder.

A GREAT SEASON: Returning to the mound in 1998 after successful off-season surgery, David went 20-7 with a 3.55 ERA in 31 starts. His 20-win total was tied for first in the American League and his opponents batted a mere .237 off his servings. His win total tied his career high and broke the Major League record for most years—ten—between 20-win seasons. David had won 20 (while losing but three) with the 1988 Mets. On June 24, he became the first Yankee pitcher since Lindy McDaniel in 1972 to get a run batted in (on a fielder's choice). In the postseason, Cone started four games, winning two, one of which was the decisive Game 6 of the ALCS versus Cleveland. David won that game despite allowing the Indians five runs in five innings.

ANOTHER GREAT YEAR: For 1999, David was 12-9 with a 3.44 ERA for second place in the American League. He finished fourth in the AL in strikeouts with 177 and opponents hit only .229 against him for second AL best. His average of 8.2 strikeouts per nine innings was good enough for the third spot. In July, David made it to his fifth All-Star Game and on the 18th versus Montreal tossed a perfect game at Yankee Stadium. At the conclusion of 1999, David ranks third in Yankee history in terms of winning percentage (.740) with a 57-20 record. Only Whitey Ford (58-17, .773) and Ron Guidry (62-19, .765) are ahead of David. In the 1999 postseason, Cone won two games, one each in the ALCS and World Series. In 14 innings of work, Cone allowed eight total hits, two earned runs (1.29 ERA) and had 13 strikeouts. He has expressed a desire to return to the Yanks in 2000. In early 2000, David signed a one-year contract with the Yankees.

ALL-TIME YANKEE LEADER: David ranks 14th in Yankee history in strikeouts (888).

DAVID CONE'S PERFECT GAME—JULY 18, 1999 AT YANKEE STADIUM—NY-6; MTL-0
88 PITCHES—68 STRIKES, 20 BALLS (PITCH-BY-PITCH)

First Inning

Wilton Guerrero: Strike one (called) (1)
Strike two (foul) (2)
Strike three (called) (3)

Terry Jones: Ball one (4)
Ball two (5)
Strike one (called) (6)
Strike two (swinging) (7)
Lined to rightfielder Paul O'Neill (8)

Rondell White: Flied deep to leftfielder Ricky Ledee (9)

Second Inning

Vladimir Guerrero: Strike one (called) (10)
Strike two (swinging) (11)
Strike three (swinging) (12)

Jose Vidro: Strike one (called) (13)
Strike two (swinging) (14)
Ball one (15)
Foul ball (16)
Foul ball (17)
Grounded to first baseman Tino Martinez unassisted (18)

Brad Fullmer: Ball one (19)
Grounded to third baseman Scott Brosius (20)

Third Inning

Chris Widger: Strike one (called) (21)
Ball one (22)
Strike two (called) (23)
Strike three (swinging) (24)

Shane Andrews: Strike one (called) (25)
Strike two (swinging) (26)
Ball one (27)
Strike three (swinging) (28)

Orlando Cabrera: Ball one (29)
Strike one (called) (30)
Strike two (foul) (31)
Strike three (swinging) (32)

Fourth Inning

Wilton Guerrero: Strike one (called) (33)
Flied to rightfielder Paul O'Neill (34)

Terry Jones: Ball one (35)
Strike one (foul) (36)
Strike two (swinging) (37)
Strike three (swinging) (38)

Rondell White: Flied to rightfielder Paul O'Neill (39)

Fifth Inning

Vladimir Guerrero: Flied to leftfielder Ricky Ledee (40)

Jose Vidro: Strike one (called) (41)
Ball one (42)
Ball two (43)
Strike two (foul) (44)
Flied to centerfielder Bernie Williams (45)

Brad Fullmer: Ball one (46)
Strike one (called) (47)
Ball two (48)
Strike two (foul) (49)
Flied to centerfielder Bernie Williams (50)

Sixth Inning

Chris Widger: Strike one (swinging) (51)
Popped to second baseman Chuck Knoblauch (52)

Shane Andrews: Strike one (called) (53)
Flied to rightfielder Paul O'Neill (54)

Orlando Cabrera: Fouled to catcher Joe Girardi (55)

Seventh Inning

Wilton Guerrero: Strike one (called) (56)
Strike two (swinging) (57)
Ball one (58)
Foul ball (59)
Foul ball (60)
Grounded to second baseman Chuck Knoblauch (61)

James Mouton: Strike one (called) (62)
Strike two (swinging) (63)
Foul ball (64)
Ball one (65)
Strike three (swinging) (66)

Rondell White: Ball one (67)
Strike one (swinging) (68)
Strike two (swinging) (69)
Strike three (swinging) (70)

Eighth Inning

Vladimir Guerrero: Fouled to catcher Joe Girardi (71)

Jose Vidro: Ball one (72)
Ball two (73)
Grounded to second baseman Chuck Knoblauch (74)

Brad Fullmer: Strike one (called) (75)
Strike two (foul) (76)
Strike three (called) (77)

Ninth Inning

Chris Widger: Strike one (swinging) (78)
Strike two (called) (79)
Strike three (swinging) (80)

Ryan McGuire: Strike one (called) (81)
Ball one (82)
Ball two (83)
Strike two (swinging) (84)
Flied to leftfielder Ricky Ledee (85)

Orlando Cabrera: Strike one (swinging) (86)
Ball one (87)
Fouled to third baseman Scott Brosius (88) to complete the second REGULAR SEASON perfect game in Yankee history on 88 pitches (68 strikes—77%). Note: Don Larsen pitched his perfect game in the 1956 World Series versus the Brooklyn Dodgers.

CONE, DAVID

Yr.	W-L	Pct.	SA	G	GS	CG	IP	H	BB	SO	SH	ERA
1995	9-2	.818	0	13	13	1	99	82	47	89	0	3.82
1996	7-2	.778	0	11	11	1	72	50	34	71	0	2.88
1997	12-6	.667	0	29	29	1	195	155	86	222	0	2.82
1998	20-7	.741	0	31	31	3	208	186	59	209	0	3.55
1999	12-9	.571	0	31	31	1	193	164	90	177	1	3.44
2000	14-4	.222	0	30	29	0	155	192	82	120	0	6.91
6 Yrs.	64-40	.615	0	145	144	7	882	829	398	888	1	4.09

Still Active

Division Series

Yr.	G	IP	BB	SO	H	W-L	SA
1995	2	15.2	9	14	15	1-0	0
1996	2	6	2	8	8	0-1	0
1997	1	3.1	2	2	7	0-0	0
1998	1	5.2	1	6	2	1-0	0
4 Yrs.	6	30.2	14	30	32	2-1	0

Still Active

Championship Series

Yr.	G	IP	BB	SO	H	W-L	SA
1996	1	6	5	5	5	0-0	0
1998	2	13	6	13	12	1-0	0
1999	1	7	3	9	7	1-0	0
2000	1	1	0	0	0	0-0	0
4 Yrs.	5	27	14	27	24	2-0	0

Still Active

World Series

Yr.	G	IP	BB	SO	H	W-L	SA
1996	1	6	4	3	4	1-0	0
1998	1	6	3	4	2	0-0	0
1999	1	7	5	4	1	1-0	0
2000	1	.3	0	0	0	0-0	0
4 Yrs.	3	19.3	12	11	16	2-0	0

Still Active

David Cone

CONROY, WID
(BORN WILLIAM EDWARD CONROY)

Yankee: 1903-08
Third Baseman, OF, SS, 2B
Born: April 5, 1877
Birthplace: Camden, NJ
Died: December 6, 1959
Bat: R; Throw: R
Ht: 5'9"; Wt: 158

CAME TO YANKS: Wid was one of several players who jumped the NL, signed with the AL, and was assigned to the Yanks (Highlanders) for the 1903 season, the first in the club's short history. In 1902 Wid hit .244 in 99 games for the Pittsburgh Pirates. Wid had his finest all-round ML season in 1903 with the Yanks

EARLY YANKEE STAR: Wid was one of the first star ballplayers on the Yanks. In the first game in the history of the franchise in New York, played on April 22, 1903, Wid played third base and batted sixth.

VERSATILE PLAYER: Wid was a versatile player who for the Yanks started at third base (1903-04, 1908) and in the outfield (1906-07), besides being an infield replacement at shortstop and second base throughout his Yankee career. With the Yanks, Wid played 402 games at third base, 231 games in the outfield, 136 games at shortstop, 15 games at second base, and nine games at first base. Wid displayed good range at third, leading AL third basemen in chances per game in 1903 (3.6) and 1908 (3.8).

CLUB LEADERSHIP: Wid led or tied for club leadership in triples in the Yanks' first five seasons (1903-07). Twice he led the Yanks in at-bats (1907-08) and walks (1904, 1906). In 1905 he led the Yanks in slugging (.395). In 1906 he led the club in HRs (four). In 1907 he led the team in games played (140). In 1908 Wid paced the Yanks in doubles (22). Three times he led the Yanks in stolen bases (1903, 1904, 1907).

ALL-TIME YANKEE LEADER: On the all-time Yankee stolen base list, Wid is tied for fifth (184). He places 18th in triples (59).

TRADED: The Yanks dealt Wid to the Washington Senators following the 1908 season.

CONROY, WID

Yr.	G	AB	R	H	2B	3B	HR	RBI	BB	SB	BA	SA
1903	126	503	74	137	23	12	1	45	32	33	.272	.372
1904	140	489	58	119	18	12	1	52	43	30	.243	.335
1905	102	385	55	105	19	11	2	25	32	25	.273	.395
1906	148	567	67	139	17	10	4	54	47	32	.245	.332
1907	140	530	58	124	12	11	3	51	30	41	.234	.315
1908	141	531	44	126	22	3	1	39	14	23	.237	.296
6 Yrs.	797	3005	356	750	111	59	12	266	198	184	.250	.338
Life.	1374	5061	605	1257	176	82	22	452	345	262	.248	.329

CREE, BIRDIE
(BORN WILLIAM FRANKLIN CREE)

Yankee: 1908-15
Outfielder
Born: October 22, 1882
Birthplace: Khedive, PA
Died: November 8, 1942
Bat: R; Throw: R
Ht: 5'6"; Wt: 150

YANKEE OUTFIELDER: Birdie played his entire ML career with the Yanks. The little guy (5' 6") made the Yanks in 1908 when he was 25 years old. Birdie was the regular Yankee leftfielder from 1910-13 but he sustained a broken wrist during the 1912 season and was sent to Baltimore of the International League. The Yanks reobtained Birdie's contract in 1913 for $5000. In 1913 Birdie led all AL outfielders in fielding (.988). He was switched to center field in 1914 and was the Yanks' fourth outfielder in 1915.

1911 SEASON: Birdie had a terrific year in 1911. He led the club in seven offensive categories: batting (.348), slugging (.513), runs scored (90), hits (181), triples (22), HRs (four) and stolen bases (48). His 22 triples has been exceeded only once by a Yankee player. Birdie was on his way to possibly a better season in 1912 when he was injured.

CLUB LEADERSHIP: Birdie led the Yanks in slugging average three times. He led the club in hits, RBIs, triples and batting average twice. Twice Birdie tied for club HR leadership. On the All-Time Yankee lists, Birdie places 15th in stolen bases (132), and 17th in triples (62).

RETIREMENT: Birdie retired as a ML player in February of 1916. He once played under the assumed name of "Burdee," hence the nickname Birdie, a name that stayed with him after his baseball career ended.

***BIRDIE CREE** (New York Yankees)*

MOST TRIPLES BY YANKEE PLAYERS IN A SEASON:
1. E. Combs, 1927 (23)
2. BIRDIE CREE, 1911 (22)
E. Combs, 1930 (22)
S. Stirnweiss, 1945 (22)

CREE, BIRDIE

Yr.	G	AB	R	H	2B	3B	HR	RBI	BB	SB	BA	SA
1908	21	78	5	21	0	2	0	4	7	1	.269	.321
1909	104	343	48	90	6	3	2	27	30	10	.262	.315
1910	134	467	58	134	19	16	4	73	40	28	.287	.422
1911	137	520	90	181	30	22	4	88	56	48	.348	.513
1912	50	190	25	63	11	6	0	22	20	12	.332	.453
1913	145	534	51	145	25	6	1	63	50	22	.272	.346
1914	77	275	45	85	18	5	0	40	30	4	.309	.311
1915	74	196	23	42	8	2	0	15	36	7	.214	.276
8 Yrs.	742	2603	345	761	117	62	11	332	269	132	.292	.398
Life.	Same.											

CROSETTI, FRANK

Nickname: "The Crow"
Yankee: 1932-48
Shortstop, 3B, 2B
Born: October 4, 1910
Birthplace: San Francisco, CA
Died: February 11, 2002
Bat: R; Throw: R
Ht: 5'10"; Wt: 165

CAME TO YANKS: In August, 1929, the Yanks purchased Frank's contract from the San Francisco Seals of the Pacific Coast League. He made the Yankee team in 1932.

WINNING BALLPLAYER: Frank was a key addition to the Yanks in 1932 when as a rookie he helped the team win the club's first World Championship in four seasons. In 17 seasons with the Bronx Bombers he was a member of nine AL pennant winners and eight World Championship clubs. Frank was a perfect example of a Yankee in the 1930s and 1940s—tough, talented and dedicated to victory. Frank was an underrated player in his prime. He was a ballplayer's ballplayer, a man who did the things to win that do not always show in the box score. He was expert at waiting out a pitcher for a walk.

YANKEE INFIELDER: Frank was the regular Yankee shortstop from 1932-40, then again in 1943 and 1945. In 1942 he played 62 games at third base, more than anyone else on the club. He retired during the 1944 season but returned in 1945. Frank was a utility infielder in 1941 and from 1946-48.

DEFENSIVE ABILITIES: Frank could make all the defensive plays that a good shortstop has to make. In 1938 he led AL shortstops in three categories: putouts (352), assists (506) and double plays (120). In 1939 he again led AL shortstops in three categories: fielding (.968), putouts (323) and double plays (118).

LEAGUE LEADER: Frank led the AL in stolen bases in 1938 (27). In 1939 he led the AL in at-bats (656). In 1938 he made 757 plate appearances, a ML record for a 154-game season.

Frank Crosetti as player (above) and coach. (New York Yankees Archives).

CLUB LEADERSHIP: In three consecutive seasons (1936-38) Frank led the Yanks in stolen bases. Twice he led the club in at-bats. In 1938 and 1939 "The Crow" played in every Yankee game.

"HIDDEN BALL TRICK": Frank was a master at pulling the "hidden ball trick." While the Yankee pitcher wasted time on the mound, Frank would casually talk to an umpire or distract the base runner on second any way possible. When the runner took his lead off second base, Frank would nail him with the ball securely hidden in his glove. The play was taught to Frank by Joe Cronin when both played for the Seals. Years later as a Yankee player, Frank pulled the "hidden ball trick" on an unsuspecting Red Sox player—Joe Cronin!

SIGN STEALER: Frank was one of the game's great sign stealers. In 1957 *The Sporting News* polled a panel of experts to pick the best 12 sign-stealers since World War I and Frank made the list. His ability to steal signs often helped the Yanks.

HIT BY PITCHED BALLS: Frank was clever at allowing himself to be hit by pitched balls. He was hit by a pitched ball 15 times in 1938, setting a Yankee club record. Frank would often wear uniform tops that were too large for him, then drape his body over the plate and allow close pitches to nick him on his shirt. Eight times he led the AL in being hit by pitched balls; 1934 (five), 1936 (12), 1937 (12), 1938 (15), 1939 (13), 1940 (10), 1942 (nine), and 1945 (10).

LEAGUE SUSPENSION: For pushing umpire Bill Summers in Game 3 of the 1942 World Series, Frank was suspended for the first 30 days of the 1943 season and fined $250, a penalty that seems to have been too harsh. Frank was intense and aggressive, but he was not mean.

ALL-TIME YANKEE LEADER: Frank is eighth on the All-Time Yankee walk list (792), tenth in runs scored (1006), games (1683), and at-bats (6277). He is 14th in triples (65), 15th in doubles (260), and 17th in hits (1541).

ALL-STAR GAME: Frank was selected to the AL All-Star team for the 1936 and 1939 All-Star Games. He pinch-hit in the 1936 game.

WORLD SERIES: As a player and coach, Frank was in uniform for 23 World Series (all as a Yankee), more times than anyone in ML history (eight times as a player, 15 times as a coach). Frank was a key reason why the Yanks won the 1936 Series. In Game 2 he scored four runs in an 18-4 Yanks rout. The next day, in Game 3, Frank's eighth-inning single knocked in the winning run for a 2-1 Yankee victory. The following day, in Game 4, "The Crow" doubled and scored the winning run as the Yanks put the New York Giants on the verge of Series elimination. Frank's only career World Series HR came off the legendary Dizzy Dean. It came at Wrigley Field in the 8th inning of Game 2 in the 1938 Series and the clout was the game winner. In the 1938 Series against the Cubs, Frank led both teams in doubles (two, tie), triples (one, tie), HRs (one, tie), RBIs (six, tie) and walks (two, tie). Frank led both clubs in runs scored (four) in the 1943 Series. His sacrifice fly in the eighth inning of Game 4 defeated the Cardinals, 2-1.

YANKEE COACH: Following the 1948 season, Frank retired for good as a player, but he stayed on with the Yanks as a coach. Until he left the Yankees after the 1968 season, "The Crow" was a fixture as the Yanks' third base coach. Frank wore the Yankee uniform consecutively longer (1932-68) than anyone in Yankee history. He was a valuable assistant to Yankee managers Harris, Stengel, Houk, Berra, and Keane. Frank doubled as an infield instructor at Yankee rookie and spring training camps. One of the first people young Mickey Mantle met when he joined the Yanks was Frank. Mantle owned a poor glove and Frank bought him a new one, a gesture much appreciated by Mickey. In 1969, Frank was a coach for the expansion Seattle Pilots. He coached for the Minnesota Twins in 1970-71 to cap a ML career that spanned 40 seasons.

GREAT SHAPE: Frank was always in great shape, even in his final years as a Yankee coach when he approached his 60th birthday. (As a coach, he could work out as hard and long as any of the players.) Frank had a good diet and hardly drank at all. He believed in long walks, early bedtimes and early risings. In short, Frank, who was also quiet, was Joe McCarthy's kind of player, and as a coach Frank was an excellent example for young players to follow. Frank had tremendous strength in his hands, making for a strong handshake. He developed a good tight grip by carrying around a rubber ball and squeezing it.

CROSETTI, FRANK

Yr.	G	AB	R	H	2B	3B	HR	RBI	BB	SB	BA	SA
1932	116	398	47	96	20	9	5	57	51	3	.241	.374
1933	136	451	71	114	20	5	9	60	55	4	.253	.379
1934	138	554	85	147	22	10	11	67	61	5	.265	.401
1935	87	305	49	78	17	6	8	50	41	3	.256	.430
1936	151	632	137	182	35	7	15	78	90	18	.288	.437
1937	149	611	127	143	29	5	11	49	86	13	.234	.352
1938	157	631	113	166	35	3	9	55	106	27	.263	.371
1939	152	656	109	153	25	5	10	56	65	11	.233	.332
1940	145	546	84	106	23	4	4	31	72	14	.194	.273
1941	50	148	13	33	2	2	1	22	18	0	.223	.284
1942	74	285	50	69	5	5	4	23	31	1	.242	.337
1943	95	348	36	81	8	1	2	20	36	4	.233	.279
1944	55	197	20	47	4	2	5	30	11	3	.239	.355
1945	130	441	57	105	12	0	4	48	59	7	.238	.293
1946	28	59	4	17	3	0	0	3	8	0	.288	.339
1947	3	1	0	0	0	0	0	0	0	0	.000	.000
<u>1948</u>	<u>17</u>	<u>14</u>	<u>4</u>	<u>4</u>	<u>0</u>	<u>1</u>	<u>0</u>	<u>0</u>	<u>2</u>	<u>0</u>	<u>.286</u>	<u>.429</u>
17 Yrs.	1683	6277	1006	1541	260	65	98	649	792	113	.245	.354

Life. Same.

World Series

Yr.	G	AB	R	H	2B	3B	HR	RBI	BA
1932	4	15	2	2	1	0	0	0	.133
1936	6	26	5	7	2	0	0	3	.269
1937	5	21	2	1	0	0	0	0	.048
1938	4	16	1	4	2	1	1	6	.250
1939	4	16	2	1	0	0	0	1	.063
1942	1	3	0	0	0	0	0	0	.000
<u>1943</u>	<u>5</u>	<u>18</u>	<u>4</u>	<u>5</u>	<u>0</u>	<u>0</u>	<u>0</u>	<u>1</u>	<u>.278</u>
7 Yrs.	29	115	16	20	5	1	1	11	.174

Life. Same.

DANIELS, BERT
(BORN BERNARD ELMER DANIELS)

Yankee: 1910-13
Outfielder
Born: October 31, 1882
Birthplace: Danville, IL
Died: June 6, 1958
Bat: R; Throw: R
Ht: 5'9"; Wt: 180

YANKEE OUTFIELDER: In 1910 27-year-old Bert began his ML career with the Yanks (Highlanders). Bert was the Yanks' regular centerfielder in 1911, the regular Yankee leftfielder in 1912 and the regular Yankee rightfielder in 1913.

1912 SEASON: Bert had a fabulous year, leading the Yanks in games played (133), runs scored (72), doubles (25), triples (11–tie), batting (.274–tie) and stolen bases (37). Bert was the Yanks' most potent offensive threat for the season.

BASE-STEALING THREAT: Bert led the Yanks in stolen bases in three of the four seasons he was a member of the club (1910, 1912, 1913). He is 13th on the all-time Yankee stolen base list (145), although he played only four years with the club.

HIT BY PITCHED BALLS: In a doubleheader played on June 20, 1913, Bert was hit by a pitched ball three times (once in the first game and twice in the second). He tied for AL leadership in being hit by pitches in 1910 (16) and led the AL by himself in the category in 1912 (18) and 1913 (18).

TRADED: In August of 1913, the Yanks traded Bert and Ezra Midkiff to Baltimore of the International League for infielder Fritz Maisel.

DANIELS, BERT												
Yr.	G	AB	R	H	2B	3B	HR	RBI	BB	SB	BA	SA
1910	95	356	68	90	13	8	1	17	41	41	.253	.343
1911	131	462	74	132	16	9	2	31	48	40	.286	.372
1912	133	496	72	136	25	11	2	41	51	37	.274	.381
1913	93	320	52	69	13	5	0	22	44	27	.216	.288
7 Yrs.	452	1634	266	427	67	33	5	111	184	145	.261	.352
Life.	523	1903	295	486	76	40	5	130	203	159	.255	.345

DAVIS, RON

Yankee: 1978-81
Pitcher
Born: August 6, 1955
Birthplace: Houston, TX
Bat: R; Throw: R
Ht: 6'4"; Wt: 205

TRADE TO YANKEES: The Yankees obtained Ron from the Cubs in June of 1978 for pitcher Ken Holtzman. The Yanks converted Ron into a reliever, and Ron began taking advantage of his devastating sidearm delivery. Pitching Coach Stan Williams taught Ron a rising fastball to complement his sinking fastball.

GETTING CHANCE WITH YANKEES: Ron was sensational at West Haven in 1978 (9-2, five saves, 1.50 ERA) and was called up to the Yankees late in the season. In 1979, Ron was called up from Columbus with the Yanks' bullpen in shambles following an injury to Goose Gossage, and Ron led the AL in relief wins (14) and broke Wilcy Moore's AL rookie record of 13 relief wins, set with the Yanks in 1927. In 1979, Ron led the Yanks in winning percentage (.875, 14-2) and games pitched (44), finished fourth in voting for Rookie of the Year and won the Rolaids Award as the Yanks' top reliever.

GOOSE'S SETUP MAN: In 1980, Gossage returned as the bullpen closer and Ron redefined the role of the No. 2 man, bringing a new respectability to one of baseball's least appreciated jobs. In 1980, Ron was second to Goose on the Yankees in games pitched (53) and was hot in September, starting the month not allowing an earned run in $20\frac{2}{3}$ innings pitched and going 4-0 with a 1.17 ERA in his final 11 games of the season. Ron emerged as a star in 1981 and pitched in the All-Star Game, replacing the injured Gossage on the team. In 1981, Ron led the Yanks in games pitched (43), and with Davis in the game, New York never lost a game they led. Ron would enter in the sixth or seventh, hold the opposition, and then turn it over to Goose in the eighth or ninth. In the combined 1980-81 seasons, the Yankees were 130-5 in games when they took a lead into the seventh inning.

STRIKEOUT ARTIST: In 1981, Ron struck out 83 batters in only 73 innings, and as late as June 4—as a reliever—he was leading the AL in strikeouts. On May 3, 1981, Ron fanned the final five Oakland batters (on 20 pitches). The next day at California, Ron faced nine batters; after Don Baylor popped up, Ron struck out the final eight batters, breaking the consecutive strikeout record for a reliever in a game of seven, held by Denny McLain. Ron fanned the first batter he faced in the next game, giving him 14 strikeouts in 15 batters faced!

POST-SEASON ACTION: There weren't many Davis-type situations in the 1980 ALCS, and Ron made only one appearance. In the post-season of 1981, Ron led the Yanks in games pitched (9) and his combined ERA was 4.63. He was great in the Division Series and didn't allow a run in three games. He was coasting in Game 1 of the ALCS when the A's Cliff Johnson excessively stalled at the plate, visibly upsetting Davis, who was soon replaced by Goose. Ron followed with a poor World Series, giving up eight runs (six earned) in $2\frac{1}{3}$ innings. Wildness (five walks) was the biggest factor in his undoing.

TRADED AWAY: Ron went on the trading block because 1) he had a poor 1981 World Series, 2) he took the Yankees to arbitration and won, and 3) in March of 1982, he gave up a HR in a one-run spring training loss to the Mets, angering George Steinbrenner. In April of 1982, the Yankees traded Ron, Greg Gagne (SS), and Paul Boris (P) to Minnesota for shortstop Roy Smalley. The trade hurt the Yanks in two areas, the bullpen and shortstop. Beginning in 1982, Davis saved 22, 30, 29 and 25 games for the Twins, although Ron never again got his ERA under 3.34 for any season.

DAVIS, RON

Yr.	W-L	Pct.	SA	G	GS	CG	IP	H	BB	SO	SH	ERA
1978	0-0	.000	0	4	0	0	2	3	3	0	0	11.57
1979	14-2	.875	9	44	0	0	85	84	28	43	0	2.85
1980	9-3	.750	7	53	0	0	131	121	32	65	0	2.95
1981	4-5	.444	6	43	0	0	73	47	25	83	0	2.71
4 Yrs.	27-10	.730	22	144	0	0	292	255	88	191	0	2.93
Life.	47-53	.470	130	481	0	0	747	735	300	597	0	4.05

Divisional Playoff

Yr.	G	IP	BB	SO	H	W-L	SA
1981	3	6	2	6	1	1-0	0
Life. Same.							

Championship Series

Yr.	G	IP	BB	SO	H	W-L	SA
1980	1	4	1	3	3	0-0	0
1981	2	3.1	2	4	0	0-0	0
1 Year	3	7.1	3	7	3	0-0	0
Life. Same.							

World Series

Yr.	G	IP	BB	SO	H	W-L	SA
1981	4	2.1	5	4	4	0-0	0
Life. Same.							

DENT, BUCKY
(BORN RUSSELL EARL O'DEY)

Yankee: 1977-82
Shortstop
Born: November 25, 1951
Birthplace: Savannah, GA
Bat: R; Throw: R
Ht: 5'9"; Wt: 170

TRADED TO YANKEES: In April of 1977, the Yankees obtained Bucky from the White Sox for Oscar Gamble (OF), LaMarr Hoyt (P), Bob Polinsky (P), and $200,000. The Yanks went to spring training preparing to give the shortstop job to rookie Mickey Klutts, but Klutts got hurt, and Dent was acquired.

EARLY PROBLEMS: Bucky replaced two popular Yankees, Gamble and the incumbent shortstop, Fred Stanley, and he was slow to assimilate. Bucky also batted ninth and was sometimes pulled for a pinch hitter, which disturbed him. On a turbulent club, it was barely noticed that Bucky nearly jumped the club in June, 1977.

ALL-STAR SHORTSTOP: Once Bucky adjusted to his new environment, he demonstrated the ability that made him an All-Star in 1975. He played in the 1980 and 1981 All-Star Games as a Yankee, and his .750 batting average (three for four) is the highest among Yankees who represented the club playing in at least two All-Star Games. He was voted to start All-Star Games in 1980 and 1981, and despite an off year in 1982, he finished second in the voting by the fans.

SOLID DEFENSIVELY: Bucky formed an excellent double-play combo with Willie Randolph. Bucky led AL shortstops in 1980 in fielding (.982). Bucky had good range and a dependable arm, and he was excellent at positioning himself; he took into account the batter, pitcher, game situation, and count.

HEROIC 1978 SEASON: In 1978, Bucky was bothered by a leg injury, and he was disabled most of July. Bucky returned to deliver key hits down the pennant stretch. In the playoff game against Boston, Bucky delivered the most important hit, a three-run HR in the seventh inning off Mike Torrez that put the Yankees ahead, 3-2. Bucky was the MVP of the World Series against the Dodgers, hitting .417 with seven RBIs and playing excellent defense. Bucky became a national celebrity and an idol with adoring teenaged girls. He had a poster and made TV and movie appearances.

DISAPPOINTMENTS: In 1979, Bucky was bothered by an unresolved contract, personal problems and a .230 batting average. He rallied in 1980 and had his best fielding year, hit .262 and was second on the club with 26 doubles. On August 30, 1981, Bucky slid hard into second base, tore ligaments in his right ring finger and was out for the year; he missed postseason too. In April of 1982, the Yankees obtained shortstop Roy Smalley, and the ensuing platoon situation was not acceptable to Bucky.

TRADED AWAY: In August of 1982, with Bucky playing less and less, and hitting .169, he was traded to Texas for Lee Mazzilli (OF-1B). Bucky finished his ML playing career in 1984 with the Royals. Bucky later developed a baseball training school in Florida, featuring a replica of Boston's Green Monster. At the opening in 1989, Bucky and pitcher Mike Torrez replayed Dent's famous 1978 playoff HR.

YANKEE MANAGER: From 1985-89, Bucky managed in the Yankee organization at Fort Lauderdale and Columbus. He managed the Yankees for the last 40 games in 1989 and the first 49 games in 1990.

BUCKY DENT

Yr.	G	AB	R	H	2B	3B	HR	RBI	BB	SB	BA	SA
1977	158	477	54	118	18	4	8	49	39	1	.247	.352
1978	123	379	40	92	11	1	5	40	23	3	.243	.317
1979	141	431	47	99	14	2	2	47	37	0	.230	.285
1980	141	489	57	128	26	2	5	57	48	0	.262	.354
1981	73	227	20	54	11	0	7	27	19	0	.238	.379
1982	59	160	11	27	1	1	0	9	8	0	.169	.188
6 Yrs.	695	2163	229	518	81	10	27	229	174	4	.239	.324
Life.	1392	4512	451	1114	169	23	40	423	328	17	.247	.321

Championship Series

Yr.	G	AB	R	H	2B	3B	HR	RBI	BB	SB	BA	SA
1977	5	14	1	3	1	0	0	2	1	0	.214	.286
1978	4	15	0	3	0	0	0	4	0	0	.200	.200
1980	3	11	0	2	0	0	0	0	0	0	.182	.182
3 Yrs.	12	40	1	8	1	0	0	6	1	0	.200	.225
Life. Same.												

World Series

Yr.	G	AB	R	H	2B	3B	HR	RBI	BB	SB	BA	SA
1977	6	19	0	5	0	0	0	2	2	0	.263	.263
1978	6	24	3	10	1	0	0	7	1	0	.417	.458
2 Yrs.	12	43	3	15	1	0	0	9	3	0	.349	.372
Life. Same.												

DICKEY, BILL

Yankee: 1928-43 (military) '46
Catcher
Born: June 6, 1907
Birthplace: Bastrop, LA
Died: November 12, 1993
Bat: L; Throw: R
Ht: 6'1"; Wt: 185

HONORS: Bill was inducted into the Baseball Hall of Fame in 1954. *The Sporting News* selected Bill to the publication's ML All-Star team in 1932, '33, '36, '38, '39, and '41 as the best catcher in baseball. In 1943 the Baseball Writers gave Bill the Sid Mercer Award. Bill wore the number "8" on his Yankee uniform and the Yanks' retired "8" in honor of Bill and Yogi Berra, who also wore the number. In 1969 Bill was named baseball's Greatest Living Catcher in a poll conducted by organized baseball. In 1980 the Yankee Foundation gave Bill the Pride of the Yankees Award.

MINOR LEAGUE STAR: In 1925 Bill began his professional baseball career with Little Rock of the Southern League, playing in three games (3 for 10, .300). In 1926 Bill played for Muskogee (.283 in 212 at-bats) and Little Rock (.391 in 46 at-bats). Bill played 101 games in 1927 for Jackson of the Cotton State League and hit a solid .297. In 1928 Bill played briefly for Buffalo of the International League (1-for-8, .125), although he spent most of the season with Little Rock (.300 in 203 at-bats). In his four-year minor league career, Bill was a good hitter for average, an excellent defensive catcher and a player who hit for little power, hitting a total of only 14 HRs.

CAME TO YANKS: When Bill was starring for Little Rock in 1928, most ML clubs assumed he would eventually play for the White Sox since Chicago at that time had a working agreement with Little Rock. But the Yanks discovered Bill was under contract only to Little Rock and not to Chicago. On the advice of Yankee scout Johnny Nee, the Yanks purchased Bill's contract from Little Rock.

YANKEE CATCHER: Bill joined the Yanks late in the 1928 season and got into 10 games. From 1929-41, Bill was the Yanks' regular catcher. In 1942, Bill shared the Yankee catching duties with Buddy Rosar. In 1943, Bill, Rollie Hemsley and Ken Sears shared the Yankee catching, with Bill appearing in the most games (71). Bill missed the entire 1944-45 seasons while serving in the military. He was a Naval lieutenant commander during World War II. In 1946 Bill returned to the Yanks, played in 39 games behind the plate, and was backup catcher at 39 years of age to Aaron Robinson.

BASEBALL'S GREATEST CATCHER: Connie Mack once named the 1938 Yanks as baseball's greatest team ever, mostly because he felt Bill was the game's greatest catcher. And Mack managed Mickey Cochrane! Mack was not the only authority who picked Bill as the all-time catcher. Bill also was selected as the all-time catcher on all-star teams picked by such experts as Ed Barrow (1939), Grantland Rice (1943) and Ty Cobb (1946). In celebration of the Yanks' 50th anniversary in 1953, the club took a poll of experts to determine the all-time Yankee all-star team. Bill was the unanimous choice for catcher, receiving all 48 votes cast.

COCHRANE'S RIVAL: Many baseball people maintain that the choice of baseball's greatest catcher is between Bill and Mickey Cochrane. The two were contemporaries, their careers paralleled, and they were catching rivals. Cochrane played 13 ML seasons (1925-37), hit 119 HRs with 832 RBIs, and had a lifetime batting average of .320 in 5169 at-bats. Bill played 17 ML seasons (1928-43, 1946), hit 202 HRs with 1209 RBIs, and had a lifetime batting average of .313 in 6300 at-bats. Bill probably had a slight edge over Mickey defensively. Both were winners; Bill played on nine AL champions and Mickey was a member of five AL champions. In their era, the debate over who was the better was constant. Ironically, Bill was catching the day at Yankee Stadium in 1937 when Mickey was beaned, prematurely ending his career. Charlie Gehringer, who played with Mickey, said in *Baseball—When the Grass Was Real* that Bill was the better thrower and had more power, and that Mickey had better speed, handled the bat better and was more aggressive.

GREAT HITTER: Bill's .313 lifetime BA is phenomenal for a catcher. If he had not experienced all the nagging catching injuries, there is no telling how high Bill could have hit. He hit more than 20 HRs with more than 100 RBIs in four consecutive seasons (1936-39), all World Championship N.Y. seasons. He hit better than .300 in 11 seasons, including every year from 1929-39 except 1935. Bill hit for average (.313), power (202 HRs) and in the clutch (1209 RBIs). Bill has the fifth highest on-base average for his career (.382) of all catchers in ML history. Being a lefthanded hitter, Bill thrived at Yankee Stadium, but he hit in all ballparks because he was a great natural hitter!

GREAT HITTING SEASONS: In 1936 Bill hit .362 in 112 games (107 as a catcher), the highest batting average in ML history by a catcher who caught in at least 100 games. It was also the first time a catcher led the Yanks in batting. The 133 RBIs Bill tallied in 1937 established the AL record for catchers.

GREAT HITTING GAMES: Against the White Sox on August 3 and 4, 1937, Bill hit grand slam HRs in consecutive games. In a game played on July 26, 1939, Bill hit three consecutive HRs.

DEFENSIVE ABILITIES: Defensively, Bill was splendid behind the plate and ranks as one of the game's best. He was an expert receiver, had great baseball sense, handled pitchers with skill, possessed a strong and accurate throwing arm and was exceptionally quick behind the plate. Bill in his day was considered tall (6'1") for a catcher, but he was anything but awkward and displayed great range around the plate. He was the first catcher to use a smaller catcher's mitt, one better suited for fielding. In the sixth inning of a game played on May 13, 1929, Bill became one of only four AL catchers to ever record three assists in one inning. He made a rare catcher's unassisted double play on June 8, 1941, against the Browns. Tiger star Charlie Gehringer once said Bill "made catching look easy."

FIELDING NUMBERS: A durable catcher, Bill caught more than 100 games in 13 consecutive seasons (1929-41), an AL record. He did not allow a single passed ball in 125 games behind the plate in 1931, an AL record. Bill frequently led AL catchers in defensive categories, including putouts (six seasons), fielding average (four seasons), assists (three seasons), and double

Bill Dickey, star Yankee catcher, is shown in action at training camp, March 16, 1937. Bill played in 1,708 games as a catcher, the most of any backstop in Yankee history. (AP/WIDE WORLD PHOTOS)

plays (one season). Bill ranks high on many all-time defensive lists for catchers—he is 13th in games caught (1708); 16th in putouts (7965) and total chances (9047); and 17th in double plays (137).

TEAM LEADER: Bill spent his entire ML career with the Yanks and influenced the team in positive ways that did not involve his bat and catcher's mitt. He was a steady, reliable, clear-thinking, quiet Yankee leader on the playing field and a gentleman off the field. Bill played the 1936 World Series with a hand fractured in two places, a fact not revealed until the next season. Bill hit only .120 in that Series but he made no excuses. He was the epitome of Yankee pride and class in the 1930s and 1940s. He was a team player in every sense of the often-used term. Bill would never think of showing up an umpire.

FRIEND OF THE GREATS: Bill was Lou Gehrig's roommate and Lou's closest friend on the Yanks. He attended Lou's small wedding and in June of 1941, Bill and Joe McCarthy left the Yanks in Detroit and returned to New York to be at Lou's funeral. It was partly Bill's idea to throw a team party for Joe DiMaggio after Joe's 56-game hitting streak in 1941. The thoughtful party was one of the highlights of Joe's baseball career. Babe Ruth, who had trouble with everyone's name fondly called Bill "Pittridge" (Babe meant the bird partridge). Like Ruth, Bill was a real outdoorsman and enjoyed bird shooting. Although he was quiet, Bill displayed his lighter side as one of the Yanks' practical jokers.

LOST TEMPER IN GAME: There is no doubt about the fact that Bill was (and is) a well-mannered gentleman. But there was one occasion when he lost his temper on the playing field. On July 6, 1932, Carl Reynolds of the Washington Senator's crashed into Bill, scoring on a squeeze play to tie the game in a rough-and-tumble play at the plate. Bill got up off the ground and broke Reynolds' jaw with a single punch. For this action he was fined $1000 AND suspended until Reynolds was able to play. After serving a 30-day suspension, Bill returned to the Yankee lineup for the first time on August 4. All Bill did in the game was blast a grand slam HR and stroke three singles.

GOOD HANDLER: Pitchers found it easy to work with Bill. He was patient with young pitchers and gave them encouragement when needed. Bill was almost always in sync with his pitcher as to what pitch should be delivered. He called a coordinated game and pitchers rarely shook him off.

ALL-TIME YANKEE LEADER: On the All-Time Yankee Top 20 list, Bill places sixth in RBI (1209), games played (1789), seventh in hits (1969), doubles (343), and batting average (.313), ninth in at-bats (6300). Also, Bill ranks tenth in triples (72), 11th in home runs (202), and 14th in runs scored (930).

ALL-STAR GAME: Bill was picked to be on the AL squad to play in the All-Star Games of 1933, '34, '36-43, and '46. (The All-Star Game was first played in 1933, so remembering that Bill was in the military in 1944 and 1945, he played in every All-Star Game for which he was eligible, except in 1935.) In the 1934 All-Star Game the NL's Carl Hubbell made baseball history by striking out Babe Ruth, Lou Gehrig, Jimmie Foxx, Al Simmons, and Joe Cronin in a row. Bill broke the legendary streak with a single.

WORLD SERIES: Bill hit .438, rapping seven singles, in his first Series (1932). Even with a fractured hand in the 1936 Series, Bill hit a three-run HR and drove in five runs in Game 2 to help the Yanks overwhelm the Giants, 18-4. His triple was an important hit in Game 3 of the 1937 Series, a 5-1 Yankee victory. In Game 1 of the 1938 Series Bill collected four singles. In Game 1 of the 1939 Series, the Yanks batted in the bottom of the 9th with the score tied, 1-1. With one out, Charlie Keller tripled and Joe DiMaggio was walked intentionally. Bad Move. Bill singled in the winning run. In Game 3 of that Series Bill hit a long HR at Cincinnati, following that with another HR in Game 4 and the Reds were swept. His two-run HR in the sixth inning of the final game of the 1943 Series gave the Yanks a 2-0 victory over the Cardinals and another World Championship. Bill is tied for eighth on the all-time World Series RBI list (24).

YANKEE MANAGER: When Bill returned to the Yanks from the military in 1946, he signed a Yankee player's contract, putting the rumor to rest that he would manage the Yanks' Newark farm club. He played his final ML season as a part-time catcher and pinch-hitter (3 for 11). On May 24, 1946, Joe McCarthy resigned as Yankee manager and Bill was named as McCarthy's replacement. Bill remained the Yanks' skipper until September 12, 1946, when he resigned.

BERRA'S TUTOR: Bill was manager of Little Rock of the Southern Association in 1947. In 1949 Yankee Manager Casey Stengel signed Bill to work exclusively with young Yogi Berra who was a poor defensive catcher. Bill proved to be a great teacher of catching skills. He worked with Berra many grueling hours in the spring of 1949 and said of Yogi, "Give him two years and he'll be the greatest catcher in the American League, by a long shot." Bill proved a good prophet as well as a good teacher when Yogi became a sensational defensive catcher. One might expect Bill to have been jealous of Yogi's success and subsequent comparison with him, but that was not the case. Bill considered Yogi his protege and rooted for Yogi. When Berra hit his 30th HR in 1952 breaking Bill's 1937 record of 29 HRs hit by a catcher, Bill jumped with joy in the first base coaching box.

YANKEE COACH: Bill was a Yankee coach under Casey Stengel from 1949 through the 1957 season. He was one of Casey's top assistants and an excellent instructor. Besides helping Berra and the other catchers, Bill was also a fine batting instructor. He helped many hitters, including Bobby Richardson whom Bill taught to be more aggressive at the plate and to drive the ball through the infield. In 1959 Bill was a Yankee scout. He returned to the Yanks in 1960 as bullpen coach but was forced to retire in July of 1960 because of illness.

DICKEY, BILL

Yr.	G	AB	R	H	2B	3B	HR	RBI	BB	SB	BA	SA
1928	10	15	1	3	1	1	0	2	0	0	.200	.400
1929	130	447	60	145	30	6	10	65	14	4	.324	.485
1930	109	366	55	124	25	7	5	65	21	7	.339	.486
1931	130	477	65	156	17	10	6	78	39	2	.327	.442
1932	108	423	66	131	20	4	15	84	34	2	.310	.482
1933	130	478	58	152	24	8	14	97	47	3	.318	.490
1934	104	395	56	127	24	4	12	72	38	0	.322	.494
1935	120	448	54	125	6	6	14	81	35	1	.279	.458
1936	112	423	99	153	26	8	22	107	46	0	.362	.617
1937	140	530	87	176	35	2	29	133	73	3	.332	.570
1938	132	454	84	142	27	4	27	115	75	3	.313	.568
1939	128	480	98	145	23	3	24	105	77	5	.302	.513
1940	106	372	45	92	11	1	9	54	48	0	.247	.355
1941	109	348	35	99	15	5	7	71	45	2	.284	.417
1942	82	268	28	79	13	1	2	37	26	2	.295	.373
1943	85	242	29	85	18	2	4	33	41	2	.351	.492
1946	54	134	10	35	8	0	2	10	19	0	.261	.366
17 Yrs.	1789	6300	930	1969	343	72	202	1209	678	36	.313	.486

Life. Same.

World Series

Yr.	G	AB	R	H	2B	3B	HR	RBI	BA
1932	4	16	2	7	0	0	0	4	.438
1936	6	25	5	3	0	0	1	5	.120
1937	5	19	3	4	0	1	0	3	.211
1938	4	15	2	6	0	0	1	2	.400
1939	4	15	2	4	0	0	2	5	.267
1941	5	18	3	3	1	0	0	1	.167
1942	5	19	1	5	0	0	0	0	.263
1943	5	18	1	5	0	0	1	4	.278
8 Yrs.	38	145	19	37	1	1	5	24	.255

Life. Same.

DiMAGGIO, JOE

Nicknames: "The Yankee Clipper" "Joltin' Joe"
      "Joe Di" "DiMag"
Yankee: 1936-42 (military) '46-51
Outfielder
Born: November 25, 1914
Died: March 8, 1999
Birthplace: Martinez, CA
Bat: R; Throw: R
Ht: 6'2"; Wt: 193

HONORS: Joe was inducted into the Baseball Hall of Fame in 1955. The Baseball Writers named Joe the AL MVP in three seasons (1939, 1941, 1947). *The Sporting News* also gave him their AL MVP Award in 1939 and 1941, besides picking him as the ML Player of the Year in 1939. In 1941 the Associated Press named Joe the Male Athlete of the Year. In 1947 *Sport* magazine gave him the publication's first Champion of the Year Award, honoring his achievements on the field. *The Sporting News* selected Joe to their ML All-Star team eight times (1937-42, '47-48), recognizing him as one of the three best outfielders in baseball. Joe won the Sid Mercer Award in 1937 and 1941, given by the Baseball Writers. Joe won the Casey Stengel "You Could Look It Up" Award in 1974, given by the Baseball Writers. His uniform number "5" was retired by the Yankees when Joe retired in 1951. On April 12, 1970, a tribute to Joe, in the form of a plaque, was placed on the center field wall of Yankee Stadium and dedicated. In 1969, during ML baseball's centennial celebration, Joe was voted baseball's Greatest Living Player. In 1976, during ML baseball's celebration of the nation's

Bicentennial, Joe's 56-game hitting streak of 1941 was voted the Most Memorable Moment in AL history. Joe is honored in the Italian-American Sports Hall of Fame in Elmwood Park, Ill.

MINOR LEAGUE STAR: Before joining the Yanks, Joe learned his baseball lessons well in the Pacific Coast League, playing for the San Francisco Seals. In 1933 Joe had a 61-game hitting streak, the longest hitting streak in professional baseball history. All the major league scouts were interested in him but in 1934 he seriously injured his knee and most scouts were scared off. In 1935 Joe was the Pacific Coast League MVP, batting .398 with 34 HRs and 154 RBIs. He learned a lot from his Seal manager, Lefty O'Doul, a great hitter himself in his time.

CAME TO YANKS: Although most AL scouts were scared away because of his 1934 injury, Yankee scouts Joe Devine and Bill Essick still recommended Joe to the Yanks. Essick, in his forceful report to owner Jacob Ruppert, was especially high on Joe. (The Yankee scouts were impressed by his going 1 for 4 in a Seal exhibition game against Satchel Paige, perhaps more of a reflection on Paige's great talent.) Joe underwent an exhaustive physical examination for the Yankee brass and his knee was pronounced strong and fit. Yankee Farm Director George Weiss wanted Joe, and against GM Ed Barrow's wishes, Jake Ruppert prepared to obtain Joe. In November of 1934, the Yanks acquired Joe from the Seals for an amount between $25,000-50,000. The Seals in turn got journeyman infielder Doc Farrell, pitcher Floyd Newkirk and minor leaguers Jim Densmore (pitcher), Les Powers (first baseman) and Ted Norbert (outfielder). Joe played with San Francisco in 1935, then joined the Yanks at the spring training camp of 1936.

COMPLETE BALLPLAYER: Many experts consider Joe to have been the best all-round baseball player in history. He excelled at every facet of the game. Joe was a sensational hitter, for average and power, a splendid, graceful, ball-hawking centerfielder, and a great thrower. He was a daring and alert base runner, a heads-up player who never missed a sign in his entire career, and a team leader. Joe was everything a manager could hope for, and his favorite manager, Joe McCarthy, for whom DiMaggio played between 1936-46, loved Joe as a player and a person. DiMaggio was the complete player, said McCarthy, who also remarked that Joe was "the best base runner I ever saw. He could have stolen 50, 60 bases a year if I had let him." A 100% effort is what Joe gave every time he stepped on the playing field. Joe was the Yanks' team leader on clubs that won 10 AL pennants and nine World Championships. Some of Joe's career statistics do not measure up to those of other greats, but one must remember when examining Joe's lifetime stats that he missed three seasons in the prime of his career because of military service (1943-45). Joe's fellow players were in awe of him and appreciated his ability. During the war, Ted Lyons of the White Sox pitched his first game on Guam for his Navy team against Joe's Army team. Joe belted a HR and afterward, Lyons said, "I left the country to get away from DiMaggio and here he is!"

DEDICATED BALLPLAYER: Joe was completely dedicated to his profession. He was constantly learning more about the game and improving himself as a player. Any teammate interested in becoming better could go to Joe and receive expert advice or information. Joe remained in the clubhouse long after the game was over while less gifted players were in a hurry to run along. Joe always kept himself in top physical shape and adhered to training rules. He was a most responsible athlete and felt responsibility to the Yanks, taking each loss as a personal failure.

CLASSIC SWING: "Joltin' Joe" simply had the most beautiful, classic, fluid batting swing the game of baseball has seen to date. He took a wide stance at the plate, and because he had tremendously strong wrists he could wait until the last instant before swinging at a pitch. Joe had as sharp a batting eye as any player in history.

POWER HITTER: The 29 HRs Joe hit in 1936 is the Yankee club rookie record. His 132 runs scored and 15 triples made in 1936 are both AL rookie records. In July of 1937, Joe cracked 15 HRs, the most ever hit in that month in ML baseball until surpassed by Albert Belle (16) in 1998. He hit 46 HRs in 1937, the most ever hit by a Yankee right-handed hitter. Joe knocked in more than 100 runs in seven consecutive seasons (1936-42). On five occasions Joe hit four or more extra base hits in a game, a ML record. The Yanks counted on Joe to be their number-one power hitter during his career, a job of considerable difficulty since Joe had to whale away into Yankee Stadium's "Death Valley" for half his games each year. Joe hit two HRs into the distant left-center field Yankee Stadium bleachers. On April 21, 1948, he hit the first HR out of Griffith Stadium.

CONSISTENT HITTER: In 1941 Joe hit safely in 56 consecutive games, a record that is still about the most awesome record in baseball history. The game after his streak was snapped, Joe began a 16-game hitting streak. Thus, Joe hit in 72 out of 73 consecutive games! His .381 batting average of 1939 is the second highest in Yankee history. Joe was a rarity in that he was a power hitter who had bat control, striking out infrequently. He had nearly as many lifetime HRs (361) as strikeouts (369)—a tremendous feat for a power hitter! He struck out just once every 18.48 at-bats and homered once per 18.89 at-bats. In 1941 Joe fanned only 13 times in 541 at-bats! His lifetime on-base average (.398) is the seventh highest in ML history for a centerfielder.

GREAT HITTING GAMES: In Joe's first ML game he stroked three hits, a triple and a pair of singles. In a game played on June 24, 1936, Joe hit two HRs in one inning. On August 27, 1938, he smacked three triples in a game. In a doubleheader played on July 13, 1940, Joe tallied nine RBIs. On September 10, 1950, Joe became the first man to hit three HRs in a game played at Washington's Griffith Stadium. Joe hit three HRs in a single game three times. Twice he hit for the batting cycle in a game.

BATTING BATTLES: The battles between Cleveland's Bob Feller, the great fastball pitcher, and Joe often highlighted Yankee-Indian contests of the late 1930s, 1940s and early 1950s. Actually, Joe did quite well in his confrontations with Feller. It was Cleveland's Mel Harder who gave "The Yankee Clipper" the greatest difficulty at the plate.

DEFENSIVE GENIUS: Joe began his rookie season of 1936 playing left field, then moved to center field midway in the season, and remained the Yanks' centerfielder until he retired

following the 1951 season. Joe's gracefulness in center field gave an easy look to tough plays. He got an immediate jump on fly balls (he always made the right first move) and never laced his catches with dramatics. In fact, Joe rarely left the ground; he was usually camped under a fly ball waiting for it to come down. Not only did Joe have great instincts in playing batted balls, but he was also a smart centerfielder who *never* threw to the wrong base. Joe was intelligent at positioning himself according to his pitcher, the batter and count. Taking all variables into account, Joe positioned himself in the right spot 90% of the time. He was a studious centerfielder and his memory and willingness to learn made him great. He was a gifted centerfielder, but he also *worked* at being great.

GREAT CATCH: Joe made many great catches in his career, but one of the most memorable came late in 1939 at Yankee Stadium. Detroit's Hank Greenberg sent a monumental blast, high and some 460 feet into the spacious center field graveyard, that Joe turned and moved on as soon as the shot was launched. Joe raced with his back to the plate and an idea as to where the ball would land. Right at the famed monuments, Joe caught the ball on the fly and everyone present agreed it was the most sensational catch ever seen. The man robbed—Greenberg—was at second base when the out was made and would have had a sure inside-the-park HR.

FIELDING NUMBERS: In 1936 Joe led all AL outfielders in assists (22). In 1937 he led AL outfielders in putouts (413). In 1941 he led AL outfielders in double plays (five). In 1947 he led AL outfielders in fielding with a .997 mark that is also the Yankee club record for centerfielders.

1949 SEASON: Joe's most heroic season was 1949. He had played in 1948 with an extremely painful right heel spur injury (calcium deposit bone chips) and he had heel surgery between the 1948-49 seasons. Joe missed the first 65 games in 1949, and there was serious concern that his career was finished. But almost miraculously, Joe woke up one morning in late June and walked without pain. He played his first 1949 game against the Giants in the Mayor's Trophy Game and pronounced himself fit. Joe made his first regular-season appearance in a key series at Boston. With a tremendous flair for the dramatic, Joe put on a rousing show, hitting four HRs with nine RBIs in a three-game Yankee sweep of the Red Sox! Even Red Sox fans, ardent Yankee haters, cheered his remarkable performance. For the remainder of l949, Joe was at his finest (.346, 14 HRs, 67 RBIs in only 272 at-bats). But in September Joe contracted pneumonia and was hospitalized. After his release, he termed himself ready for the season's final two games at the Stadium with Boston. The Yanks had to win both games to win the pennant. Although Joe was terribly weak, he was willing to give it a try. On the next to last day of the season, "Joe DiMaggio Day" was held, and Joe received many gifts. He told 69,551 Stadium fans, "I want to thank my fans, my friends, my manager, Casey Stengel, my teammates; the gamest, fightingest bunch of guys who ever lived. And I want to thank the Good Lord for making me a Yankee." [*After Joe's death on March 8, 1999, his quote "I want to thank the Good Lord for making me a Yankee," was placed all over Yankee Stadium to be viewed by players and fans alike. It was visible upon entering the Yankee offices and was prominently dis-*

A fine portrait of Joe DiMaggio, the "Yankee Clipper." As Joe stated so eloquently, "I want to thank the Good Lord for making me a Yankee."

played in the Yankee runway as a reminder to players on their way to the field dugout.] Then Joe went out and hit a crucial double in a Yankee rally, helping win the game. The next day in the year's finale, Joe was so exhausted he had to come out while Boston was batting in the ninth inning. The Yanks won the game and pennant, as Joe gave his last ounce of energy in the effort.

CLASS PLAYER: Not once in his ML career was Joe ever ejected from a game for protesting an umpire's decision! Joe was not a controversial person. He never bad-mouthed anyone. He was not involved in fights on the field or feuds with other players. Joe would not allow himself to be dragged into any seamy situations and he got along with his teammates and the Yankee front office. During his Yankee career, Joe had only one serious battle with the front office, although in 1938 he had a minor contract hassle. But after his 56-game hitting streak in 1941, Joe rightfully expected a good raise. Yet GM Ed Barrow actually wanted to cut Joe's contract by $2,500, supposedly because of the war! It was a bitter dispute and the only time Joe ever received negative publicity from the Yanks. Yankee management in the Dan Topping era thought so much of Joe that he was on hand when Casey Stengel was named Yankee manager in October 1948. There were false reports that Joe and Stengel were enemies; their relationship may have been strained, but it never affected the Yanks' performance. In fact, in Stengel's later years, Joe was very warm to Casey.

QUIET AND SHY: During his Yankee career, Joe was quiet, shy and conservative. He avoided strangers and publicity. (People who had known Joe since his Yankee career ended say Joe had grown enormously as a person. The shyness had worn off and Joe was much more comfortable at public events. Joe was a good speaker and was often witty.) When Joe first joined the Yanks, he was buddies with the other guys from the San Francisco Bay area: Tony Lazzeri, Frank Crosetti, and Lefty Gomez. His friendship with Gomez was his closest Yankee relationship. Alike in so many ways, Joe and Lou Gehrig were friends. In later years, Joe was close to Joe Page and Billy Martin. Joe was great to rookies, always making them feel part of the Yanks. When young Hank Bauer and Joe once had dinner, Joe insisted on picking up the check, telling Bauer, "When you eat with the Dago, the Dago pays."

APPRECIATIVE TEAMMATES: All Joe's teammates were fond of him and held him in awe much as the average fan did. In 1941, shortly after Joe's 56-game hitting streak ended, the guys on the Yanks organized a small party in Joe's honor. The players bought a sterling-silver cigar humidor that was inscribed, "Presented to Joe DiMaggio by his fellow players on the New York Yankees to express their admiration for his consecutive-game hitting record, 1941." All the names of the Yanks were engraved below the inscription. Joe, who had not realized how the team felt about him, was moved by the thoughtful gesture.

AUTHENTIC AMERICAN HERO: Joe was much like Babe Ruth in that both men were bigger than baseball and were idolized by the entire nation. In 1949 Joe became baseball's first $100,000 player. He could have enjoyed the same salary

for 1952, but he retired rather than play below his standards. This pride and sense of fairness to the public contributed to Joe's bigger-than-life stature. After his comeback Boston series of 1949, Joe made the cover of *Life* magazine and was the country's biggest celebrity. The nation misses watching Joe play baseball even today. As Paul Simon wrote in a song by Simon & Garfunkel in the late 1960s titled *Mrs. Robinson,* "Where have you gone Joe DiMaggio? A nation turns its lonely eyes to you." In the novel *The Old Man and the Sea,* Ernest Hemingway wrote through the main character, "I would like to take the great DiMaggio fishing. They say his father was a fisherman. Maybe he was as poor as we are and would understand."

LEAGUE LEADER: Joe won the AL batting championship in consecutive seasons (1939-40). Twice he won the HR Crown of the AL (1937, 1948). He also twice led the AL in RBIs (1941, 1948) and slugging average (1937, 1950). In 1936 Joe tied for the AL lead in triples (15). In 1937 he led the AL in runs scored (151). Joe was hit by a pitched ball eight times in 1948 to lead the AL (the first time a Yankee led the AL in HBP.)

CLUB LEADERSHIP: Joe led the Yanks in many batting categories through the years, including slugging in eight seasons and batting, HRs, RBIs and hits in seven seasons. No other Yankee has led the club more often in hits.

BASEBALL'S ALL-TIME LEADER LIST: Joe's lifetime slugging average (.579) is the seventh highest in baseball history. In his ML career, Joe averaged .89 RBI per game, the fourth best average of all time.

ALL-TIME YANKEE LEADER: Joe is among the all-time Yankee leaders in most batting categories. He is fourth in doubles (389); third in triples (131), RBIs (1537), fourth in batting (.325) and slugging (.579); fourth in runs (1390), hits (2214) and HRs (361); sixth in at-bats (6821); eighth in games played (1736) and ninth in walks (790). Joe's 361 HRs are the most ever hit by a right-handed batter in Yankee history. (Yankee Stadium is murder on right-handed power hitters.)

ALL-STAR GAME: Joe was selected to the AL All-Star team every year of his career and played in 11 All-Star Games (1936-42, 1947-50). In the 1939 All-Star Game played at Yankee Stadium, Joe's HR helped beat the NL, 3-1.

WORLD SERIES: In 1936 Joe hit .346 in his first Series. In the Yanks' seven-run ninth in the final game, he became the seventh man in World Series history to make two hits in one inning. Joe's HR in the final game of the 1937 Series helped the Yanks eliminate the Giants in a 4-2 win. In Game 2 of the 1938 Series, Joe's two-run ninth-inning HR off Dizzy Dean clinched a 6-3 Yankee victory over the Cubs. Joe tied Lou Gehrig for the most runs scored (4) in the 1938 Series. In Game 3 of the 1939 Series at Crosley Field, Joe hit a long two-run HR putting the Yanks in the lead, 4-3, in a game N.Y. won. The next day, he scored the tying run in the ninth against the Reds. Then in the tenth he scored behind Charlie Keller during Red catcher Ernie Lombardi's famous "snooze" at the plate, allowing the Yanks to sweep Cincinnati. Joe's HR won critical Game 5 of the 1947 Series for the Yanks over Brooklyn, 2-1. Joe's HR helped the

Yanks win the final game of the 1949 Series against the Dodgers. In Game 2 of the 1950 Series, Joe's tenth-inning HR into the upper left field stands at Shibe Park beat the Phillies, 2-1. After going hitless in the first three games of the 1951 Series (two of which were won by the New York Giants), Joe hit a two-run HR and a single, leading the Yanks to a 6-2 Game 4 win in a game the Yanks could not afford to lose.

WORLD SERIES LEADERS: "Joltin' Joe" is among the lifetime leaders in many World Series batting categories. He ranks third in at-bats (199); fourth in hits (54); fifth in runs scored (27), RBIs (30) and total bases (84); tied for seventh in HRs (8); and 11th in walks (19). Joe's eight HRs ties him with Bill Skowron and Frank Robinson for the most HRs by a right-handed batter in World Series history.

RETIREMENT: Most observers felt 1951 would be Joe's last season, and Joe himself realized he was slowing down when he started getting hits to right field, an indication that his bat was not as quick. On December 11, 1951, Joe officially announced his retirement as a baseball player. In 1952, Joe did his own Yankee post-game show, interviewing the Yankee star of each game. In 1953, Joe did a baseball show for kids, giving them baseball tips. Through the years, Joe went to Yankee spring training camps and served as a special instructor. He was often seen at the Stadium and rarely missed an Old Timers' Day or special event, and, as always, Joe was accorded the honor of being introduced last. In 1968-69 Joe was the Executive Vice President—Coach of the Oakland A's and helped many young players, including Reggie Jackson. A close friend of Joe, Edward Bennett Williams, bought the Baltimore Orioles in 1979 and invited Joe to get involved in the team.

THE PASSING OF THE GREAT DIMAGGIO: On March 8, 1999, just two days prior to Torre's announcement that he had prostate cancer, it was learned that Yankee great, Joe DiMaggio, had passed away after a lengthy illness. Joe was 84, and his funeral was very well-attended at St. Patrick's Cathedral in New York City. Joe eventually was laid to rest in San Francisco, his hometown. When Joe was still hospitalized, George Steinbrenner had approached DiMaggio to toss out the first pitch in the April 9 home opener and Joe seemed interested. When Joe was eventually released from the hospital in January, DiMaggio came home to find a note on his bed: "April 9, Yankee Stadium or Bust". But now with Joe's passing, that opened the way for George to ask Yogi Berra about paying a visit to Yankee Stadium to toss out the ceremonial first pitch—which eventually did come to fruition. (Yogi had not been there for 14 years due to a feud with Steinbrenner). The baseball world shared the grief that surrounded the loss of this great American icon, and on April 25 at the Stadium versus Toronto, the Yankee unveiled a new monument in honor of Joe DiMaggio prior to the game. It is the fifth such monument dedicated, the others honoring Miller Huggins, Lou Gehrig, Babe Ruth and Mickey Mantle. This monument has a beautiful inscription which reads:

JOSEPH PAUL DIMAGGIO
"THE YANKEE CLIPPER"
1914-1999

RECOGNIZED AS BASEBALL'S
"GREATEST LIVING PLAYER"

LIFETIME BATTING AVERAGE	.325
WON MVP AWARD	1939, 1941, 1947
SELECTED TO ALL-STAR GAME	13 TIMES
AMERICAN LEAGUE BATTING TITLE	1939,1940
ELECTED TO HALL OF FAME	1955

SET ONE OF BASEBALL'S MOST ENDURING RECORDS,
56-GAME HITTING STREAK
MAY 15 TO JULY 16, 1941

LED THE YANKEES TO AN INCREDIBLE NINE WORLD CHAMPIONSHIPS IN HIS 13-YEAR CAREER

A BASEBALL LEGEND AND
AN AMERICAN ICON

"HE HAS PASSED, BUT HE WILL NEVER LEAVE US"

DEDICATED BY
THE NEW YORK YANKEES
APRIL 25, 1999

Singer Paul Simon (of Simon and Garfunkel fame) was even on hand to sing "Mrs. Robinson", getting a thunderous ovation when he uttered: "Where have you gone, Joe DiMaggio? A nation turns its lonely eyes to you. What's that you say Mrs. Robinson? Joltin' Joe has left and gone away." For the remainder of 1999, Yankee players would wear Joe D's #5 on their left uniform sleeves, a great tribute for a great man. The Yanks won the game in eleven, 4-3, with reliever Jason Grimsley, picking up his first win in pinstripes. From the runway connecting the Yankee clubhouse with the field dugout, a sign was placed well in view for all to read on their way to the playing field—it read:

"I want to thank the Good Lord for making me a Yankee"
—Joe DiMaggio

DiMAGGIO, JOE

Yr.	G	AB	R	H	2B	3B	HR	RBI	BB	SB	BA	SA
1936	138	637	132	206	44	15	29	125	24	4	.323	.576
1937	151	621	151	215	35	15	46	167	64	3	.346	.673
1938	145	599	129	194	32	13	32	140	59	6	.324	.581
1939	120	462	108	176	32	6	30	126	52	3	.381	.671
1940	132	508	93	179	28	9	31	133	61	1	.352	.626
1941	139	541	122	193	43	11	30	125	76	4	.357	.643
1942	154	610	123	186	29	13	21	114	68	4	.305	.498
1946	132	503	81	146	20	8	25	95	59	1	.290	.511
1947	141	534	97	168	31	10	20	97	64	3	.315	.522
1948	153	594	110	190	26	11	39	155	67	1	.320	.598
1949	76	272	58	94	14	6	14	67	55	0	.346	.596
1950	139	525	114	158	33	10	32	122	80	0	.301	.585
1951	116	415	72	109	22	4	12	71	61	0	.263	.422
13 Yrs.	1736	6821	1390	2214	389	131	361	1537	790	30	.325	.579

Life. Same.

World Series

Yr.	G	AB	R	H	2B	3B	HR	RBI	BA
1936	6	26	3	9	3	0	0	3	.346
1937	5	22	2	6	0	0	1	4	.273
1938	4	15	4	4	0	0	1	2	.267
1939	4	16	3	5	0	0	1	3	.313
1941	5	19	1	5	0	0	0	1	.263
1942	5	21	3	7	0	0	0	3	.333
1947	7	26	4	6	0	0	2	5	.231
1949	5	18	2	2	0	0	1	2	.111
1950	4	13	2	4	1	0	1	2	.308
1951	6	23	3	6	2	0	1	5	.261
10 Yrs.	51	199	27	54	6	0	8	30	.271

Life. Same.

JOE'S 56-GAME HITTING STREAK
MAY 15 - JULY 16, 1941

MAY	AB	R	H	2B	3B	HR	RBI
15—Chicago	4	-	1	-	-	-	1
16—Chicago	4	2	2	-	1	1	1
17—Chicago	3	1	1	-	-	-	-
18—St. Louis	3	3	3	1	-	-	1
19—St. Louis	3	-	1	1	-	-	-
20—St. Louis	5	1	1	-	-	-	1
21—Detroit	5	-	2	-	-	-	1
22—Detroit	4	-	1	-	-	-	1
23—Boston	5	-	1	-	-	-	2
24—Boston	4	2	1	-	-	-	2
25—Boston	4	-	1	-	-	-	-
27—at Washington	5	3	4	-	-	1	3
28—at Washington (N)	4	1	1	-	1	-	-
29—at Washington	3	1	1	-	-	-	-
30—at Boston	2	1	1	-	-	-	-
30—at Boston	3	-	1	1	-	-	-
JUNE							
1—at Cleveland	4	1	1	-	-	-	-
1—at Cleveland	4	-	1	-	-	-	-
2—at Cleveland	4	2	2	1	-	-	-
3—at Detroit	4	1	1	-	-	1	1
5—at Detroit	5	1	1	-	1	-	1
7—at St. Louis	5	2	3	-	-	-	1
8—at St. Louis	4	3	2	-	-	2	4
8—at St. Louis	4	1	2	1	-	1	3
10—at Chicago	5	1	1	-	-	-	-
12—at Chicago (N)	4	1	2	-	-	1	1
14—Cleveland	2	-	1	1	-	-	1
15—Cleveland	3	1	1	-	-	1	1
16—Cleveland	5	-	1	1	-	-	-
17—Chicago	4	1	1	-	-	-	-
18—Chicago	3	-	1	-	-	-	-
19—Chicago	3	2	3	-	-	1	2
20—Detroit	5	3	4	1	-	-	1
21—Detroit	4	-	1	-	-	-	1
22—Detroit	5	1	2	1	-	1	2
24—St. Louis	4	1	1	-	-	-	-
25—St. Louis	4	1	1	-	-	1	3
26—St. Louis	4	-	1	1	-	-	1
27—at Philadelphia	3	1	2	-	-	1	2
28—at Philadelphia	5	1	2	1	-	-	-
29—at Washington	4	1	1	1	-	-	-
29—at Washington	5	1	1	-	-	-	1
JULY							
1—Boston	4	-	2	-	-	-	1
1—Boston	3	1	1	-	-	-	1
2—Boston	5	1	1	-	-	1	3
5—Philadelphia	4	2	1	-	-	1	2
6—Philadelphia	5	2	4	1	-	-	2
6—Philadelphia	4	-	2	-	1	-	2
10—at St. Louis (N)	2	-	1	-	-	-	-
11—at St. Louis	5	1	4	-	-	1	2
12—at St. Louis	5	1	2	1	-	-	1
13—at Chicago	4	2	3	-	-	-	-
13—at Chicago	4	-	1	-	-	-	-
14—at Chicago	3	-	1	-	-	-	-
15—at Chicago	4	1	2	1	-	-	2
16—at Cleveland	4	3	3	1	-	-	-
TOTALS	223	56	91	16	4	15	55

"MILESTONES OF THE IMPOSSIBLE STREAK"

18th Game, June 1: Joe's streak was beginning to receive publicity. On this day in Cleveland, Joe singled against Mel Harder, a very important hit because Harder usually gave Joe difficulty.

19th Game, June 2: Joe cracked two hits off Indian great Bob Feller. However, it was a sad day because when the Yankees reached Detroit they learned that Lou Gehrig had died.

21st Game, June 5: Joe got one hit off Detroit's Hal Newhouser at Briggs Stadium, a triple to keep the streak alive.

27th Game, June 14: Joe got a double off Bob Feller in two at-bats.

29th Game, June 16: Joe tied the Yankee club record held by both Roger Peckinpaugh and Earle Combs who each had hit in 29 straight games. This was Joe's first target and the national publicity was growing rapidly. Joe hit a double off the Indians' Al Milnar at Yankee Stadium.

30th Game, June 17: Joe broke the Yankee club record at Yankee Stadium on a bad-hop single off White Sox shortstop Luke Appling's shoulder. It was one of Joe's few breaks during the streak. (By the way, he never bunted.)

31st Game, June 18: Joe singled off the White Sox' Thornton Lee (a pitcher who was 22-11 with a league-leading 2.37 ERA in 1941) at Yankee Stadium. It was the fifth straight game in which Joe got just one hit. Under building pressure and with the league's best pitchers aiming to end the streak, Joe was fighting to keep it alive.

33rd Game, June 20: At that time the modern NL hitting-streak record was held by Rogers Hornsby at 33 games and it was considered a significant milestone to reach. Joe was red hot. At Yankee Stadium he banged out four hits against the Tigers, two off Bobo Newsom and two off Archie McKain. Thus Joe tied Hornsby.

34th Game, June 21: Joe passed Hornsby's streak by singling off the Tigers' Dizzy Trout.

35th Game, June 22: Joe doubled and homered off the tough Tiger twosome of Hal Newhouser and Bobo Newsom at Yankee Stadium.

36th Game, June 24: Against the St. Louis Browns at Yankee Stadium, Joe's streak was in jeopardy. But in the eighth inning he singled off Bob Muncrief. To Muncrief's credit, he refused to take the easy way to fame by walking Joe and pitched naturally to him.

38th Game, June 26: In the eighth inning the Yankees led the Browns, 3-1, but Joe was hitless. He was due to hit fourth in the bottom of the eighth. Red Rolfe walked with one out. Realizing that if he hit into a double play Joe's streak probably would be over, Tommy Henrich asked Joe McCarthy for permission to bunt. He received it and successfully sacrificed. Joe hit Eldon Auker's first pitch for a double.

40th Game, June 28: Before an Athletic-Yankee game at Shibe Park, A's pitcher Johnny Babich, always tough against the Yanks, boasted that he would end Joe's streak and by any means necessary. The first time up Joe walked. His second trip to the plate Joe laced a 3-0 pitch back up the middle through the shocked Babich's legs. Joe had tied the longest hitting streak of Ty Cobb, the second longest in AL history.

41st Game, June 29: George Sisler's 41-game hitting streak was the AL record and considered by most at the time to be the ML record. Washington's Griffith Stadium was packed to see whether Joe could tie and break the record. In the first game of the doubleheader, Joe smacked a sixth-inning double off knuckleballer Dutch Leonard to tie Sisler.

42nd Game, June 29: In the second game of the Washington doubleheader, Joe broke Sisler's record. It was far from easy. Joe was 0 for 3 when he batted in the seventh inning using Henrich's bat (his had been stolen between games) against Red Anderson. Joe singled to left. The crowd went wild.

43rd Game, July 1: The Yankees and the Red Sox played a doubleheader at Yankee Stadium. In the fourth inning Joe hit a grounder and third baseman Jim Tabor made a poor throw. It was a tough play. The official scorer, Dan Daniel, ruled a hit. It was one of the few scoring decisions Joe received in his favor. Most scorers bent over backwards to make sure Joe's hits were legitimate. (Joe eliminated any controversy, however, when he later singled.)

44th Game, July 1: While Joe was surging toward Sisler's record, it was assumed that mark was Joe's final target. But research uncovered a longer streak. In 1897 Willie Keeler, then of the NL's Baltimore Orioles, hit safely in 44 consecutive games. So that was a new obstacle in Joe's path—a somewhat unfair one some felt since Keeler had benefited from easier rules. In any event, Joe singled cleanly off Jack Wilson in the second game of the Red Sox twin-bill to tie Keeler. The game was rained out after five innings, but the game and hit were official.

45th Game, July 2: Joe broke Keeler's record, and he now held the ML record without dispute. At Yankee Stadium in the first inning, Red Sox rightfielder Stan Spence robbed Joe of a hit. The next time Joe batted, his brother Dom raced to the monuments to track down Joe's long drive and again deny Joe a hit. But in his third at-bat, Joe rocked a Dick Newsome pitch for a three-run homer. The Stadium erupted.

All-Star Game, July 8: This game did not figure in Joe's streak, which stood at 48 games. Nevertheless, Joe doubled off the Cubs' Claude Passeau, proving he could hit NL hurlers also.

55th Game, July 15: At Chicago's Comiskey Park, Joe got a pair of hits against pitcher Edgar Smith, the man of whom he had started the incredible streak back in May.

56th Game, July 16: It seemed the streak would never end. Joe was still swinging a torrid bat when the Yankees met the Indians for an afternoon game at League Park. Joe smoked a double and two singles.

July 17: The Yankees and Indians played a night game at the Indians' other ballpark, spacious Municipal Stadium, and 67,468 gathered to witness the end of Joe's great streak. Al Smith (12-13 that year) was the starting Cleveland pitcher. In the first inning Joe hit a wicked two-bouncer over third base that Ken Keltner backhanded nicely and he threw Joe out. (Keltner played on the edge of the outfield grass the whole game.) Joe walked in the fourth inning. In the seventh, Keltner made a great play on a smash by Joe which Keltner fielded brilliantly before barely throwing out Joe by a step at first base. In the eighth inning Joe faced reliever Jim Bagby Jr. (9-15 that year). Joe hit a hard grounder up the middle which shortstop Lou Boudreau fielded deftly, handling a bad hop, then tossed to second to begin a double play. It was Joe's final plate appearance of the game. The incredible consecutive-game hitting streak was over, snapped at 56 games. Joe hit .408 during his historic rampage.

DITMAR, ART

Yankee: 1957-61
Pitcher
Born: April 3, 1929
Birthplace: Winthrop, MA
Bat: R; Throw: R
Ht: 6'2"; Wt: 185

CAME TO YANKS: The Yanks acquired Art, Bobby Shantz, Clete Boyer and two others from the Kansas City A's for Irv Noren, Tom Morgan and four others in February, 1957.

YANKEE STARTER: In 1957 Art was used mostly as a relief pitcher (he was the Yanks' second best reliever) although he was also a spot starter. He had much the same job in 1958. In 1959-60 he was the Yanks' No. 2 starter behind Whitey Ford in both seasons.

CLUB LEADERSHIP: In 1957 Art tied for the club lead in games pitched (46). In 1959 he led Yankee pitchers in ERA (2.90). Art was the ace of the 1960 Yankee pitching staff, leading the club in victories (15), ERA (3.06), innings pitched (200) and complete games (8).

WORLD SERIES: In Game 6 of the 1958 Series, as the Yanks faced elimination by the Milwaukee Braves, Art pitched 3⅔ innings of scoreless ball in relief to keep the Yanks in a game that the club had to win, and did win. Art was given the starting assignment in Game 1 and again in Game 5 of the 1960 Series against the Pirates.

TRADED: The Yanks traded Art and Deron Johnson to the Kansas City A's for pitcher Bud Daley in June, 1961.

DITMAR, ART

Yr.	W-L	Pct.	SA	G	GS	CG	IP	H	BB	SO	SH	ERA
1957	8-3	.727	6	46	11	0	127	128	35	64	0	3.25
1958	9-8	.529	4	38	13	4	140	124	38	52	0	3.42
1959	13-9	.591	1	38	25	7	202	156	52	96	1	2.90
1960	15-9	.625	0	34	28	8	200	195	56	65	1	3.06
1961	2-3	.400	0	12	8	1	54	59	14	24	0	4.64
5 Yrs.	47-32	.595	11	168	85	20	723	662	195	301	2	3.24
Life.	72-77	.483	14	287	156	41	1268	1237	461	552	5	3.98

World Series

Yr.	G	IP	BB	SO	H	W-L	SA
1957	2	6	0	2	2	0-0	0
1958	1	3⅔	0	2	2	0-0	0
1960	2	1⅔	1	0	6	0-2	0
3 Yrs.	5	11⅓	1	4	10	0-2	0
Life. Same							

DOBSON, PAT

Nickname: "The Dobber"
Yankee: 1973-75
Pitcher
Born: February 12, 1942
Birthplace: Depew, NY
Bat: R; Throw: R
Ht: 6'3"; Wt: 190

CAME TO YANKS: The Yanks obtained Pat from the Atlanta Braves in June, 1973, for Wayne Nordhagen, Frank Tepedino and two minor league pitchers.

YANKEE STARTER: When Pat joined the Yanks he moved right into the starting rotation where he remained throughout his Yankee career. In 1974 he helped the Yanks make a furious run for the pennant by winning 13 of his final 17 decisions. He was the ace of the 1974 Yankee pitching staff, leading the team in innings pitched (281) and strikeouts (157) and tying for the club lead in victories (19). Pat was a finesse pitcher and a good one. He was the Yanks' fourth starter on the 1975 team.

TRADED: Pat was traded to the Indians for Oscar Gamble in November, 1975.

YANKEE RETURN: Pat returned to the Yankees as a minor-league pitching coach in the early 1980s. He also coached with the Brewers, Padres, and Royals.

DOBSON, PAT

Yr.	W-L	Pct.	SA	G	GS	CG	IP	H	BB	SO	SH	ERA
1973	9-8	.529	0	22	21	6	142	150	34	70	1	4.17
1974	19-15	.558	0	39	39	12	281	282	75	157	2	3.07
1975	11-14	.440	0	33	30	7	208	205	83	129	1	4.07
3 Yrs.	39-37	.513	0	94	90	25	631	637	192	356	4	3.65
Life.	122-129	.486	19	414	279	74	2120	2043	665	1301	14	3.54

DONALD, ATLEY

Nickname: "Swampy"
Yankee: 1938-45
Pitcher
Born: August 19, 1910
Birthplace: Morton, MS
Died: October 19, 1992
Bat: L; Throw: R
Ht: 6'1"; Wt: 186

YANKEE PROSPECT: Atley came up through the Yankee farm system, reaching Newark, the Yanks' top farm team, before he had a short stint with the Yanks in 1938. Atley was a fantastic 19-2 for Newark in 1937. In the Little World Series that year, Newark was down 3-1 in games to Columbus when Atley won Game 5 on a three-hitter, 1-0. (Newark rallied to win the Series in seven games.)

GREAT ROOKIE SEASON: Atley was 28 years old when he started his first complete ML season in 1939. From May 9 to July 25 he won 12 games in a row, an AL rookie pitcher record. That streak also tied a Yankee club record for most wins at the start of a season that stood until Ron Guidry broke it in 1978.

CONSISTENT PITCHER: Atley pitched his entire ML career with the Yanks. Between 1939-44 he was the club's fourth or fifth starter, and he was a terrific hurler to have in that position. From 1940-42, Atley was a member of one of the best pitching staffs in Yankee history (Donald, Ruffing, Gomez, Chandler, Bonham, Russo, Murphy, etc.) Atley has an outstanding lifetime winning percentage (.663). In 1945, his final ML season, he was hobbled by injuries. In his prime Atley had a great fastball.

CLUB LEADERSHIP: In 1940 Atley led Yankee pitchers in ERA (3.03). In 1945 he tied for club leadership in shutouts (two).

YANKEE SCOUT: Atley was a Yankee scout for many years. He was responsible for scouting Yankee superstar Ron Guidry and making Ron a Yankee. Atley also scouted and drafted Ron Blomberg.

DONALD, ATLEY

Yr.	W-L	Pct.	SA	G	GS	CG	IP	H	BB	SO	SH	ERA
1938	0-1	.000	0	2	2	0	12	7	14	6	0	5.25
1939	13-3	.813	1	24	20	11	153	144	60	55	1	3.71
1940	8-3	.727	0	24	11	6	119	113	59	60	1	3.03
1941	9-5	.643	0	22	20	10	159	141	69	71	0	3.57
1942	11-3	.786	0	20	19	10	148	133	45	53	1	3.11
1943	6-4	.600	0	22	15	2	119	134	38	57	0	4.60
1944	13-10	.565	0	30	19	9	159	173	59	48	0	3.34
1945	5-4	.556	0	9	9	6	64	62	25	19	2	2.97
8 Yrs.	65-33	.663	1	153	115	54	932	907	369	369	5	3.52
Life. Same.												

World Series

Yr.	G	IP	BB	SO	H	W-L	SA
1941	1	4	3	2	6	0-0	0
1942	1	3	2	1	3	0-1	0
2 Yrs.	2	7	5	3	9	0-1	0
Life Same							

DOWNING, AL

Yankee: 1961-69
Pitcher
Born: June 28, 1941
Birthplace: Trenton, NJ
Bat: R; Throw: L
Ht: 5'11"; Wt: 175

YOUNG PROSPECT: A Trenton youngster playing baseball in the backyard of the Philadelphia Phillies, Al Downing drew the attention of Phillies' scout Bill Yancey. Yancey wanted to sign Al but the Phillies, believing Al too small for baseball, refused to go along. In 1960 Yancey joined the Yankee organization and in December of that year signed Al, reportedly for a bonus of some $16,000. Al had a spectacular 1961 with the Yanks' Binghamton farm team (9-1, 1.84 ERA). The following year he pitched for Richmond in the International League and he worked the first part of the 1963 season at Richmond as well.

EARLY ML CAREER: After pitching briefly with the Yanks in 1961 and 1962, Al went down to Richmond in 1963 but was called up later in the season and had a sensational year (13-5), helping the Yanks win the AL pennant. He was the Bronx Bombers' third starter on the 1964 team and had another fine season (13-8) as the Yanks again won the pennant. Al was the Yanks' first important black starting pitcher.

STRIKEOUT ARTIST: Al was one of the hardest-throwing pitchers ever to wear a Yankee uniform. He led Yankee pitchers in strikeouts four consecutive seasons (1964-67). The 217 strikeouts Al recorded in 1964 are the fourth most ever notched by a Yankee pitcher in a season. That total also led the AL. In the second inning of a game played on August 11, 1967, Al struck out the side on nine pitches (only seven others have ever done that in the AL). In 1963 Al allowed only 5.84 hits per nine innings, a percentage that ranks in baseball's top 15.

ALL-TIME YANKEE LEADER: Al is eighth on the all-time Yankee strikeout list (1028). He is tied for 16th in ERA (3.25), and is tied for 20th in shutouts (12).

LATE YANKEE CAREER: Al was the most successful Yankee pitcher in 1967, leading Yankee pitchers in winning percentage (.583, 14-10) and tying for the club lead in shutouts (four) and complete games (10). He was selected to the AL All-Star team for the 1967 All-Star Game. Sadly, a sore arm ruined his 1968 season.

TRADED: Al, along with Frank Fernandez, was dealt to the Oakland A's in December, 1969, for Danny Cater. While finishing his ML career with the Dodgers, Al gave up Hank Aaron's record-breaking home run in 1974.

DOWNING, AL

Yr.	W-L	Pct.	SA	G	GS	CG	IP	H	BB	SO	SH	ERA
1961	0-1	.000	0	5	1	0	9	7	12	12	0	8.00
1962	0-0	.000	0	1	0	0	1	0	0	1	0	0.00
1963	13-5	.722	0	24	22	10	176	114	80	171	4	2.56
1964	13-8	.619	2	37	35	11	244	201	120	217	1	3.47
1965	12-14	.462	0	35	32	8	212	185	105	179	2	3.40
1966	10-11	.476	0	30	30	1	200	178	79	152	0	3.56
1967	14-10	.583	0	31	28	10	202	158	61	171	4	2.63
1968	3-3	.500	0	15	12	1	61	54	20	40	0	3.52
1969	7-5	.583	0	30	15	5	131	117	49	85	1	3.38
9 Yrs.	72-57	.558	2	208	175	46	1235	1014	526	1028	12	3.25
Life.	123-107	.535	3	405	317	73	2268	1946	933	1639	24	3.22

World Series

Yr.	G	IP	BB	SO	H	W-L	SA
1963	1	5	1	6	7	0-1	0
1964	3	7⅓	2	5	9	0-1	0
2 Yrs.	4	12⅓	3	11	16	0-2	0
Life.	5	16⅓	7	14	20	0-3	0

DUGAN, JOE

Nickname: "Jumping Joe"
Yankee: 1922-28
Third Baseman
Born: May 12, 1897
Birthplace: Mahanoy City, PA
Died: July 7, 1982
Bat: R; Throw: R
Ht: 5'11"; Wt: 160

CAME TO YANKS: In July of 1922, the Yanks obtained Joe and Elmer Smith from the Red Sox in a trade that sent Elmer Miller, Lefty O'Doul, Chick Fewster, and John Mitchell to Boston. The date was July 23 and Yankee-haters and St. Louis Browns' fans (the Browns were in a furious pennant race with the Yanks) howled their displeasure over what they felt was an unfair Yankee addition. (Because of the deal, a later rule was made preventing player transfers after June 15, except through waivers.) Third base was the only weak position on the 1922 Yanks, and most experts felt the Yankee acquisition of Joe was the key reason they won the AL pennant, finishing one game ahead of the Browns.

YANKEE THIRD BASEMAN: Joe was the regular Yankee third baseman from the day he joined the club until the day he left. In his seven Yankee seasons, he played on five AL pennant winners and three World Championship teams. He was a key member of the Yanks' first World Championship club in 1923 when he led the AL in at-bats (644). Twice he led the Yanks in at-bats. Knee injuries plagued Joe throughout his Yankee career. As the years went by, Joe was forced to miss more and more games. He batted second in his early Yankee days.

DEFENSIVE ABILITIES: Joe was a great man with the glove and a solid all-round defensive ballplayer. But more than just a solid defensive player, Joe was a fancy fielder in the days of small and almost useless gloves. He was an artist around third base and had a tremendous throwing arm with a quick snap throw. Joe handled bunts better than anyone of his era. In 1923 (.974) and 1925 (.970) Joe led AL third basemen in fielding. In 1924 he made four unassisted double plays, setting a ML record for third basemen.

BABE RUTH'S BUDDY: Joe was one of the Babe's best friends and shared in many of the Babe's rollicking adventures. It was Joe who tagged Ruth with the name, "Jidge," the name the Yankee players called Ruth. Joe probably knew more about the Babe than anyone and it is largely through his stories that baseball historians and fans have learned and understood Ruth. Joe was a pallbearer at the Babe's funeral. Like Ruth, "Jumping Joe" was a free spirit on the Yanks and a colorful guy. (He got his nickname in Philadelphia for his inclination to jump the Athletics team.)

1927 SEASON: Joe was one of the highest paid players on the great 1927 Yanks, making $12,000 for ethe season. He got off to a slow start at the plate, hitting around .220 for most of the season's first half, but in July Joe was torrid and finished at .269. Most of the time he hit seventh in the "Murderers' Row" lineup, following Babe Ruth, Lou Gehrig, Bob Meusel, and Tony Lazzeri.

WORLD SERIES: In Game 5 of the 1923 Series, Joe cracked four hits, including a HR, to lead the Yanks to an 8-1 victory against the Giants. The HR was the first Series HR ever hit by a Yankee player at Yankee Stadium and happened on October 14, 1923. Joe hit .333 in the 1926 Series, the third highest batting average among Yankee players. Eye and knee problems limited Joe's activity in the 1928 Series. He started Games 1 and 4, pinch-hit in Game 2, but missed Game 3 entirely.

TRADED: In December of 1928, the Yanks waived Joe to the Boston Braves because of the poor condition of Joe's knee. But Joe hit .304 for the Braves in 1929 and the Yanks were not immediately able to replace him. Result: The Yanks did not win another AL pennant until 1932.

DUGAN, JOE

Yr.	G	AB	R	H	2B	3B	HR	RBI	BB	SB	BA	SA
1922	60	252	44	72	9	1	3	25	13	1	.286	.365
1923	146	644	111	182	30	7	7	67	25	4	.283	.384
1924	148	610	105	184	31	7	3	56	31	1	.302	.390
1925	102	404	50	118	19	4	0	31	19	2	.292	.359
1926	123	434	39	125	19	5	1	64	25	2	.288	.362
1927	112	387	44	104	24	3	2	43	27	1	.269	.362
1928	94	312	33	86	15	0	6	34	16	1	.276	.381
7 Yrs.	785	3043	426	871	147	27	22	320	156	12	.286	.374
Life.	1447	5410	665	1516	277	46	42	571	250	37	.280	.372

World Series

Yr.	G	AB	R	H	2B	3B	HR	RBI	BA
1922	5	20	4	5	1	0	0	0	.250
1923	6	25	5	7	2	1	1	5	.280
1926	7	24	2	8	1	0	0	2	.333
1927	4	15	2	3	0	0	0	0	.200
1928	3	7	0	1	0	0	0	2	.143
5 Yrs.	25	91	13	24	4	1	1	9	.264
Life. Same.									

DUREN, RYNE

Yankee: 1958-61
Pitcher
Born: February 22, 1929
Birthplace: Cazenovia, WI
Bat: R; Throw: R
Ht: 6'2"; Wt: 190

HONORS: *The Sporting News* gave Ryne the AL Rookie Pitcher Award in 1958. Ryne was picked to be on the AL All-Star team for the 1958 and 1959 All-Star Games.

CAME TO YANKS: In June, 1957, the Kansas City A's traded Ryne, Suitcase Simpson and Jim Pisoni to the Yanks for Billy Martin, Ralph Terry, Woodie Held and Bob Martyn. Ryne produced a 13-2 record at the Yanks' Denver farm club in 1957.

RELIEF SPECIALIST: Ryne was used strictly out of the bullpen, and in 1958 he led the AL in saves (20). Ryne had a blazing fastball that ranks with any of the great fastballs of all time. But he did not always have control of his hummer. Ryne wore extremely thick glasses ("Coke bottles") and the combination of his speed, wildness and poor eyesight scared batters to death. In July, 1958, Ryne was beaned by Detroit's Paul Foytack and pitched only 22 innings for the rest of the season.

COLORFUL CHARACTER: Ryne was one of the most colorful people to play for the Yanks. Upon reaching the mound for a relief appearance, Ryne would usually throw his first warm-up pitch high off the home plate screen, scaring the opposition and delighting the fans. On the Yankee train celebrating the 1958 pennant clinching, there was a small incident between Ryne and coach Ralph Houk. Ryne, a little drunk, poked at Houk's cigar and the two grappled a bit, but an overzealous reporter made a bigger thing out of the incident than was called for. In the 1958 World Series, Ryne gave the umpire the choke sign and because it was seen on national TV, Commissioner Frick fined him $250. Ryne was a holdout in the spring of 1960. He came up with the novel idea of accepting the average figure reached by a poll of Yankee writers. That figure was $17,500 and Ryne and the Yanks agreed to it. Casey Stengel once said of Ryne, "He takes a drink or ten, comes in with them Coke bottles, throws one on the screen, and scares the shit out of 'em." Many years later, Ryne courageously announced that he was an alcoholic. Today he works at helping alcoholics in his native state of Wisconsin.

CLUB LEADERSHIP: In 1958 and 1959 Ryne led the Yanks in both saves and games pitched. In 1960 he tied for club leadership in games pitched (42).

ALL-TIME YANKEE LEADER: Ryne is tied for tenth on the all-time Yankee save list (43).

1958 WORLD SERIES: Ryne pitched the final two innings of Game 3 to record a save and preserve a 4-0 Yankee shutout of the Milwaukee Braves. He was the winning pitcher of Game 6, keeping the Yanks alive in the Series. He pitched 4⅔ innings of brilliant relief, fanning eight Braves.

TRADED: In May, 1961, the Yanks traded Ryne, Lee Thomas and Johnny James to the Los Angeles Angels for Bob Cerv and Tex Clevenger.

DUREN, RYNE

Yr.	W-L	Pct.	SA	G	GS	CG	IP	H	BB	SO	SH	ERA
1958	6-4	.600	20	44	1	0	76	40	43	87	0	2.02
1959	3-6	.333	14	41	0	0	77	49	43	96	0	1.88
1960	3-4	.429	9	42	1	0	49	27	49	67	0	4.96
1961	0-1	.000	0	4	0	0	5	2	4	7	0	5.40
4 Yrs.	12-15	.444	43	131	2	0	206	118	139	257	0	2.75
Life.	27-44	.380	57	311	32	2	589	443	392	630	1	3.83

World Series

Yr.	G	IP	BB	SO	H	W-L	SA
1958	3	9⅓	6	14	7	1-1	1
1960	2	4	1	5	2	0-0	0
2 Yrs.	5	13⅓	7	19	9	1-1	1
Life. Same.							

ELBERFELD, KID
(BORN NORMAN ARTHUR ELBERFELD)

Nickname: "The Tabasco Kid"
Yankee: 1903-09
Shortstop, 3B
Born: April 13, 1875
Birthplace: Pomeroy, OH
Died: January 13, 1944
Bat: R; Throw: R
Ht: 5'7"; Wt: 158

CAME TO YANKS: Elberfield was one of the five players involved in the *first* trade in Yankee history on June 10, 1903. Kid was obtained with pitcher John Deering, from Detroit, for New York's Herman Long, Ernie Courtney and Patsy Greene.

YANKEE SHORTSTOP: Kid held the job as regular Yankee shortstop for five seasons (1903-07). In 1909 he played 61 games at shortstop and 43 games at third base. On August 1, 1903, he collected four singles off A's pitcher Rube Waddell, the only Yankee hits off Waddell in the game!

YANKEE MANAGER: A leg injury ruined Kid's 1908 season, confining his play to only 19 games. During the 1908 season, Kid became the second manager in Yankee history, taking over for Clark Griffith. Kid guided the Yanks to a 27-71 record over the remainder of 1908 and returned to the club in 1909 as a player only.

FIERY BALLPLAYER: "The Tabasco Kid" was an aggressive, competitive player, and he was a great spark and a colorful attraction on those early Yankee clubs. Kid's aggressive philosophy was to win at any cost. He was notorious for getting in the way of pitched balls and was more than willing to get hit time and again in order to reach first base. Kid stole 17 bases for the Highlanders which ties him with Steve Sax for 19th place in Yankee history.

GREAT RHUBARB: Late in 1906, the Yanks were fighting for the AL pennant when Kid got into a real rhubarb. In the first game of a big doubleheader at Hilltop Park on September 3, Kid went berserk over an umpire's call and proceeded to chase the umpire all around the field trying to kick him! The police finally had to escort Kid off the field!

LEFT YANKS: The Yanks sold Kid's contract to the Washington Senators for $5000 in December of 1909.

CASEY'S BUDDY: When Kid was playing for Montgomery, Alabama, in the minors in 1912, he become good friends with a young teammate on the way up named Casey Stengel. Kid was warm to Casey and taught him a lot about baseball. In those days it was quite unusual for a 37-year-old veteran on his way out of the game to be kind to a kid, and Casey appreciated the friendship. He never forgot Kid's valuable tips.

ELBERFELD, KID

Yr.	G	AB	R	H	2B	3B	HR	RBI	BB	SB	BA	SA
1903	90	349	49	100	18	5	0	45	22	16	.287	.367
1904	122	445	55	117	13	5	2	46	37	18	.263	.328
1905	111	390	48	102	18	2	0	53	23	18	.262	.318
1906	99	346	59	106	11	5	2	31	30	19	.306	.384
1907	120	447	61	121	17	6	0	51	36	22	.271	.336
1908	19	56	11	11	3	0	0	5	6	1	.196	.250
1909	106	379	47	90	9	5	0	26	28	23	.237	.288
7 Yrs.	667	2412	330	647	89	28	4	257	182	117	.268	.333
Life.	1292	4561	647	1235	169	56	10	535	427	213	.271	.339

ESPINOZA, ALVARO

Yankee: 1988-91
Shortstop, 2B, 3B, P
Born: February 19, 1962
Birthplace: Valencia, Venezuela
Bat: R; Throw: R
Ht: 6'; Wt: 160

SIGNING WITH YANKEES: The Yankees in November 1987 signed Alvaro as a six-year minor-league free agent. Originally signed by Houston in 1978, Alvaro had played briefly with the Twins (1984-86) without particular distinction. He hit .275 at Portland in 1987 and was granted free agency. In 1988, Alvaro played mostly at the Yanks' Columbus club, hitting .246 in 119 games.

SURPRISE SUCCESS STORY: Alvaro came to the Yanks spring camp in 1989 as a nonroster longshot to make the team; he wore uniform #72 as an indication of his regard. The longshot won the regular shortstop job for New York and hit a solid .282 in 1989. Alvaro remained the regular shortstop through the 1991 season, and he also made one pitching appearance in 1991. Alvaro was a decent hitter whose skills at shortstop were average, but for three years he played above expectations, and not many of his teammates could say that.

RELEASED: The Yankees released Alvaro in March 1992. A few weeks later he was signed by Cleveland. He was a valuable part-time player for the Indians in 1994 and 1995 (their championship season).

ESPINOZA, ALVARO

Yr.	G	AB	R	H	2B	3B	HR	RBI	BB	SB	BA	SA
1988	3	3	0	0	0	0	0	0	0	0	.000	.000
1989	146	503	51	142	23	1	0	41	14	3	.282	.332
1990	150	438	31	98	12	2	2	20	16	1	.224	.274
1991	148	480	51	123	23	2	5	33	16	4	.256	.344
3 Yrs.	447	1424	133	363	58	5	7	94	46	8	.255	.317
Life.	942	2478	252	630	105	9	22	201	76	13	.254	.331

ESPINOZA, ALVARO
(Pitcher)

Yr.	W-L	Pct.	S A	G	GS	CG	IP	H	BB	SO	SH	ERA
1991	0-0	---	0	1	0	0	$^2/_3$	0	0	0	0	0.00
1 Yr.	0-0	---	0	1	0	0	$^2/_3$	0	0	0	0	0.00
Life.	Same.											

ETTEN, NICK

Yankee: 1943-46
First Baseman
Born: September 19, 1913
Birthplace: Spring Grove, IL
Died: October 18, 1990
Bat: L; Throw: L
Ht: 6'2"; Wt: 198

CAME TO YANKS: Nick was acquired from the Phillies in January, 1943, for four mediocre players and $10,000.

YANKEE STAR: Nick was the regular Yankee first baseman throughout his four-year Yankee career and he was one of the stars of the team. During the war years, the Yanks counted heavily on Nick's run production. He averaged 89.5 RBIs per season as a Yankee. Nick was a key member of the 1943 World Championship team. He was a solid, consistent first baseman for the Yanks. In 1945 Nick led AL first basemen in double plays (149).

LEAGUE LEADER: Nick was the AL HR King (22) in 1944. He also led the AL in walks (97) in 1944. In 1945 Nick led the AL in RBIs (111).

CLUB LEADERSHIP: Nick twice led the Yanks in HRs (1944-45) and RBIs (1943, '45). In 1943 he led the Yanks in doubles (35). Nick and Snuffy Stirnweiss were the only Yankee players to play in every Yankee game in 1944 and 1945.

LEFT YANKS: Nick returned to the Phillies after the 1946 season.

ETTEN, NICK

Yr.	G	AB	R	H	2B	3B	HR	RBI	BB	SB	BA	SA
1943	154	583	78	158	35	5	14	107	76	3	.271	.420
1944	154	573	88	168	25	4	22	91	97	4	.293	.466
1945	152	565	77	161	24	4	18	111	90	2	.285	.437
1946	108	323	37	75	14	1	9	49	38	0	.232	.365
4 Yrs.	568	2044	280	562	98	14	63	358	301	9	.275	.429
Life.	937	3320	426	921	167	25	89	526	480	22	.277	.423

World Series

Yr.	G	AB	R	H	2B	3B	HR	RBI	BA
1943	5	19	0	2	0	0	0	2	.105
1 Yr.	5	19	0	2	0	0	0	2	.105
Life.	Same.								

FARR, STEVE

Yankee: 1991-93
Pitcher
Born: December 12, 1956
Birthplace: Cheverly, MD
Bat: R; Throw: R
Ht: 5'10"; Wt: 190

YANKEE SIGNING: On November 26, 1990, the Yankees signed Steve as a free agent, and on December 4, 1990, Farr's role became clear as Dave Righetti signed with the Giants. Steve had toiled in the minors for over eight years until finally sticking with the Royals in 1985 and eventually replacing Dan Quisenberry as the bullpen stopper.

BULLPEN STOPPER: Steve really didn't have much of a reputation when he replaced Righetti in 1991, but his strong suits were a good slider and one of the game's best curveballs. Established new career high with 23 saves in 1991. He had his best ML season in 1992 (30 saves, 1.56 ERA) despite being on the disabled list, June 30 through July 18. Steve took the heat for the Yanks' bullpen woes in 1993, and he did have a disappointing year; his ERA was more than 2 ½ runs per game higher than in 1992. He places sixth in saves (78), which is the sixth most by a Yankee pitcher through 1999.

LEFT YANKS: Steve was granted free agency in October 1993. He played for Cleveland and Boston in 1994.

FARR, STEVE												
Yr.	W-L	Pct.	SA	G	GS	CG	IP	H	BB	SO	SH	ERA
1991	5-5	.500	23	60	0	0	70	57	20	60	0	2.19
1992	2-2	.500	30	50	0	0	52	34	19	37	0	1.56
1993	2-2	.500	25	49	0	0	47	44	28	39	0	4.21
3 Yrs.	9-9	.500	78	159	0	0	169	135	67	136	0	2.56
Life.	48-45	.516	132	509	28	1	824	751	334	668	1	3.25

FIGUEROA, ED

Nickname: "Figgy"
Yankee: 1976-80
Pitcher
Born: October 14, 1948
Birthplace: Ciales, Puerto Rico
Bat: R; Throw: R
Ht: 6'1"; Wt: 190

CAME TO YANKS: In December, 1975, the Yanks obtained Ed and Mickey Rivers from the California Angels in exchange for Bobby Bonds in a deal that helped the Yanks capture the 1976 AL pennant.

FINE STARTER: During his Yankee career, Ed was one of the most dependable right-handers in the AL. In 1976-77 Ed was the Yanks' top starter. In 1978 he had his best ML season, going 13-2 after the All-Star break and winning his last eight decisions to help the Yanks catch Boston in an amazing stretch run. However, Ed's sensational efforts were overshadowed by Ron Guidry's super year. Over the three seasons in which New York won the AL pennant (1976-78), Ed won far more games (55) than any other Yankee, averaging 18.33 victories per season. He also started more games (101), completed more games (38) and pitched more innings (749) than any Yankee during those combined championship seasons. Ed is a control pitcher with a lively fastball, a good sinker and slider, and great competitive spirit. He really bears down when the going gets tough. Ed had some disagreements with Yankee managers Martin and Howser, but he enjoyed pitching for Bob Lemon.

HERO IN PUERTO RICO: In 1976 Ed nearly became the first native-born Puerto Rican to win 20 games in the ML's. But he did become the first 20-game-winning Puerto Rican in 1978 when on September 30 he beat Cleveland, 7-0. Understandably, he is proud of the achievement. Ed is a national hero in Puerto Rico beyond comparison with anyone in the States. He had a long hard journey to the ML's, interrupted by Marine duty in Vietnam. He is a religious and serious man who now works with the youth of Puerto Rico.

SERIOUS INJURY: Ed had a painful bone spur and chips in his pitching elbow during the 1979 season. He was on the disabled list from June 25 to July 23, then attempted to pitch in pain, but had to be placed on the disabled list again on August 2 for the remainder of the year. On August 17 Ed had successful surgery. At the start of the 1980 season, Ed was in the Yankee starting rotation, but was soon sent to the bullpen in an attempt to get him back in the groove. However, he did not appreciate the demotion.

CLUB LEADERSHIP: In 1976 Ed led the Yanks in wins (19) and shutouts (four). He tied Guidry for club victory honors (16) in 1977, besides leading the Yanks in innings pitched (239) and games started (32). Ed's 35 starts in 1978 tied Guidry for the club leadership.

POST-SEASON PLAY: Ed had little success pitching in the AL Championship Series or World Series, but it is certain that the Yanks never would have reached post-season play between 1976-78 without his contributions. He did give a strong performance in Game 4 of the 1978 World Series, a game the Yanks eventually won although Ed did not get the decision. Perhaps the most disappointing time in Ed's Yankee career was the 1977 World Series. Ed was under the impression he would start Game 6 but Manager Martin told reporters he was going to start Mike Torrez. Ed learned the news from Torrez and was so upset he almost went home to Puerto Rico.

TRADED: In July 1980, the Yanks sold Ed's contract to the Texas Rangers. Ed in 1981 finished his ML career pitching two games for Oakland and Manager Billy Martin.

FIGUEROA, ED

Yr.	W-L	Pct.	SA	G	GS	CG	IP	H	BB	SO	SH	ERA
1976	19-10	.655	0	34	34	14	257	237	94	119	4	3.02
1977	16-11	.593	0	32	32	12	239	228	75	104	2	3.57
1978	20-9	.690	0	35	35	12	253	233	77	92	2	2.99
1979	4-6	.400	0	16	16	4	105	109	35	42	1	4.13
1980	3-3	.500	1	15	9	0	58	90	24	16	0	6.98
5 Yrs.	62-39	.614	1	132	126	42	912	897	305	373	9	3.53
Life.	80-67	.544	1	200	179	63	1310	1299	443	571	12	3.51

Championship Series

Yr.	G	IP	BB	SO	H	W-L	SA
1976	2	12⅓	2	5	14	0-1	0
1977	1	3⅓	2	3	5	0-0	0
1978	1	1	0	0	5	0-1	0
3 Yrs.	4	16⅔	4	8	24	0-2	0
Life. Same.							

World Series

Yr.	G	IP	BB	SO	H	W-L	SA
1976	1	8	5	2	6	0-1	0
1978	2	6⅔	5	2	9	0-1	0
2 Yrs.	3	14⅔	10	4	15	0-2	0
Life. Same.							

FISHER, RAY

Yankee: 1910-17 (military)
Pitcher
Born: October, 4, 1887
Birthplace: Middlebury, VT
Died: November 3, 1982
Bat: R; Throw: R
Ht: 5'11"; Wt: 180

HONORS: In 1959 Ray was elected to the State of Michigan Sports Hall of Fame. He is a member of the College Baseball Hall of Fame.

YOUNG PITCHING STAR: In his senior year at Middlebury College in Vermont, Ray was the team's baseball coach and pitcher. Ray was a 22-year-old ML rookie when he joined the Yanks in 1910. After the 1910 season, Ray was a Latin teacher in New Jersey, and in the following off seasons he was a teacher coach back home in Middlebury. (He was called "The Vermont School Teacher.") One of Ray's wins in his 4-3 rookie season of 1910 was against the great Big Ed Walsh.

SPITBALL PITCHER: Ray threw a legal spitball. In 1920 the spitball was banned, but the 17 ML pitchers who used the pitch were allowed to continue throwing the spitter until the end of their careers. (In Ray's case the end came after the 1920 season.) Ray was a pitching star when the Yanks played at Hilltop Park and the Polo Grounds. In 1911 he was the Yanks' 4th starter. From 1913-16, he was one of the top three Yankee starters and he was the club's fourth starter in 1917. Ray had a fantastic 1915 winning percentage (.621, 18-11) on a Yankee team that played mediocre baseball (.454, 69-83).

CLUB LEADERSHIP: Four times Ray led Yankee pitchers in shutouts. He twice led the Yanks in ERA and games started. In 1913 Ray led the club in games pitched (43), games started (31), innings pitched (246) and strikeouts (92) as the workhorse of the Yankee pitching staff.

ALL-TIME YANKEE LEADER: Ray places seventh overall in Yankee history in ERA (2.91), and is 17th in innings pitched (1380).

MILITARY DUTY AND TRADED: Ray served in the military during World War I and missed the entire 1918 baseball season. In March of 1919, the Yanks sold Ray's contract to the Cincinnati Reds. Ray finished his ML career with two successful Cincinnati seasons (1919-20). Just before the 1921 season, Ray retired to take the head coaching baseball job at the University of Michigan. But the Reds placed Ray on the ineligible list, an injustice that was not rectified until almost 60 years later thanks to the efforts of many people, including Commissioner Kuhn and President Ford. (Ford played for Ray at Michigan.) Today Ray's good name stands clear and he no longer is listed as "declared ineligible for life."

MICHIGAN HERO: From 1921-58, Ray was baseball coach at Michigan and was one of the greatest college coaches of all time. His lifetime coaching record was 661-292 and his teams won 14 Big Ten championships and one NCAA title. During the summers, Ray worked with young area pitchers and was a tremendous influence on Robin Roberts. Ray was a great pitching instructor and worked with pitchers at Michigan many years after retiring. In 1970 Michigan's ballpark was renamed Ray Fisher Stadium. Ray attends the annual Michigan Hall of Fame Induction dinners and created a stir in 1977. At the annual Michigan Hall of Fame induction dinner in 1977, President Ford went out of his way to seek out Ray, his old friend, and have a long chat.

> **STATE OF MICHIGAN SPORTS HALL OF FAME, INC.**
> (Founded in 1955. Enshrined are those who have brought honor and glory to the State of Michigan and its communities.)
>
> **RAYMOND LYLE FISHER**
> Baseball Coach
> University of Michigan 1921-1958
> Pitched for New York AL, 1910-18; Cincinnati Reds, NL, 1919-20, Coach, University of Michigan for 38 years, his teams winning 14 Big Ten Championships, and one NCAA title. Lifetime college coaching record includes 953 games played, winning 661 and losing 292 for percentage of .696. Elected to Michigan Hall of Fame in 1959.

FISHER, RAY

Yr.	W-L	Pct.	SA	G	GS	CG	IP	H	BB	SO	SH	ERA
1910	5-3	.625	1	17	7	3	92	95	18	42	0	2.92
1911	10-11	.476	1	29	22	8	172	178	55	99	2	3.25
1912	2-8	.200	0	17	13	5	90	107	32	47	0	5.88
1913	12-16	.429	0	43	31	15	246	244	71	92	1	3.18
1914	10-12	.455	1	29	26	17	209	177	61	86	2	2.28
1915	18-11	.621	0	30	28	19	248	219	62	97	4	2.11
1916	11-8	.579	2	31	21	9	179	191	51	56	1	3.17
1917	8-9	.471	0	23	18	12	144	126	43	64	3	2.19
8 Yrs.	76-78	.494	5	219	166	88	1380	1337	393	583	13	2.91
Life.	100-94	.515	7	278	208	110	1756	1667	481	680	19	2.82

FORD, RUSS

Yankee: 1909-13
Pitcher
Born: April 25, 1883
Birthplace: Brandon, Canada
Died: January 24, 1960
Bat: R; Throw: R
Ht: 5'11"; Wt: 175

YANKEE ACE: In 1909 Russ was 26 years old when he appeared in his first ML game as a Yankee (Highlander) pitcher. (It was the only game he pitched for the Yanks all season.) Russ seemingly had unlimited potential. He won 48 games over his first two complete ML seasons (1910-11). He was the Yankee pitching ace for four consecutive seasons (1910-13). After Cleveland's star pitcher Addie Joss died in 1911, an AL All-Star team was organized to play a benefit game against the Indians for Joss' widow. Russ was one of three pitchers selected to the AL team, the others being Walter Johnson and Joe Wood. Russ threw a pitch known as an "emery-ball."

1910 SEASON: The 1910 season was Russ' first full ML campaign, and he had one of the most spectacular years a Yankee pitcher ever had although he did not lead AL pitchers in a single pitching category. He did lead Yankee pitchers in eight categories (wins, winning percentage, games started, complete games, innings pitched, strikeouts, shutouts and ERA). The eight shutouts he hurled was the Yankee club record (tied by Whitey Ford in 1961) until Ron Guidry broke it in 1978. Russ allowed only 5.83 hits per nine innings for the season, a percentage that ranks in baseball's top 15 of all time. His 1.65 ERA is the second lowest ERA ever compiled by a Yankee pitcher. Only three Yankee pitchers have won more games in a season than Russ did in 1910 (26). Those 26 wins represent the ML record for a player with rookie status. The 209 strikeouts he registered ranks sixth in Yankee history.

CLUB LEADERSHIP: From 1910-13, Russ led Yankee pitchers in wins and complete games. Between 1910-12 he led the Yanks in games started, innings pitched and strikeouts. Twice Russ led the Yanks in winning percentage and ERA, also in consecutive years (1910-11). In 1912 Russ allowed 165 runs, the most in Yankee history.

HITTING UPS AND DOWNS: In three of his four complete Yankee seasons, Russ was an easy out as a batter. He had batting averages of .208 (1910), .196 (1911) and .162 (1913). But in 1912 Russ hit .286 (32 for 112). In 1910 Russ made five triples, one of the highest totals in ML history. Only three AL pitchers have made more triples in one season (Al Orth, Washington; Jesse Tannehill, Boston; and Walter Johnson, Washington).

ALL-TIME YANKEE LEADER: Russ is ranked first on the all-time Yankee ERA list (2.54) for those former pitchers who pitched at least 800 innings in a Yankee uniform. He is also 13th in complete games (100).

LEFT YANKS: Following the 1913 season, Russ left the Yanks, jumping the AL to play for Buffalo of the newly formed Federal

League. After pitching for Buffalo in 1914 (21-6) and 1915 (5-9), Russ found himself out of work when the Federal League folded following the 1915 season. He never returned to the Yanks or to ML baseball as a player.

FORD, RUSS												
Yr.	W-L	Pct.	SA	G	GS	CG	IP	H	BB	SO	SH	ERA
1909	0-0	.000	0	1	0	0	3	4	4	2	0	9.00
1910	26-6	.813	1	36	33	29	300	194	70	209	8	1.65
1911	22-11	.667	1	37	33	26	281	251	76	158	1	2.27
1912	13-21	.382	0	36	35	30	292	317	79	112	0	3.55
1913	12-18	.400	1	33	28	15	237	244	58	72	1	2.66
5 Yrs.	73-56	.566	3	143	129	100	1113	1010	287	553	10	2.54
Life.	99-71	.582	9	199	170	126	1487	1340	376	710	15	2.59

FORD, WHITEY
(BORN EDWARD CHARLES FORD)

Nickname: "The Chairman of the Board"
Yankee: 1950 (military) '53-67
Pitcher
Born: October 21, 1928
Birthplace: New York, NY
Bat: L; Throw: L
Ht: 5'10"; Wt: 178

HONORS: In 1974 Whitey was inducted into the Baseball Hall of Fame along with his good friend Mickey Mantle. Whitey won the Cy Young Award as the best pitcher in ML baseball in 1961. *The Sporting News* gave Whitey its ML Rookie Award in 1950. *The Sporting News* named Whitey the AL Pitcher of the Year in *1955,* 1961 and 1963. *The Sporting News* selected Whitey as one of three pitchers on its ML All-Star teams of 1955 and 1956 and picked him as one of two pitchers on its AL All-Star teams of 1961 and 1963. For his efforts in the 1961 World Series, Whitey won the Babe Ruth Award and *Sport* magazine's MVP Award. In 1963 the New York Baseball Writers gave Whitey the Ben Epstein "Good Guy" Award. When Whitey retired in 1967, the Yanks "retired" his uniform number, "16."

YOUNG PROSPECT: Whitey grew up in the Astoria section of Queens where he learned his baseball in the Police Athletic League and Kiwanis League. Whitey played first base for the baseball team of his high school, the Manhattan School of Aviation Trades, in the neighborhood where he was born on East 63rd Street. (Whitey's first home was on East 66th Street between 1st and 2nd Avenues.) In April of 1946, Whitey got a Yankee Stadium tryout (along with a couple hundred other kids) as a first baseman and caught the eye of Paul Krichell, the Yanks' head scout. Krichell suggested Whitey try pitching and the scout was immediately impressed with Whitey's pin-point control and natural ability to throw a curveball. Whitey did some pitching in his final year of high school, then was a tremendous pitcher in the summer sandlot leagues of New York City. In October of 1946, Krichell gave Whitey a $7,000 bonus to sign with the Yanks. (The Giants and Red Sox were outbid and the Dodgers chose not to sign Whitey, probably because of his size.)

YANKEE MINOR LEAGUER: In 1947 spring training, Whitey failed to make the Yanks' Class-A team and was sent to Edenton,

Yankee ace, Whitey Ford, brings one home at Pittsburgh's Forbes Field during the 1960 World Series. The lefty pitched his entire 16-year career in pinstripes.

N.C., where after a short trial, Manager Lefty Gomez demoted him again. Moving up through the Yanks' farm system, Whitey pitched at Butler of the Middle Atlantic League in 1947 (13-4); Norfolk of the Piedmont League in 1948 (16-8); and Binghamton of the Eastern League in 1949 (16-5) where he led the circuit in ERA (1.61). In 1950 spring training, Whitey impressed everyone with his ability and confidence. Yet he was asked by the Yanks to begin the season at Kansas City of the American Association.

ROOKIE SENSATION: Whitey was 6-3 in 1950 for the Yanks' Kansas City farm team when he was called up. Both Whitey and Casey Stengel were convinced Whitey could do the job at the ML level. He did a marvelous job! He won nine of 10 Yankee decisions, saving the pennant for the Yanks. (It took an extra-inning HR by Sam Chapman of the A's to give Whitey his one loss.) Whitey won his first ML game on July 17, 1950, when he beat the White Sox, 4-3, with relief help from Tom Ferrick. Whitey was also a World Series hero.

MILITARY DUTY: Just as Whitey became a national celebrity and a New York hero, he was called away from the Yanks and New York. On the heels of his sensational rookie debut, Whitey entered the military and missed the 1951-52 seasons. Whitey returned to the Yanks in 1953 and was the club's pitching star through 1967.

HOT STREAKS: When Whitey got into a groove he was unbeatable. In 1961 he won 14 consecutive games to tie Jack Chesbro's Yankee record established in 1904. Whitey threw back-to-back one-hitters on September 2 and 7, 1955, making him one of only two pitchers to do that in AL history. He tossed three one-hitters in his ML career. On July 20, 1956, Whitey fanned 6 straight batters on the Kansas City A's. From 1955-58, he won four Yankee Stadium home openers in a row. (He started 12 Stadium openers and was 5-6.) Whitey had a lifetime record of 30-16 against the Baltimore Orioles, making him the winningest pitcher in history against the Orioles.

INTELLIGENT PITCHER: Whitey was one of the smartest and craftiest pitchers of all time. He threw an assortment of pitches and changed speeds, always keeping batters off stride. He threw in and out, up and down, but mostly he kept the ball low. Yet, he could throw a good fastball whenever he needed one and he had a beautiful curveball. Whitey did not throw a slider until 1961 and the new pitch helped him have a great 25-4 that season, a year in which he started 39 games, the most ever by a Yankee southpaw. Under Casey Stengel (1949-60), Whitey never was a 20-game winner, mostly because Stengel often held Whitey back in the rotation to pitch against the better teams and pitchers. Whitey produced a remarkable statistic in his ML career. Not once in the 14 seasons in which he pitched more than 100 innings did he yield as many hits as the number of innings he pitched!

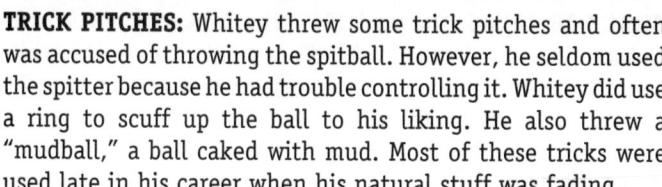

TRICK PITCHES: Whitey threw some trick pitches and often was accused of throwing the spitball. However, he seldom used the spitter because he had trouble controlling it. Whitey did use a ring to scuff up the ball to his liking. He also threw a "mudball," a ball caked with mud. Most of these tricks were used late in his career when his natural stuff was fading.

NATURAL ATHLETE: Whitey was a complete pitcher and did many things well. He was a great fielding pitcher, an underrated but important quality in a pitcher. He possibly had the finest pick-off move to first base in the history of baseball and many a base runner was caught off first in a crucial situation by a skillfully camouflaged Ford move. Whitey could swing the bat, too, making 177 hits during his ML career. He was a fine all-round athlete who possessed intelligence and a fierce determination to win.

NERVES OF STEEL: Whitey pitched his best under extreme pressure. He thrived on pressure. Yankee managers, players and fans were confident of a win whenever Whitey started a big game and the nation was used to seeing him pitch on TV in the big games. Whitey was cool in big games and was incredibly tough; he found himself in many pressure-packed situations because the Yanks always handed the ball to Whitey when it counted most. Whitey was a great competitor but he was not a cry-baby. If he lost a tough 1-0 game because of a teammate's error, Whitey would have a beer with that teammate as if nothing had happened and think about his upcoming outing. He would never berate a teammate.

FUN-LOVING: The good-natured personality and witty humor of Whitey were qualities appreciated in the Yankee clubhouse. Whitey was a good influence on the team. Whitey was great buddies with Mickey Mantle and Billy Martin, and those three loved to have fun together while with the Yanks. Whitey was always clever whenever he coyly denied throwing a spitball. He was also a classy guy throughout his career and a cooperative fellow with everyone, including the press. That old Yankee jokester, Lefty Gomez, tagged Eddie Ford with the name, "Whitey," and Elston Howard gave him the title, "The Chairman of the Board." Whitey got along splendidly with both his great catchers, Yogi Berra and Elston Howard.

HISTORIC MOMENT: On October 3, 1965, at Fenway Park, Whitey beat the Red Sox, 9-7, for his 232nd victory as a Yankee pitcher, surpassing Red Ruffing and making Whitey the winningest pitcher in Yankee history. It was not a masterpiece, but the win gave Whitey the most coveted record for a pitcher in the Yankee record book.

LEAGUE LEADER: Whitey led AL pitchers three times in wins (1955, 1961, 1963) and winning percentage (1956, 1961, 1963). Twice he led the AL in ERA (1956, 1958). In 1961 and 1963 Whitey led the AL in games started and innings pitched and in 1955 in complete games (18). Whitey led the AL in shutouts in 1958 (seven) and 1960 (four).

CLUB LEADERSHIP: Whitey led Yankee pitchers in numerous pitching categories through the years, but he was first in three categories more often than any other pitcher. In seven seasons, Whitey led the Yanks in ERA. In eight seasons, he led the Yanks

in complete games, a club record he shares with Red Ruffing. In four seasons, Whitey led the Yanks in winning percentage, a team record he shares with Mel Stottlemyre.

BASEBALL'S ALL-TIME LEADER LIST: Whitey is first on baseball's all-time winning percentage list (.690) for ML pitchers who have won at least 200 games in the 20th century. Whitey's career ERA (2.75) is one of the lowest in history for a lefthander with more than 200 wins. His winning percentage is second best in history for pitchers with at least 100 ML victories.

ALL-TIME YANKEE LEADER: Whitey is among the top 10 in most Yankee pitching categories. He is first on all-time Yankee lists for wins (236), games started (438), innings pitched (3170), strikeouts (1956), shutouts (45), and second in games pitched (498); third in winning percentage (.690—behind Chandler and Raschi); fifth in ERA (2.75); and tied for sixth in complete games (156).

ALL-STAR GAME: Whitey was selected to eight AL All-Star teams for the purpose of participating in the All-Star Game (1954, 1955, 1956, 1958, 1959, 1960, 1961, 1964). He started All-Star Games in 1955, 1961, and 1963

WORLD SERIES: Holding almost all the World Series pitching records, Whitey is first on the all-time list for wins (ten), games pitched (22), games started (22), innings pitched (146), and strikeouts (94). His $33\,^2/_3$ innings of scoreless Series pitching in the early 1960s broke Babe Ruth's most cherished record of $29\,^2/_3$ innings of scoreless Series pitching. Whitey won the final game of the 1950 Series to give the Yanks another World Championship. He won the opening games of the 1955, 1957, 1961, and 1962 Series and started more opening games in World Series history (eight) than any other pitcher. During the 1950s and early 1960s, watching Whitey Ford pitch in the World Series became a national habit.

SERIOUS INJURY: In 1964 Whitey developed a circulation problem in his left arm, and after losing Game 1 of the World Series, he was unable to continue in the Fall Classic. After the 1964 season, Whitey had an operation, but because of the circulation problem he did not sweat on his left side and experienced numbness, discomfort, pain and a clammy pitching hand when he took the mound. In 1966 Whitey was on the disabled list from August 22 through the end of the season after undergoing an operation for circulatory blockage in his left shoulder.

RETIREMENT: On May 30, 1967, Whitey was forced to retire from baseball because of his circulation trouble. He pitched 16 seasons for the Yanks, more seasons than any pitcher in Yankee history. Shortly after retiring in 1967, Mayor Lindsay proclaimed a "Whitey Ford Day" for the City of New York.

YANKEE COACH AND SCOUT: In 1964, Whitey handled the difficult dual responsibilities of being both a pitcher and pitching coach under his buddy, Manager Yogi Berra. Whitey, the wily veteran, helped his pitching comrades while taking his regular turn in the rotation. After hanging up his spikes as a player, Whitey remained in the Yankee organization. From May 30, 1967, until the season's end, Whitey was a Yankee scout and minor-league pitching coach. In 1968 he was the Yanks' first base coach. In 1974-75 Whitey was the Yanks' pitching coach.

STILL A YANKEE: Over the years, Whitey has been connected with the team in such capacities as spring-training instructor, pitching coach and scout. He stays close to the team from his Long Island home. He is still a fan favorite at Yankee Stadium events such as Old Timers Day.

FORD, WHITEY

Yr.	W-L	Pct.	SA	G	GS	CG	IP	H	BB	SO	SH	ERA
1950	9-1	.900	1	20	12	7	112	87	52	59	2	2.81
1953	18-6	.750	0	32	30	11	207	187	110	110	3	3.00
1954	16-8	.667	1	34	28	11	211	170	101	125	3	2.82
1955	18-7	.720	2	39	33	18	254	188	113	137	5	2.63
1956	19-6	.760	1	31	30	18	226	187	84	141	2	2.47
1957	11-5	.688	0	24	17	5	129	114	53	84	0	2.57
1958	14-7	.667	1	30	29	15	219	174	62	145	7	2.01
1959	16-10	.615	1	35	29	9	204	194	89	114	2	3.04
1960	12-9	.571	0	33	29	8	193	168	65	85	4	3.08
1961	25-4	.862	0	39	39	11	283	242	92	209	3	3.21
1962	17-8	.680	0	38	37	7	258	243	69	160	0	2.90
1963	24-7	.774	1	38	37	13	269	240	56	189	3	2.74
1964	17-6	.739	1	39	36	12	245	212	57	172	8	2.13
1965	16-13	.552	1	37	36	9	244	241	50	162	2	3.24
1966	2-5	.286	0	22	9	0	73	79	24	43	0	2.47
1967	2-4	.333	0	7	7	2	44	40	9	21	1	1.64
16 Yrs.	236-106	.690	10	498	438	156	3170	2766	1086	1956	45	2.75
Life. Same.												

World Series

Yr.	G	IP	BB	SO	H	W-L	SA
1950	1	8⅔	1	7	7	1-0	0
1953	2	8	2	7	9	0-1	0
1955	2	17	8	10	13	2-0	0
1956	2	12	2	8	14	1-1	0
1957	2	16	5	7	11	1-1	0
1958	3	15⅓	2	16	19	0-1	0
1960	2	18	2	8	11	2-0	0
1961	2	14	1	7	6	2-0	0
1962	3	19⅔	4	12	24	1-1	0
1963	2	12	3	8	10	0-2	0
1964	1	5⅓	1	4	8	0-1	0
11 Yrs.	22	146	34	94	132	10-8	0
Life. Same.							

GAMBLE, OSCAR

Yankee: 1976, 1979-84
Outfielder, DH
Born: December 20, 1949
Birthplace: Ramer, AL
Bat: L; Throw: R
Ht: 5'11"; Wt: 160

1976 SEASON: The Yankees obtained Oscar from Cleveland in November 1975 for pitcher Pat Dobson. Oscar had a reputation for being rebellious, which didn't at all disturb GM Gabe Paul or Mgr. Billy Martin; in fact, Oscar became one of Martin's favorite players. The Yankee front office did insist that Oscar cut off his large Afro—and he did. On April 15, 1976, in the reopening of a renovated Yankee Stadium, Oscar got three hits. Oscar platooned in right field with Lou Piniella and hit 17 HRs with 57 RBIs in only 340 AB's, playing a large role in helping the Yanks win the pennant. His relaxed style, and good natured needling, were also positive factors in the clubhouse. His wife, Juanita, sang the National Anthem at Yankee Stadium several times.

TRADE TO TEXAS: In April 1977, the Yankees traded Oscar, LaMarr Hoyt (P), Bob Polinsky (P) and $200,000 to the White Sox for Bucky Dent (SS). Oscar had his best season in 1977, hitting 31 HRs for the Chisox.

BACK TO NEW YORK: On August 1, 1979, the Rangers traded Oscar, Ray Fontenot (P), Gene Nelson (P), and Amos Lewis (3B) to the Yankees for Mickey Rivers (OF) and three minor-league pitchers (the deal was completed in October). Oscar hit .389 the rest of the season with the Yanks; for the entire year, he hit .358, the best in the AL, but his 274 AB's weren't enough to qualify for the batting title. Oscar stayed hot into the 1980 season, but on May 13 he broke his toe and didn't return to action until June 23; he still produced 50 RBIs in only 194 AB's in 1980. In 1981, Oscar had the AL's best on-base percentage for a pinch hitter (.615, 16 for 26).

POWER HITTER: Oscar played the outfield only adequately, but his stroke was perfect for Yankee Stadium. He was a low-ball hitter who crouched on top of the plate with an open stance; his short compact swing was aimed directly for the right-field porch. In 1976, he hit 11 HRs at the Stadium in only 113 AB's. In 1982, he hit 18 HRs for the season in only 316 AB's.

POST-SEASON PLAY: Oscar's bat was relatively quiet in the 1976 and 1980 post season. In the combined 1981 post season, Oscar hit .381 with two HRs and five RBIs. In the Division Series, in Game 1 he had a HR, double and single, and in Game 5 he put New York ahead for good with a HR. He didn't play much in the World Series because of the absence of the DH.

FINAL GOODBYE: In March 1985, Gamble left the Yankees as a free agent, signing with the White Sox. He hit .203 in 1985, his last ML season.

GAMBLE, OSCAR

Yr.	G	AB	R	H	2B	3B	HR	RBI	BB	SB	BA	SA
1976	110	340	43	79	13	1	17	57	38	5	.232	.426
1979	36	113	21	44	4	1	11	32	13	0	.389	.735
1980	78	194	40	54	10	2	14	50	28	2	.278	.567
1981	80	189	24	45	8	0	10	27	35	0	.238	.439
1982	108	316	49	86	21	2	18	57	58	6	.272	.522
1983	74	180	24	47	10	2	7	26	25	0	.261	.456
1984	54	125	17	23	2	0	10	27	25	1	.184	.440
7 Yrs.	540	1457	218	378	68	8	87	276	222	14	.259	.496
Life.	1584	4502	656	1195	188	31	200	666	610	47	.265	.454

Divisional Playoff

Yr.	G	AB	R	H	2B	3B	HR	RBI	BB	SB	BA	SA
1981	4	9	2	5	1	0	2	3	1	0	.556	1.333
1 Yr.	4	9	2	5	1	0	2	3	1	0	.556	1.333
Life. Same.												

Championship Series

Yr.	G	AB	R	H	2B	3B	HR	RBI	BB	SB	BA	SA
1976	3	8	1	2	1	0	0	1	1	0	.250	.375
1980	2	5	1	1	0	0	0	0	1	0	.200	.200
1981	3	6	2	1	0	0	0	1	5	0	.167	.167
3 Yrs.	8	19	4	4	1	0	0	2	7	0	.211	.263
Life. Same.												

World Series

Yr.	G	AB	R	H	2B	3B	HR	RBI	BB	SB	BA	SA
1976	3	8	1	1	0	0	0	1	0	0	.125	.125
1981	3	6	1	2	0	0	0	1	1	0	.333	.333
2 Yrs.	6	14	1	3	0	0	0	2	1	0	.214	.214
Life. Same.												

GEHRIG, LOU

Nicknames: "The Iron Horse" "Larrupin' Lou" "Columbia Lou"
"Buster Lou" "Biscuit Pants" "Pride of the Yankees"
Yankee: 1923-39
First Baseman
Born: June 19, 1903
Birthplace: New York, NY
Died: June 2, 1941
Bat: L; Throw: L
Ht: 6'; Wt: 200

HONORS: Lou was inducted into the Baseball Hall of Fame in 1939 by special election. In 1927 Lou won the League Award (the AL's MVP Award). The Baseball Writers named him the AL's MVP in 1936. *The Sporting News* gave Lou their MVP Award three times (1931, 1934, 1936). *The Sporting News* selected Lou as the first baseman on the publication's ML All-Star team six times (1927, '28, '31, '34, '36, '37). In 1931 the Baseball Writers gave him the Sid Mercer Award. Lou won the Triple Crown in 1934 to become the first Yankee ever to take that prestigious honor. When he retired as a player in 1939, the Yanks retired Lou's uniform number "4" forever. The Yanks dedicated a monument to Lou's memory and placed it in center field of Yankee Stadium. Today it rests in "Memorial Park" beyond the left field wall at the Stadium. (It was dedicated July 4, 1941, exactly two years after Lou's farewell speech.) In 1969 Lou was voted the "Greatest First Baseman Ever" in a vote celebrating baseball's centennial.

YOUNG PROSPECT: Lou grew up in New York City, the son of German immigrants who were poor monetarily, but rich in heart and love. Lou's parents came to New York from Germany in 1900. Lou was a baseball star at Commerce High School in Manhattan. In his senior year, Commerce won the city championship and went to Chicago to play Lane Tech, the champions of Chicago, at Wrigley Field. Commerce won, 12-6, thanks in part to Lou's grand slam HR. The next day the *New York Daily News* called Lou "the New York lad known as the 'Babe Ruth' of the high schools." In college Lou was a star baseball (outstanding hitter and pitcher) and football player at Columbia University. The Giants' John McGraw illegally signed Lou off the Columbia campus and sent him to the Hartford minor league club, having Lou play under an assumed name while still attending Columbia. When the ruse was discovered, Lou's Giant contract was abrogated, but he was allowed to regain his amateur status. (Lou hit .261 in 46 at-bats for Hartford in 1921.)

YANKEE PROSPECT: Famous Yankee scout Paul Krichell gave Lou a $1,500 bonus and a $3,000 salary to sign legally with the Yanks in June of 1923. In 1923 and 1924, Lou played for Hartford of the Eastern League, with whom the Yanks had a working agreement, then finished each season with the Yanks. Lou hit .304 with 24 HRs in only 227 at-bats with Hartford in 1923 and .369 with 37 HRs in 1924. On September 27, 1923, during one of Lou's brief trials with the Yanks, he hit his first ML home run off Bill Piercy at Boston's Fenway Park. For his combined Yankee trials of 1923-24, Lou made 17 hits in 38 trips to the plate (.447) and drove in 15 runs! In 1924 Lou was known as "the Babe Ruth of the rookies." He became a permanent Yankee in 1925, after impressing Manager Huggins in spring training with his booming bat.

IRON MAN: Lou was a Yankee benchwarmer for the early part of the 1925 season. On June 1 he pinch-hit for Peewee Wanninger, and the next day, regular Yankee first baseman Wally Pipp was unable to play because of a headache. Lou was sent out to play first base and did not come out of the lineup for 14 years! From June 1, 1925, through April 30, 1939, Lou played in 2130 consecutive games, a ML record quietly carved and noisily shattered in 1995 by Cal Ripken of the Baltimore Orioles. Lou is now second in consecutive games and former Yankee Everett Scott is third with 1307. Yankee Managers Huggins and McCarthy always could be certain of at least one name they would pen into the Yankee starting lineup. Yankee fans could count on seeing Lou play when they purchased a ticket. Lou in the course of his continuous play had ailments that threatened an end to his streak, including fractured fingers, charley horses, spike wounds, sore muscles, bad colds and a back pain that often bothered him. Yet he played with these handicaps. On a few occasions when Lou was not feeling well and the Yanks were on the road, McCarthy would announce Lou as the shortstop and bat him first; Lou would bat and leave the game in favor of Frank Crosetti, the regular shortstop. Lou led the AL in games played seven times (1927, 1930, 1932, 1934, 1936, 1937, 1938), more often than anyone else in AL history until Cal Ripken Jr. surpassed this mark in 1996. In 12 of 13 years between 1926 and 1938 (except 1935), Lou played in more than 150 games each year!

HOME RUN SLUGGER: Lou holds the AL record for HRs hit by a first baseman (493). When he retired in 1939, only Babe Ruth had hit more lifetime HRs than Lou's 493. Lou hit 23 career grand slam HRs, the ML record. In 1934 he hit four grand slams, a Yankee club record for 53 years until Don Mattingly hit six in 1987. Lou belted 30 HRs at Yankee Stadium in 1934, the most ever hit in one season at the Stadium. In 1931 Lou hit nine HRs in 11 games played at St. Louis. The 14 HRs Lou hit against Cleveland in 1936 represents the most HRs one player has ever hit against one club in a season in ML history. (Lou hit eight at Cleveland and six at Yankee Stadium.) In 1931 from August 28 through September 1, Lou hit a HR in six consecutive games, setting an AL record.

BIG HOME RUN DAYS: Lou enjoyed one four-HR game and three three-HR games. Thus, on four occasions he hit three or more HRs in one game, an AL record. Lou hit his first HR on September 27, 1923, off Bill Piercy at Fenway Park, and his 493rd and last HR on September 27, 1938, a shot off Washington's Dutch Leonard. On May 7, 1927, Lou blasted the first HR at enlarged and remodeled Comiskey Park, a grand slam HR off Ted Lyons that landed in the new right field pavilion. On May 1, 1929, Lou hit a tape-measure HR off Red Faber that cleared the right field roof at Comiskey.

RUN PRODUCER: In 1931 Lou set the AL record for RBIs in one season (184). In seven seasons Lou copped more than 150 RBIs (1927, 1930, 1931, 1932, 1934, 1936, 1937), a ML record. Babe Ruth and Lou are the only players in ML history to collect at least 150 RBIs in three consecutive seasons, as Lou did in 1930, 1931 and 1932. In three seasons of Lou's career (1930, 1931, 1934), he went 10 successive games in which he got at least one RBI in each game. In 13 straight years (1926-38), Lou knocked in AND scored more than 100 runs, besides totaling more than

300 bases in each season, a phenomenal accomplishment! In fact, Lou holds AL records for most 100-RBI seasons (13); most 100-runs scored seasons (13); and most seasons with at least 300 total bases (13)!

1927 SEASON: In 1927 Lou had a splendid year and was MVP of the AL. The 52 doubles he hit set the Yankee club record that stood until Mattingly hit 53 in 1986. His 117 extra-base hits are the second most ever made in ML history. Lou's slugging average of .765 is the fourth highest single season average in baseball history and the highest by anyone other than Babe Ruth (owner of the top three single-season SAs). Lou and the Babe combined for 107 HRs, the most ever hit by two players on one club until Maris and Mantle cracked 115 HRs in 1961. Lou's 1927 salary was $8,000. Lou had 175 RBIs in spite of the fact that Ruth, batting before him, cleared the bases 60 times!

OFFENSIVE THREAT: Throughout his Yankee career, Lou was a spectacular and consistent offensive performer. Jimmie Foxx once said Lou was a "more dangerous" hitter than Babe Ruth. Ruth got more good pitches to hit with big Lou waiting in the on-deck circle than he might have with a lesser batter hitting behind him. Lou was removed for a pinch-hitter eight times as a Yankee, but only twice after 1925 (by Earle Combs in 1932 and Myril Hoag in 1935). He collected more than 400 total bases in five seasons (1927, 1930, 1931, 1934, 1936), a ML record. Lou is the only player in AL history to get more than 400 total bases in consecutive years (1930-31). Lou was not a big awkward slugger by any means. In 1934 he hit 49 HRs and struck out only 31 times, the best HR-SO ratio in history for players hitting 47 or more HRs. And in 1936 Lou hit 49 HRs and fanned only 46 times. Not only was Lou a coordinated hitter, but for a big man he was also a fine base runner. He stole home plate 14 times, a Yankee club record!

GREAT DAYS: Lou once hit three triples in the first 4½ innings of a game, only to lose them officially when the game was washed out by a rainstorm. On five occasions, Lou hit four or more extra base hits in one game, a ML record. Twice he hit for the cycle in a game. He had at least 12 total bases in a game seven times! He had eight RBIs in a game three times! Lou once stole three bases in a single game. Lou never had a five-hit game, but of course he had those great multiple-HR games.

GREATEST GAME: On June 3, 1932, Lou hit four consecutive HRs against the Philadelphia A's, setting an AL record since tied only by Rocky Colavito in 1959. In Lou's fifth trip to the plate, in the ninth inning, he hit his longest shot of the day. But Al Simmons caught the ball in deep center field of Shibe Park, near the flagpole. Since 1932 was the year the Yanks finally unseated Philadelphia as champions of the AL, Lou's performance was symbolic of the changing of the guard. Unfortunately, Lou picked the wrong day to have his greatest game because on the same day, John J. McGraw, the New York Giants' famous manager of 31 years, decided to retire. McGraw was a hero in New York and somewhat of an adversary of Gehrig's. Lou never forgave McGraw for taking advantage of him in his Columbia days. In any event, the headlines of the next day were about McGraw's retirement and Lou's exploits were under-emphasized.

UNDERRATED BALLPLAYER: The McGraw retirement's getting the headlines over Lou's splendid deeds was not the first time Lou would take a publicity slight, nor would it be the last. Lou was actually an underrated player throughout his career. Looking back, that seems impossible. But it is true. Lou successfully refrained from controversy, but he was slighted when it came to publicity. When Lou permanently joined the Yanks in 1925, Babe Ruth was a national hero, and Lou remained in Ruth's considerable shadow until Ruth left the Yanks following the 1934 season. Then Joe DiMaggio joined the Yanks in 1936 and received most of the attention in New York. Even in 1935, when Lou was the club's top star, the team, fans and press lamented the loss of Ruth, while at the same time preparing for DiMaggio whose contract the Yanks had already obtained and who was tearing up the Pacific Coast League. Lou never griped publicly about his lack of exposure, but it had to hurt. But the average guy loved Lou and saw him as both a "laborer" and a "gamer" and he had his share of supporters from the people who really counted—the kids of New York.

UNDERPAID PLAYER: The Yanks did not make Lou a wealthy man. This great player's largest season salary came in either 1937 or 1938 when Lou earned somewhere between $33,000 and $39,000. (Granted, that *was* a lot of money during the Depression.) On the great 1927 team, nine players took home a larger salary than did Lou, the AL's MVP! Lou earned an estimated $400,000 as a Yankee player, considering both salary and World Series checks.

SNUB BY WRITERS: When Lou won the coveted Triple Crown in 1934, Detroit's Mickey Cochrane somehow was chosen MVP by the Baseball Writers. Cochrane led the Tigers to the AL pennant as player-manager, but his offensive statistics (.320, two HRs, 76 RBIs), paled in comparison with Lou's (.363, 49 HRs, 165 RBIs). What did Lou have to do to gain recognition?

FINALLY, RECOGNITION: Make no mistake, everyone around baseball knew Lou was a great player. The fact of his greatness just was not touted as much as it should have been. Unfortunately, it took a fatal disease for Lou to become appreciated universally as the greatest of the greats that he was. When the Yanks retired Lou's uniform Number "4" before his death, it was the first Yankee number to be so retired. At last a unique honor was accorded him. (Lou's Yankee locker was closed; no one else would ever use it.)

DEFENSIVE ABILITIES: Although Lou was not the best ever defensively at first base, he was good enough. In fact, he moved with a degree of grace around the bag. In 1938 he handled 157 double plays to lead the AL and establish the Yankee DP record for first basemen. (Lou also set the AL record which was broken a few years later.) Twice Lou led AL first basemen in putouts (1927-28). He led AL first sackers once in total chances per game (1927) and assists (1930). In seven World Series, Lou made only one error, an indication that he was a cool fielder under pressure. Lou made only 193 errors in 20,790 lifetime chances. On the all-time lists for first basemen, Lou ranks fourth in games played at first (2136); ninth in putouts (19,510), total chances (20,790) and in double plays (1574). From June 2, 1925, through September 27, 1930, Lou played in 885 consecutive games *at first base,* a ML record.

Lou Gehrig, New York Yankee first baseman who had played in 2,130 consecutive games, took the bench May 2, 1939 at his own request and looked on forlornly as his teammates warmed up for their game with the Tigers in Detroit. "I felt I wasn't helping the club by the way I was playing," Gehrig explained. The Yanks thrashed the Tigers 22 to 2. (AP/WIDE WORLD PHOTOS)

LEAGUE LEADER: Lou led the AL in games played seven times, an AL record until broken by Cal Ripken Jr. In 1934 he won the AL batting championship (.363), allowing him to win the Triple Crown. He won or tied for the AL's HR Crown in three seasons (1931, 1934, 1936). Lou led the AL five times in RBIs and on-base average. He led the AL four seasons in runs scored. He led the AL three seasons in walks. Twice he led the AL in doubles and slugging. In 1926 Lou paced the AL in triples (20). In 1931 he led the AL in hits (211).

CLUB LEADERSHIP: Through the years Lou was the seasonal leader in many batting categories, but he led the club more often than anyone in Yankee history in games played (13 times), RBIs (nine times), doubles (eight times), and batting average (eight times).

BASEBALL'S ALL-TIME LEADER LIST: Lou ranks high on some of baseball's most important slugging lists. Most importantly and impressively, he is third on the all-time RBI (1995) and slugging (.632) lists. (Aaron and Ruth are ahead of Lou in RBIs, and Lou follows Ruth and Williams in slugging.) Also on baseball's all-time lists, Lou ranks fifth in extra-base hits (1190), and sixth in on-base average (.447). Lou is eighth in runs scored (1888); 12th in total bases (5059); and 13th in walks (1508).

ALL-TIME YANKEE LEADER: Lou is first on the all-time Yankee hit (2721), extra-base hit (1190), single (1531), double (535) and triple (163) lists which about covers the hit department! Lou is also first on the Yanks' RBI list (1995). He ranks second on the at-bat (8001), games played (2164), runs scored (1888), batting (.340) and slugging (.632) lists. He is third both on the Yankee home run (493) and walk (1508) lists.

NICE GUY: Nice, quiet and conservative are three words that describe Lou. He worked hard to maintain the "Yankee Image" and certainly was the "Pride of the Yankees." Manager Joe McCarthy loved Lou, as did Lou's teammates. To players and fans alike, Lou was a most admired man. He once turned down a cigarette commercial, believing it would be a bad influence on kids. Lou never turned down the kids. He loved kids and tried to help them whenever possible. Lou was Yankee captain and he took the job seriously. He had homey interests and hobbies such as fishing and playing bridge, activities which kept him away from scandal. Lou was an unselfish man, but if he had a fault, it was his excessive frugality—the opposite of free-spending Babe Ruth. (Lou invested in real estate.)

GOOD FRIENDS: Lou was a loyal friend and he had many friends. During the 1920s Lou's closest Yankee friends were Babe Ruth, Tony Lazzeri, and Benny Bengough. In the 1930s, Lou's roommate, Bill Dickey, was probably his best friend on the Yanks. Sportswriter Fred Lieb may have been Lou's closest friend, but he had many friends representing all walks of life in the New York area. After Lou was stricken with his terrible illness, a steady procession of people, many of them famous, visited Lou's Bronx home to bring him cheer.

RELATIONSHIP WITH RUTH: While Lou kept his distance from controversy, he was involved in a few legendary feuds and

Lou Gehrig (left) and Babe Ruth are having a chat in this photo taken during the 1927 season.

these were unfortunate. When Lou joined the Yanks, Babe Ruth was his idol and he dutifully allowed the Babe to shine in the spotlight. Lou ran errands for Babe, and Ruth enjoyed the family life of the Gehrigs. The most feared batting duo in baseball history, Ruth and Gehrig, were great buddies in the 1920s. But in 1929 Lou rejected Babe's suggestion that together they hold out for more money, and a rift developed between them. There were other disagreements, the most serious stemming from a remark Lou's mother made about the Ruth family, and the great friendship was over. In Ruth's final Yankee years, the pair hardly talked and no longer did they enjoy hobbies together or go on barnstorming tours together after regular seasons. (Lou and Babe had often barnstormed together, the tours usually organized by Ruth's ghostwriter, Christy Walsh.)

FAMILY PROBLEMS: Another unpleasant subject was the relationship between Lou's mother and his wife. Lou's mother, known as Mom Gehrig, was a great cook, and her home became a meeting place for many of the Yankee players who became known as "Mom's boys." The "boys" included Ruth, Dugan, and Meusel, among others. Lou was close to his mother, a woman determined to give her son a better life, and did not marry until 1933, many years after attaining fame. Sadly, Mom never liked Lou's wife, Eleanor, and Lou had trouble bringing them together. It was not Eleanor's fault; Mom was just possessive of Lou. She had spent her life working selflessly in Lou's behalf.

ALL-STAR GAME: Lou was picked to represent the AL in the first six games in All-Star Game history (1933-38). He hit a HR in both the 1936 and 1937 All-Star Games; his 1937 HR was hit off no less than Dizzy Dean. Mickey Mantle is the only other Yankee player to hit two HRs in All-Star Game competition.

WORLD SERIES: A member of six Yankee World Championship teams, Lou was on only one World Series loser (in 1926, his first Series). He is among the leaders in most World Series batting categories, including being third in RBIs (35) and slugging (.731). Lou got at least one RBI in eight consecutive World Series games (1928, 1932), a Series record. In Game 1 of the 1926 Series, Lou's RBI single beat St. Louis, 2-1. His four hits were all for extra bases in the 1927 Series and were key hits in the first three games. In the 1928 Series, Lou was spectacular (.545, four HRs, nine RBIs) and hit two HRs in Game 3, but was slightly overshadowed by Ruth's .625. Lou was equally great in the 1932 Series sweep of Chicago (three HRs, nine runs), again hitting two HRs in Game 3. In Game 4 of the 1936 Series, Lou's two-run HR helped beat the Giants, 5-2. He hit a respectable .294 in the 1937 Series, but complained of "lumbago," an ominous signal. Playing in a weak condition in the 1938 Series, Lou managed only four singles in 14 at-bats (.286), his worst Series. Lou's batting average in the World Series (.361) ranks him 11th on the all-time list.

END OF ML CAREER: Lou had a poor spring training camp in 1939 and started the season slowly. He felt poorly, and on May 2, 1939, asked Joe McCarthy to take him out of the lineup for the good of the team—for the first time since 1925. Lou took the Yankee lineup card to home plate and the announcement was made to the Detroit crowd that his consecutive-game-playing streak was ending. Lou received a tremendous ovation and returned to the dugout with tears in his eyes. At the Mayo Clinic a few weeks later, it was discovered that Lou was suffering from the rare amyotrophic lateral sclerosis, a fatal disease. The sickness forced Lou to retire as a player, but he stayed with the club as an unofficial captain/coach for the duration of the campaign. On July 4, 1939, Yankee Stadium was packed for "Lou Gehrig Appreciation Day" and the crowd of 61,808 heard Lou give a moving speech on the most emotional day in baseball history. "I may have been given a bad break," Lou told his hushed audience, "but I have an awful lot to live for. Today I consider myself the luckiest man on the face of the earth." The Stadium rocked with chants of, "We love you, Lou."

FINAL DAYS: In 1940, New York City Mayor LaGuardia appointed Lou a special assistant to work with juvenile delinquents in New York. Lou worked at his job enthusiastically until his health would not permit him to work any longer. On June 2, 1941, Lou Gehrig died in Riverdale, a section of the Bronx, at the age of 37 (a little more than two weeks before his 38th birthday). The Yanks were in Detroit when they learned of Lou's death. Lou's fatherlike manager, Joe McCarthy, and close friend, Bill Dickey, returned to New York for the funeral. Lou's body was cremated and the urn containing his ashes was buried in a cemetery in Westchester County, N.Y. (Babe Ruth also was buried in Westchester County.)

STADIUM WORDS

The inscription on Lou's monument at Yankee Stadium reads:

HENRY LOUIS GEHRIG
June 19th, 1903 - June 2nd, 1941
A MAN, A GENTLEMAN
and
A great Ball Player
Whose amazing record
of 2,130 Consecutive Games
Should stand for all Time
This Memorial is a Tribute
From the
Yankee Players
to their beloved Captain and Team Mate
July the Fourth
1941

ON FINAL DAY

When Lou Gehrig's 2130 consecutive-game streak ended on May 2, 1939, Yankee Manager Joe McCarthy reluctantly agreed to Lou's request that he be removed from the Yankee lineup. In his *New York Times* article, James P. Dawson quoted both McCarthy and Gehrig. Here is what each said that fateful day:

McCARTHY:

"Lou just told me he felt it would be best for the club if he took himself out of the lineup. I asked him if he really felt that way. He told me he was serious. He feels blue. He is dejected.

"I told him it would be as he wished. Like everybody else I'm sorry to see it happen. I told him not to worry. Maybe the warm weather will bring him around.

"He's been a great ballplayer. Fellows like him come along once in a hundred years. I told him that. More than that, he's been a vital part of the Yankee club since he started with it. He's always been a perfect gentleman, a credit to baseball.

"We'll miss him. You can't escape that fact. But I think he's doing the proper thing."

GEHRIG:

"I decided last Saturday night on this move. I haven't been a bit of good to the team since the season started. It would not be fair to the boys, to Joe or to the baseball public for me to try going on. In fact, it would not be fair to myself.

"It's tough to see your mates on base, have a chance to win a ball game, and not be able to do anything about it. McCarthy has been swell about it all the time. He'd let me go until the cows came home, he is that considerate of my feelings, but I knew in Sunday's game that I should get out of there.

"I went up there four times with men on base. Once there were two there. A hit would have won the game for the Yankees, but I missed, leaving five stranded. Maybe a rest will do me some good. Maybe it won't. Who knows? Who can tell? I'm just hoping."

TROPHY INSCRIPTION

On July 4, 1939, "Lou Gehrig Appreciation Day" was held at Yankee Stadium and Lou was presented a trophy from his Yankee teammates engraved with these words:

We've been to the wars together,
We took our foes as they came;
And always you were the leader,
And ever you played the game.

Idol of cheering millions;
Records are yours by sheaves;
Iron of frame they hailed you,
Decked you with laurel leaves.

But higher than that we hold you,
We who have known you best;
Knowing the way you came through
Every human test.

Let this be a silent token
Of lasting friendship's gleam
And all that we've left unspoken.
—YOUR PALS ON THE YANKEE TEAM

—by John Kieran

GEHRIG, LOU

Yr.	G	AB	R	H	2B	3B	HR	RBI	BB	SB	BA	SA
1923	13	26	6	11	4	1	1	9	2	0	.423	.769
1924	10	12	2	6	1	0	0	5	1	0	.500	.583
1925	126	437	73	129	23	10	20	68	46	6	.295	.531
1926	155	572	135	179	47	20	16	112	105	6	.313	.549
1927	155	584	149	218	52	18	47	175	109	10	.373	.765
1928	154	562	139	210	47	13	27	142	95	4	.374	.648
1929	154	553	127	166	33	9	35	126	122	4	.300	.582
1930	154	581	143	220	42	17	41	174	101	12	.379	.721
1931	155	619	163	211	31	15	46	184	117	17	.341	.662
1932	156	596	138	208	42	9	34	151	108	4	.349	.621
1933	152	593	138	198	41	12	32	139	92	9	.334	.605
1934	154	579	128	210	40	6	49	165	109	9	.363	.706
1935	149	535	125	176	26	10	30	119	132	8	.329	.583
1936	155	579	167	205	37	7	49	152	130	3	.354	.696
1937	157	569	138	200	37	9	37	159	127	4	.351	.643
1938	157	576	115	170	32	6	29	114	107	6	.295	.523
1939	8	28	2	4	0	0	0	1	5	0	.143	.143
17 Yrs.	2164	8001	1888	2721	535	162	493	1995	1508	102	.340	.632

Life. Same.

World Series

Yr.	G	AB	R	H	2B	3B	HR	RBI	BA
1926	7	23	1	8	2	0	0	3	.348
1927	4	13	2	4	2	2	0	5	.308
1928	4	11	5	6	1	0	4	9	.545
1932	4	17	9	9	1	0	3	8	.529
1936	6	24	5	7	1	0	2	7	.292
1937	5	17	4	5	1	1	1	3	.294
1938	4	14	4	4	0	0	0	0	.286
7 Yrs.	34	119	30	43	8	3	10	35	.361

Life. Same.

GIBBS, JAKE
(BORN JERRY DEAN GIBBS)

Yankee: 1962-71
Catcher
Born: November 7, 1938
Birthplace: Grenada, MS
Bat: L; Throw: R
Ht: 6'; Wt: 185

BONUS BABY: Jake was a great football player at the University of Mississippi. In 1961, the Yanks signed Jake and gave him a reported bonus of $105,000.

YANKEE CATCHER: From 1962-64, Jake played briefly with the Yanks at the end of each season. He was a back-up catcher on the 1965-66 Yankee clubs. Jake missed much of the 1966 season due to a broken finger. When Elston Howard went to the Red Sox during the 1967 campaign, Jake became the regular Yankee catcher and held the job until late in the 1969 season when Thurman Munson joined the team and became the Yanks' regular catcher. Ironically, Jake hit .301 with eight HRs in only 153 at-bats in 1970, his best year at the plate. Jake was a tough, gritty catcher. 1971 was Jake's last ML season.

AFTER PLAYING DAYS: Jake was a successful head baseball coach for his alma mater, the University of Mississippi, from 1972-1990. In 1993, he returned to the Yankees as the bullpen coach. In 1994 and 1995 Jake was the minor-league manager of the Tampa Yankees. He is now retired from baseball, and was recently elected to the College Football Hall of Fame.

YANKEE CATCHERS WHO CAUGHT THE MAJORITY OF YANKEE GAMES IN EACH SEASON IN THE 30 YEARS FROM 1949-79:

Yogi Berra (1949-59)
Elston Howard (1960-66)
Jake Gibbs (1967-69)
Thurman Munson (1970-79)

GIBBS, JAKE

Yr.	G	AB	R	H	2B	3B	HR	RBI	BB	SB	BA	SA
1962	2	0	2	0	0	0	0	0	0	0	.000	.000
1963	4	8	1	2	0	0	0	0	0	0	.250	.250
1964	3	6	1	1	0	0	0	0	0	0	.167	.167
1965	37	68	6	15	1	0	2	7	4	0	.221	.324
1966	62	182	19	47	6	0	3	20	19	5	.258	.341
1967	116	374	33	87	7	1	4	25	28	7	.233	.289
1968	124	423	31	90	12	3	3	29	27	9	.213	.277
1969	71	219	18	49	9	2	0	18	23	3	.224	.283
1970	49	153	23	46	9	2	8	26	7	2	.301	.542
1971	70	206	23	45	9	0	5	21	12	2	.218	.335
10 Yrs.	538	1639	157	382	53	8	25	146	120	28	.233	.321

Life. Same.

GOMEZ, LEFTY
(BORN VERNON LOUIS GOMEZ)

Nicknames: "Goofy" "The Gay Castillion"
Yankee: 1930-42
Pitcher
Born: November 26, 1908
Birthplace: Rodeo, CA
Died: February 17, 1989
Bat: L; Throw: L
Ht: 6'2"; Wt: 173

HONORS: Lefty was inducted into the Baseball Hall of Fame in 1972. He was one of three pitchers on *The Sporting News'* 1934 and 1938 ML All-Star teams. In 1977 the New York Chapter of the Baseball Writers gave Lefty their Casey Stengel "You Could Look It Up" Award.

YOUNG PROSPECT: In 1929, the Yankees paid the San Francisco Seals of the Pacific Coast League between $35,000 and $50,000 for Lefty's contract. After going 2-5 with a 5.55 ERA as a Yankee rookie for the first half of the 1930 season, Lefty was farmed out to St. Paul of the American Association. At St. Paul, he learned the subtle skills of a complete pitcher: keeping runners close to base, backing up throws, fielding bunts, etc.

YANKEE GREAT: For 13 seasons Lefty was a Yankee star. He won more than 20 games four times (1931, '32, '34, '37), tying him with Bob Shawkey and Red Ruffing for the most 20-win seasons in Yankee history. Lefty pitched his entire ML days with the Yanks except for the one game in 1943 he pitched for the Washington Senators. Lefty and Ruffing may have been the greatest, most consistent pair of starting pitchers on one club in ML history. The duo of Gomez-Ruffing dominated the AL during the 1930s. Between 1931-41 Lefty never won fewer than 12 games a season except for 1940 when he had a sore arm. After the 1934 season, he traveled to Japan with a group of ballplayers, including Babe Ruth and Lou Gehrig. The Japanese hosts gave prizes to outstanding performers and Lefty won the pitching prize.

SLIM BUT FAST: Lefty had a fastball that belied his slimness. Yankee GM Ed Barrow annually tried to get Lefty to put on more weight, but Lefty's tremendous power actually came from his whiplash arm. The one year that he came to spring camp heavy, he had a poor season. Late in his career, "Goofy" became a control-finesse pitcher. He worked on a knuckleball and a slow curve—anything to stay in the game he loved. By then, arm problems had reduced the power of his once-great fastball with which he pitched many near no-hitters, including two one-hitters. On August 1, 1941, Lefty walked 11 men and still won a shutout game, a ML record for the most walks in a shutout win which was later tied by Yankee ace Mel Stottlemyre in 1970.

BASEBALL AND CLUB RECORDS: In 1938 Lefty allowed only three HRs in 239 innings, fewest HRs allowed in AL history for pitchers who have pitched at least 200 innings. In 1934 Lefty won 26 games, the most ever won by a Yankee southpaw. His 25 complete games of 1934 and 1937 is a Yankee record for a lefthanded pitcher, also held by Herb Pennock. Lefty allowed 22 sacrifices in 1935, a Yankee record. In his Yankee career, Lefty walked 1090 men, the most in club history. He holds the career Yankee southpaw record with 173 complete games.

FUN-LOVING, WITTY: A colorful character, Lefty loved to have a good time. When Joe DiMaggio joined the team in 1936, he became his best baseball friend. They were an unusual pair. Lefty was extroverted and happy-go-lucky; the young DiMag was introverted, reserved and even shy. But their opposite personalities seemed to strengthen their friendship. Lefty would drive Manager McCarthy to distraction when he wasn't pitching—he was a dugout fidget. But even while pitching he would get under McCarthy's skin, especially when an airplane invaded the ballpark skies. Lefty was in love with flying; so fascinated was he with passing aircraft that he would mentally abandon the game. His quotes are legendary. Once asked to explain his success as a pitcher, Lefty replied, "Clean living and a fast outfield." After a Jimmie Foxx HR off Lefty landed in Yankee Stadium's third deck, he joked, "Christ, if I was on that son of a bitch, I'd be back in California now!" Lefty may have been the wittiest Yankee.

TERRIBLE HITTER: Lefty was a terrible hitter, as his .147 lifetime batting average attests (133 for 904). He did not hit a single ML homer. His attempts at hitting were a running joke on the Yanks. Lefty, one of the best pitchers ever, was always practicing to be a slugger! Each year he bet $50 to Babe Ruth's $250 that he would get 10 hits in a season. Lefty won once. He was proud of his important World Series hits and of his pair of walks in one inning of Game 1 of the 1937 World Series (a feat not accomplished again until 1968).

LEAGUE LEADER: Lefty led the AL in strikeouts and shutouts in 3 seasons. Twice he led the AL in wins, winning percentage and ERA. In 1934 Lefty was sensational, leading the AL in wins (26), winning percentage (.839), ERA (2.33), complete games (25), innings pitched (282), strikeouts (158), and shutouts (six)!

CLUB LEADERSHIP: During his long pitching career, Lefty was the club's seasonal leader in many pitching categories; only Bob Shawkey has led the club in strikeouts as often as Lefty has—seven seasons.

ALL-TIME YANKEE LEADER: Lefty is among the top 10 in most all-time Yankee pitching categories. He is second in complete games (173); third in victories (189); fourth in games started (319), innings pitched (2498), strikeouts (1468), and in shut-outs (28); seventh in winning percentage (.652, 189-101) for those former pitchers with at least 100 Yankee decisions; and tenth in games pitched (367).

ALL-STAR GAME: Lefty was the greatest pitching performer in All-Star Game history. He was picked to the AL team in each of the first seven years of All-Star Game history (1933-39). Lefty started five All-Star Games (1933, 1934, 1935, 1937, 1938), tying a record. In three games Lefty was the winning pitcher (1933, 1935, 1937), an All-Star Game record. He pitched a total of 18 innings in All-Star Game competition, the most of any AL pitcher. He pitched six innings in the 1935 game, a Summer Classic record for a pitcher. He batted six times in All-Star Games, still another All-Star Game record for a pitcher. Lefty made only one hit himself in these affairs, but it drove in a run in the 1933 Game, the first RBI in All-Star Game history. Lefty's career mark was 3-1.

WORLD SERIES: Lefty owns a 6-0 lifetime record in World Series competition, the most wins without a loss in Series history. He won the final game of the 1936 Series with the Giants, 13-5, giving the Yanks the World Championship. Lefty in the final game of the 1937 Series pitched a complete game and won, 4-2, over the Giants to wrap up another Yankee World Championship. He knocked in the winning run with a single. Lefty won the opening game of the 1937 Series, 8-1.

LEFT YANKS: In January of 1943, the Yanks sold Lefty's contract to the Boston Braves. He never pitched for the Braves, going instead to Washington where he pitched one game for the Senators, then retired as a player.

BASEBALL AMBASSADOR: When his playing days ended, Lefty returned to the Yankee organization as a minor league manager. In 1946 and 1947, he managed the Yanks' Binghamton farm club. As his manager early in 1947, Lefty gave young Ed Ford the nickname, "Whitey" before sending him down in the farm system. He was an instructor in the Yankee farm system after leaving managing.

GOMEZ, LEFTY

Yr.	W-L	Pct.	SA	G	GS	CG	IP	H	BB	SO	SH	ERA
1930	2-5	.286	1	15	6	2	60	66	28	22	0	5.55
1931	21-9	.700	3	40	26	17	243	206	85	150	1	2.63
1932	24-7	.774	1	37	31	21	265	266	105	176	1	4.21
1933	16-10	.615	2	35	30	14	235	218	106	163	4	3.18
1934	26-5	.839	1	38	33	25	282	223	96	158	6	2.33
1935	12-15	.444	1	34	30	15	246	223	86	138	2	3.18
1936	13-7	.650	0	31	30	10	189	184	122	105	0	4.39
1937	21-11	.656	0	34	34	25	278	233	93	194	6	2.33
1938	18-12	.600	0	32	32	20	239	239	99	129	4	3.35
1939	12-8	.600	0	26	26	14	198	173	84	102	2	3.41
1940	3-3	.500	0	9	5	0	27	37	18	14	0	6.59
1941	15-5	.750	0	23	23	8	156	151	103	76	2	3.74
1942	6-4	.600	0	13	13	2	80	67	65	41	0	4.28
13 Yrs.	189-101	.652	9	367	319	173	2498	2286	1090	1468	28	3.34
Life.	189-102	.649	9	368	320	173	2503	2290	1095	1468	28	3.34

World Series

Yr.	G	IP	BB	SO	H	W-L	SA
1932	1	9	1	8	9	1-0	0
1936	2	15⅓	11	9	14	2-0	0
1937	2	18	2	8	16	2-0	0
1938	1	7	1	5	9	1-0	0
1939	1	1	0	1	3	0-0	0
5 Yrs.	7	50⅓	15	31	51	6-0	0
Life. Same.							

LEFTY'S 6-0 WORLD SERIES RECORD:
September 29, 1932 (2) Won, 5-2 vs. Cubs *
October 2, 1936 (2) Won, 18-4 vs. Giants *
October 6, 1936 (6) Won, 13-5 vs. Giants
October 6, 1937 (1) Won, 8-1 vs. Giants *
October 10, 1937 (5) Won, 4-2 vs. Giants*
October 6, 1938 (2) Won, 6-3 vs. Cubs
* = Complete Game

Lefty Gomez won 189 games as a Yankee.

GORDON, JOE

Nickname: "Flash"
Yankee: 1938-43 (military) '46
Second Baseman, 1B
Born: February 18,1915
Birthplace: Los Angeles, CA
Died: April 14, 1978
Bat: R; Throw: R
Ht: 5'10" Wt: 180

HONORS: Both the Baseball Writers and *The Sporting News* named Joe the 1942 AL MVP. In four consecutive seasons (1939-42) Joe was selected as the second baseman on *The Sporting News'* ML All-Star team.

YOUNG PROSPECT: Joe was one of the most highly touted youngsters ever to come through the Yankee farm system. Originally a shortstop, he was positioned at second base by Joe McCarthy who helped him make the transition. Thus Joe was groomed to eventually replace Tony Lazzeri. In 1937 Joe was a star on the great Newark Bear team that won the International League pennant by 25½ games. That year he hit .280 with 26 HRs. His Newark manager, Ossie Vitt, said of Joe as a second baseman: "He is better than anybody in the big leagues now, with the exception of Gehringer—and he'll catch him in a year.

ROOKIE SEASON: Joe was the regular Yankee second baseman in 1938, his rookie season. He had a fantastic year (25 HRs, 97 RBIs). Joe hit all those HRs batting mostly in the eighth spot in the Yankee order! It was important that Joe have a great rookie year, because the Yanks had traded the popular Tony Lazzeri to make room for him.

POWER HITTER: Joe was one of the few power-hitting second basemen the game has ever seen. The 253 HRs he hit during his ML career (153 of which were hit in pinstripes, places him 20th on the All-Time Yankee list) is the AL record for second basemen. The 30 HRs Joe hit in 1940 are the most ever hit by a Yankee second sacker. In his seven Yankee seasons, Joe hit more than 20 HRs four times and produced more than 100 RBIs three times. On September 8, 1940, Joe hit for the cycle. In 1942 he hit safely in 29 consecutive games.

SECOND BASEMAN: From 1938-43, Joe was the Yanks' regular second baseman. In 1941 Joe began the season at first base but the experiment was soon abandoned, and he returned to his second-base job. He missed the 1944-45 seasons while serving in the military. In 1946, Joe returned to the Yanks and resumed his duties at second base.

DEFENSIVE ABILITIES: Three times Joe led AL second basemen in assists (1939, '40, '43) and double plays (1939, '41, '42). In 1939 he led AL second basemen in putouts (370). Joe had good range and he could turn the double play perfectly. He was stylish and acrobatic. Joe is 14th on baseball's all-time double play list for second basemen (1160).

CLUB LEADERSHIP: In 1940, Joe led the Yanks in runs scored (112), doubles (32), stolen bases (18) and at-bats (616). In 1941 he led the Yanks in at-bats (588). In 1942 he led the Yanks

in batting (.322). He was the only Yankee player to participate in every Yankee game during the 1940-41 seasons.

ALL-STAR GAME: On six occasions as a Yankee player, Joe was picked to the AL team for the All-Star Game (1939-43, '46).

WORLD SERIES: In Game 3 of the 1938 Series Joe hit a HR and knocked in three runs to lead the Yanks to a 5-2 victory over the Cubs. Joe hit a HR to help the Yanks win Game 1 of the 1941 Series, 3-2, then he drove home the deciding run in the final game to wrap up the Series for the Yanks over the Dodgers. He was spectacular in that 1941 Series, leading both teams in batting (.500), slugging (.929) and walks (seven)—all five-game Series records. Joe holds a host of Series fielding records.

TRADED: In October of 1946, the Yanks traded Joe and infielder Eddie Bockman to the Indians for pitcher Allie Reynolds. Joe had some great years at Cleveland. He ended his Yankee career with exactly 1,000 hits in 1,000 games.

BASEBALL MAN: Joe spent his whole life in baseball. In later years he managed the Indians (1958-60), Tigers (1960), A's (1961) and Royals (1969). Joe also spent time in his career as a minor league manager, a batting instructor and a scout.

GORDON, JOE

Yr.	G	AB	R	H	2B	3B	HR	RBI	BB	SB	BA	SA
1938	127	458	83	117	24	7	25	97	56	11	.255	.502
1939	151	567	92	161	32	5	28	111	75	11	.284	.506
1940	155	616	112	173	32	10	30	103	52	18	.281	.511
1941	156	588	104	162	26	7	24	87	72	10	.276	.466
1942	147	538	88	173	29	4	18	103	79	12	.322	.491
1943	152	543	82	135	28	5	17	69	98	4	.249	.413
1946	112	376	35	79	15	0	11	47	49	2	.210	.338
7 Yrs.	1000	3686	596	1000	186	38	153	617	481	68	.271	.467
Life.	1566	5707	914	1530	264	52	253	975	759	89	.268	.466

World Series

Yr.	G	AB	R	H	2B	3B	HR	RBI	BA
1938	4	15	3	6	2	0	1	6	.400
1939	4	14	1	2	0	0	0	1	.143
1941	5	14	2	7	1	1	1	5	.500
1942	5	21	1	2	1	0	0	0	.095
1943	5	17	2	4	1	0	1	2	.235
7 Yrs.	23	81	9	21	5	1	3	14	.259
Life.	29	103	12	25	5	1	4	16	.243

GOSSAGE, GOOSE
(BORN RICHARD MICHAEL GOSSAGE)

Yankee: 1978-83, 1989
Pitcher
Born: July 5, 1951
Birthplace: Colorado Springs, CO
Bat: R; Throw: R
Ht: 6'3"; Wt: 180

HONORS: As a Yankee, Goose was named to represent the AL in the All-Star Game in 1978, 1980, 1981 (injured) and 1982. Goose was *The Sporting News* AL Fireman of the Year and Rolaids Relief Man of the Year in 1978. AL Pitcher of the Month, September 1979. In 1980, Goose was named to the UPI All-Star team.

SIGNING WITH YANKEES: Goose, who had broken into the ML's in 1972, was a rising star when he signed as a free agent with the Yankees in November 1977; the contract was worth a reported $2.75 million over six years. Gabe Paul, in one of his last moves with the Yanks, advised George Steinbrenner to sign Goose. The idea was for the right-handed Gossage to team with the lefthanded Sparky Lyle, but Lyle, who had won the Cy Young Award in 1977, was never receptive to the plan.

INTIMIDATION: Goose was the most awesome overpowering pitcher in baseball. He was a large, forbidding mound figure, with a whiskered face and a menacing scowl, and he got angry, and not many hitters were willing to dig in against him. In his delivery he was a bundle of flapping arms and legs, and then came his explosive fastball, moving at speeds of 90 to 100 m.p.h.—and darting and riding and rising. Hitters were especially terrified when Goose snapped a hard breaking pitch.

1978 SEASON: Goose emerged as the relief ace over Lyle and led the AL in saves (27). Goose led the Yanks in games pitched (63). His 134 innings pitched was fourth highest on the club—very high for a relief closer. In the playoff game in Boston, with the tying and winning runs on base, Goose induced Jim Rice to fly out and Yaz to pop up, ending the game. Goose also finished the clinching games in the ALCS and World Series.

1979 DISAPPOINTMENT: On April 19, Goose and teammate Cliff Johnson engaged in locker-room needling about who was the better man when they faced each other in the NL. The kidding escalated into a brief fight, and Goose suffered a torn ligament in his right thumb. Goose was on the Disabled List, April 21 through July 9, a time when the Yanks' bullpen was terrible, and the Yanks fell out of the pennant race.

1980 DOMINATION: Goose tied for the AL lead in saves (33), his career high for saves. He led the Yanks in games pitched (64). He was the difference in the division race between the Yankees and second-place Baltimore and finished third in *both* the MVP and Cy Young voting. In seven games between August 26 and September 10, he retired 28 consecutive batters, and in 18 consecutive appearances in August and September, he did not allow an earned run. After pitching six times in eight games, Goose awoke unable to raise his right arm. He may have been suffering from a tired arm when he gave up the game-winning HR to George Brett in the finale of the ALCS.

1981 SEASON: In the first half of this strike season, Goose recorded 17 saves in 18 save situations, with a 0.56 ERA. He nursed a stiff shoulder in the second half and finished with a club-leading 20 saves. Goose saved all three Yankee wins in the Division Series and Game 1 in the ALCS. Goose saved both Yankee wins in the World Series. In the combined post season, Goose pitched 14⅓ innings without allowing an earned run.

LATE YANKEE CAREER: In 1982, Goose was injured but led the Yanks in saves (30). Batters hit only .196 vs. Goose in 1982. He led the Yanks in saves (22) in 1983. Most memorable 1983 moment was giving up the HR to George Brett in the Pine Tar Game, July 24.

ALL-TIME LEADER: On the Yankee All-Time Top 20 leader lists, Goose ranks third in saves (151) and 14th in games pitched (319). On the All-Time baseball list, Goose ranks third in ML history with 115 relief wins, seventh in games pitched (1002), and 13th in saves (310).

GOING AND COMING: In January of 1984, Goose as a free agent signed with San Diego, and he helped the Padres earn their first World Series appearance that season. Goose returned to the Yankees in August 1989, as the Yanks paid the waiver price to the Giants. Goose pitched in 11 games for the Yankees before moving on. Goose retired, after 22 years in baseball, in April 1995.

GOSSAGE, GOOSE

Yr.	W-L	Pct.	SA	G	GS	CG	IP	H	BB	SO	SH	ERA
1978	10-11	.476	27	63	0	0	134	87	59	122	0	2.01
1979	5-3	.625	18	36	0	0	58	48	19	41	0	2.62
1980	6-2	.750	33	64	0	0	99	74	37	103	0	2.27
1981	3-2	.600	20	32	0	0	47	22	14	48	0	0.77
1982	4-5	.444	30	56	0	0	93	63	28	102	0	2.23
1983	13-5	.722	22	57	0	0	87	82	25	90	0	2.27
1989	1-0	1.000	1	11	0	0	14	14	3	6	0	3.77
7 Yrs.	42-28	.600	151	319	0	0	533	390	185	512	0	2.14
Life.	124-107	.537	310	1002	37	16	1809	1497	732	1502	0	3.01

Divisional Playoff

Yr.	G	IP	BB	SO	H	W-L	SA
1981	3	6.2	2	8	0	0-0	3
1 Yr.	3	6.2	2	8	0	0-0	3
Life. Same.							

Championship Series

Yr.	G	IP	BB	SO	H	W-L	SA
1978	2	4	0	3	3	1-0	1
1980	1	0.1	0	0	3	0-1	0
1981	2	2.2	0	2	1	0-0	1
3 Yrs.	5	7	0	5	7	1-1	2
Life	8	11	1	10	12	1-1	3

World Series

Yr.	G	IP	BB	SO	H	W-L	SA
1978	3	6	1	4	1	1-0	0
1981	3	5	2	5	2	0-0	2
2 Yrs.	6	11	3	9	3	1-0	2
Life	8	13.2	4	11	6	1-0	2

GRIFFEY, KEN, SR.

Yankee: 1982-86
Outfielder, 1B, DH
Born: April 10, 1950
Birthplace: Donora, PA
Bat: L; Throw: L
Ht: 5'11"; Wt: 190

TRADED TO YANKS: In November of 1981, Cincinnati traded Ken to the Yankees for Freddie Toliver (P) and Bryan Ryder (P). Ken had been the unsung star of the Big Red Machine and owned a sparkling .307 lifetime batting average. Ken had played out his option with the Reds and in a few days would be eligible for free agency; hence, the Reds getting what they could for him. Ken signed a six-year contract with the Yankees, which was Reggie Jackson's exit signal; Reggie had no desire to be a full-time DH and went into the November free-agent draft.

EXPECTATIONS: Getting Ken was part of the Yanks' plan for a more-balanced attack—more speed, and with the loss of Jackson, less power. Griffey, along with another newcomer from the Reds, Dave Collins, were supposed to ignite the running game, and Ken was still expected to provide some power.

NEGATIVES: Ken's speed wasn't the sort a team could build a running game around; so he wasn't fast enough or powerful enough to be a primary offensive player. Moreover, Yankee fans mourned the Jackson departure. Ken had difficulty changing leagues in 1982, and his timing was thrown off by all the off-speed AL pitching. Ken also had difficulty with the glare of New York, as opposed to the general calm of Cincinnati. Ken was hampered by injuries in 1982, 1983 and 1985. The Yankees never gave him his own position; Ken played left field, center field, right field, first base and designated hitter, and he was suited only for left field, so he was naturally found lacking at the other four positions.

POSITIVES: Over the last 38 games of 1982, Ken hit .341 to pull his BA from .251 on August 17 to his final mark of .277. His 13-game hitting streak, started August 18, was the club's longest in 1982. Ken kept his BA above .300 all season in 1983, finishing at .306. Ken hit all seven HRs in the second half of 1984 and .290 in the second half of 1985 to finish at a respectable .274. Hit a pair of three-run HRs vs. Minnesota in a game on July 7, 1985. In 1985, he made several great catches, going high over the left-field wall to take away HRs. Ken made the catch of the year at Yankee Stadium on August 19, 1985, when he leaped high above the left-field wall, landing in a somersault, to rob Boston's Marty Barrett of a game-tying HR in the ninth inning.

LEFT YANKS: In June of 1986, the Yankees traded Ken and Andre Robertson to Atlanta for Claudell Washington and Paul Zuvella. Ken Sr. wrapped up his 19-year ML career in 1991 as a Mariner teammate of his son, Ken Griffey, Jr., one of the best players in the game. Through 2002, Junior has a total of 468 homers in 14 seasons. The Griffeys now have a combined 620 long balls, the highest father-son total in ML history.

GRIFFITH, CLARK

Nickname: "The Old Fox"
Yankee: 1903-07
Pitcher
Born: November 20, 1869
Birthplace: Stringtown, MO
Died: October 27, 1955
Bat: R; Throw: R
Ht: 5'6"; Wt: 156

HONORS: In 1946 Clark received baseball's ultimate honor when he was inducted into the Baseball Hall of Fame.

CAME TO YANKS: In 1901 Clark jumped teams in Chicago from the NL to AL, and managed and pitched for the White Sox in 1901-02. As a reward for establishing the AL in Chicago, AL President Ban Johnson saw to it that Clark would become the first manager in Yankee-Highlander history. Clark joined the Yanks (Highlanders) as player-manager in 1903.

PITCHING GREAT: Clark's prime pitching years were behind him when he joined the Yanks. He had been a great pitcher, winning 20 or more games in eight ML seasons. He finished in ML baseball's top 50 for lifetime wins and in career winning percentage (.619, 237-146).

YANKEE HURLER: Clark was a Yankee starter in his first two seasons with the club (1903-04). He was a relief pitcher for the Yanks in 1905-07. On June 16, 1903, Clark pitched the first shutout in Yankee history, beating the White Sox, 1-0. Twice Clark led Yankee pitchers in ERA. In 1905 he led AL pitchers in games won in relief (four).

PLAYER-MANAGER: "The Old Fox" was the first Yankee manager ever hired and the first to be fired. He was released on June 24, 1908, as manager (he did not pitch in 1908).

LATER YEARS: After Clark left the Yanks, he managed the Cincinnati Reds (1909-11) and Washington Senators (1912-20). As a ML manager between 1901-20, Clark had a 1491-1367 record for 16th place in wins on the all-time managers' list. Clark later owned and operated the Senators until he died in 1955. The Griffith family, namely Clark's son Calvin, moved the Senators to Minnesota in 1961 and sold the club in 1984.

GRIFFEY, KEN, SR.

Yr.	G	AB	R	H	2B	3B	HR	RBI	BB	SB	BA	SA
1982	127	484	70	134	23	2	12	54	39	10	.277	.407
1983	118	458	60	140	21	3	11	46	34	6	.306	.437
1984	120	399	44	109	20	1	7	56	29	2	.273	.381
1985	127	438	68	120	28	4	10	69	41	7	.274	.425
1986	59	198	33	60	7	0	9	26	15	2	.303	.475
5 Yrs.	551	1977	275	563	99	10	49	251	158	27	.285	.419
Life.	2097	7229	1129	2143	364	77	152	859	719	200	.296	.431

GRIFFITH, CLARK

Yr.	W-L	Pct.	SA	G	GS	CG	IP	H	BB	SO	SH	ERA
1903	14-11	.560	0	25	24	22	213	201	33	69	2	2.70
1904	7-5	.583	1	16	11	8	100	91	16	36	1	2.87
1905	9-6	.600	3	25	7	4	103	82	15	46	2	1.67
1906	2-2	.500	2	17	2	1	60	58	15	16	0	3.02
1907	0-0	.000	0	4	0	0	8	15	6	5	0	8.64
5 Yrs.	32-24	.571	6	87	44	35	484	447	85	172	5	2.66
Life.	237-146	.619	9	452	372	337	3386	3670	774	955	22	3.31

GRIM, BOB

Yankee: 1954-58
Pitcher
Born: March 8, 1930
Birthplace: New York, NY
Died: October 23, 1995
Bat: R; Throw: R
Ht: 6'1"; Wt: 175

HONORS: Bob was named Rookie of the Year by the Baseball Writers in 1954, besides winning the AL Rookie Award given by *The Sporting News*.

YOUNG PROSPECT: Bob's minor-league statistics impressed the Yanks in the early 1950s. In 1952 he was 16-5 at the Yanks' Binghamton farm club. He missed the entire 1953 baseball season because of military service.

ROOKIE SEASON: Bob impressed Casey Stengel so much at the Yanks' 1954 instructional camp and spring training that he was kept for the regular season. He was the Yanks' fourth starter and pitched 17 games in relief. Bob had a perfect winning percentage (1.000) as a relief pitcher, a rarity, and led the AL in relief wins (8). He also led Yankee pitchers in wins and win percentage (.769, 20-6). In winning 20 games Bob became the first Yankee rookie to win 20 since Russ Ford did it in 1910. He is the only 20-game winner EVER to pitch less than 200 innings.

UNCOMPLICATED: An uncomplicated pitcher, Bob came right at the hitters with a good fastball and slider, and when he was right, both pitches worked beautifully. Bob was an uncomplicated guy, too, and although he was from Brooklyn, he preferred life away from the hustle and bustle of the city. Fishing was his favorite hobby.

ARM INJURY: If not for arm miseries, Bob might have been one of the greats. He first had arm trouble in 1955, experiencing a loss in velocity while he was pitching a game. Arm injuries continued to bother Bob, and he was unable to go longer than three or four innings at a time. Some time later, Bob lost his slider. Tendons had pulled away from the bone of his pitching arm.

RELIEF ACE: In his last three seasons with the Yanks (1956-58), Bob was used mostly out of the bullpen and was an excellent relief pitcher. In 1957 he led AL pitchers in saves (19) AND games won in relief (12), a remarkable feat. His great season was a primary reason why the Yanks of 1957 won the AL pennant. Bob was one of the few ML pitchers who was successful as a reliever and starter. Through 1999, Bob is tied for 18th place in Yankee history in saves (28).

1957 ALL-STAR GAME: Bob was a member of the 1957 AL team for the All-Star Game. He got the final NL batter out to preserve a 6-5 victory for the AL.

1955 WORLD SERIES: In Game 1 Bob pitched the ninth inning to save a 6-5 Yankee win against the Dodgers. He started Game 5 but was defeated.

TRADED: The Yanks traded Bob and Harry "Suitcase" Simpson to the Kansas City A's for Duke Maas and Virgil Trucks in June of 1958.

GRIM, BOB

Yr.	W-L	Pct.	SA	G	GS	CG	IP	H	BB	SO	SH	ERA
1954	20-6	.769	0	37	20	8	199	175	85	108	1	3.26
1955	7-5	.583	4	26	11	1	92	81	42	63	1	4.19
1956	6-1	.857	5	26	6	1	75	64	31	48	0	2.77
1957	12-8	.600	19	46	0	0	72	60	36	52	0	2.63
1958	0-1	.000	0	11	0	0	16	12	10	11	0	5.51
5 Yrs.	45-21	.682	28	146	37	10	454	392	204	282	2	3.35
Life.	61-41	.598	37	268	60	18	760	708	330	443	4	3.61

World Series

Yr.	G	IP	BB	SO	H	W-L	SA
1955	3	8⅔	5	8	8	0-1	1
1957	2	2⅓	0	2	3	0-1	0
2 Yrs.	5	11	5	10	11	0-2	1
Life. Same.							

GUETTERMAN, LEE

Yankee: 1988-92
Pitcher
Born: November 22, 1958
Birthplace: Chattanooga, TN
Bat: L; Throw: L
Ht: 6'8"; Wt: 225

TRADED TO YANKS: In December of 1987, Seattle traded Lee, Clay Parker (P) and Wade Taylor (P) to the Yankees for Steve Trout (P) and Henry Cotto (OF). The Yanks had two needs: 1) a lefthanded reliever, and 2) a middle-to-long relief man. Lee was the 3rd tallest player in ML history. He had broken into the ML's with the Mariners in 1984, and so far had pitched without any particular distinction.

1988 COLUMBUS SHUTTLE: Lee was not overly impressive early in 1988 and quickly became a regular on the New York-to-Columbus shuttle. Optioned to Columbus on May 13. Lee was the Yanks' Minor League Pitcher of the Month in July, going 5-1 with a 1.52 ERA. Recalled to the Yankees on August 5, started a game and lost badly. Made five more relief appearances, owned an ERA of 7.36 and was optioned back to Columbus on August 21. Recalled to the Yankees on September 5. Lee was a starter at Columbus (9-6, 2.76 ERA), but, curiously, he made only two starts for the Yankees in 1988, and no more thereafter.

GLIMPSES OF STARDOM: Prior to the 1989 season, Lee had little chance of making the Yankees, but he had an impressive spring training and emerged with a major bullpen role. Lee started the 1989 season by pitching 30⅔ scoreless innings. He led the AL in 1990 in relief wins (11), and he also led the Yankee pitching staff with 11 wins—without starting a single game.

TRADED AWAY: In June of 1992, the Yankees traded Lee to the Mets for Tim Burke (P), a rare Yanks-Mets swap. He pitched for the Cardinals in 1993 and the Mariners in 1995 and 1996.

GUETTERMAN, LEE

Yr.	W-L	Pct.	SA	G	GS	CG	IP	H	BB	SO	SH	ERA
1988	1-2	.333	0	20	2	0	41	49	14	15	0	4.65
1989	5-5	.500	13	70	0	0	103	98	26	51	0	2.45
1990	11-7	.611	2	64	0	0	93	80	26	48	0	3.39
1991	3-4	.429	6	64	0	0	88	91	25	35	0	3.68
1992	1-1	.500	0	15	0	0	23	35	13	5	0	9.53
5 Yrs.	21-19	.525	21	233	2	0	347	353	104	154	0	3.73
Life.	38-36	.514	25	425	23	3	658	717	222	287	1	4.33

GUIDRY, RON

Nicknames: "Gator" "Louisiana Lightning"
Yankee: 1975-88
Pitcher
Born: August 28, 1950
Birthplace: Lafayette, LA
Bat: L; Throw: L
Ht: 5'11"; Wt: 160

HONORS: Ron was the unanimous winner of the Cy Young Award in 1978. Also in 1978, he was *The Sporting News* ML Player of the Year and Man of the Year; the AP Male Athlete of the Year; *Sport* magazine's Performer of the Year; and *Baseball Digest's* ML Player of the Year. Selected as lefthanded pitcher on *The Sporting News* AL All-Star teams in 1978, 1981, 1983 and 1985. Selected to AL team for All-Star Games in 1978, 1979, 1982 and 1983. Named AL Gold Glove winner among pitchers in five consecutive seasons, 1982 through 1986. In 1984, Ron won the Roberto Clemente Award, which recognized Ron's involvement with Special Olympics. Ron and Willie Randolph were named co-captains of the Yankees on March 4, 1986.

ARRIVING IN YANKEE ORGANIZATION: Ron was the Outstanding Track Man for two years at Northside High School; his school didn't have a baseball team. At the University of Southwestern Louisiana (The Ragin' Cajuns), Ron pitched a no-hitter. Yankee Scout Atley Donald signed Ron after the Yankees made him their third-round selection in the June 1971 amateur free-agent draft, and Ron began his career at Johnson City. Ron worked his way through the farm system cast in relief because there was the feeling his size would prevent him from being durable enough to be a starter.

LACKING A PLAN: In 1975, Ron had a 2.90 ERA as a reliever at Syracuse, and he made his Yankee debut in relief against Boston July 27 at Shea Stadium. On September 22, 1975 Ron made his first ML start and was beaten by Boston. In 1976, Ron was shuttled between Syracuse and New York and became so discouraged he would have quit if his wife hadn't talked him out of it; he had a 0.68 ERA in 22 games at Syracuse and a 5.63 ERA with the Yanks. The Yankees still envisioned Ron as a reliever, and it wasn't working. The White Sox and A's tried to pry Ron away from the Yanks, but GM Gabe Paul refused to give up on Ron.

BIG BREAK IN 1977: In the spring camp of 1977, Ron was just a promising reliever; he made the team but wasn't an important factor. On April 29, when newly acquired Mike Torrez was late reporting, Manager Billy Martin gave Ron a start, asking for five good innings against Seattle; Ron turned a shutout over to Sparky Lyle in the ninth inning. With injuries to other pitchers,

Ron joined the rotation permanently in June. Ron made the leap to stardom on August 28, when he pitched a two-hitter, facing only 28 batters, and beating Texas, 1-0. Starting on August 10, 1977, through the end of the 1978 season, and including post season, Ron's record was a combined 37-4; he was most responsible for the two consecutive World Championships.

GREATNESS: Ron utilized two exceptional pitches: 1) a fastball that on good days reached 95 m.p.h., and 2) a wicked slider that became his most important pitch. He was unhittable when both pitches were clicking. The Yankee Stadium crowds began a ritual of clapping whenever Ron got two strikes on a batter. He was also a great athlete—lithe and quick—and a tremendous fielder. In 1982, Ron began altering his style a little, adding finesse, and began throwing his fastball at different speeds.

THE SEASON OF A LIFETIME: In 1978, Ron enjoyed one of baseball's greatest seasons. He began the year with 13 consecutive wins, breaking the club record set in 1939 by Atley Donald, the scout who signed Ron. At Yankee Stadium on June 17, he struck out 18 Angels, breaking the club record of 15 set by Bob Shawkey in a 1919 game. Ron set a new club record with 248 strikeouts for the year, breaking Jack Chesbro's 1904 record of 239. Ron led the AL in wins, winning percentage (25-3, .893), ERA (1.74) and shutouts (nine). Ron established a ML record for the highest winning percentage for 20 or more wins. His ERA was the lowest in the ML's since Sandy Koufax's 1.73 in 1966. Ron's nine shutouts tied the AL southpaw record set by Babe Ruth in 1916. Batters hit .191 vs. Ron. New York was 30-5 in Guidry starts, and he won 15 times following a Yankee loss. In September, he won a trio of two-hitters, including two against Boston. Ron won the division playoff at Boston, then added single wins in the ALCS and World Series.

COMING BACK TO EARTH: Ron in 1979 won his second consecutive ERA title (2.78) and may have deprived himself of another 20-win season when he volunteered to help the beleaguered bullpen after Rich Gossage was hurt; he spent a few weeks relieving before returning to the rotation. In 1979, Ron had an 11-game winning streak, and he finished third in the Cy Young voting. Ron started the 1980 season 6-0, but then he had his first ML slump as he had trouble with his slider over the summer. When Ron reached his 100th career decision, he was 72-28, trailing Whitey Ford (74-26) for the best record for the first 100 decisions. Ron's slider was awesome in August 1981 when he was AL pitcher of the Month (4-0, 0.37 ERA). In 1982, Ron was 8-1 on June 14 but didn't win again until July 18.

EXCELLENCE: Ron returned to the pinnacle in 1983, winning 21 games, leading the AL in complete games (21) and fielding a perfect 1.000. On August 7, 1984, against Chicago, Ron pitched a shutout and fanned 13; he struck out the side in the ninth on nine pitches. On August 16, 1984, suffering from inflamed rib cartilage, for the first time in his career, Ron went on the Disabled List; he didn't pitch again until September 17. In 1985, Ron led the AL in wins and winning percentage (22-6, .786) and had a 12-game winning streak from May 4 until July 31. He became only the seventh pitcher to win 20 games for the Yankees in three seasons. Ron was runner-up in the 1985 Cy Young voting.

STAYING OUT OF CONTROVERSY: Perhaps Ron's most remarkable achievement was that rarely did he get drawn into the various controversies on the Yankees. He was a total professional and kept his dignity intact, remaining a down-to-earth guy. He wasn't a whiner either, and though he stayed quiet he could easily have made an issue of his 1978 salary—$38,500. Except for Thurman Munson, who died, and Don Mattingly, who is still playing, Ron is the only star of the Steinbrenner era to play his entire career with the Yankees. When his career was over, just as he said he would, Ron simply went home to Louisiana.

WINDING DOWN: On July 2, 1986, Ron lost his seventh straight decision—the longest losing streak of his career—and was cut on his left hand by a line drive; he was out 3½ weeks. In 1987, Ron didn't sign with the Yankees by the January 8 free-agent deadline, so he couldn't re-sign until May 1, and he didn't make his first start until June 9. He displayed his old brilliance at Chicago on July 11, 1987, recording 14 strikeouts in only 6⅔ innings. In 1987, Ron's first-inning ERA was 11.12; his ERA for all other innings was 2.41. On December 8, 1987, Ron had surgery to repair a tear in a muscle that overlays the rotator cuff in the left shoulder, and he was unable to pitch for the Yankees until July 1, 1988; he later missed three weeks with a pulled hamstring. He began 1989 on the DL, and after unimpressive minor-league pitching, on July 12, 1989, Ron retired.

STAFF ACE: Ron led the Yankees in wins and strikeouts in six seasons; ERA in five seasons; and innings pitched in four seasons. He retired with a career winning record against every team in the AL. Pitched six career two-hitters.

ALL-TIME YANKEE LEADER: On the Yankees' all-time lists, Ron ranks second in strikeouts (1778); fourth in wins (170), sixth in innings pitched (2392); tied for sixth in shutouts (26); ninth in games pitched (368); and tied for eighth in winning percentage (.651). Ron also places 16th in complete games (95), and 19th overall in ERA (3.29).

POST-SEASON PLAY: Ron pitched a three-hitter to beat Kansas City in Game 2 of the 1977 ALCS, and he tried to pitch Game 5 with two days rest but left in the third inning. Ron pitched a four-hitter to beat the Dodgers in Game 4 of the 1977 World Series. He pitched eight strong innings to beat the Royals in the finale of the 1978 ALCS. Ron pitched a complete game to beat the Dodgers in Game 3 of the 1978 World Series; he was aided by the defensive heroics of Graig Nettles. Ron lost Game 1 of the 1980 ALCS to Kansas City. Ron won the opener of the 1981 World Series, with relief help from Gossage. Ron lost a 2-1 heartbreaker in Game 5 of the 1981 World Series. Recorded 15 strikeouts in 14 innings in the 1981 World Series.

GUIDRY, RON

Yr.	W-L	Pct.	SA	G	GS	CG	IP	H	BB	SO	SH	ERA
1975	0-1	.000	0	10	1	0	16	15	9	15	0	3.45
1976	0-0	.000	0	7	0	0	16	20	4	12	0	5.63
1977	16-7	.696	1	31	25	9	211	174	65	176	5	2.82
1978	25-3	.893	0	35	35	16	274	187	72	248	9	1.74
1979	18-8	.692	2	33	30	15	236	203	71	201	2	2.78
1980	17-10	.630	1	37	29	5	220	215	80	166	3	3.56
1981	11-5	.688	0	23	21	0	127	100	26	104	0	2.76
1982	14-8	.636	0	34	33	6	222	216	69	162	1	3.81
1983	21-9	.700	0	31	31	21	250	232	60	156	3	3.42
1984	10-11	.476	0	29	28	5	196	223	44	127	1	4.51
1985	22-6	.786	0	34	33	11	259	243	42	143	2	3.27
1986	9-12	.429	0	30	30	5	192	202	38	140	0	3.98
1987	5-8	.385	0	22	17	2	118	111	38	96	0	3.67
1988	2-3	.400	0	12	10	0	56	57	15	32	0	4.18
14 Yrs.	170-91	.651	4	368	323	95	2392	2198	633	1778	26	3.29

Life. Same.

Divisional Playoff

Yr.	G	IP	BB	SO	H	W-L	SA
1981	2	8.1	3	8	11	0-0	0
1981	2	8.1	3	8	11	0-0	0

Life. Same.

Championship Series

Yr.	G	IP	BB	SO	H	W-L	SA
1977	2	11.1	3	8	9	1-0	0
1978	1	8	1	7	7	1-0	0
1980	1	3	4	2	5	0-1	0
3 Yrs.	4	22.1	8	17	21	2-1	0

Life. Same.

World Series

Yr.	G	IP	BB	SO	H	W-L	SA
1977	1	9	3	7	4	1-0	0
1978	1	9	7	4	8	1-0	0
1981	2	14	4	15	8	1-1	0
3 Yrs.	4	32	14	26	20	3-1	0

Life. Same.

HADLEY, BUMP
(BORN IRVING DARIUS HADLEY)

Yankee: 1936-40
Pitcher
Born: July 5, 1904
Birthplace: Lynn, MA
Died: February 15, 1963
Bat: R; Throw: R
Ht: 5'11"; Wt: 190

CAME TO YANKS: In January of 1936, the Yanks obtained Bump and outfielder Roy Johnson from the Washington Senators in a deal that sent outfielder Jesse Hill and pitcher Jimmie DeShong to Washington.

VALUABLE PITCHER: In 1936 Bump was a valuable addition to the Yanks, a team that won the World Championship. The Yanks won the World Series in each of Bump's first four seasons with the club (1936-39). Bump was the Yanks' fifth starter in 1936, 1938 and 1939. He was the team's third starter in 1937. In 1940 Bump was a relief pitcher. He led the Yanks in 1936 in winning percentage (14-4, .778). Bump was a hard thrower.

AWFUL ACCIDENT: At Yankee Stadium on May 25, 1937, Bump beaned the Tigers' great Mickey Cochrane, fracturing his skull and nearly killing him. The ball bounced right back to Bump after hitting Cochrane's head. Yankee Stadium was known for its poor hitting background and Mickey lost the ball from the moment it was pitched. Cochrane was lucky to live, but the accident brought a premature end to his splendid playing career.

WORLD SERIES: Bump pitched a beautiful game to gain the victory in Game 3 of the 1936 Series against the New York Giants. He went eight innings, allowing ten hits but only one run. With the score tied, 1-1, in the bottom of the eighth, Red Ruffing pinch-hit for Bump during the Yanks' winning rally in the 2-1 win. Bump led all pitchers with a 1.12 ERA in the 1936 Series. In Game 3 of the 1939 Series against the Reds, Bump entered in the second inning replacing Lefty Gomez and immediately allowed two runs. But Bump shut the door the rest of the way in the 7-3 Yankee win and got the victory after turning in eight innings of great relief pitching.

LEFT YANKS: The Yanks dealt Bump to the Giants following the 1940 season. The 1941 season was Bump's last in the ML's. He was 1-0 for the Giants and 4-6 for the Philadelphia A's.

HADLEY, BUMP

Yr.	W-L	Pct.	SA	G	GS	CG	IP	H	BB	SO	SH	ERA
1936	14-4	.778	1	31	17	8	174	194	89	74	1	4.35
1937	11-8	.579	0	29	25	6	178	199	83	70	0	5.30
1938	9-8	.529	1	29	17	8	167	165	66	61	1	3.60
1939	12-6	.667	2	26	18	7	154	132	85	65	1	2.98
1940	3-5	.375	2	25	2	0	80	88	52	39	0	5.74
5 Yrs.	49-31	.613	6	140	79	29	753	778	375	309	3	4.28
Life.	161-165	.494	25	528	355	135	2946	2980	1442	1318	14	4.24

World Series

Yr.	G	IP	BB	SO	H	W-L	SA
1936	1	8	1	2	10	1-0	0
1937	1	1⅓	0	0	6	0-1	0
1939	1	8	3	2	7	1-0	0
3 Yrs	3	17⅓	4	4	23	2-1	0
Life. Same.							

HALL, MEL

Yankee: 1989-92
Outfielder, DH
Born: September 16, 1960
Birthplace: Lyons, NY
Bat: L; Throw: L
Ht: 6'; Wt: 205

TRADED TO YANKEES: In March of 1989, the Indians traded Hall to the Yankees for Joel Skinner and Turner Ward. This deal was made shortly after Dave Winfield's back problems developed in spring training. At one time, Mel had been the outstanding prospect in the Cubs' organization.

YANKEE REGULAR: Mel had been obtained for insurance, but in 1989 he became an important outfielder with Winfield sidelined all year, and Rickey Henderson unhappy and traded in mid-season. In 1989, Mel slumped and was injured, and while he was injured, Jesse Barfield was obtained to play right field.

Mel in 1989 still tied for third on the club in HRs (17); the Yankees were 15-1 in games in which Mel homered. Always known more for his bat, Mel made progress defensively in 1989 and made several great catches in left field. In 1990, Mel was a DH in 54 games; an outfielder in 50. In 1991 and 1992, he was the regular leftfielder, and in 1991 he led the club in RBIs (80).

PLAYING IN JAPAN: Mel, in 1993, took his baseball talents to Japan. Mel returned to play one more season (for the Giants) before retiring after 1996.

HALL, MEL

Yr.	G	AB	R	H	2B	3B	HR	RBI	BB	SB	BA	SA
1989	113	361	54	94	9	0	17	58	21	0	.260	.427
1990	113	360	41	93	23	2	12	46	6	0	.258	.433
1991	141	492	67	140	23	2	19	80	26	0	.285	.455
1992	152	583	67	163	36	3	15	81	29	4	.280	.429
4 Yrs.	519	1796	229	490	91	7	63	265	82	4	.273	.437
Life.	1276	4237	568	1171	229	25	134	620	267	31	.276	.437

HAMILTON, STEVE

Yankee: 1963-70
Pitcher
Born: November 30, 1933
Birthplace: Columbia, KY
Died: December 2, 1997
Bat: L; Throw: L
Ht: 6'7"; Wt: 200

CAME TO YANKS: In April of 1963, the Yanks obtained Steve from the Washington Senators in a deal that sent pitcher Jim Coates to the Senators.

RELIEF SPECIALIST: In his eight Yankee seasons, Steve made anywhere from 27-44 appearances a season as a relief pitcher, but started a combined total of only seven games. With the Yanks in 1963, Steve averaged better than a strikeout an inning in 62 innings pitched. In 1965 he had the lowest ERA in the AL (1.40), but did not record enough innings pitched to qualify for the ERA title. In 1966 Steve led the Yankee pitching staff in winning percentage (.727, 8-3). In 1968 he led the Yanks in saves (11). Steve was 31-19 as a reliever and 3-1 as a starter in his Yankee career.

CRAFTY PITCHER: Steve during his Yankee tenure acquired a distinguished appearance because of his premature grayness. His 6'7" height, coupled with his being a side-arming lefty, made Steve murder on lefthanded batters, and he was used accordingly. He threw a good curveball, had excellent control (a must for a reliever) and was a particularly intelligent pitcher. Steve was one of the best southpaw relievers in the AL during the 1960s.

BLOOPER PITCH: Late in his career, Steve on occasion served a "Folly Floater," a hesitation blooper-pitch lobbed high into the air. Steve delighted the Yankee Stadium crowd with the amusing "Folly Floater" and most batters awaited it with bemused anticipation. Tony Horton of the Indians once popped out to the catcher on a blooper and was so embarrassed that he crawled all the way back to his dugout, as the crowd, and even Tony, roared with laughter.

ATHLETIC AND SMART: From 1958-60 Steve pitched in the minors, but also played basketball in the NBA. He served as assistant basketball coach, physical education instructor, and athletic director at his alma mater, Morehead State College in Kentucky. Steve holds a Master's Degree.

ALL-TIME YANKEE LEADER: Steve ranks 15th on the all-time Yankee games pitched list (311). He also ranks 15th on the Yanks' list for saves (36).

WORLD SERIES: Steve pitched in the opening game of the 1963 Series and in two games of the 1964 Series without a decision. In the ninth inning of Game 6 in the 1964 Series, Steve came in to put out the fire and record the final two outs on a double play, ending a St. Louis rally and saving a Yankee victory.

TRADED: In September of 1970, the Yanks sold Steve's contract to the White Sox. Steve pitched for the White Sox, Giants and Cubs before retiring in 1972.

HAMILTON, STEVE

Yr.	W-L	Pct.	SA	G	GS	CG	IP	H	BB	SO	SH	ERA
1963	5-1	.833	5	34	0	0	62	49	24	63	0	2.60
1964	7-2	.778	3	30	3	1	60	55	15	49	0	3.28
1965	3-1	.750	5	46	1	0	58	47	16	51	0	1.39
1966	8-3	.727	3	44	3	1	90	69	22	57	1	3.00
1967	2-4	.333	4	44	0	0	62	57	23	55	0	3.48
1968	2-2	.500	11	40	0	0	51	37	13	42	0	2.13
1969	3-4	.429	2	38	0	0	57	39	21	39	0	3.32
1970	4-3	.571	3	35	0	0	45	36	16	33	0	2.78
8 Yrs.	34-20	.630	36	311	7	2	486	389	150	389	1	2.78
Life.	40-31	.563	42	421	17	3	663	556	214	531	1	3.05

World Series

Yr.	G	IP	BB	SO	H	W-L	SA
1963	1	1	0	1	0	0-0	0
1964	2	2	0	2	3	0-0	1
2 Yrs.	3	3	0	3	3	0-0	1
Life. Same.							

HARTZELL, ROY

Yankee: 1911-16
Outfielder-Infielder
Born: July 6, 1881
Birthplace: Golden, CO
Died: November 6, 1961
Bat: L; Throw: R
Ht: 5'8"; Wt: 155

CAME TO YANKS: Roy came to the Yanks from the St. Louis Browns for cash before the 1911 season.

VERSATILE PLAYER: Roy could play almost anywhere. In 1911 he was the Yanks' starting third baseman. In 1913 he was the team's regular second baseman. And in 1914-15 Roy was the regular Yankee leftfielder.

CLUB LEADERSHIP: In 1911 Roy led the Yanks in RBIs (91). That was the highest RBI total by a Yankee player in the club's first 13 years of existence (1903-15), until Wally Pipp had 93 RBIs in 1916. Roy led the Yanks in walks in consecutive seasons (1911-12).

LEFT YANKS: The 1916 season was Roy's final campaign in the ML's. In July, 1916, the Yanks released Roy to Baltimore of the International League.

HARTZELL, ROY

Yr.	G	AB	R	H	2B	3B	HR	RBI	BB	SB	BA	SA
1911	144	527	67	156	17	11	3	91	63	22	.296	.387
1912	123	416	50	113	10	11	1	38	64	20	.272	.356
1913	141	490	60	127	18	1	0	38	67	26	.259	.300
1914	137	481	55	112	15	9	1	32	68	22	.233	.308
1915	119	387	39	97	11	2	3	60	57	7	.251	.313
1916	33	64	12	12	1	0	0	7	9	1	.188	.203
6 Yrs.	697	2365	283	617	72	34	8	266	328	98	.261	.330
Life.	1288	4548	503	1146	112	55	12	397	455	182	.252	.309

HENDERSON, RICKEY

Yankee: 1985-89
Outfielder, DH
Born: December 25, 1958
Birthplace: Chicago, IL
Bat: R; Throw: L
Ht: 5'10"; Wt: 180

YANKEE HONORS: Rickey represented the AL team in the All-Star game as a Yankee in 1985, 1986, 1987 and 1988. In 1985, he was an outfielder on the AL All-Star teams selected by *The Sporting News* and the Associated Press. Rickey won a Silver Slugger Award as an AL outfielder in 1985.

TRADED TO THE YANKEES: In December of 1984, Oakland traded Rickey, Bert Bradley (P) and cash to the Yankees for Stan Javier (OF), Jay Howell (P), Jose Rijo (P), Eric Plunk (P) and Tim Birtsas (P). Rickey later signed a five-year contract with the Yanks.

1985 SEASON: Rickey sprained his left ankle on March 17, and his much anticipated debut with the Yankees was postponed until April 22. Rickey was fabulous, leading the AL in SBs (80) and runs (146), the most runs scored by a Yankee since Joe DiMaggio scored 151 runs in 1937. Rickey scored 56 runs of Don Mattingly's 145 RBIs. In June, Rickey hit .416 with six HRs and 22 SBs and was named AL Player of the Month.

1986 SEASON: Again Rickey led the AL in runs (130) and SBs (87), setting an AL record for the most consecutive years having 50 or more SBs (seven). Rickey established career highs in HRs (28), doubles (31) and RBIs (74). And he did all this even though the umpires reinterpreted his strike zone this year and disregarded his deep crouch; Rickey chased more bad pitches in his uncertainty about the exact dimensions of his strike zone.

STOLEN BASE KING: In 1985, Rickey's 80 SBs broke Fritz Maisel's club record of 74, set in 1914; Rickey broke his own club record with 87 SBs in 1986; he broke it again with 93 SBs in 1988. He led the AL in SBs three times as a Yankee. On June 4, 1988, Rickey stole his 249th base as a Yankee breaking Hal Chase's club record. Rickey finished with 326 SBs as a Yankee and remains first on the club's all-time list. Rickey currently holds the all-time single-season SB record (130 with Oakland in 1982) and the career record (1403 through 2002).

POWER AND SPEED: Nobody has ever dominated a game on the basepaths like Rickey, and he is perhaps the greatest leadoff man the game has ever known. In 1986, he set an AL record for the most leadoff HRs in a season (nine), and on April 14, 1987, he broke the AL record for career leadoff HRs, which was 28 and held by Eddie Yost; Rickey later went on to set the ML record. In 1985, Rickey was the first American Leaguer to have 20 HRs and 50 SBs (24/80), and he duplicated this feat in 1986 (28/87).

FIELDING: Rickey's only weakness as a player was his just-average throwing arm. He played center field in 1985, 1986 and 1987, and returned to his best position, left field, in 1988. He was famous for making a snatch catch on easy fly balls; he swatted at the ball as if it were a bug.

FALL FROM GRACE: Rickey's star starting burning out in New York in 1987, a season when he didn't lead the AL in SBs. He was going great up until June 4, 1987, when he left a game with a pulled right hamstring; he was never healthy the rest of the year and was on the Disabled List most of June, and then again, July 26 through September 1. He suffered from an unexpected power shortage in 1988, as his HR output dropped to six. During the 1989 season, he was asking for a new contract and setting a timetable, and he seemed to play halfheartedly at times; once on a ball kicked by him in left field, he barely bothered to jog after it.

BACK TO OAKLAND: On June 21, 1989, the Yankees traded Rickey back to Oakland for Eric Plunk (P), Greg Cadaret (P) and Luis Polonia (OF). Rickey spurted in the second half, led the AL in three categories, won the MVP Award in the ALCS, and hit .474 in the World Series. Rickey has had four separate stints with the Athletics and two with the Padres. He has also played for the Angels, Mets, Mariners, and Red Sox during a 24-year career.

HENDERSON, RICKEY

Yr.	G	AB	R	H	2B	3B	HR	RBI	BB	SB	BA	SA
1985	143	547	146	172	28	5	24	72	99	80	.314	.516
1986	153	608	130	160	31	5	28	74	89	87	.263	.469
1987	95	358	78	104	17	3	17	37	80	41	.291	.497
1988	140	554	118	169	30	2	6	50	82	93	.305	.399
1989	65	235	41	58	13	1	3	22	56	25	.247	.349
5 Yrs.	596	2302	513	663	119	16	78	255	406	326	.288	.455

Life. Still Active

HENRICH, TOMMY

Nicknames: "Old Reliable" "The Great Debater"
Yankee: 1937-42 (military) 1946-50
Outfielder, 1B
Born: February 20, 1913
Birthplace: Massillon, OH
Bat: L; Throw: L
Ht: 6'; Wt: 180

HONORS: In 1949 *The Sporting News* named Tommy to its ML All-Star team as the best first baseman in baseball.

CAME TO YANKS: In 1937 Tommy, who had signed originally with the Cleveland Indians in 1934, became convinced that the Indians were deliberately keeping him in the minors. In his three minor league seasons, Tommy had hit .326, .337 and .346, the final mark made at the highest minor league classification. Late in the 1936 season, Cleveland GM Cy Slapnicka called up another outfielder, Jeff Heath, and later had Tommy's contract sold to Milwaukee, a team in the Indian chain. Following the sale he read conflicting stories about his future. One report had Milwaukee selling his contract to the Boston Braves and another had the Indians trading Tommy to the Browns. It appeared that a violation of baseball's rules was imbedded in the confusion. Tommy wrote a letter explaining his dissatisfaction to Commissioner Landis who held a hearing, eventually ruling against Cleveland and his adversary, Slapnicka. Tommy became a free agent and a unique auction was held. Eight ML teams expressed an interest in Tommy with the Browns pushing hard, but Tommy did not want to play for a loser. As a kid he was a Yankee fan and now he wanted to play for the best, the Yanks. Tommy finally signed with the Yanks for a $25,000 bonus.

ROOKIE SEASON: Tommy began the 1937 season at the Yanks' Newark farm club. When Yankee Manager Joe McCarthy became disenchanted with outfielder Roy Johnson early in the season, he had GM Ed Barrow bring Tommy up to the Yanks. Although Tommy was injured part of the 1937 season, he had a great rookie season as the Yanks' fifth outfielder (.320, eight HRs, 42 RBIs in 206 at-bats).

OUTFIELDER-FIRST BASEMAN: Tommy was the Yanks' regular rightfielder in 1938. He was the club's fourth outfielder in 1939-40. He was the Yanks' regular rightfielder in 1941-42. He joined the Coast Guard in the final month of the 1942 season and missed the World Series. Like so many of the Yankee players of the 1940s, Tommy missed three baseball seasons during the prime of his career (1943-45) while serving in the military. When Tommy returned to the Yanks, he was the club's rightfielder from 1946-48. He was the Yankee first baseman, besides playing 61 games in the outfield, in 1949. He played part of the season with a broken bone in his back. A knee injury limited his 1950 season to 34 games at first base and pinch-hitting duty (7 for 33).

WINNING BALLPLAYER: Tommy not only was a tremendous ballplayer but a leader as well. He was a key member of seven Yankee World Championship teams. He had the mental toughness that helped make the Yanks winners. When the pressure was the most intense, Tommy performed his best. Sportswriter Red Smith once wrote that Tommy "got more pure joy out of baseball than any player I ever knew."

GREAT HITTER: Tommy was one of the best clutch hitters in Yankee history. In four different seasons Tommy scored more than 100 runs and he hit more than 20 HRs in a season four times. He hit four grand slam HRs in 1948, tying a Yankee club record. The Yanks counted on Tommy's booming bat and he always produced.

LEAGUE LEADER: In consecutive seasons (1947-48) Tommy led the AL in triples. In 1948 he led the AL in runs scored (138). In 1946 he led the AL in being hit by pitched balls (7).

CLUB LEADERSHIP: Tommy led the Yanks in doubles three times. Twice he led the Yanks in runs scored. In 1946 he led the club in games played (150) and at-bats (565). In 1947 he led the team in RBIs (98). In 1949 he led the Yanks in HRs (24), batting (.287), slugging (.526) and walks (86).

DEFENSIVE ABILITIES: Tommy was a tremendous defensive rightfielder. He made only two errors in 1946 when he fielded .992, second highest fielding average in Yankee history for a rightfielder. He played 1017 games in the outfield and 189 games at first base during his ML career, entirely with the Yanks.

ALL-TIME YANKEE LEADER: Tommy is eighth on the all-time Yankee triple list (73). He is tenth on the club's all-time bases on balls list (712). His lifetime slugging average (.491) is the 11th highest in Yankee history for those players with at least 1500 Yankee at-bats. Tommy is 14th in all-time Yankee HRs (183); 14th in doubles (269); 15th in RBI (795); and 15th in runs scored (901).

ALL-STAR GAME: Tommy was selected to the AL team for five All-Star Games (1942, '47-50).

WORLD SERIES: One of the most bizarre plays in Series history involved Tommy. In Game 4 of the 1941 Series, Tommy fanned to apparently end the game. But the ball got by Dodger catcher Mickey Owen and Tommy alertly raced to first base. The Yanks rallied to win the game and the Series. He capped a fantastic 1947 Series (10 for 31, .323) by knocking in the winning run in a 5-2 Game 7 victory over the Dodgers. In the bottom of the ninth inning of Game 1 of the 1949 Series Tommy hit a HR to win the game for Allie Reynolds, 1-0.

RETIREMENT: In December of 1950, Tommy officially retired as a ballplayer. Tommy was a Yankee coach for the 1951 season, and he worked hard, long hours teaching Mickey Mantle some of the subtle skills of being an outfielder. After coaching in 1951, he did some sports broadcasting. He was a New York Giant coach in 1957. Before the San Francisco bound Giants' final game in New York, played on September 29, 1957, Tommy resigned saying, "I don't think it would be fair to my family to uproot them." His 20-year association with New York baseball was over. Tommy also places 12th in doubles (269), and 14th in runs scored (901).

HENRICH, TOMMY												
Yr.	G	AB	R	H	2B	3B	HR	RBI	BB	SB	BA	SA
1937	67	206	39	66	14	5	8	42	35	4	.320	.553
1938	131	471	109	127	24	7	22	91	92	6	.270	.490
1939	99	347	64	96	18	4	9	57	51	7	.277	.429
1940	90	293	57	90	28	5	10	53	48	1	.307	.539
1941	144	538	106	149	27	5	31	85	81	3	.277	.519
1942	127	483	77	129	30	5	13	67	58	4	.267	.431
1946	150	565	92	142	25	4	19	83	87	5	.251	.411
1947	142	550	109	158	35	13	16	98	71	3	.287	.485
1948	146	588	138	181	42	14	25	100	76	2	.308	.554
1949	115	411	90	118	20	3	24	85	86	2	.287	.526
1950	73	151	20	41	6	8	6	34	27	0	.272	.536
11 Yrs.	1284	4603	901	1297	269	73	183	795	712	37	.282	.491
Life. Same.												

World Series

Yr.	G	AB	R	H	2B	3B	HR	RBI	BA
1938	4	16	3	4	1	0	1	1	.250
1941	5	18	4	3	1	0	1	1	.167
1947	7	31	2	10	2	0	1	5	.323
1949	5	19	4	5	0	0	1	1	.263
4 Yrs.	21	84	13	22	4	0	4	8	.262
Life. Same.									

HOGG, BILL

Nickname: "Buffalo Bill"
Yankee: 1905-08
Pitcher
Born: September 11, 1881
Birthplace: Canada
Died: December 8, 1909
Bat: R; Throw: R
Ht: 6'; Wt: 200

UNKNOWN BACKGROUND: Not much is known about Bill who died in 1909 at the age of 28 in New Orleans, Louisiana. It is a known fact that "Buffalo Bill" played his entire ML career with the Yanks (Highlanders). His date of birth, in Canada not Michigan, was recently discovered as September 11, 1881.

KEY YANKEE PITCHER: From 1905-07, Bill was one of the top three Yankee pitchers. Besides being the Yanks' No. 4 starter in 1905, Bill led AL pitchers in relief wins (four). He was the No. 3 starter on the 1906 team and a big reason why the Yanks were in the fight for the AL pennant, finishing just three games behind the White Sox. In 1907 he led the Yanks in winning percentage (.556, 10-8) as the club's No. 4 starter. In 1908 "Buffalo Bill" was again the fourth starter but was a hard luck pitcher. He lost nine games in a row, a Yankee club record that was tied in 1967, although he had an excellent ERA for the season (3.01).

HOGG, BILL											
Yr.	W-L	Pct.	SA	G	GS	CG	IP	H	BB	SO	SH	ERA
1905	9-13	.409	1	39	22	9	205	178	101	125	3	3.20
1906	14-13	.519	0	28	25	15	206	171	72	107	3	2.93
1907	11-8	.579	0	25	21	13	167	173	83	64	0	3.08
1908	4-15	.211	0	24	21	7	152	155	63	72	0	3.01
4 Yrs.	38-49	.437	1	116	89	44	730	677	319	368	6	3.06
Life. Same.											

HOWARD, ELSTON

Nickname: "Ellie"
Yankee: 1955-67
Catcher, OF, 1B
Born: February 23, 1929
Birthplace: St. Louis, MO
Died: December 14, 1980
Bat: R; Throw: R
Ht: 6'2"; Wt: 200

HONORS: The Baseball Writers selected Elston the MVP of the AL in 1963. *The Sporting News* picked him as the catcher on its AL All-Star team in 1961, 1963 and 1964. In 1964 the New York Chapter of the Baseball Writers gave Elston the Ben Epstein "Good Guy" Award.

YOUNG PROSPECT: In July of 1950, the Yanks purchased Ellie's contract for about $30,000 from the Kansas City Monarchs of the old Negro Leagues. Elston was hitting .375 at the time. (He once roomed with Hall-of-Famer Ernie Banks while with the Monarchs.) Elston finished the 1950 season at Muskegon of the Central League, then missed the 1951-52 baseball seasons while serving in the military. In 1953 Ellie played for the Class-AAA Kansas City Blues (.286, 10 HRs, 70 RBIs). In the spring training camp of 1954, Yankee great Bill Dickey worked with Elston on catching, a position he was just learning to play. Elston had a sensational 1954 season at Toronto (.330, 22 HRs, 109 RBIs) and was named the MVP of the International League.

BREAKS YANKEE COLOR LINE: Elston became the first black player in Yankee history when he made the club in the spring of 1955, his ML rookie season. Though Yank management (Weiss) was racially prejudiced, there was probably less prejudice among Yankee players than anywhere in baseball. All the players made Ellie feel welcome, especially Phil Rizzuto. Casey Stengel sometimes made unfortunate racial remarks. But he showed how he really felt toward Elston when he said, "You can substitute, but you can rarely replace. With Howard, I have a replacement, not a substitute." The reference was to Yogi Berra. In Elston's first several spring training camps at St. Petersburg, FL, he had to live with a black family in the segregated part of town. Ellie was the only player not staying at the Yanks' hotel. (He spent a lot of time with another black player, Bill White, of the St. Louis Cardinals who also trained at St. Pete). Though Elston was not militant about gaining his rights, he worked for change in his own way—quietly and with dignity.

VERSATILE BALLPLAYER: In his first five seasons with the Yanks (1955-59), Elston played in the outfield, at first base and was second-string catcher behind Yogi Berra. Elston progressively had more at-bats in each of his first five Yankee campaigns. By 1960, at the age of 31, he had become the regular Yankee catcher, a job he held for seven seasons (1960-66). Over his Yankee career, Elston played in 1029 games as catcher, 265 games as outfielder and 85 games as first baseman.

WINNER AND LEADER: Elston was an important member of the AL pennant-winning Yankee teams in nine of his first 10 seasons with the club! (Only in 1959 did the Yanks fail to win the flag.) Ellie played on World Championship teams in 1956, 1958, 1961 and 1962. He was a leader on the Yanks, especially in 1963 when Mickey Mantle was hurt and missed most of the season. Everyone on the club respected Elston as both a player and a man. He was a consistent player both offensively and defensively, a player his teammates could count on. Both his easygoing manner off the field and competitive spirit on the field were good influences on the Yankee team.

DEFENSIVE ABILITIES: In the 1960s, Elston was the best all-round catcher in baseball. He was an outstanding defensive catcher (especially since he did not become a regular at the position until he was 31) and a great handler of pitchers. He won the Gold Glove Award as the best defensive catcher in the AL in 1963 and 1964. In 1964 Elston led AL catchers in fielding (.998) and putouts (939), both marks also being Yankee club fielding records for catchers. His 939 putouts and 1008 total chances of 1964 each rank seventh on baseball's all-time lists for catchers. Perhaps Elston's most impressive defensive statistic is his lifetime fielding average as a catcher (.993)—the second highest in baseball history! Ellie was tops at catching foul pops of all baseball's catchers. Mickey Mantle said he never missed one and he never had a finger broken, so skillful was he at handling foul tips and pitches.

GREAT HITTER: In 1961 Elston hit .348 in 446 at-bats, an unbelievable mark for a catcher. (He batted .315 against right-handers and .405 hitting against lefties!) Five times Ellie led the Yanks in batting (for those players with at least 350 at-bats in a season). In 1963, his MVP year, Ellie led the Yanks in HRs (28), batting (.287) and slugging (.528). In 1964, he led the club in doubles (27). Elston had good power to all fields. Like fellow right-hander Bill Skowron, he had the ability to hit HRs into the short right field porch at Yankee Stadium. He hit more than 20 HRs three straight seasons (1961-63).

ALL-TIME YANKEE LEADER: It is probably because he did not get enough at-bats during the Stengel years that Elston is not in any of the top 10 lists on the Yanks. But he does rank in the top 20 on the all-time Yankee lists for games played, RBIs, at-bats, hits, doubles and HRs. He is 15th in games played (1492) and 17th in RBIs (733). Only three right-handed hitters (DiMaggio, Lazzeri, Skowron) hit more Yankee HRs than Ellie (161). Ellie ranks 20th in homers (161) in Yankee history; 19th in at-bats (5044) and 20th in hits (1405).

ALL-STAR GAME: Elston was selected to the AL team for the All-Star Game in nine consecutive seasons (1957-65). He played in six games from 1960-64.

WORLD SERIES: Elston is among the leaders in many lifetime World Series statistics. He ranks third in games played (54); seventh in runs scored (25); eighth in at-bats (171); tied for ninth in hits (42); and 12th in total bases (66). In Game 1 of the 1955 Series Elston became the sixth man in Series history to hit a HR in his first Series at-bat. He hit a HR in the Yanks' 9-0 Game 7 victory over the Dodgers in the 1956 Series. The Baseball Writers gave Elston the Babe Ruth Award (MVP) for his work in the 1958 Series. He made a great catch in left field to lead the Yanks to a crucial Game 5 victory; then in Game 7, Elston's RBI single broke a 2-2 tie, leading the Yanks to that final game win.

Elston Howard was the first African-American to play for the Yankees. Ellie's debut in pinstripes was on April 14, 1955.

In the 1960 Series, Ellie led both clubs in batting (.462). In Game 1 of the 1961 Series, Elston hit an opposite-field solo HR at the Stadium to help Whitey Ford defeat the Reds, 2-0. His five runs scored and three doubles led all hitters in the 1961 Series. Ellie's .333 batting average was the best by the Yanks in the 1963 Series. (He was the only regular to hit above .250). In lifetime Series play, Elston was hit by a pitched ball three times, tying a World Series record. Ellie played four positions in World Series play, a record he shares with three others.

TRADED: In August of 1967, Elston was dealt to the Red Sox for pitchers Ron Klimkowski and Peter Magrini. The Sox were weak in the catching corps and Ellie helped them win the 1967 AL pennant. He played for Boston again in 1968, then retired.

YANKEE COACH: After his retirement, Elston returned to the Yanks as a coach. From 1969-78, Elston was an important Yankee coach who had a positive influence on many Yankee players. He worked in the first-base coaching box and the bullpen. He had dreams of becoming Yankee manager and had hoped to be offered the job in 1973 when Ralph Houk stepped down. But his ambition never interfered with his relationships with those who did hold the job. He got along well with all of them.

YANKEE EXECUTIVE: Elston missed the entire 1979 baseball season because of a serious heart illness. He was hospitalized for some time. In February 1980, Elston was named an administrative assistant to principal owner George Steinbrenner.

TRAGIC DEATH: In early December 1980, Elston was hospitalized again. He died of heart failure on December 14, 1980. At Ellie's funeral, moving eulogies were delivered by Whitey Ford, Reggie Jackson, and Yankee broadcaster Bill White. Many baseball people attended the funeral of the man Ford said "had so much dignity, so much class." At Opening Day 1981 ceremonies, Elston's family was honored, and on July 21, 1984, in a joint ceremony at Yankee Stadium, the uniform numbers of Elston (32) and Roger Maris (nine) were retired and plaques in their honor added to Monument Park. Elston was the first black Yankee player; the first black MVP in the AL; and the AL's first black coach. He was a great man and a great Yankee.

HOWARD, ELSTON

Yr.	G	AB	R	H	2B	3B	HR	RBI	BB	SB	BA	SA
1955	97	279	33	81	8	7	10	43	20	0	.290	.477
1956	98	290	35	76	8	3	5	34	21	0	.262	.362
1957	110	356	33	90	13	4	8	44	16	2	.253	.379
1958	103	376	45	118	19	5	11	66	22	1	.314	.479
1959	125	443	59	121	24	6	18	73	20	0	.273	.476
1960	107	323	29	79	11	3	6	39	28	3	.245	.353
1961	129	446	64	155	17	5	21	77	28	0	.348	.549
1962	136	494	63	138	23	5	21	91	31	1	.279	.474
1963	135	487	75	140	21	6	28	85	35	0	.287	.528
1964	150	550	63	172	27	3	15	84	48	1	.313	.455
1965	110	391	38	91	15	1	9	45	24	0	.233	.345
1966	126	410	38	105	19	2	6	35	37	0	.256	.356
1967	66	199	13	39	6	0	3	17	12	0	.196	.271
13 Yrs.	1492	5044	588	1405	211	50	161	733	342	8	.279	.436
Life.	1605	5363	619	1471	218	50	167	762	373	9	.274	.427

World Series

Yr.	G	AB	R	H	2B	3B	HR	RBI	BA
1955	7	26	3	5	0	0	1	3	.192
1956	1	5	1	2	1	0	1	1	.400
1957	6	11	2	3	0	0	1	3	.273
1958	6	18	4	4	0	0	0	2	.222
1960	5	13	4	6	1	1	1	4	.462
1961	5	20	5	5	3	0	1	1	.250
1962	6	21	1	3	1	0	0	1	.143
1963	4	15	0	5	0	0	0	1	.333
1964	7	24	5	7	1	0	0	2	.292
9 Yrs.	47	153	25	40	7	1	5	18	.261
Life.	54	171	25	42	7	1	5	19	.246

HOWE, STEVE

Yankee: 1991-96
Pitcher
Born: March 10, 1958
Birthplace: Pontiac, MI
Bat: L; Throw: L
Ht: 6'2"; Wt: 198

Steve Howe

SIGNED BY YANKS: A one-time Dodger star who sustained six suspensions for drug abuse, was out of baseball altogether in 1988 and 1989 and was reduced to pitching for Class A Salinas in 1990. Then, in February, 1991, Howe walked into the Yankees' Spring camp, fired his 90-plus-m.p.h. fastball, and was signed. The southpaw was practically unhittable in 1991 until suffering a left elbow injury in the season. His ERA in 37 games was 1.68; lefthanded batters hit only .128 against him.

ANOTHER DRUG SUSPENSION: Howe in 1992 received his seventh drug-related suspension from the Baseball Commissioner. He was reinstated by an arbitrator in November, but had a poor 1993 season (3-5, 4.97, 4 saves), missing a month early in the campaign because of an ankle injury. He returned to form in 1994. After several would-be closers failed, Howe rose to become the closer the Yankees needed. He recorded 15 saves, his ERA in 20 games at Yankee Stadium was 0.89, and opponents hit only .194 against him. Something happened in 1995 to the zip in Howe's fastball and slider, however. His ERA ballooned to 4.96, and opponents hit .324 against him.

FINAL MAJOR LEAGUE SEASON: Howe was granted free agency in late 1995 and was again signed by the Yankees for the 1996 season. Yankee owner George Steinbrenner believed in Steve and Howe was given yet another chance to prove himself. In 1996, Steve was 0-1 with a lone save in 25 games with a terrible ERA of 6.35, allowing 12 earned runs in 17 innings. His stuff, which proved so promising for so many years, was gone, and he was released by the Yankees on June 24, 1996. The former National League Rookie of the Year in 1980 was to never pitch again in baseball after 12 seasons in the Majors. Steve's total of 30 saves ranks 17th overall in Yankee history.

HOWE, STEVE

Yr.	W-L	Pct.	SA	G	GS	CG	IP	H	BB	SO	SH	ERA
1991	3-1	.750	3	37	0	0	48	39	7	34	0	1.68
1992	3-0	1.000	6	20	0	0	22	9	3	12	0	2.45
1993	3-5	.375	4	51	0	0	51	58	10	19	0	4.97
1994	3-0	1.000	15	40	0	0	40	28	7	18	0	1.80
1995	6-3	.667	2	56	0	0	49	66	17	28	0	4.96
1996	0-1	.000	1	25	0	0	17	19	6	5	0	6.35
6 Yrs.	18-10	.643	31	229	0	0	227	219	50	116	0	3.57
Life.	47-41	.534	91	497	0	0	606	586	139	328	0	3.03

Division Series

Yr.	G	IP	BB	SO	H	W-L	SA
1995	2	1.0	0	0	4	0-0	0
Life.	4	3.0	0	2	5	0-0	0

HOYT, WAITE

Nickname: "The Brooklyn Schoolboy"
Yankee: 1921-30
Pitcher
Born: September 9, 1899
Birthplace: Brooklyn, NY
Died: August 25, 1984
Bat: R; Throw: R
Ht: 6'; Wt: 180

HONORS: In 1969, Waite was inducted into the Baseball Hall of Fame. He was selected as one of two pitchers on *The Sporting*

News' 1928 ML All-Star team. In 1966, the Baseball Writers of New York gave Waite the Casey Stengel "You Could Look It Up" Award.

EARLY STARDOM: Waite was a great high school pitcher for Erasmus Hall in Brooklyn—hence the nickname, "The Brooklyn Schoolboy." Giant Manager John J. McGraw signed Waite as a 16-year-old phenom. Waite pitched one game for the Giants in 1918, then was a promising pitcher in 1919-20 for the Red Sox. He became a real pitcher in Boston, and at the age of 20 pitched 11 perfect innings in an extra-inning game against the Yanks.

CAME TO YANKS: In December of 1920, the Yanks obtained Waite, Wally Schang, Mike McNally and Harry Harper from the Red Sox in exchange for Del Pratt, Muddy Ruel, Sammy Vick and Hank Thormahlen.

YANKEE STAR PITCHER: Waite was a major factor in the Yanks' winning their first AL pennant in 1921. He was the team's No. 2 starter and second biggest winner (19-13). Every year from 1921-29 Waite was one of the Yanks' top three starters. He was the most consistent Yankee hurler in the 1920s, starring on the Yanks' first six pennant-winning teams (1921-23, 1926-28). He won more games (116), averaging 19.33 wins per season, than any other Yankee over those years. In 1927 Waite was the undisputed ace on what may have been the greatest team of all time. On the World Championship teams of 1927-28, Waite's combined record was 45-14!

INTERESTING MAN: Waite was a ballplayer with unusually sophisticated tastes; he was talented and picturesque. He was a painter, writer and a singer. (He sang at the great New York Palace Theatre.) He was also a mortician for a while and was a baseball broadcaster after retiring as a player. Waite was a high-class guy who understood his worth. In the spring of 1928, he was a holdout. (After all, for his super 1927 season, Waite was paid a whopping $12,000 salary!) He was a ML star with the Yanks before his 22nd birthday. Waite was a proud player and occasionally was temperamental. He had several disagreements with Manager Miller Huggins (though it must be noted he felt Huggins was a great manager). Playing in New York, Waite took advantage of all the cultural and entertainment avenues open to him. He was a popular guy on the Yanks, and he was an especially good friend of Babe Ruth.

BABE RUTH'S BUDDY: Waite understood the Babe, his personality and his mystique better than anyone. They were close friends but Waite was one of the few people who did not bow to Babe's every wish. In 1923 Waite and Babe had a spat and did not speak for a year. Then they nearly fought when Waite accused Babe of dogging it in going after a fly ball, and they did not talk to each other for another year. Finally, Babe came to Waite, offered a beer and asked to be friends again. Waite and Babe did have a close friendship, working toward incredible successes on the field and good times off the field. Still, when Waite was traded from the Yanks in 1930 and Babe came to offer his goodbye, his very words were, "Take care of yourself—Walter."

LEAGUE LEADER: In 1927 Waite led the AL in wins (22) and winning percentage (.759, 22-7). His 2.63 ERA in 1927 was the lowest of all starting pitchers in the AL. In 1928 Waite led the AL in saves (eight).

CLUB LEADERSHIP: Although Waite was used mostly as a starter, he led the Yanks in saves three times (1924-25, 1928). He led the club in shutouts three times (1922, 1926-27). Twice he led the team in strikeouts (1926-27) and winning percentage (1927-28). He was a workhorse, leading the Yanks in innings pitched in 1927 and in games pitched in 1924. In 1923 his 3.02 ERA led all Yankee pitchers. In 1927 his 32 games started and 23 games complete led the Yanks in both categories.

ALL-TIME YANKEE LEADER: Waite is among the lifetime Yankee pitching leaders in many categories. He is sixth on the all-time Yankee games started list (275); seventh on the innings pitched (2272) and tied for sixth in complete games(156); and eighth on the win (157) and 11th on the games pitched (365) lists. Waite also ranks 15th in winning percentage (.616); 17th in strikeouts (713); 17th in shutouts (15); and tied for 18th in saves (28).

WORLD SERIES: Waite was one of the best big-game pitchers in Yankee history. He is among the leaders in many lifetime World Series pitching categories, including wins (fifth with six wins) and innings pitched (fifth with 84 innings). Only Whitey Ford started more World Series games than did Waite (11). He pitched 27 innings (three complete games) without allowing an earned run in the 1921 Series, although the Yanks lost to the New York Giants in eight games. In Game 2, Waite shut out the Giants, 3-0, on two singles. In Game 5, he allowed only six hits and won, 3-1. Unfortunately, he lost the final game (Game 8) by a 1-0 score, though the lone Giant run was unearned. In Game 4 of the 1926 Series, the first Series game in which Ruth hit three HRs, Waite defeated the Cardinals. Waite won Game 1 of the 1927 Series, 5-4, getting the Yanks off and running to a four-game sweep of the Pirates. He was a star of the 1928 Series sweep of the Cardinals. He pitched complete game victories in Game 1 and Game 4. (The Yanks used only three pitchers for the entire Series!) In four of his six Yankee Series (1921, 1922, 1926, 1928), Waite compiled an ERA under 1.50!

TRADED: In May of 1930, the Yanks traded Waite and shortstop Mark Koenig to the Tigers for three obscure players (outfielder Harry Rice, infielder Yats Wuestling and pitcher Ownie Carroll). The Yanks made a mistake dealing away Waite; he won 70 more ML games after leaving New York.

BASEBALL MAN: Waite remained associated with baseball after retiring as a player in 1938. He was a beloved broadcaster for the Cincinnati Reds, 1941-65. He was a grand gentleman, gracious, a valuable baseball historian, and involved with baseball until his death in Cincinnati, his adopted hometown.

Waite Hoyt—Yankee pitcher from 1921-1930. (New York Yankees Archives)

HOYT, WAITE

Yr.	W-L	Pct.	SA	G	GS	CG	IP	H	BB	SO	SH	ERA
1921	19-13	.594	3	43	32	21	282	301	81	102	1	3.09
1922	19-12	.613	0	37	31	17	265	271	76	95	3	3.43
1923	17-9	.654	1	37	28	19	239	227	66	60	1	3.02
1924	18-13	.581	4	46	32	14	247	295	76	71	2	3.79
1925	11-14	.440	6	46	30	17	243	283	78	86	1	4.00
1926	16-12	.571	4	40	27	12	218	224	62	79	1	3.84
1927	22-7	.759	1	36	32	23	256	242	54	86	3	2.63
1928	23-7	.767	8	42	31	19	273	279	60	67	3	3.36
1929	10-9	.526	1	30	25	12	202	219	69	57	0	4.24
1930	2-2	.500	0	8	7	2	48	64	9	10	0	4.53
10 Yrs.	157-98	.616	28	365	275	156	2272	2405	631	713	15	3.48
Life.	237-182	.566	52	674	422	226	3762	4037	1003	1206	26	3.59

World Series

Yr.	G	IP	BB	SO	H	W-L	SA
1921	3	27	11	18	18	2-1	0
1922	2	8	2	4	11	0-1	0
1923	1	2 1/3	1	0	4	0-0	0
1926	2	15	1	10	19	1-1	0
1927	1	7 1/3	1	2	8	1-0	0
1928	2	18	6	14	14	2-0	0
6 Yrs.	11	77 2/3	22	48	74	6-3	0
Life.	12	83 2/3	22	49	81	6-4	0

HUNTER, CATFISH
(BORN JAMES AUGUSTUS HUNTER)

Yankee: 1975-79
Pitcher
Born: April 8, 1946
Birthplace: Hertford, NC
Died: September 9, 1999
Bat: R; Throw: R
Ht: 6'; Wt: 190

New York Yankees' Catfish Hunter fires to the plate against the Toronto Blue Jays, September 27, 1978 in New York. Hunter, the Hall of Fame pitcher who ushered in baseball's era of big bucks for free agents, died September 9, 1999 at age 53 after battling the disease named after another New York Yankees great, Lou Gehrig. (AP/WIDE WORLD PHOTOS, Ray Stubblebine)

CAME TO YANKS: After the 1974 season, Catfish was declared a free agent because Oakland A's owner Charlie Finley had failed to honor certain obligations in his contract. Every ML club was eligible to sign Catfish who eventually narrowed his choices to the Padres and Yankees. He chose the Yanks for the value of the five-year contract offered (estimated at $3.5 million), the Yanks' good chances at winning the pennant and because he liked Yankee tradition. The signing was announced on the New Year's Eve heralding 1975. The package included a bonus, a ten-year retirement plan, life insurance policies for the family and provision for legal fees. The actual cash outlay, therefore, was far less than $3.5 million.

MOVING IN BIG COMPANY: Catfish was one of the game's greatest pitchers whose best seasons were with the A's. When Catfish was 23-14 for the Yanks in 1975 he joined Walter Johnson and Lefty Grove as the only AL pitchers to win 20 games five years in a row. Late in the 1976 season Catfish became the fourth pitcher in the 20th century to win his 200th ML game before his 31st birthday, joining Cy Young, Christy Mathewson and Walter Johnson!

SMART PITCHER: When Catfish was pitching his game he had hitters completely off balance. He moved the ball around the strike zone brilliantly, working quickly, relying on pinpoint control and mixing up his pitches. Catfish had a good moving fastball. He had a lifetime 26-24 record against Baltimore, recording the second most wins (behind Whitey Ford) in history over the competitive Orioles.

WORKHORSE: Starting in 1970 with the A's, Catfish pitched more than 250 innings in every year through 1976. In 1974 (A's) and 1975-76 (Yanks), he pitched a total of 945 innings and completed 74 games—a lot of strain on a pitching arm. In 1975 he pitched 30 complete games, the most pitched in the AL since Bob Feller's 36 in 1946. Only three times has a Yankee pitcher started more games than Catfish did in 1975 (39). The total of 328 innings he hurled in 1975 was the most by a Yankee pitcher since 1921 when Carl Mays pitched 337 innings. For the Yanks over the combined 1975-76 seasons, Catfish pitched 627 innings; and his mediocre record after 1976 might be attributable to overwork.

UPS, DOWNS AND UPS: In 1975 and 1976 Catfish was the Yanks' No. 1 starter. Beginning in 1977 he was plagued by arm miseries. He spent extended periods of time on the disabled list in 1977 because of arm problems and was confined to the role of fifth starter. In 1978 Catfish was again the Yanks' fifth starter, but he staged an amazing comeback. After beginning the year bothered by the same nagging injuries, Catfish had a great second half, winning 10 of his last 13 decisions, including a 6-0 August, and leading the Yanks to a miracle pennant win over Boston. His last season (1979) was a disappointing one.

LEAGUE AND CLUB LEADERSHIP: As a Yankee in 1975, Catfish led AL pitchers in wins (23), complete games (30) and innings pitched (328). He also led Yankee pitchers in 1975 in ERA (2.58), shutouts (seven) and winning percentage (.622, 23-14). In both 1975-76, Catfish led the Yanks in games started, complete games and strikeouts.

CLASS GUY: Catfish, in the time he was with the Yankees, may have been the classiest guy on the team. He was easily the most popular Yankee among his teammates, the fans and the press. He always did what was in his power to help the club—he was the team player. During his Yankee career, it was discovered that he was a diabetic, but he never complained and served as an inspiration to other diabetics. It is no accident that the Yanks became big winners after Catfish's arrival. Just before he retired, the Yanks held "Catfish Hunter Day" at the Stadium and he received many gifts. (He was an enthusiastic hunter and the Remington Arms Company presented him with a Remington gun.)

ALL-STAR GAME: As a Yankee, Catfish was selected to the AL team for the 1975 and 1976 All-Star Games. He pitched in each game, losing the 1975 Summer Classic.

AL CHAMPIONSHIP SERIES: In Game 1 of the 1976 playoffs, Catfish pitched a masterful five-hitter, beating the Royals, 4-1. (It was the Yanks' first post-season victory in 12 years.) He pitched six strong innings in Game 3 of the 1978 playoffs, a game the Yanks won.

WORLD SERIES: Catfish lost a 4-3 heartbreaker in Game 2 of the 1976 Series to Cincinnati (the Reds' ninth-inning run was unearned). In Game 6, the final game, of the 1978 Series, he scattered six hits in seven innings to beat the Dodgers, 7-2, and wrap up the World Championship for New York. Fitting that he got the win that ended the miracle season!

RETIREMENT: Catfish retired following the 1979 season and left baseball gracefully. He returned to his native North Carolina and worked his 230-acre farm, and settled down to enjoy his family, coach Little League, and hunt and fish. In 1987, Catfish was inducted into the Baseball Hall of Fame.

THE TRAGIC DEATH OF CATFISH HUNTER: During an off day on September 9, 1999, the Yankee family was devastated by the news of the death of Jim "Catfish" Hunter. Hunter, who was 53, had been diagnosed with ALS, commonly known as Lou Gehrig's Disease, in November of last year. His condition had been deteriorating over the past several weeks. Catfish, a nickname given him for his Southern heritage by Athletics owner Charles O. Finley, spent 15 years in the Majors, the last five with the Yankees. Having 224 career victories, Jim posted 63 of those in the Yankee win column. He was elected on the first ballot to the Baseball Hall of Fame in Cooperstown, New York in 1987, along with the Cubs' Billy Williams. Hunter never pitched in the minors and became the first pitcher to toss a perfect game since 1922, when he defeated the Minnesota Twins on May 8, 1968. Catfish won 20-plus games in five consecutive seasons beginning in 1971. His streak came to an end after his 23-14 mark in 1975, his first year as a Yankee, when he tossed 308 innings and completed a league-high 23 games. Hunter became the first multimillionaire player ever when declared a free agent on a technicality after the 1974 season. He eventually agreed to terms with the Yankees, signing a five-year deal worth $3.75 million. This contract was announced on New Year's Eve 1974 for tax reasons, and he put into motion the concept of full-scale free agency, which began after the 1976 season. Jim's funeral was held on September 13 in his hometown of Hertford, North Carolina. It was attended by many people, including ex-

Yankees Reggie Jackson and Lou Piniella. Jim was laid to rest in a cemetery that was behind the field where he played baseball for his high school. As a tribute to Hunter, the Yankees added a black circle on their field jersey, just below the number five, honoring Joe DiMaggio, who had passed in March. Catfish, you will never be forgotten!

HUNTER, CATFISH

Yr.	W-L	Pct.	SA	G	GS	CG	IP	H	BB	SO	SH	ERA
1975	23-14	.622	0	39	39	30	328	248	83	177	7	2.58
1976	17-15	.531	0	36	36	21	299	268	68	173	2	3.53
1977	9-9	.500	0	22	22	8	143	137	47	52	1	4.71
1978	12-6	.667	0	21	20	5	118	98	35	56	1	3.58
1979	2-9	.182	0	19	19	1	105	128	34	34	0	5.31
5 Yrs.	63-53	.543	0	137	136	65	993	879	267	492	11	3.58
Life.	224-166	.574	1	500	476	181	3449	2958	954	2012	42	3.26

Championship Series

Yr.	G	IP	BB	SO	H	W-L	SA
1976	2	12	1	5	10	1-1	0
1978	1	6	3	5	7	0-0	0
2 Yrs.	3	18	4	10	17	1-1	0
Life.	10	69⅓	18	37	57	4-3	0

World Series

Yr.	G	IP	BB	SO	H	W-L	SA
1976	1	8⅔	4	5	10	0-1	0
1977	2	4⅓	0	1	6	0-1	0
1978	2	13	1	5	13	1-1	0
3 Yrs.	5	26	5	11	29	1-3	0
Life.	12	63	17	33	57	5-3	1

JACKSON, REGGIE

Nickname: "Mr. October"
Yankee: 1977-81
Outfielder, DH
Born: May 18, 1946
Birthplace: Wyncote, PA
Bat: L; Throw: L
Ht: 6'; Wt: 195

HONORS AS A YANKEE: Reggie represented the AL for the All-Star Game in every season that he was a Yankee (1977-81). Reggie was the 1977 World Series MVP. In 1980, he was the rightfielder and designated hitter on the AL All-Star team selected by *The Sporting News,* and he won a Silver Slugger Award. Reggie was inducted into the Baseball Hall of Fame in 1993, and he chose to be wearing a Yankee cap on his plaque.

ON THE ROAD TO NEW YORK: Reggie broke into the ML's with the A's in 1967. He became a star in 1969, hitting 47 HRs; won the AL MVP Award in 1973; and led Oakland to three straight World Championships (1972-74). Besides talking with his bat, Reggie became exceptionally good at self promotion; he was not only articulate but at times poetic. Teammate Catfish Hunter once said of Reggie: "He'd give you the shirt off his back. Of course, he'd call a press conference to announce it." For years he had looked longingly at New York and once predicted there would be a candy bar named after him if he played in the Big Apple. In April 1976, as the new free-agent system loomed, Oakland traded Reggie to Baltimore; Reggie reported four weeks late and still hit 27 HRs with 91 RBIs. The Orioles refused to pay

Reggie the money he was asking, so in November 1976 Reggie entered the first free agent re-entry draft.

YANKEE SIGNING: GM Gabe Paul wasn't interested in signing Reggie (Gabe wanted Bobby Grich), and Billy Martin really didn't want Reggie (Martin wanted Joe Rudi), but George Steinbrenner on his own went after Reggie. Steinbrenner charmed Reggie and took him to the fanciest clubs in New York City. On November 29, 1976, Reggie signed a five-year contract, worth approximately $3 million, to play for the Yankees, and the reason he did, Reggie said, was because Steinbrenner "outhustled everybody else."

1977 SPRING TRAINING: When Reggie arrived for spring training, Reggie and Steinbrenner held a press conference—Martin wasn't invited—and Reggie called his bat "the Dues Collector," boasting that his bat "now helps the Yankees intimidate every other team in baseball." Martin was feeling slighted and threatened by the Jackson-Steinbrenner friendship, and he grew more and more resentful; he needed to let Reggie know that this was Billy's team, and he began embarrassing Reggie in ways such as batting Reggie fifth when Reggie wanted to bat fourth. Additionally, Reggie wasn't warmly welcomed by his new teammates because 1) they felt they had done just fine without him in 1976 and didn't need "the Dues Collector" to make them a good team, and 2) many of them were having difficulty prying more money away from the owner who gave it so freely to Reggie. Reserve catcher Fran Healy was the only Yankee attempting to make Reggie feel at home.

THE *SPORT* ARTICLE: Reggie was feeling especially lonely one day in spring training when he was interviewed by Robert Ward, saying: "I'm the straw that stirs the drink. It all comes back to me. Maybe I should say me and Munson, but really he doesn't enter into it. Munson thinks he can be the straw that stirs the drink, but he can only stir it bad." When the story came out in *Sport* on May 23, 1977, Thurman Munson was furious, as were his teammates. That night when Reggie crossed the plate after hitting a home run, and teammates awaited the customary handshaking, Reggie turned sharply and headed for the other end of the dugout without shaking anyone's hand; Reggie's relations with the team went into a deep freeze.

THE BOSTON EXPLOSION: The Yankees were in Boston in June 1977 for a high-profile series, and the Saturday afternoon game was carried on national TV. As the Red Sox were enjoying a big inning, Reggie, playing right field, moved cautiously toward a Jim Rice blooper, and Rice hustled it into a double. Martin was livid, viewing the play as a lack of hustle, and he immediately sent Paul Blair out to replace Reggie. Humiliated, Reggie jogged into the dugout and confronted Martin; they nearly fought in full view of the TV camera. Martin nearly lost his job, and the tension between Billy and Reggie was now very thick.

THE BEST TEAM MONEY COULD BUY: The publicity the Yankees and Reggie received in 1977 was unbelievable. There was a fear among many fans that the rich Yankees would use the new free-agent system to dominate baseball, and Reggie represented the greed of the new system. There were many fans who wanted to see Reggie fail, especially in Baltimore; his defection as a free agent was probably the number one factor

A smiling Reggie Jackson—Did he just blast one into the centerfield bleachers?!

that mobilized Baltimore into a "baseball town." In the end, his powerful bat helped drive the Yanks to the division title; he hit 32 HRs and led the club in RBIs (110), doubles (39), walks (75) and slugging (.550).

1977 ALCS: Reggie hit only .125 against the Royals, and Martin benched him in Game 5 against southpaw Paul Splittorff. Reggie delivered a pinch-hit run-scoring single in the eighth as the Yanks closed to within 3-2 (and rallied to win in the ninth).

1977 WORLD SERIES: In Game 6 at Yankee Stadium, Reggie hit three consecutive HRs, all on the first pitch, as the Yankees beat the Dodgers to wrap up the club's first World Championship since 1962. After the third HR, the Stadium was rocking with chants of "Reggie! Reggie! Reggie!" Babe Ruth, who had done it twice, is the only other to hit three HRs in a World Series game. He set World Series records for most HRs (five), total bases (25) and runs (ten), and his 1.250 slugging average set a record for a six-game Series. Reggie was the toast of the city in a ticker tape parade that followed.

OPENING DAY 1978: The Yankees beat Chicago, 4-2, as Reggie delivered a three-run homer in the first inning. A new candy bar named after Reggie had just come out, and fans had been given free samples. When Reggie hit the HR, the fans chanted Reggie's name and showered the field with Reggie Bars.

SUSPENSION: On July 17, 1978, Reggie attempted a sacrifice bunt with two strikes and struck out; he chose to bunt even after Billy Martin had ordered Reggie to hit away. The Yankees lost, and soon fell 14 games behind Boston, and Reggie lost the test of wills; he was suspended five days for insubordination. On July 23, Martin told two sportswriters that Reggie and George Steinbrenner "deserve each other" and that "one's a born liar, the other's convicted." The next day, Martin tearfully resigned as manager.

1978 COMEBACK: Reggie and the Yankees concentrated on baseball the rest of 1978, made up 14 games and finished in a first-place tie with Boston, and Reggie tied Graig Nettles for club leadership in HRs (27) and led the club in RBIs (97) and slugging (.477). Reggie hit a HR in the Yanks' 5-4 playoff win at Boston. In the combined games against Boston, Kansas City and Los Angeles in the post season, Reggie hit .400 with 5 HRs and 15 RBIs in 11 games. Reggie reached base safely five times in Game 1 of the ALCS. In Game 2 of the World Series, won by the Dodgers, 4-3, Reggie batted against rookie Bob Welch in the ninth with two outs and two runners on base; Reggie fouled off many pitches before striking out. In Game 6, the Yanks won, 7-2, and captured the Series, and Reggie delivered the coup de grace with a two-run homer off Welch.

CHANGING FRIENDSHIPS: The Yankees started slow in 1979, and in June Billy Martin returned as Yankee manager, which instigated a break in the Jackson-Steinbrenner friendship, as Reggie felt he should have been told what George was planning, and George was angry that a ballplayer would inject an opinion about front-office matters. As Reggie broke away from the owner, he became closer with his teammates, including Munson, and as Martin grew closer to Steinbrenner, Billy stopped hating Reggie. In 1979, Reggie led the Yankees in HRs (29), RBIs (89) and slugging (.544).

GREATEST YANKEE SEASON: Reggie in 1980 shared the AL HR Crown with Milwaukee's Ben Oglivie, and his total of 41 HRs were the most by a Yankee since 1961. Reggie hit .300 on the dot—his only .300 season in his career. Reggie led the Yanks in hits (154), RBIs (111) and slugging (.597); the most RBIs by a Yankee since Mickey Mantle's 111 in 1964 and the highest slugging average since Mantle's .605 in 1962. On October 4, he homered in his fourth consecutive game, as the Yankees won and clinched the division title. Reggie finished second to George Brett in the MVP voting.

FINAL YANKEE SEASON: Reggie reported to spring training in 1981 a couple days later than Steinbrenner wanted, and contract negotiations were cut off for the remainder of the year. Reggie's mood sank as he felt the owner was giving him the cold shoulder, and Reggie's impending free agency hung over the club all season. Reggie was hitting only .199 with six HRs when the players went on strike June 12, and he needed to hit well in September to finish at .237 with 15 HRs (tying Nettles for club HR lead). Reggie was already planning his Yankee exit by late season.

1981 POST-SEASON: In the Game 5 finale of the Division Series, Milwaukee took an early lead, 2-0, but then Reggie unloaded a two-run homer, and the Yanks went on to win. Reggie pulled a calf muscle in Game 2 of the ALCS, left the game and didn't return to the ALCS. During the ALCS victory celebration, he got into a scuffle with Nettles, which further angered Steinbrenner. Reggie didn't play in the World Series until Game 4, when he reached base safely five times—homer, two singles and two walks. Also in Game 4, Reggie lost a fly ball in the sun that bounced off his chest for a critical error. Reggie felt he was physically ready to play in Game 3, but that the owner had kept him from playing. When the Dodgers won the Series in Game 6, he cleared out his locker for good.

LEAVING THE YANKEES: In January of 1982, Reggie signed as a free agent with the Angels. Reggie made a triumphant return to Yankee Stadium on April 27, 1982, hitting a long HR to the delight of the crowd. In 1982, Reggie led the AL with 39 HRs and led the Angels to an AL West title. Reggie played through 1987. In 1993, Reggie rejoined the Yankees as a special advisor and had a "Reggie Jackson Day" at Yankee Stadium on August 14; his number 44 uniform was retired.

PLACE IN HISTORY: Among baseball's all-time leader lists, Reggie ranks first in strikeouts (2597) and eighth in HRs (563). He was one of the game's greatest sluggers and most exciting personalities. Fielding was the weakest part of his game, but he made some great catches and he had a tremendous throwing arm. He was a winner, playing on 11 division champions, six pennant winners and five World Champions. On the All-Time World Series Lists, Reggie ranks first in slugging (.755); tied with Lou Gehrig for fifth in HRs (10); tied with three other Yankees, Gil McDougald, Hank Bauer, and Bill Dickey, for eighth in RBIs (24); 12th in batting (.357); and tenth in runs (21). "Some people call October a time of pressure," Reggie once said. "I call it a time of character."

JACKSON, REGGIE

Yr.	G	AB	R	H	2B	3B	HR	RBI	BB	SB	BA	SA
1977	146	525	93	150	39	2	32	110	74	17	.286	.550
1978	139	511	82	140	13	5	27	97	58	14	.274	.477
1979	131	465	78	138	24	2	29	89	65	9	.297	.544
1980	143	514	94	154	22	4	41	111	83	1	.300	.597
1981	94	334	33	79	17	1	15	54	46	0	.237	.428
5 Yrs.	653	2349	380	661	115	14	144	461	326	41	.281	.526
Life.	2820	9864	1551	2584	463	49	563	1702	1375	228	.262	.490

Divisional Playoff

Yr.	G	AB	R	H	2B	3B	HR	RBI	BB	SB	BA	SA
1981	5	20	4	6	0	0	2	4	1	0	.300	.600
1 Yr.	5	20	4	6	0	0	2	4	1	0	.300	.600
Life. Same.												

Championship Series

Yr.	G	AB	R	H	2B	3B	HR	RBI	BB	SB	BA	SA
1977	5	16	1	2	0	0	0	1	2	1	.125	.125
1978	4	13	5	6	1	0	2	6	3	0	.462	1.000
1980	3	11	1	3	1	0	0	0	1	0	.273	.364
1981	2	4	1	0	0	0	0	1	1	1	.000	.000
4 Yrs.	14	44	8	11	2	0	2	8	7	2	.250	.432
Life.	45	163	16	37	7	0	6	20	17	4	.227	.380

World Series

Yr.	G	AB	R	H	2B	3B	HR	RBI	BB	SB	BA	SA
1977	6	20	10	9	1	0	5	8	3	0	.450	1.250
1978	6	23	2	9	1	0	2	8	3	0	.391	.696
1981	3	12	3	4	1	0	1	1	2	0	.333	.667
3 Yrs.	15	55	15	22	3	0	8	17	8	0	.400	.891
Life.	27	98	21	35	7	1	10	24	15	1	.357	.755

JETER, DEREK

Yankee: 1995-2002
Shortstop
Born: June 26, 1974
Birthplace: Pequannock, NJ
Bat: R; Throw: R
Ht: 6'3"; Wt: 185

PHENOMENAL PROSPECT: Derek was selected *by Baseball America, The Sporting News,* and *USA Today Baseball Weekly* as the Minor League Player of the Year in 1994. He had been considered a prized jewel in the New York Yankee farm system. Derek was the first-round draft selection in 1992 and made rapid improvements at the plate. In 1994, he hit .329 in Class A (Tampa), .377 in Class AA (Albany) and .349 in Class AAA (Columbus). The Yankees did not want to rush Jeter, but he was called up in 1995, making his Major League debut on May 29 after Tony Fernandez, the starting Yankee shortstop, was placed on the disabled list. For 1995, he played in 15 games and batted .250.

STARTING SHORTSTOP: With Tony Fernandez out for the 1996 season, Derek made his presence known in the Yankee infield, being the first rookie shortstop to start on opening-day since Tom Tresh in 1962. Both players (shortstops Tresh and Jeter) would be named American League Rookie of the Year. Jeter hit his first Major League homer in that April 2 opener at Cleveland. Derek would play in 157 games (156 at short), leading the Yanks with 185 hits, batting .314. He had the longest hitting streak (17) by a Yankee rookie since Joe DiMaggio had one of

18 in 1936. In the postseason, Jeter hit a controversial game-tying homer off Armando Benitez of Baltimore in the eighth inning of Game 1 of the ALCS, when a young fan reached over the wall. The Yankees would go on to win, 5-4, in 11 innings on a dramatic leadoff homer by Bernie Williams.

CONTINUES TO SHINE: After his Rookie of the Year season in 1996, Derek continued to play rock steady, batting .291 with 10 homers and 70 RBI in 159 games, all starts at shortstop. He led the AL with 748 plate appearances in 1997 and finished in the top five in several offensive categories. Derek scored 100+ runs in each of his first two full seasons, only the second Yankee to accomplish this (DiMaggio was the first, 1936-37). He hit .333 (7 for 21) with two home runs in the Division Series versus Cleveland, topping off another great season. In 1998, Jeter continued to shine, batting .324 with 19 homers and 84 RBI, finishing third in voting for American League Most Valuable Player. He set career highs in six batting categories and became the second Yankee shortstop to have 200+ hits in one season with 203 safeties. The other is Hall of Famer Phil Rizzuto, who had exactly 200 in his 1950 MVP season. Derek became the first Yankee to have 50 or more hits in a month since DiMaggio had 53 in July, 1941, during the midst of his awesome 56-game hitting streak. Jeter's month was August, getting 50 hits in 131 at bats in 32 games, a .386 average. Also in that month, Derek had 22 RBI, 30 runs scored, nine doubles and four home runs. He started each of the 13 Yankee postseason games and batted a lofty .353 versus San Diego in the World Series.

A SPECTACULAR SEASON: In 1999, Derek would set career highs in nearly every offensive category: Batting average (.349), runs (134), hits (219), home runs (24), RBI (102), doubles (37), triples (nine) and walks (91). He finished first in the AL in hits (219) and multi-hit games (67); he placed second in: batting average (.349), runs (134) and triples (nine-tied); he was also third in the league in on-base percentage (.438) and fourth in total bases (346-tied). Derek is currently ranked fifth on the all-time Yankee list of batting averages with a .318 mark; he trails only Babe Ruth (.349), Lou Gehrig (.340), Earle Combs (.325) and Joe DiMaggio (.325)—pretty good company that Derek keeps! Derek reached base in each of the first 53 Yankee games of 1999, a record for players since 1961. He became the first Yankee shortstop ever to hit 20+ homers in a season, blasting 24 in 1999. Along with Bernie Williams (202), they became the first Yankee duo to each collect 200+ hits in a season, since Joe DiMaggio and Lou Gehrig did it back in 1937! He has now led his club in hits for the fourth straight season. Was named to his second All-Star Team. In 12 postseason games, Derek hit .375 (18 for 48) and scored ten runs. Hopefully, Derek, now 25, will remain a Yankee for many more seasons to come—but first, the Yankees must sign him to a new contract, which the Yankees did prior to the 2000 season.

ALL-TIME-YANKEE LEADER: Derek ranks fifth in Yankee history in lifetime batting average (.317). At his current pace, Derek's name will undoubtedly be found on most All-Time Yankee lists.

A pensive Derek Jeter hits one high and far.

JETER, DEREK

Yr.	G	AB	R	H	2B	3B	HR	RBI	BB	SB	BA	SA
1995	15	48	5	12	4	1	0	7	3	0	.250	.375
1996	157	582	104	183	25	6	10	78	48	14	.314	.430
1997	159	654	116	190	31	7	10	70	74	23	.291	.405
1998	149	626	127	203	25	8	19	84	57	30	.324	.481
1999	158	627	134	219	37	9	24	102	91	19	.349	.552
2000	148	593	119	201	31	4	15	73	68	22	.339	.481
2001	150	614	110	191	35	3	21	74	56	27	.311	.480
2002	157	644	124	191	26	0	18	75	73	32	.297	.421
8 Yrs.	1093	4388	839	1390	214	38	117	563	470	167	.317	.463

Life. Same.

Division Series

Yr.	G	AB	R	H	2B	3B	HR	RBI	BB	SB	BA	SA
1996	4	17	2	7	1	0	0	1	0	0	.412	.471
1997	5	21	6	7	1	0	2	2	3	1	.333	.667
1998	3	9	0	1	0	0	0	0	2	0	.111	.111
1999	3	11	3	5	1	1	0	0	2	0	.455	.727
2000	5	19	1	4	0	0	0	2	2	0	.211	.211
2001	5	18	2	8	1	0	0	1	1	0	.444	.500
2002	4	16	6	8	0	0	2	3	2	0	.500	.875
7 Yrs.	29	111	20	40	4	1	4	9	12	1	.360	.523

Life. Same.

Championship Series

Yr.	G	AB	R	H	2B	3B	HR	RBI	BB	SB	BA	SA
1996	5	24	5	10	2	0	1	1	0	2	.417	.625
1998	6	25	3	5	1	1	0	2	2	3	.200	.320
1999	5	20	3	7	1	0	1	3	2	0	.350	.550
2000	6	22	6	7	0	0	2	5	6	1	.318	.591
2001	5	17	0	2	0	0	0	2	2	0	.118	.118
5 Yrs.	27	108	17	31	4	1	4	13	12	6	.287	.454

Life. Same.

World Series

Yr.	G	AB	R	H	2B	3B	HR	RBI	BB	SB	BA	SA
1996	6	20	5	5	0	0	0	1	4	1	.250	.250
1998	4	17	4	6	0	0	0	1	3	0	.353	.353
1999	4	17	4	6	1	0	0	1	1	3	.353	.412
2000	5	22	6	9	2	1	2	2	3	0	.409	.863
2001	7	27	3	4	0	0	1	1	0	0	.148	.259
5 Yrs.	26	103	22	30	3	1	3	6	11	4	.291	.427

Life. Same.

JOHN, TOMMY

Nickname: "TJ"
Yankee: 1979-82, 1986-89
Pitcher
Born: May 22, 1943
Birthplace: Terre Haute, IN
Bat: R; Throw: L
Ht: 6'3"; Wt: 180

LONGEVITY: Tommy's ML career spanned 26 seasons—every year from 1963 through 1989 except 1975. He suffered a serious elbow injury with the Dodgers in 1974, and on September 25, 1974, in the first operation of its kind, a tendon was taken from his right forearm and used in the reconstruction of his left elbow. Now whenever a pitcher has this type of operation, it is called "Tommy John" surgery. Tommy missed the entire 1975 season, but returned with the Dodgers in 1976 to win 10 games and go 20-7 in 1977. In baseball history, Tommy ranks 17th in innings pitched (4707); and 22nd in wins (288).

SIGNING WITH YANKEES: In November of 1978, the Yankees signed Tommy to a five-year contract, worth more than $1

million. Tommy had played out his contract with the Dodgers, whom the Yankees had beaten in the World Series a month earlier.

1979 SEASON: Tommy started with nine straight wins on his way to a 21-9 record, becoming the eighth pitcher to win 20 games in both leagues. Tommy was AL Pitcher of the Month in April (4-0, 1.12 ERA) and pitched four consecutive complete games in May. Tommy was selected to the AL team for the All-Star Game, and he finished second to Mike Flanagan in the Cy Young Award voting. Tommy led the Yankees in wins, games started, complete games, innings pitched and shutouts.

1980 SEASON: Tommy started with seven consecutive wins on his way to a 22-9 record. Tommy led the AL in shutouts with six—three against Chicago in three starts—and he led the Yanks in wins, games started, complete games and innings pitched. Losing pitcher in All-Star Game. Tommy was picked as the lefthanded pitcher on the All-Star team picked by *The Sporting News*. On August 15, Tommy beat the Orioles in a critical game, halting the Baltimore charge. Tommy left in the seventh inning of Game 3 of the 1980 ALCS, leading, 2-1, but Rich Gossage couldn't hold the lead.

CLASSY PITCHER: Tommy had a great sinkerball, a good curveball and excellent control. He "threw grounders" and relied on double plays to avoid trouble. He resembled Whitey Ford in 1) fluid motion, 2) classy style, and 3) making sluggers look silly. In a 1980 complete-game victory, Tommy used only 81 pitches. He once said of pitching: "I was always taught the art of pitching was to throw as close to the plate as possible without it being a strike."

1981 SEASON: Tommy won two Opening Days, both against Texas, the scheduled one on April 9, and the August 10 game that started the Second Season after a two-month strike. On August 13, his 2½-year-old son, Travis, fell from a third story window and was in a coma 14 days; he eventually made a fine recovery. Tommy pitched five consecutive complete games in September. Tommy won the Lou Gehrig Memorial Award in 1981. He won Game 1 of the ALCS and Game 2 of the World Series. In Game 6 of the World Series, with the score 1-1 in the fourth inning, Manager Bob Lemon replaced Tommy with pinch-hitter Bobby Murcer; the TV camera caught Tommy's unrestrained anger about the decision. Tommy's ERA for 13 innings in the World Series was 0.69.

FALL FROM GRACE: Through 1981 Tommy had good relations with George Steinbrenner, and he often publicly praised the owner. Hard working, conservative and religious, Tommy stayed out of controversy. This changed in February 1982 when he took the Yankees to arbitration before accepting an extra year on his contract; he was no longer the golden boy. With Tommy struggling, Manager Gene Michael sent Tommy to the bullpen in July 1982, and he responded by demanding a trade—but only to Boston, Milwaukee, Kansas City or California. On July 31, 1982, Tommy nearly came to blows with club executive Bill Bergesch; Tommy angrily confronted Bergesch about remarks Bergesch reportedly made about Tommy's lack of appreciation for what the Yankees had done for the Johns when their son was in critical condition in 1981. Tommy continued to make statements that seemed to be designed to force a trade.

DUMPED: On August 29, 1982, Tommy pitched a three-hitter against Toronto. Two days later the Yankees traded Tommy to California for a player to be named later. In November 1982, the Yankees got pitcher Dennis Rasmussen.

RETURNING TO NEW YORK: Tommy in 1986 came to spring training with the Yankees as a non-roster invitee. He made the team, but an injury prevented him from pitching until May 2. It was an injury-riddled season; he was disabled two months with a strained Achilles tendon, and on September 3 he was lost for the year with a fractured left thumb after falling off the bullpen mound in Oakland.

COMEBACK SEASONS: In 1987, at the age of 44, Tommy went 13-6 and was the club's workhorse; he led the Yanks in games started (33) and innings pitched (187). In 1988, Tommy again led the Yanks in games started (32). On July 27, 1988, Tommy tied a ML record by making three errors on one play. He pitched the season opener in 1989, but he was released after making 10 starts.

ALL-TIME YANKEE LEADER: Tommy ranks 20th in Yankee history in winning percentage (.603), 19th in innings pitched (1367) and wins (91), and is tied for 20th in shutouts (12).

JOHN, TOMMY

Yr.	W-L	Pct.	SA	G	GS	CG	IP	H	BB	SO	SH	ERA
1979	21-9	700	0	37	36	17	276	268	65	111	3	2.96
1980	22-9	.710	0	36	36	16	265	270	56	78	6	3.43
1981	9-8	.529	0	20	20	7	140	135	39	50	0	2.63
1982	10-10	.500	0	30	26	9	187	190	34	54	2	3.66
1986	5-3	.625	0	13	10	1	71	73	15	28	0	2.93
1987	13-6	.684	0	33	33	3	188	212	47	63	1	4.03
1988	9-8	.529	0	35	32	0	176	221	46	81	0	4.49
1989	2-7	.222	0	10	10	0	64	87	22	18	0	5.80
8 Yrs.	91-60	.603	0	214	203	53	1367	1456	324	483	12	3.59
Life.	288-231	.555	4	760	700	162	4707	4783	1259	2245	46	3.34

Divisional Playoff

Yr.	G	IP	BB	SO	H	W-L	SA
1981	1	7	2	0	8	0-1	0
1	1	7	2	0	8	0-1	0
Life. Same.							

Championship Series

Yr.	G	IP	BB	SO	H	W-L	SA
1980	1	6.2	1	3	8	0-0	0
1981	1	6	1	3	6	1-0	0
2 Yrs.	2	12.2	2	6	14	1-0	0
Life	7	47.2	15	27	40	4-1	0

World Series

Yr.	G	IP	BB	SO	H	W-L	SA
1981	3	13	0	8	11	1-0	0
1 Yr.	3	13	0	8	11	1-0	0
Life.	6	33.2	7	21	34	2-1	0

JOHNSON, BILLY

Nickname: "The Bull"
Yankee: 1943 (military) 1946-51
Third Baseman, 1B
Born: August 30, 1918
Birthplace: Montclair, NJ
Bat: R; Throw: R
Ht: 5'9"; Wt: 180

HONORS: *The Sporting News* selected Billy as the third baseman on its 1943 ML All-Star team. Billy was picked to the AL team for the 1947 All-Star Game.

YOUNG PROSPECT: The Yanks signed Billy as a kid in 1937 for $100. He spent six years working his way up through the Yankee farm system before reaching the Yanks in 1943.

ROOKIE SEASON: Billy started at third base in his rookie season and played in all 155 Yankee games that year. Billy was a star at the plate, leading the Yanks in batting (.280), hits (166) and at-bats (592). He was the second biggest run producer on the club with 94 RBIs. He was equally sensational defensively, leading AL third basemen in putouts (183), assists (326) and double plays (32). Billy also hit into 27 double plays as a batter, an AL record. But all things considered, Billy had a terrific rookie season.

MILITARY DUTY: Billy missed the 1944-45 baseball seasons while serving in the military.

AFTER THE WAR: In 1946 Billy returned to the Yanks and was the club's regular third baseman in 1947-48. His 95 RBIs in 1947 were the most by a Yankee third baseman until Graig Nettles knocked in 107 runs in 1977. Casey Stengel platooned Billy with Bobby Brown at third base in 1949-50. In 1949 Billy was 6-for-13 as a Yankee pinch-hitter.

WORLD SERIES: Billy is tied with Tommy Leach and Tris Speaker for the most lifetime World Series triples (four). In Game 3 of the 1943 Series, Billy's three-run triple was the key hit in a 6-2 Yankee win. The eight runs Billy scored in the 1947 Series led both teams and the three triples he rapped is a record for an AL player in one Series. His eight runs tied a seven-game Series record for most runs

TRADED: In the spring of 1950, "The Bull" had a bitter salary dispute with the Yankee front office and became a holdout. Holdouts in those days were usually headed for a trade. In May, 1951, the Yanks dealt Billy to the Cardinals for first baseman Don Bollweg and $15,000.

JOHNSON, BILLY

Yr.	G	AB	R	H	2B	3B	HR	RBI	BB	SB	BA	SA
1943	155	592	70	166	24	6	5	94	53	3	.280	.367
1946	85	296	51	77	14	5	4	35	31	1	.260	.382
1947	132	494	67	141	19	8	10	95	44	1	.285	.417
1948	127	446	59	131	20	6	12	64	41	0	.294	.446
1949	113	329	48	82	11	3	8	56	48	1	.249	.374
1950	108	327	44	85	16	2	6	40	42	1	.260	.376
1951	15	40	5	12	3	0	0	4	7	0	.300	.375
7 Yrs.	735	2524	344	694	107	30	45	388	266	7	.275	.395
Life.	964	3253	419	882	141	33	61	487	347	13	.271	.391

World Series

Yr.	G	AB	R	H	2B	3B	HR	RBI	BA
1943	5	20	3	6	1	1	0	3	.300
1947	7	26	8	7	0	3	0	2	.269
1949	2	7	0	1	0	0	0	0	.143
1950	4	6	0	0	0	0	0	0	.000
4 Yrs.	18	59	11	14	1	4	0	5	.237

Life. Same.

JOHNSON, HANK
(BORN HENRY WARD JOHNSON)

Yankee: 1925-26,'28-32
Pitcher
Born: May 21, 1906
Birthplace: Bradenton, FL
Died: August 20, 1982
Bat: R; Throw: R
Ht: 5'11"; Wt: 175

EARLY ML CAREER: Hank came up to the Yanks as a 19-year-old rookie phenom in 1925. He spent the 1926 season in the minors, but did appear in one Yankee game and recorded a save.

1928 SEASON: In 1928 Hank made the Yanks for good. He was extremely valuable to the Yanks; over the season he beat the Philadelphia A's five times. (The Yanks won the AL pennant, finishing 2½ games ahead of the A's.) On September 11, Hank beat the A's and Lefty Grove, 5-3, in an important contest. (Babe Ruth's two-run HR won the game.) This win took the fight out of the A's. On August 1, he went 5 for 5 in a game (all singles). Hank led the AL in hitting batters (12).

YANKEE STARTER: From 1928-31, Hank was one of the top four Yankee starters. He was also used often as a relief pitcher. Only 48% of his Yankee career appearances were as a starter. A back injury ruined his 1929 season. In 1930 Hank led AL pitchers in games won in relief with nine. Hank was a good friend of Babe Ruth, and the Ruths were guests at the Johnson's Florida home during one spring training camp. Hank and Babe enjoyed hunting together.

CLUB LEADERSHIP: Hank tied for club leadership in games pitched in 1930 (44) and 1931 (40). In 1931 he led the Yanks in saves (four).

RETIREMENT: Hank retired during the 1932 season. He returned to the mound to pitch for the Red Sox (1933-35) and later for the A's (1936) and Cincinnati Reds (1939).

JOHNSON, HANK

Yr.	W-L	Pct.	SA	G	GS	CG	IP	H	BB	SO	SH	ERA
1925	1-3	.250	0	24	4	2	67	88	37	25	1	6.85
1926	0-0	.000	1	1	0	0	1	2	2	0	0	18.00
1928	14-9	.609	0	31	22	10	199	188	104	110	1	4.30
1929	3-3	.500	0	12	8	2	43	37	39	24	0	5.06
1930	14-11	.560	2	44	15	7	175	177	104	115	1	4.67
1931	13-8	.619	4	40	23	8	196	176	102	106	0	4.72
1932	2-2	.500	0	5	4	2	31	34	15	27	0	4.88
7 Yrs.	47-36	.566	7	157	76	31	713	702	403	407	3	4.84
Life.	63-56	.529	11	249	116	45	1066	1107	567	568	4	4.76

JONES, SAD SAM

Nickname: "Sad Sam"
Yankee: 1922-26
Pitcher
Born: July 26, 1892
Birthplace: Woodsfield, OH
Died: July 6, 1966
Bat: R; Throw: R
Ht: 6'; Wt: 170

CAME TO YANKS: In December of 1921, the Yanks obtained "Sad Sam," along with "Bullet Joe" Bush and Everett Scott, from the Red Sox in a deal that sent Roger Peckinpaugh, Jack Quinn, Rip Collins and a minor leaguer to Boston.

DURABLE GREAT: Sam pitched 22 consecutive seasons in the AL, an unbroken string of seasons that represents an AL record, also held by Cy Young. Sam pitched for the Indians (1914-15), Red Sox (1916-21), Yankees (1922-26), Browns (1927), Senators (1928-31) and White Sox (1932-35). The Tigers and A's were the only teams of the then-eight-team AL for which Sam did not work.

YANKEE STAR: The 1922 Sam was the Yanks' fifth starter but he was especially valuable as a relief pitcher. His eight saves led the AL. Sam was the star of the 1923 Yankee pitching staff. In 1924 he was the Yanks' fifth starter and his disappointing season was a factor in the Yanks' second-place finish. "Sad Sam" and Herb Pennock were the righty-lefty aces of the 1925 Yankee pitching staff in a season in which Sam allowed 127 earned runs, the most in Yankee history. In 1926 Sam was the Yanks' fourth starter.

TOUGH LOSS: On May 20, 1922, Sam took the mound before a capacity crowd at Yankee Stadium for an important encounter with the St. Louis Browns. Sam entered the ninth inning with a 2-1 lead and seemingly secured the third out by receiving a throw at first base after a ground ball. In fact, the umpire signaled the end of the game and the crowd charged onto the field. But Sam had dropped the ball, the runner was safe, and after the field was cleared, play was resumed. The Browns scored seven runs and won the heartbreaker, 8-2. Sam understandably was so upset that he had several poor outings following this game.

1923 SEASON: Sam was the ace of the Yankee pitching staff in 1923, the first year the Yanks won the World Championship. He was used as both a starter and reliever. He led the club in wins (21) AND saves (four). He also led the team in games pitched (39) and shutouts (three). "Sad Sam" capped a fantastic season by pitching a no-hitter against the Philadelphia A's on September 4, winning, 2-0.

CLUB LEADERSHIP: Three times Sam led Yankee pitchers in saves. Twice he led the Yanks in games pitched. In 1922 Sam tied for the club leadership in complete games (21) and in 1925 he tied for the club leadership in games started (31).

WORLD SERIES: In Game 3 of the 1923 Series Sam pitched a beautiful game but lost to the New York Giants, 1-0, when Casey Stengel hit a seventh inning HR. Sam pitched two scoreless innings in relief to record a save in the final game of the 1923 Series to clinch the Yanks' first World Championship.

TRADED: Sam was dealt to the St. Louis Browns in February, 1927. The Yanks got outfielder Cedric Durst and pitcher Joe Giard in the trade.

STARS THE YANKEES OBTAINED FROM THE RED SOX BETWEEN 1918-23:

Duffy Lewis, OF (1919)
Carl Mays, P (1919)
Babe Ruth, OF (1920)
Wally Schang, C (1921)
Waite Hoyt, P (1921)
Everett Scott, SS (1922)
SAD SAM JONES, P (1922)
Joe Bush, P (1922)
Joe Dugan, 3B (1922)
Herb Pennock, P (1923)

JONES, SAM

Yr.	W-L	Pct.	SA	G	GS	CG	IP	H	BB	SO	SH	ERA
1922	13-13	.500	8	45	28	21	260	270	76	81	0	3.67
1923	21-8	.724	4	39	27	18	243	239	69	68	3	3.63
1924	9-6	.600	3	36	21	8	179	187	76	53	3	3.63
1925	15-21	.417	2	43	31	14	247	267	104	92	1	4.63
1926	9-8	.529	5	39	23	6	161	186	80	69	1	4.98
5 Yrs.	67-56	.545	22	202	130	67	1089	1149	405	363	8	4.06
Life.	229-217	.513	31	647	487	250	3883	4084	1396	1223	36	3.84

World Series

Yr.	G	IP	BB	SO	H	W-L	SA
1922	2	2	1	0	1	0-0	0
1923	2	10	2	3	5	0-1	1
1926	1	1	2	1	2	0-0	0
3 Yrs.	5	13	5	4	8	0-1	1
Life.	6	22	10	9	15	0-2	1

KAMIENIECKI, SCOTT

Nickname: Kamie
Yankee: 1991-96
Pitcher
Born: April 19, 1964
Birthplace: Mt. Clemens, MI
Bat: R; Throw: R
Ht: 6'; Wt: 195

DRAFTED BY YANKEES: Scott was selected by the Yanks in the 1986 free-agent draft. After spending four seasons in the minor leagues, Scott was brought up to the Big Show in June, appearing in nine games with a 4-4 record for the Yanks. In 1992, Scott broke into the regular starting rotation tossing 28 games and finishing with a record of 6-14. He had his most productive season for New York in 1993, going 10-7 in 20 games started, with a 4.06 ERA.

DISABLED LIST: During his six-year stint with the Yankees, Kamie spent much of the time on the disabled list. In his last two years with the Yanks (1995 and 1996), Scott spent two months on the DL in 1995 and appeared in only seven games in 1996, not pitching again after July. Kamie was granted free-

agency in December, 1996, being signed by the Baltimore Orioles for 1997. After three seasons with Baltimore, Scott split his last season (2000) between Cleveland and Atlanta.

KAMIENIECKI, SCOTT

Yr.	W-L	Pct.	SA	G	GS	CG	IP	H	BB	SO	SH	ERA
1991	4-4	.500	0	9	9	0	55	54	22	34	0	3.90
1992	6-14	.300	0	28	28	4	188	193	74	88	0	4.36
1993	10-7	.588	1	30	20	2	154	163	59	72	0	4.08
1994	8-6	.571	0	22	16	1	117	115	59	71	0	3.76
1995	7-6	.538	0	17	16	1	90	83	49	43	0	4.01
1996	1-2	.333	0	7	5	0	23	36	19	15	0	11.12
6 Yrs.	36-39	.480	1	113	94	8	627	644	282	323	0	4.33
Life.	53-59	.473	5	250	138	8	975.2	1006	446	542	0	4.52

Division Series

Yr.	G	IP	BB	SO	H	W-L	SA
1995	1	5.0	4	4	9	0-0	0

Life. Still active through 1999.

Scott Kamieniecki

KEATING, RAY

Yankee: 1912-16, 1918
Pitcher
Born: July 21, 1891
Birthplace: Bridgeport, CT
Died: December 29, 1963
Bat: R; Throw: R
Ht: 5'11"; Wt: 185

EARLY PROMISE: In 1912 Ray was a promising 21-year-old ML rookie pitcher in the Yankees' last season at Hilltop Park. He was the Yanks' No. 4 starter in 1913 when he tied for the club leadership in shutouts (2). In 1914 Ray was the Yanks' No. 2 starter and led the Yankee pitching staff in strikeouts (109).

FINAL YANKEE YEARS: Ray was used less in 1915 (fifth starter) and 1916 (seventh starter) than in his previous Yankee years. In 1917 Ray was out of the ML's, and in 1918 the Yankees used him sparingly and mostly in long relief.

LEFT YANKS: In March of 1919, the Yanks sold Ray's contract to the Boston Braves. Ray ended his ML career with the Braves in 1919.

KEATING, RAY													
Yr.	W-L	Pct.	SA	G	GS	CG	IP	H	BB	SO	SH	ERA
1912	0-3	.000	0	6	5	3	36	36	18	21	0	5.80
1913	6-12	.333	0	28	21	9	151	147	51	83	2	3.21
1914	7-11	.389	1	34	25	14	210	198	67	109	0	2.96
1915	3-6	.333	0	11	10	8	79	66	45	37	1	3.63
1916	5-6	.455	0	14	12	6	91	91	37	35	0	3.07
1918	2-2	.500	0	15	6	1	48	39	30	16	0	3.91
6 Yrs.	23-40	.365	1	108	79	41	616	577	248	301	3	3.36
Life.	30-51	.370	1	130	93	50	752	706	293	349	4	3.29

KEELER, WILLIE
(BORN WILLIAM HENRY KEELER)

Nickname: "Wee Willie"
Yankee: 1903-09
Outfielder
Born: March 3, 1872
Birthplace: Brooklyn, NY
Died: January 1, 1923
Bat: L; Throw: L
Ht: 5'4"; Wt: 140

HONORS: In 1939 Willie was inducted into the Baseball Hall of Fame, baseball's ultimate honor.

CAME TO YANKS: After hitting .333 for Brooklyn in 1902, the lure of a bigger salary enticed Willie to jump the NL for the AL. In the raiding war with the NL that was waged by AL President Ban Johnson, the signing of Willie may have been the junior circuit's biggest catch. Willie in 1903 joined the Yanks (Highlanders) for the club's first season of play. He was one of the game's great gate attractions and one of the first players to earn $10,000. (The NL salary limit was $2,400.)

1903 SEASON: On April 22, 1903, the Yanks played the first game in the club's history and Willie batted second in the order and played right field. In the first inning, Willie scored the first run in the team's history. He had a somewhat poor 1903 season, his .313 batting average his lowest since 1893, but still led the Yanks in batting, hits and runs scored. Willie was the club's first star among players who played every day.

GREAT PLAYER: Willie was an established ML star when he joined the Yanks, and indeed most of his great seasons were behind him. Willie was a NL star for New York (1892-93), Brooklyn (1893), Baltimore (1894-98) and Brooklyn (1899-1902). He batted .300 or better in 16 seasons! For the Yanks, Willie was the club's regular rightfielder in the first seven seasons of the franchise (1903-09).

BAT CONTROL: With the Orioles, Willie and John McGraw invented the hit-and-run play and Willie was expert at handling the bat in the play. Willie was an excellent place hitter. In fact, he was the best place hitter in the era of place hitters. Handling the bat skillfully, Willie almost always put the ball into play. He was a fantastic bunter. When infields played him deep, he bunted for hits, and when the fielders played in, he hit the ball over their heads. He just had tremendous bat dexterity. Willie swung the shortest bat (30½") ever used in ML baseball and used the entire ballpark, hitting to all fields.

BATTING-EYE: Once questioned about hitting, Willie offered an explanation that was to become famous: "I hit 'em where they ain't." A great batting-eye also helped Willie. He struck out only .019 times per at-bat for his ML career, making him the second hardest man (behind Joe Sewell) in ML history to strike out. The tiny guy was a great pure hitter, a smart hitter with a sensitive batting eye. Only in 1907 did "Wee Willie" make fewer than 100 hits (99) over a season in which he appeared in 100 or more games.

YANKEE RECORDS: In 1905 Willie made 42 sacrifices, setting a Yankee club record that has stood for over 90 seasons and is unlikely to ever be broken. In 1906 Willie cracked 166 singles, another Yankee record, until Steve Sax had 171 in 1989.

CLUB LEADERSHIP: In three consecutive seasons (1903-05) Willie led the Yanks in batting average and hits. He led the club in games played and runs scored in 1903, 1905 and 1906. Twice he led the team in at-bats. In 1904 Willie led the Yanks in slugging (.409).

BASEBALL'S ALL-TIME LEADER LIST: Willie's .345 lifetime batting average is the tied for seventh highest in ML history for those players with at least 4000 at-bats. Willie is 21st on baseball's all-time runs scored list (1720). He is 29th on baseball's hit list (2932).

ALL-TIME YANKEE LEADER: Willie is tied for 17th in batting average (.294) in Yankee history, and is 20th in steals (118).

LEFT YANKS: "Wee Willie" was dealt from the Yanks to the New York Giants following the 1909 season. He played in 19 games for the Giants in 1910 and that was the end of his ML career.

KEELER, WILLIE

Yr.	G	AB	R	H	2B	3B	HR	RBI	BB	SB	BA	SA
1903	132	512	95	160	14	7	0	32	32	24	.313	.367
1904	143	543	78	186	14	8	2	40	35	21	.343	.409
1905	149	560	81	169	14	4	4	38	43	19	.302	.363
1906	152	592	96	180	9	3	2	33	40	23	.304	.340
1907	107	423	50	99	5	2	0	17	15	7	.234	.255
1908	91	323	38	85	3	1	1	14	31	14	.263	.288
1909	99	360	44	95	7	5	1	32	24	10	.264	.319
7 Yrs.	873	3313	482	974	66	30	10	206	220	118	.294	.341
Life.	2123	8591	1719	2932	242	145	33	810	524	495	.341	.415

KEICH, MIKE

Yr.	W-L	Pct.	SA	G	GS	CG	IP	H	BB	SO	SH	ERA
1969	4-6	.400	1	28	13	1	105	91	49	66	0	4.54
1970	6-3	.667	0	26	14	1	99	103	55	63	0	4.83
1971	10-9	.526	0	37	24	3	170	167	82	93	0	4.07
1972	10-13	.435	0	29	28	2	175	172	76	78	0	3.70
1973	1-1	.500	0	5	4	0	15	20	14	4	0	9.20
5 Yrs.	31-32	.492	1	125	83	7	564	553	276	304	0	4.31
Life.	39-51	.433	6	235	112	8	861	875	442	497	1	4.59

KELLER, CHARLIE

Nickname: "King Kong"
Yankee: 1939-43 (military) '45-49, '52
Outfielder
Born: September 12, 1916
Birthplace: Middletown, MD
Died: May 23, 1990
Bat: L; Throw: R
Ht: 5'10"; Wt: 185

KEKICH, MIKE

Yankee: 1969-73
Pitcher
Born: April 2, 1945
Birthplace: San Diego, CA
Bat: R; Throw: L
Ht: 6'2"; Wt: 200

CAME TO YANKS: Mike began his ML career pitching for the Los Angeles Dodgers in 1965 (0-1) and 1968 (2-10). In December of 1968 the Dodgers traded Mike to the Yanks for outfielder Andy Kosco.

VERSATILE PITCHER: Throughout his Yankee career, Mike handled the difficult chore of being a spot starter and long reliever. He was the club's sixth starter in 1969; fifth starter in 1970 and 1971; and fourth starter in 1972. A leg injury hampered Mike during the 1970 campaign. In 1971 Mike hurled a one-hitter.

FAMILY EXCHANGE: A scandal of sorts involved Mike and teammate Fritz Peterson before the 1973 season. Mike honestly disclosed that he and Peterson had switched families, exchanging wives, children, pets and all. Some critics were unable to accept such an interpretation of the time's new morality, and both men and their families were hit with negative publicity. Eventually, Peterson married Susanne Kekich and kept the two Kekich girls. But Mike did not marry Marilyn Peterson. The episode had a dreadful effect on Mike, who lost many friends and was on the verge of a breakdown.

TRADED: In June of 1973, the Yanks traded Mike to the Indians for pitcher Lowell Palmer. (Palmer never appeared for the Yankees.) Mike spent most of 1973 in therapy. He was 1-4 for Cleveland in 1973 and 0-0 for Texas in 1975.

COURAGEOUS MAN: On top of his emotional problems, after leaving the Yanks, Mike had a serious motorcycle accident, abdominal surgery from which he nearly died, and bouts with food poisoning. Attempting a comeback to the ML's, Mike played in the minors, Japan and South America. He remarried in June 1977 and his luck returned. In 1977 he made a comeback with Seattle (5-4). As a Yankee, Mike was known as a fun lover and practical joker. He was pilot, motorcyclist, skier and hot-air balloner. In 1981 Mike was a pitcher in Mexico, where he also attended medical school.

GREAT PROSPECT: Charlie was a powerful home run slugger at the University of Maryland when the Yanks signed him, reportedly for a bonus of about $10,000. Charlie was immediately called "the next Babe Ruth." The 1937 season was his first in professional baseball, and the 20-year-old played at the Yanks' top farm club, the Newark Bears. Charlie hit .353, led the Bears to a Little World Series championship and was named the Minor League Player of the Year by *The Sporting News*. In 1938 he again played right field for Newark and hit .365. Charlie is a member of the International League Hall of Fame for his two

Charlie "King Kong" Keller played 11 seasons with the Yanks.

years of tremendous play for Newark. One of the best prospects ever to come through the Yankee farm system, Charlie joined the Yanks as a 22-year-old rookie in 1939.

POPULAR YOUNG STAR: In his rookie season of 1939, Charlie immediately became a popular player with his teammates and the Yankee fans. He was dubbed "King Kong" in jest, a tribute to his muscular frame and bushy eyebrows, but it was a nickname that Charlie hated. He was sensational in his first seven ML seasons and certainly one of the game's true stars. Charlie was also one of the great hustlers on the field in baseball history. He played his heart out in every game.

LATER YEARS IN BASEBALL: Charlie probably would have become an all-time baseball great except for some unfortunate circumstances that intervened. Charlie missed the 1944 season and much of 1945 while serving in the Merchant Marines. In 1947 he slipped a disk in his back, forcing him to miss most of the season. He had surgery for a back ailment, a problem that would never again allow him to be 100% healthy as a baseball player. Charlie missed much of the 1948 season because of a broken hand. He was a part-time outfielder and pinch-hitter in 1949.

FEARED SLUGGER: Charlie was an awesome slugger and possibly the strongest player of his era. In the International League he hit with power to all fields, but as a Yankee rookie in 1939 he hit just 11 HRs because his shots to left and center fields stayed in mammoth Yankee Stadium. Manager Joe McCarthy worked with him on pulling the ball toward the Stadium's right field "porch" and some high home-run totals followed for Charlie. Three times he hit more than 30 HRs in a season. Pitchers feared Charlie and walked him more than 100 times in each of five seasons. Casey Stengel said of Charlie, "That boy thought he could hit, and showed it the way he stood up at the plate, and he COULD hit." Charlie homered in consecutive pinch-hit appearances on September 12 and 14, 1948.

OUTFIELDER: For most of his first two Yankee seasons (1939-40), Charlie played right field. He was switched to left field in 1941. In the 143 games that he played in the outfield in 1943, Charlie made just two errors. He fielded 1.000 in 1945, playing 44 games in the outfield.

CLUB LEADERSHIP: Charlie led the Yanks in many seasons in offensive categories, including walks five times; HRs four times; slugging three times; and triples and runs scored twice. In 1946 he led the Yanks in games played (150-tie), runs (98), hits (148), doubles (29), triples (10), HRs (30), RBIs (101), walks (113) and slugging (.533). The time he missed while in the Merchant Marines had not left Charlie rusty!

LEAGUE LEADER: In 1940 and 1943 Charlie led the AL in walks. His HR percentage led all AL sluggers in 1943 (6.1).

ALL-TIME YANKEE LEADER: Charlie's Yankee career slugging average (.518) is the sixth highest in Yankee history for those players with at least 1500 at-bats as a Yankee. He is ninth on the all-time Yank walk list (760). Charlie ranks 13th on the Yankee HR list (184). Keller also ranks 11th in triples (69) and 18th in RBI (723).

ALL-STAR GAME: Charlie was picked to the AL All-Star team for five All-Star Games (1940, '41, '43, '46, '47). He hit a HR in the 1946 All-Star Game.

ON-BASE AVERAGE: Charlie's lifetime on-base average (.410) is one of the highest of all time, ranking 29th. Only five ML leftfielders (Ted Williams, Joe Jackson, Stan Musial, Jesse Burkett and Ed Delahanty) have higher lifetime on-base averages than Charlie's.

WORLD SERIES: Charlie is near the top-10 on the all-time World Series slugging list (.611). In his first Series, the 1939 Series, he personally tore the Cincinnati Reds apart. He led both teams in batting (.438), hits (seven), HRs (three), runs (eight) and RBIs (six). In Game 3 Charlie cracked two HRs and had four RBIs, leading the Yanks to a 7-3 win. Then in the tenth inning of Game 4, the final game, Charlie scored while cracking into Cincinnati catcher Ernie Lombardi at home plate, and while the dazed Lombardi "snoozed" (the press's term) Joe DiMaggio also scored, and the Yanks wrapped up another World Championship. In Game 4 of the 1941 Series with Brooklyn, Charlie doubled home the winning runs in the ninth inning after Tommy Henrich fanned with two outs but reached first base on a passed ball.

FINAL PLAYING DAYS: In December of 1949, the Yanks released Charlie who signed with the Tigers. He was used mainly as a pinch-hitter by Tiger Manager Red Rolfe, a former Yankee teammate. Charlie hit .314 in 1950 and .258 in 1951. The Yanks re-signed Charlie in September of 1952 after his release from Detroit. He played in two Yankee games, and then retired as a player after the close of the 1952 season.

MARYLAND HORSEMAN: In 1957, Charlie was the Yanks' first base coach. He had a couple sons who were prospects in the Yankee minors. After retiring as a player, and until he died in 1990, Charlie was mostly devoted to running his successful horse farm located in the beautiful countryside near Frederick, MD. The farm was named "Yankeeland," and many of the famous race horses bred there had Yankee in their names.

KELLER, CHARLIE

Yr.	G	AB	R	H	2B	3B	HR	RBI	BB	SB	BA	SA
1939	111	398	87	133	21	6	11	83	81	6	.334	.500
1940	138	500	102	143	18	15	21	93	106	8	.286	.508
1941	140	507	102	151	24	10	33	122	102	6	.298	.580
1942	152	544	106	159	24	9	26	108	114	14	.292	.513
1943	141	512	97	139	15	11	31	86	106	7	.271	.525
1945	44	163	26	49	7	4	10	34	31	0	.301	.577
1946	150	538	98	148	29	10	30	101	113	1	.275	.533
1947	45	151	36	36	6	1	13	36	41	0	.238	.550
1948	83	247	41	66	15	2	6	44	41	1	.267	.417
1949	60	116	17	29	4	1	3	16	25	2	.250	.379
1952	2	1	0	0	0	0	0	0	0	0	.000	.000
11 Yrs.	1066	3677	712	1053	163	69	184	723	760	45	.286	.518
Life.	1170	3790	725	1085	166	72	189	760	784	45	.286	.518

World Series

Yr.	G	AB	R	H	2B	3B	HR	RBI	BA
1939	4	16	8	7	1	1	3	6	.438
1941	5	18	5	7	2	0	0	5	.389
1942	5	20	2	4	0	0	2	5	.200
1943	5	18	3	4	0	1	0	2	.222
4 Yrs.	19	72	18	22	3	2	5	18	.306

Life. Same.

KELLY, PAT

Yankee: 1991-97
Second Baseman
Born: October 14, 1967
Birthplace: Philadelphia, PA
Bat: R; Throw: R
Ht: 6'; Wt: 160

CAME FROM THE YANKEE FARM SYSTEM: Kelly, a ninth-round 1988 draft selection by the Yankees, had been a shortstop at West Chester State, but the Yankees immediately turned the Philadelphia native into a second baseman. In working his way through the Yankee farm system, Kelly impressed observers with his fielding acrobatics.

JOINS THE YANKEES: When Kelly was called up in May, 1991, the Yankees made room at second base by moving Steve Sax to third. Within a week, however, Sax pulled his rank and switched positions with Kelly. The rookie coped bravely with having to learn the foreign position, hit .242 in 96 games, and was 12 for 13 in stolen-base attempts. Sax was traded and Kelly became the regular second baseman in 1992. He battled injuries—left thumb, right knee—and hit only .226. He was sidelined by a hamstring pull for most of the 1993 season's final weeks, but he did hit a solid .273 and was an excellent fielder. He was especially proficient at inside baseball—the kind made famous by John McGraw—leading the Yankees in stolen bases, 14; sacrifice bunts, 10; and bunt singles, 14.

BEST SEASON WITH THE YANKS: Kelly hit .280, his big-league career high in 1994. No longer did he seem overpowered by the league's tougher right-handed pitchers. He was a more relaxed hitter, more patient, stroking the ball to all fields, and developing extra-base power to the gaps. He led the league with 14 sacrifice bunts. Defensively, he made use of his outstanding range, sure hands, and excellent ability in turning the double play. Pat lost his job to Randy Velarde, who in November, 1995 signed as a free agent from California, having been lured with the chance to play daily. There was talk that either Roberto Alomar or Craig Biggio of Houston were possible acquisitions for second base. But Biggio re-signed with Houston, and Alomar accepted a huge contract offer from Baltimore.

SUSCEPTIBLE TO INJURIES: Kelly's problem throughout his career with the Yanks was his susceptibility to injuries. Disabled for long stretches in 1995 (as well as in 1996 and 1997), he hit only .237 and gave way to Velarde. In November, 1995, he underwent arthroscopic surgery to repair a muscle tear in his right shoulder. In 1996, Pat played in only 13 games, spending much time in the minors for rehabilitation purposes.

MAKES YANKEE EXIT: In 1997, Kelly had to share his second-base duties with others due to ongoing rehab. Pat played in 67 games, batting a lowly .242. After seven seasons in pinstripes, Pat finished his career with the Cardinals in 1998 and the Blue Jays in 1999.

KELLY, PAT

Yr.	G	AB	R	H	2B	3B	HR	RBI	BB	SB	BA	SA
1991	96	298	35	72	12	4	3	23	15	12	.242	.339
1992	106	318	38	72	22	2	7	27	25	8	.226	.374
1993	127	406	49	111	24	1	7	51	24	14	.273	.389
1994	93	286	35	80	21	2	3	41	19	6	.280	.399
1995	89	270	32	64	12	1	4	29	23	8	.237	.333
1996	13	21	4	3	0	0	0	2	2	0	.143	.143
1997	67	120	25	29	6	1	2	10	14	8	.242	.358
7 Yrs.	591	1719	218	431	97	11	26	183	122	56	.251	.365
Life.	681	1988	253	495	109	11	36	217	145	61	.249	.369

Division Series

Yr.	G	AB	R	H	2B	3B	HR	RBI	BB	SB	BA	SA
1995	5	3	3	0	0	0	0	1	1	0	.000	.000
Life.	Same											

KELLY, ROBERTO

Yankee: 1987-92
Outfielder
Born: October 1, 1964
Birthplace: Panama City, Panama
Bat: R; Throw: R
Ht: 6'2"; Wt: 180

PRIME PROSPECT: In February 1982, Yankee Scout Fred Ferreira signed Roberto in Panama. Roberto broke into the Yankee farm system as a 17-year-old in 1982, hitting .198 at Bradenton. Roberto didn't develop into a hitter until 1986 when he hit .291 at Albany-Colonie. His first display of power came in 1987 at Columbus when he hit 13 HRs; he also stole 51 bases. Columbus Manager Bucky Dent said: "I've never seen a player improve more than Roberto, and part of the reason is his willingness to listen."

Pat Kelly

DIFFICULTY GETTING ESTABLISHED: Roberto was impressive in two brief trials with the Yankees in 1987, and the Yankees rejected several trade offers for him in the off-season. The plan for 1988 was to put Roberto in center, taking advantage of his range and exceptional fielding, and moving Rickey Henderson to left, but on May 21, with Roberto hitting .254, he was optioned to Columbus. Roberto was recalled to New York on June 24, but on June 28 he ran into the centerfield wall trying to catch a triple and suffered a sprained left wrist and a bruised right knee; he was on the Disabled List until September 1 and couldn't bat the remainder of the year because of the wrist injury. Claudell Washington had done a fine job replacing Kelly, but the Yankees let Washington move on as a free agent over the winter, and once again in 1989 the centerfield job was open for Kelly to win.

A STAR IS BORN: Roberto in the spring of 1989 earned back his centerfield job—he kept it four seasons—and played like a potential superstar, hitting .302, stealing 35 bases and catching everything in center; and he did all this while being concerned about unrest in his native Panama. In 1990, Roberto led the Yankees in games (162), ABs (641), runs (85), hits (183), doubles (32) triples (four) and batting (.285). He led AL outfielders with 430 total chances in 1990. Although Roberto in 1991 was disabled from July 6 through August 13, he still popped 20 HRs and led the team with 32 SBs. Roberto doubled in the 1992 All-Star Game. In 1992, Roberto led the Yanks in SBs (28) and set a ML season record for most times reaching base on catcher's interference (eight).

TRADED: In November of 1992, the Yankees traded Roberto to Cincinnati for Paul O'Neill (OF) and Joe DeBerry (1B). He left the Yanks tied with Horace Clarke for ninth place on the club's stolen-base list (151). He was hitting .319 when he was hurt in July 1993 and out for the season. Roberto was traded to Atlanta in 1994. Early in the season, Roberto was traded again. From Atlanta he went to Montreal, and then the Expos sent him to the Dodgers about a month later. He later played for the Twins, Mariners, and Rangers.

IN THE YANKEE FOLD AGAIN: Roberto was signed to a minor league Yankee contract for the 2000 season. Roberto appeared in 10 games for the Yankees in 2000 before being released.

KEY, JIMMY

Yankee: 1993-96
Pitcher
Born: April 22, 1961
Birthplace: Huntsville, AL
Bat: R; Throw: L
Ht: 6'1"; Wt: 185

SIGNS WITH YANKEES: After breaking in with Toronto in 1984, Key built a solid career with the Blue Jays—his crowning glory was a 2-0 record in the 1992 World Series—and in December, 1992, he signed a four-year contract with the Yankees. He came to New York with a great curveball, slider and change-up. Also, he is a master of control, induces double plays and discourages home runs.

A SOLID ACQUISITION: Key in 1993 immediately got into the groove, pitching 23 consecutive scoreless innings. He had an eight-game winning streak from May until July and pitched in the All-Star Game. When the season ended, Key was the Yankee leader in wins (18), ERA (3.00), games started (34), innings pitched (236 2/3) and strikeouts (173); and he was 11-3 in games following a Yankee defeat. He also led the league in fewest walks allowed per nine innings pitched (1.6). He had an even better 1994. He led the league in wins (17-with four losses), winning percentage (.810) and games started (25). He personally snapped all three of the Yankees' four-game losing streaks. Don Mattingly said he found the Yankees were playing with the same confidence behind Key that they once had behind Ron Guidry. Key was named American League Pitcher of the Year by *The Sporting News,* and he was runner-up to David Cone in the Cy Young Award voting.

KELLY, ROBERTO

Yr.	G	AB	R	H	2B	3B	HR	RBI	BB	SB	BA	SA
1987	23	52	12	14	3	0	1	7	5	9	.269	.385
1988	38	77	9	19	4	1	1	7	3	5	.247	.364
1989	137	441	65	133	18	3	9	48	41	35	.302	.417
1990	162	641	85	183	32	4	15	61	33	42	.285	.418
1991	126	486	68	130	22	2	20	69	45	32	.267	.444
1992	152	580	81	158	31	2	10	66	41	28	.272	.384
2000	10	25	4	3	1	0	1	1	1	0	.120	.280
7 Yrs.	648	2302	324	641	111	12	57	259	169	151	.278	.411
Life.	1337	4797	687	1390	241	30	124	585	317	235	.290	.430

Lefty Jimmy Key won 48 games in four seasons as a Yankee.

FINAL TWO SEASONS WITH THE YANKS: Jimmy ended his 1995 early with an arm injury, going on the disabled list from mid-May to the end of the season. Key pitched in only five games in '95, going 1-2. He required rotator-cuff surgery and in 1996 had a 12-11 record and a 4.68 ERA in 30 games started. After his mediocre 1996 season, Key was granted free agency and signed with Baltimore in December, 1996. He retired after the 1998 season.

KEY, JIMMY

Yr.	W-L	Pct.	SA	G	GS	CG	IP	H	BB	SO	SH	ERA
1993	18-6	.750	0	34	34	4	237	219	43	173	2	3.00
1994	17-4	.810	0	25	25	1	168	177	52	97	0	3.27
1995	1-2	.333	0	5	5	0	30	40	6	14	0	5.64
1996	12-11	.522	0	30	30	0	169	171	58	116	0	4.68
4 Yrs.	48-23	.676	0	94	94	5	604	607	159	400	2	3.68
Life.	186-117	.614	10	470	389	34	2592	2518	668	1538	13	3.51

Division Series

Yr.	G	IP	BB	SO	H	W-L	SA
1996	1	5.0	1	3	5	0-0	0
Life.	2	9.2	1	7	13	0-1	0

Championship Series

Yr.	G	IP	BB	SO	H	W-L	SA
1996	1	8.0	1	5	3	1-0	0
Life.	8	38.2	11	21	37	2-1	0

World Series

Yr.	G	IP	BB	SO	H	W-L	SA
1996	2	11.1	5	1	15	1-1	0
Life.	4	20.1	5	7	21	3-1	0

KLEINOW, RED
(BORN JOHN PETER KLEINOW)

Nickname: "Doc"
Yankee: 1904-10
Catcher, Inf.
Born: July 20, 1879
Birthplace: Milwaukee, WI
Died: October 9, 1929
Bat: R; Throw: R
Ht: 5'10"; Wt: 185

FIRST REGULAR YANKEE CATCHER: Red began his ML career playing for the Yanks (Highlanders) in 1904. From 1904-09 he shared the Yankee catching chores. (In those days, most clubs regularly used a pair of catchers.) Red was the first regular catcher over an extended period of time in Yankee history. In 1906 Red led AL catchers in double plays (eight). During his Yankee career, Red also played in nine games at infield positions.

TRADED: Early in the 1910 season, the Yanks dealt Red and Clyde Engle to the Red Sox for outfielder Harry Wolter. He had gotten off to a great start at the plate with the Yanks (five for 12, .417). Red wrapped up his ML playing career in 1911 with the Phillies.

KLEINOW, RED

Yr.	G	AB	R	H	2B	3B	HR	RBI	BB	SB	BA	SA
1904	68	209	12	43	8	4	0	16	15	4	.206	.282
1905	88	253	23	56	6	3	1	24	20	7	.221	.281
1906	96	268	30	59	9	3	0	31	24	8	.220	.276
1907	90	269	30	71	6	4	0	26	24	5	.264	.316
1908	96	279	16	47	3	2	1	13	22	5	.168	.204
1909	78	206	24	47	11	4	0	15	25	7	.228	.320
1910	6	12	2	5	0	0	0	2	1	2	.417	.417
7 Yrs.	522	1496	137	328	43	20	2	127	131	38	.219	.279
Life.	584	1665	146	354	45	20	3	135	153	42	.213	.269

KLINE, STEVE

Yankee: 1970-74
Pitcher
Born: October 6, 1947
Birthplace: Wenatchee, WI
Bat: R; Throw: R
Ht: 6'3"; Wt: 205

YOUNG PROSPECT: In the June, 1966 amateur free-agent draft, Yankee scout Eddie Taylor made Steve the Yanks' seventh selection. Between 1966-70, Steve pitched at Yankee farm clubs at Johnson City, Fort Lauderdale, Greensboro, Binghamton and Syracuse. He was having a great 1970 campaign at Syracuse (8-2, 2.54 ERA), and the Yanks called him up to the big club.

YANKEE STARTER: At 22, Steve was the Yanks' fourth starter in 1970. He was fourth again in 1971 and became the third starter on the 1972 Yankee pitching staff. He was the most consistent starter in 1972 (16-9, 2.40 ERA). In 1972's. Yankee Stadium opener, Steve beat the Brewers, 2-0. In 1973 Steve was bothered by an elbow injury. Unfortunately, that injury was a permanent one and it prematurely ended a promising pitching career.

TRADED: In April of 1974 the Yanks traded Steve, along with three other pitchers (Fritz Peterson, Tom Buskey, Fred Beene), to the Indians in exchange for Chris Chambliss, Dick Tidrow and Cecil Upshaw.

KLINE, STEVE

Yr.	W-L	Pct.	SA	G	GS	CG	IP	H	BB	SO	SH	SA
1970	6-6	.500	0	16	15	5	100	99	24	49	0	3.41
1971	12-13	.480	0	31	30	15	222	206	37	81	1	2.96
1972	16-9	.640	0	32	32	11	236	210	44	58	4	2.40
1973	4-7	.364	0	14	13	2	74	76	31	19	1	4.01
1974	2-2	.500	0	4	4	0	26	26	5	6	0	3.46
5 Yrs.	40-37	.519	0	97	94	33	659	617	141	213	6	2.96
Life.	43-45	.489	1	129	105	34	750	708	184	240	6	3.26

KNIGHT, JACK
(BORN JOHN WESLEY KNIGHT)

Nickname: "Schoolboy"
Yankee: 1909-11, '13
Shortstop, 1B, 2B, 3B
Born: October 6, 1885
Birthplace: Philadelphia, PA
Died: December 19, 1965
Bat: R; Throw: R
Ht: 6'2"; Wt: 180

COMING AND GOING: Before the 1909 season, the Yanks picked up Jack on waivers from the Red Sox. They dealt Jack to Washington after the 1911 season, and in July of 1913 the Yanks reobtained him on waivers from the Senators.

VERSATILE INFIELDER: Jack played all the infield positions. He was the Yankee shortstop for the majority of the club's games from 1909-11. In 1913 Jack played more Yankee games at first base than anyone else on the club. In his four Yankee seasons he played 239 games at shortstop; 119 games at first base; 67 games at second base; and five games at third base. His salary in 1911 was $4,500, an extremely high figure in those days.

CLUB LEADERSHIP: In 1910 Jack led the Yanks in batting (.312) and doubles (25).

RELEASED: The Yanks released Jack following the 1913 season, ending his ML career.

KNIGHT, JACK

Yr.	G	AB	R	H	2B	3B	HR	RBI	BB	SB	BA	SA
1909	116	360	46	85	8	5	0	40	37	15	.236	.286
1910	117	414	58	129	25	4	3	45	34	23	.312	.413
1911	132	470	69	126	16	7	3	62	42	18	.268	.351
1913	70	250	24	59	10	0	0	24	25	7	.236	.276
4 Yrs.	435	1494	197	399	59	16	6	171	138	63	.267	.340
Life.	767	2664	301	636	96	24	14	270	211	86	.239	.309

KOENIG, MARK

Yankee: 1925-30
Shortstop, 3B
Born: July 19, 1902
Birthplace: San Francisco, CA
Died: April 22, 1993
Bat: Both; Throw: R
Ht: 6'; Wt: 180

CAME TO YANKS: In 1925, the Yanks bought Mark's contract for $35,000 from St. Paul of the American Association. Scout Paul Krichell and Manager Miller Huggins had seen Mark play and urged Yankee management to obtain him.

YANKEE SHORTSTOP: Mark played 28 games at shortstop for the Yanks at the end of the 1925 season. He was the Yanks' regular shortstop for three years (1926-28), in every one of which the Yanks won the AL pennant. In 1929, Mark was the Yanks' utility infielder, playing 61 games at shortstop, 37 games at third base and one game at second base. Mark played 19 games at shortstop in 1930 before the Yanks traded him. He could play all three bases and also could pitch (as he did in five ML games after leaving the Yankees.)

ROOKIE SEASON: The 1926 season was Mark's first full ML season and he had a few problems. He made 52 errors, leading AL shortstops. While the number of errors was high, it must be noted that Mark was handicapped by the tiny gloves that were used in his time. He had good range and was the glue of the Yankee infield. Mark had to get used to playing with second baseman Tony Lazzeri who was also a rookie in 1926. (It was a phenomenal achievement for the Yanks to win the pennant with rookies at second and shortstop.) Mark hit well (.271), but had a rough World Series, hitting .125, striking out seven times and making four errors.

1927 SEASON: Mark may have been ML baseball's most improved player in 1927. He became a great gloveman and teamed with Lazzeri to form a splendid double-play combination. His batting average leaped to .285 and he was a "Murderers' Row" member who was to be reckoned with. Capping a great year, he was the World Series hero with his .500 batting average. The 1927 Yanks could never have been as great as they were without a large contribution from Mark. The Yanks paid him a $7000 salary this year.

CONTACT HITTER: His best ML season at the plate was 1928 when he hit .319. He was a good spray-hitting batsman. In 1926 he led the Yanks in at-bats (617). He usually batted second in the order, between Combs and Ruth, and handled the bat well. From 1926-28, Mark scored 281 runs, averaging 93.66 runs per season. Although Mark was a good friend of Babe Ruth, he proved to the Babe once that he could make good contact with his fists, too. During a 1926 exhibition game, Mark took exception to some critical remarks made by Ruth and popped the Babe a few times in the dugout.

WORLD SERIES: Mark was the star hitter of the 1927 Series, leading all batters in batting (.500), at-bats (18), hits (nine) and doubles (2-tie). A bruised heel hobbled Mark in the 1928 Series but he played anyway, limping through the four-game Yankee sweep of St. Louis.

TRADED: In May of 1930, the Yanks dealt Mark and pitcher Waite Hoyt to the Tigers for three less talented ballplayers (outfielder Harry Rice, infielder Yats Wuestling and pitcher Ownie Carroll).

WORLD SERIES HISTORY: During the summer of 1932, Mark joined the Chicago Cubs, a team in the midst of a torrid pennant race, and hit .353 over the season's final 33 games. Cub Manager Charlie Grimm, among others, credited Mark's brilliant play with bringing Chicago the NL pennant. But the Cub players voted Mark only a half share of the World Series money. The 1932 Series between the Yanks and Cubs was a bitter one, and one reason was the attack by the players on the Cubs for withholding a full share from Mark. The ex-Yankee was very popular among the Yankee players who felt he had been dealt a slight by the Cubs. There was bad blood and hostility in the background as Babe Ruth, who led the defense of Mark, hit his famous "called shot" HR.

KOENIG, MARK

Yr.	G	AB	R	H	2B	3B	HR	RBI	BB	SB	BA	SA
1925	28	110	14	23	6	1	0	4	5	0	.209	.282
1926	147	617	93	167	26	8	5	62	43	4	.271	.363
1927	123	526	99	150	20	11	3	62	25	3	.285	.382
1928	132	533	89	170	19	10	4	63	32	3	.319	.415
1929	116	373	44	109	27	5	3	41	23	1	.292	.416
1930	21	74	9	17	5	0	0	9	6	0	.230	.297
6 Yrs.	567	2233	348	636	103	35	15	241	134	11	.285	.382
Life.	1162	4271	572	1190	195	49	28	443	222	31	.279	.367

World Series

Yr.	G	AB	R	H	2B	3B	HR	RBI	BA
1926	7	32	2	4	1	0	0	2	.125
1927	4	18	5	9	2	0	0	2	.500
1928	4	19	1	3	0	0	0	0	.158
3 Yrs.	15	69	8	16	3	0	0	4	.232
Life.	20	76	9	18	3	1	0	5	.237

KUBEK, TONY

Yankee: 1957-65
Shortstop, OF, 3B
Born: October 12, 1936
Birthplace: Milwaukee, WI
Bat: L; Throw: R
Ht: 6'3"; Wt: 190

HONORS: In 1957, Tony won both the Baseball Writers' AL Rookie of the Year and the AL Rookie Award given by *The Sporting News*. In the 1957 Yankee spring training camp, Tony won the James P. Dawson Award, honoring the most outstanding rookie in camp. *The Sporting News* selected Tony to their AL All-Star team in 1961 as the best shortstop in the League.

YOUNG PROSPECT: The Yanks signed Tony in September 1953, one month before his 17th birthday. The youngster hit .344 at Owensboro in 1954 and .334 at Quincy in 1955. Playing for Manager Ralph Houk in 1956, Tony was a star on the Denver club, hitting .331, and was picked as shortstop on the American Association's All-Star team. In 1957 spring training, Tony impressed Casey Stengel who took a big interest in the potential star. Gil McDougald also helped Tony learn shortstop skills, and Tony appreciated the help.

ROOKIE SEASON: Tony was especially valuable in 1957 because of his versatility; he played 50 games in the outfield, 41 games at shortstop, 38 games at third base and one game at second base. Stengel had the confidence in the 20-year-old Tony to play him at different positions and the youngster did the job at the plate as well (.297).

YANKEE SHORTSTOP: Beginning in 1958, Tony was the regular Yankee shortstop for eight seasons (1958-65), although he still played in the outfield or at third base when called upon. Tony missed the first two-thirds of the 1962 season while serving in the military, but he excelled when he returned to the Yanks, hitting .314 in 45 games. As a shortstop, Tony displayed excellent range and teamed with good friend Bobby Richardson to provide some of the best defense up the middle of the infield in Yankee history. In 1963 he fielded .980, the fifth best fielding mark by a shortstop in Yankee history.

CLUB LEADERSHIP: Twice Tony led the Yanks in doubles (1959, 1961) and at-bats (1958, 1960). His 38 doubles in 1961 is a Yankee club record for shortstops. In 1961 he tied for club leadership in triples (six).

DRAMATIC RETURN: After missing the first four months of the 1962 season because of military service, Tony rejoined the Yanks on August 4 and in his first game, on August 7 against the Minnesota Twins, hit a three-run HR in his first at-bat!

QUIET GUY: One guy on the team that Yankee GM George Weiss did not worry about getting into trouble was Tony. He neither smoked nor drank, and he avoided publicity. He and his pal Bobby Richardson were quiet, conservative and religious. They both enjoyed reading and other sports (ping pong, etc.). Casey Stengel once said of Tony, "Here's a boy who sits on the bench without opening his mouth so you don't know which side he's on. But when he goes out on the field, you know."

ALL-STAR GAME: Tony was selected to the AL team for All-Star Games in 1958, 1959 and 1961.

WORLD SERIES: The 1957 World Series had to be a thrill, though an ironic one, for Tony, who was just a few days away from his 21st birthday. The Yanks' opponents were the Braves of Tony's hometown of Milwaukee. Milwaukee fans were rabid,

Tony Kubek (New York Yankees Archives)

and they were obsessed in their desire to beat the Yanks. Garbage was thrown on the lawn of Tony's parents and a sign said "Get Out of Town, You Bush Traitor. " In Game 3, the first Series game ever played in Milwaukee, Tony cracked two HRs to lead the Yanks to a 12-3 romp. (He also had four RBIs in that game.) In the eighth inning of Game 7 of the 1960 Series, Tony got an unlucky break when a sharply hit ground ball hit by Bill Virdon took a terrible hop and struck him in the throat, putting Tony, who was unable to talk, in the hospital. The Pirates went on to a big inning and to eventually win the Series. The Yanks won Game 7 of the 1962 Series, 1-0, and the only run of the game came when Tony hit into a double play, scoring Bill Skowron from third. Tony missed the end of the 1964 season and Series because of a sprained wrist, besides having a back injury. Tony played four positions in World Series play, a record he shares with four others.

RETIREMENT: Back and neck ailments bothered Tony in his final years as a ML baseball player, and after the 1965 season he was informed by doctors that further play would risk paralysis. Faced with that warning, Tony retired as a player at the age of 29, ending a distinguished Yankee career. Since his retirement as a player, Tony has been an excellent baseball broadcaster on network TV. In 1990, Tony began broadcasting Yankee games for the Madison Square Garden Network (cable TV) and during the strike of 1994, upset with the condition of baseball, he retired.

KUBEK, TONY

Yr.	G	AB	R	H	2B	3B	HR	RBI	BB	SB	BA	SA
1957	127	431	56	128	21	3	3	39	24	6	.297	.381
1958	138	559	66	148	21	1	2	48	25	5	.265	.317
1959	132	512	67	143	25	7	6	51	24	3	.279	.391
1960	147	568	77	155	25	3	14	62	31	3	.273	.401
1961	153	617	84	170	38	6	8	46	27	1	.276	.395
1962	45	169	28	53	6	1	4	17	12	2	.314	.432
1963	135	557	72	143	21	3	7	44	28	4	.257	.343
1964	106	415	46	95	16	3	8	31	26	4	.229	.340
1965	109	339	26	74	5	3	5	35	20	1	.218	.295
9 Yrs.	1092	4167	522	1109	178	30	57	373	217	29	.266	.364
Life. Same.												

World Series

Yr.	G	AB	R	H	2B	3B	HR	RBI	BA
1957	7	28	4	8	0	0	2	4	.286
1958	7	21	0	1	0	0	0	1	.048
1960	7	30	6	10	1	0	0	3	.333
1961	5	22	3	5	0	0	0	1	.227
1962	7	29	2	8	1	0	0	1	.276
1963	4	16	1	3	0	0	0	0	.188
6 Yrs.	37	146	16	35	2	0	2	10	.240
Life. Same.									

KUCKS, JOHNNY

Yankee: 1955-59
Pitcher
Born: July 27, 1933
Birthplace: Hoboken, NJ
Bat: R; Throw: R
Ht: 6'3"; Wt: 190

HONORS: Johnny was picked for the AL All-Star team for the 1956 All-Star Game.

YOUNG PROSPECT: Johnny's first season in the Yankee organization was a spectacular one. That year, in 1952, he was 19-6 at Norfolk in the Class B Piedmont League and recorded a 2.55 ERA. He missed the 1953-54 seasons because of military service. In the instructional camp of 1955, Johnny impressed Casey Stengel and was invited to spring training at St. Petersburg. When Johnny made the Yanks that spring, it meant he jumped from Class B minor league ball to the big leagues with only one year of professional experience!

STARTER AND RELIEVER: As a Yankee rookie in 1955, Johnny was impressive as the club's fifth starter and a long relief man. Fifty-eight percent of his Yankee career appearances were as a starter. John was primarily a sinkerball pitcher.

1956 SEASON: The 1956 season was Johnny's best in the ML's. He was the Yanks' second biggest winner (18-9) that year behind Whitey Ford. He led the Yanks in games started (31) and shutouts (three).

WORLD SERIES: In Game 7 of the 1956 Series Johnny pitched a three-hit shutout to beat the Dodgers at Ebbetts Field, 9-0, enabling the Yanks to regain the World Championship the club had lost the year before to Brooklyn. In 19 innings of World Series pitching he compiled a splendid 1.89 ERA.

TRADED: Johnny was dealt to the Kansas City A's, along with Tom Sturdivant and Jerry Lumpe, while the A's sent Ralph Terry and Hector Lopez to the Yanks in May, 1959.

KUCKS, JOHNNY

Yr.	W-L	Pct.	SA	G	GS	CG	IP	H	BB	SO	SH	ERA
1955	8-7	.533	0	29	13	3	127	122	44	49	1	3.41
1956	18-9	.667	0	34	31	12	224	223	72	67	3	3.85
1957	8-10	.444	2	37	23	4	179	169	59	78	1	3.56
1958	8-8	.500	4	34	15	4	126	132	39	46	1	3.93
1959	0-1	.000	0	9	1	0	17	21	9	9	0	8.64
5 Yrs.	42-35	.545	6	143	83	23	673	667	223	249	6	3.82
Life.	54-56	.491	7	207	123	30	938	970	308	338	7	4.10

World Series

Yr.	G	IP	BB	SO	H	W-L	SA
1955	2	3	1	1	4	0-0	0
1956	3	11	3	2	6	1-0	0
1957	1	$^2/_3$	1	1	1	0-0	0
1958	2	$4^1/_3$	1	0	4	0-0	0
4 Yrs.	8	19	6	4	15	1-0	0
Life. Same.							

KUZAVA, BOB

Nickname: "Sarge"
Yankee: 1951-54
Pitcher
Born: May 28, 1923
Birthplace: Wyandotte, MI
Bat: B; Throw: L
Ht: 6'2"; Wt: 202

CAME TO YANKS: In June of 1951, the Yanks acquired Bob and pitcher Bob Ross from the Washington Senators for pitchers Bob Porterfield, Tom Ferrick and Fred Sanford.

VALUABLE PITCHER: The Yanks used Bob as a relief pitcher and spot starter. Although he received little publicity, Bob was a key member of the Yankee pitching staffs of the early 1950s. He gave the Yanks great depth in the pitching department. "Sarge" had good control, changed speeds nicely and, though a southpaw, was effective against right-handed batters because his ball tailed away from them.

BIGGEST GAME: In the second game of an important August, 1953 doubleheader against the White Sox, who were then still in the pennant race, Bob, before about 68,000 fans on a Ladies' Day at the Stadium, took a no-hitter into the ninth inning. He retired the first White Sox batter in the ninth. Then Bob Boyd ripped a hit to left-center to end the no-hit bid. Bob finished with a one-hitter, a 3-0 shutout, and an important Yankee win.

WORLD SERIES: In the ninth inning of Game 6 of the 1951 Series, Bob entered the game with the bases full of Giants, no one out and the Yanks leading, 4-1. Bob allowed three long fly balls but each was caught, two for sacrifice flies, and Bob had saved a 4-3 Yankee win. More importantly, the win gave the Yanks four wins in the Series and the World Championship. Again "Sarge" was the hero in the final game of the 1952 Series, this time in Game 7. He came in to retire the final eight Dodger batters (escaping another bases-loaded jam in the seventh inning) to save a 4-2 Yankee victory and assure another celebration. The game was played at Ebbets Field, and fans thought Casey Stengel was crazy to bring in Bob, a southpaw, at such a cozy, right-handed hitting ball park. But Bob, taming the potent Dodger bats, proved that Stengel's confidence in him was justified.

LEFT YANKS: In August of 1954, the Yanks waived Bob to the Orioles.

KUZAVA, BOB												
Yr.	W-L	Pct.	SA	G	GS	CG	IP	H	BB	SO	SH	ERA
1951	8-4	.667	5	23	8	4	82	76	27	50	1	2.40
1952	8-8	.500	3	28	12	6	133	115	63	67	1	3.45
1953	6-5	.545	4	33	6	2	92	92	34	48	2	3.31
1954	1-3	.250	1	20	3	0	40	46	18	22	0	5.45
4 Yrs.	23-20	.535	13	104	29	12	347	329	142	187	4	3.39
Life.	49-44	.527	13	213	99	34	862	849	415	446	7	4.05

World Series							
Yr.	G	IP	BB	SO	H	W-L	SA
1951	1	1	0	0	0	0-0	1
1952	1	2⅔	0	2	0	0-0	1
1953	1	⅔	0	1	2	0-0	0
3 Yrs.	3	4⅓	0	3	2	0-0	2
Life. Same.							

LAKE, JOE

Yankee: 1908-09
Pitcher
Born: December 6, 1881
Birthplace: Brooklyn, NY
Died: June 30, 1950
Bat: R; Throw: R
Ht: 6'; Wt: 185

1908 SEASON: In 1908, Joe's ML rookie season, he was the Yanks' (Highlanders) No. 2 starter. He led the AL in losses (22), establishing the Yankee club record for defeats in a season.

1909 SEASON: In 1909 Joe was the ace of the Yankee pitching staff, leading the club in wins (14), ERA (1.88), strikeouts (117), games started (26) and shutouts (three-tie). In December 1909, the Yankees traded Joe to the St. Louis Browns for catcher Lou Criger; Criger would hit .188 for the Yanks in 1910, while Lake won 11 games for the Browns.

LAKE, JOE												
Yr.	W-L	Pct.	SA	G	GS	CG	IP	H	BB	SO	SH	ERA
1908	9-22	.290	0	38	27	19	269	252	77	118	2	3.17
1909	14-11	.577	1	31	26	17	215	180	59	117	3	1.88
2 Yrs.	23-33	.411	1	69	53	36	485	432	136	235	5	2.60
Life.	62-90	.408	5	199	139	96	1318	1329	332	594	8	2.85

LaPORTE, FRANK

Nickname: "Pot"
Yankee: 1905-08,'09-10
Infielder, OF
Born: February 6, 1880
Birthplace: Uhrichsville, OH
Died: September 25, 1939
Bat: R; Throw: R
Ht: 5'8"; Wt: 175

COMING AND GOING: Frank was a 25-year-old rookie when he broke into the ML's with the Yanks (Highlanders) in 1905. He was dealt to the Red Sox early in the 1908 season. He returned to the Yanks before the 1909 season. Then he was traded to the St. Louis Browns before the 1911 season.

VERSATILE PLAYER: In 1906, Frank was the regular Yankee third baseman. In 1907 he played 64 games at third base and 63 games in the outfield. Frank played only at second base for the Yanks in 1909, but in 1910 he played 79 games at second, 24 games in the outfield, and 15 games at third.

CLUB LEADERSHIP: In 1907 Frank led the Yanks in slugging (.360) and triples (11-tie).

LaPORTE, FRANK

Yr.	G	AB	R	H	2B	3B	HR	RBI	BB	SB	BA	SA
1905	11	40	4	16	1	0	1	12	1	1	.400	.500
1906	123	454	60	120	23	9	2	54	22	10	.264	.368
1907	130	470	56	127	20	11	0	48	27	10	.270	.360
1908	39	145	7	38	3	4	1	15	8	3	.262	.359
1909	89	309	35	92	19	3	0	31	18	5	.298	.379
1910	124	432	43	114	14	6	2	67	33	16	.264	.338
6 Yrs.	516	1850	205	507	80	33	6	227	109	45	.274	.363
Life.	1194	4212	501	1185	198	79	15	560	288	101	.281	.377

LARSEN, DON

Nicknames: "Night Rider" "Gooneybird"
Yankee: 1955-59
Pitcher
Born: August 7, 1929
Birthplace: Michigan City, IN
Bat: R; Throw: R
Ht: 6'4"; Wt: 225

HONORS: In 1973, the Baseball Writers gave Don the Casey Stengel "You Could Look It Up" Award. Don's 1956 World Series perfect game was voted the Most Memorable Moment in World Series/All-Star Game competition in baseball's 1976 voting conducted in honor of the nation's Bicentennial celebration.

CAME TO YANKS: In November of 1954, the Yanks obtained Don from the Orioles as part of an 18-player transaction, the largest ML trade in history.

YANKEE STARTER: In 1954, the year before joining the Yanks, Don was 3-21 for Baltimore, but Yankee GM Weiss realized Don's tremendous potential and was happy to obtain him. In 1955-56 Don was the Yanks' fourth starter. He split his time in 1955 between New York and the Yanks' Class-AAA Denver team, going 9-2 in New York and 9-1 at Denver for a combined 18-3 season. In 1957 he was the Yanks' fifth starter. Though hampered by an elbow injury in 1958, Don was the Yanks' third starter. In all his Yankee seasons except 1958, Don was also used as a reliever. He compiled an outstanding winning percentage as a Yankee pitcher (.652) compared to his combined winning percentage with all his other ML teams (.350). Don had a good fastball and slider and also used a knuckleball and a change of pace.

GOOD HITTER: Don had a lifetime batting average of .242 with 14 HRs and 72 RBIs in 596 at-bats. His .371 lifetime slugging average is the 10th highest by a 20th century ML pitcher. Don's bat helped him win games with the Yanks and he hit eight Yankee HRs. On August 22, 1956, he hit a grand slam HR against Boston. On August 17, 1958, he hit a pinch-hit HR. In 1958 Don hit .306 and belted four HRs.

"NIGHT RIDER": Don liked the nightlife. His fellow players called him "Night Rider" and "Gooneybird," and a former manager of Don's, Jimmy Dykes, once said, "The only thing Larsen fears is sleep." In the spring training camp of 1956, Don had a car accident at 4 a.m. and GM George Weiss wanted to trade him, but Casey Stengel stuck up for him and Don remained on the Yanks, thus preserving his date with destiny. When asked why Don was out at such an hour, Casey joked, "He was mailing a letter." But Don had another reputation that tarnished his image, and that was that he was erratic in tight games. But in September of 1956, Don lived up to his potential, winning all four of his starts that month and all on four-hitters. An experiment with a no-windup delivery paid dividends.

WORLD SERIES: On October 8, 1956, Don hurled the only no-hitter—in fact, it was a perfect game—in World Series history. The Brooklyn Dodgers sent 27 men to the plate and 27 Dodgers went back to the dugout after making outs. It was not only the most dramatic game in baseball history, but many believe it was the greatest single achievement in the history of American sports. Don's perfect game came at a critical point, the victory giving the Yanks a 3-2 Series lead over Brooklyn. For his heroics in the 1956 Series, Don won both *Sport* magazine's MVP Award and the Babe Ruth Award given by the Baseball Writers. In Game 3 of the 1957 Series, his first Series outing since his game of perfection, he pitched $7^1/_3$ innings of solid relief to beat the Braves, 12-3. He retired the first four batters he faced, giving him an incredible World Series record of $11^1/_3$ consecutive innings of perfect pitching. In another clutch effort, Don went seven shutout innings, beating the Braves in Game 3 of the 1958 Series at a time when the Yanks were down two games to zero.

TRADED: In December of 1959, the Yanks traded Don, Hank Bauer, Norm Siebern and Marv Throneberry to the Kansas City A's for Roger Maris, Joe DeMaestri and Kent Hadley.

LARSEN, DON

Yr.	W-L	Pct.	SA	G	GS	CG	IP	H	BB	SO	SH	ERA
1955	9-2	.818	2	19	13	5	97	81	51	44	1	3.06
1956	11-5	.688	1	38	20	6	180	133	96	107	1	3.26
1957	10-4	.714	0	27	20	4	140	113	87	81	1	3.74
1958	9-6	.600	0	19	19	5	114	100	52	55	3	3.07
1959	6-7	.462	0	25	18	3	125	122	76	69	1	4.33
5 Yrs.	45-24	.652	3	128	90	23	655	549	362	356	7	3.50
Life.	81-91	.471	23	412	171	44	1548	1442	725	849	11	3.78

World Series

Yr.	G	IP	BB	SO	H	W-L	SA
1955	1	4	2	2	5	0-1	0
1956	2	$10^2/_3$	4	7	1	1-0	0
1957	2	$9^2/_3$	5	6	8	1-1	0
1958	2	$9^1/_3$	6	9	9	1-0	0
4 Yrs.	7	$33^2/_3$	17	24	23	3-2	0
Life.	10	36	19	24	24	4-2	0

New York Yankees catcher Yogi Berra leaps into the arms of pitcher Don Larsen after Larsen struck out the last Brooklyn Dodgers batter to complete his perfect game during the World Series game 5 on October 8, 1956. (AP/WIDE WORLD PHOTOS)

DON LARSEN'S PERFECT GAME—OCTOBER 8, 1956 GAME 5, WORLD SERIES—NY-2; BKN-0
97 PITCHES (PITCH-BY-PITCH)

First Inning

Jim Gilliam:	Ball one (1)
	Strike one (foul ball) (2)
	Ball two (3)
	Strike two (called) (4)
	Strike three (called) (5)
Pee Wee Reese:	Strike one (foul ball) (6)
	Ball one (7)
	Strike two (called) (8)
	Ball two (9)
	Ball three (10)
	Strike three (called) (11)
Duke Snider:	Ball one (12)
	Strike one (swinging) (13)
	Ball two (14)
	Lined out to rightfielder Hank Bauer (15)

Second Inning

Jackie Robinson:	Strike one (called) (16)
	Smashed a liner off third baseman Andy Carey's glove that ricochetted to shortstop Gil McDougald who threw out Jackie by a step (17)
Gil Hodges:	Ball one (18)
	Strike one (swinging) (19)
	Strike two (called) (20)
	Strike three (whiffed on a low outside curve) (21)
Sandy Amoros:	Strike one (swinging) (22)
	Strike two (foul ball) (23)
	Ball one (24)
	Ball two (25)
	Popped to second baseman Billy Martin (26)

Third Inning

Carl Furillo:	Strike one (called) (27)
	Flied to rightfielder Hank Bauer (28)
Roy Campanella:	Ball one (29)
	Strike one (called) (30)
	Strike two (swinging) (31)
	Strike three (swinging) (32)
Sal Maglie:	Lined out to centerfielder Mickey Mantle (33)

Fourth Inning

Jim Gilliam:	Grounded to second baseman Billy Martin (34)
Pee Wee Reese:	Rolled weakly to second baseman Billy Martin (35)
Duke Snider:	Ball one (36)
	Ball two (37)
	Strike one (long foul ball) (38)
	Strike two (called) (39)
	Foul ball (40)
	Strike three (called) (41)

Fifth Inning

Jackie Robinson:	Ball one (42)
	Strike one (foul ball) (43)
	Strike two (swinging) (44)
	Long foul ball (45)
	Flied deep to rightfielder Hank Bauer (46)

Gil Hodges:	Strike one (called) (47)
	Strike two (called) (48)
	Ball one (49)
	Ball two (50)
	Crushed a liner deep to left-center that Mickey Mantle ran down, making a tremendous backhanded catch (51)
Sandy Amoros:	Ball one (52)
	Strike one (called) (53)
	Strike two (long foul ball) (54)
	Ball two (55)
	Grounded to second baseman Billy Martin (56)

Sixth Inning

Carl Furillo:	Strike one (foul ball) (57)
	Popped to Billy Martin in short right field (58)
Roy Campanella:	Popped to Billy Martin in short center field (59)
Sal Maglie:	Strike one (swinging) (60)
	Strike two (swinging) (61)
	Ball one (62)
	Foul ball (63)
	Foul ball (64)
	Ball two (65)
	Strike three (swinging) (66)

Seventh Inning

Jim Gilliam:	Strike one (called) (67)
	Ball one (68)
	Strike two (foul ball) (69)
	Grounded hard to shortstop Gil McDougald (70)
Pee Wee Reese:	Strike one (foul ball) (71)
	Flied to Mickey Mantle in deep center (72)
Duke Snider:	Ball one (73)
	Flied to leftfielder Enos Slaughter (74)

Eighth Inning

Jackie Robinson:	Strike one (called) (75)
	Strike two (foul ball) (76)
	Grounded back to Larsen on the mound (77)
Gil Hodges:	Strike one (called) (78)
	Ball one (high) (79)
	Strike two (swinging) (80)
	Ball two (outside) (81)
	Lined to third baseman Andy Carey who made a great catch (82)
Sandy Amoros:	Strike one (called) (83)
	Flied to Mickey Mantle in deep center (84)

Ninth Inning

Carl Furillo:	Strike one (foul ball) (85)
	Strike two (foul ball) (86)
	Ball one (high) (87)
	Foul ball (into first base box seats) (88)
	Foul ball (into right field box seats) (89)
	Flied to rightfielder Hank Bauer (90)
Roy Campanella:	Strike one (foul ball) (91)
	Grounded to second baseman Billy Martin (92)
Dale Mitchell: (batting for Maglie)	Ball one (outside) (93)
	Strike one (called) (94)
	Strike two (swinging) (95)
	Foul ball (into left field stands) (96)
	Strike three! (called) (97)

LARY, LYN

Nickname: "Broadway"
Yankee: 1929-34
Infielder
Born: January 28, 1906
Birthplace: Armona, CA
Died: January 9, 1973
Bat: R; Throw: R
Ht: 6'; Wt: 165

CAME TO YANKS: In January, 1928, the Yanks purchased Lyn and infielder Jimmy Reese from Oakland of the Pacific Coast League for $150,000.

YANKEE UTILITY INFIELDER: Lyn began his ML career with the Yanks in 1929. He was one of the best utility infielders in Yankee history and was the Yanks' regular shortstop in 1930 and 1931, playing in every Yankee game in 1931. Babe Ruth was godfather to Lyn's son. In 1931 Lyn had 484 assists, sixth most by a Yankee shortstop.

GOOD HITTER: Lyn knocked in 107 runs in 1931, the most RBIs ever produced by a Yankee shortstop in a season. He was one of six Yankee players to score at least 100 runs in 1931. In that 1931 season, Lyn led the Yanks in doubles (35).

TRADED: In May, 1934, the Yanks traded Lyn to the Red Sox for infielder Fred Muller and $20,000.

TOP YANKEE SHORTSTOPS' BEST RBI SEASONS:

    LYN LARY—107 (1931)
    D. Jeter—102 (1999)
    D. Jeter—84 (1998)
    F. Crosetti—78 (1936)
    D. Jeter—78 (1996)

LARY, LYN

Yr.	G	AB	R	H	2B	3B	HR	RBI	BB	SB	BA	SA
1929	80	236	48	73	9	2	5	26	24	4	.309	.428
1930	117	464	93	134	20	8	3	52	45	14	.289	.386
1931	155	610	100	171	35	9	10	107	88	13	.280	.416
1932	91	280	56	65	14	4	3	39	52	9	.232	.343
1933	52	127	25	28	3	3	0	13	28	2	.220	.291
1934	1	0	0	0	0	0	0	0	1	0	.000	.000
6 Yrs.	496	1717	322	471	81	26	21	237	238	42	.274	.388
Life.	1302	4604	805	1239	247	56	38	526	705	162	.269	.372

LAZZERI, TONY

Nickname: "Poosh 'Em Up"
Yankee: 1926-37
Second Baseman, 3B, SS
Born: December 6, 1903
Birthplace: San Francisco, CA
Died: August 6, 1946
Bat: R; Throw: R
Ht: 5'11"; Wt: 170

HONORS: In 1932 *The Sporting News* selected Tony for its ML All-Star team as the best second baseman in baseball. Tony was picked to the AL team for the first All-Star Game ever played, in 1933. In 1936 the New York Chapter of the Baseball Writers gave Tony the Sid Mercer Award. In 1991, at long last, Tony was inducted into the Baseball Hall of Fame.

MINOR LEAGUE STAR: Tony was a legendary performer in the Pacific Coast League in the days when the P.C.L. played a 200-game schedule. At Salt Lake City, Tony in 1925 established P.C.L. records with 60 HRs and 222 RBIs. His 202 runs scored that year is a record for professional baseball. Tony was a shortstop.

CAME TO YANKS: The Yanks purchased Tony's contract from Salt Lake City for $60,000 in 1925 on the advice of head scout Paul Krichell. When Tony came to the Yanks' 1926 spring training camp in St. Petersburg, FL, it was his first trip east of the Rocky Mountains. In camp, Yankee Manager Miller Huggins worked hard with Tony, who at Salt Lake City was a shortstop, teaching him the skills involved in turning the double play at second base.

SECOND SACKER: For his entire 12-season Yankee career (1926-37), Tony was the club's regular second baseman. He was the starter at second base longer than anyone in Yankee history. He also often played at third base (1930-31,1934) and shortstop (1927, 1929). In all, Tony played 1441 Yankee games at second, 144 at third and 62 at shortstop. In 1927 Tony fielded .971, one point behind the league-leader at second base, Bucky Harris. In 1929 Tony led AL second basemen in double plays (101).

GREAT HITTER: A great offensive player, Tony was an especially good clutch hitter. He was a key member, and the chief right-handed power hitter, in the famed "Murderers' Row" line-up. The son of a blacksmith, Tony had wrists that generated enormous power. Seven times Tony knocked in more than 100 runs and five times he batted .300 or better. He was one of the most proficient power-hitting second basemen in history.

HOT STREAK: From May 21-24 of 1936, Tony hit seven HRs in four consecutive games (hitting at least one HR in each game) for an AL record. On May 24, 1936, Tony hit three HRs and had 11 RBIs in one game, also an AL record. In that game he hit two grand slam HRs, becoming the first player in AL history to accomplish that feat. Over successive games (May 23-24, 1936), Tony knocked in 15 runs, a ML record. Twice in his ML career, Tony hit three HRs in a single game.

SILENT MAN: Tony was so quiet that one sportswriter said interviewing Tony "is like trying to mine coal with a nail file and a pair of scissors." Reporter Jack Mahon said he once saw Tony, Frank Crosetti and Joe DiMaggio, all silent types, sit quietly in a hotel lobby for 80 minutes. Finally, DiMaggio cleared his throat. "What did you say?" asked Crosetti. "He didn't say nothing. Shut up," snapped Tony. Again there was silence. In 1936 Tony, Crosetti and rookie DiMaggio drove to spring training in Florida all the way from San Francisco, and not more than a few sentences were spoken the lengthy trip. Tony's voice often sounded angry and sometimes he was surly.

He had a bad temper occasionally, especially with reporters. But many of his teammates remember him differently. Tony liked to kid around in the clubhouse, breaking tension by giving "hot foots" or by playing other practical jokes on teammates. Mostly, Tony let his bat and glove do his talking for him.

POPULAR PLAYER: Tony's skills and popularity in New York were very much responsible for getting people of Italian descent interested in baseball. At Yankee Stadium, Italian fans would yell, "Poosh 'Em Up, Tony," asking Tony to hit them a ball in the stands whenever Tony batted. On September 9, 1927, "Tony Lazzeri Day" was held at Yankee Stadium.

SMART PLAYER: Some experts believe Tony was the smartest player ever to play the game. And Tony did not let the fact he was an epileptic hinder his baseball career. He had tremendous baseball instincts, was clever and was tough as nails. An article in the *New York Times* once compared Tony to Christopher Columbus, saying, "He didn't discover America, but Columbus never went behind third for an overthrow to cut-off the tying run in the ninth inning." For his great 1927, Tony was paid a salary of $8,000.

CLUB LEADERSHIP: Twice Tony led the Yanks in stolen bases. In 1929 he led the club in batting (.354) and doubles (37). In 1932 he led the team in triples (16).

ALL-TIME YANKEE LEADER: Tony ranks high on many of the all-time Yankee leader lists. He is fifth in triples (115) and sixth in walks (831); seventh in RBIs (1154); ninth in doubles (327); tenth in hits (1784); 12th in runs scored (952); 11th in at-bats (6094); and 13th in both stolen bases (147) and games played (1659). Tony ranks 17th in HRs (169), and 18th in batting average (.293) in Yankee history.

WORLD SERIES: In the seventh inning of Game 7 of the 1926 Series, Grover Cleveland Alexander struck out Tony, then a rookie, with the bases loaded to preserve a 3-2 Cardinal victory. Before fanning, Tony hit an apparent HR that barely went foul. He played all four games of the 1928 Series with a shoulder so severely injured that he could not throw overhand. But he gutted it out and gave his best effort. In Game 4, the final game, of the 1932 Series, Tony hit a pair of two-run HRs to power the Yanks to a 13-6 victory over the Cubs and a Series sweep. In Game 2 of the 1936 Series, Tony hit the second grand slam HR in World Series history, leading the Yanks to an 18-4 romp against the Giants. He hit safely in all five games of the 1937 Series and led both clubs in batting (.400).

RELEASED: After the 1937 season, Chicago Cubs' owner Phil Wrigley let Yankee management know that he would like to have the aging Lazzeri. The Yanks had a tremendous prospect at Newark in Joe Gordon and they were anxious to play Joe. So somewhat reluctantly, the Yanks released Tony a few days following the completion of the 1937 World Series and Tony signed with the Cubs. Tony's leadership qualities were an important factor in Chicago's winning the 1938 NL pennant.

FINAL ML DAYS: After playing for the Cubs in 1938, Tony played in 1939 for the Brooklyn Dodgers and New York Giants. On June 7, 1939, Tony played third base in a 7-1 Giants loss to the Cubs and made two errors. It turned out to be Tony's last ML game; Giant Manager Bill Terry released him and five days later Tony was signed to manage Toronto of the International League.

LAZZERI, TONY

Yr.	G	AB	R	H	2B	3B	HR	RBI	BB	SB	BA	SA
1926	155	589	79	162	28	14	18	114	54	16	.275	.462
1927	153	570	92	176	29	8	18	102	69	22	.309	.482
1928	116	404	62	134	30	11	10	82	43	15	.332	.535
1929	147	545	101	193	37	11	18	106	69	9	.354	.561
1930	143	571	109	173	34	15	9	121	60	4	.303	.462
1931	135	484	67	129	27	7	8	83	79	18	.267	.401
1932	142	510	79	153	28	16	15	113	82	11	.300	.506
1933	139	523	94	154	22	12	18	104	73	15	.294	.486
1934	123	438	59	117	24	6	14	67	71	11	.267	.445
1935	130	477	72	130	18	6	13	83	63	11	.273	.417
1936	150	537	82	154	29	6	14	109	97	8	.287	.441
1937	126	446	56	109	21	3	14	70	71	7	.244	.399
12 Yrs.	1659	6094	952	1784	327	115	169	1154	831	147	.293	.467
Life.	1740	6297	986	1840	334	115	178	1191	870	148	.292	.467

World Series

Yr.	G	AB	R	H	2B	3B	HR	RBI	BA
1926	7	26	2	5	1	0	0	3	.192
1927	4	15	1	4	1	0	0	2	.267
1928	4	12	2	3	1	0	0	0	.250
1932	4	17	4	5	0	0	2	5	.294
1936	6	20	4	5	0	0	1	7	.250
1937	5	15	3	6	0	1	1	2	.400
6 Yrs.	30	105	16	28	3	1	4	19	.267
Life.	32	107	16	28	3	1	4	19	.262

LEYRITZ, JIM

Yankee: 1990-96, 1999-2000
Catcher
Born: December 27, 1963
Birthplace: Muncie, IN
Bat: R; Throw: R
Ht: 5'10"; Wt: 175

COMES UP THROUGH THE FARM SYSTEM: Signed by Bill Livsey in 1985, Leyritz bashed his way through the Yankee farm system. After leading the Eastern League in 1989 with a .315 batting average, he was summoned to the Yankees in 1990, and he delivered a ninth-inning game-tying pinch-hit single in his Major League debut on June 8. He was asked to plug a large hole at third base, but in two months' time it was apparent that he lacked an everyday third baseman's fielding ability, and he spent most of 1991 at Columbus.

VERSATILE PLAYER: In 1992, Leyritz extended his services to five different positions—catcher, right field, third base, first base and second base—and was a designated hitter as well. In 1993, he emerged as a productive offensive player, batting .309 with 14 homers and 53 RBI in only 259 at bats. And in 1994 he set career highs in home runs (17) and RBI (58). The value of Jim to the Yankees lies in his versatility and solid right-handed hitting. In fact, he had a 1.000 fielding average accepting 297 chances with no errors, splitting his time between catching and first base. A very talkative person, Leyritz doesn't mind putting himself in the spotlight or out on a limb, vowing he could hit 25 to 30 homers in a season if given the chance. Then he went out and hit 31 homers in 508 at bats over the combined 1993-94 seasons.

DRAMATIC POSTSEASON HOME RUN: Versatility, not catching, remains Leyritz's strength, but in 1995 Andy Pettitte preferred throwing to Leyritz, and so he caught on days the then-rookie southpaw pitched. This is why Leyritz was in the lineup at Yankee Stadium in Game 2 of the playoffs against Seattle. He had been 0 for 5 and trashed the clubhouse after grounding out in the 13th inning. But in the 15th, he homered, ending the marathon at 1:22 a.m., and triumphantly circled the bases. It was a great moment for Jim, whose numbers had dropped off in 1995, having only seven homers and 37 RBI. His numbers were very similar in 1996 and he continued to contribute in the field, playing every position but shortstop and pitcher. In December, 1996, Jim was traded to the Anaheim Angels for two players to be named later.

RETURNS TO YANKEES IN 1999: In 1999, Leyritz returned to his club of origin on July 31 after being acquired from the National League Champion San Diego Padres just before the trading deadline. Of Leyritz's return to the Yankees, Manager Joe Torre said: "I could use some help managing this team." In 31 games since joining the Yankees, he batted .227, with no homers and five RBI. In the postseason, he appeared in four games, going one for three, his only hit—you guessed it—a home run! Jim's homer came in Game 4 of the World Series versus Atlanta, giving the Yankees an insurance run in their 4-1 win! Incredibly, Jim now has 13 hits in the playoffs and eight of them have been for home runs. Jim started the 2000 season with the Yankees, but was later traded to the Dodgers.

LEYRITZ, JIM

Yr.	G	AB	R	H	2B	3B	HR	RBI	BB	SB	BA	SA
1990	92	303	28	78	13	1	5	25	27	2	.257	.356
1991	32	77	8	14	3	0	0	4	13	0	.182	.221
1992	63	144	17	37	6	0	7	26	14	0	.257	.444
1993	95	259	43	80	14	0	14	53	37	0	.309	.525
1994	75	249	47	66	12	0	17	58	35	0	.265	.518
1995	77	264	37	71	12	0	7	37	37	1	.269	.394
1996	88	265	23	70	9	1	8	26	28	7	.235	.410
1999	81	200	25	47	10	0	7	40	30	2	.264	.381
2000	24	55	2	12	1	0	1	4	7	0	.218	.273
9 Yrs.	627	1816	230	475	80	2	66	273	228	7	.262	.417
Life.	903	2527	325	667	107	2	90	387	337	7	.264	.415

Division Series

Yr.	G	AB	R	H	2B	3B	HR	RBI	BB	SB	BA	SA
1995	2	7	1	1	0	0	1	2	0	0	.143	.571
1996	2	3	0	0	0	0	0	1	0	0	.000	.000
1999	2	2	0	0	0	0	0	1	1	0	.000	.000
3 Yrs.	6	12	1	1	0	0	1	4	1	0	.083	.333
Life.	10	22	4	5	0	0	4	9	1	0	.227	.773

Championship Series

Yr.	G	AB	R	H	2B	3B	HR	RBI	BB	SB	BA	SA
1996	3	8	1	2	0	0	1	2	1	0	.250	.625
1 Yr.	3	8	1	2	0	0	1	2	1	0	.250	.625
Life.	8	20	2	4	0	0	2	6	1	0	.200	.500

World Series

Yr.	G	AB	R	H	2B	3B	HR	RBI	BB	SB	BA	SA
1996	4	8	1	3	0	0	1	3	4	1	.375	.750
1999	2	1	1	1	0	0	1	2	1	0	1.000	4.000
2 Yrs.	6	9	2	4	0	0	2	5	5	1	.444	1.111
Life.	10	19	2	4	0	0	2	5	6	1	.211	.526

LINDELL, JOHNNY

Yankee: 1941-50
Outfielder, P, 1B
Born: August 30, 1916
Birthplace: Greeley, CO
Died: August 27, 1985
Bat: R; Throw: R
Ht: 6'4"; Wt: 217

YOUNG PROSPECT: The Yanks signed Johnny to a contract in 1936, and he began working his way through the Yankee farm system as a promising pitcher. In 1941, at the Yanks' Newark farm club in the International League, Johnny was named the Minor League Player of the Year by *The Sporting News*.

YOUNG ML PITCHER: Johnny played in one game with the Yanks at the end of the 1941 season. He reached the ML's for good as a 25-year-old Yankee rookie in 1942, producing a 2-1 record with one save in 23 games, including two starts.

YANKEE OUTFIELDER: The Yanks converted Johnny to an outfielder in 1943 to take advantage of his potent bat. In 1943-44, while Joe DiMaggio was in the military, Johnny was the Yanks' centerfielder. Most of the 1945 season Johnny himself spent in the military. John was the regular Yankee leftfielder in 1947-48. He was a reserve outfielder in 1946 and 1949.

Jim Leyritz

DEFENSIVE ABILITIES: The former pitcher had a great throwing arm for an outfielder. In 1944 he led AL outfielders in putouts (468). That is also the most putouts ever made by a Yankee outfielder in a season.

FINE HITTER: In a game on August 17, 1944, Johnny hit four consecutive doubles (one of eight AL players to perform that feat). He led the AL in triples in 1943 (12) and he tied for the AL lead in triples in 1944 (16). He led the 1944 Yanks in RBIs (103) and slugging (.500).

TEAM PLAYER: Johnny was great to have on a club. He was a hustling player who gave 100% every time he stepped on the field. He also was a fun-loving guy, and his pranks kept the team loose. He was talented; he was picked for the AL team in the 1943 All-Star Game. All his teammates loved Johnny, the mischievous rogue.

MOST IMPORTANT HIT: On October 1, 1949, the Red Sox came to Yankee Stadium leading the Yanks by one game with two games left to play. On the next to last day of the season, the Red Sox and Yanks were in one of their classic struggles. With the score tied, 4-4, in the bottom of the eighth inning, Johnny pulled a HR to beat the Red Sox, 5-4, and tie Boston for the AL lead. (The Yanks won the next day to win the pennant.)

WORLD SERIES: Johnny was the hitting star of the 1947 Series, leading both clubs in batting (.500), RBIs (seven) and doubles (three).

LEFT YANKS: In May, 1950, the Yanks sold Johnny's contract to the Cardinals.

LINDELL, JOHNNY

Yr.	G	AB	R	H	2B	3B	HR	RBI	BB	SB	BA	SA
1941	1	1	0	0	0	0	0	0	0	0	.000	.000
1942	27	24	1	6	1	0	0	4	0	0	.250	.292
1943	122	441	53	108	17	12	4	51	51	2	.245	.365
1944	149	594	91	178	33	16	18	103	44	5	.300	.500
1945	41	159	26	45	6	3	1	20	17	2	.283	.377
1946	102	332	41	86	10	5	10	40	32	4	.259	.410
1947	127	476	66	131	18	7	11	67	32	1	.275	.412
1948	88	309	58	98	17	2	13	55	35	0	.317	.511
1949	78	211	33	51	10	0	6	27	35	3	.242	.374
1950	7	21	2	4	0	0	0	2	4	0	.190	.190
10 Yrs.	742	2568	371	707	112	45	63	369	250	17	.275	.428
Life.	854	2795	401	762	124	48	72	404	289	17	.273	.429

World Series

Yr.	G	AB	R	H	2B	3B	HR	RBI	BA
1943	4	9	1	1	0	0	0	0	.111
1947	6	18	3	9	3	1	0	7	.500
1949	2	7	0	1	0	0	0	0	.143
3 Yrs.	12	34	4	11	3	1	0	7	.324
Life. Same.									

LINDELL, JOHNNY
(Pitcher)

Yr.	W-L	Pct.	SA	G	GS	CG	IP	H	BB	SO	SH	ERA
1942	2-1	.667	1	23	2	0	53	52	22	28	0	3.76
Life.	8-18	.308	1	55	28	15	252	247	161	146	1	4.47

LOPAT, ED

Nicknames: "Steady Eddie," "Junkman"
Yankee: 1948-55
Pitcher
Born: June 21, 1918
Birthplace: New York, NY
Died: June 15, 1992
Bat: L; Throw: L
Ht: 5'10"; Wt: 185

CAME TO YANKS: The Yanks acquired Ed from the White Sox for catcher Aaron Robinson and pitchers Bill Wight and Fred Bradley in February, 1948.

SMART PITCHER: Ed was one of the smartest, cleverest pitchers in baseball history. He was not a thrower; he was a pitcher who made a science of pitching. Ed consistently kept batters off stride with his assortment of off-speed pitches. Yet, if a batter disregarded Ed's fastball, he could sneak a fastball by him. He was just a master at setting up hitters. Casey Stengel loved to open a series with his fastball pitchers, Reynolds and Raschi, then change the pace with Ed. Ed roomed with Allie Reynolds, who was amazed that he could be successful without a blazing fastball. Through Ed, Allie learned many of the secrets of pitching and became better for it.

NICKNAMES: Mel Allen tagged Ed "Steady Eddie" because of his assortment of junk pitches, Ben Epstein of the *New York Mirror* nicknamed Ed "Junkman."

WINNING PITCHER: Ed was a vital pitcher during the record five straight Yankee World Championship years (1949-53), averaging 16 wins a season. He was a team leader on those great Yankee teams. In 1952 a shoulder injury limited his pitching time, yet he was 10-5 in only 19 starts. In his career, Ed had a 40-12 record against Cleveland.

LEAGUE LEADER: In 1953, Ed was the AL's ERA champ (2.42), besides leading AL pitchers in winning percentage (.800, 16-4). In 1951, Ed tied Bob Lemon for most HRs hit by an AL pitcher (3).

CLUB LEADERSHIP: Twice Ed tied for club leadership in games started. In consecutive seasons (1949-50) he led Yankee pitchers in shutouts, and in 1951 he paced the Yanks in wins (21-tie), ERA (2.91) and complete games (20).

ALL-TIME YANKEE LEADER: Ed's winning percentage (.657, 113-59) is the sixth best for Yankee pitchers with at least 100 decisions. He is 11th on the all-time Yankee shutout list (20). Also, Ed ranks 13th in wins (113); 15th in innings pitched (1497); 16th in ERA (3.19); and 18th with 91 complete games.

1951 HOLDOUT: Ed was a holdout in the spring of 1951. After having a fine 1950 season (18-8), Ed deservedly felt that a $10,000 raise on his $26,000 salary was in order. However, Yankee GM George Weiss offered only a $2000 raise. Following a tough fight, Weiss compromised and upped Ed's salary by $5000.

MOST IMPORTANT REGULAR SEASON WIN: On September 14, 1952, with the Yanks holding a slim half-game lead on Cleveland, Ed beat the Indians, 7-1, to win the biggest game of the year for the Yanks.

ALL-STAR GAME: As a Yankee pitcher, Ed was selected to the AL team for the 1951 All-Star Game. Unfortunately, he was the losing pitcher.

WORLD SERIES: Ed was a tremendous pitcher in Series play (4-1, 2.60 ERA). He started and won Game 4 of the 1949 Series. He pitched two complete game victories in the 1951 Series, allowing only 10 hits and one earned run in those 18 innings. He beat the Giants, 3-1, in Game 2, then won Game 5, 13-1. In Game 2 of the 1953 Series, Ed beat the Dodgers, 4-2, in another complete game.

LEFT YANKS: Midway through the 1955 season, the Yanks released Ed to the Baltimore Orioles.

LATER CAREER: After his retirement as a player in 1955, Ed stayed in baseball as a coach, manager and general manager. He was the Yankee pitching coach in 1960. In 1963 and 1964 he managed the Kansas City A's. Ed's leadership qualities made him successful in all his baseball endeavors. He was also general manager of the A's, after managing the club. In the late 1980s, Ed scouted the NL for the Yankees.

CAME TO YANKS: In May of 1959, the Yanks obtained Hector and Ralph Terry from the Kansas City A's in exchange for Johnny Kucks, Tom Sturdivant and Jerry Lumpe. For the remainder of the 1959 season, Hector was the Yanks' regular third baseman, playing 76 games at third and 35 games in the outfield.

YANKEE OUTFIELDER: Hector had been a third baseman and second baseman—second almost exclusively in the minors and majors, but he was not a top fielding infielder and was switched to the outfield with the Yanks. He drew criticism for his fielding, but improved once he became accustomed to the outfield. In 1960, Hector was the Yanks' regular leftfielder. He was platooned in left field in 1961-62. He was a regular in 1963 and a reserve his last three seasons (1964-66).

BENCH STRENGTH: Hector played his highest total of Yankee games in 1963 and had his most Bronx at-bats. It was important that Hector produce because Mickey Mantle and Roger Maris were hurt most of the season. He did produce (14 HRs, 52 RBIs in 433 ABs), and, together with Johnny Blanchard, Phil Linz, Harry Bright and veteran Yogi Berra, gave the Yanks tremendous depth. In 1965, Hector often played in right field. Mostly Hector was a valuable fourth outfielder and a manager's dream as a player able to produce in any situation (regular play, platoon play, occasional play, or pinch-hitting). In 1962, when Tony Kubek returned from the army to play shortstop and rookie sensation Tom Tresh was switched to Hector's left field position, he accepted a more limited role without complaint. Hector was an important member of five consecutive Yankee AL champions (1960-64). He was a winner, and in 1960 played on two champions; after helping the Yanks win, he returned to Panama and was a member of the champion Cervesa Balboa team.

GOOD HITTER: Hector was a good natural hitter who from a closed stance hit with power to all fields. He was a strong late inning, extra-base, opposite-field clutch hitter. With the A's in June 1958, Hector hit three HRs in one game. In 1959, Hector finished near the top of most of the Yanks' offensive categories. Only Mickey Mantle and Elston Howard had more RBIs than Hector's 69; for the complete season he had 22 HRs and 93 RBIs. In 1964 he hit .318 (7 for 22) as a pinch-hitter and in 1966 he hit .350 (7 for 20) as a pinch-hitter. As he entered the 1966 season, Hector's .271 lifetime batting average was third highest on the Yanks behind Mantle and Howard.

LOPAT, ED

Yr.	W-L	Pct.	SA	G	GS	CG	IP	H	BB	SO	SH	ERA
1948	17-11	.607	0	33	31	13	227	246	66	83	3	3.65
1949	15-10	.600	1	31	30	14	215	222	69	70	4	3.26
1950	18-8	.692	1	35	32	15	236	244	65	72	3	3.47
1951	21-9	.700	0	31	31	20	235	209	71	93	4	2.91
1952	10-5	.667	0	20	19	10	149	127	53	56	2	2.53
1953	16-4	.800	0	25	24	9	178	169	32	50	3	2.42
1954	12-4	.750	0	26	23	7	170	189	33	54	0	3.55
1955	4-8	.333	0	16	12	3	87	101	16	24	1	3.74
8 Yrs.	113-59	.657	2	217	202	91	1497	1507	405	502	20	3.19
Life.	166-112	.597	3	340	318	164	2439	2464	650	859	27	3.21

World Series

Yr.	G	IP	BB	SO	H	W-L	SA
1949	1	5⅔	1	4	9	1-0	0
1950	1	8	0	5	9	0-0	0
1951	2	18	3	4	10	2-0	0
1952	2	11⅓	4	3	14	0-1	0
1953	1	9	4	3	9	1-0	0
5 Yrs.	7	52	12	19	51	4-1	0
Life. Same.							

LOPEZ, HECTOR

Yankee: 1959-66
Outfielder, 3B, 2B
Born: July 8, 1932
Birthplace: Colon, Panama
Bat: R; Throw: R
Ht: 5'11"; Wt: 174

WORLD SERIES: Like all the Yanks, Hector hit well (.429) in the 1960 Series. His seven RBIs in only four games and nine at-bats in the 1961 Series is just one RBI short of the record for a five-game Series. Hector got all seven RBIs in the last two games! His two-run seventh inning single iced Game 4 for the Yanks. The next day in the finale, Hector hit a three-run HR and had five RBIs at Crosley Field as the Yanks romped over the Reds, 13-5, sewing up the World Championship. In the third inning of Game 2 in the 1963 Series, Roger Maris hurt his knee and Hector replaced him. Hector got two ground-rule doubles—one that bounced into the right field stands and one that bounced into the left field stands at the Stadium.

RETIREMENT: In 1966 Hector played in his fewest Yankee games, as young Roy White replaced him as the Yanks' fourth outfielder. The Yanks released Hector in October of 1966 and he retired from ML baseball. He was a Yankee scout in the early 1970s. In 1993, he was hired as a coach for the Tampa Yankees of the Gulf Coast League. In 1994 and 1995, Hector managed in the Yankee farm system, running the Gulf Coast League Yankees.

LOPEZ, HECTOR

Yr.	G	AB	R	H	2B	3B	HR	RBI	BB	SB	BA	SA
1959	112	406	60	115	16	2	16	69	28	3	.283	.451
1960	131	408	66	116	14	6	9	42	46	1	.284	.414
1961	93	243	27	54	7	2	3	22	24	1	.222	.305
1962	106	335	45	92	19	1	6	48	33	0	.275	.391
1963	130	433	54	108	13	4	14	52	35	1	.249	.395
1964	127	285	34	74	9	3	10	34	24	1	.260	.418
1965	111	283	25	74	12	2	7	39	26	0	.261	.392
1966	54	117	14	25	4	1	4	16	8	0	.214	.368
8 Yrs.	864	2510	325	658	94	21	69	322	224	7	.262	.399
Life.	1450	4644	623	1251	193	37	136	591	418	16	.269	.415

World Series

Yr.	G	AB	R	H	2B	3B	HR	RBI	BA
1960	3	7	0	3	0	0	0	0	.429
1961	4	9	3	3	0	1	1	7	.333
1962	2	2	0	0	0	0	0	0	.000
1963	3	8	1	2	2	0	0	0	.250
1964	3	2	0	0	0	0	0	0	.000
5 Yrs.	15	28	4	8	2	1	1	7	.286
Life. Same.									

LYLE, SPARKY
(BORN ALBERT WALTER LYLE)

Nickname: "The Count"
Yankee: 1972-78
Pitcher
Born: July 22, 1944
Birthplace: DuBois, PA
Bat: L; Throw: L
Ht: 6'1"; Wt: 182

HONORS: Sparky won the AL's Cy Young Award in 1977. In 1972 *The Sporting News* named him the AL Fireman of the Year. Three times Sparky was picked to the AL team for the All-Star Game (1973, '76, '77) as a Yankee. Rolaids gave him the Yankee Relief Man Award in 1976 and 1977.

CAME TO YANKS: Sparky was traded to the Yanks from the Red Sox for Danny Cater and Mario Guerrero in March, 1972, in one of the best Yankee trades in history.

GREAT RELIEF PITCHER: Sparky was one of the greatest relief pitchers in Yankee history. He possessed a tremendous slider that he used almost exclusively. In the tightest situations Sparky stayed cool. His 35 saves in 1972 was a Yankee club record until 1990. His 72 games pitched in 1977 was also a Yankee record until 1985. Sparky in 1977 became the first relief pitcher in AL history to win the Cy Young Award. On August 29, 30 and 31, 1977, he won three straight games in relief, an AL record. Sparky was a great favorite of Yankee Stadium fans, especially in his early years with the club when "Pomp and Circumstance" was played at the Stadium when he came in to relieve. He helped other pitchers, and he aided Ron Guidry in developing his slider. The Yanks could count on Sparky in a pinch. When the Yanks signed free agent Rich Gossage after the 1977 season, Sparky was upset. Rightly or wrongly, he felt he was the bullpen ace and wanted commensurate pay.

LEAGUE LEADER: Sparky led AL relief pitchers in saves in 1972 (35) and 1976 (23). In 1977, he led the AL in games pitched (72).

CLUB LEADERSHIP: In six consecutive seasons (1972-77) Sparky led the Yanks in games pitched. Five times he led the Yanks in saves. Four times he led Yankee pitchers in ERA and twice led in winning percentage (those with at least 10 decisions and 100 innings pitched).

PRACTICAL JOKE EXPERT: One of baseball's all-time pranksters, Sparky's specialty was sitting in cakes in his birthday suit. Once he came to camp with his arms and legs in casts, scaring the Yanks to death, and once during a team meeting he came out of a coffin Dracula-style. There was little he would not do in the Yankee clubhouse.

BASEBALL'S ALL-TIME LEADER LIST: Lyle retired after the 1982 season. He leads the AL in career games finished with 599 through the 2002 season. Sparky is among the leaders in many lifetime pitching statistics. Sparky ranks in the top 25 in most game appearances by a reliever and saves. He is in baseball's top 20 in relief wins and in the category known as wins plus saves.

ALL-TIME YANKEE LEADER: Sparky is fourth on the all-time Yankee save list (141). He is sixth on the all-time Yankee games pitched list (420).

Sparky Lyle

AL CHAMPIONSHIP SERIES: Sparky pitched the ninth inning of Game 3 of the 1976 playoffs to preserve a 5-3 victory over the Kansas City Royals, as Sparky recorded a save in a crucial game. He was magnificent in the 1977 playoffs against the Royals, winning both Games 4 and 5 to wrap up the AL pennant for the Yanks. He was especially brilliant in Game 4 when he pitched 5⅓ innings of scoreless ball to win, 6-4.

WORLD SERIES: In Game 1 of the 1977 Series Sparky pitched the final 3⅔ innings of scoreless ball to get the win in a game that went 12 innings. (It was the first Series win for the Yankees since 1964.)

TRADED: In November 1978, the Yankees traded Sparky to Texas as part of a ten-player deal that netted Dave Righetti for the Yanks. Shortly thereafter, Sparky's book, *The Bronx Zoo*, came out and infuriated Yankee management. Sparky was never again a star and completed his ML career in 1982.

YANKEES ACQUIRED BY TRADES THAT HELPED TO MOLD THE GREAT CHAMPIONSHIP CLUBS (1976-78):

1972—SPARKY LYLE (RED SOX)
1973—Graig Nettles (Indians); Fred Stanley (Padres)
1974—Lou Piniella (Royals); Chris Chambliss (Indians); Dick Tidrow (Indians)
1976—Mickey Rivers (Angels); Ed Figueroa (Angels); Oscar Gamble (Indians); Willie Randolph (Pirates); Dock Ellis (Pirates)
1977—Paul Blair (Orioles); Bucky Dent (White Sox); Mike Torrez (A's); Cliff Johnson (Astros)

LYLE, SPARKY

Yr.	W-L	Pct.	SA	G	GS	CG	IP	H	BB	SO	SH	ERA
1972	9-5	.643	35	59	0	0	108	84	29	75	0	1.92
1973	5-9	.357	27	51	0	0	82	66	18	63	0	2.51
1974	9-3	.750	15	66	0	0	114	93	43	89	0	1.66
1975	5-7	.417	6	49	0	0	89	94	36	65	0	3.12
1976	7-8	.467	23	64	0	0	104	82	42	61	0	2.26
1977	13-5	.722	26	72	0	0	137	131	33	68	0	2.17
1978	9-3	.750	9	59	0	0	112	116	33	33	0	3.47
7 Yrs.	57-40	.588	141	420	0	0	746	666	234	454	0	2.41
Life.	99-76	.566	238	899	0	0	1390	1292	481	873	0	2.88

Championship Series

Yr.	G	IP	BB	SO	H	W-L	SA
1976	1	1	1	0	0	0-0	1
1977	4	9⅓	0	3	7	2-0	0
1978	1	1⅓	0	0	3	0-0	0
3 Yrs.	6	11⅔	1	3	10	2-0	1
Life. Same.							

World Series

Yr.	G	IP	BB	SO	H	W-L	SA
1976	2	2⅔	0	3	1	0-0	0
1977	2	4⅔	0	2	2	1-0	0
2 Yrs.	4	7⅓	0	5	3	1-0	0
Life. Same.							

MAISEL, FRITZ
(BORN FREDERICK CHARLES MAISEL)

Nickname: "Flash"
Yankee: 1913-17
Third Baseman, 2B, OF
Born: December 23, 1889
Birthplace: Catonsville, MD
Died: April 22, 1967
Bat: R; Throw: R
Ht: 5'7"; Wt: 170

MINOR LEAGUER: In 1910, Fritz broke into professional baseball playing third base for Elgin (.287) and Wheeling (.238). Playing for the Baltimore Orioles of the International League in 1911 (.233), 1912 (.276) and 1913 (.283), Fritz played shortstop and third base, and stole 124 bases over the three seasons. He led the I.L. in runs scored (119) in 1913.

CAME TO YANKS: In August of 1913, Baltimore traded Fritz to the Yanks for outfielder Bert Daniels and third baseman Ezra Midkiff. A native of the Baltimore area, Fritz was a friend of Baltimore Oriole owner Jack Dunn. In fact, early in 1914 while a member of the Yanks, Fritz was with Dunn when the Oriole owner made the historic signing of Babe Ruth.

YANKEE INFIELDER: Fritz was a 23-year-old rookie third baseman with the Yanks in 1913. He was the Yanks' regular third baseman in 1914-15 and a utility player in 1916, playing 26 games in the outfield, 11 games at third and four games at second. In 1917 Fritz was the Yankee second baseman. Fritz made 206 putouts in 1914, the most ever recorded by a Yankee third baseman.

BASE STEALER: His 74 stolen bases in 1914, besides leading the AL that year, established the Yankee club record for over 70 years. Fritz was probably the second greatest base-stealing threat in Yankees history. He is seventh on the all-time Yankee stolen base list (183), although he was on the club only 4½ seasons.

CLUB LEADERSHIP: Fritz led the Yanks in stolen bases three times. Twice he led the Yanks in runs scored.

TRADED: In January of 1918, the Yanks traded Fritz, Joe Gedeon, Les Nunamaker and pitchers Urban Shocker and Nick Cullop to the St. Louis Browns for second baseman Del Pratt and pitcher Eddie Plank. (Hall of Famer Plank refused to report to the Yanks and retired.)

BALTIMORE STAR: Fritz played third base for the Browns in 1918, his final ML season. From 1919-28, Fritz played again for Baltimore of the International League, and hit .300 or better in 8 of 10 seasons. Fritz holds I.L. records for runs scored (1379) and stolen bases (383) in an I.L. career. Fritz also spent time as manager of the Orioles, and years later when Baltimore became an AL team, he was a scout for the big-league Orioles.

BALTIMORE FAMILY: The Maisels always were important people in the baseball community of Baltimore. Fritz's brother George played four seasons of ML baseball and Fritz's son Bob was a longtime sports editor of *The Baltimore Sun*. Bob often called his father "the little round man."

MAISEL, FRITZ

Yr.	G	AB	R	H	2B	3B	HR	RBI	BB	SB	BA	SA
1913	51	187	33	48	4	3	0	12	34	25	.257	.310
1914	150	548	78	131	23	9	2	47	76	74	.239	.325
1915	135	530	77	149	16	6	4	46	48	51	.281	.357
1916	53	158	18	36	5	0	0	7	20	4	.228	.259
1917	113	404	46	80	4	4	0	20	36	29	.198	.228
5 Yrs.	502	1827	252	444	52	22	6	132	214	183	.243	.305
Life.	591	2111	295	510	56	24	6	148	260	194	.242	.299

MANNING, RUBE
(BORN WALTER S. MANNING)

Nickname: "Speedy"
Yankee: 1907-10
Pitcher
Born: April 29, 1883
Birthplace: Chambersburg, PA
Died: April 23, 1930
Bat: R; Throw: R
Ht: 6'; Wt: 180

CAREER YANKEE: Rube pitched his entire ML career with the Yanks (Highlanders). In 1908 he was the club's No. 3 starter and second biggest winner (13) on the staff behind Jack Chesbro. He and Chesbro got little support from their last-place team. In 1909 Rube was the Yanks' No. 5 starter. He had a career record of 5-2 as a relief pitcher.

MANNING, RUBE

Yr.	W-L	Pct.	SA	G	GS	CG	IP	H	BB	SO	SH	ERA
1907	0-1	.000	0	1	1	1	9	8	3	3	0	3.00
1908	13-16	.448	1	41	26	19	245	228	86	113	2	2.94
1909	7-11	.389	1	26	21	11	173	167	48	71	2	3.17
1910	2-4	.333	0	16	9	4	75	80	25	25	0	3.70
4 Yrs.	22-32	.407	2	84	57	35	502	483	162	212	4	3.14
Life. Same.												

MANTLE, MICKEY

Nicknames: "The Commerce Comet" "The Mick"
Yankee: 1951-68
Outfielder, 1B
Born: October 20, 1931
Birthplace: Spavinaw, OK
Died: August 13, 1995
Bat: Both; Throw: R
Ht: 6'; Wt: 200

HONORS: In 1974 Mickey was inducted into the Baseball Hall of Fame in his first year of eligibility. Three times the Baseball Writers named Mickey MVP of the AL (1956, 1957, 1962). In 1956 Mickey captured the AL Triple Crown and *Sport* magazine named him its "Man of the Year," the Associated Press gave Mickey its Male Athlete of the Year Award and Mickey won the Hickok Belt as the Top Professional Athlete of the Year. Also in 1956, he was named ML Player of the Year by *The Sporting News*. In 1962 *The Sporting News* named Mickey AL Player of the Year.

Mickey was selected as an outfielder to *The Sporting News*' ML All-Star team in 1952, 1956 and 1957 and the AL All-Star squad in 1961, 1962, and 1964. The New York Baseball Writers gave Mickey their Sid Mercer Award in 1956 and 1961. (Roger Maris also got the award the latter year.) In 1956 Mickey won the "Sultan of Swat" Award. Mickey won the prestigious Hutch Award (honoring courage in baseball) in 1965, the first year it was given. Mickey won many other awards and honors during his baseball career from organizations all over the country. Upon his retirement as a player, Mickey's famous number "7" uniform was retired by the Yankee club. On April 12, 1970, a plaque honoring Mickey's Yankee achievements was dedicated at Yankee Stadium. In 1978 Mickey was presented with the Pride of the Yankees Award, given each year by the Yankee Foundation.

MICKEY'S FATHER: Tom Greenwade, Harry Craft, Casey Stengel and Ralph Houk were all important factors in the development of Mickey as a player and person. But the man who had the greatest influence on Mickey was his dad, Mutt Mantle. Mr. Mantle was a knowledgeable and passionate baseball fan, and he was dedicated to making his first son a ML ballplayer. His favorite player in 1931 was Mickey Cochrane, so he named his son Mickey. From the time Mickey was a young child, Mr. Mantle worked hard teaching the game to the boy, a game that would keep Mickey out of the rough life in the lead mines that was his father's. (But swinging a sledge hammer while working in the mines as a teenager developed Mickey's powerful arms.) Mr. Mantle converted his son, a natural right-handed hitter, into a switch-hitter.

SENSATIONAL PROSPECT: As a high schooler in Commerce, OK, Mickey played semipro baseball for the Baxter Springs Whiz Kids. In 1948, Yankee scout Tom Greenwade got his first look at Mantle, who was then known as "Little Mickey." In 1949, Whiz Kid Manager Barney Barnett and umpire Kay Jacobson arranged for Mickey to have a tryout with the Yanks' Joplin, Missouri farm club. Joplin Manager Johnny Sturm was impressed and mentioned Mickey to Greenwade. When Greenwade saw Mickey he was shocked to discover Mickey had put on plenty of solid weight and had grown several inches. Following Mickey's high school graduation, the Yankee scout met with Mickey and his father after a Whiz Kid game, and, sitting in a car during a rainstorm, signed Mickey to an $1,100 bonus and a $400 fee for playing the rest of the season. Greenwade claimed Mickey was a doubtful prospect, but shortly thereafter Mickey read Greenwade compared him to Ruth and DiMaggio. Both St. Louis clubs blew chances to sign Mickey. The Browns showed little interest when Mickey visited St. Louis and Cardinals Scout Runt Marr—the first scout to contact Mickey—failed to return to Mickey, apparently because the Cards did not want to give him bonus money.

MINOR LEAGUE STAR: After Tom Greenwade signed him in 1949, Mickey was sent to the Yanks' Class-D club at Independence and had a good season (.313, 7 HRs, 63 RBIs) as a shortstop. In 1950 Mickey played shortstop for Joplin and had a sensational year at the plate (.383, 26 HRs, 136 RBIs). At the end of 1950, Mickey traveled with the Yanks, although he was not on the active roster. By 1950 Mickey was known in baseball circles as a phenom, a player who combined tremendous power

The great Mickey Mantle flexes his muscles for the camera, demonstrating his powerful swing.

and speed. One of the most intelligent men in baseball history, Branch Rickey, then Pirate GM, stated that Mickey was the best prospect he had ever set his eyes on. Rickey offered the top power hitter of the NL and a future Hall of Famer, Ralph Kiner, AND $500,000 to the Yanks for Mickey! The Yanks declined the offer.

1951 SEASON: At the Yanks' "instructional school," Mickey made daily headlines with his remarkable skills. Hitting from either side of the plate, he knocked balls eye-popping distances through the thin Arizona air. So impressed was Casey Stengel that he had Mickey stay with the big club for spring training. Just before the season opened, Stengel decided to keep Mickey on the Yanks, although Mickey was only 19 years old! The first job was giving Mickey a crash course in playing the outfield. Since he had been a minor league shortstop (and not a very good one), it was a big adjustment for the kid to make. But Casey, Joe DiMaggio and Tommy Henrich all helped Mickey learn the art of playing in the outfield. But because Mickey was striking out too often early in the 1951 campaign, the Yanks sent him down to their top farm club at Kansas City. Casey told Mickey, "Don't feel bad about this. You got a round-trip ticket. You'll be back with us before the season is over." Mickey continued to slump at Kansas City, but after a talk with his father, went on a hitting rampage and had great statistics at KC in only 166 at-bats (.361, 11 HRs, 50 RBIs). Mickey finished the 1951 season with the Yanks and produced well (.267, 13 HRs, 65 RBIs). For the season with the Yanks, Mickey played right field next to the great DiMaggio, who was in his last season as Yankee centerfielder. He made $7,000 for his rookie year, $1,000 more than the minimum, because Stengel urged GM Weiss to give Mickey the "extra" money.

YANKEE SUPERSTAR: When Joe DiMaggio retired following the 1951 campaign, Mickey won the job as the Yankee centerfielder and played the position from 1952-66, although occasionally he played left or right to save himself from too much running when his injuries were severe. In 1967-68, Mickey's final two seasons, he played first base to save wear on his aching legs. Mickey was a superstar in every sense of the word and was the top drawing card of the AL during his career. He was a member of 12 AL pennant-winning teams and seven World Champions. He was the greatest switch-hitter in the history of baseball. He hit .300 or better 10 times in his career and only the fact that he played his final four seasons on sheer guts prevented him from having a lifetime batting average well above .300. He finished at .298.

RESPECTED PLAYER: Mickey was loved by his teammates, respected by his foes and liked by all baseball people. Other players were in awe of his abilities. Lou Boudreau said of Mickey, "Ted Williams could never hit the ball as hard as

Mickey Mantle taking a mighty swing.

Mantle." The great Stan Musial once stated, "If Mantle hits .400 and 60 home runs some year. I can't say I'll be surprised." Once in the early 1960s, Tiger star Al Kaline was signing autographs in a Detroit store when a boy told him, "You're not half as good as Mickey Mantle." Replied Kaline, "Son, NOBODY is half as good as Mickey Mantle." Managers around the AL also held Mickey in great respect. Al Lopez said, "Mantle has more power than Ruth." Paul Richards once said of Mickey, "He can hit better than anyone else, he can throw better, and he can run better. What else is there?"

HOME RUNS: Mickey hit 373 HRs batting lefthanded and 163 HRs from the right side during regular season ML play. He hit 266 HRs at Yankee Stadium (the Yankee Stadium record) and 270 HRs on the road. The park where Mickey hit the most road HRs was Detroit's Tiger Stadium where he blasted 42 HRs. He hit 16 HRs in May, 1956, the most ever hit in that month in ML history. In 1961, Mickey and Roger Maris staged a dramatic run at Babe Ruth's single-season HR record and their combined HR total of that year (115) is the record for two players on a team, breaking the Ruth-Gehrig mark set in 1927 (107). The 54 HRs Mickey hit in 1961 were the most ever hit by a runner-up to a league HR champion until surpassed by Sammy Sosa (66) in 1998, the year Mark McGwire blasted 70 home runs. It also stands as the all-time high for a switch-hitter. His Home Run ratio of 1961 was 10.5 HRs per 100 at-bats. September injuries prevented Mickey from catching Ruth's HR record in 1961. In games played on July 4 and July 6 of 1962, Mickey hit four consecutive HRs, a record matched by few others. On May 13,1955 he hit three HRs in a game. His first ML HR was a 450-foot shot off the White Sox' Randy Gumpert at Comiskey Park on May 1, 1951 and on September 10, 1962, he hit the 400th HR of his career against Detroit. On May 13, 1967, Mickey hit his 500th HR off Baltimore's Stu Miller. A plaque with a bust of Mantle was installed where the ball landed, but was stolen during Yankee Stadium's renovation in the 1970s. Missing for nearly 20 years, in 1995 it was recovered by the FBI and private investigators hired by Major League Baseball. A former security guard at the Stadium was charged in the case. On September 20, 1968, Mickey hit his 535th HR, putting him ahead of Jimmie Foxx on the all-time list. Detroit's Denny McLain apparently gave Mickey a sweet pitch to hit on purpose. Mickey hit HRs from both sides of the plate in the same game 10 times, an AL record. In a 1965 exhibition game, he hit the first HR ever hit at Houston's Astrodome. In a 1966 hot streak, he hit 11 HRs in 14 games.

TAPE MEASURE HOME RUNS: Mickey hit some of the longest HRs ever hit and fans throughout the AL flocked to see him send one into orbit. On two occasions Mickey nearly became the first man to hit, a fair ball out of Yankee Stadium: 1) May 30, 1956—He hit a HR off Washington's Pedro Ramos that struck the facade, just a few feet from clearing the right field roof. 2) May 22, 1963—Batting lefthanded again, Mickey hit a HR off Kansas City's Bill Fischer that struck the facade at almost the exact spot as the previous shot. However, this ball was still rising! He hit the first HR to go over the old black screen (that served as the hitters' back-drop) to the right of the 461 ft. sign at Yankee Stadium. That shot came on June 21, 1955, off southpaw Alex Kellner and the ball landed in the ninth row of the bleachers, 486 feet from home plate. Mickey hit a change-

up! On August 12, 1964, Mickey hit the longest HR ever measured inside Yankee Stadium. Batting lefty against Chicago's Ray Herbert, he drove the ball over the 461 ft. sign in center field, a 502-foot swat! Batting right-handed, Mickey in 1953 hit a 565-foot HR over the left field wall at Griffith Stadium in Washington off Chuck Stobbs. The HR ushered in the age of the tape measure. In Game 2 of the 1960 World Series, Mickey hit two of the longest HRs ever seen at Pittsburgh's Forbes Field. Both were hit right-handed and the second HR, hit off Joe Gibbon, sailed beyond the 457 ft. sign in dead center field, making Mickey the first righty to clear that sign in Forbes' history. Batting lefty at Minnesota's Metropolitan Stadium, Mickey hit a HR that cleared a double fence in right field, a 480-foot blast. Batting right-handed at Chicago's Comiskey Park, he hit the base of a light tower on top of the left field roof. Mickey hit one of the longest HRs ever seen at Cleveland's Municipal Stadium—a 470-foot drive to center field—over the fence and against the old bleachers on one hop. Several times he cleared the right field roof of Tiger Stadium in Detroit. These are but a few of Mickey's tape-measure HRs. Seldom, in fact, did he hit a cheap one.

SPEED: Before his many leg injuries slowed him down, Mickey was one of the fastest men to ever play the game. Running out of the lefthanded batter's box, Mickey once ran from home plate to first base in 3.1 seconds, the fastest time ever clocked. In 1961 he grounded into only two double plays all season, setting a Yankee club record. He was a smart and daring base runner. On several occasions Mickey scored from second base on a wild pitch. He led the Yanks in stolen bases eight times. Sometimes his speed even helped his power totals. Mickey hit six inside-the-park HRs in his career. In his first 12 seasons, he stole 133 bases in 163 attempts for a remarkable .816 percentage. Mickey brought back the forgotten art of the drag bunt from the lefthanded box and he was almost impossible to get out. When he was in a slump, Mickey could snap out of it with a drag-bunt hit.

LEAGUE LEADER: Mickey won the HR Crown of the AL four times (1955, '56, '58, '60). He won the AL slugging title four times (1955, '56, '61, '62) and led the AL in runs scored in six seasons (1954, '56, '57, '58, '60, '61). His leading the AL in runs scored three years in a row (1956-58) tied an AL record. For batters with at least 500 at-bats a season, Mickey led the AL in fewest times grounding into double plays three times (1954, '56, '61), tying an AL record. In 1956 Mickey won the Triple Crown, leading the AL in HRs (52), RBIs (130) and batting (.353); thus making him the only other Yankee besides Lou Gehrig to ever win the Triple Crown. In 1956 Mickey also led the AL in total bases (376), runs scored (132), slugging (.705) and HR ratio (9.8 HRs per 100 at-bats). Thrice Mickey led the AL in HR ratio (1954, '56, '61). Mickey led the AL in walks five times (1955, '57, '58, '61, '62). In 1955 he led the AL in triples (11). Mickey's 1956 slugging mark of .705 has been topped only three times in the AL since then. Mickey's 1957 batting mark of .365 was the highest BA by a runner-up to a batting champ (Williams) in 20 years and remains the highest BA ever recorded by a switch-hitter in AL history.

Mickey Mantle (New York Yankees Archives)

CLUB LEADERSHIP: Mickey led the Yanks in different offensive categories many times in many seasons. But he led the club in walks 14 times and runs scored 10 times, more often than anyone in Yankee history in both.

GETTING ON BASE: Because Mickey walked so often (pitchers were afraid of him and he had a great-batting eye) and was a good hitter for average, he had great on-base averages (OBA). His .515 on-base average of 1957 is the ninth highest in ML history. In 1964 his .426 on-base average was 20 points higher than anyone else's in the AL. Mickey's lifetime on-base average (.423) is tied for 18th highest in ML history. Only three centerfielders (Billy Hamilton, Ty Cobb, Tris Speaker) have lifetime OBAs that are higher than Mickey's.

BASEBALL'S ALL-TIME LEADER LIST: Mickey is among baseball's all-time leaders in many offensive categories. He is seventh in walks (1734); tied for seventh with Willie Mays and seventh in career HR ratio (6.6 HRs per 100 at-bats); tenth in HRs (536); 33rd in total bases (4511); and 32nd in extra base hits (952). Mantle is tied for 13th in multiple-homer games (46) and second in times hitting a home run from both sides of the plate in the same game (10).

ALL-TIME YANKEE LEADER: Mickey is at or near the top of team lists in major offensive categories. He is first in Yankee games played (2401) and at-bats (8102); second in HRs (536) and walks (1734); third in runs scored (1677) and hits (2415); fourth in RBIs (1509) and slugging (.557); sixth in doubles (344); ninth in stolen bases (153); and ninth in triples (72). His batting average (.298) ranks him 13th in Yankee history.

INJURIES: Mickey played his entire ML career with an assortment of serious injuries, especially knee injuries. Even before he had played his first ML game he was afflicted with osteomyelitis, a bone disease which Mickey contracted in high school after he was kicked in the shin playing football. Mickey courageously played with pain throughout his 18-year Yankee career. His first major injury as a Yankee occurred in the 1951 World Series when he stepped on a water sprinkler in Yankee Stadium's right field. Several injuries limited Mickey's play in different World Series. In 1962 he badly hurt his knee again, and in 1963 he missed 96 games because of a broken bone in a foot that got caught in the fence in Baltimore. A shoulder injury ruined his 1965 season. Following a shoulder operation before the 1966 season, Mickey reported he was ready for Opening Day, 1966! There were many other injuries in Mick's career, yet he played hurt better than all of baseball's healthy players. Once at an All-Star Game, Hall of Famer Early Wynn watched Mickey dress and said, "I watched him bandage that knee—that whole leg—and I saw what he had to go through every day to play. Seeing those legs, his power becomes unbelievable." Mickey had a real fear of dying young due to the fact that his father and father's brother both died young. Mickey felt he would not live to be middle-aged, and he sometimes abused himself, reflecting a live-for-today attitude. In June 1995 Mantle underwent a liver transplant with the initial prognosis being very favorable, but he died of cancer August 13, 1995.

DEFENSIVE ABILITIES: Mickey was a great defensive centerfielder. His speed (before his numerous leg injuries) enabled him to track down balls in Yankee Stadium's spacious center field. He had a strong and accurate throwing arm. In 1962 Mickey won a Gold Glove for his play in center field. The Mick led all AL outfielders in assists in 1954 (20). He led AL outfielders in fielding in 1955 (.995) and 1959 (.995). In 1966 he fielded 1.000 in 97 games in the outfield. In 1952 Mickey led AL outfielders in double plays (five). He made numerous sensational catches, some of the best in baseball history, during his career. In 1967 and 1968 he played first base (in an effort to save his legs) and did an excellent job, to the amazement of many experts who said the switch would be impossible.

EARLY MISUNDERSTANDINGS: The first half of his ML career, basically the entire decade of the 1950s, was tough for Mickey. New York fans and press were occasionally brutal with him. When Mickey arrived in New York in 1951, it was with much publicity and fanfare. The fans immediately expected the second coming of Babe Ruth, and because Mickey was not an immediate superstar, they felt let down and took to booing him in the worst ways. Mickey, being a shy youngster, was not demonstrative on the field, and the fans mistook this lack of flair for conceit. Another problem stemmed from his replacing the legendary Joe DiMaggio, who was incredibly popular in New York. Many DiMaggio fans refused to accept the fact that anyone could take Joe's place either in center field or as the star of the Yanks. To make matters worse, Casey Stengel believed that Mickey was not living up to his potential as the game's greatest player ever. Mickey's father died early in Mickey's Yankee career, and Casey became sort of a father figure. But a stern father figure he could be. No matter how well Mickey did, Casey expected more. Following the 1958 season, in which Mickey won the HR Crown (42) besides hitting .304, Casey was upset and said, "I never saw a ballplayer who had greater promise. He could be the best there ever was. Name me one thing he can't do. You can't. And listen to me. Every year he ought to lead the league in everything. Nobody hits the ball farther, right or lefthanded. Nobody is faster running to first base, or stealing. There ain't nothing wrong with his arm, and he can catch anything out there, except when he gets careless, which he does when he starts thinking about the foreign situation, the national debt and maybe his putting." All these circumstances could have kept him from becoming a great player, but none did. He survived all criticism, even the nonsense that he was a stupid player. Once the Dodger players were sitting around telling stories to support their view that Mickey was immature. Said Jackie Robinson: "Hell, we've got plenty of guys that stupid. But we don't have anyone that good." It must also be remembered that Mickey was only 19 when he came to New York from Oklahoma. No two worlds could have been more different, and Mickey was still only 27 in 1959, his ninth ML season! The pressures on such a young man in strange surroundings must have been immense. His friendships with Whitey Ford and Billy Martin were probably comforting.

TEAM LEADER: Mickey was the undisputed leader of the Yanks during the 1960s. In 1960 things changed between Mickey and the fans. In an August game, Mickey failed to run out a double-play grounder in which Roger Maris hurt himself trying to break up the play at second base. Mickey heard the worst booing of his career, especially the next night when he was introduced at the Stadium before an important game against Baltimore. Mickey hit two HRs to win the game, and the cheers were deafening. The New York press wrote the next day of all Mickey's attributes, including his courage in playing with painful injuries, and he was never again booed at the Stadium. As Mickey became the darling of the fans, it was Maris who began to absorb the terrible booing. Mickey's efforts in 1960 were also enough to finally please Casey. Though Maris eventually won the MVP Award, at the end of the season, Casey declared that Mantle deserved that honor. Because of his courage, grit, ability, competitiveness and friendliness with his teammates, Mickey was the most popular guy of the Yanks. In fact, few players in baseball ever said anything negative about Mickey. With the fans, in New York and on the road, Mickey was a hero during the decade of the 1960s. By the end of his career, Mickey may have been the most popular player in Yankee history with the club's fans. Mickey played the game to win, and his teammates, the fans and press came to appreciate that. And the Yanks won behind Mickey's leadership. The saying was, "As Mantle goes, so go the Yankees."

ALL-STAR GAME: Mickey was selected to the AL team for every All-Star Game season from 1952-68, except in 1966. He hit a HR in the 1955 All-Star Game off Robin Roberts and the next year cracked an All-Star HR off Warren Spahn. Roberts and Spahn were two of the dominant pitchers the NL had in the 1950s.

WORLD SERIES: Mickey holds the World Series records for most lifetime HRs (18), RBIs (40), runs scored (42), walks (43), extra-base hits (26) and total bases (123). Mickey was badly injured in Game 2 of the 1951 Series when he wrenched his knee after going 1-for-5 at the plate. He hit a HR in both Game 6 and Game 7 of the 1952 Series to ensure Yankee wins and the World Championship. His HR won Game 2 of the 1953 Series, then he hit the fourth grand slam in Series history in Game 5. Mickey saved Don Larsen's perfect game in the 1956 Series by making a fantastic catch of a drive hit in the left-centerfield alley by Gil Hodges. He also hit a HR in Larsen's support. Besides hitting two tape-measure HRs in Game 2 of the 1960 Series, Mickey made a great base running play in the ninth inning of Game 7 to allow the Yanks to tie the game. Mickey batted .400 in that Series. His valiant HR in Game 4 of the 1963 Series tied the game, 1-1, before the Dodgers won, 2-1, to sweep the Series. Mickey hit a ninth-inning HR at Yankee Stadium to beat the Cardinals, 2-1, in Game 3 of the 1964 Series. He hit a HR in each of his last two Series games (Game 6 and Game 7 of the 1964 Series). He had at least one HR in nine Series, two HRs in six Series and three HRs in three Series—all World Series records.

RETIREMENT: On March 1, 1969, at the Yanks' spring training camp in Fort Lauderdale, FL, Mickey announced his retirement as a ballplayer. On June 8, 1969 Yankee Stadium was packed and thundering for "Mickey Mantle Day," as the club officially retired Mickey's number 7.

FACING LIFE WITHOUT BASEBALL: Mickey's popularity never waned, and he stayed connected with the Yanks as a spring-training instructor and with annual visits on Old Timers Day. Mickey badly missed the game and had recurring dreams about being locked out of Yankee Stadium as he was being announced

to hit. He continued his close friendship with Billy Martin, and over the years the two of them sank deeper and deeper into alcoholism. Billy was killed in 1989, but Mickey in 1994 received treatment. When Mickey left The Betty Ford Treatment Center, he seemed spiritually renewed, and soon thereafter, he coped, sober, with the death of a son. This was Billy, who died at age 36 after a battle with Hodgkin's disease. The Mantles, who separated, had four sons in all. Merlyn Mantle disclosed that she had been a heavy drinker, too. Joining a program for recovering alcoholics "saved my life," she told the *New York Daily News.* "In getting help for myself, I think I probably made my family aware that there is help out there. My two sons got sober and Mick got sober, too."

TWO FINAL HOME RUNS: But Mickey's body had undergone years of abuse from his drinking. On June 8, 1995 he underwent a liver transplant at Baylor University Medical Center in Dallas, which appeared to be successful. Then, in early August, cancer was detected in his lungs. He was readmitted and he died August 13. But before he went, he did two generous things. He warned America's youth not to take him for a role model. "Don't be like me," he said. And he raised awareness for the need for organ donations. His funeral was attended by some 1,500 friends, teammates, and relatives. "We were best friends," Merlyn Mantle said. "He was my best friend. Even though Mick and I didn't live together, we were very close. He loved me and I loved him."

MANTLE, MICKEY

Yr.	G	AB	R	H	2B	3B	HR	RBI	BB	SB	BA	SA
1951	96	341	61	91	11	5	13	65	43	8	.267	.443
1952	142	549	94	171	37	7	23	87	75	4	.311	.530
1953	127	461	105	136	24	3	21	92	79	8	.295	.497
1954	146	543	129	163	17	12	27	102	102	5	.300	.525
1955	147	517	121	158	25	11	37	99	113	8	.306	.611
1956	150	533	132	188	22	5	52	130	112	10	.353	.705
1957	144	474	121	173	28	6	34	94	146	16	.365	.665
1958	150	519	127	158	21	1	42	97	129	18	.304	.592
1959	144	541	104	154	23	4	31	75	94	21	.285	.514
1960	153	527	119	145	17	6	40	94	111	14	.275	.558
1961	153	514	132	163	16	6	54	128	126	12	.317	.687
1962	123	377	96	121	15	1	30	89	122	9	.321	.605
1963	65	172	40	54	8	0	15	35	40	2	.314	.622
1964	143	465	92	141	25	2	35	111	99	6	.303	.591
1965	122	361	44	92	12	1	19	46	73	4	.255	.452
1966	108	333	40	96	12	1	23	56	57	1	.288	.538
1967	144	440	63	108	17	0	22	55	107	1	.245	.434
<u>1968</u>	<u>144</u>	<u>435</u>	<u>57</u>	<u>103</u>	<u>14</u>	<u>1</u>	<u>18</u>	<u>54</u>	<u>106</u>	<u>6</u>	<u>.237</u>	<u>.398</u>
18 Yrs. Life. Same.	2401	8102	1677	2415	344	72	536	1509	1734	153	.298	.557

World Series

Yr.	G	AB	R	H	2B	3B	HR	RBI	BA
1951	2	5	1	1	0	0	0	0	.200
1952	7	29	5	10	1	1	2	3	.345
1953	6	24	3	5	0	0	2	7	.208
1955	3	10	1	2	0	0	1	1	.200
1956	7	24	6	6	1	0	3	4	.250
1957	6	19	3	5	0	0	1	2	.263
1958	7	24	4	6	0	1	2	3	.250
1960	7	25	8	10	1	0	3	11	.400
1961	2	6	0	1	0	0	0	0	.167
1962	7	25	2	3	1	0	0	0	.120
1963	4	15	1	2	0	0	1	1	.133
<u>1964</u>	<u>7</u>	<u>24</u>	<u>8</u>	<u>8</u>	<u>2</u>	<u>0</u>	<u>3</u>	<u>8</u>	<u>.333</u>
12 Yrs. Life. Same.	65	230	42	59	6	2	18	40	.257

MARIS, ROGER
(BORN ROGER EUGENE MARAS)

Yankee: 1960-66
Outfielder
Born: September 10, 1934
Birthplace: Hibbing, MN
Died: December 14, 1985
Bat: L; Throw: R
Ht: 6'; Wt: 200

HONORS: Roger was voted the MVP of the AL by the Baseball Writers in consecutive seasons (1960-61). In 1961 *The Sporting News* named Roger the ML Player of the Year. The Associated Press gave Roger their Male Athlete of the Year Award in 1961. He won the Hickok Belt as the Top Professional Athlete of 1961. Also in 1961 *Sport* magazine voted Roger their "Man of the Year" and *Sports Illustrated* named Roger their "Sportsman of the Year," the only time a Yankee has won that prestigious award. Finally, in 1961, Roger shared the Sid Mercer Award with Mickey Mantle, given by the Baseball Writers. *The Sporting News* named Roger the AL Player of the Year in 1960. He was selected to *The Sporting News* 1960 ML All-Star team and to its 1961 AL All-Star team, both years as an outfielder. Roger won the "Sultan of Swat" Award in 1960 and 1961.

CAME TO YANKS: Roger was traded to the Yanks from the Kansas City A's along with Joe DeMaestri and Kent Hadley in December of 1959. In return, the A's received Hank Bauer, Don Larsen, Norm Siebern and Marv Throneberry.

YANKEE OUTFIELDER: Roger was the Yankee rightfielder from 1960-66. Injuries kept Roger to only 86 games in the outfield in 1963. In 1965, leg injuries and a hand injury limited Roger's play to 43 games in the outfield. Roger was a shadow of his former self in 1966 when he played 95 outfield games.

Roger Maris (above) (New York Yankees Archives)

1961 SEASON: This was the season that made Roger the new single-season HR king. In one of the most dramatic assaults on a baseball record ever, Roger caught, then surpassed Babe Ruth's famous HR record of 60. Roger hit 61 HR, but struck out only 67 times for a fine HR-SO ratio. (Ironically, he was not once intentionally walked all year.) Roger hit his 50th HR on August 22, becoming the first player ever to hit his 50th HR in August. At Baltimore on September 20, in the Yanks 154th game, Roger blasted HR No. 59. At Yankee Stadium on September 26, Roger hit No. 60 off Oriole Jack Fisher. On October 1 at Yankee Stadium, Roger rocketed No. 61 off Red Sox pitcher Tracy Stallard in the season's final game. (The HR also gave Roger the RBI title—142 to 141 by Oriole Jim Gentile.) Incredibly, only 23,154 fans paid to witness the famous event. Sal Durante retrieved the historic HR in the right field grandstands and won $5000. Roger actually hit 62 HRs during the year, but he lost one HR to a game that did not become official because of rain. He hit 30 of his HRs at Yankee Stadium, tying the Stadium record. Roger hit 13 HRs against the White Sox, the most ever hit against one club since ML baseball expanded in 1961. In June Roger hit 15 HRs, the most ever hit in that month in ML history until shattered by Sammy Sosa in June of 1998, blasting 20 home runs. In a July 25 doubleheader, Roger belted four roundtrippers. From August 11-16 Roger hit a HR in each of six games in a row, tying an AL record. He was simply sensational!

1961 AFTERMATH: Roger electrified the baseball world and the nation in 1961, and it should have been—it DESERVED to be—Roger's finest moment. Unfortunately, the memory of this unprecedented national exposure was not a happy one for Roger, mostly because of the unfair pressure placed on him by the press, fans, and even the commissioner. The press asked him the same questions day after day and many members were not satisfied with the same honest answers. Roger was often portrayed as surly, when in reality he just wanted to do his job in peace. Roger was so besieged, that by the end of the season his hair was falling out. Roger and Mickey Mantle were chasing Ruth's record together. Mickey and Roger were close friends and even shared an apartment with Bob Cerv, but a competition was built up between them by the fans, egged on by the press. Through no fault of his own, Mickey was the people's choice, and Roger was unfairly branded the usurper. To make matters worse, Commissioner Frick ruled Roger had to set the record in the same 154 games Ruth played in. Any other new record would be one with an asterisk. Why? Perhaps because Frick had been close to Ruth and, in fact, was one of Ruth's ghostwriters. Even today, many baseball historians are reluctant to give Roger his rightful due. The fact that 1961 was an expansion year, which allowed at least 20 new pitchers into the AL is often waved around. Yet, Roger hit only two HRs off pitchers new to the AL, Jim Archer and Norm Bass, both of the Kansas City A's! One fact works in Roger's favor. As every year went by, his record became more and more impressive until the emergence of McGwire and Sosa. The old adage in sports that records are made to be broken was in full force in 1998 when *both* Mark McGwire and Sammy Sosa shattered Maris' record with 70 and 66 homers, respectively! In 1999, both players *again* topped the 60-homer mark, McGwire beating Sammy Sosa by two with 65 homers. Barry Bonds (73) and Sosa (64) combined for 137 homers in 2001.

A shot of Roger Maris preparing to shag some flies.

IN THE WORDS OF CASEY: Stengel, for whom Roger played only one year (1960), was once asked to evaluate Roger's baseball skills. Said Casey in that unique way of his: "I give the man a point for speed. I do this because Maris can run fast. Then I can give him a point because he can slide fast. I give him another point because he can bunt. I also give him a point because he can field. He is very good around fences—sometimes on top of fences. Next, I give him a point because he can throw. A rightfielder has to be a thrower or he's not a rightfielder. So I add up my points and I've got five for him before I even come to his hitting. I would say this is a good man." Casey knew a complete ballplayer when he saw one.

OFFENSIVE ABILITIES: Roger was one of the most feared power hitters in baseball in the early 1960s. In the five consecutive seasons that the Yanks won the AL flag (1960-64), Roger averaged 36.4 HRs a year. In three straight seasons (1960-62) he knocked in more than 100 runs a year, each year leading the Yanks in RBIs. AL pitchers learned to respect Roger. In a 12-inning game played on May 22, 1962, he was intentionally walked four times, an AL record. Roger was a good and daring base runner who made many heads-up plays on the base paths. He had above average speed, and he always hustled on the playing field.

DEFENSIVE ABILITIES: Roger was a tremendous defensive rightfielder, possessing a cannon arm. In 1960 he won a Gold Glove Award. He often dove into Yankee Stadium's right field seats to rob opponents of HRs. Roger's 1964 fielding average (.996) is the highest ever recorded by a Yankee rightfielder. One would not be far from the truth in stating that Roger was the greatest fielding rightfielder in Yankee history.

LEAGUE LEADER: In 1960 Roger led the AL in RBIs (112) and slugging (.581). In 1961 he led the AL in runs scored (132-tie), HRs (61) and RBIs (142). That was the last time a Yankee player won a RBI title until 1985.

ALL-TIME YANKEE LEADER: Roger ranks seventh on the all-time Yankee slugging list (.515). He is tenth on the Yanks' all time HR list (203).

ALL-STAR GAME: In 1960, 1961 and 1962, Roger was picked to the AL team for the All-Star Game.

WORLD SERIES: In Game 1 of the 1960 Series, Roger became the seventh man in Series history to hit a HR in his first Series at-bat. Roger won crucial Game 3 of the 1961 Series with a ninth inning HR against the Reds. He saved Game 7 and the 1962 Series when he ran down Willie Mays' ninth-inning double and held Matty Alou, the potential tying run, at third (from which he did not score). It was a great hustling play, and the Yanks beat the Giants, 1-0. Roger is sixth on the all-time World Series runs scored list (26).

SAD FINAL YEARS: Roger's last few Yankee seasons were unhappy for him. The fans treated him badly and the club was unfair with him. Roger suffered a hand fracture in May of 1965, and numerous x-rays were taken, but according to Roger, he was never told of the break and was urged to work out in an effort to get back into the line-up. Of course, there was no way that Roger could perform up to his standards, but it was not until September that he found out he had a broken hand. During the 1966 season, Roger informed Manager Ralph Houk of his plans to retire after that season. Houk convinced him to wait until the following spring training to announce his decision. After the 1966 season, Roger was assured by Yankee GM Lee MacPhail that the Yanks had no plans for trading him, and that the club would allow him to retire as wished.

TRADED: In one of the worst trades in Yankee history, the Yanks traded Roger to the Cardinals for Charley Smith in December of 1966. Roger helped the Cardinals to a World Series title in 1967, and a NL Pennant winner in 1968 before retiring as a player. He was offered a beer distributorship from Anheiser-Busch in October 1968. Roger was finally talked into returning to the Yankee Old-Timer games in the 1980s. His number "9" was retired by the Yankees in a ceremony at Yankee Stadium on July 21, 1984. Roger died after a long fight with cancer on December 14, 1985.

Maris' 61 HRs—1961

Date	No.	Pitcher	At
April 26	1	Foytack, Det.	Detroit
May 3	2	Ramos, MN	Minnesota
May 6	3	Grba, L.A.	Los Angeles
May 17	4	Burnside, WA	Yankee Stadium
May 19	5	J. Perry, Cleve.	Cleveland
May 20	6	Bell, Cleve.	Cleveland
May 21	7	Estrada, Balt.	Yankee Stadium
May 24	8	Conley, Bos.	Yankee Stadium
May 28	9	McLish, Chi.	Yankee Stadium
May 30	10	Conley, Bos.	Boston
	11	Fornieles, Bos.	
May 31	12	Muffett, Bos.	Boston
June 2	13	McLish, Chi.	Chicago
June 3	14	Shaw, Chi.	Chicago
June 4	15	Kemmerer, Chi.	Chicago
June 6	16	Palmquist, MN	Yankee Stadium
June 7	17	Ramos, MN	Yankee Stadium
June 9	18	Herbert, K.C.	Yankee Stadium
June 11	19	Grba, L.A.	Yankee Stadium
	20	James, L.A.	
June 13	21	J. Perry, Cleve.	Cleveland
June 14	22	Bell, Cleve.	Cleveland
June 17	23	Mossi, Det.	Detroit
June 18	24	Casale, Det.	Detroit
June 19	25	Archer, K.C.	Kansas City
June 20	26	Nuxhall, K.C.	Kansas City
June 22	27	Bass, K.C.	Kansas City
July 1	28	Sisler, Wash.	Yankee Stadium
July 2	29	Burnside, Wash.	Yankee Stadium
	30	Klippstein, Wash.	
July 4	31	Lary, Det.	Yankee Stadium
July 5	32	Funk, Cleve.	Yankee Stadium
July 9	33	Monbouquette, Bos.	Yankee Stadium
July 13	34	Wynn, Chi.	Chicago
July 15	35	Herbert, Chi.	Chicago
July 21	36	Monbouquette, Bos.	Boston
July 25	37	Baumann, Chi.	Yankee Stadium
	38	Larsen, Chi.	
	39	Kemmerer, Chi.	
	40	Hacker, Chi.	
August 4	41	Pascual, MN	Yankee Stadium
August 11	42	Burnside, Wash.	Washington
August 12	43	Donovan, Wash.	Washington
August 13	44	Daniels, Wash.	Washington
	45	Kutyna, Wash.	
August 15	46	Pizarro, Chi.	Yankee Stadium
August 16	47	Pierce, Chi.	Yankee Stadium
	48	Pierce, Chi.	
August 20	49	J. Perry, Cleve.	Cleveland
August 22	50	McBride, L.A.	Los Angeles
August 26	51	Walker, K.C.	Kansas City
September 2	52	Lary, Det.	Yankee Stadium
	53	Aguirre, Det.	
September 6	54	Cheney, Wash.	Yankee Stadium
September 7	55	Stigman, Cleve.	Yankee Stadium
September 9	56	Grant, Cleve.	Yankee Stadium
September 16	57	Lary, Det.	Detroit
September 17	58	Fox, Det.	Detroit
September 20	59	Pappas, Balt.	Baltimore
September 26	60	Fisher, Balt.	Yankee Stadium
October 1	61	Stallard, Bos.	Yankee Stadium

HRs BY MONTHS:

April	—	1
May	—	11
June	—	15
July	—	13
Aug.	—	11
Sept.	—	9
Oct.	—	1

WHERE HIT:

Yankee Stadium—30	Kansas City—4
Chicago—5	Washington—4
Cleveland—5	Los Angeles—2
Detroit—5	Baltimore—1
Boston—4	Minnesota—1

PITCHERS ROGER HIT HARD:

Burnside, Washington — 3 HRs
Lary, Detroit — 3 HRs
J. Perry, Cleveland — 3 HRs
9 pitchers allowed 2 HRs each

NUMBER OF HRs HIT AGAINST EACH AL TEAM:

TEAM	NUMBER
Chicago	13
Washington	9
Cleveland	8
Detroit	8
Boston	7
Kansas City	5
Los Angeles	4
Minnesota	4
Baltimore	3

MARIS, ROGER

Yr.	G	AB	R	H	2B	3B	HR	RBI	BB	SB	BA	SA
1960	136	499	98	141	18	7	39	112	70	2	.283	.581
1961	161	590	132	159	16	4	61	142	94	0	.269	.620
1962	157	590	92	151	34	1	33	100	87	1	.256	.485
1963	90	312	53	84	14	1	23	53	35	1	.269	.542
1964	141	513	86	144	12	2	26	71	62	3	.281	.464
1965	46	155	22	37	7	0	8	27	29	0	.239	.439
1966	119	348	37	81	9	2	13	43	36	0	.233	.382
7 Yrs.	850	3007	520	797	110	17	203	548	413	7	.265	.515
Life.	1463	5101	826	1325	195	42	275	851	652	21	.260	.476

World Series

Yr.	G	AB	R	H	2B	3B	HR	RBI	BA
1960	7	30	6	8	1	0	2	2	.267
1961	5	19	4	2	1	0	1	2	.105
1962	7	23	4	4	1	0	1	5	.174
1963	2	5	0	0	0	0	0	0	.000
1964	7	30	4	6	0	0	1	1	.200
5 Yrs.	28	107	18	20	3	0	5	10	.187
Life.	41	152	26	33	5	0	6	18	.217

MARTIN, BILLY
(ALFRED MANUEL MARTIN)

Nicknames: "Billy the Kid", "The Brat"
Yankee: 1950-53 (military) 1955-57
Second Baseman, SS, 3B
Born: May 16, 1928
Birthplace: Berkeley, CA
Died: December 25, 1989
Bat: R; Throw: R
Ht: 5'11"; Wt: 165

YOUNG PROSPECT: In the late 1940s, Billy was with Oakland of the Pacific Coast League. Oaks' Manager Casey Stengel, after taking the Yankee helm, had the Yanks obtain Billy, who began his ML career in 1950 after impressing everyone at spring training camp.

AGGRESSIVE PLAYER: Casey Stengel loved him, because Billy was an aggressive, hustling player who always gave 100% effort. Billy was brash and cocky. He hung around Joe DiMaggio on his first day in a Yankee uniform, an unprecedented achievement. Joe and Billy became good friends. Sometimes Billy got into scraps with opposing players and some of the fights were aimed at awakening a slumping Yankee team. His most memorable fights were against Clint Courtney of the Browns and Jimmy Piersall of the Red Sox. By most accounts, little Billy was undefeated. Stengel kept pushing Billy to be more and more aggressive. After DiMaggio retired, Billy became one of the leaders of the team. He was quite popular on the Yankee club and established friendships with such Yankee greats as Mickey Mantle, Whitey Ford, Yogi Berra and Phil Rizzuto. Whenever an opposing player attempted to intimidate the slight Rizzuto, he had to answer to Billy. A frustrated Brooklyn Dodger Manager Charlie Dressen once called Billy "the All-American out."

YANKEE SECOND BASEMAN: Billy was a Yankee utility infielder in 1950 and 1951. Early in his rookie season, he was sent to the Yanks' Kansas City farm club for seasoning. He spent a month there before returning in June, 1950. He was the regular Yankee second baseman in 1952, 1953 and 1956. (Billy missed the 1954 season and most of the 1955 campaign while serving in the military.) He was a fine defensive second baseman. In 1953 he led AL second basemen in turning double plays (121). During a doubleheader played on September 24, 1952, Billy handled 24 chances cleanly at second base, tying an AL record.

GOOD HITTER: Billy was a good contact hitter who occasionally hit for power. In his first ML game, played on April 18, 1950, he stroked two hits in the eighth inning, a ML record for hits in one inning of a player's first ML game. Billy was always a tough out in a clutch situation, thriving on pressure. In 1953 he led the Yanks in games played (149) and at-bats (587). Because of his fine all-round play in 1956, Billy was picked to the AL team for the All-Star Game.

WORLD SERIES: Billy was spectacular in World Series play. He is tied for fourth on the all-time Series list for triples (three). His .333 lifetime Series batting average is fourth (with at least 75 ABs) on the all-time Series list. Martin is tied for fourth (with several other players) in triples with three. Billy's three-run HR lead the Yanks to a 7-1 win over the Dodgers in Game 2 of the 1952 Series. He saved the 1952 Series for the Yanks in Game 7 when he made a great lunging catch of a windblown infield pop-up late in the game with two outs and the bases loaded with Dodgers. Billy was the hitting star of the 1953 Series (.500, 23 total bases—third most in Series history) and for his efforts he won the Babe Ruth Award as the Series MVP. His single in the bottom of the ninth inning of Game 6 of the 1953 Series decided the game, giving the Yanks a record fifth straight World Championship. As the Yankee players mobbed each other, Stengel was the first to jump out of the Yankee dugout and bearhug Billy in the pair's most jubilant moment together.

Billy Martin (right), with Mickey Mantle (center), and Whitey Ford in a comedic baseball moment.

TRADED: On the night of May 16, 1957, Billy was one of six Yankee players partying (most were accompanied by their wives) at the Copacabana Club in New York City. An argument ensued between the Yanks and a group of drunken bowlers and one of the bowlers was roughed up. (It is almost a certainty that this bowler was hit by a bouncer.) The story received much publicity, and Yankee GM Weiss, who disliked Martin, blamed Billy for the incident. Weiss was very wrong about Billy's involvement, but he had made up his mind to trade Billy anyway. On June 15, 1957, the Yanks traded Billy, Ralph Terry, Woodie Held, and Bob Martyn to the Kansas City A's for pitcher Ryne Duren, second baseman Milt Graff, and outfielders Harry "Suitcase" Simpson and Jim Pisoni. Weiss used the excuse that Billy was a bad influence on Yankee stars as the reason he was included in the deal. A bad influence? Billy had roomed with Phil Rizzuto, Yogi Berra, and Mickey Mantle in years when each of them won an MVP Award!

YANKEE MANAGER: Billy managed successfully with Minnesota, Detroit, Texas, and Oakland, but it was as Yankee manager that he was best known. Billy managed the Yankees five times—1975-78, 1979, 1983, 1985 and 1988—and won two AL pennants and one World Series. He remained popular with Yankee fans, although he was greeted with less enthusiasm each time he returned.

MARTIN, BILLY

Yr.	G	AB	R	H	2B	3B	HR	RBI	BB	SB	BA	SA
1950	34	36	10	9	1	0	1	8	3	0	.250	.361
1951	51	58	10	15	1	2	0	2	4	0	.259	.345
1952	109	363	32	97	13	3	3	33	22	3	.267	.344
1953	149	587	72	151	24	6	15	75	43	6	.257	.395
1955	20	70	8	21	2	0	1	9	7	1	.300	.371
1956	121	458	76	121	24	5	9	49	30	7	.264	.397
1957	43	145	12	35	5	2	1	12	3	2	.241	.324
7 Yrs.	527	1717	220	449	70	18	30	188	112	19	.262	.376
Life.	1021	3419	425	877	137	28	64	333	188	34	.257	.369

World Series

Yr.	G	AB	R	H	2B	3B	HR	RBI	BA
1951	1	0	1	0	0	0	0	0	.000
1952	7	23	2	5	0	0	1	4	.217
1953	6	24	5	12	1	2	2	8	.500
1955	7	25	2	8	1	1	0	4	.320
1956	7	27	5	8	0	0	2	3	.296
5 Yrs.	28	99	15	33	2	3	5	19	.333
Life. Same.									

MARTINEZ, TINO

Yankee: 1996-2001
First Baseman
Born: December 7, 1967
Birthplace: Tampa, FL
Bat: L; Throw: R
Ht: 6'2"; Wt: 210

JOINS THE YANKEES: New Yankee first baseman, Tino Martinez, a member of the 1988 U. S. Olympic baseball team, broke into the major leagues with Seattle in 1990. He became their regular first sacker in '92, hitting 16, 17 and 20 home runs over the next three seasons. He blossomed in 1995, hitting .293 with 31 homers and 111 RBI, and he hit .409 (nine for 22) with one homer and five RBI against the Yankees in the Division Series. The deal that brought Tino to New York cost promising left-handed pitcher Stirling Hitchcock and third baseman Russ Davis. Besides Martinez, the Yankees gained a couple of pitchers in the transaction. Good or bad, the deal diminished the uncertainties surrounding first base at Yankee Stadium. No one ever had a tougher act to follow than replacing Don Mattingly, a first-base mainstay with the Yankees for 14 seasons.

FIRST SEASON WITH THE YANKS: In 1996, Tino hit .292 with 25 homers and a team-high 117 RBI in his first season as a Yankee. He did a Mattingly-like accomplishment by leading all American League first basemen in fielding (.996). Tino had a disappointing postseason, batted a collective .188 (nine for 48), with six runs scored and nary a home run or RBI. He was a dismal one for 11 (.091) in the World Series, striking out five times.

A SEASON PLAYERS DREAM ABOUT: Tino enjoyed a career season in 1997. He had career-high stats in batting average (.296), homers (44) and RBI (141) and led the Yankees in many offensive categories. His home-run total was the highest by a Yankee first baseman since Lou Gehrig whacked 49 roundtrippers in 1936. Tino sizzled in April, setting a new Major League record for RBI in that month with 34—the prior mark was 32 set by Barry Bonds of the Giants in 1996. He was the starting first sacker for the AL All-Star team, going 0-for-2. For his efforts

Tino Martinez replaced Don Mattingly at first base in 1996.

Yankee first sacker, Tino Martinez, takes a rip at a pitch.

in '97, Martinez was named to *The Sporting News* All-Star Team and won the Louisville Slugger/*Sporting News* Silver Slugger Award for AL first basemen. Tino continued his postseason woes, hitting .222 (4 for 18) versus Cleveland.

ANOTHER SOLID SEASON: In 1998, Tino had another solid year, batted .281 and leading the club with 28 homers and 123 RBI. This was his fourth overall consecutive season with 100+ RBI and third since joining the Yankees. He joined a very elite group of Yankee legends (Ruth, Gehrig and DiMaggio) by driving in at least 120 runs in two straight seasons. After mediocre Division and Championship Series, Tino's bat was rejuvenated versus San Diego in the World Series, hitting .385 (5-for-13) with four RBI and a homer, all coming on a Game 1 grand slam versus Mark Langston, capping a seven-run seventh in the Yankees 9-6 victory. Tino's slammer was the 17th overall in the Fall Classic and the eighth by a Yankee.

HIS 1999 SEASON: Tino hit .263 with 28 homers and 105 RBI in 159 games. He started 151 of those at first. He has now reached the 25+ and 100+ RBI plateaus for the fifth year in a row (fourth as a Yankee), becoming the first Yankee to hit those plateaus in his first four seasons as a Yankee since Joe DiMaggio's streak of six consecutive seasons (1936-41)...the only other Yankees with four-year streaks are Lou Gehrig (12 years, 1927-38) and Babe Ruth (eight years, 1926-33). Tino has 407 RBI in his first 500 games as a Yankee...only two players had more than Tino in their first 500 games: Babe Ruth (483) and Joe DiMaggio (475)...Lou Gehrig also had 407 RBI in his first 500 games. In the postseason, Martinez batted .244 (11 for 45), scored eight runs, had eight RBI and two homers.

LAST TWO YANKEE SEASONS: Although Tino fell off in the 2000 regular season, he was ready for the postseason. He was "Mr. Consistent" with eight hits in each of the playoff series. His overall playoff batting average for 2000 was .364 during the 16 postseason games. Tino had a great 2001 regular season with 34 HRs, 113 RBIs, while sporting a .280 batting average. He hit one of the two dramatic game-tying home runs in the 2001 World Series. With the Yankees choosing to sign Jason Giambi after the 2001 season, Tino filed for free agency and moved to the National League by inking a contract with the Cardinals.

MARTINEZ, TINO

Yr.	G	AB	R	H	2B	3B	HR	RBI	BB	SB	BA	SA
1996	155	595	82	174	28	0	25	117	68	2	.292	.466
1997	158	594	96	176	31	2	44	141	75	3	.296	.577
1998	142	531	92	149	33	1	28	123	61	2	.281	.505
1999	159	589	95	155	27	2	28	105	69	3	.263	.458
2000	155	569	69	147	37	4	16	91	52	4	.258	.422
2001	154	589	89	165	24	2	34	113	42	1	.280	.501
6 Yrs.	923	3467	523	966	180	11	175	690	367	15	.279	.488
Still Active.												

Division Series

Yr.	G	AB	R	H	2B	3B	HR	RBI	BB	SB	BA	SA
1996	4	15	3	4	2	0	0	0	4	0	.267	.400
1997	5	18	1	4	1	0	1	4	2	0	.222	.444
1998	3	11	1	3	0	0	0	0	0	0	.273	.455
1999	3	11	1	2	0	0	0	0	2	0	.182	.182
2000	5	19	2	8	2	0	0	4	1	0	.421	.526
2001	5	18	1	2	0	0	1	2	1	0	.111	.278
6 Yrs.	25	92	9	23	7	0	3	10	10	0	.250	.424
Still Active.												

Championship Series

Yr.	G	AB	R	H	2B	3B	HR	RBI	BB	SB	BA	SA
1996	5	22	3	4	1	0	0	0	0	0	.182	.227
1998	6	19	1	1	1	0	0	1	6	2	.105	.158
1999	5	19	3	5	1	0	1	3	2	0	.263	.474
2000	6	25	5	8	2	0	1	1	2	0	.320	.520
2001	5	21	3	5	1	0	1	3	0	0	.250	.450
5 Yrs.	27	106	15	24	6	0	3	8	10	2	.226	.368
Still Active.												

World Series

Yr.	G	AB	R	H	2B	3B	HR	RBI	BB	SB	BA	SA
1996	6	11	0	1	0	0	0	0	2	0	.091	.091
1998	4	13	4	5	0	0	1	4	6	0	.385	.615
1999	4	15	3	4	0	0	1	5	2	0	.267	.467
2000	5	22	3	8	1	0	0	2	1	0	.364	.409
2001	6	21	1	4	0	0	1	3	2	0	.190	.333
5 Yrs.	25	82	11	22	1	0	3	14	13	0	.268	.390
Still Active.												

MATTINGLY, DON

Yankee: 1982-95
First Baseman
Born: April 20, 1961
Birthplace: Evansville, IN
Bat: L; Throw: R
Ht: 6'; Wt: 200

EXCELLENT YANKEE PROSPECT: A native of Evansville, IN, Mattingly was a three-sport high school star who was signed for the Yankees by scouts Jax Robertson and Gus Poulos following his selection in the 19th round of the 1979 draft. He quickly proved he was an excellent hitter. He moved through the farm system: 1979, he batted .349 with Oneonta (A); 1980, led Greensboro (A) to the pennant, batting a league-high .358 and was named MVP of the South Atlantic League; 1981, batted .316 with AA Nashville; and 1982, had an average of .315 with Columbus (AAA).

MAJOR LEAGUE DEBUT: He also played seven games for the Yankees in 1982, making his Major League debut on September 8 versus Baltimore as a left fielder, replacing future Hall-of-Famer Dave Winfield. The following Spring he won the James P. Dawson Award as the top rookie in Spring training camp. He made the team but then was sent down to Columbus in mid-April. Following the retirement of Bobby Murcer, he was recalled in June and hit .283 in 91 games.

ESTABLISHED AS A GREAT PLAYER: Mattingly put together four great seasons in a row, starting in 1984 when he became the first Yankee batting champion since 1956 when Mickey Mantle had his triple-crown MVP season. Don won the crown in dramatic fashion, rapping out four hits in the season finale to nudge out teammate Dave Winfield, .343 to .340. Mattingly was also named as a reserve to the AL All-Star team during his first full season in the Major Leagues. He also led the league with 207 hits and 44 doubles and was its outstanding defensive first baseman with a .996 fielding average. Donnie was even better in 1985, leading the Majors in RBI (145) and doubles (48); and he led the American League in total bases (370) and extra-base hits (86). He was second in the league in hits (211), third in batting (.324), and fourth in homers with 35. Defensively, he again led league first baseman in fielding with a .995 percentage. For all this, he deservedly won the American League Most Valuable Player Award.

CONTINUES TO IMPROVE!: Mattingly in 1986 hit .352 with 31 homers and 113 RBI, and led the Majors in: hits (238), total bases (388), extra-base hits (86), doubles (53) and in slugging percentage (.573). Shattering two prestigious Yankee club records standing since the legendary 1927 season, Don's 238 hits eclipsed Earle Combs' 231 and his 53 doubles surpassed Lou Gehrig's 52. Like Combs and Gehrig, Mattingly was now considered a great Yankee, too! In 1987, Don tied one big-league record and set another. First, between July 8 and 18, he hit at least one home run in eight consecutive games, tying Dale Long's 1956 record. Also, he hit six grand slams, breaking the season record set by Ernie Banks (five with the 1955 Chicago Cubs) and later matched in 1961 by Baltimore's Jim Gentile. Don had his fourth straight 100-RBI season, and he had a league-leading season in fielding. But in a pre-game workout he injured his back fielding grounders and was sidelined for just a matter of weeks, but tests would later reveal a disc problem.

CAREER DECLINES: Then, for the first time in his career, Mattingly slid backwards. In 1988, he hit .311 with 18 homers and 88 RBI—top-level play but disappointing when compared to his previous four seasons. Next season was better; he hit .303—joining Combs, Dickey, DiMaggio, Gehrig and Ruth as Yankees with six consecutive .300 seasons—and he had 23 homers and 113 RBI. The 1990 season signaled a marked decline. Suffering from back spasms and pain, he missed 54 games and had his worst season—.256, five homers and 42 RBI in 102 games. On February 28, 1991, Donnie was named as the 10th Yankee Captain, the first so-named since Ron Guidry in 1986. His numbers swelled somewhat in 1991, but so did his unhappiness; in August, he was benched because he wouldn't get a haircut. It was almost the last straw for Mattingly, who, having been stuck with three poor New York teams in a row, considered leaving the Yankees.

RENEWED CONFIDENCE: Donnie's problems were resolved in October, 1991, when his old minor-league teammate, Buck Showalter, became the Yankees manager. Showalter was able to reset the Yankees' course with purpose and direction, earning Mattingly's respect, and baseball in New York became fun again for Donnie Baseball. With renewed vigor, Mattingly in 1992 made 40 doubles for the first time since 1986. It was his fourth 40-double season, the third most in Yankee history behind Gehrig (7) and Bob Meusel (5). During the tight division race in 1993, Don's blistering bat carried the Yankees from late June through late August, producing 56 RBI in 51 games in that span. But he was bothered by tendinitis in his right wrist (this would require surgery in November), and he hit only .250 in September. He finished the 1993 season batting .291 with 17 homers and 86 RBI, and he set the club fielding record (.998) for first baseman.

FINAL TWO SEASONS AS A YANKEE: Mattingly in 1994 improved his batting average to .304, hitting .340 with runners in scoring position. A year after drawing a career-high 61 walks, he had 60 and would have established a new career high had it not been for the season-shortening strike. Don is respected for his fielding skills and work ethic. Through 1994, his career fielding average (.996) was the highest in American League history, and he has led the league in fielding six times while winning nine Gold Gloves. No one has ever made a 3-6-3 double play look any smoother. In fact, through the 1999 season, Donnie remains first in AL history with that .996 fielding mark. Don is a tireless worker, and at one point seemed to be spending half his life in the batting cage. One wonders if his back problems aren't somehow related to the stress he put upon himself. But his work habits rubbed off on his teammates, always setting a great example as Yankee Captain. Tiring of the endless back exercises necessary to stay in playing condition, Mattingly began hinting of retirement in 1994, but in early March, 1995, after months of working daily at his sports restaurant in Evansville, he itched to play again. He had injuries, and an eye ailment, and occasionally was belittled for lack of production, but in the closing days of the 1995 season, Yankee fans displayed their support for him with generous cheers. Although Donnie was short on power (seven homers, 49 RBI), he hit a respectable .288 and had 32 doubles. And when he finally got into his first postseason action versus Seattle in the Division Series, he rose to the occasion, going 10 for 24 (.417) with five extra-base hits.

ANNOUNCES RETIREMENT: The deal for Tino Martinez in December, 1995 appeared to draw the curtain on the reign of Don Mattingly at first base for the New York Yankees. Although Mattingly hadn't officially retired, he had apparently decided not to return for the 1996 season. He told New York to make plans without him, and General Manager Bob Watson and field Manager Joe Torre weren't exactly begging him to come back. In fact, the Yankee brass acted as if he weren't in their plans, Don covering himself by filing for free agency in November 1996. Don did not play ball in 1996 and in a press conference on January 22, 1997, he announced his official retirement from baseball after an illustrious 14-year career with the Yankees. Don still holds the AL league record for the highest fielding percentage by a first baseman (.996). It will be interesting to see whether the Hall of Fame welcomes this great player into their fold upon eligibility. Well, Donnie gets my vote of confidence. Thanks, Don, for your many years of consistent play in pinstripes!

ALL-TIME YANKEE LEADER: Don's name appears prominently on the Top 20 Yankee batting lists. He ranks second in doubles (442); fifth in at-bats (7003) and hits (2153); seventh in games played (1785). Don is eighth in home-runs (222) and RBIs (1099), ninth in runs (1007), and tenth in batting average (.307)

MATTINGLY, DON

Yr.	G	AB	R	H	2B	3B	HR	RBI	BB	SB	BA	SA
1982	7	12	0	2	0	0	0	1	0	0	.167	.167
1983	91	279	34	79	15	4	4	32	21	0	.283	.409
1984	153	603	91	207	44	2	23	110	41	1	.343	.537
1985	159	652	107	211	48	3	35	145	56	2	.324	.567
1986	162	677	117	238	53	2	31	113	53	0	.352	.573
1987	141	569	93	186	38	2	30	115	51	1	.327	.559
1988	144	599	94	186	37	0	18	88	41	1	.311	.462
1989	158	631	79	191	37	2	23	113	51	3	.303	.477
1990	102	394	40	101	16	0	5	42	28	1	.256	.335
1991	152	587	64	169	35	0	9	68	46	2	.288	.394
1992	157	640	89	184	40	0	14	86	39	3	.288	.416
1993	134	530	78	154	27	2	17	86	61	0	.291	.445
1994	97	372	62	113	20	1	6	51	60	0	.304	.411
1995	128	458	59	132	32	2	7	49	40	0	.288	.413
14 Yrs.	1785	7003	1007	2153	442	20	222	1099	588	14	.307	.471

Life. Same.

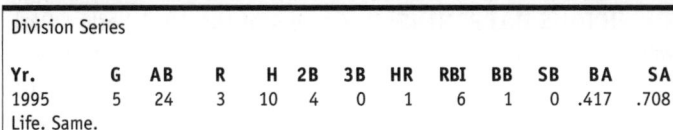

Division Series

Yr.	G	AB	R	H	2B	3B	HR	RBI	BB	SB	BA	SA
1995	5	24	3	10	4	0	1	6	1	0	.417	.708
Life. Same.												

MAY, RUDY

Nickname: "The Dude"
Yankee: 1974-76, 1980-83
Pitcher
Born: July 18, 1944
Birthplace: Coffeyville, KS
Bat: L; Throw: L
Ht: 6'2"; Wt: 205

STYLISH PITCHER: Rudy threw a hard, rising fastball, a hard and slow curve—at times he had the best curve in the AL—and a change-up, and he was able to pitch to different locations as well. Rudy broke into the ML's with the Angels in 1965 and stuck with the Angels for good in 1969, but he had only one winning season with the Angels and didn't match the club's expectations.

OBTAINED BY THE YANKEES: In June of 1974, the Yankees obtained Rudy's contract from California for cash, perhaps nearly $100,000. The Angels had given up on Rudy, whose confidence was shaken.

PENNANT RACE: On June 23, 1974, at Shea Stadium in his Yankee debut against Detroit, Rudy four-hit the Tigers in a rainstorm, a game he later called, "the greatest thing that ever happened to me," as he proved he could still pitch, and in his next start he four-hit Baltimore. In his fourth Yankee game, he hurt his hip diving on artificial turf (Kansas City), and he was on the Disabled List from July 11 through August 1. He returned with a two-hitter against Boston. He was the Yanks' best pitcher over the final two months. He pitched five four-hitters in 1974.

PITCHING FOR MARTIN: After a decent 1975 season as the Yanks' third starter, on April 15, 1976, Rudy started the first game at renovated Yankee Stadium; he fell behind, 4-0, but got no decision when the Yankees rallied to win, 11-4. In late May 1976, Manager Billy Martin removed Rudy from a game, and afterwards Rudy wanted to talk about it; Martin reacted instead with anger and Rudy thus gained entrance into Billy's doghouse.

TRADED TO BALTIMORE: In June of 1976, the Yankees traded Rudy, Tippy Martinez (P), Scott McGregor (P), Dave Pagan (P) and Rick Dempsey (C) to the Orioles for Ken Holtzman (P), Doyle Alexander (P), Grant Jackson (P), Ellie Hendricks (C) and Jimmy Freeman (P). This is one of the most talked about Yankee trades; the Yanks did okay in the short run, but were burned in the long run.

RETURNING TO NEW YORK: In November of 1979, the Yankees signed Rudy as a free agent. The three-year contract was for about $1 million, and some thought the Yanks were wasting money.

SWING MAN: In 1980, Rudy had his best season (15-5), filling the void left by the departed Dick Tidrow; Rudy was used in long, middle and short relief and starting roles. He led the AL in ERA (2.47) in 1980. By early August 1980, Rudy was in the starting rotation, and he was the club's best starter over the final two months; he won his last eight decisions. He pitched a complete game but lost Game 2 of the 1980 ALCS, 3-2. On April 25, 1981, Rudy's 11-game winning streak was snapped. In 1981, Rudy led the Yankees in games started (22) and innings pitched (148). He started Game 2 of the 1981 ALCS, but did not pitch long enough to get the win.

RELIEVER: In 1982, Rudy spent most of the year in the bullpen—he was also on the Disabled List for most of June with a sore left shoulder—and had excellent control; he had 85 strikeouts and only 14 walks for a ratio of better than six to one. In June 1983, he hurt his back while packing and was on the DL until September 9; he made four relief appearances for the Yanks in September—and his 16-year ML career was over.

MAY, RUDY

Yr.	W-L	Pct.	SA	G	GS	CG	IP	H	BB	SO	SH	ERA
1974	8-4	.667	0	17	15	8	114	75	48	90	2	2.28
1975	14-12	.538	0	32	31	13	212	179	99	145	1	3.06
1976	4-3	.571	0	11	11	2	68	49	28	38	1	3.57
1980	15-5	.750	3	41	17	3	175	144	39	133	1	2.46
1981	6-11	.353	1	27	22	4	148	137	41	79	0	4.14
1982	6-6	.500	3	41	6	0	106	109	14	85	0	2.89
1983	1-5	.167	0	15	0	0	18	22	12	16	0	6.87
7 Yrs.	54-46	.574	7	184	102	30	842	715	281	586	5	3.12
Life.	152-156	.494	12	535	360	87	2622	2314	958	1760	24	3.46

Divisional Playoff

Yr.	G	IP	BB	SO	H	W-L	SA
1981	1	2	0	1	1	0-0	0
1 Yr.	1	2	0	1	1	0-0	0
Life. Same							

Championship Series

Yr.	G	IP	BB	SO	H	W-L	SA
1980	1	8	3	4	6	0-1	0
1981	1	3.1	0	5	6	0-0	0
2 Yrs.	2	11.1	3	9	12	0-1	0
Life. Same							

World Series

Yr.	G	IP	BB	SO	H	W-L	SA
1981	3	6.1	1	5	5	0-0	0
1981	3	6.1	1	5	5	0-0	0
Life. Same.							

MAYS, CARL

Nickname: "Sub"
Yankee: 1919-23
Pitcher
Born: November 12, 1891
Birthplace: Liberty, KY
Died: April 4, 1971
Bat: L; Throw: R
Ht: 5'11"; Wt: 195

CAME TO YANKS: On July 13, 1919, Carl pitched his last game for the Red Sox. Disgusted with the lack of hitting, he jumped the team. He should have been suspended, but Boston owner

Harry Frazee was anxious to gain monetary compensation for his star pitcher. On July 29, the Sox sent Carl to the Yanks for $40,000 and pitchers Al Russell and Bob McGraw. AL President Ban Johnson, convinced that the Sox should have suspended Carl instead of selling his contract, was outraged and invoked the suspension. A legal battle between Johnson and the Yanks ensued. The Yanks won, and Carl on August 9, 1919 pitched his first game as a Yankee after a court clash that nearly tore apart the AL.

YANKEE ACE: From August 9 through the end of the 1919 season, Carl was spectacular (9-3, 1.65 ERA). He was the Yanks' ace pitcher in 1920 and 1921, winning a combined total over the two seasons of 53 games! The 27 wins Carl recorded in 1921 has only been exceeded once by a Yankee pitcher. He pitched in 337 innings in 1921, a total that NO Yankee pitcher has surpassed since. Carl faced 1406 batters in 1921, the most ever faced by a Yankee pitcher. He was the club's fourth starter in 1922, yet Miller Huggins hardly used him in 1923. On baseball's all-time double-play list for pitchers, Carl is tied for 14th with 56.

TRAGIC ACCIDENT: In a game played on August 16, 1920, at the Polo Grounds, Carl beaned Cleveland's Ray Chapman, killing him. (This remains the only death on a ML baseball field.) Carl, who often used the brush-back pitch, swore that he did not deliberately throw at Chapman. In fact, the pitch he threw was a curve ball. Most people believe the tragedy was an accident, and some recall that Chapman froze when the pitch approached and made no effort to avoid it.

LEAGUE LEADER: In 1920, Carl led the AL in shutouts (six). He was the best pitcher in the AL in 1921, leading AL pitchers in wins, winning percentage (27-9, .750), games pitched (49), innings pitched (337) and saves (seven).

CLUB LEADERSHIP: Carl led the Yanks in complete games and win percentage three times in each category. Twice he led the club in wins, ERA, innings pitched and games pitched.

ALL-TIME YANKEE LEADER: Carl is fifth on the all-time Yankee win percentage list for those pitchers with at least 100 Yankee decisions (.670,79-39). Carl is ranked 18th in ERA (3.25) overall in Yankee History.

CONTROVERSIAL SORT: Carl was a controversial player in his era, tending to have problems with management wherever he went. He was also known to have a few fights with his teammates, especially when he lost his temper over errors made by fielders behind him. Babe Ruth, for one, did not like Carl's show of anger, and the two often came close to fighting. Other Yankees resented Carl, too, but he did have his friends on the team. Manager Miller Huggins hated Carl, and on July 17, 1923, Huggins kept him in a game against Cleveland while Carl allowed 13 runs and 20 hits. (Several Yankees were upset over this public humiliation.) Carl was scheduled to travel on Babe Ruth's infamous 1921 barnstorming tour, but Commissioner Landis talked him out of going. Even Carl's pitching motion was controversial. He had a very unusual underarm delivery; he dipped so low that his arm sometimes scraped the ground.

SUSPICIOUS HAPPENING: In Game 4 of the 1921 Series, Carl was coasting in the late innings, protecting a 1-0 lead, when the Giants scored three quick runs in the top of the eighth inning enroute to a 4-2 series-tying victory. That night sportswriter Fred Lieb brought a man to see Commissioner Landis who claimed that Carl had been induced to throw the game. Landis assigned a detective agency to investigate but no evidence was found to substantiate the claim. However, years later, Col. Til Huston told Lieb that he still suspected Mays, and Miller Huggins also had no use for him. Yet, the accusations against Carl were never proved.

PHILADELPHIA HEX: Carl had a particular hold on the Philadelphia A's, winning 23 consecutive games against the A's between 1918-23 while pitching for the Red Sox and Yanks.

GOOD HITTER: Carl's .268 lifetime batting average (291 for 1085) is the tenth highest for a ML pitcher in the 20th century. In his full Yankee seasons, Carl hit .239 (1920), .343 (1921), .250 (1922) and .148 (1923). His 49 hits in 1921 ranks as the third most in ML history made by a pitcher. Carl hit two HRs in 1921 and one HR in 1923.

WORLD SERIES: In Game 1 of the 1921 Series, Carl shut out the New York Giants on five hits, winning 3-0. Thus, Carl was the winning pitcher in the first World Series game in Yankee history. He pitched 26 innings without allowing a walk, a World Series record.

LEFT YANKS: In December of 1923, the Yanks asked waivers on Carl but none of the other seven AL teams was interested. Finally, the Yanks sold Carl's contract to the Cincinnati Reds for the interleague waiver price of $7500. In 1924 Carl proceeded to go 20-9 for the Reds while the Yanks finished a close second to Washington. With Carl, the Yanks assuredly would have won the AL pennant.

MAYS, CARL

Yr.	W-L	Pct.	SA	G	GS	CG	IP	H	BB	SO	SH	ERA
1919	9-3	.750	0	13	13	12	120	96	37	54	1	1.65
1920	26-11	.703	2	45	37	26	312	310	84	92	6	3.06
1921	27-9	.750	7	49	38	30	337	332	76	70	1	3.05
1922	12-14	.462	2	34	29	21	240	257	50	41	1	3.60
1923	5-2	.714	0	23	7	2	81	119	32	16	0	6.20
5 Yrs.	79-39	.670	11	164	124	91	1090	1114	279	273	9	3.25
Life.	207-126	.622	31	490	325	231	3021	2912	734	862	29	2.92

World Series

Yr.	G	IP	BB	SO	H	W-L	SA
1921	3	26	0	9	20	1-2	0
1922	1	8	2	1	9	0-1	0
2 Yrs.	4	34	2	10	29	1-3	0
Life.	8	57⅓	8	17	47	3-4	1

McDANIEL, LINDY
(BORN LYNDALL DALE McDANIEL)

Yankee: 1968-73
Pitcher
Born: December 13, 1935
Birthplace: Hollis, OK
Bat: R; Throw: R
Ht: 6'3"; Wt: 195

CAME TO YANKS: In July of 1968, the Yanks obtained Lindy from the San Francisco Giants in a trade that sent Bill Monbouquette to the Giants.

RELIEF SPECIALIST: Lindy was one of baseball's greatest relief pitchers. His 29 saves in 1970 ranks as a tie for tenth among relief pitchers in Yankee history. His bread and butter pitch was the forkball. In his six seasons with the Yanks, Lindy was an important member of a great Yankee bullpen. He worked with such fine relievers as Steve Hamilton, Jack Aker and Sparky Lyle. Since the AL began using the designated hitter in 1973, Lindy is the only Yankee pitcher to bat as many as two times in regular season play (and both times he made outs).

CLUB LEADERSHIP: In three successive seasons (1969-71), Lindy led the Yanks in games pitched. Twice Lindy led the club in saves (1970, 1971) and ERA (1970, 1973).

BASEBALL'S ALL-TIME LEADER LIST: Through the 2002 season, Hoyt Wilhelm is the only pitcher in ML history to have won more games as a relief pitcher than Lindy (119). Only eight ML pitchers have pitched in more games than did Lindy (987).

ALL-TIME YANKEE LEADER: Lindy ranks ninth on the all-time Yankee save list (58).

TRADED: In December of 1973, the Yanks traded Lindy to the Kansas City Royals in a deal that brought outfielder Lou Piniella and pitcher Ken Wright to the Yanks.

McDANIEL, LINDY												
Yr.	W-L	Pct.	SA	G	GS	CG	IP	H	BB	SO	SH	ERA
1968	4-1	.800	10	24	0	0	51	30	12	43	0	1.75
1969	5-6	.455	5	51	0	0	84	84	23	60	0	3.55
1970	9-5	.643	29	62	0	0	112	88	23	81	0	2.01
1971	5-10	.333	4	44	0	0	70	82	24	39	0	5.01
1972	3-1	.750	0	37	0	0	68	54	25	47	0	2.25
1973	12-6	.667	10	47	3	1	160	148	49	93	0	2.86
6 Yrs	38-29	.567	58	265	3	1	545	486	156	363	0	2.89
Life.	141-119	.542	172	987	74	18	2139	2099	623	1361	2	3.45

McDOUGALD, GIL

Nickname: "Smash"
Yankee: 1951-60
Infielder
Born: May 19, 1928
Birthplace: San Francisco, CA
Bat: R; Throw: R
Ht: 6'; Wt: 175

HONORS: In 1951, Gil was voted the AL Rookie of the Year by the Baseball Writers. In 1957, he was selected as the shortstop on *The Sporting News'* ML All-Star team.

MINOR LEAGUER: Gil began playing in the Yankee organization in 1948, hitting .340 in 101 games at Twin Falls of the Pioneer League. He enjoyed a spectacular 1949 season (.344, 13 HRs, 116 RBIs) at Victoria. In 1950 he played at Beaumont under Manager Rogers Hornsby and had another tremendous year at the plate (.336, 13 HRs, 115 RBIs). That year Gil was the MVP of the Texas League and the circuit's all-star second baseman.

ROOKIE SEASON: At the February 1951 Yankee instructional school camp, Casey Stengel was impressed with both Gil's ability and attitude, and Gil was kept on the big club for spring training, eventually making the team. Gil, a month before his 23rd birthday, was the third baseman in the Yanks' starting lineup on Opening Day, 1951. Late in July, Jerry Coleman was benched, and Gil was switched to second base. Gil played 82 games at third and 55 games at second. He led the Yanks in batting (.306). Along with fellow rookies Mickey Mantle, Tom Morgan and Jackie Jensen, he was a great addition to the club—both in the field and at the plate—and it was Gil who was the Rookie of the Year.

VERSATILE INFIELDER: Gil is the only man in Yankee history to start regularly at third base (1952, 1953, 1960), second base (1954, 1955, 1958) and shortstop (1956, 1957). As a team player, Gil was willing, confident and gutty enough to repeatedly make the switch of positions around the infield, and his versatility allowed Stengel to juggle the infield to suit his wishes. Late in the 1955 season, Billy Martin returned from the army and Gil was moved from second to third to make room for Billy. During the Yanks' 1955 post-season trip to Japan, Stengel allowed Gil to play shortstop, and Gil was great. The next year he was the AL's best shortstop! His versatility was on display in 1959 when he played 53 games at second, 52 games at shortstop and 25 games at third.

DEFENSIVE ABILITIES: Gil did not just play second, third and shortstop; he mastered all three positions. In his career he was the best in the AL at whatever position he played. Three times he led the AL in making double plays—and at three different positions! In 1955 Gil led AL second sackers in fielding (.985).

BATTING THREAT: Gil hit for both average and power. Twice he hit higher than .300, and only seven right-handed hitters in Yankee history have hit more HRs than Gil's 112. On May 3, 1951, Gil knocked in six runs in the ninth inning, tying an AL record for most RBIs in one frame. In the inning, Gil tripled home a pair of runs and hit a grand slam HR. Together with Mantle, Berra, Skowron and Bauer, Gil helped form a 1950s version of "Murderers' Row."

BATTING STANCE: For the first half of his ML career, Gil was successful hitting out of a unique batting stance that no one has ever copied. He had a wide stance with his left foot aimed at the pitcher and his chest facing the pitcher, and he allowed his bat to fall below parallel to the ground although he held his hands high. But the weird stance served Gil well until 1955 when Casey Stengel forced him to change because pitchers were getting him out on outside-corner pitches. Gil's average rose, and in 1956 he hit hard line drives to all fields with his new, more orthodox stance.

TERRIBLE ACCIDENT: On May 7, 1957, Gil hit a wicked liner up the middle that struck Indian pitcher Herb Score near the right eye with a sickening thud. Three bones were broken in Score's face, and he never regained his outstanding form. Gil was terribly shaken, vowed to quit baseball if Score had lost his eye and visited Herb in the hospital. Score eventually recovered, but the aggressive style in Gil's play was gone, although he was obviously not at fault for the accident. But he stopped trying to hit up the middle and his batting suffered. The emotional turmoil Gil experienced shows how compassionate a man he is.

CLASS BALLPLAYER: In his 10 Yankee seasons, Gil was an important member of eight AL champions and five World Championship clubs. Gil was a scrappy and fearless performer (a pitcher was foolish to throw at him because Gil became more determined and was good as an angry player). He played the game with the intensity Stengel loved to see in his players. Off the field, Gil was a class guy and one of the best when it came to accommodating fans (giving autographs, etc.) Young Yankee infielders were pleasantly surprised to find that Gil would go out of his way to help them. He roomed with another class player, Hank Bauer.

UNPUBLICIZED STAR: Although he was one of the top players in the game, Gil at times was overlooked by the media. Sometimes circumstances kept him out of the limelight. He had a great year in 1956, hitting .311, and finishing second in the MVP voting. But Mickey Mantle won the Triple Crown that year. And in 1958 Gil was performing in MVP style until he encountered back spasms that he kept secret. He hit around .200 for the final two months, tainting his year. President Eisenhower once gave him an autographed ball that said, "To Joe McDougald. Best wishes."

CLUB LEADERSHIP: Gil led the Yanks in batting in 1951 (.306) and hits (154) in 1953. Three times he led the club in triples and in 1957 tied for the AL lead (9). In 1957 he also led the Yanks in at-bats (539). Twice he paced the team in doubles. Through 1999, Gil ranks 20th in games played (1336).

ALL-STAR GAME: Gil was picked to the AL team for All-Star Games in five seasons (1952, 1956, 1957, 1958, 1959). He was an All-Star Game starter at second base, third base and shortstop.

WORLD SERIES LEADERS: Gil is among the leaders in most lifetime World Series offensive categories. He is tied at fourth with Hank Bauer in games played (53); fifth in at-bats (190); eighth in runs scored (23) and RBIs (24); and tenth in total bases (72).

WORLD SERIES: In Game 5 of the 1951 Series, Gil hit the third grand slam HR in World Series history in a 13-1 Yankee rout of the New York Giants. He led both clubs in RBIs (7) in that Series. At Ebbets Field in Game 4 of the 1953 Series, Gil hit a two-run HR and the next day he blasted a solo HR in an 11-7 Yankee win. He got three of the Yanks' eight hits off Johnny Podres in Brooklyn's win in Game 7 of the 1955 Series. In that Series, Gil led the Yanks in at-bats (27). He made a great play to keep Don Larsen's perfect game intact in the 1956 Series. In the second inning, fleet Jackie Robinson smashed a liner off third baseman Andy Carey's glove, and Gil recovered the ball in time to nip Robinson at first base. It was a play Carey and McDougald had pulled several times during the season. In Game 5 of the 1958 Series, Gil led the Yanks to a 7-0 win over Milwaukee with a solo HR and a two-run double. Then in Game 6 he rapped a clutch tenth-inning HR, leading the Yanks to a 4-3 win.

RETIREMENT: Before the 1960, season Gil informed Stengel it would be his last. He played 84 games at third, sharing the job

with Clete Boyer, and saw action in 42 games at second. Gil also hit .450 (9-for-20) as a pinch-hitter! In the expansion draft following the 1960 season, the Los Angeles Angels drafted Gil off the Yanks' roster and offered him a big contract. But Gil decided to retire as a player while he was still on top.

BASEBALL MAN: Gil left baseball in 1960 to devote his full energies to his successful maintenance company, but he remained associated with the game. He coached baseball at Fordham University in the Bronx and co-authored (with Fred McMane) *Baseball: The Sports Playbook,* an instructional book on baseball strategy.

McDOUGALD, GIL

Yr.	G	AB	R	H	2B	3B	HR	RBI	BB	SB	BA	SA
1951	131	402	72	123	23	4	14	63	56	14	.306	.488
1952	152	555	65	146	16	5	11	78	57	6	.263	.369
1953	141	541	82	154	27	7	10	83	60	3	.285	.416
1954	126	394	66	102	22	2	12	48	62	3	.259	.416
1955	141	533	79	152	10	8	13	53	65	6	.285	.407
1956	120	438	79	136	13	3	13	56	68	3	.311	.443
1957	141	539	87	156	25	9	13	62	59	2	.289	.442
1958	138	503	69	126	19	1	14	65	59	6	.250	.376
1959	127	434	44	109	16	8	4	34	35	0	.251	.353
1960	119	337	54	87	16	4	8	34	38	2	.258	.401
10 Yrs.	1336	4676	697	1291	187	51	112	576	559	45	.276	.410

Life. Same.

World Series

Yr.	G	AB	R	H	2B	3B	HR	RBI	BA
1951	6	23	2	6	1	0	1	7	.261
1952	7	25	5	5	0	0	1	3	.200
1953	6	24	2	4	0	1	2	4	.167
1955	7	27	2	7	0	0	1	1	.259
1956	7	21	0	3	0	0	0	1	.143
1957	7	24	3	6	0	0	0	2	.250
1958	7	28	5	9	2	0	2	4	.321
1960	6	18	4	5	1	0	0	2	.278
8 Yrs.	53	190	23	45	4	1	7	24	.237

Life. Same.

MEDICH, DOC
(BORN GEORGE FRANCIS MEDICH)

Yankee: 1972-75
Pitcher
Born: December 9, 1948
Birthplace: Aliquippa, PA
Bat: R; Throw: R
Ht: 6'5"; Wt: 225

HONORS: In 1973, Doc was picked as the right-handed pitcher on the ML All-Rookie team selected by *Baseball Digest.*

YOUNG PROSPECT: In the June, 1970 amateur draft, the Yanks picked Doc in the 29th round. Yankee scout Randy Gumpert made the selection. In 1970 and 1971, Doc pitched at Oneonta, Manchester and Kinston. Doc had a great year at West Haven, a AA team in the Eastern League in 1972 (11-3, 1.44 ERA), prompting the Yanks to call him up at the end of the season.

YOUNG PITCHING STAR: In 1973, Doc's ML rookie season, he was the Yanks' No. 2 starter and the second best starter on the pitching staff behind Mel Stottlemyre. Doc was the Yanks' ace pitcher in 1974, and he was the AL's Player of the Month for

July. He had a disappointing 1975 season. That year he allowed 15 sacrifice flies, the most in Yankee history.

CLUB LEADERSHIP: In 1973 Doc led Yankee pitchers in strikeouts (145). In 1974 he led the Yanks in wins (19-tie), complete games (17) and shutouts (4).

DOCTOR: Doc was a medical student at the University of Pittsburgh during the winters of his Yankee career. Today he is a doctor. He has helped people who were ill at the ballpark a few times during his ML career.

TRADED: Doc was traded to the Pirates in December, 1975, for Willie Randolph, Dock Ellis, and Ken Brett. Before retiring after the 1982 season, Medich pitched for five other ML teams, including a one-game stint with the Mets.

MEDICH, DOC

Yr.	W-L	Pct.	SA	G	GS	CG	IP	H	BB	SO	SH	ERA
1972	0-0	.000	0	1	1	0	0	2	2	0	0	0.00
1973	14-9	.609	0	34	32	11	235	217	74	145	3	2.95
1974	19-15	.559	0	38	38	17	280	275	91	154	4	3.60
1975	16-16	.500	0	38	37	15	272	271	72	132	2	3.50
4 Yrs.	49-40	.551	0	111	108	43	787	765	239	431	9	3.40
Life.	124-105	.541	2	312	287	71	1996	2036	624	955	16	3.78

MEUSEL, BOB

Nicknames: "Long Bob" "Languid Bob"
Yankee: 1920-29
Outfielder, 3B
Born: July 19, 1896
Birthplace: San Jose, CA
Died: November 28, 1977
Bat: R; Throw: R
Ht: 6'3"; Wt: 190

MINOR LEAGUE STAR: Bob began his pro career playing in the Pacific Coast League. Playing for Vernon of the P.C.L., Bob hit .311 in 164 at-bats in 1917; .375 in eight at-bats in 1918; and .337 in 655 at-bats (221 hits) in 1919. He was on his way to the Yankees for the 1920 season.

ROOKIE SEASON: He had a fantastic rookie season with the Yanks in 1920 (11 HRs, 83 RBIs, .328). He served notice right away that he was a sensational hitter. Bob played 45 games at third base before the Yanks switched him to the outfield.

DEFENSIVE ABILITIES: Bob possessed one of the great outfield throwing arms in baseball history. In consecutive seasons (1921-22) he led all AL outfielders in assists. AL base runners learned not to run on him. Bob had 28 assists in 1921, setting a Yankee club record for outfielders. His eight double plays in 1921 tied a Yankee outfielders' record. In the second game of a doubleheader played on September 5, 1921, Bob had four assists, tying an AL outfielders' record. In 1921-22 Bob was the regular rightfielder and from 1923-29 the Yanks' leftfielder.

GREAT HITTER: Bob was an original Yankee superstar and a key member of "Murderers' Row." He led the AL in HRs (33) and RBIs (138) in 1925. (That was the only year between 1920-33 that Babe Ruth did not have at least a share of the HR Crown.) Five

times Bob knocked in more than 100 runs for the Yanks. He hit for the cycle (single, double, triple, HR in a game) three different times in his career (in 1921, '22, '28), an AL record. In a game played on September 15, 1926, Bob hit three sacrifice flies, an AL record he holds with four others (including Don Mattingly). The 47 doubles he hit in 1927 has only been exceeded three times (Lou Gehrig in that same year and Don Mattingly in 1985 and 1986) by a Yankee player. Bob made $13,000 for his great 1927 season. Bob hit .309 lifetime and his brother, Irish, hit .310 lifetime! Lou Gehrig is the only Yankee to have ever hit at least 40 doubles in a season more often than Bob's five times.

CLUB LEADERSHIP: Bob ran well for a big man, leading the Yanks in stolen bases five times. Twice he led the club in at-bats and triples. In 1924 he led the club in doubles (40). Bob was the only Yankee to play in every Yankee game in 1925 (156).

LAID-BACK CALIFORNIAN: Bob was a laid-back Californian long before the expression became popular. He had tremendous baseball talent, but Miller Huggins, Bob's Yankee manager, complained that his attitude was "one of just plain indifference." He liked to hang around with Babe Ruth, and it is said that Bob would do whatever the Babe asked him to do. (Babe and Bob had many barnstorming tours together.) Throughout his Yankee career, Bob was quiet and occasionally surly with the press. But he mellowed considerably near the end of his playing days. Sportswriter Frank Graham observed of Bob, "He's learning to say hello when it's time to say goodbye."

SUSPENSIONS: Bob was under suspension for the first six weeks of the 1922 season by order of Commissioner Landis. The commissioner suspended both Bob and Babe Ruth for their barnstorming tour after the 1921 World Series in violation of big league rules. In June of 1924, AL President Ban Johnson suspended Bob for 10 days and fined him $100 for his part in a riot in Detroit during a Yankee-Tiger game. The incident started when he was hit by a pitch by Bert Cole and ended with Tiger fans all over the field as players and fans fought. (The Yanks were awarded a forfeit victory.) Bob, Cole and Babe Ruth were punished by the AL office for their roles in the melee.

ALL-TIME YANKEE LEADER: On the All-Time Yankee Top 20 Lists, Bob ranks eighth in doubles (338) and triples (87), ninth in RBI (1005) and batting average (.311) 16th in hits (1565), 19th in steals (130), runs scored (764), and 20th in at-bats (5032).

WORLD SERIES: In three consecutive World Series (1921-23), Bob played against his brother, Irish, of the Giants. In Game 2 of the 1921 Series, Bob stole home. Bob's .300 batting mark in the 1922 Series was the highest on the Yanks. His two-run triple was the key hit in a six-run Yankee rally that helped the Yanks beat the Giants, 8-4, in critical Game 4 of the 1923 Series. His eighth inning hit in Game 6 of the 1923 Series helped the Yanks clinch the club's first World Championship. In Game 1 of the 1928 Series, his two-run HR led the Yanks to a 4-1 win over the Cardinals, and in Game 3 of that Series, he stole home for the second time in his World Series career, making him the only player in World Series history to steal home twice. It was a perfect double steal with Tony Lazzeri taking second as Bob broke for home.

Bob Meusel

MEUSEL, BOB

Yr.	G	AB	R	H	2B	3B	HR	RBI	BB	SB	BA	SA
1920	119	460	75	151	40	7	11	83	20	4	.328	.517
1921	149	598	104	190	40	16	24	135	34	17	.318	.559
1922	121	473	61	151	26	11	16	84	40	13	.319	.522
1923	132	460	59	144	29	10	9	91	31	13	.313	.478
1924	143	579	93	188	40	11	12	120	32	26	.325	.494
1925	156	624	101	181	34	12	33	138	54	10	.290	.542
1926	108	413	73	130	22	3	12	81	37	16	.315	.470
1927	135	516	75	174	47	9	8	103	45	24	.337	.510
1928	131	518	77	154	45	5	11	113	39	6	.297	.467
1929	100	391	46	102	15	3	10	57	17	1	.261	.391
10 Yrs.	1294	5032	764	1565	338	87	146	1005	349	130	.311	.500
Life.	1407	5475	826	1693	368	95	156	1067	375	139	.309	.497

World Series

Yr.	G	AB	R	H	2B	3B	HR	RBI	BA
1921	8	30	3	6	2	0	0	3	.200
1922	5	20	2	6	1	0	0	2	.300
1923	6	26	1	7	1	2	0	8	.269
1926	7	21	3	5	1	1	0	0	.238
1927	4	17	1	2	0	0	0	1	.118
1928	4	15	5	3	1	0	1	3	.200
6 Yrs.	34	129	15	29	6	3	1	17	.225
Life. Same.									

LEFT YANKS: In October of 1929, the Yanks sold Bob's contract to the Cincinnati Reds. Bob hit .289 in 113 games for the Reds in 1930, his final ML season as a player.

THE 1955 STREET AND SMITH YEARBOOK'S LIST OF BASEBALL'S 10 MIGHTIEST ARMS:
—by Ken Smith

1. BOB MEUSEL (YANKEES)
2. Babe Ruth (Yankees)
3. Chick Hafey (Cards, Reds)
4. Willie Mays (Giants)
5. Tris Speaker (Red Sox, Indians)
6. Tom Griffith (Dodgers)
7. Joe Birmingham (Indians)
8. Ron Northey (Phillies)
9. Joe DiMaggio (Yankees)
10. Carl Furillo (Dodgers)

MICHAEL, GENE

Nickname: "The Stick"
Yankee: 1968-74
Shortstop, 2B, 3B, P
Born: June 2, 1938
Birthplace: Kent, OH
Bat: Both; Throw: R
Ht: 6'2"; Wt: 183

CAME TO YANKS: In November of 1967, the Yanks purchased Gene's contract from the Los Angeles Dodgers.

YANKEE SHORTSTOP: In 1968, Gene was a reserve shortstop, playing at that position in 43 Yankee games. From 1969-73 he was the Yanks' regular shortstop. In 1974 he was the club's utility infielder, playing 45 games at second base, 39 at shortstop and two at third. In a 1968 game against Detroit, Manager Ralph Houk had him pitch three innings in an emergency. Gene allowed five hits but no runs and the Yanks won, although Gene did not figure in the decision. (He also fanned three batters!)

DEFENSIVE ABILITIES: Gene was a classy shortstop with the glove. He had good range and a fine throwing arm. In 1971 he averaged 5.4 chances per game, the highest average of any regular AL shortstop. Gene was a master at the "hidden ball trick," nailing base runners with that deceptive maneuver five times!

STUDIOUS PLAYER: Relying on his wits, Gene was a heady and intelligent player. He was a student of the game and liked to talk baseball with Yankee third baseman Bobby Cox. (The left side of the Yanks' infield in 1968-69—Michael and Cox—both later became ML managers.) Gene, who received a teaching degree from Kent State, roomed with Thurman Munson, another smart and scrappy Yankee. Gene was a consistent and popular Yankee player, and was once honored with a "day" by his many New York area friends.

SCRAPPY PLAYER: Besides being smart, Gene was a tough player and he was fearless. He was hardnosed on the field, his aggressive play sometimes leading to fights. On May 6, 1968, he brawled with Cleveland's Tony Horton after first baseman Horton made a hard tag on him at first base. Both players were ejected from the game after the fight. Gene also had the guts to fight at contract time, once taking owner George Steinbrenner to arbitration over his salary. He lost the fight and was forced to accept management's offer.

LEFT YANKS: Before the 1975 season, the Yanks dealt Gene to the Tigers. Gene ended his ML playing career with Detroit in 1975, although he later had a brief stint with the Red Sox.

BACK WITH THE YANKS: Gene served in many capacities with the Yankees after returning to the club in 1976. He was special scout and coach (1976); administrative assistant (1977); first-base coach (1977); manager of Columbus (1979); general manager (1980); and manager (1981, 1982). Gene later managed the Cubs (1986-87). He served with success as the Yanks' general manager from 1990 to after the close of the 1995 season. Gene is now Vice President of Major League Scouting in the Baseball Operations Department of the Yankees Front Office.

MICHAEL, GENE												
Yr.	G	AB	R	H	2B	3B	HR	RBI	BB	SB	BA	SA
1968	61	116	8	23	3	0	1	8	2	3	.198	.250
1969	119	412	41	112	24	4	2	31	43	7	.272	.364
1970	134	435	42	93	10	1	2	38	50	3	.214	.255
1971	139	456	36	102	15	0	3	35	48	3	.224	.276
1972	126	391	29	91	7	4	1	32	32	4	.233	.279
1973	129	418	30	94	11	1	3	47	26	1	.225	.278
1974	81	177	19	46	9	0	0	13	14	0	.260	.311
7 Yrs.	789	2405	205	561	79	10	12	204	215	21	.233	.289
Life.	973	2806	249	642	86	12	15	226	234	22	.229	.284

MICHAEL, GENE (Pitcher)												
Yr.	W-L	Pct.	SA	G	GS	CG	IP	H	BB	SO	SH	ERA
1968	0-0	---	0	1	0	0	3	5	1	3	0	0.00
1 Yr.	0-0	---	0	1	0	0	3	5	1	3	0	0.00
Life. Same.												

MOGRIDGE, GEORGE

Yankee: 1915-20
Pitcher
Born: February 18, 1889
Birthplace: Rochester, NY
Died: March 4, 1962
Bat: L; Throw: L
Ht: 6'2"; Wt: 165

YANKEE STARTER: After a two-year absence from ML baseball, George joined the Yanks in 1915. He was the Yanks' third starter from 1916-18. He was the club's fourth starter in 1919 and the fifth starter in 1920.

NO-HITTER: On April 24, 1917, George pitched a no-hitter against the Red Sox, winning 2-1. It was the second no-hitter in Yankee history and the first time a Yankee pitcher threw a hitless game and won. Incredibly, George accomplished this feat at Fenway Park, the field that eats up lefthanded pitching!

DEFENSIVE ABILITIES: In 1917 George fielded 77 chances without making an error, setting a Yankee fielding record for pitchers.

1918 SEASON: Only in 1918 did George's true talent show while he was on the Yanks. That year he led the AL in games pitched (45) and games saved (seven). He also led the Yankee pitching staff in wins (16), ERA (2.18) and innings pitched (239).

TRADES: In January, 1921, the Yanks traded George and Duffy Lewis (OF) to Washington for Braggo Roth (OF). George won 18 games for the Senators in both 1921 and 1922. George was traded to the Browns in 1925. In March 1926, the Yanks reacquired George and cash from the Browns for Wally Schang (C). George did not appear in any games with the Yanks in 1926; the Yanks waived him to the Boston Braves in June. He retired from baseball after the 1927 season.

MOGRIDGE, GEORGE												
Yr.	W-L	Pct.	SA	G	GS	CG	IP	H	BB	SO	SH	ERA
1915	2-3	.400	0	6	6	3	41	33	11	11	1	1.76
1916	6-12	.333	0	30	21	9	195	174	45	66	2	2.31
1917	9-11	.450	0	29	25	15	196	185	39	46	1	2.98
1918	16-13	.552	7	45	19	13	239	232	43	62	1	2.18
1919	10-7	.588	0	35	18	13	169	159	46	58	3	2.82
1920	5-9	.357	1	26	15	7	125	146	36	35	0	4.31
6 Yrs.	48-55	.476	8	171	104	60	966	929	220	278	8	2.74
Life.	133-130	.506	20	398	261	137	2266	2350	565	679	20	3.22

MOORE, WILCY
(BORN WILLIAM WILCY MOORE)

Nickname: "Cy"
Yankee: 1927-29, 1932-33
Pitcher
Born: May 20, 1897
Birthplace: Bonita, TX
Died: March 29, 1963
Bat: R; Throw: R
Ht: 6'; Wt: 195

CAME TO YANKS: In August of 1926, the Yanks purchased Wilcy's contract for a reported $3,500 from Greenville of the Sally League. Yankee GM Ed Barrow made the purchase sight unseen after reading in *The Sporting News* that "Cy" was 20-1 at one point during the year before. Reminded of the humble status of the Sally League in those days, Barrow remarked, "Anyone who has a 20-1 record anywhere is worth taking a look at." Wilcy finished the 1926 season at 30-4 for Greenville. Barrow was convinced Wilcy had been buried in the minors and gave him a good shot at making the Yanks in the spring camp of 1927.

ROOKIE SEASON: "Cy" was a 30-year-old ML rookie on the 1927 Yanks and he had a spectacular year on perhaps the greatest team in baseball history. He was not overpaid, making all of $3000 for the season. He was used mostly as a relief pitcher but he also spot-started. Wilcy led the AL in saves (13), games won in relief (13), and he posted the lowest ERA in the league (2.28), although he did not qualify for the ERA championship. Not only did "Cy" lead the Yanks in games pitched (50), he also set the 154-game AL record for most games pitched by a rookie. After Lou Gehrig, Babe Ruth and Waite Hoyt, Wilcy was probably the fourth most valuable player in the AL. The Yanks in Wilcy enjoyed a tremendous lift from an unexpected source.

OTHER SEASONS: There is no doubt that Wilcy was the first great relief pitcher in Yankee history, but he had a disappointing sophomore season. During the winter of 1927-28, "Cy" fell off a barn and hurt his pitching arm. He tried to pitch in 1928 but had problems, and returned to his farm with his career in doubt. He made a fine comeback in 1929 and once again took his place as the ace of the Yankee bullpen. He did not pitch ML baseball in 1930, and the Yanks sold his contract to the Red Sox. With Boston, he was 11-13 in 1931 and was 4-10 in 1932, when late in the campaign the Red Sox sold his contract back to the Yanks. Wilcy had a great finish in 1932 with the Yanks and performed splendidly as the Yanks' bullpen stopper in 1933.

THE PITCHER AND THE MAN: Wilcy had a tremendous sidearm sinkerball, and when he was pitching well the ball really dipped. He needed the good sinker because his curveball was only average. One of his real strengths was his coolness under pressure. "Cy" was not a pitcher who got nervous while on the mound. Wilcy was a cotton farmer from Oklahoma. He was carefree and happy-go-lucky. The Yankee players enjoyed the wit of this clever and funny man.

BET WITH RUTH: Wilcy became a good friend of Babe Ruth upon joining the Yanks. Because Wilcy was such a terrible hitter (lifetime: 21 for 205, .102 BA), in the spring of 1927 Ruth bet Wilcy a few hundred dollars that he would not make more than three hits all year. Wilcy made six (in 75 at-bats for a .080 BA) and with his winnings he bought two mules for his Oklahoma farm. He told Babe that one mule was named "Babe" and the other "Ruth."

CLUB LEADERSHIP: "Cy" led Yankee pitchers in saves four times. Twice he led the club in games pitched.

WORLD SERIES: Wilcy had a great lifetime World Series ERA (0.56). He gave up only one earned run in 10²/₃ innings pitched in the 1927 Series. In Game 1 of the 1927 Series, Wilcy recorded a save in a 5-4 Yankee victory, then he returned to hurl a complete game as a starter to win Game 4, 4-3, finishing the sweep of the outclassed Pittsburgh Pirates. As a relief pitcher, Wilcy won Game 4 of the 1932 Series, the Yankee win that completed a sweep of the Chicago Cubs.

RELEASED: The Yanks released Wilcy in December of 1933. Wilcy was just five months shy of his 37th birthday and never again pitched ML baseball. For Wilcy, fame was fast and fleeting, but for a man who did not reach the ML's until late in his baseball life, he had a great career.

MORGAN, TOM

Nickname: "Plowboy"
Yankee: 1951-52 (military) 1954-56
Pitcher
Born: May 20, 1930
Birthplace: El Monte, CA
Died: January 13, 1987
Bat: R; Throw: R
Ht: 6'1"; Wt: 180

YOUNG PROSPECT: Tom began in the Yanks' farm system in 1949, pitching for Ventura of the California League (12-9). In 1950 he was the pitching star of the Yanks' Binghamton team in the Eastern League (17-8). In the Yanks' 1951 spring exhibition season Tom pitched 25 consecutive scoreless innings and made the big club, along with Mickey Mantle, Gil McDougald and Jackie Jensen. (Tom did pitch briefly at Kansas City of the American Association in 1951, posting a 2-1 record.)

VERSATILE PITCHER: As a 21-year-old rookie pitcher in 1951, Tom was the Yanks' fourth starter and showed great promise. He missed part of the 1952 season and all of the 1953 season while serving in the military. In 1954 Tom was the sixth starter on the Yankee pitching staff. Over the 1955-56 seasons, Tom was a successful relief pitcher, appearing in more games (81) and saving more games (21) than any other Yankee for those combined campaigns. Tom threw a hard sinkerball that was perfect for getting double-play grounders. On June 30, 1954, he hit three batters in the third inning, tying several others for the most hit batsmen in one inning in AL history. In the 1954 home opener, Tom blanked the A's, 3-0.

CLUB LEADERSHIP: In 1951, Tom led Yankee pitchers in winning percentage (.750, 9-3). In 1954 he tied for the club leadership in shutouts (four), although he made only 17 starts he led Yankee pitchers in saves (11) in 1956. Tom is tied for 20th in save totals (26) in Yankee history.

BASEBALL'S ALL-TIME LEADER LIST: Tom's lifetime winning percentage as a relief pitcher (.615, 40-25) ranks among baseball's top 20 for relief pitchers. (He was 17-11, .607, as a Yankee relief pitcher.)

GREATEST GAME: In a game played on May 16, 1956, against the Indians, Tom entered the game in the fourth inning and retired all 17 batters he faced, winning the game. Never again were the Yanks out of first place in the AL standings that season.

NICKNAME: Mel Allen nicknamed Tom "Plowboy" because he took so long in walking to the mound from the bullpen.

TRADED: In February, 1957, the Yanks traded Tom, outfielder Irv Noren and four others to the Kansas City A's for pitchers Bobby Shantz and Art Ditmar, infielder Clete Boyer and two other infielders. Morgan retired as a player in 1963 after also pitching for Detroit, Washington, and the Los Angeles Angels.

YANKEE COACH AND SCOUT: Tom returned to the Yankees in 1979 as Manager Bob Lemon's pitching coach. In 1980 Tom was a Yankee scout out of his Rancho Palos Verdes, Calif. home.

MOORE, WILCY											
Yr.	W-L	Pct.	SA	G	GS	CG	IP	H	BB	SO	SH	ERA
1927	19-7	.731	13	50	12	6	213	185	59	75	1	2.28
1928	4-4	.500	2	35	2	0	60	71	31	18	0	4.18
1929	6-4	.600	8	41	0	0	62	64	19	21	0	4.06
1932	2-0	1.000	4	10	1	0	25	27	6	8	0	2.52
1933	5-6	.455	8	35	0	0	62	92	20	17	0	5.52
5 Yrs.	36-21	.632	35	171	15	6	422	439	135	139	1	3.30
Life.	51-44	.537	49	261	32	14	692	732	232	204	2	3.69

World Series

Yr.	G	IP	BB	SO	H	W-L	SA
1927	2	10²/₃	2	2	11	1-0	1
1932	1	5¹/₃	0	1	2	1-0	0
2 Yrs.	3	16	2	3	13	2-0	1

MORGAN, TOM

Yr.	W-L	Pct.	SA	G	GS	CG	IP	H	BB	SO	SH	ERA
1951	9-3	.750	2	27	16	4	125	119	36	57	2	3.68
1952	5-4	.556	2	16	12	2	94	86	33	35	1	3.07
1954	11-5	.688	1	32	17	7	143	149	40	34	4	3.34
1955	7-3	.700	10	40	1	0	72	72	24	17	0	3.25
1956	6-7	.462	11	41	0	0	71	74	27	20	0	4.16
5 Yrs.	38-22	.633	26	156	46	13	505	500	160	163	7	3.48
Life.	67-47	.588	64	443	61	18	1023	1040	300	364	7	3.61

World Series

Yr.	G	IP	BB	SO	H	W-L	SA
1951	1	2	1	3	2	0-0	0
1955	2	3⅔	3	1	3	0-0	0
1956	2	4	4	3	6	0-1	0
3 Yrs.	5	9⅔	8	7	11	0-1	0
Life. Same.							

MUNSON, THURMAN

Yankee: 1969-79
Catcher, OF
Born: June 7, 1947
Birthplace: Akron, OH
Died: August 2, 1979
Bat: R; Throw: R
Ht: 5'11"; Wt: 190

TRAGIC DEATH: There is no more tragic date in Yankee history than August 2, 1979. On that date Thurman was practicing takeoffs and landings in his new twin-engine jet, a Cessna Citation, at the Akron-Canton Airport on a Yankee off-day. Approaching the runway, Thurman's plane clipped a tree and crashed before the runway. (The cause of the crash is still not known.) Two companions left the burning plane safely, but Thurman was trapped inside. The news of Thurman's death brought sorrow to the nation and the baseball community and was a sad and painful loss to the Yankees. The entire Yankee team attended Thurman's funeral in Canton. Lou Piniella and Bobby Murcer gave moving eulogies to their best friend and teammate. That night in New York the Yanks beat the Orioles, 5-4, as Murcer drove in all five runs.

HONORS: In 1970, the Baseball Writers selected Thurman as the AL Rookie of the Year. In 1976 the Baseball Writers voted Thurman the MVP of the AL. In 1976 *The Sporting News* picked him as the AL Player of the Year. *The Sporting News* selected him as their catcher on the publication's AL All-Star team four years in a row (1973-76). Thurman was catcher on the Associated Press' ML All-Star team in 1976. The Yanks retired Thurman's Number "15" uniform following his untimely death. A plaque in Yankee Stadium was dedicated on September 20, 1980, in his honor. Munson's locker in the Yankee Clubhouse remains empty as an ongoing tribute to Thurman's #15.

YOUNG PROSPECT: Thurman was a baseball star at Kent State University where he was scouted by former Yankee star Gene Woodling. In the June, 1968, amateur Free Agent Draft, Woodling made Thurman the Yanks' No.1 pick. Thurman received a $75,000 bonus. He had only played at Binghamton (.301) in 1968 and at Syracuse (.363) in 1969. He had played only 99 minor league games when the Yanks called him up in the 1969 season.

CAPTAIN AND LEADER: Thurman impressed the Yanks immensely in the time he spent with the club in 1969. In spring training, 1970, he won the starting job as catcher, which he held until the day he died. Early in his Yankee career, he established himself as the backbone of a budding young club. He was the best catcher in the AL during the 1970s without a doubt. In the spring of 1976, Thurman was named the first Yankee captain since Lou Gehrig. On the Yankee teams that won three AL pennants in a row (1976-78) and two World Championships, Thurman was the undisputed leader and the most respected man on the Yanks. Especially in his final years, he played with an assortment of painful injuries that would have kept a less dedicated player out of the lineup. However, Thurman was a "gamer"; if he could walk he played. He also was a hustler on the playing field.

DEFENSIVE ABILITIES: He was a tremendous defensive catcher. In three consecutive seasons (1973-75) Thurman won the Gold Glove Award as the best defensive catcher in the AL. In 1971 he led AL catchers in fielding (.998), a mark that tied the Yankee club record for catchers. His 1971 fielding average is the tenth highest in ML history for a catcher. He led AL catchers in assists in 1970 (80), 1973 (80) and 1974 (75) and AL catchers in double plays in 1973 (11) and 1975 (14). Thurman was exceptional in all the physical catching fundamentals. He threw with one of the quickest releases ever seen, blocked the plate tenaciously, and pounced on bunts like a cat. He was also brilliant in the mental aspects of catching. Yankee pitchers always appreciated the way he called a game, and Thurman was an expert at handling pitchers and controlling the different personalities on the pitching staff.

SITUATION HITTER: In his prime Thurman was the best clutch hitter in the AL. He was a smart hitter and a "situation" hitter, one who hit for power, but one who had the bat control to hit to all fields. From 1975-77 Thurman knocked in more than 100 runs and hit better than .300 in each of those three seasons to become the first player since the Indians' Al Rosen (1952-54) to accomplish that feat. He batted third in the lineup for most of his career because he was the Yanks' best bat. He hit the first Yankee HR in the "new" Yankee Stadium.

FINE BASE RUNNER: Thurman was a smart, aggressive base runner—one of the finest base-running catchers the game has ever seen. Ed Sweeney is the only catcher in Yankee history to steal more bases in a season (19 in 1914) than Thurman did in 1976 (14).

CLUB LEADERSHIP: Twice Thurman led the Yanks in hits, RBIs and batting. In 1973 he led the club in triples (four) and tied for the club leadership in doubles (29), besides leading the team in slugging (.487). In 1975 he led the Yanks in games played (157) and at-bats (597). Yogi Berra is the only other catcher to ever lead the Yanks in those two categories.

ALL-TIME YANKEE LEADER: On the Top 20 Yankee Batting lists, Thurman ranks 16th in hits (1558); 18th in games played (1423) and at-bats (5344); 19th in RBI (701); and 20th in batting average (.292).

ALL-STAR GAME: Thurman was selected to the AL team for seven All-Star Games (1971, '73-78).

AL CHAMPIONSHIP SERIES: Thurman enjoyed outstanding playoffs in 1976 (.435) and 1977 (.286). He delivered the most important hit of the 1978 Championship Series. With one out in the bottom of the eighth inning of Game 3 and the Royals ahead, 5-4, Thurman, who had only six HRs all year, hit a booming 440-foot HR to win the game, 6-5.

WORLD SERIES: Thurman led the Yanks in batting in the 1976 Series (.529) and tied a Series record by making six straight hits. In the bottom of the eighth inning of Game 4 of the 1978 Series, he doubled home the tying run to send the game into extra-innings in a game that the Yanks won, 4-3. Thurman drove in five runs in Game 5 of the 1978 Series, leading the Yanks to a 12-2 win over the Dodgers. His lifetime Series batting average (.373) is the sixth highest of all time, tied with Hall-of-Famer, George Brett.

RESPONSIBLE MAN: Thurman was a misunderstood man. A tough, gruff exterior was seen by the press and public but actually he was warm and completely dedicated to his family. In 1978 he was given the Father of the Year Award. He was a professional baseball player but he was a family man first—he kept his priorities straight. Thurman was also a friendly man with his associates and one of the most popular players in baseball. Thurman's son Michael was signed by the Yankees to a minor league contract in July 1995.

HALL OF FAME CREDENTIALS: Thurman is a likely inductee into the Baseball Hall of Fame. If catching is the most important job on the field, and if Thurman was one of the best, his election is a formality. There are only a handful of catchers in Thurman's class—Cochrane, Hartnett, Campanella, Bench, Fisk, and former Yankees' Dickey, Berra, and Howard. In a total of 30 post-season games (AL playoffs, World Series) Thurman posted a combined batting average of .357. When the situation was important, he showed his importance to the Yankees.

MUNSON, THURMAN

Yr.	G	AB	R	H	2B	3B	HR	RBI	BB	SB	BA	SA
1969	26	86	6	22	1	2	1	9	10	0	.256	.349
1970	132	453	59	137	25	4	6	53	57	5	.302	.415
1971	125	451	71	113	15	4	10	42	52	6	.251	.368
1972	140	511	54	143	16	3	7	46	47	6	.280	.364
1973	147	519	80	156	29	4	20	74	48	4	.301	.487
1974	144	517	64	135	19	2	13	60	44	2	.261	.381
1975	157	597	83	190	24	3	12	102	45	3	.318	.429
1976	152	616	79	186	27	1	17	105	29	14	.302	.432
1977	149	595	85	183	28	5	18	100	39	5	.308	.462
1978	154	617	73	183	27	1	6	71	35	2	.297	.373
1979	97	382	42	110	18	3	3	39	32	1	.288	.374
11 Yrs.	1423	5344	696	1558	229	32	113	701	438	48	.292	.410

Life. Same.

Championship Series

Yr.	G	AB	R	H	2B	3B	HR	RBI	BA
1976	5	23	3	10	2	0	0	3	.435
1977	5	21	3	6	1	0	1	5	.286
1978	4	18	2	5	1	0	1	2	.278
3 Yrs.	14	62	8	21	4	0	2	10	.339

Life. Same.

World Series

Yr.	G	AB	R	H	2B	3B	HR	RBI	BA
1976	4	17	2	9	0	0	0	2	.529
1977	6	25	4	8	2	0	1	3	.320
1978	6	25	5	8	3	0	0	7	.320
3 Yrs.	16	67	11	25	5	0	1	12	.373

Life. Same.

Yankee catcher, Thurman Munson, blocks the plate as George Scott tries to beat the throw.

MURCER, BOBBY

Yankee: 1965-66, 1969-74, 1979-83
Outfielder, DH, 3B, SS
Born: May 20, 1946
Birthplace: Oklahoma City, OK
Bat: L; Throw: R
Ht: 5'11"; Wt: 160

Bobby Murcer

TOP PROSPECT: Bobby hit .458 in his senior year at Oklahoma City's Southeast High School, and at about the time of his June 2, 1964, graduation, was signed by Yankee Scout Tom Greenwade for a reported $20,000 bonus. Bobby quickly became the crown jewel in a depleted Yankee farm system. In 1964, he hit .365 at Johnson City. In 1965, he hit .322 at Greensboro and was named Carolina League Player of the Year. In 1966, he played mostly at Toledo and hit 15 HRs.

YANKEE DEBUT: Bobby was called up to the Yankees in September 1965; he was 19, looked even younger, was quiet and more than a little scared—and in awe of his famous Yankee teammates. At the time Bobby was being groomed as Tony Kubek's successor at shortstop. On September 14, 1965, at Washington's D.C. Stadium (later renamed Robert F. Kennedy Stadium), he hit his first ML homer. Bobby returned briefly with the Yanks in 1966 but hit only .174.

UNCLE SAM CALLS: On March 6, 1967 Bobby was inducted into the Army. He missed the 1967 and 1968 seasons. He later said his Army experience helped him become more responsible and taught him discipline. He was more mature when he returned to the Yankees in 1969. He was also clean cut and well behaved.

COMPARISONS TO MANTLE: Mickey Mantle had retired before the 1969 season, and with no more Mantle to write about, the sportswriters in 1969 spring training began building up Bobby, who hit .380 in the exhibition season, comparing him with Mantle. Murcer and Mantle did have these similarities: 1) both were Oklahomans, 2) both were signed by Tom Greenwade, 3) both began as shortstops, 4) both later became centerfielders, and 5) both played in the ML's at age 19. The Yankees even gave Mantle's locker to Bobby.

FINDING A POSITION: Bobby didn't play shortstop up to ML caliber, so the great experiment of early 1969 was his shift to third base; it didn't work, Bobby making 14 errors in 31 games. His biggest problem was overthrowing. After making three wild throws in a game, Bobby fielded a grounder and a fan was heard to scream, "Look out, he's got it again!" Manager Ralph Houk moved him to the outfield—first to right field and then to center—and Bobby was more comfortable.

YANKEE STAR: On April 7, 1969, Opening Day in Washington, with President Nixon watching, Bobby homered and led the Yankees to an 8-4 win; it was the first game for Bobby as the team's Big Guy, and he would remain the Big Guy for six seasons. He led the Yankees in RBIs in five seasons; homers and hits in four seasons; and runs, doubles, slugging and batting in three seasons. He was an outfielder on *The Sporting News* AL All-Star teams in 1971, 1972 and 1973. In 1971, Bobby began hitting more to left field and battled Tony Oliva into the final week for the batting championship, finishing at .331, six points behind Oliva. In 1972, Bobby hit a career-high 33 HRs and led the AL in runs (102) and total bases (314). In 1973, he became the youngest player in AL history to earn $100,000, and the first Yankee to do so since Mantle.

GREAT GAMES: In a doubleheader against Cleveland at Yankee Stadium on June 24, 1970, Bobby hit homers in four consecutive official at-bats (with a walk in between), starting with his last AB in the first game. On June 3, 1972, Bobby scored five runs—the 11th Yankee to ever do so—in an 18-10 win over Chicago. On August 29, 1972, in an 11-inning game against Texas, he became the first Yankee since Mantle in 1957 to hit for the cycle. On July 13, 1973, against Kansas City at Yankee Stadium, he hit three homers off Gene Garber—a three-run homer and two solos—and the Yanks won, 5-0.

ALL STAR: Bobby started four consecutive All-Star Games, 1971-74. He started in center in 1971 (replacing the injured Tony Oliva), 1972 and 1974, and in left in 1973. Bobby hit only .091 (1 for 11) as a Yankee in All-Star Games.

PLAYING THE OUTFIELD: Bobby wasn't in Mantle's league, but he had some defensive accomplishments, including winning a Gold Glove in 1972. Bobby also tied for the AL lead in outfield assists in 1970 (15) and 1973 (14), and in 1972 he led AL outfielders in total chances (396) and putouts (382). Manager Bill Virdon in May 1974 boldly inserted Elliott Maddox in center field and moved Bobby to right; the Yankee pitchers were happy because Bobby had lost a step or two and Maddox was one of the game's best centerfielders. Bobby did an excellent job in right and in 1974 led AL outfielders in assists (21).

THE SHEA WOES: Bobby had a lefthanded stroke that was perfect for Yankee Stadium, but while the Stadium was being renovated, the Yankees in 1974 played their home games in Shea Stadium, a more difficult home-run park for lefthanded hitters. He hit many fly balls to the middle of the warning track and beyond, but he didn't hit his first homer at Shea until the next-to-last week of the season. It became a mental burden; the longer he went homerless at Shea, the more he was asked about it, and the harder he would swing. He finished the year with only 10 homers. The Yankees stayed in an exciting pennant race until getting eliminated on October 1, the season's next-to-last day; Bobby didn't play as he had been hurt trying to break up a hotel lobby fight between teammates Rick Dempsey and Bill Sudakis.

SHOCKING TRADE: Yankee fans, as well as Bobby, were shocked on October 22, 1974, when the Yankees traded Bobby to the Giants for Bobby Bonds. Yankee GM Gabe Paul engineered the deal; he was looking for right-handed power (Bonds) to protect against all the southpaw pitching the Yankees saw in 1974.

YANKEE RETURN: In June of 1979, the Yankees re-acquired Bobby from the Cubs for Paul Semall (P) and cash. Murcer had been preparing for a day game at Wrigley Field when he was informed of his trade to the Yankees. He hurriedly caught a flight to Toronto and arrived only 20 minutes before the game with the Blue Jays. Billy Martin had Bobby in the starting lineup, and Murcer responded by singling twice during the eventual 11-2 Yankee victory. Bobby received a tremendous ovation upon his return to Yankee Stadium. He was 33; his skills slightly eroded with time.

MUNSON'S DEATH: One of the joys for Bobby in returning to the Yankees was reuniting with close friend, Thurman Munson, but on August 2, 1979, Munson was killed in a plane crash. On August 6, the Yankees attended the funeral in Canton, OH, and Bobby gave an eulogy. Then the Yanks returned to Yankee Stadium for a game that night against Baltimore. The Orioles led, 4-0, in the seventh when Bobby delivered a three-run homer. In the ninth, with runners on second and third, Bobby drilled a two-run single, giving the Yanks a moving 5-4 victory.

PART TIMER: In 1980, Bobby was a part-time outfielder, DH and pinch hitter and produced 13 HRs and 57 RBIs in only 297 AB's. He had 13 game-winning RBI in 1980, and delivered several clutch hits down the stretch as the Yankee won the division. At Yankee Stadium on Opening Day 1981, he delivered a pinch-hit grand slam, and he went on to lead AL pinch hitters with three HRs and 12 RBIs. He was a part-time DH in 1982.

RETIREMENT: Bobby's final ML game was June 11, 1983, as a pinch hitter. Bobby retired on June 20, 1983—Don Mattingly took his place on the roster—and began a new career with the Yankee broadcasting team. Bobby continues to be part of the Yankee game broadcasts.

ALL-TIME YANKEE LEADER: Bobby ranks 13th in home runs (175), and 19th in RBI (687) in Yankee history.

MURCER, BOBBY

Yr.	G	AB	R	H	2B	3B	HR	RBI	BB	SB	BA	SA
1965	11	37	2	9	0	1	1	4	5	0	.243	.378
1966	21	69	3	12	1	1	0	5	4	2	.174	.217
1969	152	564	82	146	24	4	26	82	50	7	.259	.454
1970	159	581	95	146	23	3	23	78	87	15	.251	.420
1971	146	529	94	175	25	6	25	94	91	14	.331	.543
1972	153	585	102	171	30	7	33	96	63	11	.292	.537
1973	160	616	83	187	29	2	22	95	50	6	.304	.464
1974	156	606	69	166	25	4	10	88	57	14	.274	.378
1979	74	264	42	72	12	0	8	33	25	1	.273	.409
1980	100	297	41	80	9	1	13	57	34	2	.269	.438
1981	50	117	14	31	6	0	6	24	12	0	.265	.470
1982	65	141	12	32	6	0	7	30	12	2	.227	.418
1983	9	22	2	4	2	0	1	1	1	0	.182	.409
13 Yrs.	1256	4428	641	1231	192	29	175	687	491	74	.278	.453
Life.	1908	6730	972	1862	285	45	252	1043	862	127	.277	.445

Divisional Playoff

Yr.	G	AB	R	H	2B	3B	HR	RBI	BB	SB	BA	SA
1981	2	1	0	0	0	0	0	0	1	0	.000	.000
1 Yr.	2	1	0	0	0	0	0	0	1	0	.000	.000
Life. Same.												

Championship Series

Yr.	G	AB	R	H	2B	3B	HR	RBI	BB	SB	BA	SA
1980	1	4	0	0	0	0	0	0	0	0	.000	.000
1981	1	3	0	1	0	0	0	0	1	0	.333	.333
2 Yrs.	2	7	0	1	0	0	0	0	1	0	.143	.143

World Series

Yr.	G	AB	R	H	2B	3B	HR	RBI	BB	SB	BA	SA
1981	4	3	0	0	0	0	0	0	0	0	.000	.000
1 Yr.	4	3	0	0	0	0	0	0	0	0	.000	.000
Life. Same.												

MURPHY, JOHNNY

Nicknames: "Grandma" "Fireman", "Fordham Johnny"
Yankee: 1932, '34-43 (retired) '46
Pitcher
Born: July 14, 1908
Birthplace: New York, NY
Died: January 14, 1970
Bat: R; Throw: R
Ht: 6'2"; Wt: 190

EARLY ML CAREER: After pitching just two games for the Yanks in 1932, Johnny joined the club permanently in 1934 and was the Yanks' fourth starter in 1934. When the Yanks asked him to become a relief pitcher in 1935, Johnny naturally was reluctant. He was afraid his salary would suffer; at the time, relief specialists were not held in high regard.

RELIEF SPECIALIST: His fears about being a reliever were put to rest as he acquired great fame and made relief pitching respectable in baseball circles. Johnny was the greatest righthanded relief pitcher in Yankee history, at least until Goose Gossage came along. The curve was his "out" pitch. He saved so many games for Lefty Gomez that the newspapers often referred to a Yankee victory as a Gomez-Murphy win. Over the combined 1937-38 seasons, Johnny compiled a fantastic 21-6 record with 20 relief wins. He would have had many more saves had it not been for his era's strict definition of a save. His success paved the way for other young hurlers to become bullpen specialists as the art of relief pitching blossomed.

NICKNAMES AND SUPERSTITIONS: It was because of his rocking-chair pitching motion that Johnny was tagged "Grandma," a nickname he hated. "Fireman" was a name that future relievers would acquire—their job was to putout the fire. "Fordham Johnny," of course, came from the university he attended. He was a superstitious player who sat at the same place on the bench in certain game situations.

TEAM LEADER: Johnny always thought of the team first, doing anything he could to bring it together for the purpose of winning. Becoming a reliever for the Yanks' betterment took a lot of guts. In 1941 he made arrangements for the Yankee party the players gave Joe DiMaggio after his 56-game hitting streak. When the ML players and owners in 1946 had the important meeting to establish a players' contract, Johnny was one of three AL players selected to the committee, and his intelligence and leadership were a force in that historic gathering.

HITTING GAME: Johnny was only a .154 lifetime hitter, but on August 28, 1936 he erupted for five singles in five at-bats—good for five RBIs and three runs scored! It was an unusual accomplishment for a relief pitcher to even bat five times in a game. He batted .361 (13 for 36) in 1936.

LEAGUE LEADER: In four seasons (1938-39, 1941-42), Johnny led the AL in saves. He led AL pitchers in games won in relief six times (1935, 1937, 1938, 1940, 1941, 1943).

CLUB LEADERSHIP: Johnny led the Yanks in many pitching categories through the years, but he led the club in two categories more often than anyone else in Yankee history. He led in saves ten times, five times more than the nearest Yankee, Sparky Lyle. Nine times he led the club's pitchers in games pitched, also more times than any Yankee pitcher.

BASEBALL'S ALL-TIME LEADER LIST: Johnny ranks near baseball's all-time top 20 lists for relief wins (73), winning percentage in relief (.635, 73-42) and wins plus saves (180). Among inactive relief pitchers with 200 or more appearances, he ranks first in the percentage of game appearances resulting in either a win or save (48%; 73 wins plus 107 saves=180 in 375 relief games). Bruce Sutter, Rollie Fingers, and Goose Gossage are all either just above or below him.

ALL-TIME YANKEE LEADER LIST: Johnny is fifth on the all-time Yankee save list (104). Johnny is eighth on the all-time Yankee games pitched list (383). In Yankee history, Johnny ranked 13th in winning percentage (.637) and 17th in victories (93).

ALL-STAR GAME: In 1937 and 1939 Johnny was selected to the AL team for each season's All-Star Game, a rarity for a relief pitcher in those days.

WORLD SERIES: Johnny is tied for second on the all-time World Series save list (four). As a relief pitcher, Johnny appeared in at least one game in six World Series, a Series record. In fact, he won or saved a game in relief in all six World Series he was involved in. In Game 6, the final game, of the 1936 Series, Johnny got the final eight Giant outs (allowing only a harmless solo HR), recording a save and handing the Yanks the World Championship. He got the final out of Game 3 in the 1937 Series. He threw a pair of shutout innings to save Game 2 of the

1938 Series, as the Yanks won, 6-3. In Game 4 of the 1939 Series, Johnny was the winning pitcher as the Yanks finished a sweep of the Reds, giving New York its fourth straight World Championship. He pitched the last couple of innings in Game 4 of the 1941 Series, recording a win in a 7-4 Yankee victory against the Dodgers. In Game 3 of the 1943 Series, "Fordham Johnny" pitched the ninth inning to save an important 6-2 Yankee win over the Cardinals.

IN AND OUT OF RETIREMENT: After the 1943 season, Johnny retired as a player. He returned to the Yanks in 1946 and pitched like he had never left the game (4-2, 7 saves, 3.40 ERA). He was released in April of 1947 and he signed with the Red Sox. Johnny pitched 32 games for Boston in 1947 (0-0, three saves), then retired as a player permanently.

BASEBALL MAN: Once his playing career ended, he remained associated with baseball. His most successful post was as general manager of the New York Mets, a club Johnny helped make a winner in the late 1960s. The "Miracle Mets" were still celebrating their 1969 World Championship in January of 1970 when he died.

MURPHY, JOHNNY

Yr.	W-L	Pct.	SA	G	GS	CG	IP	H	BB	SO	SH	ERA
1932	0-0	.000	0	2	0	0	3	7	3	2	0	16.20
1934	14-10	.583	4	40	20	10	208	193	76	70	0	3.12
1935	10-5	.667	5	40	8	4	117	110	55	28	0	4.08
1936	9-3	.750	5	27	5	2	88	90	36	34	0	3.38
1937	13-4	.765	10	39	4	0	110	121	50	36	0	4.17
1938	8-2	.800	11	32	2	1	91	90	41	43	0	4.24
1939	3-6	.333	19	38	0	0	61	57	28	30	0	4.40
1940	8-4	.667	9	35	1	0	63	58	15	23	0	3.69
1941	8-3	.727	15	35	0	0	77	68	40	29	0	1.98
1942	4-10	.286	11	31	0	0	58	66	23	24	0	3.41
1943	12-4	.750	8	37	0	0	68	44	30	31	0	2.51
1946	4-2	.667	7	27	0	0	45	40	19	19	0	3.40
12 Yrs.	93-53	.637	104	383	40	17	990	944	416	369	0	3.54
Life.	93-53	.637	107	415	40	17	1045	985	444	378	0	3.50

World Series

Yr.	G	IP	BB	SO	H	W-L	SA
1936	1	2⅔	1	1	1	0-0	1
1937	1	⅓	0	0	0	0-0	1
1938	1	2	1	1	2	0-0	1
1939	1	3⅓	0	2	5	1-0	0
1941	2	6	1	3	2	1-0	0
1943	2	2	1	1	1	0-0	1
6 Yrs.	8	16⅓	4	8	11	2-0	4
Life. Same.							

NETTLES, GRAIG

Nickname: "Puff"
Yankee: 1973-83
Third Baseman
Born: August 20, 1944
Birthplace: San Diego, CA
Bat: L; Throw: R
Ht: 6'; Wt: 180

TRADE TO YANKS: In November of 1972, the Yankees obtained Graig and Jerry Moses (C) from Cleveland for Jerry Kenney (3B) and three of the Yanks' best young players/prospects—John Ellis, Charlie Spikes and Rusty Torres. As the 1972 season ended, Yankee Manager Ralph Houk said the Yanks needed a power hitter in the middle of the lineup, and GM Lee MacPhail made the deal. In announcing the deal, MacPhail said: "We traded tomorrow for today. Our fans have waited long enough." The subsequent achievements by Nettles would far exceed those of others involved in the trade.

HIGH EXPECTATIONS: Graig had broken into the ML's with the Twins in 1967 and became a regular with the Indians in 1970, with HR totals in Cleveland of 26, 28, and 17. Graig was given uniform No. 9, the same number Roger Maris had worn, and expectations were for him to put up Maris-like offensive numbers. He hit 22 HRs in 1973, but his BA was only .234. Graig set an AL record for April HRs in 1974, with 11, but he finished with only 22 HRs. It took Graig a couple years to adjust to the Yankees and the expectations of the club and fans. He started turning it around with an excellent year defensively in 1974.

AMONG BASEBALL'S GREATEST THIRD BASEMEN: In 1974, as Brooks Robinson faded, Graig emerged as the AL's best fielding third baseman. As best all-round third baseman in the AL, Graig was sandwiched between two others holding that distinction who were adored in their cities—Robinson in Baltimore and George Brett in Kansas City—and even playing in New York City he sometimes lacked the high profiles of the other two. He was the best all-round third baseman in Yankee history. On July 21, 1980, Graig hit his 267th homer as an AL third baseman, passing Brooks Robinson for the AL record; eventually he stretched his record to 319 homers. Graig's 37 homers and 107 RBIs in 1977 are both single-season records for Yankee third basemen.

POWER HITTER: Graig led or tied for home-run leadership on the Yankees in six seasons. In 1976, he led the AL with 32 HRs; it was the first time a Yankee led the AL since Maris in 1961. Graig led the AL in 1975 in sacrifice flies (11). In the AL for the decade of the 1970s, Graig trailed only Carl Yastrzemski and Reggie Jackson in total RBIs. In 1978, Graig led the Yanks with 14 game-winning RBIs. In Game 4 of the 1978 ALCS, Graig's HR helped clinch the pennant. Graig had RBIs in 10 consecutive games in April 1974, one short of Babe Ruth's club record, and on the Yanks' all-time lists, he ranks sixth in HRs (250) and tenth in RBIs (834).

GREAT FIELDER: Graig had great reflexes, a strong and accurate arm, a sure glove, diving ability, and was apt at keeping his eyes glued on the ball. He played further away from the third-base line than other third basemen, allowing him to reach more balls hit in the hole; he was still able to protect the line because he was great at going to his right; consequently, he covered more ground than others at third. Graig won Gold Gloves in 1977 and 1978. He ranks with Clete Boyer as the best fielding third baseman in Yankee history (but, of course, Boyer wasn't as dangerous a hitter).

ALL-TIME YANKEE LEADER: On the Yankee Top 20 lists, Craig ranks 13th in games played (1535); 16th in at-bats (5519); and 20th in runs scored (750).

FIELDING STATISTICS: As an Indian player in 1971, he set ML records for third basemen with 412 assists and 54 double plays. With the Yankees, his 410 assists in 1973 tied Brooks Robinson for second most in ML history. Graig set a Yankee record for third basemen in fielding in 1978 (.975). As a Yankee, he led AL third baseman in assists in three seasons; total chances and double plays twice; and putouts once.

FIELDING IN 1978 WORLD SERIES: Graig had a defensive World Series that was comparable to Brooks Robinson's in the 1970 World Series, and, finally, Graig got the acclaim he deserved as a fielder. The Yankees dropped the first two games to the Dodgers, and put ace Ron Guidry on the mound for Game 3. Guidry won a complete game, 5-1, but didn't have his best stuff; Graig saved him with at least four sensational plays, all coming in key situations. The first gem came in the third inning; two more came in the fifth, including one with the bases loaded; and the final one came with two outs and the bases loaded in the sixth. The Guidry/Nettles heroics turned the momentum and ignited four straight Yankee wins.

FIELDING IN THE 1981 WORLD SERIES: On the first play of Game 1, Graig dove for a sharp grounder down the line, pounced on the ball, leaped to his feet and threw out Davey Lopes by an eyelash. Later in the game he speared a liner down the line, robbing Steve Garvey of a double and halting a promising Dodger rally, as the Yanks won, 5-3. Afterwards, Dodger Manager Tom Lasorda called the Nettles show at third "so great that it makes me sick to my stomach to watch him." The Dodgers' big break came in Game 2 when Graig suffered a hairline fracture of his glove thumb attempting another diving stop, and Graig sat out Games 3-4-5, all won by Los Angeles. He got two hits in Game 6 but had to leave for a pinch runner.

SMART PLAYER: Graig was baseball smart and a student of Billy Martin; he played for Martin in the minors at Denver and gained knowledge and confidence from Martin. Graig wasn't fast, but he was an excellent base runner; he was daring and knew when to try for the extra base, seldom getting caught. He was the first one to notice George Brett's pine-tar bat in the famous 1983 game, and the Yanks temporarily won a rule interpretation. Martin once said, "Having Nettles on your team is like having a manager on your team at all times."

FIGHTING BOSTON: Graig was a scrapper and got into a few baseball fights. The most famous was at Yankee Stadium against Boston on May 20, 1976. Lou Piniella and Carlton Fisk came up fighting after a play at the plate, and in the melee that followed, Graig picked up pitcher Bill Lee and hurled him to the ground; Lee fell on his pitching shoulder, resulting in torn ligaments and a trip to the Disabled List. Lee was only 5-7 in 1976 after going 17-9 in 1975, a key factor in Boston not contending in 1976. Lee always held a grudge against Nettles and the Yankees and talked negatively about them whenever possible.

PUFF: Known for his clubhouse wit, teammates called him "Puff" because Graig had the habit of talking with teammates, interjecting a wisecrack, and then disappearing—gone like a puff of smoke. In 1978 alone he got off three memorable lines: 1) When he was fined $500 for missing a mandatory luncheon, he said: "If this club wants somebody to play third base, they've got me. If they want somebody to go to luncheons, they should hire George Jessel." Old-time comedian Jessel sent Graig a telegram reading, "Thanks for getting my name in the paper." 2) As controversy swirled around the club, Graig noted: "When I was a little boy, I wanted to be a baseball player and join a circus. With the Yankees, I've accomplished both." 3) As Sparky Lyle sank deeper in the bullpen, Graig observed: "In one year Sparky Lyle has gone from Cy Young to sayonara."

ALL-STAR: Graig was selected to the AL team for All-Star Games in 1975, 1977, 1978, 1979 and 1980. He hit .222 (two for nine) as a Yankee. He also made the NL team in 1985. Graig was picked to the AL All-Star team selected by *The Sporting News* three times.

1981 ALCS: Graig won the MVP Award as the Yankees swept Oakland in three games. Graig set a three-game ALCS record with nine RBIs—he had one three-run hit in each game—and he batted .500 (6 for 12). He moved into first place on the all-time ALCS RBI list (17), passing Reggie Jackson, with whom he had a brief fight during the victory party. Jackson took back the ALCS RBI lead in 1982.

LATE YANKEE CAREER: In July 1980, Graig was diagnosed with hepatitis, and he didn't play until the final two games of the season; he was badly missed, as the Yankees nearly blew an 8½ game lead. Graig returned for the 1980 ALCS and legged out an inside-the-park homer. On January 29, 1982, Graig was named the team captain. He missed several weeks in 1982 with a fractured left thumb. In 1983, Graig had his best season since 1978 (20 HRs, 75 RBIs).

TRADED TO PADRES: In March of 1984, the Yankees traded Graig to San Diego, his hometown, for pitchers Dennis Rasmussen and Darin Cloninger. Graig hit 20 homers in 1984 and helped the Padres win their first pennant. He finished his ML career in 1988 and rejoined the Yankees as a coach in 1991. In 1995 Graig was the third-base coach for the San Diego Padres where he remained for one season.

NETTLES, GRAIG

Yr.	G	AB	R	H	2B	3B	HR	RBI	BB	SB	BA	SA
1973	160	552	65	129	18	0	22	81	78	0	.234	.386
1974	155	566	74	139	21	1	22	75	59	1	.246	.403
1975	157	581	71	155	24	4	21	91	51	1	.267	.430
1976	158	583	88	148	29	2	32	93	62	11	.254	.475
1977	158	589	99	150	23	4	37	107	68	2	.255	.496
1978	159	587	81	162	23	2	27	93	59	1	.276	.460
1979	145	521	71	132	15	1	20	73	59	1	.253	.401
1980	89	324	52	79	14	0	16	45	42	0	.244	.435
1981	103	349	46	85	7	1	15	46	47	0	.244	.398
1982	122	405	47	94	11	2	18	55	51	1	.232	.402
1983	129	462	56	123	17	3	20	75	51	0	.266	.446
11 Yrs.	1535	5519	750	1396	202	20	250	834	627	18	.253	.433
Life.	2700	8986	1193	2225	328	28	390	1314	1088	32	.248	.421

Divisional Playoff

Yr.	G	AB	R	H	2B	3B	HR	RBI	BB	SB	BA	SA
1981	5	17	1	1	0	0	0	1	3	0	.059	.059
1 Yr.	5	17	1	1	0	0	0	1	3	0	.059	.059

Life. Same.

Championship Series

Yr.	G	AB	R	H	2B	3B	HR	RBI	BB	SB	BA	SA
1976	5	17	2	4	1	0	2	4	3	0	.235	.647
1977	5	20	1	3	0	0	0	1	0	0	.150	.150
1978	4	15	3	5	0	1	1	2	0	0	.333	.667
1980	2	6	1	1	0	0	1	1	0	0	.167	.667
1981	3	12	2	6	2	0	1	9	1	0	.500	.917
5 Yrs.	19	70	9	19	3	1	5	17	4	0	.271	.557
Life.	24	85	10	22	3	1	5	19	5	0	.259	.494

World Series

Yr.	G	AB	R	H	2B	3B	HR	RBI	BB	SB	BA	SA
1976	4	12	0	3	0	0	0	2	3	0	.250	.250
1977	6	21	1	4	1	0	0	2	2	0	.190	.238
1978	6	25	2	4	0	0	0	1	0	0	.160	.160
1981	3	10	1	4	1	0	0	0	1	0	.400	.500
4 Yrs.	19	68	4	15	2	0	0	5	6	0	.221	.250
Life.	24	80	6	18	2	0	0	7	11	0	.225	.250

NOREN, IRV

Yankee: 1952-56
Outfielder, 1B
Born: November 29, 1924
Birthplace: Jamestown, NY
Bat: L; Throw: L
Ht: 6'; Wt: 190

HONORS: Irv was on the AL All-Star team as a Yankee player in the 1954 All-Star Game.

CAME TO YANKS: The Yanks obtained Irv from the Washington Senators early in the 1952 season in a trade that sent Jackie Jensen, Spec Shea, and two others to the Senators.

YANKEE OUTFIELDER: Irv was the regular Yankee leftfielder during the 1954-55 seasons. He was a valuable fourth outfielder in 1952-53.

DEFENSIVE ABILITIES: Irv was an outstanding defensive outfielder. In 1952 he played 60 games in the Yankee outfield without making an error, and in 1953 he made only two errors in 96 games. In fact, Irv made only 12 errors in the 408 games he played as a Yankee outfielder. He could also play first base.

GOOD HITTER: He was a good contact hitter. In 1954 he led the Yanks in batting (.319). That year Irv was leading the AL in batting, hitting around .350, but slumped in September.

INJURIES: It is possible that Irv could have been one of the all-time Yankee greats, but he was constantly plagued with knee problems. Irv courageously played with pain throughout his Yankee career. He had operations on both knees.

TRADED: The Yanks traded Irv and five others to the Kansas City A's in February, 1957, for Art Ditmar, Bobby Shantz and Clete Boyer (plus two others). Irv was a coach for the Oakland A's during their championship seasons in 1971-74. He coached for the Chicago Cubs in 1975.

NOREN, IRV

Yr.	G	AB	R	H	2B	3B	HR	RBI	BB	SB	BA	SA
1952	93	272	36	64	13	2	5	21	26	4	.235	.353
1953	109	345	55	92	12	6	6	46	42	3	.267	.388
1954	125	426	70	136	21	6	12	66	43	4	.319	.481
1955	132	371	49	94	19	1	8	59	43	5	.253	.375
1956	29	37	4	8	1	0	0	6	12	0	.216	.243
5 Yrs.	488	1451	214	394	66	15	31	198	166	16	.272	.402
Life.	1093	3119	443	857	157	35	65	453	335	34	.275	.410

World Series

Yr.	G	AB	R	H	2B	3B	HR	RBI	BA
1952	4	10	0	3	0	0	0	1	.300
1953	2	1	0	0	0	0	0	0	.000
1955	5	16	0	1	0	0	0	1	.063
3 Yrs.	11	27	0	4	0	0	0	2	.148

Life. Same.

O'NEILL, PAUL

Yankee: 1996-2001
Outfielder
Born: February 25, 1963
Birthplace: Columbus, OH
Bat: L; Throw: L
Ht: 6'4"; Wt: 215

COMES TO YANKS FROM CINCINNATI: The Yankees obtained Paul in November 1992 from the Reds for outfielder Roberto Kelly. Paul really did not want to leave Cincinnati, but later stated that coming to the Yankees was the best thing to happen to his major league career. Not only did he develop into one of the best defensive outfielders for the Yankees, he also made adjustments in his swing to turn him into a better all-around hitter. Hitting left handed pitching used to be a problem for Paul, but he learned to sit on the breaking ball and then adjust to the fastball with his great bat speed.

PRODUCTIVE SEASONS: In 1993, his first New York season, Paul hit a then career high .311 to go with a .504 slugging percentage. Most players drop off the first season they switch leagues, but not Paul. He quickly won over the hearts of the Yankee fans with his steady style of hard playing. Chants of "O'Neill, O'Neill" and "Paulie, Paulie, Paulie" quickly became common among the Yankee Stadium faithful during the late innings. In 1997, at the age of 34, Paul started a four-season run of 100 or better RBI totals. He batted a career high .324 that

season, and reached additional career numbers in doubles (42) and RBI (117). During those four seasons, he averaged 175 hits, with a career high in safeties (191) coming in 1998. He had a 235 game errorless string snapped on May 7, 1997.

ALL-STAR: Paul represented the Yankees on the AL All-Star squad in 1994, 1995, 1997, and 1998. He was the starting right-fielder for the AL in the 1998 contest at Coors Field in Denver.

POSTSEASON: Paul appeared in 17 postseason series with the Yankees. His over-the-shoulder game saving catch for the final out in Game 5 of the 1996 World Series made up for a poor playoff batting average that year. His best Yankee postseason batting numbers occurred in the 1997 Division Series (.421 BA and .842 SA), the 2001 ALCS (.417 BA and .917 SA), and the 2000 World Series (.474 BA). That World Series victory against the Mets also showed Paul could still provide the long hit for total bases as his slugging percent was .789 for the five games. Paul's dad passed away just before Game 4 of the 1999 World Series. It was his father who had convinced Paul after the 1992 trade from the Reds that going to the Yankees would be good for his son's career. Paul hit 10 of his 11 career postseason home runs while wearing Yankee pinstripes.

ALL-TIME YANKEE LEADER: In Yankee history, Paul is 11th in RBI (858); 12th in home runs (185), doubles (304) and batting average (.303); and 19th in hits (1426).

RETIRED: Paul retired after the 2001 season, but he remains with the Yankees as part of their broadcasting team.

Paul O'Neill averaged .303 in his nine seasons with the Yanks.

O'NEILL, PAUL

Yr.	G	AB	R	H	2B	3B	HR	RBI	BB	SB	BA	SA
1993	141	498	71	155	34	1	20	75	44	2	.311	.504
1994	103	368	68	132	25	1	21	83	72	5	.359	.603
1995	127	460	82	138	30	4	22	96	71	1	.300	.526
1996	150	546	89	165	35	1	19	91	102	0	.302	.474
1997	149	553	89	179	42	0	21	117	75	10	.324	.514
1998	152	602	95	191	40	2	24	116	57	15	.317	.510
1999	153	597	70	170	39	4	19	110	66	11	.285	.459
2000	142	566	79	160	26	0	18	100	51	14	.283	.424
2001	137	510	77	136	33	1	21	70	48	22	.267	.459
9 Yrs.	1254	4700	720	1426	304	14	185	858	586	80	.303	.492
Life.	2053	7318	1041	2105	451	21	281	1269	892	141	.288	.370

Division Series

Yr.	G	AB	R	H	2B	3B	HR	RBI	BB	SB	BA	SA
1995	5	18	5	6	0	0	3	6	5	0	.333	.833
1996	4	15	0	2	0	0	0	0	0	0	.133	.133
1997	5	19	5	8	2	0	2	7	3	0	.421	.842
1998	3	11	1	4	2	0	1	1	1	0	.364	.818
1999	2	8	2	2	0	0	0	0	1	0	.250	.250
2000	5	19	4	4	1	0	0	0	2	0	.211	.263
2001	3	11	1	1	1	0	0	0	0	0	.091	.182
7 Yrs.	27	101	18	27	6	0	6	14	12	0	.267	.504
Life. Same.												

Championship Series

Yr.	G	AB	R	H	2B	3B	HR	RBI	BB	SB	BA	SA
1996	4	11	1	3	0	0	1	2	3	0	.273	.545
1998	6	25	6	7	2	0	1	3	3	2	.280	.480
1999	5	21	2	6	0	0	0	1	1	0	.286	.286
2000	6	20	0	5	0	0	0	5	1	0	.250	.250
2001	5	12	2	5	0	0	2	3	1	0	.417	.917
5 Yrs.	26	89	11	26	2	0	4	14	9	0	.292	.449
Life.	31	106	12	34	5	0	5	18	10	1	.321	.509

World Series

Yr.	G	AB	R	H	2B	3B	HR	RBI	BB	SB	BA	SA
1996	5	12	1	2	2	0	0	0	3	0	.167	.333
1998	4	19	3	4	1	0	0	0	1	0	.211	.263
1999	4	15	0	3	0	0	0	4	2	0	.200	.200
2000	5	19	2	9	2	2	0	2	3	0	.474	.789
2001	5	15	1	5	1	0	0	0	2	0	.333	.400
5 Yrs.	13	46	4	9	3	0	0	4	6	0	.196	.261
Life.	17	58	6	10	3	0	0	5	11	1	.172	.224

ORTH, AL

Nickname: "The Curveless Wonder"
Yankee: 1904-09
Pitcher
Born: September 5, 1872
Birthplace: Tipton, IN
Died: October 8, 1948
Bat: L; Throw: R
Ht: 6'; Wt: 200

CAME TO YANKS: The Yanks (Highlanders) obtained Al from the Washington Senators for pitcher Long Tom Hughes in July of 1904.

PITCHING STAR: Al was one of the best pitchers of his era and was an established nine-year veteran when he joined New York. He was ill much of the 1904 season, a factor in Jack Chesbro's heavy workload. In 1905-06 Al was the Yanks' No. 2 starter. In 1907 he was the club's No. 1 starter. At the age of 35, Al in 1908 was the Yanks' fifth starter, his career winding down. Al was called "The Curveless Wonder" because he was successful in spite of an almost total reliance on the fastball.

1906 SEASON: This was Al's best ML season. He and Chesbro were a great 1-2 pitching combination—together they won 51 games. Al and Chesbro together pitched in 664 of the season's 1358 innings. Thus, one or the other was on the mound 49% of the time! Only once has a Yankee pitcher won more games than Al did in 1906 (27). Al led the AL in wins, complete games (36) and innings pitched (339). On August 12, Al had 11 assists in a game, an AL record he shares with three other pitchers.

GOOD HITTER: Al was a fine hitting pitcher, as his lifetime batting average of .273 and 12 lifetime HRs attest. As a pitcher, he hit .278 lifetime, the fifth highest career BA by a pitcher with at least 500 at-bats. Again as a pitcher, Al had a lifetime .380 slugging average, the eighth highest of 20th-century pitchers with at least 500 at-bats. Al led ML pitchers in hitting in 1907 (.324) and 1908 (.290). As one of the best hitting pitchers in the first decade of the 20th century, Al was often used as a pinch-hitter. From 1904-09, he was 12 for 47 (.255) as a pinch-hitter. He went 5-for-13 (.385) in 1909. Al played five games in the outfield and six games at second base for the Yanks.

CLUB LEADERSHIP: Al led Yankee pitchers in innings pitched and complete games three times in each category. In consecutive years (1906-07), he led the Yanks in victories. In 1905 Al led the club in shutouts (four). He led the Yanks in 1907 in games pitched (36).

ALL-TIME YANKEE LEADER: Al's Yankee career ERA (2.72) is the third lowest in Yankee history for those pitchers with at least 800 innings pitched as a Yankee. Al ranks 12th in complete games (102) on the All-Time Yankee list.

LEFT YANKS: The 1909 season was Al's last in the ML's. He was 0-0, pitching in one Yankee game. In 1909 he also pitched for Lynchburg of the Virginia League and was 1-2. Al finished his pitching career with Indianapolis of the American Association in 1910 as a 4-8 pitcher. Al later spent some years as an umpire, including a stint in the NL (1913-16).

ORTH, AL

Yr.	W-L	Pct.	SA	G	GS	CG	IP	H	BB	SO	SH	ERA
1904	11-6	.647	0	20	18	11	138	122	19	47	2	2.68
1905	18-16	.529	0	40	37	26	305	273	61	121	6	2.86
1906	27-17	.614	0	45	39	36	339	317	66	133	3	2.34
1907	14-21	.400	0	36	33	21	249	244	53	78	2	2.61
1908	2-13	.133	0	21	17	8	139	134	30	22	1	3.42
1909	0-0	.000	0	1	1	0	3	6	1	1	0	12.00
6 Yrs.	72-73	.497	0	163	145	102	1173	1096	230	402	14	2.72
Life.	205-189	.520	5	440	394	324	3355	3564	661	948	31	3.37

PAGE, JOE

Nicknames: "Fireman", "The Gay Reliever"
Yankee: 1944-50
Pitcher
Born: October 28, 1917
Birthplace: Cherry Valley, PA
Died: April 21, 1980
Bat: L; Throw: L
Ht: 6'3"; Wt: 200

HONORS: In 1949 Joe was one of three pitchers selected to *The Sporting News* ML All-Star team. He was also picked to the AL All-Star team for three All-Star Games (1944, 1947, 1948).

EARLY ML CAREER: Joe pitched for a small mine-town team before getting his Yankee break. Joe began his ML career with the Yanks in 1944. That year he was the Yanks' fifth starter. In 1945 he was used infrequently, mostly as a spot starter. Joe was the Yanks' third starter in 1946, although he was also used almost as much in relief. Joe's first three Yankee seasons, when he was used 60% of the time as a starter, were not at all spectacular. In fact, there did not seem to be a regular job on the pitching staff for him.

TURNING POINT: After pitching inconsistently early in the 1947 season, Joe was on the verge of being sent down to Newark. Then in a game played on May 26, 1947, against the Red Sox, he was brought in to pitch early in the game with the Yanks trailing, 3-1. With the bases loaded, Joe ran the count to 3-0 to both Rudy York and Bobby Doerr, but struck out both of them. He got the third out, the Yanks went on to win 9-3, and Joe's whole career changed. For the next four seasons, he was the best relief pitcher in baseball.

LATER ML CAREER: The Yanks were desperately looking for a replacement for Johnny Murphy when Joe became the club's bullpen ace in 1947. Joe had a great fastball which he used in extricating the Yanks from tough situations. Although he did not win the MVP Award in 1949, Joe was probably most responsible for the Yankee pennant, producing the best season of any Yankee relief pitcher to that date. His 27 saves in 1949 are the 11th most in Yankee history.

GREATEST GAME: The Yanks beat the Red Sox on October 1, 1949, the next-to-last day of the season, to tie Boston for first place. Joe came into the game in the third inning with the bases loaded and walked in two runs as Boston got a 4-0 lead. But Joe found himself, holding the Sox to just one hit and no runs over the last 6²/₃ innings. The Yanks won, 5-4!

TOUGH COMPETITOR: When Joe took the mound, he was all business. He scowled at the batter, then gave him his best fastball. Casey Stengel said Joe "could get the fire out quick. He just came in and blasted the ball in there." During Joe's Yankee tenure, there was a continuing debate in baseball concerning who was the better player—Joe DiMaggio or Ted Williams. DiMaggio was Page's hero so he really bore down when he faced Ted in an effort to prove DiMaggio the better player. To his delight, Page usually retired Williams. Joe saved so many games for Allie Reynolds that the newspapers often called a Yankee win a Reynolds-Page victory.

FREE SPIRIT: Joe was a free-spirited, fun-loving player. He stayed out late at night but his pitching did not usually seem affected. When they played together on the Yanks, Joe and Joe DiMaggio were great pals. Page had the ability to make DiMaggio comfortable. He was DiMaggio's disciple. Page was a lively Irishman, friendly and always smiling.

LEAGUE LEADER: In 1947 and 1949 Joe led the AL in both saves and games won in relief. In consecutive seasons (1948-49) he led the AL in games pitched. Joe led the AL in games finished 3 straight years (1947-49), an AL record.

CLUB LEADERSHIP: Joe led Yankee pitchers in saves and games pitched in four straight seasons (1947-50). He had the lowest ERA (2.59) on the 1949 Yankee pitching staff.

ALL-TIME YANKEE LEADER: Joe is seventh on the all-time Yankee save list (76), and is 19th overall in games pitched (278).

WORLD SERIES: In Game 1 of the 1947 Series, Joe pitched the final four innings to save a 5-3 victory over the Dodgers. Then he won Game 7, pitching five shutout innings (only one Dodger hit) in a 5-2 Yankee victory. Joe won the Babe Ruth Award as the Series best player in 1949. In the 1949 Series Joe saved Game 2, won Game 3, then returned to finish Game 5 to wrap up the World Championship for the Yanks.

END OF CAREER: Joe while pitching in the 1951 spring training camp had a mound mishap in which he tore a throwing arm muscle. Casey Stengel was forced to release the injured pitcher. Joe's ML career was over except for a brief stint with the Pirates in 1954.

PAGE, JOE

Yr.	W-L	Pct.	SA	G	GS	CG	IP	H	BB	SO	SH	ERA
1944	5-7	.417	0	19	16	4	103	100	52	63	0	4.56
1945	6-3	.667	0	20	9	4	102	95	46	50	0	2.82
1946	9-8	.529	3	31	17	6	136	126	72	77	1	3.57
1947	14-8	.636	17	56	2	0	141	105	72	116	0	2.48
1948	7-8	.467	16	55	1	0	108	116	66	77	0	4.26
1949	13-8	.619	27	60	0	0	135	103	75	99	0	2.59
1950	3-7	.300	13	37	0	0	55	66	31	33	0	5.04
7 Yrs.	57-49	.538	76	278	45	14	780	711	414	515	1	3.44
Life.	57-49	.538	76	285	45	14	790	727	421	519	1	3.53

World Series

Yr.	G	IP	BB	SO	H	W-L	SA
1947	4	13	2	7	12	1-1	1
1949	3	9	3	8	6	1-0	1
2 Yrs.	7	22	5	15	18	2-1	2
Life. Same.							

PAGLIARULO, MIKE

Nickname: "Pags"
Yankee: 1984-89
Third Baseman
Born: March 15, 1960
Birthplace: Medford, MA
Bat: L; Throw: R
Ht: 6'2"; Wt: 195

YANKEE PROSPECT: At Medford High School, Mike was All State (MA) for two years in baseball and soccer. Mike was selected by the Yankees in the sixth round of the June 1981 draft and signed by Yankee Scout Fred Ferreira. Mike broke into pro ball hitting .216 at Oneonta. He hit 22 HRs at Greensboro in 1982 and 19 HRs at Nashville in 1983. He was considered an outstanding fielder; the question was whether he would hit ML pitching. In 1984, Mike hit .212 at Columbus; he was called up to the Yankees when Toby Harrah got hurt and made his ML debut on July 7.

YANKEE THIRD BASEMAN: Mike became the Yankees' regular third baseman in July 1984 and held the job until 1989. He had a good glove and was a hard-nosed player. In May 1986, he was hit in the face with a pitch, suffered a hairline fracture of his nose, missed just one game, and returned with homers in three consecutive games; the players began calling him "Rambo." He was hardworking; some blamed his frequent September slumps on his overly zealous work habits.

POWER HITTER: The first four years with the Yankees, Mike improved in HRs each year: seven to 19 to 28 to 32. He was hitting .165 with two homers on June 9, 1985, and then he seemed to find himself; the rest of the year he hit .263 with 17 HRs. In 1987, Mike reached career highs in HRs (32) and RBIs (87); he led the team in homers—second best in club history for a third sacker behind the 37 hit by Graig Nettles in 1977—and game-winning RBI (12).

HEADING DOWNHILL: Mike suffered from a sore right elbow in September 1987—he didn't homer in his final 20 games—and had arthroscopic surgery on October 8. On July 6, 1988, Mike left a game with a pulled hamstring and played sporadically through mid-August; he hit only .195 the rest of the season and

missed the final week when he re-pulled the hamstring. These were the first steps backwards for Mike as a Yankee. On October 14, 1988, he underwent surgery to relocate the ulnar nerve in his right elbow.

LEFTHANDED PITCHING: Mike always had trouble with lefthanded pitching. In 1986, Mike hit .196 (32 for 163) with two HRs against lefties, and .258 (88 for 341) with 26 HRs against righties; he started the year 0-for-17 vs. lefties. In 1987, Mike hit only four of his 32 homers against southpaws. He hit his first three homers of 1988 against southpaws, sparking hope, but in mid-April he went 0-for-18 with 12 strikeouts against lefties; he finished the year hitting .170 (18 for 106) against lefties.

TRADED AWAY: In 1989, Dallas Green, often critical of his players, managed the Yankees, and he lost confidence in Mike; Pags was in a platoon situation and pressed more and more. Mike was hitting .197 with four homers when in July of 1989 he was traded along with Don Schulze to San Diego for pitchers Walt Terrell and Freddie Toliver (Toliver completing the deal in September, although he never appeared in a game for the Yanks). The Yankees were left with a big hole at third base. Mike later played for Minnesota (1991-93) and Baltimore (1993). On December 1, 1993, he signed with the Seibu Lions of the Japan Pacific League. His Japanese baseball career was short-lived as Mike signed and played with the Texas Rangers in 1995, his last season in the Majors.

PAGLIARULO, MIKE

Yr.	G	AB	R	H	2B	3B	HR	RBI	BB	SB	BA	SA
1984	67	201	24	48	15	3	7	34	15	0	.239	.448
1985	138	380	55	91	16	2	19	62	45	0	.239	.442
1986	149	504	71	120	24	3	28	71	54	4	.238	.464
1987	150	522	76	122	26	3	32	87	53	1	.234	.479
1988	125	444	46	96	20	1	15	67	37	1	.216	.367
1989	74	223	19	44	10	0	4	16	19	1	.197	.296
6 Yrs.	703	2274	291	521	111	12	105	337	223	7	.229	.427
Life.	1246	3901	462	942	206	18	134	505	343	18	.241	.407

PEARSON, MONTE
(BORN MONTGOMERY MARCELLUS PEARSON)

Yankee: 1936-40
Pitcher
Born: September 2, 1909
Birthplace: Oakland, CA
Died: January 27, 1978
Bat: R; Throw: R
Ht: 6'; Wt: 175

CAME TO YANKS: In December of 1935, the Indians traded Monte and fellow pitcher Steve Sundra to the Yanks for pitcher Johnny Allen.

WINNING PITCHER: The Yanks in Monte's first four seasons with the club (1936-39) won the World Championship each year, and a key reason was Monte's consistent pitching. Ranking just behind Yankee greats Red Ruffing and Lefty Gomez, Monte was the third most important starter on the great 1936-39 Yankee clubs. (Ruffing won 82 games, Gomez 64 and Pearson 56.)

1936 SEASON: This was Monte's best ML season. He led the AL in winning percentage (.731, 19-7). He led Yankee pitchers in ERA (3.71) and strikeouts (118). Ruffing won just one more game than Monte to lead the Yanks in victories.

NO-HITTER: On August 27, 1938, Monte hurled a no-hitter against his former teammates, the Cleveland Indians. In fact, he faced the minimum number of 27 batters with two Indians who had walked wiped out on double plays. It was the first no-hitter ever pitched at Yankee Stadium, New York winning, 13-0.

AT THE PLATE: Monte's lifetime batting average is only .228, but he was on occasion a good hitter. Monte hit .253 (23 for 91) and one HR in 1936 and .321 (17 for 53) in 1939. He helped himself at the plate on June 17, 1936, banging out four hits and four RBIs, and beating Cleveland, 12-2.

ALL-STAR GAMES: Monte was selected to the AL team for the All-Star Games of 1936 and 1940.

WORLD SERIES: Monte was a super pitcher in World Series action. His 4-0 World Series record includes three complete games. He allowed an average of only 4.79 hits per nine innings in World Series games, the second lowest average in Fall Classic history. His lifetime World Series ERA (1.01) is the seventh lowest in World Series history for pitchers with at least 25 innings pitched, and he is the only Yankee pitcher ranking in the top 10. In Game 4 of the 1936 Series, Monte beat the Giants, 5-2, on a seven-hitter. Monte won Game 3 of the 1937 Series, 5-1. The Cubs fell to Monte, 5-2, in Game 3 of the 1938 Series, as Monte pitched a complete-game give-hitter. In Game 2 of the 1939 Series, he had a no-hitter in progress until the eighth inning, when Ernie Lombardi singled over second base with one out. But Monte finished with a masterful two-hit shutout, beating the Reds, 4-0, in his final World Series game.

TRADED: In December of 1940, the Yanks traded Monte to Cincinnati for infielder Don Lang and $20,000. Lang never played with the Yanks and Monte pitched in only seven games with a 1-3 record for the Reds in 1941, his final ML season.

PEARSON, MONTE

Yr.	W-L	Pct.	SA	G	GS	CG	IP	H	BB	SO	SH	ERA
1936	19-7	.731	1	33	31	15	223	191	135	118	1	3.71
1937	9-3	.750	1	22	20	7	145	145	64	71	0	3.17
1938	16-7	.696	0	28	27	17	202	198	113	98	1	3.97
1939	12-5	.706	0	22	20	8	146	151	70	76	0	4.49
1940	7-5	.583	0	16	16	7	110	108	44	43	1	3.69
5 Yrs.	63-27	.700	2	121	114	54	826	793	426	406	4	3.82
Life.	100-61	.621	4	224	191	94	1430	1392	740	703	5	4.00

World Series

Yr.	G	IP	BB	SO	H	W-L	SA
1936	1	9	2	7	7	1-0	0
1937	1	8⅔	2	4	5	1-0	0
1938	1	9	2	9	5	1-0	0
1939	1	9	1	8	2	1-0	0
4 Yrs	4	35⅔	7	28	19	4-0	0
Life. Same.							

PECKINPAUGH, ROGER

Yankee: 1913-21
Shortstop
Born: February 5, 1891
Birthplace: Wooster, OH
Died: November 17, 1977
Bat: R; Throw: R
Ht: 5'10"; Wt: 165

CAME TO YANKS: In May, 1913, the Yanks obtained Roger from the Indians for shortstop Bill Stumpf and outfielder Jack Lelivelt.

YANKEE SHORTSTOP: In all nine seasons with the Yanks (1913-21) Roger was the regular shortstop. A solid player, Roger was the glue of the first great Yankee teams. When the Yanks won their first AL pennant in 1921. Roger was the team's senior member—he had been a member of the Yanks continuously longer than anyone else. He was durable, playing in every Yankee game in 1914, the first time a Yankee player had ever played in every game of a season. Roger was a field general and leader. He was captain of the Yanks for some time.

DEFENSIVE ABILITIES: Although Roger made a lot of errors, he was still a fine defensive player. As a Yankee player, Roger led AL shortstops in assists three times and in turning double plays twice. In a doubleheader played on September 8, 1919, he handled 24 chances, tying an AL record for shortstops. On baseball's all-time fielding lists for shortstops, Roger ranks

tenth in assists (6337); 12th in games played at shortstop (1983) and total chances (10,809); and 14th in putouts (3919).

CLUB LEADERSHIP: Three times Roger led the Yanks in walks. Twice he led the Yanks in HRs. In 1913 he led the club in triples (seven). In 1914 he led the team in RBIs (51). In 1918 he led the Yanks in stolen bases (12). Roger led the Yanks in runs (89), walks (59) and batting (.305) in 1919.

ALL-TIME YANKEE LEADER: Roger ranks 15th in steals (143).

BATTING THREAT: Between June 11 and July 9 of 1919, Roger batted safely in 29 consecutive games, establishing the Yankee club record which was not broken until Joe DiMaggio's 56-game streak of 1941. Late in his Yankee career, Roger batted second in the order, just ahead of Babe Ruth. Walter Johnson considered Roger a very dangerous hitter in the clutch, in some respects more dangerous than Ruth.

YANKEE MANAGER: Yankee owners Frank Farrell and Bill Devery realized Roger's leadership qualities and made him Yankee manager for the final 17 games of the 1914 season. At 23 years of age, Roger was the youngest ML manager in history.

TRADED: In December of 1921, the Yanks dealt Roger and pitchers Jack Quinn and Rip Collins to the Red Sox for Sad Sam Jones, Bullet Joe Bush and Everett Scott in a blockbuster trade. The Red Sox then sent Roger to the Washington Senators where he was a star player. Roger won the League Award in 1925. (At the time the League Award was considered the MVP Award.) Roger never appreciated the fact that the Yanks unloaded him and always played especially hard against New York. In later years Roger managed the Cleveland Indians (1928-33, '41).

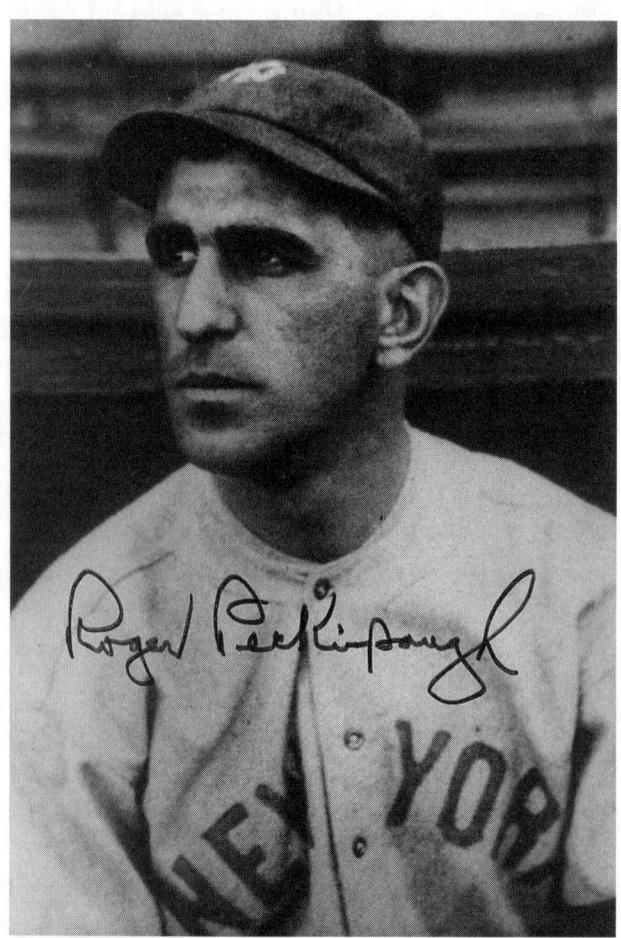

Roger Peckinpaugh

PECKINPAUGH, ROGER

Yr.	G	AB	R	H	2B	3B	HR	RBI	BB	SB	BA	SA
1913	95	340	35	91	10	7	1	32	24	19	.268	.347
1914	157	570	55	127	14	6	3	51	51	38	.223	.284
1915	142	540	67	119	18	7	5	44	49	19	.220	.307
1916	146	552	65	141	22	8	4	58	62	18	.255	.346
1917	148	543	63	141	24	7	0	41	64	17	.260	.330
1918	122	446	59	103	15	3	0	43	43	12	.231	.278
1919	122	453	89	138	20	2	7	33	59	10	.305	.404
1920	139	534	109	144	26	6	8	54	72	8	.270	.386
1921	149	577	128	166	25	7	8	71	84	2	.288	.397
9 Yrs.	1220	4555	670	1170	174	53	36	427	508	143	.257	.342
Life.	2012	7233	1006	1876	256	75	48	739	814	207	.259	.335

World Series

Yr.	G	AB	R	H	2B	3B	HR	RBI	BA
1921	8	28	2	5	1	0	0	0	.179
1 Yr.	8	28	2	5	1	0	0	0	.179
Life.	19	64	4	16	4	0	1	4	.250

PENNOCK, HERB

Nickname: "The Knight of Kennett Square"
Yankee: 1923-33
Pitcher
Born: February 10, 1894
Birthplace: Kennett Square, PA
Died: January 30, 1948
Bat: Both; Throw: L
Ht: 6'; Wt: 160

HONORS: Herb was inducted into the Baseball Hall of Fame in 1948. *The Sporting News* selected him as one of three pitchers on its 1926 ML All-Star team. In 1932 the New York Chapter of the Baseball Writers gave Herb the Sid Mercer Award.

CAME TO YANKS: In January of 1923, the Yanks purchased his contract from the Red Sox in a deal that also sent three unheralded players to Boston. Herb was thought to be over the hill (at age 29).

LONGEVITY RECORD: For 22 consecutive seasons, 11 of them with the Yanks (and excepting 1918 when he was serving in the military), Herb pitched ML baseball. That is a ML record that Herb shares with four others. Although he pitched many years for other clubs, it is for his years with the Yanks that he is most remembered.

YANKEE STAR: Herb was the ace Yankee pitcher from 1924-26, winning a combined total of 60 games for an average of 20 wins per season. Between 1923-29 Herb was one of the Yanks' top three starters. In 1925 he lost 17 games, the most ever lost by a Yankee southpaw. Herb was in the midst of a great 1928 campaign, when in mid-August he developed a sore arm and did not pitch the rest of the year. He never completely recovered. He was used increasingly less over his last four Yankee seasons (1930-33) when he was 36-39 years old.

FINE GENTLEMAN: In Herb's era, it was generally felt that only two AL pitchers—Herb and Walter Johnson (another gentleman)—would not throw at a hitter. Herb was refined, an unusual quality for a ballplayer of his era. He went to the best prep schools, loved flowers, and cut a royal figure while fox hunting near his spacious Pennsylvania home. Herb, in fact, raised silver foxes at his country home near Kennett Square, Pa. As a person, Herb was good-looking, graceful, friendly, quiet and courageous, not unlike the way he pitched. He was the All-American boy without being stuffy or conceited. Herb loved baseball, but he certainly did not need the income. Because he did not need the sport for the money, he had leverage on management that his teammates did not enjoy at contract time, and in 1927 made $17,500, the second highest salary on that great Yankee team. Herb was simply a class person and was responsible in club matters. He was a pallbearer at Miller Huggins' funeral and when the body was taken to Cincinnati for burial, Herb was there to represent the Yankee players. (Huggins once called him "the greatest lefthander of all time.")

THE BABE'S PAL: Babe Ruth and Herb were close friends, beginning with their playing days on the Red Sox and continuing in New York, even though they were opposite personalities—sort of the Odd Couple of baseball. Herb hunted quail with the Babe, and when Ruth visited Herb's Pennsylvania home, Herb took the Babe on fox hunts!

CLASSY PITCHER: Babe Ruth called him the smartest southpaw he had ever seen, and in 1934 Ruth picked Herb as one of three pitchers on his all-time all-star team. Herb was slight but durable because he conserved energy by using a beautiful, graceful, pitching motion. He used his brains when pitching, and the words "classy" and "stylish" best describe him. Besides pitching smartly and seemingly without effort, Herb was an artist with a lot of heart. Thus, he had style, head and heart. Herb had some speed on his fastball and a fine curveball. Definitely not a strikeout artist, he was a splendid control pitcher. Herb starred on five pennant-winning Yankee teams (1923, '26-28, '32). He was a model pitcher; youngsters were urged to study his style.

CONFUSED TIGER: During the 1920s, the Tigers' Fats Fathergill was a fine right-handed hitter in the AL (.326 lifetime) who was sure there was not a southpaw alive who could consistently get him out. Once, after going 0-for-4 against Herb, Fats asked teammate Harry Heilman, "What the hell happened?" Heilman, a Hall of Famer, answered, "You didn't face a lefthander. You faced Herb Pennock." Herb studied each situation and dealt with each hitter differently. Thus, no one could help Fats.

LEAGUE LEADER: In 1923 Herb led AL pitchers in winning percentage (.760, 19-6). In 1925 he led the AL in innings pitched (277). In 1928 he led the AL in shutouts (five).

CLUB LEADERSHIP: Herb led Yankee pitchers in shutouts five times. He led the pitching staff in ERA and winning percentage three seasons. In each of the years 1924, 1925 and 1926, Herb led the Yanks in wins, innings pitched, shutouts and complete games. In 1925 he led the club in games pitched (47).

ALL-TIME YANKEE LEADER: Herb is in or near the top 10 on the all-time Yankee pitching list for many categories, including being fourth in complete games (164); seventh in wins (162); eighth in games started (268) and innings pitched (2190); and is 11th in winning percentage (.643, 162-90); 13th in games pitched (346). Herb's 25 complete games of 1924 is a Yankee record for a lefthander, tied twice by Lefty Gomez. In 1924 Herb hurled 286 innings, the most ever in a season by a Yankee southpaw. Herb ranks 12th in shutouts (19) overall in Yankee history, and 18th in strikeouts (700).

WORLD SERIES: Herb is another of the many Yankee pitching stars who performed superbly under World Series pressure. Only Lefty Gomez has won more World Series games without a loss than did Herb who tallied a 5-0 World Series record, all with the Yanks. Herb also had three lifetime saves. He won critical Game 2 of the 1923 Series, pitching a complete game and winning, 4-2. He returned in Game 6 to beat the New York Giants and deliver the first World Championship in Yankee history. In the 1926 Series, Herb pitched a pair of beautiful complete game wins but the Yanks lost a seven-game Series to St. Louis. In Game 3 of the 1927 Series against the Pirates, Herb had a perfect game in progress for 7⅓ innings before Pie Traynor singled. Herb finished with a three-hit victory that was all the more remarkable because Pittsburgh had a reputation for murdering southpaw pitchers. In the twilight of his career, Herb saved the final two games of the 1932 Series, completing the Yanks' sweep of the Cubs.

LEFT YANKS: In January of 1934, the Yanks released Herb a month before his 40th birthday. Upon his release, Herb was asked by sportswriters how he felt he had been treated by the Yanks. "Royal," answered Herb.

BASEBALL MAN: In 1934, Herb pitched for the Red Sox, had a 2-0 record and retired as a ML ballplayer. He remained associated with the game until his death. He was a Red Sox coach (1936-40) and supervisor of the Red Sox farm system (1941-43). From 1944-48, Herb was general manager of the Philadelphia Phillies. But in January of 1948, Herb died suddenly of a stroke and the baseball world mourned his loss. A short time after his death he was voted into the Baseball Hall of Fame. He was given a final tribute in 1950, when the "Whiz Kids" won a surprising NL pennant, for it was Herb who was most responsible for building that Phillies club.

PENNOCK, HERB												
Yr.	W-L	Pct.	SA	G	GS	CG	IP	H	BB	SO	SH	ERA
1923	19-6	.760	3	35	27	21	224	235	68	93	1	3.33
1924	21-9	.700	3	40	34	25	286	302	64	101	4	2.83
1925	16-17	.485	2	47	31	21	277	267	71	88	2	2.96
1926	23-11	.676	2	40	33	19	266	294	43	78	1	3.62
1927	19-8	.704	2	34	26	18	210	225	48	51	1	3.00
1928	17-6	.739	3	28	24	18	211	215	40	53	5	2.56
1929	9-11	.450	2	27	23	8	158	205	28	49	1	4.91
1930	11-7	.611	0	25	19	11	156	194	20	46	1	4.32
1931	11-6	.647	0	25	25	12	189	247	30	65	1	4.28
1932	9-5	.643	0	22	21	9	147	191	38	54	1	4.60
1933	7-4	.636	4	23	5	2	65	96	21	22	1	5.54
11 Yrs.	162-90	.643	21	346	268	164	2190	2471	471	700	19	3.56
Life.	241-162	.598	32	617	419	247	3558	3900	916	1227	35	3.61

World Series							
Yr.	G	IP	BB	SO	H	W-L	SA
1923	3	17⅓	1	8	19	2-0	1
1926	3	22	4	8	13	2-0	0
1927	1	9	0	1	3	1-0	0
1932	2	4	3	4	2	0-0	2
4 Yrs.	9	52⅓	8	21	37	5-0	3
Life.	10	55⅓	8	24	39	5-0	3

PEPITONE, JOE

Nickname: "Pepi"
Yankee: 1962-69
First Baseman, OF
Born: October 9, 1940
Birthplace: Brooklyn, NY
Bat: L; Throw: L
Ht: 6'2"; Wt: 195

HONORS: In 1963 Joe was the first baseman on *The Sporting News* AL All-Star team. Joe was picked for the AL All-Star team for three consecutive All-Star Games (1963-65).

YOUNG PROSPECT: In August, 1958, the 17-year-old Joe was given a bonus of between $20,000 and $25,000 to sign with the club. From 1958-61 the Brooklyn native played in the Yankee farm system at such stops as Auburn, Fargo-Moorhead, Binghamton, and Amarillo. Joe had a great 1961 at Amarillo in the Texas League (21 HRs, 87 RBIs, .316) and in 1962 split his time between the Yanks and Richmond. In the 8th inning of a May 23 Yankee game he hit two HRs. He impressed the club so much that Moose Skowron was traded to make room for Joe at first base for the 1963 season.

YANKEE STAR: Joe held the regular Yankee first baseman's job from 1963-69, except in '67-68 when he spelled Mickey Mantle

in center field (Mickey held down first). Joe had a natural HR stroke, especially for Yankee Stadium. As a Yankee, he hit more than 25 HRs in each of four seasons.

DEFENSIVE ABILITIES: He was smooth and agile around first base. He won a Gold Glove Award for his defensive play in three seasons (1965, '66, '69). Joe led AL first basemen in fielding three times; putouts twice; assists once; and double plays once. In 1965 he established the Yankee first basemen's fielding record (.997). In 1964 he made 121 assists, another Yankee club record for first basemen. Both of these club records have been surpassed by Don Mattingly.

CLUB LEADERSHIP: Three times Joe led the Yanks in RBIs and games played. Twice he led the club in HRs. In 1966 he led the team in slugging (.463). Joe ranks 16th in home-runs (166) in Yankee history.

COLORFUL CHARACTER: As both a player and a personality, Joe was distinctive, colorful and individualistic. He was the first ML player to have long hair and to bring a hair dryer into the locker room. In his style and attitudes, Joe was a reflection of many of the changes taking place in American society in the late 1960s and early 1970s. His was a magnetic personality, drawing fans—and antagonists, too—all around the AL. Joe was always in search of fun and he usually found it. He was a young man making the most of life and becoming somewhat legendary in the process. All the same, it is commonly believed that a more disciplined Joe Pepitone could possibly have been one of baseball's all-time greats. He had that much talent.

BEAN BALL RIOT: The Yanks in 1963 were on track for a routine AL championship when Joe injected some excitement into the season. In an August 21 game, Joe took exception to some close pitches from the Indians' Gary Bell. Joe charged Bell while Cleveland first baseman Fred Whitfield attempted to restrain him. He decked Whitfield, and both teams emptied onto the field for a baseball fight that actually saw some good punches. The *Newark Evening News* the next day asked in a headlin

Joe Pepitone (New York Yankees Archives)

: "Pepitone: New Breed at Stadium?" Hardly the traditional self-controlled Yankee, but he was creating excitement.

1964 WORLD SERIES: In Game 6 of the 1964 Series, Joe cracked a grand-slam HR to lead the Yanks to an 8-3 victory over the Cardinals.

TRADED: The Yanks dealt Joe to the Houston Astros for outfielder Curt Blefary in December, 1969.

YANKEE RETURN: Joe's ML career ended in 1973 and a few years later he was a player and star attraction in a professional slow-pitch softball league. In the autumn of 1980, the Yanks signed Joe as a minor-league instructor, working with youngsters on hitting, defense and base running (all strong suits in Joe's play). In 1988, Joe served time in jail on a four-month sentence for criminal possession of drugs and weapons, and as part of a work-release program, he worked in the Yankee front office. Later he worked for the Yankees as a special assistant and remained in that capacity through 2002.

PEPITONE, JOE												
Yr.	G	AB	R	H	2B	3B	HR	RBI	BB	SB	BA	SA
1962	63	138	14	33	3	2	7	17	3	1	.239	.442
1963	157	580	79	157	16	3	27	89	23	3	.271	.448
1964	160	613	71	154	12	3	28	100	24	2	.251	.418
1965	143	531	51	131	18	3	18	62	43	4	.247	.394
1966	152	585	85	149	21	4	31	83	29	4	.255	.463
1967	133	501	45	126	18	3	13	64	34	1	.251	.377
1968	108	380	41	93	9	3	15	56	37	8	.245	.403
1969	135	513	49	124	16	3	27	70	30	8	.242	.442
8 Yrs.	1051	3841	435	967	113	24	166	541	223	31	.252	.423
Life.	1397	5097	606	1315	158	35	219	721	302	41	.258	.432

World Series									
Yr.	G	AB	R	H	2B	3B	HR	RBI	BA
1963	4	13	0	2	0	0	0	0	.154
1964	7	26	1	4	1	0	1	5	.154
2 Yrs.	11	39	1	6	1	0	1	5	.154

PEREZ, MELIDO

Yankee: 1992-95
Pitcher
Born: February 15, 1966
Birthplace: Costa Verde, Dominican Republic
Bat: R; Throw: R
Ht: 6'4"; Wt: 210

BECOMES A YANKEE: The Yankees obtained Melido in a blockbuster trade with the White Sox in January, 1992, the Yanks giving up a faded Steve Sax and cash for Perez, Bob Wickman and Domingo Jean. Perez became the Yankee ace in 1992, leading the club in most pitching categories. He owned an impressive 2.87 ERA, a 13-16 record notwithstanding, and his 218 strikeouts were the third most in Yankee history.

SUFFERS A DIFFICULT SEASON: After straining his left hip flexor in Spring training, Perez endured an injury-plagued 1993 season. His record slipped to 6-14, his ERA shot up to 5.19 and he had zero complete games—after pitching 10 in 1992. He missed the final month and had surgery on his pitching shoulder.

REBOUNDS: In 1994, Perez rebounded with a 9-4 record. He seemed to be maturing and becoming a more complete pitcher, throwing strikes and getting more groundouts and fewer strikeouts. He didn't throw as hard and this put less pressure on his right shoulder.

FINAL SEASON WITH THE YANKS: In 1995, Perez' shoulder didn't hold up. When he was able to pitch, he wasn't fluid and seemed tentative. He made only 12 starts and finished 5-5 with a 5.58 ERA. Melido was on the disabled list for two full months beginning in July, being sent to the minors for rehab. After nine years in the Majors, Perez would never pitch again.

PEREZ, MELIDO												
Yr.	W-L	Pct.	SA	G	CS	CG	IP	H	BB	SO	SH	ERA
1992	13-16	.448	0	33	33	10	247.2	212	93	218	1	2.87
1993	6-14	.300	0	25	25	0	163	173	64	148	0	5.19
1994	9-4	.692	0	22	22	1	151.1	134	58	109	0	4.10
1995	5-5	.500	0	13	12	1	69.1	70	31	44	0	5.58
4 Yrs.	33-39	.458	0	93	92	12	631.1	589	246	519	1	4.06
Life.	78-85	.479	1	243	201	20	1354.2	1268	551	1092	5	4.17

PETERSON, FRITZ
(BORN FRED INGELS PETERSON)

Yankee: 1966-74
Pitcher
Born: February 8, 1942
Birthplace: Chicago, IL
Bat: Both; Throw: L
Ht: 6'; Wt: 190

HONORS: The Baseball Writers gave Fritz the Ben Epstein "Good Guy" Award in 1970. Fritz was selected to the AL team for the 1970 All-Star Game.

YOUNG PROSPECT: Yankee scout Lou Maguolo signed Fritz to a Yankee contract in 1963. (A graduate of Northern Illinois University, Fritz gave up a promising hockey career to sign with

Yankee starter Melido Perez, won 33 games in pinstripes in his four seasons.

Yanks.) After pitching at Harlan in 1963 and Shelby in 1964, Fritz had a sensational 1965 season at Greensboro (11-1, 1.50 ERA) and Columbus, Ga. (5-5, 2.18 ERA). Minor league pitching coach Cloyd Boyer helped Fritz become a skilled pitcher. He made the Yanks in spring training, 1966.

STAR YANKEE PITCHER: Fritz was one of the strongest and most durable lefthanded pitchers in Yankee history. As a 24-year-old rookie, Fritz in 1966 was the Yanks' No. 2 starter. He was one of the top three Yankee starters for eight consecutive seasons (1966-73). From 1969-72 Fritz was one of the premier pitchers in the AL. Mike Cuellar, Mickey Lolich and Dave McNally were the only lefthanders to win more games in the AL over those four seasons than did Fritz. He had the misfortune of pitching for the Yanks during the club's bleakest years. He was a popular Yankee, his elaborate practical jokes furnishing his teammates with welcome entertainment.

CLUB LEADERSHIP: Fritz led Yankee pitchers in strikeouts in three consecutive seasons (1969-71). Three times he led the Yanks in wins, including his rookie year when he tied for the club lead with 12. He twice led the club in games started, shutouts and complete games. In 1969 Fritz led the team in ERA (2.55) and in 1970 he led Yankee pitchers in winning percentage (.645, 20-11). In 1971 he led the Yanks in innings pitched (274).

HOME OPENERS: In the 1969 Yankee Stadium opener, Fritz defeated the Washington Senators, 8-2. Fritz was beaten by the Indians, 3-1, in the 1973 home opener (the last opener of the "old" Stadium).

ALL-TIME YANKEE LEADER: Fritz is ninth on the all-time Yankee games started list (265). He is tenth on the all-time Yankee innings pitched list (1857). Peterson ranks 11th in ERA (3.10); 13th in strikeouts (893); 14th in wins (109) and shutouts (18); and 18th in games pitched (288).

TRADED: In April, 1974, Fritz and three other Yankee pitchers were traded from the Yanks to the Indians for Chris Chambliss, Dick Tidrow and Cecil Upshaw.

LEGACY: Fritz ended his ML career in 1976. Although he was an excellent pitcher, he is perhaps best remembered for revealing publicly before the 1973 season that he and teammate Mike Kekich had exchanged wives; in fact, they announced, they had exchanged families. Later, Fritz became a devoutly religious man and became very active in the Baseball Chapel, an organization of Christian ballplayers.

PETERSON, FRITZ											
Yr.	W-L	Pct.	SA	G	GS	CG	IP	H	BB	SO	SH	ERA
1966	12-11	.522	0	34	32	11	215	196	40	96	2	3.31
1967	8-14	.364	0	36	30	6	181	179	43	102	1	3.47
1968	12-11	.522	0	36	27	6	212	187	29	115	2	2.63
1969	17-16	.515	0	37	37	16	272	228	43	150	4	2.55
1970	20-11	.645	0	39	37	8	260	247	40	127	2	2.90
1971	15-13	.536	1	37	35	16	274	269	42	139	4	3.05
1972	17-15	.531	0	35	35	12	250	270	44	100	3	3.24
1973	8-15	.348	0	31	31	6	184	207	49	59	0	3.95
1974	0-0	.000	0	3	1	0	8	13	2	5	0	4.70
9 Yrs.	109-106	.507	1	288	265	81	1857	1796	332	893	18	3.10
Life.	133-131	.504	1	355	330	90	2218	2217	426	1015	20	3.30

ANDY PETTITTE

Yankee: 1995-2002
Pitcher
Born: June 15, 1972
Birthplace: Baton Rouge, LA
Bat: L; Throw: L
Ht: 6'5"; Wt: 235

COMES UP THROUGH THE MINORS: In May, 1991, Andy was signed by the Yankees as a free agent. He progressed well, and after a 1994 season in which he was a combined 14-4 at Albany and Columbus, his four-year minor league record stood at 42-20 with a 2.56 ERA. In 1994, Andy was named the organization's Minor-League Pitcher of the Year after that 14-4 split season between Albany (AA) and Columbus (AAA). He is a deceptive pitcher; although large (6'5", 235 pounds), he isn't particularly overpowering. He mixes pitches well and has excellent control. In 1995, he made his Major League debut on April 29 at Kansas City, pitching $2/3$ of an inning and allowing two earned runs. Pettitte did not waste his opportunity, improving in his starts. For the season, Andy pitched in 31 games, starting 26, finishing 12-9 with a 4.17 ERA. For his efforts, Andy placed third in AL Rookie of the Year voting. He did start Game 2 of the Division Series versus Seattle, having a no-decision, pitching seven innings and allowing four earned runs.

WINS 55 GAMES OVER NEXT THREE SEASONS: In 1996, Andy had a record of 21-8 (.724), leading the American League in wins in 34 starts and was eighth in ERA with 3.87. On April 9, Pettitte became the youngest pitcher since "Hippo" Vaughn to start a Yankee home opening-day game. Vaughn took the mound at New York on April 14, 1910. Having an excellent move to first with a runner on, Andy led the Majors with 11 pickoffs. He did finish second to Toronto's Pat Hentgen in the American League Cy Young Award voting and was named to The Sporting News All-Star Team. In the postseason, Pettitte started five total games, having a record of 2-1 and 4.78 ERA. In Game 5 of the World Series versus Atlanta, lefty Andy outdueled ace John Smoltz, tossing $8^{1/3}$ innings of a 1-0 Yankee win. In 1997, Andy probably had his best season to date, going 18-7 with a 2.88 ERA in 35 starts, the latter stat leading the league. He set career-highs for: ERA, starts, shutouts (one), innings pitched (240.1) and strikeouts (166). He again led AL pitchers with 14 pickoffs and started the season with a 5-0 mark in April. Andy struggled in the Division Series versus Cleveland, losing two games and having an inflated ERA of 8.49 (11 earned runs in $11^{2/3}$ innings pitched). In the Yankees' record-breaking 1998 season, Pettitte continued to establish himself as one of the premier lefties in the Majors. He went 16-11 in 32 starts with an 4.24 ERA. In three seasons from 1996 through 1998, Andy has posted 55 victories, which ranks first in the American League over that period and second in the Majors to John Smoltz (56 wins) of Atlanta. His career winning percentage (.657) ranks second highest of all active Major League pitchers with at least 100 starts, only Mike Mussina of Baltimore having a better mark with .667 (118-59). In the playoffs, Pettitte started three games, having a decision in each, going 2-1. His crowning achievement was winning Game 4 of the World Series versus San Diego, pitching $7^{1/3}$ innings of shutout ball and getting the well-deserved victory. Relievers Jeff Nelson and Mariano Rivera came in to preserve the 3-0 New York victory and more importantly helped to clinch the 24th World Series crown for the Yankees in 35 visits.

CONTINUES TO WIN: Andy has had eight straight winning seasons for the Yankees. Strangely, though, Andy was almost traded in 1999 just before the August 1st deadline. Joe Torre and GM Brian Cashman met with principal owner George Steinbrenner to convince him of Andy's continued benefit to the team. Andy had been struggling before then, but when he saw he was still a Yankee, he posted a personal-high five victories in that month. He has followed that up with 19-9, 15-10, and 13-5 seasons in 2000-2002. His 3.27 ERA in 2002 was his best since 1997, but his mound innings were limited to 134.2 pitched.

POSTSEASON: Andy has a 10-7 record in 25 postseason starting assignments. He was 2-0 in the 2001 ALCS and selected as the series MVP when the Yankees eliminated the heavy-hitting Seattle Mariners club. He has struggled in his last three postseason games against Arizona in the 2001 World Series (0-2, 10.00 ERA in 9 IP) and in the 2002 Division Series versus Anaheim (12.00 ERA in 3 IP).

ALL-STAR: Andy represented the Yankees on the AL All-Star squad in 1996 and 2001. He pitched the fourth inning in the 2001 All-Star game at Seattle's Safeco Field allowing one hit and striking out one.

ALL-TIME YANKEE LEADER: Andy ranks on the Top 20 All-Time Yankee pitching list as follows: tenth in winning percentage (.646); seventh in strikeouts (1095); and tied for tenth in wins (128).

Yankee lefty Andy Pettitte.

PETTITTE, ANDY

Yr.	W-L	Pct.	SA	G	GS	CG	IP	H	BB	SO	SH	ERA
1995	12-9	.571	0	31	26	3	175	183	63	114	0	4.17
1996	21-8	.724	0	35	34	2	221	229	72	162	0	3.87
1997	18-7	.720	0	35	35	4	240	233	65	166	1	2.88
1998	16-11	.593	0	33	32	5	216	226	87	146	0	4.24
1999	14-11	.560	0	31	31	0	191	216	89	121	0	4.70
2000	19-9	.679	0	32	32	3	2-4.2	219	80	125	1	4.35
2001	15-10	.600	0	31	31	2	200.2	224	41	164	0	3.99
2002	13-5	.722	0	22	22	3	134.2	144	32	97	1	3.27
8 Yrs.	128-70	.646	0	250	243	22	1584.1	1674	529	1095	3	3.93

Life. Same.

Division Series

Yr.	G	IP	BB	SO	H	W-L	SA
1995	1	7	3	0	9	0-0	0
1996	1	6.1	6	3	4	0-0	0
1997	2	11.2	1	5	15	0-2	0
1998	1	7	0	8	3	1-0	0
1999	1	7.1	0	5	7	1-0	0
2000	2	11.1	3	7	9	1-0	0
2001	1	6.2	2	4	7	0-1	0
2002	1	3	0	1	8	0-0	0
8 Yrs.	10	60.1	15	33	62	3-3	0

Life. Same.

Championship Series

Yr.	G	IP	BB	SO	H	W-L	SA
1996	2	15	5	7	10	1-0	0
1998	1	4.2	3	1	8	0-1	0
1999	1	7.1	1	5	8	1-0	0
2000	1	6.2	1	2	9	1-0	0
2001	2	9	2	8	11	2-0	0
5 Yrs.	9	48	12	23	46	5-1	0

Life. Same.

Worlds Series

Yr.	G	IP	BB	SO	H	W-L	SA
1996	2	10.2	4	5	11	1-1	0
1998	1	7.1	3	4	5	1-0	0
1999	1	3.2	1	1	10	0-0	0
2000	2	13.2	4	9	16	0-0	0
2001	2	9	2	9	12	0-2	0
5 Yrs.	8	44.1	14	28	54	2-3	0

Life. Same.

PINIELLA, LOU

Nickname: "Sweet Lou"
Yankee: 1974-84
Outfielder, DH
Born: August 28, 1943
Birthplace: Tampa, FL
Bat: R; Throw: R
Ht: 6'; Wt: 185

TRADED TO YANKEES: In December of 1973, the Yankees obtained Lou and pitcher Ken Wright from the Royals for pitcher Lindy McDaniel. Lou had been signed in 1962 by Cleveland Scout Spud Chandler, the former Yankee star, and had bounced around with several organizations before winning Rookie of the Year in 1969 with the Royals.

EMOTIONAL PLAYER: In 1974, Lou played left field, hit .305 and began a love affair with Yankee fans. He was consistent, hit in the clutch, and wasn't afraid to show emotion on the field. He was a throwback to an old rough-and-tumble player in the mold of Hank Bauer or Enos Slaughter—a combination of baseball smarts and old-fashioned desire. Yankee fans ate it up and expressed their affection with chants of "Looou, Looou." Lou kept a running feud going with Baltimore Manager Earl Weaver, who had managed him at Elmira in 1965 and whom Lou felt had been responsible for his leaving the Orioles' organization. On May 20, 1976, on a play in which Lou was thrown out, Lou and Boston's Carlton Fisk came up fighting, and a brawl ensued; it was a signal to take Lou and the Yankees seriously. Lou gave a heartfelt eulogy at Thurman Munson's funeral on August 6, 1979.

INNER EAR PROBLEM: In April 1975, Lou developed an inner ear infection that made him dizzy. After several failed treatments, he had surgery, missed several weeks and returned to the roster July 6. He was still disoriented, dizzy and couldn't hear in his right ear, and he didn't travel with the team because he couldn't fly. He played occasionally and finished with a BA of .196. He was still bothered with the problem the following spring; his career was in jeopardy. All of a sudden the problem went away, and Lou in 1976 hit .281 platooning in right with Oscar Gamble; he was runner-up to teammate Dock Ellis for Comeback Player of the Year.

SWEET STROKE: A reliable outfielder and a smart baserunner, Lou first and foremost was a great pure hitter. He was a student of hitting fundamentals. He hit a career high .330 in 1977 and led the Yankees in batting (for those players having at least 350 ABs) in 1974 (.305) and 1978 (.314) and tied in 1979 (.297). In 1982, he led all DHs with a .344 BA; as a DH he hit .361 with men in scoring position; and he hit .360 as a pinchhitter. On September 4, 1982, he concluded a streak of seven consecutive hits over two games. In the 1981 postseason, Lou hit a combined .387 (12 for 31). For all players with at least 500 games as a Yankee, Lou's .295 Yankee career BA ranks 15th.

BAD RAP AS FIELDER: Early in his career, Lou had a reputation as a poor outfielder. While he wasn't graceful, he was usually dependable as a Yankee outfielder. He tied a ML record with two assists in the third inning on May 27, 1974. One misplay kept the "poor fielder" tag alive: On October 1, 1974, the Yankees led in Milwaukee, 2-0, with one out in the eighth, when Bob Hansen lofted a fly ball to right field. Lou called off the centerfielder, but at the last instant pulled away, and the ball fell for a triple, igniting a game-tying rally; the Brewers won in extra innings, and the Yankees were eliminated from the division race.

QUICK THINKING: Lou more than made up for the Milwaukee play with a play he made in the division playoff in Boston on October 2, 1978. It was the bottom of the ninth, one out, and the Yankees leading, 5-4, and in right field Lou was looking into a mean sun. With Rick Burleson on first base, Jerry Remy hit a line drive that Lou lost in the sun. But Lou didn't panic and didn't display his problem to Burleson, who watched to see whether Lou would make the catch. At the last instant Lou saw the ball and made a saving one-hop stab, and Burleson stopped at second. Burleson never scored, but he would have had he gone to third on Remy's hit, because the next batter hit a long fly ball.

POSTSEASON: Lou batted .333 and hit safely in all five games of the 1977 ALCS. Lou homered in defeat in Game 1 of the 1980 ALCS. In the 1981 Division Series, Lou homered in the Yanks'

3-0 win in Game 2. He hit a three-run homer in the Yanks' 13-3 win in Game 2 of the 1981 ALCS.

WORLD SERIES: Lou hit safely in all six games of the 1978 World Series, and his two-out tenth-inning single knocked in the winning run in Game 4, evening the Series with the Dodgers at two games apiece. Lou's World Series hitting streak reached nine games in 1981. In the 1981 World Series, Lou led the Yanks in batting (.438), tied for most hits on the club (seven) and was in the middle of most rallies.

LATE CAREER: Lou started playing less left field in 1980. In 1981, he became a part-time rightfielder and saw more action as a DH and pinch hitter. He seemed to be fading in 1981 but rebounded with a .307 average in 1982. He was disabled in April 1983 with a sore left shoulder, and he was bothered by it much of the year.

RETIRING AS A PLAYER: While he was still a player, on August 24, 1982, Lou added the duties of batting instructor. On June 17, 1984, he retired as a player and became a coach. Lou Piniella Day was celebrated at Yankee Stadium on August 5, 1984. Lou was a Yankee coach again in 1985 and when Billy Martin took over as manager in 1985, he said he was under a management requirement to groom Lou as his replacement.

MANAGER: Lou replaced Martin and managed the Yankees in 1986 and 1987. He started 1988 as general manager, with Billy managing again, but when Martin was fired Lou finished up the year as manager. Lou moved on to Cincinnati as manager, 1990-92, and led the Reds to a World Championship in 1990. He became manager of the Mariners in 1993. He successfully managed Seattle to their first-ever ML playoff appearance in 1995. Included was the one-game playoff victory against the Angels, and a thrilling triumph in the best-of-five division series with the Yankees, before Seattle was eliminated by the Indians. Lou was named as the 1995 AL Manager of the Year. Lou remained manager of the Mariners through the 2002 season. He signed on as the skipper of the Tampa Bay Devil Rays for 2003. Since 1993, he has brought his club to the playoffs six times with no World Series appearances.

PINIELLA, LOU

Yr.	G	AB	R	H	2B	3B	HR	RBI	BB	SB	BA	SA
1974	140	518	71	158	26	0	9	70	32	1	.305	.407
1975	74	199	7	39	4	1	0	22	16	0	.196	.226
1976	100	327	36	92	16	6	3	38	18	0	.281	.394
1977	103	339	47	112	19	3	12	45	20	2	.330	.510
1978	130	472	67	148	34	5	6	69	34	3	.314	.445
1979	130	461	49	137	22	2	11	69	17	3	.297	.425
1980	116	321	39	92	18	0	2	27	29	0	.297	.361
1981	60	159	16	44	9	0	5	18	13	0	.277	.428
1982	102	261	33	80	17	1	6	37	18	0	.307	.448
1983	53	148	19	43	9	1	2	16	11	1	.291	.405
1984	29	86	8	26	4	1	1	6	7	0	.302	.407
11 Yrs.	1037	3291	392	971	178	20	57	417	215	10	.295	.413
Life.	1747	5867	651	1705	305	41	102	766	368	32	.291	.409

Divisional Playoff

Yr.	G	AB	R	H	2B	3B	HR	RBI	BB	SB	BA	SA
1981	4	10	1	2	1	0	1	3	0	0	.200	.600
1 Yr.	4	10	1	2	1	0	1	3	0	0	.200	.600
Life. Same.												

Championship Series												
Yr.	G	AB	R	H	2B	3B	HR	RBI	BB	SB	BA	SA
1976	4	11	1	3	1	0	0	0	0	0	.273	.364
1977	5	21	1	7	3	0	0	2	0	0	.333	.476
1978	4	17	2	4	0	0	0	0	0	0	.235	.235
1980	2	5	1	1	0	0	1	1	2	0	.200	.800
1981	3	5	2	3	0	0	1	3	0	0	.600	1.200
5 Yrs.	18	59	7	18	4	0	2	6	2	0	.305	.475
Life. Same.												

World Series												
Yr.	G	AB	R	H	2B	3B	HR	RBI	BB	SB	BA	SA
1976	4	9	1	3	1	0	0	0	0	0	.333	.444
1977	6	22	1	6	0	0	0	3	0	0	.273	.273
1978	6	25	3	7	0	0	0	4	0	1	.280	.280
1981	6	16	2	7	1	0	0	3	0	1	.438	.500
4 Yrs.	22	72	7	23	2	0	0	10	0	2	.319	.347
Life. Same.												

PIPGRAS, GEORGE

Nickname: "The Danish Viking"
Yankee: 1923-24,'27-33
Pitcher
Born: December 20, 1899
Birthplace: Ida Grove, IA
Died: October 19, 1986
Bat: R; Throw: R
Ht: 6'1"; Wt: 185

YOUNG PROSPECT: When George got out of the army in 1918, he pitched semipro ball in Minnesota. The White Sox signed him but because he couldn't get his pitches under control in the minors they released him. In 1922 George enjoyed a fine year at Charleston, SC, his contract then under the control of the Red Sox who in January of 1923 traded George and outfielder Harvey Hendrick to the Yanks for catcher Al DeVormer.

EARLY ML CAREER: George reported to the Yanks' 1923 spring training camp, but the Yanks had great starters in Waite Hoyt, Herb Pennock, Bob Shawkey, Sam Jones and Joe Bush, and there was little room for a 23-year-old flamethrower who had trouble throwing strikes. "Up for a cup of coffee" with the Yanks in 1923-24, George was used sparingly in both seasons. In 1925 he was farmed out to Nashville of the Southern League, and in 1926 he pitched for St. Paul of the American Association.

1927 SEASON: George was practically a rookie on the 1927 Yankees, perhaps the greatest team of all time. He got his big break one day when Dutch Ruether was ill and unable to pitch. Miller Huggins handed the ball to George, who won the game and replaced Ruether in the starting rotation. George was the fifth starter on the 1927 club.

YANKEE STAR: From 1928-30 George was the Yanks' ace pitcher. He had a great fastball. No right-handed pitcher on the Yanks has since won more games than George's 24 wins of 1928. After a poor 1931 season, George's 1932 comeback was very much responsible for the Yanks winning the World Championship. He was the Yanks' third starter in 1932. An elbow injury hampered his efforts in the 1933 campaign.

IMPORTANT VICTORY: On September 28,1928, George defeated the Tigers, 11-6, clinching the Yanks' third consecutive AL pennant.

LEAGUE LEADER: In 1928 George led the AL in wins (24), games started (38) and innings pitched (301). In 1930 he led AL hurlers in shutouts (3).

ALL-TIME YANKEE LEADER: On the Top 20 Yankee lists, George ranks 18th in wins (93); 18th in shutouts (14); strikeouts (656), 20th in complete games (84) and innings pitched (1352).

CLUB LEADERSHIP: George led the Yanks in innings pitched, complete games, games started and wins in three consecutive seasons (1928-30). Twice he led the Yanks in games pitched, strikeouts and shutouts. In 1930 he led the club in ERA (4.11) in a season when the baseball was extremely juiced up.

WORLD SERIES: George started three World Series games in his career and won them all. Urban Shocker was scheduled to pitch Game 2 of the 1927 Series, but late in Game 1 Huggins gave the assignment to George. He beat the Pirates, 6-2, pitched a complete-game seven-hitter and served only three curveballs to a Pirate team anticipating breaking balls. In Game 2 of the 1928 Series, George dazzled the Cardinals with curveballs and beat them and Grover Cleveland Alexander, 9-3, on a neat four-hitter. (In 1928 the Yanks used only three pitchers to sweep the Cards—Pipgras, Hoyt and Tom Zachary.) George went eight innings to beat the Cubs, 7-5, in Game 3 of the 1932 Series.

LEFT YANKS: In May of 1933, the Yanks sold the contracts of George and infielder Billy Werber to the Red Sox for $100,000. He had a combined 11-10 record in 1933, but broke his arm in a freak accident while pitching against Detroit. It was an injury (suffered while he was actually throwing the ball) that brought a premature end to his pitching career. George was 0-0 (two games) in 1934 and 0-1 (five games) in 1935 for Boston.

BASEBALL UMPIRE: George loved baseball and wanted to stay in the game after he was forced to retire as a player. Red Sox owner Tom Yawkey suggested umpiring and arranged for George to umpire in the old NY-PA League (now known as the Eastern League), a job he held from 1936-38. From 1939-45 George was an AL umpire, officiating at All-Star and World Series games as one of the game's best umpires. He was tough, too. During a White Sox-Browns game he once kicked out 17 players! George was a minor league supervisor of umpires from 1946-49. In later years, he worked as a Red Sox scout.

PIPGRAS, GEORGE												
Yr.	W-L	Pct.	SA	G	GS	CG	IP	H	BB	SO	SH	ERA
1923	1-3	.250	0	8	2	2	33	34	25	12	0	5.94
1924	0-1	.000	1	9	1	0	15	20	18	4	0	9.98
1927	10-3	.769	0	29	21	9	166	148	77	81	1	4.11
1928	24-13	.649	3	46	38	22	301	314	103	139	4	3.38
1929	18-12	.600	0	39	33	13	225	229	95	125	3	4.23
1930	15-15	.500	4	44	30	15	221	230	70	111	3	4.11
1931	7-6	.538	3	36	14	6	138	134	58	59	1	3.79
1932	16-9	.640	0	32	27	14	219	235	87	111	2	4.19
1933	2-2	.500	0	4	4	3	33	32	12	14	0	3.27
9 Yrs.	93-64	.592	11	247	170	84	1352	1376	545	656	14	4.04
Life.	102-73	.583	12	276	189	93	1488	1529	598	714	16	4.09

World Series

Yr.	G	IP	BB	SO	H	W-L	SA
1927	1	9	1	2	7	1-0	0
1928	1	9	4	8	4	1-0	0
1932	1	8	3	1	9	1-0	0
3 Yrs	3	26	8	11	20	3-0	0
Life. Same.							

PIPP, WALLY
(BORN WALTER CLEMENT PIPP)

Nickname: "Pipp the Pickler"
Yankee: 1915-25
First Baseman
Born: February 17, 1893
Birthplace: Chicago, IL
Died: January 11, 1965
Bat: L; Throw: L
Ht: 6'1"; Wt: 180

CAME TO YANKS: Wally, who joined the Yankees in 1915, had played 12 games for the Detroit Tigers in 1913, hitting .161 (5-for-31), so the Yanks in acquiring Wally were picking up a player with little ML experience. Reportedly, AL President Ban Johnson had something to do with arranging Wally's becoming a Yankee. (Johnson had promised the new Yankee owners good players, although Jake Ruppert and Til Huston could not have been too impressed with Wally's ML record.)

YANKEE FIRST SACKER: For 10 seasons (1915-24), Wally was the Yanks' regular first baseman although he missed the second half of the 1918 season, while serving in the military. He was a durable player and in 1917, 1921 and 1924 he played in every Yankee game. Besides being durable and consistent, he was a feisty player as well. Late in the 1922 season, he decked Babe Ruth right on the dugout bench after Ruth criticized his defensive play.

FINE HITTER: Wally was a good clutch hitter. He teamed with Babe Ruth and Bob Meusel to form the heart of the first powerful Yankee clubs that won three straight AL pennants (1921-23). In 1921 and 1923, the Yankee batting order usually had Ruth hitting third, Meusel fourth and Wally fifth. In 1922 the order usually was Ruth, Pipp (fourth) and Meusel. Wally knocked in 90 or more runs in a season five times for the Yanks.

LEAGUE LEADER: In consecutive seasons (1916-17), Wally was the HR king of the AL. In 1924 he led the AL in triples (19).

CLUB LEADERSHIP: Wally led the Yanks in triples seven times, more often than anyone else in Yankee history. In his first three Yankee seasons (1915-17), Wally led the club in RBIs each season. He led the Yanks in doubles three times. Twice he led the club in HRs, runs, hits and slugging average. In 1916 and 1922 Wally led the Yanks in batting (.262 and .329).

DEFENSIVE ABILITIES: Wally was a fine defensive first baseman. Twice he led AL first basemen in fielding (1915, 1924). Four times he led AL first basemen in chances accepted, putouts and double plays, all AL records. The 1667 putouts Wally made in 1922 is the Yankee club record for first basemen. Wally is 14th

on the all-time first basemen's putout (18,779) and total chances (20,099) lists. He is 20th on the all time first basemen's assist list (1152).

ALL-TIME YANKEE LEADER: Wally is fourth on the All-Time triples list (121). He also ranks 13th in RBI (825); 14th in hits (1577); 15th in at-bats (5594); 16th in games played (1488); and 17th in runs (820).

WORLD SERIES: Wally led the Yanks in at-bats (21), hits (six) and RBIs (three) in the 1922 Series when the Yanks failed to win a single game against the New York Giants. Two weeks prior to the 1923 Series, Wally cracked a rib and the Yanks asked Commissioner Landis if Lou Gehrig could replace him on the roster for the Series. Landis agreed, but Giant Manager John McGraw refused to let Gehrig play because Lou had not been on the team long enough to qualify for Series competition. (Only players on the ML roster before September 1 are eligible.) Wally was forced to play; wrapped in tape, he played with pain, displayed courage, and performed well.

HISTORIC MOMENT: Early in the 1925 season, Wally was struck in the head by a pitched ball. Not long after that, on June 2, he complained of a headache and was rested. Miller Huggins played Gehrig (who had pinch-hit the day before) at first base. The red-hot-hitting Gehrig did not come out of the lineup until 1939. Most baseball fans know how Wally Pipp lost his job, but not everyone remembers that Wally was a great ballplayer in his own right. He is far more than a trivia note.

TRADED: The Yanks dealt Wally to Cincinnati following the 1925 season. Wally had three fine seasons with the Reds (1926-28) and retired from ML baseball with a fine .281 lifetime batting mark and an RBI total just shy of 1000.

PIPP, WALLY

Yr.	G	AB	R	H	2B	3B	HR	RBI	BB	SB	BA	SA
1915	136	479	59	118	20	13	4	60	66	18	.246	.367
1916	151	545	70	143	20	14	12	93	54	16	.262	.417
1917	155	587	82	143	29	12	9	70	60	11	.244	.380
1918	91	349	48	106	15	9	2	44	22	11	.304	.415
1919	138	523	74	144	23	10	7	50	39	9	.275	.398
1920	153	610	109	171	30	14	11	76	48	4	.280	.430
1921	153	588	96	171	35	9	8	97	45	17	.296	.427
1922	152	577	96	190	32	10	9	90	56	7	.329	.466
1923	144	569	79	173	19	8	6	108	36	6	.304	.397
1924	153	589	88	174	30	19	9	113	51	12	.295	.457
1925	62	178	19	41	6	3	3	24	13	3	.230	.348
11 Yrs.	1488	5594	820	1577	259	121	80	825	490	114	.282	.414
Life.	1872	6914	974	1941	311	148	90	996	596	125	.281	.408

World Series

Yr.	G	AB	R	H	2B	3B	HR	RBI	BA
1921	8	26	1	4	1	0	0	2	.154
1922	5	21	0	6	1	0	0	3	.286
1923	6	20	2	5	0	0	0	2	.250
3 Yrs.	19	67	3	15	2	0	0	7	.224
Life. Same.									

POWELL, JACK

Nickname: "Red"
Yankee: 1904-05
Pitcher
Born: July 9, 1874
Birthplace: Bloomington, IL
Died: October 17, 1944
Bat: R; Throw: R
Ht: 5'11"; Wt: 195

CAME TO YANKS: Jack came to the Yanks (Highlanders) before the 1904 season from the St. Louis Browns. The Browns received pitcher Harry Howell, catcher Jack O'Connor, and cash.

1904 SEASON: In 1904 Powell and Jack Chesbro nearly carried the Yanks to an AL pennant as they combined for 64 victories! Jack and Chesbro started 96 of the Yanks' 151 games! Jack's 45 starts, 38 complete games and 390 innings pitched are the second highest total for each category in Yankee history. Only Jack Chesbro's 1904 statistics in those three categories are higher. Throughout his ML career, Jack was a genuine workhorse, but he never worked as hard in any season as he did in 1904.

BASEBALL'S ALL-TIME LEADER LIST: Jack is 14th on baseball's all-time complete game list (422). He is 35th on baseball's all-time games started (516) and 26th in innings pitched (4389) lists.

TRADED: Jack was in the midst of a disappointing 1905 season when the Yanks dealt him back to the Browns late in the year. The Browns bought Jack's contract.

```
YANKEE COMPLETE GAME LEADERS
1. J. Chesbro—48 (1904)
2. JACK POWELL—38 (1904)
3. A. Orth—36 (1906)
4. J. Chesbro—33 (1903)
5. R. Ford—32 (1912)
```

POWELL, JACK

Yr.	W-L	Pct.	SA	G	GS	CG	IP	H	BB	SO	SH	ERA
1904	23-19	.548	0	47	45	38	390	340	92	202	3	2.44
1905	8-13	.381	1	36	23	13	203	214	57	84	1	3.50
2 Yrs.	31-32	.492	1	83	68	51	593	554	149	286	4	2.81
Life.	245-256	.489	14	577	516	422	4389	4319	1021	1621	47	2.97

PRATT, DEL

Yankee: 1918-20
Second Baseman
Born: January 10, 1888
Birthplace: Walhalla, SC
Died: September 30, 1977
Bat: R; Throw: R
Ht: 5'11"; Wt: 175

CAME TO YANKS: In January, 1918, the Yanks obtained Del and Eddie Plank (the Hall of Fame pitcher refused to report to the Yanks and retired) from the St. Louis Browns for Urban Shocker, Nick Cullop, Les Nunamaker, Fritz Maisel, and Elmer Gedeon.

YANKEE SECOND BASEMAN: Del was the regular second baseman in all three of his Yankee seasons. He was one of the best second basemen of his era. Del was durable, playing in every Yankee game in 1918 and 1920, and a fine contact hitter. In 1920 he was tremendous. His 97 RBIs that season were second only to Babe Ruth on the Yanks.

DEFENSIVE ABILITIES: As a Yankee player, Del twice led AL second basemen in assists and double plays. In 1918 he led AL second basemen in putouts (340) and double plays (82). Del's 515 assists in 1920 is the Yankee club record for second basemen. He is 13th on baseball's all-time total chances list (9525) for second basemen.

CLUB LEADERSHIP: Twice Del led the Yanks in stolen bases and doubles. In 1918 he tied for the club leadership in runs scored (65). In 1920 he led the team in hits (180), making eight more hits than Ruth.

TRADED: In December, 1920, the Yanks traded Del, Hank Thormahlen, Muddy Ruel and Sammy Vick to the Red Sox for Waite Hoyt, Wally Schang, Harry Harper and Mike McNally. Del accepted the head coaching job at the University of Michigan, but just before the 1921 season he quit Michigan and returned to the Red Sox. He ended his ML career playing for Boston (1921-22) and Detroit (1923-24).

PRATT, DEL

Yr.	G	AB	R	H	2B	3B	HR	RBI	BB	SB	BA	SA
1918	126	477	65	131	19	7	2	55	35	12	.275	.356
1919	140	527	69	154	27	7	4	56	36	22	.292	.393
1920	154	574	84	180	37	8	4	97	50	12	.314	.427
3 Yrs.	420	1578	218	465	83	22	10	208	121	46	.295	.394
Life.	1835	6826	856	1996	392	117	43	966	513	246	.292	.403

QUINN, JACK
(BORN JOHN QUINN PICUS)

Yankee: 1909-12, '19-21
Pitcher
Born: July 5, 1883
Birthplace: Janesville, PA
Died: April 17, 1946
Bat: R; Throw: R
Ht: 6'; Wt: 196

EARLY YANKEE CAREER: Jack was acquired after he went 14-0 for the Virginia League's Richmond club in 1908, his second season in professional baseball. He was a spot starter and reliever with the Yanks in 1909, his rookie season during which Jack was ill much of the time. Jack was the Yanks' No. 2 starter in 1910 and their second biggest winner. The Yanks sold Jack's contract in July of 1912 to Rochester of the International League.

LEAGUE CONTROVERSY: Jack played for Baltimore of the rival Federal League in 1914-15, before pitching for Vernon of the

Pacific Coast League from 1916-18. The 1918 P.C.L. season ended in July because of the war and the White Sox signed Jack. The Yanks in the meantime acquired Jack's contract from Vernon. He finished the 1918 season with the White Sox (5-1) but the Yanks maintained that he belonged to them. Late in 1918 the National Commission ruled in the Yanks' favor. Because AL President Ban Johnson cast the deciding vote in New York's favor, Chicago owner Charles Comiskey never forgave Johnson and a rift in the AL developed.

VALUABLE PITCHER: Jack was the No. 1 starter and workhorse on the 1919 Yankee pitching staff. In 1920 he was the Yanks' third starter. In 1921, the Yanks' first pennant-winning season, Jack was a valuable pitcher in both a starting and relieving role. Late in the 1921 season, the Yankee pitching staff collectively selected Jack to pitch a crucial game.

CLUB LEADERSHIP: Twice Jack led Yankee pitchers in winning percentage. In 1919 he led the Yanks in innings pitched (264), games started (31) and shutouts (four).

SPITBALL PITCHER: Jack was a colorful spitball pitcher, a breed of pitcher the fans enjoyed coming out to see. He threw a legal spitter. In 1920 the spitball was banned, but the 17 ML pitchers who threw it were allowed to continue using the pitch. Jack was a spitballer until he retired in 1933, using the pitch legally longer than just about everyone except Burleigh Grimes.

BASEBALL'S ALL-TIME LEADER LIST: Counting his two years in the short-lived Federal League, Jack ranks 28th on baseball's all-time games pitched list (756). His 1240 assists are the eighth most by a pitcher in baseball history.

1921 WORLD SERIES: In the 1921 Series, Jack became the first pitcher in Yankee history to lose a Series game. The Giants bombed him in Game 3, the key game of the Series, which he entered as a relief pitcher.

TRADED AGAIN: In December, 1921, the Yanks traded Jack, pitchers Rip Collins and Bill Piercy and shortstop Roger Peckinpaugh to the Red Sox for shortstop Everett Scott and pitchers Sad Sam Jones and Bullet Joe Bush. Jack was traded apparently because Miller Huggins and Ed Barrow felt he was too old at age 38. However, old Jack fooled them by continuing to pitch successfully in the ML's until 1933! Jack's record of pitching in 23 ML seasons stood 50-plus years until finally eclipsed by current Yankee broadcaster, Jim Kaat, who pitched his 24th season in 1982.

ALL-TIME YANKEE LEADER: Jack ranks 15th overall in Yankee history in ERA (3.16).

QUINN, JACK												
Yr.	W-L	Pct.	SA	G	GS	CG	IP	H	BB	SO	SH	ERA
1909	9-5	.643	1	23	11	8	119	110	24	36	0	1.97
1910	18-12	.600	0	35	31	20	236	214	58	82	0	2.44
1911	8-10	.444	2	40	16	7	175	203	41	71	0	3.76
1912	5-7	.417	0	18	11	7	103	139	23	47	0	5.79
1919	15-14	.517	0	38	31	18	266	242	65	97	4	2.61
1920	18-10	.643	3	41	31	16	253	271	48	101	2	3.20
1921	8-7	.533	0	33	13	6	119	158	32	44	0	3.73
7 Yrs.	81-65	.555	6	228	144	82	1270	1337	291	478	6	3.16
Life.	247-218	.531	57	755	443	242	3926	4238	860	1329	28	3.28

World Series							
Yr.	G	IP	BB	SO	H	W-L	SA
1921	1	3⅔	2	2	7	0-1	0
1 Yr.	1	3⅔	2	2	7	0-1	0
Life.	3	10⅔	4	5	17	0-1	0

RAMOS, PEDRO
(BORN PEDRO RAMOS Y GUERRA)

Nickname: "Pete"
Yankee: 1964-66
Pitcher
Born: April 28, 1935
Birthplace: Pinar del Rio, Cuba
Bat: B; Throw: R
Ht: 6'; Wt: 175

CAME TO YANKS: In September, 1964, the Yanks acquired Pedro from the Indians for Ralph Terry, who went to the Indians following the 1964 season, and cash.

1964 SEASON: Pedro joined the Yanks late in the 1964 season when the club was in a furious pennant race with the White Sox and Orioles. He was brilliant down the stretch, saving eight games and probably the AL pennant for the Yanks who finished just one game ahead of the White Sox. On the next to last day of the season, he pitched a perfect ninth inning to clinch the AL flag. Because he was obtained after September 1, Pedro was ineligible for the 1964 World Series and his absence badly hurt the Yanks.

RELIEF SPECIALIST: In 1965 and 1966 Pedro led Yankee relief pitchers in saves. The 65 games (1965) in which he appeared established the Yankee games-pitched record for right-handers that stood until 1991 when John Habyan appeared in 66. During his entire Yankee career, Pedro was the club's ace relief pitcher. He threw what he called a "Cuban palm ball" but some swore it was a "wet one." Pedro was not the most stable personality, but he knew how to pitch in a tough situation. Pedro was fast and occasionally he was used as a pinch-runner.

ALL-TIME YANKEE LEADER: Pedro ranks 14th on the all-time Yankee save list (40).

TRADED: In February of 1967, the Yanks dealt Pedro to the Phillies in a trade that brought pitcher Joe Verbanic to New York. He pitched for Philadelphia (1967), Pittsburgh (1969), Cincinnati (1969) and Washington (1970) before leaving ML baseball.

RAMOS, PEDRO											
Yr.	W-L	Pct.	SA	G	GS	CG	IP	H	BB	SO	SH	ERA
1964	1-0	1.000	8	13	0	0	22	13	0	21	0	1.25
1965	5-5	.500	19	65	0	0	92	80	27	68	0	2.92
1966	3-9	.250	13	52	1	0	90	98	18	58	0	3.61
3 Yrs.	9-14	.391	40	130	1	0	204	191	45	147	0	3.04
Life.	117-160	.422	55	582	268	73	2356	2364	724	1305	13	4.08

RANDOLPH, WILLIE

Yankee: 1976-88
Second Baseman
Born: July 6, 1954
Birthplace: Holly Hill, SC
Bat: R; Throw: R
Ht: 5'11"; Wt: 165

HONORS: Willie won the James P. Dawson Award as the best rookie in the Yankees' spring camp in 1976. In 1976, he made ML All-Rookie All-Star teams picked by Topps and *Baseball Digest*. He was selected to the AL team for All-Star Games in 1976, 1977 (setting a record for second baseman with six assists), 1980, 1981 and 1987 (and he made the NL team in 1989). Selected as second baseman on AL All-Star team picked by *The Sporting News* in 1977 and 1978. In 1980, Willie won a Silver Bat Award as the AL's best-hitting second baseman. In 1985, he was given the Good Guy Award by the New York Press Photographers Association. On March 4, 1986, Willie was named co-captain of the Yankees, along with Ron Guidry.

TRADE TO YANKEES: In December of 1975, the Yankees obtained Willie, Dock Ellis (P) and Ken Brett (P) from Pittsburgh for Doc Medich. Willie, who had been born in SC and moved as a baby to the Brownsville section of Brooklyn where he played baseball at Tilden High School, had been drafted by the Pirates in 1972. In spring training of 1975, the Yankees and Pirates played six games, and Willie strongly impressed Yankee scouts, especially with his speed and fielding. In 1975, Willie hit .339 at Charleston and played 30 games for the Pirates. The Pirates were willing to let Willie go because they were happy with their regular second baseman, Rennie Stennett.

ROOKIE SEASON: In the spring camp of 1976, Willie beat out Sandy Alomar for the second-base job. It wasn't given to him; he performed well under pressure and close observation, and he kept the job for 13 seasons. He was the first rookie to have his name placed on the All-Star Game ballot; he made the team but was scratched due to injury. On Opening Day at a renovated Yankee Stadium, Willie had two singles, a stolen base and made a great catch of a foul pop down the right-field line. Willie kept his BA above .300 into June. He kept to himself and was quiet, almost invisible among his high-profile teammates, but he displayed unusual poise for a rookie. He also had these positive characteristics: 1) he had a great-batting eye, especially for a rookie, 2) he made very few mistakes, and 3) he had good work habits. The Yankees won their first pennant in 12 years in 1976.

DEFENSIVE STAR: Willie in his era rivaled Kansas City's Frank White as the AL's best defensive second basemen, and he was the best since Bobby Richardson on the Yankees. In 1979, he led AL second sackers in putouts (355), assists (478), total chances (846) and double plays (128). In 1984, he led AL second basemen in double plays (112). On September 13, 1986, Willie played in his 1447th game at second for the Yanks, passing Tony Lazzeri and becoming the club's all-time leader in games played at second. Willie had great range, quick hands, made smart plays, and hung in there bravely in turning double plays. Even late in his career, after hundreds of runners blasted him at second base, Manager Lou Piniella, commenting on

Willie's 1986 performance, said: "He turned the double play better than anybody in baseball as far as I'm concerned."

GETTING ON BASE: After initially batting near the bottom of the order, Willie became an excellent lead-off man, but when the Yankees had Mickey Rivers or Rickey Henderson, Willie batted second. Because he drew so many walks, Willie's on-base percentages were usually more impressive than his batting averages; his best on-base percentage was .429 in 1980, ranking second in the AL behind George Brett. In 1980, Willie led the AL in walks with 119—he walked in each of his final 15 games—the most ever drawn by a Yankee second baseman and the most by a Yankee since Mickey Mantle had 122 walks in 1962. Willie's walk total of 119 in 1980 is the most ever by a Yankee right-handed batter through the 1999 season. Willie led the Yanks in walks in seven seasons. Since Willie wasn't much of a long-ball threat, he achieved his high total of walks strictly because he had perhaps the best batting eye in baseball. Willie ranks fourth on the Yanks' all-time list for walks (1005).

SOLID HITTER: Willie was a consistent hitter, normally hitting between .270 and .300. He never had a bad year until 1981 (.232), and he hit a Yankee career high of .305 in 1987. In the pressure-packed 1978 season, he hit .320 with runners on base. He developed good extra-base power to right-center field. His 13 triples in 1979 were the most by a Yankee since 1948. On the Yankees' all-time leader lists, Willie ranks eighth in at-bats (6303), ninth in games (1694) and 11th in hits (1731).

ALL-TIME YANKEE LEADER: Willie ranks 16th in doubles (259), and 19th in triples (58) on the all-time Yankee batting list.

BOSTON MASSACRE: The biggest series of the year in 1978 was the Yankees sweeping four games in Boston in early September, and in the opener on September 7, Willie drove in five runs in the 15-3 rout. Willie finished the series going 8-for-16 (.500) and scoring six runs.

STOLEN BASES AND RUNS: In five seasons, between 1978 and 1982, Willie led the Yankees each year in stolen bases and runs scored. He also led the club in runs in 1987. On the Yankees' all-time leader lists, Willie ranks second in SBs (251) and seventh in runs scored (1027).

INJURIES: Some of Willie's speed was sapped by knee and leg injuries. In 1978, Willie was disabled three weeks early in the summer with a bruised right knee, and on September 29, he pulled his left hamstring beating out an infield hit, and he was sidelined for the rest of the season and the post season. In 1983, Willie was out from June 27 until August 5 with a pulled hamstring that he reinjured when attempting to come back in July. He was going great in 1987 when on July 15 he tore cartilage in his left knee; he had arthroscopic surgery on July 17 and was out until mid-August, and he was in and out of the lineup the rest of the season. He suffered through an injury-plagued 1988 season.

QUIET LEADER: Willie was quietly confident, thoroughly professional and a good citizen. He steadfastly avoided controversy and kept a detached dignity. As turmoil swirled around the club in 1977, Thurman Munson said Willie was the only happy player on the Yankees. Young players on the club would say it was Willie who made them feel part of the team. "I've become a little more vocal over the years," said Willie in 1986. "But I try to do most of my talking on the field."

CHAMPIONSHIP SERIES: In dramatic Game 5 of the 1977 ALCS, when the Yankees rallied to go ahead of the Royals in the top of the ninth, Willie's sacrifice fly was the game winner. Although he hit .385 in the 1980 ALCS, Willie's role is best remembered for an eighth-inning play in Game 2. With the Yanks losing, 3-2, two outs and Willie on first base, Bob Watson lined a double that bounced to the base of the left-field wall. When the Royals leftfielder (Willie Wilson) overthrew the primary cut-off man, Willie was waved home by third base coach Mike Ferraro. Third baseman George Brett grabbed the errant outfield throw and pegged a strike to catcher Darrell Porter whose tag just beat a diving Randolph at the plate. After the Yanks lost the game 3-2, many of their fans (including Steinbrenner who wanted to immediately fire Ferraro) blamed the coach, but Willie later stated that he would have tried to score even if Ferraro had held him up. In Game 3 of the 1981 ALCS, Willie broke a scoreless tie with a long sixth-inning homer, and he ended the 4-0 win with a leaping catch in shallow center, as the Yanks swept Oakland.

WORLD SERIES: In Game 1 of the 1977 Series, Willie homered, and later in the bottom of the 12th, he led off with a double and scored the winning run on a single by Paul Blair. Willie homered in Games 4 and 6 of the 1981 Series, and he set a six-game World Series record with nine walks.

LEAVING THE YANKEES: In November of 1988, the Yankees signed second baseman Steve Sax as a free agent, and on Dec. 10, 1988, Willie signed with Sax's old club, the Dodgers, as a free agent. In 1989, both Sax and Randolph went to the All-Star Game representing their respective new leagues. Willie went on to play for Oakland in the 1990 World Series, hit a career high .327 in 124 games with Milwaukee in 1991, and finished his ML career with the Mets in 1992.

YANKEE COACH: In 1995, his name was mentioned in connection with the open managerial position, which went to Joe Torre in November 1995. Willie just completed his ninth season as the Yankees third base coach.

RANDOLPH, WILLIE

Yr.	G	AB	R	H	2B	3B	HR	RBI	BB	SB	BA	SA
1976	125	430	59	115	15	4	1	40	58	37	.267	.328
1977	147	551	91	151	28	11	4	40	64	13	.274	.387
1978	134	499	87	139	18	6	3	42	82	36	.279	.357
1979	153	574	98	155	15	13	5	61	95	33	.270	.368
1980	138	513	99	151	23	7	7	46	119	30	.294	.407
1981	93	357	59	83	14	3	2	24	57	14	.232	.305
1982	144	553	85	155	21	4	3	36	75	16	.280	.349
1983	104	420	73	117	21	1	2	38	53	12	.279	.348
1984	142	564	86	162	24	2	2	31	86	10	.287	.348
1985	143	497	75	137	21	2	5	40	85	16	.276	.356
1986	141	492	76	136	15	2	5	50	94	15	.276	.346
1987	120	449	96	137	24	2	7	67	82	11	.305	.414
1988	110	404	43	93	20	1	2	34	55	8	.230	.300
13 Yrs.	1694	6303	1027	1731	259	58	48	549	1005	251	.275	.357
Life.	2202	8018	1239	2210	316	65	54	687	1243	271	.276	.351

Divisional Playoff

Yr.	G	AB	R	H	2B	3B	HR	RBI	BB	SB	BA	SA
1981	5	20	0	4	0	0	0	1	1	0	.200	.200
1 Yr.	5	20	0	4	0	0	0	1	1	0	.200	.200

Life. Same.

Championship Series

Yr.	G	AB	R	H	2B	3B	HR	RBI	BB	SB	BA	SA
1976	5	17	0	2	0	0	0	1	3	1	.118	.118
1977	5	18	4	5	1	0	0	2	1	0	.278	.333
1980	3	13	0	5	2	0	0	1	1	0	.385	.538
1981	3	12	2	4	0	0	1	2	0	0	.333	.583
4 Yrs.	16	60	6	16	3	0	1	6	5	1	.267	.367
Life.	22	70	8	19	3	0	1	9	6	1	.271	.357

World Series

Yr.	G	AB	R	H	2B	3B	HR	RBI	BB	SB	BA	SA
1976	4	14	1	1	0	0	0	0	1	0	.071	.071
1977	6	25	5	4	2	0	1	1	2	0	.160	.360
1981	6	18	5	4	1	1	2	3	9	1	.222	.722
3 Yrs.	16	57	11	9	3	1	3	4	12	1	.158	.404
Life.	20	72	11	13	3	1	3	4	13	2	.181	.375

RASCHI, VIC

Nickname: "The Springfield Rifle"
Yankee: 1946-53
Pitcher
Born: March 28, 1919
Birthplace: West Springfield, MA
Died: October 14, 1988
Bat: R; Throw: R
Ht: 6'1"; Wt: 205

HONORS: *The Sporting News* selected Vic as one of three pitchers on its 1950 ML All-Star team.

TURBULENT YANKEE ARRIVAL: The Yanks called Vic up from the Newark farm club along with Yogi Berra and Bobby Brown in September of 1946. All three were in the starting lineup their first day on the club which was in a turbulent swirl. On that day Bill Dickey, the Yanks' second manager of the year, went to the front office and resigned. Johnny Neun took over so on Neun's first day as manager, Vic started his first ML game. Yet he won the game amid all the confusion, proving immediately his ability to handle pressure.

WINNING PITCHER: After his Yankee pitching of late 1946 (two starts, two wins), Vic was a starter in 1947, and a star by 1948. During the height of the Yanks' success, Vic was the Yanks' No. 1 starter (1948-52). Vic pitched two one-hitters during his Yankee career. On September 28, 1951, he beat the Red Sox, 11-3, to clinch the AL pennant for the Yanks. On August 3, 1953, Vic beat the Tigers, 15-0, and drove in seven runs himself, an AL record for pitchers. On May 3, 1950, he balked four times, an AL record. In the 1951 home opener, he blanked Boston, 5-0.

BIGGEST REGULAR SEASON WIN: On the final day of the 1949 season, the Yanks and Red Sox were tied for first place in the AL. Casey Stengel handed the ball to Vic and Vic pitched a complete game, defeating Boston, 5-3, enabling the Yanks to win the pennant by one game.

GUTTY PERFORMER: Vic was probably the hardest working ballplayer of his era, always pushing himself to higher peaks. He was a fierce competitor, possessing a blazing fastball. His unshaven, bristly beard and mean scowl made him a forbidding figure on the mound. During the last few years of his Yankee career, he pitched in pain with severely damaged knees. Speaking of Vic, Casey Stengel once remarked, touching his head, his arm and his heart, "He wins because he pitched from here, here, and here." He was a tremendous battler who was as responsible as anyone for making the Yanks a winning team. (He was also superstitious and refused to be photographed before a game.)

LEAGUE LEADER: Twice he led the AL in games started. In 1950 he led the AL in winning percentage (.724, 21-8) and in 1951 he led the AL in strikeouts (164).

CLUB LEADERSHIP: In four consecutive seasons (1948-51) Vic led the Yanks in wins. In three straight years he led the club in innings pitched (1949-51) and complete games (1948-50). Twice he led the team in shutouts. Vic led or tied for club leadership in games started in every year from 1948-52.

BASEBALL'S ALL-TIME LEADER LIST: Vic is fifth on baseball's all-time win percentage list (.667, 132-66) for those pitchers with at least 100 ML victories.

ALL-TIME YANKEE LEADER: Vic's Yankee career win percentage (.706, 120-50) is the second highest in Yankee history. He is ninth on the all-time Yankee shutout list (24). His 120 wins ranks 12th in Yankee history. Vic is 14th in both innings pitched (1537) and complete games (99) and 15th in strikeouts (832).

ALL-STAR GAME: Vic was selected to the AL All-Star team for four All-Star Games (1948-50, '52). Vic was the winning pitcher in the 1948 All-Star Game, the last time that a Yankee pitcher won an All-Star Game, and started the 1950 and 1952 All-Star Games.

WORLD SERIES: In Game 5, the final game, of the 1949 Series, Vic was the winning pitcher as the Yankees sewed up a Yankee World Championship. He had lost a 1-0 heartbreaker in Game 2. In Game 1 of the 1950 Series Vic threw a brilliant two-hit shutout at the Phillies to win, 1-0. His Game 6 win against the New York Giants in the 1951 Series brought another World Championship to the Yanks. In Game 2 of the 1952 Series Vic pitched a three-hitter to beat Brooklyn, 7-1, before he returned to defeat the Dodgers again in Game 6. (He shared hero's honors in that Series with Allie Reynolds, Johnny Mize and Billy Martin.)

POOR TRADE: Vic and Yankee GM George Weiss annually battled over Vic's salary, sometimes bitterly. In February of 1954 the Yanks sold Vic's contract to the Cardinals for a reported $85,000. This move was perhaps Weiss' most incompassionate; Vic had ruined his knees helping the Yanks win six AL pennants and World Championships. The deal went over badly with Yankee players, but Weiss won the desired results. All Yankee holdouts were quick to sign.

RASCHI, VIC

Yr.	W-L	Pct.	SA	G	GS	CG	IP	H	BB	SO	SH	ERA
1946	2-0	1.000	0	2	2	2	16	14	5	11	0	3.94
1947	7-2	.778	0	15	14	6	105	89	38	51	1	3.87
1948	19-8	.704	1	36	31	18	223	208	74	124	6	3.84
1949	21-10	.677	0	38	37	21	275	247	138	124	3	3.34
1950	21-8	.724	1	33	32	17	257	232	116	155	2	4.00
1951	21-10	.677	0	35	34	15	258	233	103	164	4	3.27
1952	16-6	.727	0	31	31	13	223	174	91	127	4	2.78
1953	13-6	.684	1	28	26	7	181	150	55	76	4	3.33
8 Yrs.	120-50	.706	3	218	207	99	1537	1347	620	832	24	3.47
Life.	132-66	.667	3	269	255	106	1819	1666	727	944	26	3.72

World Series

Yr.	G	IP	BB	SO	H	W-L	SA
1947	2	1⅓	0	1	2	0-0	0
1949	2	14⅔	5	11	15	1-1	0
1950	1	9	1	5	2	1-0	0
1951	2	10⅓	8	4	12	1-1	0
1952	3	17	8	18	12	2-0	0
1953	1	8	3	4	9	0-1	0
6 Yrs.	11	60⅓	25	43	52	5-3	0
Life.	Same.						

Vic Raschi loosens up.

RASMUSSEN, DENNIS

Yankee: 1984-87
Pitcher
Born: April 18, 1959
Birthplace: Los Angeles, CA
Bat: L; Throw: L
Ht: 6'7"; Wt: 230

EARLY TRADES: In 1982, Dennis had an 11-8 record pitching for Spokane in the Angels' organization. On August 31, 1982, the Yankees traded pitcher Tommy John to the Angels for a player to be named later; in November, California sent Dennis to the Yankees to complete the deal. In 1983, Dennis went 13-10 for the Yanks' Columbus farm club. On August 26, 1983, the Yankees obtained pitcher John Montefusco from San Diego for two players to be named later; on September 12, the Yanks sent Dennis and Edwin Rodriguez to the Padres to complete the deal. Dennis made his ML debut with the Padres in September 1983.

SECOND TRADE TO YANKS: On March 30, 1984, the Yankees traded third baseman Graig Nettles to San Diego for Dennis and pitcher Darin Cloninger (who completed the deal in April). Dennis began the 1984 season at Columbus (4-1, 3.09 ERA).

GETTING ESTABLISHED: He was called up to the Yankees in May 1984 and made his Yankee debut on May 23 against Seattle; he pitched eight shutout innings, struck out 10 batters and earned his first ML win. He tied for the third most starts on the club in 1984. In July 1985, George Steinbrenner joined Howard Cosell in the broadcast booth for an ABC Game of the Week. "If Dennis Rasmussen doesn't pitch well today," said Steinbrenner to Cosell and the TV audience, "I'm going to send him to the minors." He was bombed in the fifth inning, and the next day he was optioned to Columbus. Dennis returned to the Yankees in September and made four relief appearances.

THE 1986 STAFF ACE: Dennis, given a slim shot of making the club in the spring of 1986, barely made the rotation as the fifth starter, and ended up as the staff ace; he led the club in wins, winning percentage (18-6, .750), games started (31) and innings pitched (202). Batters hit only .217 against Dennis. He won six consecutive starts between June 24 and July 22, including his first ML shutout on July 5. He won on July 22, but he was hit by a seventh-inning line drive and left with a severe bruise above his left elbow; he was out almost two weeks, and when he returned he slumped until winning his last three starts.

LEAVING YANKEES: Dennis was not as effective in 1987 and was even banished to Columbus for one game in mid-season. In August of 1987, the Yankees traded him to Cincinnati for pitcher Bill Gullickson. Dennis continued to bounce around with mixed success; he was on the Disabled List much of 1993. In 1994, he pitched in the minors for Phoenix and Omaha. Rasmussen pitched in five games with the Kansas City Royals in 1995.

RASMUSSEN, DENNIS

Yr.	W-L	Pct.	SA	G	GS	CG	IP	H	BB	SO	SH	ERA
1984	9-6	.600	0	24	24	1	147.2	127	60	110	0	4.57
1985	3-5	.375	0	22	16	2	101.2	97	42	63	0	3.98
1986	18-6	.750	0	31	31	3	202	160	74	131	1	3.88
1987	9-7	.563	0	26	25	2	146	145	55	89	0	4.75
4 Yrs.	39-24	.619	0	103	96	8	597.1	529	231	393	1	4.28
Life.	91-77	.542	0	256	235	21	1461	1424	522	835	5	4.15

RAWLEY, SHANE

Yankee: 1982-84
Pitcher
Born: July 27, 1955
Birthplace: Racine, WI
Bat: R; Throw: L
Ht: 6'; Wt: 170

TRADED TO YANKEES: On April 1, 1982, the Yankees obtained Shane from Seattle for Bobby Brown (OF), Gene Nelson (P) and Bill Caudill (P). Since breaking in with Seattle in 1978, Shane had been primarily a reliever. The Rawley acquisition made Ron Davis expendable, and the Yankees traded Davis shortly thereafter, which was unfortunate because Shane was converted to a starter.

CONVERSION: Shane struggled as a reliever early in 1982. Coach Jeff Torborg suggested to Manager Clyde King that Shane try starting, and he made a July 5 start; 12 days later he pitched his first complete-game victory. Starting allowed him to use his complete assortment of pitches. He had a smooth effortless motion that made pitching look easy, and he was more impressive than his 11-10 record of 1982. In 1983, Shane led the Yankees in games started (33). He preferred starting because it gave him more time to warm up. "We clock him, and he throws faster in the late innings than he does in the early innings," said Torborg in 1984. "We never realized it took him so long to get warmed up."

TRADED TO PHILLIES: In June of 1984, the Yankees traded Shane to Philadelphia for Marty Bystrom (P) and Keith Hughes (OF). It was an unfortunate trade for the Yankees, because, starting in 1984, Shane won 10, 13, 11, and 17 games for the Phillies.

RAWLEY, SHANE

Yr.	W-L	Pct.	SA	G	GS	CG	IP	H	BB	SO	SH	ERA
1982	11-10	.524	3	47	17	3	164	165	54	111	0	4.06
1983	14-14	.500	1	34	33	13	238.1	246	79	124	2	3.78
1984	2-3	.400	0	11	10	0	42	46	27	24	0	6.21
3 Yrs.	27-27	.500	4	92	60	16	444.1	457	160	259	2	4.11
Life	111-118	.485	40	469	230	41	1871	1934	734	991	7	4.02

RENIFF, HAL

Nickname: "Porky"
Yankee: 1961-67
Pitcher
Born: July 2, 1938
Birthplace: Warren, OH
Bat: R; Throw: R
Ht: 6'; Wt: 215

YOUNG PROSPECT: Hal began in the Yankee organization in 1956. From 1956-61 he played at Kearney, Modesto, Salem, Amarillo, Binghamton, and Richmond. His best minor league season was 1959 when he was 21-7 at Modesto.

RELIEF SPECIALIST: Hal became a member of the Yankee bullpen as a rookie in 1961. He was strictly a relief specialist and never started a game in his entire ML career. Hal had a good curveball and fine control. A military stint and a sore arm ruined his 1962 baseball season. He had an outstanding season in 1963 when he was the ace of the Yankee bullpen.

CLUB LEADERSHIP: Twice Hal led the Yankee pitchers in games pitched. In 1963 he led the Yanks in saves (18).

ALL-TIME YANKEE LEADER: Hal is tied for 12th on the all-time Yankee save list (41).

Yankee righty Allie Reynolds, pitched two no-hitters for the Yanks in 1951.

LEFT YANKS: In June 1967, in a rare Yankees-Mets transaction, the Yanks sold Hal's contract to the Mets. Hal finished his ML career, in 1967 with the Mets going 3-3 with four saves.

RENIFF, HAL

Yr.	W-L	Pct.	SA	G	GS	CG	IP	H	BB	SO	SH	ERA
1961	2-0	1.000	2	25	0	0	45	31	31	21	0	2.58
1962	0-0	.000	0	2	0	0	4	6	5	1	0	7.36
1963	4-3	.571	18	48	0	0	89	63	42	56	0	2.62
1964	6-4	.600	9	41	0	0	69	47	30	38	0	3.12
1965	3-4	.429	3	51	0	0	85	74	48	74	0	3.80
1966	3-7	.300	9	56	0	0	95	80	49	79	0	3.21
1967	0-2	.000	0	24	0	0	40	40	14	24	0	4.28
7 Yrs.	18-20	.474	41	247	0	0	428	341	219	293	0	3.26
Life	21-23	.477	45	276	0	0	471	383	242	314	0	3.27

World Series

Yr.	G	IP	BB	SO	H	W-L	SA
1963	3	3	1	1	0	0-0	0
1964	1	⅓	0	0	2	0-0	0
2 Yrs.	4	3⅓	1	1	2	0-0	0
Life.	Same.						

REYNOLDS, ALLIE

Nickname: "Superchief"
Yankee: 1947-54
Pitcher
Born: February 10, 1915
Birthplace: Bethany, OK
Died: December 26, 1994
Bat: R; Throw: R
Ht: 6'; Wt: 195

HONORS: *The Sporting News* selected Allie as one of three pitchers on its 1951 and 1952 ML All-Star teams. In 1951 Allie won the Hickok Belt as the Top Professional Athlete of the Year. The Baseball Writers gave him the Sid Mercer Award that same year.

CAME TO YANKS: In October, 1946, the Yanks obtained Allie from the Indians for second baseman Joe Gordon and infielder Ed Bockman. It was on the advice of Joe DiMaggio that the Yanks went after Allie.

VERSATILE ACE PITCHER: Allie was known as a great "two-way pitcher," that is, as both a starter and relief pitcher. His versatility as a pitcher is unmatched in Yankee history. Of his Yankee career appearances, 71% were as a starting pitcher. In 86 Yankee career relief appearances, Allie saved 41 games and won 15 others. In the 1947-48 seasons he was the Yanks' No. 1 starter and he was a member of the Yanks' "Big 3" from 1948-52 (Allie, Vic Raschi, and Ed Lopat). In 1952 Allie finished second in the AL MVP voting to Bobby Shantz, then of the Philadelphia A's. He was the Yankee relief ace in 1953, besides being a spot starter. His games were divided exactly in half between starting and relieving in 1954, Allie's final ML season at the age of 39. Allie had a tremendous fastball. In 1951 Casey Stengel said of Allie, "He don't run to the bullpen for the weak ones. But when it's the Red Sox, Indians, Tigers, or White Sox, even when he started the day before, you look beside you and the guy ain't there any more. He's in the bullpen. There's no use kidding about it. That big guy comes close to being the most valuable pitcher in baseball right now."

1951 NO-HITTERS: In 1951 Allie hurled two no-hitters! No other Yankee has ever pitched two no-hitters in the same year. On July 12, 1951, Allie no-hit Cleveland in a night game, winning 1-0. He fanned four and allowed three walks. On September 28, 1951, he pitched a no-hitter against Boston, winning 8-0, in a Yankee Stadium day game, fanning nine, walking four and retiring Ted Williams "twice" to end the game. Catcher Yogi Berra dropped a Williams foul pop, but caught a second one.

LEAGUE LEADER: In 1947 Allie officially led AL pitchers in winning percentage (.704, 19-8). He led the AL in shutouts in 1951 (seven). In 1952 Allie led the AL in ERA (2.06), strikeouts (160) and shutouts (six). Allie led the AL in shutouts two years in a row (1951-52), tying a ML record.

CLUB LEADERSHIP: He led Yankee pitchers in shutouts four times. He led the Yanks in innings pitched, games pitched and strikeouts, each three times. Twice he led the club in wins, saves, games started and complete games.

ALL-TIME YANKEE LEADER: Allie's Yankee winning percentage (.686, 131-60) is the fourth highest in Yankee history for those pitchers with at least 100 Yankee decisions. He is fifth on the all-time Yankee shutout list (27), ninth on the Yanks' strikeout list (967), ninth on the club's win (131) and 12th on the save (41-tie with Hal Reniff) lists, and 12th on the all-time Yankee games started list (209). Allie is also 12th in innings pitched (1700); 17th in games pitched (295); 15th in complete games (96); and 20th overall in ERA (3.30).

POPULAR, INTELLIGENT: Allie, part Creek Indian, was extremely popular with Yankee fans and teammates. The Oklahoma A&M alumnus was also an intelligent, professional athlete who invested in oil wells that became quite profitable. He came to the Yanks tagged with the reputation of failing under pressure. Allie continually proved that tag a falsehood. As a matter of fact, the New Yorkers never had a pitcher who was better in the clutch. He often pitched with serious injuries. Allie roomed with Ed Lopat and the two talked constantly about pitching and he learned from Lopat, one of the craftiest pitchers ever. In 1954 when the ML players formally organized the ML Baseball Players Association, Allie was the AL Player Representative. He brought the same powerful presence that he had on the mound to his union responsibility. In short, he was all business.

ALL-STAR GAME: As a Yankee pitcher, Allie was selected to five AL teams for All-Star games played in 1949, 1950, 1952, 1953 and (at the age of 39) 1954. Allie was the losing pitcher in the 1953 All-Star Game.

WORLD SERIES LEADER: He is among the leaders in almost all the lifetime World Series pitching categories. He is second on the all-time win (seven) and save (four) lists; third in games pitched (15) and strikeouts (62); fourth in shutouts (two); sixth in games started (nine); eighth in innings pitched (77); and 10th in complete games (five). Ranking tenth on the all-time list, Allie struckout 7.22 batters per nine innings in World Series play. In 15 World Series games, he had a batting average of .308 (8 for 26). The only pitcher with more World Series hits than Allie is Christy Mathewson (nine).

WORLD SERIES GAMES: Allie was one of the Yankees' best clutch pitchers in World Series action. In Game 2 of the 1947 Series, Allie struck out six Dodgers and won easily, 10-3. Game 1 of the 1949 Series saw Allie fan nine Dodgers to outduel Don Newcombe in a 1-0 Yankee victory. Reynolds was then brought in to relieve Game 4 with two outs in the sixth inning, and he proceeded to retire the last 10 batters (five on strikes) to save a 6-4 Yankee win. In Game 2 of the 1950 Series he went 10 innings, beating the Phillies, 2-1. Then he returned in relief to get the final out in Game 4 to complete the four-game Yankee sweep. Allie hurled a four-hit shutout and fanned 10 Dodgers in Game 4 of the 1952 Series. He came back in Game 7 and won that game as a relief pitcher, then won the final game (Game 6) of the 1953 Series in relief, giving the Yanks their record fifth consecutive World Championship.

RETIREMENT: Allie hurt his back in a freak accident in 1953 when the Yankee team bus hit a railroad overpass in Philadelphia. That injury forced him to retire before the 1955 season; Allie went out with his customary class. On August 26, 1989, a plaque honoring Allie's Yankee achievements was added to Monument Park at Yankee Stadium.

REYNOLDS, ALLIE

Yr.	W-L	Pct.	SA	G	GS	CG	IP	H	BB	SO	SH	ERA
1947	19-8	.704	2	34	30	17	242	207	123	129	4	3.20
1948	16-7	.696	3	39	31	11	236	240	111	101	1	3.77
1949	17-6	.739	1	35	31	4	214	200	123	105	2	4.00
1950	16-12	.571	2	35	29	14	241	215	138	160	2	3.74
1951	17-8	.680	7	40	26	16	221	171	100	126	7	3.05
1952	20-8	.714	6	35	29	24	244	194	97	160	6	2.06
1953	13-7	.650	13	41	15	5	145	140	61	86	1	3.41
1954	13-4	.765	7	36	18	5	157	133	66	100	4	3.32
8 Yrs.	131-60	.686	41	295	209	96	1700	1500	819	967	27	3.30
Life.	182-107	.630	49	434	309	137	2492	2193	1261	1423	36	3.30

World Series

Yr.	G	IP	BB	SO	H	W-L	SA
1947	2	11⅓	3	6	15	1-0	0
1949	2	12⅓	4	14	2	1-0	1
1950	2	10⅓	4	7	7	1-0	1
1951	2	15	11	8	16	1-1	0
1952	4	20⅓	6	18	12	2-1	1
1953	3	8	4	9	9	1-0	1
6 Yrs.	15	77⅓	32	62	61	7-2	4
Life. Same.							

RICHARDSON, BOBBY

Yankee: 1955-66
Second Baseman, 3B, SS
Born: August 19, 1935
Birthplace: Sumter, SC
Bat: R; Throw: R
Ht: 5'9"; Wt: 170

HONORS: For six consecutive seasons (1961-66), Bobby was selected as second baseman on *The Sporting News'* AL All-Star team. Bobby was named to the AL team for All-Star Games played in seven different years (1957, 1959, 1962-66).

YOUNG PROSPECT: Bobby began playing in the Yankee farm system in 1953 at Norfolk (.211 in 27 games) and Olean (.412 in 32 games). As a regular at Binghamton in 1954 he hit .310. In 1955-56 he played at Denver under Manager Ralph Houk, hitting .296 and .328, respectively. The Yanks called 19-year-old Bobby up from the minors briefly in 1955 and quickly recognized the talent of the young infielder who was already fielding in ML fashion. Bobby also had a 25-game stint at Richmond in 1955 (.280). He got into five Yankee games in 1956.

YANKEE SECOND BASEMAN: After brief Yankee trials in 1955-56, Bobby made the big club for good in 1957. He played 93 games at second base, more than Jerry Coleman, Billy Martin (who was traded in mid-season) and Gil McDougald, other second sackers. In 1958 Bobby was backup second baseman to McDougald. He was also the kind of three-way infielder (2B-3B-SS) Casey Stengel liked. In 1959 Bobby became the Yanks' permanent second baseman and held the job for eight consecutive seasons (1959-66). During that time he was the best second baseman in the AL.

DEFENSIVE ABILITIES: Bobby was one of the greatest fielding second basemen in the history of baseball. Five years in a row (1961-65) he won the Gold Glove Award as the finest fielding second sacker in the AL. Bobby teamed with his good buddy Tony Kubek to form an excellent double play combo. Four times Bobby led AL second basemen in making double plays and twice he led in putouts. He had an outstanding glove, great quickness and excellent range. Bill Skowron had trouble with pop-ups so Bobby caught almost all of them hit to the infield's right side. No second baseman started the double play better than Bobby. With no time to shift his feet on grounders, Bobby fielded the ball, twisted hard to his right so that his right knee hit the dirt, and fired the ball accurately to the shortstop racing across the bag. It was beautiful to watch, and he consistently made the play look easy. He was smooth.

TABLE-SETTER: Bobby was a fine offensive player. He had good bat control and was a good base runner with fair speed. Bill Dickey taught him to be more aggressive at the plate. In 1962 Bobby made 209 hits; it was the first 200-hit season by a Yankee since Phil Rizzuto had 200 in 1950. Bobby had his best offensive season in 1962 when he finished second to Mickey Mantle in the MVP voting. Bobby batted at the top of the Yankee lineup (first or second) and his job was to get on base so that the big boys could knock him in. He seldom struck out.

IRON MAN: Under Manager Ralph Houk, he was rarely rested. He was reliable, made the lineup day in and day out and occasionally played with injuries. From 1960-65 Bobby played in 150 or more games each season. From 1961-66 Bobby batted over 600 times in each season. His 692 at-bats in 1962 is the AL record. On June 24, 1962, Bobby batted 11 times in one game, tying an AL record for an extra-inning contest.

TAKING CRITICISM: Many young players were damaged by cutting criticism from Casey Stengel in "The Old Professor's" later Yankee years. But not Bobby. Stengel once told the press, "Look at him. (Richardson) Don't drink. Don't smoke. Nothing. But he still can't hit .220." Once, after Kubek and Bobby each made an error in a game, Stengel called them "Little Rock" and "Big Rock." He survived these cutdowns and his performance

improved. He may have had a baby face, but he was mentally tough. (It should be added that Stengel also made statements in support of Bobby.)

CLASS AND RELIGION: The clean-living Bobby represented most of the traditional Yankee values. He was a great competitor but a clean player. His strong Christian beliefs were nurtured in the Bible Belt of South Carolina. On the Yanks, Bobby proved his Christianity by practicing rather than preaching, and his teammates respected his feelings. (Once after striking out, Bill Skowron interrupted his dugout cussing by excusing himself to Bobby.) Bobby never once made his teammates feel uncomfortable, and they accepted him as one of them. Bobby held religious services for the team on Sundays. In 1958 Yankee GM George Weiss hired detectives to trail goodtiming Yankee players. Bobby, Kubek, and several others were followed to the Detroit YMCA for a night of ping-pong.

HELPING YOUTH: Throughout his Yankee career, Bobby liked to work with kids. In 1965 the Greater New York YMCA honored Bobby for his long work with the YMCA in Sumter, S.C., and YMCA organizations around the country. Bobby enjoyed speaking to youth groups, and Ralph Houk advised him that sticking with baseball would give Bobby a vehicle in which to better get his message across to kids.

LEAGUE LEADER: Bobby led the AL in at-bats for three consecutive seasons (1962-64). In 1962 he led the AL in hits (209).

CLUB LEADERSHIP: Bobby led the Yanks in at-bats six times. He led the Yanks in hits five times. He was the team leader in stolen bases and games played three times. In 1959 Bobby was the only Yankee to reach the .300 mark, hitting .301. In 1962 he led the Yanks in runs (99), doubles (38), hits (209), stolen bases (11) and at-bats (692).

ALL-TIME YANKEE LEADER: On the Top 20 Yankee list, Bobby ranks 17th in at-bats (5386); 18th in hits (1432), and 19th in games played (1412).

WORLD SERIES: From October 5, 1960, through October 15, 1964, Bobby played in 30 consecutive World Series games, a record. He was a tremendous World Series performer. Bobby is the only player on a losing team to ever win *Sport Magazine's* MVP Award, winning it in 1960 after making 12 RBIs to set a record. In Game 3 of the 1960 Series, Bobby hit a grand-slam HR and knocked in six runs, setting a single-game record, and in Game 6 he made two triples, tying a record. In the 1961 Series, Bobby led both clubs in hits (nine). In Game 7 of the 1962 Series, with the Yanks protecting a 1-0 lead with two outs in the bottom of the ninth, the San Francisco Giants had men on second and third when Bobby speared Willie McCovey's screaming line drive to end the game. The Yanks were World Champs once again. Bobby's 13 hits in the 1964 Series stand as a World Series record (twice tied, by Lou Brock in 1968 and by Marty Barrett in 1986).

LOYALTY AND RETIREMENT: Kubek and Bobby as friends and roommates agreed they would not burden the Yanks by retiring together, so when Kubek was forced to retire after the 1965 season, Bobby came back for one last year even though he probably wanted to leave the game. On September 17, 1966, "Bobby Richardson Day" was held at Yankee Stadium and Bobby at the season's close retired at the age of 31. He took a job as an insurance company publicist.

BASEBALL COACH: In 1970 Bobby became baseball coach at the University of South Carolina. Bobby had many fine teams at South Carolina, including 1975 when he took a 47-4-1 record into the College World Series. Bobby has also shared his love for Christ in his book, *Grand Slam*. He unsuccessfully ran for Congress in his native South Carolina where he serves as a church and civic leader.

RICHARDSON, BOBBY											
Yr.	G	AB	R	H	2B	3B	HR	RBI	BB	SB	BA	SA
1955	11	26	2	4	0	0	0	3	2	1	.154	.154
1956	5	7	1	1	0	0	0	0	0	0	.143	.143
1957	97	305	36	78	11	1	0	19	9	1	.256	.298
1958	73	182	18	45	6	2	0	14	8	1	.247	.302
1959	134	469	53	141	18	6	2	33	26	5	.301	.377
1960	150	460	45	116	12	3	1	26	35	6	.252	.298
1961	162	662	80	173	17	5	3	49	30	9	.261	.316
1962	161	692	99	209	38	5	8	59	37	11	.302	.406
1963	151	630	72	167	20	6	3	48	25	15	.265	.330
1964	159	679	90	181	25	4	4	50	28	11	.267	.333
1965	160	664	76	164	28	2	6	47	37	7	.247	.322
1966	149	610	71	153	21	3	7	42	25	6	.251	.330
12 Yrs.	1412	5386	643	1432	196	37	34	390	262	73	.266	.335
Life. Same.											

World Series									
Yr.	G	AB	R	H	2B	3B	HR	RBI	BA
1957	2	0	0	0	0	0	0	0	.000
1958	4	5	0	0	0	0	0	0	.000
1960	7	30	8	11	2	2	1	12	.367
1961	5	23	2	9	1	0	0	0	.391
1962	7	27	3	4	0	0	0	0	.148
1963	4	14	0	3	1	0	0	0	.214
1964	7	32	3	13	2	0	0	3	.406
7 Yrs.	36	131	16	40	6	2	1	15	.305
Life. Same.									

RIGHETTI, DAVE

Nickname: "Rags"
Yankee: 1979, 1981-90
Pitcher
Born: November 28, 1958
Birthplace: San Jose, CA
Bat: L; Throw: L
Ht: 6'4"; Wt: 195

HONORS: In 1981, Dave was selected as AL Rookie of the Year by the Baseball Writers and AL Rookie Pitcher of the Year by *The Sporting News*. In 1986 and 1987, Dave won both the Rolaids AL Relief Man of the Year and *The Sporting News* AL Fireman of the Year (co-winner with Jeff Reardon in 1987). Dave was selected to *The Sporting News* All-Star team in 1986. Dave pitched in both the 1986 and 1987 All-Star Games.

TRADED TO THE YANKEES: In November of 1978, the Yankees obtained Dave, Mike Griffin (P), Paul Mirabella (P) and Greg Jemison (P) from Texas for Sparky Lyle (P), Dave Rajsich (P), Larry McCall (P), Mike Heath (C), Domingo Ramos (INF) and cash. Texas had signed Dave out of San Jose City College, and

he had been one of their top prospects. Yankee GM Al Rosen said Dave was the key to making the deal, and some began calling Dave "the next Ron Guidry."

YANKEE FARM HAND: In 1979, Dave was impressive at both West Haven and Columbus. He made his ML debut on September 16, 1979, which was Catfish Hunter Day at Yankee Stadium; he pitched well, no decision. Billy Martin liked what he saw in Dave. In the spring of 1980, a *The Sporting News* survey identified him as the ML's best rookie prospect. But Dave never made it to New York in 1980; instead, he battled control problems in Columbus and had a poor year (6-10, 4.63 ERA).

ROOKIE OF THE YEAR: In 1981, Dave gained control of his blazing fastball and excellent curveball and consistently got ahead of the hitters. He started the season at Columbus (5-0) and was recalled to New York on May 21. He was 3-0 with a 1.50 ERA when the players' strike halted play in June. He had only one poor start in 15 starts and allowed only one home run—hit by Gorman Thomas. Dave's 2.06 ERA would have led the AL, but he was $1\frac{1}{3}$ innings shy of qualifying for the title. He was the first Yankee to be named Rookie of the Year since Thurman Munson in 1970.

1981 POST-SEASON PLAY: In Game 2 of the Division Series against Milwaukee, Dave got the win, pitching six innings, striking out 10, and combining with Ron Davis and Goose Gossage on a shutout. Dave pitched three solid innings in the middle-inning relief to win Game 5, the clincher, of the Division Series. In Game 3 of the ALCS against Oakland, Dave again won the clinching game, and again combined with Davis and Gossage on a shutout. In Game 3 of the World Series against Los Angeles, he started against Fernando Valenzuela, only the fourth rookie match-up in Series history; Dave lasted only two innings but escaped with no decision. So, for the post season, Dave was 3-0 with a 2.12 ERA, but somehow pitched only two innings in the World Series!

SOPHOMORE JINX: Dave lost his control in 1982 and led the AL in walks (108). Laboring with a 5-5 record, on June 26, Dave was sent down to Columbus. His father, Leo, who played shortstop in the Yankee farm system, was informed in a call from George Steinbrenner. After four games at Columbus, Dave returned to the Yankees. One of the problems Dave experienced was not knowing whom to listen to for help, as the Yankees had multiple managers and pitching coaches in 1982. He regained his control in 1983.

THE NO-HITTER: On July 4, 1983, before a holiday crowd of 41,077, including Richard Nixon, and with the temperature a sweltering 94 degrees, Dave pitched a no-hitter against Boston at Yankee Stadium. He made 132 pitches. He struck out nine and walked four (the only base runners) and faced only 29 batters (one pickoff and one double-play erasing two of the four walks). No great fielding play was necessary to preserve the no-hitter, although rightfielder Steve Kemp made a great eighth-inning catch on a foul ball. Dave got the final out by fanning Wade Boggs—who would win the batting crown at .361—and the fans erupted in holiday celebration. It was the first Yankee no-hitter since Don Larsen's in the 1956 World Series; the first regular-season Yankee no-hitter since two by

Allie Reynolds in 1951; the first no-hitter by a Yankee southpaw since George Mogridge in 1917; and the first no-hitter *ever* pitched by a lefthander at Yankee Stadium.

REPLACING GOSSAGE: With Goose Gossage having departed the Yankees, in 1984 Dave moved to the bullpen, sparking a continually lively debate about the wisdom of ending such a promising career as a starter. Dave saw it as a challenge and responded with 31 saves in 40 save situations. His competitive fire and heart made him a natural for pitching in the late innings with a game on the line. He did need to learn how to warm up quickly and to be ready to pitch almost daily. He was unique among most relievers in that he had a full assortment of pitches. In 1985, he was selected AL Pitcher of the Month for August (4-0, 5 saves, 1.17 ERA). Also in 1985, he led the AL in relief wins (12), and he set a Yankee record with 74 games pitched.

THE GREATEST YEAR: In 1986, Dave set a then-ML record with 46 saves, breaking the mark of 45 set by Dan Quisenberry in 1983 and tied by Bruce Sutter in 1984. From July 3 through the end of the season, Dave converted 29 saves in 30 save situations. He broke the record in style in Boston on October 4, the season's final day, by saving both ends of a doubleheader. With 46 saves and eight wins, Dave contributed to 54 of the Yanks' 90 wins—or 60%. Dave also tied his own club record with 74 games pitched.

ALL-TIME SAVE LEADER: On July 24, 1988, Dave recorded his 151st save as a Yankee and surpassed Gossage as the club's all-time save leader. Dave remained the save leader until he was passed by Mariano Rivera during the 2002 season.

ALL-TIME YANKEE LEADER: Dave has appeared in more games (522) as a pitcher than any other in Yankee history. Of those games, he started 76 with the remaining 446 in relief, finishing 379 of them. Dave also ranks tenth in strikeouts (940), and 13th in ERA (3.11).

LATE YANKEE CAREER: Dave continued to be the Yankee stopper through 1990, and he continued to be effective, but he became progressively less dominant. He did strike out seven straight batters over two games against Baltimore in September 1988.

LEAVING THE YANKEES: Rags in December 1990 signed with the Giants as a free agent. His saves dropped from 36 in 1990 to 24, 3 and 1 over the next three seasons. He finished 1994 with Toronto and then resurfaced with the Chicago White Sox starting nine games during the 1995 season. Recently, Dave has served as the pitching coach of the San Francisco Giants.

RIGHETTI, DAVE

Yr.	W-L	Pct.	SA	G	GS	CG	IP	H	BB	SO	SH	ERA
1979	0-1	.000	0	3	3	0	17	10	10	13	0	3.63
1981	8-4	.667	0	15	15	2	105	75	38	89	0	2.05
1982	11-10	.524	1	33	27	4	183	155	108	163	0	3.79
1983	14-8	.636	0	31	31	7	217	194	67	169	2	3.44
1984	5-6	.455	31	64	0	0	96	79	37	90	0	2.34
1985	12-7	.632	29	74	0	0	107	96	45	92	0	2.78
1986	8-8	.500	46	74	0	0	107	88	35	83	0	2.45
1987	8-6	.571	31	60	0	0	95	95	44	77	0	3.51
1988	5-4	.556	25	60	0	0	87	86	37	70	0	3.52
1989	2-6	.250	25	55	0	0	69	73	26	51	0	3.00
1990	1-1	.500	36	53	0	0	53	48	26	43	0	3.57
11 Yrs.	74-61	.548	224	522	76	13	1137	999	473	940	2	3.11
Life	82-79	.509	252	718	89	13	1404	1287	591	1112	2	3.46

Divisional Playoff

Yr.	G	IP	BB	SO	H	W-L	SA
1981	2	9	3	13	8	2-0	0
1 Yr.	2	9	3	13	8	2-0	0
Life. Same.							

Championship Series

Yr.	G	IP	BB	SO	H	W-L	SA
1981	1	6	2	4	4	1-0	0
1 Yr.	1	6	2	4	4	1-0	0
Life Same							

World Series

Yr.	G	IP	BB	SO	H	W-L	SA
1981	1	2	2	1	5	0-0	0
1 Yr.	1	2	2	1	5	0-0	0
Life. Same.							

RIVERA, MARIANO

Yankee: 1995-2002
Pitcher
Born: November 29, 1969
Birthplace: Panama City, Panama
Bat: R; Throw: R
Ht: 6'2"; Wt: 168

SIGNED OUT OF PANAMA: Yankee scout Herb Raybourn signed Mariano out of Panama, and the right-hander broke into pro ball spectacularly in 1990. At Tampa (Rookie League), he allowed only one earned run in 52 innings pitched, a 0.17 ERA! He had success at Greensboro (Class A), too, but he had surgery on his right elbow in 1992 and was injury-riddled in 1993. Rebounding in 1994, Rivera was a combined 10-2 with Tampa, Albany, and Columbus. His ERA for his minor-league career through 1994 was a sensational 2.04. Mariano was called up to the Yankees in 1995, making his Major League debut on May 23 at California. In that debut, Rivera took the 10-0 Yankee loss, allowing five earned runs in 3 1/3 innings pitched. Shuttling from Columbus (AAA) to the Yanks, Rivera posted a 5-3 record in 19 games, starting in ten. He was 1-0 with a 0.00 ERA in the Division Series versus Seattle and won in his postseason debut in Game 2. Mariano pitched the final 3 1/3 innings of that historic game at Yankee Stadium won by the Yankees in the 15th inning on that dramatic Jim Leyritz homer.

BECOMES DOMINANT PITCHER: In 1996, Mariano became one of the most dominant pitchers in baseball with an ERA of 2.09, an 8-3 record and five saves. Of the 61 games in which he appeared, mostly as a middle reliever, Rivera recorded the most ever strikeouts by a Yankee non-starter with 130 (in 107 $^{2}/_{3}$ innings), surpassing the previous mark of 122 set by Goose Gossage in 1978. In eight games of postseason play, Mariano was 1-0 with a spectacular 0.63 ERA, allowing but one earned run in 14 $^{1}/_{3}$ innings! Rivera became strictly a closer in the 1997 season, going 6-4 with a 1.88 ERA, posting 43 saves in 66 games. He ranked second among American League relievers in both ERA and saves. That save total was tied for the second most in Yankee history, John Wetteland posting the same number in 1996. In two relief efforts versus Cleveland in the Division Series, he had a 4.50 ERA with one save. Mariano continued to shine with yet another impressive season in 1998. He was 3-0 with a spectacular ERA of 1.91, saving 36 in 54 appearances. His save total of 35 tied Dave Righetti (1990) as the third highest in Yankee history. Rivera was phenomenal in the '98 postseason: in 10 games, he allowed NO RUNS in 13 $^{1}/_{3}$ innings, saving three of four Yankee wins against San Diego in the World Series. To culminate his season, Mariano had the privilege of retiring Mark Sweeney on a ground ball for the final out of the Series.

CONTINUES TO SHINE IN: Mariano had great seasons in 1999-2001 with 66, 66, and 71 appearances, respectively. With Games Saved totals being 45, 36, and 50 in those seasons, Mariano quickly moved up in the team leadership in categories that past Yankee relievers had held for many years. He was the first Yankee pitcher to have three 40+ saves in a season (1997, 1999, and 2001). In 1999, Rivera amazingly did not allow a run in his final 28 appearances of the season (30.2 IP) while converting 22 saves in the process. Three stints on the Disabled List in 2002 dropped Mariano's numbers, but he still managed another 28 saves in 45 games.

POSTSEASON: The decision to make Mariano the Yankee closer looks even better when the best face the best in October. Mariano has a 6-1 mark, with 25 saves in 80 innings pitched. His postseason ERA is 0.90 with 62 strikeouts and only 12 walks. He had three saves in the 1998 World Series while his dominance of the Braves in the 1999 World Series led him to named MVP of the Fall Classic. His ERA in the 1998 and 1999 postseasons was 0.00 for the 18 games he appeared in. He continued this scoreless run in the 2000 Division Series and saved all three wins against Oakland. Even with the two runs he allowed in the 2001 World Series loss to Arizona in Game 7, Mariano still sports a 1.67 ERA for the 18 World Series games he has appeared in.

ALL-STAR: Mariano has appeared in the All-Star game in 1997, 2000, and 2002. He was also selected by Joe Torre for the 1999 squad but declined to take care of personal business in Panama.

ALL-TIME YANKEE LEADER: Mariano ranks first in saves (243) and second in games pitched on the all-time Yankee pitching list.

RIVERA, MARIANO

Yr.	W-L	Pct.	SA	G	GS	CG	IP	H	BB	SO	SH	ERA
1995	5-3	.625	0	19	10	0	67	71	30	51	0	5.51
1996	8-3	.727	5	61	0	0	107.2	73	34	130	0	2.09
1997	6-4	.600	43	66	0	0	71.2	65	20	68	0	1.88
1998	3-0	1.000	36	54	0	0	61.1	48	17	36	0	1.91
1999	4-3	.571	45	66	0	0	69	43	18	52	0	1.83
2000	7-4	.636	36	66	0	0	75.2	58	25	58	0	2.85
2001	4-6	.400	50	71	0	0	80.2	61	12	83	0	2.34
2002	1-4	.250	28	45	0	0	46	35	11	41	0	2.74
8 Yrs.	38-27	.585	243	448	10	0	579	454	167	519	0	2.60

Life. Same.

Division Series

Yr.	G	IP	BB	SO	H	W-L	SA
1995	3	5.1	1	8	3	1-0	0
1996	2	4.2	1	1	0	0-0	0
1997	2	2	0	1	2	0-0	1
1998	3	3.1	1	2	1	0-0	2
1999	2	3	0	3	1	0-0	2
2000	3	5	0	2	2	0-0	3
2001	3	5	0	4	4	0-0	2
2002	1	1	0	0	1	0-0	1
8 Yrs.	19	29.1	3	21	14	1-0	10

Life. Same.

Championship Series

Yr.	G	IP	BB	SO	H	W-L	SA
1996	2	4	1	5	6	1-0	0
1998	4	5.2	1	5	0	0-0	1
1999	3	4.2	0	3	5	1-0	2
2000	3	4.2	0	1	4	0-0	1
2001	4	4.2	1	3	2	0-0	2
5 Yrs.	16	23.2	3	17	17	3-0	6

Life. Same.

World Series

Yr.	G	IP	BB	SO	H	W-L	SA
1996	4	5.2	3	4	4	0-0	0
1998	3	4.1	0	4	5	0-0	3
1999	3	4.2	1	3	3	1-0	2
2000	4	6	1	7	4	0-0	2
2001	4	6.1	1	7	6	1-1	1
5 Yrs.	18	27	6	25	22	2-1	8

Life. Same.

Mariano Rivera

RIVERS, MICKEY
(BORN JOHN MILTON RIVERS)

Nickname: "Mick the Quick"
Yankee: 1976-79
Outfielder
Born: October 31, 1948
Birthplace: Miami, FL
Bat: L; Throw: L
Ht: 5'10"; Wt: 165

HONORS: *The Sporting News* selected Mickey as an outfielder on its 1976 AL All-Star team. He was also on the AL team for the 1976 All-Star Game. The Associated Press picked Mickey as an outfielder on its ML All-Star team in 1976.

CAME TO YANKS: In December, 1975, the Yanks acquired Mickey and pitcher Ed Figueroa from the California Angels for outfielder Bobby Bonds.

SPEED MERCHANT: Mickey was probably the fastest man ever to play for the Yanks. He was the leadoff hitter on the team and when he got on base the Yankee offense rolled. His speed distracted infielders when he was at-bat and pitchers when he was on base. Mickey's 43 stolen bases in 1976 were the most by a Yankee player since Snuffy Stirnweiss stole 55 bases in 1944. Unfortunately, Mickey was hampered by various leg injuries that prevented him from stealing as many bases in his final three Yankee seasons. In 1977 Mickey grounded into only two double plays, tying a Yankee record set by Mickey Mantle in 1961. He was a blur when he ran the bases aggressively.

YANKEE CENTERFIELDER: Mickey was the Yanks' regular centerfielder the entire time he was on the club (1976-79). Defensively, he patrolled spacious Yankee Stadium center field in the best tradition of Combs, DiMaggio and Mantle. It takes a man with Mickey's great speed to cover all the Stadium's real estate, and Mickey covered it like a blanket. He did not have a strong arm, yet he had the ability to position himself so that he put his body into a throw, resulting in an accurate throw delivered quickly.

GOOD HITTER: Mickey provided a good stick and delivered many key Yankee hits. For his first three Yankee seasons, he hit a combined .301. He also could hit the long ball occasionally. In 1976 Mickey hit in 20 consecutive games. (It was at the time the longest Yankee team hitting streak since Joe Gordon's 29 straight games in 1942.)

GREAT ABILITY: When Mickey put his mind to baseball he was a player to behold; he was one of the most exciting players ever to wear the Yankee uniform. If Mickey had one fault, it was that he was not always in the mood for baseball. Personal problems seemed to weigh on his mind and the fans, his manager and the front office tended to question his baseball commitment. But Mickey's teammates liked him. Some suggested that Mickey just needed gentler handling. The Yanks were an awesome team when Mickey was at his best. Mickey is a fun-loving guy who enjoyed going to the race track, often with his pal Ken Holtzman when the two were Yankee teammates.

LEAGUE LEADER: Mickey led the AL in fewest times grounding into double plays (for batters with at least 500 at-bats) two successive years, tying an AL record for most successive years.

CLUB LEADERSHIP: In 1976 and 1977 he led the Yanks in batting and stolen bases. Twice he led the Yanks in triples. In 1977 he led the Yanks in hits (184).

AL CHAMPIONSHIP SERIES: In Game 4 of the 1977 Series Mickey rapped four hits, leading the Yanks to a 6-4 victory over the Royals. The next day, with the AL pennant on the line, the Yanks entered the top of the ninth inning losing, 3-2. Mickey was one of the heroes of that Yankee uprising when his single tied the game and the Yanks went on to win. He never hit below .348 in three Championship Series!

WORLD SERIES: In Game 3 of the 1977 Series, Mickey stroked three hits, including two doubles, leading the Yanks to a key 5-3 win over the Dodgers. Mickey's three hits in Game 5 of the 1978 Series helped the Yanks rout the Dodgers, 12-2.

TRADED: In August 1979, the Yanks traded Mickey to the Texas Rangers for outfielder Oscar Gamble. (The trade originally called for minor leaguers coming to the Yanks but Commissioner Kuhn vetoed that feature. The Yanks then accepted Gamble in the deal.) Several minor leaguers exchanged clubs in October 1979, completing the deal.

RIVERS, MICKEY

Yr.	G	AB	R	H	2B	3B	HR	RBI	BB	SB	BA	SA
1976	137	590	95	184	31	8	8	67	13	43	.312	.432
1977	138	565	79	184	18	5	12	69	18	22	.326	.439
1978	141	559	78	148	25	8	11	48	29	25	.265	.397
1979	74	286	37	82	18	5	3	25	13	3	.287	.416
4 Yrs.	490	2000	289	598	92	26	34	209	73	93	.299	.422
Life.	1467	5629	785	1660	247	71	61	499	266	267	.295	.397

Championship Series

Yr.	G	AB	R	H	2B	3B	HR	RBI	BA
1976	5	23	5	8	0	1	0	0	.348
1977	5	23	5	9	2	0	0	2	.391
1978	4	11	0	5	0	0	0	0	.455
3 Yrs.	14	57	10	22	2	1	0	2	.386
Life. Same.									

World Series

Yr.	G	AB	R	H	2B	3B	HR	RBI	BA
1976	4	18	1	3	0	0	0	0	.167
1977	6	27	1	6	2	0	0	1	.222
1978	5	18	2	6	0	0	0	1	.333
3 Yrs.	15	63	4	15	2	0	0	2	.238
Life. Same.									

RIZZUTO, PHIL

Nickname: "Scooter"
Yankee: 1941-42 (military) '46-56
Shortstop
Born: September 25, 1917
Birthplace: Brooklyn, NY
Bat: R; Throw: R
Ht: 5'6"; Wt: 150

Phil Rizzuto, New York Yankee shortshop, works out prior to an exhibition game in St. Petersburg against the St. Louis Cardinals, March 16, 1942. (AP/WIDE WORLD PHOTOS)

HONORS: *The Sporting News* in 1940 named Phil the Minor League Player of the Year for Phil's outstanding play at the Yanks' Kansas City farm team. With the Yanks in 1941, Phil was "Rookie of the League" (before the official rookie awards as we know them today were given). He also won the Catholic Youth Organization's "most popular Yankee" award. In 1950 the Baseball Writers selected Phil as the MVP of the AL and the same year *The Sporting News* picked him as the ML Player of the Year. Phil in 1950 also won the first Hickok Belt Award as the Top Professional Athlete of the Year. Phil had won the New York Chapter of the Baseball Writers' 1949 Sid Mercer Award. *The Sporting News* named him to that publication's ML All-Star team as the best shortstop in baseball four years in a row (1949-52). Phil was selected to the AL team for five All-Star Games (1942, 1950-53). In 1981 Phil was presented with the Pride of the Yankees Award, given each year by the Yankee Foundation.

YOUNG PROSPECT: Following his 1936 graduation from Brooklyn's Richmond Hill High School, he tried out with the Dodgers and Giants who said he was too small. (Casey Stengel of the Dodgers broke the news harshly.) Yankee scout Paul Krichell saw him play a semi-pro game at Floral Park on Long Island, was impressed, and invited him to a Yankee Stadium tryout. After several days of workouts, and several more days of anxious waiting, Krichell signed Phil (almost waiting too long and allowing the Red Sox to sign him). Yankee GM Ed Barrow once said of Phil's signing, "Rizzuto cost me 15 cents, ten for postage and five for a cup of coffee we gave him the last day he worked out at the Stadium."

MINOR LEAGUER: Phil began playing in the Yanks' farm system at about $75 a month in 1936, playing in Bassett, Va., where his career almost came to an end. A leg injury incurred when he stepped in a gopher hole, became infected and gangrene set in. For a time Phil was threatened with the loss of the leg. Later he played in Norfolk, Va., and in 1939 went to Kansas City. Under Norfolk Manager Ray White, Phil hit .336 (1938) and under Kansas City Manager Billy Meyer, he hit .316 (1939) and .347 (1940) against top-notch minor league pitching. Billy Hitchcock, a K.C. teammate, nicknamed Phil "Scooter" in 1939. The double play combination at K.C. was Phil and Gerry Priddy, perhaps the best DP combo in minor-league history. Both were invited to the Yanks' 1941 spring camp and both made the big club. By the time Phil's minor league days were over, he had proved the Dodgers and Giants terribly wrong—not about his size, but about his ability.

YANKEE SHORTSTOP: As a rookie in 1941, he was the Yanks' regular shortstop and hit a robust .307. He was Yankee shortstop every year from 1941-54, except for his years of Navy service (1943-45). He was a Yankee in 1955-56 but played less than regularly.

MILITARY SERVICE: In August of 1942, Phil enlisted in the Navy. He was given a leave of absence until October 6, allowing him to finish the 1942 baseball season. The Cardinals beat the Yanks in Game 5 to wrap up the World Series on October 5. If a Game 6 had been necessary, Phil would have been unable to play. In the Navy, he contracted malaria and the sickness continued to plague him during the first three seasons upon his return to the Yanks (1946-48).

YANKEE SPARK PLUG: Phil was a key member of nine Yankee pennant-winning teams and seven World Champions; some would say he was the backbone of those great teams. Joe McCarthy once said of him, "For a little fellow to beat a big fellow he has to be terrific, he has to have everything, and Rizzuto's got it." He brought that talent and determination to the Yanks. From his hospital bed in 1949, Tommy Henrich said, "We have nothing to worry about as long as Rizzuto remains healthy. He's the team's spark plug." Late in the 1949 campaign, Boston's Ted Williams pointed to Phil and told Henrich, "If we had that little squirt, we'd be out in front by 10 games now."

COMPLETE BALLPLAYER: The 200 hits Phil collected in 1950 is a Yankee club record for shortstops. Besides being a fine hitter, he was a great defensive player, and he did all the things characteristic of a smart, heads-up player. He was durable, had good speed, and may have been the best base runner of his era. He was one of the game's greatest bunters. In 1951, Ty Cobb said that two players, Phil and Stan Musial, were the only mid-century players who Cobb felt would have been stars in his time. Cobb pointed to Phil's ability to hit to any field, to his great bunting skills and his all-round defensive genius. Phil was a master at handling the bat. He led the ML's in sacrifice hits four straight years (1949-52). In 1947 Phil was hit by a pitched ball eight times, leading the AL.

FEARS: Phil overcame many fears to play ML baseball. He was terrified of flying. He was afraid of being on a baseball diamond (or anywhere else) during an electrical storm. He was frightened of snakes or anything that crawls. His fear was so apparent that teammates were naturally given to practical jokes; Phil was sometimes a willing victim—provided the joke did not involve a real crawler. He found so many unpleasant things tucked in his glove that he was one of the first players to bring his glove to the dugout between innings. The popular Phil somehow found a way to keep his active fears in check during his playing career. It should be added that Phil was fearless on the field, holding his ground as rugged runners barreled into second base.

GREAT OFFENSIVE PLAY: Phil made the most important play of the 1951 season on September 17, a suicide squeeze bunt in the bottom of the ninth to score Joe DiMaggio and beat the Indians, 2-1, putting the Yanks into first place for good. After the game, an admiring Casey Stengel remarked, "Only Rizzuto could have bunted that ball successfully the way it was pitched, high and inside." The Indian pitcher, realizing that a squeeze was probably on, hurled the toughest possible pitch to bunt, and Phil still executed the play to perfection.

GREAT DEFENSIVE PLAY: In another late-season game in 1951, Cleveland's Jim Hegan blooped a fly between left field and the infield. Phil dashed into shallow left and with his back to the plate snatched the ball in the air with his bare hand! He stumbled, fell and rolled into foul territory, but Phil kept the ball in his bare hand for the out!

DEFENSIVE ABILITIES: He was a marvelously graceful shortstop. Known for his acrobatics around second base, he worked brilliantly on the double play with five different regular Yankee second basemen (Joe Gordon, Snuffy Stirnweiss, Jerry Coleman,

Billy Martin and Gil McDougald) in his Yankee career. Casey Stengel once said of Phil, "He is the greatest shortstop I have ever seen in my entire baseball career, and I have watched some beauties. Honus Wagner was a better hitter, sure, but I've seen this kid make plays Wagner never did. If I were a retired gentleman, I would follow the Yankees around just to see Rizzuto work those miracles every day."

FIELDING NUMBERS: In one streak, he accepted 289 straight chances without making an error. He led AL shortstops in fielding in consecutive seasons (1949-50). Twice he led AL shortstops in double plays and putouts, and in 1952 he led AL shortstops in assists (458). Phil helped turn 123 double plays in 1950, setting a Yankee club record for shortstops. Phil ranks 11th on baseball's all-time shortstop double play list (1217).

CLUB LEADERSHIP: Phil led the Yanks in stolen bases eight times, more often than any Yankee player in history except Mickey Mantle who tied him. Five times Phil led the Yanks in games played. He led the club in at-bats three times. Twice he led the team in runs, hits, doubles and triples. In 1950 Phil led the Yanks in seven major offensive categories (runs, hits, doubles, walks, stolen bases, batting and at-bats).

ALL-TIME YANKEE LEADER: Phil is in 11th place on the all-time Yankee games played list (1661). He is in 12th place on the stolen base list (149); 13th on both the hit (1588) and at-bat lists (5816); 16th on both the run scored (877) and triple (62) lists; and 20th in doubles (239).

WORLD SERIES: Phil ranks among the leaders in most lifetime World Series offensive categories. He is third in stolen bases (10) and fourth in walks (30) on those all-time Series lists. In the 1942 Series, Phil led both competing clubs in batting (.381) and hits (eight). In Game 5 of the 1942 Series, Phil's HR almost rallied the Yanks in a 4-2 loss to St. Louis. His two-run HR in Game 5 of the 1951 Series, helped rout the New York Giants, 13-1.

RELEASE: The Yanks released Phil in August of 1956, ending his tremendous 13-year ML career with an abrupt stroke, although it was a most difficult decision for GM Weiss and Manager Stengel to make. (Stengel was never Phil's favorite manager; Joe McCarthy was.) Despite the August release, the Yankee players showed their feelings for Phil by voting him a full World Series paycheck.

YANKEE BROADCASTER: In 1957, Phil joined Mel Allen and Red Barber in the Yankee broadcast booth and was a fixture there for nearly 39 years. His presence bridged the generations, from the DiMaggio era to the Mattingly era, and his voice, or even the mention of his name, usually triggered a smile or a warm response. On August 4, 1985, "Phil Rizzuto Day" at Yankee Stadium, the Yankees retired Phil's number 10 uniform and dedicated a plaque in the Scooter's honor in Monument Park. Finally, in 1994, Phil was inducted into the Baseball Hall of Fame. (His general baseball excellence and particularly brilliant defensive play had gained deserved recognition at last.) Phil tossed aside a suggestion that he might also enter the Hall one day as a broadcaster, saying he is "not a professional." Whatever, he is beloved by many who looked

forward to his return to the WPIX mike in 1996. But after the death of his friend Mickey Mantle in August 1995, Phil began to think that maybe he should spend more time at home. He wasn't talking with WPIX. Was he asserting a stance? If so, wrote Richard Sandomiv in *The New York Times,* you couldn't blame him for wanting to "dictate his terms, unlike his playing retirement, forced upon him in 1956 by the Yankees." Rizzuto left the Yankee broadcast team after the 1996 season ending a 57-year affiliation with the Yanks both as a player and a broadcaster. Thank you, Phil, for your years of dedicated service—and Scooter, "Holy Cow," you were the greatest!

RIZZUTO, PHIL

Yr.	G	AB	R	H	2B	3B	HR	RBI	BB	SB	BA	SA
1941	133	515	65	158	20	9	3	46	27	14	.307	.398
1942	144	553	79	157	24	7	4	68	44	22	.284	.374
1946	126	471	53	121	17	1	2	38	34	14	.257	.310
1947	153	549	78	150	26	9	2	60	57	11	.273	.364
1948	128	464	65	117	13	2	6	50	60	6	.252	.328
1949	153	614	110	169	22	7	5	65	72	18	.275	.358
1950	155	617	125	200	36	7	7	66	91	12	.324	.439
1951	144	540	87	148	21	6	2	43	58	18	.274	.346
1952	152	578	89	147	24	10	2	43	67	17	.254	.341
1953	134	413	54	112	21	3	2	54	71	4	.271	.351
1954	127	307	47	60	11	0	2	15	41	3	.195	.251
1955	81	143	19	37	4	1	1	9	22	7	.259	.322
1956	31	52	6	12	0	0	0	6	6	3	.231	.231
13 Yrs.	1661	5816	877	1588	239	62	38	563	650	149	.273	.355

Life. Same.

World Series

Yr.	G	AB	R	H	2B	3B	HR	RBI	BA
1941	5	18	0	2	0	0	0	0	.111
1942	5	21	2	8	0	0	1	1	.381
1947	7	26	3	8	1	0	0	2	.308
1949	5	18	2	3	0	0	0	1	.167
1950	4	14	1	2	0	0	0	0	. 143
1951	6	25	5	8	0	0	1	3	.320
1952	7	27	2	4	1	0	0	0	. 148
1953	6	19	4	6	1	0	0	0	.316
1955	7	15	2	4	0	0	0	1	.267
9 Yrs.	52	183	21	45	3	0	2	8	.246

Life. Same.

ROLFE, RED
(BORN ROBERT ABIAL ROLFE)

Yankee: 1931, '34-42
3B, SS
Born: October 17, 1908
Birthplace: Penacook, NH
Died: July 8, 1969
Bat: L; Throw: R
Ht: 5'11"; Wt: 170

HONORS: *The Sporting News* selected Red as the third baseman on its ML All-Star team in three consecutive seasons (1937-39).

EARLY ML CAREER: Red played his first ML game in 1931 as the Yankee shortstop. It was the only ML game he played until 1934 when he became the Yanks' reserve shortstop and third baseman.

McCARTHY'S SHIFT: Red's original position was shortstop. But Manager Joe McCarthy believed third base would suit him better. McCarthy felt Red did not have the arm to play shortstop, but that he possessed a terrific glove. In Red's first game at third base, a hot smash blackened his eye, but he worked hard and quickly learned his new position.

YANKEE THIRD BASEMAN: In 1935 Red became the regular Yankee third baseman. He was a vital member on four straight Yankee World Championship teams (1936-39). In 1935 and 1939 he played in every Yankee game. A quiet man, Red was greatly respected by his Yankee teammates. He was a disciple of Joe McCarthy and he was typical of the disciplined Yanks of the 1930s. He knew his job and performed it to the best of his ability. He roomed with Joe Gordon, both later to become ML managers. He was the Yanks' regular third baseman for seven seasons (1935-41). Ed Barrow once called Red "the best third sacker the Yankees ever had." (Barrow died in 1953.)

DEFENSIVE ABILITIES: Red was not only a steady defensive third baseman; he often made sensational plays. He led AL third basemen in fielding in 1935 (.964) and 1936 (.957).

GOOD CONTACT HITTER: Although Red was not a power hitter, he was an excellent contact hitter. He led the AL in triples in 1936 (15). In 1939 he was fantastic, pacing the AL in hits (213), doubles (46) and runs scored (139). Red had the ability to be on base during a Yankee rally, scoring more than 100 runs in seven consecutive years (1935-41). For those seasons he averaged 120.85 runs scored per season, a remarkable average. From August 9-25, 1939, Red scored at least one run in 18 consecutive games, setting an AL record. (He scored 30 runs during that streak.) Hitting better than .300 in seasons times and spraying the ball all around enabled Red to get on base for the big sluggers to bring home.

CLUB LEADERSHIP: Red led the Yanks in hits and at-bats three times. Twice he led the club in runs scored, doubles and triples.

ALL-TIME YANKEE LEADER: Red is 12th on the All-Time Yankee triple (67) list. He is 13th on the runs scored (942) list, and 18th in doubles (257).

ALL-STAR GAME: Red was picked as a member of the AL team for four All-Star Games in consecutive seasons (1937-40).

WORLD SERIES: Red hit better than .300 in four of his six World Series. His 10 hits in the 1936 Series tied teammate Jake Powell for the most hits in that Series. Red's 10 hits were all singles, a six-game Series record for one-base hits. In the 1942 Series, his final Fall Classic, Red led all players in runs scored (five).

RETIREMENT: Following the 1942 campaign, Red retired as a Yankee player to return to his native New Hampshire and coach baseball at Dartmouth College. He had a fine baseball mind and was naturally called back to ML duty as a Yankee coach in 1946. Red then managed the Tigers from 1949-52 and did a good job with a mediocre team.

ROLFE, RED

Yr.	G	AB	R	H	2B	3B	HR	RBI	BB	SB	BA	SA
1931	1	0	0	0	0	0	0	0	0	0	.000	.000
1934	89	279	54	80	13	2	0	18	26	2	.287	.348
1935	149	639	108	192	33	9	5	67	57	7	.300	.404
1936	135	568	116	181	39	15	10	70	68	3	.319	.493
1937	154	648	143	179	34	10	4	62	90	4	.276	.378
1938	151	631	132	196	36	8	10	80	74	13	.311	.441
1939	152	648	139	213	46	10	14	80	81	7	.329	.495
1940	139	588	102	147	26	6	10	53	50	4	.250	.366
1941	136	561	106	148	22	5	8	42	57	3	.264	.364
1942	69	265	42	58	8	2	8	25	23	1	.219	.355
10 Yrs.	1175	4827	942	1394	257	67	69	497	526	44	.289	.413

Life. Same.

World Series

Yr.	G	AB	R	H	2B	3B	HR	RBI	BA
1936	6	25	5	10	0	0	0	4	.400
1937	5	20	3	6	2	1	0	1	.300
1938	4	18	0	3	0	0	0	1	.167
1939	4	16	2	2	0	0	0	0	.125
1941	5	20	2	6	0	0	0	0	.300
1942	4	17	5	6	2	0	0	0	.353
6 Yrs.	28	116	17	33	4	1	0	6	.284

Life. Same.

RUFFING, RED
(BORN CHARLES HERBERT RUFFING)

Yankee: 1930-42 (military) '45-'46
Pitcher
Born: May 3, 1904
Birthplace: Granville, IL
Died: February 17, 1986
Bat: R; Throw: R
Ht: 6'2"; Wt: 205

HONORS: In 1967 Red was inducted into the Baseball Hall of Fame. He was one of two pitchers on *The Sporting News* 1937 ML All-Star team and one of three pitchers on that publication's 1938 and 1939 ML All-Star teams.

CAME TO YANKS: In May of 1930, the Yanks obtained Red from the Red Sox in exchange for Cedric Durst and $50,000. The deal is considered one of the biggest "steals" in Yankee history. But consider this: Red's ML record at the time of the trade was 39-96 and he had led the AL in losses in both 1928 (10-25) and 1929 (9-22), although he was certainly a hard-luck pitcher in Boston. Red had to be good to lose so many.

YANKEE ACE: Red's career changed completely after he joined the Yanks. With the Bronx Bombers and a great defensive team behind him, he became a great right-handed pitcher, the greatest in Yankee history. During the Yanks' string of four consecutive World Championships (1936-39), Red won at least 20 games in each season. No Yankee pitcher has ever won 20 games in a row as often. (Bob Shawkey and Lefty Gomez are the only other Yanks to win 20 games four times.) Red was a big, strong fellow with a fastball that really hummed. He was also a tremendous competitor. There were those who said that Red sometimes coasted in games, but others felt he was gifted at pacing himself, and in the late innings he was firing his best stuff. In any event, Red was pitching in a brutal era for AL pitchers, the age of the great sluggers.

SOBER CHAP: Many outsiders thought Red was a stern and cold person who did not have a sense of humor, but in reality he just had a very businesslike attitude on the mound. Off the field, Red, who was also known as Charley, was one of the guys and was involved in many of the club's practical jokes.

DYNAMITE DUO: During the 1930s, Red teamed with southpaw Lefty Gomez, forming the best and most consistent one-two punch in baseball history. Together Ruffing and Gomez won 408 games between 1930-42, averaging $31\frac{1}{3}$ wins per season for their combined win total.

ENDURANCE RECORDS: Red pitched ML baseball from 1924-47. Excepting the years 1943-44 when he was serving in the military, Red pitched 22 consecutive seasons in the ML's. Of those 22 seasons, Red spent 15 in a Yankee uniform. He pitched 200 or more innings in 13 consecutive seasons (1928-40), an AL record he shares with Eddie Plank.

GREATEST GAME: On August 7, 1938, Red had a no-hitter in progress in the ninth inning against Cleveland. But with one out, Roy Weatherly doubled to ruin the bid. Red won the game anyway, 7-0.

LOST TOES: Red was an all-round athlete. As a youngster he was a power hitter seemingly destined to become a great outfielder until the day a mining accident cost four toes on his left foot. But Red was young and he courageously overcame the handicap by turning to pitching, a position where the missing toes did not hinder him as much as a position where more running is required.

TREMENDOUS HITTER: Red may have been the best all-around hitting pitcher of all time. Red set a ML record, hitting better than .300 in eight seasons as a pitcher; six of them as a Yankee (1930, 1931, 1932, 1935, 1939, and 1941). Red led ML pitchers in hitting four times (1930, 1931, 1932, and 1941). His 98 career doubles are the most in history by a pitcher. His 273 RBIs (he also had 273 wins) is a modern ML record for a pitcher. The only pitchers to hit more HRs than Red's 36 are Wes Ferrell (38) and Bob Lemon (37). Red's lifetime slugging average (.389) ranks fourth highest in history for a pitcher and he is 19th on the pitcher's batting list (.269) in the 20th century for those with at least 500 at-bats. His slugging mark in 1930 (.582) is the third best ever for a pitcher.

PINCH-HITTER: His hitting ability helped win many games. Joe McCarthy seldom pinch-hit for Red, allowing him the chance to pick up wins in close games. Indeed, Red was a Yankee pinch-hitter 206 times, getting his 45 hits in 181 at-bats (.249) with 18 walks. His 58 career pinch-hits rank second for a pitcher. In 1935 Red led all hitters in the ML's in pinch-hitting average with a .444 mark (8-for-18). On June 5, 1937, Red delivered a pinch-hit HR. One year Red was a holdout, asking for more pay for his valuable work as a pinch-hitter.

HITTING AND PITCHING: Twice Red hit two HRs in a single game (September 18, 1930 and June 17, 1936). On August 13, 1932, Red's tenth-inning HR won his own game, 1-0! In that game Red permitted only three Washington hits and fanned ten Senators. He truly did it all in that contest and saved the Yanks'

streak of games in which they were not shutout, a streak that eventually ran to 308 games. On August 14, 1933, Red's grand-slam HR in the bottom of the ninth defeated Boston, 6-2. It was the first grand slam ever hit by a Yankee pitcher. On June 17, 1936, Red beat Cleveland, 15-4, and made four hits, including two HRs. In that game Red hit for 10 total bases, setting an AL record for a pitcher which still stands through 1999. On August 13, 1939, he blanked Philadelphia, 21-0, and led the assault with four hits.

LEAGUE LEADER: In 1932 Red led the AL in strikeouts (190). In 1938 he led the AL in wins, winning percentage (21-7, .750) and shutouts (four). In 1939, Red led the AL in shutouts (five). He fielded 1.000 in 1941, leading AL pitchers in fielding. And proving he was a three-way threat, Red tied for the lead among ML pitchers in hitting HRs in 1930 (four), 1932 (three) and 1936 (five).

CLUB LEADERSHIP: Red led Yankee pitchers in complete games eight times and wins seven times, tying for the most seasons to lead the Yanks in each category. He also led the club six times in shutouts; five times in innings pitched; four times in games started; and three times in ERA.

BASEBALL'S ALL-TIME LEADER LIST: Red ranks 28th on baseball's all-time win list (273).

ALL-TIME YANKEE LEADER: Red has won more games; pitched, started and completed more games; pitched more innings; and struck out more batters than any right-hander in Yankee history. Red ranks in the top 10 on all-time Yankee lists for many categories. He is first in complete games (261) by a wide margin; second in wins (231), games started (391), and innings pitched (3169), tied for second in shutouts (40); third in games pitched (426) and in strikeouts (1526); and tied for ninth in winning percentage for those pitchers with at least 100 Yankee decisions (.651, 231-124).

ALL-STAR GAMES: As a Yankee pitcher, Red was selected to the AL team for six All-Star Games. He started the All-Star Games in 1939 and 1940.

WORLD SERIES: Red was a clutch pitcher in the World Series. He is among the lifetime leaders in most Series pitching statistics. He is tied for second in wins (seven). Red consistently got the Yanks off to good Series starts. He started the opening game of a Series six times and he won five of them (1932, '38, '39, '41, '42). Red also won the final game of the 1938 Series. In Game 1 of the 1932 Series he pitched a complete-game victory. In Game 2 of the 1937 Series he beat the Giants, 8-1, and helped himself with three RBIs. Red won two games in the 1938 Series, allowing only four runs in 18 innings, as he led the Yanks to a four-game sweep of the Cubs. Red won Game 1 of the 1939 Series against the Reds, 2-1, by pitching a masterful four-hitter. He held the Dodgers to six hits in Game 1 of the 1941 Series, winning 3-2. His victory over the Cardinals in Game 1 of the 1942 Series was the only Yankee win of that Fall Classic.

END OF ML CAREER: In December, 1942, Red was inducted into the U.S. Army Air Corps and missed the 1943 and 1944 baseball seasons. In July of 1945, Red came back from the service at the age of 41. He was used sparingly in 1946, although his ERA was a brilliant 1.77. Because Red had bad memories of his flights in the Army Air Corps, he was one of several Yankees who would not take team flights in 1946 and Joe McCarthy allowed him to arrange his own transportation. In late September, 1946, the Yanks released Red. The White Sox signed Red in December of 1946 and Red, at age 43, went 3-5 for Chicago in the 1947 season. Red was a coach for the Mets during their inaugural 1962 season.

RUFFING, RED

Yr.	W-L	Pct.	SA	G	GS	CG	IP	H	BB	SO	SH	ERA
1930	15-5	.750	1	34	25	12	198	200	62	117	2	4.14
1931	16-14	.533	2	37	30	19	237	240	87	132	1	4.41
1932	18-7	.720	2	35	29	22	259	219	115	190	3	3.09
1933	9-14	.391	3	35	28	18	235	230	93	122	0	3.91
1934	19-11	.633	0	36	31	19	256	232	104	149	5	3.93
1935	16-11	.593	0	30	29	19	222	201	76	81	2	3.12
1936	20-12	.625	0	33	33	25	271	274	90	102	3	3.85
1937	20-7	.741	0	31	31	22	256	242	68	131	5	2.98
1938	21-7	.750	0	31	31	22	247	246	82	127	3	3.31
1939	21-7	.750	0	28	28	22	233	211	75	95	4	2.93
1940	15-12	.556	0	30	30	20	226	218	76	97	3	3.38
1941	15-6	.714	0	23	23	13	186	177	54	60	2	3.54
1942	14-7	.667	0	24	24	16	194	183	41	80	4	3.21
1945	7-3	.700	0	11	11	8	87	85	20	24	1	2.89
1946	5-1	.833	0	8	8	4	61	37	23	19	2	1.77
15 Yrs.	231-124	.651	8	426	391	261	3169	2995	1066	1526	40	3.47
Life.	273-225	.548	16	624	536	335	4344	4284	1541	1987	45	3.80

World Series

Yr.	G	IP	BB	SO	H	W-L	SA
1932	1	9	6	10	10	1-0	0
1936	2	14	5	12	16	0-1	0
1937	1	9	3	8	7	1-0	0
1938	2	18	2	11	17	2-0	0
1939	1	9	1	4	4	1-0	0
1941	1	9	3	5	6	1-0	0
1942	2	17⅔	7	11	14	1-1	0
7 Yrs.	10	85⅔	27	61	74	7-2	0
Life. Same.							

RUSSELL, ALLAN

Nickname: "Rubberarm"
Yankee: 1915-19
Pitcher
Born: July 31, 1893
Birthplace: Baltimore, MD
Died: October 20, 1972
Bat: R; Throw: R
Ht: 5'11"; Wt: 165

CAME TO YANKS: In August of 1915, the Yanks bought Allan's contract from Jersey City of the International League.

STARTER AND RELIEVER: The Yanks used Allan as both a starting and relief pitcher. Half of his Yankee games were in each category. He was the Yanks' fifth starter in 1916. In 1917 Allan led the Yanks in saves (two). He was the Yanks' fourth starter in 1918. Al's brother Lefty pitched for the A's from 1910-12.

SPITBALL PITCHER: Allan threw a legal spitball. In 1920 the spitball was banned, but the 17 ML pitchers who threw one were allowed to continue using it until they retired.

TRADED: In July of 1919, the Yanks sent Allan, pitcher Bob McGraw and $40,000 to the Red Sox for star pitcher Carl Mays.

RUSSELL, ALLAN

Yr.	W-L	Pct.	SA	G	GS	CG	IP	H	BB	SO	SH	ERA
1915	1-2	.333	0	5	3	1	27	21	21	21	0	2.67
1916	6-10	.375	6	34	18	8	171	138	75	104	1	3.20
1917	7-8	.467	2	25	10	6	104	89	39	55	0	2.24
1918	7-11	.389	4	27	18	7	141	139	73	54	2	3.26
1919	5-5	.500	1	23	9	4	91	89	32	50	1	3.47
5 Yrs.	26-36	.419	13	114	58	26	534	476	240	284	4	3.05
Life.	70-76	.479	42	345	110	54	1394	1382	610	603	5	3.52

RUSSO, MARIUS

Nicknames: "Lefty" "Red "
Yankee: 1939-43 (military) '46
Pitcher
Born: July 19, 1914
Birthplace: Brooklyn, NY
Bat: L; Throw: L
Ht: 6'1"; Wt: 190

HONORS: Marius was selected to the AL All-Star team for the 1941 All-Star Game.

YOUNG STAR PITCHER: Marius played his entire ML career with the Yanks. As a 25-year-old rookie in 1939, he began his ML career very impressively (8-3, 2.41 ERA). During the combined 1940-41 seasons, only Red Ruffing won more Yankee games than Marius (28 wins). In 1941 Marius was probably the Yanks' most effective pitcher. A sore arm ruined his 1942 season. Then he missed the 1944-45 seasons while serving in the military. Marius returned to the Yanks in 1946 and completed his ML career.

PENNANT CLINCHER: On September 16, 1939, his win clinched the Yanks' fourth consecutive AL pennant.

GREATEST GAME: On June 26, 1941, George McQuinn's seventh-inning HR was the only St. Louis Brown hit off Marius in a game that Marius won, 4-1.

CLUB LEADERSHIP: In 1939 Marius led the Yanks in ERA (2.41). In 1941 he led the Yanks in innings pitched (210), games started (27), complete games (17) and strikeouts (105).

WORLD SERIES: Marius won critical Game 3 of the 1941 Series, pitching a complete game four-hitter to beat Brooklyn, 2-1. In Game 4 of the 1943 Series, he pitched a complete game, defeating the Cardinals, 2-1. Marius scored the winning run after doubling.

RUSSO, MARIUS

Yr.	W-L	Pct.	SA	G	GS	CG	IP	H	BB	SO	SH	ERA
1939	8-3	.727	2	21	11	9	116	86	41	55	2	2.41
1940	14-8	.636	1	30	24	15	189	181	55	87	0	3.28
1941	14-10	.583	1	28	27	17	210	195	87	105	3	3.09
1942	4-1	.800	0	9	5	2	45	41	14	15	0	2.78
1943	5-10	.333	1	24	14	5	102	89	45	42	1	3.72
1946	0-2	.000	0	8	3	0	19	26	11	7	0	4.34
6 Yrs.	45-34	.570	5	120	84	48	681	618	253	311	6	3.13
Life. Same.												

World Series

Yr.	G	IP	BB	SO	H	W-L	SA
1941	1	9	2	5	4	1-0	0
1943	1	9	1	2	7	1-0	0
2 Yrs.	2	18	3	7	11	2-0	0

RUTH, BABE
(BORN GEORGE HERMAN RUTH)

Nicknames: "The Sultan of Swat", "The Bambino", "Jidge"
(also "The Colossus of Clout")
Yankee: 1920-34
Outfielder, 1B, P
Born: February 6, 1895
Birthplace: Baltimore, MD
Died: August 16, 1948
Bat: L; Throw: L
Ht: 6'2"; Wt: 215

HONORS: Babe is one of the five charter members of the Baseball Hall of Fame. (The Hall opened in 1936.) He won the League Award (the AL's MVP) in 1923. He was an outfielder selection in the first six seasons that *The Sporting News* picked a ML All-Star team (1926-31). The Baseball Writers gave Babe the William J. Slocum Award in 1931. He was selected to the AL All-Star team for the first and second All-Star Games in 1933 and 1934. In balloting conducted by baseball, Babe was named baseball's "Greatest Player Ever" in 1969. In a nationwide poll celebrating the Bicentennial year of 1976, Babe was voted baseball's "Most Memorable Personality."

CAME TO YANKS: Late in 1919 Red Sox owner Harry Frazee, in need of cash, let Jacob Ruppert and Til Huston know that Ruth's contract might be for sale. The Yankee owners wanted Babe desperately and on December 26, 1919, the most important date in Yankee history, Babe Ruth became a Yankee, the Red Sox receiving $125,000, a $300,000 loan against a mortgage on Fenway Park and other considerations. (The deal was actually announced on Jan. 3, 1920.)

RUTH'S IMPACT ON BASEBALL: Whether he was the greatest baseball player ever is a matter of continuing debate. But there is no question that Babe had the greatest impact on the game. He personally saved professional baseball (with an assist from Commissioner Landis) after the devastating Black Sox scandal of 1919. The excitement Babe generated kept people interested in the positive side of big-league baseball. Of course, it was largely because of Babe that the Yanks became the most successful and famous team in history. By hitting HRs by the score, he dramatically changed the game of baseball, transforming it to the power game we know today. Babe was more than a great baseball player. He was the most well-known man in American society for 30 years. But to the American sports-loving community, he was the most esteemed of athletic heroes. It was because of his presence, his "draw," that the Yanks were able to build Yankee Stadium. Many people wanted the Stadium, which opened in 1923, to be named after Ruth but the attribution, "The House That Ruth Built" was recognition enough. Certainly a piece of the Stadium bore his name; the right field stands were called "Ruthville" during Babe's tenure. Babe's Yankee salaries were commensurate with his importance to the game and to the Yankees, climbing to a peak of $80,000 in 1930—in those days a fortune! Babe made $70,000 in 1927 when the average Yankee salary was $11,000. All players' salaries improved because of Babe.

HOME RUNS: Babe brought the HR and the HR swing to baseball. The 54 HRs he hit in 1920 broke—by 25—the ML record (29) which he set just the year before. He set a new HR record four times, capping off the power climb with 60 in 1927. Babe hit 50 or more HRs in four seasons (tied by Mark McGuire in 1999) and 40 or more in 11 seasons, the latter an achievement that remains unmatched. In just two seasons, (1927, '28) he hit an incredible 114 HRs. In each of 11 seasons, Babe hit a HR in every park in the AL (one of those seasons as a Red Sox player). Seventy-two times in his career (including Red Sox and Brave action) Babe hit two or more HRs in one game, a ML record. In June, 1930, he hit 15 HRs, the most ever hit in that month in the ML's. In September, 1927, he hit 17 HRs, the most ever hit in that month in ML history. Babe hit 32 HRs on the road in 1927, a ML record. In his career he hit 16 extra-inning HRs, an AL record. Babe cracked 32 HRs at the Polo Grounds in 1921, the most ever hit by a Yankee player at the club's home park. Appropriately, Babe hit the first HR ever hit in Yankee Stadium, "The House That Ruth Built." In 1933 he hit the first HR in All-Star Game history. On seven different occasions Babe hit three HRs in a doubleheader. Twice he hit three HRs in a regular-season contest. He hit 259 Yankee Stadium HRs. Only Mickey Mantle has hit more there, and Mickey played 18 years at the Stadium while Babe played only 12. After Babe hit his 700th HR on July 13, 1934, *The New York Times* had a headline reading "Ruth's Record of 700 Home Runs Likely to Stand for All Time in Major Leagues." When Babe retired with 714 HRs, he had more than twice the number of his closest rival. Babe was the oldest HR king in AL history in 1931. When the season ended he was 36 years and 231 days old. Babe hit some of the longest HRs on record and his blasts were always a wondrous sight.

SLUGGING RECORDS: Babe's slugging averages of 1920 (.847), 1921 (.846) and 1927 (.772) are the three highest slugging averages in baseball history! Babe had at least a .600 slugging average in 13 seasons (1919-24, '26-32), the most times in ML history. He had at least a .700 slugging average in nine seasons (1920-21, '23-24, '26-28, '30-31), another ML record. Babe is the only man in ML history to ever produce a .800 slugging mark, and he did it twice (1920-21).

SINGLE-SEASON RECORDS: The most famous record in sports, Babe's 60 HRs in 1927, stood until 1961 when Roger Maris walloped 61. But Babe retains other single-season records. In 1921 Babe scored 177 runs, the most in ML baseball in the 20th century. (Billy Hamilton scored 192 runs in 1894.) Babe's 170 walks in 1923 is the undisputed ML record. That season Babe reached base 379 times, more times than anyone in ML history, and he had the unheard of on-base percentage of .542! In 1921 he registered 457 total bases, clouting 119 extra-base hits, both ML records. His HR percentage of 1920 (11.8 times per 100 at-bats) is the highest in ML history. His .847 slugging average of 1920 is a ML record with plenty to spare. In 1921, Ruth almost equalled his 1920 slugging mark, this time .846! The best consecutive seasons in history!

CONSISTENCY: Not just a power hitter enjoying a few spectacular years, Babe was great throughout his career, with the exception of 1925 when he was hampered by illness. He and Lou Gehrig are the only men in ML history to reach 150 RBIs in three

The patented upper-cut swing of the great Babe Ruth.

consecutive seasons. (Babe did it from 1929-31.) In six different seasons Babe scored more than 150 runs (1920, '21, '23, '27, '28, '30). No one in baseball history has equalled that record. His HR records also are a mark of consistency. Babe was not only a man who smashed a baseball a country mile—he also made hits consistently, and considering the many walks given up by terrified pitchers, that is an accomplishment! His .393 batting average in 1923 is the highest mark in Yankee history. Four times he led the Yanks in hits and he had 200 or more hits in three seasons.

SUPER HOT STREAKS: For all his consistency, Babe had his streaks, and when he was hot, no pitcher in the world could stop him. From June 10-14, 1921, Babe hit seven HRs in five straight games, an AL record. From August 28—September 5, 1921, he hit at least one extra-base hit in nine consecutive games, an AL record. In September, 1927, and again in August, 1929, he hit grand slam HRs in consecutive games. During an 11-game streak of the 1931 season, he got at least one RBI per game in 11 straight games, setting a Yankee club record. From May 18-24, 1930, Babe hit nine HRs in one week!

LEAGUE LEADER: Babe led the AL in HRs a dozen times (10 seasons as a Yankee), a ML record. As a Yankee player, he led the AL in walks 11 times, a ML record. Over 13 seasons (11 as a Yankee), he led the AL in slugging, by far more often than any other player. He also led the AL in slugging seven years in a row (1918-24), another AL record. In eight seasons (seven as a Yankee), Babe led the AL in runs scored, a ML record. He also shares the record for most consecutive years leading the AL in runs scored (three) (from 1919-21 and again 1926-28). In six seasons (five as a Yankee), Babe was his league's RBI champ, still another ML record. He led the AL in extra-base hits four straight years (1918-21), an AL record. He led the AL in total bases in 1921, 1923, 1924, 1926 and 1928. As a Yankee player, Babe led the AL in HR percentage 11 times (every year from 1920-31 except 1925). In 1924 Babe won his only batting championship when he hit .378.

CLUB LEADERSHIP: He was first among his teammates in numerous offensive categories through the years, but in two categories he was particularly outstanding—in HRs and slugging. He was the club leader in these categories in 13 seasons, more often than anyone else in Yankee history.

DEFENSIVE ABILITIES: Babe was a fine defensive outfielder, possessing a strong and accurate throwing arm. He played right field for the Yanks except in 1921 and 1922 when he was the leftfielder. (He also played 14 Yankee games at first base.) He made many great catches in the Yankee Stadium outfield and covered a lot of ground (before he became overweight). In 1923 he made 378 putouts, setting a Yankee rightfielders' record. He was also a durable outfielder, playing in every Yankee game in 1923, 1924 and 1928.

BASE RUNNER: Babe was an intelligent, daring base runner. He had good speed, especially before he became overweight late in his career. Three times he led the Yanks in stolen bases and twice he stole 17 bases in a season. One of the few base-running mistakes he ever made came in Game 7 of the 1926 World Series when he tried to steal second base in the bottom of the ninth inning with the Yanks trailing the Cardinals, 3-2.

Babe was thrown out to end the Series. It was not a smart play, but the story serves to indicate the daring Babe used on the base paths. (He was not a station-to-station base runner.)

GETTING ON BASE: Only Ted Williams has a higher lifetime on-base average than Babe's .474. Babe led the AL in OBA ten times. He has five of the best 11 single-season OBA's. His .545 in 1923 ranks third; .530 in 1920, fourth; .516 in 1926, eighth; .513 in 1924, tenth; and .512 in 1921, 11th.

YANKEE PITCHER: When Babe pitched for the Red Sox, he was probably the best lefthander in the AL. Babe pitched in only five games as a Yankee. His record: 5-0! On September 28, 1930, after not having pitched in nine years, Babe pitched a complete game and beat the Red Sox, 9-3! On October 1, 1933, he pitched and beat Boston, 6-5. He also hit the game-winning HR!

MAGNETIC PERSONALITY: Because of his colorful, magnetic personality, Babe was the center of attention wherever he went throughout his life, and naturally he thrived in New York City. He was loved by the fans, press, his teammates—by all who knew him. The stories of Babe's exploits and adventures on and off the field number in the hundreds. One thing is for sure, he lived life to the fullest. His Yankee teammates were fond of him and held him in awe, not only for his baseball ability but for the force and color of his personality. Through the years, Joe Dugan, Waite Hoyt, and Whitey Witt were especially close to Babe, but almost all his teammates were his friends. Babe was a lovable character in spite of his inclination to be stubborn and selfish. He loved kids and would do anything to help them. Shortly before his death, Babe established the Babe Ruth Foundation Inc., set up to provide funds for the education (mental and physical) of needy boys. He never forgot his own bleak childhood. Babe was dynamic and graphic; he was fun-loving and unpredictable, and the public loved it. He once hit three consecutive HRs in a game (May 22, 1930). When he came to bat for the fourth time in that game, the fans were amazed and delighted to see him batting right-handed! He went down on strikes.

GEHRIG FEUD: Because Babe always had to have his own way, he was embroiled in controversies. Perhaps his saddest feud was the one he had with Lou Gehrig. Babe was close to Lou (they were bridge partners, fishing chums, devotees of the cooking of Mom Gehrig, and barnstorming buddies) until their well-publicized quarrel late in Babe's career. The families of both men were involved in the unfortunate situation that apparently stemmed from a comment made by Lou's mother and which melted away years later, on "Lou Gehrig Day" at Yankee Stadium, when Babe impulsively threw his arms around Lou. The warm embrace was captured in one of the most famous photographs in sports journalism.

BUCKING THE SYSTEM: Babe could be stubborn and belligerent and was disdainful of authority. After the 1921 World Series, he organized and headed a group of ballplayers to barnstorm the country. Commissioner Landis warned Babe that the trip would be in violation of ML rules (World Series players were not allowed to barnstorm after the Series), but Babe made his tour anyway. Landis responded by suspending Babe for the first six weeks of the 1922 campaign. (Yankee star Bob Meusel

Locker Room Talk—Following Old Timers' Day ceremonies at Yankee Stadium, Babe's locker was shipped to the Baseball Hall of Fame. Babe (right) shows his old locker to former teammates, Bob Meusel (left) and Mark Koenig. (New York Yankees Archives)

Hero Chores—Babe Ruth dutifully performing the chores required of America's greatest sports hero. Photo taken around 1927. (New York Yankees Archives)

was also suspended.) When Babe finally joined the team in late spring, he was again suspended, this time for throwing dirt at an umpire. He was also suspended in 1922 for chasing a fan through the Polo Grounds (the Bambino lost his Yankee captaincy for this one). The Babe in 1922 also found time to have a dugout fight with Wally Pipp and to have a picture taken in a speakeasy (for which he was fined). All in all, it was not an uneventful year for Babe.

RELATIONSHIP WITH MILLER HUGGINS: Through the years, Babe had some legendary battles with Yankee Manager Miller Huggins. Huggins liked Ruth and appreciated his enormous importance to the Yanks. What Huggins did not appreciate was Babe's endless night life. Late in the 1925 season (the year the Babe was bothered by illness, a stomach disorder), Huggins suspended Babe indefinitely for insubordination. The irate Ruth, who was also fined $5,000, went over Huggins' head, but GM Ed Barrow and owner Jake Ruppert supported Huggins and Babe was forced to make peace with his tiny manager. Once he realized he did not run the Yanks, his relationship with Huggins became more harmonious. The two men respected and liked each other. When Huggins died suddenly in 1929, Babe was deeply sorrowed.

RELATIONSHIP WITH JOE McCARTHY: Babe was not so affectionate toward Joe McCarthy, his Yankee manager from 1931-34. McCarthy's assignment to the Yankee helm upset him because he felt the job should have been his. The resentful Babe frequently belittled McCarthy during their time together, although he was most gracious in his praise of McCarthy when the Yanks won the 1932 World Series. Babe always wanted to be Yankee manager. He was well liked by Jake Ruppert. The Yankee owner and the Babe got along well. However, to Ruppert and Barrow, Babe appeared too undisciplined to be manager.

TEAM PLAYER: His run-ins did not owe to petulance. To the contrary, his feuds with Gehrig, Landis, Huggins, and McCarthy reflected his spirited and emphatic personality. In time, Babe resolved almost all his misunderstandings, except perhaps with McCarthy. When he was wrong, he knew it; he could be big-spirited, and usually he would make amends. The fact is that Babe was a tremendous team player whose first objective was to bring to the Yankees AL pennants and World Championships. Babe was the Yanks' leader and he was a smart, team-minded player. He had only two seasons, 1922 and 1925, when his life style, for all of its extravagance, hurt the club. In all other seasons, Babe delivered a home run or a bunt, whatever helped the team.

BASEBALL'S ALL-TIME LEADER LIST: Babe is ranked first on baseball's all-time slugging (.690) and walk (2056) lists. He is second on the all-time HR (714), RBI (2213) and runs scored (2174) lists. He is third on the extra-base hit list (1356). He is fifth in total bases (5793). His lifetime batting mark (.342) ties him for eighth highest in baseball history. His career HR ratio (8.5 HRs per 100 at-bats) is easily the best in ML history, even surpassing Mark McGwire's and Barry Bonds's recent home run rampage.

ALL-TIME YANKEE LEADER: Babe ranks first on the all-time Yankee HR (659), runs scored (1959), walk (1847), total bases (5131), batting (.349) and slugging (.711) lists. He is second on the all-time Yankee RBI (1971), hits (2518) and third on the double (424) lists. He is fourth on both the club's games played (2084) and at-bat (7217) lists. He is sixth on the team's triple list (106).

WORLD SERIES: Babe was spectacular in his seven Yankee World Series, four of which were won by the Yanks. His HR ratio (11.6 HRs per 100 at-bats) is the highest in Series history. Babe is second on the all-time Series HR (15), walk (33) and slugging (.744) lists, besides being a leader in most other offensive categories. In Game 4 of the 1921 Series, Babe hit the first HR by a Yankee in Series history. Babe hit his blast off the Giants' Paul Douglas at the Polo Grounds. In Game 2 of the 1923 Series, Babe hit two monstrous HRs leading the Yanks to a 4-2 victory and evening the Series with the Giants. It was also a "must win" for the Yanks who had trailed 1-0 in games after losing the Series to the Giants in 1921 and 1922. Babe became the first player to hit three HRs in a Series game, this feat accomplished in Game 4 of the 1926 Series against the St. Louis Cardinals. In that Series he led both clubs in HRs (four), runs scored (six),

walks (11—a Series record), and stole the only base for the Yanks. In Game 7 he walked four times. After hitting a three-run HR to help the Yanks win Game 3 of the 1927 Series, "The Sultan of Swat" belted a two-run blast in Game 4 to lead the Yanks to a sweep of the Pirates. His batting average in the 1928 Series (.625) is the second highest in Series history, and his 22 total bases is a four-game Series record. In Game 4 of the Series Babe hit three HRs for the second time in Series history, leading the Yanks to a Series sweep of the Cardinals. In Game 3 of the 1932 Series he pulled the most dramatic stunt of his career, hitting his famous "called shot" HR off the Cubs' Charlie Root. (Babe hit two HRs in the game.) Between the 1927-32 Series Babe scored a run in nine consecutive games, a Series record. Babe hit better than .300 in six Series, another Series record.

END OF CAREER: As his playing career waned, Babe pleaded to become Yankee manager. But Ruppert and GM Barrow refused to give him the job, and it became obvious that the 1934 season would be Babe's last as a Yankee player. He was 39 years old and the speed had left his legs and bat. On September 24, 1934, he played his final game at Yankee Stadium. He walked in the first inning and was replaced by a pinch-runner. On September 30, 1934, while on the road, Babe played his last game as a Yankee. He went 0-for-3 and walked. After the 1934 season, he demanded to be made Yankee manager. The club continued to turn him away, and when Babe was presented with an opportunity by the Boston Braves, the Yanks did not stand in his way. The Yankees and the Babe parted on reasonably amicable terms. He was given his unconditional release to sign with the Braves as a player, coach and club vice president. (Babe was sure that a managing job was to follow.) But he did not find the job to his liking and he retired in June, 1935. A ML managing job was never offered him.

FINAL YEARS: For part of the 1938 season Babe was a coach with the Brooklyn Dodgers. That was his last official connection with baseball. During his retirement, Babe saw many games at Yankee Stadium and even suited up a few times. On August 23, 1942, Babe put on the Yankee uniform for a War Bonds benefit exhibition before the regular game. Before 69,000 fans at Yankee Stadium he faced the great Walter Johnson. Babe hit the first and 21st pitch Johnson threw into the right-field stands. With the second blast, the Babe showed the Stadium fans for the final time his distinctive home run trot. On April 27, 1947, "Babe Ruth Day" ceremonies were held at Yankee Stadium, and Babe gave a short speech to an adoring throng of 60,000. He was very sick with throat cancer. On June 13, 1948, Babe made his last Yankee Stadium appearance at the Yanks' Old Timers' Game. His illness made it difficult to take part in the festivities, but he was pleased to see old friends. Also, the Yanks finally retired Babe's uniform Number "3." Babe died of throat cancer on August 16, 1948. His body lay in state for 1½ days at Yankee Stadium and more than 100,000 people paid their last respects. More than 6,500 jammed into St. Patrick's Cathedral in New York for the funeral. Cardinal Spellman celebrated the mass. Waite Hoyt, Joe Dugan, Whitey Witt, Connie Mack, and sportswriter Fred Lieb were pallbearers. It was a hot day and Joe Dugan turned to Waite Hoyt and remarked, "I'd give my right arm for a beer, it's that hot." Hoyt answered, "So would the Babe." Babe is buried in Mount Pleasant, N.Y.

BABE RUTH'S BEST TOTALS:

Games—154 (1928)	HRs—60 (1927)
At-Bats—540 (1921,'27)	RBIs—170 (1921)
Runs—177 (1921)*	SBs—17(1921, 23)
Hits—205 (1923)	Walks—170 (1923)*
Doubles—45 (1923)	BA—.393 (1923)†
Triples—16 (1921)	SA—.847 (1920)*

* ML record
† Yankee record

BABE'S 60 HRs—1927

Date	No.	Pitcher	At
April 15	1	Ehmke, Phil	Yankee Stadium
April 23	2	Walberg, Phil	Philadelphia
April 24	3	Thurston, Wash	Washington
April 29	4	Harriss, Bos	Boston
May 1	5	Quinn, Phil	Yankee Stadium
	6	Walberg, Phil	
May 10	7	Gaston, St L	St. Louis
May 11	8	Nevers, St L	St. Louis
May 17	9	Collins, Det	Detroit
May 22	10	Karr, Cleve	Cleveland
May 23	11	Thurston, Wash	Washington
May 28	12	Thurston, Wash	Yankee Stadium
May 29	13	MacFayden, Bos	Yankee Stadium
May 30	14	Walberg, Phil	Philadelphia
May 31	15	Quinn, Phil	Philadelphia
	16	Ehmke, Phil	
June 5	17	Whitehill, Det	Yankee Stadium
June 7	18	Thomas, Chi	Yankee Stadium
June 11	19	Buckeye, Cleve	Yankee Stadium
	20	Buckeye, Cleve	
June 12	21	Uhle, Cleve	Yankee Stadium
June 16	22	Zachary, St L	Yankee Stadium
June 22	23	Wiltse, Bos	Boston
	24	Wiltse, Bos	
June 30	25	Harriss, Bos	Yankee Stadium
July 3	26	Lisenbee, Wash	Washington
July 8	27	Hankins, Det	Detroit
July 9	28	Holloway, Det	Detroit
	29	Holloway, Det	
July 12	30	Shaute, Cleve	Cleveland
July 24	31	Thomas, Chi	Chicago
July 26	32	Gaston, St L	Yankee Stadium
	33	Gaston, St L	
July 28	34	Stewart, St L	Yankee Stadium
Aug. 5	35	G. Smith, Det	Yankee Stadium
Aug. 10	36	Zachary, Wash	Washington
Aug. 16	37	Thomas, Chi	Chicago
Aug. 17	38	Connally, Chi	Chicago
Aug. 20	39	Miller, Cleve	Cleveland
Aug. 22	40	Shaute, Cleve	Cleveland
Aug. 27	41	Nevers, St L	St. Louis
Aug. 28	42	Wingard, St L	St. Louis
Aug. 31	43	Welzer, Bos	Yankee Stadium
Sept. 2	44	Walberg, Phil	Philadelphia
Sept. 6	45	Welzer, Bos	Boston
	46	Welzer, Bos	
	47	Russell, Bos	
Sept. 7	48	MacFayden, Bos	Boston
	49	Harriss, Bos.	
Sept. 11	50	Gaston, St. L.	Yankee Stadium

Date	No.	Pitcher	At
Sept. 13	51	Hudlin, Cleve.	Yankee Stadium
	52	Shaute, Cleve.	
Sept. 16	53	Blankenship, Chi.	Yankee Stadium
Sept. 18	54	Lyons, Chi.	Yankee Stadium
Sept. 21	55	Gibson, Det.	Yankee Stadium
Sept. 22	56	Holloway, Det.	Yankee Stadium
Sept. 27	57	Grove, Phil.	Yankee Stadium
Sept. 29	58	Lisenbee, Wash.	Yankee Stadium
	59	Hopkins, Wash.	
Sept. 30	60	Zachary, Wash.	Yankee Stadium

HRs BY MONTHS:

April	—	4
May	—	12
June	—	9
July	—	9
August	—	9
September	—	17

WHERE HIT:

Yankee Stadium	— 28
Boston	— 8
Philadelphia	— 5
Cleveland	— 4
Detroit	— 4
St. Louis	— 4
Washington	— 4
Chicago	— 3

PITCHERS BABE HIT HARD:

Walberg, Philadelphia — 4 HRs
Gaston, St. Louis — 4 HRs
Harriss, Boston — 3 HRs
Welzer, Boston — 3 HRs
Zachary, St. Louis/Washington — 3 HRs
Thurston, Washington — 3 HRs
Holloway, Detroit — 3 HRs
Thomas, Chicago — 3 HRs
Shaute, Cleveland — 3 HRs

NUMBER OF HOME RUNS HIT AGAINST EACH AL TEAM:

Boston	11
Cleveland	9
Philadelphia	9
St. Louis	9
Detroit	8
Washington	8
Chicago	6

A BABE RUTH CHART

Babe's Parents' Business: Saloon Keepers in Baltimore, MD.
Orphanage Where Babe Was Placed As a Boy: St. Mary's Industrial School for Boys, Baltimore, MD. (Babe had both parents, but was termed "incorrigible.")
Where Babe Was Discovered As a Baseball Pitcher: Mount St. Mary's College, Emmitsburg, MD. (Jack Dunn, owner of the Baltimore Orioles, learned of an outstanding young pitcher named George Herman Ruth who pitched impressively at an exhibition at the college. A Joe Engle told Dunn about him.)

Babe's Professional Baseball Career Before Joining Yankees in 1920: 1914-Pitched for Baltimore and Providence of the International League (combined record: 22-9). Late 1914-1919—Pitched and played outfield for the Boston Red Sox.

When and Why He Was Given the Name "Babe": Spring training, 1914. The Oriole players began calling Ruth "Dunn's Babe" because of his youth and early publicity. The name stuck.

Sold from Baltimore to the Red Sox: Babe, Ernie Shore, and Ben Egan were sold to Boston for $25,000 in 1914.

Early Nicknames Given Babe in Boston: "The Mauler," "The Mightiest Slugger of Them All," "Tarzan."

Name Yankee Players Called Babe: "Jidge" (a form of George first used by Joe Dugan).

Babe and Lou Gehrig Were Known in the Yankee Line-Up As: "The Home Run Twins."

Babe Addressed Most People This Way: "Hey, kid!"

Babe's Two Wives: He married Helen Woodford on October 17, 1914. He married Claire Merritt Hodgson on April 17, 1929.

Favorite Hobbies of the Babe: Golf, Hunting, and Fishing.

Longest Golf Drive Reportedly Hit by Babe: A 340-yard drive hit in Los Angeles in 1919.

Babe's Most Famous Food and Drink: Hot dogs and beer.

Possibly Babe's Biggest Meal Ever (unofficially): An omelet made of 18 eggs, three big slices of ham, six slices of buttered toast, and four cups of coffee.

Babe's Mouth Was Always Busy With Such Things as: Food, drink, chewing gum, a cigar, and a pipe.

Some of Babe's Baseball Superstitions: He carried a silver dollar as a good-luck charm. He used a favorite hotel door on good days but would switch his door entrance on bad days. The sight of a butterfly meant luck to him. He had several others.

Babe Was a Bilingual Speaker: He was fluent in German, besides English.

Babe's Religion: He became a Catholic at St. Mary's.

The Most Famous Speeding Ticket Given Babe: One he got on June 8, 1921, for speeding on Riverside Drive, New York City. Babe was fined $100 and sentenced to a day in jail.

The Babe's Cure for the Common Cold: Gnaw on an onion.

Babe's Way to Keep Cool During a Hot Day Game: Putting wet cabbage leaves under the baseball cap.

Babe's Best Business Deals: Investments in annuities and insurance.

Babe's Worst Business Deals: A clothing store on Broadway which closed after six months (Babe Ruth's for Men). His Babe Ruth's Home Run Candy was forced out of business because the name was too similar to that of the Baby Ruth candy bar.

The Record for Most League Suspensions in a Year Held by Babe: five suspensions in 1922.

The Shortest Term as Yankee Captain Held by Babe: six games in 1922.

Babe's Most Celebrated Feuds Were With: Commissioner Landis, Miller Huggins, and Lou Gehrig.

Babe's Most Famous Snub: In 1928 he refused to have his picture taken with Herbert Hoover, because Babe was supporting Al Smith for President. (Later, a photo was taken of Hoover and Babe together to appease Republicans.)

Babe's Agent, Ghostwriter and One of His Closest Friends: Christy Walsh (a sports cartoonist).

Famous Ghostwriters of the Babe: Christy Walsh, William J. Slocum, Ford Frick, and Westbrook Pegler.

Babe's Yankee Roommates: Ping Bodie, Bob Meusel, and Jimmie Reese.

Man Who Has Roomed With Both Babe and Frankie Frisch: Jimmie Reese.

Pitcher Who Gave Babe the Most Legendary Trouble: Hub Pruett. Babe struck out 13 of his first 21 at-bats against Pruett.

Only Pitcher to Ever Pitch to Both Babe and Mickey Mantle: Al Benton.

Pitcher Who Gave Up the Most Babe Ruth Home Runs: Rube Walberg. Babe hit 17 lifetime HRs against Walberg.

Only Person to Ever Pinch-Hit for Babe on the Yankees: Bobby Veach in 1925. (Veach flied out.)

Player Babe Copied His Batting Style and Swing from: Shoeless Joe Jackson, one of the game's greatest natural hitters.

Names of the Bats Babe Used in 1927: "Black Betsy" used to hit HR No. 59, "Beautiful Bella" used to hit No. 60, and "Big Bertha."

Heaviest Bat Babe Used: 54 ounces. That is supposedly the heaviest bat EVER used by anyone.

Usual Weight of a Babe Ruth Bat: 44 ounces.

Most Bats Used by Babe in a Season: Reportedly, he used 170 bats one season. Babe gave away many to fans.

Babe's Poor Lifetime Pinch-Hit Record: 13 for 67 (.194).

Biggest Baseball Boast Made by Babe: Babe once stated, "I could have hit a .600 lifetime average easy. But I would have had to hit them singles. The people were paying to see me hit them home runs."

Yankee Rightfielder That Babe Replaced in 1920: Sammy Vick. (A popular myth that George Halas, the famous football coach, was replaced by Babe is not true. Halas played only six games in the Yankee outfield in 1919.)

Most Imaginative Defensive Play Made by Babe: In a late 1920s game at Detroit's Navin Field, Babe chased a long fly to the outfield wall and pretended it was going over for a HR. The runner on second base, Charlie Gehringer, started trotting home, but Babe caught the ball and threw to second to double-up Gehringer.

Most Consistent Habit of Babe's at the Plate: Babe knocked dirt out of his spikes after every strike.

Smallest Bet Won by Babe on Most Famous Event: Babe won a mere $10 from Tony Lazzeri after hitting his 60th HR in 1927.

Yankee Players That Babe Disliked: Very few, if any. But it was known that Babe shied away from Carl Mays and Leo Durocher.

Babe's Yankee Uniform Number: He wore "3" because he batted third in the Yankee lineup (1929-34).

People who wore Uniform Number "3" on the Yankees after Babe: George Selkirk, Allie Clark, Bud Metheny, Cliff Mapes, and Ducky Medwick (in spring training). The Yanks finally retired Number "3" in 1948.

Special prayers given for Babe on "Babe Ruth Day" at Yankee Stadium in 1947: Francis Cardinal Spellman gave a special prayer. Mel Allen was the announcer. Babe gave a short speech.

Most Famous Face of the Roaring '20s: Babe Ruth's "moon face."

People Who Could Get Babe To Do Anything: Photographers.

Group of People whom Babe Loved the Most: Kids. Babe would do anything for them. He visited them all the time.

Babe's Most Crowd-Pleasing Performance With a Kid: In 1920 at the Polo Grounds, a kid came on the field to snap Babe's photo. Babe took the camera, handed it to a teammate, put his arm around the boy and had that picture taken as the crowd roared its approval.

Babe's Most Famous Home Run Hit for a Sick Kid: Babe promised to hit a home run for Johnny Sylvester, who was mildly ill, and the Babe came through as promised. (The story was a bit overplayed.)

Most Famous Babe Ruth Legend That Did Not Happen: Babe DID NOT hold Miller Huggins off the back of a moving train and threaten to drop him.

Biggest Yankee Publicity Stunt Involving Babe: On the last day of the 1933 season, in a meaningless game, Babe pitched and beat the Red Sox, 6-5, before about 25,000 at Yankee Stadium.

Name Sometimes Given Babe's Barnstorming Teams: The "Bustin' Babes." (Gehrig's team was the "Larrapin' Lous.")

Babe's Funniest Barnstorming Strikeout: As a joke, promoter Joe Engle arranged for Jackie Mitchell, a girl pitcher, to strike out Babe, Gehrig, and Lazzeri in order.

Country Where Babe Was Best Known Outside the U.S.A.: Japan. Babe took barnstorming teams there and they loved him.

Favorite Japanese Shout in World War II: "To hell with Babe Ruth!"

Babe's Most Famous Injury: The "bellyache heard 'round the world"—his spring training illness of 1925.

Babe's Funniest Injury: In 1931 Babe cut his finger on a chicken-wire fence going after a ball in the outfield. Holding his hand in pain, Babe LIMPED all the way to the dugout. When told that his nail would have to be clipped, Babe cried, "Not without gas!"

Dramatic Injuries to the Babe: He led the league every year in being carried off the field injured.

Most Unusual Financial Arrangement with Club: In the spring of 1928 the Yanks made $60,000 touring Texas and Oklahoma. Babe received 10% of the gate.

Amount of Money Yankees Reportedly Spent to Insure Babe's Life: $300,000.

Babe's Highest Baseball Salary: The Yanks paid him $80,000 in 1930.

The Numbers Most Associated With Babe: "60" — He hit 60 home runs in 1927. "714"—He hit 714 home runs lifetime.

Babe's Most Unusual Base on Balls: In 1923 Babe was once walked intentionally with the bases loaded!

Babe's Best Season Statistically: 1921.

Year Babe Came the Closest to Winning the Triple Crown: 1924.

Reason Babe Won Only One League Award (MVP in 1920s): A ballplayer was allowed to win the League Award just once. After Babe won it in 1923 he was ineligible for further consideration.

Babe's First Big League Home Run: As a Red Sox player on May 6, 1915, Babe hit his first HR off the Yanks' Jack Warhop at the Polo Grounds. The ball landed in Seat 26 of Section 3 in the second deck of the right field grandstand. Babe was the first batter of the third inning and he hit the first pitch. It was Babe's 18th career at-bat and his fifth hit. (Less than a month later, Babe hit an even longer HR off Warhop at the Polo Grounds.)

Babe's Most Famous Regular Season Home Run: His 60th HR of 1927 hit off Tom Zachary at Yankee Stadium.

Babe's Most Famous World Series Home Run: His "called shot" HR of the 1932 Series hit off Charlie Root at Wrigley Field.

Babe's Longest Home Run: His 602-foot HR in 1926 that soared out of Navin Field in Detroit at center field.

The First All-Star Game Home Run in History and Hit by Babe: His HR off Bill Hallahan in the 1933 game.

Babe's Typical Home Run Gestures and Trot: He had a broad grin, tipped his cap and took those baby steps around the bases. Occasionally he took a bow.

Babe's Most Difficult Home Run Trot: After hitting HR No. 56 in 1927, he carried his bat with him as he rounded the bases. As Babe circled third base, a boy grabbed his bat. Babe pulled both the bat and boy with him until he crossed the plate.

Babe's Favorite Response to a Standing Ovation: Several snappy military salutes.

Biggest Challenge By a Catcher to Babe's Home Runs: After Babe hit a pair of HRs on June 11, 1927, Cleveland catcher Luke Sewell asked the home plate umpire to inspect Babe's bat when he next came to bat. The bat was ruled legal, but Babe struck out.

Most Unusual Rule That Did Not Benefit Babe in 1927: In those days a hit that bounced over the fence into the stands was ruled a HR. But every one of Babe's 60 HRs cleared the fence.

Most Legendary Myth Concerning a Line Drive Hit by Babe: The one that says Babe hit a liner through the legs of Senator pitcher Hod Lisenbee that eventually rose to clear the center field fence for a HR! In reality, the ball fell beyond second base for a single after passing through Lisenbee's legs.

Most Stolen Bases by Babe in a World Series Inning: Two. In the fifth inning of Game 2 of the 1921 Series, Babe walked with two outs and promptly stole second and third. He was left stranded.

Babe's Most Controversial Decision on the Field: His two-out attempt to steal second in the ninth inning of Game 7 of the 1926 World Series. Babe was called out and the Series was over with St. Louis victorious.

Incident Proving Babe Possessed Good Speed: He once beat teammate Joe Dugan easily in a foot race for a $10 bet. And Dugan was fast.

Babe's Biggest Baseball Thrill: The 1928 World Series when he hit three HRs in one game. He hit one when Bill Sherdel tried to "sneak pitch." He also made a great catch to end the Series.

Babe's Record He Was Most Proud of: His 29 consecutive scoreless innings pitched in World Series action as a Red Sox player. (Whitey Ford broke it in 1961.)

World Series Record of Babe's That Was Broken by Willie Randolph: In 1923 Babe set a six-game Series record by walking eight times. The record stood until 1981 when Willie Randolph broke it by walking nine times.

The Day Babe Was an Indian: In a 1927 game against Cleveland, Babe accepted an Indian bonnet and wore it for an inning.

Most Startled Babe Ruth Autograph Seeker: After allowing Babe's HR No. 58 in September 1927, pitcher Hod Lisenbee entered the Yanks' clubhouse in civilian clothes and asked Babe to autograph the ball he had hit. Babe obliged but did not know Lisenbee had just pitched against him.

The Most Serious Charge Ever Made Against Babe: He was accused of hitting a cripple in New York City late on the night of July 4 in 1927. But Babe proved he was in Newark, NJ, at the time.

Creaming the Competition: 1921—Babe led AL in runs with 177. Runner-up Jack Tobin had 132. 1921—Babe led AL in slugging with .846 mark. Runner-up Harry Heilmann had a .606 mark. 1923—Babe led AL in walks with 170. Runner-up Joe Sewell had 98. 1920—Babe led AL in homers with 54. Runner-up George Sisler had 19.

On Whether Babe Would Have Been a Good Manager: Three great Yankee pitchers—Bob Shawkey, Waite Hoyt, and Lefty Gomez—in the past made comments on the subject. Shawkey and Hoyt

Ted Williams, left, former Boston Red Sox outfielder and home run king of the previous two seasons, chooses up in the best sandlot style with the one and only Babe Ruth before the start of a hitting contest at a Field Day in Boston July 12, 1943. Williams is a Naval Air Cadet at Chapel Hill. (AP/WIDE WORLD PHOTOS)

did not believe Babe had managerial potential, but Gomez stated Babe would have made a fine manager.

World War II Fund Raiser: Babe worked for the Red Cross, bought war bonds and did benefits at Yankee Stadium.

Babe's Writing Experience: He covered every World Series for the papers between 1921-36. Each year he put out "Babe Ruth's Annual All-Star Team."

Babe's Movie Career: In 1920 he did a motion picture called "The Babe Comes Home." He played himself in the movie about Lou Gehrig, "Pride of the Yankees."

Actors Who Played Babe in Movies About His Life: William Bendix, Max Gail, Stephen Lang, and John Goodman.

Writer Who Wrote Babe's Autobiography With Babe: Bob Considine.

Babe's Last Yankee Stadium Appearance: June 13, 1948.

Date Babe's Yankee Stadium Monument Was Dedicated: July 19, 1949.

Greatest Lecture to America's Greatest Sports Hero: At a dinner in November of 1922, New York State Senator Jimmy Walker (later mayor of New York City) addressed the crowd and asked Babe:

> "Babe, a kid just stopped me on the street and asked me for a dime. He wanted to make up a quarter and buy a Babe Ruth cap. Don't you think you owe something to that kid and others like him?"

The speech moved Babe to tears and he promised to straighten up his act.

LONG HOME RUNS HIT BY BABE RUTH

In New York Babe hit several homers of great distance, including many that cleared the right field roof at the Polo Grounds. He hit one tremendous shot into the Polo Grounds' center field bleachers and at Yankee Stadium he blasted a homer off the distant right-field scoreboard. Here are some of his longest homers hit away from New York:

- As a Red Sox player in April of 1919, Babe hit a HR that was paced off at 587 feet in Tampa, FLa. It was hit off the Giants and in full view of John J. McGraw.
- Before the right-field wall was built at Washington's Griffith Stadium, Babe hit a HR off Walter Johnson that traveled some 525 feet to right field.
- In June of 1926 at Detroit's Navin Field, Babe hit a HR that flew over the low right-field wall, bounced off the top of a parked car and finally came to rest two blocks away on Plum Street. It traveled 602 feet on a fly and stopped rolling some 800-850 feet away from home plate.
- Babe hit another tremendous HR at Navin Field in July of 1934. His 700th HR soared over the right field wall and rolled several hundred feet down a street leading to the ballpark.
- In Game 4 of the 1926 World Series at St. Louis' Sportsman's Park, Babe hit a gigantic HR deep into the center field bleachers.
- At remodeled-enlarged Comiskey Park in Chicago in August of 1927, Babe creamed a HR that cleared the new right field roof and traveled at least 475 feet. It was the first fair ball hit out of the "new" Comiskey. (Second decks were built in the outfield stands before the 1927 season.)
- Babe cleared the right-field retaining wall at Cleveland's

League Park in August of 1929. It was Babe's 500th HR.

- In Game 3 of the 1932 World Series at Chicago's Wrigley Field, Babe hit his famous "called shot" HR. The blast sailed 448 feet, over the bleacher screen in deepest center field. It was the longest Wrigley HR to that date.
- As a Brave player at Pittsburgh's Forbes Field in May of 1935, Babe hit the first HR to clear Forbes' right field roof. It was a blast estimated at close to 600 feet. Also, it was Babe's third HR of the game and his 714th—and last—of his big-league career.

RUTH—AARON HOME RUN CHART

Babe Ruth: Born in Baltimore, MD, February 6, 1895. ML career, 1914-35. Became a regular outfielder in 1919 at the age of 24. Retired at the age of 40.

Hank Aaron: Born in Mobile, AL, February 5, 1934. ML career 1954-76. Became a regular outfielder in 1954 at the age of 20 Retired at the age of 42.

	Ruth	Aaron
Years in Major Leagues	22	23
Games Played	2,503	3,298
At-Bats	8,399	12,364
Bases on Balls	2,056	1,402
Total Home Runs	714	755
Home Runs in Seasons as Outfielder	688 (1919-34)	733 (1954-74)
Avg. No. of HRs Per Season as OF	43 (1919-34)	35 (1954-74)
Avg. No. of HRs Per Season in Life	32.45	32.83
Home Run Percentage (HRs per 100 ABs)	8.5	6.1
HRs Hit in His 20s	284	342
HRs Hit in His 30s	424	371
HRs Hit in His 40s	6	42
League Home Run Championships Won	12	4
Seasons Hitting 20 or More HRs	16	20
Seasons Hitting 30 or More HRs	13	15
Seasons Hitting 40 or More HRs	11	8
Seasons Hitting 50 or More HRs	4	0
Seasons Hitting 60 HRs	1	0

GREAT TRIBUTES TO BABE RUTH

After Babe hit his 60th home run, Paul Gallico wrote:

> "Once he had that 59, that number 60 was as sure as the setting sun. A more determined athlete than George Herman Ruth never lived. He is one of the few utterly dependable news stories in sports."

Jimmy Cannon wrote of the Babe:

> "He was a parade all by himself, a burst of dazzle and jingle, Santa Claus drinking his whiskey straight and groaning with a bellyache caused by gluttony. Babe Ruth made the music that his joyous years danced to in a continuous party. What Babe Ruth is comes down, one generation handing it to the next, as a national heirloom."

Red Smith wrote of the Babe:

> "Now that Babe is gone, what's to be said that hasn't been said? Nothing, when you come down to it. Just that he was Babe Ruth."

The author compiled much of the Babe Ruth biography from the following books: Robert Creamer's Babe: The Legend Comes to Life, *Marshall Smelser's* The Life That Ruth Built, *and Babe's autobiography (as told to Bob Considine).* The Babe Ruth Story. *Each of these books gives a fascinating view of America's greatest athlete and of the persons around him. Each is must reading for anyone interested in the great Babe. The author is indebted to Mr. Creamer, Mr. Smelser, and Mr. Considine.*

RUTH, BABE

Yr.	G	AB	R	H	2B	3B	HR	RBI	BB	SB	BA	SA
1920	142	458	158	172	36	9	54	137	148	14	.376	.847
1921	152	540	177	204	44	16	59	171	144	17	.378	.846
1922	110	406	94	128	24	8	35	99	84	2	.315	.672
1923	152	522	151	205	45	13	41	131	170	17	.393	.764
1924	153	529	143	200	39	7	46	121	142	9	.378	.739
1925	98	359	61	104	12	2	25	66	59	2	.290	.543
1926	152	495	139	184	30	5	47	146	144	11	.372	.737
1927	151	540	158	192	29	8	60	164	138	7	.356	.772
1928	154	536	163	173	29	8	54	142	135	4	.323	.709
1929	135	499	121	172	26	6	46	154	72	5	.345	.697
1930	145	518	150	186	28	9	49	153	136	10	.359	.732
1931	145	534	149	199	31	3	46	163	128	5	.373	.700
1932	133	457	120	156	13	5	41	137	130	2	.341	.661
1933	137	459	97	138	21	3	34	103	114	4	.301	.582
1934	125	365	78	105	17	4	22	84	103	1	.288	.537
15 Yrs.	2084	7217	1959	2518	424	106	659	1971	1847	110	.349	.711
Life.	2503	8399	2174	2873	506	136	714	2213	2056	123	.342	.690

World Series

Yr.	G	AB	R	H	2B	3B	HR	RBI	BA
1921	6	16	3	5	0	0	1	4	.313
1922	5	17	1	2	1	0	0	1	.118
1923	6	19	8	7	1	1	3	3	.368
1926	7	20	6	6	0	0	4	5	.300
1927	4	15	4	6	0	0	2	7	.400
1928	4	16	9	10	3	0	3	4	.625
1932	4	15	6	5	0	0	2	6	.333
7 Yrs.	36	118	37	41	5	1	15	30	.347
Life.	41	129	37	42	5	2	15	33	.326

Pitching

Yr.	W-L	Pct.	SA	G	GS	CG	IP	H	BB	SO	SH	ERA
4 Yrs.	5-0	1.000	0	5	4	2	31	40	16	5	0	5.52
10 Yrs.	94-46	.671	4	163	148	107	1221	974	441	488	17	2.28

SAIN, JOHNNY

Nickname: "The Man of a 1000 Curves"
Yankee: 1951-55
Pitcher
Born: September 25, 1917
Birthplace: Havana, AR
Bat: R; Throw: R
Ht: 6'2"; Wt: 200

HONORS: In 1953 Johnny was selected as an AL pitcher for the All-Star Game.

CAME TO YANKS: In August, 1951, the Yanks obtained Johnny from the Boston Braves, where he had been a star pitcher, for pitcher Lew Burdette and $50,000.

ACE RELIEF PITCHER: Although Johnny had been a very successful starter in the NL, he became the Yanks' ace relief pitcher. Besides coming out of the bullpen, he was the Yanks' fourth starter in 1952 and 1953. He was used strictly as a relief

pitcher in 1954 and he was the best in the AL. On September 26, 1952, Johnny won the Yankee pennant clincher in a game that went into extra innings.

LEAGUE LEADER: Johnny led AL relief pitchers in saves in 1954 (22).

CLUB LEADERSHIP: Twice he led Yankee pitchers in saves (1952, '54), and twice he led the Yanks in games pitched (1952-tie, '54).

ALL-TIME YANKEE LEADER: Johnny is 14th on the all-time Yankee save list (39).

WORLD SERIES: In Game 1 of the 1953 Series Johnny pitched the final 3²/₃ innings to record a victory, as the Yanks downed the Dodgers, 9-5.

TRADED: The Yanks traded Johnny and Enos Slaughter to the Kansas City A's for pitcher Sonny Dixon and cash in May, 1955.

YANKEE PITCHING COACH: After retiring as a pitcher, Johnny became one of baseball's best pitching coaches. He coached the Yanks in the early 1960s (1961-63) and was credited with helping many of the pitchers, especially with the slider. (He taught it to Ralph Terry for one.) After leaving the Yanks, Johnny was successful at other ML coaching stops.

SAIN, JOHNNY

Yr.	W-L	Pct.	SA	G	GS	CG	IP	H	BB	SO	SH	ERA
1951	2-1	.667	1	7	4	1	37	41	8	21	0	4.14
1952	11-6	.647	7	35	16	8	148	149	38	57	0	3.47
1953	14-7	.667	9	40	19	10	189	189	45	84	1	3.00
1954	6-6	.500	22	45	0	0	77	66	15	33	0	3.16
1955	0-0	.000	0	3	0	0	5	6	1	5	0	7.20
5 Yrs.	33-20	.623	39	130	39	19	457	451	107	200	1	3.31
Life.	139-116	.545	51	412	245	140	2126	2145	619	910	16	3.49

World Series

Yr.	G	IP	BB	SO	H	W-L	SA
1951	1	2	2	2	4	0-0	0
1952	2	6	3	3	6	0-1	0
1953	2	5²/₃	1	1	8	1-0	0
3 Yrs.	5	13²/₃	6	6	18	1-1	0
Life.	6	30²/₃	6	15	27	2-2	0

SAX, STEVE

Yankee: 1989-91
Second Baseman
Born: January 29, 1960
Birthplace: Sacramento, CA
Bat: R; Throw: R
Ht: 5'11"; Wt: 185

YANKEE SIGNING: In November of 1988, Steve signed with the Yankees as a free agent, several weeks after helping the Dodgers beat the A's in the World Series. Steve had broken in with the Dodgers in 1981; his best season was in 1986 when he hit .332 with 40 stolen bases.

YANKEE STAR: Steve replaced Willie Randolph as Yankee second baseman in 1989 and made the AL team for the All-Star Game (Randolph making the NL team with the Dodgers). Steve in 1989 was one of the few bright stories for the Yankees; he led the club in batting (.315), hits (205), runs (88), stolen bases (43) and games (158); he led the AL with 651 at-bats. He led AL second basemen in 1989 in double plays with 117. He was a scrappy and determined throwback to a time when players loved to get their uniforms dirty; he was visibly enthusiastic about playing baseball. Steve slumped to .260 in 1990, but he went to the All-Star Game and led the Yanks in SBs (43). In 1991, Steve led the Yanks in games (158), ABs (652), runs (85), hits (198), doubles (38) and BA (.304). Steve's 117 stolen bases rank him 19th in the All-Time Yankee list.

TRADED TO CHISOX: In January of 1992, the Yankees traded Steve (and possibly cash) to the White Sox for three pitchers—Melido Perez, Bob Wickman and Domingo Jean. The timing of the trade was good; the Yanks got pitching improvement, and Sax slumped to .236 in 1992, his last season as a regular player.

SAX, STEVE

Yr.	G	AB	R	H	2B	3B	HR	RBI	BB	SB	BA	SA
1989	158	651	88	205	26	3	5	63	52	43	.315	.387
1990	155	615	70	160	24	2	4	42	49	43	.260	.325
1991	158	652	85	198	38	2	10	56	41	31	.304	.414
3 Yrs.	471	1918	243	563	88	7	19	161	142	117	.294	.376
Life.	1769	6940	913	1949	278	47	54	550	556	444	.281	.358

SCHANG, WALLY
(BORN WALTER HENRY SCHANG)

Yankee: 1921-25
Catcher
Born: August 22, 1889
Birthplace: South Wales, NY
Died: March 6, 1965
Bat: B; Throw: R
Ht: 5'11"; Wt: 165

CAME TO YANKS: In December of 1920, the Yanks obtained Wally, pitchers Waite Hoyt and Harry Harper and infielder Mike McNally from the Red Sox for second baseman Del Pratt, catcher Muddy Ruel, pitcher Hank Thormahlen and outfielder Sammy Vick.

YANKEE CATCHER: Wally was the first of a long line of great Yankee catchers. He was the Yanks' regular catcher on the club's first three AL pennant-winning teams (1921-23). Groin and rib injuries limited his playing time in 1923. He was first-string catcher on the Yanks in 1924 and second-string in 1925. Ed Barrow said Wally was the strongest man in baseball. Wally was supposed to go on Babe Ruth's ill-fated 1921 barnstorming tour, but Commissioner Landis convinced him not to go.

STAR PLAYER: Wally was an excellent hitter and a good defensive backstop. In 1921 and 1922, Wally was one of four Yankee starters to hit better than .300. He is tied with Gary Carter for eighth on baseball's all-time double play list (149), and he is tenth on the assists list (1420) for all the catchers in baseball history. In 1922 Wally was one of the highest paid Yankees, making $10,000.

ALL-TIME YANKEE LEADER: Wally's Yankee career batting average (.297) is the 14th highest in Yankee history for players with at least 500 or more games.

GETTING ON BASE: Perhaps surprisingly, Wally owns the second highest lifetime on-base average (.393) of all catchers in ML history. Only Mickey Cochrane's lifetime OBA is higher. Wally was hit by a pitched ball 107 times in his ML career, placing him in the top 30 on the all-time list in the 20th century.

WORLD SERIES: In the 1921 Series, Wally stroked the first triple in a World Series game by a Yankee player. In the 1923 Series, the first World Series ever won by the Yanks, Wally contributed with a fine .318 batting average.

TRADED: In March of 1926, the Yanks traded Wally to the St. Louis Browns for pitcher George Mogridge and cash.

SCHANG, WALLY

Yr.	G	AB	R	H	2B	3B	HR	RBI	BB	SB	BA	SA
1921	134	424	77	134	30	5	6	55	78	7	.316	.453
1922	124	408	46	130	21	7	1	53	53	12	.319	.412
1923	84	272	39	75	8	2	2	29	27	5	.276	.342
1924	114	356	46	104	19	7	5	52	48	2	.292	.427
1925	73	167	17	40	8	1	2	24	17	3	.240	.335
5 Yrs.	529	1627	225	483	86	22	16	213	223	29	.297	.406
Life.	1840	5306	769	1506	264	90	59	710	849	122	.284	.401

World Series

Yr.	G	AB	R	H	2B	3B	HR	RBI	BA
1921	8	21	1	6	1	1	0	1	.286
1922	5	16	0	3	1	0	0	0	.188
1923	6	22	3	7	1	0	0	0	.318
3 Yrs.	19	59	4	16	3	1	0	1	.271
Life.	32	94	8	27	4	2	1	8	.287

SCOTT, EVERETT

Nickname: "Deacon"
Yankee: 1922-25
Shortstop
Born: November 19, 1892
Birthplace: Bluffton, IN
Died: November 2, 1960
Bat: R; Throw: R
Ht: 5'8"; Wt: 148

CAME TO YANKS: In December of 1921, Everett was traded to the Yanks, along with pitching stars Sam Jones and Joe Bush, from the Red Sox. In return the Yanks sent shortstop Roger Peckinpaugh and pitchers Jack Quinn and Rip Collins to Boston.

YANKEE SHORTSTOP: From 1922-24, Everett was the regular Yankee shortstop. He played in every Yankee game in 1922, 1923 and 1924. He was a clever player, besides being durable. He always wore a stern appearance—hence the nickname, "Deacon." Everett was the Yankee team captain. He was known as "the smartest bridge player in baseball."

PLAYING STREAK: From June 20, 1916 through May 5, 1925, Everett played in 1307 consecutive games, the longest consecutive-game playing streak by a shortstop in ML history. He started the streak as a member of the Red Sox and finished it as a Yankee player. On May 6, 1925, Yankee Manager Miller

Huggins benched Everett, snapping Everett's playing skein, because Huggins felt "Deacon" was playing poorly. Pee Wee Wanninger replaced Everett in the Yankee lineup. At the time Everett concluded his streak it was the longest in ML history, and the record stood until Lou Gehrig broke it. The 1,307 straight games Everett played in still stands as the third longest playing streak in ML history.

DEFENSIVE ABILITIES: Everett was the best fielding shortstop of his era in the AL. He was reliable and consistent. Everett led AL shortstops in fielding in 1922 (.964) and 1923 (.961). The 1923 infield of the Yanks was one of the best fielding infields in Yankee history. Everett, second baseman Aaron Ward and third baseman Joe Dugan all led the AL in fielding at their respective positions. In 1922 he led AL shortstops in assists (538). That total is also the Yankee club record for shortstops. Everett was the glue of the 1923 team, the first Yankee team to win the World Championship.

WORLD SERIES: In Game 4 of the 1923 Series, Everett's two-run bases-loaded single highlighted the Yanks' six-run second inning, helping the Yanks beat the New York Giants, 8-4, and squaring the Series at two games each.

TRADED: Soon after his playing streak ended during the 1925 season, the Yanks dealt Everett to the Washington Senators.

SCOTT, EVERETT

Yr.	G	AB	R	H	2B	3B	HR	RBI	BB	SB	BA	SA
1922	154	557	64	150	23	5	3	45	23	2	.269	.345
1923	152	533	48	131	16	4	6	60	13	1	.246	.325
1924	153	548	56	137	12	6	4	64	21	3	.250	.316
1925	22	60	3	13	0	0	0	4	2	0	.217	.217
4 Yrs.	481	1698	171	431	51	15	13	173	59	6	.254	.325
Life.	1654	5837	552	1455	208	58	20	549	243	69	.249	.315

World Series

Yr.	G	AB	R	H	2B	3B	HR	RBI	BA
1922	5	14	0	2	0	0	0	1	.143
1923	6	22	2	7	0	0	0	3	.318
2 Yrs.	11	36	2	9	0	0	0	4	.250
Life.	27	90	3	14	0	1	0	6	.156

SELKIRK, GEORGE

Nickname: "Twinkletoes"
Yankee: 1934-42 (military)
Outfielder
Born: January 4, 1908
Birthplace: Huntsville, Ontario, Canada
Died: January 19, 1987
Bat: L; Throw: R
Ht: 6'1"; Wt: 182

YOUNG PROSPECT: George began playing minor league ball in 1927 and, in November of 1931, the Yanks purchased George's contract from Jersey City of the International League. George was a great player at Jersey City. In fact, he is enshrined in the International League Hall of Fame. During the 1934 season, the Yanks called George up from Jersey City.

BABE RUTH'S REPLACEMENT: When he was called up to the Yanks in 1934, it was understood that George would be Babe Ruth's eventual replacement in right field. George had an outstanding rookie season in 1934 as a reserve outfielder (.313). After the 1934 season, Ruth left the Yanks and George was given the difficult chore in 1935 of playing Ruth's right field position. George even wore Ruth's number, "3." George responded in 1935 by being the Yanks' second most run-producing hitter, behind Lou Gehrig. George initially heard boos from Ruth loyalists at the Stadium, but he reacted as a true professional and was accepted.

YANKEE OUTFIELDER: George was the regular Yankee rightfielder in 1935 and 1936. In 1937 a broken collarbone kept him on the sidelines for much of the season. George was the Yanks' regular leftfielder from 1938-40. He was a reserve outfielder in 1941 and 1942. Unfortunately, George never fully recovered from the severe collarbone injury he sustained in a fall.

GREAT HITTER: George was a power-hitting member of the great Bronx Bomber clubs of the late 1930s. He was an excellent hitter, batting better than .300 in each of his first four ML seasons. George really helped the Yanks win AL pennants in 1936 (18 HRs, 107 RBIs, .308) and 1939 (21 HRs, 101 RBIs, .306). He had a tremendous slugging average in 1937 (.629) in only 256 at-bats. He had a fine batting eye.

DEFENSIVE ABILITIES: In 1939 George led all AL outfielders in fielding (.989). He led AL outfielders in making double plays in 1940 (6). Obviously, George was not just a slugger.

CLUB LEADERSHIP: In 1935 George led the Yanks in triples (12). In 1939 he led the club in walks (103).

ALL-STAR GAME: George was selected to the AL All-Star team for the All-Star Games in 1936 and 1939.

WORLD SERIES: In Game 1 of the 1936 Series George became the fourth man in Series history to hit a HR in his first World Series at-bat. His solo clout accounted for the only run scored by the Yanks. He added another HR in Game 5 of this Series, although it also came in a losing cause. George hit a two-run bases-loaded single to help the Yanks beat the Giants, 8-1, in Game 1 of the 1937 Series. In the 1937 Series, George led all hitters with six RBIs. He led or tied all players in walks in three different Series (1936, '38, '39).

MILITARY SERVICE: Following the 1942 baseball season, George entered the Navy and missed the baseball seasons of 1943, '44 and '45. He was discharged from the Navy in 1946, but at the age of 38 his ML playing days were over. George's entire ML playing career was with the Yanks.

BASEBALL MAN: George was involved in baseball for 45 years, starting in 1924 when he was Rochester's bat-boy. In 1946 George became manager of the Yanks' top farm club, the Newark Bears. Later George was a Yankee scout and managed Yankee farm clubs at Binghamton and Kansas City, doing a fine job at each stop. In the 1950s George was a manager in the Milwaukee Braves farm system, before serving as Kansas City

A's farm director. He spent 1961 with the Baltimore Orioles. In 1962 George became GM of the Washington Senators and made several great trades for that club. He left in 1969 when egotistical owner Bob Short arrived in Washington.

SELKIRK, GEORGE

Yr.	G	AB	R	H	2B	3B	HR	RBI	BB	SB	BA	SA
1934	46	176	23	55	7	1	5	38	15	1	.313	.449
1935	128	491	64	153	29	12	11	94	44	2	.312	.487
1936	137	493	93	152	28	9	18	107	94	13	.308	.511
1937	78	256	49	84	13	5	18	68	34	8	.328	.629
1938	99	335	58	85	12	5	10	62	68	9	.254	.409
1939	128	418	103	128	17	4	21	101	103	12	.306	.517
1940	118	379	68	102	17	5	19	71	84	3	.269	.491
1941	70	164	30	36	5	0	6	25	28	1	.220	.360
1942	42	78	15	15	3	0	0	10	16	0	.192	.231
9 Yrs.	846	2790	503	810	131	41	108	576	486	49	.290	.483

Life. Same.

World Series

Yr.	G	AB	R	H	2B	3B	HR	RBI	BA
1936	6	24	6	8	0	1	2	3	.333
1937	5	19	5	5	1	0	0	6	.263
1938	3	10	0	2	0	0	0	1	.200
1939	4	12	0	2	1	0	0	0	.167
1941	2	2	0	1	0	0	0	0	.500
1942	1	1	0	0	0	0	0	0	.000
6 Yrs.	21	68	11	18	2	1	2	10	.265

Life. Same.

SEWELL, JOE

Yankee: 1931-33
Third Baseman
Born: October 9, 1898
Birthplace: Titus, AL
Died: March 6, 1990
Bat: L; Throw: R
Ht: 5'7"; Wt: 155

HONORS: Joe was inducted into the Baseball Hall of Fame in 1977.

CAME TO YANKS: In October, 1930, the Yanks signed Joe after the Indians had released him. Joe had been an outstanding shortstop and third baseman with Cleveland for 11 seasons.

YANKEE THIRD BASEMAN: Joe was the regular Yankee third baseman in each of his three seasons with the club (1931-33). When he joined the Yanks he brought much needed stability to the Yankee infield. He was a valuable member of the 1932 Yankee World Championship team that boasted eight future Hall of Famers!

DIFFICULT TO STRIKE OUT: Joe was the hardest man in baseball history to strike out. He had tremendous bat control. He holds baseball's lifetime record for fewest strikeouts per at-bat (.016). In his ML career, he fanned only 114 times in 7132 official at-bats (not including walks, etc.), the fewest times in ML history for players with at least 7000 at-bats. Joe fanned only 15 times in 1511 official Yankee at-bats, an average of only one strikeout per 100.7 at-bats. As a Yankee in 1932, he struck out only three times in 503 official at-bats, setting a 20th-century ML record for fewest strikeouts per at-bat (.010). In

Joe Sewell

1932, Joe did not strike out until his 68th game (July 28), having come to bat some 263 times prior to that first whiff. Joe's final two fans occurred on August 19 (first game—his 86th game), and September 18 (first game—his 119th game). What an incredible batting eye! Reportedly, Joe could actually see the pitch meet his bat. When asked his secret, Joe said, "It's very simple, just keep your eye on the ball."

SCORING RUNS: With the Yanks, Joe's offensive job was to reach base so that the heavy bats behind him could knock him in. He did his job well. Sandwiched between Earle Combs and Babe Ruth, Joe usually batted second in the Yanks' lineup. In 1931 Joe was one of six Yankees to score at least 100 runs. For his three Yankee seasons, Joe averaged 94.7 runs scored per season. Joe's lifetime on-base average (.391) ranks among the top 10 for either third basemen or shortstops, his two ML positions.

RETIREMENT: In January of 1934, the Yanks released Joe, the greatest of three Sewell brothers to play ML baseball, and Joe retired as a player. In 1934 and 1935 Joe was a Yankee coach. He became associated with Cleveland in 1953 and scouted for the Indians for many years.

SEWELL, JOE

Yr.	G	AB	R	H	2B	3B	HR	RBI	BB	SB	BA	SA
1931	130	484	102	146	22	1	6	64	62	1	.302	.388
1932	125	503	95	137	21	3	11	68	56	0	.272	.392
1933	135	524	87	143	18	1	2	54	71	2	.273	.323
3 Yrs.	390	1511	284	426	61	5	19	186	189	3	.282	.367
Life.	1903	7132	1141	2226	436	68	49	1051	844	74	.312	.413

World Series

Yr.	G	AB	R	H	2B	3B	HR	RBI	BA
1932	4	15	4	5	1	0	0	3	.333
1 Yr.	4	15	4	5	1	0	0	3	.333
Life.	11	38	4	9	1	0	0	3	.237

SHANTZ, BOBBY

Yankee: 1957-60
Pitcher
Born: September 26, 1925
Birthplace: Pottstown, PA
Bat: R; Throw: L
Ht: 5'6"; Wt: 142

HONORS: As a Yankee pitcher Bobby was selected to the AL All-Star team for the 1957 All-Star Game.

CAME TO YANKS: In February, 1957, the Yanks acquired Bobby, Art Ditmar, Clete Boyer and three others from the Kansas City A's in exchange for Irv Noren, Tom Morgan and four others.

VERSATILE PITCHER: Bobby was successful with the Yanks as both a starter and relief pitcher. This was a very classy little pitcher. In 1957, as the Yanks' fourth starter, Bobby won the AL ERA championship (2.45). He was a spot starter and long relief man in 1958. In 1959 Bobby was used almost exclusively out of the Yankee bullpen. He was the ace of the Yankee bullpen in 1960.

GREAT FIELDING PITCHER: Bobby was one of the greatest fielding pitchers of all time. In 1957, when only one Gold Glove Award was given at each position for both leagues, Bobby was selected as the best defensive pitcher in ML baseball. (He also was the first Yankee player to win a Gold Glove,) winning the award three times, 1958-60.

CLUB LEADERSHIP: In 1957, Bobby tied for Yankee club leadership in complete games (nine). In 1960 he led Yankee pitchers in saves (11) and he tied for club leadership in games pitched (42).

WORLD SERIES: Bobby started Game 2 of the 1957 Series. In Game 2 of the 1960 Series he got the final two outs to record a save. He threw five beautiful innings of relief pitching in Game 7 of the 1960 Series and was on his way toward becoming a Series hero before some bad breaks knocked him out of the box. (The Yanks eventually lost in a game characterized by unusual events.)

TRADED: The Yanks lost Shantz on December 14, 1960 to the expansion Washington Senators who had made Bobby their top

selection in the American League special draft. Two days later Shantz was traded to the Pittsburgh Pirates after the Senators had been deluged with trade offers for him. Bobby later played for Houston, St. Louis, Chicago Cubs, and Philadelphia before retiring after the 1964 season.

SHANTZ, BOBBY

Yr.	W-L	Pct.	SA	G	GS	CG	IP	H	BB	SO	SH	ERA
1957	11-5	.688	5	30	21	9	173	157	40	72	1	2.45
1958	7-6	.538	0	33	13	3	126	127	35	80	0	3.36
1959	7-3	.700	3	33	4	2	95	64	33	66	2	2.38
1960	5-4	.556	11	42	0	0	68	57	24	54	0	2.79
4 Yrs.	30-18	.625	19	138	38	14	461	405	132	272	3	2.73
Life.	119-99	.546	48	537	171	78	1936	1795	643	1072	15	3.38

World Series

Yr.	G	IP	BB	SO	H	W-L	SA
1957	3	6⅔	2	7	8	0-1	0
1960	3	6⅓	1	1	4	0-0	0
2 Yrs.	6	13	3	8	12	0-1	0
Life. Same.							

SHAWKEY, BOB
(BORN JAMES ROBERT SHAWKEY)

Nickname: "Sailor Bob"
Yankee: 1915-27
Pitcher
Born: December 4, 1890
Birthplace: Sigel, PA
Died: December 31, 1980
Bat: R; Throw: R
Ht: 5'11"; Wt: 168

CAME TO YANKS: In July of 1915, the Yanks paid a reported $85,000 to the Philadelphia A's for Bob's contract. It was a great deal for the Yanks. The first great Yankee pitching staffs were built around Bob, the first man voted into the Pennsylvania Hall of Fame.

YANKEE ACE PITCHER: Bob was one of the great pitchers in Yankee history and a major reason why the Yanks became a championship team. Bob won 20 or more games for the Yanks in four seasons, tying Lefty Gomez and Red Ruffing for the most 20-win seasons in Yankee history. From 1916-20 he was the peerless ace of the Yankee pitching staff. In the first three years that the Yanks won AL pennants (1921-23), Bob won 54 games, averaging 18 wins per season.

GREAT GAMES: On seven occasions in his Yankee career, Bob won a 1-0 shutout, a Yankee club record. Twice Bob pitched one-hitters as a Yankee hurler. On September 27, 1919, Bob struck out 15 members of the Philadelphia A's, the club record until broken by Ron Guidry in 1978.

SUPERSTITION, SERVICE AND FRIENDS: Bob always wore his "lucky" red sweatshirt regardless of the weather. Still, misfortune struck. He was hobbled by a leg injury in 1921 and another leg injury, a foot fracture, limited his service in 1926. He missed nearly all of the 1918 season while serving in the military during World War I. Bob was a very slow worker on the mound. He was a popular member of the Yanks and a golf buddy of Babe Ruth. Bob was also a fisherman.

YANKEE STADIUM OPENER: On April 18, 1923, Bob started the first game ever played at Yankee Stadium. He went the distance in beating the Red Sox on 3 hits, 4-1. Bob also belted a HR, becoming the second man (behind Babe Ruth) to hit a HR in the new ballpark.

LEAGUE LEADER: In 1916 Bob led AL pitchers in saves (eight) and games won in relief (seven). In 1920 he won the AL ERA championship (2.45).

CLUB LEADERSHIP: Seven times Bob led Yankee pitchers in strikeouts, tying him with Lefty Gomez for the most times leading the club in strikeouts. Three times he led the Yanks in wins, games started and innings pitched. Twice he led the club in ERA, saves, games pitched and complete games.

ALL-TIME YANKEE LEADER: Bob is fifth on the all-time Yankee win list (168) and seventh on the games pitched (415) list. He is fifth on the all-time Yankee complete games (161), innings pitched (2489) and sixth on the strikeout (1163) lists. He is seventh on the Yankee games started (274) list. He is tied for eighth on the club's shutout (26) list. Bob is also tenth in ERA (3.12), and 20th in saves (26).

WORLD SERIES: Bob started Game 3 of the 1921 Series. He pitched all ten innings in one of the most controversial games in Series history, Game 2 of the 1922 Series. The game was called after 10 innings because of darkness, although there was still plenty of daylight. Bob pitched heroically but had only a 3-3 tie to show for his efforts. In Game 4 of the 1923 Series Bob was the winning pitcher, beating the New York Giants, 8-4, a victory that the Yanks needed to even the Series. (The Yanks went on to win the club's first World Series.)

YANKEE COACH AND MANAGER: In November, 1927, the Yanks released Bob and he retired as a player. Bob remained with the Yanks in 1928 and 1929 as one of Miller Huggins' coaches. In 1930 he was Yankee manager but was fired by the Yanks, shabbily and unfairly, following the season.

BASEBALL MAN: After leaving the Yanks, Bob managed minor-league teams at Jersey City (1931), Scranton (1932-33), top Yankee farm club Newark (1934-35), Watertown (1947) and Tallahassee (1949). Bob pitched a little for Montreal in 1928 (9-9), Jersey City in 1931 (0-1) and Newark in 1934 (0-1).

YANKEE LOYALTY: In 1973 Bob threw out the first ball at Yankee Stadium's "Golden Anniversary Day" ceremonies. When the Stadium reopened in April of 1976, Bob again threw out the first ball, 53 years after he pitched the first game at the "old" Stadium. Through the years, Bob attended many special Stadium events and he especially enjoyed Old Timers' Day. Bob was a Yankee fan, living in Syracuse, and a great story teller. He especially liked talking about his days with the Ruth-Gehrig Yanks. Bob Shawkey died a few weeks past his 90th birthday on New Year's Eve 1980, and the Yanks lost an old and loyal friend.

SHAWKEY, BOB

Yr.	W-L	Pct.	SA	G	GS	CG	IP	H	BB	SO	SH	ERA
1915	4-7	.364	0	16	9	5	86	78	35	31	1	3.26
1916	24-14	.632	8	53	27	21	277	204	81	122	4	2.21
1917	13-15	.464	1	32	26	16	236	207	72	97	2	2.44
1918	1-1	.500	0	3	2	1	16	7	10	3	1	1.13
1919	20-11	.645	4	41	27	22	261	218	92	122	3	2.72
1920	20-13	.606	2	38	31	20	268	246	85	126	5	2.45
1921	18-12	.600	2	38	31	18	245	245	86	126	3	4.08
1922	20-12	.625	1	39	33	19	300	286	98	130	3	2.91
1923	16-11	.593	1	36	31	17	259	232	102	125	1	3.51
1924	16-11	.593	0	38	25	10	208	226	74	114	1	4.12
1925	6-14	.300	0	33	20	9	186	209	67	81	1	4.11
1926	8-7	.533	3	29	10	3	104	102	37	63	1	3.62
1927	2-3	.400	4	19	2	0	44	44	16	23	0	2.89
13 Yrs.	168-131	.562	26	415	274	161	2489	2304	855	1163	26	3.12
Life.	196-150	.566	28	488	332	194	2937	2722	1018	1360	33	3.09

World Series

Yr.	G	IP	BB	SO	H	W-L	SA
1921	2	9	6	5	13	0-1	0
1922	1	10	2	4	8	0-0	0
1923	1	7⅔	4	2	12	1-0	0
1926	3	10	2	7	8	0-1	0
4 Yrs.	7	36⅔	14	18	41	1-2	0
Life.	8	41⅔	16	18	45	1-3	0

SHOCKER, URBAN
(BORN URBAIN JACQUES SHOCKCOR)

Yankee: 1916-17, '25-28
Pitcher
Born: August 22, 1890
Birthplace: Cleveland, OH
Died: September 9, 1928
Bat: R; Throw: R
Ht: 5'10"; Wt: 170

MINOR LEAGUE STAR: In 1913 Urban began his professional baseball career pitching for Windsor of the Border League, logging a 6-7 record. He was 20-8 and 19-10 in 1914 and 1915 respectively, pitching for Ottawa of the Canadian League.

EARLY YANKEE DAYS: The Yanks obtained Urban in 1916 and that year Urban split time between the Yanks (5-3) and Toronto (15-3, 1.31 ERA) of the International League. In 1916 Urban was a 26-year-old rookie spot starter for the Yanks. In 1917 he was the Yanks' sixth starter. In January of 1918, the Yanks traded Urban, Fritz Maisel, Les Nunamaker, Nick Cullop and Joe Gedeon to the St. Louis Browns for Del Pratt and Eddie Plank. (The Yanks were burned badly in the trade. Hall of Fame pitcher Plank refused to join the Yanks, electing to retire. Meanwhile, Urban was sensational with the Browns. From 1920-23, Urban won 20, 27, 24 and 20 games!)

BACK WITH YANKS: In December of 1924, the Yanks reobtained Urban from the Browns. The Yanks sent Bullet Joe Bush and two less successful pitchers to St. Louis in exchange for Urban. Urban rejoined the Yanks with the reputation as one of the best pitchers in baseball, but the Browns foolishly gave him up because they felt Urban was a troublemaker.

YANKEE STAR: Urban was the Yanks' third starter in 1925 and he was the only Yankee starter to achieve a .500 record (12-12) in that disappointing Yankee campaign. Again he was the club's third starter in 1926 and 1927. As one of the Yanks' "big three" (along with Waite Hoyt and Herb Pennock) in 1927, Urban combined with Hoyt and Pennock for a 59-21 record! Urban practiced voodoo rites before pitching a game. He started and lost to the Cardinals in Game 2 of the 1926 World Series.

SPITBALL PITCHER: Urban threw a legal spitball and it was a wicked one. In 1920 the spitball was banned, but the 17 pitchers who used the pitch, including Urban, were allowed to throw wet ones until retiring. Urban was a spitball pitcher his entire ML career.

DEFENSIVE ABILITIES: Urban was a fine fielding pitcher. His ML career fielding average (.980) ranks 13th on baseball's all-time list for pitchers.

CLUB LEADERSHIP: In 1925 Urban tied for the club leadership in shutouts (two). He had his greatest Yankee season in 1926, leading the Yanks in ERA (3.38), games pitched (41), games started (33) and complete games (19).

COURAGEOUS MAN: Quite possibly Urban was the most courageous man in sports history. Ill with a swollen heart, Urban fought bravely in his last few years to play baseball and indeed for life itself. His heart problem was so serious that he could not sleep lying down. His illness became so severe in the spring of 1928 that Urban, having pitched in only one game, was forced to leave the team and he voluntarily retired. Urban was released by the Yanks in July of 1928—he was a very sick man. Reportedly, he knew he was terminally ill before the 1927 season started and yet had an 18-6 record!

TRAGIC DEATH: On September 9, 1928, Urban succumbed to heart failure. At the time of Urban's death, the Yanks were in a furious pennant race with the Philadelphia A's. But the news of the popular pitcher's death shocked and saddened the Yankee players and for the moment the pennant race was forgotten. Even the Yankees had not known the seriousness of Urban's illness, and his death shed new light on Urban's courageous battle to live and to pitch. Urban died in Denver where he had gone to try to recuperate, but his condition was complicated by pneumonia.

SHOCKER, URBAN												
Yr.	W-L	Pct.	SA	G	GS	CG	IP	H	BB	SO	SH	ERA
1916	4-3	.571	0	12	9	4	82	67	32	43	1	2.62
1917	8-5	.615	1	26	13	7	145	124	46	68	0	2.61
1925	12-12	.500	2	41	30	15	244	278	58	74	2	3.65
1926	19-11	.633	2	41	33	19	258	272	71	59	0	3.38
1927	18-6	.750	0	31	27	13	200	207	41	35	2	2.84
1928	0-0	.000	0	1	0	0	2	3	0	0	0	0.00
6 Yrs.	61-37	.622	5	152	112	58	932	951	248	279	5	3.14
Life.	187-117	.615	25	411	319	202	2682	2709	657	983	28	3.16

World Series							
Yr.	G	IP	BB	SO	H	W-L	SA
1926	2	7⅔	0	3	13	0-1	0
1 Yr.	2	7⅔	0	3	13	0-1	0
Life. Same.							

SKOWRON, BILL

Nickname: "Moose"
Yankee: 1954-62
First Baseman, 3B
Born: December 18, 1930
Birthplace: Chicago, IL
Bat: R; Throw: R
Ht: 5'11"; Wt: 195

HONORS: Bill was the Minor League Player of the Year in 1952, playing for Kansas City in the American Association. In 1960 *The Sporting News* selected him for its ML All-Star team as baseball's best first baseman. On August 27, 1960, "Moose Skowron Day" was celebrated at Yankee Stadium. In 1980 Bill was elected to the National Polish-American Hall of Fame in Orchard Lake, MI.

GREAT PROSPECT: Bill played football and baseball at Purdue University. He was an All-American and hit .500 in his final Purdue season. The Yanks signed Bill in 1950, and before being sent to the minors, in the final weeks of the season Bill and Mickey Mantle roomed together on the Yanks, traveling as non-roster players. They worked out with the club but could not play—and went to the movies together every day as they experienced the world of pro ball for the first time. In 1951, Bill played at Binghamton (.246 in 21 games) and Norfolk, capturing the Class-B Piedmont League batting title (.334). Bill was also converted from a shortstop to a third baseman. In 1952 with the Kansas City Blues, Bill hit .341 and led the A.A. in HRs (31) and RBIs (134). Bill hit .318 for the Blues in 1953.

EARLY ML CAREER: In 1954, Bill made the Yanks and his rookie season was little short of spectacular—he hit .340 in 87 games! Bill worked hard at becoming a first baseman. With the Blues he had played first, third and the outfield, but in 1954 he played 61 games at first, five games at third and two games at second. Bill played 12 games in his Yankee career at third, but none after 1958. Casey Stengel platooned Bill with Joe Collins at first base in 1954-55.

YANKEE STAR: From 1956-62 Bill was the Yanks' regular first baseman and a key player on four World Championship clubs (1956, 1958, 1961, 1962). Bill was one of the best players of his era, a power-hitting star who hit for high batting average. In his first four ML seasons, Bill hit higher than .300 each year for a combined .314 average. Bill was also a fine, underrated defensive first baseman. In 1958 he led AL first basemen in fielding (.993). Injuries plagued him in 1957-58. In 1959 he had a torn thigh muscle and then on July 25 Bill broke his arm in two places reaching for a bad throw and having the runner, Coot Veal, run into him. Bill was out of action for the remainder of the season. The 1961 season was the first and only year in which he appeared in as many as 150 games.

POWER HITTER: "Moose" was a big, muscular Yankee who wore a menacing scowl, but who in reality was a gentle and kindly athlete. He was an extremely strong player, hitting more than 20 HRs in each of four seasons. He hit some awesome HRs, but being a right-handed hitter and swinging into Yankee Stadium's "Death Valley," he had fence-clearing woes. He did hit many of his HRs to right field at the Stadium. As a noted "wrong field" hitter, he had the amazing ability to drive any type of pitch to right field, and he took advantage of the Stadium's short right-field porch. Bill was one batter who hit better without any pre-knowledge of what pitch was coming. In 1961, the trio of Maris-Mantle-Skowron hit a total of 143 HRs ("Moose" hit 28), the most ever hit by a threesome on one ML club. Bill hit right-handers well, hitting 22 of his 28 HRs in 1961 off righties. On April 20, 1957, Bill became the third man to hit a HR to centerfield out of Boston's Fenway Park. Joe DiMaggio, Tony Lazzeri, and Dave Winfield are the only strictly right-handed batters who have hit more Yankee HRs than Bill's 165.

CLUB LEADERSHIP: In 1960, Bill led the Yanks in batting (.309), hits (166) and doubles (34). In 1962, he led the club in triples (six). Twice he led the team in doubles.

ALL-TIME YANKEE LEADER: Bill's Yankee career slugging average (.496) is the eighth highest in Yankee history for those players with at least 1500 Yankee at-bats. Moose ranks 19th in home-runs (165) and 17th in batting average (.294).

ALL-STAR GAME: As a Yankee player, Bill was picked to be on the AL All-Star team for the All-Star Game in five consecutive years (1957-61). Wearing the Yankee uniform, Bill was 6-for-14 (.429) in All-Star Games, the best batting performance in the Summer Classic by any Yankee player.

WORLD SERIES: On the all-time World Series lists, Bill ranks sixth in RBIs (29), seventh in HRs (eight) and 11th in total bases (69). In Game 6 of the 1955 Series, Bill's first-inning three-run HR led the Yanks to a 5-1 win over Brooklyn, keeping the Yanks alive in the Series. In Game 7 of the 1956 Series, Bill became the sixth player in World Series history to hit a grand slam HR, icing a 9-0 win and the World Championship for the Yanks. Bill entered the 1957 Series with a painful back injury. He grounded out in the first inning of Game 1 and had to leave the game. He did not return to the lineup until Game 7, and third baseman Eddie Mathews robbed him of a bases-loaded extra-base hit to end the Series. In Game 6 of the 1958 Series, Bill's tenth-inning single provided the winning margin for the Yanks. He came back the next day to belt a three-run HR, clinching the Yanks' 6-2 win and capping a remarkable Yankee comeback Series decision over the Milwaukee Braves. Bill led both clubs in hits (12) in the 1960 Series. In Game 1 of the 1961 Series, Bill hit a HR in support of Whitey Ford's 2-0 shutout of Cincinnati.

TRADED: In November of 1962, the Yanks traded Bill to the Los Angeles Dodgers for pitcher Stan Williams. Bill hit .385 against the Yanks in the 1963 World Series. He later played for Washington, Chicago White Sox, and California.

ALL-TIME YANKEE RIGHTHANDED HR HITTERS
(NO SWITCHERS)
1. Joe DiMaggio (361)
2. Dave Winfield (205)
3. Tony Lazzeri (169)
4. BILL SKOWRON (165)
5. Elston Howard (161)

SKOWRON, BILL

Yr.	G	AB	R	H	2B	3B	HR	RBI	BB	SB	BA	SA
1954	87	215	37	73	12	9	7	41	19	2	.340	.577
1955	108	288	46	92	17	3	12	61	21	1	.319	.524
1956	134	464	78	143	21	6	23	90	50	4	.308	.528
1957	122	457	54	139	15	5	17	88	31	3	.304	.470
1958	126	465	61	127	22	3	14	73	28	1	.273	.424
1959	74	282	39	84	13	5	15	59	20	1	.298	.539
1960	146	538	63	166	34	3	26	91	38	2	.309	.528
1961	150	561	76	150	23	4	28	89	35	0	.267	.472
1962	140	478	63	129	16	6	23	80	36	0	.270	.473
9 Yrs.	1087	3748	517	1103	173	44	165	672	278	14	.294	.496
Life.	1658	5547	681	1566	243	53	211	888	383	16	.282	.459

World Series

Yr.	G	AB	R	H	2B	3B	HR	RBI	BA
1955	5	12	2	4	2	0	1	3	.333
1956	3	10	1	1	0	0	1	4	.100
1957	2	4	0	0	0	0	0	0	.000
1958	7	27	3	7	0	0	2	7	.259
1960	7	32	7	12	2	0	2	6	.375
1961	5	17	3	6	0	0	1	5	.353
1962	6	18	1	4	0	1	0	1	.222
7 Yrs.	35	120	17	34	4	1	7	26	.283
Life.	39	133	19	39	4	1	8	29	.293

STAFFORD, BILL

Yankee: 1960-65
Pitcher
Born: August 13, 1939
Birthplace: Catskill, NY
Died: September 19, 2001
Bat: R; Throw: R
Ht: 6'2"; Wt: 193

THROUGH THE YANKEE FARM SYSTEM: The Yanks signed Bill as a kid in 1957. For the next four seasons Bill moved up through the Yankee farm system, playing at St. Petersburg (Florida State League), Binghamton (Eastern League) and Richmond (International League). Midway through the 1960 season, the Yanks called Bill up from Richmond and Bill got off to an impressive start (3-1, 2.25 ERA with the Yanks on the year).

YOUNG PITCHING STAR: Bill was one of the Yankees' promising pitching prospects in the early 1960s. He was the Yanks' third starter in 1961 when he posted the league's second best ERA (2.68). With that kind of ERA, his win percentage (.609) with any luck should have been at least equal to the team's win percentage (.673). Bill was 14-9 on the year. He tied Whitey Ford for club leadership in shutouts (three). Bill repeated as the Yanks' third starter in 1962 when he, Whitey Ford and Ralph Terry combined to start 109 of the Yankees' 162 games.

LATER YANKEE CAREER: In 1963 Bill was the Yanks' sixth starter and also was used in relief. He was used strictly as a relief pitcher in 1964. A sore arm plagued him in 1965, although he was the club's fifth starter.

WORLD SERIES: Bill started and pitched 6⅔ innings of Game 3 of the 1961 Series in a game that the Yanks won, although Bill did not receive the decision. In Game 3 of the 1962 Series, Bill pitched a brilliant four-hitter to beat the San Francisco Giants, 3-2.

TRADED: In June, 1966, the Yanks traded Bill, pitcher Gil Blanco and outfielder Roger Repoz to the Kansas City A's for pitcher Fred Talbot and catcher Billy Bryan.

STAFFORD, BILL

Yr.	W-L	Pct.	SA	G	GS	CG	IP	H	BB	SO	SH	ERA
1960	3-1	.750	0	11	8	2	60	50	18	36	1	2.25
1961	14-9	.609	2	36	25	8	195	168	59	101	3	2.68
1962	14-9	.609	0	35	33	7	213	188	77	109	2	3.67
1963	4-8	.333	3	28	14	0	90	104	42	52	0	6.02
1964	5-0	1.000	4	31	1	0	61	50	22	39	0	2.67
1965	3-8	.273	0	22	15	1	111	93	31	71	0	3.56
6 Yrs.	43-35	.551	9	163	96	18	730	653	249	408	6	3.48
Life	43-40	.518	9	186	104	18	786	707	270	449	6	3.52

World Series

Yr.	G	IP	BB	SO	H	W-L	SA
1960	2	6	1	2	5	0-0	0
1961	1	6⅔	2	5	7	0-0	0
1962	1	9	2	5	4	1-0	0
3 Yrs.	4	21⅔	5	12	16	1-0	0
Life.	Same.						

STIRNWEISS, SNUFFY
(BORN GEORGE HENRY STIRNWEISS)

Yankee: 1943-50
Infielder
Born: October 26, 1918
Birthplace: New York, NY
Died: September 15, 1958
Bat: R; Throw: R
Ht: 5'8"; Wt: 175

HONORS: The Baseball Writers gave Snuffy the Sid Mercer Award in 1945. *The Sporting News* selected him for its ML All-Star team as the best second baseman in baseball in 1945. Snuffy was picked as a third baseman to be on the AL team for the 1946 AL All-Star Game.

YANKEE INFIELDER: Snuffy began his ML career as a reserve shortstop on the Yanks in 1943. In 1944-45 he was the Yanks' star second baseman, playing every Yankee game in each season at second base. In 1946 he played the majority of the Yankee games at third base. He returned as the regular Yankee second baseman in 1947-48. Snuffy was a reserve Yankee second baseman in 1949.

EXCITING PLAYER: Snuffy was one of the most exciting and popular players to wear the Yankee uniform. He possessed great speed and was a tremendous base runner, especially early in his career. (He was bothered by injuries late in his career.) His 22 triples in 1945 fell only one shy of the Yankee club record. The 55 bases he stole in 1944 is the sixth highest total by a player in Yankee history. He was a key member of three Yankee World Championship clubs (1943, '47, '49). He was a beloved free spirit, both with the fans and players.

DEFENSIVE ABILITIES: As a defensive infielder, he was sensational at second, third and shortstop. He led AL second basemen in fielding in 1944 (.982) and 1948 (.993). His 1948 fielding mark of .993 set the Yankee club record for second basemen. Snuffy also led AL second basemen in assists (481)

and putouts (433) in 1944. Those 433 putouts is the Yankee second baseman's record. In 1945 he led AL second basemen in putouts (432) and double plays (119).

LEAGUE LEADER: In 1944 Snuffy led the AL in hits (205), triples (16), runs (125) and stolen bases (55). In 1945 he had a spectacular season, leading the AL in batting (.309), slugging (.476), at-bats (632), runs (107), hits (195), triples (22) and stolen bases (33), yet somehow he was denied the MVP Award.

ALL-TIME-YANKEE LEADER: Snuffy ranks 13th in triples (66), and 19th in steals (130) on the All-Time Yankee Top 20 lists.

CLUB LEADERSHIP: Snuffy led the Yanks in stolen bases four years in a row (1943-46). Three times he led the club in at-bats. Not including his AL-leading statistics, he twice led the Yanks in batting, walks, and doubles. (In 1944 and 1945 he led the Yanks in about every offensive category except HRs and RBIs.)

WORLD SERIES: In the 1947 Series, Snuffy led both clubs in walks (eight).

TRADED: The Yanks traded Snuffy, three others and $50,000 to the St. Louis Browns in June, 1950. In the trade, the Yanks obtained pitchers Joe Ostrowski, Tom Ferrick and Sid Schacht and third baseman Leo Thomas.

TRAGIC DEATH: In September, 1958, Snuffy died in a Newark Bay, N.J., train derailment.

STIRNWEISS, SNUFFY

Yr.	G	AB	R	H	2B	3B	HR	RBI	BB	SB	BA	SA
1943	83	274	34	60	8	4	1	25	47	11	.219	.288
1944	154	643	125	205	35	16	8	43	73	55	.319	.460
1945	152	632	107	195	32	22	10	64	78	33	.309	.476
1946	129	487	75	122	19	7	0	37	66	18	.251	.318
1947	148	571	102	146	18	8	5	41	89	5	.256	.342
1948	141	515	90	130	20	7	3	32	86	5	.252	.336
1949	70	157	29	41	8	2	0	11	29	3	.261	.338
1950	7	2	0	0	0	0	0	0	0	0	.000	.000
8 Yrs.	884	3281	562	899	140	66	27	253	468	130	.274	.382
Life.	1028	3695	604	989	157	68	29	281	541	134	.268	.371

World Series

Yr.	G	AB	R	H	2B	3B	HR	RBI	BA
1943	1	1	1	0	0	0	0	0	.000
1947	7	27	3	7	0	1	0	3	.259
1949	1	0	0	0	0	0	0	0	.000
3 Yrs.	9	28	4	7	0	1	0	3	.250
Life.	Same								

STOTTLEMYRE, MEL

Yankee: 1964-74
Pitcher
Born: November 13, 1941
Birthplace: Hazelton, MO
Bat: R; Throw: R
Ht: 6'1"; Wt: 178

HONORS: In 1965 Mel was named as one of two pitchers on *The Sporting News* AL All-Star team.

YOUNG PROSPECT: In 1960 Mel was pitching for Yakima Valley College where the Yanks' Northwest scout, a short, bespectacled man named Eddie Taylor, saw him. Taylor was impressed with Mel's sinker and his determination. He signed Mel for the Yanks, giving the 19-year-old a small bonus. In 1961 Mel pitched for Harlan and Auburn. He was 17-9 at Greensboro in 1962 before starring at Richmond of the AAA International League in 1963 and 1964. *The Sporting News* named Mel the 1964 Minor League Player of the Year (the last Yankee prospect so honored) on the basis of his outstanding Richmond record (13-3, 1.42 ERA).

ROOKIE SENSATION: In August, 1964, the faltering Yankees called Mel up from Richmond. He rescued the AL pennant for the Yanks, posting a 9-3 record during a tight pennant race. On September 26, 1964, he went 5-for-5 at-bat and pitched a two-hitter to beat the Washington Senators, 7-0, in another crucial Yankee victory. In his ML debut on August 12 he beat the White Sox, 7-3, on a seven-hitter in a "must win" for the third place Yanks, then three games behind Baltimore and 1½ behind Chicago.

YANKEE ACE: Mel was the Yankee pitching ace the entire time that he was on the Yanks. It was unfortunate that he joined the Yanks just when the great dynasty was crumbling. He won at least 20 games three times, pitching for mediocre Yankee clubs. If he had pitched for some of the championship Yankee teams, there is no telling how successful Mel's career would have been. Mel was a tremendous sinkerball pitcher, an outstanding fielding pitcher and sometimes a dangerous hitter. From April 10, 1967, through June 11, 1974, Mel had 272 starting assignments in a row.

GREAT MOMENTS: In 1972 Mel won four consecutive shutout games from the California Angels, an AL record for a 12-club league. On July 20, 1965, Mel hit an inside-the-park grand slam HR against the Red Sox at Yankee Stadium. In 1970 he pitched an 11-walk shutout! Mel started four Yankee Stadium home openers and had a 2-2 record in those games.

LEAGUE LEADER: In 1965 Mel led AL pitchers in innings pitched (291) and complete games (18). In 1969 he led the AL in complete games (24).

CLUB LEADERSHIP: Mel led Yankee pitchers in numerous pitching categories through the years, but in five categories he was especially dominating. He led the Yanks in games started (nine times), innings pitched (eight times) and shutouts (seven times), more often than any pitcher in Yankee history. Mel led the club in wins seven times, tying with Red Ruffing for the most times leading the Yanks in wins. Mel led the Yanks in winning percentage four times, tying him with Whitey Ford for the most times to lead the team in that statistic.

ALL-TIME YANKEE LEADER: Mel is second on the all-time Yankee shutout list (40). He is third on the all-time Yankee games started (356) and innings pitched (2662) lists. He is fifth on the Yankee strikeout list (1257). He is sixth on the Yankee win list (164); eighth on the complete game (152) list. He is 12th in games pitched (360), and eighth overall in ERA (2.97). His 139 defeats are the most in Yankee history.

ALL-STAR GAME: Mel was selected to the AL team for five All-Star Games (1965, '66, '68, '69, '70). He was the AL's starting pitcher in the 1969 All-Star Game played at Washington's RFK Stadium.

1964 WORLD SERIES: In his only World Series action, Mel started in three games for the Yanks. He beat the Cardinals, 8-3, in Game 2, pitching a beautiful seven-hit complete game. In Game 5, he pitched seven good innings and was relieved (the Yanks lost, 5-2, no decision for Mel). Bob Gibson beat Mel in Game 7. (Mel in all three games was pitted against the great Gibson, but Mel held his own.)

CAREER-ENDING INJURY: A serious shoulder injury ended Mel's 1974 season prematurely. Had he remained healthy for the entire 1974 season, the Yanks probably would have won the East Division of the AL. The shoulder problem forced Mel to retire in spring training, 1975. It was unfortunate that the classy veteran, who had been "the franchise" during the club's bleakest years, was unable to be part of the Yankee success that soon followed his retirement.

BASEBALL FAMILY: The Mel Stottlemyres produced two sons who pitched in the ML's, Mel Jr. (1990) and Todd, who has been pitching in the ML's since 1988. Mel returned to New York in the 1980s and served several years as Mets pitching coach. In 1994 and 1995, Mel was pitching coach for the Astros. Mel returned to the Yankees in 1996, and just completed his seventh season as the Yankees pitching coach.

STOTTLEMYRE, MEL

Yr.	W-L	Pct.	SA	G	GS	CG	IP	H	BB	SO	SH	ERA
1964	9-3	.750	0	13	12	5	96	77	35	49	2	2.06
1965	20-9	.690	0	37	37	18	291	250	88	155	4	2.63
1966	12-20	.375	1	37	35	9	251	239	82	146	3	3.80
1967	15-15	.500	0	36	36	10	255	235	88	151	4	2.96
1968	21-12	.636	0	36	36	19	279	243	65	140	6	2.45
1969	20-14	.588	0	39	39	24	303	267	97	113	3	2.82
1970	15-13	.536	0	37	37	14	271	262	84	126	0	3.09
1971	16-12	.571	0	35	35	19	270	234	69	132	7	2.87
1972	14-18	.438	0	36	36	9	260	250	85	110	7	3.22
1973	16-16	.500	0	38	38	19	273	259	79	95	4	3.07
1974	6-7	.462	0	16	15	6	113	119	37	40	0	3.58
11 Yrs.	164-139	.541	1	360	356	152	2661	2435	809	1257	40	2.97

Life. Same.

World Series

Yr.	G	IP	BB	SO	H	W-L	SA
1964	3	20	6	12	18	1-1	0
1 Yr.	3	20	6	12	18	1-1	0

Life. Same.

STURDIVANT, TOM

Nickname: "Snake"
Yankee: 1955-59
Pitcher
Born: April 28, 1930
Birthplace: Gordon, KS
Bat: L; Throw: R
Ht: 6'; Wt: 186

CONVERTED PITCHER: Famous Yankee scout Tom Greenwade scouted and signed Tom as a kid. In the minor leagues Tom was converted from an outfielder to a pitcher. Tom made the Yanks as a relief pitcher in 1955.

IMPORTANT YANKEE STARTER: Tom was the Yanks' most pleasant surprise of the 1956 season, as the club's fifth starter and third biggest winner (16-8). In 1956 Tom hit .313 (20 for 64), a remarkable batting average for a pitcher. In 1957 Tom was the Yanks' No. 1 starter and ace pitcher. A sore arm ruined his 1958 season. He tried to keep the ball hit to the middle of the baseball field where the great Yankee defense could make the play. Tom was a fun-loving guy who liked to play practical jokes on his Yankee teammates.

LEAGUE LEADER: His winning percentage (.727, 16-6) led AL pitchers in 1957.

CLUB LEADERSHIP: In 1957, Tom led Yankee pitchers in wins (16), games started (28) and innings pitched (202).

WORLD SERIES: In Game 4 of the 1956 Series Tom pitched a terrific six-hit complete game, beating the Dodgers, 6-2, in a Yankee "must win." He started Game 4 of the 1957 Series.

TRADED: The Yanks traded Tom, pitcher Johnny Kucks and infielder Jerry Lumpe to the Kansas City A's for pitcher Ralph Terry and outfielder Hector Lopez in May, 1959.

STURDIVANT, TOM

Yr.	W-L	Pct.	SA	G	GS	CG	IP	H	BB	SO	SH	ERA
1955	1-3	.250	0	33	1	0	68	48	42	48	0	3.16
1956	16-8	.667	5	32	17	6	158	134	52	110	2	3.30
1957	16-6	.727	0	28	28	7	202	170	80	118	2	2.54
1958	3-6	.333	0	15	10	0	71	77	38	41	0	4.20
1959	0-2	.000	0	7	3	0	25	20	9	16	0	4.97
5 Yrs.	36-25	.590	5	115	59	13	524	449	221	333	4	3.20
Life.	59-51	.536	17	335	101	22	1137	1029	449	704	7	3.74

World Series

Yr.	G	IP	BB	SO	H	W-L	SA
1955	2	3	2	0	5	0-0	0
1956	2	9⅔	8	9	8	1-0	0
1957	2	6	1	2	6	0-0	0
3 Yrs.	6	18⅔	11	11	19	1-0	0
Life. Same.							

SWEENEY, JEFF
(BORN EDWARD FRANCIS SWEENEY)

Yankee: 1908-15
Catcher, 1B
Born: July 19, 1888
Birthplace: Chicago, IL
Died: July 4, 1947
Bat: R; Throw: R
Ht: 6'1"; Wt: 200

YANKEE CATCHER: Jeff began his ML career with the Yanks (Highlanders) in 1908. He was a reserve catcher in 1908-09. From 1910-14 he was the club's first-string catcher, although only twice did he catch at least 100 games. (Not many catchers in those days caught 100 games in a season.) Jeff was the Yanks' reserve catcher in 1915.

DEFENSIVE ABILITIES: In 1912, Jeff led AL catchers in putouts (548). In 1913, he led AL catchers in assists (180). That total is also the Yankee club record for catchers' assists. His 167 assists in 1912 is the second highest number of assists by a catcher in Yankee history.

OFFENSIVE THREAT: Jeff was one of the best base-running catchers in Yankee history. His 19 stolen bases in 1914 is the single season Yankee record for a catcher. He tied for club leadership in HRs in 1913 (two).

LEFT YANKS: The 1915 season was Jeff's last with the Yanks. He did not return to the ML's until 1919, playing for the Pirates.

BEST STOLEN BASE SEASONS FOR TOP YANKEE CATCHERS:

J. Sweeney—12 (1910)	Y. Berra—5 (1951)
JEFF SWEENEY—19 (1914)	E. Howard—3 (1960)
W. Schang—12 (1922)	T. Munson—14 (1976)
B. Dickey—7 (1930)	J. Girardi—13 (1996)

SWEENEY, JEFF

Yr.	G	AB	R	H	2B	3B	HR	RBI	BB	SB	BA	SA
1908	32	82	4	12	2	0	0	2	5	0	.146	.171
1909	67	176	19	47	3	0	0	21	16	3	.267	.284
1910	78	215	25	43	4	4	0	13	17	12	.200	.256
1911	83	229	17	53	6	5	0	18	14	8	.231	.301
1912	110	351	37	94	12	1	0	30	27	6	.268	.308
1913	117	351	35	93	10	2	2	40	37	11	.265	.322
1914	87	258	25	55	8	1	1	22	35	19	.213	.264
1915	53	137	12	26	2	0	0	5	25	3	.190	.204
8 Yrs.	627	1799	174	423	47	13	3	151	176	62	.235	.281
Life.	644	1841	174	427	48	13	3	151	181	63	.232	.277

TARTABULL, DANNY

Yankee: 1992-95
Designated Hitter, OF
Born: October 30, 1962
Birthplace: Miami, FL
Bat: R; Throw: R
Ht: 6'1"; Wt: 204

DEVELOPING POWER HITTER: In 1985 Danny hit 43 homers with Calgary of the Pacific Coast League, and he hit 25 with the Seattle Mariners in 1986. He was traded to the Royals, and in 1987 he hit his career high of 34 homers. His best all-round season was in 1991 (31 HRs, 100 RBIs, and .316 BA). His father, Jose, who played in the majors for nine seasons (1962-70), hit only two homers.

BIG-NAME ACQUISITION: When the Yankees signed Danny as a free agent in January 1992 to a five-year multimillion dollar deal, they were adding a recognized Big Guy. At the age of 29, Danny seemed primed for big-city stardom. He became the cleanup man and rightfielder. His Yankee career was destined, however, to be somewhat disappointing, and subsequent injuries were major factors.

DISAPPOINTING INITIAL SEASON: Even before the 1992 season opened, Danny suffered an injury to his right wrist. He went on the Disabled List in April with a strained left hamstring and again in July with back spasms. He missed 39 games altogether. However, he finished strong; in his final 66 games, he hit 19 of his club-leading 25 homers.

ONE MEMORABLE GAME: Danny had a great night on September 8, 1992. After spending the afternoon at the Smithsonian Institute in Washington, D.C., he went up the road to Baltimore, where he had five hits in as many trips, including two homers and a double. More impressively, he had nine RBIs, the second highest in a game ever made by a Yankee, second only to Tony Lazzeri's 11 RBIs in a 1936 game.

BEST YANKEE SEASON: Danny enjoyed his best Yankee season in 1993, leading the club in homers (31), RBIs (102), runs (87), and walks (92). He also set a club record with 156 strikeouts, which wasn't so glaring in light of his overall production. He battled injuries once again, missing three weeks in May and June with a kidney bruise. But the most meaningful injury to his career came on July 15, 1993, when he hurt his throwing shoulder. The tear required surgery in November, and Danny was never able to throw again as well as he did before the injury. This would play a large role in Danny later moving out of rightfield and becoming the DH.

LESS PRODUCTIVE: Danny in 1994 was relatively healthy but experienced a poor season. He had difficulty making contact at the plate in the early months and was leaving too many runners on base. He was hitting .233 on June 17 when Manager Showalter dropped him temporarily to sixth in the batting order, Danny hit .288 the rest of the year. He hit a mighty .339 against lefthanded pitching, but only .219 against righthanders. He was fourth in the AL with 111 strikeouts. Danny seemed to be losing bat speed, but he refused to cut down his swing when he had two strikes.

LIMITATIONS: What had made Danny valuable was his home runs and his consistently high RBI per AB rate. These abilities usually had made up for the following limitations: 1) He made

too little contact with frequent strikeouts. 2) He was slow of foot, clogging up the base paths. 3) He had very poor range in right field. 4) His throwing had deteriorated after the 1993 shoulder injury. By 1994 he was primarily a DH, and his limitations were beginning to outweigh his attributes.

LEAVING THE YANKEES: In 1995, Danny wasn't even hitting for power anymore. He had become a liability. He was a cloud in the clubhouse and no ray of sunshine to the fans either, and with his big contract, he was a pain in the backside of George Steinbrenner. Danny was hitting .224 with six homers in 59 games when the Yankees traded him to Oakland for Ruben Sierra. Danny was unhappy about his treatment in New York, and though his treatment may have been unfair, the bottom line is once his power production dropped, he was no longer a valuable player. In January 1996, Danny was traded by the Athletics to the White Sox. Danny ended his career in 1997 after a few games with the Phillies.

TARTABULL, DANNY												
Yr.	G	AB	R	H	2B	3B	HR	RBI	BB	SB	BA	SA
1992	123	421	72	112	19	0	25	85	103	2	.266	.489
1993	138	513	87	128	33	2	31	102	92	0	.250	.503
1994	104	399	68	102	24	1	19	67	66	1	.256	.464
1995	59	192	25	43	12	0	6	28	33	0	.224	.380
4 Yrs.	424	1525	252	385	88	3	81	282	294	3	.252	.473
Life.	1406	5011	756	1366	289	22	262	925	768	37	.273	.496

TERRY, RALPH

Yankee: 1956-57, '59-64
Pitcher
Born: January 9, 1936
Birthplace: Big Cabin, OK
Bat: R; Throw: R
Ht: 6'3"; Wt: 195

HONORS: In 1962, *The Sporting News* selected Ralph as one of two pitchers on the publication's AL All-Star team. Also in 1962, he was named to the AL team for the All-Star Game.

OUTSTANDING YOUNG PROSPECT: As an 18-year-old in 1954, Ralph was scouted and signed by famous Yankee scout Tom Greenwade. But the Cardinals contended they had signed Ralph. Commissioner Ford Frick ruled in favor of the Yanks and Ralph began his pro career at Binghamton. From 1954-56 Ralph pitched at Binghamton and Denver. He was 13-4 at Denver in 1956 when he was called up to the Yanks for a brief stint.

COMING AND GOING: In June, 1957, the Yanks traded Ralph, along with Billy Martin, Woodie Held and Bob Martyn, to the Kansas City A's for Ryne Duren, Harry "Suitcase" Simpson, Jim Pisoni, and Milt Graff. The Yanks reacquired Ralph, along with Hector Lopez, in May, 1959, from the A's for Tom Sturdivant, Johnny Kucks and Jerry Lumpe. Following the 1964 season the Yanks dealt Ralph to the Indians, completing the deal that brought Pedro Ramos to the Yanks in September, 1964.

STAR YANKEE PITCHER: Ralph had excellent stuff, and he mixed up all four major pitches well (fastball, change of pace, curve and slider). After rejoining the Yanks in 1959, he was the

Danny Tartabull

Yanks' sixth starter. In 1960 he was the Yanks' fourth starter and he won the AL pennant clincher at Boston. Ralph became the No. 3 Yankee starter in 1961, behind the ace of the staff, Whitey Ford. Ralph's 1961 winning percentage (.842, 16-3) was topped only by Ford in the entire AL. In 1962 Ralph had his most sensational year and he became the ace of the Yankee pitching staff. Including his two World Series wins, Ralph had 25 victories in the 1962 season, which happened to be the most wins by a Yankee right-hander since George Pipgras won 24 in 1928. Ralph allowed 40 HRs in 1962, the most in Yankee history. Ralph and Whitey Ford were the workhorses of the 1963 squad Yankee coach Johnny Sain taught him how to throw the slider. The slider became Ralph's bread and butter pitch, enabling him to become one of the best right-handers in Yankee history. In 1964 Ralph was dropped down to the fourth Yankee starter.

LEAGUE LEADER: In 1962 Ralph led the AL in wins (23), games started (39) and innings pitched (299). He led the AL in games started (37) and complete games (18) in 1963.

ALL-TIME YANKEE LEADER: Ralph ranks 19th in Yankee history in shutouts (14), and 20th in strikeouts (615).

CLUB LEADERSHIP: Besides his AL leading stats in 1962, Ralph also led Yankee pitchers in complete games (14), strikeouts (176) and shutouts (three). Twice he led the Yanks in strikeouts.

WORLD SERIES: In Game 7 of the 1960 Series, Ralph had the misfortune of giving up the famous ninth-inning game-winning HR hit by Bill Mazeroski that won the Series for Pittsburgh. Actually, Ralph lost his stuff in the bullpen because he had been asked to warm up at least four times before coming in. He started a pair of games in the 1961 Series. Ralph had the guts to redeem his 1960 mistake by being the hero of the 1962 Series. He was tremendous in the 1962 Series, winning *Sport Magazine's* MVP Award and the Babe Ruth Award. After losing a 2-0 heartbreaker in Game 2, he returned to beat the San Francisco Giants, 5-3, in a complete game victory in Game 5. Then with the Series on the line in Game 7, Ralph pitched a heroic four-hitter to defeat the Giants, 1-0!

TIDROW, DICK

Nickname: "Dirt"
Yankee: 1974-79
Pitcher
Born: May 14,1947
Birthplace: San Francisco, CA
Bat: R; Throw: R
Ht: 6'4"; Wt: 220

CAME TO YANKS: In April, 1974, the Yanks obtained Dick, first baseman Chris Chambliss and relief pitcher Cecil Upshaw from the Indians in a deal that sent pitchers Fritz Peterson, Steve Kline, Tom Buskey, and Fred Beene to Cleveland.

VERSATILE PITCHER: During his stay with the Yanks, Dick was one of the most valuable players on the club, performing every job asked of a pitcher. In 1974 he was the Yanks' No. 3 starter and the club's third biggest winner (11-9). From 1975-77 Dick held the most difficult job on a pitching staff. He was the long relief man, a spot starter and also a short reliever. Thus, Dick never knew exactly when he was going to pitch or in what situation he would find himself on the mound, yet he produced splendidly. Over the combined 1975-77 seasons, Dick won 21 games and saved 20 others. Late in the 1977 pennant race, when the Yanks needed a starter badly, Dick started seven games and the Yanks won them all. In 1978 he was the Yanks' No. 3 starter. When renovated Yankee Stadium reopened on April 15, 1976, Dick was the winning pitcher in relief against the Twins.

TEAM PLAYER: Dick was a great guy to have on a club. He was one of the leaders on the Yanks. He was helpful to young pitchers and he was an especially good buddy of Ron Guidry's. Dick was well respected by his Yankee teammates who knew firsthand of his unpublicized contribution to the Yankee cause.

POST-SEASON PLAY: Dick was the winning pitcher in relief, hurling the 9th inning in Game 5 of the 1976 AL Championship Series as the Yanks won the club's first AL pennant in 12 years. Lost in the excitement of the Yanks' comeback extra-inning victory in Game 4 of the 1978 World Series was Dick's beautiful three innings of scoreless relief pitching that kept the Yanks in the game.

TRADED: In May 1979, the Yankees traded Dick to the Cubs for pitcher Ray Burris. It was a poor trade for the Yanks, as Dick had a few good years left; he finished his ML career with the Mets in 1984.

TERRY, RALPH

Yr.	W-L	Pct.	SA	G	GS	CG	IP	H	BB	SO	SH	ERA
1956	1-2	.333	0	3	3	0	13	17	11	8	0	9.45
1957	1-1	.500	0	7	2	1	21	18	8	7	1	3.05
1959	3-7	.300	0	24	16	5	127	130	30	55	1	3.39
1960	10-8	.556	1	35	23	7	167	149	52	92	3	3.40
1961	16-3	.842	0	31	27	9	188	162	42	86	2	3.15
1962	23-12	.657	2	43	39	14	299	257	57	176	3	3.19
1963	17-15	.531	1	40	37	18	268	246	39	114	3	3.22
1964	7-11	.389	4	27	14	2	115	130	31	77	1	4.54
8 Yrs.	78-59	.569	8	210	161	56	1198	1109	270	615	14	3.44
Life.	107-99	.519	11	338	257	75	1849	1748	446	1000	20	3.62

World Series

Yr.	G	IP	BB	SO	H	W-L	SA
1960	2	6⅔	1	5	7	0-2	0
1961	2	9⅓	2	7	12	0-1	0
1962	3	25	2	16	17	2-1	0
1963	1	3	1	0	3	0-0	0
1964	1	2	0	3	2	0-0	0
5 Yrs.	9	46	6	31	41	2-4	0
Life.	Same.						

TIDROW, DICK

Yr.	W-L	Pct.	SA	G	CG	GS	IP	H	BB	SO	SH	ERA
1974	11-9	.550	1	33	25	5	191	205	53	100	0	3.87
1975	6-3	.667	5	37	0	0	69	65	31	38	0	3.12
1976	4-5	.444	10	47	2	0	92	80	24	65	0	2.63
1977	11-4	.733	5	49	7	0	151	143	41	83	0	3.16
1978	7-11	.389	0	31	25	4	185	191	53	73	0	3.84
1979	2-1	.667	2	14	0	0	23	38	4	7	0	7.94
6 Yrs.	41-33	.554	23	211	59	9	711	722	206	366	0	3.61
Life.	100-94	.515	55	620	138	32	1747	1705	579	975	5	3.68

Championship Series

Yr.	G	IP	BB	SO	H	W-L	SA
1976	3	7⅓	4	0	6	1-0	0
1977	2	7	3	3	6	0-0	0
1978	1	5⅔	2	1	8	0-0	0
3 Yrs.	6	20	9	4	20	1-0	0
Life.	7	23	12	7	21	1-0	0

World Series

Yr.	G	IP	BB	SO	H	W-L	SA
1976	2	2⅓	1	1	5	0-0	0
1977	2	3⅔	0	1	5	0-0	0
1978	2	4⅔	0	5	4	0-0	0
3 Yrs.	6	10⅔	1	7	14	0-0	0
Life. Same.							

TRESH, TOM

Yankee: 1961-69
Outfielder, SS, 3B
Born: September 20, 1937
Birthplace: Detroit, MI
Bat: Both; Throw: R
Ht: 6'; Wt: 191

HONORS: The Baseball Writers selected Tom as the AL's Rookie of the Year in 1962. *The Sporting News* also gave Tom its AL Rookie Award in 1962. In spring training, 1962, Tom was given the James P. Dawson Award as the best Yankee rookie in camp. In 1962 *The Sporting News* selected Tom to the publication's AL All-Star team as the best shortstop in the circuit. In 1962 Tom was shortstop on Topps ML Rookie All-Star team. In 1962 and 1963, Tom was a member of the AL team for the All-Star Game.

YOUNG PROSPECT: Tom, whose dad, Mike, was a ML catcher for 12 seasons, signed with the Yankees in 1958 and in 1958-61 was on the Yankee farm teams at New Orleans, St. Petersburg, Greensboro, Binghamton, Amarillo, and Richmond. By the time he got to St. Petersburg he was an established switch-hitter. But in his first action at St. Pete, an exhibition game, he rapped four hits off a rightie while batting right-handed. He told his manager, Tom Hamilton, that he felt he should swing from the right side exclusively. Hamilton phoned New York and relayed the Tresh proposal. He received a one-word answer: "No!" At Richmond in 1961 Tom hit .315 and was named International League rookie of the year. The Yankees called him up at the end of that season for a brief look.

ROOKIE STAR: Yankee shortstop Tony Kubek was in the Army for most of the 1962 season, and Tom, after waging a furious spring training battle with Phil Linz, was made shortstop until Kubek returned in August. Tom did a tremendous job at shortstop, and his bat was exceptionally potent. When Tom was switched to left field, a position unfamiliar to him, he played like a seasoned veteran. He was the biggest Yankee story of the 1962 season.

SWITCH-HITTING SLUGGER: Tom was a power-hitting switch-hitter. He hit 20 or more HRs in four seasons as a Yankee player. On three different occasions he hit HRs from both sides of the plate in one game. In a game against the White Sox played on June 6, 1965, he hit three consecutive HRs.

STOLEN BASE RECORD: Tom had good speed and was a smart base runner. In 1964 he was 13 for 13 in stolen base attempts.

DEFENSIVE ABILITIES: After being the Yanks' shortstop for most of the 1962 season, Tom played left field from late in the 1962 season through the 1965 season. He was one of the best defensive outfielders in the game. In 1964 he led all AL outfielders in fielding (.996). Tom won a Gold Glove Award in 1965 as the best defensive leftfielder in the AL. Because the Yanks were hurting so badly in the infield in 1966, Tom played 64 games at third base. (He was a team player.) He was the leftfielder again in 1967. Tom was Yankee shortstop in 1968 and 1969 before he was traded.

CLUB LEADERSHIP: Tom led the Yanks in doubles three times. Twice he led the club in runs scored and walks. The two years (1963, '66) that Tom led the team in walks were the only years between 1954-68 that Mickey Mantle did not lead the Yanks in that category. In 1964 Tom led the Yanks in stolen bases (13). In 1965 he led the club in HRs (26), RBIs (74), runs (94), hits (168), doubles (29), triples (six) and slugging (.477).

WORLD SERIES: In the 1962 Series he led the Yanks in batting (.321) and he led both clubs in hits (nine) and runs scored (five). His three-run HR in the bottom of the eighth inning beat the San Francisco Giants, 5-3, in Game 5 of the 1962 Series. He made a great catch in Game 7 to help win the final game of the Series. He hit a two-run HR off Sandy Koufax in Game 1 of the 1963 Series. With two outs in the bottom of the 9th inning of Game 5 of the 1964 Series, Tom hit a two-run HR to tie the game that the Yanks eventually lost in 10 innings.

TRADED: Tom was traded from the Yanks to the Tigers for outfielder Ron Woods in June, 1969.

TRESH, TOM

Yr.	G	AB	R	H	2B	3B	HR	RBI	BB	SB	BA	SA
1961	9	8	1	2	0	0	0	0	0	0	.250	.250
1962	157	622	94	178	26	5	20	93	67	4	.286	.441
1963	145	520	91	140	28	5	25	71	83	3	.269	.487
1964	153	533	75	131	25	5	16	73	73	13	.246	.402
1965	156	602	94	168	29	6	26	74	59	5	.279	.477
1966	151	537	76	125	12	4	27	68	86	5	.233	.421
1967	130	448	45	98	23	3	14	53	50	1	.219	.377
1968	152	507	60	99	18	3	11	52	76	10	.195	.308
1969	45	143	13	26	5	2	1	9	17	2	.182	.266
9 Yrs.	1098	3920	549	967	166	33	140	493	511	43	.247	.413
Life.	1192	4251	595	1041	179	34	153	530	550	45	.245	.411

World Series

Yr.	G	AB	R	H	2B	3B	HR	RBI	BA
1962	7	28	5	9	1	0	1	4	.321
1963	4	15	1	3	0	0	1	2	.200
1964	7	22	4	6	2	0	2	7	.273
3 Yrs.	18	65	10	18	3	0	4	13	.277
Life. Same.									

TURLEY, BOB

Nickname: "Bullet Bob"
Yankee: 1955-62
Pitcher
Born: September 19, 1930
Birthplace: Troy, IL
Bat: R; Throw: R
Ht: 6'2"; Wt: 215

HONORS: In 1958 Bob won the Cy Young Memorial Award as the best pitcher in the ML's. *The Sporting News* selected Bob as the AL Pitcher of the Year and the ML Player of the Year in 1958, and the Baseball Writers gave Bob the Sid Mercer Award. He also won the Hickok Belt as the Top Professional Athlete of the Year in 1958, and *The Sporting News* selected him as one of three pitchers on the publication's 1958 ML All-Star team.

CAME TO YANKS: In November, 1954, Bob came to the Yanks from the Baltimore Orioles as part of an 18-player trade, the largest trade in ML history. (Don Larsen also came to the Yanks, and Gene Woodling went to the Orioles.)

FASTBALL PITCHER: "Bullet Bob" possessed a scorching, lively fastball, and when he was on the top of his game (as he was during the entire 1958 season), Bob was as tough to hit as any pitcher in history. Mickey Mantle stated he never saw a harder thrower than Bob when he was right. Bob had a good curveball, but he used it as his waste pitch and for setting up batters. To be effective in a game, Bob needed his blazing fastball, and a lot of strikeouts indicated he had his speed. Sometimes Bob was wild. In 1955 he walked 177 batters, the most ever by a Yankee right-hander, and he led the AL in walks in 1955 and 1958 (128). Only four times has a Yankee pitcher recorded more strikeouts than Bob's 210 in 1955. For his ML career, Bob fanned 6.65 batters per nine innings, which ties him for the 40th best ratio in ML history. For his ML career, Bob allowed only 7.18 hits per nine innings, the tenth best ratio in ML history. Bob got his childhood pitching practice throwing pears in his back yard.

YANKEE STAR: As a Yankee pitcher, Bob hurled three one-hitters, tying him with Whitey Ford for the most in Yankee history. In his best Yankee seasons (1955, 1958), he was the Yanks' ace starter. He was the club's third starter in 1956 and the second starter in 1957. In the 1959 Yankee Stadium home opener, Bob beat the Red Sox, 3-2, but his 8-11 record in 1959 was disappointing on the heels of his splendid 1958 season. Bob and Whitey Ford teamed to form an excellent right-left combination for the Yanks in the late 1950s. In 1960 Bob was the Yanks' third starter, and although his 9-3 record was not sensational, the Yanks won 14 of the 15 games in which he was relieved after starting. A sore arm ruined his 1961 campaign. He attempted to pitch with constant arm pain, but finally was placed on the disabled list for much of the season, then had surgery. He was used mostly in relief in 1962.

FINE GENTLEMAN: Although Bob's fastball was frighteningly quick, batters were not usually intimidated, because they knew that Bob was too much of a gentleman to throw at a hitter. On the Yanks, he was known as a serious, religious fellow, but one who was quite friendly and liked by his teammates. There was one bit of deception, though, at which Bob was especially adept. He could discover telltale signs in other pitchers that allowed him to know what kind of pitch was to be delivered. As soon as he learned the pitch, Bob quickly relayed the information (usually by whistling) to the Yankee batter who gained a great advantage. Mickey Mantle hit many HRs after being tipped by Bob.

LEAGUE LEADER: In 1958 Bob led AL pitchers in wins, winning percentage (21-7, .750) and complete games (19).

CLUB LEADERSHIP: Besides his AL leading stats in 1958, Bob also led the Yanks in innings pitched (245). Three times he led the Yanks in strikeouts and shutouts. Bob led the club in complete games in two straight seasons (1957-58). Twice he led the team in games started.

ALL-TIME YANKEE LEADER: Bob is tenth on the all-time Yankee shutout list (21). He is 12th on the all-time Yankee strikeout list (909); 19th overall in winning percentage (.612); and 20th in victories (82).

ALL-STAR GAME: Bob was selected to the AL team for the 1955 and 1958 All-Star Games. He started the 1958 All-Star Game.

WORLD SERIES: In Game 6 of the 1956 Series, Bob fanned 11 Dodgers, the most ever recorded by a losing pitcher in a World Series game. Bob lost a 1-0 heartbreaker in the 10th inning when a ball was misplayed in the outfield. In Game 6 of the 1957 Series, he pitched a four-hitter to beat Milwaukee, 3-2. Bob was the hero of the 1958 Series, winning *Sport Magazine's* MVP Award. With the Yanks trailing three games to one, Bob kept the Yanks alive by blanking the Braves, 7-0, in Game 5. He returned in Game 6 in relief to get the final Brave out, recording a save. Then in Game 7 Bob won again, 6-2, to give the Yanks a remarkable Series comeback conquest. In Game 2 of the 1960 Series, he beat Pittsburgh, 16-3.

LEFT YANKS: Following the 1962 season, the Yanks sold Bob's contract to the Los Angeles Angels. In 1963 Bob was 2-7 for the Angels and 1-4 for the Red Sox in his last ML season.

TURLEY, BOB

Yr.	W-L	Pct.	SA	G	GS	CG	IP	H	BB	SO	SH	ERA
1955	17-13	.567	1	36	34	13	247	168	177	210	6	3.06
1956	8-4	.667	1	27	21	5	132	138	103	91	1	5.05
1957	13-6	.684	3	32	23	9	176	120	85	152	4	2.71
1958	21-7	.750	1	33	31	19	245	178	128	168	6	2.97
1959	8-11	.421	0	33	22	7	154	141	83	111	3	4.32
1960	9-3	.750	5	34	24	4	173	138	87	87	1	3.27
1961	3-5	.375	0	15	12	1	72	74	51	48	0	5.75
1962	3-3	.500	1	24	8	0	69	68	47	42	0	4.57
8 Yrs.	82-52	.612	12	234	175	58	1269	1025	761	909	21	3.62
Life.	101-85	.543	12	310	237	78	1713	1366	1068	1265	24	3.64

World Series

Yr.	G	IP	BB	SO	H	W-L	SA
1955	3	5⅓	4	7	7	0-1	0
1956	3	11	8	14	4	0-1	0
1957	3	11⅔	6	12	7	1-0	0
1958	4	16⅓	7	13	10	2-1	1
1960	2	9⅓	4	0	15	1-0	0
5 Yrs.	15	53⅔	29	46	43	4-3	1
Life. Same.							

VELARDE, RANDY

Yankee: 1987-95, 2001
Infielder
Born: November 24, 1962
Birthplace: Midland, TX
Bat: R; Throw: R
Ht: 6'; Wt: 192

BECOMES A YANKEE: Randy was in the White Sox organization when the Yankees obtained him in a trade involving minor-league pitchers. His first three seasons with the Yanks (1987, 1988, 1989) were spent splitting his time between Columbus (the Yankee AAA club) and New York. He was the Yanks' utility man in 1990 and 1991, and in 1992, he was the regular shortstop, hitting .272 in 121 games.

VERSATILE INFIELDER: Randy became valuable to the Yanks because of his versatility. He wasn't good enough defensively to hold a regular infield position, however, and he didn't hit for enough power to play in the outfield. In 1993, Randy began to develop into of the game's best all-purpose players. He worked on his different roles. Manager Buck Showalter plugged him in wherever needed—usually shortstop, third base or left field—and he responded with a batting average of .301 in 1993 and .279 in 1994.

LAST SEASON WITH THE YANKS: Velarde took over at second base for much of 1995, and he did a decent job defensively while hitting .278 in 111 games. But he did hit a meek .176 in the playoffs, although he put New York ahead in the 11th inning of the finale against Seattle with a run-scoring single off ace Randy Johnson. A month later, he signed with the Angels.

RETURNS: After playing with the Angels, Athletics, and Rangers, Randy returned to the Yankees for part of the 2001

season and participated in the postseason games. It was a short-lived stint though as he signed with Oakland for the 2002 season.

VELARDE, RANDY											
Yr.	G	AB	R	H	2B	3B	HR	RBI	BB	SB	BA	SA
1987	8	22	1	4	0	0	0	1	0	0	.182	.182
1988	48	115	18	20	6	0	5	12	8	1	.174	.357
1989	33	100	12	34	4	2	2	11	7	0	.340	.480
1990	95	229	21	48	6	2	5	19	20	0	.210	.319
1991	80	184	19	45	11	1	1	15	18	3	.245	.332
1992	121	412	57	112	24	1	7	46	38	7	.272	.386
1993	85	226	28	68	13	2	7	24	18	2	.301	.469
1994	77	280	47	78	16	1	9	34	22	4	.279	.439
1995	111	367	60	102	19	1	7	46	55	5	.278	.392
2001	15	46	4	7	3	0	0	1	5	2	.152	.217
10 Yrs.	673	1981	267	518	102	10	43	209	191	24	.261	.388

Still Active.

Division Series											
Yr.	G	AB	R	H	2B	3B	HR	RBI	BB	SB	BA	SA
1995	5	17	3	3	0	0	0	1	6	0	.176	.176
2001	4	5	1	3	1	0	0	1	0	0	.600	.800
2 Yrs.	9	22	4	6	1	0	0	2	6	0	.273	.318

Still Active.

Championship Series											
Yr.	G	AB	R	H	2B	3B	HR	RBI	BB	SB	BA	SA
2001	1	1	0	0	0	0	0	0	0	0	.000	.000
1 Yr.	1	1	0	0	0	0	0	0	0	0	.000	.000

Still Active.

World Series											
Yr.	G	AB	R	H	2B	3B	HR	RBI	BB	SB	BA	SA
2001	1	3	0	0	0	0	0	0	1	0	.000	.000
1 Yr.	1	3	0	0	0	0	0	0	1	0	.000	.000

Still Active.

Randy Velarde played his first nine Major League seasons in pinstripes.

WARD, AARON

Yankee: 1917-26
Infielder
Born: August 28, 1896
Birthplace: Booneville, AK
Died: January 30, 1961
Bat: R; Throw: R
Ht: 5'10"; Wt: 160

CAME TO YANKS: In June of 1917, the Yanks purchased Aaron's contract from Louisville of the Southern League. In the summer of 1917, Aaron was a 21-year-old rookie reserve shortstop for the Yanks. He spent most of the 1918 season serving in the military. In limited playing time in 1919, Aaron played all four infield positions.

YANKEE INFIELDER: After having been a part-time utility player for three seasons, in 1920 Aaron became the Yanks' regular third baseman, playing 114 games at third and 12 at shortstop. In 1921 he was shifted to second base for 123 games and played 33 at third. Aaron was the Yanks' regular second baseman from 1921-25, although a leg injury forced him to miss some games in 1924. Tony Lazzeri became the second sacker in 1926 and Aaron was used sparingly. Only Gil McDougald in the 1950s was as versatile an infielder as was Aaron.

DEFENSIVE ABILITIES: Aaron had good range and was a consistent, hardworking second baseman. In two consecutive games (April 20, 21) of the 1921 campaign, he handled 18 chances to tie an AL third baseman's record. He led AL second basemen in assists in 1922 (489) and again in 1923 (493). He also led AL second basemen in fielding in 1923 (.980).

MEMBER OF YANKEE PENNANT WINNERS: Aaron was a key member of the first Yankee championship clubs. He played in every game in each of the first three Yankee AL pennant-winning years (1921, '22, '23). Besides being a valuable defensive player, Aaron was a capable hitter. His best year at the plate was 1921 (.306, 75 RBIs).

WORLD SERIES: In the 1923 Series he was outstanding, leading both clubs in hits (ten) and batting (.417). He hit a HR to help the Yanks beat the New York Giants, 4-2, in Game 2 of the 1923 Series. He wasn't derelict in the previous (1922) Series, either, hitting the Yanks' only two HRs.

TRADED: The Yanks traded Aaron to the White Sox in January of 1927 for catcher Johnny Grabowski and infielder Ray Morehart. In 1927 Aaron hit .270 in 145 games for the White Sox and the following season he got into six games for the Indians in his last ML season.

WARD, AARON

Yr.	G	AB	R	H	2B	3B	HR	RBI	BB	SB	BA	SA
1917	8	26	0	3	0	0	0	1	1	0	.115	.115
1918	20	32	2	4	1	0	0	1	2	1	.125	.156
1919	27	34	5	7	2	0	0	2	5	0	.206	.265
1920	127	496	62	127	18	7	11	54	33	7	.256	.387
1921	153	556	77	170	30	10	5	75	42	6	.306	.423
1922	154	558	69	149	19	5	7	68	45	7	.267	.357
1923	152	567	79	161	26	11	10	82	56	8	.284	.422
1924	120	400	42	101	13	10	8	66	40	1	.253	.395
1925	125	439	41	108	22	3	4	38	49	1	.246	.337
1926	22	31	5	10	2	0	0	3	2	0	.323	.387
10 Yrs.	908	3139	382	840	133	46	45	390	275	31	.268	.382
Life.	1059	3611	457	966	158	54	50	446	339	37	.268	.383

World Series

Yr.	G	AB	R	H	2B	3B	HR	RBI	BA
1921	8	26	1	6	0	0	0	4	.231
1922	5	13	3	2	0	0	2	3	.154
1923	6	24	4	10	0	0	1	2	.417
3 Yrs.	19	63	8	18	0	0	3	9	.286
Life.	Same.								

WARHOP, JACK
(BORN JOHN MILTON WARHOP)

Nicknames: "Crab", "Chief"
Yankee: 1908-15
Pitcher
Born: July 4, 1884
Birthplace: Hinton, WV
Died: October 4, 1960
Bat: R; Throw: R
Ht: 5'9"; Wt: 168

YANKEE STARTER: Jack played his entire ML career with the Yanks. From 1909-15, Jack was one of the top three Yankee starters, except in 1913 when he was bothered by a sore arm

and only started seven games. He was a submarine pitcher, throwing "underhand subterfuges."

HITTING BATTERS: Jack hit 120 batters in his lifetime, ranking 12th on the all-time list for the 20th century. In 1909 Jack hit 26 batsmen. Besides 1909, Jack also led the AL in hitting batters in 1910 (18). Hitters had difficulty picking up pitches from Jack's unorthodox delivery.

STEALING HOME: Jack is the only Yankee pitcher to ever successfully steal home plate twice. Against Chicago on August 27, 1910, he stole home. He stole home again on July 12, 1912, in a game against St. Louis.

BAD LUCK: In 1914 Jack was a hard-luck pitcher, losing five 1-0 games! He remains one of six pitchers holding that unwanted ML record. With any hitting support at all, Jack could easily have been 15-8 instead of 8-15 in 1914.

TROUBLE WITH RUTH: Jack was very much responsible for the first fuss made over Babe Ruth's slugging ability. On May 6, 1915, he took the mound for the Yanks at the Polo Grounds and faced a young Red Sox pitcher named Babe Ruth. In the contest, Ruth took Jack deep for his first ML homer, a mammoth blast which landed in the second tier of the right field grandstand. (Jack had no decision in the extra-inning game.) A few weeks later on June 2, 1915, Babe again connected off Jack at the Polo Grounds, and this time he sent a HR more than 10 feet farther up the second deck than the previous blast. (Pitcher Ruth beat Jack, 7-1.) It bothered Jack that the Babe, a pitcher no less, had bombed him twice. The HRs received a lot of publicity and Jack could have claimed credit for making Babe Ruth a famous slugger.

CLUB LEADERSHIP: Jack led the Yanks in games pitched four times. He was the club leader in saves three times. Often the workhorse of the Yanks' pitching staff, he twice led the club in innings pitched. In 1909 Jack led the team's pitchers in complete games (21).

ALL-TIME YANKEE LEADER: Jack ranks 11th in Yankee history in complete games (105); tied for 14th in ERA (3.12); and is 17th in innings pitched (1413).

WARHOP, JACK

Yr.	W-L	Pct.	SA	G	GS	CG	IP	H	BB	SO	SH	ERA
1908	1-2	.333	0	5	4	3	36	40	8	11	0	.4.46
1909	13-15	.464	2	36	23	21	243	197	81	95	3	2.40
1910	14-14	.500	2	37	27	20	243	219	79	75	0	3.00
1911	12-13	.480	0	31	25	17	210	239	44	71	1	4.16
1912	10-19	.345	3	39	22	16	258	256	59	110	0	2.86
1913	4-6	.400	0	15	7	1	62	69	33	11	0	3.75
1914	8-15	.348	0	37	23	15	217	182	44	56	0	2.37
1915	7-9	.438	0	21	19	12	143	164	52	34	0	3.96
8 Yrs.	69-93	.426	7	221	150	105	1413	1366	400	463	4	3.12
Life.	Same.											

WELLS, ED

Nickname: "Satchelfoot"
Yankee: 1929-32
Pitcher
Born: June 7, 1900

Birthplace: Ashland, OH
Died: May 1, 1986
Bat: L; Throw: L
Ht: 6'1"; Wt: 183

CAME TO YANKS: From 1923-27 Ed had a 24-28 record pitching for the Detroit Tigers, and in 1928 he was 25-7 for the Birmingham Barons of the Southern League. Late in the 1928 season, the Yanks purchased Ed's contract and Ed reported to the Yanks' spring training camp at St. Petersburg, Fla., in 1929.

BEING A YANKEE: Ed was a good pal of Babe Ruth. He roomed with Hall of Fame pitcher Herb Pennock on road trips all four years he was a Yankee (1929-32) and developed a close friendship with Pennock. Ed had a good overhand fastball. In May of 1929, he made his first Yankee start and beat Hall of Famer Ted Lyons and the White Sox, 1-0, at Yankee Stadium. Against the Senators at Yankee Stadium, Ed once just missed a no-hitter. Washington's only hit was a grounder Lyn Lary failed to make a play on, but Ed won the game, 2-0.

YANKEE STARTER: In 1929 Ed was the Yanks' third starter and the second biggest winner on the pitching staff (13-9). He tied for the club leadership in shutouts in 1929 (three). In 1930 he was again the Yanks' third starter and his winning percentage (.800, 12-3) led all Yankee hurlers with at least 10 decisions.

YANKEE RELIEVER: Ed was used mostly as a relief pitcher in 1931 and 1932, working out of the Yankee bullpen with Hank Johnson, George Pipgras and Wilcy Moore. He was a member of the 1932 World Championship Yankee team, but he did not appear in the World Series.

LEFT YANKS: The day before the 1933 season opened, the Yanks held a Yankee Stadium workout, and afterward Joe McCarthy informed Ed that he had been dealt from the Yanks to the Browns. Ed's record for the Browns was 7-21 for the combined 1933-34 seasons and then he returned to the minors. His pro career ended in New Orleans, in 1937, a career that produced more than 150 wins in the ML's and minors over 15 years.

WELLS, ED												
Yr.	W-L	Pct.	SA	G	GS	CG	IP	H	BB	SO	SH	ERA
1929	13-9	.591	0	31	23	10	193	179	81	78	3	4.33
1930	12-3	.800	0	27	21	7	151	185	49	46	0	5.20
1931	9-5	.643	2	27	10	6	117	130	37	34	0	4.32
1932	3-3	.500	2	22	0	0	32	38	12	13	0	4.26
4 Yrs.	37-20	.649	4	107	54	23	492	532	179	171	3	4.59
Life.	68-69	.496	13	291	140	54	1232	1417	468	403	7	4.65

WETTELAND, JOHN

Yankee: 1996-97
Pitcher
Born: August 21, 1966
Birthplace: San Mateo, CA
Bat: R; Throw: R
Ht: 6'2"; Wt: 215

BECOMES A YANKEE: Wetteland became available to the Yankees before the 1995 season, because lost revenue from the 1994 baseball strike forced Montreal to trim its payroll. Thus, the Expos sent Wetteland to New York mostly for cash. He saved 37, 43 and 25 games for Montreal in the seasons prior to 1995. General Manager Gene Michael reportedly told George Steinbrenner that Wetteland was a fireballer in the mold of Goose Gossage. Steinbrenner shelled out the bucks and later wondered whether he had received his money's worth.

TWO SEASONS WITH THE YANKEES: In 1995, Wetteland had a good year. He saved 31 games and opponents hit only .185 off him. But he allowed a half dozen home runs that were hit at the most inopportune time. Worse, he was absolutely hammered in the playoffs versus Seattle (0-1, 14.55 ERA). John in 1996 saved 43 (the most in the American League) of the 66 games in which he appeared, finished 58, and struck out 69 in 63 $^2/_3$ innings. He proved to be a formidable force for the Yankees throughout the regular season as well as in the postseason. Appearing in 12 total games in the postseason, John saved seven of them and had an overall ERA of 2.19 in 12 $^1/_3$ innings. In the World Series versus Atlanta, Wetteland earned a save in each of the four Yankee victories and was deservedly named the Most Valuable Player. John had indeed made his mark with the Yankees, proving that he WAS a most valuable player when the Yanks landed him prior to the 1995 season. In November, 1996, John was granted free agency and was signed by the Texas Rangers. Thank you, John, for your fine efforts as a Yankee!

ALL-TIME YANKEE LEADER: John, in his two seasons as a Yankee, ranks eighth overall in saves (74).

John Wetteland had seven saves for the Yankees in the 1996 postseason.

WETTELAND, JOHN

Yr.	W-L	Pct.	SA	G	GS	CG	IP	H	BB	SO	SH	ERA
1996	1-5	.167	31	60	0	0	61.1	40	14	66	0	2.93
1997	2-3	.400	43	62	0	0	63.2	54	21	69	0	2.83
2 Yrs.	3-8	.273	74	122	0	0	125	94	35	135	0	2.88
Life.	48-45	.516	330	618	17	0	765	616	252	804	0	2.93

Division Series

Yr.	G	IP	BB	SO	H	W-L	SV
1995	3	4.1	2	5	8	0-1	0
1996	3	4	5	4	2	0-0	2
4 Yrs.	8	10.1	8	11	10	0-1	2
Life.	10	12.1	9	13	10	0-1	2

Championship Series

Yr.	G	IP	BB	SO	H	W-L	SV
1996	4	4.0	1	5	2	0-0	1
Life. Same.							

World Series

Yr.	G	IP	BB	SO	H	W-L	SV
1996	5	4.1	1	6	4	0-0	4
Life. Same.							

WHITE, ROY

Yankee: 1965-79
Outfielder, 3B, 1B, 2B, DH
Born: December 27, 1943
Birthplace: Los Angeles, CA
Bat: Both; Throw: R
Ht: 5'10"; Wt: 172

HONORS: In 1966, Roy won the James P. Dawson Award as the best rookie in Yankee spring training camp. He was selected to the AL team for the All-Star Games in 1969 and 1970. The Baseball Writers gave Roy the Ben Epstein "Good Guy" Award in 1976.

YOUNG PROSPECT: Yankee scout Tuffy Hashem signed 18-year-old Roy to begin playing in the Yankee organization in 1962. He played at Greensboro (.204) and Fort Lauderdale (.286) in 1962. In 1963 Roy hit .309 for Greensboro. In 1964 he hit .257 for Columbus, Ga. Roy was the Southern League's MVP in 1965, hitting .300 with 19 HRs. At the end of the 1965 season, he was called up to the Yanks and hit .333 (14 for 42). In 1966 Roy was the Yanks' fourth outfielder and hit .225. He began the 1967 season playing for Spokane of the Pacific Coast League and terrorized that league's pitchers for half a season (.343) before the Yanks called him up for good.

YANKEE OUTFIELDER: Roy was a second baseman in the minors, but he became an outfielder once he joined the Yanks. From the time he rejoined the Yanks during the 1967 season through the 1977 season, he was the Yanks' regular leftfielder, except for 1974 when he was mainly used as a designated hitter. In 1967 he played 17 games at third base and in 1975 he played seven games at first base. Roy was platooned with Lou Piniella in left field in 1978 and was a reserve outfielder in 1979. Roy twice played in 162 games (1970, 1973). He is the only Yankee player to do that twice.

SWITCH-HITTING STAR: Roy was one of the AL's best offensive players during his 15-year Yankee career. He was one of the most consistent of the fine players in which Yankee history is so rich. Only the great Mickey Mantle was a more productive switch-hitter than was Roy, who besides being a fine clutch hitter, hit for both power and average. Roy hit HRs batting right-handed and lefthanded in the same game on five occasions—only Mantle, Reggie Smith, and Eddie Murray have accomplished the feat more often in the ML. Roy's 17 sacrifice flies in 1971 set the AL record for SF's. For some time Roy batted fourth in the Yankee lineup. But he also had the speed to bat first, the bat control to bat second, and the hitting talent to bat third. In fact, Roy batted in every spot in the order. His most productive season was 1970 (22 HRs, 94 RBIs, .296, 109 runs scored).

COMPLETE OFFENSIVE THREAT: Roy probably had the best batting eye on the Yanks during the 1970s. He had great speed and was a daring and smart base runner. He could deliver the type of hit that any situation called for and was a good bunter. Roy did a lot of things that did not show up in the box score. He was an expert at hitting behind runners, moving runners, and executing the hit-and-run play. In good times and bad, Roy did it all.

CLUB LEADERSHIP: Roy led the Yanks in stolen bases six times and the team in walks five times. He led the club in games played, runs and triples four times. For three straight seasons (1968-70) Roy was the team leader in doubles. Roy twice led the team in hits, RBIs, batting and slugging.

LEAGUE LEADER: Roy led the AL in walks (99) in 1972, in at-bats (639) in 1973 and in runs scored (104) in 1976.

ALL-TIME YANKEE LEADER: Roy ranks fourth on the all-time Yankee stolen base list (233), fifth on the all-time Yankee walk list (934), fifth on the club's most games played list (1881), seventh on the at-bat list (6650), ninth on the most hits list (1803), 11th in runs scored list (964), and 13th on the all-time Yankee doubles list (300). Roy also ranks 16th in RBI (758).

DEFENSIVE ABILITIES: A weak throwing arm was his only baseball shortcoming and the only reason he could not be classified as a superstar. Even with a poor arm, Roy was one of the best defensive leftfielders of his era. His good speed and judgment served Roy well in the outfield, and he seldom misplayed a ball. He also knew where to throw the ball once he retrieved it. Through the years, Roy made great over-the-fence catches to rob opponents of numerous HRs. Roy fielded 1.000 in 145 outfield games in 1971, setting the Yankee single-season fielding record for outfielders. His lifetime fielding average in the outfield is among the top 20 in baseball history. In 1976 Roy made 380 putouts, the Yankee club record for leftfielders.

CLASS GUY: Roy's soft-spoken, sophisticated manner added class to the Yankee club. Intelligent and dignified, he was most cooperative with the press and Yankee fans. Roy's last couple of Yankee seasons were tough ones—he saw himself being phased out. Always popular with true Yankee fans, Roy enjoyed standing ovation after standing ovation at Yankee Stadium in 1979. In 1974 Yankee Manager Bill Virdon said of Roy, "He's a professional. I don't say that about a lot of people."

MOST IMPORTANT HIT: Roy delivered the biggest hit of the 1977 season. The Red Sox came to Yankee Stadium on June 24 leading the Yanks by four games. With the Yankees trailing 5-3 and appearing to be dead and slipping out of the pennant race, Willie Randolph tripled with two out and no one on in the bottom of the ninth. Roy then came to the plate and sent out a booming HR to tie the score. The 54,940 fans made enough noise to be heard in Boston! The Yanks went on to win the game in extra innings, to sweep the series—and to climb back into the pennant race.

AL CHAMPIONSHIP SERIES: In the final game of the 1976 playoffs, Roy scored two key runs in the Yanks' 7-6 victory. The Yanks rallied for ninth inning runs to win Game 5 of the 1977 playoffs and Roy's pinch-hit walk was a key to the rally. He eventually scored the winning run. Roy's sixth inning HR in Game 4 of the 1978 playoffs beat the Royals, 2-1, to give the team their third straight AL pennant.

WORLD SERIES: Roy had disappointing Series in 1976 and 1977. He was sensational in the 1978 Series (.333), leading both clubs in runs scored (nine). After the Yanks lost the first two games in Los Angeles, Roy got the Yanks off to a good start in Game 3 at the Stadium, which the Yanks won, 5-1, with a first-inning HR. In the bottom of the tenth inning of Game 4, Roy scored the winning run in a 4-3 Yankee victory. In the Game 5 12-2 rout of the Dodgers, Roy knocked in three runs.

LEFT YANKS: After the 1979 season, Roy, unsigned with the Yanks, elected to enter the free-agent reentry draft. Reportedly, he was given many offers to play with other ML teams. But late in the winter Roy decided to play the 1980 season in Japan. He left the Yanks as he played with the Yanks—with class.

AFTER PLAYING DAYS: Roy played in Japan through 1982 before retiring as a player. Roy was a Yankee coach in 1983-84 and 1986. In 1995, he was named as a roving outfield instructor for the Yankees.

WHITE, ROY

Yr.	G	AB	R	H	2B	3B	HR	RBI	BB	SB	BA	SA
1965	14	42	7	14	2	0	0	3	4	2	.333	.381
1966	115	316	39	71	13	2	7	20	37	14	.225	.345
1967	70	214	22	48	8	0	2	18	19	10	.224	.290
1968	159	577	89	154	20	7	17	62	73	20	.267	.414
1969	130	448	55	130	30	5	7	74	81	18	.290	.426
1970	162	609	109	180	30	6	22	94	95	24	.296	.473
1971	147	524	86	153	22	7	19	84	86	14	.292	.469
1972	155	556	76	150	29	0	10	54	99	23	.270	.376
1973	162	639	88	157	22	3	18	60	78	16	.246	.374
1974	136	473	68	130	19	8	7	43	67	15	.275	.393
1975	148	556	81	161	32	5	12	59	72	16	.290	.430
1976	156	626	104	179	29	3	14	65	83	31	.286	.409
1977	143	519	72	139	25	2	14	52	75	18	.268	.405
1978	103	346	44	93	13	3	8	43	42	10	.269	.393
1979	81	205	24	44	6	0	3	27	23	2	.215	.288
15 Yrs.	1881	6650	964	1803	300	51	160	758	934	233	.271	.404
Life.	Same.											

Championship Series

Yr.	G	AB	R	H	2B	3B	HR	RBI	BA
1976	5	17	4	5	3	0	0	3	.294
1977	4	5	2	2	2	0	0	0	.400
1978	4	16	5	5	1	0	1	1	.313
3 Yrs.	13	38	11	12	6	0	1	4	.316
Life.	Same.								

World Series

Yr.	G	AB	R	H	2B	3B	HR	RBI	BA
1976	4	15	0	2	0	0	0	0	.133
1977	2	2	0	0	0	0	0	0	.000
1978	6	24	9	8	0	0	1	4	.333
3 Yrs.	12	41	9	10	0	0	1	4	.244
Life. Same.									

WICKMAN, BOB

Yankee: 1992-96
Pitcher
Born: February 6, 1969
Birthplace: Green Bay, WI
Bat: R; Throw: R
Ht: 6'1"; Wt: 212

JOINS THE YANKS: The Yankees got Wickman with Melido Perez and Domingo Jean from the Chicago White Sox for Steve Sax and cash in January, 1992. Wickman in 1992 was 12-5 as starter at Columbus (the Yankee AAA club) when he was called up to the Yankees in August. He started eight games and was 6-1 with an ERA of 4.11.

PHYSICALLY CHALLENGED: The right-hander, who as a child lost the tip of his right index finger in a farm accident, won his first eight decisions in 1993, which, when added to his carryover wins from the previous year, gave him an 11-game winning streak—the longest by a Yankee right-hander since Jim Coates won 13 consecutive games in 1959-60. In 19 starts, Wickman built a 14-4 record, but it was a record that owed more to the Yankees' offense (they scored an average of 7.3 runs for him) than to his pitching (4.63 ERA). In July, Manager Buck Showalter sent him to the bullpen to become a set-up man.

IMPROVES IN 1994: Bob developed a knack for the set-up, establishing himself as a first-rate pitcher in his new role. He led the league in 1994 with 52 games pitched, his ERA was a solid 3.09, and he stranded 72 percent of the runners he

Bob Wickman

inherited, the best percentage among Yankee relievers. In 1995, Bob's ERA rose to 4.05 and his season was generally uninspiring, going 2-4 in 63 contests. After going 4-1 in 58 games in 1996 and with an ERA of 4.67, Wickman's days as a Yankee were through. In August, he was traded with New Orleans native Gerald Williams to the Milwaukee Brewers for Graeme Lloyd and Pat Listach. The latter never appeared in a Yankee game. After several seasons with Milwaukee, Bob is now the closer for the Cleveland Indians.

WICKMAN, BOB

Yr.	W-L	Pct.	SA	G	GS	CG	IP	H	BB	SO	SH	ERA
1992	6-1	.857	0	8	8	0	50.1	51	20	21	0	4.11
1993	14-4	.778	4	41	19	1	140	156	69	70	1	4.63
1994	5-4	.556	6	53	0	0	70	54	27	56	0	3.09
1995	2-4	.333	1	63	1	0	80	77	33	51	0	4.05
1996	4-1	.800	0	58	0	0	79	94	34	61	0	4.67
5 Yrs.	31-14	.689	11	223	28	1	419.1	432	183	259	1	4.21

Still Active.

Division Series

YR	G	IP	BB	SO	H	W-L	SV
1995	3	3.0	0	3	5	0-0	0

Still Active.

WILLIAMS, BERNIE

Yankee: 1991-2002
Outfielder
Born: September 13, 1968

Bernie Williams

Birthday: San Juan, Puerto Rico
Bat: BOTH; Throw: R
Ht: 6'2"; Wt: 205

SIGNED BY THE YANKS IN PUERTO RICO: Bernie was just turning 18 in his native Puerto Rico in 1985 when he was signed by the Yankees. Williams finally reached the Yankees in July, 1991 and was the centerfielder the rest of the season. He struggled, hitting .238, and in one August game struck out five times in five at-bats. But on the positive side, he covered great gobs of center-field territory, hit .343 with runners in scoring position, and finished the season with a five-hit game. He spent most of the 1992 season with Columbus (the Yankee AAA club), but in August once again became the Yankee centerfielder. This time he was better prepared, reaching base safely in 48 of his final 49 games, and the Yankees traded away Roberto Kelly. Playing centerfield all season in 1993, Bernie hit 12 home runs, had 68 RBI, and his 21-game hitting streak in August helped him salvage a .268 batting average.

STEADILY IMPROVES: He started slowly in 1994, but then hit .316 in July and .327 in August, finishing with an overall .289 average. His numbers for only 108 games in the strike-shortened season were impressive: 29 doubles, 12 homers, 57 RBI, 80 runs, 61 walks and 16 stolen bases. Already an elite defensive outfielder, Bernie was becoming a more confident hitter. In 1995 Williams was one-for-two in the improvement department. He stole only eight bases and was thrown out six times. But he was able to actually boost his lefthanded batting average (.310, 114 for 368) above his right-handed average (.303, 59 for 195). And in the playoffs, he became the first player in postseason history to homer from both sides of the plate in one game. The 1995 season didn't begin well for Williams, who was hitting a dismal .194 at one point. But he got hot—he became incredible—and finished with a .307 batting average with 93 runs scored and 82 RBI. He followed this by hitting .429 (9 for 21) in the playoffs.

EMERGES AS A GREAT PLAYER: In 1997, Bernie batted .328 with 21 homers and 100 RBI, finishing in the top ten of many American League offensive categories. He also found time to win his first Rawlings Gold Glove Award for his outfield work in the center garden at Yankee Stadium. He was placed on the disabled list on two separate occasions during the season, causing him to play in just 129 of the scheduled 162 games. He did win AL Player of the Month honors in August, batting .395 with eight homers and 23 RBI in 29 games. Bernie did not fare well in postseason play, batting .118 with no homers and one RBI in five games versus the Cleveland Indians in the 1997 Division Series. In 1998, Bernie became (now get this!) the first player ever to win a batting title, Gold Glove Award and World Series Championship in the same season. He won his first batting title (.339), edging out Boston's Mo Vaughn (.337) on the final day of the season and won his second straight Gold Glove Award for his centerfield brilliance. He did miss 31 total games due to injuries, which did not assist him in a statistical sense. Bernie had a game of historic import in Yankee history when he went 4-for-5 on the 50th Anniversary of the death of Babe Ruth. In that August 16 game at The Stadium versus Texas, Williams blasted a truly dramatic game-winning solo homer in the bottom of the ninth, the Yankees winning 6-5.

Indeed, the 50,304 on hand were witness to a most memorable event!

CONSISTENT SEASONS CONTINUE: Bernie has been a dominant force in the Yankee line up since the 1995 season. He was a good hitter up until then, but what looked as a career year in 1995 has simply become a signature now for Bernie. He has seven straight seasons of 100+ runs scored. In five seasons, since 1996, Bernie has produced 100 or more RBIs. The only other Yankees to have more seasons of combined 100 runs scored to go with 100 or more RBI are Lou Gehrig (14 times), Babe Ruth (11), and Joe DiMaggio (8). Get the picture! Bernie surpassed Mickey Mantle in this endeavor as "The Mick" had three of these seasons. Bernie and Derek Jeter each had 200+ hits in 1999. They were the first Yankee teammates to pull this off since Gehrig and DiMaggio did in 1937. Even when Bernie is having an off-day at the plate, he patrols center field with the skillful measure that has earned him four AL Gold Glove awards.

POSTSEASON: While it's true that Bernie has had some poor offensive numbers in several of the postseason series, he also has had more than a few stellar performances in the playoffs. He has hit 17 postseason home runs and driven in 56 runs. He has had two "walk-off" postseason home runs (1996 ALCS-Game 1 and 1999 ALCS-Game 2) for a MLB playoff record in that category. In the 1996 Division Series versus Texas he not only hit for a .467 BA, but lashed out a 1.067 SA. Bernie has had a .600 or better SA in seven of the postseason series he has appeared in. He pounded Texas pitching once again in the 1999 Division Series by knocking in six runs (the Yankees scored eight) in the Game 1 victory to provide the impetus for another sweep of the overmatched Rangers.

ALL-STAR: Bernie has represented the Yankees on the AL All-Star squad in 1997, 1999, 2000, and 2001. Bernie was also on *The Sporting News* All-Star team in 2000 and 2002.

ALL-TIME YANKEE LEADER: Bernie ranks on the top 20 all-time Yankee batting lists as follows: fifth in doubles (353); seventh in home runs (226) and runs scored (1066); ninth in batting average (.308); tenth in RBI's (998); 12th in at-bats (5958); and 15th in stolen bases (138).

WILLIAMS, BERNIE

Yr.	G	AB	R	H	2B	3B	HR	RBI	BB	SB	BA	SA
1991	85	320	43	76	19	4	3	34	48	10	.238	.350
1992	62	261	39	73	14	2	5	26	29	7	.280	.406
1993	139	567	67	152	31	4	12	68	53	9	.268	.400
1994	108	408	80	118	29	1	12	57	61	16	.289	.453
1995	144	563	93	173	29	9	18	82	75	8	.307	.487
1996	143	551	108	168	26	7	29	102	82	17	.305	.535
1997	129	509	107	167	35	6	21	100	73	15	.328	.544
1998	128	499	101	169	30	5	26	97	74	15	.339	.575
1999	158	591	116	143	28	6	25	115	100	9	.342	.536
2000	141	537	108	165	37	6	30	121	71	13	.307	.566
2001	146	540	102	166	38	0	26	94	78	11	.307	.522
2002	154	612	102	204	37	2	19	102	83	8	.333	.493
12 Yrs.	1537	5958	1066	1833	353	52	226	998	827	138	.308	.498
Life. Same.												

Division Series

Yr.	G	AB	R	H	2B	3B	HR	RBI	BB	SB	BA	SA
1995	5	21	8	9	2	0	2	5	7	1	.429	.810
1996	4	15	5	7	0	0	3	5	2	1	.467	1.067
1997	5	17	3	2	1	0	0	1	4	0	.118	.176
1998	3	11	0	0	0	0	0	0	1	0	.000	.000
1999	3	11	2	4	1	0	1	6	1	0	.364	.727
2000	5	20	3	5	3	0	0	1	1	0	.250	.400
2001	5	18	4	4	3	0	0	5	3	0	.222	.389
2002	4	15	4	5	1	0	1	3	3	0	.333	.600
7 Yrs.	34	128	29	36	11	0	7	26	22	2	.281	.531
Life. Same.												

Championship Series

Yr.	G	AB	R	H	2B	3B	HR	RBI	BB	SB	BA	SA
1996	5	19	6	9	3	0	2	6	5	1	.474	.947
1998	6	21	4	8	1	0	0	5	7	1	.381	.429
1999	5	20	3	5	1	0	1	2	2	1	.250	.450
2000	6	23	5	10	1	0	1	3	2	1	.435	.609
2001	5	17	4	4	0	0	3	5	5	0	.235	.765
5 Yrs.	27	100	22	36	6	0	7	21	21	4	.360	.630
Life. Same.												

World Series

Yr.	G	AB	R	H	2B	3B	HR	RBI	BB	SB	BA	SA
1996	6	24	3	4	0	0	1	4	3	1	.167	.292
1998	4	16	2	1	0	0	1	3	2	0	.063	.250
1999	4	13	2	3	0	0	0	0	4	1	.231	.231
2000	5	18	2	2	0	0	1	1	5	0	.111	.278
2001	7	24	2	5	1	0	3	9	18	2	.208	.250
5 Yrs.	26	95	11	15	1	0	3	9	18	2	.158	.263
Life. Same.												

WILLIAMS, JIMMY

Nickname: "Buttons"
Yankee: 1903-07
Second Baseman
Born: December 20, 1876
Birthplace: St. Louis, MO
Died: January 16, 1965
Bat: R; Throw: R
Ht: 5'9"; Wt: 175

GETTING TO NEW YORK: In 1899, Jimmy broke into the NL with the Pittsburgh club with a bang, hitting .355 (219 for 617) and leading the NL in triples (27). When the AL became a big league in 1901, Jimmy was a member of the Baltimore Orioles in their inaugural AL season. He led the AL with 21 triples in both 1901 and 1902. When the Baltimore franchise was shifted to New York for the 1903 season, Jimmy was one of only six players (and one of two regulars) to make the transfer with the club to New York. In getting Jimmy, the Yanks (Highlanders) were landing one of the game's best young players.

YANKEE SECOND BASEMAN: Jimmy was the first regular second baseman in Yankee history, and he never played any other position for the Yanks. He was a fixture at second base in the first five seasons of the club's existence (1903-07). On April 22, 1903, "Buttons" batted fourth in the first game ever played by the Yanks.

DEFENSIVE ABILITIES: In 1903 Jimmy led AL second basemen in assists (438), a feat he repeated in 1904 (465). He led AL second sackers in turning double plays in 1904 (52) and 1905 (51). Jimmy was durable, consistent, possessed good range and turned the double play skillfully as the pivot man. Unfortunately, Jimmy made a big throwing error against Boston in the game that eliminated the Yanks from pennant contention in 1904. The play allowed Boston to tie the score, 2-2, in the seventh inning, and Jack Chesbro later wild pitched the winning run home.

CLUB LEADERSHIP: Jimmy led the Yanks in doubles in the club's first four seasons (1903-06). In 1903 he led the Yanks in doubles (30), triples (12), RBIs (82), slugging (.392) and games played (132). In 1904 he led the club in games played (146), at-bats (559) and doubles (31). In 1905 he paced the team in doubles (20), HRs (four), RBIs (60) and walks (50). In 1906 Jimmy led the Yanks in doubles (25) and RBIs (77). He led the club in triples in 1907 (11).

LEFT YANKS: The Yanks dealt Jimmy to the St. Louis Browns following the 1907 season. For St. Louis, Jimmy hit .236 in 148 games in 1908 and .195 in 110 games in 1909, Jimmy's last ML campaign.

WILLIAMS, JIMMY

Yr.	G	AB	R	H	2B	3B	HR	RBI	BB	SB	BA	SA
1903	132	502	60	134	30	12	3	82	39	9	.267	.392
1904	146	559	62	147	31	7	2	74	38	14	.263	.354
1905	129	470	54	107	20	8	6	62	50	14	.228	.343
1906	139	501	62	139	25	7	3	77	44	8	.277	.373
1907	139	504	53	136	17	11	2	63	35	14	.270	.359
5 Yrs.	685	2536	291	663	123	45	16	358	206	59	.261	.364
Life.	1456	5481	781	1507	242	138	49	796	474	151	.275	.396

WINFIELD, DAVE

Nickname: "Winny"
Yankee: 1981-88, 1990
Outfielder, DH
Born: October 3, 1951
Birthplace: St. Paul, MN
Bat: R; Throw: R
Ht: 6'6"; Wt: 220

GREAT ATHLETE: At the University of Minnesota, Dave played basketball and was the star pitcher, and he was the MVP of the 1973 College World Series. He was drafted by four teams in three sports—Atlanta Hawks (NBA), Utah Stars (ABA), Minnesota Vikings (NFL), and San Diego Padres. Dave signed with the Padres, bypassed the minors and hit safely in his first six ML games in 1973. Dave developed into one of the game's best players but was stuck in the relative obscurity of San Diego.

SIGNING WITH THE YANKEES: In December of 1980, Dave signed as a free agent with the Yankees; it was a ten-year deal worth about $23 million, and at the time was called the most lucrative contract in team sports history. George Steinbrenner didn't realize how lucrative it was; soon after the deal was inked, Steinbrenner realized he had incorrectly interpreted the contract's cost of living escalator and that Dave was going to cost him much more than he had expected. George asked Dave to rewrite the contract, and Dave refused; they were adversaries from then on.

HONORS: With the Yankees, Dave won Gold Gloves in 1982, 1983, 1984, 1985 and 1987. He won Silver Bats every year from 1981 through 1985. He was an outfielder on *The Sporting News* AL All-Star team in 1982, 1983, and 1984.

NEW YORK DEBUT: In 1981, Dave led the Yankees in RBIs (68), hits (114), doubles (25), slugging (.464), games (105) and at-bats (388). He sailed through the Division Series, hitting .350 and tying Bob Watson for club lead in hits (seven). But then he hit only .154 in the ALCS. Worst of all, he hit .045 (one for 22) in the World Series. He kept his sense of humor. After breaking a 0-for-16 start with a single, he jokingly asked for the ball. This World Series failure stuck with him until he won the 1992 World Series with a hit for Toronto.

DEFENSIVE GENIUS: Dave had perhaps the best outfielder arm in the game, and in 1982 he led AL outfielders in assists (17). He had a unique way of digging his cleats into the Yankee Stadium outfield wall padding to propel him above the wall and steal home runs; he did this many times. Late in the 1981 season, Dave robbed Baltimore's Doug DeCinces with a play that left all who saw it awestruck. The ball seemed headed for the fourth or fifth row of the left-field seats, but Dave ran hard, dug in his cleats, timed his leap perfectly, fully extended his body and pulled in the ball before it reached the seats. Only slightly less spectacular was a similar catch he made in the 1981 ALCS, robbing Tony Armas of a homer.

DARING BASE RUNNER: Dave won more than a few games every year with aggressive base running. He turned normal singles into doubles, and needed only about seven or eight huge strides to cover the ground between first and second.

RIGHT-HANDED POWER: Dave may well have been the club's second greatest ever right-handed hitter after Joe DiMaggio. In 1982, he hit 37 homers, the most ever by a right-handed-hitting Yankee except DiMaggio, who hit 39 in 1948 and 46 in 1937. Dave was the first Yankee to have five consecutive 100-RBI seasons (1982-86) since DiMaggio had seven in a row (1936-42).

HITTING MACHINE: Dave was AL Player of the Month for September 1982 (11 HRs, 22 RBIs). In 1983, he led the Yankees in nine offensive categories. In 1984, he had a 20-game hitting streak. In June 1984, he had three five-hit games, tying Ty Cobb for the most five-hit games in one month. He hit .351 in 1987 with runners in scoring position and .347 under the same conditions in 1988. He was AL Player of the Month in April 1988 when he set a new ML record with 29 RBIs.

1984 BATTING RACE: Dave shortened his stroke and battled teammate Don Mattingly for the batting crown. Going into the last day of the season, Dave was ahead, .3410 to .3394; but Mattingly went 4-for-5 and Dave went 1-for-4, and Mattingly won, .343 to .340.

ALL-STAR GAMES: Dave played in 12 All-Star Games; four with San Diego (1977-80) and eight with the Yankees (1981-88). He got three hits in the 1983 Game. He played all 13 innings of the 1987 Game. In 1988, he made his eighth start and 12th consecutive All-Star Game appearance. Lifetime, he hit .361 and holds All-Star Game records for most doubles (seven) and most consecutive All-Star Games with at least one hit (seven).

SEAGULLS BEWARE: On August 4, 1983, in Toronto, where seagulls sometimes swarmed the ballpark, Dave was finishing between-inning warm-ups with a ball boy and tried to bounce a ball near a seagull to get it to leave the field. Instead, the ball fatally beaned the bird. The fans roundly booed, and the Toronto police were waiting in the clubhouse and charged Dave with cruelty to animals. Down at the station, where authorities had the bird, its feet upright, Dave posted $500 bail. Charges were later dropped, and sanity prevailed.

BATTLES WITH STEINBRENNER: Dave feuded with Steinbrenner most of his Yankee career, and often the trigger was George not paying the Winfield Foundation—Dave's charitable organization that assisted community youth groups—the $300,000 he was supposed to pay each year, as a condition of Dave's contract. In 1985, Dave sued Steinbrenner for the payment, and late in the season, George called him "Mr. May" (as opposed to Reggie Jackson, who was Mr. October). Mentally tough, he resisted all attempts to trade him. In January of 1989, Dave sued Steinbrenner for failing to make his payment to the Winfield Foundation, and a short time later George countersued and talked about having information about wrongdoing inside the Foundation. No wrongdoing was ever proven, but Steinbrenner was barred from baseball in 1990 for having paid a known gambler $40,000 for information on Dave.

LATE YANKEE CAREER: In 1988, Dave reached base safely in 44 of his first 48 games, and although he hit only .266 in September and October, he finished with perhaps his finest season (.322. 25 HRs, 107 RBIs); Don Mattingly called him the club's MVP. On March 19, 1989, Dave went on the Disabled List and missed the entire 1989 season. He had surgery for a herniated disk.

TRADED AWAY: In May of 1990, the Yankees traded Dave to the Angels for pitcher Mike Witt. Dave ended up winning *The Sporting News* AL Comeback Player of the Year in 1990, as he finished with 21 homers and 78 RBIs. He had a better year in 1991 and even better with Toronto in 1992 (26 HRs, 108 RBIs). He hit 21 homers for the Twins in 1993 and finished 1995 with the Indians.

ALL-TIME LEADER: On baseball's all-time leader lists, Dave ranks eighth in at-bats (11,003) and games played (2973); tenth in total bases (5221); 12th in RBI's (1833); 15th in extra-base hits (1093; 18th in hits (3110); and 25th in home runs (465). He was the first 40-year-old in baseball history to amass 108 RBIs in a season. He retired in February 1996, after a 23-year career.

ALL-TIME YANKEE LEADER: On the Yankees' all-time leader lists, Dave ranks ninth in home runs (205); 14th in RBIs (818), and 20th in doubles (236).

WINFIELD, DAVE

Yr.	G	AB	R	H	2B	3B	HR	RBI	BB	SB	BA	SA
1981	105	388	52	114	25	1	13	68	43	11	.294	.464
1982	140	539	84	151	24	8	37	106	45	5	.280	.560
1983	152	598	99	169	26	8	32	116	58	15	.283	.513
1984	141	567	106	193	34	4	19	100	53	6	.340	.515
1985	155	633	105	174	34	6	26	114	52	19	.275	.471
1986	154	565	90	148	31	5	24	104	77	6	.262	.462
1987	156	575	83	158	22	1	27	97	76	5	.275	.457
1988	149	559	96	180	37	2	25	107	69	9	.322	.530
1990	20	61	7	13	3	0	2	6	4	0	.213	.361
9 Yrs.	1172	4485	722	1300	236	35	205	818	477	76	.290	.495
Life.	2973	11003	1669	3110	540	88	465	1833	1216	223	.283	.475

Divisional Playoff

Yr.	G	AB	R	H	2B	3B	HR	RBI	BB	SB	BA	SA
1981	5	20	2	7	3	0	0	0	1	0	.350	.500
1 Yr.	5	20	2	7	3	0	0	0	1	0	.350	.500

Life. Same.

Championship Series

Yr.	G	AB	R	H	2B	3B	HR	RBI	BB	SB	BA	SA
1981	3	13	2	2	1	0	0	2	2	1	.154	.231
1 Yr.	3	13	2	2	1	0	0	2	2	1	.154	.231
Life.	9	37	9	8	2	0	2	5	6	1	.216	.432

World Series

Yr.	G	AB	R	H	2B	3B	HR	RBI	BB	SB	BA	SA
1981	6	22	0	1	0	0	0	1	5	1	.045	.045
1 Yr.	6	22	0	1	0	0	0	1	5	1	.045	.045
Life.	12	44	0	6	1	0	0	4	7	1	.136	.159

WITT, WHITEY
(LAWTON WALTER WITT)

Birth Name: Ladislaw Waldemar Wittkowski
Yankee: 1922-25
Outfielder
Born: September 28, 1895
Birthplace: Orange, MA
Died: July 14, 1988
Bat: L; Throw: R
Ht: 5'7"; Wt: 150

CAME TO YANKS: The Yanks obtained Whitey from the Philadelphia A's before the 1922 season.

YANKEE CENTERFIELDER: Whitey became the Yankees' centerfielder in 1922, making $4,000 as a star player on the pennant-winning team of that year. He was an important member of the 1923 team, the Yankees' first World Championship club, and he played centerfield in 1924. Whitey was a popular Yankee and was one of Babe Ruth's best friends. He was a pallbearer for the Babe's funeral.

DEFENSIVE ABILITIES: As the Yankee centerfielder, Whitey could really go get the ball in the spacious outfields of the Yanks' home parks, the Polo Grounds, then Yankee Stadium. He led all AL outfielders in fielding in 1923 (.979).

GREAT LEADOFF MAN: Whitey was one of the best leadoff men in Yankee history. In his day he was probably the fastest man from home plate to first in baseball. He also had an excellent batting eye. In 1922 Whitey led the AL in walks (89). He had a great on-base percentage, enabling him to score runs in abundance. From 1922-24 he scored 299 runs, an average of 99.6 runs per season. In 1922 he led the Yanks in runs scored (98). On April 18, 1923, Yankee Stadium opened and Whitey as leadoff man became the first Yankee to bat at Yankee Stadium.

COURAGEOUS EFFORT: The Yankees went to St. Louis in September, 1922, for a crucial three-game series with the Browns over whom they held a half-game lead. They won the first game in the late innings during which a bottle came from a crowd that had grown ugly, striking Whitey and knocking him unconscious. After losing the second game, the Yankees won the finale of the series with Whitey Witt, his head bandaged, knocking in the runs that produced the most important victory of the year.

LEFT YANKS: In July, 1925, the Yanks released Whitey. He played with the Brooklyn Dodgers in 1926, then retired.

WITT, WHITEY

Yr.	G	AB	R	H	2B	3B	HR	RBI	BB	SB	BA	SA
1922	140	528	98	157	11	6	4	40	89	5	.297	.364
1923	146	596	113	187	18	10	6	56	67	2	.314	.408
1924	147	600	88	178	26	5	1	36	45	9	.297	.362
1925	31	40	9	8	2	1	0	0	6	1	.200	.300
4 Yrs.	464	1764	308	530	57	22	11	132	207	17	.300	.376
Life.	1139	4171	632	1195	144	62	18	302	489	78	.287	.364

World Series

Yr.	G	AB	R	H	2B	3B	HR	RBI	BA
1922	5	18	1	4	1	1	0	0	.222
1923	6	25	1	6	2	0	0	4	.240
2 Yrs.	11	43	2	10	3	1	0	4	.233
Life.	Same.								

WOMACK, DOOLEY
(BORN HORACE GUY WOMACK)

Yankee: 1966-68
Pitcher
Born: August 25, 1939
Birthplace: Columbia, SC
Bat: L; Throw: R
Ht: 6'; Wt: 170

LONG JOURNEY TO YANKS: Dooley began in the Yankee organization in September, 1958. He spent eight seasons in the Yankee farm system before making the big club in 1966.

RELIEF SPECIALIST: In 1966 Dooley had a strong rookie year, pitching mostly in long relief. He was the ace of the Yankee bullpen in 1967 when he led the Yanks in saves (18) and games pitched (65). In 1967 and 1968, Dooley led the club in games pitched. In 1968 Dooley was used mostly in long relief. On June 3, 1968, he began a triple play, the most recent Yankee triple play.

TRADED: In December, 1968, the Yanks traded Dooley to the Houston Astros for outfielder Dick Simpson.

WOMACK, DOOLEY

Yr.	W-L	Pct.	SA	G	GS	CG	IP	H	BB	SO	SH	ERA
1966	7-3	.700	4	42	1	0	75	52	23	50	0	2.64
1967	5-6	.455	18	65	0	0	97	80	35	57	0	2.41
1968	3-7	.300	2	45	0	0	62	53	29	27	0	3.21
3 Yrs.	15-16	.484	24	152	1	0	234	185	87	134	0	2.70
Life.	19-18	.514	24	193	1	0	302	253	111	177	0	2.95

WOODLING, GENE

Yankee: 1949-54
Outfielder
Born: August 16, 1922
Birthplace: Akron, OH
Died: June 2, 2001
Bat: L; Throw: R
Ht: 5'10"; Wt: 195

MINOR LEAGUE STAR: For several years Gene terrorized pitchers in the minors, winning a batting title in the Ohio State League (.398) and two in the Eastern League. He was a reserve outfielder in the ML's in 1943 and 1946 with Cleveland and in 1947 with Pittsburgh. In 1948 Gene played for the San Francisco Seals of the Pacific Coast League. He led the P.C.L. with a .385 batting average and was named Minor League Player of the Year.

CAME TO YANKS: While managing the Oakland Oaks in the P.C.L. in 1948, Casey Stengel's attention was attracted to Gene's hitting exploits. When Stengel became Yankee manager, he encouraged Yankee GM George Weiss to obtain Gene, and the deal was made before the 1949 season.

PLATOON SYSTEM: It is often mentioned that Gene was an integral member of Stengel's platoon system. The statement is probably true but only for the 1949 season when Gene *was* platooned extensively. However, Gene would have to be considered a regular in all his other Yankee seasons, except in 1954 when he was hampered by a hand injury.

GREAT HITTER: Gene used an open stance in the minors, but he had trouble hitting in his first ML stint. Seal Manager Lefty O'Doul had Gene take a more comfortable stance, and Gene hit from a crouch, crowded the plate and looked as if he were hiding as he wound up and peered at the pitcher from over his right shoulder. From 1949-62, Gene was one of the game's best hitters. He was a tremendous pure hitter and a magician with a bat. He creamed inside pitches from his wound-up crouch. He was a smart hitter and swore he never got a hit without at least one strike on him. And because he was coachable, he allowed himself to improve at the plate.

WINNING BALLPLAYER: Gene is one of only 12 Yankee players who were members of all five World Championship teams in a row (1949-53), a record. Gene was a ferocious competitor, the epitome of the winning attitude. On the Yanks, he was known as a very honest player and one of the few Yanks who would engage in words with Stengel when he felt he was not being used properly.

DEFENSIVE ABILITIES: Known as a great hitter, Gene's defensive abilities were vastly underrated and overlooked. His lifetime fielding average in the outfield (.989) is among the top 20 in ML history. Gene played an outstanding left field. He led AL outfielders in fielding over three straight seasons (1951-tie, 1952, 1953), an AL record. His fielding marks of 1952 (.996) and 1953 (.996) were especially impressive, because Gene made only one error in each season. One play that stuck with Gene came in the final game of the 1950 World Series when a ball that would have been the final out was lost in the sun and a pair of runs scored. The Yanks won, but Gene's play was remembered best.

CLUB LEADERSHIP: Gene led or tied for club leadership in triples three years in a row (1949-51). Twice he led the Yanks in walks. In 1953, he paced the Yanks in batting (.306).

WORLD SERIES: Gene was an outstanding performer under World Series pressure as his .318 lifetime average in Series action attests. He is tied for tenth on the all-time World Series runs scored (21) list, and is 11th in walks (19). In the 1949 Series, he tied Jerry Coleman for most doubles (three). In the 1950 Series, he tied Philadelphia's Granny Hamner for most hits (six) and highest batting average (.429). In Game 3 Gene scored the winning run in the bottom of the ninth inning after singling and coming around to score on two hits. (Yanks won, 3-2). In the 1951 Series, Gene led all players in runs scored (six). His HR helped the Yanks defeat Brooklyn, 4-2, in Game 7 of the 1952 Series. Gene's blast went over the right field screen at Ebbets Field and gave the Yanks a 2-1 lead in the fifth. He led all players in walks (six) in the 1953 Series.

LAST YANKEE GAME: In a game played on August 21, 1954, Gene broke his thumb, ending his season. It proved to be his last game as a Yankee player.

TRADED: In November of 1954, the Yanks traded Gene to the Baltimore Orioles as part of an 18-player transaction. The Yanks obtained Bob Turley and Don Larsen as part of the deal. In 1962, he became the second former Yankee to play for the expansion Mets. He was the first-base coach for the Baltimore Orioles from 1964-67 under Hank Bauer.

YANKEE SCOUT: Gene was a Yankee scout in the 1960s and 1970s. His best known recruit was the late great Yankee catcher, Thurman Munson. Gene's report to the Yanks on Thurman simply stated: "GET HIM."

THE 12 YANKEES WHO PLAYED ON ALL FIVE CHAMPIONSHIP TEAMS, 1949-53:

Hank Bauer	Johnny Mize
Yogi Berra	Vic Raschi
Jerry Coleman	Allie Reynolds
Joe Collins	Phil Rizzuto
Ralph Houk	Charlie Silvera
Eddie Lopat	GENE WOODLING

WOODLING, GENE

Yr.	G	AB	R	H	2B	3B	HR	RBI	BB	SB	BA	SA
1949	112	296	60	80	13	7	5	44	52	2	.270	.412
1950	122	449	81	127	20	10	6	60	69	5	.283	.412
1951	120	420	65	118	15	8	15	71	62	0	.281	.462
1952	122	408	58	126	19	6	12	63	59	1	.309	.473
1953	125	395	64	121	26	4	10	58	82	2	.306	.468
1954	97	304	33	76	12	5	3	40	53	3	.250	.352
6 Yrs.	698	2272	361	648	105	40	51	336	377	13	.285	.434
Life.	1796	5587	830	1585	257	63	147	830	920	29	.264	.431

World Series

Yr.	G	AB	R	H	2B	3B	HR	RBI	BA
1949	3	10	4	4	3	0	0	0	.400
1950	4	14	2	6	0	0	0	1	.429
1951	6	18	6	3	1	1	1	1	.167
1952	7	23	4	8	1	1	1	1	.348
1953	6	20	5	6	0	0	1	3	.300
5 Yrs.	26	85	21	27	5	2	3	6	.318
Life. Same.									

WYNEGAR, BUTCH
(BORN HAROLD DELANO WYNEGAR)

Yankee: 1982-86
Catcher
Born: March 14, 1956
Birthplace: York, PA

Bat: B; Throw: R
Ht: 6'1"; Wt: 190

TRADED TO YANKEES: On May 11, 1982, Rick Cerone, the Yanks' regular catcher, broke his thumb, and the next day, the Yanks obtained Butch and pitcher Roger Erickson from Minnesota for shortstop Larry Milbourne, pitchers John Pacella and Pete Filson, and cash. Butch had broken in with the Twins in 1976 and made the All-Star team in each of his first two seasons. Butch's father was a longtime Yankee fan, and Butch had become a switch-hitter "because I wanted to be just like Mantle."

DEFENSIVE SKILLS: Butch had good tools behind the plate. He blocked balls in the dirt well, and he was soothing to pitchers, offering encouragement as needed. Butch caught Dave Righetti's no-hitter on July 4, 1983.

SHARING CATCHING CHORES: Butch was the Yanks' catcher in 1982 until Cerone returned July 15; 10 days later Butch was disabled with a devastating viral infection that kept him sidelined until September. Butch and Cerone fairly evenly split the catching in 1983, with Butch catching in 93 games and Cerone 78; Butch had a bruised left arm in May and a sore foot in September.

REGULAR CATCHER: Butch established himself as the regular catcher in 1984, and Cerone was traded to the Atlanta Braves. Butch started strong in 1985, catching well and hitting near .300. Then, in Baltimore, on June 17, while waiting in the on-deck circle, he was hit in the batting helmet with a foul ball; he was disabled through early July, and on July 22 he went back on the DL with a sprained lower back. His season continued unraveling, and he finished the year hitting only .196 at Yankee Stadium. His biggest Yankee moment came in Toronto on October 4, 1985, when his two-out ninth-inning homer off Tom Henke tied a game that the Yankees went on to win, and the Yanks moved to within two games of the first-place Blue Jays.

LEAVING THE YANKEES: Butch's woes continued in 1986, as he hit only .181 lefthanded and split the catching with Joel Skinner and Ron Hassey. Butch grew increasingly unhappy and aloof and finally left the Yanks on July 31, 1986. He had physical and mental tests done, and eventually returned to his Florida home and entered therapy. The Yanks put him on the Restricted List on August 1 and stopped paying his salary. Butch said he had become unhappy playing under the high-key managing styles of Billy Martin and Lou Piniella. In December of 1986, the Yankees traded Butch to California for pitcher Ron Romanick. Various foot problems sped Butch's decline, and he played his last ML season in 1988. In 1995, Butch was a minor-league manager in the Texas Rangers organization.

WYNEGAR, BUTCH

Yr.	G	AB	R	H	2B	3B	HR	RBI	BB	SB	BA	SA
1982	63	191	27	56	8	1	3	20	40	0	.293	.393
1983	94	301	40	89	18	2	6	42	52	1	.296	.429
1984	129	442	48	118	13	1	6	45	65	1	.267	.342
1985	102	309	27	69	15	0	5	32	64	0	.223	.320
1986	61	194	19	40	4	1	7	29	30	0	.206	.345
5 Yrs.	449	1437	161	372	58	5	27	168	251	2	.259	.363
Life	1301	4330	498	1102	176	15	65	506	626	10	.255	.347

THE
LONG PINSTRIPED LINE

Joseph Paul DiMaggio takes a
practice swing.

The list that follows includes every player who ever performed in a major league game wearing a Yankee uniform. The essential information shown for each former player (non-pitcher) covers his years as a Yankee, positions played, hits, at-bats, batting average and number of games played. For former pitchers, the won-loss totals and the number of Yankee games pitched are given. An asterisk(*) preceding the name of a player indicates he is the subject of a biographical sketch with complete statistical treatment in Chapter 2. Through 2002, 1,304 players have appeared in at least one game for the Yankees.

COMPLETE YANKEE PLAYER LIST (1903-2002)

Abbott, Jim (1993-94) Pitcher: 20-22 in 56 games. Pitched a no-hitter against Cleveland on 9/4/93. Otherwise a disappointing Yankee career.

Ables, Harry (1911) Pitcher: 0-1 in 3 games.

Adams, Spencer (1926) 2B-3B: 3 for 25, .120; played in 28 games. Played in 1926 World Series without an at-bat, pinch-running in two games.

Adkins, Doc (1903) Pitcher: 0-0 in two games.

Adkins, Steve (1990) Pitcher: 1-2 in five games.

Aguayo, Luis (1988) 3B-2B-SS: 35 for 140, .250; played in 50 games.

*Aker, Jack (1969-72) Pitcher: 16-10 in 124 games.

Aldrete, Mike (1996) OF-1B: 17 for 68, .250; 32 games. 0-0 in one game as a pitcher in 1996.

Alexander, Doyle (1976, 1982-83) Pitcher: 11-14 in 43 games. Went 10-5 in 1976. Started and lost Game 1 of the 1976 World Series.

Alexander, Walt (1915-17) Catcher: 44 for 197, .223; played in 81 games.

Allen, Bernie (1972-73) 3B-2B: 63 for 277, .227; played in 101 games.

*Allen, Johnny (1932-35) Pitcher: 50-19 in 94 games. Pitched for all three NY teams-Yankees, Dodgers, and Giants.

Allen, Neil (1985, 1987-88) Pitcher: 6-4 in 66 games.

Almanzar, Carlos (2001) Pitcher: 0-1 in 10 games.

Almonte, Erick (2001) SS-DH: 2 for 4, .500; played in 8 games.

Alomar, Sandy (1974-76) 2B-SS-3B: 231 for 931, .248; played in 294 games. Starting second baseman from July 1974 until Willie Randolph took over in spring training 1976. Led AL second basemen in fielding (.985) in 1975. Father of Roberto and Sandy Alomar, Jr.

Alou, Felipe (1971-73) 1B-OF: 289 for 1065, .271; played in 344 games. Regular rightfielder in 1971, platooned at first base in 1972 and regular first baseman in 1973. Brother of Matty and Jesus Alou. Father of Moises Alou.

Alou, Matty (1973) OF-1B: 147 for 497, .296; played in 123 games. Brother of Felipe and Jesus Alou.

Alston, Del (1977-78) OF: 13 for 43, .302; played in 25 games.

Amaro, Ruben (1966-68) SS-1B-3B: 103 for 481, .214; played in 191 games.

Anderson, John (1904-05) OF-1B: 178 for 657, .271; played in 175 games.

Anderson, Rick (1979) Pitcher: 0-0 in one game.

Andrews, Ivy (1931-32, 1937-38) Pitcher: 8-6 in 41 games.

Appleton, Pete (1933) Pitcher: 0-0 in one game.

Aragon, Angel (1914, 1916-17) INF-OF: 9 for 79, .114; played in 33 games.

Ardizoia, Rugger (1947) Pitcher: 0-0 in 1 game.

Arias, Alex (2002) SS-3B: 0 for 7, .000; played in 6 games.

Armstrong, Mike (1984-86) Pitcher: 3-3 in 52 games.

Arnsberg, Brad (1986-87) Pitcher: 1-3 in eight games.

*Arroyo, Luis (1960-63) Pitcher: 22-10 in 127 games.

Ashford, Tucker (1981) 2B: 0 for 0, .000; played in three games.

Assenmacher, Paul (1993) Pitcher: 2-2 in 26 games.

Ausanio, Joe (1994-95) Pitcher: 4-1 in 41 games.

Austin, Jimmy (1909-10) 3B-SS: 195 for 869, .224; played in 269 games. Regular third baseman in 1909 and 1910. Led NY in stolen bases (30) in 1909.

Autry, Chick (1924) Catcher: 0 for 0; played in two games.

Azocar, Oscar (1990) OF: 53 for 214, .248; played in 65 games.

Babe, Loren (1952-53) 3B: 8 for 39, .205; played in 17 games. Longtime Yankee coach, minor league manager and scout.

*Bahnsen, Stan (1966, 1968-71) Pitcher: 55-52 in 153 games.

Bailey, Bill (1911) OF-3B: 1 for 9, .111; played in five games.

*Baker, Frank "Home Run" (1916-19, 1921-22) 3B: 735 for 2548, .288; played in 676 games.

Baker, Frank (1970-71) SS: 38 for 196, .194; played in 78 games.

Balboni, Steve (1981-83, 1989-90) DH-1B: 164 for 766, .214; played in 295 games. Hit 41 HRs as a Yankee.

Ball, Neal (1907-09) SS-2B: 125 for 519, .241; played in 155 games.

Bankhead, Scott (1995) Pitcher: 1-1 in 20 games.

Banks, Willie (1997-98) Pitcher: 4-1 in 14 games.

Barber, Steve (1967-68) Pitcher: 12-14 in 37 games.

Barfield, Jesse (1989-92) OF: 300 for 1296, .232; played in 396 games. Regular rightfielder in 1989 and 1990. Injured in 1991 and 1992.

Barger, Cy (1906-07) Pitcher: 0-0 in three games.

Barker, Ray (1965-67) 1B-3B: 68 for 306, .222; played in 176 games. Hit pinch-hit HRs in consecutive games in June of 1965, making him one of only 14 men in AL history to accomplish this feat.

Barnes, Frank (1930) Pitcher: 0-1 in two games.

Barnes, Honey (1926) Catcher: 0 for 0, .000; played in one game.

Barney, Ed (1915) OF: 7 for 36, .194; played in 11 games.

Batten, George (1912) 2B: 0 for 3, .000; played in one game.

*Bauer, Hank (1948-59) OF: 1326 for 4784, .277; played in 1406 games.

Baumann, Paddy (1915-17) INF-OF: 156 for 566, .276; played in 204 games.

*Baylor, Don (1983-85) DH-OF-1B: 401 for 1504, .267; played in 420 games.

Beall, Walter (1924-27) Pitcher: 4-5 in 33 games.

Beattie, Jim (1978-79) Pitcher: 9-15 in 40 games. Started and won Game 1 of the 1978 Championship Series. Pitched his first ML complete game to win Game 5 of the 1978 World Series.

Beck, Rich (1965) Pitcher: 2-1 in three games.

Beck, Zinn (1918) 1B-3B: 0 for 8, .000; played in 11 games.

Beene, Fred (1972-74) Pitcher: 7-3 in 54 games.

Beggs, Joe (1938) Pitcher: 3-2 in 14 games. Record of 21-4 for the great 1937 Newark Bears.

Bell, Rudy (also Jack) (1907) OF: 11 for 52, .212; played in 17 games.

Bella, Zeke (1957) OF: 1 for 10, .100; played in five games.

Bellinger, Clay (1999-2001) 3B-1B-DH-OF-2B-SS: 60 for 310, .194; played in 181 games.

Bengough, Benny (1923-30) Catcher: 217 for 846, .257; played in 317 games. Capable backup catcher for most of eight seasons; regular in 1925. After 36 games in 1926, he was hitting .381 when he was hit by a pitch, resulting in a broken arm; he was out for the year.

Ron Blomberg

Beniquez, Juan (1979) OF: 36 for 142, .254; played in 62 games.

Berberet, Lou (1954-55) Catcher: 4 for 10, .400; played in seven games.

Bergman, Dave (1975, 1977) OF-1B: 1 for 21, .048; played in 12 games.

Bernhardt, Juan (1976) OF-3B: 4 for 21, .190; played in 10 games.

Bernhardt, Walter (1918) Pitcher: 0-0 in one game.

Berra, Dale (1985-86) 3B-SS: 50 for 217, .230; played in 90 games. Yogi's son; his father managed him early in 1985 season.

*Berra, Yogi (1946-63) Catcher-OF: 2148 for 7546, .285; played in 2116 games. Yankee Manager, 1964, 1984-85.

*Bevens, Bill (1944-47) Pitcher: 40-36 in 96 games.

Beville, Monte (1903-04) Catcher-1B: 56 for 280, .200; played in 91 games.

Billiard, Harry (1908) Pitcher: 0-0 in six games.

Bird, Doug (1980-81) Pitcher: 8-1 in 39 games.

Blackwell, Ewell (1952-53) Pitcher: 3-0 in 13 games. Started Game 5 of 1952 World Series (no decision).

Bladt, Rick (1975) OF: 26 for 117, .222; played in 52 games.

Blair, Paul (1977-79, 1980) OF-INF: 66 for 296, .223; played in 172 games. Delivered clutch hits in Game 5 of Championship Series and Game 1 of World Series in 1977. Great defensive centerfielder.

Blair, Walter (1907-11) Catcher-OF-1B: 115 for 587, .196; played in 216 games. Used mostly as a reserve catcher.

Blanchard, John (1955, 1959-65) Catcher-OF-1B: 260 for 1063, .245; played in 454 games. Hit 64 HRs, including 21 in 1961. Over three games, July 21-26, 1961, he hit 4 HRs in four consecutive ABs, a ML record; two were pinch-hit HRs. Delivered two HRs in 1961 World Series, including a pinch-hit HR to tie Game 3.

Blanco, Gil (1965) Pitcher: 1-1 in 17 games.

Blasingame, Wade (1972) Pitcher: 0-1 in 12 games.

Blateric, Steve (1972) Pitcher: 0-0 in one game.

Blaylock, Gary (1959) Pitcher: 0-1 in 15 games.

Blefary, Curt (1970-71) OF-1B: 64 for 305, .210; played in 120 games.

Bliss, Elmer (1903-04) P-OF: 1-0 as a pitcher and 0 for 4 at-bat; pitched one game in 1903 and played one game in OF in 1904.

Blomberg, Ron (1969, 1971-76) 1B-OF: 355 for 1177, .302; played in 400 games. NY's first pick in 1967 draft. Great lefthanded hitter vs. righthanded pitching. On April 6, 1973, Ron became first DH in ML history. Injuries cut short his promising career.

Blowers, Mike (1989-91) 3B: 44 for 217, .203; played in 76 games.

Bockman, Eddie (1946) 3B: 1 for 12, .083; played in four games. Yanks traded him and Joe Gordon to Cleveland for Allie Reynolds.

Bodie, Ping (1918-21) OF: 369 for 1357, .272; played in 385 games. Regular leftfielder in 1918 and the centerfielder in 1919 and 1920. In 1919, he led NY in slugging (.406) and doubles (27). Roomed with Babe Ruth, but made the statement: "I don't room with Babe Ruth, I room with Babe Ruth's suitcase."

Boehmer, Len (1969, 1971) INF: 19 for 113, .168; played in 48 games.

Boehringer, Brian (1995-97, 2001) Pitcher: 5-10 in 78 games.

*Boggs, Wade (1993-97) 3B-1B-DH-P: 702 for 2240, .313; played in 602 games. Pitched in one game in 1997, a no-decision game finished, one inning, four batters faced, no runs, one walk and one strikeout.

Bollweg, Don (1953) 1B: 46 for 155, .297; played in 70 games. Went 0 for 2 in 1953 World Series.

Bonds, Bobby (1975) OF: 143 for 529, .270; played in 145 games. Obtained from Giants for Bobby Murcer. Led NY in HRs (32), stolen bases (30), runs (93) walks (89), and slugging (.512) in 1975. Started 1975 All-Star Game. Played hurt in 1975. Traded to Angels for Mickey Rivers and Ed Figueroa. Father of Barry Bonds.

Bones, Ricky (1996) Pitcher: 0-0 in four games.

*Bonham, Ernie (1940-46) Pitcher: 79-50 in 158 games.

Bonilla, Juan (1985, 1987) 2B: 16 for 71, .225; played in 31 games.

Boone, Luke (1913-16) 2B-3B-SS: 197 for 937, .210; played in 287 games. Regular second baseman in 1914 and 1915.

Bordagaray, Frenchy (1941) OF: 19 for 73, .260; played in 36 games. Played in 1941 World Series without an at-bat, pinch-running in Game 2. Colorful character.

Bordi, Rich (1985, 1987) Pitcher: 9-9 in 67 games.

Borowski, Joe (1997-98) Pitcher: 1-1 in nine games.

*Borowy, Hank (1942-45) Pitcher: 56-30 in 107 games.

Borton, Babe (1913) 1B: 14 for 108, .130; played in 33 games.

Boston, Daryl (1994) OF-DH: 14 for 77, .182; played in 52 games.

*Bouton, Jim (1962-68) Pitcher: 55-51 in 197 games.

*Boyer, Clete (1959-66) 3B-SS: 882 for 3658, .241; played in 1068 games.

Bradley, Ryan (1998) Pitcher: 2-1 in five games.

Bradley, Scott (1984-85) DH-Catcher-OF: 14 for 70, .200; played in 28 games.

Brady, Neal (1915, 1917) Pitcher: 1-0 in four games.

Bragg, Darren (2001) OF-DH: 1 for 4, .250; played in 5 games.

Branca, Ralph (1954) Pitcher: 1-0 in five games.

Branch, Norm (1941-42) Pitcher: 5-2 in 37 games.

Brant, Marshall (1980) 1B-DH: 0 for 6, .000; played in three games.

Braxton, Garland (1925-26) Pitcher: 6-2 in 40 games.

Brennan, Don (1933) Pitcher: 5-1 in 18 games.

Brenneman, Jim (1965) Pitcher: 0-0 in three games.

Brett, Ken (1976) Pitcher: 0-0 in two games. Brother of Hall-of-Famer George Brett.

Breuer, Marv (1939-43) Pitcher: 25-26 in 86 games. Fifth starter, 1940-42. In Game 4 of the 1941 World Series, Marv relieved and held Brooklyn scoreless between the fifth and 8th innings, and the Yanks rallied to win.

Brewer, Billy (1996) Pitcher: 1-0 in four games.

Brickell, Fritzie (1958-59) SS-2B: 10 for 39, .256; played in 20 games.

Brideweser, Jim (1951-53) SS-2B: 16 for 49, .327; played in 51 games.

Bridges, Marshall (1962-63) Pitcher: 10-4 (19 saves) in 75 games. In 1962, he led the Yanks in saves (18) and games pitched (52), and he probably saved the pennant.

Bright, Harry (1963-64) 1B-3B: 38 for 162, .235; played in 64 games. Struck out to end Game 1 of the 1963 World Series as Sandy Koufax notched his 15th strikeout to set a Series record (since broken).

Brinkman, Ed (1975) INF: 11 for 63, .175; played in 44 games.

*Broaca, Johnny (1934-37) Pitcher: 40-27 in 99 games.

Brockett, Lew (1907, 1909, 1911) Pitcher: 13-15 in 50 games. Tied for club lead in shutouts (three) in 1909. Remained a holdout for the entire 1910 season.

Bronstad, Jim (1959) Pitcher: 0-3 in 16 games.

Brookens, Tom (1989) 3B-SS-2B: 38 for 168, .226; played in 66 games.

Brosius, Scott (1998-2001) 3B-1B-OF-DH: 507 for 1901, .267; played in 540 games. Was the MVP in the 1998 World Series versus San Diego, going 8-for-17 (.471) with six RBI and assisted in making the final out of the '98 series.

Brower, Bob (1989) OF: 16 for 69, .232; played in 26 games.

Brown, Boardwalk (1914-15) Pitcher: 7-11 in 39 games.

*Brown, Bobby (1946-52, 1954) 3B-SS-2B-OF: 452 for 1619, .279; played in 548 games.

Brown, Bobby (1979-81) OF: 138 for 542, .255; played in 198 games. Hit 14 HRs and had 27 stolen bases in 1980. In the post-season of 1981, he played seven games, went 1 for 2, and scored three runs.

Brown, Curt (1984) Pitcher: 1-1 in 13 games.

Brown, Hal (1962) Pitcher: 0-1 in two games.

Brown, Jumbo (1932-33, 1935-36) Pitcher: 19-16 in 80 games. Weighed 295 lbs. Hit .313 (10 for 32) in 1935 and .000 (0 for 19) in 1936.

Bruske, Jim (1998) Pitcher: 1-0 in three games.

Bryan, Bill (1966-67) Catcher-1B: 17 for 81, .210; played in 43 games.

Buckles, Jess (1916) Pitcher: 0-0 in two games.

Buddie, Mike (1998-99) Pitcher: 4-1 in 26 games.

Buhner, Jay (1987-88) OF: 18 for 91, .198; played in 32 games.

Burbach, Bill (1969-71) Pitcher: 6-11 in 37 games.

Burdette, Lew (1950) Pitcher: 0-0 in 2 games. Destroyed Yanks with 3 wins in 1957 World Series.

Burke, Tim (1992) Pitcher: 2-2 in 23 games.

Burns, George (1928-29) 1B: 2 for 13, .154; played in 13 games.

Burr, Alex (1914) OF: 0 for 0; played in one game.

Burris, Ray (1979) Pitcher: 1-3 in 15 games.

Bush, Homer (1997-98) 2B-DH-3B-SS: 31 for 82, .378; played in 55 games.

*Bush, Joe (1922-24) Pitcher: 62-38 in 115 games.

Buskey, Tom (1973-74) Pitcher: 0-2 in 12 games.

Buxton, Ralph (1949) Pitcher: 0-1 in 14 games.

Buzas, Joe (1945) SS: 17 for 65, .262; played in 30 games.

Byrd, Harry (1954) Pitcher: 9-7 in 25 games.

Byrd, Sammy (1929-34) OF: 321 for 1143, .281; played in 565 games. Late in Babe Ruth's career, Sammy was often Ruth's late-inning OF replacement or pinch-runner; hence, his nickname, "Babe Ruth's Legs." In 1934, he led AL outfielders in fielding (.988). Later, he joined the pro golf tour and won 23 tour events.

*Byrne, Tommy (1943, 1946-51, 1954-57) Pitcher: 72-40 in 221 games.

Bystrom, Marty (1984-85) Pitcher: 5-4 in 15 games.

Cadaret, Greg (1989-92) Pitcher: 22-23 in 188 games.

Caldwell, Charlie (1925) Pitcher: 0-0 in three games.

*Caldwell, Ray (1910-18) Pitcher: 95-99 in 248 games.

Callison, Johnny (1972-73) OF: 95 for 411, .231; played in 137 games.

Camp, Howie (1917) OF: 6 for 21, .286; played in five games.

Campaneris, Bert (1983) 2B-3B: 46 for 143, .322; played in 60 games.

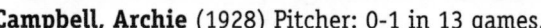

Campbell, Archie (1928) Pitcher: 0-1 in 13 games.

Candelaria, John (1988-89) Pitcher: 16-10 in 35 games. Knee injury both years.

Cantwell, Mike (1916) Pitcher: 0-0 in one game.

Canseco, Jose (2000) OF-DH: 27 for 111, .243; played in 37 games.

*Carey, Andy (1952-60) 3B-SS: 567 for 2130, .266; played in 688 games.

Carlyle, Roy (1926) OF: 20 for 53, .377; played in 35 games.

Carmel, Duke (1965) 1B: 0 for 8, .000; played in six games.

Carroll, Dick (1909) Pitcher: 0-0 in two games.

Carroll, Ownie (1930) Pitcher: 0-1 in 10 games.

Carroll, Tommy (1955-56) 3B-SS: 8 for 23, .348; played in 50 games. Bonus Baby from Notre Dame.

Cary, Chuck (1989-91) Pitcher: 11-22 in 60 games. Injured in 1989 and 1990.

Casey, Hugh (1949) Pitcher: 1-0 in four games.

Castillo, Alberto (2002) Catcher: 5 for 37, .135; played in 37 games.

Castleton, Roy (1907) Pitcher: 1-1 in three games.

Castro, Bill (1981) Pitcher: 1-1 in 11 games.

Cater, Danny (1970-71) 1B-3B-OF: 293 for 1010, .290; played in 276 games. Regular first baseman in 1970 and hit .301. In March, 1972, the Yanks traded Cater and Mario Guerrero to Boston for Sparky Lyle. Cerone pitched in 1987 (0-0). No runs in two innings. Finished both games; no saves; one walk; one strikeout; and one balk; faking seven batters.

*Cerone, Rick (1980-84, 1987, 1990) C-INF-P: 459 for 1842, .249; played in 587 games. Not to be confused with Rick Cerrone, the head of Yankee Media Relations, who spells his name with two R's. Pitched in two games in 1987 with no decisions. Faced seven batters, two innings, no runs. Finished both games.

Cerv, Bob (1951-56, 1960, 1961-62) OF: 205 for 772, .266; played in 379 games. Valuable reserve outfielder. Hit a double off 457-foot sign at Yankee Stadium. Hit 26 HRs; 8 as a pinch-hitter. Went 3 for 3 as a pinch-hitter in World Series games. Hit pinch-hit HR in 1955 World Series. Made 2 hits in 1 inning in 1960 World Series.

*Chambliss, Chris (1974-79, 1988) 1B: 954 for 3383, .282; played in 885 games.

Chance, Frank (1913-14) 1B: 5 for 24, .208; played in 12 games. Activated himself while managing the club in 1913 and 1914.

*Chandler, Spud (1937-47) Pitcher: 109-43 in 211 games.

Channell, Les (1910, 1914) OF: 7 for 20, .350; played in seven games.

Chapin, Darrin (1991) Pitcher: 0-1 in three games.

*Chapman, Ben (1930-36) OF-3B-2B: 1079 for 3539, .305; played in 909 games.

Chartak, Mike (1940, 1942) OF: 2 for 20, .100; played in 16 games.

*Chase, Hal (1905-13) 1B-OF-2B: 1182 for 4158, .284; played in 1059 games. Managed club in 1910 and 1911. First Yankee Captain. Pitched in one game (0-0) in 1908.

*Chesbro, Jack (1903-09) Pitcher: 129-91 in 269 games.

Choate, Randy (2000-2002) Pitcher: 3-2 in 77 games.

Christiansen, Clay (1984) Pitcher: 2-4 in 24 games.

Cicotte, Al (1957) Pitcher: 2-2 in 20 games.

Clark, Allie (1947) OF: 25 for 67, .373; played in 24 games. Went 1 for 2 with a walk in 1947 World Series. Pinch-hitting for Yogi Berra in Game 7, Allie singled home an important insurance run. Wore Babe Ruth's number 3 before it was retired.

Clark, George (1913) Pitcher: 0-1 in 11 games.

Clark, Jack (1988) DH-OF-1B: 120 for 496, .242; played in 150 games. Hit 27 HRs with 93 RBIs.

*Clarke, Horace (1965-74) 2B-SS-3B: 1213 for 4723, .257; played in 1232 games.

Clarkson, Walter (1904-07) Pitcher: 14-10 in 59 games. Led Yanks in ERA (2.32) in 1906.

Clay, Ken (1977-79) Pitcher: 6-14 in 81 games. Pitched $3\frac{2}{3}$ hitless innings to save Game 1 of 1978 ALCS. Pitched in two games of 1977 World Series and 1 game of 1978 World Series (no decisions).

Clemens, Roger (1999-2002) Pitcher: 60-27 in 124 games.

Clements, Pat (1987-88) Pitcher: 3-3 in 61 games. Also 7 saves.

Clevenger, Tex (1961-62) Pitcher: 3-1 in 42 games.

Clinton, Lu (1966-67) OF: 37 for 163, .227; played in 86 games.

Closter, Alan (1971-72) Pitcher: 2-2 in 16 games.

Coakley, Andy (1911) Pitcher: 0-1 in 2 games. Coached Lou Gehrig at Columbia.

*Coates, Jim (1956, 1959-62) Pitcher: 37-15 in 167 games.

Cockman, Jim (1905) 3B: 4 for 38, .105; played in 13 games.

Coggins, Rich (1975-76) OF: 28 for 111, .252; played in 58 games.

Colavito, Rocky (1968) OF: 20 for 91, .220; played in 39 games. Came into a game as a relief pitcher, did not allow a run in $2\frac{2}{3}$ innings, and was the winning pitcher.

Cole, King (1914-15) Pitcher: 14-12 in 43 games. Died during the winter following the 1915 season.

Coleman, Curt (1912) 3B: 9 for 37, .243; played in 12 games.

*Coleman, Jerry (1949-57) 2B-SS-3B: 558 for 2119, .263; played in 723 games. Yankee TV-Radio broadcaster for many years.

Coleman, Michael (2001) OF-DH: 8 for 38, .211; played in 12 games.

Coleman, Rip (1955-56) Pitcher: 5-6 in 39 games. Pitched in relief in Game 4 of 1955 World Series (no decision).

Collins, Bob (1944) Catcher: 1 for 3, .333; played in three games.

Collins, Dave (1982) OF-1B: 88 for 348, .253; played in 111 games.

*Collins, Joe (1948-57) 1B-OF: 596 for 2329, .256; played in 908 games.

Collins, Orth (1904) OF: 6 for 17, .353; played in five games.

*Collins, Pat (1926-28) Catcher: 182 for 667, .269; played in 264 games. Led AL catchers in double plays (14) in 1926. Caught the majority of games on the 1927 Yankees and hit .275. Hit a combined .500 (4 for 8) in three World Series.

Collins, Rip (1920-21) Pitcher: 25-13 in 64 games. Went 14-8 in 1920 and 11-5 in 1921, and he pitched two one-hitters. Hit hard in relief in Game 3 of 1921 World Series.

Colman, Frank (1946-47) OF: 7 for 43, .163; played in 27 games.

Colson, Loyd (1970) Pitcher: 0-0 in one game.

*Combs, Earle (1924-35) OF: 1866 for 5748, .325; played in 1454 games. Yankee coach.

*Cone, David (1995-2001) Pitcher: 64-40 in 144 games. Second Yankee pitcher to toss a regular-season perfect game on July 18, 1999 versus the Montreal Expos of the National League (David Wells pitched his perfect game in 1998). **For a pitch-by-pitch account of David's game, see page 55.**

David Cone

Connelly, Tom (1920-21) OF: 1 for 6, .167; played in five games.

Connor, Joe (1905) Catcher-1B: 5 for 22, 227; played in eight games.

*Conroy, Wid (1903-08) INF-OF: 750 for 3005, .250; played in 797 games.

Cook, Andy (1993) Pitcher: 0-1 in four games.

Cook, Doc (1913-16) OF: 282 for 1028, .274; played in 286 games. Yanks' regular rightfielder in 1914 and 1915. In 1914, he led NY in batting (.283), slugging (.326), and hits (133).

Cooke, Dusty (1930-32) OF: 68 for 255, .267; played in 122 games.

Coomer, Ron (2002) 3B-1B-DH: 39 for 148, .264; played in 55 games.

Cooney, Johnny (1944) OF: 1 for 8, .125; played in 10 games.

Cooney, Phil (1905) 3B: 0 for 3, .000; played in one game.

Cooper, Don (1985) Pitcher: 0-0 in seven games.

Cooper, Guy (1914) Pitcher: 0-0 in one game.

Costello, Dan (1913) PH: 1 for 2, .500, pinch-hit in two games.

Cotto, Henry (1985-87) OF: 69 for 285, .242; played in 137 games.

Cottrell, Ensign (1915) Pitcher: 0-1 in seven games.

Courtney, Clint (1951) Catcher: 0 for 2, .000; played in one game. First to wear glasses behind the plate. Got into several fights with Yankees after leaving club.

Courtney, Ernie (1903) 1B-SS-2B: 21 for 79, .266; played in 25 games.

Coveleski, Stan (1928) Pitcher: 5-1 in 12 games. The great Hall of Famer made a contribution to the Yankees' 1928 World Championship in his last ML season.

Cowan, Billy (1969) OF-1B: 8 for 48, .167; played in 32 games.

Cowley, Joe (1984-85) Pitcher: 21-8 in 46 games. Yanks' fourth starter in 1985.

Cox, Bobby (1968-69) 3B-2B: 141 for 628, .225; played in 220 games. Spent several years in the Yankee organization as a minor league manager and Yankee coach. Has been Atlanta Braves' manager since 1990, making 11 playoff appearances; going 1-4 in the World Series.

Cox, Casey (1972-73) Pitcher: 0-1 in six games.

*Cree, Birdie (1908-15) OF-INF: 761 for 2603, .292; played in 742 games.

Criger, Lou (1910) Catcher: 13 for 69, .188; played in 27 games.

Crompton, Herb (1945) Catcher: 19 for 99, .192; played in 36 games.

*Crosetti, Frank (1932-48) SS-3B-2B: 1541 for 6277, .245; played in 1683 games. Yankee coach for 20 seasons.

Cruz, Ivan (1997) DH-1B-OF: 5 for 20, .250; played in 11 games.

Cruz, Jose (1988) DH-OF: 16 for 80, .200; played in 38 games.

Cullen, Jack (1962, 1965-66) Pitcher: 4-4 in 19 games.

Cullenbine, Roy (1942) OF: 28 for 77, .364; played in 21 games. Batted third in every game of the 1942 World Series and hit .263 (5 for 19). Scored three runs, walked once, stole one base, hit one double, and had two RBIs. Played right field.

Cullop, Nick (1916-17) Pitcher: 18-15 in 58 games. No. 2 starter in 1916; led Yanks in winning percentage (.667, 12-6) and ERA (2.05).

Cullop, Nick (1926) PH: 1 for 2, .500; pinch-hit in two games. Known as "Babe Ruth of the Minors," he hit 420 HRs and 1856 RBIs in the minors. Broke into MLs with Yanks.

Cumberland, John (1968-70) Pitcher: 3-4 in 18 games. Signed on with Texas for 2000.

Curry, Jim (1911) 2B: 2 for 11, .182; played in four games.

Curtis, Chad (1997-99) OF-DH: 255 for 971, .263; played in 340 games.

Curtis, Fred (1905) 1B: 2 for 9, .222; played in two games.

Dahlgren, Babe (1937-40) 1B-3B: 283 for 1143, .248; played in 327 games. Hit .340 for great Newark Bears of 1937. Replaced Lou Gehrig at 1B when Lou retired in 1939 and hit 15 HRs with 89 RBIs. Hit a double and HR in Game 2 of the 1939 World Series.

Daley, Bud (1961-64) Pitcher: 18-16 in 80 games. Won final game of 1961 World Series, pitching 6⅔ innings in relief. A sore arm derailed his career in 1963.

Daley, Tom (1914-15) OF: 50 for 199, .251; played in 77 games.

*Daniels, Bert (1910-13) OF-3B-1B: 427 for 1634, .261; played in 455 games.

Davidson, Bobby (1989) Pitcher: 0-0 in one game.

Davis, Chili (1998-99) DH: 158 for 579, .273; played in 181 games.

Davis, George (1912) Pitcher: 1-4 in 10 games.

Davis, Kiddo (1926) OF: 0 for 0; played in one game.

Davis, Lefty (1903) OF-SS: 88 for 372, .237; played in 104 games.

*Davis, Ron (1978-81) Pitcher: 27-10 in 144 games.

Davis, Russ (1994-95) 3B-DH; 29 for 112, .259; played in 44 games.

Dayett, Brian (1983-84) OF-DH: 37 for 156, .237; played in 75 games.

Deering, John (1903) Pitcher: 4-3 in nine games.

Deidel, Jim (1974) Catcher: 0 for 2, .000; played in two games.

DeJesus, Ivan (1986) SS: 0 for 4, .000; played in seven games.

Delahanty, Frank (1905-06, 1908) OF-1B: 111 for 459, .242; played in 138 games. Had four brothers who played ML ball, including Hall of Famer Ed Delahanty.

Delgado, Wilson (2000) 2B-SS-3B: 11 for 45, .244; played in 31 games.

Del Greco, Bobby (1957-58) OF: 4 for 12, .333; played in 20 games.

Delsing, Jim (1949-50) OF: 11 for 30, .367; played in 21 games.

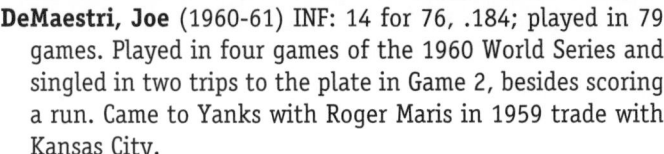

DeMaestri, Joe (1960-61) INF: 14 for 76, .184; played in 79 games. Played in four games of the 1960 World Series and singled in two trips to the plate in Game 2, besides scoring a run. Came to Yanks with Roger Maris in 1959 trade with Kansas City.

Demmitt, Ray (1909) OF: 105 for 427, .246; played in 123 games.

Dempsey, Rick (1973-76) Catcher-OF: 71 for 307, .231; played in 141 games.

*Dent, Bucky (1977-82) SS: 518 for 2163, .239; played in 695 games. Yankee manager, 1989-90.

Derrick, Claud (1913) INF: 19 for 65, .292; played in 23 games.

Derry, Russ (1944-45) OF: 86 for 367, .234; played in 116 games.

Deshaies, Jim (1984) Pitcher: 0-1 in two games. Was the 1000th Yankee player to appear in a regular season game.

DeShong, Jimmie (1934-35) Pitcher: 10-8 in 60 games.

Destrade, Orestes (1987) 1B-DH: 5 for 19, .263; played in nine games. Great prospect in NY organization.

Devens, Charlie (1932-34) Pitcher: 5-3 in 16 games. Yanks signed him out of Harvard University as a potential superstar.

DeVormer, Al (1921-22) Catcher: 29 for 108, .269; played in 46 games. Went 0 for 1 in 1921 World Series. Yanks traded him to Red Sox for George Pipgras (and another player).

*Dickey, Bill (1928-43, 1946) Catcher: 1969 for 6300, .313; played in 1789 games. Yankee manager, 1946. Yankee coach under Casey Stengel. Yankee scout.

Dickson, Murry (1958) Pitcher: 1-2 in six games. Pitched in relief in Games 2 and 4 of the 1958 World Series (no decisions).

*DiMaggio, Joe (1936-42, 1946-51) OF: 2214 for 6821, .325; played in 1736 games.

Dineen, Kerry (1975-76) OF: 10 for 29, .345; played in 11 games.

Dingman, Craig (2000) Pitcher: 0-0 in 10 games.

*Ditmar, Art (1957-61) Pitcher: 47-32 in 168 games.

Dixon, Sonny (1956) Pitcher: 0-1 in three games.

*Dobson, Pat (1973-75) Pitcher: 39-37 in 94 games; Yankee minor league coach, 1980s.

Dolan, Cozy (1911-12) 3B: 33 for 129, .256; played in 37 games.

*Donald, Atley (1938-45) Pitcher: 65-33 in 153 games. Yankee scout.

Donovan, Mike (1908) 3B: 5 for 19, .263; played in five games.

Donovan, Wild Bill (1915-16) Pitcher: 0-3 in 10 games. Yankee manager, 1915-17.

Dorsett, Brian (1989-90) Catcher-1B: 13 for 57, .228; played in 22 games.

Dotson, Rich (1988-89) Pitcher: 14-14 in 43 games.

Dougherty, Patsy (1904-06) OF: 248 for 922, .269; played in 234 games. Regular leftfielder in 1904 and 1905. Led AL in runs (113) and ABs (647), playing for both Red Sox and Yankees in 1904.

Dowd, John (1912) SS: 6 for 31, .194; played in 10 games. O'Dowd was his birth name, but he played under the name Dowd.

*Downing, Al (1961-69) Pitcher: 72-57 in 208 games.

Doyle, Brian (1978-80) 2B-SS: 27 for 159, .170; played in 93 games. Hit .286 (2 for 7) in three games of 1978 ALCS. Hit .428 (7 for 16), including his first ML extra-base hit, and starred at second base in 1978 World Series, playing in every game.

Doyle, Jack (1905) 1B: 0 for 3, .000; played in one game. Played for all three NY teams: Yankees, Dodgers, and Giants.

Doyle, Slow Joe (1906-10) Pitcher: 22-21 in 70 games. On August 25 and 30, 1906, he pitched shutouts in his first two ML games. Led Yanks in strikeouts (94) in 1907.

Drabek, Doug (1986) Pitcher: 7-8 in 27 games. Yanks traded him to Pittsburgh in 1986; he won NL Cy Young Award in 1990.

Drescher, Bill (1944-46) Catcher: 37 for 139, .266; played in 57 games.

Drews, Karl (1946-48) Pitcher: 8-10 in 52 games. Pitched in relief in Games 3 and 6 of the 1947 World Series (no decisions).

Dubiel, Monk (1944-45) Pitcher: 23-22 in 56 games. No. 2 starter in 1944 and tied for club leadership in complete games (19) and shutouts (3). No. 3 starter in 1945.

*Dugan, Joe (1922-28) 3B: 871 for 3043, .286; played in 785 games.

Duncan, Mariano (1996-97) 2B-3B-OF-DH: 178 for 572, .311; played in 159 games.

*Duren, Ryne (1958-61) Pitcher: 12-15 in 131 games.

Durocher, Leo (1925, 1928-29) SS-2B: 164 for 638, .257; played in 210 games. Utility infielder in 1928 and regular SS in 1929. Babe Ruth thought Leo was the cockiest rookie he ever saw. Leo walked out during a contract dispute with GM Ed Barrow after 1929 season, and Barrow soon got rid of him. From 1939-73, he managed the Dodgers, Giants, Cubs and Astros.

Durst, Cedric (1927-30) OF-1B: 121 for 485, .249; played in 239 games. Went 0 for 1 in the 1927 World Series. Hit .375 (3 for 8) in the 1928 World Series, playing all four games in center field, replacing the injured Earle Combs. Cedric scored three runs, had two RBIs, and hit a HR in Game 4. Yanks traded him in 1930 to Red Sox for Red Ruffing.

Easler, Mike (1986-87) DH-OF: 195 for 657, .297; played in 211 games.

Eastwick, Rawly (1978) Pitcher: 2-1 in eight games. Yanks signed him to lucrative free-agent contract.

Edwards, Doc (1965) Catcher: 19 for 100, .190; played in 45 games. Yankee minor league manager.

Edwards, Foster (1930) Pitcher: 0-0 in two games.

Eenhoorn, Robert (1994-96) 2B-3B-SS: 5 for 32, .156; played in 20 games.

Eiland, Dave (1988-91, 1995) Pitcher: 6-10 in 36 games.

Einertson, Darrell (2000) Pitcher: 0-0 in 11 games.

*Elberfeld, Kid (1903-09) SS-3B: 647 for 2412, .268; played in 667 games. Yankee Manager, 1908.

Elliot, Gene (1911) OF-3B: 1 for 13, .077; played in five games.

Ellis, Dock (1976-77) Pitcher: 18-9 in 35 games. No. 3 starter in 1976; led Yankees in winning percentage (.688, 17-8) and was *The Sporting News* AL Comeback Player of the Year. Won Game 3 of 1976 ALCS.

Ellis, John (1969-72) Catcher-1B-3B: 172 for 662, .260; played in 235 games. Won James P. Dawson Award as spring training's best rookie in 1970. Part of trade to Indians for Graig Nettles.

Elster, Kevin (1994-95) SS: 2 for 37, .054; played in 17 games.

Embree, Red (1948) Pitcher: 5-3 in 20 games.

Engle, Clyde (1909-10) OF: 140 for 505, .277; played in 140 games.

Tom Ferrick

Enright, Jack (1917) Pitcher: 0-1 in one game.

Erdos, Todd (1998-2000) Pitcher: 0-0 in 20 games.

Erickson, Roger (1982-83) Pitcher: 4-6 in 21 games.

Espino, Juan (1982-83, 1985-86) C-SS-2B-3B-P: 16 for 73, .219; played in 49 games.

*Espinoza, Alvaro (1988-91) SS: 363 for 1424, .255; played in 447 games. Pitched in 1 game (0-0) in 1991; $\frac{2}{3}$ innings; two batters faced. One game finished; no hits or runs.

Estalella, Bobby (2001) Catcher: 0 for 4, .000; played in three games.

*Etten, Nick (1943-46) 1B: 562 for 2044, .275; played in 568 games.

Evans, Barry (1982) INF: 8 for 31, .258; played in 17 games.

Fallon, Charles (1905) Pinch-runner (0 for 0): played in one game, no runs scored.

*Farr, Steve (1991-93) Pitcher: 9-9 in 159 games.

Farrell, Doc (1932-33) INF: 36 for 156, .231; played in 70 games.

Ferguson, Alex (1918, 1921, 1925) Pitcher: 7-3 in 39 games.

Fernandez, Frank (1967-69) Catcher-OF: 80 for 392, .204; played in 149 games.

Fernandez, Tony (1995) SS-2B: 94 for 384, .245; played in 108 games.

Ferraro, Mike (1966, 1968) 3B: 19 for 115, .165; played in 33 games. Yankee minor league manager and Yankee coach.

Ferrell, Wes (1938-39) Pitcher: 3-4 in eight games.

Ferrick, Tom (1950-51) Pitcher: 9-5 in 39 games. Saved nine games during second half of 1950 season, helping Yanks win pennant. Won Game 3 of the 1950 World Series in relief.

Fewster, Chick (1917-22) OF-INF: 174 for 642, .271; played in 228 games. Went 2 for 10 (.200) in the 1921 World Series,

including a 2-run HR in Game 6. Scored three runs in that Series. Colorful character.

Fielder, Cecil (1996-97) DH-1B: 146 for 561, .260; played in 151 games.

Figga, Mike (1997-99) DH-Catcher: 1 for 8; played in five games.

*Figueroa, Ed (1976-80) Pitcher: 62-39 in 132 games.

Filson, Pete (1987) Pitcher: 1-0 in seven games.

Finneran, Happy (1918) Pitcher: 3-6 in 23 games.

Fischlin, Mike (1986) SS-2B: 21 for 102, .206; played in 71 games.

Fisher, Brian (1985-86) Pitcher: 13-9 in 117 games. Saved 20 games.

Fisher, Gus (1912) Catcher: 1 for 10, .100; played in four games.

*Fisher, Ray (1910-17) Pitcher: 76-78 in 219 games.

Fitzgerald, Mike (1911) OF: 10 for 37, .270; played in 16 games.

Foli, Tim (1984) INF: 41 for 163, .252; played in 61 games.

Fontenot, Ray (1983-84) Pitcher: 16-11 in 50 games.

Foote, Barry (1981-82) Catcher: 33 for 173, .191; played in 57 games.

Ford, Ben (2000) Pitcher: 0-1 in four games.

*Ford, Russ (1909-13) Pitcher: 73-56 in 143 games.

*Ford, Whitey (1950, 1953-67) Pitcher: 236-106 in 498 games. Yankee minor league instructor, coach, and scout.

Fossas, Tony (1999) Pitcher: 0-0 in five games.

Foster, Eddie (1910) SS: 11 for 83, .133; played in 30 games.

Fournier, Jack (1918) 1B: 35 for 100, .350; played in 27 games.

Fox, Andy (1996-97) 2B-3B-SS-DH-OF: 44 for 220, .200; played in 135 games.

Francis, Ray (1925) Pitcher: 0-0 in four games.

Frazier, George (1981-83) Pitcher: 8-9 in 140 games. Led NY in games pitched in 1982 and 1983. Saved 12 games. Won Game 1 of 1981 ALCS. Losing Pitcher in three games of 1981 World Series.

Freeman, Mark (1959) Pitcher: 0-0 in one game.

French, Ray (1920) SS: 0 for 2, .000; played in two games.

Frey, Lonny (1947-48) 2B: 5 for 28, .179; played in 25 games. Played for all three NY teams: Yankees, Dodgers, and Giants.

Friend, Bob (1966) Pitcher: 1-4 in 12 games.

Frill, John (1910) Pitcher: 2-2 in 10 games.

Fulton, Bill (1987) Pitcher: 1-0 in 3 games.

Fultz, Dave (1903-05) OF-3B: 257 for 1056, .243; played in 306 games. In club's first game on April 22, 1903, he batted 3rd and played OF and got first hit in club history. Regular centerfielder in 1904 and 1905. Led club in stolen bases in 1905 (44).

Funk, Liz (1929) 0 for 0; played in one game as a pinch-runner.

Gabler, John (1959-60) Pitcher: 4-4 in 24 games.

Gallagher, Joe (1939) OF: 10 for 41, .244; played in 14 games.

Gallego, Mike (1992-94) SS-2B-3B: 231 for 882, .262; played in 261 games. Disabled much of the 1992 season. Regular shortstop in 1993 and 1994 and played excellent defense. He also hit 10 HRs in 1993.

*Gamble, Oscar (1976, 1979-84) OF-DH: 378 for 1457, .259; played in 540 games.

Ganzel, John (1903-04) 1B: 253 for 941, .269; played in 259 games. On May 11, 1903, he hit the first HR in Yankee history. Led Yanks in HRs (6) in 1904. Regular 1B in 1903 and 1904. In 1903, he led AL 1B in fielding (.988).

Burleigh Grimes

Garbark, Mike (1944-45) Catcher: 116 for 475, .244; played in 149 games.

Garcia, Damaso (1978-79) 2B-SS: 18 for 79, .228; played in 29 games.

Garcia, Karim (2002) OF: 1 for 5, .200; played in two games.

Gardner, Billy (1961-62) 3B-2B: 21 for 100, .210; played in 45 games. Lined out as a pinch hitter to end Game 2 of the 1961 World Series.

Gardner, Earle (1908-12) 2B: 249 for 948, .263; played in 273 games. Played semi-regularly at second base in 1910 and 1911.

Gardner, Rob (1970, 1971-72) Pitcher: 9-5 in 23 games.

Garlick, Stephen (also "Stibby") (1958-63) OF-SS-3B: 187 for 636, .294; played in 162 games. Was 11 for 39 (.282) in 17 World Series games.

Garvin, Ned (1904) Pitcher: 0-1 in two games.

Gaston, Milt (1924) Pitcher: 5-3 in 29 games.

Gazella, Mike (1923, 1926-28) 3B-SS-2B: 85 for 352, .241; played in 160 games. Played in 1926 World Series without an at-bat (used briefly at 3B in Game 5). Yankee scout.

Gedeon, Joe (1916-17) 2B: 120 for 552, .217; played in 155 games.

*Gehrig, Lou (1923-39) 1B-OF-SS: 2721 for 8001, .340; played in 2164 games. Played 8 games in the outfield and one game in 1934 at shortstop.

Geren, Bob (1988-91) Catcher: 147 for 620, .237; played in 249 games.

Gettel, Al (1945-46) Pitcher: 15-15 in 53 games. Yanks' No. 5 starter in 1945 (9-8).

Giambi, Jason (2002) 1B-DH: 176 for 560, .314, played in 155 games.

Giard, Joe (1927) Pitcher: 0-0 in 16 games.

*Gibbs, Jake (1962-71) Catcher: 382 for 1639, .233; played in 538 games. College head coach, Yankee bullpen coach and minor league manager from 1972-1995.

Gibson, Paul (1993-94, 1996) Pitcher: 3-1 in 54 games.

Gibson, Sam (1930) Pitcher: 0-1 in two games.

Gilhooley, Frank (1913-18) OF: 251 for 907, .277; played in 250 games. Regular rightfielder in 1918 and led AL outfielders in double plays (eight). Also led Yanks in walks (53) in 1918.

Girardi, Joe (1996-99) Catcher-DH: 349 for 1283, .272; played in 379 games.

Glade, Fred (1908) Pitcher: 0-4 in five games.

Gleich, Frank (1919-20) OF: 6 for 45, .133; played in 29 games.

Glenn, Joe (1932-33, 1935-38) Catcher: 97 for 385, .252; played in 138 games. Backup catcher in his six-year Yankee career. Caught Babe Ruth's final game as a pitcher.

*Gomez, Lefty (1930-42) Pitcher: 189-101 in 367 games. Yankee minor league pitching instructor and farm manager.

Gonder, Jesse (1960-61) Catcher: 6 for 19, .316; played in 22 games.

Gonzalez, Fernando (1974) 2B-3B-SS: 26 for 121, .215; played in 51 games.

Gonzalez, Pedro (1963-65) INF-OF: 38 for 143, .266; played in 101 games. Went 0-for-1 in the 1964 World Series.

Good, Wilbur (1905) OF-P: 3 for 8 in 6 games, .375; Pitcher: 0-2 in five games.

Gooden, Dwight (1996-97, 2000) Pitcher: 24-14 in 67 games. Pitched a no-hitter against Seattle on 5/14/96.

Goodwin, Art (1905) Pitcher: 0-0 in one game.

*Gordon, Joe (1938-43, 1946) 2B-1B: 1000 for 3686, .271; played in 1000 games.

Gorman, Tom (1952-54) Pitcher: 10-7 in 75 games. Pitched in relief in Game 3 of the 1952 World Series and Game 4 of the 1953 World Series (no decisions).

*Gossage, Goose (1978-83, 1989) Pitcher: 42-28 in 319 games.

Gossett, Dick (1913-14) Catcher: 20 for 126, .159; played in 49 games.

Gowell, Larry (1972) Pitcher: 0-1 in two games.

Grabowski, Johnny (1927-29) Catcher: 114 for 456, .250; played in 167 games. Split the catching chores with Pat Collins on the great 1927-28 teams. Went 0 for 2 in the 1927 World Series.

Granger, Wayne (1973) Pitcher: 0-1 in seven games.

Gray, Ted (1955) Pitcher: 0-0 in one game.

Grba, Eli (1959-60) Pitcher: 8-9 in 43 games. Yanks lost him to Angels in 1960 expansion draft.

Greene, Todd (2001) Catcher-DH: 20 for 96, .208; played in 35 games.

Greene, Willie (also Patsy) (1903) 3B-SS: 4 for 13, .308; played in 4 games.

*Griffey Sr., Ken (1982-86) OF-1B: 563 for 1977, .285; played in 551 games. Father of Ken Griffey, Jr.

Griffin, Mike (1979-81) Pitcher: 2-4 in 18 games.

*Griffith, Clark (1903-07) Pitcher: 32-24 in 87 games. Managed club, 1903-08.

*Grim, Bob (1954-58) Pitcher: 45-21 in 146 games.

Grimes, Burleigh (1934) Pitcher: 1-2 in 10 games. The Great Hall of Famer ended his ML career with the Yanks. Yankee minor league instructor and scout.

Grimes, Oscar (1943-46) INF: 246 for 926, .266; played in 281 games. Regular Yankee third baseman in 1944 and 1945. Led Yanks in walks in 1945 (97). In 1945, he led AL third basemen in double plays (35).

Grimsley, Jason (1999-2000) Pitcher: 10-4 in 118 games. Also one save.

Jason Grimsley

Grissom, Lee (1940) Pitcher: 0-0 in five games.

Guante, Cecilio (1987-88) Pitcher: 8-8 in 79 games. Also 12 saves.

***Guetterman, Lee** (1988-92) Pitcher: 21-19 in 233 games.

***Guidry, Ron** (1975-88) Pitcher: 170-91 in 368 games. Played in 2 games in the outfield (1979, 1983).

Gulden, Brad (1979-80) Catcher: 16 for 95, .168; played in 42 games. Took over as Yankee catcher in 1979 following the death of Thurman Munson.

Gullett, Don (1977-78) Pitcher: 18-6 in 30 games. 1st Yankee signed in new free-agent system, November 1976. Went 14-4 in 1977 and led Yanks in win pct. (.778). Started Game 1 of 1977 World Series and left after 8 $\frac{1}{3}$ innings with Yanks ahead, 3-2. Disabled much of 1978 with a double tear in his rotator cuff of pitching shoulder, a career-ending injury.

Gullickson, Bill (1987) Pitcher: 4-2 in eight games.

Gumpert, Randy (1946-48) Pitcher: 16-4 in 72 games. Yanks' No. 5 starter in 1946 and led club in win pct. (.786, 11-3). Pitching for White Sox, he gave up Mickey Mantle's first HR in 1951. Yankee scout.

Gura, Larry (1974-75) Pitcher: 12-9 in 34 games.

Habyan, John (1990-93) Pitcher: 11-9 in 164 games. Also 10 saves.

***Hadley, Bump** (1936-40) Pitcher: 49-31 in 140 games.

Hadley, Kent (1960) 1B: 13 for 64, .203; played in 55 games. Came to Yanks with Roger Maris in 1959 trade with Kansas City.

Hahn, Eddie (1905-06) OF: 53 for 182, .291; played in 54 games.

Hahn, Noodles (1906) Pitcher: 3-2 in six games.

Haines, Hinkey (1923) OF: 4 for 25, .160; played in 28 games. Went 0 for 1 at-bat in the 1923 World Series, playing in two games. As a pinch-runner, he scored a crucial run in Game 6, the final game of that Series. Pro quarterback for NY Giants (1925-28) and Staten Island Stapletons (1929-31).

Halas, George (1919) OF: 2 for 22, .091; played in 12 games. One of the founders and immortals of the National Football League.

Hale, Bob (1961) 1B: 2 for 13, .154; played in 11 games.

Hall, Jimmie (1969) OF-1B: 50 for 212, .236; played in 80 games.

***Hall, Mel** (1989-92) OF-DH: 490 for 1796, .273; played in 519 games.

Hambright, Roger (1971) Pitcher: 3-1 in 18 games.

***Hamilton, Steve** (1963-70) Pitcher: 34-20 in 311 games. Played in the NBA with the Minneapolis Lakers (1958-60).

Handiboe, Mike (1911) OF: 1 for 15, .067; played in five games.

Hanley, Jim (1913) Pitcher: 0-0 in 1 game.

Hannah, Truck (1918-20) Catcher-1B: 173 for 736, .235; played in 244 games. Caught more games than anyone else in the club during his three seasons with the Yanks.

Hansen, Ron (1970-71) INF: 57 for 236, .242; played in 120 games.

Hanson, Joe (1913) Catcher: 0 for 2, .000; played in one game.

Hardin, Jim (1971) Pitcher: 0-2 in 12 games.

Hargrave, Bubbles (1930) Catcher: 30 for 108, .278; played in 45 games.

Harper, Harry (1921) Pitcher: 4-3 in 8 games. Started Game 6 in the 1921 World Series, but he was knocked out in the second inning (no decision).

Harrah, Toby (1984) 3B: 55 for 253, .217; played in 88 games.

Harris, Greg (1994) Pitcher: 0 for 1 in three games.

Harris, Joe (1914) OF-1B: 0 for 1, .000; played in two games.

Hart, Jim Ray (1973-74) DH: 87 for 358, .243; played in 124 games.

***Hartzell, Roy** (1911-16) OF-INF: 617 for 2365, .261; played in 697 games.

Hassett, Buddy (1942) 1B: 153 for 538, .284; played in 132 games. Regular first baseman in 1942. Injured during World Series. Entered military after 1942 World Series. Minor league manager.

Hassey, Ron (1985-86) Catcher-DH-1B: 136 for 458, .297; played in 156 games. Hit 19 HRs as a Yankee.

Hawkins, Andy (1989-91) Pitcher: 20-29 in 66 games. In 1989, he led the Yanks in wins (15), games started (34), complete games (five), innings pitched (208), strikeouts (98), and shutouts (two). Yanks' fourth starter in 1990. Lost an eight-inning no-hitter to the White Sox on 7/1/90.

Hawks, Chicken (1921) OF: 21 for 73, .288; played in 41 games.

Hayes, Charlie (1992, 1996-97) 3B-2B-1B: 241 for 929, .259; played in 262 games. Caught a foul ball for the final out of the 1996 World Series.

Healy, Fran (1976-78) Catcher: 47 for 188, .250; played in 74 games. Played peacekeeper role on '77 Yanks and befriended Reggie Jackson. Spent several years as a Yankee radio broadcaster, teaming well with Phil Rizzuto.

Heath, Mike (1978) Catcher: 21 for 92, .228; played in 33 games. Caught briefly in Game 5 of the 1978 World Series without an at-bat.

Heaton, Neal (1993) Pitcher: 1-0 in 18 games.

Heffner, Don (1934-37) INF-OF: 135 for 526, .257; played in 161 games.

Hegan, Mike (1964, 1966-67, 1973-74) 1B-OF: 72 for 346, .208; played in 141 games. Went 0 for 1 in the 1964 World Series, playing in three games. Son of Yankee coach Jim Hegan.

Heimach, Fred (1928-29) Pitcher: 13-9 in 48 games.

Held, Woodie (1954, 1957) 3B-SS: 0 for 4, .000; played in five games.

Hemphill, Charlie (1908-11) OF: 335 for 1238, .271; played in 386 games. Regular centerfielder in 1908 and 1910. In 1908, he led the Yanks in games (142), runs (62), hits (150), triples (nine), RBIs (44), walks (59), stolen bases (42), batting (.297), and slugging (.356).

Hemsley, Rollie (1942-44) Catcher: 144 for 549, .262; played in 174 games. Played in the 1944 All-Star Game (0 for 2 at-bats).

Henderson, Bill (1930) Pitcher: 0-0 in three games.

*Henderson, Rickey (1985-89) OF-DH: 663 for 2302, .288; played in 596 games.

Hendrick, Harvey (1923-24) OF: 38 for 142, .268; played in 77 games. Went 0-for-1 in the 1923 World Series.

Hendricks, Elrod "Ellie" (1976-77) Catcher: 15 for 64, .234; played in 36 games. Singled as pinch-hitter in the 1976 ALCS and went 0 for 2 as a pinch-hitter in the 1976 World Series.

Hendryx, Tim (1915-17) OF: 124 for 495, .251; played in 153 games.

*Henrich, Tommy (1937-42, 1946-50) OF-1B: 1297 for 4603, .282; played in 1284 games. Yankee coach.

Henry, Bill (1966) Pitcher: 0-0 in 2 games.

Henson, Drew (2002) DH: 0 for 1, .000; played in three games.

Hernandez, Adrian (2001-02) Pitcher: 0-4 in eight games.

Hernandez, Leo (1986) 3B-2B: 5 for 22, .227; played in seven games.

Hernandez, Orlando (1998-2002) Pitcher: 53-38 in 124 games. Named MVP in 1999 American League Championship Series.

Hernandez, Xavier (1994) Pitcher: 4-4 in 31 games. Saved six games.

Herrmann, Ed (1975) DH-Catcher: 51 for 200, .255; played in 80 games.

High, Hugh (1915-18) OF: 295 for 1179, .250; played in 345 games. Regular centerfielder in 1915 and regular leftfielder in 1916 and 1917. Released in April 1919.

Hildebrand, Oral (1939-40) Pitcher: 11-5 in 34 games. Started Game 4 of the 1939 World Series and pitched four strong innings (no decision).

Hill, Glenallen (2002) OF-DH: 44 for 132, .333; played in 40 games. Hit 16 HRs in part of one season with Yanks.

Hill, Jesse (1935) OF: 115 for 392, .293; played in 107 games.

Hillegas, Shawn (1992) Pitcher: 1-8 in 21 games.

Hiller, Frank (1946, 1948-49) Pitcher: 5-6 in 29 games.

Hillis, Mack (1924) 2B: 0 for 1, .000; played in one game.

Hinton, Rich (1972) Pitcher: 1-0 in seven games.

Hitchcock, Sterling (1992-95, 2002) Pitcher: 17-17 in 69 games.

Hoag, Myril (1931-32, 1934-38) OF: 349 for 1228, .284; played in 471 games. On June 6, 1934, he got 6 singles in six at-bats, a 9-inning game ML record. Regular rightfielder in 1937. In Game 5 of the 1937 World Series, he hit an important HR in the Yanks' 4-2 clinching victory, and his six hits for the Series tied several Yankees for most hits on the club. Hit .320 in three World Series.

Hobson, Butch (1982) DH-1B: 10 for 58, .172; played in 30 games.

Hoff, Red (1911-13) Pitcher: 0-2 in 12 games. The last living member of the New York Highlanders (the early Yankees) died in 1998 at the age of 107. Red was the oldest living Highlander, er, Yankee.

Hoffman, Danny (1906-07) OF: 213 for 837, .254; played in 236 games. Regular centerfielder in both seasons. In 1906, he led Yanks in stolen bases (32). In 1907, he led the Yanks in runs (81), HRs (5), and walks (42).

Hofman, Solly (1916) OF: 8 for 27, .296; played in six games.

Hofmann, Fred (1919-25) Catcher: 143 for 584, .245; played in 213 games. Reserve catcher. Went 0 for 1 in two pinch-hit at-bats in the 1923 World Series; he walked in the middle of the Yanks' 8th-inning rally in Game 6.

*Hogg, Bill (1905-08) Pitcher: 37-50 in 116 games.

Hogue, Bobby (1951-52) Pitcher: 4-5 in 34 games. Pitched strongly in relief in Games 1 and 3 of the 1951 World Series (no decisions).

Holcombe, Ken (1945) Pitcher: 3-3 in 23 games.

Holden, Bill (1913-14) OF: 46 for 218, .211; played in 68 games.

Holland, Al (1986-87) Pitcher: 1-0 in 28 games.

Holloway, Ken (1930) Pitcher: 0-0 in 16 games.

Holmes, Darren (1998) Pitcher: 0-3 in 34 games.

Holmes, Fred (1903) 1B: 0 for 0, played in one game.

Holt, Roger (1980) 2B: 1 for 6, .167; played in two games.

Holtzman, Ken (1976-78) Pitcher: 12-10 in 44 games.

Honeycutt, Rick (1995) Pitcher: 0-0 in three games.

Hood, Don (1979) Pitcher: 3-1 in 27 games.

Orlando Hernandez

Hood, Wally (1949) Pitcher: 0-0 in two games.

Hopp, Johnny (1950-52) 1B-OF: 26 for 115, .226; played in 80 games. Delivered many clutch hits in final weeks of the 1950 pennant race.

Horan, Shags (1924) OF: 9 for 31, .290; played in 22 games.

Houk, Ralph (1947-54) Catcher: 43 for 158, .272; played in 91 games. Delivered a pinch-hit single in Game 6 of the 1947 World Series. Served the Yanks as a minor league manager, coach, manager and general manager.

***Howard, Elston** (1955-67) Catcher-OF-1B: 1405 for 5044, .279; played in 1492 games. Yankee coach and front office executive.

Howard, Matt (1996) 2B-3B: 11 for 54, .204; played in 35 games.

***Howe, Steve** (1991-96) Pitcher: 18-10 in 229 games.

Howell, Harry (1903) Pitcher: 9-6 in 25 games.

Howell, Jay (1982-84) Pitcher: 12-12 in 86 games. Knee injury in 1983. Went 9-4 with 7 saves in 1984.

Howser, Dick (1967-68) INF: 63 for 299, .211; played in 148 games. Yankee coach (1969-78) and manager (1980).

***Hoyt, Waite** (1921-30) Pitcher: 157-98 in 365 games. Pitched for all three NY teams: Yankees, Dodgers, and Giants.

Hudler, Rex (1984-85) INF: 9 for 58, .155; played in 29 games.

Hudson, Charlie (1987-88) Pitcher: 17-13 in 63 games. Went 11-7 in 1987 and led the Yanks in complete games (six) and shutouts (three). Shoulder injury in 1988.

Hughes, Keith (1987) PH: 0 for 4, .000; pinch-hit in four games.

Hughes, Long Tom (1904) Pitcher: 7-11 in 19 games.

Hughes, Tom (1906-07, 1909-10) Pitcher: 17-17 in 54 games. Pitched the first Yankee no-hitter on August 30, 1910; allowed a 10th inning hit and lost in the 11th to Cleveland.

Hummel, John (1918) OF-1B-2B: 18 for 61, .295; played in 22 games.

Humphreys, Mike (1991-93) OF-DH-3B: 15 for 85, .176; played in 54 games.

Hunt, Ken (1959-60) OF: 10 for 34, .294; played in 31 games. Yanks lost him to Angels in 1960 expansion draft.

Hunter, Billy (1955-56) SS-3B: 79 for 330, .239; played in 137 games.

***Hunter, Catfish** (1975-79) Pitcher: 63-53 in 137 games.

Hutton, Mark (1993-94, 96) Pitcher: 1-3 in 21 games.

Hyatt, Ham (1918) OF-1B: 30 for 131, .229; played in 53 games.

Incaviglia, Pete (1997) DH: 4 for 16, .250; played in five games.

Irabu, Hideki (1997-99) Pitcher: 29-20 in 74 games. First Yankee player to appear in a game whose last name begins with the letter "I".

Jacklitsch, Fred (1905) Catcher: 0 for 3, .000; played in one game.

Jackson, Grant (1976) Pitcher: 6-0 in 21 games. In 1976 postseason, he pitched in relief in three games (no decisions).

***Jackson, Reggie** (1977-81) OF-DH: 661 for 2349, .281; played in 653 games.

James, Dion (1992-93, 1995-96) OF-DH: 214 for 709, .302; played in 273 games.

James, Johnny (1958, 1960-61) Pitcher: 5-1 in 30 games.

Javier, Stan (1984) OF: 1 for 7, .143; played in seven games.

Jean, Domingo (1993) Pitcher: 1-1 in 10 games.

Jefferson, Stan (1989) OF: 1 for 12, .083; played in 10 games.

Jensen, Jackie (1950-52) OF: 64 for 257, .249; played in 108 games. Used as a pinch runner in 1950 World Series. Football star of University of California. MVP with Boston in 1958.

Jerzembeck, Mike (1998) Pitcher: 0-1 in 3 games.

***Jeter, Derek** (1995-2002) SS-DH: 1390 for 4388, .317; played in 1093 games.

Jimenez, D'Angelo (1999) 3B-2B: 8 for 20, .400; played in seven games.

Jimenez, Elvio (1964) OF: 2 for 6, .333; played in one game.

Jodie, Brett (2001) Pitcher: 0-1 in one game.

***John, Tommy** (1979-82, 1986-89) Pitcher: 91-60 in 214 games.

Johnson, Alex (1974-75) DH-OF: 37 for 147, .252; played in 62 games.

***Johnson, Billy** (1943, 1946-51) 3B-1B: 694 for 2524, .275; played in 735 games.

Johnson, Cliff (1977-79) Catcher-1B: 91 for 380, .239; played in 160 games. Hit .400 (6 for 15) in the 1977 ALCS, including a tremendous Game 2 (HR, double, two RBIs, two runs). Went 0 for 3 in combined 1977-78 World Series. Hit three HRs in a June 30, 1977 game, with two HRs in one inning.

Johnson, Darrell (1957-58) Catcher: 14 for 62, .226; played in 26 games. Yankee scout.

Johnson, Deron (1960-61) 3B: 4 for 23, .174; played in 19 games.

Johnson, Don (1947, 1950) Pitcher: 5-3 in 23 games.

Johnson, Ernie (1923-25) INF: 107 for 327, .327; played in 159 games. In 1923 World Series, he was used as a defensive replacement at shortstop and a pinch runner.

Derek Jeter

*Johnson, Hank (1925-26, 1928-32) Pitcher: 47-36 in 157 games.

Johnson, Jeff (1991-93) Pitcher: 8-16 in 38 games.

Johnson, Johnny (1944) Pitcher: 0-2 in 22 games.

Johnson, Ken (1969) Pitcher: 1-2 in 12 games.

Johnson, Lance (2000) OF-DH: 9 for 30, .300; played in 18 games.

Johnson, Nick (2001-02) 1B-OF-DH: 105 for 445, .236; played in 152 games.

Johnson, Otis (1911) INF: 49 for 209, .234; played in 71 games.

Johnson, Roy (1936-37) OF: 54 for 198, .273; played in 75 games. Went 0 for 1 in the 1936 World Series, playing in two games.

Johnstone, Jay (1978-79) OF: 27 for 113, .239; played in 59 games. Played two games in right field in the 1978 World Series without an at-bat.

Jones, Darryl (1979) OF: 12 for 47, .255; played in 18 games.

Jones, Gary (1970-71) Pitcher: 0-0 in 14 games.

Jones, Jimmy (1989-90) Pitcher: 3-3 in 28 games.

Jones, Ruppert (1980) OF: 73 for 328, .223; played in 83 games. Missed much of the season and all of the ALCS due to illness and injury.

*Jones, Sad Sam (1922-26) Pitcher: 67-56 in 202 games.

Jordon, Tim (1903) 1B: 1 for 8, .125; played in two games.

Jorgens, Art (1929-39) Catcher: 176 for 738, .238; played in 307 games. Spent his entire career as Bill Dickey's backup. Sometimes called "the luckiest man in baseball" because he took home five World Series checks without ever playing in a World Series game.

Jose, Felix (2000) OF-DH: 7 for 29, .241; played in 20 games.

Juden, Jeff (1999) Pitcher: 0-1 in two games.

Jurewicz, Mike (1965) Pitcher: 0-0 in two games.

Justice, David (2000-01) OF-DH: 176 for 656, .268; played in 189 games.

Kaat, Jim (1979-80) Pitcher: 2-4 in 44 games. Won 283 games in ML's over four decades (1950s-60s-70s-80s).

*Kamieniecki, Scott (1991-96) Pitcher: 36-39 in 113 games.

Kammeyer, Bob (1978-79) Pitcher: 0-0 in eight games.

Kane, Frank (1919) PH: 0 for 1, .000; pinch-hit in one game.

Karlon, Bill (1930) OF: 0 for 5, .000; played in two games.

Karpel, Herb (1946) Pitcher: 0-0 in two games.

Karsay, Steve (2002) Pitcher: 6-4 in 78 games.

Kauff, Benny (1912) OF: 3 for 11, .273; played in five games.

Kaufman, Curt (1982-83) Pitcher: 1-0 in 11 games.

Kearse, Eddie (1942) Catcher: 5 for 26, .192; played in 11 games.

*Keating, Ray (1912-16, 1918) Pitcher: 23-40 in 108 games.

Keefe, Bobby (1907) Pitcher: 3-5 in 19 games.

*Keeler, Willie (1903-09) OF: 974 for 3313, .294; played in 873 games. First of 13 players to appear for all three NY teams: Yankees, Dodgers, and Giants.

Keisler, Randy (2000-01) Pitcher: 2-2 in 14 games.

*Kekich, Mike (1969-73) Pitcher: 31-32 in 125 games.

*Keller, Charlie (1939-43, 1945-49, 1952) OF: 1053 for 3677, .286; played in 1066 games.

*Kelly, Pat (1991-97) 2B-3B-DH: 431 for 1719, .251; played in 591 games.

*Kelly, Roberto (1987-92,2000) OF-DH: 640 for 2302, .278; played in 648 games.

Kemp, Steve (1983-84) OF-DH: 181 for 686, .264; played in 203 games.

Kennedy, John (1967) INF: 35 for 179, .196; played in 78 games.

Kenney, Jerry (1967, 1969-72) 3B-SS-OF: 321 for 1353, .237; played in 460 games. Missed 1968 season due to military service. Regular third baseman, 1969-71. Part of November 1972 trade to Cleveland for Graig Nettles.

Keough, Matt (1983) Pitcher: 3-4 in 12 games.

Key, Jimmy (1993-96) Pitcher: 48-23, played in 94 games.

Kiefer, Steve (1989) 3B: 1 for 8, .125; played in five games.

Kingman, Dave (1977) DH: 6 for 24, .250; played in eight games. Blasted 4 HRs and struck out 13 times. Ineligible for post-season play.

Kingman, Harry (1914) 1B: 0 for 3, .000; played in four games.

Kipp, Fred (1960) Pitcher: 0-1 in four games.

Kitson, Frank (1907) Pitcher: 4-0 in 12 games.

Kittle, Ron (1986-87) DH: 63 for 239, .264; played in 89 games. Hit 16 HRs.

Kleinhans, Ted (1936) Pitcher: 1-1 in 19 games.

*Kleinow, Red (1904-10) Catcher-INF: 328 for 1496, .219; played in 522 games.

Klepfer, Ed (1911, 1913) Pitcher: 0-1 in 10 games.

Klimkowski, Ron (1969-70, 1972) Pitcher: 6-10 in 64 games.

*Kline, Steve (1970-74) Pitcher: 40-37 in 97 games.

Klutts, Mickey (1976-78) 3B-SS: 6 for 20, .300; played in eight games.

Knickerbocker, Bill (1938-40) INF: 64 for 265, .242; played in 97 games.

Knight, Brandon (2001-02) Pitcher: 0-0 in 11 games.

*Knight, John (1909-11, 1913) INF: 399 for 1494, .267; played in 435 games.

Knoblauch, Chuck (1998-2001) 2B-OF-DH: 579 for 2127, .272; played in 539 games.

*Koenig, Mark (1925-30) SS-3B: 636 for 2233, .285; played in 567 games.

Konstanty, Jim (1954-56) Pitcher: 8-3 in 62 games. In 1955, he led Yanks in saves (11) and games pitched (45). Recorded 15 saves in all with NY.

Kosco, Andy (1968) OF-1B: 112 for 446, .240; played in 131 games. Cracked 15 HRs.

Kraly, Steve (1953) Pitcher: 0-2 in five games.

Kramer, Jack (1951) Pitcher: 1-3 in 19 games.

Krueger, Ernie (1915) Catcher: 5 for 29, .172; played in 10 games. Played for all three NY teams: Yankees, Dodgers, and Giants.

Kryhoski, Dick (1949) 1B: 52 for 177, .294; played in 54 games.

*Kubek, Tony (1957-65) SS-OF-3B: 1109 for 4167, .266; played in 1092 games.

*Kucks, Johnny (1955-59) Pitcher: 42-35 in 143 games.

Kunkel, Bill (1963) Pitcher: 3-2 in 22 games. Became an AL umpire after his playing career.

*Kuzava, Bob (1951-54) Pitcher: 23-20 in 104 games.

*Lake, Joe (1908-09) Pitcher: 23-33 in 69 games.

Lamar, Bill (1917-19) OF: 38 for 167, .228; played in 50 games.

Lanier, Hal (1972-73) INF: 40 for 189, .212; played in 95 games.

LaPoint, Dave (1989-90) Pitcher: 13-19 in 48 games. Shoulder injury in 1989.

*LaPorte, Frank (1905-07, 1908-10) INF-OF: 507 for 1850, .274; played in 516 games.

LaRoche, Dave (1981-83) Pitcher: 8-3 in 52 games. Occasionally threw a dazzling blooper known as LaLob.

*Larsen, Don (1955-59) Pitcher: 45-24 in 128 games.

*Lary, Lyn (1929-34) INF: 471 for 1717, .274; played in 496 games.

Lawton, Marcus (1989) OF: 3 for 14, .214; played in 10 games.

Layden, Gene (1915) OF: 2 for 7, .286; played in three games.

*Lazzeri, Tony (1926-37) 2B-3B-SS: 1784 for 6094, .293; played in 1659 games. Played for all three NY teams: Yankees, Dodgers, and Giants.

Leary, Tim (1990-92) Pitcher: 18-35 in 77 games. Led AL with 19 losses in 1990. Led Yanks in 1990 in games started (31), innings pitched (208), and strikeouts (138).

Ledee, Ricky (1998-99) OF-DH: 134 for 520, .258; played in 192 games.

Lefebvre, Joe (1980) OF: 34 for 150, .227; played in 74 games. Hit HRs in his first 2 ML games. Played in one game without an at-bat in ALCS.

Leiter, Al (1987-89) Pitcher: 7-8 in 22 games. Finger injury in 1988.

Leiter, Mark (1990) Pitcher: 1-1 in 8 games.

Leja, Frank (1954-55) 1B: 1 for 7, .143; played in 19 games. A Bonus Baby whom Paul Krichell thought would be "the next Lou Gehrig."

Lelivelt, Jack (1912-13) OF: 60 for 177, .339; played in 54 games.

Leon, Eddie (1975) SS: 0 for 0; played in one game.

LeRoy, Louis (1905-06) Pitcher: 3-1 in 14 games.

Levy, Ed (1942, 1944) OF-1B: 42 for 194, .216; played in 53 games.

Lewis, Duffy (1919-20) OF: 251 for 924, .272; played in 248 games. Regular leftfielder in 1919 and 1920. Led Yanks in RBIs (89) in 1919. Knee injury in 1920.

Lewis, Jim (1982) Pitcher: 0-0 in one game.

Ley, Terry (1971) Pitcher: 0-0 in six games.

*Leyritz, Jim (1990-96, 1999-2000) Catcher-INF-OF-DH: 443 for 1682, .263; played in 577 games.

Lilly, Ted (2000-02) Pitcher: 8-12 in 49 games.

Lindblad, Paul (1978) Pitcher: 0-0 in 7 games. Pitched in relief in Game 1 of the 1978 World Series (no decision).

*Lindell, Johnny (1941-50) OF-1B-P: 707 for 2568, .275; played in 742 games. As a pitcher in 1942, he compiled a 2-1 record in 23 games.

Linz, Phil (1962-65) INF-OF: 238 for 968, .246; played in 354 games. Valuable utility player. His harmonica playing on team bus in 1964 started a celebrated confrontation with Manager Yogi Berra. Hit two HRs in 1964 World Series.

Little, Bryan (1986) 2B: 8 for 41, .195; played in 14 games.

Little, Jack (1912) OF: 3 for 12, .250; played in three games

Llewellyn, Clem (1922) Pitcher: 0-0 in one game.

Lloyd, Graeme (1996-98) Pitcher: 4-3 in 109 games.

Locklear, Gene (1976-77) OF: 10 for 37, .270; played in 14 games.

Lollar, Sherm (1947-48) Catcher: 15 for 70, .214; played in 33 games. Hit .750 (3 for 4) with three runs scored in the 1947 World Series.

Lollar, Tim (1980) Pitcher: 1-0 in 14 games.

Lombardi, Phil (1986-87) OF-Catcher: 11 for 44, .250; played in 25 games.

Long, Dale (1960, 1962-63) 1B: 46 for 150, .307; played in 81 games. In 1960 World Series, he delivered a pinch-hit single in Game 7, a key hit in the Yanks' game-tying ninth-inning rally. Hit .200 (1 for 5) with an RBI in the 1962 World Series; he played two games at first base.

Mickey Mantle

Long, Herman (1903) SS: 15 for 80, .188; played in 22 games.

*Lopat, Ed (1948-55) Pitcher: 113-59 in 217 games. Yankee coach and scout.

Lopez, Art (1965) OF: 7 for 49, .143; played in 38 games.

*Lopez, Hector (1959-66) OF-INF: 658 for 2510, .262; played in 864 games. Yankee minor league coach and manager.

Louden, Baldy (1907) 3B: 1 for 9, .111; played in four games.

Love, Slim (1916-18) Pitcher: 21-17 in 91 games. Led Yanks in games started (29) and strikeouts (95) in 1918, when he went 13-12.

Lovullo, Torey (1991) 3B: 9 for 51, .176; played in 22 games.

Lowell, Mike (1998) 3B-DH: 4 for 15, .267; played in eight games.

Lucadello, Johnny (1947) 2B: 1 for 12, .083; played in 12 games.

Lucey, Joe (1920) 2B-SS: 0 for 3, .000; played in three games.

Luebbe, Roy (1925) Catcher: 0 for 15, .000; played in eight games.

Luke, Matt (1996) Pinch-runner: played in one game, one run scored.

Lumpe, Jerry (1956-59) 3B-SS: 120 for 442, .271; played in 159 games. Hit .286 (4 for 14, 2 RBIs, 1 walk) in the 1957 World Series; went 2 for 3 as a pinch-hitter. Hit .167 (2 for 12, one walk) in the 1958 World Series; went 0 for 3 as a pinch-hitter.

Lusader, Scott (1991) OF-DH: 1 for 7, .143; played in 11 games.

*Lyle, Sparky (1972-78) Pitcher: 57-40 in 420 games.

Lyons, Al (1944, 1946-47) Pitcher: 1-1 in 19 games.

Lyttle, Jim (1969-71) OF: 71 for 295, .241; played in 164 games.

Maas, Duke (1958-61) Pitcher: 26-12 in 96 games. Second biggest winner on the 1959 Yankees behind Whitey Ford; had a 14-8 record.

Maas, Kevin (1990-93) DH-1B: 276 for 1191, .232; played in 384 games. Hit 64 HRs. Hit 21 HRs in only 254 ABs in 1990, his rookie year. Hit 23 HRs in 500 ABs in 1991.

MacDonald, Bob (1995) Pitcher: 1-1 in 33 games.

MacFayden, Danny (1932-34) Pitcher: 14-10 in 64 games.

Mack, Ray (1947) Pinch-runner: 0 for 0; played in one game; no runs scored.

Madden, Tommy (1910) PH: 0 for 1, .000; pinch-hit in one game.

Maddox, Elliott (1974-76) OF-INF: 218 for 730, .299; played in 210 games. Went 2 for 9 (.222, 1 RBI) in the 1976 ALCS and played three games in right field. Went 1 for 5 (.200, one walk) in the 1976 World Series; he played right field in Game 1 and DH in Game 2. Excellent defensive outfielder and hit .303 in 1974. Suffered serious knee injury in 1975.

Madison, Dave (1950) Pitcher: 0-0 in one game.

Magee, Lee (1916-17) OF: 169 for 683, .247; played in 182 games. Regular centerfielder until traded during summer of 1917.

Maglie, Sal (1957-58) Pitcher: 3-1 in 13 games. Last of 13 players to appear for all three NY teams: Yankees, Dodgers, and Giants. Sal was the losing Brooklyn pitcher in Don Larsen's perfect game in the 1956 World Series.

Magner, Stubby (1911) SS-2B: 7 for 33, .212; played in 13 games.

Magnuson, Jim (1973) Pitcher: 0-1 in 8 games.

*Maisel, Fritz (1913-17) 3B-2B-OF: 444 for 1827, .243; played in 501 games.

Majeski, Hank (1946) 3B: 1 for 12, .083; played in eight games.

Makosky, Frank (1937) Pitcher: 5-2 in 26 games.

Roger Maris article in The Sporting News (1960).

Malone, Pat (1935-37) Pitcher: 19-13 in 92 games. In 1936, he led AL pitchers in saves (9) and relief wins (8). In 1936 World Series, he saved Game 3 and lost Game 5 in relief.

Maloney, Pat (1912) OF: 17 for 79, .215; played in 22 games.

Mamaux, Al (1924) Pitcher: 1-1 in 14 games.

*Manning, Rube (1907-10) Pitcher: 22-32 in 84 games.

*Mantle, Mickey (1951-68) OF-1B: 2415 for 8102, .298; played in 2401 games.

Manto, Jeff (1999)1B-3B: 1 for 8, .125; played in six games.

Manzanillo, Josias (1995) Pitcher: 0-0 in 11 games.

Mapes, Cliff (1948-51) OF: 196 for 799, .245; played in 317 games. Had a great throwing arm. Replaced an injured Joe DiMaggio in center field for much of the 1949 season. Wore #3 until it was retired in Babe Ruth's honor. Wore #7 in Mickey Mantle's rookie year before Mantle took the number. Cliff went 1 for 14 in the 1949-50 World Series.

*Maris, Roger (1960-66) OF: 797 for 3007, .265; played in 850 games.

Markle, Cliff (1915-16, 1924) Pitcher: 6-6 in 21 games.

Marquis, Jim (1925) Pitcher: 0-0 in two games.

Marsans, Armando (1917-18) OF: 49 for 211, .232; played in 62 games.

Marshall, Cuddles (1946, 1948-49) Pitcher: 6-4 in 45 games.

*Martin, Billy (1950-53, 1955-57) 2B-3B-SS: 449 for 1717, .262; played in 527 games. Managed Yankees five times between 1975 and 1988.

Martin, Hersh (1944-45) OF: 208 for 736, .283; played in 202 games. Regular leftfielder in 1944 and 1945, and he hit .302 in 1944.

Martin, Jack (1912) INF: 52 for 231, .225; played in 69 games.

*Martinez, Tino (1996-2001) 1B-DH: 966 for 3467, .279; played in 923 games.

Martinez, Tippy (1974-76) Pitcher: 3-2 in 44 games. Led club in saves (eight) in 1975.

Mason, Jim (1974-76) SS: 183 for 880, .208; played in 339 games. Regular shortstop in 1974. Became the 14th player to hit a homer in his first World Series at-bat in 1976; it was also his only World Series at-bat.

Mata, Vic (1984-85) OF: 24 for 77, .312; played in 36 games.

*Mattingly, Don (1982-95) 1B-OF-DH-3B: 2153 for 7003, .307; played in 1785 games.

May, Carlos (1976-77) DH-OF: 121 for 469, .258; played in 152 games. In 1976, he hit .200 (2 for 10) in the ALCS and .000 (0 for 9) in the World Series.

*May, Rudy (1974-76, 1980-83) Pitcher: 54-46 in 184 games.

Mayberry, John (1982) 1B-DH: 45 for 215, .209; played in 69 games.

*Mays, Carl (1919-23) Pitcher: 80-39 in 164 games.

Mazzilli, Lee (1982) 1B-DH-OF: 34 for 128, .266; played in 37 games. Yankee coach starting in 2000 season.

McCall, Larry (1977-78) Pitcher: 1-2 in seven games.

McCarthy, Joe (1905) Catcher: 0 for 2, .000; played in one game. Not to be confused with the great Yankee manager.

McCauley, Pat (1903) Catcher: 1 for 19, .053; played in six games.

McClure, Larry (1910) OF: 0 for 1, .000; played in one game.

McConnell, George (1909, 1912-13) Pitcher: 13-28 in 60 games. In 1912, he was the Yanks' No. 4 starter, led the staff in ERA (2.75), and hit .297 (27 for 91).

McCormick, Mike (1970) Pitcher: 2-0 in nine games.

McCullers, Lance (1989-90) Pitcher: 5-3 in 63 games.

***McDaniel, Lindy** (1968-73) Pitcher: 38-29 in 265 games.

McDermott, Mickey (1956) Pitcher: 2-6 in 23 games. Pitched in relief in Game 2 of the 1956 World Series (no decision).

McDevitt, Danny (1961) Pitcher: 1-2 in eight games.

McDonald, Dave (1969) 1B: 5 for 23, .217; played in nine games.

McDonald, Donzell (2001) OF: 1 for 3, .333; played in five games.

McDonald, Jim (1952-54) Pitcher: 16-12 in 69 games. Started and won Game 5 of the 1953 World Series.

***McDougald, Gil** (1951-60) 2B-3B-SS: 1291 for 4676, .276; played in 1336 games.

McDowell, Jack (1995) Pitcher: 15-10 in 30 games. Was 0-2 in the 1995 Division Series.

McDowell, Sam (1973-74) Pitcher: 6-14 in 29 games.

McEvoy, Lou (1930-31) Pitcher: 1-3 in 34 games.

McFarland, Herm (1903) OF: 88 for 362, .243; played in 103 games.

McGaffigan, Andy (1981) Pitcher: 0-0 in two games.

McGlothen, Lynn (1982) Pitcher: 0-0 in four games.

McGraw, Bob (1917-19, 1920) Pitcher: 1-2 in 24 games.

McGuire, Deacon (1904-07) Catcher: 160 for 695, .230; played in 225 games. Split the catching chores with Red Kleinow on the 1904-06 teams. Only non-pitcher to play in 26 seasons, 25 as a catcher.

McHale, Marty (1913-15) Pitcher: 12-27 in 51 games. Teamed with Giants' Mike Donlin in a vaudeville act. A singer, he was known as "the Caruso of baseball."

McIlveen, Irish (1908-09) OF: 36 for 172, .209; played in 48 games.

McIntosh, Tim (1996) C-1B-3B: 0 for 3 in three games.

McKechnie, Bill (1913) INF: 15 for 112, .134; played in 45 games. A Hall of Fame manager.

McKinney, Rich (1972) 3B: 26 for 121, .215; played in 37 games.

McManus, Frank (1904) Catcher: 0 for 7, .000; played in four games.

McMillan, Norm (1922) OF-3B: 20 for 78, .256; played in 33 games. Went 0 for 2 in the 1922 World Series.

McMillan, Tommy (1912) SS: 34 for 149, .228; played in 41 games.

McNally, Mike (1921-24) INF: 117 for 465, .252; played in 202 games. Hit .200 (4 for 20, 3 runs, 1 RBI) in the 1921 World Series; he played every game but the last at third base. In Game 1, he stole two bases, including a steal of home.

McQuaid, Herb (1926) Pitcher: 1-0 in 17 games.

McQuinn, George (1947-48) 1B: 232 for 819, .283; played in 238 games. A farm-system product in the 1930s, he had Lou Gehrig ahead of him and escaped to the Browns. Regular NY first baseman in 1947 and 1948. Led AL in batting for much of 1947 before trailing off and finishing at .304. He made the AL All-Star team both years.

Meacham, Bobby (1983-88) SS-2B-3B: 324 for 1371, .236; played in 457 games. Regular shortstop in 1984 and 1985. Stole 25 bases in 1985.

Meara, Charlie (1914) OF: 2 for 7, .286; played in four games.

Mecir, Jim (1996-97) Pitcher: 1-5 in 51 games.

***Medich, Doc** (1972-75) Pitcher: 49-40 in 111 games.

Melvin, Bob (1994) Catcher: 4 for 14, .286; played in nine games.

Mendoza, Ramiro (1996-2002) Pitcher: 54-34 in 277 games.

Merkle, Fred (1925-26) 1B: 5 for 15, .333; played in eight games. Played for all three NY teams: Yankees, Dodgers, and Giants.

Messersmith, Andy (1978) Pitcher: 0-3 in six games.

Metcalf, Tom (1963) Pitcher: 1-0 in eight games.

Metheny, Bud (1943-46) OF: 344 for 1390, .247; played in 376 games. Regular rightfielder in 1943, 1944, and 1945. Hit .125 (1 for 8) in the 1943 World Series. Hit 14 HRs in 1944.

Meulens, Hensley (1989-93) OF-DH-3B-1B: 101 for 457, .221; played in 159 games. Hit 12 HRs. Struck out 149 times. Highly-touted HR-hitting prospect.

***Meusel, Bob** (1920-29) OF-3B: 1565 for 5032, .311; played in 1294 games.

Meyer, Bob (1964) Pitcher: 0-3 in seven games.

***Michael, Gene** (1968-74) SS-2B-3B-P: 561 for 2405, .233; played in 789 games. Yankee coach, minor league manager, Yankee manager, General Manager, and Scouting Executive. In 1968, pitched as a reliever in one game (0-0); three innings, five hits, no earned runs, one sacrifice hit, and hit one of the 16 batters he faced. No walks, strikeouts, or saves.

Midkiff, Ezra (1912-13) 3B-SS-2B: 77 for 370, .208; played in 104 games.

Mikkelsen, Pete (1964-65) Pitcher: 11-13 in 91 games. Ace of bullpen in 1964, leading club in saves (12) and games pitched (50). Won the pennant clincher. Appeared in four games of the 1964 World Series.

Milbourne, Larry (1981-82, 1983) INF: 69 for 260, .265; played in 106 games.

Militello, Sam (1992-93) Pitcher: 4-4 in 12 games.

Miller, Bill (1952-54) Pitcher: 6-8 in 36 games.

Miller, Elmer (1915-18, 1921-22) OF: 308 for 1230, .250; played in 357 games. Regular rightfielder in 1917. Shared center-field duties in 1921, and he played center in every game of the 1921 World Series; he hit only .161 (5 for 31).

Miller, John (1966) OF-1B: 2 for 23, .087; played in six games. On Sept. 11, 1966, he hit a HR in his first ML at-bat, the only Yankee to ever accomplish that feat.

Mills, Alan (1990-91) Pitcher: 2-6 in 42 games.

Mills, Buster (1940) OF: 25 for 63, .397; played in 34 games.

Milosevich, Mike (1944-45) SS-2B: 92 for 381, .241; played in 124 games.

Mirabella, Paul (1979) Pitcher: 0-4 in 10 games.

Miranda, Willie (1953-54) SS-2B: 42 for 174, .241; played in 140 games.

Mitchell, Bobby (1970) OF: 5 for 22, .227; played in 10 games.

Mitchell, Fred (1910) Catcher: 45 for 196, .230; played in 68 games.

Mitchell, Johnny (1921-22) SS-2B: 11 for 46, .239; played in 17 games.

Mize, Johnny (1949-53) 1B: 230 for 870, .264; played in 375 games. Hall of Famer. Led the AL in pinch hits in 1951, 1952, and 1953, and he hit .429 (9 for 21) as a pinch hitter in 1951. On Sept. 15, 1950, he hit three HRs in a game against Detroit. Hit 25 HRs in only 274 ABs in 1950. Hitting star of the 1952 World Series (.400, three HRs) and won the Babe Ruth Award as MVP. Hit 44 HRs as a Yankee.

Mmahat, Kevin (1989) Pitcher: 0-2 in four games.

***Mogridge, George** (1915-20) Pitcher: 50-55 in 171 games.

Mohorcic, Dale (1988-89) Pitcher: 4-3 in 45 games.

Mole, Fenton (1949) 1B: 5 for 27, .185; played in 10 games.

Monbouquette, Bill (1967-68) Pitcher: 11-12 in 50 games. Yankee scout.

Mondesi, Raul (2002) OF-DH: 65 for 270, .241; played in 71 games.

Johnny Mize

Monroe, Ed (1917-18) Pitcher: 1-0 in 10 games.

Monroe, Zack (1958-59) Pitcher: 4-2 in 24 games. Pitched in relief in Game 2 of the 1958 World Series (no decision).

Montefusco, John (1983-86) Pitcher: 10-3 in 24 games. Neck injury in 1984. Hip injury in 1985 and 1986.

Monteleone, Rich (1990-93) Pitcher: 17-9 in 120 games.

Moore, Archie (1964-65) OF-1B: 11 for 40, .275; played in 40 games.

Moore, Earl (1907) Pitcher: 2-6 in 12 games.

*Moore, Wilcy (1927-29, 1932-33) Pitcher: 36-21 in 171 games.

Morehart, Ray (1927) 2B: 50 for 195, .256; played in 73 games.

Moreno, Omar (1983-85) OF-DH: 143 for 573, .250; played in 199 games.

Morgan, Mike (1982) Pitcher: 7-11 in 30 games.

*Morgan, Tom (1951-52, 1954-56) Pitcher: 38-22 in 156 games. Yankee coach and scout.

Moriarty, George (1906-08) INF-OF: 249 for 982, .254; played in 292 games. Served as an umpire after his playing career.

Moronko, Jeff (1987) 3B-SS-OF: 1 for 11, .091; played in seven games.

Morris, Hal (1988-89) OF-1B-DH: 7 for 38, .184; played in 30 games.

Moschitto, Ross (1965, 1967) OF: 6 for 36, .167; played in 110 games.

Moses, Jerry (1973) DH-Catcher: 15 for 59, .254; played in 21 games.

Mulholland, Terry (1994) Pitcher: 6-7 in 24 games. Expected to be a primary starter, but his ERA was a horrendous 6.49.

Mullen, Charlie (1914-16) 1B-2B-OF: 147 for 559, .263; played in 192 games.

Mumphrey, Jerry (1981-83) OF: 311 for 1063, .293; played in 286 games. Centerfielder in 1981 and 1982 and in 1983 until Aug. 10, 1983 trade to Houston for Omar Moreno. Led Yanks in triples (five), stolen bases (14), and batting (.307) in 1981. In 1981, post-season, he hit .095 (2 for 21) vs. Milwaukee, .500 (6 for 12) vs. Oakland and .200 (3 for 15) vs. Los Angeles. Led Yanks in 1983 in triples (10) and batting (.300) in 1982; also had broken finger in 1982.

Muncrief, Bob (1951) Pitcher: 0-0 in two games.

Munoz, Bobby (1993) Pitcher: 3-3 in 38 games.

*Munson, Thurman (1969-79) Catcher-OF: 1558 for 5344, .292; played in 1423 games.

*Murcer, Bobby (1965-66, 1969-74, 1979-83) OF-DH-3B-SS: 1231 for 4428, .278; played in 1256 games.

*Murphy, Johnny (1932, 1934-43, 1946) Pitcher: 93-53 in 383 games.

Murphy, Rob (1994) Pitcher: 0-0 in three games.

Murray, Dale (1983-85) Pitcher: 3-6 in 62 games.

Murray, George (1922) Pitcher: 4-2 in 22 games.

Murray, Larry (1974-76) OF: 1 for 12, .083; played in 20 games.

Mussina, Mike (2001-02) Pitcher: 35-21 in 67 games.

Narron, Jerry (1979) Catcher: 21 for 123, .171; played in 61 games. Caught first game after the death of Thurman Munson.

Naulty, Dan (1999) Pitcher: 1-0 in 33 games.

Neagle, Denny (2000) Pitcher: 7-7 in 16 games.

Nekola, Bots (1929) Pitcher: 0-0 in nine games.

Nelson, Gene (1981) Pitcher: 3-1 in eight games.

Nelson, Jeff (1996-2000) Pitcher: 22-19 in 307 games.

Nelson, Luke (1919) Pitcher: 3-0 in nine games.

*Nettles, Graig (1973-83) 3B: 1396 for 5519, .253; played in 1535 games.

Neuer, Tex (1907) Pitcher: 4-2 in seven games.

Nevel, Ernie (1950-51) Pitcher: 0-1 in four games.

Newkirk, Floyd (1934) Pitcher: 0-0 in one game.

Newsom, Bobo (1947) Pitcher: 7-5 in 17 games. Most traveled pitcher in ML history. Played for all three NY teams: Yankees, Dodgers, and Giants. Started and lost Game 3 of 1947 World Series; also relieved (no decision) in Game 6.

Newton, Doc (1905-09) Pitcher: 20-25 in 78 games. Club's fifth starter in 1906, 1907, and 1908. On August 4, 1905, he was half of an all-physician battery, teaming with catcher Mike Powers.

Niarhos, Gus (1946, 1948-50) Catcher: 82 for 311, .264; played in 153 games. Caught briefly in Game 2 of the 1949 World Series.

Niekro, Joe (1985-87) Pitcher: 14-15 in 36 games. Brother of Phil Niekro.

Niekro, Phil (1984-85) Pitcher: 32-30 in 65 games. Famous knuckleball pitcher. Won 318 games in a ML career spanning 24 seasons.

Nielsen, Jerry (1992) Pitcher: 1-0 in 20 games.

Nielsen, Scott (1986, 1988-89) Pitcher: 6-6 in 19 games.

Niles, Harry (1908) 2B-OF: 90 for 361, .249; played in 96 games.

Nixon, Otis (1983) OF: 2 for 14, .143; played in 13 games.

Nokes, Matt (1990-94) Catcher-DH: 342 for 1376, .249; played in 452 games. Regular catcher in 1991 and 1992. Hit 24 HRs in 1991 and 22 HRs in 1992.

*Noren, Irv (1952-56) OF-1B: 394 for 1451, .272; played in 488 games.

Nottebart, Don (1969) Pitcher: 0-0 in four games.

Nunamaker, Les (1914-17) Catcher-1B: 282 for 1076, .262; played in 369 games. Caught the bulk of Yankee games each season, 1914-17. In the second inning on August 3, 1914, he threw out 3 runners attempting to steal, setting a ML record.

Oates, Johnny (1980-81) Catcher: 17 for 90, .189; played in 49 games. Began coaching at Yanks' Columbus farm club in 1981. As Texas manager, faced the Yankees three times in the Division Series, losing all 3, winning but 1 of 9 games.

O'Berry, Mike (1984) Catcher: 8 for 32, .250; played in 13 games.

O'Connor, Andy (1908) Pitcher: 0-1 in one game.

O'Connor, Jack (1903) Catcher: 43 for 212, .203; played in 64 games.

O'Connor, Paddy (1918) Catcher: 1 for 3, .333; played in one game.

Odom, Heinie (1925) 3B: 1 for 1, 1.000; played in one game.

O'Doul, Lefty (1919-20, 1922) Pitcher-OF: 0-0 in 11 games. After leaving the Yanks, he became one of the great hitters of all time; hit .349 lifetime. Hit .243 (9 for 37) in 40 games with the Yanks. Played for all three NY teams: Yankees, Dodgers, and Giants.

Office, Rowland (1983) OF: 0 for 2, .000; played in two games.

Ojeda, Bobby (1994) Pitcher: 0 for 0 in two games.

Paul O'Neill

Oldring, Rube (1905, 1916) OF-SS: 46 for 188, .245; played in 51 games.

Oliver, Bob (1975) 1B-DH: 5 for 38, .132; played in 18 games.

Oliver, Joe (2001) Catcher: 9 for 36, .250; played in 12 games.

Oliver, Nate (1969) DH: 0 for 1, .000; pinch-hit in one game.

*O'Neill, Paul (1993-2001) OF-DH-1B: 1426 for 4700, .303; played in 1254 games; hit .474 in 2000 World Series.

O'Neill, Steve (1925) Catcher: 26 for 91, .286; played in 35 games.

O'Rourke, Queenie (1908) OF-INF: 25 for 108, .231; played in 34 games.

*Orth, Al (1904-09) Pitcher: 72-73 in 163 games.

Osteen, Champ (1904) INF: 21 for 107, .196; played in 28 games.

Ostrowski, Joe (1950-52) Pitcher: 9-7 in 75 games. Pitched strongly in relief in Game 3 of the 1951 World Series (no decision).

Otis, Bill (1912) OF: 1 for 17, .059; played in four games.

Overmire, Stubby (1951) Pitcher: 1-1 in 15 games.

Owen, Spike (1993) SS: 78 for 334, .234; played in 103 games.

Pacella, John (1982) Pitcher: 0-1 in three games.

Paddock, Del (1912) 3B: 45 for 156, .288; played in 46 games.

Pagan, Dave (1973-76) Pitcher: 2-4 in 40 games.

*Page, Joe (1944-50) Pitcher: 57-49 in 278 games.

*Pagliarulo, Mike (1984-89) 3B: 521 for 2274, .229; played in 703 games.

Pall, Donn (1994) Pitcher: 1-2 in 26 games.

Parker, Christian (2001) Pitcher: 0-1 in one game.

Parker, Clay (1989-90) Pitcher: 5-6 in 27 games.

Paschal, Ben (1924-29) OF: 232 for 750, .309; played in 346 games. Replaced an ill Babe Ruth for much of the 1925 season. Hit 2 inside the park HRs at Yankee Stadium in 1925. Led the Yanks in stolen bases (14) in 1925. Replaced the injured Earle Combs in center for most of the 1928 World Series and hit .200 (2 for 10).

Pasqua, Dan (1985-87) OF-DH-1B: 187 for 746, .251; played in 275 games. Hit 42 HRs.

Patterson, Gil (1977) Pitcher: 1-2 in 10 games.

Patterson, Jeff (1995) Pitcher: 0-0 in three games.

Patterson, Mike (1981-82) OF: 5 for 25, .200; played in 15 games.

Pavlas, Dave (1995-96) Pitcher: 0-0 in 20 games.

*Pearson, Monte (1936-40) Pitcher: 63-27 in 121 games.

*Peckinpaugh, Roger (1913-21) SS: 1170 for 4555, .257; played in 1220 games. Manager, final weeks of 1914 season.

Peek, Steve (1941) Pitcher: 4-2 in 17 games.

Pena, Hipolito (1988) Pitcher: 1-1 in 16 games.

*Pennock, Herb (1923-33) Pitcher: 162-90 in 346 games.

*Pepitone, Joe (1962-69) 1B-OF: 967 for 3841, .252; played in 1051 games. Currently a special assistant in Business Development for the Yankees.

Perez, Marty (1977) 3B: 2 for 4, .500; played in one game.

*Perez, Melido (1992-95) Pitcher: 33-39 in 93 games.

Perez, Pascual (1990-91) Pitcher: 3-6 in 17 games. Shoulder injury in 1990 and 1991.

Perez, Robert (2001) OF-DH: 4 for 15, .267; played in six games.

Perkins, Cecil (1967) Pitcher: 0-1 in two games.

Perkins, Cy (1931) Catcher: 12 for 47, .255; played in 16 games. Yankee coach in the 1930s.

Perry, Gaylord (1980) Pitcher: 4-4 in 10 games. Hall of Famer.

*Peterson, Fritz (1966-74) Pitcher: 109-106 in 288 games.

*Pettitte, Andy (1995-99) Pitcher: 81-46 in 165 games.

Phelps, Ken (1988-89) DH-1B: 70 for 292, .240; played in 131 games. Hit 17 HRs.

Phillips, Eddie (1932) Catcher: 9 for 31, .290; played in nine games.

Phillips, Jack (1947-49) 1B: 38 for 129, .295; played in 62 games. Went 0 for 2 in the 1947 World Series.

Pieh, Cy (1913-15) Pitcher: 9-9 in 43 games.

Piercy, Bill (1917, 1921) Pitcher: 5-5 in 15 games. Pitched in relief in Game 6 of the 1921 World Series (no decision). Lost his 1921 World Series check and was suspended the first six weeks of 1922 for going on Babe Ruth's barnstorming tour.

Pillette, Duane (1949-50) Pitcher: 2-4 in 16 games.

*Piniella, Lou (1974-84) OF-DH: 971 for 3291, .295; played in 1037 games. Coach, manager, and general manager of the Yanks.

*Pipgras, George (1923-24, 1927-33) Pitcher: 93-64 in 247 games.

*Pipp, Wally (1915-25) 1B: 1577 for 5594, .282; played in 1488 games.

Pisoni, Jim (1959-60) OF: 4 for 26, .154; played in 37 games.

Plunk, Eric (1989-91) Pitcher: 15-13 in 117 games.

Polley, Dale (1996) Pitcher: 1-3 in 32 games.

Polonia, Luis (1989-90, 1994-95) OF-DH: 249 for 837, .297; played in 239 games. Came to Yanks in June 1989 trade that sent Rickey Henderson to Oakland. Luis hit .313 for the Yanks in 1989. Yanks traded him to California in April 1990 for Claudell Washington and Rich Monteleone. Signed by Yanks in December 1993. He was an excellent lead-off man in 1994, hitting .311, and he led the Yanks in stolen bases in 1994 and 1995. Yanks let him go after signing Darryl Strawberry during the 1995 season.

Porterfield, Bob (1948-51) Pitcher: 8-9 in 40 games. His promotion from Newark in 1948 was at the heart of the Weiss-Harris dispute.

Posada, Jorge (1995-2002) Catcher-DH-1B: 653 for 2439, .268; played in 724 games.

Pose, Scott (1997) OF-DH: 19 for 87, 218; played in 54 games.

*Powell, Jack (1904-05) Pitcher: 31-32 in 83 games.

Powell, Jake (1936-40) OF: 263 for 966, .272; played in 272 games. Regular outfielder in 1936 and 1937. Received a 10-day suspension for racist remarks he made on the radio in July 1938. Beaned by a pitch, suffered a severe concussion, and missed much of the 1940 season. Led or tied all players in the 1936 World Series in batting (.455), runs (8), hits (10), and walks (four) and hit a two-run HR in the finale.

Powers, Mike (1905) 1B-Catcher: 6 for 33, .182; played in 11 games. Was a practicing physician.

*Pratt, Del (1918-20) 2B: 465 for 1578, .295; played in 420 games.

Priddy, Gerry (1941-42) INF: 90 for 363, .248; played in 115 games. Hit .100 (1 for 10), one double, one walk, in the 1942 World Series, playing the final three games at first base. Reached Yanks as half of great minor league double-play combination with Phil Rizzuto.

Priest, Johnnie (1911-12) 2B-3B: 4 for 23, .174; played in nine games.

Pulido, Alfonso (1986) Pitcher: 1-1 in 10 games.

Puttmann, Ambrose (1903-05) Pitcher: 6-7 in 29 games.

Queen, Mel (1942, 1944, 1946-47) Pitcher: 8-4 in 33 games.

Quick, Eddie (1903) Pitcher: 0-0 in one game.

*Quinn, Jack (1909-12, 1919-21) Pitcher: 81-65 in 228 games.

Quirk, Jamie (1989) Catcher: 2 for 24, .083; played in 13 games.

Raines, Tim (1996-98) OF-DH: 237 for 793, .299 in 242 games. Tim retired prior to the start of the 2000 season.

Rajsich, Dave (1978) Pitcher: 0-0 in four games.

Ramos, Bobby (1982) Catcher-DH: 1 for 11, .091; played in four games.

Ramos, Domingo (1978) SS: 0 for 0; played in one game.

Ramos, John (1991) Catcher-DH: 8 for 26, .308; played in 10 games.

Aurelio Rodriguez

*Ramos, Pedro (1964-66) Pitcher: 9-14 in 130 games.

Randle, Lenny (1979) DH-OF: 7 for 39, .179; played in 20 games.

*Randolph, Willie (1976-88) 2B: 1731 for 6303, .275; played in 1694 games. Yankee coach.

*Raschi, Vic (1946-53) Pitcher: 120-50 in 218 games.

*Rasmussen, Dennis (1984-87) Pitcher: 39-24 in 103 games.

*Rawley, Shane (1982-84) Pitcher: 27-27 in 92 games.

Reardon, Jeff (1994) Pitcher. 1-0 in 11 games.

Reed, Jack (1961-63) OF: 30 for 129, .233; played in 222 games. His only ML HR on June 25, 1962 won for the Yanks a seven-hour, 22-inning game at Detroit. Used as a defensive replacement in center field in three games of the 1961 World Series. Often used as a defensive replacement for Mickey Mantle to rest Mickey's legs. Yankee minor league manager.

Reese, Jimmie (1930-31) 2B-3B: 124 for 433, .286; played in 142 games. Babe Ruth's roommate. Coached Angels into the 1990s. History's greatest handler of a fungo bat.

*Reniff, Hal (1961-67) Pitcher: 18-20 in 247 games.

Renna, Bill (1953) OF: 38 for 121, .314; played in 61 games.

Rensa, Tony (1933) Catcher: 9 for 29, .310; played in eight games.

Repoz, Roger (1964-66) OF: 63 for 262, .240; played in 127 games.

Reuschel, Rick (1981) Pitcher: 4-4 in 12 games. Missed 1982 season with a shoulder injury.

Revering, Dave (1981-82) 1B: 34 for 159, .214; played in 59 games.

*Reynolds, Allie (1947-54) Pitcher: 131-60 in 295 games.

Reynolds, Bill (1913-14) Catcher: 2 for 10, .200; played in nine games.

Rhoden, Rick (1987-88) Pitcher: 28-22 in 60 games. In 1987, he led Yanks in wins (16) and strikeouts (107). Led Yanks in innings pitched (197) in 1988. Batted (0 for 1) in a 1988 game.

Rhodes, Gordon "Dusty" (1929-32) Pitcher: 7-9 in 41 games.

Rice, Harry (1930) OF-1B: 103 for 346, .298; played in 100 games.

*Richardson, Bobby (1955-66) 2B-3B-SS: 1432 for 5386, .266; played in 1412 games.

Richardson, Nolen (1935) SS: 10 for 46, .217; played in 12 games.

Rickey, Branch (1907) OF-Catcher-1B: 25 for 137, .182; played in 52 games. While catching on June 28, 1907, he allowed 13 stolen bases, an AL record. Tremendous general manager with the Cardinals and Dodgers; elected into the Baseball Hall of Fame.

*Righetti, Dave (1979, 1981-90) Pitcher: 74-61 in 522 games. Yankee leader with 522 games pitched.

Rijo, Jose (1984) Pitcher: 2-8 in 24 games.

Rios, Danny (1997) Pitcher: 0-0 in two games.

Rivera, Juan (2001-02) OF: 22 for 87, .253; played in 31 games.

*Rivera, Mariano (1995-2002) Pitcher: 38-27 in 448 games; Yankee leader with 243 saves; 0.90 ERA in postseason career. Named MVP in 1999 World Series.

Rivera, Ruben (1995-96) OF: 25 for 89, .281; played in 51 games. Cut by Yankees during 2002 Spring Training for an alleged clubhouse theft.

*Rivers, Mickey (1976-79) OF: 598 for 2000, .299; played in 490 games.

*Rizzuto, Phil (1941-42, 1946-56) SS: 1588 for 5816, .273; played in 1661 games. Yankee broadcaster from 1957 to 1997.

Roach, Roxey (1910-11) SS-OF-2B: 57 for 260, .219; played in 83 games.

Roberts, Dale (1967) Pitcher: 0-0 in two games.

Robertson, Andre (1981-85) SS-2B-3B: 182 for 724, .251; played in 254 games.

Robertson, Gene (1928-29) 3B-2B: 165 for 560, .295; played in 173 games. Went 1 for 8 (.125, one run, two RBIs, one walk) in the 1928 World Series, playing third base in the final three games.

Robinson, Aaron (1943, 1945-47) Catcher: 211 for 743, .284; played in 233 games. Batted once in 1943, then entered the military. Returned during the 1945 season. Caught the majority of Yankee games in 1946 and hit 16 HRs in only 330 ABs. Made AL team for 1947 All-Star Game. Shared Catching with Yogi Berra in 1947.

Robinson, Bill (1967-69) OF: 187 for 906, .206; played in 310 games. Obtained by Yanks in November 1966 from Atlanta for Clete Boyer. Much heralded when he joined the Yanks in 1967. Great throwing arm. Didn't hit the way the Yanks had expected; he later became a good hitter in the NL.

Robinson, Bruce (1979-80) Catcher: 2 for 17, .118; played in 10 games.

Robinson, Eddie (1954-56) 1B: 85 for 369, .230; played in 199 games. Went 2 for 3 with two walks and 1 RBI in the 1955 World Series; he pinch-hit in three games and played first base in Game 5. Hit 16 HRs in only 173 at-bats in 1955.

Robinson, Hank (1918) Pitcher: 2-4 in 11 games.

Robinson, Jeff (1990) Pitcher: 3-6 in 54 games.

Rodriguez, Aurelio (1980-81) 3B-2B-1B: 54 for 216, .250; played in 79 games. Hit .333 (2 for 6) in 1980 ALCS, playing in two games. Played in one game in the 1981 ALCS. Hit .417 (5 for 12) in the 1981 World Series.

Rodriguez, Carlos (1991) SS-2B: 7 for 37, .189; played in 15 games.

Rodriguez, Eddie (1982) 2B: 3 for 9, .333; played in three games.

Rodriguez, Ellie (1968) Catcher: 5 for 24, .208; played in nine games.

Rodriguez, Henry (2001) DH: 0 for 8, .000; played in five games.

Roenicke, Gary (1986) OF-DH: 36 for 136, .265; played in 69 games.

Roettger, Oscar (1923-24) Pitcher: 0-0 in six games.

Rogers, Jay (1914) Catcher: 0 for 8, .000; played in five games.

Rogers, Kenny (1996-97) Pitcher: 18-15 in 61 games.

Rogers, Tom (1921) Pitcher: 0-1 in five games. Pitched in relief in Game 3 of the 1921 World Series (no decision).

Roland, Jim (1972) Pitcher: 0-1 in 16 games.

*Rolfe, Red (1931, 1934-42) 3B-SS: 1394 for 4827, .289; played in 1175 games.

Rosar, Buddy (1939-42) Catcher: 205 for 751, .273; played in 252 games. At Yanks' Newark farm team, he hit .332 in 1937 and .387 in 1938. Spent four seasons with the Yanks as Bill Dickey's backup catcher. Selected to AL team for the 1942 All-Star Game. Delivered a pinch-hit in the 1942 World Series, his only at-bat in World Series play.

Rosenthal, Larry (1944) OF: 20 for 101, .198; played in 36 games.

Roser, Steve (1944-46) Pitcher: 5-4 in 31 games.

Roth, Braggo (1921) OF: 43 for 152, .283; played in 43 games. His brother, Frank, was a Yankee coach in 1921.

Royster, Jerry (1987) 3B: 15 for 42, .357; played in 18 games.

Ruel, Muddy (1917-20) Catcher: 130 for 517, .251; played in 172 games. Split the catching chores with Truck Hannah in 1919 and 1920.

Ruether, Dutch (1926-27) Pitcher: 15-9 in 32 games. Babe Ruth said Dutch's 2 wins saved the 1926 pennant. Lost Game 3 of the 1926 World Series. Won 13 games as Yanks' fourth starter in 1927 and tied for club lead in shutouts (three).

*****Ruffing, Red** (1930-42, 1945-46) Pitcher: 231-124 in 426 games; 18 walks. Pinch-hit 206 times as a Yankee, getting 45 hits in 181 at-bats (.249) with 8 walks.

*****Russell, Allan** (1915-19) Pitcher: 26-36 in 114 games.

*****Russo, Marius** (1939-43, 1946) Pitcher: 45-34 in 120 games.

*****Ruth, Babe** (1920-34) OF-1B-P: 2518 for 7217, .349; played in 2084 games. As a pitcher, he compiled a 5-0 record in five games with the Yanks; four games started; two completed.

Ryan, Blondy (1935) SS: 25 for 105, .238; played in 30 games.

Ryan, Rosy (1928) Pitcher: 0-0 in three games. Pitched for all three NY teams: Yankees, Dodgers, Giants.

*****Sain, Johnny** (1951-55) Pitcher: 33-20 in 130 games. Yankee pitching coach.

Sakata, Lenn (1987) 3B-2B: 12 for 45, .267; played in 19 games. Ankle injury. While with Baltimore in 1982, he was replaced at SS by Cal Ripken, Jr.

Salas, Mark (1987) Catcher: 23 for 115, .200; played in 50 games.

Saltzgaver, Jack (1932, 1934-37) INF: 161 for 647, .249; played in 226 games. On April 12, 1932, he walked four times in his first ML game, a ML record. Regular third baseman in 1934.

Sample, Billy (1985) OF: 40 for 139, .288; played in 59 games.

Sanchez, Celerino (1972-73) 3B-SS-OF-DH: 76 for 314, .242; played in 105 games.

Sanchez, Rey (1997) 2B-SS: 43 for 138, .312; played in 38 games.

Sanders, Deion (1989-90) OF: 32 for 180, .178; played in 71 games. Starred in the NFL for Atlanta, San Francisco, and Dallas.

Sanders, Roy (1918) Pitcher: 0-2 in six games.

Sanderson, Scott (1991-92) Pitcher: 28-21 in 67 games. In 1991, he led the Yanks in wins (16), games started (34), complete games (two), innings pitched (208), strikeouts (130), and shutouts (two). Only Yankee chosen for the 1991 All-Star Game.

Sands, Charlie (1967) PH: 0 for 1, .000; pinch-hit in one game.

Sanford, Fred (1949-51) Pitcher: 12-10 in 66 games.

Santana, Rafael (1988) SS: 115 for 480, .240; played in 148 games. Regular Yankee shortstop. Missed all of 1989 season with an elbow injury.

Savage, Don (1944-45) 3B-OF: 76 for 297, .256; played in 105 games.

Sawyer, Rick (1974-75) Pitcher: 0-0 in five games.

*****Sax, Steve** (1989-91) 2B: 563 for 1918, .294; played in 471 games.

Scarborough, Ray (1952-53) Pitcher: 7-3 in 34 games. Pitched in relief in Game 1 of the 1952 World Series (no decision).

Schaefer, Germany (1916) OF: 0 for 1, .000; played in one game.

Schaeffer, Harry (1952) Pitcher: 0-1 in five games.

Schalk, Roy (1932) 2B: 3 for 12, .250; played in three games.

Schallock, Art (1951-55) Pitcher: 3-2 in 28 games. Pitched in relief in Game 4 of the 1953 World Series (no decision).

*****Schang, Wally** (1921-25) Catcher: 483 for 1627, .297; played in 529 games.

Schmidt, Bob (1965) Catcher: 10 for 40, .250; played in 20 games.

Schmidt, Butch (1909) Pitcher: 0-0 in one game.

Schmitz, Johnny (1952, 1953) Pitcher: 1-1 in eight games.

Schneider, Pete (1919) Pitcher: 0-1 in seven games.

Schofield, Dick (1966) SS: 9 for 58, .155; played in 25 games.

Schreiber, Paul (1945) Pitcher: 0-0 in 2 games. Yankee batting practice pitcher; he had not pitched in the ML's in 22 years when he was activated at age 42.

Schult, Art (1953) 0 for 0; played in 7 games as pinch-runner, scoring 3 runs.

Schulz, Al (1912-14) Pitcher: 9-17 in 47 games.

Schulze, Don (1989) Pitcher: 1-1 in two games.

Schwarz, Bill (1914) Catcher: 0 for 1, .000; played in one game.

Schwert, Pi (1914-15) Catcher: 5 for 23, .217; played in 11 games.

*****Scott, Everett** (1922-25) SS: 431 for 1698, .254; played in 481 games.

Scott, George (1979) DH-1B: 14 for 44, .318; played in 16 games.

Scott, Rodney (1982) SS-2B: 5 for 26, .192; played in 10 games.

Scurry, Rod (1985-86) Pitcher: 2-2 in 36 games.

Seabol, Scott (2001) DH: 0 for 1, .000; played in one game.

Sears, Ken (1943) Catcher: 52 for 187, .278; played in 60 games.

Seeds, Bob (1936) OF-3B: 11 for 42, .262; played in 13 games. Game 5 of the 1936 World Series ended when as a pinch-runner Bob was out attempting to steal second base. Hit .305 on great 1937 Newark Bears team. Always a great minor league hitter, he couldn't produce in the majors.

Segrist, Kal (1952) 2B: 1 for 23, .043; played in 13 games.

*****Selkirk, George** (1934-42) OF: 810 for 2790, .290; played in 846 games. Yankee minor league manager.

Sepkowski, Ted (1947): 0 for 0; played in two games as a pinch-runner; 1 run scored.

Severeid, Hank (1926) Catcher: 34 for 127, .268; played in 41 games. Hit .273 (6 for 22, one double, one run, 1 RBI, one walk) in the 1926 World Series; he played catcher in all seven games.

*****Sewell, Joe** (1931-33) 3B: 426 for 1511, .282; played in 390 games. Yankee coach. Most difficult player to strike out in ML history. Fanned only 15 times in 1511 at-bats as a Yankee.

Shanks, Howard (1925) 3B-2B-OF: 40 for 155, .258; played in 66 games.

Shantz, Billy (1960) Catcher: 0 for 0; played in one game. Brother of Bobby.

*****Shantz, Bobby** (1957-60) Pitcher: 30-18 in 138 games. Brother of Billy.

*****Shawkey, Bob** (1915-27) Pitcher: 168-131 in 415 games. Yankee coach in late 1920s. Yankee manager, 1930.

Shea, Spec (1947-49, 1951) Pitcher: 29-21 in 100 games. As a rookie in 1947, he led the Yanks in winning percentage (.737, 14-5) and was the winning pitcher in the All-Star Game. Won 2 games in the 1947 World Series; he won Game 1 and pitched a four-hitter to win Game 5. Dropped to 9-10 in 1948.

Shealy, Al (1928) Pitcher: 8-6 in 23 games.

Shears, George (1912) Pitcher: 0-0 in four games.

Enos Slaughter

Sheehan, Tom (1921) Pitcher: 1-0 in 12 games. Went on Babe Ruth's unapproved barnstorming tour after the 1921 World Series, but was not punished because he had not pitched in the Series.

Sheldon, Rollie (1961-62, 1964-65) Pitcher: 23-15 in 91 games. Jumped from Class-D to the Yanks in 1961, and in 1961 and 1962, he was the Yanks' fourth starter. He had an 11-5 record in 1961. Made two relief appearances in the 1964 World Series.

Shelton, Skeeter (1915) OF: 1 for 40, .025; played in 10 games.

Sherid, Roy (1929-31) Pitcher: 23-24 in 87 games. Yanks' fifth starter as a rookie in 1929. Third starter in 1930 and had a 12-13 record.

Sheridan, Pat (1991) OF: 23 for 113, .204; played in 62 games.

Sherrill, Dennis (1978, 1980) INF-DH: 1 for 5, .200; played in five games.

Shields, Ben (1924-25) Pitcher: 3-0 in six games.

Shields, Steve (1988) Pitcher: 5-5 in 39 games.

Shirley, Bob (1983-87) Pitcher: 14-20 in 165 games. High-priced free-agent signee who was used mostly in middle-to-long relief and spot starts.

*Shocker, Urban (1916-17, 1925-28) Pitcher: 61-37 in 152 games.

Shopay, Tom (1967, 1969) OF: 12 for 75, .160; played in 36 games.

Shore, Ernie (1919-20) Pitcher: 7-10 in 34 games.

Short, Bill (1960) Pitcher: 3-5 in 10 games.

Siebern, Norm (1956, 1958-59) OF: 274 for 1002, .273; played in 308 games. Yanks' 4th outfielder in 1956. In 1957, he was the Minor League Player of the Year at Denver (24 HRs, 118 RBIs, .349). Regular Yankee leftfielder in 1958 and hit .300. Hit .125 (1 for 8) in the 1958 World Series. Yanks' leftfielder again in 1959 and in December 1959, he was traded to the A's in deal that brought Roger Maris to the Yanks.

Sierra, Ruben (1995-96) DH-OF: 149 for 575, .259; played in 152 games.

Silvera, Charlie (1948-56) Catcher: 125 for 429, .291; played in 201 games. Backup catcher to Yogi Berra. Went 0 for 2 in World Series play, but he was a member of six World Series championships.

Silvestri, Dave (1992- 95) INF-DH: 14 for 73, .192; played in 43 games.

Silvestri, Ken (1941, 1946-47) Catcher: 18 for 71, .254; played in 33 games.

Simmons, Hack (1912) 2B-1B-SS: 96 for 401, .239; played in 110 games.

Simpson, Dick (1969) OF: 3 for 11, .273; played in six games.

Simpson, Harry (1957-58) OF-1B: 67 for 275, .244; played in 99 games. Hit .083 (1 for 12, 1 RBI) in the 1957 World Series, playing four games at first base and pinch hitting in another game. Nicknamed "Suitcase" as he played for five clubs in his 8-year career.

Sims, Duke (1973-74) Catcher-DH: 5 for 24, .208; played in nine games. On September 30, 1973, he hit the last Yankee HR in the "old" Yankee Stadium.

Skiff, Bill (1926) Catcher: 1 for 11, .091; played in six games. Spent many years in the Yankee organization as scout, roving farm supervisor, special coach, and minor league manager.

Skinner, Camp (1922) OF: 6 for 33, .182; played in 27 games.

Skinner, Joel (1986-88) Catcher: 119 for 556, .214; played in 206 games. Given starting job after mid-season trade to NY in 1986, but he lost it while hitting .137 in 1987.

Skizas, Lou (1956) OF: 1 for 6, .167; played in six games.

*Skowron, Bill (1954-62) 1B-3B: 1103 for 3748, .294; played in 1087 games.

Slagle, Roger (1979) Pitcher: 0-0 in one game.

Slaught, Don (1988-89) Catcher: 179 for 672, .266; played in 214 games. Regular catcher both years. Groin injury in 1988.

Slaughter, Enos (1954-55, 1956-59) OF: 168 for 663, .253; played in 350 games. Broken wrist in 1954. In 1958, he led the AL in pinch-hit ABs (48) and at age 42, he hit .304. Delivered key three-run HR in Game 3 of the 1956 World Series. Tied for most runs scored (6) in the 1956 World Series. Hall of Famer, mostly for his Cardinal career.

Smalley, Roy (1982-84) INF-DH: 299 for 1146, .261; played in 339 games. Regular shortstop in 1982 and 1983. Hit 20 HRs in 1982 and 18 HRs in 1983.

Smallwood, Walt (1917, 1919) Pitcher: 0-0 in eight games.

Smith, Charley (1967-68) 3B: 111 for 495, .224; played in 181 games. Yanks traded Roger Maris to St. Louis for him.

Smith, Elmer (1922-23) OF: 61 for 210, .290; played in 91 games. Went 0 for 2 pinch hitting in the 1922 World Series.

Smith, Joe (1913) Catcher: 5 for 32, .156; played in 14 games.

Smith, Keith (1984-85) SS: 0 for 4, .000; played in six games.

Smith, Klondike (1912) OF: 5 for 27, .185; played in seven games.

Smith, Lee (1993) Pitcher: 0-0 in eight games. Saved three games.

Smythe, Harry (1934) Pitcher: 0-2 in eight games.

Snow, J.T. (1992) 1B: 2 for 14, .143; played in seven games. Highly regarded prospect. Traded for Jim Abbott.

Soderholm, Eric (1980) DH-3B: 79 for 275, .287; played in 95 games.

Sojo, Luis (1996-99, 2000-01) INF-DH: 192 for 733, .262, played in 271 games; Had .400 BA in 11 World Series games for Yanks.

Solaita, Tony (1968) 1B: 0 for 1, .000; played in one game.

Soriano, Alfonso (1999-2002) 2B-3B-SS-DH: 373 for 1328, .281; Led AL with 209 hits in 2002.

Souchock, Steve (1946, 1948) 1B: 50 for 204, .245; played in 91 games. Spent many years in the Yankee organization as a scout, special scout and troubleshooter, minor league manager, minor league camp coordinator, and instructional school coordinator.

Spencer, Jim (1978-81) 1B-DH: 189 for 767, .246; played in 299 games. Hit 45 Yankee HRs. Hit .167 (2 for 12) but scored three runs in the 1978 World Series. Went 0 for 1 as a pinch hitter in the 1980 ALCS.

Spencer, Shane (1998-2002) OF-DH-1B: 287 for 1091, .263; played in 345 games. Was a combined 6 for 19 (.263) in six games in the 1998 postseason.

Spikes, Charlie (1972) OF: 5 for 34, .147; played in 14 games. Part of trade to Indians for Graig Nettles.

Springer, Russ (1992) Pitcher: 0-0 in 14 games.

*Stafford, Bill (1960-65) Pitcher: 43-35 in 163 games.

Stahl, Jake (1908) OF-1B: 70 for 274, .255; played in 75 games.

Staiger, Roy (1979) 3B: 3 for 11, .273; played in four games.

Stainback, Tuck (1942-45) OF: 163 for 646, .252; played in 211 games. Used twice as a pinch runner in the 1942 World Series. He got thrown out at third in a key play of Game 2. Hit .176 (3 for 17) in the 1943 World Series, playing all five games in the outfield.

Staley, Gerry (1955-56) Pitcher: 0-0 in three games.

Stanceu, Charley (1941, 1946) Pitcher: 3-3 in 25 games.

Stankiewicz, Andy (1992-93) SS-2B: 107 for 409, .262; played in 132 games. Regular shortstop in 1992.

Stanley, Fred (1973-80) SS-2B-3B: 224 for 1008, .222; played in 521 games. Shared shortstop position in 1975. He was the regular shortstop in 1976 and set Yankee record with .983 fielding average. Hit .333 in 1976 ALCS but only .167 in the World Series. Beat Boston with a grand slam in a critical game in 1978.

Stanley, Mike (1992-95, 1997) Catcher-DH-1B: 391 for 1372, .285; played in 426 games. Chosen for the 1995 All-Star game.

Stanton, Mike (1997-2002) Pitcher: 30-12 in 428 games.

Starr, Dick (1947-48) Pitcher: 1-0 in five games.

Stegman, Dave (1982) DH: 0 for 0; played in two games.

Sterrett, Dutch (1912-13) OF-1B-2B-Catcher: 67 for 265, .253; played in 87 games.

Stewart, Bud (1948) OF: 1 for 5, .200; played in six games.

Stine, Lee (1938) Pitcher: 0-0 in four games.

*Stirnweiss, Snuffy (1943-50) 2B-3B-SS: 899 for 3281, .274; played in 884 games.

Stoddard, Tim (1986-88) Pitcher: 10-6 in 109 games. Saved 11 games.

*Stottlemyre, Mel (1964-74) Pitcher: 164-139 in 360 games.

Stowe, Hal (1960) Pitcher: 0-0 in one game.

Strawberry, Darryl (1995-99) DH-OF: 169 for 662, .255; played in 231 games. Only player to have played with the Yankees, Mets, Giants and Dodgers. Was suspended for the 2000 season due to drug violation.

Street, Gabby (1912) Catcher: 16 for 88, .182; played in 29 games.

Stuart, Marlin (1954) Pitcher: 3-0 in 10 games.

Stumpf, Bill (1912-13) INF: 37 for 158, .234; played in 54 games.

*Sturdivant, Tom (1955-59) Pitcher: 36-25 in 115 games.

Sturm, Johnny (1941) 1B: 125 for 524, .239; played in 124 games. Regular first baseman on a World Championship team in his only ML season. Hit .286 (6 for 21) in the World Series and got a base hit in his first World Series at-bat. Missed four seasons while serving in the military (1942-45). Later managed in the Yankee farm system.

Sudakis, Bill (1974) DH-1B-3B-Catcher: 60 for 259, .232; played in 89 games.

Sundra, Steve (1936, 1938-40) Pitcher: 21-11 in 77 games. Had 15-4 record for Newark in 1937. Best Yankee season was 11-1 in 1939. Pitched well over middle innings in Game 4 of the 1939 World Series, which the Yanks won to complete the sweep.

Sveum, Dale (1998) 1B-3B-DH: 9 for 58, .155; played in 30 games.

*Sweeney, Jeff (1908-15) Catcher: 423 for 1799, .235; played in 627 games.

Swoboda, Ron (1971-73) OF-DH: 69 for 294, .235; played in 152 games.

Talbot, Fred (1966-69) Pitcher: 14-24 in 89 games. Yanks' fourth starter in 1966 and 1967. Record of 1-9 in 1968. Traded for Jack Aker in May 1969.

Tamulis, Vito (1934-35) Pitcher: 11-5 in 31 games. Was 18-6 on the great Newark Bears of 1937.

Tanana, Frank (1993) Pitcher: 0-2 in three games.

Tannehill, Jesse (1903) Pitcher: 15-15 in 32 games. Number two starter on the Yanks'—Highlanders'—first team.

Tarasco, Tony (1999) OF: 5 for 31, .161; played in 14 games.

*Tartabull, Danny (1992-95) DH-OF: 385 for 1525, .252; played in 424 games.

Taylor, Wade (1991) Pitcher: 7-12 in 23 games. Yanks' third starter.

Taylor, Zack (1934) Catcher: 1 for 7, .143; played in four games. Played for all three NY teams: Yankees, Dodgers, Giants.

Tepedino, Frank (1967, 1969-71, 1972) OF-1B: 17 for 77, .221; played in 52 games.

Terrell, Walt (1989) Pitcher: 6-5 in 13 games.

*Terry, Ralph (1956-57, 1959-64) Pitcher: 78-59 in 210 games.

Tessmer, Jay (1998-2000, 2002) Pitcher: 1-0 in 22 games.

Tettelbach, Dick (1955) OF: 0 for 5, .000; played in two games.

Tewksbury, Bob (1986-87) Pitcher: 10-9 in 31 games. Yanks gave up on him before he developed into an excellent pitcher.

Thames, Marcus (2002) OF: 3 for 13, .231; played in seven games.

Thomas, Ira (1906-07) Catcher-1B: 63 for 323, .195; played in 124 games.

Thomas, Lee (1961) OF: 1 for 2, .500; played in two games.

Thomas, Myles (1926-29) Pitcher: 14-12 in 71 games. Yanks' No. 5 starter in 1926. Made two appearances in the 1926 World Series (no decisions). Went 7-4 and hit .333 (9 for 27) in 1927.

Thomas, Stan (1977) Pitcher: 1-0 in three games.

Thomasson, Gary (1978) OF: 32 for 116, .276; played in 55 games. Went 1 for 5 in the post season. Caught a fly ball for the final out of the ALCS.

Thompson, Homer (1912) Catcher: 0 for 0; played in one game. Brother of Tommy Thompson.

Thompson, Ryan (2002) OF: 13 for 50, .260; played in 33 games.

Thompson, Tommy (1912) Pitcher: 0-2 in seven games.

Thoney, Jack (1904) 3B-OF: 24 for 128, .188; played in 36 games.

Thormahlen, Hank (1917-20) Pitcher: 28-20 in 76 games. Led Yanks in shutouts (3) in 1918. Yanks' third starter in 1919 and went 13-10. Traded to Boston in December 1920 in the deal that brought Waite Hoyt to the Yanks.

Throneberry, Marv (1955, 1958-59) 1B-OF: 82 for 344, .238; played in 141 games. Went 0 for 1 as a pinch hitter in the 1958 World Series. Became a legendary defensive liability with the Mets and was made nationally famous for a series of television beer commercials he appeared in long after his playing days were over. In May 1962, "Marvelous Marv" became the first of over 50 Yankees to also play for the Mets.

Thurman, Mike (2002) Pitcher: 1-0 in 12 games.

Tiant, Luis (1979-80) Pitcher: 21-17 in 55 games. Signed as a free agent from Red Sox; he had lifetime 22-14 record vs. the Yanks. In 1979, he was the Yanks' third starter, went 13-8, and on July 8, 1979, he one-hit the A's. Hurt for part of 1980 season, then left the Yanks as a free agent.

*Tidrow, Dick (1974-79) Pitcher: 41-33 in 211 games.

Tiefenauer, Bobby (1965) Pitcher: 1-1 in 10 games.

Tiemeyer, Eddie (1909) 1B: 3 for 8, .375; played in three games.

Tift, Ray (1907) Pitcher: 0-0 in four games.

Tillman, Bob (1967) Catcher: 16 for 63, .254; played in 22 games.

Tillotson, Thad (1967-68) Pitcher: 4-9 in 50 games.

Tipple, Dan (1915) Pitcher: 1-1 in three games.

Tolleson, Wayne (1986-90) INF: 187 for 837, .223; played in 355 games. Regular shortstop in 1987. Shoulder and leg injuries in 1988. Utility infielder in 1989-90.

Torgeson, Earl (1961) 1B: 2 for 18, .111; played in 22 games.

Torres, Rusty (1971-72) OF: 52 for 225, .231; played in 89 games.

Torrez, Mike (1977) Pitcher: 14-12 in 31 games. Led Yanks in complete games (15). Pitched 6 consecutive complete game wins down the pennant stretch. Won two games in the World Series, including the finale. After the season, he signed with Boston as a free agent.

Tovar, Cesar (1976) 2B-DH: 6 for 39, .154; played in 13 games.

*Tresh, Tom (1961-69) OF-SS-3B: 967 for 3920, .247; played in 1098 games.

Triandos, Gus (1953-54) 1B-Catcher: 8 for 52, .154; played in 20 games.

Trout, Steve (1987) Pitcher: 0-4 in 14 games.

Trucks, Virgil (1958) Pitcher: 2-1 in 25 games.

Truesdale, Frank (1914) 2B-3B: 46 for 217, .212; played in 77 games.

*Turley, Bob (1955-62) Pitcher: 82-52 in 234 games.

Turner, Chris (2000) Catcher-1B: 21 for 89, .236; played in 37 games.

Turner, Jim (1942-45) Pitcher: 11-9 in 88 games. Led the Yanks in both saves and games pitched in both 1944 and 1945. Led AL in saves (10) in 1945. Saved 19 games as a Yankee. Manager in the Yankee minors. Yankee pitching coach and Casey Stengel's righthand man (1949-59) and pitching coach again from 1966 into the early 1970s.

Uhle, George (1933-34) Pitcher: 8-5 in 22 games.

Underwood, Tom (1980-81) Pitcher: 14-13 in 47 games. Went 13-9 in 1980 and pitched two scoreless innings in the 1980 ALCS.

Unglaub, Bob (1904) 3B-SS: 4 for 19, .211; played in six games.

Upshaw, Cecil (1974) Pitcher: 1-5 in 36 games.

Valo, Elmer (1960) OF: 0 for 5, .000; played in eight games.

Van Atta, Russ (1933-35) Pitcher: 15-9 in 59 games. On April 25, 1933, he cracked four singles, making him the first pitcher to get four hits in his first 9-inning ML game.

Vance, Dazzy (1915, 1918) Pitcher: 0-3 in 10 games. Went on to a spectacular Hall of Fame career after leaving the Yanks.

Vance, Joe (1937-38) Pitcher: 1-0 in five games. Played for Brooklyn Dodgers of NFL in 1931.

Vander Wal, John (2002) OF-DH-1B: 57 for 219, .260; played in 84 games.

Vaughn, Bobby (1909) 2B-SS: 2 for 14, .143; played in five games.

Vaughn, Hippo (1908, 1910-12) Pitcher: 23-29 in 73 games. Hand injury ruined his rookie season in 1908. Yanks' fourth starter in 1910; he went 12-11 and had a 1.83 ERA. Illness impeded him in 1911. Yanks sold his contract to Washington in June 1912. Hippo later became a five-time 20-game winner for the Cubs.

Veach, Bobby (1925) OF: 41 for 116, .353; played in 56 games. The only man to ever pinch-hit for Babe Ruth while Babe was on the Yanks.

*Velarde, Randy (1987-95, 2001) INF, OF-DH: 518 for 1981, .261; played in 673 games.

Velez, Otto (1973-76) OF-1B-DH-3B: 56 for 246, .228; played in 105 games. Went 0 for 4 as a pinch hitter in the 1976 post season.

Ventura, Robin (2002) 3B-1B: 115 for 465, .247; played in 141 games.

Verbanic, Joe (1967-68, 1970) Pitcher: 11-10 in 75 games.

Verdi, Frank (1953) SS: 0 for 0; played in one game. Manager in Yankee minors.

Vick, Sammy (1917-20) OF: 139 for 564, .246; played in 169 games. The last regular Yankee rightfielder before Babe Ruth joined the team.

Vizcaino, Jose (2000) 2B-3B-SS-DH: 48 for 174, .276; played in 73 games.

Wade, Jake (1946) Pitcher: 2-1 in 13 games.

Wakefield, Dick (1950) PH: 1 for 2, .500; pinch-hit in three games (1 walk). After Yanks traded him to the White Sox in April 1950, Dick refused to report unless he was given a $5,000 raise by Chicago as compensation for the World Series check he expected to miss with the Yanks. Commissioner Chandler ordered Dick back to the Yanks.

Walewander, Jim (1990) INF: 1 for 5, .200; played in nine games.

Walker, Curt (1919) PH: 0 for 1, .000; pinch-hit in one game.

Walker, Dixie (1931, 1933-36) OF: 104 for 388, .268; played in 131 games. Hit 15 HRs in 1933. He later was one of Brooklyn's favorite stars.

Wallace, Mike (1974-75) Pitcher: 6-0 in 26 games.

Walsh, Jimmy (1914) OF: 26 for 136, .191; played in 43 games.

Walsh, Joe (1910-11) Catcher: 4 for 13, .308; played in 5 games.

Walters, Roxy (1915-18) Catcher-OF: 138 for 568, .243; played in 193 games.

Walton, Danny (1971) OF: 2 for 14, .143; played in five games.

Waner, Paul (1944-45) PH: 1 for 7, 143; pinch-hit in 10 games (three walks). The great Hall of Famer concluded his ML career with the Yanks.

Wanner, Jack (1909) SS: 1 for 8, .125; played in three games.

Wanninger, Pee Wee (1925) SS-3B: 95 for 403, .236; played in 117 games. Replaced Everett Scott in May 1925, ending Scott's long playing streak, and he was the player Lou Gehrig pinch-hit for in June 1925, starting Gehrig's remarkable playing streak.

*Ward, Aaron (1917-26) 2B-3B-SS: 840 for 3139, .268; played in 908 games.

Ward, Gary (1987-89) OF-DH-1B: 188 for 777, .242; played in 245 games. Regular outfielder in 1987 when he hit 16 HRs with 78 RBIs.

Ward, Joe (1909) 2B: 5 for 28, .179; played in nine games.

Ward, Pete (1970) 1B: 20 for 77, .260; played in 66 games. Yankee minor league manager and scout.

*Warhop, Jack (1908-15) Pitcher: 69-93 in 221 games.

Washburn, George (1941) Pitcher: 0-1 in one game.

Washington, Claudell (1986-88, 1990) OF-DH: 272 for 982, .277; played in 315 games. Valuable reserve outfielder in 1987. Hit .308 as a regular in 1988. Signed with the Angels as a free agent in January 1989. Traded back to the Yanks for Luis Polonia in April 1990. Suffered finger injury in 1990 and hit only .163. Hit the 10,000th home run in Yankee franchise history on April 20, 1988.

Waslewski, Gary (1970-71) Pitcher: 2-3 in 50 games.

Watson, Allen (1999-2000) Pitcher: 4-0 in 38 games.

Watson, Bob (1980-82) 1B-DH: 181 for 642, .282; played in 196 games. Regular first baseman in 1980 and 1981. In 1980, he hit .307 with 13 HRs and 68 RBIs. Hit .500 in the 1980 ALCS and led the Yanks with six hits. Groin injury reduced his playing time in 1981. In 1981 post season, he hit .438 (seven for 16) in the Division Series, .250 (3 for 12) in the ALCS, and .318 (7 for 22) in the World Series. Led Yanks with seven RBIs in the World Series. Hired as Yankee General Manager in November 1995; resigned in 1998.

Weatherly, Ray (1943, 1946) OF: 75 for 282, .266; played in 79 games. Went 0 for 1 in the 1943 World Series.

Weathers, David (1996-97) Pitcher: 0-3 in 21 games.

Weaver, Jeff (2002) Pitcher: 5-3 in 15 games.

Weaver, Jim (1931) Pitcher: 2-1 in 17 games.

Wehrmeister, Dave (1981) Pitcher: 0-0 in five games.

Weinert, Lefty (1931) Pitcher: 2-2 in 17 games.

Wells, David (1997-98, 2002) Pitcher: 53-21 in 93 games. Became first Yankee pitcher to toss a regular-season perfect game on May 17, 1998 versus Minnesota (Don Larsen pitched his in the 1956 World Series versus the Brooklyn Dodgers). **For a pitch-by-pitch account of David's game, see page 263.**

*Wells, Ed (1929-32) Pitcher: 37-20 in 107 games.

Wensloff, Butch (1943, 1947) Pitcher: 16-12 in 40 games. No. 2 starter on the 1943 Yankees when he was 13-11. Pitched strongly in relief in Game 6 of the 1947 World Series (no decision).

Wera, Julie (1927, 1929) 3B: 15 for 54, .278; played in 43 games.

Werber, Bill (1930, 1933) SS-3B: 4 for 16, .250; played in seven games.

Werth, Dennis (1979-81) 1B-OF-DH-Catcher: 27 for 124, .218; played in 76 games.

Westbrook, Jake (2000) Pitcher: 0-2 in three games.

*Wetteland, John (1995-96) Pitcher: 3-8 in 122 games. Named MVP in 1996 World Series, saving four of the five games.

Wever, Stefan (1982) Pitcher: 0-1 in one game.

Whitaker, Steve (1966-68) OF: 142 for 615, .231; played in 181 games. Regular rightfielder in 1967 and hit 11 HRs.

White, Rondell (2002) OF-DH: 109 for 455, .240; played in 126 games.

*White, Roy (1965-79) OF-INF-DH: 1803 for 6650, .271; played in 1881 games.

Whitehurst, Wally (1996) Pitcher: 1-1 in two games.

Whiteman, George (1913) OF: 11 for 32, .344; played in 11 games.

Whiten, Mark (1997) OF-DH: 57 for 215, .265; played in 69 games. Hit four HRs in one game in 1993 while playing with the Cardinals.

Whitfield, Terry (1974-76) OF: 23 for 86, .267; played in 31 games.

Whitson, Ed (1985-86) Pitcher: 15-10 in 44 games. Had a memorable brawl with Billy Martin during the heat of the pennant race in September 1985.

Wicker, Kemp (1936-38) Pitcher: 9-5 in 24 games. Pitched in relief in Game 4 of the 1937 World Series (no decision).

Wickland, Al (1919) OF: 7 for 46, .152; played in 26 games.

*Wickman, Bob (1992-96) Pitcher: 31-14 in 223 games.

Widger, Chris (2002) Catcher: 19 for 64, .297, played in 21 games.

Wiesler, Bob (1951, 1954-55) Pitcher: 3-6 in 26 games.

Wight, Bill (1946-47) Pitcher: 3-2 in 15 games.

Wilborn, Ted (1980) OF: 2 for 8, .250; played in eight games.

Wilkinson, Ed (1911) OF-2B: 3 for 13, .231; played in 10 games.

*Williams, Bernie (1991-2002). OF-DH: 1833 for 5958, .308; played in 1537 games; Has 17 career postseason HRs.

Bernie Williams

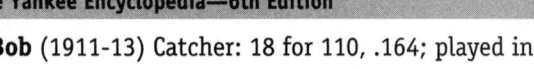

Williams, Bob (1911-13) Catcher: 18 for 110, .164; played in 46 games.

Williams, Gerald (1992-96, 2001-02) OF-DH: 159 for 659, .241; played in 384 games. Only one of 2 Yankees (the other: Myril Hoag in 1934) with 6 hits in a game, getting six safeties in a 15-inning affair at Batimore, on May 1, 1996.

Williams, Harry (1913-14) 1B: 50 for 260, .192; played in 86 games.

*****Williams, Jimmy** (1903-07) 2B: 663 for 2536, .261; played in 685 games.

Williams, Stan (1963-64) Pitcher: 10-13 in 50 games. Pitched strongly in relief in Game 1 of the 1963 World Series. Yankee pitching coach and minor league coach.

Williams, Todd (2001) Pitcher: 1-0 in 15 games.

Williams, Walt (1974-75) OF-DH-2B: 58 for 238, .244; played in 125 games. His nickname, "No Neck," was among the most descriptive in Yankee history.

Wilson, Archie (1951-52) OF: 1 for 6, .167; played in seven games.

Wilson, Enrique (2001-02) INF-OF-DH: 43 for 204, .211; played in 108 games.

Wilson, George (also Ted) (1956) OF: 2 for 12, .167; played in 11 games. Went 0 for 1 in the 1956 World Series.

Wilson, Pete (1908-09) Pitcher: 9-8 in 20 games.

Wiltse, Snake (1903) Pitcher: 0-3 in four games.

Windhorn, Gordon (1959) OF: 0 for 11, .000; played in seven games.

*****Winfield, Dave** (1981-88, 1990) OF: 1300 for 4485, .290; played in 1172 games. Missed 1989 season due to injury.

Witasick, Jay (2001) Pitcher: 3-0 in 32 games.

Witek, Mickey (1949) PH: 1 for 1, 1.000; pinch-hit in one game.

Witt, Mike (1990-91, 1993) Pitcher: 8-9 in 27 games. Traded to the Yanks for Dave Winfield. Elbow injury in 1990 and 1991. Missed all of 1992 season. Shoulder injury in 1993.

*****Witt, Whitey** (1922-25) OF: 530 for 1764, .300; played in 464 games.

Wohlers, Mark (2001) Pitcher: 1-0 in 31 games.

Wolfe, Bill (Also Barney) (1903-04) Pitcher: 6-12 in 27 games.

Wolter, Harry (1910-13) OF: 379 for 1370, .277; played in 396 games. Regular rightfielder in 1910 and 1911. Made eight double plays in 1911, setting a record for Yankee outfielders. Missed most of 1912 with a broken leg. Centerfielder in 1913. In 1910, he led the Yanks in games (135), runs (84), HRs (four) and walks (66). Twice he led the club in walks.

Wolverton, Harry (1912) 3B: 15 for 50, .300; played in 34 games. Managed Yankees in 1912.

*****Womack, Dooley** (1966-68) Pitcher: 15-16 in 152 games.

*****Woodling, Gene** (1949-54) OF: 648 for 2272, .285; played in 698 games. Yankee scout.

Woods, Ron (1969-71) OF: 89 for 428, .208; played in 192 games.

Woodson, Dick (1974) Pitcher: 1-2 in eight games.

Workman, Hank (1950) 1B: 1 for 5, .200; played in two games.

Wright, Ken (1974) Pitcher: 0-0 in three games.

Wuestling, Yats (1930) SS-3B: 11 for 58, .190; played in 25 games.

Wyatt, John (1968) Pitcher: 0-2 in seven games.

*****Wynegar, Butch** (1982-86) Catcher: 372 for 1437, .259; played in 449 games.

Wynn, Jim (1977) DH-OF: 11 for 77, .143; played in 30 games. Hit a tape measure HR in the 1977 opener; not much thereafter.

Yarnall, Ed (1999-2000) Pitcher: 1-0 in seven games.

Yeager, Joe (1905-06) INF: 144 for 524, .275; played in 172 games.

York, Jim (1976) Pitcher: 1-0 in three games.

Young, Curt (1992) Pitcher: 3-0 in 13 games. Leg injury.

Young, Ralph (1913) SS: 1 for 15, .067; played in seven games.

Zachary, Tom (1928-30) Pitcher: 16-4 in 36 games. Best remembered for allowing Babe Ruth's 60th HR pitching for Washington in 1927. Waived to Yanks in August 1928. Surprise starter in Game 3 of the 1928 World Series and beat the Cardinals with a complete game. In 1929, his 12-0 record set a ML record for the most games won without a loss in a season. Also led Yanks in 1929 in ERA (2.47).

Zalusky, Jack (1903) Catcher-1B: 5 for 16, .313; played in seven games.

Zeber, George (1977-78) 2B-3B-SS: 21 for 71, .296; played in 28 games. Went 0 for 2 in the 1977 World Series.

Zeider, Rollie (1913) SS-2B-1B-3B: 37 for 159, .233; played in 50 games.

Zinn, Guy (1911-12) OF: 109 for 428, .255; played in 115 games. On Aug. 15, 1912, he stole home twice in one game, making him one of five players in the AL to accomplish this feat.

Zuber, Bill (1943-46) Pitcher: 18-23 in 66 games; used mostly as a spot starter. Went 8-4 on the 1943 World Champions. Hard-luck 5-11 in 1945; he was beaten by shutout seven times, a Yankee club record.

Zuvella, Paul (1986-87) SS-2B-INF: 10 for 82, .122; played in 35 games.

DAVID WELLS' PERFECT GAME MAY 17, 1998 AT YANKEE STADIUM—NY-4; MN-0
120 PITCHES—79 strikes, 41 balls (PITCH-BY-PITCH)

FIRST INNING

Matt Lawton:
Ball one (1)
Strike one (called) (2)
Ball two (3)
Flied to leftfielder Chad Curtis (4)

Brent Gates:
Strike one (called) (5)
Strike two (swinging) (6)
Foul ball (7)
Flied to centerfielder Bernie Williams (8)

Paul Molitor:
Grounded to second baseman Chuck
Knoblauch to first baseman Tino Martinez (9)

SECOND INNING

Marty Cordova:
Ball one (10)
Strike one (called) (11)
Strike two (swinging) (12)
Foul ball (13)
Grounded to David Wells (P) to 1B Martinez (14)

Ron Coomer:
Ball one (15)
Strike one (swinging) (16)
Ball two (17)
Strike two (foul ball) (18)
Strike three (swinging) (19)

Alex Ochoa:
Ball one (20)
Strike one (called) (21)
Fouled to catcher Jorge Posada (22)

THIRD INNING

Jon Shave:
Strike one (foul ball) (23)
Ball one (24)
Strike two (foul ball) (25)
Ball two (26)
Strike three (called) (27)

Javier Valentin:
Ball one (28)
Strike one (swinging) (29)
Ball two (30)
Strike two (foul ball) (31)
Foul ball (32)
Ball three (33)
Foul ball (34)
Foul ball (35)
Strike three (called) (36)

Pat Meares:
Strike one (called) (37)
Strike two (swinging) (38)
Ball one (39)
Ball two (40)
Strike three (swinging) (41)

FOURTH INNING

Matt Lawton:
Ball one (42)
Ball two (43)
Ball three (44)
Strike one (called) (45)
Grounded to SS Jeter to 1B Martinez (46)

Brent Gates:
Strike one (called) (47)
Strike two (called) (48)
Foul ball (49)
Foul ball (50)
Foul ball (51)
Strike three (swinging) (52)

Paul Molitor:
Strike one (foul ball) (53)
Strike two (swinging) (54)
Ball one (55)
Flied to leftfielder Chad Curtis (56)

FIFTH INNING

Marty Cordova:
Strike one (called) (57)
Strike two (foul ball) (58)
Strike three (called) (59)

Ron Coomer:
Strike one (called) (60)
Ball one (61)
Strike two (swinging) (62)
Strike three (swinging, dropped by catcher
Jorge Posada to first baseman Tino
Martinez) (63)

Alex Ochoa:
Ball one (64)
Ball two (65)
Strike one (called) (66)
Strike two (swinging) (67)
Grounded to 2B Knoblauch to 1B Martinez (68)

SIXTH INNING

Jon Shave:
Strike one (foul ball) (69)
Ball one (70)
Strike two (foul ball) (71)
Strike three (foul tip) (72)

Javier Valentin:
Ball one (73)
Strike one (swinging) (74)
Strike two (called) (75)
Strike three (called) (76)

Pat Meares:
Strike one (foul ball) (77)
Ball one (78)
Ball two (79)
Flied to centerfielder Williams (80)

SEVENTH INNING

Matt Lawton: Ball one (81)
                   Ball two (82)
                   Flied to centerfielder Williams (83)

Brent Gates: Ball one (84)
                   Strike one (swinging) (85)
                   Ball two (86)
                   Strike two (foul ball) (87)
                   Ball three (88)
                   Grounded to 1B Martinez (unassisted) (89)

Paul Molitor: Ball one (90)
                   Strike one (called) (91)
                   Ball two (92)
                   Ball three (93)
                   Strike two (called) (94)
                   Strike three (swinging) (95)

EIGHTH INNING

Marty Cordova: Ball one (96)
                   Strike one (foul ball) (97)
                   Ball two (98)
                   Grounded to SS Jeter to 1B Martinez (99)

Ron Coomer: Ball one (100)
                   Strike one (foul ball) (101)
                   Ball two (102)
                   Grounded to 2B Knoblauch, who
                   bobbled the ball briefly, to 1B Martinez (the
                   most challenging play of the game!) (103)

Alex Ochoa: Ball one (104)
                   Strike one (swinging) (105)
                   Ball two (106)
                   Flied to first baseman Martinez (107)

NINTH INNING

Jon Shave: Ball one (108)
                   Strike one (foul ball) (109)
                   Strike two (called) (110)
                   Foul ball (111)
                   Ball two (112)
                   Foul ball (113)
                   Flied to rightfielder Paul O'Neill (114)

Javier Valentin: Ball one (115)
                   Strike one (called) (116)
                   Strike two (foul ball) (117)
                   Strike three (foul tip) (118)

Pat Meares: Strike one (foul ball) (119),
                   Flied to rightfielder O'Neill to complete
                   the first REGULAR SEASON perfect game in
                   Yankee Stadium history on pitch #120!!

(NOTE: Pitch-by-pitch accounts of the perfect games by David Cone and Don Larson may be found on pages 55 and 129, respectively.)

4

THE MANAGERS

The great tactician Casey Stengel averaged 96 wins a season in 12 years at the Yankee helm.

The Yankees have been fortunate to have employed Miller Huggins, Joe McCarthy, and Casey Stengel, three of baseball's greatest managers, and some might add two others—Billy Martin and Joe Torre—to this list. It is the players, of course, who have the most to do with field success or failure, but managers still play key roles; roles that almost without exception are terminated by firing.

THE BOSSES ON THE FIELD

INTRODUCTION

To the youngster growing up in the 1930s, Joe McCarthy had always been, and always would be, the manager of the New York Yankees. Nothing else seemed quite so lasting. But, as the saying goes, managers are hired to be fired, especially since George Steinbrenner became the owner in 1973 and changed managers 20 times.

But even prior to Steinbrenner, Yankee managers usually departed unhappily. Miller Huggins died on the job. Probably only Art Fletcher left the position entirely of his own free will. The remainder were either discharged outright or resigned under pressure.

Getting along with the front office is a requirement of managerial security. Bucky Harris couldn't get along with General Manager George Weiss and was replaced by Casey Stengel, who enjoyed a fine relationship with Weiss. Billy Martin continually resisted front-office authority and even defied the owner—and Steinbrenner fired him five times.

Like Steinbrenner, the first Yankee owners, Frank Farrell and Bill Devery, fought with almost all their managers. As a consequence, six managerial changes were made over the turbulent years from 1903 to 1914.

Jake Ruppert, club owner from 1915 to 1939, was one of the most patient employers. He had only five managers and was unhappy with only his first, Wild Bill Donovan. Ruppert replaced Donovan with Miller Huggins, and he would support Huggins in the face of the outright hostility shown toward Huggins by Ruppert's partner, Til Huston.

Following Huggins' death in 1929, it was Ruppert's hope that Art Fletcher, serving as interim manager, would occupy the managing position permanently. But Fletcher preferred his former coaching job, and a shocked Ruppert allowed him to be a coach instead. Bob Shawkey managed in 1930, and then Joe McCarthy became available. McCarthy became manager despite Babe Ruth's strong campaign for the job.

McCarthy and General Manager Ed Barrow were a perfect fit for each other. They had the solid support of Ruppert, and they settled into an efficient long-term period of tranquility and championships.

Then came 1945, and the arrival of Larry MacPhail as part owner, president, and general manager of the Yankees. It was the dawn of turmoil.

The following year, 1946, for the first time, the Yankees used three managers in one season—McCarthy, Bill Dickey, and Johnny Neun. McCarthy, it was quickly apparent, was not a

perfect fit with MacPhail. Bucky Harris, on the other hand, worked well with MacPhail and won the World Series in 1947.

Then MacPhail suddenly left the club, and co-owners Dan Topping and Del Webb delegated the managing matter to General Manager George Weiss. Weiss was frustrated with Harris in 1948 and replaced him with Casey Stengel in 1949. There could not have been two more dissimilar personalities than Weiss and Stengel, yet they worked together beautifully, orchestrating Yankee success after success.

Weiss and Stengel were fired after the 1960 World Series, as Topping turned to his man, Ralph Houk, to replace Stengel. It was no secret that Houk had Topping's ear on all Yankee matters. Houk won three straight pennants, and in 1964 he became General Manager and named Yogi Berra manager. Yogi, however, was undermined by Houk. Somehow Yogi rallied his players to win the pennant and barely lost a seven-game World Series to the Cardinals.

Everyone was shocked with what happened following the 1964 World Series. Berra was fired, and in his place the Yankees hired Johnny Keane, who had just beaten them as manager of the Cardinals. Keane turned out to be a poor match for the Yankees, and in 1966 Houk returned to the dugout to run the team. Houk was the first to have two separate stints as the Yankee manager. He had good working relationships with Lee MacPhail and Mike Burke, his front-office bosses, and serenity ruled. But it wasn't forever.

In January of 1973, George Steinbrenner became the principal owner of the Yankees, and the days of serenity and job security were over. The Billy Martin terms are known as I through V as an amusing accommodation to history. But Bob Lemon, Gene Michael, and Lou Piniella each had two shots at managing the Yankees, too. Not many managers actually got fired in the old-fashioned sense; they were usually assigned elsewhere in the organization.

It is interesting to note that Steinbrenner has slowed up his firing pace, and that the Yankees have been relatively stable since 1991. There have been only three managerial changes in the decade; the second, the October 1991 hiring of Buck Showalter seemed fruitful, as Showalter and General Manager Gene Michael led the Yankees back into baseball's upper echelon. They both departed, however, soon after the Yankees lost in the playoffs in 1995.

Some great baseball men have managed the Yankees. Thirty-one in all. Nine are in the Baseball Hall of Fame. What follows is an up-close look at all of them.

Yet, it is notable that the most successful Yankee managers had excellent relations with the front office. Huggins got along well with Ruppert and Barrow (though he was in conflict with Huston), as did McCarthy. Stengel was in complete harmony with Weiss. Houk was given a free hand, first by Topping and later by Burke.

What is even more impressive is the number of managers who have bitten the dust in spite of field successes. Harris, Stengel, Berra, Martin, Dick Howser, and Gene Michael were all winners (the first four won pennants, Howser a division title, and Michael had the Yanks in first at the end of 1981's First Season—Remember, '81 had a split season due to a strike) only to be separated from their jobs, and in each case-management owner problems were to blame. Winning is not necessarily everything, as Howser learned in 1980, when after winning 103 games he elected to resign because of difficulties with Steinbrenner. Even the great McCarthy resigned in part because of difficulties with Larry MacPhail.

While the firings of Berra and Stengel may have been singularly unjust and unfeeling, none of the long list of Yankee skippers ever has been more shabbily treated than Shawkey, who had no idea he was being let go the day he arrived at the Stadium to encounter a commotion over Joe McCarthy—the new manager.

Who were these 31 men who had the temerity to take the reins of the dynamic Yankees? From where did they come?

They were, for the most part, Anglo-Americans who came from America's heartland. None have been black. Elston Howard dearly wanted to manage the Yankees, and as a valued member of the Yankee organization one day might have had a shot at the job but for his untimely death in 1980. In 1995, Willie Randolph was mentioned as the replacement for Buck Showalter before Joe Torre was hired. Wild Bill Donovan and Joe McCarthy were Irish, Yogi Berra and Billy Martin Italian, and Casey Stengel and Ralph Houk German, but by and large New York's skippers fell outside any "ethnic" designation.

Twelve of the Yankee helmsmen were born in the interior states: Ohio (the most with five), Missouri (four), Illinois (one), Kansas (one), and Michigan (one). Eight were native to the Northeast: Pennsylvania (two), New York (two), Maryland (one), Delaware (one), Massachusetts (one), and Maine (one). Seven were born in the South: Florida (three), Georgia (one), Louisiana (one), and North Carolina (one). Moving West, there were no managers from Kansas to the Pacific Ocean, North to South, except for California, which numbered four. Not a single Yankees manager had come from the New York Metropolitan area until the arrival of Joe Torre, a Brooklyn native.

The three managers who lasted the longest with the club and who are generally considered the best, Miller Huggins, Joe McCarthy, and Casey Stengel, all hailed from large cities—Huggins from Cincinnati, McCarthy from Philadelphia, and Stengel from Kansas City, Mo. But with the exception of a handful of other managers from the larger cities (St. Louis, Baltimore, Miami) the typical New York skipper has been the product of a farm town in the Midwest, West, or South.

Seven of the first eight Yankees managers (George Stallings being the lone exception) were player-managers. Since their time, only Bill Dickey has served as an active player while managing the Yankees. All but four of the managers, McCarthy, Johnny Keane, Stump Merrill and Buck Showalter, played in at least one big-league game.

The 31 managers brought 31 personalities to the job. Some—Kid Elberfield and Billy Martin—were fiery; others—Miller Huggins and Joe McCarthy—exerted a more sober leadership. Easily the funniest were Casey Stengel and Yogi Berra, although Yogi as manager was less than his naturally humorous self, so intent was he on getting the 1964 Yanks untracked. Yogi was well liked by the press, but Donovan and Stengel were the most popular Yankees managers with the press. Bob Lemon and Dick Howser were regarded by the press as decent men; the New York Chapter of the Baseball Writers conferred on each its Ben Epstein "Good Guy" Award.

Bob Shawkey, Bill Dickey, Ralph Houk, Yogi Berra, Billy Martin, Dick Howser, and Gene Michael all wore pinstripes as ballplayers, too. Bucky Harris, Casey Stengel, Johnny Keane, Bill Virdon, and Bob Lemon were tough competitors against New York before joining the Yankees. Harris managed against the Bronx Bombers during his many years with Washington, Detroit, and Boston before taking over in New York. In 1924, his first season as a manager, the "Boy Wonder" led the Senators to a surprising pennant, edging the favored Yankees and breaking hearts in New York.

Stengel hit two memorable home runs as a Giant against the Yankees in the 1923 World Series; Keane beat the Yanks in the 1964 World Series as manager of the Cardinals; Virdon made two circus catches at critical times to help the Pirates defeat the Yankees in the 1960 World Series; and Lemon was a relentless rival of the Yanks while pitching in Cleveland from 1946 to 1958.

Many Yankees managers became fierce rivals of the Yanks after leaving New York. As owner of the Washington Senators, Clark Griffith struggled (mostly in vain) to compete with the Yankees. Frank Chance managed against the Yankees as ruler of Fenway Park in 1923. Roger Peckinpaugh fought bitterly against New York both as a player and manager after being traded from the Yanks. Joe McCarthy, as Beantown king from 1948 to 1950, warred against his old team as did Bucky Harris with Washington and Detroit during the 1950s. Stengel, Yogi Berra, Joe Torre and Dallas Green as managers of the New York Mets, waged a battle with the Yankees for the attention and affection of the media and fans of the New York area. Also, after managing the Yankees, Ralph Houk (Tigers and Red Sox), Billy Martin (A's), and Dick Howser (Royals) aimed to shoot down the Bronx Bombers, and Lou Piniella did as Seattle manager in the 1995 playoffs.

Nine of the 31 men who have managed the Yankees have plaques in their honor hanging in the Baseball Hall of Fame. But only three—Huggins, McCarthy, and Stengel—are in the Hall chiefly because of their Yankee managing. Clark Griffith, the first Yankees manager, made the Hall mainly because of his great pre-1900 pitching career and later years as a Washington Senators' owner. Frank Chance was inducted because of his playing and managing days with the Chicago Cubs. (His two years in New York, in fact, were disappointing.) Bill Dickey and Yogi Berra are Hall-of-Famers because of outstanding catching careers. Bucky Harris' Hall of Fame plaque cites his 40 years in the game, only two of which were with the Yankees. Bob Lemon is enshrined because of his tremendous Cleveland Indian pitching career. (Lemon is the only Yankees manager who was a Hall-of-Famer before piloting the club.)

What follows is an up-close look at the men who have led the Yanks on the field—an attempt to provide the baseball background, Yankees managerial history, and some of the managerial principles of each of the Yankees' skippers.

MANAGER PROFILES

GRIFFITH, CLARK

Nicknames: "The Old Fox" "Griff"
Manager: 1903-08
Born: November 20, 1869
Birthplace: Clear Creek, MO
Died: October 27, 1955

Clark Griffith, who would one day become the owner of the Washington Senators, was the first manager of the Yankees (Highlanders). Griffith had been a great pitcher. As a big-league rookie in 1891, he was a 20-game winner pitching in the American Association. Pitching for Hall of Famer Cap Anson's Chicago National League club between 1893-1900, Griffith won 20 or more games in six successive seasons (1894-99), winning more than 150 games for the Chicago club.

In 1901, Griffith jumped leagues in the "Windy City," joining up with the new league—the American League—created by Ban Johnson. "Griff" had a pair of successful years as the player- manager of the Chicago White Sox (he had a mound record of 24-7 in 1901), while at the same time developing a friendship with Johnson, the all-powerful ruler of the circuit. In 1902, John J. McGraw, manager of the American League's franchise in Baltimore, was under the impression that he would accompany the team to New York when Johnson shifted the franchise there. But Johnson and McGraw, two strong-willed men, had some run-ins concerning the league's umpiring, and their relationship became strained. Johnson respected Griffith, trusted him, and decided to reward "Griff" for getting the league a good start in Chicago by giving him the New York job. Word leaked out of Johnson's plan in the summer of 1902; McGraw quit Baltimore and went to New York to manage the Giants, his relationship with Johnson forever being an adversarial one.

It was as a player-manager that Clark joined the New York Highlanders in 1903. He faced a difficult task in attempting to gain a legion of fans. The New York Giants were an established team with established fans, and in his first full season as Giant Manager, McGraw brought home a team that had finished last in 1902 to a second-place National League standing. And the Giants had two exciting 30-game winners in Iron Man Joe McGinnity and the immortal Christy Mathewson. At the same time, the National Leaguers claimed that there was no room for another club in New York and declared war on the Highlanders.

Yet, in the face of all these odds, "Griff" and his team gave McGraw and his boys a run for the money. When Griffith left the Highlanders in 1908, American League baseball was solidly fixed in New York City, as the club was followed by a small but hard-core band of dedicated fans. And Griffith's Highlander teams had some field successes, most notably in the seasons of 1904 and 1906.

In only its second year of existence, Griffith's 1904 team nearly won the pennant, losing out to Boston on the final day of the season. After a less successful 1905 campaign, Griffith in 1906 led New York to another surprising second-place league ranking—only three games to the rear of the legendary "Hitless Wonders," the Chicago White Sox. The Highlanders dropped to fifth place in 1907 with Clark, in addition to running the club, continuing to do mound duty; he compiled a 31-23 pitching record from 1903-07.

Griffith's nickname, "The Old Fox" was attributable to such baseball tactics as used in a 1907 game with Chicago. The White Sox were leading 4-1 when it began to rain in the fifth inning, before the game had reached official length. Griffith put himself into the game as relief pitcher and in warming up, stalled unconscionably. A delay was called, but it lasted only 10 minutes. Yet skies still threatened and Griffith, having instructed his players to deliberately make errors, served up

YANKEE MANAGERS SINCE 1903

Clark Griffith	Bob Shawkey	Billy Martin
Kid Elberfeld	Joe McCarthy	Bob Lemon
George Stallings	Bill Dickey	Dick Howser
Hal Chase	Johnny Neun	Gene Michael
Harry Wolverton	Bucky Harris	Clyde King
Frank Chance	Casey Stengel	Lou Piniella
Roger Peckinpaugh	Ralph Houk	Dallas Green
Wild Bill Donovan	Yogi Berra	Bucky Dent
Miller Huggins	Johnny Keane	Stump Merrill
Art Fletcher	Bill Virdon	Buck Showalter
		Joe Torre

easy pitches. It got to the point where players were refusing to make putouts, specifically Hal Chase at first base. Finally Umpire John Sheridan ordered Chase to make a putout or face a Highlander forfeiture of the game. Griffith was forced to instruct his team to play the game the way Doubleday intended, and the White Sox were 8-1 winners when the game was called the following inning. Their pitcher, Ed Walsh, had a shortened no-hitter.

Griffith neglected to follow up on a tip in 1907. Had he been quicker to investigate a fast-balling youngster from out west whose talents were described to him in a letter from a traveling salesman, the course of baseball might have changed. Clark was interested in the "scouting report" but was slow-acting, while the Washington Senators were quick to sign the talented kid. That kid was Walter Johnson, the immortal pitcher who won more games against the Yankees (60) than anyone in history. Of course, Griffith benefited from his mistake when he later took control of the Senators.

The 1908 Highlanders began the season poorly, and on June 24, "The Old Fox" was released. The imprudence of the decision to let him go is suggested by a comparison of New York's standing and record at the time of the firing (sixth place, 24-32) with its ultimate position and post-Griffith record (last place, 27-71). The Highlanders had sunk so low that they missed seventh place by a full 17 games. As for Griffith, his career blossomed. He managed at Cincinnati (1909-11) before buying some stock in the Washington Senators at Ban Johnson's request. Clark managed the Senators for nine seasons (1912-20) and then became owner-president of the club, a position he held for 35 years (1920-55). Although he reigned over the only pennant-winning clubs in Washington history (1924, 1925, 1933), Clark toiled mostly unsuccessfully for years attempting to beat his former club, the Yankees. This was always difficult, especially in 1927. Griffith picked the 1927 Yankees as baseball's greatest team.

Clark Griffith, who died in 1955, is recognized as one of the great pioneers in professional baseball, as one of those who helped make the game an important American experience. He spent 67 years in the game after beginning his career in 1888 pitching for Bloomington. He died with his place in the Baseball Hall of Fame secure; he was inducted into the Hall in 1946.

YANKEE MANAGER RECORD FOR CLARK GRIFFITH

Years	Won	Lost	Percentage	Standing
1903	72	62	.537	4th
1904	92	59	.609	2nd
1905	71	78	.477	6th
1906	90	61	.596	2nd
1907	70	78	.473	5th
1908	24	32	.429	incomplete season
6 Yrs.	419	370	.531	0 pennants

ELBERFELD, KID

Nickname: "The Tabasco Kid"
Manager: 1908
Born: April 13, 1875
Birthplace: Pomeroy, OH
Died: January 13, 1944

Norm "Kid" Elberfeld was named interim manager of the Yankees (Highlanders) the day Clark Griffith was fired, June 24, 1908. "The Tabasco Kid" was the team's star shortstop, who this season was hobbled by injuries. The Yankees under Elberfeld were horrendous (27-71). He finished out the year but was not rehired to manage for 1909, although he did return to the team as a player.

YANKEE MANAGER RECORD FOR KID ELBERFELD

Years	Won	Lost	Percentage	Standing
1908	27	71	.276	incomplete season
1 Yr.	27	71	.276	0 pennants

STALLINGS, GEORGE

Nickname: "The Miracle Man"
Manager: 1909-10
Born: November 17, 1867
Birthplace: Augusta, GA
Died: May 13, 1929

George Stallings took over as Yankees (Highlander) manager with the start of the 1909 season. The Yankees took a gamble on Stallings, a fringe ballplayer in the 1890s for the National League Brooklyn and Philadelphia clubs (he played in just seven big league games), and a short-term skipper with the Philadelphia Phillies (1897-98) and Detroit Tigers (1901). It was with the inept 1898 Phillies that George is said to have coined the term "bonehead," a term he probably had occasion to use with the 1909 Yankees, although he improved the club's American League standing from eighth to fifth.

The 1910 season should have been a rewarding experience for Stallings. He had the team playing excellent ball; the Yankees were in second place, although they were 15 games behind the strong Philadelphia A's. Yet, after losing to the Cleveland Indians on September 23, Stallings, disturbed by front office interference, resigned. It was his star player, Hal Chase, who cost Stallings his job.

Stallings was the first baseball person of importance to accuse Chase of throwing games for gambling purposes. American League President Ban Johnson did not appreciate George's frank comments about one of his league's best drawing cards, and while he never launched an investigation of Chase, Johnson saw fit to blast Stallings. Chase and Stallings never got along, and after a mid-season 1910 game in St. Louis, the Yankees pilot openly charged Hal with trying to throw the game. As Chase remained in Stallings' doghouse, the tension mounted. On September 20, *The New York Times* reported that if Chase remained a Yankee, Stallings planned to quit. The situation was brought to a head when owner-president Frank Farrell recalled George from a road trip to question him about the Chase allegations. But Farrell, like Ban Johnson, was on

Chase's side, and the forced resignation of Stallings resulted. And it was Chase who replaced Stallings as manager!

Besides the Chase episode, Stallings is associated with coarseness, resourcefulness, and a superstitious nature. He has been depicted in one report as a vulgar-tongued, contentious bully. He is also portrayed as exceptionally resourceful. He rented an apartment near Hilltop Park's outfield fence and there kept a spy who was equipped with field glasses. The spy would pick up signals and, using a mirror, would let Yankee hitters know what to expect. This advantage was discovered in time and Stallings was forced to reposition the signaling spy in an outfield fence billboard that advertised a whiskey. His superstitious side was exemplified by his firm belief that loose paper in the dugout was a bad omen. Whenever a piece of harmless paper floated to the dugout, the ballplayers would watch with amusement as Stallings seethed.

Leaving the Yankees was the best thing that ever happened to George Stallings. He managed the Boston Braves for eight campaigns (1913-20) and gained undying fame as skipper of the 1914 Miracle Braves, a team that made up a 14-game deficit to win the National League title and then swept the favored Athletics in the World Series. The imaginative leadership of Stallings is generally credited with making the miracle happen: hence Stallings received the title, "The Miracle Man."

During the 1920s, "The Miracle Man" was a minor league manager. It was widely rumored in June of 1925 that Stallings, then managing Rochester of the International League, would be named to replace Miller Huggins as Yankees manager. The rumor was unfounded, and less than four years later, George Stallings died at the age of 61.

Smiling Skipper—In two years of managing the Highlanders, George Stallings improved the team's AL standing from eighth to second. But he was forced to resign in September of 1910 when club brass would not back him in George's battle with star player Hal Chase. (New York Yankees Archives)

YANKEE MANAGER RECORD FOR GEORGE STALLINGS				
Years	Won	Lost	Percentage	Standing
1909	74	77	.490	5th
1910	79	61	.564	incomplete season
2 Yrs.	153	138	.526	0 pennants

CHASE, HAL

Nickname: "Prince Hal"
Manager: 1910-11
Born: February 13, 1883
Birthplace: Los Gatos, CA
Died: May 18, 1947

It was September 24, the day after the abrupt and forced resignation of Manager George Stallings with only two weeks remaining in the 1910 season, that Hal Chase was named Yankees manager. Chase, the team's star first baseman, was the victor, and Stallings, who made the first strong allegations that "Prince Hal" was throwing games, was the loser. Not only were Stallings' charges ignored by league and club officials, but he was chastised for making them.

Reportedly, Chase had wanted to be manager since Clark Griffith departed. Some of those close to the scene believed Hal sabotaged Stallings and positioned himself for the job. New York finished the 1910 season strongly under Chase (9-2) and he was made player-manager for 1911. The deal he got was more than fair; it was lucrative. Yankees owners Farrell and Devery

agreed to pay Hal $6000, making him probably the highest paid player in the league.

But the 1911 season was an unhappy one, with the New Yorkers dropping to sixth place (after finishing second in 1910) with a record of 76-76. As a player Chase had one of his best years at the plate (.315), but led league first basemen in errors (36), an unexpected statistic for one of the smoothest fielders of all time. On November 21, 1911, "Prince Hal" stepped down as manager and returned in the role of player only for the 1912 season.

YANKEE MANAGER RECORD FOR HAL CHASE				
Years	Won	Lost	Percentage	Standing
1910	9	2	.818	incomplete season
1911	76	76	.500	6th
2 Yrs.	85	78	.521	0 pennants

WOLVERTON, HARRY

Manager: 1912
Born: December 6, 1873
Birthplace: Mt. Vernon, OH
Died: February 4, 1937

Harry Wolverton had the misfortune of managing the 1912 Yankees (50-102), the worst team in Yankees history. So poor was this team that it sank below the inept St. Louis Browns, claiming exclusive occupancy of the American League basement. Wolverton's lack of success as a helmsman contrasted sharply with his playing career. He was a fine third baseman, working for four different major league clubs (1898-1905), and in three campaigns hitting better than .300. He was still an able batter in 1912; the New York manager sent himself to the plate 50 times and hit well, particularly when in the role of a pinchhitter (.385—10 for 26). Quite impressive for a 38-year-old who in seven years had not swung a bat at big-league pitching! But Wolverton could not make winners of his charges and was let go after the 1912 season had run its painful course. It was Wolverton's only season as a major league manager.

YANKEE MANAGER RECORD FOR HARRY WOVERTON				
Years	Won	Lost	Percentage	Standing
1912	50	102	.329	8th
1 Yr.	50	102	.329	0 pennants

CHANCE, FRANK

Nicknames: "Husk" "The Peerless Leader"
Manager: 1913-14
Born: September 9, 1877
Birthplace: Fresno, CA
Died: September 14, 1924

Frank Chance's service as manager of the New York Yankees contributed little to his 1946 induction into the Baseball Hall of Fame. He was inducted because of his .297 lifetime batting average compiled over 17 major-league seasons between 1898-1914 (15 of them with the Chicago Cubs), because he was the first base anchor in the Cubs' famed Tinker-to-Evers-to-Chance double-play aggregation, and because of his managerial tenure in Chicago, where in one five-year stretch, he led the Cubs to four National League pennants (1906, '07, '08, '10). In 1906 the Cubs were victorious in 116 games, the most in big-league history.

His induction into the Hall of Fame was actually in spite of his role with the Yankees, which began amid great hope and excitement, for Frank Chance was one of the respected men in baseball in the dawning years of the 20th century. To Yankees owners Frank Farrell and Bill Devery, the January 8, 1913 signing of Chance was a real coup. Indeed, it had been Chance's intention to retire from baseball to his California orange grove after severing connections with the Cubs following the 1912 season. But the Yankees made Frank a tremendously lucrative offer, a three-year contract reportedly close to $40,000 a year. How could Chance refuse? The Yankees owners believed Chance was the latest answer to the Giants' popular skipper, John J. McGraw. After all, Chance had as many sportswriter friends in New York City as did McGraw, and Chance's name was readily recognizable with the fans.

As a ballplayer, "The Peerless Leader" was tough as nails. He was one of the first to use a plastic plate insert in his baseball cap when batting. And he was wise to do so because rival pitchers so often succeeded in aiming at his head that many believe Chance died prematurely (at 47) as a result of all the beanings he experienced. Frank was a fierce competitor, displaying a self-confident sneer on the playing field, and he was just as tough as a manager. He was a fighter all right, but one widely respected for his fairness and fair play. And Chance

was a natural leader, a quality he displayed when he played baseball at the University of Washington. There he was a catcher and nicknamed "Husk" because of his large physique.

One of Chance's best managerial qualities was his ability to get his ballplayers to play over their heads—he got the most out of his team. His fighting spirit was mirrored by his teams. Umpires were baited, and tricks were used. One of "Husk's" favorite maneuvers was delaying a game so his beleaguered pitcher could regain his poise.

Unfortunately, "The Peerless Leader" was saddled with a 1913 Yankees team so inferior that his managerial skills could not drive it above seventh place. The dismal performance continued in 1914 and on September 15, with the Yankees lagging in sixth place, Chance resigned. Thus was brought to a close what was, perhaps, an impossible situation for Chance. He was convinced that first baseman Hal Chase was throwing games, and in 1913 Chase, the Yanks' best player, was dealt to the White Sox. Chance was rid of a problem but was left with a damaged relationship with the club's owners and an unfortunate residual effect of the Chase departure. His club was now weaker than ever. Chance's own efforts to help the 1913 team at the plate were not up to his usual standards (5 for 24, .208).

Chance returned to baseball in 1916 as the owner-manager of the Los Angeles club in the Pacific Coast League. After two years there, he again dropped out of baseball only to return for a one-year stint as manager of the Boston Red Sox in 1923. He died the following year.

YANKEE MANAGER RECORD FOR FRANK CHANCE				
Years	Won	Lost	Percentage	Standing
1913	57	94	.377	7th
1914	60	74	.448	incomplete season
2 Yrs.	117	168	.411	0 pennants

PECKINPAUGH, ROGER

Manager: 1914
Born: February 5, 1891
Birthplace: Wooster, OH
Died: November 17, 1977

Roger Peckinpaugh took over as Yankees manager on September 16, 1914, succeeding the released Frank Chance. For the remainder of the season, the team won ten and lost ten under the 23-year-old Peckinpaugh, who was a natural leader. But Peckinpaugh was not named manager for the 1915 season. Jacob Ruppert and Til Huston, having acquired the Yankees in January of 1915, had their own ideas on who should lead the team, and Peckinpaugh was returned to his shortstop position. Thus ended the brief reign of the youngest manager in Major League history. But it was not before Peckinpaugh gained an experience that would stand him in good stead later. For after his retirement as a player, he would manage the Cleveland Indians for seven seasons (1928-33, 1941).

YANKEE MANAGER RECORD FOR ROGER PECKINPAUGH				
Years	Won	Lost	Percentage	Standing
1914	10	10	.500	incomplete season
1 Yr.	10	10	.500	0 pennants

DONOVAN, WILD BILL

Manager: 1915-17
Born: October 13, 1876
Birthplace: Lawrence, MA
Died: December 9, 1923

Jake Ruppert and Til Huston began their search for a new Yankees manager with their purchase of the club in January 1915. As always, the problem was to find a name and personality that would give the Giants' John J. McGraw some competition. The search led to Wild Bill Donovan.

Wild Bill had an outstanding reputation in baseball. In his major-league pitching career, which began in 1898, he had 187 wins and 139 losses. He pitched in the National League for Washington (1898) and Brooklyn (1899-1902) and in the American League for Detroit (1903-12, 1918) and New York (1915-16). Wild Bill was 25-15 in 1901 and 25-4 in 1907, his two best seasons. Although Donovan was only 1-4 over the World Series of 1907, 1908, and 1909, pitching for the Tigers, he completed five of his six starts. His greatest Series game was Game 1 in 1907 when he went the full 12 innings and fanned 12 Cubs, only to settle for a 3-3 tie. The Tigers failed to score as Wild Bill lost the final game of both the 1908 and 1909 Series.

Donovan was probably the best base-stealing pitcher the majors ever saw. He stole the most bases (36), stole the only base in World Series history by a pitcher (in 1908), twice stole home plate, and after singling in a May 1906 game stole second, third and then home!

Wild Bill managed Providence of the International League in 1913 and 1914. One of his star pitchers in 1914 was none other than Babe Ruth. The two developed a warm relationship, and Donovan is given some credit for Ruth's maturation as a ballplayer. In fact, the Yankees owners were attracted by Donovan's reputation as a teacher and motivator of young players.

As a manager in the majors, Donovan's rookie year of 1915 was unimpressive, the Yanks finishing fifth. They did a little better in 1916, coming in fourth, but fell back to sixth in 1917. Still, the makings of a good club (Pipp, Peckinpaugh, Baker, Shawkey, Caldwell, Mogridge, Shocker) were there and Donovan, at the helm longer than anyone since Griffith, lent badly needed continuity and stability. All the same, the impatient owners after the 1917 season fired Donovan, who was an extremely popular figure in New York. The firing did not sit well with the press.

Wild Bill, who made 10 pitching appearances and recorded a 0-3 mark while managing New York, returned to pitching in 1918. (He was 1-0 in two games for Detroit at the age of 41.) In 1919 and 1920, he managed Jersey City of the International League, before taking the helm of the Philadelphia Phillies for the first half of the 1921 season. In 1922 Wild Bill led George Weiss' New Haven club to the Eastern League championship. He also managed New Haven in 1923. The following December Wild Bill Donovan died in Forsyth, N.Y., at the age of 47.

YANKEE MANAGER RECORD FOR WILD BILL DONAVAN				
Years	Won	Lost	Percentage	Standing
1915	69	83	.454	5th
1916	80	74	.519	4th
1917	71	82	.464	6th
3 Yrs.	220	239	.479	0 pennants

HUGGINS, MILLER

Nicknames: "Hug", "The Mighty Mite", "The Lawyer",
       "Little Mr. Everywhere", "Rabbit"
Manager: 1918-29
Born: March 27, 1879
Birthplace: Cincinnati, OH
Died: September 25, 1929

Miller Huggins was the first of the great Yankees managers. He came to New York in 1918 after five seasons in St. Louis as manager of the Cardinals. Thus, Huggins was a well-known baseball figure when he joined the Yankees.

In 1899 Huggins began a minor-league playing career that included three years at St. Paul (1901-03) where he hit better than .300 in each season. He joined his hometown team, the Cincinnati Reds, in 1904, and performed as a fine second baseman for the Reds (1904-09), not only as a sensational defensive player but also as a fine leadoff hitter. In a seven-inning game in 1904 he hit three triples. Earning nicknames such as "Little Mr. Everywhere" and "Rabbit," Huggins was recognized as an outstanding baserunner, and an innovative one, too. He was one of the first to use and perfect the delayed steal. Miller crouched at the plate, shortening his already small strike zone, and thus drew many walks. After leaving the Reds, Miller played for St. Louis (1910-16) and became the Cardinals' player-manager in 1913, a year St. Louis finished in the National League cellar. But the next year, with Huggins beautifully orchestrating the league's best pitching staff, the Cardinals jumped up to third place. A couple of mediocre seasons passed, and in 1917 "Hug" again brought St. Louis up to third place. One reason for the renewed success of the Cardinals was the rapid development of infielder Rogers Hornsby, an unlikely prospect whose mercurial rise to stardom Hornsby later acknowledged was largely due to Huggins' guidance.

Meanwhile, the Yankees owners Jake Ruppert and Til Huston were looking for a new manager for the 1918 season and consulted American League President Ban Johnson who suggested that they hire Miller Huggins away from the Cardinals and the National League (taking from the Nationals was an ingrained inclination with Johnson). Huston wanted to hire Wilbert Robinson, the popular and rotund character who in 1917 completed the fourth of his 18 seasons as manager of the Brooklyn Dodgers. But Ruppert felt "Uncle Robbie" was too old at age 50. On the other hand, he was not enthusiastic about Huggins whose dress and manner suggested the embodiment of the dingier aspects of the lowly working class. When Jake met Miller, however, he came away convinced of Huggins' baseball genius. Because of this favorable impression and the great respect Jake at this time had for Johnson's opinion, and in the absence of Huston who had been taken to France by World War I, Ruppert went ahead and offered Huggins the Yankees job. However, it was not easy to convince Miller to take the job of running one of baseball's most mediocre franchises. In fact, when Huggins was approached by the Yankees about the job, he was in New York representing St. Louis at the National League meeting, and he told the Yankees he felt their position would be a step down for him. Huggins was not interested. But Ban Johnson, a most determined man once he set his sights, badly wanted Huggins in New York working as the antithesis of the loud Giant manager hero, John

Miller Huggins on October 2, 1928. The manager of the New York Yankees (1918-29) guided them to six AL pennants and three World Series titles. Elected to the Hall of Fame, 1964.(AP/WIDE WORLD PHOTOS)

McGraw. So Johnson pulled some strings. J.G. Taylor Spink, publisher of *The Sporting News,* urged his good friend Huggins to give the Yankees a chance and negotiate with Ruppert. Apparently Miller, after meeting with the Yankees owner, was impressed with Ruppert's presentation, dedication, and desire to transform the Yankees into a championship team, and on October 26, 1917, Miller Huggins signed a two-year contract to manage the Yankees. The New York press was instantly at odds with Huggins because he took the job away from the popular Wild Bill Donovan. But Miller was not bothered by the bad press and anti-Huggins feelings that he experienced during his first three Yankee seasons (1918-20). It was not until Huggins was a proven winner with three straight pennants in the bag (1921-23) and a World Championship (1923) that the press and some of the public changed their attitude about Huggins' being an inferior leader. By the late 1920s, Huggins enjoyed a good press and had a special place in the public's heart.

In Miller Huggins, the Yankees had a law school graduate from the University of Cincinnati (Miller studied law during his off-seasons as a player and was admitted to the bar), a brilliant baseball mind, and a tough but fair man. He was a plain man to be sure, but a levelheaded person who possessed a great amount of common sense. He was smart in his judgments of players as talents and men. Grantland Rice felt that Miller handled a pitching staff better than any manager he ever encountered. But perhaps more importantly, Huggins was similar to Vince Lombardi in this respect—each player who ever had an association with Miller learned something about life from the little big man. Not that Miller's talents were conspicuous or that he was a fountain of charisma. He was consigned to the shadows of his more famous players (at least in the public eye) and the other manager in town, the heralded McGraw. Miller once said, "McGraw and I could enter a crowded room at the same time and be introduced—and in two minutes the crowd would be all around McGraw and nobody would even remember I was there." But Huggins knew baseball, loved the game, and was an ethical man.

Yet, there was another side of Miller Huggins that disturbed some of his players. Besides being tough but fair, Miller could be stubborn and often was irritable. Some of Huggins' grumpiness can be attributed to the many medical problems "The Mighty Mite" experienced in his lifetime. He had chronic neuritis, bad nerves, dental troubles, sinus headaches, and often suffered from indigestion. Still, it is possible that Miller was too overbearing with his talented, free-spirited ballplayers. He tried to keep a tight hold on the reins, possibly imposing an excess of discipline. At spring training camps, "Hug" stayed angry as he watched his ballplayers party whenever the chance presented itself. Some Yankees felt Miller was mean, cold, and selfish, but it must be remembered that it was a two-way street and many ballplayers brought trouble on themselves.

Miller's life with the Yankees was as laden with conflict as it was rich in glory. And yet he was such a little man, standing only 5'6" and weighing a mere 140 lbs. "The skinny little scrap of a fellow," said Gerald Holland, "who did not seem to be able to find a uniform small enough to fit him..." Miller could be tough. His confrontations with the great Ruth are legendary. He had the courage to impose discipline and he had the respect of most of his players. But he was, all the same, so slight a man, and the Yankees were, to be sure, well stocked with rowdies, and the mixture inevitably bred disciplinary problems, especially in the early years of Hug's regime. Ruth and Meusel in particular would show disdain for Huggins to his face. The 1922 season was

especially turbulent, the Yanks having weekly fights among themselves, often right on the bench. These Yankees teams of the early 1920s were some of the drinkingest teams in baseball history, and this contributed to the problem. (Himself a nondrinker, "Hug" did get drunk on whiskey—and lost his false teeth—in the train celebration after the 1928 World Series triumph.) Miller once remarked, "I wouldn't go through the years from 1919 to 1923 again for all the money in the world." (Besides unruly players, Yankee Owner Til Huston was riding Huggins' back.) The Yankees manager rarely called clubhouse meetings to iron out problems (possibly a blessing), and some of his quarrels with players demonstrated childishness on both sides. But it was the $5000 fine and indefinite suspension Huggins hung on Ruth in 1925 that established Huggins as a man in control of his charges. "Hug" won the battle with Ruth with the support of Ruppert and General Manager Ed Barrow, and his final four Yankee seasons went relatively smoothly.

Of all the wild and crazy Yankees of the Roaring 20s, four were particularly disruptive to the serenity of Miller Huggins— Babe Ruth, Bob Meusel, Carl Mays, and Bullet Joe Bush. Huggins enjoyed the Babe's flamboyance as much as anyone and really liked Ruth, respecting him as a person and a baseball player. He just could not tolerate Ruth's endless night life and sporadic disobedience. After the 1925 incident, however, relations between Ruth and Huggins improved decisively. Miller's problems with Meusel stemmed from his belief that the outfielder was an underachiever lost in the bowels of indifference.

Besides, Meusel did whatever Ruth did, so trouble occasionally found him. But Huggins never held anything against Meusel who, indifferent or not, was a truly fine ballplayer. Meusel sometimes argued with Huggins, but "The Lawyer" held few grudges against those who argued with him. (In a heated moment late in the 1920 campaign, outfielder Sammy Vick punched Miller, but the next day Miller told the apprehensive Vick that he liked Vick's spirit.)

In fact, the only two ballplayers that the decent and kindhearted Huggins disliked were pitchers Mays and Bush. Mays disobeyed Huggins at a key moment of the 1921 World Series and the two were cast at odds. In 1923 Mays saw limited action (81 innings) and complained until Huggins started him in a game against Cleveland. The Indians rocked Mays, knocking in 13 runs on 20 hits, but Huggins made Mays pitch the entire nine innings. Joe Bush cursed Huggins from the mound during the 1922 World Series; it was an outrageous display and one of several times he rebelled against Huggins' authority, and the Yankees manager never forgave him. Of all the wild Yankees of the 1920s, only Mays and Bush remained permanently in Huggins' doghouse.

There were actually two Yankee dynasties during the Miller Huggins years. In each of the first three seasons under his leadership, the Yanks improved in the standings—from sixth in 1917 (the year before Huggins arrived) to fourth in 1918 to third in 1919 and 1920. Of course the club was greatly strengthened in 1920 with the purchase from Boston of Babe Ruth, and the Yankees glory years began in 1921 when Huggins won the first American League pennant in Yankees history. The Yankees won another pennant in 1922, and in 1923 the club copped their first World Championship.

A couple of years of disappointment followed. In 1924, the Yanks finished in second place, but only two games behind the Washington Senators. The 1925 season was a disaster. Miller should have known that when he was jailed in Daytona, FL, during spring training. He was charged with hotel burglary and held for eight hours before he finally proved he was the Yankees manager. Huggins entered the 1925 season confident the Yanks would win the pennant, but the Yanks finished in seventh place with a dismal 69-85 record. Miller fought with the Babe all year, and during an August western road trip, "Hug" had a detective follow Ruth in Chicago and St. Louis. A tremendous fine and suspension followed. But Ruth was not the only Yankees player in Huggins' disfavor. Many played lazily and felt antagonistic toward the skipper, and others were simply well past their prime. After the season, Huggins unloaded the undesirables and malcontents (excepting Ruth of course). The Yankees organization made some excellent personnel decisions, and Huggins embarked on his second string of successes in 1926.

Although given virtually no chance to win the flag in 1926, Miller's Yankees finished first and pushed the Cardinals to seven games in the World Series before losing. The 1927 Yankees, baseball's most famous team, were incredible, posting a record of 110-44. In the consecutive World Series of 1927 and 1928, the "Hugmen" swept the Pirates and Cardinals respectively in four straight games. Six league pennants and three World Championships during the 1920s gave the name of Miller Huggins well-earned respect.

Miller Huggins was more than just a manager to the Yankees. In the final months of 1919, Miller strongly urged Jake Ruppert and Til Huston to purchase Babe Ruth when that possibility became known. Immediately after the Yanks obtained Ruth, Huggins journeyed to California and met with the vacationing Babe. Salary was discussed and Miller laid down some rules of conduct for Ruth. "Hug" was correctly convinced that Babe would turn the Yankees into a great team.

In the days of Huggins, the Yankees had a thin scouting staff, and Huggins journeyed the country in the off-season doubling as a scout. He was involved in the planning of Yankee trades and purchases, besides scanning the minor leagues for talent. Most of the young Yankee stars of the 1920s had been studied by Huggins before reaching the Yanks. Once these ballplayers donned the Yankees uniform, they received expert training from Miller, especially the infielders. When Tony Lazzeri joined the team in 1926, he was instructed by Huggins in the art of turning the double play.

Many changes were made to the Yankees from the time Huggins took over in 1918 to the Yanks' first pennant-victory of 1921. Only Roger Peckinpaugh, Wally Pipp, Aaron Ward, and Bob Shawkey lasted the four years of building. The checkbook of Ruppert and Huston, the front office brilliance of Barrow and the talent-discovering ability of head scout Paul Krichell were all instrumental in keeping the Yanks on top of the ladder during the 1920s. But besides managing the club, Huggins was a valuable complement to the front office and scouting team of Ruppert, Huston, Barrow, and Krichell. However, Huggins and Barrow did make mistakes concerning player personnel. Huggins played catcher Muddy Ruel sparingly and allowed him to be traded after the 1920 season. Ruel subsequently had some great years with the Boston Red Sox and Washington Senators. After making a critical error in the final game of the 1921 World Series, Peckinpaugh was traded by the Yanks to the Red Sox and then to the Senators where he enjoyed five splendid years including 1925 when he won the League Award (MVP). Pitcher Jack Quinn was also dealt to the Red Sox after the 1921 season at the age of 37 but the aging hurler pitched successfully in the big leagues for 12 more years. Huggins shipped the hated Carl

Mays to Cincinnati after the 1923 season, and the move may have cost the Yanks the 1924 pennant. Mays was 20-9 for the Reds in 1924, but it is impossible to predict what the temperamental star would have done in New York. (After all, Mays was 3-5 for the Reds in 1925.) These are some of the mistakes made by Huggins, and indeed Barrow. Successful the Yankee brass may have been; infallible they were not.

Miller Huggins ranks with Col. Jacob Ruppert, Edward Barrow and, of course, George Herman Ruth, as the most influential men in the building of the greatest dynasty in the story of baseball. Huggins enjoyed good working relationships with both Ruppert and Barrow. That was not the case with Til Huston, who criticized Miller whenever the opportunity presented itself. On the final Yankee western road trip of 1920, Huston told all who would listen that the pennant was being lost because Huggins had mismanaged his pitching staff (an ironic complaint considering Grantland Rice's comments on the subject). After the Yanks' humiliating 1922 World Series defeat, Huston told reporters, "Miller Huggins has managed the Yankees for the last time." But Ruppert and Barrow backed Huggins, and it was Huston who was soon to separate from the Yankees. Once Ruppert assumed complete ownership and control of the club in 1923, Miller's job was secure and everyone knew it, and Miller had more confidence in his authority over his ballplayers. He ran the club his way and his managing naturally improved. Only two Yankee managers, Joe McCarthy and Casey Stengel, have won more games as the team's skipper than Huggins' 1067 victories. Yet, critics of Miller's era claimed that Ruppert bought pennants for Huggins during the 1920s (sound familiar?). Sadly and unfairly, it was not until after Huggins' tragic death in 1929 that the talents of "The Mighty Mite" were fully appreciated.

The 1929 season was one of the saddest in Yankee history. "Hug" desperately wanted to become the first American League manager to win four pennants in a row, but he watched that goal slip away during a summer of lethargic Yankees baseball. Miller tried everything in an attempt to get the Yanks on track, including seldom-before-used clubhouse meetings, goadings, pleadings, and words of encouragement, but nothing awoke the overconfident team. Huggins believed the players had become fat cats, satisfied with their prior successes. As the Yanks continued to perform sluggishly, Huggins' unhappiness with the team's play increased and he was often ill, forcing him to miss a number of games. He had insomnia, other illnesses and reportedly was depressed about some bad advice he had given friends who lost money after buying land in Florida. Never a big eater, Miller's appetite vanished completely and he developed an ugly sore under one eye. Yankees coach and dear friend Art Fletcher insisted that Miller consult a doctor, but Huggins refused asking Fletcher, "Go to a doctor because I've got a red spot on my face? Me, who took the spikes of Frank Chance and Fred Clarke?" Following a game on September 20, 1929, Huggins made the short walk from Yankee Stadium to his nearby apartment. He felt terrible and a doctor was called. Although his sore was diagnosed merely as a carbuncle, Huggins was hospitalized at St. Vincent's. His temperature rose to 105°, he received daily blood transfusions and he made his will. On September 25, 1929, Miller Huggins died from erysipelas, a form of blood poisoning, at the age of 50. The Yankee players were informed of Huggins' death before a game in Boston, and several of them broke down and cried, including Ruth who the day before had publicly asked for prayers for the recovery of his manager. Said the Babe when told of the tragic news, "You know what I thought of Miller Huggins, and you know what I owe to him." Services were held in New York City on September 27 and Miller was buried in his hometown of Cincinnati on September 29.

Miller Huggins' funeral was one that touched all New Yorkers, and the pallbearers represented the best of the Yankees—loyal coaches Art Fletcher, Charley O'Leary and Bob Shawkey; and star players Babe Ruth, Lou Gehrig, Earle Combs, Herb Pennock and Tony Lazzeri. The New York Baseball Writers honored Miller by naming him winner of the William J. Slocum Award in 1929, the first year it was given. For several years following Huggins' death, a number of New York sportswriters made an annual trip to Cincinnati to place a wreath on Miller's grave. The Yankees honored the memory of Miller Huggins by placing a monument to him in center field of Yankee Stadium, holding the dedication ceremonies on May 30, 1932. It was the first monument, soon to be joined by monuments honoring Gehrig and Ruth. In 1964, Miller Huggins was paid the ultimate baseball tribute with his long overdue induction into the Baseball Hall of Fame. The day the Huggins plaque was hung in the Hall, another great Yankees manager, Joe McCarthy, said a few words in Miller's honor. Of Huggins, McCarthy stated, "This is the man who cut the Yankees' pennant pattern."

YANKEE MANAGER RECORD FOR MILLER HUGGINS

Years	Won	Lost	Percentage	Standing
1918	60	63	.488	4th
1919	80	59	.576	3rd
1920	95	59	.617	3rd
1921	98	55	.641	1st
1922	94	60	.610	1st
1923	98	54	.645	1st
1924	89	63	.586	2nd
1925	69	85	.448	7th
1926	91	63	.591	1st
1927	110	44	.714	1st
1928	101	53	.656	1st
1929	82	61	.573	incomplete season
12 Yrs.	1067	719	.597	6 pennants

World Series

Years	Outcome	Won	Lost	Opponent
1921	Lost	3	5	New York Giants
1922	Lost	0	4 (1 Tie)	New York Giants
1923	Won	4	2	New York Giants
1926	Lost	3	4	St. Louis Cardinals
1927	Won	4	0	Pittsburgh Pirates
1928	Won	4	0	St. Louis Cardinals
6 Yrs.	3-3	18	15 (1 Tie)	

FLETCHER, ART

Manager: 1929
Born: January 5, 1885
Birthplace: Collinsville, IL
Died: February 6, 1950

Art Fletcher assumed the managerial duties of the Yankees on September 20, 1929, following the hospitalization of Miller Huggins who died five days later. Fletcher had been a Yankees coach for three seasons and was well known in New York, having

been the Giants' shortstop from 1909 through 1919. He was the Giants' captain for part of that time, and in all he had 13 major league seasons under his belt as a player. He had a career average of .277 and was known as a fighting, competitive player on the field and a gentleman off. Art ranks 15th (141) on the All-Time hit-by-pitch list, leading the National League five times in that category (1913, 1914, 1916, 1917, 1918). He stayed in baseball after his playing days and managed the Philadelphia Phillies for four years before joining the Yanks in 1927. Fletcher took the Yankees through the last two difficult weeks of the 1929 season but refused to manage beyond that, turning down General Manager Barrow's offer of the job on a permanent basis. Fletcher insisted he wanted to remain a coach. Owner Jake Ruppert wanted Fletcher as his skipper and never could understand why Art would turn down the job. As a coach, Fletcher did outstanding work and remained in that position with the Yankees through the 1945 season. He functioned mostly in the third-base coaching box. He was Joe McCarthy's lieutenant for many years, and when McCarthy fell ill during the 1945 season, Art ran the team. He was valued for his knowledge of baseball in general and his understanding of the Yankees team in particular.

Art had great concentration and "X-ray" eyes. He was expert at picking up telling nuances in opposing pitchers' moves. Many Yankee players worked an arrangement with Fletcher in which he would relay the forthcoming pitch to the batter. He was reliable, probably the best ever at picking up signs. Many a Yankee homer was hit with knowledge of what pitch was coming, thanks to Art Fletcher. In 1957 *The Sporting News* polled a panel of experts to determine the 12 best sign-stealers since World War I, and Art naturally made the list.

YANKEE MANAGER RECORD FOR ART FLETCHER

Years	Won	Lost	Percentage	Standing
1929	6	5	.545	incomplete season
1 Yr.	6	5	.545	0 pennants

SHAWKEY, BOB

Manager: 1930
Born: December 4, 1890
Birthplace: Sigel, PA
Died: December 31, 1980

On October 23, 1929, Bob Shawkey was named manager of the Yankees, after an 18-year association with professional baseball. Shawkey was a fireman on the Pennsylvania Railroad before becoming a professional ballplayer in 1911. He joined the Philadelphia Athletics in 1913 and had a combined 30-19 record for the A's over three seasons, when in June of 1915 the A's sold Bob's contract to the Yankees. Between 1915-27, Shawkey posted a 168-131 Yankees record and proved himself one of the great pitchers in the club's history. After closing out his active career in 1927, Bob remained with the Yankees in 1928 and 1929 as pitching coach. Bob, in fact, was one of the first specialized pitching coaches in big league history. He also coached and managed in the minors, and when Art Fletcher declined to become manager for 1930, GM Ed Barrow offered the Yankees job to Shawkey, who accepted. However, Shawkey reportedly was not one of owner Jacob Ruppert's three top choices for manager.

The Yankees under Shawkey had an 86-68 record in 1930 and finished third in the American League, 16 games behind the powerful Philadelphia A's. Shawkey's crew was one of the hardest-hitting Yankee clubs ever, but the pitching staff was one of the poorest. But then there was that baseball they played with in 1930, probably the juiciest ever used. The team's third-place finish was in no way related to Shawkey's ability as manager—this team just had too many holes to win it all. Bob's relationship with his players was that of good buddy, and there were reports that some players abused his good nature. Shawkey denied any problems existed, and most players liked Bob. Babe Ruth was a close pal of Shawkey, a golfing buddy, and although he wanted the job of managing the Yanks himself, Ruth was not resentful of Shawkey. Because Shawkey did not overmanage, Yankee players were allowed to play their game naturally (Ruth was never given signals), and the result was an exciting team. Yankees home attendance in 1930 (1,169,230) was the highest since 1921 when the Yankees played in the Polo Grounds, and was the best Yankee Stadium attendance from the year it opened in 1923 until 1946. Interest was high in the Yankees, and most baseball people thought Shawkey did a creditable job with the material he had in 1930.

Yet Ruppert and Barrow found fault with Shawkey and jumped at the chance to hire Joe McCarthy after he was fired by the Cubs. In one of the most unethical moves the Yankee club ever made, McCarthy was hired to be Yankees manager before Shawkey was fired. Bob was naturally shocked to learn of the change when he came to Yankee Stadium and saw the commotion over the McCarthy signing.

It was an unbelievably shabby thing to do to a man who had been so loyal to the Yankee organization. Although he realized an injustice had been committed against him, Shawkey was too big a man to remain bitter. Until the day he died—December 31, 1980, New Year's Eve—Bob Shawkey, who lived to be 90, attended all Yankee events. He was a monument of unrequited loyalty. His importance to the game is documented by the fact that his obituary appeared in *Time* magazine, a general news publication.

Shawkey remained in baseball after being released by the Yankees. He managed at Jersey City (1931), Scranton (1932-33), and Newark (1934-35). Newark of the International League was then the Yanks' top farm club, and by giving Shawkey a job considered a most important one in the organization, the Yankees showed they thought highly of Bob despite the unpleasantness of his firing of 1930. Bob was away from the game until 1947 when he managed at Watertown. He also managed at Tallahassee in 1949. Shawkey pitched a little with Jersey City in 1931 (0-1) and Newark in 1934 (0-1).

YANKEE MANAGER RECORD FOR BOB SHAWKEY

Years	Won	Lost	Percentage	Standing
1930	86	68	.558	3rd
1 Yr.	86	68	.558	0 pennants

McCARTHY, JOE

Nicknames: "Marse Joe", "Pushbutton Joe"
Manager: 1931-46
Born: April 21, 1887
Birthplace: Philadelphia, PA
Died: January 13, 1978

Joe McCarthy became Yankees manager following the 1930 season, replacing Bob Shawkey who had been under the impression that his services would be continued. But when the Chicago Cubs fired McCarthy, Yankees General Manager Ed Barrow, long a McCarthy admirer, quickly signed him to a contract.

McCarthy is one of a relative few to manage in the major leagues without ever having played big-league ball; he spent 15 seasons as a minor-league player. (Joe's big-league success as a manager did much to change the attitude of baseball people that major-league playing experience was a necessary requirement to become a big-league skipper.) Beginning his minor-league career in 1907, Joe, who was a second baseman, third baseman and outfielder, played at Wilmington, Franklin, Toledo, Wilkes-Barre, Buffalo and Louisville. He hit better than .300 only twice, his best season being 1913 when he hit .325 for Wilkes-Barre of the New York State League where he served as player-manager. McCarthy managed again at Louisville of the American Association from 1919 through 1925, continuing also as a player the first three of those years before retiring as a player. As manager of Louisville, Joe won two pennants in seven seasons.

After paying his dues with a distinguished minor-league record, in 1926 McCarthy was selected to manage the Chicago Cubs. He proceeded to turn the cellar-dwelling Cubs of 1925 into a winning team. The Cubs finished fourth in 1926, fourth in 1927, third in 1928, and in 1929 Joe led the club to a National League pennant. However, the Cubs lost the 1929 World Series in five games to Connie Mack's Philadelphia Athletics in a Series made famous because of Game 4, when the A's overcame an 8-0 deficit with a ten-run seventh inning. Cub President William Veeck, Sr. blamed McCarthy for losing the Series, and Joe's Chicago days were numbered. Joe was not happy with the Cubs anyway. Veeck interfered in team matters, which were McCarthy's domain, and Joe was uneasy during the entire 1930 season. The Cubs dropped to second place in 1930 and McCarthy was released on September 24, four games before the end of the season. Cub owner William Wrigley said Joe lacked the ability to bring the desired World Championship to Chicago. The Boston Red Sox reportedly offered McCarthy their managerial post but "Marse Joe" declined. Ed Barrow also disagreed with the Cubs' opinion of McCarthy's abilities and the stage was set for McCarthy's Yankee employment. In mid-October of 1930, Joe McCarthy was hired as Yankees manager. Years later, his Yankee boss, Barrow, would term McCarthy the greatest manager in baseball history. Barrow is not alone in that judgment.

A difficult situation faced McCarthy in New York. Upon joining the Yankees, owner Jacob Ruppert told Joe, "I don't like finishing second, McCarthy." Replied Joe confidently, "Neither do I, Colonel." The Yankees were a veteran team, perhaps even over-aged at certain positions, and rather set in their ways. McCarthy was a strong, authoritative manager, and a conflict of egos threatened. Also, the rivalry between the American and National Leagues was intense, and McCarthy was naturally viewed as a National Leaguer. Among some Yankees, Joe McCarthy was resented as an interloper from the enemy league. Babe Ruth, Tony Lazzeri, and others were cool toward Joe at first.

With the cards stacked against him, Joe McCarthy won his biggest Yankee victory in the first months of his first Yankee season. Joe handled a sensitive situation with skill and earned the respect of his club. He won the respect and cooperation of most of the team's established stars—Lazzeri, Lou Gehrig, Earle Combs, and Herb Pennock. New stars such as Bill Dickey, Red Ruffing, and Lefty Gomez followed the older players' lead. Only one man was steadfast in his disdain for McCarthy, and that man was Ruth. The Babe, who wanted the manager's job for himself, was at first resentful of McCarthy and later openly critical of him. Ruth could not believe that McCarthy deserved to be Yankee manager since Joe had never played in the big leagues. In fact, Ruth had pitched to McCarthy in the International League and was not impressed with Joe's skills. That the great "Bambino" was passed over for the Yankee job for a two-bit bush leaguer was an insult the Babe could never accept.

McCarthy was well aware of Ruth's feelings and dealt with the four-year problem (1931-34) in the best way he could—he ignored the Babe as much as possible, refusing to make big waves out of little ones. Joe and Babe seldom saw each other off the playing field; each was jealous of the other, but McCarthy refused to allow their relationship to divide the team. Joe proved his diplomatic prowess in 1931 when he named Ruth the greatest ballplayer in baseball history in a poll conducted by the *Philadelphia Public Ledger*, although Joe was often heard to say he considered Frankie Frisch the best player he had ever seen. (Years later McCarthy would change his answer to Joe DiMaggio.) In the winter of 1934-35, when Ruth was campaigning to replace McCarthy, Joe offered to step down. But Barrow strongly supported McCarthy and would always choose Joe over Babe if a choice had to be made. And Jake Ruppert followed Barrow's advice.

From 1931-34, there were two sets of rules on Yankee clubs, one for Ruth and one for the other 24 players. That's the way it had always been and McCarthy accepted it, the players accepted it, and Ruth's big bat continued to produce. That situation changed after the Babe's Yankee departure. Stars received no special privileges from Joe, and men like Gehrig, DiMaggio, and Dickey did not ask for any. With the loss of Babe Ruth, McCarthy in 1935 assumed complete control over the Yankees. He became a better manager, much the way Miller Huggins improved once he was free of Til Huston. And the Yankees were a better team for it.

By 1931, most of the free-spirited players of the 1920s were gone, leaving behind a Yankee team that had a distinctively conservative air. Talented but troublesome personalities such as Johnny Allen and Ben Chapman eventually left the Yankees. (Both Allen and Chapman were Southerners and hot-tempered. Reportedly, McCarthy did not like Southern ballplayers because he felt their hot tempers hurt on-the-field performance. Yet, McCarthy was happy to have on his team such Hall of Fame Southerners as Earle Combs, Bill Dickey, and Joe Sewell as well as other fine players from Dixie. It is possible that McCarthy was not prejudiced against the South or its people, but just did not like hot-tempered players no matter where their roots.) Joe himself had a terrible temper, but he was wise enough to

control it on most occasions. Gehrig, Lazzeri, Combs, and Dickey, among others, were the kind of players McCarthy loved: superbly talented but undemonstrative men, serious in work and quiet in leisure. The public's image of the Yanks during the McCarthy era (1931-46) was one that mixed greatness with something akin to dignity (although some would replace "dignity" with "colorlessness"). To McCarthy's satisfaction, and due partly to his influence, the men who joined the Yankees during the 1930s were for the most part quiet and conservative: Frank Crosetti in 1932, Red Rolfe in 1934, and Joe DiMaggio and Jake Powell in 1936, among others. These were McCarthy's type, and relatively few were his personnel problems. As "Marse Joe" once said, "Give a boy a bat and a ball and a place to play, and you'll have a good citizen."

McCarthy wanted his ballplayers to be gentlemen. He wanted them to abide by moral codes, and he insisted that training rules be strictly adhered to. One of Joe's first acts as manager was to break the card table in the Yankee clubhouse. Explained Joe, "This is a clubhouse, not a clubroom, and I want players in here to think of baseball and nothing else." Shaving was not allowed in Joe's clubhouse, because that business was supposed to be taken care of before coming to work. McCarthy made sure a dress code was followed. The code required a dining player to wear jacket and tie. Joe did not conduct a bed check on the road, but players were expected in the dining room by 8:30 each morning when their condition would be observed by McCarthy as he peered from his morning newspaper. Joe frowned on hijinks and loud celebrations in public or for that matter even in the clubhouse, believing such histrionics to be "bush" or "college." To put it simply, Joe McCarthy expected his men to act like professionals at all times. He drove his teams hard and expected much from them. He was tough and firm, but not a tyrant. No one (excepting Ruth) was immune from discipline. (Grover Cleveland Alexander discovered that in 1926 with the Cubs. The winner of 373 big-league games broke training rules, and McCarthy traded him to St. Louis.)

Almost immediately, Joe McCarthy proved his worth to the Yankees. In only his second Yankee campaign, he won the 1932 American League pennant in a runaway, thus becoming the first manager in history to win pennants in both leagues (only Yogi Berra, Al Dark, Sparky Anderson, and Dick Williams have since duplicated the feat). In the 1932 World Series, the Yankees won four straight games from the Cubs, the team that two years earlier fired McCarthy, and Joe had sweet revenge. But the Yankees faced three years of frustration. The clubs of this period (1933-35) were excellent, and Joe enjoyed watching the emergence of Gehrig as the game's best player, but the Yankees finished a no-cigar second in each of these seasons. Sportswriters referred to McCarthy as "Second-Place Joe," an unflattering nickname that did not sit well with McCarthy.

Beginning in 1936, there followed a remarkable string of Yankee successes that established McCarthy as a great manager in everyone's eyes. The Yankees won a phenomenal seven American League pennants in eight years, losing out to Detroit in 1940. Perhaps even more impressive is the fact that of the seven World Series in which the Yankees were thus cast, New York won all but one, losing only to the St. Louis Cardinals in 1942. Under McCarthy, the Yankees won a then-record four straight World Championships (1936-39). In those four World Series, the Yankees lost a total of three games! These were probably the hardest-hitting clubs in history, a tribute to Joe's

Joe McCarthy: The manager with the highest winning percentage in baseball history

belief in the "power game" philosophy, an antithesis of John McGraw's "inside baseball." In 1941 and 1943, McCarthy's men easily won the World Series. His teams from 1941-43 were power-packed also, but McCarthy continued to win mainly because of his excellent and deep pitching staff. Joe won the World Championship in 1943, though many of his stars were called into military service. In all, McCarthy won eight league pennants and seven World Championships. His skein of six straight World Series triumphs in as many efforts (1932, 1936, 1937, 1938, 1939, 1941) has never been equaled, and his total of seven World Championships has been matched only by Casey Stengel.

But the glory years of Joe McCarthy were not without detraction. He was often called "Pushbutton Joe" in reference to the wealth of talent at his disposal. Actually, White Sox Manager Jimmy Dykes in a moment of jest labeled Joe "the pushbutton manager." Dykes respected McCarthy, knowing full well the tremendous ability of the Yankee manager, but Joe's critics used the phrase to hurt McCarthy who hated both the phrase and the nickname. His face would burn beet red, and his Irish temper would flare whenever the pushbutton tag was uttered in Joe's presence. The fact is that the Yanks were loaded with talent. So great was this talent, many fans believed that McCarthy would win no matter how he managed—skillfully or badly. (In an All-Star Game, McCarthy benched his Yankee players and won anyway as proof of his ability.) It was an unfair view of a man who was an alert and astute dugout manager and who had every quality a great manager must have. He continued to win during years when the Yankees were changing personnel, and he had to contend with the same problems as

other managers—injuries, pitching uncertainties, advancing age at key positions—all challenges he successfully met. In fact, McCarthy personally molded the Yankee infield of the late 1930s. He was convinced that Joe Gordon, a young shortstop, could become a second baseman and helped Gordon make the transition before he reached the Yankees. A few years earlier McCarthy made a similar move with Red Rolfe, another promising shortstop. Joe believed Red did not have the arm to play shortstop, yet recognized Rolfe's great glove. So McCarthy moved Rolfe to third base where he excelled. Thus, McCarthy was able to keep his best fielding shortstop, Frank Crosetti, in the lineup, flanked by two former shortstops, and the result was an excellent defensive infield with hitting punch. And it was McCarthy's clever creation.

Joe McCarthy not only made changes when necessary; he quickly recognized talent. During the spring training camp of 1939, the Yankees and Dodgers barnstormed north together. On the train one night McCarthy sat next to a Dodger youngster (who would not play in the majors until the next season) and declared: "Reiser, you're going to play for me." Pete Reiser was incredulous. "How can I play for you? I'm with the Dodgers." Said Joe, "We'll get you. I'll tell Ed Barrow and you'll be a Yankee." The Yankees offered $100,000 and five players for Reiser, but Brooklyn wisely would not part with "Pistol Pete" the National League batting champ in 1941. (Reiser was injury-plagued or might have become an all-time great.)

The public sometimes perceived Joe as being dull. He was poor news copy. He never explained his managerial moves. He never called attention to himself or made himself the star of the Yankees (as possibly Stengel did). Few personality traits were attached to Joe, excepting perhaps his cigar-smoking and long-sleeved uniforms. But to baseball insiders, Joe was a personality. He enjoyed talking and his favorite subject was old vaudeville acts.

The record of Joe McCarthy speaks for itself. But for World War II, McCarthy might have established an untouchable managerial record. Beginning in 1942, key Yankee stars were called into the military. The Yankees finished third in 1944 and fourth in 1945, much to McCarthy's distress. Additionally, he found out in 1945 that he did not enjoy the same close rapport with the new Yankee owners (MacPhail, Topping, Webb) that he had with Jacob Ruppert and Ed Barrow. Illness forced Joe to miss a few games in 1945, and his health was not good. Early in the 1946 season, Joe suffered a mild breakdown. He relinquished the managerial reins on May 24, 1946, and went home to rest, apparently especially happy to be disassociated from Larry MacPhail. Joe had once said of managing, "Sometimes I think I'm in the greatest business in the world. Then I lose four straight and want to change places with a farmer." And that is exactly what McCarthy did. After all the years of pressure, he retired to live quietly on his farm and let the competitive juices still. But soon the juices flowed again, and in 1948 Joe returned to the dugout of the Boston Red Sox, a team he managed for three seasons. He lost a one-game playoff to the Indians in 1948, and the Yanks beat him on the final two days of the 1949 season to rob him of a pennant.

Joe DiMaggio once declared, "Never a day went by when you didn't learn something from McCarthy. You finally think you know something about this game, and then McCarthy tells you something you never even expected." Needless to say, DiMaggio, whom some consider the game's greatest player, was an admirer (and friend) of McCarthy. "Marse Joe" paid tremendous attention to detail, missed nothing that happened on the field, and had an amazing memory. He remembered everything about both his players and his opponents, and he never made the same mistake twice. A disciple of sound fundamentals, McCarthy also stressed mental alertness. Thus, Yankee players more often made the right play and the quick-thinking play than other teams. Seldom did a Yankee player throw to the wrong base or disregard a coaching signal. If a player made a foolish mistake, the tough disciplinarian McCarthy would reprimand his man one-to-one and usually in private. Yankee players respected and appreciated the latter consideration. Joe drove his team hard, never letting overconfidence set in and kept the pressure to win on his Yankee players. But Joe also kept complete harmony on his Bronx Bomber teams. He wanted his players fighting the opposition rather than themselves or umpires, and that is how the Yankees responded. Pitcher Wes Ferrell, who late in the 1938 season was released by Washington and picked up by the Yankees, was welcomed by McCarthy with the warning: "We've got one rule around here. We don't second-guess the manager." On the other hand, Spud Chandler said in *Baseball When The Grass Was Real* that he never heard McCarthy second-guess a pitcher. Joe demanded respect and got it. Ferrell thought him very professional, all business and all baseball. And Ferrell had seen a good deal of major-league ball. (He pitched from 1927 to 1941, had a record of 193-168, was a 20-game winner six times while with the Indians and Red Sox, and pitched for four other teams.)

Joe McCarthy is remembered as one of baseball's best skippers. Famous sportswriter Grantland Rice felt McCarthy, John McGraw, and Connie Mack were the three best managers he ever set his eyes on. And those three Irishmen are always quickly mentioned whenever the subject of the game's greatest is discussed. McCarthy won more games (1460) with the Yanks than did any other Yankee manager. He owns the highest winning percentage (.627) of all Yankee managers with at least 105 wins. In fact, in Joe's complete 24-year major league career, he compiled the highest winning percentage (.615) of any manager in baseball history. Of his 24 teams, none ever ended up in the standings lower than fourth. (He never knew what it was to have a second division club.) McCarthy's complete major- league record was 2125-1333, placing him fifth on baseball's all-time victory list for managers. *The Sporting News* named Joe the Major League Manager of the Year three times (1936, 1938, 1943), and in 1939 "Marse Joe" shared a portion of the William J. Slocum Award given by the New York chapter of the Baseball Writers. In 1957, Joe McCarthy received baseball's highest honor, induction into the Baseball Hall of Fame. Many times McCarthy was asked which was his greatest team. Joe felt that his 1938 Yankee club was not only his best team but the greatest team in the history of baseball.

It is difficult to find a bad word about Joe McCarthy. Almost all of his players respected him, most liked him, and some were devoted to him. When Lou Gehrig became fatally ill in 1939, Joe reacted to the news as a father might have. The Yanks were in Detroit in 1941 when word of Gehrig's death reached McCarthy, and Joe and Bill Dickey hustled back to New York for Lou's funeral. He was very close to other players, also, including DiMaggio. Those few who disliked him, understood him. Relief pitcher Joe Page, whose battles with McCarthy in 1946 contributed to the manager's unhinging, once said of McCarthy, "I

hated his guts, but there never was a better manager." Joe, a native of Germantown, Pennsyvania, and his wife retired to a farm outside of Buffalo, N.Y. He lived to the ripe old age of 90 and died on January 13, 1978.

JOE McCARTHY'S TEN COMMANDMENTS OF BASEBALL

1. Nobody ever became a ballplayer by walking after a ball.
2. You will never become a .300 hitter unless you take the bat off your shoulder.
3. An outfielder who throws back of a runner is locking the barn after the horse is stolen.
4. Keep your head up and you may not have to keep it down.
5. When you start to slide, S-L-I-D-E. He who changes his mind may have to change a good leg for a bad one.
6. Do not alibi on bad hops. Anybody can field the good ones.
7. Always run them out. You can never tell.
8. Do not quit.
9. Do not find too much fault with the umpires. You cannot expect them to be as perfect as you are.
10. A pitcher who hasn't control hasn't anything.

YANKEE MANAGER RECORD FOR JOE McCARTHY

Years	Won	Lost	Percentage	Standing
1931	94	59	.614	2nd
1932	107	47	.695	1st
1933	91	59	.607	2nd
1934	94	60	.610	2nd
1935	89	60	.597	2nd
1936	102	51	.667	1st
1937	102	52	.662	1st
1938	99	53	.651	1st
1939	106	45	.702	1st
1940	88	66	.571	3rd
1941	101	53	.656	1st
1942	103	51	.669	1st
1943	98	56	.636	1st
1944	83	71	.539	3rd
1945	81	71	.533	4th
1946	22	13	.629	incomplete season
16 Yrs.	1460	867	.627	8 pennants

World Series

Years	Outcome	Won	Lost	Opponent
1932	Won	4	0	Chicago Cubs
1936	Won	4	2	New York Giants
1937	Won	4	1	New York Giants
1938	Won	4	0	Chicago Cubs
1939	Won	4	0	Cincinnati Reds
1941	Won	4	1	Brooklyn Dodgers
1942	Lost	1	4	St. Louis Cardinals
1943	Won	4	1	St. Louis Cardinals
8 Yrs.	7-1	29	9	

DICKEY, BILL

Manager: 1946
Born: June 6, 1907
Birthplace: Bastrop, LA
Died: November 12, 1993

The May 24, 1946 resignation of Joe McCarthy as Yankee manager brought to the helm Bill Dickey, the great Baseball Hall of Fame catcher (1928-46) who compiled a .313 lifetime batting average.

Dickey answered the call to duty in the difficult days following McCarthy's resignation, serving as manager until September 12, 1946, when he himself resigned. Apparently, Bill wanted a new contract for the 1947 season, but General Manager Larry MacPhail would not agree to a new pact until the 1946 campaign was completed. During a meeting in MacPhail's office, Dickey resigned. The Yankees were 57-48 (.543) under Dickey and never got into the race for the pennant, which the Red Sox ran away with. After managing Little Rock of the Southern Association in 1947, Bill returned to the Yankees as a coach, a job he held until the late 1950s. He served as a scout in 1959, then returned as a coach only to have illness force him to quit the club in July of 1960. Bill was a trusted aide of Casey Stengel. One of his strong suits was teaching; he tutored an unpolished Yogi Berra for many long hours in the art of catching during the spring of 1949. Bill remarked to many nonbelievers, "Give him two years and he'll be the greatest catcher in the American League, by a long shot." Bill proved to be right, of course, and he never once was jealous of Berra's surpassing his own reputation. Dickey was Berra's biggest supporter. Bill was a fine hitting instructor, too, and helped many players, including Bobby Richardson.

YANKEE MANAGER RECORD FOR BILL DICKEY

Years	Won	Lost	Percentage	Standing
1946	57	48	.543	incomplete season
1 Yr.	57	48	.543	0 pennants

NEUN, JOHNNY

Manager: 1946
Born: October 28, 1900
Birthplace: Baltimore, MD
Died: March 28, 1990

The 1946 season was a difficult one for the Yankees. First Joe McCarthy, then Bill Dickey resigned as Yankee manager. On September 12, Yankee coach Johnny Neun became the club's third manager of the season. Neun played first base for the Detroit Tigers (1925-28) and Boston Braves (1930-31) and had a .289 lifetime average. He brought the Yankees home over the final days of the 1946 season with an 8-6 record. But in the mind of General Manager Larry MacPhail, Johnny was hired as an interim manager. MacPhail, meanwhile, conducted a search for an experienced skipper and settled finally on Bucky Harris as the Yankees' manager. Neun went to Cincinnati and managed the Reds in 1947 and 1948. Johnny later rejoined the Yanks, serving many years as a scout and as coordinator of Yankee spring training camp. During the 1950s, Johnny

toured Yankee farm clubs, instructing both managers and players. Besides being an instructor at the famous "instructional school" camps conducted, by Casey Stengel, Neun managed in the Yankee minors, and he was a key Yankee scout in the 1960s. He is one of only two major-league first basemen to own an unassisted triple play. Johnny accomplished the feat on May 31, 1927, while with the Tigers.

YANKEE MANAGER RECORD FOR JOHNNY NEUN

Years	Won	Lost	Percentage	Standing
1946	8	6	.571	incomplete season
1 Yr.	8	6	.571	0 pennants

HARRIS, BUCKY

Manager: 1947-48
Born: November 8, 1896
Birthplace: Port Jervis, NY
Died: November 8, 1977

In his first year as Yankee manager, 1947, Bucky Harris won the World Championship for the Yankees. Yankee President Larry MacPhail, as shrewd a baseball man as there ever was, said he was responsible for bringing Harris to the Yankees. And Bucky's patience and calmness helped to mold the Yanks, after their year of turmoil, into a more united team. Harris was almost a legendary baseball figure when he joined the Yankees.

He was an outstanding second baseman for 12 seasons (1919-31), playing almost exclusively for the Washington Senators and hitting .274 lifetime. But Bucky became famous in 1924 as the "Boy Wonder" manager—at the ripe old age of 27—of the only World Championship team in Washington Senator history. From that initial success Harris went on to manage over 20 seasons, field-bossing the Senators, Tigers, Red Sox, and Phillies, and serving most recently as general manager of the Buffalo club in the International League. The Yanks on November 5, 1946, announced that they had obtained the services of this experienced and respected baseball man who the following year, after leading the Yankees to an easy pennant, would be named Manager of the Year by *The Sporting News*.

The club finished 12 games ahead of the second-place Tigers, then beat the Brooklyn Dodgers in a memorable seven-game World Series. Bucky kept a loose rein on the club, and the Yankee players, even the McCarthy loyalists, took a strong liking to him. But in 1948, while the Yankees were in the midst of a pennant struggle, Harris began having differences with the front office, especially with GM George Weiss who faulted Bucky's failure to enforce a player curfew. The Yanks finished in third place, only two games behind deadlocked Cleveland and Boston, but Weiss' mind was already made up: Harris would go. Weiss and Harris both used poor judgment in their relationship, Weiss hired private detectives behind Harris' back to trail certain players, then had Harris read the detectives' reports to the team. Bucky rightfully was angry and joked with his players about the silliness of it all. On the other hand, Bucky was foolish in his dealings with Weiss. As Harris' boss, Weiss did, after all, find it impossible to contact Harris away from the ballpark. (Communication is an essential requisite of a good manager-general manager relationship.) In his calls to Bucky's room, Weiss resented the invariable report that Harris was "out" (The dog races were a favorite Harris pastime.) Bucky also had an unlisted phone number and became known as "the four-hour manager." Both sides, in a relationship that begged for collaboration, were dug in. The case of pitcher Bob Porterfield was an example. Harris wanted him in New York and Weiss wanted him in Newark. Yankee executives fell to choosing sides before Harris got Porterfield. His differences with Weiss not-withstanding, Bucky Harris was shocked when the Yankees on October 6, 1948, announced that his contract would not be renewed.

There is no doubt that Bucky was a fine manager, and the Baseball Writers seemed to side with him in the dispute with Weiss, naming him winner of the William J. Slocum Award for 1948. Harris had no trouble finding another job in baseball. He managed the Senators from 1950-54 (his third tour of duty with them) and the Tigers in 1955-56. In his later years Bucky was a big league scout, staying in the game he loved for more than half a century. In 1975 Harris was inducted into the Baseball Hall of Fame and rightfully so. Bucky Harris ranks third all-time in games managed (4408), and fourth overall in wins (2157). Bucky Harris managed some excellent teams and some very poor ones, but he was never seduced by self-importance. Reflecting on his managing career, Bucky often remarked, "I was no genius. If you don't have the players, you can't win." Bucky neglected to mention his role in the development of players. Yogi Berra is a case in point. While blessed with a couple of excellent defensive catchers, Harris as Yankee skip-per knew he needed Berra's bat. As GM at Buffalo, he had witnessed what Berra, who was with the International League's Newark club, could do with the bat. Bucky brought Yogi along slowly behind the plate, putting him in as many games as possible. But he positioned Yogi mainly in the outfield. Bucky has therefore been given much of the credit for developing Yogi into a good major league hitter.

YANKEE MANAGER RECORD FOR BUCKY HARRIS

Years	Won	Lost	Percentage	Standing
1947	97	57	.630	1st
1948	94	60	.610	3rd
2 Yrs.	191	117	.620	1 Pennant

World Series				
Years	Outcome	Won	Lost	Opponent
1947	Won	4	3	Brooklyn Dodgers
1 Yr.	1-0	4	3	

STENGEL, CASEY

Nickname: "The Old Perfessor"
Manager: 1949-60
Born: July 30, 1890
Birthplace: Kansas City, MO
Died: September 29, 1975

On October 12, 1948, the Yankees shocked the baseball world by announcing that a much-traveled and colorful—some would say clownish—Casey Stengel would succeed popular Bucky Harris as Yankee manager. Yankee GM George Weiss had known and trusted Stengel for more than 20 years. He was impressed with Stengel's success as a minor-league manager

and was understanding about Casey's poor managerial record in the majors, a record Weiss knew to be undermined by player ineptitude. But skeptics felt Casey was hired to provide some humor while Weiss rebuilt the club for a solid manager. Babe Ruth, who liked Casey, once called him "one of the daffiest guys I ever met."

Casey began his baseball career in 1910. (Following high school, he had entered Western Dental College in his hometown of Kansas City, Missouri, but soon he got the itch to play baseball, his real love in life.) After seasoning as an outfielder in the minors (Kankakee, Maysville, Aurora, Montgomery), Stengel joined the Brooklyn Dodgers in 1912. (Soon thereafter, Charles Dillon "Dutch" Stengel acquired the name Casey, a name to which he only occasionally answered, after his K.C. home.) Over 14 seasons Casey traveled from the Dodgers to the Pirates, Phillies, Giants and finally the Braves. He was as accomplished as he was traveled, batting .284 lifetime and .393 for three World Series. He made his biggest impact as a player by hitting two game-winning home runs for the Giants against their archrivals, the Yankees, in the 1923 World Series. These were the first World Series four baggers hit at Yankee Stadium and the first was an inside-the-parker. As he rounded the bases, Casey was heard shouting encouragement to himself. "Go legs, go!" he pleaded.

Stengel bought a small piece of the Worcester, Massachu-setts, Eastern League club in 1925 and was installed as president, general manager and player-manager. (It was at this time that he and George Weiss, who was also associated with the Eastern League, became friends.) When he was offered a better managing job with Toledo in the superior American Association, Casey released himself as a player, fired himself as manager, resigned as president and general manager, and sold his interest in the club.

Casey managed six seasons at Toledo (1926-31), winning the American Association pennant in 1927. There Stengel raised ballplayers for his former manager, John McGraw, and in return McGraw's Giants supplied the Mud Hens with players they could not use. (Throughout Casey's minor-league manag-ing career, he was teaching, scouting and wheeling-dealing—buying and selling ballplayers.) Stengel returned to Brooklyn as a coach in 1932, and in 1934 was named the Dodgers' manager. The Dodgers were the doormat of the National League and finished no better than fifth in Casey's three years as field boss. Next stop was Boston where Casey piloted the Braves from 1938 to 1943. Again he was saddled with a sorry club and again he was able to finish no better than fifth. He managed Milwaukee in the American Association in 1944. He won the pennant but quit because he was sure owner Bill Veeck would fire him on his return from the military. Weiss then hired him to manage the Yankees' Kansas City farm team, and from there it was on to the Oakland Oaks of the Pacific Coast League, a job Weiss helped him land. In his third season at Oakland, Casey's Oaks won 114 games and the pennant, and *The Sporting News* named him the Minor League Manager of the Year (1948).

Thus Casey's managerial resume on the eve of his Yankee hiring showed experience with seven organizations, two of them in the majors—Brooklyn and Boston—and five in the minors—Worcester, Toledo, Milwaukee, Kansas City and Oak-land. His recent managerial past, at least, was creditable, but his future in baseball was uncertain. He could be financially independent. His wife Edna had done well in business and real

Although Riska never played a game for the Yankees, the young pitching prospect went on to become the Executive Director of the Heisman Memorial Trophy at the Downtown Athletic Club in New York City.

Casey Stengel in his first five seasons (1949-53) as a Yankee manager led his charges to five consecutive World Series titles, an astounding feat that may never be duplicated.

estate in California, where the Stengels made their home, and Casey's own investments (oil wells) proved most profitable. But George Weiss wanted a good baseball man on whom he could count for an agreeable working relationship, and his thoughts turned to Stengel. Weiss' good feelings toward Casey were reinforced by some glowing reports on Stengel's recent work. Moreover, he was certain that Stengel's success with an able Oakland team better reflected his managerial abilities than did his poor record with the inept National League clubs. He decided to take a chance on Ol' Case, and Del Webb and Dan Topping went along, although the latter required some convincing. Topping was not the only skeptic. Yankee fans and New York sportswriters questioned the hiring (the sportswriters were, however, happy over the prospects of having an entertaining subject). Casey had a reputation for clownishness, not for brilliance. The players, too, regarded Stengel with suspicion; the veterans among them maintained strong loyalties toward McCarthy and Harris.

But Casey answered his critics by leading an injury-riddled Yankee team to an unexpected pennant and World Series victory in 1949. He manipulated players, installing a platoon system at certain positions to get the most out of his personnel. In view of the fact that the 1949 Yanks were plagued by no less than 71 disabling injuries, including one that drydocked Joe DiMaggio for the first half of the season, this managing job must be rated as one of the best in the history of the game. In the course of the season, Stengel used seven different first basemen! He was as easygoing a manager in 1949 as he was resourceful, feeling his way around on a new job in a new league. A marked difference in his command emerged in 1950, however, and lasted until the day he and the Yankees separated. He became a dominant (some would say dictatorial) force. He ruled on the field with a sharp tongue and an iron hand, although off the field he let his players raise a little hell. (He was a hell-raiser as a player himself, after all.) Casey ran the dugout like a general. Everyone knew HE was in command.

He followed his initial success in 1949 with American League pennants and World Series triumphs in 1950, 1951, 1952 and 1953. Thus he managed the only team to ever win five consecutive World Championships, achieving this remarkable feat in his first five seasons as Yankee manager! The celebrated clown of baseball had become the sport's undisputed genius. *Sport* magazine in 1953 named him the "Man of the Year," an incredible honor for someone who had no occasion to either swing a bat or throw a ball.

Stengel's 1954 Yankees won 103 games (most ever won by a Stengel team), but Cleveland's success was even more spectacular, and the Yankees' five-year reign was ended. New York returned to the top perch the following year, the first of four straight American League championship years (1955-58) during which the Stengelmen also garnered two World Championships (1956,1958). But in 1959 the Yankees finished third, and it was apparent that Stengel, now 69, no longer was the manager he once was. He tended toward crankiness, and in the late innings of doubleheaders he would occasionally come close to dozing off. Once a great instructor to the younger players, he had little time for them now and even less patience with their mistakes. Indications were that the 1960 season would be his last.

Stengel drove the Yankees to a relatively easy pennant victory, but in a tough, seven-game World Series, they bowed to the Pittsburgh Pirates. They set numerous Series batting records, so badly did they pummel the Pirates in three of the seven games, but the other four games—all close ones—went to Pittsburgh. Casey's managerial moves were questioned. Particularly, he was second-guessed for his pitching assignments, for getting only two Series starts out of Whitey Ford who in ranking third on the staff in wins (12-9) was hardly the Yankees' ace, but who nevertheless hurled two shutouts in the Series. His pitching changes in Game 7 were very debatable and Ralph Terry, who gave up the game-winning home run, was up in the bullpen on at least four occasions. By the time he got to the mound he appeared to have lost something. Casey's handling of Terry and his general Series performance—may have sealed his fate.

In any case, the ownership decided to release Casey. He had been paid $90,000, the highest salary ever paid a manager to that date, to manage in 1960, and generous financial treatment would be accorded him on his departure. On October 15, 1960, two days after the close of the Series, Stengel's retirement was announced. It may have been the Yankees' only option but it was handled insensitively, and the public and press regarded the decision as cold and heartless. The press conference for Stengel's "retirement" went poorly. The irrepressible Stengel let it be known that he was leaving the Yanks against his free will. Blurted he to a sympathetic press: "I guess this means they fired me. I'll never make the mistake of being 70 again."

In 1962, the National League's New York Mets came into existence and scored a major coup by hiring Stengel as their first manager. Casey managed this hapless but lovable team for four seasons before a hip injury in the 1965 season forced his retirement. His association with the Met misfits and castoffs seemed to underscore his own attractive humanity and added to his tremendous popularity. But make no mistake; Stengel played each game to win and took each inevitable loss considerably harder than did the Mets' New Breed fans.

Stengel was a unique manager in many ways and a great one in all ways. His hero, fatherlike figure, and managerial model was John McGraw, for whom he once played. For three seasons, McGraw was to Stengel what Stengel would be to young Billy Martin years later. Casey soaked up what he could from McGraw. He adopted such techniques as that of constantly berating his team when it was playing well and backing off during losing streaks. Like McGraw, Casey attended to the smallest details. His platooning of players at certain positions was not a novel idea. Several managers—among them McGraw who had platooned Stengel—had engaged in the practice, but Stengel was the first in many years to platoon successfully. Casey reasonably figured that if he could get, say, 15 home runs and 60 RBIs out of each of two players platooned, he had an offensively productive position. Casey kept charts in his head of each player's abilities, especially his performance against specific opposition. And Casey did not always platoon only on the basis of opposing a left-handed or right-handed pitcher. That was only one variable in his reasoning. Hank Bauer and Gene Woodling were sometimes platooned, but they were often in the same game, too. A tough pitcher, however, might force one or the other to the bench.

Uncanny was Stengel's ability to shuttle lineups successfully and make the correct pitching change. He perfected the art of thinking several steps ahead of the action during a game. Possessing such a terrific grasp of each individual game, Casey more often than not out-managed the other team. He almost always had the pitcher or pinch-hitter he wanted in the game when he wanted him. And with the knowledge of his players' strengths and weaknesses so precise, Casey was a brilliant dugout manager.

Platooning is usually done in the outfield and at first base, but Stengel also regularly juggled the infield positions of second, third and shortstop. Mostly because Gil McDougald was able to play any of the three infield positions equally well, Stengel could constantly make long-term and short-term changes in his infield. As circumstances varied, he shook up his infield over the years (1949-60), plugging in or pulling out four first basemen (Henrich, Mize, Collins and Skowron); four second basemen (Coleman, Martin, McDougald and Richardson); six third basemen (Johnson, Brown, McDougald, Carey, Lopez and Boyer); and four shortstops (Rizzuto, Hunter, McDougald and Kubek). The one constant amid the changing faces was Yankee success. Stengel worked his entire 25-man roster, probably using his bench as well as any manager ever. And he was an excellent judge of talent. Two Pacific Coast Leaguers, Gene Woodling and Billy Martin, came to the Yanks on his recommendation and proved to be outstanding. Casey was wise enough to switch Mickey Mantle from shortstop to the outfield and bring Bill Skowron in from the outfield to first base. Both moves helped each player and ultimately the team.

The Yankees under Stengel stressed fundamentals, "The Old Perfessor" believing that most games are lost, not won. Stengel had lineups with such typically sound all-round players as Henrich, Rizzuto, Coleman, Martin, Bauer, Woodling, Mapes, McDougald, Noren, Skowron, Howard, Richardson, Kubek, and Maris. The pitchers were in the same mold.

One intangible all Stengel-led Yankee teams possessed was complete confidence in themselves as a collective unit. Casey instilled that confidence into the players. He was a great leader of men, and his Yankee teams were never inclined to play scared. Nor did they ever foolishly underestimate an opponent. The Yanks merely EXPECTED to win. Also, Stengel kept his club alert. He constantly asked his players game-situation questions, drilling valuable baseball information into his students.

Ol' Case was great with the youngsters before becoming somewhat irascible in his later years; he was fatherlike in his relationships with Mickey Mantle and Billy Martin. But not all the Yankee players were charmed by Casey. Joe DiMaggio was not enamored with him and was upset by a few of his decisions, including Stengel's moving him to the first-base position for a game in 1950. Joe was upset during a 1951 game when Casey sent Cliff Mapes out to center field to replace DiMaggio while an inning was in progress, and Joe waved Mapes back to the dugout. When the inning was over, DiMaggio took himself out of the game. Another time Stengel took DiMaggio out of the cleanup spot without the courtesy of an explanation to one of the game's greats. Some others did not warm to Stengel, either (mostly those loyalists of McCarthy and Harris), but the press and public liked him. Casey was a winner. He was colorful and accessible and he spoke a funny language known as "Stengelese." Make no mistake about this fact: Casey only spoke Stengelese when he wanted to and usually only to the press. His players understood Casey perfectly. Casey was great copy for the print medium (a quote from Stengel was always at hand) and the relationship between Stengel and the press was a case of lasting love, Casey viewing the press as "my writers."

Casey Stengel, the personality, was bigger than the Yankees or baseball. But it must be remembered that the funny image of Casey portrayed by an adoring press was often a facade. True, he was basically a warmhearted, kindly and humorous man, but there were other sides to Casey. He could be mean and intimidating, and by 1960 he had abused the sensitivities of many players, especially the younger ones. Some were damaged irreparably by his sharp tongue, and many resented Casey's public criticism of them. But, in his own eyes, Stengel was critical of his players in an effort to promote individual improvement, and he attacked only those he felt talented enough to improve. Yet, his targets did not take kindly to what was perceived as abuse.

His use of the word "nigger" did not often offend people. Like others born in his time and place, Stengel probably thought of blacks in stereotyped terms, but he was not a racist. He made Elston Howard feel like a Yankee, and he ensured that Howard got the same treatment as any other player. He looked at a player through color-blind eyes; he looked for ability.

He could be compassionate, hating to release proven veterans or send young players back to the minors. On occasion he would fight with Weiss for salary increases for his players. Of course, players so defended could be counted on for loyalty, something Stengel needed as badly as the players needed money. Casey sometimes dipped into his own pocket, buying his players presents, long-distance phone calls and other niceties.

Casey was an authentic nonstop talker. The verbal stream was not a gimmick, not an image-cultivating invention. He was an endurance drinker, too, but was probably never drunk as a Yankee manager. That's where his other habit saved him; while others were drinking, Casey was talking. He simply used drinking as a social outlet to talk late into every night.

Casey Stengel was one of the game's greatest managers, ranking in fame and success with John McGraw, Connie Mack, Miller Huggins and Joe McCarthy. The 10 pennants he won tied him with McGraw as baseball's winningest manager. More impressive is the fact that Casey won his 10 pennants in only 12 seasons as Yankee manager! His seven World Championships tied him with McCarthy in that category. Even with all the poor teams Casey managed, he finished with a record of 1905-1842 (.508) as a Major League manager, ranking eighth all-time in victories. His 37 wins in World Series competition is unsurpassed.

Awards descended on Casey aplenty. *The Sporting News* named him Major League Manager of the Year in 1949, 1953 and 1958, and the New York Baseball Writers gave Casey the "William J. Slocum Award" in 1950, the Ben Epstein "Good Guy" Award in 1960, and the Casey Stengel "You Could Look It Up" Award in 1970. His uniform Number "37" was appropriately retired by the Yankees and the Mets. In 1966 "The Old Perfessor" won the ultimate laurel with his induction into the Baseball Hall of Fame. He was selected three years later during baseball's centennial celebration in 1969 as the game's "Greatest Living Manager." He was praised, to be sure, by the baseball community, and he was loved by the public. Quite possibly, Casey Stengel held the affection of the public more than any other figure in baseball history. Simply put, Casey Stengel was one of the best things to ever happen to the game of baseball. He was an authentic Baseball Ambassador, making the game fun for millions of Americans.

YANKEE MANAGER RECORD FOR CASEY STENGEL

Years	Won	Lost	Percentage	Standing
1949	97	57	.630	1st
1950	98	56	.636	1st
1951	98	56	.636	1st
1952	95	59	.617	1st
1953	99	52	.656	1st
1954	103	51	.669	2nd
1955	96	58	.623	1st
1956	97	57	.630	1st
1957	98	56	.636	1st
1958	92	62	.597	1st
1959	79	75	.513	3rd
1960	97	57	.630	1st
12 Yrs.	1149	696	.623	10 pennants

World Series

Years	Outcome	Won	Lost	Opponent
1949	Won	4	1	Brooklyn Dodgers
1950	Won	4	0	Philadelphia Phillies
1951	Won	4	2	New York Giants
1952	Won	4	3	Brooklyn Dodgers
1953	Won	4	2	Brooklyn Dodgers
1955	Lost	3	4	Brooklyn Dodgers
1956	Won	4	3	Brooklyn Dodgers
1957	Lost	3	4	Milwaukee Braves
1958	Won	4	3	Milwaukee Braves
1960	Lost	3	4	Pittsburgh Pirates
10 Yrs.	7-3	37	26	

HOUK, RALPH

Nickname: "The Major"
Manager: 1961-63; 1966-73
Born: August 9, 1919
Birthplace: Lawrence, KS

Ralph Houk had served the Yankees as a minor-league player, a third-string catcher in New York, a Yankee coach and a minor-league manager in the Yankee farm system. He was a loyal and dedicated member of the organization, and the opinion was long held that when Casey Stengel retired, Houk would succeed him. One of the reasons Stengel was squeezed out in October 1960 was the fear that the Yanks would lose Houk to another team, several of whom had approached him about managing.

Houk began playing in the Yankee farm system at Neosho when he was 19 years old. He was progressing through the Yankee organization when his career was interrupted by World War II. Houk was a war hero, earning the Award of the Silver Star and advancing to the rank of major before being discharged and joining the Yankee farm team in Beaumont, Texas, in 1946. He joined the parent club the following year where he played until 1952. He saw limited action, catching 89 games and hitting .272 in 158 at-bats. But Stengel and others felt that "The Major" had leadership qualities, and Houk was made a Yankee coach for 1953 and 1954. In 1955 he was named manager of the Yanks' Denver farm club and he remained in Denver for three seasons. There he won a Little World Series (1957) and helped mold such future Yankees as Tony Kubek, Bobby Richardson, John Blanchard, Ralph Terry and Ryne Duren. Everything about his work in Denver was impressive, and he returned to the Yankees in 1958 to coach and to undergo final preparation for the manager's post. In October of 1960, Stengel was retired, and Ralph replaced him as manager. No mistake about it, Houk was Dan Topping's man.

Houk quickly established a rapport with the Yankee players during spring training for the 1961 season and induced a genuinely good spirit in camp. He did away with Stengel's elaborate platoon system and decided against shuttling players around from position to position. The players appreciated the stability of a set team, and the pitchers were enthusiastic over Houk's regular starting rotation. The team jelled into one of the strongest in Yankee history and stormed to 109 wins and an easy five-game World Series conquest of the Cincinnati Reds. (The World Series victory made Houk the third rookie manager in history to win the World Championship.)

Houk's strong suit throughout his managerial career was his ability to hold a team together, to keep its parts working in relative harmony. He was optimistic in outlook and understanding with his players, preferring to heap praise rather than belittle. He did loads for the confidence of a number of players on the 1961 club, including Mickey Mantle, who had occasionally been hurt by Stengel's criticism. Houk told Mickey that he was the best player alive, the leader of the team, and Mantle responded with an outstanding season. All the Yankees responded to Houk's approving manner, which verged on outright insulation from the negative, in those first three seasons. His press relations were a bit different. The press, indeed, was frequently the butt of Houk's temper. The notion could be entertained that this was in the team's interest—better for the press to see the darker side of Houk than his players.

The 1962 team also won the World Series, and when the Houk Yankees captured their third straight American League pennant in 1963, Ralph became the first man in 54 years to win pennants in his first three seasons as a major league manager. (Detroit's Hughie Jennings won three straight American League pennants in 1907, '08, '09.) Houk, however, left the managerial job after the 1963 season to become the Yankee general manager, a move made on the eve of a disaster that was soon to bring the once proud Yankee dynasty tumbling down. The collapse came in 1965. When the 1966 season got off badly (4-16), Manager Johnny Keane was fired and Houk was reinstalled as manager. It was obvious that the Yanks were in a long rebuilding process, and in many ways Ralph Houk was successful. He helped develop such stars as Roy White, Bobby Murcer, Thurman Munson, Ron Blomberg, Fritz Peterson, Stan Bahnsen and Doc Medich. His patience made him a good manager for a young, developing team. Perhaps his greatest season as manager was in 1970 when he led a mediocre but hustling team to 93 wins, and the Yanks had fun along the way.

Ralph Houk resigned as Yankee manager on the final day of the 1973 season, apparently because of disenchantment with the new Yankee ownership. "The Major" went on to manage the Tigers from 1974 to 1978. He started that job saddled with an aging team, but retired from the job after the 1978 season with the Tigers apparently endowed with the nucleus of a solid team for the future. In 1979 and 1980, Ralph was a consultant for the Tiger organization. He completed his long career managing the Red Sox from 1981 through 1984.

Baseball legend Joe DiMaggio, second from right, donned his uniform again to serve as an aide in spring training, March 9, 1961 in St. Petersburg, FL. From left are: Yogi Berra, Mickey Mantle, DiMaggio and manager Ralph Houk, who played on the Yankees when DiMaggio retired. (AP Photo/WIDE WORLD PHOTOS)

YANKEE MANAGER RECORD FOR RALPH HOUK

Years	Won	Lost	Percentage	Standing
1961	109	53	.673	1st
1962	96	66	.593	1st
1963	104	57	.646	1st
1966	66	73	.475	incomplete season
1967	72	90	.444	9th
1968	83	79	.512	5th
1969	80	81	.497	5th (EAST)
1970	93	69	.574	2nd (EAST)
1971	82	80	.506	4th (EAST)
1972	79	76	.510	4th (EAST)
1973	80	82	.494	4th (EAST)
11 Yrs.	944	806	.539	3 pennants

World Series

Years	Outcome	Won	Lost	Opponents
1961	Won	4	1	Cincinnati Reds
1962	Won	4	3	San Francisco Giants
1963	Lost	0	4	Los Angeles Dodgers
3 Yrs.	2-1	8	8	

BERRA, YOGI

Manager: 1964, 1984-85
Born: May 12, 1925
Birthplace: St. Louis, MO

Yogi Berra, one of the greatest players in Yankee history, spent the 1963 season as a player-coach and became manager in 1964 when Ralph Houk moved up to become General Manager according to a preordained plan. Early in the 1963 spring training camp, Yogi, Houk, Roy Hamey, and Dan Topping met on Topping's yacht and Berra was told the plan, which was to give Yogi the manager's job as Houk became GM. Yogi asked for time to talk it over with his wife and was given 24 hours. His answer was affirmative, but the news was kept from the public until after the 1963 World Series. The announcement was made on October 22, 1963, in a press conference in the Crystal Suite of the Sheraton-Plaza Hotel in New York.

The 1964 season found Berra and the Yankees in a tight late-season pennant race with the Baltimore Orioles and the Chicago White Sox. New York had spent much of the season in third place before getting red hot in September (22-6) to finish one game ahead of the White Sox and two games ahead of the Orioles. Berra never gave up and must be given much of the credit

Yogi Berra

for the September resurgence. The sluggish play of the team during the summer could not be laid at Berra's feet but was attributable to the reality that the Yankees were injury-burdened and aging and a year from collapse. Berra's 1964 edition was the dynasty's last stand.

The World Series was exciting, and Berra handled it well, but the St. Louis Cardinals defeated the Yankees in seven games. The day after the Series ended, the Yankees shocked everyone by firing Berra, then hiring St. Louis Manager Johnny Keane. It was a move that angered many Yankee fans. Berra, in spite of his field success, had found little support from the front office, for good reason. GM Houk had decided during the season to fire Yogi for an alleged lack of communication with and control over his players. This brought to mind the Phil Linz incident—the time Berra and utility infielder Linz got into a loud argument over Linz's playing his harmonica aboard the team bus following a Yankee defeat. But years later, Joe Pepitone said that Yogi got more out of him than did any other manager. Remembering that Pepitone was one of the most individualistic of players, Berra had to have something as a manager.

After getting canned by the Yankees, Berra hooked up with Casey Stengel, his former manager, as a Mets coach in 1965. Yogi managed the Mets from 1972-75, and his 1973 club captured the National League pennant; Berra thus joined Joe McCarthy as only the second manager to win pennants in both leagues.

Berra, who was inducted into the Baseball Hall of Fame in 1972, returned to the Yankees in 1976 as a coach under Billy Martin, his old teammate. Billy in his Yankee career may have ignored or humiliated some of his other coaches, but he listened to Yogi. Berra remained a coach through several managing changes.

On December 16, 1983, Martin was fired for the third time, and Berra was thrust into the manager's hot seat. "People change—but I don't think Yogi will," predicted Willie Randolph that day. "You can talk to him."

Indeed, the players always felt comfortable with Yogi. They trusted him. There was less pressure because Yogi tried to shield them from the owner. And, as Randolph said, Yogi listened.

Yogi had one last goal to achieve in baseball. He wanted another crack at winning a World Series as a manager. It wouldn't be in 1984, as Detroit preempted a pennant race by bursting out of the starting gate with an amazing 35-5 record. Yogi, blending youngsters with veterans, led the Yankees to baseball's best record, 51-30, after the All-Star break. The Yankees, however, still finished third, and Berra narrowly averted getting fired.

In December 1984, the Yankees obtained Yogi's son, Dale, from Pittsburgh, and Yogi became only the second man to manage his son in big-league history. Connie Mack played his son, Earl, in five games with the Philadelphia A's.

"Yogi will be the manager the entire season, win or lose," stated George Steinbrenner in the spring training of 1985. But Yogi felt the owner's heat early, especially when Yogi refused to schedule a mandatory workout. When the Yankees slipped to 6-10, Steinbrenner axed Berra and brought back Martin.

The Yankee players were angry with the Berra firing. Don Baylor kicked a trash can across the clubhouse. Don Mattingly threw shampoo. When Yogi stepped off the team bus to return home, the players gave him a tremendous ovation. "We had become a family under Yogi," explained Baylor.

"If they liked Berra so much," said Steinbrenner, "they should have won for him." Bitter, Yogi would later say he wouldn't ever come back to Yankee Stadium as long as Steinbrenner owned the Yankees. Yogi finished his glorious career coaching with Houston. Yogi had a change of heart and returned to throw out the first pitch for the 1999 opener at Yankee Stadium.

YANKEE MANAGER RECORD FOR YOGI BERRA				
Years	Won	Lost	Percentage	Standing
1964	99	63	.611	1st
1984	87	75	.537	3rd (EAST)
1985	6	10	.375	incomplete season
3 Yrs.	192	148	.565	1 Pennant

World Series				
Years	Outcome	Won	Lost	Opponent
1964	Lost	3	4	St. Louis Cardinals
1 Yr.	0-1	3	4	

KEANE, JOHNNY

Manager: 1965-66
Born: November 3, 1911
Birthplace: St. Louis, MO
Died: January 6, 1967

Johnny Keane had the misfortune of being the New York Manager in 1965 when the Yankee dynasty came crashing down. And less than a year before, it seemed to him clearly the best job in baseball.

Keane was one of those rare big-league managers who never played a game in the major leagues. He became manager of the St. Louis Cardinals in the middle of the 1961 season and his record (47-33) was decisively better than that of his predecessor, Solly Hemus (33-41). By 1963 Keane had nudged St. Louis into second place. However, the Cards were languishing in fifth place in 1964 when owner Gussie Busch fired his general manager, Bing Devine, and made signals that Keane was to follow. But lame-duck Manager Keane led the Cardinals to the National League pennant, then an exciting seven-game World Series win over the Yankees.

Yankee GM Ralph Houk coveted Keane, who announced his resignation as St. Louis manager the day after the World Series. When Houk fired Yogi Berra that same day, Keane was ready to step in as the Yankees' field boss. Keane was eager to make the move to New York, but in reality he was inheriting a Yankee team that was old, hurt and not about to bloom with new stars. Moreover, Keane did not fit in with his players, New York, or the American League. He was a likable, religious man on the one hand, and on the other the target of resentment from players who were forced by Keane to play with injuries. It was a bad situation for all concerned. The Yanks limped home in sixth place in 1965, and when the club got off to a poor start in 1966 (4-16), Keane was relieved of his managerial duties by Houk who came down from the front office to take over. Sadly, Johnny Keane was afflicted with a heart ailment and died on January 6, 1967, eight months after leaving the Yankees.

YANKEE MANAGER RECORD FOR JOHNNY KEANE

Years	Won	Lost	Percentage	Standing
1965	77	85	.475	6th
1966	4	16	.200	incomplete season
2 Yrs.	81	101	.445	0 pennants

VIRDON, BILL

Manager: 1974-75
Born: June 9, 1931
Birthplace: Hazel Park, MI

When the Yankees, following the 1973 season, were blocked by the Oakland A's in their attempt to sign Dick Williams to replace Ralph Houk, the club turned to quiet, bespectacled Bill Virdon. Without doubt, Virdon had the necessary credentials.

He was an outstanding prospect in the Yankee organization in the early 1950s, until he and two other players were traded to the St. Louis Cardinals for Enos Slaughter in April of 1954. Virdon hit .281 and had 17 home runs with the Cards in 1955 and was voted the National League's Rookie of the Year. From 1957 to 1965 he played for the Pittsburgh Pirates, ending his 12-year major-league career with a .267 lifetime batting average. But Virdon is best remembered as a great defensive centerfielder. No Yankee fan will ever forget the two spectacular catches he made at critical points of the 1960 World Series to help the Pirates defeat the Yankees.

Virdon began his major-league managing career in style in 1972, winning the National League East title by 11 games for the Pirates (and losing to Cincinnati in a thrilling five-game playoff series). But the Pirates were laboring just under the

.500 mark (67-69) in 1973 when Virdon was replaced by the man *he* had replaced, Danny Murtaugh.

The Yankees had themselves a fine manager in Bill Virdon who in 1974, his first season at the helm, nearly claimed a pennant. In fact, for a time in September the Yankees led the American League East and ended the season only two games behind the division champion Baltimore Orioles. *The Sporting News* saw fit to name Virdon the Major League Manager of the Year. He was honest in his dealings with the players, management and the press. He also made at least one courageous stand. Although mindful that Bobby Murcer was regarded as the continuation of a Yankee tradition of Hall of Fame centerfielders, from Combs to DiMaggio to Mantle, Virdon went ahead and put Elliott Maddox, a defensive genius, in center and moved Murcer to right.

In 1975 the Yankees regressed, and Virdon was fired in early August, the New York record at the time 53-51. Bill Virdon left the Yanks without a bad word spoken, and the Houston Astros quickly hired him. Virdon, in 1979, led the Astros in the club's first serious assault on a division title. It wasn't until the final week of the season that the Astros were knocked out of the race. In 1980 the Astros indeed won the National League West and then lost an extremely exciting Championship Series to the Phillies. Virdon turned Houston, once justifiably thought to be a poor baseball city, into a community of Astro zealots. By 1980's end, Bill was accepting various "Manager of the Year" awards. Virdon's Astros made the playoffs again in 1981. Bill has continued to coach in the majors, mainly with the Pirates.

YANKEE MANAGER RECORD FOR BILL VIRDON

Years	Won	Lost	Percentage	Standing
1974	89	73	.549	2nd (EAST)
1975	53	51	.510	incomplete season
2 Yrs.	142	124	.534	0 pennants

MARTIN, BILLY

Nicknames: "Billy the Kid" "The Brat"
Manager: 1975-78; 1979; 1983; 1985; 1988
Born: May 16, 1928
Birthplace: Berkeley, CA
Died: December 25, 1989

Billy Martin, the scrapper, became manager of the Yankees on August 2, 1975. He was always a scrapper, according to one account—a tough, street-brawling kid from Berkeley, Calif. But he is also portrayed as having been a good boy who read the Bible and regularly attended church. He was loyal to his family, made money for his family, and was always regarded by his mother as a good boy. In any case, Billy—not a one-dimensional boy and not a one-dimensional man—in succeeding Bill Virdon was stepping into a job he had dreamed of. Now he would patrol the Yankee dugout as did his fatherlike hero, Casey Stengel. The gravely ill Casey, who would soon die, wept with joy when he learned of Billy's appointment.

Billy's career began with farm clubs of the Oakland Oaks and blossomed with the Oaks under Stengel in 1947 and 1948. Billy, Casey and the Oaks won a Pacific Coast League pennant in 1948 and Casey became Yankee manager in 1949. On Casey's recommendation, Martin followed him to New York in 1950. With the Yanks, Billy sustained the reputation he made in Oakland as a scrappy, hustling, aggressive player. He was the Yankees' second baseman from 1950 through 1957 (missing 1954 and most of the 1955 season while in the military), hitting .262 overall (his lifetime average was .257). He excelled in the pressure games, including the seventh game of the 1952 World Series when his lunging catch saved the game and the Series for New York. In the 1953 World Series he hit a dazzling .500. He had close friendships with Mickey Mantle and Whitey Ford. He loved Stengel and was, in turn, Stengel's favorite player, and he was loved by Yankee fans. So Billy took it hard when he was traded in 1957 following a Copacabana nightclub incident for which Martin was unfairly blamed. He was peddled to the Kansas City A's and later played for the Tigers, Indians, Reds, Braves and Twins, performing as a player until 1961. But the spark that characterized his play was gone after Billy left New York.

Minnesota released Billy during the 1962 spring training. He made the Twins' payroll ($10,000 a year) as a scout and troubleshooter in 1963 and 1964, and in 1965 worked as the Twins' third-base coach. He got along well with the players and seemed to have a special rapport with Spanish-speaking players. The Twins won the American League pennant in 1965. Martin again served as coach in 1966 and 1967 and was named manager of the Twins' Denver club for 1968. In 1969 he moved up to manage the Twins. His managerial career was similar to his playing career—successful but well traveled, usually because of battles with the front office. He led the Twins to an American League West title in his first year as skipper. Billy piloted the Tigers from 1971-73 and led that team to an American League East title in 1972. "Billy the Kid" next went to Texas late in the 1973 campaign to lead the Rangers to a last-place finish. But the following year he brought them up to second place. It was in July of 1975, a couple of weeks before Billy's Yankee hiring was announced at Old Timers' Day in New York, that the Rangers canned him.

The naming of Martin as Yankee manager brought about a most satisfying reunion: Billy was back with the Yankees, back with the New York fans. He had as much "Yankee Pride" as anyone, and he implanted his own fierce desire to win in his team. Billy's acuity as a strategist and his ability to run a ball club became apparent in 1976 with the Yankees' surprisingly easy conquest of the American League East. By playing aggressive, Billy Martin-type baseball, the Yanks finished 10 games ahead of the Orioles and defeated the Royals in the playoffs for the league pennant. But the Yanks lost to Cincinnati in four straight games in the World Series; Martin was so upset that he forced the umpires to eject him before the final game was over. The 1976 Yankees were an aggressive, hustling club, the kind Martin liked and seemed to do best with. He liked the hit-and-run play, and the suicide squeeze was one of his favorites. He was better with running, base-stealing clubs than he was with power teams. The 1977 edition of the Yankees was power-wealthy. Martin and the Yankees were expected to win every-thing, and team tensions flared through most of the season. Billy had problems with the front office and with Reggie Jackson, the recently signed free-agent slugger. Jackson was owner George Steinbrenner's man, in Billy's view, and he seemed to regard Reggie as having been thrust on him and his

team. He let Reggie know that the field boss of the New York Yankees was Billy Martin. In his managerial past, Billy had several run-ins with management. He always insisted, rightly or wrongly, in managing his own way. The 1977 Yankees withstood their internal problems and went on to win the World Series, one of two achievements for which Martin must be credited—the other being his ability to somehow retain his sanity. Injuries decimated the Yankees of 1978, and by July they were 14 games behind the Red Sox. Billy was again having problems with Jackson, but he had not given up on catching Boston. Just as the Yanks were on a five-game winning streak, Billy made an uncomplimentary remark in a Chicago airport about Jackson and owner George Steinbrenner. On July 24, 1978, in a tearful statement, Billy stepped down as Yankee manager. A few days later it was dramatically announced, again to an Old Timers' Day crowd at the Stadium, that Billy Martin would return as manager in 1979. The fans went wild with delight.

Billy remained associated with the Yanks following his resignation (special scout, etc.) and when the Yanks started the 1979 season poorly, Bob Lemon, who had succeeded Martin, stepped aside to make way for Billy. The Stadium throng gave Martin a long, loud standing ovation as Billy brought out his first lineup card in 11 months. But the Yankees had too many injuries, too many players having off-performances, and too solid an opponent in Baltimore to get back into the pennant race. The Yanks, in fact, finished in fourth place in the American League East, although their record (89-71) was better than that of the champions of the West, the Angels. Yet there were good signs. Martin made peace with Jackson and kept the team together. The team won its final eight games, and if the right improvements were made, the Yanks and Martin could have high hopes for 1980.

The 1979 season was barely over when Billy got into a barroom disagreement with a marshmallow salesman. One thing led to another, and Billy sucker punched the guy. When the story was reported, Billy tried to cover up the truth. It was the deception that most angered Steinbrenner, and on October 28, 1979, he fired Billy again.

Martin managed Oakland in 1980 and drove his young A's to a completely unexpected second-place standing. Berkeley Billy had returned home, breathed life into a moribund franchise and won the hearts of the Bay Area with exciting baseball, which they called Billyball. The Associated Press named Martin Manager of the Year in 1980, and again in 1981, giving him a total of four in eight seasons, including 1974 with Texas and 1976 with New York. Martin's A's in 1981 won the AL West and met the Yankees in the Championship Series. The Yankees rained on Martin's parade, sweeping the Series in three games.

Martin was unhappy in 1982, and at times he acted like he almost wanted to be fired. In October, he *was* fired by the A's, and in January 1983 he was hired to manage the Yankees for a third time. Billy III it was called. Steinbrenner spent lavishly to get Billy back: A four-year contract guaranteeing upwards of $400,000 per year, a signing bonus, a free apartment, a car, and the dangling possibility that Billy might one day become a Yankee executive with real power. Billy was even allowed to have his right-hand man, pitching coach Art Fowler; Billy and George had fought many times over Fowler.

Early in 1983 Martin and Steinbrenner concentrated on battling the umpires, but in June Martin had a voluntary

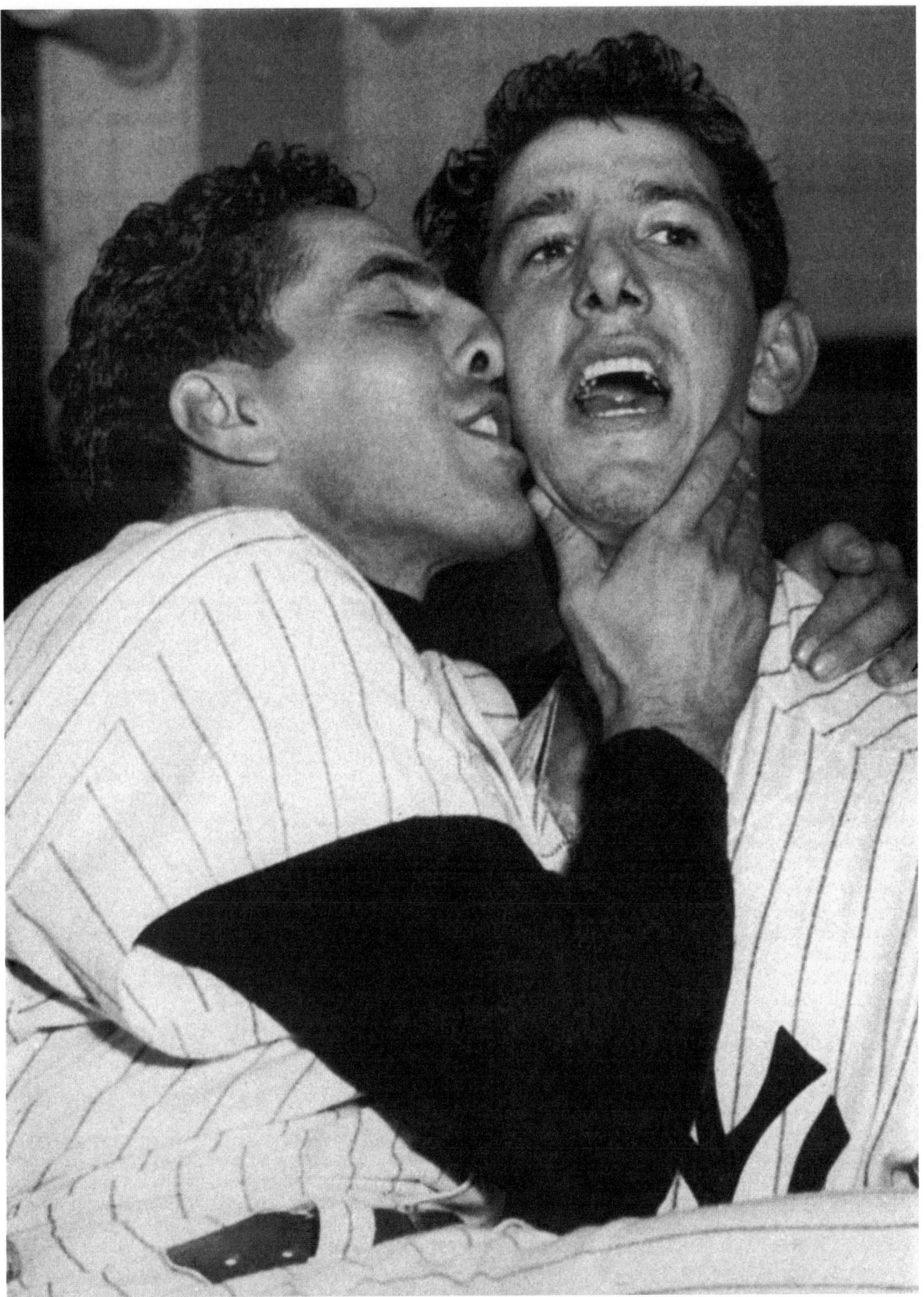

Phil Rizzuto lays one on Billy Martin to celebrate the Yankees' fifth consecutive World Championship after beating the Dodgers in the 1953 World Series. (AP/WIDE WORLD PHOTOS)

workout that Steinbrenner had expected would be mandatory, and as punishment, George fired Fowler in July . Billy, drinking heavily, and suspecting that Fowler's replacements were spying for the owner, mismanaged the bullpen. The July 24 Pine Tar Game, and the subsequent ruling against the Yankees, also took some steam out of the club. "We felt we had a game taken away from us," said Martin. The Yankees finished third with 91 wins.

Steinbrenner in any case wasn't happy, and in December 1983 he replaced Martin with Yogi Berra. Billy hung around collecting $400,000 as a scout in 1984. Martin returned as manager—Billy IV—on April 28, 1985, when Steinbrenner canned Berra after 16 games. The players were loyal to Berra, so Billy kept cool and slowly won them over with winning baseball. The club established itself as a serious contender.

But as the season unfolded, Martin was once again overwhelmed by his regular problems—alcohol, women and friction with Steinbrenner. Billy had a mediocre pitcher, Ed Whitson, who felt misused by Martin all season—and he was angry about it.

In September, Martin and Whitson had it out in the hotel bar at the Cross Keys Inn in Baltimore. Billy entered the bar in time to see Whitson attacking another patron, and when he tried to break it up, Whitson turned on him. Billy punched his pitcher in the face. Teammates pulled Whitson into the lobby, with Martin giving chase. Whitson broke Martin's arm with a kick. Whitson was dragged by others outside, with Martin again in pursuit. When security men finally broke it up, Martin had a bloody nose, two cracked ribs and the broken arm. It took the efforts of many people to keep the snarling Martin and Whitson separated the rest of the night.

It was an ugly scene and a signal that Billy was unraveling. Yet, the Yankees were still in the race when they went to Toronto for the final three games of the season. The Yanks needed to sweep the series to force a playoff with the Blue Jays, but New York won only two of the games. Billy was satisfied with his efforts. On the final day he told reporters that since Earl Weaver and Sparky Anderson hadn't made it to the playoffs and had lucrative contracts, then he, Billy Martin, deserved $500,000 in 1986—or he might not return.

Steinbrenner wasn't amused. "Billy's talking a half million dollars?" asked George. "Well, let's see. That'll be $200,000 for managing the team and $300,000 for being the first challenger to Michael Spinks."

A few weeks later Steinbrenner replaced Martin with Lou Piniella, and Billy joined the Yankee broadcasting team in 1986 and 1987. His contract was extended four more years. Billy even was given a "Day" at Yankee Stadium on August 10, 1986, when his number 1 uniform was retired.

Martin climbed back into the number 1 uniform as manager in 1988. When Billy V was announced on October 19, 1987, a lot of people were laughing. "The last laugh is going to be mine," vowed Martin. He had Fowler back, he seemed healthy, and he would claim that his January 1988 marriage was a good influence on him.

Billy's marriage wasn't all that happy, and his health didn't last long either. While the Yankees were in Texas on May 7, Billy visited a sleazy strip bar where a rough crowd hung out. Something Billy said or did caught the attention of some tough guys who beat Billy to a pulp in the men's room. Billy needed 80 stitches to close his wounds.

The Yankees were in first place most of May, but Billy was disintegrating. On May 30, he ended an argument with Umpire Dale Scott by scooping up a pile of dirt and throwing it on Scott. Billy was soon fined and suspended three games, but the umpires thought he got off too light. Billy threatened to sue the umpires. Finally, on June 7, Commissioner Ueberroth made Martin apologize.

Billy wasn't happy that the front office hadn't gotten rid of Tim Stoddard, and in one game he allowed Stoddard to stay in and take a beating. Acting General Manager Clyde King, never a Martin fan, interpreted Billy's behavior as a slap in the face, and he advised Steinbrenner to make a change.

Billy's last three games were all last-at-bat losses in Detroit, knocking the Yankees out of first place. On June 23, 1988, Martin was replaced by Piniella. Steinbrenner said he was worried about Billy's drinking and eroding managerial skills. In 1989 Billy was a roving scout for the Yankees and hoped to get another chance at the helm. On Christmas day, after an afternoon of drinking in a bar, Martin was killed when he wrecked his truck.

A complicated man, Billy grew up on the wrong side of the tracks and was always trying to prove himself. He was fiery, combative, daring, a brilliant baseball strategist, and a guy who would help out ex-ballplayers down on their luck. He was also crude, sometimes slurring ethnic and racial groups, and a bully. He hated anyone having any control over him, but in the end alcohol was his master.

YANKEE MANAGER RECORD FOR BILLY MARTIN

Years	Won	Lost	Percentage	Standing
1975	30	26	.536	incomplete season
1976	97	62	.610	1st (EAST)
1977	100	62	.617	1st (EAST)
1978	52	42	.553	incomplete season
1979	55	40	.579	incomplete season
1983	91	71	.562	3rd (EAST)
1985	91	54	.628	incomplete season
1988	40	28	.588	incomplete season
8 Yrs.	556	385	.591	2 pennants

World Series

Years	Outcome	Won	Lost	Opponent
1976	Lost	0	4	Cincinnati Reds
1977	Won	4	2	Los Angeles Dodgers
2 Yrs.	1-1	4	6	

LEMON, BOB

Manager: 1978-79; 1981-82
Born: September 22, 1920
Birthplace: San Bernardino, CA
Died: January 11, 2000

Bob Lemon on September 6, 1981, returned to manage the Yankees for a second time and won an American League pennant. But it is the first stint that Lemon served at the Yankee helm that is truly one of baseball's most remarkable stories. Lemon was named to replace Billy Martin after Martin's July 24, 1978 resignation. Just a few weeks before, Bob was fired as the White Sox manager. He became the first American League manager to win a pennant after taking over in mid-season.

The 1978 Yankees had fallen behind the first-place Red Sox by as many as 14 games and were 10 games back when Lemon took the managerial reins. Lemon knew the kind of personality situation he was getting into in New York. In fact, when asked about the Yanks' internal problems in 1977, the then-Chicago manager quipped: "It's like Mary Hartman, Mary Hartman"— a pointed reference to the popular soap opera of the day. Internal discontent had the Yanks by the throat as Lemon took over, but Bob's low-key approach seemed to stabilize the team. Most of the real and imagined problems were soon settled or pushed aside and forgotten. Not only was the climate improved, but injured players began to return to the lineup. Soon the Yankees were playing good baseball. The Red Sox, meanwhile, were faltering. Finally New York pulled ahead of Boston. But then the Red Sox rallied, tying the Yankees on the last day of the season and forcing a one-game playoff.

Because of Lemon's good planning, Ron Guidry was ready to pitch for the Yankees at Fenway Park and the Yanks beat Boston, 5-4, winning the AL East title and capping the greatest comeback in baseball history. Bob Lemon deserved and was given much of the credit for the miracle. The Yankees then beat the Royals and Dodgers to capture the World Championship. In less than three months as Yankee manager, Bob Lemon had himself a World Championship. Lemon helped the team by getting Thurman Munson out of the outfield and returning him to everyday catcher, by making Reggie Jackson the regular rightfielder and cleanup hitter, and by pitching Ed Figueroa every fourth day instead of every fifth. But mostly Lemon just let the Yankees play, and slowly their assorted wounds responded. Lemon believes a team plays best when its members are comfortable and allowed to perform without worry. He was cool and collected, and the Yanks turned red hot.

Lemon was accorded the kind of acclaim he won as a great right-handed pitcher for the Cleveland Indians (1946-58). His lifetime record was a brilliant 207-128 for a winning percentage of .618. He was a fierce competitor with a hot temper, but a respected and well-liked teammate. Bob remained in baseball following his playing career. He was a scout for the Indians (1959); a coach for the Indians (1960), Phillies (1961) and Angels (1967-70); and a minor-league manager at Honolulu (1964) and Seattle (1965-66), both of the Pacific Coast League. *The Sporting News* named him the Minor League Manager of the Year in 1966.

Lemon's first managing job in the majors was with Kansas City (1970-72). In 1971 he took his young Royals to a surprising second-place finish in the AL West. Making his way to New York, Lemon did an excellent job as Yankee pitching coach in 1976, the Yanks' pitching staff recording the league's lowest ERA. (Bob's greatest job as a mentor may have been in the early 1950s when he coached actor Ronald Reagan for the Grover Cleveland Alexander movie, "The Winning Team." He also played a small role, portraying Jesse Haines in Game 7 of the 1926 World Series.) Lemon in 1977 became the White Sox manager and turned Chicago into the year's surprise team with a 90-72 record (contrasted to a 64-97 mark the previous year). But Chicago got off to a lackluster start in 1978 and on June 30, Bill Veeck fired Lemon. Yankee President Al Rosen, a close friend and former Cleveland teammate, knew immediately whom he wanted to be Yankee manager when Billy Martin resigned a few weeks later.

Ten days after his Yankees won the 1978 World Series, Bob Lemon experienced a deep personal tragedy. His 26-year-old son, Jerry, was killed in an automobile accident. Understandably, Bob was not as intense in his managerial duties in 1979 as he had been the previous season. The Yanks started slowly, and in late June, Yankee principal owner George Steinbrenner replaced Lemon with Billy Martin. Said Lemon: "It's not that I didn't want to win, but when I lost, it didn't bother me as much." He left New York with dignity and without a bad word for anyone. The New York Baseball Writers gave Lemon their Ben Epstein "Good Guy" Award for 1979, and at the ceremonies Lemon joked, "I was only here a year. I wasn't around long enough for the writers to find out what kind of guy I really am."

Lemon left New York but not the Yankees; he remained in the Yankee organization with a contract that ran through the 1982 season. Bob scouted for the Yanks from 1979-81 out of his home in Long Beach, Calif., and turned down several offers from other teams to manage. But in early September 1981, Steinbrenner and Yankee Manager Gene Michael became embroiled in a dispute that led to a change of managers. A self-confessed "company man," Lemon was summoned to Tampa, where Steinbrenner offered him the Yankee managerial job. He accepted and even let on that his release in 1979 was for his own good.

Lemon inherited a Yankee team that lacked incentive, having already qualified for the expanded playoff plan by winning the First Season of 1981. The Yanks' 11-14 finish under Bob is not indicative of his talents. In fact, Lemon had the Yanks primed and ready for the playoffs. After knocking off Milwaukee, the Yankees polished off Oakland in three consecutive games, leading Lemon to joke about "Bobbyball." In both series, the Yankees had the right man in the right place at the right time, thanks to Lemon.

But the 1981 World Series against the Dodgers turned into a nightmare for Lemon. The Yankees easily won the first two games before dropping three one-run games in a row in Los Angeles. Each defeat was hard to take and each was a second guesser's dream. But Lemon's moves in those games were nothing compared to the emphatic, gambling decision he made in fateful and final Game 6. With the score tied, 1-1, in the bottom of the fourth, and with two outs and two on, Lemon pinchhit for Tommy John. New York failed to score, and a succession of Yankee relievers failed to do the job. The Yanks were pummeled, 9-2, and lost the Series. But some of the Yankee players failed to produce and other circumstances, most notably Lemon's rustiness in developing strategies pinned to the absence of a designated hitter and the need to bat the pitcher, conspired to undermine the cause.

Steinbrenner promised Lemon he would manage a full season in 1982 "no matter what." The plan was for Lemon to retire after the season and pass the job back to Gene Michael. But on April 25, after the Yankees won and improved their record to 6-8, the impatient Steinbrenner made the change six months early. Michael became the manager, and Lemon returned to scouting, a position he still held with the Yankees in 1994.

Lemon had at least four factors working against him in 1982: 1) Reggie Jackson in January signed with the Angels, and the Yankees missed his power. 2) The new players, Ken Griffey and Dave Collins, weren't fitting in the picture. 3) The decision to open spring training two weeks early had left the players unhappy and resentful. 4) The trading of reliever Ron Davis for shortstop Roy Smalley hurt the club in the bullpen, defensively at shortstop, and with morale, as Bucky Dent stewed.

What can't be taken away from Lemon is his status as one of the game's greats. He received baseball's highest honor in

1976 when he was inducted into the Baseball Hall of Fame for his pitching greatness. Bob's Jersey (#21) was retired by the Cleveland Indians in 1998. He died January 11, 2000.

YANKEE MANAGER RECORD FOR BOB LEMON				
Years	Won	Lost	Percentage	Standing
1978	48	20	.706	incomplete season
1979	34	31	.523	incomplete season
1981	11	14	.440	incomplete season
1982	6	8	.429	incomplete season
4 Yrs.	99	73	.576	2 pennants

World Series				
Years	Outcome	Won	Lost	Opponent
1978	Won	4	2	Los Angeles Dodgers
1981	Lost	2	4	Los Angeles Dodgers
2 Yrs.	1-1	6	6	

HOWSER, DICK

Manager: 1980
Born: May 14, 1937
Birthplace: Miami, FL
Died: June 17, 1987

Dick Howser became Yankee manager on October 28, 1979, following the sudden dismissal of Billy Martin. He had been with the Yankees as a player and a coach since 1967.

Howser began his major-league playing career with the Kansas City A's in 1961 when he hit .280, stole 37 bases, and won *The Sporting News'* American League Rookie Award. He played shortstop for the A's and Indians before the Yanks obtained him from Cleveland in December 1966 for pitcher Gil Downs and money. Howser had built a reputation as a fine glove man, and the Yankees used him as a utility infielder in 1967 and 1968. Howser, who had a lifetime batting average of .248, went 63 for 299 with New York (.211). He was released as a player in October 1968 and immediately signed as a Yankee coach.

Replacing the legendary Frank Crosetti, who retired, Howser was the Yankee third base coach from 1969 to 1978. He worked harmoniously with four managers (Houk, Virdon, Martin, Lemon) and got along equally well with the Yankee players. Howser was reportedly offered the manager's job when Martin's position with the Yankees was in jeopardy. He is said to have declined the offer because of his friendship with Billy, but he was acting manager for a few days in 1978—after Martin resigned and before Bob Lemon could take up the reins.

Howser returned to his alma mater, Florida State University, as baseball coach following the 1978 World Series. His 1979 FSU team had a 43-17 record and made it to the NCAA Regional Playoffs. So Howser was doing well in his native Sunshine State when the Yankees contacted him in October of 1979.

Dick Howser said yes, thus becoming the 23rd Yankee manager. Managing the Yanks, he said, "was the only job I would have taken. I've had a couple of feelers from other organizations in the last few months but I never considered them. But this is the New York Yankees. How can I turn it down?"

Howser enjoyed a great season as rookie manager in 1980, becoming only the fourth manager in big-league history to win at least 100 games in his initial campaign (joining Mickey

Cochrane, Ralph Houk and Sparky Anderson). Only the 109 victories registered by Houk with the 1961 Yankees are more by a first-year skipper than Howser's 103 triumphs of 1980. Dick ran a tight ship—there was no question he was in charge—but he brought a much-needed lighter atmosphere to Yankee business. Perhaps his greatest contribution in 1980 was reestablishing the winning attitude in the Yankee clubhouse, dugout and on the playing field. There is no question that some talented veterans resented Howser's extensive platooning system, but with the gifted, deep bench at his call, Dick would have been foolish not to make the most of it. He did. Perhaps some players' roles were not defined clearly enough to suit them, but in Dick's first year he was entitled to some rookie mistakes. And Dick probably made a few strategical errors from the dugout. But what manager doesn't? Overall, Howser did an outstanding job, and the proof is in the Yanks' 103 wins.

Howser got the most out of the 1980 Yankees even when faced with serious and long-term injuries to, among others, his centerfielder Ruppert Jones and his third baseman Graig Nettles. Howser drove his team to an early season lead largely because of the great attitude of the club. He weathered the disturbing events of late summer when Baltimore appeared ready to surge past the Yanks. And Dick was strong enough not to panic, letting his team and Goose Gossage put together a powerful final five-week run to win the division. The three-game playoff loss to Kansas City was an unpleasant ending to a marvelous year.

In the face of all his accomplishments, Dick Howser resigned on November 21, 1980. His troubles with principal owner George Steinbrenner, which became public in August when the Yankee owner publicly denounced his manager after an embarrassing series in Baltimore, were irreconcilable. In the playoff loss to the Royals, the controversial decision by third-base coach Mike Ferraro, Howser's man, to send home Willie Randolph to be thrown out in Game 2, was to Steinbrenner vindication that he was correct about Ferraro's poor third-base coaching judgment. Several weeks later, Steinbrenner announced that deposed Boston manager Don Zimmer was welcome to the Yanks' third-base coaching job if the position suited Zimmer. Howser stated publicly that he wanted the courtesy of approving his coaches, and the fireworks started. Howser's Yankee days were numbered, and he reluctantly relinquished the reins after some soul-searching. The reason given for Howser's resignation was that a business offer too good to pass up was made to Dick back home in Tallahassee, Florida. The entire situation was an unhappy and distasteful one for all concerned. In losing Dick Howser, the Yankees lost a decent man who had given years of loyal service to the club. The New York chapter of the Baseball Writers Association of America showed what they thought of Howser when in the winter of 1980-81 they awarded him the Ben Epstein "Good Guy" Award for 1980.

Howser remained with the Yankees as director of scouting in the southeast until August 1981 when he was named manager of the Kansas City Royals. The Royals qualified for the expanded strike-season playoffs, and lost three straight games. Howser's Royals lost the ALCS in 1984—again, in three straight games. At this point, Howser was 0-9 in postseason play, and he had a lot of baseball people and fans pulling for him.

The Royals won their division again in 1985 and met Toronto in the ALCS. Kansas City lost the first two games, extending Howser's playoff losing streak to 11 games. Finally, the Royals broke through with a win, and with the monkey off their backs, they went on to win the ALCS. When the Royals defeated the Cardinals in the World Series, Howser quickly had gone from a pitied man to a world champion manager.

Two days after managing the American League to an All-Star Game victory in 1986, Howser was diagnosed as having a brain tumor. He left the club, bravely but unsuccessfully attempted a comeback in the spring training of 1987, and died in June at age 50.

YANKEE MANAGER RECORD FOR DICK HOWSER

Years	Won	Lost	Percentage	Standing
1978	0	1	.000	incomplete season
1980	103	59	.636	1st (EAST)
2 Yrs.	103	60	.632	0 pennants

MICHAEL, GENE

Nickname: "Stick"
Manager: 1981, 1982
Born: June 2, 1938
Birthplace: Kent, OH

With Dick Howser's resignation on November 21, 1980, principal owner George Steinbrenner named Gene Michael the Yankee manager for 1981. Michael had served as the club's general manager since October of 1979. His association with the Yankees began in 1968 when he came over from the Dodgers as a shortstop.

A fine athlete at Kent State University where he earned a degree in education, Gene had a basketball opportunity (the New York Knicks of the NBA were interested in signing him) but opted for a career in baseball. He signed with Pittsburgh and spent eight seasons in the Pirate farm system before getting his chance with the big club in 1966 (5 for 33, .152, in 30 games). In 1966 he was dealt to Los Angeles where he saw more playing time, hitting .202 in 98 games. But the biggest break of Michael's career came on November 30, 1967, when the Dodgers sold his contract to the Yankees.

Michael spent seven Yankee seasons (1968-74) as a skillful and heady defensive player; he was a conspicuously successful practitioner of the hidden ball trick, pulling the deceptive play five times. He was a popular and consistent Yankee, a fiery player wont to get into scraps, and a student of the game. "Stick" was not much with the stick (his 1969 season, when he hit .272, was the only season he ever hit over .260). But he was a vital piece of the Yankee rebuilding effort.

Displaying as much courage off the field as on, Michael is one of the few Yankee players to ever take owner Steinbrenner to arbitration over a salary dispute. He lost and was forced to accept management's figure (though it was only about $10,000 below what Gene demanded). His playing career ended with the Tigers in 1975, although he later had a brief trial with the Red Sox, and he returned to the Yankees as a special scout and coach. He coached briefly in 1976 and then moved into the Yankee front office as an administrative assistant. In one of his roles in 1976-77, he would use a walkie-talkie to reach the Yankee dugout and from a vantage point in the stands participate in the positioning of fielders. The tactic caused a stir around baseball but many teams have since followed the Yankee lead.

After serving as the Yanks' first-base coach in 1978, he managed the club's Class-AAA team in Columbus to an International League championship in 1979. He then became the Yankee GM. In short, Gene Michael had been under Yankee grooming.

Toward the end of the 1980 season, Steinbrenner began dropping hints that "Stick" might become the next Yankee skipper. Columbus executive George Sisler once told him, Steinbrenner informed the press, that Michael had the makings of a great manager. Without doubt, the excellent working relationship Michael and Steinbrenner enjoyed was unique in the Yankee inner circle. And it did not seem attributable to subservience on Michael's part. Gene, on assuming the manager's job insisted that he spoke his own mind and was no rubber stamp for the owner. He was to prove as good as his word.

Gene met with the press on August 28 after 1981's Second Season (due to a player's strike) had gotten off to a dreary start and aired grievances he had with the club's owner. He was tired of working under constant threats of dismissal, he said, adding, "I told him (Steinbrenner) to quit threatening me. If he wants me to go, make the move—don't wait." Michael said that he listened to Steinbrenner's suggestions but he could not agree with all of them. "I can't take it any longer," he told the press.

Steinbrenner appeared to have been both stunned and hurt by Michael's remarks and waited nine days for an apology. Gene refused and on September 6 Steinbrenner said he had no alternative but to fire him. The situation was rich in irony. What Steinbrenner liked in Michael, besides his considerable baseball knowledge—what was perhaps the main reason for Michael's hiring—was Gene's disciplined toughness and fighting spirit, the latter a product of his intense desire to excel. Michael could do battle on the playing field and win Steinbrenner's approving admiration, but the fight and spirit in Gene Michael ultimately cost him his job.

The Yankees went into the 1981 playoffs based on the First Season title they won under Michael. Bob Lemon, Michael's replacement, received the credit for winning the pennant (but also the blame for losing the World Series).

Once his anger subsided, Steinbrenner decided that fairness dictated he give Michael another chance. Michael became the manager in waiting, and in April 1982, Lemon was replaced by Michael. Now Michael was stuck with an overrated unhappy club, soon to be decimated even further by injuries and constantly changing personnel. On August 3, the White Sox swept the Yankees in a doubleheader, fans at Yankee Stadium were offered an apology and free tickets, and the Yankees fell to 50-50 for the season—and Michael was replaced by Clyde King. Steinbrenner blamed the players. "I don't really blame Stick," said the Boss. "It's just that I have to do what I have to do."

Michael coached for the Yankees, and in June 1986 he was hired as Cubs manager by General Manager Dallas Green. Green was as unrelenting as Steinbrenner. By the end of the 1986 season, Green was saying Michael wasn't being tough enough. Stick quit in 1987 before Green could fire him.

Michael later rejoined the Yankees, and on August 20, 1990, on Steinbrenner's final day as general partner before serving his ban from baseball, Steinbrenner named Michael the club's general manager. Stick did an outstanding job in rebuilding the Yankees but seemed to fall from favor again in 1995. After being asked to take a salary cut following the 1995

Gene Michael (New York Yankees Archives)

season, Stick stepped down as general manager and is now an executive in the Yakees scouting department.

YANKEE MANAGER RECORD FOR GENE MICHAEL				
Years	Won	Lost	Percentage	Standing
1981	48	34	.585	incomplete season
1982	44	42	.512	incomplete season
2 Yrs.	92	76	.548	0 pennants

KING, CLYDE

Manager: 1982
Born: May 23, 1925
Birthplace: Goldsboro, NC

Clyde King managed the Yankees from August 1982 through the end of the season. He was the club's third manager of the season, and he accepted the position "reluctantly, but willingly." At one point in 1982, King had been the team's pitching coach—one of five the Yankees had in 1982.

King played baseball and basketball at the University of North Carolina, pitched in the majors between 1944 and 1953, mostly with Brooklyn, and managed the Giants (1969-70) and Braves (1974-75). He joined the Yankees in 1975 and became a troubleshooter, doing whatever George Steinbrenner asked of him.

King was named Yankee pitching coach on June 11, 1982, and he returned to front-office special assignments on July 19. On August 4, as a favor to Steinbrenner, he became manager. King insisted at the time that Steinbrenner said he could manage in 1983, too, although King was often called an interim manager. Steinbrenner was hoping King would "light a spark."

None was lit. The club played no better for King than it had for Bob Lemon or Gene Michael. In late September, the Yankees

were granted permission by the A's to speak with Martin, but King said he wanted to remain manager. He talked about having had a "positive" meeting with the owner.

So it had to hurt in January 1983 when King was replaced by Billy Martin. Clyde returned to the front office as a scout and advisor to Steinbrenner—he was GM from 1984 to 1986—and he continued as a special advisor with the Yankees through 1995.

YANKEE MANAGER RECORD FOR CLYDE KING				
Years	Won	Lost	Percentage	Standing
1982	29	33	.468	incomplete season
1 Yr.	29	33	.468	0 pennants

PINIELLA, LOU

Nickname: "Sweet Lou"
Manager: 1986-87, 1988
Born: August 28, 1943
Birthplace: Tampa, FL

On October 27, 1985, Lou Piniella, one of the most popular Yankees ever, and a .295 Yankee-career hitter, was named Yankee manager, replacing Billy Martin. Piniella accepted a one-year contract for $200,000. He had been groomed for the job since becoming a batting instructor while still playing in 1981. He had been a Yankee coach since retiring as a player in June 1984. He wanted to become manager but had been uncomfortable with his manager-in-waiting status.

When Martin returned as manager in April 1985, Billy and Lou talked. "Look Lou," said Martin. "I talked to George. He wants me to take this club over now. He also wants me to take you under my wing. He wants me to teach you. He wants you to manage this baseball team. You'll probably be the next one."

Martin expected to move into a front-office decision-making position, and Piniella believed Martin was committed to the plan. He began learning game tactics from Martin. Things went smoothly. Then, in mid-season, Martin was hospitalized and George Steinbrenner asked Piniella to run the club in Billy's absence. It was a disaster. Angry that he wasn't consulted or informed, Martin ran the club from his hospital phone. Billy got the credit in the press for the first two wins; Lou got the blame for the next three losses. A few Yankees openly defied Lou's authority. Lou felt it was a bad joke—and played at his expense.

Piniella told General Manager Clyde King he was quitting. The next day Martin called Lou, asked him to return and admitted he should have allowed Piniella to run the club. And Lou learned a valuable lesson, too; he was no longer one of the guys, he was management.

"Remember, you're in charge," Steinbrenner told Piniella at their first meeting after Lou was named manager. "You make the rules, but be sure you enforce them."

Piniella somehow coaxed 90 wins and a second-place standing out of the Yankees in 1986. His pitching staff was terrible; the Yankees allowed more than four earned runs per game for the first time in 36 years, and Dennis Rasmussen was the only double-figures winner. Billy Martin was watching from the broadcast booth. "I think Lou Piniella did a fantastic job," said Martin. "The way he kept the team in the race, with all the pitching problems he faced, I think he deserved to be Manager of the Year." Lou was rewarded with a new two-year contract.

At the All-Star break in 1987, Piniella's Yankees were in first place with a record of 55-34. However, New York fell apart in the throes of an 11-17 August, and eventually finished fourth. The team's ERA was a horrendous 4.36. The Yankees used 15 different starting pitchers but couldn't find the answer to their problem.

During a 2-8 road trip in August, Piniella missed a phone call from Steinbrenner. Things got tense. A few days later Steinbrenner said the following in an interview: "Lou Piniella has no reason to be hurt. I do. I've made every player move he's asked for since Day One, and this is what happens. If anyone should be hurt, it's me. I've done everything for this guy. I gave him a chance to manage the New York Yankees without going to the minors first. In retrospect, maybe that was a mistake."

The handwriting was on the wall—Lou was out. Actually, he got promoted. In October 1987, Martin was named manager and Piniella became the General Manager. Now Piniella was really caught between a rock and a hard place, namely Martin and Steinbrenner. Lou resigned on May 29, 1988. Soon thereafter, however, on June 23, George replaced Martin as manager with Piniella. Lou took over a 40-28 club two games out of first place and drove it back into first briefly in late July. But the club swooned with an awful 9-20 August. The Yankees finished only 3½ games behind first-place Boston, but the signs were evident that the Yankees were declining.

Steinbrenner was still looking for a quick fix—and more discipline. He replaced Piniella with Dallas Green in October 1988. In November 1989, Piniella was named manager of Cincinnati, and in 1990 he led the Reds to an upset World Series sweep over the powerful A's.

In 1993, Piniella moved on to manage Seattle and was reunited with General Manager Woody Woodward, with whom he had worked closely on the Yankees. Lou did a great job in 1995. Basically with five outstanding players—Randy Johnson, Ken Griffey Jr., Jay Buhner, Edgar Martinez and Tino Martinez—and little else but a cast of mediocre players, Lou was able to rally his club from a two-games-to-none deficit and beat the Yankees. The storybook season ended in a playoff series loss to Cleveland, but Piniella's stock as one of the game's best motivators soared.

Lou's Mariner teams continued to excel with subsequent playoff appearances in 1997, 2000, and 2001. In 2001 he guided Seattle to an AL Record 116 wins during the regular season. His 2000 and 2001 teams were both eliminated in the ALCS by the Yankees. Citing a desire to move closer to his family, Lou left the Mariners after the 2002 season to take over the Tampa Bay Devil Rays.

YANKEE MANAGER RECORD FOR LOU PINIELLA

Years	Won	Lost	Percentage	Standing
1986	90	72	.556	2nd (EAST)
1987	89	73	.549	4th (EAST)
1988	45	48	.484	incomplete season
3 Yrs.	224	193	.537	0 pennants

GREEN, DALLAS

Manager: 1989
Born: August 4, 1934
Birthplace: Newport, DE

Dallas Green became the Yankee manager on October 7, 1988. A career National Leaguer, Green was the first manager hired by George Steinbrenner having no previous connection to the Yankees, and Green brought an entirely new coaching staff with him to New York. "I'm coming in here as a new guy because everybody who supposedly knew all about these guys hadn't gotten the job done," explained Green. His friendship with Steinbrenner extended 30 years when they used to hang out in the same bar in Buffalo; George was building ships, Green pitching in the minors.

Most of his career Green had been with the Phillies. He served as pitcher, minor-league executive, and manager, and as manager in 1980 he led the Phillies to their first-ever World Series championship. He was also general manager of the Cubs, 1981-87. He was an imposing 6'5" and at least 245 pounds, and he ran things like a drill sergeant. On the surface, Green seemed to be the enforcer Steinbrenner had always coveted. "I'm a screamer, a yeller and a cusser," he once said. "I never hold back."

Green in 1989 inherited a miserable pitching staff. Additionally, Jack Clark had been traded, Dave Winfield was sidelined all year, and Rickey Henderson was unhappy and traded in mid-season. Green platooned Mike Pagliarulo, who pressed when he played. Green was correct in assessing Pags' weakness against lefthanded pitching, but he was the first Yankee manager unable to get overall offensive production from Pags. When Pagliarulo was traded, the Yankees were left with a huge hole at third base.

Tough, caustic and quick to criticize his players, Green preached game-situation baseball. After losing a May game, 4-3, in 11 innings, he paced the clubhouse for 10 minutes and complained that the Yankees "need 10 hits, 16 passed balls and 10 errors before we can score a run." Added Green: "It's pretty obvious the guys don't understand what game-situation baseball is. We had a chance to win that game 50 times."

But besides bullying his players, Green began finding fault with the owner, who in turn found fault with the manager. They bickered through the press for weeks. When Steinbrenner second-guessed him, Green called him "Manager George." Steinbrenner attacked some of Green's coaches, particularly batting coach Frank Howard, and George was angry when Dallas said the Yankees hadn't had a scouting report on a young pitcher who mowed them down because the club didn't have any scouts on the road.

Finally, on August 18, 1989, with the Yankees slumbering at 56-65, Steinbrenner replaced Green with Bucky Dent. Green told reporters that in a meeting with Steinbrenner earlier in the day George had said he was firing four of Green's coaches. Green suggested he fire the manager instead—and Green *and* the coaches (Charlie Fox, Pat Corrales, Lee Elia and Frank Howard) were canned.

Steinbrenner, however, insisted the firing "had nothing to do with coaching changes." It was about their deteriorating relationship, said George. "I was beginning to read in the papers he was saying a lot of personal things," explained the Boss. "I told him it was very disappointing to me."

Green replaced a struggling Jeff Torborg as the Mets manager in 1993. Dallas was replaced by Bobby Valentine in 1996, as the Mets remained below .500 during Green's tenure.

YANKEE MANAGER RECORD FOR DALLAS GREEN

Years	Won	Lost	Percentage	Standing
1989	56	65	.463	incomplete season
1 Yr.	56	65	.463	0 pennants

DENT, BUCKY

Manager: 1989-90
Born: November 25, 1951
Birthplace: Savannah, GA

On August 18, 1989, Columbus Manager Bucky Dent received a phone call from George Steinbrenner. "My plane will be there at 12:30, be on it." With that, Dent was whisked off to Detroit to join the Yankees as their new manager. He flew into a mess.

The Yankees were lousy, a far cry from the proud Yankee teams Dent played on between 1977 and 1982. Dent's most profound contribution to the club's success had been his three-run homer off Mike Torrez in the Yanks' 5-4 playoff win in Boston in 1978. In 1989, Dent opened a baseball school in Florida and built a replica of Fenway Park's Green Monster, and when it opened, Dent and Torrez recreated the 1978 homer. Dent, unlike his predecessor, Dallas Green, understood Yankee tradition.

Dent started managing in the Yankee farm system in 1985 and had performed well at Fort Lauderdale and Columbus. "Who knows how long it will last," he said upon taking over the Yankees, "but I'm going to be here as long as I can."

When the Yankees suddenly won nine consecutive games, the Yankees announced that Dent would remain as manager. The Yankees finished the season 74-87, and 18-22 under Dent.

The biggest concern about Dent was whether he could be vocal enough to be a strong leader. He had been rather quiet as a player. "I really am a fiery guy," he insisted in the spring of 1990.

But as Bucky surveyed his team early in 1990 he must have known he didn't have the tools to win. His starting pitching was terrible, and he had no established bullpen closer. His only hope seemed to be outscoring the opposition.

As the early season unfolded, the pitching *was* bad, but so was the run production. The Yankees, in fact, were scoring the fewest runs in the majors. On June 6, 1990, with the Yankees having lost nine of ten games, including four straight, and owning baseball's worst record (18-31), Dent was dismissed as manager. "He's been made the scapegoat," said catcher Rick Cerone. "We're the ones who got him fired. We're the ones with the worst record in baseball."

Other players were more critical of Dent. Some felt he didn't communicate well. "Bucky listened to too many people," said one unidentified player. "He didn't do a bad job, but he managed scared. But managing in New York, I couldn't blame him."

There was a gloomy feeling that the Yankees had reached one of their lowest points in history.

YANKEE MANAGER RECORD FOR BUCKY DENT

Years	Won	Lost	Percentage	Standing
1989	18	22	.450	incomplete season
1990	18	31	.367	incomplete season
2 Yrs.	36	53	.404	0 pennants

MERRILL, STUMP

Manager: 1990-91
Born: February 25, 1944
Birthplace: Brunswick, ME

Stump Merrill's dream came true on June 6, 1990, when he was rewarded for 14 hard-working seasons in the Yankee organization with his promotion to Yankee manager. Merrill got a hint as early as May 13 when George Steinbrenner went to Columbus, where Merrill was managing, and told Stump there might be a change and that Stump was being considered.

Carl Harrison Merrill, a Maine native, played baseball at the University of Maine. After spending six years catching in the Phillie farm system (1966-71)—he never reached the majors but did celebrate his first of two professional homers by sliding into home—Merrill returned to the University of Maine, earned a Master's degree and was an assistant baseball and football coach.

Merrill in 1977 joined the Yankee organization as the pitching coach at West Haven. The next year Stump began a managing journey that took him to West Haven, Nashville, Fort Lauderdale and Columbus. He earned respect everywhere.

Yankee Manager Yogi Berra in 1985 chose Merrill as first-base coach. When Billy Martin replaced Berra early in the season, Merrill was swept out and returned to managing Columbus. Manager Lou Piniella brought Merrill back as administrative coach in 1986 and first-base coach in 1987. Merrill over the next two years was minor-league coordinator, advance major-league scout, and minor-league manager at Prince William.

Stump broke Steinbrenner's New York-needs-a-big-name rule. Stump wasn't dramatic, or even colorful. He was a feisty fireplug, and a no-nonsense guy who watched helplessly as the Yankees lost their first four games under him, extending their losing streak to eight games. The weak Yankees finished the 1990 season dead last.

Yet, Merrill was enthusiastic in the 1991 spring camp. He thought the Yankees might surprise people, and he was striving for daily improvement. He seemed on the right track when the Yankees surged above .500 in July, but the club folded badly and finished 71-91.

Sadly, Merrill was sabotaged by some of his players. They whined, used anonymous quotes and questioned his ability as a tactician. Others believed Stump wasn't enough of a force. When Stump did lay down the law, it was with the wrong person, Don Mattingly, and over a silly matter. He benched Mattingly on August 15 over Don's refusal to get a haircut.

General Manager Gene Michael shared some of the blame for the Mattingly fiasco, but nevertheless he relieved Merrill of the managing job on October 7, 1991. When he was asked if the negative quotes from his players had hastened his exit, Stump replied, "Sure it did."

YANKEE MANAGER RECORD FOR STUMP MERRILL				
Year	Won	Lost	Percentage	Standing
1990	49	64	.434	incomplete season
1991	71	91	.438	5th (EAST)
2 Yrs.	120	155	.436	0 pennants

SHOWALTER, BUCK

Manager: 1992-1995
Born: May 23, 1956
Birthplace: DeFuniak Springs, FL

When Stump Merrill was fired on October 7, 1991, Buck Showalter was one of the coaches let go, too. That, combined with General Manager Gene Michael's assertion that he wanted a manager with prior major-league experience, seemed to leave Buck out of the picture. That is until the Yankee ownership partners met on October 18 and strongly urged Michael to reconsider Showalter over some of the retread candidates Michael had in mind.

George Steinbrenner was at the partners meeting, which was allowed in the agreement he had with the commissioner banning him from the day-to-day activities. The question is how much of a role, if any, Steinbrenner had in the Showalter hiring. It is known that Showalter had become one of Steinbrenner's favorites inside the organization. If the Boss indeed made the choice, it may have been his wisest decision as owner.

On October 29, 1991, Michael introduced Showalter as the new manager. When he was asked if Buck had been his first choice, Michael replied, "He is now." Showalter, the youngest manager in the majors and the youngest Yankee manager since 1914, impressed everyone with the way he made an uncomfortable situation somehow comfortable. "There is no one in this room who feels any better vibes about the organization than me," said Buck.

Buck made it a point to start patching the club's damaged relationship with Don Mattingly, who wasn't sure he wanted to stay with the Yankees. Showalter and Mattingly had been minor-league teammates, and Don would say later that the Yankees turned for the better the day Buck became manager.

Born William Nathaniel Showalter III, Buck was raised in Florida and graduated from Mississippi State University in 1979. He was selected by the Yankees in the fifth round of the June 1977 draft, and though he was a good hitter—he hit .324 with Nashville in 1980—he never played in the majors. He started managing in the Yankee farm system in 1985. His two-year record at Oneonta was 114-41; he was the New York-Penn League's Manager of the Year in 1985. In 1987 and 1988, he managed Ft. Lauderdale, and in 1989, as manager of Albany-Colonie, he was the Manager of the Year in the Eastern League. Along the way, he developed a reputation as a great game tactician.

Showalter was a Yankee coach in 1990 and 1991, the first year as the Eye in the Sky administrative coach and the next season as third-base coach.

As Yankee manager, Showalter quickly developed a good working relationship with Gene Michael. They kept the club stable and focused on winning baseball, and they played and evaluated their young players. Buck was selected as a coach for the 1992 All-Star Game, the first Yankee manager so honored since Ralph Houk was selected in 1970. The Yankees finished 76-86, a five-game improvement over 1991.

George Steinbrenner resumed command of the Yankees on March 1, 1993. "He's tough," Steinbrenner said when asked about Showalter. "He's detail oriented, and I think he did a very creditable job last year." Buck later would also describe George as "tough," but he never complained publicly and seemed to learn the fine art of not fighting the Boss.

Showalter in 1993 led the Yankees into a genuine pennant race. As late as September 9, the Yankees and Blue Jays were tied for first place, but then Toronto got hot while New York slumped, and the Yankees finished seven games out. No one blamed Showalter, who finished second in Manager of the Year voting by the Baseball Writers. He had brought a new harmony to the clubhouse, and the Yankees enjoyed a winning season for the first time since 1988.

Not that Buck let the players do their own thing. Buck and Gene Michael moved in quickly to deal with problems or problem players, but they kept the problems internal. Complainers weren't tolerated. Early in the 1994 season, veteran reliever Jeff Reardon complained openly about a mop-up assignment, and he was released. Buck was molding a *team.* "When Buck looks at a player, he doesn't ask if he can hit, if he can throw, he asks what kind of guy he is," said catcher Mike Stanley in 1993. "He's looking for winning personalities."

Indeed, in 1994, the Yankees were very much winners. Showalter guided the team to a 70-43 record and a 6½-game lead in the American League East when the players' strike halted the season in August. Showalter was selected Manager of the Year.

Buck Showalter

Showalter was faced with many adversities in 1995, not the least of which was losing his injured pitching ace, Jimmy Key, early in the season. Although the Yankees struggled most of the season, Buck was able to rally the club for a strong September and qualify for the playoffs as a wildcard entry. He managed without flair in the playoffs, but he was handicapped with an ineffective bullpen.

One of Steinbrenner's best moves ever may have been the grooming and development of Showalter, who has become one of the most respected managers in the game. George had once encouraged Buck to take on a bit more color, but the only thing the manager took on was more work. Often he would sleep in his Yankee Stadium office. He may have been short on color, but he gave Steinbrenner what the owner always wanted—a manager willing to spend 24 hours a day at Yankee Stadium.

Showalter was also very respectful—properly respectful—of the Boss, to whom he referred in the press as Mr. Steinbrenner. Unlike other Yankee managers who would complain on the record about Steinbrenner's meddling ways, Buck never did, at least not on the record.

But it wasn't enough to save his job. If it weren't for fleas, a dog wouldn't know he's a dog; if it weren't for the ability to hire and fire, a boss would not know he's the boss. Five days before his contract was to expire as Yankee manager, Showalter was out the door. What really happened, however, remains unclear.

The press release issued by the Yankees on October 26, 1995, had Steinbrenner saying that Showalter, rejecting an offer for a new two-year, $1.05 million contract, had said he would not return in 1996. Showalter disagreed with this account, saying he never resigned but only rejected the offer in the context of contract negotiations. Murray Chass of *The New York Times*, in a phone interview with Showalter who was at home in Pensacola, Fla., asked Showalter if he had resigned or ever said the word. "Heavens, no," said Buck. "I was hopeful to the end that something would work out."

If it was a misunderstanding, neither party was anxious to reopen the door. In fact, one was left believing that either Showalter was purposely looking for a way out, or he was tricked into leaving by the owner. Possibly another unresolved matter had forced the issue. According to unidentified Yankee officials in printed accounts, Steinbrenner had wanted to fire at least two of Buck's coaches.

Aced out or not, Showalter immediately became a leading candidate for several managing positions. A few weeks later, he was signed to a long-term contract by the Arizona Diamondbacks. Buck served at the minor league level prior to Arizona's entry into the National League in 1998. After a 65-97 inaugural season with the Diamondbacks in 1998, Buck turned them around in the very next campaign. The D'Backs won 100 games and were in the playoffs earlier than any expansion team in baseball history. Buck was released though after Arizona slipped to 85-77 in 2000. Arizona then won the 2001 World Series, just as the Yankees had done in 1996 after Showalter was let go. Buck appeared on ESPN as a baseball analyst for two years before he accepted the Texas Rangers manager position for 2003.

YANKEE MANAGER RECORD FOR BUCK SHOWALTER

Years	Won	Lost	Percentage	Standing
1992	76	86	.469	4th (EAST-tied)
1993	88	74	.543	2nd (EAST)
1994	70	43	.619	1st (EAST)
1995	79	65	.549	2nd (EAST)
4 Yrs.	313	268	.539	1 wildcard

TORRE, JOE

Manager: 1996-
Born: July 18, 1940
Birthplace: Brooklyn, NY

Joe Torre was born in New York, played major league baseball in New York, and managed in New York. Nothing new about New York for the new Yankee manager. Except the Yankees; he has never had any previous connection with them—never even played against them.

As a player, Joseph Paul broke in with the Milwaukee Braves in 1960, the year his older brother Frank Joseph left Milwaukee to join the Phillies. Joe moved with the Braves to Atlanta in 1966 and swatted 36 home runs. He would never again display that kind of power, but he was an exceptional hitter. With St. Louis in 1971 he was the league's Most Valuable Player, leading the circuit in batting (.363), RBIs (137), and hits (230).

Torre, who spent his early and middle playing years behind the plate and his latter years playing the infield corners, joined the Mets in 1975. He finished his playing career in 1977.

Torre has the distinction of having been asked to manage all three major league teams he played for—Mets (1977-81), Braves (1982-84), and Cardinals (1990-95). In five seasons managing the Mets, Torre was unable to lift the club above fifth place. He did take the 1982 Braves to the NLCS, losing to St. Louis. His best year with the Cardinals was a second-place finish in 1991. He was fired by the Cards in June 1995 and finished the season in the broadcast booth as a television commentator.

Hired as manager by the Yankees in November 1995 on the heels of Buck Showalter's strange departure, Torre was said to be the only candidate interviewed—although the names Willie Randolph, Chris Chambliss, and Sparky Anderson were also mentioned—and perhaps the pivotal point in Torre's favor was his friendship with the new general manager, Bob Watson. Torre would take home $1.05 million a year on a two-year contract to shoulder perhaps baseball's toughest job.

Introduced at Yankee Stadium, Torre chose his words diplomatically. Did he know what was in store working for George Steinbrenner? "Hopefully," he said, "you go out and win, and when you win, everybody's happy."

In his first season (1996) at the Yankee helm (92-70), Joe Torre, the 31st Yankee manager, guided his club to its first World Series visit since 1981. In six games, the Yankees defeated the Atlanta Braves, a team possessing one of the most formidable pitching staffs in all of baseball history. The Yanks had won their 23rd World Series title since their first in 1923! It was Joe's first trip to the Fall Classic in his baseball career that began with the Milwaukee Braves in 1960. After a combined 4,268 games played (2,209) and managed (2,059), Torre did not have to chase his dream any longer–he had made it to the World

Series. An enormous ticker-tape parade was held in New York City to celebrate Joe and his club's victorious march through the playoffs–congratulations, Joe! For his efforts, Joe was named BBWAA Co-Manager of the Year, sharing the honors with Johnny Oates of the Texas Rangers.

In 1997, Torre managed the Yankees to four more victories than the previous year (96). However, his club would be defeated in the first-round Division Series by the Cleveland Indians. No one could have dreamed the kind of season that was looming on the horizon for the Yankees in 1998!

Beginning his third season with Yankees, the Bronx Bombers had "THE" season for the ages. After all was said and done, the Yankees had won a then AL record 114 games, finishing 22 full games (a new Yankee record) over Boston, who themselves had won a very respectable total of 92 games. The Yankees marched through the playoffs, dismantling Texas with a three-game sweep in the Division Series and then defeating Cleveland in the league Championship Series in six. The Yankees then attained their crown jewel by not only defeating the San Diego Padres in the World Series–but by sweeping them in four straight! They had won their 24th World Series in 35 attempts! All in all, the '98 Yanks had won an astonishing 125 total games (114 regular season and 11 in the postseason) and certainly this club WILL go down in history as one of the greatest ever assembled! Ring number two for Joe in three seasons and another ticker-tape parade–a guy could certainly get used to this! Torre was deservedly named the BBWAA Manager of the Year and also won the Associated Press Manager of the Year Award.

Before the 1999 season began, Joe Torre was diagnosed with prostate cancer, having to miss his team's first 36 games. Joe underwent surgery in St. Louis on March 18 and slowly began the healing process. In Joe's absence, Don Zimmer took the reigns, finishing with a 21-15 ledger when Joe returned at Boston on May 18. The Yankees found themselves in a pennant-race with Boston for most of the season, but the Bombers prevailed by four games over the Red Sox, who had won the "wildcard" slot in the playoffs. The Yanks finished with a 98-64 record, and Joe had managed his team to exactly 400 victories in his first four years–a 100-win average per season! In the postseason, the Bronx Bombers swept the Rangers again for the second straight year in the Division Series, and in five, defeated their long-standing rivals, the Boston Red Sox, in the ALCS. Facing Atlanta again in the World Series (the 36th for the Yankees), New York swept Ted Turner's club in four straight! Where was Atlanta, anyway, in this series?! That relentless tomahawk chopping by their fans must be affecting them!! The Yankees now had a four-game sweep (their eighth overall since 1927) in consecutive seasons! They were the first team to accomplish a back-to-back sweep since the Yankees of 1938-39. The Yanks had also won a record-tying 12 World Series games in a row, a record that was dated back to the days of Ruth and Gehrig! They were "The Team of the Century", having won their 25th World Series!

Torre's 2000 Yankee team won the AL East by 2½ games over the Red Sox. The Yankees took possession of first place just after the All-Star break, and had a nine game lead before it came down to the unimpressive season ending numbers. Their 2000 record of 87-74 (.540) was just the fifth best in the AL. In the division series, the Yankees defeated the A's, 3 games to 2 in a hard fought round of contests. Joe then piloted the Yanks

to their 37th AL pennant in the ALCS against Lou Piniella and the Mariners. After winning games 2, 3, and 4, the Yankees clinched another flag with a 9-7 victory to win the playoffs by a 4 games to 2 edge. The World Series of 2000 against Bobby Valentine and the Mets had the baseball world buzzing about the renewal of the Subway Series. Torre and the Yankees did not let the media hype go to their heads as they took care of the Mets in five games for their 26th World Series championship.

In 2001, Torre once again led the Bronx Bombers to a first-place season. The Yankees went into the top spot in the AL East during an early July series in Baltimore and had built their lead to 13 games by the second week of September. The 9/11 tragedy shook the world, but the New York community was in utter shock by the attack on the World Trade Center and the deaths of so many city fire fighters and police officers during the rescue attempt. After resuming the season in Chicago on September 18th, Torre ended up in October with another division title by way of a 95-65 (.594) record. Although they sputtered in the first two games of the division series against the A's, Joe pushed his charges through by winning the next three games and again eliminating Art Howe and the Oakland team. Next in line stood the Mariners who had just won an AL record 116 games in the regular season. Torre and the Yanks charged through Seattle in five games with the clincher being a 12-3 thrashing of Lou Piniella's squad. The Yankees had just won their 38th AL pennant and went up against the Arizona Diamondbacks in the World Series. The Yankees were down to their last out in Games 4 and 5, but they were able to pull out

Joe Torre, the only New York City Native to manage the Yankees.

each game. With a 2-1 lead going into the 9th inning in Game 7, it appeared another World Series title was going to be engineered by Joe. The wheels came off though as the D'Backs rallied for a 3-2 victory and sent Torre and Yanks back home unhappy.

The 2002 season ended with Joe watching the Yankees being eliminated in the division series for the first time since 1995. A great regular season under Torre's command of 103-58 (.640) was cast aside by the red-hot Anaheim Angels as they disposed of the Yankees in four games.

On the Yankee manager list Joe is behind only Joe McCarthy (7) and Casey Stengel (7) in World Series titles (4). He is fifth on the Yankee manager list in winning percentage at .606.

YANKEE MANAGER RECORD FOR JOE TORRE

Years	Won	Lost	Percentage	Standing
1996	92	70	.568	1st (EAST)
1997	96	66	.593	2nd (EAST)
1998	114	48	.704	1st (EAST)
1999	98	64	.605	1st (EAST)
2000	87	74	.540	1st (EAST)
2001	95	65	.594	1st (EAST)
2002	103	58	.640	1st (EAST)
7 Yrs.	685	445	.606	5 pennants

World Series

Years	Outcome	Won	Lost	Opponent
1996	Won	4	2	Atlanta Braves
1998	Won	4	0	San Diego Padres
1999	Won	4	0	Atlanta Braves
2000	Won	4	1	New York Mets
2001	Lost	3	4	Arizona Diamondbacks
5 Yrs.	4-1	19	7	

YANKEE MANAGERS IN REVIEW

IMPORTANT DATES

March 12,1903: The New York Highlanders are officially approved as members of the American League, the franchise having moved from Baltimore where in 1902 Wilbert Robinson was manager. Robinson does not accompany the team to New York. Instead, the former great pitcher, Clark Griffith, joins the Highlanders as player-manager.

June 24, 1908: With the Highlanders mired in sixth place, Griffith is released as the club's manager. Star Highlander shortstop Kid Elberfeld is named interim manager.

Winter of 1908-09: It is decided that Elberfeld will return only as a Highlander infielder in 1909, and George Stallings is named the club's third manager. Stallings is a former player and comes with big-league managerial experience.

September 23-24, 1910: The Yankees are in second place but Stallings, upset with front office interference, resigns as manager. The next day the Yankees' star first baseman, Hal Chase, is named Yankee manager.

November 21, 1911: It is decided that Chase will return only as a player in 1912 and the former fine third baseman, Harry Wolverton, is named the Yanks' fifth manager.

January 8, 1913: Following the release of Wolverton as Yankee manager (he had the misfortune of managing the worst team in club history), Yankee management scores a major victory by inducing heralded Frank Chance to step aboard as Yankee manager. Chance had been an outstanding player and manager of the Cubs, and his signing is applauded.

September 15-16, 1914: The Yankees are in sixth place and Chance resigns. Yankee shortstop Roger Peckinpaugh is named interim manager, at 23 the youngest manager in big-league history.

Winter of 1914-15: It is decided that Peckinpaugh will return as shortstop in 1915. Wild Bill Donovan, a former pitching star and, in 1914, manager of Providence, is named the eighth manager of the Yankees by new owners Jake Ruppert and Til Huston.

October 26, 1917: Having released Donovan, the Yankees hire Miller Huggins who for the previous five seasons managed the St. Louis Cardinals.

September 20, 1929: Huggins is hospitalized, and his loyal coach, Art Fletcher, assumes the managerial duties.

September 25, 1929: Miller Huggins dies. Fletcher is named manager of the Yankees for the rest of the season.

Winter of 1929-30: Fletcher is offered the job of Yankee manager but prefers coaching. The former Yankee pitching great and the club's pitching coach the previous two seasons, Bob Shawkey, is named the Yankees' 11th manager.

October 14 1930: Before Shawkey is officially informed of his release, the Yankees hire Joe McCarthy as Yankee manager. McCarthy had been fired as Cub manager on September 23.

May 24, 1946: In need of some much deserved rest, McCarthy resigns for reasons of health and because of problems with the front office. Yankee catcher and star, Bill Dickey, is named the 13th manager in the history of the club.

September 12, 1946: After a meeting with Yankee General Manager Larry MacPhail, Dickey resigns. Yankee coach Johnny Neun is named interim manager.

November 5, 1946: Bucky Harris is hired as the 15th Yankee manager, replacing Neun. Harris had plenty of previous major league managerial experience. In 1946 he was general manager at Buffalo.

October 6, 1948: The Yankees release Harris in a surprise move. Harris had his differences with General Manager George Weiss.

October 12, 1948: The Yankees shock the baseball world by hiring funnyman Casey Stengel as their new manager. In 1948 Stengel managed the Oakland Oaks.

October 15, 1960: Stengel is released for reasons of age and because of anxieties in the front office that the man groomed to succeed him, Yankee coach Ralph Houk, might be lured away by another club. Houk becomes the Yankees' 17th manager.

October 22, 1963: Shortly after the Yanks' World Series loss to the Dodgers, it is announced that Houk will move upstairs to become the club's general manager and that Yogi Berra, a player-coach on the team in 1963, will take over in 1964 as Yankee field boss. This decision was made in spring training and was kept secret all season.

October 1964: In the days that followed the World Series, a bizarre series of events take place. The day after the Yanks' Game 7 loss to St. Louis (October 16), Berra is released. Cardinal manager and St. Louis hero Johnny Keane resigns his post and four days after is hired as the Yankees' 19th manager.

May 6, 1966: After the Yankees start the season with a 4-16 record, Keane is released. Stepping down from General Manager to become Yankee manager for the second time is Ralph Houk.

September 30, 1973: On the final day of the season, Houk resigns as Yankee manager, apparently because of problems with the new Yankee ownership of George Steinbrenner.

December 21, 1973: American League President Joe Cronin rules that Oakland A's Manager Dick Williams is still bound to the A's and that the contract he signed earlier with the Yankees is not to be honored. The Yankees are still managerless.

Winter of 1973-74: Bill Virdon is named the Yankees' 20th manager. He was fired as manager of the Pirates during the 1973 season.

August 2, 1975: Virdon is released as Yankee manager and former Yankee star second baseman Billy Martin is announced to a cheering Yankee Stadium Old Timers' Day throng as Virdon's replacement. A successful big-league manager with many teams, Martin had recently been fired by the Texas Rangers.

September 29, 1975: Casey Stengel, the great Yankee manager of a bygone era, dies.

January 13, 1978: Joe McCarthy, another great Yankee manager of a bygone era, dies.

July 24, 1978: Martin resigns as Yankee manager a day after he criticizes owner George Steinbrenner and rightfielder Reggie Jackson. His remarks were reported in the press and sparks were flying. Named to replace Martin is Bob Lemon who was fired a few weeks earlier as manager of the White Sox.

July 28, 1978: Before a shocked, cheering Old Timers' Day crowd at Yankee Stadium, it is announced that Billy Martin will return to the Yankee helm, beginning in 1980.

June 18, 1979: With the Yankees struggling badly, Lemon is released as Yankee manager and is replaced by Billy Martin.

October 28, 1979: Five days after having an altercation in a Minnesota hotel-bar with a marshmallow salesman, Martin is released as Yankee manager. Dick Howser, former Yankee player and coach, leaves his position as baseball coach at Florida State University to become the 23rd manager in Yankee history.

November 21, 1980: Howser resigns as Yankee manager after several months of discord with owner George Steinbrenner. Yankee General Manager Gene Michael steps down to field level, becoming the Yankees' 24th manager.

September 6, 1981: Michael is released as Yankee manager and replaced by former Yankee skipper, Bob Lemon. Michael had told the press he was tired of having Steinbrenner threaten his job. Steinbrenner waited nine days for a Michael apology, and when none was forthcoming, made the managerial change.

April 25, 1982: Lemon is replaced by Michael after the Yankees beat Detroit, 3-1, improving their record to 6-8. This was a change that was planned for after the season, but Steinbrenner couldn't wait.

August 3-4, 1982: Michael is fired after losing both ends of a late-night doubleheader to the White Sox, and Yankee Stadium fans are offered free tickets as an amends by management. Clyde King, a Steinbrenner advisor, becomes manager "reluctantly, but willingly."

January 11, 1983: What has been rumored since October when Oakland fired Billy Martin has come to pass. Martin is named Yankee manager, returning for Billy III.

December 16, 1983: Billy III ends, as Martin is fired and replaced by Yogi Berra. Berra has been a Yankee coach continuously since 1976.

April 28, 1985: Billy IV opens, as Martin returns again as Yankee manager. Yogi Berra is fired after only 16 games. His players are angry, and Yogi will vow never to set foot in Yankee Stadium again as long as Steinbrenner owns the club. Yogi did eventually return to Yankee Stadium in 1999.

October 27, 1985: Billy IV ends, as Martin is replaced by Lou Piniella. Martin's undoing was a brutal barroom brawl he had with pitcher Ed Whitson in September. Piniella has been groomed for his new position while coaching with the Yankees.

October 19, 1987: Billy V opens, as Martin replaces Piniella. As the Yankees stumbled over the final two months of the 1987 season, Steinbrenner had complained about Lou's lack of experience. Piniella is promoted to general manager.

June 23, 1988: Billy V closes, as Martin exits for the final time. His drinking and behavior are out of control. Piniella, who recently resigned as general manager, becomes the manager for the second time.

October 7, 1988: Dallas Green replaces Piniella as Yankee manager. Green, recently the Cubs general manager, comes from outside the organization. He is known as a tough disciplinarian, which is Steinbrenner's number-one requirement.

August 18, 1989: Green, locked in a war of words with Steinbrenner, whom Green calls "Manager George," is fired. Bucky Dent is promoted to Yankee manager from his post managing Columbus. But the Yankees will have a losing season.

December 25, 1989: Five-time Yankee manager Billy Martin dies in a one-car wreck near his Binghamton, New York, home. Martin had spent Christmas day drinking in a bar.

June 6, 1990: As the Yankees occupy the cellar in the AL East, Dent is replaced by Stump Merrill. Merrill has been faithfully working in the organization since 1977, most recently as manager at Columbus. The Yankees will lose their first four games under Merrill, extending a losing streak to eight games.

October 7, 1991: Merrill is fired after a 71-91 season. A significant factor was the whining and backstabbing of some of his players, who complained to the press about Stump's abilities, or lack of ability, in some of the players' views.

October 29, 1991: Buck Showalter is named the 30th man to manage the Yankees. General Manager Gene Michael is forced to change gears, as he had been saying the Yankees were looking for someone with big-league managing experience. But the ownership partners urged Michael to reconsider Showalter, a hard-working farm-system manager since 1985, and a Yankee coach over the past two seasons.

October 26, 1995: Buck Showalter's return of a contract is viewed as a resignation. Showalter characterized his rejection of the offer as part of the negotiation process. But George Steinbrenner said his manager had instead indicated he would not be returning for the 1996 season.

November 2, 1995: Joe Torre, fired as manager of the Cardinals in June, is named the 31st manager of the Yankees. Torre, who managed the Mets, Braves, and Cardinals, is a longtime friend of the new Yankees general manager Bob Watson.

October 26, 1996: Joe Torre, in his first year as Yankee skipper, guides the Bombers to their 23rd World Series Championship and first since 1978!

September 25, 1998: Joe Torre leads his club to their 112th win of the season, setting a new American League record. The Yankees would finish the year with a record of 114-48, a winning percentage of .704.

October 21, 1998: Torre, in his third season as Yankee manager, guides the Yankees to a four-game sweep in the World Series versus San Diego. It is the Yankees' 24th World Series title since their first in 1923. In the postseason, the Bombers were 11-2 versus the best clubs in baseball.

March 1999: Joe Torre announces that he has prostate cancer for which he undergoes successful surgery. Joe misses the first 36 games of the season. Don Zimmer is the acting manager in Torre's absence and is not credited with any of the wins or losses during his 36-game tenure. Joe returns to the club on May 18 at Boston and eventually leads his charges to their 36th American League pennant, since winning their first in 1921. He finishes the 1999 season with 400 wins in his first four years as a Yankee manager!

April 9, 1999: After 14 years of shunning Yankee Stadium, Yogi Berra and George Steinbrenner heal old wounds as Yogi throws out the first pitch. *[Joe DiMaggio was originally scheduled to do the honors, but his death made that impossible.]*

October 27, 1999: Torre, in his fourth season as Yankee manager, leads the Yanks to their 25th World Series title, a sweep of the Atlanta Braves. The sweep was their second consecutive, winning the previous year in four against San Diego. The Yankees have a record-tying 12 straight World Series victories. The Yanks were 11-1 in the postseason, now having a two-year record of 22-3 (.880) against the best opposition baseball has to offer. The World Series was clinched at Yankee Stadium, the site of the final baseball game of the 20th century! How fitting!

October 26, 2000: Joe Torre pilots the Yankees to their 26th World Series title after a 4-2 victory in Game 5 at Shea Stadium. In Game 1, the Yankees broke the consecutive World Series games won record (13) after they came from behind in the 9th and won in the 12th inning, 4-3. They extended this record to 14 consecutive World Series game wins the next night with a 6-5 victory in Game 2. The Yankees start the new century the way they finished the last one with another World Series title.

Joe Torre

YANKEES WIN LIST (Regular Season)

1. Joe McCarthy   —   1460
2. Casey Stengel   —   1149
3. Miller Huggins   —   1067
4. Ralph Houk   —   944
5. Joe Torre   —   685
6. Billy Martin   —   556
7. Clark Griffith   —   419
8. Buck Showalter   —   313
9. Lou Piniella   —   224
10. Wild Bill Donovan   —   220
11. Yogi Berra   —   192
12. Bucky Harris   —   191
13. George Stallings   —   153
14. Bill Virdon   —   142
15. Stump Merrill   —   120
16. Frank Chance   —   117
17. Dick Howser   —   103
18. Bob Lemon   —   99
19. Gene Michael   —   92
20. Bob Shawkey   —   86
21. Hal Chase   —   85
22. Johnny Keane   —   81
23. Bill Dickey   —   57
24. Dallas Green   —   56
25. Harry Wolverton   —   50
26. Bucky Dent   —   36
27. Clyde King   —   29
28. Kid Elberfeld   —   27
29. Roger Peckinpaugh   —   10
30. Johnny Neun   —   8
31. Art Fletcher   —   6
        1903 through 2002:   8777

YANKEE WINNING PERCENTAGE LIST

1. Dick Howser   —   .632
2. Joe McCarthy   —   .627
3. Casey Stengel   —   .623
4. Bucky Harris   —   .620
5. Joe Torre   —   .606
6. Miller Huggins   —   .597
7. Billy Martin   —   .591
8. Bob Lemon   —   .576
9. Johnny Neun   —   .571
10. Yogi Berra   —   .565
11. Bob Shawkey   —   .558
12. Gene Michael   —   .548
13. Art Fletcher   —   .545
14. Bill Dickey   —   .543
15. Ralph Houk   —   .5394
16. Buck Showalter   —   .5387
17. Lou Piniella   —   .537
18. Bill Virdon   —   .534
19. Clark Griffith   —   .531
20. George Stallings   —   .526
21. Hal Chase   —   .521
22. Roger Peckinpaugh   —   .500
23. Wild Bill Donovan   —   .479
24. Clyde King   —   .468
25. Dallas Green   —   .463
26. Johnny Keane   —   .445
27. Stump Merrill   —   .436
28. Frank Chance   —   .411
29. Bucky Dent   —   .404
30. Harry Wolverton   —   .329
31. Kid Elberfeld   —   .276

AL PENNANTS AND WORLD SERIES CHAMPIONSHIPS

	AL Pennants Won	World Series Won
Casey Stengel	10	7
Joe McCarthy	8	7
Miller Huggins	6	3
Joe Torre	5	4
Ralph Houk	3	2
Billy Martin	2	1
Bob Lemon	2	1
Bucky Harris	1	1
Yogi Berra	1	0
GRAND TOTALS	36	25

Dick Howser won a division championship in 1980.

Gene Michael won a First Season championship in the split-season of 1981, but Bob Lemon managed in the playoffs when the pennant was won.

Buck Showalter finished first in the strike-shortened 1994 season, and in 1995 he won the AL's first wildcard playoff spot.

MANAGERS' RECORDS

Manager	Years	Complete Seasons	Won	Lost	Percentage
Clark Griffith	1903-08	5	419	370	.531
Kid Elberfeld	1908	0	27	71	.276
George Stallings	1909-10	1	153	138	.526
Hal Chase	1910-11	1	85	78	.521
Harry Wolverton	1912	1	50	102	.329
Frank Chance	1913-14	1	117	168	.411
Roger Peckinpaugh	1914	0	10	10	.500
Wild Bill Donovan	1915-17	3	220	239	.479
Miller Huggins	1918-29	11	1067	719	.597
Art Fletcher	1929	0	6	5	.545
Bob Shawkey	1930	1	86	68	.558
Joe McCarthy	1931-46	15	1460	867	.627
Bill Dickey	1946	0	57	48	.543
Johnny Neun	1946	0	8	6	.571
Bucky Harris	1947-48	2	191	117	.620
Casey Stengel	1949-60	12	1149	696	.623
Ralph Houk	1961-63, 1966-73	10	944	806	.539
Yogi Berra	1964, 1984-85	2	192	148	.565
Johnny Keane	1965-66	1	81	101	.445
Bill Virdon	1974-75	1	142	124	.534
Billy Martin	1975-78, 1979 1983, 1985, 1988	3	556	385	.591
Bob Lemon	1978-79, 1981-82	0	99	73	.576
Dick Howser	1978 (1 game), 1980	1	103	60	.632
Gene Michael	1981, 1982	0	92	76	.548
Clyde King	1982	0	29	33	.468
Lou Piniella	1986-87, 1988	2	224	193	.537
Dallas Green	1989	0	56	65	.463
Bucky Dent	1989-90	0	36	53	.404
Stump Merrill	1990-91	1	120	155	.436
Buck Showalter	1992-95	4	313	268	.539
Joe Torre	1996-2002	7	685	445	.606
GRAND TOTALS:			**8777**	**6548**	**.572**

YANKEE MANAGERS AND COACHES—PAST AND PRESENT

Buck Showalter—Yankees Manager from 1992-1995. (New York Yankees Archives)

Brian Butterfield—1994-1995 Yankees first base coach. (New York Yankees Archives)

Wally Moses—Yankee batting coach (1961-1962) who helped many hitters on the great 1961 team.

Rick Down—1993-1995, 2002 Yankees batting coach. (New York Yankees Archives)

Billy Connors—1989-1990 and 1994-1995 Yankees pitching coach. (New York Yankees Archives)

Willie Randolph—Yankee third base coach since 1994. (New York Yankees Archives)

5

OWNERS AND TOP EXECUTIVES

Judge Kenesaw Mountain Landis heard all about Joe DiMaggio's tonsillectomy today when the two met at Yankee Stadium before a game between the Yankees and the Washington Senators on April 20, 1937. The beaming gentleman in the center is Col. Jake Ruppert, owner of the world champions. (AP/WIDE WORLD PHOTOS)

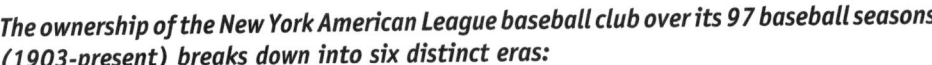

The ownership of the New York American League baseball club over its 97 baseball seasons (1903-present) breaks down into six distinct eras:

1903-15—Frank Farrell and Bill Devery.
1915-39—Jacob Ruppert (in the first eight years, Tillinghast L'Hommedieu Huston was co-owner with Ruppert).
1939-45—The interim period following Ruppert's death when the club was owned by Ruppert heirs and controlled by Yankee President Ed Barrow.
1945-64—Dan Topping and Del Webb. They had a third partner, Larry MacPhail, for the first three years.
1964-72—The Columbia Broadcasting System, the only corporate owner in Yankee history.
1973-present—George Steinbrenner and his limited partners.

THE YANKEE BRASS

INTRODUCTION

Yankee owners through history have been diverse in their personalities but all share a common quality: success in business. Ruppert, Webb, and Steinbrenner easily qualify as multimillionaires and the others, though less well-heeled, qualify as wealthy. Almost all have been self-made men. True, Steinbrenner entered the business world through his family's shipping firm, but it was by his own enterprise that he attained his present business stature. Through hard work, the owners lived the American dream of financial success. Jacob Ruppert, the only owner with an old-money background (the Ruppert brewery wealth), was the lone exception.

The others built their own fortunes—Devery in business and politics, Farrell in horse racing and gambling, Huston in construction, and Topping as an entrepreneur in many ventures. Webb scored in construction and Steinbrenner in shipbuilding. Although it might be difficult to document that the complete line of Yankee owners has been impeccably upright, it is just as true that none has brought lasting disgrace to the New York Yankees. Because of their gambling backgrounds, however, Farrell and Devery almost certainly would not be approved as owners by the American League were they to buy the club today.

Some owners were involved in the sports business before buying the Yankees. For Farrell it was horse racing and for Larry MacPhail it was baseball. MacPhail had been an executive of two big league clubs. Topping had owned two professional football clubs, and Steinbrenner once owned a professional basketball team.

They were involved in sports in more than just a business way. Devery was a boxer. Ruppert was a sandlot pitcher and Webb pitched professionally. Topping played both college football and baseball and was a good golfer. Steinbrenner in college ran track and played football. He later coached high school football and basketball and was a college football coach. (Mike Burke, who ran the club for CBS, played college football.)

The Topping-Webb era was easily the smoothest of those in which there was co-ownership. Topping and Webb were novices in baseball when, with MacPhail, they bought the Yankees in 1945, and they let the expert MacPhail run the club. Following the 1947 World Series, MacPhail sold out after arguing with his partners, although there were many reasons for his departure. Topping and Webb then collaborated in a relationship unique for its harmony. That old baseball law, and indeed a rule of business, that says there can be only one boss was violated. Topping and Webb together, in quiet and cooperative partnership, guided the Yankees during the club's most successful period.

Other two-man Yankee ownerships were less free of controversy. Farrell and Devery, both flamboyant men (as were most Yankee owners), fought often and their battles hurt the club. The Ruppert-Huston years were contentious, although the two managed to collaborate in the building of the foundation of the Yankee dynasty. That situation stabilized when the likable Huston sold his interest to Ruppert.

The one-boss rule has worked well for the Yankees. From 1923 until his death in January of 1939, when Ruppert was for all purposes the sole owner (Barrow owned a small portion of the club), the Yankees won eight pennants and seven World Championships. (In Barrow's short tenure—1939-45—as sole boss, the Yanks won four pennants and three World titles.) The club was sagging when Larry MacPhail took over and MacPhail single-handedly put the Yanks back on the track that brought them the World Championship in 1947. Steinbrenner in 1973 took over an aimless, leaderless outfit and reestablished the winning Yankee tradition with five American League East titles in the six years between 1976-81, four league pennants (1976-78, 1981) and back-to-back World Championships (1977-78). Since Steinbrenner took ownership of the Yankees in 1973, the Bronx Bombers are 7-1 in American League Championship Series Play, and have won five of seven World Series titles.

Owners such as the Devery-Farrell tandem, Larry MacPhail and Steinbrenner firmly planted themselves as chief decision makers. Others like Ruppert, Topping-Webb, and the CBS Corporation delegated much of the decision making to hired hands.

Traditionally, club presidents and/or general managers have been the decision makers in the day-to-day operations. The Yankees have employed two of the greatest general managers in history—Ed Barrow and George Weiss. Barrow had a free hand in club matters, thanks to Ruppert, and Weiss ran the show for Topping and Webb.

Tracking the Yankee organizational structure wasn't too difficult until the George Steinbrenner era. Ever-changing executive titles and frequent personnel turnover has wreaked havoc on the traditional front-office structure and has blurred the record of the Steinbrenner regime. But it really doesn't matter because Steinbrenner himself has set the course and made all the directional changes. His "baseball people," as he calls them, have two purposes: 1) advisory roles, and 2) implementing the directives of the Boss. The most important of these "baseball people" are summarized under Steinbrenner in the biographical sketches that follow.

THE YANKEE BRASS PROFILES

WILLIAM S. DEVERY

Bill Devery and Frank Farrell were the first owners of the New York American League franchise—a franchise that had resided in Baltimore as the Orioles since 1901. They bought the club in 1903 and moved it to New York.

American League President Ban Johnson supported the purchase transaction and the intercity transfer. Johnson was an enemy of New York Giants Manager John McGraw; he wanted Devery and Farrell to battle McGraw for the hearts of New York's baseball fans—for the New York baseball market. Johnson was able to funnel star players to the infant New York club, but year after year the team struggled. The Highlanders were perennially low in league standings.

William S. Devery, also known as "Big Bill," had a colorful background as a bartender, prize fighter and police officer. Some people thought Devery was more than just colorful, that he and Farrell were involved in illegal activities and corruption. But these accusations were never proved.

Though he was not as active in team affairs as was his partner, Devery was interested in the club and wanted a winner. Thus he was in step with Farrell in running out of patience with the team's performances. As the years slipped by, the two owners' frustration became tougher and tougher to handle with grace. They fought with their managers, firing them in rapid order. Actually, Devery and Farrell fought with everyone and ended up at each other's throats. Devery had no serious money problems but the Yankees became an annoying operation, and a small one at that, to Bill. Also, the rise in player salaries caused by the competition from the Federal League (1914-15) disturbed Devery. The two disgusted owners, Devery and Farrell, sold the Yankees early in 1915 to Jacob Ruppert and Til Huston for $460,000. They had paid $18,000 for the franchise 12 years earlier.

looked on Farrell as a shady character. Nevertheless, Frank was quite acceptable to American League President Ban Johnson, who wanted staying power behind the franchise Farrell and Devery acquired in 1903 and moved from Baltimore to New York. Johnson was certain the upstart American League would never be considered "major" without a team representing New York.

In the early years of the franchise in New York, Farrell took a stronger personal interest in the team than did Devery. He also assumed more control, and in 1907 replaced Joe Gordon as club president. He developed close relationships and strong loyalties with his players. When in 1910 Yankee Manager George Stallings accused star player Hal Chase of throwing games, Farrell ended up firing Stallings and making Chase manager! When sportswriter Haywood Broun wrote a story in 1913 saying that Chase was not playing 100 percent, Farrell, a known gambler himself, jumped all over Broun for his innuendos. A few days after the Broun incident, however, Chase was traded.

Farrell could be a generous man. In spite of the bitter war that engulfed the Yanks and New York Giants since the American Leaguers "invaded" New York in 1903, Farrell offered the Giants the use of Hilltop Park after a fire in April of 1911 burned down much of the Giants' home field, the Polo Grounds. Farrell's offer was readily accepted by the Giants, and a truce befell the two New York clubs (to be broken when Babe Ruth came to New York in 1920 with a resultant Yankee eclipse of the Giants that the latter found too damaging to cheerfully bear).

Despite his best efforts to turn his team into a winner, Farrell was unsuccessful. Dissatisfied with the club, pressed by financial reversals, and lacking a good relationship with Devery, Farrell in January of 1915 was disposed to sell, and he and Devery sold the club to Ruppert and Huston.

FRANK J. FARRELL

Frank Farrell and his partner, Bill Devery, became the first owners of New York's American League baseball club. Farrell, a former bartender and saloonkeeper and a man of some means, was the owner of a racing stable and ran a gambling house. In fact, he was a gambling tycoon, and there were those who

JOSEPH W. GORDON

Joe Gordon was the first president of New York's American League baseball club. It has been speculated that he may have influenced the selection of the team's original nickname—the Highlanders—after Gordon's Highlanders, the famous British army regiment.

Gordon was in the coal business and was a man American League President Ban Johnson used as a middle man between himself and Frank Farrell and Bill Devery when the franchise was being shifted from Baltimore to New York. Gordon thus became associated with Farrell and Devery in the front office of the new club. The new Highlander management, especially Gordon, faced a tough fight in New York because the established Giants were backed by a powerful big shot in Tammany Hall who felt, as the Giants did, that New York City was being "invaded" by an American League enemy. When Gordon led a group searching for a ballpark site, he was told by a politician, "No matter where you go, the City will decide to run a street car over second base." Gordon and the Highlander owners, however, were persistent and finally found their site in Washington Heights.

Gordon was the president of the Highlanders from the establishment of the club in New York in 1903 until 1907. He was replaced by co-owner Farrell who developed a strong interest in club operations and who took the job of club president for himself.

COL. TILLINGHAST L'HOMMEDIEU HUSTON

Til Huston was a key figure in making the New York Yankees the world's most famous baseball team. His is a name associated with the Yankees' acquisition of Babe Ruth and the construction of magnificent Yankee Stadium.

Born in Ohio in 1869, Huston became an engineer and for his first career job, he journeyed to Cincinnati and became city engineer. Til went to Cuba as a captain in a volunteer regiment of engineers during the Spanish-American War (he earned his title of colonel in World War I) and afterwards acquired a measure of wealth in the Cuban construction business. Three major harbors in Cuba were improved under Huston's supervision. In Cuba, Huston met New York Giants' Manager John McGraw and, being both rich and a lover of the game, allowed as how he would like to buy a baseball franchise.

Huston and Jacob Ruppert had never met until McGraw brought them together, but they had a common interest in owning a big-league club. They at first tried to buy the Giants, and only when they were unsuccessful in this effort did they turn to the Yankees, a team that McGraw told them could be acquired. On January 11, 1915, Huston and Ruppert bought the Yankees from Frank Farrell and Bill Devery for $460,000, each putting up half the money. At the final meeting closing the sale of the Yankees, Ruppert discovered that Huston was a man of decisive action when Til astounded Jake and all present by slapping on the table his half of the Yankee purchase money—230 $1000 bills!

Til Huston was a big, overweight, affable man who loved to drink beer and talk the hours away. He was a big eater and a man of simple tastes. Unlike Ruppert, Til was not a city slicker or a fancy dresser. Hunting and the outdoors appealed to Huston. His baseball friends, such as Harry Frazee and Wilbert Robinson, were men of similar tastes who enjoyed drinking with Huston. Til got along well with ballplayers and had many pals in the press. His friends called him "Cap," having been a captain in the army when he bought the Yanks.

After buying the Yankee club, Ruppert and Huston, the new president and vice president, respectively, set out to build a championship team. However, the Yanks struggled during the first few years under the new ownership. To Huston it was not a disheartening time, however; he found happiness in his close association with his players and his active participation in club affairs. And although he could not have known it, booming success stood just around the corner in the person of Babe Ruth. When Boston Red Sox owner Harry Frazee decided to sell Ruth, he approached friend and drinking companion, Til Huston, initiating an elaborately arranged transaction that in 1920 brought the Babe to New York.

The best friend Babe Ruth ever had in Yankee management was Til Huston. Besides the outward similarity with weight problems, the two were extroverts, adventuresome and alike in many ways. They both enjoyed eating and drinking, and if Til started to lecture the Babe about an excessive lifestyle, Babe would remind "Cap" that they shared the same high living. (Then they would laugh.) In fact, everyone in Yankee management liked to give Ruth advice, but "Cap" could not do it seriously. Til and Babe socialized, traveled together and each had a desire to be popular. Huston did for Ruth what no other management figure would do—he lavished praise on the Babe and made the big guy feel even bigger. Til was genuinely concerned for Ruth's welfare and even hired detectives to check the Babe's associates to make sure they were honest and suitable business partners for Ruth. During Ruth's infamous 1921 barnstorming tour, Til reached Babe in Scranton, PA, and convinced Babe to quit the tour. Not many people could have so persuaded the strong-willed Babe. Til and Babe were so easy in their dealings that they once flipped a coin to settle a salary dispute. When Huston left the Yankees in 1923, Ruth lost his only close friend in Yankee management. (There were rumors during the 1930s that Huston was going to buy the Dodgers and name Ruth manager.)

Huston proved himself to be an astute baseball businessman in an age when many management people had old-fashioned ideas about the business of baseball. While other owners believed that their city's "civic pride" was strong enough to pull fans to the ballpark to root for the hometown team, Huston had the correct opinion that only winners attracted attention. He felt the only way for the Yankees to be financially successful was to be successful in the league standings. Working toward that goal, Til knew the purchase of Ruth's contract would make the Yankees a winning and colorful team. For that reason, Huston and Ruppert paid the Red Sox comparatively the same price that they had for the entire Yankee franchise. The Yankee acquisition of Ruth was the best investment in baseball history. Besides being a friend of Ruth, Huston completely understood the Babe's business worth to the Yankees.

Being a self-made man of means, Til Huston held the same conservative views espoused by many of the self-made. Were he a baseball franchise owner today he would doubtless join the collection of conservative owners desperately fighting the upward surge in player salaries. With everyone except Ruth, Huston took a hard line concerning pay. In 1919 "Cap" was part of an owner conspiracy, the intent of which was to hold down player salaries.

By the time Ruth came to New York in 1920, Huston's relationship with Ruppert was afflicted by an irreparable rift. The cause of the trouble was Ruppert's hiring of Manager Miller Huggins in October of 1917 when Huston was in France.

Ruppert took the action without consulting Huston who wanted his buddy Uncle Wilbert Robinson for the job. When Til heard from Ruppert that Huggins was going to be hired, he sent a cable from France stating his disapproval of Huggins. Ruppert proceeded to sign his man and Huston's outrage returned with him from overseas. He felt back-stabbed. He never forgave Ruppert and never passed up a chance to criticize Huggins. Til kept an open ear for players' complaints against Huggins, reducing Miller's ability to lead, and told the press often of his unhappiness with the manager's performance.

A Huston-Huggins showdown was preempted when Til's attention was diverted from Huggins and directed toward American League President Ban Johnson and his club-owning cronies. Huston joined Ruppert in waging war on Johnson, who promised the two partners when they purchased the Yankees that he would deliver quality ballplayers. Ban's promises were still unkept in 1919, and Huston and Ruppert broke from Johnson and camp to become leaders of a group of owners known as "the Insurrectionists." In the end this group was successful in stripping Johnson of his power and establishing Judge Kenesaw Mountain Landis as baseball's first commissioner. This was one occasion during the eight-year partnership that Huston and Ruppert were united. They fought alongside each other and were rewarded with a joint—and indeed monumental—victory.

Huston and Ruppert also worked as a well-oiled tandem in planning and building Yankee Stadium. In May of 1921 they bought land in the Bronx for the purpose of fulfilling a dream—a stadium of their own. Huston, an experienced construction man and an engineer, supervised the building process himself. He is reported to have overseen the pouring of every ton of concrete.

But the fundamental disquiet of the Huston-Ruppert relationship still smoldered. Til and Jake rarely agreed on important club matters, with Jake usually winning the argument. (Ruppert was more tenacious than the amiable Huston.) They disagreed completely on the merits of their manager. When the humiliated Yankees finally succumbed to the Giants in the 1922 World Series without winning so much as a single game for their side, Huston announced that "Miller Huggins has managed the Yankees for the last time." Although GM Ed Barrow and Huston were good friends—it was because of his friendship with Huston that Barrow in 1920 joined the Yanks—Barrow sided with Ruppert in support of Huggins.

With the deck stacked against him, "Cap" decided to sell his share of the club. From the close of the 1922 World Series until the following May, he and Ruppert were in negotiations. On May 21, 1923, Huston accepted $1.5 million from Ruppert (some in cash and part in notes to be paid off later) and walked away from an unpalatable situation—carrying with him substantially more than a $1 million gain for his eight-year investment. It is said that Ruppert was afraid Huston would buy another baseball team and that this concern was a factor in the long negotiations.

But Til Huston was content to leave baseball. He was in 1923 the national commander of the Veterans of Foreign Wars and he regarded that position as a full-time job. He was 54. "I'm old and tired" he said. "The Yankees are a good team and the Stadium is nearly finished. It looks as if my work is about done." Reports circulated on the heels of Til's Yankee exit that he would buy the Red Sox. But Til Huston was never to return to baseball.

COL. JACOB RUPPERT

At one time, Jacob Ruppert had the longest tenure (24 years) of any Yankee owner until surpassed in 1998 by George Steinbrenner, who purchased the Bombers in 1973. Ruppert was president of the Yankees from 1915, when he and Til Huston bought the club from Frank Farrell and Bill Devery, until his death in January of 1939.

Ruppert was blessed with the wealth of his family's successful brewery business. In fact, his interest in buying the team was spurred by an advertising scheme; he made it known that the team would be called the New York Knickerbockers—after the Rupperts' most popular beer. But the managing editors of all 13 New York newspapers refused to accept the name because of the difficulty of fitting it into headlines, and the Yankees stayed the Yankees. Ruppert bought the team anyway.

Jake's grandfather came from Bavaria and had his own New York brewery by 1851. Jake's father entered the family business in 1867, the same year Jake was born. Jake did well at Columbia Grammar School and could have furthered his education, but his role in life was already established, and his father insisted Jake enter the family brewery business. The Ruppert business was lucrative and Jake also did well in real estate. He was rich from birth and, having inherited much of his wealth and sense of values and tastes, could be called a bona fide plutocrat.

Few men have lived as interesting a life as Jacob Ruppert. In addition to his business interests, Jake was a social and political figure. He was well mannered and well dressed (it is to him that the Yankees owe their pinstripes and blue stockings). He enjoyed the finer things of life, and as a lifelong gentleman bachelor indulged himself in his interests—horses, the Jockey Club, show dogs, and women, among whom he had many friends. (When Jake died, he left about $100 million. His estate was divided equally among two relatives and a former chorus girl the press had never heard of.) Jake belonged to at least seven clubs, including the Seventh Regiment, a unit for rich military hobbyists. Jake also enjoyed yachting and raced cars in the early days of the automobile. He had a stable of racing horses, a herd of Percheron draft horses, pedigreed dogs and a score of monkeys. In 1934 Admiral Richard Byrd journeyed to the South Pole, thanks in part to Ruppert, who gave Byrd $250,000. Byrd in turn named his flagship the *Jacob Ruppert*. Jake had a huge (12-room) town apartment on Fifth Avenue with five people serving him, besides having a house on the Hudson River. With all of his business, sporting and social interests, Jake somehow found time to serve four terms in Congress as the representative of a Manhattan district that was predominantly Republican. And Ruppert was a Democrat!

Ruppert was a frustrated baseball player in his youth. He was a sandlot pitcher from New York City's East Side who failed in his attempt to make the New York Giants baseball club. Instead he became a serious fan and yearned to own a team himself. In 1900 Jake tried to buy the Giants for $150,000, but John T. Brush purchased the team at the same price. In 1912 Jake could have bought the Chicago Cubs but he said he was not interested "in anything so far from Broadway." He did not follow the Yankees and had never seen the Yanks play until they moved into the Polo Grounds in 1913, and then he went to see the Yanks only because he wished to watch opponents such as Ty Cobb of the Tigers and Walter Johnson of the Senators. Ruppert was a diehard Giant fan.

Both American League President Ban Johnson and Boston Red Sox owner Joseph Lannin wanted Ruppert in the American League. In 1914, Johnson told Ruppert if he bought the Yankees he could obtain Eddie Collins from the Philadelphia Athletics for $50,000. At about the same time, Til Huston, who also wanted to own a team, entered the picture. After Ruppert and Huston unsuccessfully tried to buy the Giants, both Giant Manager John McGraw and Bill Fleischmann, a Cincinnati friend of Ruppert, suggested that Ruppert and Huston purchase the New York Yankees. Jake researched the Yankees and was shocked at the unprofessional condition of the club books in the Yankee office. He seriously considered buying an Indianapolis minor-league club and moving it to New York, but Ban Johnson discouraged him. While relaxing at his playground in French Lick, Ind., Ruppert announced his decision to buy the Yankees. Ruppert and Huston each coughed up $230,000 and on January 11, 1915, they became owners of the Yankees, a franchise in dire need of repair. Ruppert did not kid himself about what he had bought. As he said, he owned "an orphan ball club, without a home of its own, without players of outstanding ability, without prestige."

Jake loved baseball and he grew to love the Yankees with a fervor, especially during winning seasons. He once said a perfect afternoon at Yankee Stadium was "when the Yankees score eight runs in the first inning and then slowly pull away." Ruppert loved the excitement of being around the Yankees and often worked out with the team at spring training. The Yankees were mostly fun for him, but as he poured money into the team in increasing amounts through the years, Jake came to understand that the club was another million-dollar business. But Jake enjoyed the many frolics and battles he waged on behalf of his Yankees. To be sure, Jake took himself seriously; he was convinced of his importance to baseball. And considering some of the other owners who are enshrined in the Baseball Hall of Fame, it seems a mistake that Ruppert is not a member of the Hall.

Perhaps one reason Jacob Ruppert is not more recognized for his contributions is that he was not an innovator. In 1922, the St. Louis Cardinal farm system of Branch Rickey (and owner Sam Breadon) was born. It immediately proved successful, but Ruppert was slow in following the Cardinal lead. Ten years later, in 1932, Jake bought the minor-league franchise in Newark and instructed his general manager, Ed Barrow, to establish a first-class farm system. George Weiss was hired as farm director, and Ruppert proceeded to buy other minor-league franchises in a number of small towns and cities, including Kansas City. The Yankee farm system became the best in the game, but it remained an invention of the Cardinals. Jake did have the best uniformed team in baseball, and possibly the biggest innovation Ruppert brought to big-league baseball concerned uniforms. In 1923, the Yankees, already the game's best dressers, became the first team to step on the field in a clean uniform each game, as Ruppert bought two extra sets of uniforms.

Make no mistake, however, Ruppert was a shrewd baseball man, and he improved with age. His first important step in making the Yankees winners came in October of 1917 when he hired Miller Huggins to manage the Yankees—an action to which partner Huston, in France at the time, took strong exception. Jake considered Huggins a working hand but was convinced of Huggins' baseball knowledge after talking with Ban Johnson, who urged Ruppert to hire Huggins, and after meeting with Huggins.

Under Huggins the Yanks improved in 1918 and 1919 and were gaining in strength. Yet they still lacked something in Ruppert's view. While it was Huston who was first approached in the Babe Ruth acquisition, it was Ruppert who worked out the cash deal during the winter of 1919-20 that made Ruth a Yankee.

With Ruth in the lineup in 1920, the Yankees outdrew the New York Giants in the latter's own ballpark. The Giants' owner, Charley Stoneham, against his better judgment, ordered the Yanks to vacate the Polo Grounds. Ironically, in 1919, Ruppert approached Stoneham about his plan to have both the Yankees and Giants abandon the Polo Grounds and together build a huge sports stadium to seat almost 100,000 fans. Stoneham was uninterested. So when the Yankees were given notice, Ruppert and Huston bought land in the Bronx for $600,000, and on this tract built a stadium for $2.5 million. The stadium would be known, on Ruppert's insistence, as Yankee Stadium, no matter the clamor to name it after Ruth.

Ruppert and Huston, meanwhile, could not overcome the friction stemming from Huggins' hiring. When Huston's friend, Yankee GM Ed Barrow, stood by Ruppert in the defense of Huggins, Til Huston knew his Yankee days were numbered. Ruppert was especially upset about Huston's public criticism of a sell out and on May 21, 1923, after negotiating with Ruppert for about seven months, he traded his half of the Yankees to Ruppert for $1.5 million. (The value of the Yankees had appreciated considerably because of the consecutive pennants the Yanks had won, the presence of Ruth and the playing of baseball on Sunday in New York.) Following Huston's departure, Jake allowed Huggins to have complete control over his charges. When the sale was announced, the Yankee team was in Chicago and received a telegram. It read: "I am now the sole owner of the Yankees. Miller Huggins is my manager"—Jacob Ruppert. From that point on, the Yanks were a better team.

One of the reasons Ruppert's Yankees were so successful was Jake's willingness to remove himself from the everyday operations of the team. Jake spent his ample bank account lavishly and wisely on the Yankees. But he got excellent people to work for him, and for the most part let them call the shots. Both Miller Huggins and Joe McCarthy managed the Yankees for long periods of time, each was successful and neither had interference from Ruppert. General Manager Ed Barrow came from the Red Sox in 1920 (Red Sox owner Harry Frazee let Barrow go, but did he have any choice since the Yankee owners held the mortgage on Fenway Park, an outcome of the Ruth deal!) Barrow ran affairs the way he saw fit. Although Ruppert called Ed "Barrows," he usually deferred to Barrow's judgment. After Huston left the scene, Barrow purchased a small percentage of the Yankees from Ruppert, and Ruppert was assured of sound financial decisions from Barrow. And in the 1930s, Ruppert had George Weiss running his farm system. With Huggins, McCarthy, Barrow, and Weiss, all Baseball Hall of Famers, Ruppert's Yankee empire was in good hands.

But again, Jake Ruppert was a good baseball man and did not avoid major decisions when he alone had to make them. On several occasions he was drawn into difficult matters—usually salary disputes with Ruth, who for the most part enjoyed fair treatment at Ruppert's hands. After a Ruth holdout in 1930, Jake agreed to pay the famed slugger and crowd builder the astronomical salary of $80,000. But when Huggins and Ruth battled, there was no doubt where Ruppert stood, and that was squarely behind his manager. When the Babe made his him-or-me position public against Huggins in 1925, Jake stated, "Huggins will be the manager as long as he wants to be. You can see where we stand and where Ruth stands."

On another occasion Ruppert made his acuity felt. He had spent loads of money expanding the Yankee farm chain and improving the ballparks of his farm clubs, but his most important decision concerning a prospect involved Joe DiMaggio, who was developed outside the organization. When Barrow decided against obtaining an injured DiMaggio from the San Francisco Seals, Ruppert sided with scout Bill Essick and Weiss, and countermanded Barrow. To the Yanks' good fortune, he "gambled" on DiMag. Jacob Ruppert was not known as the "Master Builder in Baseball" for nothing!

The relationship between Jake Ruppert and Babe Ruth was a compatible one. They did not socialize, but Jake was usually more than fair with the Babe. Sometimes Jake was required to remind Ruth that he, Ruth, did not run the Yankees and to mind his manager. But Jake was generous with Babe. He even paid extra money to Ruth for playing in spring training exhibitions, which brought the Yankees a substantial income. As did Huston, Ruppert shielded Ruth from dishonest businessmen, caring about his star performer. Jake understood the importance of Ruth to the Yankees, both in the standings and financially. A prediction Jake made prior to the 1927 season indicates Ruppert believed in the saying, "as Ruth goes, so go the Yankees." Jake said the Yankees would win the 1927 pennant because the Babe was "ready to have his greatest year." When Ruth remarried in April of 1929, Jake asked Claire Ruth to travel with the Yankees, an extremely unusual request in baseball. But Jake knew Claire would make Babe behave.

Ruppert—everyone—was well aware of Ruth's desire to ultimately manage the Yankees. But Jake felt, as did almost all management people in baseball, that Babe's lack of discipline eliminated him from managerial consideration. He may also have thought, as Connie Mack did, that Mrs. Ruth would soon be running any team managed by the Babe. When Babe came to Jake following the 1929 season (when the Yanks were in search of a manager) and asked to be manager, Jake, perhaps rationally answered, "You can't manage yourself, 'Root.' How do you expect to manage others?" It was a line Ruppert repeated whenever the Babe approached him on the managing subject, and probably an unfair one considering the maturation Babe had developed since 1925. Certainly Barrow was against the idea of Ruth as Yankee manager. But perhaps Jake had a different, more logical, even human reason for not hiring the Babe. A baseball axiom, more truthful than any other, states: baseball managers are hired to be fired. If Ruth were hired to manage the Yankees, inevitably he would be fired. How do you fire the greatest player of all time, the greatest sports hero New York City or America ever had? Maybe Jake thought about that, and maybe Babe's popularity ultimately cost him the job he wanted most.

After the 1933 season, Jake wanted Babe to retire, but Babe wanted to play another year. Jake offered Babe the Newark managing job, but Ruth, citing the fact that other big-league stars began their managing careers in the majors, felt managing Newark would be too big a step down for him. Babe had rejected Jake's final offer. Ruppert and Barrow refused again after the 1934 season to accommodate Ruth by making him Yankee manager (they were pleased with McCarthy), but

Ruppert went out of his way to work out a deal that enabled Ruth to join the Boston Braves in February of 1935. For the greatest drawing card in baseball history, Ruppert received not a cent—he was most generous to the exiting Babe Ruth.

Being a dignified man, Ruppert was not prone to unruly behavior. He did, however, give his team grand victory parties, usually at the Commodore Hotel. And Ruppert naturally celebrated every pennant-clinching and World Series victory. Many rich people feel it is their duty to be generous, and Jake was one. When the Yankees won, the entire organization was rewarded. One memorable celebration occurred on the train bringing the Yankees home from St. Louis after sweeping the Cardinals in four straight games. Ruth and other Yankees grabbed Ruppert and playfully ripped his pajama top apart.

But there was a darker side of Jacob Ruppert. He could be sneaky. In part he was sneaky when he dealt with Ruth, maneuvering Babe into gladly accepting the Braves' offer in 1935 when Ruppert may or may not have known that Babe was heading for a bad situation in Boston. But Jake was at his sneakiest in 1922 when he hired detective Jimmy Kelly to spy on Yankee players. Kelly, after becoming friendly with the Yankee team, took some team members to an illegal brewery near Chicago. There a group photo was taken of Ruppert's players holding beer. Kelly gave the photo to Ruppert who used it against his men. (This is an ironic story since Jake was in the brewery business himself.) In fact, Ruppert went to pains attempting to keep his team out of trouble. In the spring training of 1920, the Yankees partied hard every night in south Florida, and while he was owner, Jake never took his club to south Florida again.

When Ruppert and Huston entered the league in 1915, American League President Ban Johnson welcomed them with open arms. He was still in search of a successful Yankee franchise to battle the Giants for New York City hearts, and Johnson liked the ambition of the new owners. However, it was not long before a series of events had Johnson wishing he had never set eyes on Ruppert and Huston. Johnson did not keep his promise of sending Ruppert-Huston quality players. Eddie Collins, for one, did not become a Yankee, and by 1919 Ruppert had lost his respect for Johnson and went about building the Yankees on his own.

The most serious confrontation between the league president and Ruppert and Huston was the Carl Mays case of 1919. After the Yanks obtained Mays from the Red Sox in mid-season, Johnson ordered him back to Boston. He suspended Mays for his alleged jumping of the Red Sox. Ruppert, however, won a temporary court injunction restraining Johnson and his office from interfering with Mays' right to pitch for New York. This was the first serious challenge to Johnson's authority by a member of the league Ban had organized and single-handedly ruled. Naturally he was furious. When the 1919 season ended, Detroit owner Frank Navin argued that Mays' Yankee wins should not be counted, a notion that would have allowed the Tigers instead of the Yankees to grab third-place money. The National Commission withheld Yankee World Series shares until the New York Supreme Court awarded the Yankees a permanent injunction, ruling that big league clubs had the right to regulate their business without Johnson's interference.

Following the Mays case, the American League was divided into two armed camps. Ban Johnson had the support of the ownership of Detroit, Cleveland, Washington, Philadelphia, and St. Louis. Charles Comiskey of Chicago (still furious that Johnson allowed Jack Quinn to become a Yankee in a 1918 decision), Harry Frazee of Boston and the New York ownership of Ruppert-Huston were the opposition. They were known as "the Insurrectionists," and the group's leaders were Ruppert and Huston.

At a league meeting following the Yankee court victory, Johnson and his boys unseated "the Insurrectionists" (Ruppert, Frazee and Comiskey) on the five-man league board of directors and replaced them with Johnson loyalists. A string of legal fights ensued, capped by a $500,000 lawsuit the Yankee owners brought against Johnson, claiming an attempt was made to drive them out of baseball.

Obviously, the league could not continue to function under such a set of circumstances. A showdown league meeting was held on February 10, 1920. Ruppert and Huston won that fight, too. Johnson lost most of his power, Carl Mays was reinstated honorably and the Yankees' 1919 third-place standing became official. Also, a two-man board of reviews was created to examine large fines and long suspensions made by the league. The board was Jacob Ruppert and Clark Griffith of Washington.

The settlement was understandably not to Ban Johnson's favor. He became merely a figurehead until retiring seven years later. Actually, the most significant achievement of "the Insurrectionists" was the pressure they generated to make Judge Kenesaw Mountain Landis baseball's first commissioner. The Yankees, Red Sox and White Sox aligned themselves with the National League and threatened a new 12-team National League (adding another city) unless Landis was made commissioner. Whether the threat was or was not sincere, it worked. The other five American League clubs and Johnson were forced to accept Landis, who became commissioner early in 1921, thus abolishing the unsatisfactory ruling body known as the National Commission. Remarkably, Yankee owners Col. Jacob Ruppert and Col. Til Huston had won just about every battle in the long war against the American League hierarchy. But Ruppert was also a victim of his own victory. In 1922, Jake could not fight Commissioner Landis on Babe Ruth's suspension. After all, Ruppert was chiefly responsible for the Commissioner's creation, and Jake had urged his fellow owners to accept all Landis' decisions without complaint.

During spring training camp in St. Petersburg, FL, in 1938, Jake caught a bad cold that stayed with him throughout the entire baseball season, keeping him from the Stadium for all but a couple of games. He had a number of medical problems and then developed phlebitis. On January 13, 1939, Jacob Ruppert died at the age of 71. Excepting relatives and brewery associates, Babe Ruth was the last to visit Ruppert just before Jake's death. During the visit, Jake, who had always called Babe by his surname, which sounded like "Root" because of Ruppert's slight German accent, looked up from his hospital bed and murmured, "Babe, Babe." Ruth was deeply moved.

Jacob Ruppert, who gained his honorary military title of colonel at the age of 22 while serving on the staff of the governor of New York, could be said in retrospect to have earned a second and perhaps more substantial title: Father of the Yankees. It was he who more than any other nurtured the style and winning tradition of the Yankees. In his two dozen years of club ownership, the Yanks were tops in the American League 10 times and the holders of World Championships seven times. On April 23, 1940, a plaque in memory of Jacob Ruppert was unveiled in Yankee Stadium's center field. Ruppert's memory lives on.

HARRY SPARROW

Harry Sparrow, who joined the Yankee organization in 1915, previously worked for the New York Giants and was a close friend and bodyguard of John McGraw.

He was hired by co-owners Jacob Ruppert and Til Huston to perform the duties of business manager (general manager). Sparrow died suddenly while at work in May of 1920. He was succeeded by Ed Barrow.

EDWARD G. BARROW

Ed Barrow was 52 when he joined the Yankees on October 29, 1920, yet he would be associated with the New York club for a quarter century and would come to be seen as the architect of the great Yankee dynasty.

Barrow's association with the Yankees was so strong as to eclipse a successful baseball career starting some three decades before his Yankee affiliation. His life began in America's pioneering days. Ed was born in a covered wagon heading west on May 10, 1868, in Springfield, Ill. He grew up near Des Moines, Iowa, and worked in Chicago before teaming with Harry Stevens to run the scoreboard and a soda concession business at Exposition Park, the Pirates' ballpark. In 1894, Barrow and Stevens bought the club in Wheeling, W.V. (Interstate League), and Barrow was both manager and business manager. A year later, Barrow moved on, becoming owner of the Paterson, N.J. team of the newly organized Atlantic League. There he signed and developed Honus Wagner, whose contract Ed later sold to the Pittsburgh Pirates. In 1897, Ed was elected president of the Atlantic League, a position he held for three years. In 1900, he bought an interest in the Toronto club, became team manager, and led it to a pennant in 1902. The following year Barrow was named manager of the Detroit Tigers but resigned in 1904 after a dispute with Frank Navin. The next few years, Barrow managed at Indianapolis, Montreal and again at Toronto. In 1910, he became president of the Eastern League, which he later renamed the International League.

Barrow in 1918 was named manager of the Boston Red Sox. He gave Boston a World Championship that same year and began converting Babe Ruth from pitcher to outfielder. While he felt Ruth was as good as any southpaw pitcher he had ever seen, Barrow wanted the Babe's big bat in the lineup, and he saw Ruth as an excellent defensive outfielder. The Red Sox had a dismal 1919 season under Barrow, dropping to sixth place, although Ruth had his first great hitting season. When Barrow learned that Boston owner Harry Frazee had sold Ruth's contract to the Yankees during the winter of 1919-20, he was furious. And although the Red Sox improved their record, moving up a notch to fifth place in 1920, Ed was anxious to leave Boston. Frazee had said of the Ruth deal, "I believe the sale of Ruth will ultimately strengthen the team." That is exactly the kind of thinking Barrow was seeking to escape. The Red Sox were in for several years of mediocrity, and the club's ownership and management was hated by Beantown press and fans alike.

Yankee co-owner Til Huston, Frazee, and Barrow were all close friends. After the 1920 season, it was apparent to all three that because of the financial pressures weighing on Frazee, the Boston club, once so powerful, had eroded miserably and that the Yankees were gaining in strength. In other words, the balance of power had shifted from Boston to New York in the American League. Huston and Jacob Ruppert wanted Barrow, and with the advice and consent of Frazee, Barrow joined the Yankee front office following the 1920 season. The man known as "Cousin Egbert" or "Cousin Ed" in his pre-Yankee days moved to New York where he became tagged "The Yankee Empire Builder." And it was in New York that Ed first impressed on the baseball world the fact that winning teams are created by a good front office. Rival owners and executives often tried to pry from Barrow his success formula. Barrow's success stemmed from the fact that he outworked his rivals. Yet besides hard work, Ed knew the game and business of baseball, and he hired people just as smart as he was. The winning of championships was the result of a well-put-together front office.

Ed Barrow entered a favorable situation and had a great opportunity upon joining the Yankees. In New York his title was at first business manager-secretary—the equivalent of today's general manager. Barrow came to town a most purposeful man. His will was to instill the winning spirit and a winning atmosphere into the Yankee organization, which had yet to win a pennant. His first act as GM was to shift Yankee spring training camp from Jacksonville, Fla., where the Yankees had enjoyed the partying life, to Shreveport, La., for the 1921 camp. (Shreveport proved to be just as much fun to the Yankee hellraisers.) One of his first acts in New York, bringing scout Paul Krichell to the Yanks, had more long-range benefits.

The first great Yankee teams were built around ex-Red Soxer Babe Ruth. Barrow bought or traded for a number of the stars he had at Boston and gave the Red Sox in all the deals only one player, catcher Muddy Ruel, who developed into a star. After a dozen years of buying, selling and trading, Barrow (and Ruppert), impressed by Branch Rickey's success with the St. Louis Cardinal farm system—the first in baseball history—hired George Weiss to establish and operate a Yankee farm system. Soon New York had the best farm chain in baseball, and the future successes of the Yankees were all but guaranteed.

Barrow was one of a handful of people to have monumental influence on Yankee success. In his 25-year tenure he saw New York claim 14 league pennants and 10 World Championships. And he built the Yankee steamrollers both by going into the market and by growing his own through a finely wrought farm system.

A cold and icy man who seldom cracked a joke—that's one way Ed Barrow has been described. A sense of humor was definitely not a Barrow trademark and any attempt at humor was registered with a sharp tongue. He was a tough man both mentally and physically and he had many fist fights through the years. Reportedly, Ed never lost one. (As the Babe's Boston skipper, Ed once challenged Ruth to a fight, but Ruth declined the invitation.) Next to baseball, Barrow enjoyed the sport of boxing. He hated golf, thinking it a sissy game, and hated to see his ballplayers waste their strength on the links. (But Ed never prevented his players from playing golf as did John J. McGraw.) Barrow was a supreme commander, running a tight ship from Yankee Stadium and his 42nd Street office. Because he hated phonies, or phoniness of any kind, all of Ed's friends were close ones. Some people who worked for Barrow disliked

Edward Barrow, architect of the Yankee dynasties of the '20s, '30s and '40s.

him because Ed had perfected the art of making underlings feel inferior and replaceable. (Harry Frazee called Barrow, "Simon," as in Simon Legree.) Ed had thick, dark, menacing eyebrows, and when he lost his temper, which was often, he turned crimson and had trouble with his speech.

Under the circumstances of the Barrow personality, one can only wonder how a ballplayer felt when he came into Barrow's office to ask for a raise. Needless to say, the young man was not whistling a sunny tune. For on top of everything else, Barrow was a hard-line baseball man from the old-old school, who worked long hours and believed in high levels of team discipline and above all else: LOW levels of player compensation. (Barrow himself gave the appearance of being underpaid, his attire usually including a sweater full of holes.) He believed a player had to be kept lean and hungry for that World Series check. The sight of those menacing eyebrows, the ominous cold stare and the threat of violence, or at least the explosion of a terrible temper, kept most ballplayers from arguing contracts with Barrow. Besides, in Barrow's era, a player could either sign his contract or not play baseball. He had no choice in the matter. However, occasionally a brave soul would defy Ed. When Leo Durocher came to Barrow asking for a raise following the 1929 season, Ed made an offer that moved Leo to turn and walk out. "If you go out that door," the composed Barrow coldly warned, "you'll go out of the American League." Durocher walked and was never again associated with the American League. Barrow directed the Yankees with an iron hand, but he felt that was the only way a successful club could be run.

Barrow's conflicts with players over money included a legendary contract dispute with Joe DiMaggio in the spring of 1942. Joe had good reason to expect a raise from his $37,500 salary in view of his 56-game hitting streak in 1941. But Barrow wanted DiMaggio to take a $5,000 cut! An ugly public battle ensued, with Barrow bringing in World War II and the paltry $21 a month paid the soldier. It was a tawdry tactic but one that had some fans against "The Yankee Clipper" for the only time in his career. DiMaggio eventually signed for $43,750, but he was hurt by the episode.

Ruling the Yanks in dictatorial style was Barrow's way, but it also was the way of all successful baseball executives. Ed had little room for sentiment and was all business, bowing only to Jacob Ruppert in Yankee operations. His values, ethics and morals were shaped by the 19th century. (Ed was born three years after the Civil War and was 32 when the 20th century began.) Barrow was conservative, once ordering a woman to put out a cigarette during a game in the 1920s. He refused to install lights at the Stadium, believing baseball was meant to be played under the sun. (Ironically, on July 4, 1896, Ed arranged for his Paterson club to play a night game in Wilmington, DE). Novelties and lights at the ballpark were thought of as phony gimmicks by Ed, and consequently there were no game promotions or home night games in Ed's Yankee tenure. To Barrow's way of thinking, baseball alone drew fans to his ballpark. And the better the team, Ed felt, the higher the attendance figures.

Realizing that a manager must have complete control of his team, Barrow protected his skippers from interference. He persuaded the enthusiastic Ruppert and Huston to stay out of the Yankee clubhouse; this was the manager's domain, he insisted. (A familiar ploy of the Yankee owners was to question Miller Huggins immediately after a defeat.) Barrow, himself a minor owner after Ruppert sold him 5-10 percent of the club for $300,000 when Huston departed, refused to interfere with his managers. Ed never entered the Yankee clubhouse unless invited by his manager (and then usually only to offer congratulations on another pennant or World Series victory) and he never stepped on the playing field with the players. Barrow stayed in the background. Before every game at the Stadium, Ed would go to a kitchen on the grandstand floor and order a cheese sandwich and a glass of buttermilk. Then his manager (Miller Huggins or Joe McCarthy) would meet him and the two would chat about Yankee business. Usually these brief, informal get-togethers were the only meetings necessary.

Yankee Managers Huggins and McCarthy knew they had the support of their superior, Barrow, who in turn knew he had the support of his boss, owner Ruppert. In fact, Ruppert had complete confidence in Barrow, and the two were friendly besides being business associates. They occasionally socialized and vacationed together. Ed felt McCarthy was the greatest manager in baseball history, and during the 1930s when the delineation of power was Ruppert-Barrow-McCarthy, the Yankees ran smoothly.

While Barrow confined himself to the business end of club operations, he had sound baseball instincts and a shrewdness about the game and its practitioners. He brought the Yanks' first great relief ace to the Stadium scene in 1927 in the person of Wilcy Moore, an aging Sally League pitcher whose impressive statistics Ed had read in *The Sporting News*. (Sportswriters joked that Barrow found Moore in the Sears-Roebuck catalog.) Barrow bought Moore's contract sight unseen and cheaply, although he was told that Moore was an over-the-hill pitcher whose record (he was 20-1 at one point the previous year)

reflected the weakness of the Sally League. Moore went 19-7 with 13 saves for the Yankees in 1927!

Many of the players whose contracts Barrow bought were players whom he had never seen. But he trusted his excellent scouts, led by Paul Krichell, and had considerable acuity of his own when it came to baseball. When the Yankees badly needed infielders in 1925, Barrow had the minor leagues searched and found and obtained Tony Lazzeri, Mark Koenig, and Leo Durocher. A number of Yankee scouts, including Krichell and Huggins, had watched these three play, but the final decision to bring them to New York was made by Barrow. Baseball Hall of Fame immortal Branch Rickey once said of Ed, "Many men can scout an individual player; others can scout a whole team as a unit. Barrow could do both. Not many men can."

But for all his baseball savvy, Barrow did commit one perceptual error. When Ruth was the toast of the nation in the early 1920s because of his home run feats, Barrow predicted that once the Babe learned how to hit, his average would rise to around .400, and he would not be remembered for all those silly home runs.

The entire Barrow-Ruth relationship was unusual, and in some ways it was weird. Their careers paralleled, and Barrow was in a way responsible for Ruth's path toward success. Barrow was a father figure to Ruth, some felt, but that was probably not the case. Ed believed Ruth was a marvelously gifted ballplayer but never understood Babe's significance to the game or to the country for that matter. In Boston the two disagreed often and came close to fighting on more than one occasion. In fact, they never got along well, but it is inaccurate to say they hated each other. Babe brought fowl from hunting conquests as presents to Ed, and Barrow, who would not have done this for most people, worked closely with Ruth's agent, Christy Walsh, in a plan that withheld some of Ruth's salary. This was in Babe's interest and designed by Walsh, so that spendthrift Babe could not blow all his money. In other ways, Barrow protected Ruth. Barrow and Ruth, however, were vastly different personalities, and their styles and attitudes often clashed. Ed loved Babe's big bat (as Huggins did) but not Ruth's colorfulness (as Huggins did not). But one can only speculate on the question: Did Barrow like Ruth as a person, as did Huggins, who genuinely liked Babe? During the winter of 1933-34, Barrow offered the Newark managing position to Ruth, indicating that success at Newark would mean a promotion (and the only higher job was managing the Yankees). Babe (probably foolishly) rejected the offer, but one wonders whether Barrow was sincere with the Babe. Barrow NEVER gave serious thought to the Babe's becoming Yankee manager. After enjoying good working relationships with Huggins and McCarthy, Barrow did not need a crystal ball to foresee a stormy Ruth-Barrow working relationship. If Jacob Ruppert (who also never gave serious consideration to hiring Ruth) had hired Ruth as manager, Barrow probably would have soon left the Yanks or campaigned to have Ruth fired. However, in the end, following Babe's 1948 Yankee Stadium farewell, Ruth embraced 80-year-old Barrow much the way he had embraced Lou Gehrig at the Stadium nine years earlier.

Remembering that Ed Barrow had his run-ins with Babe Ruth at both Boston and New York, it is still difficult to believe the order of Barrow's picks as the five best ballplayers in baseball history, published in *The New York Times* by John Kieran in 1925. Here is Barrow's ranking:

1. Honus Wagner
2. Ty Cobb
3. Nap Lajoie
4. Babe Ruth
5. Tris Speaker

Barrow actually picked Lajoie over Ruth! And even in 1925 Ruth's feats were recognized as incredible and he was given credit (or discredit in the view of some, possibly Barrow included) for having changed the way baseball was played. In Barrow's autobiography, written after he left the game, he still maintained Wagner was the greatest player of all time. (Remember, Wagner was a Barrow discovery.)

Barrow did not consider Ruth a dumb ballplayer. In fact, he felt Babe's unsuccessful steal attempt that ended Game 7 of the 1926 World Series was Babe's only "dumb play" in his career. Years after Kieran listed Barrow's player ranking, Barrow said, "I never saw the Babe make a mistake in a ball game. Ruth always knew, instinctively, what to do on a ball field." But Ed did not realize Babe's impact on baseball and the way it is played. Somewhere along the line, Barrow made the transition from the pre-Ruth game of "inside baseball" to the power game personified by the Bronx Bomber teams Ed put together. There was a very special place in his heart, however, for the game he knew in his first 50 years.

Following Jacob Ruppert's death in 1939, Ed Barrow was named Yankee club president, and in the absence of Ruppert was the only one who mattered in the Yankee front office. Yankee success continued with Barrow as president, the Bronx Bombers winning four pennants in five seasons and copping the World Championship in the alternate years of 1939, 1941 and 1943. Barrow held the job until the trio of MacPhail, Topping and Webb purchased the Yankees from the Ruppert estate in January of 1945, at which time Ed became chairman of the board. Two years later, Ed Barrow retired at the age of 79.

Upon retiring from the Yankees, Barrow named his final all-time Yankee team. It had Bill Dickey and Benny Bengough as catchers in the traditional two-catcher system; Lou Gehrig at first; Joe Gordon at second; Joe Dugan at third; Frank Crosetti at shortstop; Babe Ruth, Bob Meusel and Joe DiMaggio in the outfield; and Jack Chesbro, Urban Shocker, Herb Pennock, Lefty Gomez and Red Ruffing representing his five-man pitching staff. In his autobiography, Barrow named his most famous creation, the 1927 Yankee club, as his best Yankee team. But curiously, he did not name the 1927 Yanks as the greatest team in baseball history. He gave that honor, surprisingly, to the Chicago White Sox, the most infamous team the game has ever seen and one forever known as the Black Sox after some of its members threw the 1919 World Series.

Barrow received much praise and many honors through the years. *The Sporting News* named him the Major League Executive of the Year in 1937 and 1941, and in 1940 the New York chapter of the Baseball Writers presented him with the William J. Slocum Award. In September of 1953, the Committee on Veterans named him to the Baseball Hall of Fame, an action that preceded Ed Barrow's death by only three months. On April 15, 1954, a plaque dedicated to his memory was unveiled on the center field wall in Yankee Stadium.

Even after Barrow's Yankee departure and death, his executive baseball philosophy was kept alive at Yankee Stadium by his successor and protege, George Weiss, who learned some valuable baseball lessons from his former boss. And when the list of outstanding baseball executives is voiced, the names of Ed Barrow and George Weiss, along with Branch Rickey, lead the list.

LARRY (LELAND S.) MACPHAIL, SR.

Larry MacPhail became president and general manager of the Yankees after he, Dan Topping and Del Webb bought the team from the heirs of Jacob Ruppert on January for the sum of $2.8 million 26, 1945. MacPhail had had his sights set on the Yankees for some time. In the autumn of 1942, he reenlisted in the U.S. Army, serving in World War II, and leaving his executive post with the Brooklyn Dodgers. Larry was 52 years old at the time. After becoming a high-ranking officer, MacPhail returned from the Army with the thought of buying the Yankees, a club that had been up for sale for several years. With his partners Topping and Webb, MacPhail wrapped up the deal, purchasing the Yankees, Yankee Stadium and the franchise's farm chain for a little less than $3 million. It was a steal!

MacPhail came to the Bronx with a record of success behind him and a reputation for progressivism and individualism. Born in Cass City, Mich., on February 3, 1890, MacPhail displayed interesting and daring qualities long before he entered professional baseball in 1930 at the age of 40. As a captain in World War I, Larry was part of an operation designed to capture Kaiser Wilhelm of Germany. Although the raid failed, MacPhail captured the Kaiser's ashtray! MacPhail first made his mark on baseball as president and general manager of the Columbus, Ohio, club in the American Association (1930-32). He built fine big-league clubs as general manager at Cincinnati (1933-37) and as vice-president and president at Brooklyn (1938-42).

Perhaps MacPhail is best remembered for his pioneering of night baseball. In 1932 Larry had lights installed at the home ballpark of the Columbus Redbirds. Big-league history was made on May 24, 1935, in Cincinnati, when MacPhail introduced night baseball to the majors. Just before that night's game between the Reds and Phillies, President Roosevelt turned on the switch for the first big-league night game, and because of the success of night ball in Cincinnati, the course of baseball history was changed. In 1938, upon joining the Dodgers, Larry lighted the Ebbets Field playing field. And continuing in the same progressive vein in the Bronx, Larry had lights installed atop Yankee Stadium in 1946 and scored great success at the gate.

MacPhail built fine teams at Cincinnati and Brooklyn, but Yankee fans might be more interested in Larry's association with Babe Ruth. The Babe during the 1930s was anxious to become a big-league manager and MacPhail was one of the few men considering Ruth for a job. In 1934 he almost hired the Babe at Cincinnati, and in 1938 he made Ruth a Brooklyn coach. MacPhail thought Ruth managerial material but negative remarks by Leo Durocher (about Babe's signal-relaying inability) killed Ruth's chances with MacPhail. (In 1946 when Larry was with the Yankees, Ruth asked him for the Newark job, but Larry so hemmed and hawed that the Babe got the negative message.) Without Ruth, MacPhail's Dodgers of 1941 won the National League pennant, sending Brooklyn into a frenzy.

In MacPhail's short three-year Yankee residence (1945-47), he completely revitalized the franchise. The public responded to MacPhail's unique, energetic and imaginative front office operation, and fans flocked to Yankee Stadium in droves. Night baseball was at the root of the attendance increase, although it must be recognized that the Yanks of the mid-1940s were highly popular and that the public in general was baseball hungry following the war. In MacPhail's three years as club president, the Yankees drew 5,326,295 fans and made more money than any team did in TEN years, let alone three.

Under MacPhail, the Yankees became the first major-league team to regularly travel by air. (When a coal strike tied up the railroad, Larry contracted with an airline for a 44-passenger airplane to fly the Yanks.) MacPhail sent a spring training squad to Panama by air. Flying baseball trips were made commonplace after Larry's lead. Before spring training in 1947, Larry organized a Yankee tour that included exhibitions at San Juan, Puerto Rico; Caracas, Venezuela; and Havana, Cuba.

MacPhail was a pioneer of radio and television coverage in baseball. He brought regular radio broadcasts to Brooklyn and on August 26, 1939, he was the brain behind the first telecast of a baseball game, an experiment that brought the Dodgers-Reds doubleheader to the few television sets in the New York City area. With the Yankees in 1946, Larry sold the first commercial television rights. Dumont paid $75,000 for season rights to televise Yankee games, although the New York City area had no more than 500 TV sets.

Larry was progressive in the social arena as well. When Jackie Robinson joined Brooklyn as the first black in the majors in 1947, MacPhail instituted a system to scout the Negro Leagues for outstanding ballplayers. He fully intended to bring black athletes to the Yankees, an intention that withered under his successor, George Weiss, who ignored the scouting system. (Put simply, MacPhail wanted the best players on the Yanks, and Weiss wanted the best WHITE players.) Larry's Hall of Fame plaque honors him for "helping set up employee and player pension plans." And MacPhail required his players to wear batting helmets for their own protection.

In general, Larry MacPhail aroused excitement in New York City over the Yankees, the kind of excitement that had been missing since the departure of Babe Ruth. (Of course, the Great Depression and World War II had made it difficult for people to get excited about sports.) A showman with flair, MacPhail was a shrewd talent scout, a great promoter and a financial genius. He offered entertainment acts at the Stadium. He had women ushers, and for women he promoted fashion shows, gave away nylon stockings on Ladies' Day and established a womens' lounge at the Stadium. For season ticket holders, the luxurious Stadium Club was created (an idea that quickly spread to other sports facilities). The team received a new clubhouse, and the press was also given new facilities. In short, MacPhail gave everyone a little something. For himself and the Yankee image, Larry moved the club's business offices to fashionable Fifth Avenue.

MacPhail had some differences with the great Joe McCarthy, the manager he inherited in 1945. The two were completely dissimilar personalities, and it was inevitable that they would part. McCarthy left the team in 1946, a tumultuous year in which MacPhail went through three managers (McCarthy, Dickey and Neun) before settling on the experienced Bucky Harris for the 1947 campaign. A successful MacPhail-Harris relationship developed, similar to the familiar Barrow-Huggins and Barrow-McCarthy tandems of the past (and the Weiss-Stengel partnership of the future). The MacPhail-Harris combi-

nation, however, was never given a chance to become famous.

A solid baseball executive was Larry MacPhail. At the same time, the red-haired fighting genius could be abrasive with his loud and argumentative manner. (He fired Leo Durocher several times when the two were together at Brooklyn.) MacPhail was not above hiring private detectives, as he once did, to follow Yankee players suspected of not getting to bed on time. Larry drank a bit. He would fight with anyone and everyone at any time. Through the years, Larry had disagreements with Commissioner Chandler, other club owners, and sometimes battled verbally in the press box and team clubhouse. MacPhail was occasionally rough with his own son, Lee, who was then a Yankee minor-league executive. Lee MacPhail was President of the American League from 1974-1983. Nor was the responsible and thoughtful Joe DiMaggio beyond Larry's reach; MacPhail once fined Joe for missing a Yankee promotion. Brilliant and volatile, Larry MacPhail was the Charley Finley of his era. (By the way, long before Finley suggested using orange baseballs at night, MacPhail experimented with yellow baseballs.)

Larry MacPhail also had a soft side. On the final day of the 1947 season, he assembled a great collection of old-time stars to play two innings of baseball before the regular game for the benefit of the Babe Ruth Foundation Inc. Both the Yankees and Connie Mack's Athletics turned the day's gate receipts over to the Foundation. Babe was sincerely grateful to MacPhail, and 25,000 fans came to see such old Yankee favorites as Frank Baker, Duffy Lewis, Wally Schang, Wally Pipp, Herb Pennock, Bob Meusel, Earle Combs, Waite Hoyt, Lefty Gomez, Red Ruffing, Red Rolfe, George Selkirk, Roger Peckinpaugh, Buddy Hassett, and Johnny Sturm. Baseball greats Tris Speaker, Al Simmons, George Sisler, Jimmie Foxx, Mickey Cochrane, Lefty Grove, Chief Bender, Cy Young, Ed Walsh and many more attended. (Del Webb picked up Ty Cobb in a private plane in Las Vegas and brought him to New York for the festivities.) It was a fine gesture on MacPhail's part and one of baseball's few genuine acts on behalf of the Babe in his final years. It was also MacPhail who popularized Old Timers' Day, the bringing back of old ballplayers for a day at the ballpark.

The 1947 season was most difficult for Larry. It began with the bizarre Havana, Cuba, misunderstanding with Leo Durocher, Branch Rickey, and the Dodgers. The complete story has never been learned because Commissioner Chandler put a gag on all participants, and in later years all parties gave different versions of the incident, investigation, rulings, and reasons behind the rulings. In any event, Durocher, who supposedly made remarks about MacPhail being seated with gamblers, remarks that were completely false (MacPhail explained that the Yankees and Dodgers changed sides of the field and after sitting in the box meant for Rickey, he found himself next to a gambler and casino manager), was suspended for the year. Most insiders felt Chandler was after Durocher because of previous incidents, the slugging of a fan for one. Ironically, MacPhail went to bat for Leo and was called in to see Chandler a few times for violating his gag order.

Reportedly, Chandler was anxious to have MacPhail out of baseball. Rumor had it that the Commissioner had several meetings with Topping and Webb, both of whom assured Chandler that they planned to buy out Larry's Yankee ownership.

Throughout the 1947 season, Larry was temperamental, screaming at Yankee players and knocking them in public. MacPhail and Rickey, rivals for years, had an irreparable

Larry MacPhail, SR. (New York Yankees Archives)

argument during the 1947 World Series, and Larry was disgusted. Also, unknown to the public, MacPhail's doctor had urged Larry to leave the hectic baseball life.

In the Yankee locker room following the seventh game of the 1947 World Series in which the Yankees beat the Dodgers, MacPhail announced that he was leaving the Yankee organization. There was also a report that at a victory party, marked by some heavy drinking, MacPhail got into a heated argument with his partners. In any event, Larry sold his one-third share to Topping-Webb for $2 million—a figure not far from the $2.8 million that transferred ownership from the Rupperts.

Larry MacPhail was inducted into the Baseball Hall of Fame in 1978, three years after he died (October 1, 1975) at the age of 85. His contributions to the game in New York and elsewhere were astute and imaginative; Larry was one of the outstanding baseball executives in the history of the game. No other executive made as big an impact on the New York Yankees in as short a time as Larry MacPhail. It is hard to believe that he did so much in the space of less than three years.

DANIEL R. TOPPING

Dan Topping was one of a triumvirate that assumed ownership of the Yankees in 1945. Although he was himself an athlete of some distinction—he played baseball and football in college and was a fine golfer—he was not an avid baseball fan.

A millionaire, Topping was an officer in the American Canteen Company. His business interests were many, and they included two football teams, the Brooklyn Dodgers and later the New York Yankees of the All-American Conference.

Topping stayed out of the day-to-day operations of the Yankees as much as possible, letting one of his partners,

President and General Manager Larry MacPhail, manage the club, and his players grab the headlines. When MacPhail sold out to Topping and third partner Del Webb following the 1947 season, Topping became president, named George Weiss general manager, and continued his policy of noninterference over the next 13 years.

Topping's detachment extended to Weiss' refusal to acquire black players in the early 1950s (Weiss was biased against blacks) even though he personally was not opposed to the idea, and in fact had black players on his Dodger football team.

Dan in a fight could be tough as he showed in the movement to unseat Commissioner Chandler. In spite of his general popularity, Chandler's contract was not renewed at the end of 1950. Topping and Webb were not leaders of the anti-Chandler attack, but they were influential within the minority of club owners who wanted Chandler out. The Yankee owners resented Chandler's so-called "Gestapo methods" that included investigations of the owners and the keeping of background files on them. Topping was also involved in a running feud with Bill Veeck and in time won that battle, too.

Topping was an ardent admirer of Joe DiMaggio and was fair with the Yankee Clipper at contract time, making DiMaggio baseball's first $100,000-a-year player (in 1949). He respected DiMaggio's judgment. When, after the 1946 season, Cleveland's overtures to the Yanks for Joe Gordon, their sensational second baseman, narrowed down to one of two pitchers, Red Embree and Allie Reynolds, Topping consulted DiMag. He was advised to take Reynolds, and Reynolds became one of the outstanding pitchers in Yankee history. Topping thought so much of DiMaggio that when the Yanks were searching for a manager following the 1948 season, Dan seriously considered asking Joe to be a player-manager. Weiss, however, was against it, and finally convinced a reluctant Topping to accept Casey Stengel.

It was through Topping, a man of considerable charm, that Manager Casey Stengel in 1950 asked DiMaggio to take a stab at playing first base. It was something of a twist—a manager asking an owner to ask a superstar to change his position. It was also an experiment that failed to warm DiMaggio's heart and indeed failed outright. But DiMaggio held nothing against Topping, who each year in the autumn of Joe's career would plead with him to continue playing baseball. DiMaggio finally said no following the 1951 season. He was to say no once more—in 1954 when Topping asked him to return to the team as a coach with the prospect of becoming manager on Stengel's eventual retirement. DiMaggio had no interest in managing.

Even without DiMaggio, the 1950s were pleasant and rewarding for Topping and the Yanks, who won eight American League pennants and six World Championships. It was the most successful decade in the team's history, and it was juxtaposed in time with what was to be a decade of painful disappointment for the Yanks and their fans—the 1960s.

Dan Topping found himself in a dilemma as the latter decade opened. The popular Stengel and the successful Weiss were getting on in years (Stengel turned 70 in July of 1960, and Weiss was in the same age bracket) and this fact, along with other considerations, spelled forced retirement. Actually, after the 1959 season, Topping wanted to let both Stengel and Weiss go, but he was afraid of the adverse reaction that was likely from public and press. He decided to consider the 1960 season a rebuilding year, then bring in his old favorites, Ralph Houk and Roy Hamey, to get the Yanks back on track again. Although the "rebuilding year" of 1960 turned into another championship season, Topping proceeded with his housecleaning, and Stengel and Weiss were doomed. Topping and the Yankees were dealt heaping criticism from the press and the public when the axes fell. The "retirements" were poorly handled and were probably the biggest blunder of the Topping era. Said Topping at the time: "Twelve years ago we were ridiculed when we hired Casey Stengel. Today, when Casey is leaving, we are ridiculed again."

But the Yankees' great team strength continued through 1961. New York won 109 games, the American League championship and the World Series, dispatching Cincinnati in five games. Topping gained a measure of redemption, and *The Sporting News* named him the Major League Executive of the Year.

Topping's health began to slip badly the following year, in 1962. He developed both emphysema and a heart condition and underwent surgery for the removal of part of his stomach. Several heart attacks followed, and Topping and Webb decided that they would sell the team when the opportunity arose. Once so disposed, the two owners spent little money to maintain the high quality of the franchise, and they all but ignored the farm system. Good player prospects were signing with other clubs for the bonus money Topping and Webb declined to offer.

One of the last major decisions Topping made as owner came in the spring of 1963. Following the 1962 World Series, GM Roy Hamey told Topping that he wished to retire and that the 1963 season would be his last as general manager. Topping was faced with two problems. On the one hand, he had to replace a general manager. On the other, he had an even more serious problem. Because of Casey Stengel, the crosstown Mets were winning hearts and stealing attention and valuable newspaper space. Yankee Manager Ralph Houk, who had Topping as his biggest booster, did not have the personality to compete with Casey. Topping took the natural action, killing two birds with one stone. He decided to reward Houk for a job well done by making him general manager and to replace Houk with the colorful and popular Yogi Berra to battle the equally loved Stengel for the attention of New York. Dan reasoned Berra would bring the fans back to the Bronx in 1964, and he was not concerned about Berra's lack of managerial experience. The whole scheme was unloaded on a shocked Berra aboard Topping's yacht during the spring camp of 1963, and the plan was kept secret all season.

In August of 1964, Topping and Webb sold the Yankees to the Columbia Broadcasting System for $14.4 million. Actually, CBS purchased 80 percent of the club for $11.2 million but later bought the remaining 20 percent. (Topping, Webb and MacPhail had paid the heirs of Jacob Ruppert $2.8 million for the team in 1945, and MacPhail sold his share to his partners three years later for $2 million.) Topping continued as club president until September of 1966 when CBS bought Topping's remaining stock and installed Mike Burke as president.

Dan Topping and co-owner Del Webb were the most successful owners in baseball history. They made money and they enjoyed incredible successes on the field. In their 20 years with the Yankees, their team won 15 American League pennants and 10 World Championships!

DEL E. WEBB

Del Webb loved to show off his Yankees. Not only did the Yanks play the game he happened to love, but they played it spectacularly well; over the 20 years (1945-64) in which Webb was a major owner, New York claimed 15 American League pennants and 10 World Championships.

Webb bought into the club along with Dan Topping and Larry MacPhail, the latter of whom three years later sold his one-third interest to Webb and Topping, making them co-owners of the franchise. The ownership brought all three financial and psychic rewards. Webb took particular pleasure in the team.

In his youth, Webb played professional baseball and showed promise as a pitcher before arm problems intervened. Later, after a serious illness, he moved to Phoenix and went into the construction business. Soon he had built the Del. E. Webb Corporation into one of the country's largest and most successful construction companies, a firm responsible for much of the construction of the Southwest and partly responsible for making Las Vegas what it is today. For multimillionaire Webb, the Yankees were a welcome diversion from his often hectic business life.

He enjoyed showing off the club to friends and associates, and in 1951 arranged with Horace Stoneham, the owner of the New York Giants, to have the Yanks and Giants switch training sites for the year. Thus the Giants went to St. Petersburg, Florida, while the Yankees traveled to Phoenix. Webb's friends were properly impressed by this great Yankee team.

The Yankees to Webb were more than a plaything, to be sure. Webb took a serious interest in club business, and in 1954 joined Topping as club president. (The two held the position jointly until they sold the franchise.) He was an important factor in the signing of Casey Stengel. Although the decision to hire Stengel was primarily that of GM George Weiss, Webb, who was impressed with the way Casey had managed the farm club at Kansas City, lent his strong support to the decision. As a matter of fact, Webb had long before idolized Casey—when Casey was a player. Ironically, the task of telling Stengel that he was to "retire" following the 1960 season fell to Webb.

Webb was a strong supporter of Ralph Houk and was afraid Houk would be lost to another club if he were not soon given the manager's job in New York. He was, accordingly, the chief decision-maker in the Houk-for-Stengel change. He was not supportive of Yogi Berra as manager, a proposal made to him before the 1963 season (with Berra to manage in 1964) by Topping and soon-to-be GM Houk. Berra could do the job technically, Webb felt, but neither he nor anyone else would discipline players long his friends. Webb liked Berra, but felt Yogi needed to gain experience first managing in the minors. And Webb did not like Houk's insinuation that he would control Yogi. Berra got the job, but as things turned out, Webb was not exactly off the mark in his reservations about the situation, even though Yogi won the pennant in 1964.

But Del enjoyed himself in his Yankee association. In the locker room following Don Larsen's perfect game in the 1956 World Series, Webb happily proclaimed that "this will set spring training back forever," a reference to Larsen's early morning car accident during spring training for the 1956 campaign.

Webb could have become the sole owner of the Yankees. The ailing Topping offered to sell him his share in 1962, but Webb was too absorbed in the construction business to allow adequate attention to the franchise. The two decided they would sell jointly, and in the meantime make no expenditures in maintaining the franchise that did not have to be made. Thus the club deterioration that followed was more by omission than by design. But it did not appear to impact on the $14.4 million price CBS eventually paid (CBS bought 80 percent of the club in August of 1964, and six months later Webb sold CBS his final 10 percent of the Yanks) for a team Topping, MacPhail and Webb had acquired in 1945 from the heirs of Jacob Ruppert for $2.8 million. This was a money-making team, and the financial success of the venture was attributable in large measure to the business acuity of Del Webb, the Yankee owner whose chief reward for ownership lay more in kicks than in bucks.

GEORGE M. WEISS

Lifelong baseball man George Weiss was general manager of the Yankees from January of 1948 to November of 1960—the most successful period in the history of the franchise.

Weiss was born June 23, 1894, in New Haven, Conn. After graduating from Yale University in New Haven, George began his baseball career as manager of the New Haven High School baseball team. There he established a pretty good semi-pro baseball team built around many of his former high school stars. As a young businessman, Weiss was able to bring such drawing cards as the Yankees, Ty Cobb and Walter Johnson to New Haven to play against his team in Sunday exhibitions. In 1919 Weiss became owner of the Eastern League franchise in New Haven and there developed Weiss Park and many ballplayers for the majors, and in the process drew the attention of Yankee GM Ed Barrow. In 1928, Weiss became vice president-general manager of the International League's Baltimore Orioles and there continued to impress baseball insiders with his shrewd baseball business dealings. (George sold ballplayers for an estimated $500,000 in his combined New Haven and Baltimore tours.)

After having met and impressed Jake Ruppert in February of 1932 at a minor-league convention in West Baden, Ind., George Weiss was asked by Barrow to direct the Yankees' newly established farm system in the manner of the network Branch Rickey had built for the St. Louis Cardinals. Weiss accepted the post of assistant secretary and farm director, which entailed some time as president of the Yanks' top farm club, the Newark Bears, a club Weiss was responsible for turning into a tremendously powerful and successful club. George built the farm system into baseball's most profitable in terms of both money and talent produced. During the 1930s, Ruppert bought minor-league franchises in Newark, N.J.; Kansas City, Mo.; Butler, Pa.; Norfolk, Va.; Springfield, Mass.; Augusta, Ga.; Bassett, Va.; Beaumont, Tex.; Akron, Ohio; Portland, Oreg.; Binghamton, N.Y., and other cities and towns. The system became a huge network, and Weiss supervised every detail of its operation.

Weiss and Barrow, both of German descent, worked well together in making the Yanks an awesome power. They did not always share the same lens, however. In fact, Barrow became aware of the business toughness of Weiss in their very first dealing. It was in the early 1920s when Weiss, through Barrow, booked New Haven for an exhibition game with the Yankees. When the main gate attraction, Babe Ruth, failed to appear, Weiss withheld payment. Commissioner Landis supported Weiss, and Barrow's respect for Weiss and his steadfastness in business matters grew. While working together, the two found occasion to differ. When Barrow lost interest in obtaining an injured San Francisco Seal named Joe DiMaggio in 1934, Weiss went to owner Ruppert and begged him to sign DiMag. Ruppert did, and the Yankees landed one of the game's greatest players.

As farm system director, Weiss kept close watch on his scouts and their prospects. Occasionally, George got a lead himself. In 1942, he received a letter from an old associate, Leo Browne, then the head of the American Legion baseball program in St. Louis, telling Weiss of a fine, though unrefined, prospect named Yogi Berra. Weiss seldom missed a chance to sign a good prospect, and this was no exception. He had Yankee coach Johnny Schulte investigate Berra and gave Schulte permission to sign Berra. The rest is history. (Yogi, by the way, was one of the few players who won contract battles with Weiss when Weiss became general manager.)

Weiss not only ran a good farm system but a conservative one. Only the St. Louis Cardinals spent less money on getting and keeping minor-league players than did Weiss. He was rewarded for his good and thrifty work by being named Yankee general manager in 1948.

The 1948 season was not a good one for New York—the Yankees finishing in third place—and was a particularly mettlesome one for George Weiss. The problem was Manager Bucky Harris. Besides the usual topics of conversation between a general manager and a manager, Weiss and Harris had other problems to talk about, but talking was impossible. Harris could not be reached. Calls to his room during road trips produced an invariable response: Harris was "out." Harris was fired in October of 1948, and Casey Stengel was hired in his stead.

Weiss and Stengel were old friends, and Stengel had managed the Yankee farm team at Kansas City in 1945. While many questioned the hiring of Stengel, Weiss knew he had both a good manager and a field boss with whom he could work cooperatively. He was right; for the next dozen years, the two complemented each other and worked in splendid collaboration. Weiss would get for Stengel the players he needed, drawing from the farm system or seeking talent elsewhere through purchase or trade. Weiss tended to acquire such aging National League stars as Johnny Mize, Enos Slaughter, Johnny Sain, Jim Konstanty, Johnny Hopp, Ewell Blackwell, Ralph Branca, and Johnny Schmitz, all of whom made significant contributions to the Yankee cause.

Stengel's outgoing personality also benefited Weiss by drawing attention from the GM. Weiss was shy and he avoided publicity. It is said that he was so shy he preferred to court enmity in preference to active interpersonal relationships, the establishment and maintenance of which were of considerable discomfort to "Lonesome George," as he was sometimes called. His wife was the only close friend that he had. (While Weiss and Stengel had a friendly relationship, they were primarily business partners.) Weiss, in order to avoid having to talk with strangers, insisted that his wife remain at his side at social events and baseball gatherings he was forced to attend.

Weiss had no hobbies. He was quiet, humorless, drab, tireless, and mistake-free. His single interest—his entire life—was the franchise. To him there were two reasons for the Yankees' existence, and these were to win championships and to make money. He took a tough stand on player salaries, and he could be stubborn, ruthless, vengeful and even cruel in dealing with Yankee personnel. George led the fight by the owners during the 1950s to control salary surges that had baseball executives quaking. Weiss was always ready to cut the salary of any Yankee star.

Perhaps Weiss was difficult with players at contract time for one simple reason: it is believed he was given a top budget for the annual payroll by Topping and Webb, and when he came in under the ceiling, he was rewarded with a percentage of the money saved. Weiss, in negotiating with Yankee players, had the audacity to figure in their World Series checks in their salary totals! Such practices were harsh indeed, but in fairness it should be said they were not atypical of the way organized baseball was run in those days.

Weiss and Vic Raschi had a bitter contract fight before the 1954 season. (The two hassled *every* year over Raschi's contract.) When it was convenient for Weiss to get rid of Raschi, who the previous year pitched his heart out in the face of serious, disabling injuries, Weiss did exactly that. And on Old Timers' Day in 1956, he heartlessly cut from the team an outstanding and loyal Yankee of a decade and a half, shortstop Phil Rizzuto.

He could be especially cruel in dealings with players he had no fondness for. He hated Billy Martin and resented Martin's hero roles in the 1952 and 1953 World Series. When Weiss got his chance in 1957, Martin—the proud Yankee—was unceremoniously unloaded.

Weiss wanted players who were conservative, compliant and quiet. The nocturnal types were expendable, that is, not indispensable to his twin objectives, and in due time found themselves separated from the team. He would have detectives follow suspected stay-ups. He preferred to absorb criticism over the all-white Yankees than to bring black players to the team. Finally, Elston Howard broke the ice in 1955, but Weiss was slow to add other black players to the team. In 1953, on the television program "Youth Wants to Know," Jackie Robinson

Light Moment—Yankee General Manager George Weiss (right) breaks into a rare grin in the presence of Yankee shortstop Phil Rizzuto. Here they admire Scooter's No. 10 jersey. (New York Yankees Archives)

created quite an uproar when he accused the Yankee front office of being prejudiced. If Robinson meant Weiss, he was absolutely correct and no one who knew Weiss should have been shocked. George continually said that if a black player were found who was good enough and fit the "Yankee image," that player would be welcomed by the Yankees. This was nonsense. The Yanks had several black prospects in the early 1950s, the best of whom probably was Vic Power. Presumably Weiss traded Power because he did not have the "Yankee image," because Power certainly had the talent. The Yankees did not shake the lily-white image until after Weiss had departed and a number of black players joined the Yanks. Apparently the word was sent by Weiss to Yankee scouts (it could have come only from Weiss) that they were not to search earnestly for black prospects. Late to sign blacks, the Yanks paid dearly in the 1960s on the field for their closed-door policy, long after Weiss had left the team.

His shortcomings aside, Weiss was a keen judge of baseball talent. His record as a trader was enviable. His first deal as Yankee GM brought pitcher Eddie Lopat to the Yanks, and his final deal brought Roger Maris from the A's. In between were many skillful transactions. George had a sweetheart relationship with the A's. When Philadelphia was left by the A's for Kansas City, Parke Carroll, who had worked for Weiss as general manager of the Yanks' Kansas City farm club, became the new Kansas City A's general manager. For several years, Carroll acted as if Weiss were still his boss, sending player after player to New York to help the Yankees. It may have been coincidental, but it seemed to most onlookers that after each player transfer, the new Yankees performed considerably better than the former Yanks in Kansas City. And sometimes a player moved back and forth a few times. The rest of the American League cried foul, but Weiss was properly indignant whenever the question was raised.

George Weiss was the most respected brain in baseball during his tenure as Yankee GM, although it is doubtful his methods would work with today's players. The *Sporting News* named him the Major League Executive of the Year in 1950, 1951, 1952 and 1960.

But in November of 1960 the Yankees announced that Weiss was "retiring." Weiss broke down and cried in his first public display of emotion. Baseball was his life—baseball, period—and he could not accept a termination of his role in the game.

Fully aware of what was in store for her, Mrs. Weiss commented after his firing, "I married him for better or worse, but not for lunch."

Weiss was not finished in baseball, however, becoming the New York Mets' first president and general manager in 1961, positions he held until 1966. He was largely responsible for building the club that in 1969 won the World Series, and he remained associated with the club as an advisor until December of 1971. George died August 13, 1972.

It could be argued that Weiss was the most astute baseball man in the history of the game. For all his faults and inadequacies, he was certainly successful—the record testifies to that. George Weiss won the baseball community's supreme accolade in 1971 when he was inducted into the Baseball Hall of Fame.

ROY HAMEY

A lifelong baseball man, Roy Hamey spent a total of 19 seasons in the New York organization, serving the Yankees at various times between 1934 and 1963 and attaining the position of general manager before illness forced him to retire.

Hamey started in baseball in 1925 as a business manager in his home town of Springfield, Ill. He joined the Yankee organization in 1934 as business manager of the Binghamton, N.Y., farm club and became the Yanks' GM in November of 1960, succeeding George Weiss. In between he served as business manager at Kansas City, president of the American Association, GM at Pittsburgh and Philadelphia, and Yankee farm director and assistant GM to Weiss in New York.

During Hamey's three-year tenure as the Yankees' GM, New York won three American League pennants and two World Championships. Hamey came down with hepatitis in 1962, and after the World Series victory by the Yankees over the Giants, Roy decided that he would retire at the close of the 1963 season. Besides his poor health, the strain of being Yankee GM had Hamey yearning for a quieter way of life. He remained with the Yankee organization for many years, scouting out of his Arizona home.

RALPH HOUK

Ralph Houk was named vice president and general manager of the New York Yankees in October of 1963. As GM he succeeded Roy Hamey. Houk had given the Yankees years of service as a player, minor league manager, and coach and manager of the parent club. He had, as manager, just won his third American League pennant in as many years.

He was an inspiring manager; he emphasized a player's good points—made him feel good about himself—and as a consequence got more from his personnel than might have been expected.

He also won the players' warm affection by his supportive, virtue-finding approach. But as GM, one of Houk's responsibilities at contract time was to bring the players back to earth. This turnaround did not sit well with some of the Yankees.

The Yankees won the 1964 American League pennant after which Houk hired Johnny Keane to manage the club for the 1965 campaign, a move that puzzled many Yankees and disturbed not a few. For it was not apparent why Yogi Berra was removed from the post after having led the team to the pennant in 1964. In truth, Houk had decided to fire Berra during the 1964 season with the Yanks at the time playing lackluster ball. The hiring of Keane spelled disaster from start to finish—the Yankees finished in sixth place in 1965 and with the team off to a bad 4-16 start in 1966, Keane was fired and Houk returned to managing. He seemed to do a better job as field boss, anyway.

But in fairness to Houk's stint as general manager, it must be noted that he became GM under the most difficult circumstances. Owners Topping and Webb had decided they would sell the club at the opportune time and in the meantime put a moratorium on expenditures designed to keep the organization—and the team—in the best of tone. Talent was drying up. Ever the optimist, Ralph Houk insisted that the Yanks had plenty of great prospects. The failure of enough of these prospects to plug the holes of deficiency ultimately washed the happy Houk portrayals with the harsh light of reality.

MICHAEL BURKE

It was on September 20, 1966, at the close of the Yankees' most dismal season, that Mike Burke became Yankee president. Burke was named to fill the post of the departing Dan Topping, who had just sold the remainder of his Yankee stock to CBS. A network vice president, Burke was 50 years old. At the University of Pennsylvania, Mike had been a football player.

The Yankees finished the 1966 season in tenth place, their first last-place finish since 1912 when the then-Highlanders placed eighth. The circumstances surrounding Burke's presidency were not all that bright, either, for Mike was chief executive under a CBS ownership that expected to reap financial and psychic benefits from its possession of the club but in actuality had invested in a white elephant. The Yankees were in dilapidation; players were aging and the farm system was dry. To develop the organization necessary to make the Yankees winners again required more money than CBS was willing to put into the franchise.

Yet, the Yankees under Burke had become respectable by 1973—the foundation was there for a new, more aggressive ownership to build upon. And a change in ownership was dictated the previous year when CBS instructed Mike to either sell the club or buy it himself. (Word came from CBS Chairman William Paley.)

Gabe Paul, then vice president and general manager of the Cleveland Indians, brought Burke and George Steinbrenner together, and the two formed a group that bought the Yankees from CBS in January of 1973. The night before the press conference announcing the new ownership, Burke learned Steinbrenner was adding another limited partner—Gabe Paul. Burke should have been concerned.

In spring training, the wife of a front-office employee loyal to Burke overheard a breakfast conversation Steinbrenner was having with friends at the next table. He hadn't taken control yet. "When we get this club," the wife told her husband she heard George say, "we'll make that Irish son-of-a-bitch flap in the breeze!" He meant Burke, of course, and Burke bought Steinbrenner's explanation when he confronted George.

But Burke soon got the message and offered his resignation on April 28, 1973. Quoting from the poem, "An Irish Airman Foresees His Death," Burke made an eloquent departure. Steinbrenner in November would install his man, Gabe Paul, as club president. Burke was made a public-relations consultant and kept a small financial interest in the Yankees, and he later became president of Madison Square Garden. In 1981, he retired in Ireland. He died in 1987.

Possibly the greatest contribution Mike Burke made to the Yankees was his determination to keep the Yankees in Yankee Stadium. Burke resisted strong New Jersey efforts to lure the Yankees across the Hudson, as the football Giants were lured, and he convinced important New York City people that the renovation of the Stadium was essential.

LEE (LELAND S.) MacPHAIL

The 1966 season was one of turbulence for the last-place Yankees. First, Ralph Houk stepped down as general manager in May, returning to the dugout as manager. In September Dan Topping sold his remaining Yankee interest to CBS, stepped down as club president, and was replaced as president by CBS' own man, Mike Burke. In October the shake-up was completed as Lee MacPhail, the veteran baseball executive, was named general manager of the Yankees.

The son of Larry MacPhail, former Yankee part-owner, president and GM (1945-47), Lee was considered an outstanding baseball man in his own right. A decade or so earlier, he worked under Yankee GM George Weiss as the Yanks' minor-league director, beginning his employment in the Yankee farm department in the mid-1940s. It was during this time that the lower leagues produced some of the Yankees' best prospects.

His one and only—Mike Burke (right), the Yankee team president in the late 1960s and early 1970s, with the only manager he ever employed, Ralph Houk. (New York Yankees Archives)

MacPhail went to Baltimore in 1959 to become president and general manager of the Orioles, remaining there until 1965 and laying the foundation for some fine Oriole teams. He faced a tough situation on his New York return in the spring of 1966.

The Yankees were an aging team. The farm system could no longer deliver. And the corporate ownership, CBS, lacked the Jacob Ruppert brand of personal involvement. MacPhail in this set of circumstances did the best that he could. Most of his early trades, some of them involving Yankee stars (Roger Maris for Charley Smith, for instance), did not pan out. But some of his later trades were excellent. Trades that made Yankees of Graig Nettles and Sparky Lyle were beautifully engineered.

Lee MacPhail had a personality the opposite of his father, Larry, who was the earlier baseball version of George Steinbrenner. In any case, when Steinbrenner took over the Yankees in 1973, Lee must have been aware of the similarities between George and his father. Lee left the Yankees after the 1973 season. He was elected president of the American League and served in that capacity from 1974-84.

As American League president, MacPhail's biggest brush with Steinbrenner came in 1983 when Lee reversed his umpires and ruled against the Yankees in the famous Yankees-Royals Pine Tar Game. Steinbrenner suggested MacPhail uproot from New York and go house-hunting in Kansas City.

After stepping down as league president, MacPhail became president of the Major League Player Relations Committee, which represented the owners in negotiations with the Players Association.

GEORGE M. STEINBRENNER

At a press conference on January 3, 1973, Mike Burke announced that he and a consortium had bought the New York Yankees from CBS for $10 million. Burke and George Steinbrenner were the general partners; they had 12 limited partners. Steinbrenner reportedly put up 30 percent of the price tag. "We plan absentee ownership as far as running the Yankees is concerned," Steinbrenner told the press. "We're not going to pretend to be something we aren't. I'll stick to building ships."

The price was an incredible steal. Franchises in Cleveland and Seattle had recently sold for about the same amount. Thirty-plus years after the purchase, the Yankees are probably worth 40 to 50 times what the club cost in 1973.

When CBS Chairman William Paley in 1972 decided to sell the Yankees, he offered the club to Burke, who was running the club for CBS and had found his association with the Yankees to be extremely satisfying. Gabe Paul of the Indians introduced Burke to Steinbrenner, and Burke and Steinbrenner sought Yankee ownership together. George rounded up more partners, Burke gave the group the inside track, and the deal was closed.

Burke was soon aced out of the picture, and after the 1973 season, Manager Ralph Houk and General Manager Lee MacPhail left the scene, too. It was becoming all too apparent to everyone associated with the team that there was only one Boss—George Steinbrenner. Gabe Paul became the Yankees' president and general manager, but Steinbrenner settled into the role of chief decision maker.

John McMullen was a limited partner who later owned the Houston Astros. "Nothing is more limited than being a limited partner of George's," he once said.

Lee MacPhail, son of Larry MacPhail (New York Yankees Archives)

Over the years Steinbrenner has turned three pet issues into major conflicts with his hired hands: a mandate against long hair, mandatory workouts and the coaching staffs selected by his managers. After the home opener in 1973, he drew first blood over haircuts. He wrote down the uniform numbers of Yankee players whose hair was too long and gave the list to Manager Houk. The players laughed uproariously as Houk read off the numbers in mocking fashion. It started a pattern of feeling among the players, managers and coaches, lasting over 25 years, that Steinbrenner wasn't one of them; he wasn't a baseball person, and his silly rules didn't fit the game.

Steinbrenner *did* understand what plays, and sells, in New York City. He calls New York "a star vehicle town," demanding famous names, colorful personalities and bold headlines. To this aim, Steinbrenner in 1975 hired the combative Billy Martin as manager, and George staged the announcement for maximum exposure and emotional appeal—on Old Timers' Day.

Actually, Steinbrenner was serving a suspension when Martin was hired in 1975. George made illegal contributions to Nixon's Committee to Re-Elect the President (CREEP), a charge he admitted to and a violation for which, on November 27, 1974, he was fined $15,000 by the courts and later suspended from baseball for two years by Commissioner Bowie Kuhn. Kuhn reinstated him on March 1, 1976, reducing the suspension for good behavior.

The details of George's illegal political contributions smack of the unsavory Watergate affair. George was a Democrat, close friends with leaders of the party and a hard-working fund raiser. He raised about $2 million for Democratic Congressional candidates in Cleveland for the 1970 elections, a fact that did not go unnoticed by those in Nixon's camp. In 1972, Steinbrenner was threatened with a range of harassments, including antitrust investigations of American Shipbuilding Company and Internal Revenue Service audits, unless he went along with the Nixon people who wanted money and dirt on certain Democrats. Steinbrenner gave $75,000 to CREEP and $25,000 bonuses to each of several American Shipbuilding executives, who in turn passed the money on to CREEP. Steinbrenner in April 1973 was indicted on 14 counts of violating the campaign funding law. Steinbrenner was later pardoned by President Reagan.

Steinbrenner officially returned to the Yankees in 1976 for an exciting season in a brand newly renovated Yankee Stadium. Martin led the Yankees to their first pennant in 12 years, which was won on a dramatic homer by Chris Chambliss, and Thurman Munson was the league's MVP. Everything was perfect, except the Yankees were swept by Cincinnati in the World Series. Steinbrenner wasn't happy.

On his own, against the wishes of Gabe Paul and Billy Martin, Steinbrenner, surveying the first free-agent crop, inherently understood that Reggie Jackson would bring the Yankees the most excitement, and he personally wooed Jackson. Reggie, impressed with the Steinbrenner charm and willingness to "outhustle" the competition, signed with the Yankees. The 1977 season was a wild rollercoaster ride as Jackson, Munson, Martin and Steinbrenner shoved each other aside for attention. There were times when Reggie's only friends on the team were reserve catcher Fran Healy and Steinbrenner, who stuck by Jackson and was rewarded when Jackson won the deciding game of the World Series with three home runs.

Steinbrenner was accused of "buying pennants," but he adapted the best to the new free-agent era. Besides Jackson, in the next few years, Steinbrenner landed Don Gullett, Goose Gossage, Tommy John, Luis Tiant, Bob Watson, Rudy May and Dave Winfield—and all delivered. George had already signed Catfish Hunter in 1975 when Hunter was set free because A's owner Charlie Finley hadn't complied with contractual conditions owed Hunter. Ironically, Steinbrenner had been against the idea of free agency. "It can ruin baseball," he once said.

The theater and winning continued in 1978. Martin and Jackson still couldn't get along, but Steinbrenner backed his manager when he suspended Reggie for insubordination. Billy, however, resigned after calling both Reggie and George liars. Four days later, Steinbrenner capitalized once again on the dramatic; Martin was introduced to a stunned and cheering Old Timers Day crowd at Yankee Stadium as the returning manager in 1980. When Martin came back earlier than planned, in 1979, Jackson and Steinbrenner ended their friendship. Reggie felt deceived, and George didn't believe he needed to run anything by Reggie before he changed managers.

But in 1978 the Yankee owner watched the Yankees make up a 14-game deficit, beat the Red Sox in a playoff, march through the ALCS, and beat the Dodgers in the World Series for the second consecutive year. George was giving Yankee fans what they wanted, and he was riding high. The franchise had been restored to full glory.

George Steinbrenner was born July 4, 1930, in the wealthy Cleveland suburb of Bay Village, Ohio. He was a rich kid, but his strict father, Henry, refused to give him an allowance, encouraging his son to earn the money instead. Henry was the real Boss—probably the only man George ever deferred to—but even so, when they were later in business together, George could be heard at times screaming at his father. His father, of course, was screaming just as loudly at George. Henry was unhappy when George in the 1960s bought into a professional basketball team; it was a waste of time and money to Henry.

At 13, George entered Culver Military Academy in Indiana and ran hurdles in track and played end in football. At Williams College in Massachusetts, he ran varsity low hurdles and played halfback. He was an English major, perhaps surprisingly, and was especially interested in Shakespeare. He was glee-club president, wrote a sports column for the school newspaper and wrote his senior thesis on the heroines of Thomas Hardy novels.

It seemed George would stay out of the family shipping business. During peacetime military duty in Columbus, Ohio, George served as a general's aide. He coached high-school football and basketball in Columbus, and in 1955 he became an assistant football coach under Lou Saban at Northwestern University. Later he served as backfield coach at Purdue University.

But the family business, a Great Lakes shipping company known as Kinsman Marine Transit Company, was in trouble. In 1960, George was asked by Henry to join him, and together the Steinbrenners aggressively went after new business. They outworked and outhustled the opposition. After three years of tireless work, Kinsman Transit signed an important contract, and success was won.

In 1967, George was part of a group that bought the American Shipbuilding Company, which George revitalized as chairman. It became Steinbrenner's major business interest. But he also has had investments in a wide range of ventures, including producing with James Nederlander the Tony Award winning musical, "Applause." George has invested in thoroughbred race horses since 1969 and owns an 800-acre stud farm in Ocala, Fla. He owns the Bay Harbor Inn in Tampa, Fla., where he maintains a home.

In its September 13, 1993 issue, *Sports Illustrated* ranked the 93 professional team owners by net worth, and Steinbrenner was ranked 34th with a net worth of $225 million. The story cited among Steinbrenner's holdings: 55 percent ownership of the Yankees; the horse farm in Ocala; several hotels; two million shares of American Shipbuilding Company; a towing and barge operation in Tampa; and a Great Lakes shipping interest.

But on November 4, 1993, American Shipbuilding Company filed for protection from its creditors after losing money over four consecutive years. The biggest blow was the Navy canceling a contract. The Yankees, once a vehicle for fun and fame, may now be holding up the Steinbrenner empire.

Steinbrenner was a loyal Indian fan as a boy growing up in Cleveland, but he loved the excitement of the Yankees coming to town. He has said that "owning the Yankees is like owning the Mona Lisa." Owning the Yankees has enabled him to become a player in the whole New York City scene. He stimulated the city early in his ownership, and attendance at Yankee Stadium in 1980 increased for the eighth straight year. He became one of America's most recognizable personages. His style annoyed some, but his combination of winning and theater were absorbing. But he was walking a fine line, and he crossed it in the 1980s.

Steinbrenner, who has always admitted he is difficult to work for, became nearly impossible to please. The managerial changes he has made currently number 19, and in the 1980s he went through managers, pitching coaches and general managers like Kleenexes. Once Steinbrenner, who has called himself "the principal owner with a lot of input," is displeased, he can be ruthless in setting up an employee for dismissal. One of the ways he could always goad Billy Martin was to take away Billy's favorite coach, the pitching coach, Art Fowler.

Steinbrenner hasn't tolerated mistakes from coaches, whom traditionally in baseball come with the manager as a package. George was furious in Game 2 of the 1980 ALCS when third-base coach Mike Ferraro sent home Willie Randolph, who was out at the plate in a critical play. George had been critical of Manager Dick Howser during the season, even though Howser would win 103 games, the second most by the Yankees in the Steinbrenner era. Ferraro was important to Howser. A few weeks after the Yankees were swept in the ALCS, Steinbrenner announced that Don Zimmer was welcome to the Yanks' third-base coaching job if he wanted it. Howser said he wanted the right to approve his coaches. Steinbrenner squeezed the issue until Howser resigned. Hiring and firing Billy Martin five times was one thing—a clash of strong personalities and a manager who continually pushed his luck—but it was hard to defend the public humiliation of Howser, a good man who had done a first-rate job.

Steinbrenner was feisty in the postseason of 1981. When the Yankees lost Game 4 in their battle with Milwaukee for the division title, Steinbrenner was waiting in the locker room for his defeated players. He became embroiled in a shouting match with Rick Cerone. Steinbrenner was upset with his catcher all year. He resented Cerone's taking a contract dispute to arbitration—and winning.

Steinbrenner broke up a victory-party fight after the ALCS sweep of Oakland between Graig Nettles and Reggie Jackson. There were times when either man would have longed to punch out George. And following Game 5 of the World Series in Los Angeles, while riding in an elevator in the Hyatt-Wilshire Hotel, Steinbrenner was accosted by two detractors of the Yankees. Punches were thrown, and George was later sporting a swollen lip and a broken hand under his cast. Or at least that was how George explained it to the press.

Following the bitter 1981 World Series defeat in six games, after the Yankees had won the first two games, Steinbrenner issued a press release, saying in part: "I want to sincerely apologize to the people of New York and to the fans of the New York Yankees everywhere for the performance of the Yankee team in the World Series." Gracious losing is not George's strong suit.

Reggie Jackson wasn't apologizing to anyone after the World Series. He was the one who felt slighted. He had been hurt and unable to play Games 1 and 2, but he felt ready to play Game 3. That he wasn't in the lineup Reggie attributed to Steinbrenner's desire for him to be "invisible" in the World Series. Steinbrenner let Jackson play out his contract, making no serious attempt to sign him.

Steinbrenner miscalculated. Reggie signed with the Angels and had a big year in 1982. In April, he made a triumphant return to Yankee Stadium and hit a home run, and the fans responded with cheers and the serenading of Steinbrenner's name with obscenities. George would later publicly admit regretting allowing Jackson to leave. In 1993, he made Reggie a special advisor and had Reggie's number 44 uniform retired.

Other proud Yankees were similarly discarded. Lou Piniella was probably the closest Yankee to George, but Lou escaped the circus atmosphere and managed Cincinnati to a World Championship in 1990. Meanwhile, Steinbrenner in 1990 fired his manager, the popular Bucky Dent, and the angered New York press called the Boss names like "scourge of the city" and "the Pinstriped monster." The theater wasn't as much fun when the winning stopped.

The Yankees were baseball's overall winningest team in the 1980s (they were akin to the Atlanta Braves of the 90s—lots of winning with little to show for it), although they won zero titles after 1981, but in efforts to recapture the magic, the future was mortgaged. Over-the-hill veterans were obtained to plug holes, and good prospects were traded away. Minor-league and scouting directors came and went. General managers and managers were juggled routinely. There was a general atmosphere of instability. By 1989, the Yankees disintegrated completely. The only constant in the club's demise was Steinbrenner.

The Boss even lost his edge in the free-agent game. He spent millions on inferior free-agent pitchers such as Bob Shirley, Ed Whitson, Andy Hawkins and Dave LaPoint. Many free agents spurned Yankee offers, choosing not to enter the tense atmosphere around the Yankees. George also took a pass on some quality free agents, such as Jack Morris. Steinbrenner, who in 1993 stated his support of a salary cap, more than any other owner was responsible for the escalating player salaries. The Yankees' payroll in the 1980s—a reported $137.8 million—was $21 million higher than the next highest payroll in the league, belonging to the Angels.

By the time 1990 rolled around, Steinbrenner's popularity had plummeted. Forgotten were many of the charitable contributions he has made. In 1980, for instance, he gave $125,000 to the Save Amateur Sports campaign helping high school athletic programs in New York City. George has also founded the Silver Shield Foundation in New York City and the Gold Shield Foundation in Tampa; these organizations provide college educations for all children of police officers and firefighters killed in the line of duty. George has always been a soft touch for a good cause.

Steinbrenner in 1990 watched the Yankees finish last with a horrible 67-95 record. Actually, he *couldn't* be at the games to watch; he was banned from the day-to-day operations of the club, an indirect consequence of his 10-year feud with Dave Winfield.

George Steinbrenner, Principal Owner of the Yankees. (New York Yankees Archives)

In December 1980, Steinbrenner signed Winfield to a 10-year $23-million contract as a free agent. When George realized the potential value of the complicated contract, he asked Dave to rewrite it; Winfield refused. George never eased up in making war against Winfield.

Winfield in the early 1980s had a gambler named Howard Spira working for the Winfield Foundation, a charitable organization helping community youth groups. Spira also worked for Top Hat, a promotional corporation founded by Winfield's agent, Al Frohman, who died in 1987. Spira in January 1989 went public with his claim that Winfield had lent him $15,000 in 1981. Winfield denied it. Spira produced a photocopy of the check. Winfield then acknowledged he had made the loan but couldn't remember why he had given Spira the money. Albert Whitton, a chauffeur for Top Hat in the early 1980s, later told *Sports Illustrated* that Frohman and Winfield knew Spira gambled and that Frohman told Whitton "the money was to pay off [Spira's] gambling debts."

Steinbrenner already knew much of the story. As early as December 1986, Spira had informed Steinbrenner that he had damaging information on Winfield. Steinbrenner began investigating Spira's charges. Commissioner Peter Ueberroth in September 1987 became aware of the Steinbrenner-Spira relationship, when Ueberroth at Steinbrenner's urging, sent Baseball's Director of Security, Kevin Hallinan, to Yankee Stadium to meet with Steinbrenner representatives. Hallinan was given several documents with Spira's charges against Winfield. There was no adequate follow-up by Baseball. It was only after Spira kept approaching the commissioner's staff that Hallinan finally interviewed Spira in February 1989.

In January 1989, Winfield sued Steinbrenner for failing to make a contractual payment of $300,000 to the Winfield Foundation. Four days later, George countersued, charging the Winfield Foundation with "fraud, wrongdoing and misappropriations." The public was beginning to get the picture.

Baseball began an investigation of Steinbrenner in March 1990 after Steinbrenner admitted paying Spira $40,000. In June, Baseball's Chief Investigator, John Dowd, reported his findings to Commissioner Fay Vincent. On July 5 and 6, Vincent held a closed hearing with Steinbrenner and his lawyers. Steinbrenner maintained that because he had to make payments to the Winfield Foundation he had every right to investigate it. George said Spira told him, among other things, that Winfield lent him $15,000 in 1981 at a usurious rate to help cover Spira's gambling debts, and that a death threat made on Winfield in the 1981 World Series had been concocted by Frohman in order to explain Winfield's poor performance. Steinbrenner never denied he knew Spira was a gambler.

One of Steinbrenner's problems in the whole sordid affair was that he kept changing his story as to why he gave Spira $40,000. This led Spira's attorney, David Greenfield, to quip at one point: "This guy changes the story about what happened more often than he changes managers."

On July 30, 1990, Steinbrenner went to Vincent's office for the commissioner's decision. Vincent told George he was suspended two years. George didn't like the word suspension; he thought it might jeopardize his position as vice-president on the U.S. Olympic Committee. Vincent scratched suspension and revised the penalty to mean Steinbrenner was permanently banned from the day-to-day operations of the Yankees. Steinbrenner was satisfied, but he insisted he and Vincent had made an *agreement*.

The "agreement" stated that Steinbrenner was leaving the Yankees because he maintained an "undisclosed working relationship" with an admitted gambler, Spira, who brought Steinbrenner potentially damaging information on Winfield. And that Steinbrenner in January 1990 compounded his guilt by paying the gambler $40,000.

Steinbrenner regrouped and went after Vincent and Dowd, claiming the investigation had been unfair. Indeed, it seemed Baseball was tenacious in investigating Steinbrenner, but rather casual in investigating leads about others. Winfield, who had associated with Spira and paid him money, too, was cleared without much of an investigation. Vincent said the investigation was confined to Steinbrenner. Incredibly, Vincent in October 1990 told *Sports Illustrated*: "I am not trying to find every person in baseball who has done something illegal, such as place a bet with a bookie."

Dowd was also vulnerable to Steinbrenner counterattacks. Steinbrenner charged that Dowd made numerous changes in the transcripts of testimony, and three witnesses claimed that the investigation team inaccurately summarized their statements. Dowd denied making any deal with Spira, but it sounded fishy when Dowd explained giving Spira's attorney the name of a law firm in Florida "as a professional courtesy." Spira in March 1990 was indicted in Tampa on charges that included an extortion attempt on Steinbrenner (Spira had demanded an additional $110,000 he said Steinbrenner owed him), and he was later convicted and imprisoned.

It was no wonder Steinbrenner thought there was a concerted effort against him. Lawsuits flew everywhere over the next two years. Finding a successor to Steinbrenner proved a difficult task. There was early speculation that Steinbrenner might try making his son, Hank, the new managing general partner, but Hank declined. The next in line, Leonard Kleinman, the chief operating officer, was blocked by Vincent because of a pending hearing on Kleinman's role in the Spira affair.

Steinbrenner resigned as managing general partner on August 20, 1990. In his last official decision, he named Gene Michael to replace Harding "Pete" Peterson as general manager. Finally, on September 13, 1990, Robert E. Nederlander was appointed managing general partner. Nederlander resigned on December 5, 1991. On December 31, 1991, Daniel R. McCarthy was elected managing general partner, but McCarthy was later rejected by Vincent; McCarthy had sued Vincent in 1990 trying to prevent Steinbrenner's forced departure. On March 22, 1992, Joseph A. Molloy, Steinbrenner's son-in-law, was elected managing general partner.

Steinbrenner was desperately trying to regain control of the Yankees. Yankee representatives had initiated three lawsuits against Vincent. In April 1992, Kleinman announced he would drop his suit, paving the way for George's return.

On July 24, 1992, Vincent, in one of his final acts before his September forced resignation, reduced Steinbrenner's exile to 30 months and said George could return March 1, 1993, provided all the lawsuits were dropped.

The Boss seemed slightly more mellow. He was looser, sometimes going home early to hit tennis balls, and he was lighter, having shed 14 pounds. He was excited about baseball again, but following his March 1, 1993 return, he stayed uncharacteristically in the background. Gene Michael and Buck Showalter were doing their jobs well and rebuilding the Yankees into a powerhouse again.

George's biggest complaint was with Yankee Stadium and attendance. The Yankees had twice peaked at 2.6 million home fans—in 1980 and again in 1988. But both times there was a subsequent drop in attendance, and this was in an era when several smaller markets, such as Baltimore and Toronto, were beginning to draw better crowds. Steinbrenner used the long-standing argument that South Bronx crime and poor parking were at the roots of the Yankees' attendance problems. He once again talked about moving to the New Jersey Meadowlands. He challenged Yankee fans to respond with increased numbers.

The Boss was back. No doubt the world would have heard a lot more from him in 1994 as the Yankees built up a comfortable lead and seemed headed for postseason play until it all came to a screeching halt with the players' strike.

He was less than laid back in 1995 when things on the field were not so rosy. A drunk-driving charge against Gene Michael during spring training cost the GM some of his shine with the Boss, and Showalter was too colorless for Steinbrenner's liking. Steinbrenner was sore at both, moreover, for not supporting him publicly in his faultfinding with Danny Tartabull, the high-priced Michael acquisition who went flat in New York. Neither Michael nor Showalter wanted to damage Tartabull's tradeworthiness, but Steinbrenner felt himself out on a limb, abandoned.

Additionally, he kept saying he had a high-priced club that just wasn't getting the job done. "If you have the highest payroll, you should be in this thing. Atlanta and Cincinnati are still there," he said, referring to the playoffs.

Low attendance at Yankee Stadium (the baseball strike left a bad taste nationwide) bugged him too. A shortened 144-game season it was, but still, an attendance of 1.7 million wasn't exactly gratifying. Deep into September, with the Yanks in the thick of the wildcard scramble, they averaged only 17,000 in a four-game set with Toronto.

You knew the fireworks were there, ready to pop. Michael on October 18 was reassigned to a new position, that of director of major-league scouting, and Bob Watson was brought in to take his place. Then Buck Showalter was separated. Steinbrenner reportedly wanted two of Showalter's coaches fired, and Buck wouldn't go along. The Yankees said Showalter left by his own volition, but Showalter in returning a proffered contract said it was a step in the negotiation process and not a resignation. Joe Torre was brought in to backfill for Showalter.

Steinbrenner vowed the Yankees would be "much closer to budget in 1996." Among those with whom they then dickered in building a team for 1996 was Roberto Alomar, who wanted to become the highest paid player in ML history.

George Steinbrenner hired Joe Torre as the Yankees' 31st manager on November 2, 1995. Joe became the first New York City native (Brooklyn) to manage the Yankees. Torre would go on to win World Series titles in 1996, 1998, 1999, and 2000. Under Steinbrenner's tenure, the Bronx Bombers have won six World Series titles in eight tries since he purchased the team in January, 1973. Steinbrenner now possesses the longest tenure of ownership in Yankee history. In 1998, GM Bob Watson resigned and was replaced by then 30-year-old Brian Cashman, the youngest GM in Yankee history.

Steinbrenner makes all the big decisions with the help of his "baseball people." His advisors are not always part of the Yankee organization, and some of those within the organization, having come up on the business side, are not baseball authorities in the technical sense. Sketches of past and present high-level organization people follow. In January, 2003, Steinbrenner celebrated the 30th anniversary of his ownership of the Yankees. He was also ranked as #1 on the list of the most powerful people in sports on the annual list compiled by *The Sporting News*.

GABE PAUL

It was Gabe Paul who initially brought Mike Burke and George Steinbrenner together late in 1972, and when the purchase of the Yankees was made in 1973; Paul was a limited partner. Later in the year, Gabe became president and general manager, remaining in the posts until December 1977 when he returned to the Indians to work for Steve O'Neill, who had been a limited partner in the Yankees. Gabe retired in Tampa in 1987.

Gabe started in baseball in 1925 as a 16-year-old batboy for Rochester. He eventually became chief decision maker for Cincinnati, Houston and Cleveland. He had left the Reds the year before they won the pennant in 1961 but received much of the credit for assembling that team.

With the Yankees, when it came to trading, Gabe could pull the trigger. The players initially resented him, calling him "Dial-a-Deal," but Gabe swept out the country club and brought in the players who won the 1976 pennant. In December 1975, Gabe traded Doc Medich to Pittsburgh for Willie Randolph, Dock Ellis and Ken Brett. Randolph was the key to the deal, but it is revealing that Gabe traded the man who was the club's golden boy—Medich—for the player with one of the game's worst reputations—Ellis. Gabe didn't care about reputation or public image; he wanted talented, aggressive players.

Gabe liked the way Billy Martin managed, and he was able to prevent Steinbrenner from interfering in 1976. He wasn't so successful in that regard in 1977, but he was able to save Martin's job after the nationally televised blowout with Reggie Jackson in June.

Perhaps Gabe's best Yankee decision was his refusal not to trade Ron Guidry. Steinbrenner in 1977 was anxious to close a deal with the White Sox for Bucky Dent, and Chicago wanted Guidry. Steinbrenner might have sacrificed Guidry, but Gabe held firm, and the deal was finally made without including Guidry.

AL ROSEN

Al Rosen became club president in March 1978. Rosen had no previous front-office experience, but he had been a friend of Steinbrenner's since 1966. He also had been a great third baseman for the Indians, with whom he had five consecutive 100-RBI seasons (1950-54) and was league MVP in 1953. He was tough, having suffered 11 broken noses as an amateur boxer, and he was honorable.

Rosen made two important contributions to the Yankees. First, when Billy Martin resigned in July 1978, Al turned to his old friend from the Indians, Bob Lemon, and the new manager and Rosen stabilized the club, setting the stage for the Yankees' great comeback. Also, Rosen in November 1978 made a 10-player deal with Texas. The Yanks gave up a declining Sparky Lyle and got a developing Dave Righetti, whom Rosen predicted "could be the next Ron Guidry."

The 1979 season turned sour early. In May, Steinbrenner, upset with a poor performance by Dick Tidrow, ordered Rosen to trade him. Rosen, sadly, complied, and got poor value in return. In June, Steinbrenner replaced Lemon with Martin. Rosen took it personally, feeling bad for his friend.

Rosen and Martin had never liked each other. Martin ignored Rosen and dealt instead with Cedric Tallis. Rosen OK'ed a July 13 game in California to be rescheduled for a 5:15 start to accommodate national TV, and in the twilight, the Yankee batters managed only one hit off Nolan Ryan. When Steinbrenner found out Rosen had given the permission for the time change, he verbally abused Rosen on the phone. Rosen took a deep breath, called friends in Atlantic City and was offered a job in the casino business.

On July 19, 1979, Rosen resigned from the Yankees and became executive vice president of Bally's in Atlantic City. In October 1980, he became president and general manager of the Astros. He later took the same positions with the Giants and helped San Francisco go from last place in 1985 to a division title in 1987.

CEDRIC TALLIS

Cedric Tallis came to the Yankees with the reputation as the genius who had built up the Royals franchise. He had been in baseball since 1948, and he had roles in the construction of Anaheim Stadium, the opening of Royals Stadium and the renovation of Yankee Stadium. He served briefly as Yankee general manager between December 1977 and November 1979, but remained several years thereafter as a vice president. His role with the Yankees was always low key.

GENE MICHAEL

Gene "Stick" Michael has spent 28 years in the Yankee organization. The only years since 1968 that he wasn't with the Yankees were 1975, when he was finishing his playing career with Detroit, and 1986-87, when he managed the Chicago Cubs. Stick, as a Yankee, has been a player, 1968-74; coach, 1976, 1978 and 1983-86; administrative assistant, 1976-77; Columbus manager, 1979; Yankee general manager, 1980; Yankee manager, 1981 and 1982; and after returning to the Yankees in 1988, a scout, coach, and director of major league scouting.

On August 20, 1990, as he was stepping down as managing general partner, George Steinbrenner named Michael general manager. The promotion meant more this time because Michael would be running the club while Steinbrenner was banned from baseball. There had always been a perception that Michael was a Steinbrenner "yes man," but over the next two years Michael established his own legacy.

Michael had a great year in 1992. In January, he signed free agents Danny Tartabull and Mike Gallego; obtained by trade Melido Perez and Bob Wickman; and signed reserve catcher Mike Stanley. In November, he obtained Paul O'Neill by trade. In December, he signed free agents Jimmy Key and Wade Boggs, and obtained Jim Abbott by trade. Stick picked up nine important players, and the only regular player he lost was Roberto Kelly (although the jury is still out on giving up prospect J.T. Snow).

There are two ways of describing the team Michael and Manager Buck Showalter have built. One is bland. The other is a low-key, team-oriented winning approach in which problems are dealt with internally—not publicly. Stick often begins his morning reading the newspaper and noting any quotes that might stir up trouble. Along with Showalter, Michael in the spring camp of 1994 confronted Sterling Hitchcock who seemed to be complaining about the Yankees' renowned impatience with young pitchers. Michael likes to nip that kind of talk in the bud.

When Steinbrenner returned to the Yankees on March 1, 1993, Michael and Showalter had a team ready for contention in an exciting 1993 pennant race. Steinbrenner continued staying mostly in the background—at least publicly—and in August 1994, the Yankees were in first place when the players' strike ended the season.

But the principal owner was stirred up in 1995, and at the conclusion of the season shifted Michael to another job. Michael was named director of major league scouting (a position he still holds going into the 2000 season)—a newly created job for which Steinbrenner was allowing him to write his own job description. He was to also serve as an advisor to Steinbrenner and as a talent evaluator. Michael, who played a big role in getting the Yankees into postseason play in 1995 for the first time in 14 years, was said to be in favor of his reassignment. Gene continues in that role going into the 2000 season.

LOU SABAN

Steinbrenner developed a friendship with Lou Saban in 1955 when George was an assistant football coach under Saban at Northwestern. Saban, a well traveled but successful football coach in college and the pros, had a brief stint as president of the Yankees in 1981-82.

BILL BERGESCH

As a Cardinal scout, Bill Bergesch signed Bob Gibson, established the farm system for the expansion New York Mets, and worked for the Yankees between 1963-67 as traveling secretary and stadium manager. He returned to the Yankees in 1978 as director of scouting, and between 1980-84 he was in charge of baseball operations, meaning he had some of the duties normally performed by a general manager. His most famous incident came in 1982 when he nearly had a clubhouse fistfight with Tommy John, who was angry that Bergesch reportedly said John should have been more grateful to the Yankees than the way John was acting. Bergesch was a special advisor to the club in 1995.

GENE McHALE

Gene McHale, a Fordham graduate, in December 1972 joined the Yankees as an employee of CBS, and he remained as the club's controller after Steinbrenner bought the team. He became a vice president, and on January 5, 1983, he was named club president. Steinbrenner credited McHale with progress the Yankees had made in communications and marketing. McHale served three years as president.

MURRAY COOK

Murray Cook's baseball career began in the early 1960s as a minor-league player, and he went on to run the Pittsburgh farm system. He joined the Yankees in January 1983 as director of player development, and five months later, he was promoted to general manager. He held the job less than a year.

CLYDE KING

When Clyde King joined the Yankees in 1975, he was primarily a troubleshooter, roaming wherever Steinbrenner felt there was a need. King would fill three Yankee positions notorious for turning over personnel—pitching coach, manager and general manager. He was also a scout.

On April 9, 1984, at age 59, King was named general manager by Steinbrenner, who called him "a great company man." King was squeezed out in 1986, but he was in charge of evaluating the Billy Martin situation after Lou Piniella quit as general manager in May 1988. King, a southern gentleman, and Billy Martin didn't like each other. Billy always suspected that King was spying on him for Steinbrenner, and in a way that was what King did, since King went where the problems were, and evaluated the problems, and there were usually problems around Martin.

In June 1988, King traveled with the Yankees, and he watched one game in which Martin allowed reliever Tim Stoddard to take a beating from the Indians. Billy had been trying to get rid of Stoddard, and King interpreted Billy's unprofessional behavior as showing up the front office. King advised Steinbrenner to change managers, and on June 23 Lou Piniella replaced Martin. King continued to serve as special advisor in 1995.

WOODY WOODWARD

Before joining the Yankees in October 1984 as vice president of baseball operations, Woody Woodward had played nine years in the majors (1963-71), coached at Florida State (1975-78), and had worked in the farm system and front office of the Cincinnati Reds. Woodward's initial duties with the Yankees included negotiating player contracts, evaluating players and supervising the minor-league system.

On October 10, 1986, Woodward was named general manager, and he developed a good working relationship with Manager Lou Piniella. Woodward was the odd man out on October 19, 1987, when he was replaced by Piniella as general manager. Woodward moved on to run the Seattle Mariners and hired Piniella as his manager.

LOU PINIELLA

On October 19, 1987, Lou Piniella became general manager of the Yankees. Piniella and Manager Billy Martin didn't work well together, and Lou was constantly caught in the middle of the Steinbrenner-Martin power struggles. He stepped down in May 1988, and a month later he replaced Martin as manager.

BOB QUINN

Bob Quinn—his father and grandfather were famous baseball general managers—in 1967 and 1969 was named Minor League Executive of the Year, served the Indians from 1973-85, and in 1986 joined the Yankees as a vice president. Quinn was named general manager of the Yankees on June 8, 1988, shortly after Lou Piniella resigned, but Quinn lasted in the job only one year. In 1995, he was general manager of the Giants.

RICK BAY

Shortly before the 1988 season, Rick Bay was named chief operating officer of the Yankees; he was in the job less than a year. He had been athletic director at Ohio State (1984-87) and the University of Oregon (1981-84), and in the 1970s he was an outstanding wrestling coach.

SYD THRIFT

Syd Thrift in the early 1950s was a part-time Yankee scout while teaching high school. In 1957, he was put in charge of Pittsburgh's scouting, and in 1967 he joined the expansion Royals and became the director of the Royals Baseball Academy, which was highly praised inside baseball. He was with the A's briefly, and in 1985 he became general manager of the Pirates. He was fired in 1988 but received much of the credit for putting together the Pirate team that in 1990 began winning division titles.

It was considered a coup when Steinbrenner brought in Thrift in 1989. With Thrift, there was hope for a long-range plan. But Thrift became a casualty after only months in his Yankee job, apparently for his failure to give vocal support to Steinbrenner's August firing of Manager Dallas Green.

GEORGE BRADLEY

George Bradley came to the Yankees in 1988 as vice president of player development and scouting. Since 1968 he had worked in the scouting systems of the A's, Phillies, Tigers and Angels. He was supposedly responsible for overseeing the Yankees' minor-league and scouting operations, but his powers extended to the big club along the way. In October 1989, Harding Peterson became general manager, but Peterson and Bradley did not always work in unison.

HARDING "PETE" PETERSON

In October 1989, Steinbrenner hired Harding Peterson as general manager. Peterson later said he was "co-GM" with George Bradley, and it became increasingly unclear as to who was in charge of the day-to-day operation (although Steinbrenner was a good guess). There was an embarrassing incident when Bradley was in the team office in Tampa, talking to reporters by phone and drumming up a big deal he said he was close to making, while Peterson at the same time was in New York telling reporters nothing was happening on the trade front. Steinbrenner's last move before going into exile on August 20, 1990, was to replace Peterson with Gene Michael.

LEONARD KLEINMAN

In the late 1980s, the Yankees' position of chief operating officer passed quickly from Rick Bay to Mike Luczkovich to Leonard Kleinman. When Steinbrenner was preparing to step down in August 1990, he wanted Kleinman to become managing general partner, but Commissioner Vincent called it "inappropriate" because Vincent was preparing a hearing on Kleinman's involvement in the Howard Spira case. Kleinman answered with a lawsuit. In November 1990, Vincent cleared Kleinman of any wrongdoing. Kleinman finally dropped his lawsuit in 1992, paving the way for Steinbrenner's return.

JOSEPH A. MOLLOY

Joe Molloy, George Steinbrenner's son-in-law, in March 1992 succeeded Daniel McCarthy as managing general partner. He remained in the position even after his father-in-law returned to the Yankees in March 1993. Molloy, a native of the Tampa area who joined the Yankees in 1987, has received some of the credit for the stabilization of the Yankees. He also played a role in the building of the Yankees' baseball complex in Tampa.

BOB WATSON

Bob Watson, the Yankees' general manager who was hired after the 1995 season, had no illusions about working for George Steinbrenner. He was asked about this. "I played for the man," he said. "I have an understanding of how demanding he is."

Watson, 50, came to New York from Houston where he served as the Astros' GM for two years. But he was not new to New York, having played for the Yankees as a first baseman and designated hitter, 1980 through a piece of the 1982 season. He was highly regarded in New York as a gentleman and team player.

His contract was for two years beginning in 1995 with two years more at the team's option. He was approached October 23 by Joe Molloy, managing general partner, and, as he himself said, his hiring was "very sudden." He was signed the next day as Gene Michael's replacement.

Bob was an outstanding hitter with the Houston Astros for many years before joining the Yankees as a free agent in 1980, after spending the last half of 1979 in Boston. In 1980 he led the Yankees with a .307 average. Injuries and age began impairing his performance, and he had a weak 1981 season

until the postseason when, between the playoffs and World Series, he hit a combined .340.

Watson finished his playing career in Atlanta in 1984. His Braves manager was Joe Torre, the man Watson hired as Yankee manager in November 1995.

In 1996, Watson engineered some important acquisitions that aided the Yankees' pennant-clinching cause, and eventually culminated in their first World Series championship since 1978.

On February 3, 1998, Watson announced his resignation in a press conference at Yankee Stadium. Bob had been instrumental in developing the team that won the World Series title in 1996.

BRIAN CASHMAN

Brian Cashman was hired as the new Yankee general manager the same day that former GM, Bob Watson, announced his resignation. Cashman, just 30 years old, had served in the capacity of assistant general manager for the San Diego Padres in 1993.

Within a month of his appointment, Cashman named a lady, Kim Ng, to the position of assistant GM. Kim was only the second woman to hold such a position in baseball, the first being Elaine Weddington Steward, the assistant GM of the Boston Red Sox named in 1990.

Brian has been instrumental in the development of the current Yankee Club into a formidable force in baseball, winning two consecutive World Series titles since his appointment as GM prior to the 1998 season. Again, ex-GM, Bob Watson, should be given some credit for these successes as should Brian Cashman.

Brian Cashman

MAJOR SALES OF THE YANKEE CLUB

Date	Former Owner(s)	New Owner(s)	Estimated Price
January 9, 1903	Baltimore club	B. Devery F. Farrell	$18,000
January 11, 1915	B. Devery F. Farrell	T. Huston J. Ruppert	$460,000
May 21, 1923	T. Huston (sells his 50%)	J. Ruppert (E. Barrow has small %)	$1.5 million (50% of club)
January 26, 1945	Ruppert Heirs	L. MacPhail D. Topping D. Webb	$2.8 million
October 7, 1947	L. MacPhail	D. Topping D. Webb (now co-owners)	$2 million (33⅓% of club)
August 1964	D. Topping D. Webb	CBS	$14.4 million
January 3, 1973	CBS	G. Steinbrenner (and limited partners)	Between $10-12 million

IMPORTANT DATES IN THE YANKEE FRONT OFFICE
(OWNERS, PRESIDENTS, GENERAL MANAGERS)

January 9, 1902: New Yorkers Frank Farrell and Bill Devery buy the American League franchise in Baltimore for $18,000 and announce their desire to move the team to New York.

March 12, 1903: The American League approves by vote the shift of the Baltimore franchise to New York. The New York club will be known as the Highlanders and will play in brand new Hilltop Park (also called Highlander Park and American League Park). Club owners Frank Farrell and Bill Devery name Joe Gordon to be the first club president.

1907: Co-owner Farrell makes himself president of the Highlanders.

January 11, 1915: Farrell and Devery sell the Yankees to Jacob Ruppert and Til Huston for $460,000. Ruppert takes the office of president of the Yankees.

May 7, 1920: Yankee Business Manager Harry Sparrow dies.

October 29, 1920: Ed Barrow, after leaving the Red Sox, becomes Yankee business manager-secretary (a job now known as general manager).

May 21, 1923: Huston sells his half of the Yankees to Ruppert for $1.5 million, leaving Ruppert sole owner of the club. (Barrow later purchases a small interest in Yanks.)

January 13, 1939: Col. Jacob Ruppert, owner of the Yankees, dies. Barrow replaces him as president of the Yankees.

January 26, 1945: The Ruppert heirs sell the Yankees to the trio of Larry MacPhail, Dan Topping and Del Webb for $2.8 million.

February 21, 1945: Larry MacPhail replaces Barrow, three months shy of his 77th birthday, as president-general manager of the Yankees.

October 7, 1947: MacPhail sells his one-third share of the Yankees to Topping and Webb for $2 million. Topping becomes president of the Yankees.

January 1948: George Weiss is rewarded for years of Yankee service by being named general manager of the Yankees.

December 15, 1953: Ed Barrow, former Yankee general manager and president, dies.

1954: Co-owner Webb becomes co-president of the Yankees as an equal partner with Topping.

November 2, 1960: Weiss is "retired" as Yankee general manager. Roy Hamey succeeds Weiss.

October 22, 1963: Hamey retires as general manager of the Yankees after three seasons. Former Yankee Manager Ralph Houk moves upstairs to succeed him.

August 14, 1964: CBS purchases 80 percent of the Yankees from Topping and Webb. (The total sale price of 100 percent of the team reaches close to $14.4 million.) Topping remains with the Yankees as club president.

March 1, 1965: Webb sells his remaining 10 percent interest in the Yankees to CBS.

May 7, 1966: Houk steps down as general manager to return to the dugout as Yankee manager.

September 20, 1966: Mike Burke becomes president of the Yankees under the CBS ownership. He succeeds Topping, who sells his remaining Yankee interest to CBS.

October 13, 1966: Lee MacPhail is named new Yankee general manager, filling the job last held by Houk. (Dan Topping Jr. had served as interim GM between Houk and MacPhail.)

August 14, 1972: George Weiss, former Yankee general manager, dies.

January 3, 1973: George Steinbrenner and Mike Burke head a group of partners who buy the Yankees from CBS for about $10 million. From this moment on, Steinbrenner will make the major decisions about the club.

April 28, 1973: Burke resigns as president of the Yankees. He kept an unimportant title and a small financial interest in the club.

October 21, 1973: Lee MacPhail leaves the Yankees and will become president of the American League.

August 20, 1990: Steinbrenner goes into a forced exile as a result of the Howard Spira affair and names Gene Michael as general manager. The managing general partner position will be passed from Robert E. Nederlander to Daniel R. McCarthey to Joseph A. Molloy.

March 1, 1993: Steinbrenner returns from exile as the self-described "Principal Owner with a lot of input."

October 18, 1995: The Yankees announce that Gene Michael, general manager since 1990, has been reassigned to the position of director of major league scouting.

October 24, 1995: Bob Watson, formerly the general manager of the Houston Astros, becomes general manager of the Yankees.

February 3, 1998: Bob Watson formally announces his resignation as general manager at a Yankee Stadium Press Conference. Later that same day, the Yankees announce the naming of 30-year-old Brian McGuire Cashman as the new general manager. Brian had served for five years as assistant general manager prior to his new appointment.

THE PEOPLE BEHIND THE SCENES

Mel Allen, voice of the Yankees for 25 seasons. How about that?!

The executives in the front office and the ballplayers on the field are supported and surrounded by many low-profile people. Occasionally, however, some of them edge up to the limelight, and, in the cases of Paul Krichell, Mel Allen, Bob Sheppard, and Pete Sheehy, some even grab it.

THE SUPPORT AND SATELLITE CAST

Baseball isn't a game, the more sage among us instruct; it's a business. Whatever, it's *interesting* in its many dimensions. Extending way beyond the playing field, these dimensions can be as engaging as what transpires on the field. Jack Mann's book of nearly 30 years ago, *The Decline and Fall of the New York Yankees,* remains hard to put down and yet seldom deals with the actual playing of the game.

Elephants in the circus of yesteryear pulled a flat, heavy canvas into circus-tent form, and wonderfully indifferent roustabouts staked it to earth with musically rhythmic sledge-hammer blows. The get-ready process was nearly as fascinating as the great three-ring show. Construction today is somewhat like that; baseball is definitely like that.

The scale of big-league baseball is immense. The spectrum of talents necessary to stage it embraces many and varied actors—scouts, coaches, farm managers, nuts and bolts managers for travel and other logistics, trainers, clubhouse attendants, instructors, communicators, marketing strategists, merchandisers, turf managers, security specialists, hawkers, even organ players.

What all of these actors do in the broadest sense is *accommodate.* They accommodate the players and they accommodate the fans.

The fans are accommodated first and foremost with wins, and toward that objective, the Yankees through history have fielded some pretty good teams. They have been blessed with good horses—some roped through trades and negotiation, and others corralled by scouts.

The scouts are hard to notice and harder yet to read. Who knows what they accomplish? They are like the members of a chorus, a writer once noted. No listener knows how—or even if—a given chorus member is contributing.

Some search-and-find men stand out from the chorus, however. Paul Krichell is one. Krichell from 1920 until his death in 1957 did as much to make the Yankee fans happy as did any one player except for Babe Ruth. He was a discerner of baseball potential wherever found, and sometimes that was right under New York's nose.

It was Krichell who brought the big Columbia University athlete, Lou Gehrig, into the Yankee fold. While Lou had conspicuous talents, these all the same had to be impressed on General Manager Ed Barrow so that the chances of getting the strapping prospect didn't slip away. Krichell's excitement over Gehrig as he described him to Barrow was such that it hindered his speech. Finally, he uttered something about "another Ruth" only to leave Barrow incredulous—until he had a chance to see Gehrig for himself.

Far less obvious as a promising prospect was little Phil Rizzuto. Diminutive Phil seemed an unlikely candidate for the big leagues, but Krichell had the ability to strip away negatives and see through to potential. A smallish New Yorker himself, Krichell signed Phil and later signed still another smallish New Yorker, Whitey Ford.

Krichell joined the Yankees with Ed Barrow, who in his book, *My Fifty Years in Baseball,* called him "the best judge of baseball players I ever saw." It takes a good judge to judge a good judge, and Barrow by his own words considered himself pretty good. It is hard to understand what made Krichell so astute, the way Barrow tells it. Barrow barked the orders and Krichell did the running, pausing only long enough to amuse the builder of the great Yankee Empire by noting the confinement of his vocabulary to "immediately" and "at once."

Krichell wouldn't let size, reputation or other "externals" get in the way of his positive appraisals. His recommendation that a questionable, clownish Casey Stengel be hired as Yankee manager was without qualification.

His scouting is associated with three-quarters of the great 1927 team's infield—Gehrig, Mark Koenig, and Tony Lazzeri, although in Barrow's version, the Krichell role in Lazzeri's recruitment was limited and cautionary.

Another scout, Tom Greenwade, is best known for his discovery of Mickey Mantle. Yankee scouts "knew what they were looking for," wrote Mann, and they worked at it. "You find a Mickey Mantle because you have a Tom Greenwade out hunting for him."

Krichell, Greenwade (who also discovered Bobby Murcer in Oklahoma), Bill Essick (Joe DiMaggio), Joe Devine (a role in the DiMaggio acquisition), Bob Connery (his best work was for the Cardinals—Rogers Hornsby), Harry Hesse (who combined with Gene Woodling for Thurman Munson), Eddie Taylor (Mel Stottlemyre), Atley Donald (Ron Guidry) and others contributed scouting excellence over the years. And some Yankee players, such as Bill Dickey, who was recruited by Johnny Nee, later became scouts themselves.

Many a baseball man has moved in and out of scouting. And scouting roles are sometimes performed by non-scouts. Connery was president of the St. Paul team when he helped appraise Lazzeri for Barrow, and Johnny Schulte was a Yankee coach when he scouted Yogi Berra.

The vital importance of scouting was suggested by Gabe Paul in 1965. At the time a Cleveland Indians executive, Paul noted that the once-formidable Yankee scouting system had sunk to a sorry state prior to the fall of the Yankee Dynasty.

Until 1965, young prospects were fair game on the open market, and the teams with the best scouting departments, such as the Yankees and the Dodgers, gobbled up most of the talent. The drafting of amateur prospects, imposed in 1965, was intended to provide parity. The Yankees managed to pluck a gem in the 19th round of the June 1979 draft when they selected a youngster out of high school in Evansville, Ind.—Don Mattingly. He was signed by Yankee scouts Jax Robertson and Gus Poulos.

Besides Krichell, the Yankee scouts of 1934 were Nee, Devine, Essick and Gene McCann—a total of five. Sixty-five years later, Yankee scouts include the following—a total of 38: Wade Taylor, Craig Nettles, Ron Hansen, Ron Brand and Frank Dolson, all major-league scouts; Damon Oppenheimer and Donny Rowland, national cross-checkers; Ket Barber and Mike Naples, special assignment scouts; Joe Arnold, Mike Baker, Mark Batchko, Bobby DeJardin, Lee Elder, Tim Kelly, Greg Orr, Scott Pleis, Cesar Presbott, Gus Quattlebaum, Joe Robison, Phil Rossi, Steve Webber, J. Leon Wurth and Bill "Yogi" Young, all area supervisor scouts; Dick Groch, Coordinator of Canadian Scouting; Manuel Duran, Karl Heron, Ricardo Heron, Ruddy Jabalera, Victor Mata, Manuel Tomas Medina, Roberto Morillo, Raul Ortega, Jim Patterson, Jose "Tito" Quintero, Luis Ramos, Edgar Rodriguez and Arquimedes Rojas, all foreign scouts.

The major-league scouts track major-league personnel for game preparation and for possible future trades and signings. The increasing number of foreign scouts is indicative of the abundant talent in Latin America, which is still governed by a free market.

You can spot scouts at minor-league ballparks and at college ballgames if you take the trouble to search them out. By and large, though, the talent-seekers are an engrossed and inconspicuous lot.

Yankee prospects, when signed, enter the farm system and there, undergo the kind of training and experience which they and the club hope will carry them to the top.

The farm system dates from 1932 and owes to the determination of owner Jacob Ruppert. The brewer's baseball experts didn't want it, Barrow relates. Barrow, Krichell, McCann and Manager Joe McCarthy tried to talk Ruppert out of the farm

idea. The Colonel had been reading about Branch Rickey's farm system for the Cardinals and was "very agitated that we might be missing something," according to Barrow.

They thought they had succeeded, until some weeks later when the Colonel announced to Barrow his purchase of the team and ballpark in Newark. Barrow said he couldn't run things in Newark, too, that they'd have to get someone to run the club, and that's how George Weiss entered the Yankee scene. Nominated by Barrow, Weiss was accepted by Ruppert and became the bossman at Newark.

The farm system grew, reaching its heyday in 1952, then falling into decline in the 1960s, but whether growing or declining, was studded with outstanding teachers, motivators and developers of talent. Important minor-league managers have included Oscar Vitt, Billy Meyer, Mayo Smith, Rogers Hornsby, Steve Souchock and Loren Babe. Johnny Neun and Ralph Houk were for years the only farm-system managers to earn promotions to managing the parent club. However, more recent Yankee managers—Gene Michael, Bucky Dent, Stump Merrill and Buck Showalter—were all groomed in the Yankee minors.

Instruction has come from such fine baseball men as Bill Skiff, Ben Tincup and Jim Gleeson. The talent grew, too, sometimes to amazing proportions, but nowhere more so than down on the original spread.

The Newark Bears, the Yankees' top farm team for a couple of decades, nudged out the Montreal Royals for the International League title in 1937 by a mere 25½ games. They then went on to sweep Syracuse and Baltimore on their way to the Little World Series, which they also won after spotting Columbus three games.

The Bears were loaded for bear with Charlie Keller, Joe Gordon, Babe Dahlgen, Atley Donald, George McQuinn, Marius Russo and a fistfull of other future big leaguers. Keller, the top Bear, didn't go up immediately, however, what with the parent club loaded in the outfield and the pipeline clogged. As for McQuinn, it appeared that as a first baseman he might be mired indefinitely with the peerless, ceaseless Gehrig in front of him. He finally made a name for himself with the St. Louis Browns and returned to the Yankees in 1947.

Manager Ossie Vitt, a teammate of Ty Cobb in his playing days, had an engaging public presence, but with his players, he was a manager who pushed hard at conditioning and fundamentals. His successes in 1937 landed him the manager's job in Cleveland, where he had a pretty good 1938 and an equally good 1939, the year Keller broke in big with the Yankees and became King Kong Keller. (The flattering "King" was eschewed as the short form, with "Kong" preferred.)

Back in Newark, the Bears fell into decline. The 1937 team, called by Mann the greatest in minor-league history, was becoming a memory. Vitt's own memories of his Newark club were fond memories, which didn't help him in 1940 when much was expected of the talent-laden Indians.

Along about the middle of the season, the Indians hit a rough spot, and a dozen players—Bob Feller was in the forefront—asked the Cleveland management to fire Ossie. The so-called "Cleveland Crybabies" said they were being undermined by Vitt's sarcasm and that he was transferring his "jitters" to them. The dispute was smoothed over but when the season ended—Cleveland finishing second by a single game—Vitt was let go.

One of the allegations the players leveled against him was that he persisted in comparing the Indians unfavorably with minor-league teams, "notably the Newark Bears of 1937," according to Ronald A. Mayer's book, *The 1937 Newark Bears.*

Newark's attendance fell off to 88,000 in 1948, and the Yankees put the club up for sale. The Chicago Cubs picked up the team in 1950 and moved it to Springfield, Mass. Weiss, now the Yankees' general manager, explained that "attendance did not warrant our continuance of the Newark club." The reasons for the gate decline were several, but radio and television combined to form one. "The romance of the airwaves is part of the romance of the game," as network broadcaster Bob Costas once wrote. Radio was still king, but television was coming on, and the Bears were not the only club to feel the double whammy.

Ossie Vitt cut a high profile, but generally Yankee coaches have greater visibility than the farm skippers. The coaches have included such big names as Bob Shawkey, Joe Sewell, Earle Combs, Charlie Dressen, Art Fletcher, Jim Hegan (who coached as his son, Mike, played for the Yankees), Bill Dickey, Tommy Henrich, Charlie Keller, Wally Moses, Johnny Sain, Yogi Berra, Johnny Schulte, Jim Turner, Elston Howard, Dick Howser, Gene Michael, Clyde King, Tom Morgan, Stan Williams, Art Fowler and Mel Stottlemyre. The last-named five are among countless pitching coaches used in the Steinbrenner era.

Fowler, Billy Martin's right-hand man, was often the instrument that measured Steinbrenner's anger with Martin.

When George was hot, he threatened to fire Fowler; when he was livid, Fowler was gone. And Martin was a sure bet to act out his anger in reaction.

Frank Roth and Charley O'Leary coached under Miller Huggins on the first pennant-winning team of 1921. Frank Crosetti was a fixture at third base from the late 1940s through 1968, and, in fact, took home 15 World Series checks as a coach to go with his eight as a player.

Coaches like Crosetti are visible parts of the organization. They are, after all, in New York and not in Rattlesnake Glen. But to most fans, no one is more visible than the broadcasters. The institution, the team, fuses with the broadcaster, and the broadcaster fuses with the listener or viewer into whose audio/visual range he enters by invitation.

Not everyone cares to go to the ballpark and not everyone can go. To have the game, complete with expert interpretation, and maybe a yuk or two brought to them is a treat of no small measure.

Yankee games have been broadcast by the great Mel Allen and a number of other outstanding voices—most notably, those of Red Barber and Phil Rizzuto—but to fans of middle age and beyond, certainly Allen's melodious intonations rush to mind at the mention of Yankee broadcasting.

Allen, an Alabaman, is the son of Julius Allen Israel and Anna Leibovitz. He holds a law degree, but got into broadcasting and changed his name to Allen at his employer's request.

Eddie Layton, Yankee Stadium organist since 1968. He has recorded 25 albums.

He began broadcasting for the Yankees in 1939 and spent exactly a quarter of a century at the mike before the Bombers bombed him. Somebody on high had decided to quiet the "voice of the Yankees"—Allen never knew who or why—and that was that. The voice that *was* the Yankees was silenced.

Allen was a Yankee advocate, but he didn't come off as a cheerleader or "homer." (Like having a Methodist minister comment on Methodism; you'd expect, naturally, that the comments would be favorable.) Moreover, Mel didn't have to cheer his Yankees on. They did the job, leaving him only to report the deed. His book, *You Can't Beat the Hours*, written on the eve of his firing, noted that the Yankees "haven't done badly, for a fact. In the first 25 years of my broadcasting for them, they managed to win 18 pennants and 13 world championships. How about that?"

An Allen call—How about that! Another was his home run signature—Going, going, gone! The first "going" reported the possibility, the second gave it heightened excitement and credence. The "gone" (when the ball was safely over the fence) confirmed the event.

Allen, who at the peak of his popularity in New York received 1,000 letters a week from admiring fans, stayed in sports broadcasting after his separation from the Yankees. While the firing was not handled well and was unjustified, there was healing over the years, and Allen kept an association with the club until he died in 1996.

He was teamed up for some years with Red Barber, who left the Brooklyn Dodgers in 1954 with bitterness and was brusquely fired from the Yankees. But Barber's 1966 dismissal didn't leave him reeling as Allen's did him, although Red, too, failed to find absolute peace of mind, as a card he sent to well-wishers indicated: "My removal from (Yankee President) Mike Burke's peerage is a blessing," it said.

Barber considered himself a reporter; reporters report—they don't obscure or rationalize, and that is what may have got him into trouble with the Yankee brass—or sealed his fate at least.

On September 22, 1966, only 413 payees showed up at Yankee Stadium. No doubt there were jokes about maybe joining the players in the dugout, but from the club perspective, it was a dreary day and the less made of it the better. What was important to Barber, however, was the story line—the ocean of empty seats in once-proud Yankee Stadium.

Red couldn't get the TV cameras to pan those banks of empty seats. So he served his viewers by *telling* them what they were prevented, apparently under orders from Burke, from seeing. "I don't know what the paid attendance is today—but whatever it is, it is the smallest crowd in the history of Yankee Stadium, and this crowd is the story, not the game," he said.

Days later, Barber had a breakfast meeting with Burke at which he expected to get a new contract. Instead he was served a pink slip, a "favor" as he was to regard it, setting him free. "I was like a squirrel in a cage and didn't know it," Red was quoted as saying in Curt Smith's *Voices of the Game*. Ironically, Burke sought to bring sunshine into the Yankee citadel of secrecy, and here he was, lopping off the head of candor.

Burke's side of the story was that he "inherited" the decision to let Barber go. He agreed with the decision, he said, noting that Barber *was* great, but adding that every man arrives at a point when it's time to step aside.

Phil Rizzuto, the former Yankee shortstop, broke into the broadcast booth with Allen and Barber in 1957 replete with

dems and *dos* and sounding like road-repair equipment. But the growth potential he showed in baseball showed again, Phil quickly becoming a pleasant-voiced, engaging announcer—even if, on occasion, he became so engrossed in a field happening that he forgot he had listeners listening.

Phil is not without his detractors, especially among the barbarous legions of Yankee haters. His supporters see him as witty, self-effacing and kind-spirited and, of course, knowing in the game of baseball. Trademark expression: Holy Cow! It's used when Phil is incredulous, which he is often in spite of his 82 years. Phil is perpetually childlike, happy to be amazed.

When Roger Maris hit his 61st homer in 1961, Phil was at the mike. "Hit deep to right," he said, his voice rising. "This could do it! Way back there! Holy Cow, he did it! Sixty-one home runs!"

The August 13, 1995 death of Mickey Mantle impacted Rizzuto, nudging him to reflect on life generally, as well as on his family obligations. He seemed in a retiring mood, kindling speculation that he might not be back at the mike again in 1996. Rizzuto fans hoped he would sign up once more with WPIX.

The Yankee's great broadcast names have included Graham McNamee (well-known sportscaster in the early days of radio), Philips Carlin, Arch McDonald, Curt Gowdy, Russ Hodges, Jerry Coleman, Joe Garagiola, Tony Kubek, Frank Messer, Bill White, Fran Healy (who played off wonderfully against Rizzuto), Jay Johnstone, Bobby Murcer, Rick Cerone (the player, not that media guy), DeWayne Staats, and Tom Seaver. Current broadcasters include John Sterling (TTTHHHEEE YANKEES WIN!!), the personable Michael Kay (SEE YAAA!), Al Trautwig, Jim Kaat, Ken Singleton, Paul O'Neill, Charley Steiner and Suzyn Waldman. The last name on that list, Ms. Waldman, is a lady who made sports history. In 1995, she became the first woman to work a nationally televised baseball game when she covered the Yankees-Rangers game for the Baseball Network. In 1996, Suzyn became the first woman ever to call the play-by-play for any Major-league team when she worked with Bobby Murcer and Rick Cerone on a Yankee broadcast through WPIX-TV. Her broadcasting career goes back to 1987, when she began with WFAN-Radio in New York City, and she is currently the longest tenured beat reporter of the Yankees.

The airwaves people communicate directly. Within the bowels of the citadel, other communicators have struggled to get the word out, to keep the Yankees in the bosom of free advertising, as a cynic might put it, or to accommodate the baseball public with legitimate news, as a more idealistic observer might view it.

Robert O. Fishel served the Yankees as public relations director from 1954 to 1973 when he was named a Yankee vice president, a job he held for two years before becoming executive vice president of the American League. He worked with diligence writing news releases, arranging press conferences, answering media queries—in short, doing all the things a PR man does and more, like serving as a statistician. He was as thoughtful as he was hardworking as a member of the Yankee support cast.

In his book, *The Decline and Fall of the New York Yankees*, Jack Mann rated Fishel high as a PR man and "high among human beings in general," adding: "There was this sports editor who was fired...and to a PR man there is nothing quite as out of style as an unfrocked sports editor. What good can he do for you? This sports editor in his period of unemployment received about 10 calls from publicity people and four or five invitations to lunch. They were all from Bob Fishel."

Fishel died in 1988, and the following year the Yankee Stadium pressroom was renamed the "Robert O. Fishel Press Room." The inscription on the plaque in that room says: "With compassion, integrity and dignity, he elevated his profession."

Fishel had replaced another outstanding PR man in Red Patterson. A sportswriter on the old *New York Herald Tribune* before becoming Yankee publicity director in 1946, Patterson was resourceful and imaginative and is thought to have fathered the "tape-measure home run" idea.

This was in 1953 when Mickey Mantle blasted a long one out of old Griffith Stadium in Washington, D.C. Using a tape measure, after determining where the ball had landed, Patterson added to the ballpark's known dimensions and reckoned the Mick's homer traveled 565 feet.

PR men come and go—all kinds of field hands come and go—but the voice of the Yankees' public address system stays to grace the wonderful ballpark in the Bronx as it has for over 40 years.

What an incredibly distinctive, modulated and clear voice it is. And why not; it has a master's degree in speech from Columbia University.

The voice belongs to Bob Sheppard who became interested in voice control and diction as a teenager. At St. John's University, he won a gold medal in public speaking and was a member of the debating team. He was also quarterback of the football team and first baseman on the baseball team.

He did the PA for some football games before joining the Yankees. He worked out an arrangement to cover his teaching responsibilities, which, as time went on and more and more weekday games were played at night, collided less and less with his Yankee Stadium job.

As Mel Allen was the Yankees, Bob Sheppard in a way has become Yankee Stadium, the aural equivalent of the Gothic arches that symbolize the Stadium.

Sheppard is a voice, but not a presence. He could in all probability stand outside the ballpark after a game and never be recognized. He brings to mind another Yankee organization luminary of even lower profile, the late Pete Sheehy.

Sheehy, who died in 1985, missed four seasons while serving in the military during World War II, but outside of this, he was with the club every day of every season since the day in 1926 when he tried to sneak in Yankee Stadium, failed and was given a proposition by the clubhouse manager: He could see the game free *if* he helped move some trunks. Pete did, was asked to come back the next day, and from then on remained a member of the organization until his death some 59 years later.

Sheehy hewed close to the locker-room axiom: "All that is seen here, all that is heard here, stays here." He was scrupulous in keeping the confidences of the clubhouse. He would never agree to collaborate on writing a book, although he doubtless had a wealth of inside Yankee information.

Through the years, Pete dealt with big names in baseball—Ruth, Gehrig, DiMaggio, Mantle. He liked all the Yankees but was a particularly close friend of the late Thurman Munson, whose sudden death dealt a harsh blow to him. He saw Babe Ruth hit No. 60 in 1927 and Roger Maris hit No. 61 in 1961.

When the renovated Yankee Stadium was opened in 1976, Pete was a special guest at the opening ceremonies, and the home locker room in the new facility was named the "Pete Sheehy Clubhouse."

Bob Sheppard, P.A. announcer at Yankee Stadium for over 40 years.

The Yankees have had some memorable traveling secretaries, too. Mark Roth, one of the early holders of the job, had been a baseball writer and is credited with being one of the first newspapermen to call the Highlanders "Yankees." It was Roth who wrote, when the Yankees unloaded Hal Chase for two Chicago players, one foot-sore and the other short on skill: "The Yankees traded Chase to Chicago for a bunion and an onion."

Another holder of the travel job was Frank Scott, who seemed to be popular with everyone but George Weiss and was finally forced to leave the organization. Scott became a player agent, the first of a new breed, and for a standard 10 percent, represented such clients as Rizzuto, Gil McDougald, Allie Reynolds, Ed Lopat, Mickey Mantle and Yogi Berra, who had been something of a problem one night when Scott was still road secretary. Berra didn't have a bed, although he actually did—it was in the wall. It was a Murphy bed, Scott explained. But the problem didn't go away. A bed that can come down can go up, and Yogi wasn't about to wake up in the middle of the night stuck in a wall. Scott got him a room with a regular bed.

The club also has had some outstanding trainers. Perhaps the best known has been Gus Mauch, who was very close to Casey Stengel. Gene Monahan has been head trainer since 1973. The Yankees have had excellent team physicians as well, notably Dr. Sidney S. Gaynor, team physician from 1946 to 1976. He was considered a pioneer in the treatment of athletic injuries.

Major-league baseball requires human skills of many stripes and is about much more than a balance sheet. A steel executive, it is said, once asked a job applicant what the company made, and when the young man said steel, the executive said, no, the answer is money. Baseball may be a business, but it is doubtful that its reason for being will ever be so narrowly focused—for the good of the business, if for no other reason.

7 SEASON SUMMARIES

Miller Huggins, manager of the New York Yankees with Bill McKechnie, left, manager of the St. Louis Cardinals, before the first game of the World Series in New York, October 4, 1928. (AP/WIDE WORLD PHOTOS)

The New York Yankees have played baseball in the American League for 99 seasons. The seasonal summaries that follow single out Yankee heroes and highlights and identify the key reasons why the Yankees won (36 times) or failed to win the American League pennant.

But the Yankees, before they could play, first had to be. How did they come to be?

YANKEE HISTORY, SEASON BY SEASON FROM 1903

ORIGINS AND BIRTH

The story of how the Yankees came to be touches three teams—the Baltimore Orioles, the New York Giants and, in a less direct sense, the Cincinnati Redlegs—and as many men—Ban Johnson, John T. Brush and John J. McGraw.

As a boy growing up in Ohio, Johnson loved baseball and became a catcher for Marietta College from which he was graduated in 1887. He became a sportswriter for the *Cincinnati Commercial-Gazette* and covered the Cincinnati Redlegs. While covering baseball, he formed ideas on baseball management and in 1893 became president of the Western League. The Western League developed into one of baseball's most financially successful circuits under Johnson's leadership.

The Western League was renamed the American League in 1900, and following the baseball season of that year, Johnson announced that the league was withdrawing from the National Agreement, a pact that governed all of professional baseball and acknowledged the National League as baseball's only major-league. Thus, the AL entered the 1901 season as baseball's second major-league. The new "big" league had teams in Chicago, Boston, Detroit, Philadelphia, Baltimore, Washington, Cleveland and Milwaukee and was getting big-name players as Johnson and wealthy owners of AL franchises raided the senior circuit of established stars, using offers of higher salaries to entice exciting players to jump to the AL. Raiding was facilitated by an NL salary ceiling of $2,400.

Baltimore's 1901 AL Orioles were reborn birds. The original Orioles were NL Orioles. In their short life (1892-99), the NL Orioles were the toast of baseball, winning championships under Manager Ned Hanlon in 1894, 1895 and 1896. Those clubs were famous for their scrappy, spirited and brilliant baseball. They boasted such future Hall of Famers as John McGraw, Wilbert Robinson, Wee Willie Keeler, Hugh Jennings, Joe Kelley and Dan Brouthers. The team also shaped the way baseball was played; with McGraw its leading proponent, "inside baseball"

ruled until Babe Ruth revolutionized the game. But Baltimore was dropped from the NL in 1900 when the league trimmed its franchises from 12 to eight. Ban Johnson and the AL Orioles in 1901 scored a major coup by signing several popular players who had been with the old Oriole club, and they included McGraw, Robinson and Iron Man Joe McGinnity.

McGraw was player-manager (and part owner) of the 1901 Orioles and as a part-time third baseman hit .352. Robinson hit .299 and McGinnity had a 26-20 record. But the real stars were leftfielder Mike Donlin (.341, 67 RBIs), second baseman Jimmy Williams (.317, 96 RBIs) and shortstop Bill Keister (.328, 93 RBIs), who played for the NL Orioles in 1899. This talent and the McGraw genius notwithstanding, Baltimore finished fifth in the league's inaugural major-league season. Somewhere along the line, League President Johnson decided to move the franchise to New York. McGraw was said to have been assured he would accompany the club to New York as manager.

The events of the 1901 and 1902 seasons intervened, however Johnson was determined to equip his umpires with both complete authority and protection from physical abuse. The man who most often refused to conform to this code of conduct, new to baseball, was McGraw.

"Mugsy" McGraw was a vicious umpire baiter who sometimes resorted to physical violence to settle a dispute. He was brought up that way in the NL, and, refusing to change his ways, drew a host of suspensions and fines. Finally, in the middle of the 1902 season, he was suspended indefinitely by Johnson, an act that put the Johnson-McGraw relationship under severe strain. On top of this, McGraw was said to have learned that Johnson had decided Clark Griffith, another famous league jumper who was in Johnson's good graces for helping to establish a strong AL club in Chicago, would become manager of the AL's future New York club.

McGraw wanted out. He quit as Oriole manager and began negotiations that led to Brush's buying not just McGraw's share but the entire Baltimore package. This was John T. Brush, chairman of the National League's Executive Committee! The John T. Brush who at the close of the 1902 season would buy the controlling interest in the New York Giants!

The Orioles, meanwhile, finished dead last. What else? The team was destroyed by its new owner, Brush having released his players so they could sign with NL teams. The enemy was entrenched in the camp of the fledgling AL; a crisis was at hand. It got so bad that on July 17, 1902, Baltimore was unable to field enough players to play St. Louis. Johnson revoked the franchise, filled out the Orioles' roster with players from other league clubs, ran the team on league funds, and somehow kept the club together until the season's end. He prevailed in keeping the league's schedule and integrity intact. More important, he was now in a position to move the forsaken franchise to New York.

Johnson rightfully reckoned that if true major-league status was to be gained for his league, it would have to have a team in New York. He also had two other reasons for wanting to penetrate the New York market. One was McGraw and the other was Brush. McGraw left Baltimore in the summer of 1902 to become manager of the senior circuit's New York Giants, a job he would hold until 1932. From the moment "Little Napoleon" bailed out of Johnson's upstart major-league to rejoin the establishment (and perhaps earlier), John J. and Ban were enemies. Later in the same year, 1902, Brush bought controlling interest in the Giants. So Johnson's war with the NL was not just a business crusade—he hated John J. and John T. with unadulterated, turn of-the-century passion.

Ban Johnson and John T. Brush had crossed swords before the Baltimore episode. Brush owned the Redlegs (1891-1902) that Johnson covered as a sportswriter (1887-1893). He deeply resented criticisms Johnson had written for the *Cincinnati Commercial-Gazette*. The antagonism between the two intensified when Johnson began his league rivalry. And, of course, Brush's attempted sabotage of the Orioles was not exactly an act of peace. So heavy was the hatred that the pennant-winning Giants of 1904 refused to compete in the World Series against what Brush and McGraw called "unworthy" and "inferior" AL opponents. (The fact that the AL a year earlier won the first World Series ever played simply was not acknowledged in the Giant camp!)

So revenge joined the business motivation behind Ban Johnson's resolve to put a franchise in New York. Those with some say in the two-year-old AL gathered in New York's Fifth Avenue Hotel on March 12, 1903, to vote to transfer the Baltimore club to New York. The vote was rubberstamp approval of Johnson's design. Johnson even before the New York club was officially established was rounding up players for the club, seeing to it that the brightest stars collected in the NL raids found their way to New York.

As expected, Clark Griffith was brought to New York as manager-pitcher, giving the club a recognizable name to compete with that of McGraw. Jack Chesbro (28-6 in 1902) was raided from Pittsburgh, as were Jesse Tannehill (20-6 in 1902), third baseman Wid Conroy, leftfielder Lefty Davis and catcher Jack O'Connor. Wee Willie Keeler (.338 in 1902) was signed away from Brooklyn. Sister clubs in the junior circuit contributed players as well. Only six players came up from Baltimore,

among them second baseman Jimmy Williams, centerfielder Herm McFarland and pitcher Handsome Harry Howell.

The raiding of the NL was so successful that the senior circuit was forced to seek an inter-league agreement. A treaty that ended the raiding was signed in January of 1903, the NL for its part allowing the AL to keep all the NL players it had signed up to that time. The pact provided that the AL not "invade" Pittsburgh; if the Americans would stay out of Pittsburgh, the NL would allow the AL to have a club in New York. Peace was established and happiness reigned in all quarters except for the Giant camp, which was furious over the final decision. The Giants would be made a lot unhappier before the young century reached the quarter mark by an AL competitor they regarded as despicable.

In retrospect, Johnson's behavior was unbelievable. In raiding players for the New York club, he was acting like the owner of one of the teams he was to impartially preside over as league president. And he was more interested in making his New York team competitive with the Giants than with the rest of the American League. Bucking the Giants would not be easy, however.

A melancholy time for the Giants, who finished eighth in 1900, seventh in 1901 and eighth in 1902, had come to an end now that the great John J. McGraw was their skipper. The 1902 dismantling of Baltimore's AL Orioles didn't hurt either, the Giants acquiring many of the players Brush released. Suddenly, the Giants in 1903 were second-place finishers and in 1904 the champions of the league. To thank for their rush of success, they had in 1904 such former AL Orioles as Manager McGraw, first baseman Dan McGann (.286, 71 RBIs), rightfielder George Browne (.284) and centerfielder Roger Bresnahan (.284). And then there was the fabulous Iron Man Joe McGinnity (35-8, 1.61 ERA) whose not-uncommon chain of employment was the NL Orioles (1899), the Brooklyn Dodgers* (1900), the AL Orioles (1901-02) and the New York Giants (1902-08). (Incidentally, also going to the Brooklyn Dodgers from the disbanded NL Orioles for at least the 1900 season were four other players including Handsome Harry Howell.) Between them in 1904, McGinnity and Christy Mathewson won 68 games! The Giants' pennant-winning margin was 13 games!

Attendance was on the rise, and the Giants' popularity seemed boundless. Indeed, the New York Giants would be the most successful NL team for the next 30 years. What a head of steam they were building! And the irony of it! Had John T. Brush not broken up that old AL gang in Baltimore, the Bresnahans and McGinnitys might well have been starring for another New York organization, speaking of which...

For their $18,000, Frank Farrell and Bill Devery, the owners of the new American League club in New York, got one, a franchise, and two, thanks to Johnson, a respectable measure of player talent. Now for a place to display this baseball wealth.

Finding a site for a new ballpark posed a problem. Former Giant owner Andrew Freedman was an active owner who served as club president from 1895-1902 and who hired John McGraw shortly before selling the team to Brush. Freedman maintained his close Giant connection and shared Brush's disdain for the "invading" American Leaguers. And Freedman, a subway contractor and a roguish sort, had political influence. He had enough political clout, in fact, to make Farrell and Devery feel unwelcome in their own town. McGraw and Brush were also

---

When the NL Orioles disbanded after the 1899 season, several Orioles followed Manager Ned Hanlon to Brooklyn.

close to the city's controlling political organization, Tammany Hall. "No matter where you go," Farrell and Devery were told, "the City will decide to run a street car over second base."

But suddenly there it was—a brand new Hilltop Park in the upper Manhattan neighborhood of Washington Heights. As might be expected, Johnson, Farrell and Devery had connections, too. The Highlanders had a home, and though it was as impermanent as their name (they would officially become known as the Yankees in 1913), a home it was all the same. The AL was both established and housed in the nation's greatest city.

1903

Highlander Manager Clark Griffith on April 22 led his charges onto a Washington, D.C. field before 11,950 fans for the first game in Highlander-Yankee history. The first run scored in Highlander history, and the club's only run of the game (Washington won, 3-1), was scored by Wee Willie Keeler.

The Highlanders played their first home opener at Hilltop Park on April 30 before 16,293, and behind the pitching of Jack Chesbro won 6-2. John Ganzel on May 11 hit the first Highlander home run. In a regulation game played on May 17, the Highlanders and Griffith, who pitched as well as managed, were defeated by Cleveland in a game notable for the fact that it was played in neither New York nor Cleveland—it was a Sunday game, and because Sunday ball at the time was prohibited in Cleveland, it had to be played in Columbus, Ohio. Cleveland Hall of Famer Addie Joss won, 9-2.

The Highlanders did well in their maiden season, finishing in fourth place. American League President Ban Johnson made sure the franchise had a quality player roster. (The 1903 Highlanders were jokingly called the New York All-Stars.) There was a degree of disappointment, nevertheless. The Highlanders' 72-62 record put them 17 games behind first-place Boston.

And while the club finished eight games ahead of Detroit, the Tigers out hit (.268 to .249) and out pitched (2.75 to 3.08 ERA) the New Yorkers.

How the Highlanders gained a fourth-place finish is indeed hard to square with their having only the seventh-best ERA in an eight-team league and the fifth-best batting average. Many of their "all-stars" had mediocre years.

A total of 28 players got into Highlander games but only 15 saw appreciable action. Of the six who came to New York from a gutted Baltimore franchise, only Jimmy Williams, Herm McFarland and Handsome Harry Howell were regulars. Part-time shortstop Ernie Courtney, who played in one Baltimore game in 1902, was traded in mid-season, and Tim Jordan, who also played in one Baltimore game in 1902, appeared in just two Highlander games. Pitcher Snake Wiltse, who was 7-11 for Baltimore in 1902, was 0-3 for the Highlanders.

Generally, the Highlander lineup had Monte Beville and Jack O'Connor sharing the catching; Ganzel at first base; Williams at second base; Wid Conroy at third base; Kid Elberfeld, acquired in mid-season from Detroit, at shortstop; Lefty Davis in left field; McFarland in center; and Keeler in right. Five pitchers handled almost all the mound chores: Chesbro, Jesse Tannehill, Griffith, Howell and Bill Wolfe.

Neither of the club's catchers, Beville (.194) nor O'Connor (.203) hit a lick, but well-respected batsmen also failed, and they included the top four outfielders. Playing for the Philadel-

phia A's in 1902, Dave Fultz, the Highlanders' fourth outfielder this year, hit .302 and led the league in runs scored. But in New York, Fultz's average dropped 78 points to .224. Davis had hit .280 the previous year for Pittsburgh, but slumped to .237, a drop of 43 points. (He also led AL outfielders in errors with 19.) McFarland hit .306 for the White Sox and Orioles in 1902, but his average took a 63-point drop to .243 in 1903, his final big-league season. Keeler, the other outfielder and the team's star, led the Highlanders in batting, hits and runs scored, but his .318 batting average was his lowest since 1893. One of the finest young players in the game, second baseman Williams, led the Highlanders in several offensive categories but slumped to .267 after hitting .313 in 1902 (and after breaking into the "bigs" in 1899 hitting .355). But he was excellent defensively with good range. Elberfeld hit .287 in 90 Highlander games, but he started the campaign hitting .341 in 35 Tiger games. Only Ganzel (.277) and Conroy (.272) hit better than expected.

The pitching staff was almost as perplexing. To be sure, Chesbro was outstanding (21-15, 2.77 ERA), and for the third year in a row was a 20-game winner. The 29-year-old right-hander pitched 325 innings. But Tannehill, who finished his career with a 197-117 record, had a disappointing 15-15 season. He had been a 20-game winner in 1898, 1899, 1900 and 1902 for Pittsburgh and he would win a total of 43 games for the AL Boston club in 1904 and 1905. Manager Griffith came through with a great effort (14-10, 2.70 ERA) as the third starter and Handsome Harry Howell (10-6) had one of his best years. Rookie Wolfe was respectable (6-9, 2.97 ERA), but the pitching staff lacked top-notch quality, especially when compared with some others around the league. And with Keeler the only .300 hitter, the club lacked the offense to make up for its mediocre pitching. New York's run production was helped by a total of 160 stolen bases (third most in the AL), but base stealing would not be the formula for future Yankee successes.

In spite of their reputational luster and respectable showing, the Highlanders failed to draw well either at home (211,808) or on the road. The New York Giants of John McGraw were rebuilding successfully (with a wealth of ex-Orioles) and were fast becoming baseball's best team. Not only were the Giants good, but they were colorful, exciting, glamorous and extremely popular. They *owned* New York. The Highlanders and their small band of followers lived in the deep, extended shadows of McGraw and Company.

1904

The Highlanders lost the race on the last day of the season when ace Jack Chesbro uncorked a wild pitch in the ninth inning that allowed Boston to score the game's winning run and capture the AL pennant. The last days of the season were thrilling.

On Friday, October 7, Chesbro beat Boston at Hilltop Park for his 41st victory, putting the Highlanders a half game ahead of the Pilgrims (to be renamed the Red Sox). A doubleheader in Boston was scheduled for the next day and Highlander Manager Clark Griffith wanted Chesbro to stay home and rest. But Chesbro traveled to Boston on his own and was allowed to pitch Saturday's first game. Bad decision. The Pilgrims hammered "Happy Jack," 13-2, and went on to take the nightcap and a 1½-game lead over New York.

On Monday the Highlanders and Pilgrims played a double-header at Hilltop Park. New York needed a sweep to win the pennant and the pitching match-up was Chesbro against Bill Dineen (23-14 this year) in the first game. With the score tied, 2-2, Lou Criger led off the Boston ninth with an infield hit. Dineen sacrificed Criger to second and the baserunner then reached third on a groundout. With two down, Chesbro got ahead on the count to Fred Parent, 0-2, but his third pitch went over catcher Red Kleinow's head, allowing Criger to score what was to be the pennant-clinching run. Boston prevailed, 3-2, the winning run having been scored without a ball hit out of the infield.

The gritty New Yorkers went on to win the second game, 1-0, to bring a measure of satisfaction to the some 28,000 Highlander fans who crowded Hilltop Park to see their heroes fail by a slim 1½ game margin. For Chesbro it was an unfitting finish to one of the greatest individual seasons in the history of baseball.

His 41 victories (against 12 losses) still stand—and seem likely to endure—as the most single-season wins of the 20th century. Chesbro also set modern major-league records for games started (51) and complete games (48), besides establishing the Yankee club record for innings pitched (455). And this was not a fluke season for "Happy Jack," who, after winning at least 21 games for the fourth year in a row, was considered one of the two best pitchers in the AL, the other being Cy Young.

Jack Powell (23-19, 2.44 ERA) combined with Chesbro to win 64 games, another AL record that still stands. But aside from Chesbro and Powell, the Yankee pitching staff lacked pennant-winning depth. As a result, the tandem of aces was overworked, pitching a combined total of 845 innings—enough work for an entire starting rotation! The number-three starter, Al Orth (11-6, 2.68 ERA, 138 innings pitched), obtained early in the season from Washington, was ill much of the year. Long Tom Hughes (7-11, 3.70 ERA) and the aging Griffith (7-5, 2.87 ERA) each contributed what he could.

But Boston had more balanced production from five pitchers, including three 20-game winners: Cy Young was 26-16, and Dineen was 23-14 and former Highlander Jesse Tannehill 21-11. (The pennant may have been decided in the previous off-season when Tannehill was transferred to the Pilgrims. That New York would help Boston win a pennant, in retrospect, is something of a switch. Had Tannehill been a Highlander in 1904, New York would have walked away with the pennant.)

Willie Keeler (.343) again led the Highlanders' offense, and once more was the team's only regular to hit better than .300. Third baseman Wid Conroy (.243) led the team in stolen bases (30), a vital statistic on a running club (their 163 stolen bases ranking third in the AL). The lineup was basically the same as in 1903, except that Deacon McGuire (.208) and Red Kleinow (.206) were brought in to do the catching, Dave Fultz (.274) moved from a reserve role into center field, and Patsy Dougherty (.283) was obtained early in the season from the Pilgrims to play left field. Dougherty led the AL in runs scored (113) and at-bats (647). Roving outfielder-first baseman John Anderson (.278) led the team in RBIs (82).

Defensively, the Highlanders were weak, finishing seventh in the AL in team fielding (.958). But the club did generate some excitement in New York, as evidenced by the fact that attendance doubled from the previous year's, rising to 438,919. A few

blocks away at the Polo Grounds, John McGraw was showing off one of his finest teams ever, featuring 30-game winners Iron Man Joe McGinnity and Christy Mathewson. Most of New York was enthralled with this Giant team, easy winners of the NL pennant; most of the excitement was at the Polo Grounds.

1905

Manager Clark Griffith's Highlanders had a disappointing year, finishing sixth with a 71-78 record. Jack Chesbro (19-15) and Al Orth (18-16) were quality pitchers, but otherwise New York's pitching was weak. The Highlanders had the highest team ERA (2.92) in the AL.

Willie Keeler hit .302, making him the only Highlander regular to better the .300 mark for the third consecutive season. Outfielder Dave Fultz stole 44 bases, and the rookie sensation at first base, Hal Chase (.249), were the only other bright spots in the lineup. New York had drafted Hal from the Pacific Coast League the previous autumn and eventually signed Chase after a hassle with the P.C.L. He immediately became a fan favorite in New York because he was a ballplayer who was both talented and heads-up.

The slick double-play combination of Jimmy Williams (.228) and Kid Elberfeld (.262) both fell off badly at the plate, as did Patsy Dougherty (.263) and Fultz (.232). Catchers Red Kleinow (.221) and Deacon McGuire (.219) and third baseman Joe Yeager (.267) also swung quiet sticks. The Highlanders led the AL in stolen bases (200), but they scored 36 fewer runs than their pitching staff allowed.

Perhaps even worse for club co-owners Frank Farrell and Bill Devery was the fact that attendance at Hilltop Park sagged nearly 30 percent from the previous season. The club's two crowd-drawing stars, the 33-year-old rightfielder, Keeler, and the 31-year-old spitballer, Chesbro, both were popular enough but they were growing old before their time, and the 22-year-old Chase verged on becoming the club's center of attention.

Meanwhile, just down the block at the Polo Grounds, the royal Giants were capping their season by winning the World Series.

A few notes on the season: On August 4 the Highlander battery was made up of Doc Newton (3-2) and reserve catcher Mike Powers, a pair of physicians. In a 5-3 Detroit win over New York on August 30, 18-year-old Ty Cobb made his ML debut and hit a double off Chesbro.

1906

Again the Highlanders fought for the AL pennant and again they fell short. The Chicago White Sox, immortalized in baseball history as the incredible "Hitless Wonders," rode the crest of a late-season 19-game winning streak and finished in first place three games ahead of New York. The White Sox pennant claim defied a team batting average of only .230 (easily the lowest in the league), compared with the Highlanders' .266 (second highest in the league).

In early August, Chicago was in fourth place behind Philadelphia, New York and Cleveland. But then came the great Chicago winning streak that bolted the White Sox out of the pack and into first place. The Athletics slumped and the month of September saw a two-team race between Chicago and New

York. The Highlanders were not eliminated until the final week of the season.

Something of a pattern had been established by the Highlanders: In 1903 and 1905 many important players had unusually poor seasons and the team was disappointing, and in 1904 and this season most players played up to their potential, as the Highlanders barely missed winning the pennant.

Al Orth (27-17) and Jack Chesbro (24-16) paced the Highlander pitching staff, fifth best (2.78 ERA) in the AL. But "Buffalo Bill" Hogg (14-13) was the only other New York pitcher winning in double figures. In his first two major-league games, on August 25 and August 30, "Slow Joe" Doyle pitched shutouts, a feat accomplished by only three others in AL history. Unfortunately, Doyle failed to win another game all season.

Hal Chase (.323, 76 RBIs), who hit three triples and one double in a 9-8 victory over the Senators on August 30, Kid Elberfeld (.306) and "Wee Willie" Keeler (.304) were all consistently excellent batsmen. Jimmy Williams (.277) provided clutch hitting, leading the club in RBIs (77). The Highlanders finished a league second in RBIs (528) and runs scored (641). Outfielder-shortstop Wid Conroy (.245) and new regulars, third baseman Frank LaPorte (.264), Danny Hoffman (.256) and Frank Delahanty (.238), all contributed.

The team successfully sacrificed 178 times, a team record that stands to this day, and the Highlanders put together a winning streak of 15 games which on only three occasions has been exceeded by the club. Incredibly, the team also won both ends of five consecutive doubleheaders from August 30 to September 4, a major-league record.

In the midst of the pennant race, the Highlanders on September 3 swept a wild doubleheader from the Philadelphia A's before more than 20,000 at Hilltop Park. In the first game, Highlander shortstop Elberfeld went crazy over a close play at third base and tried to attack umpire Mike O'Loughlin after the umpire had ruled the A's Danny Murphy safe. Elberfeld proceeded to chase O'Loughlin around the field, while the crowd, a large percentage of which was Irish, booed this bush tantrum. Finally, the police escorted "The Tabasco Kid" off the field. In the second game, another argument erupted and the A's walked off the field, giving New York a forfeit victory and a sweep of the doubleheader.

The next day the Highlanders recorded their fifth successive twin-bill sweep, downing Boston, 7-0 and 1-0, behind the shutout pitching of Walter Clarkson (9-4) and Orth. However, the 10 Highlander victories in six calendar days proved to be academic; the improbable "Hitless Wonders," one of the least likely pennant winners in history, were not to be denied. Chicago's team ERA of 2.13, as compared to New York's 2.78, was probably the key factor in determining the league champion in one of the wildest years in AL history.

1907

The Highlanders finished in fifth place in a depressing season that seemed all the more so, following as it did the thrilling pennant race of the previous year.

An ankle injury bothered ace hurler Jack Chesbro (10-10) and the slack was not taken up by the remainder of the mound corps. Although Al Orth won 14 games to lead the club, he also tied for the lead among AL pitchers in defeats (21). Only Bill Hogg (9-8) had a winning record among the regular five Highlander starters. However, Slow Joe Doyle (11-11, 2.65 ERA) pitched better than his .500 record indicates.

A 25-year-old utility player, Branch Rickey, played 52 games for New York without anyone's sensing the impact he was to have on baseball. As a catcher, Rickey on June 28 allowed 13 Washington stolen bases, an AL record, in the Senators' 16-5 thrashing of New York. Rickey's .182 season batting average typified the Highlanders' impotence. The club failed to produce a single .300 hitter among its players. (Pitcher Orth, who hit .324, was probably the club's biggest threat at the plate.)

While the infield hit respectably—first baseman Hal Chase hit .287, third baseman George Moriarty .277, shortstop Kid Elberfeld .271, second baseman Jimmy Williams .270 and third baseman-outfielder Frank LaPorte .270—no regular outfielder, where productive hitting is most expected, hit better than Danny Hoffman's .253. It was a miserable season for 35-year-old Willie Keeler who hit a lowly .234 and failed in collecting 100 hits for the first year since 1893.

On July 15, the White Sox dealt the Highlanders the worst shutout loss in club history, 15-0.

Making matters worse, New York was the league's worst defensive team (.947), erring a league-leading 334 times (a horrendous average of 2.25 errors per game). In a June 12 game against Detroit, New York committed 11 errors.

One bright spot: the team stole 206 bases, second best in the AL behind Washington's 223.

1908

The Highlanders hit rock bottom, finishing in the cellar for the first time in club history. Kid Elberfeld, "The Tabasco Kid," took over as manager from Clark Griffith early in the season but could not lift the team.

Among the slings and arrows along the way was the no-hitter Cy Young, the winningest pitcher in baseball history, pitched against the Highlanders June 30 to give the Red Sox an 8-0 win. Highlander pitchers Rube Manning, Doc Newton and Joe Lake were rocked in the contest, as even the 41-year-old Young stroked a trio of hits. But it wasn't only the old-timers who could beat the Highlanders in this dreadful year of 51-103 Highlander baseball.

Young Big Ed Walsh, who had a 40-15 record pitching for the White Sox, feasted on the Highlanders by beating them nine times! And 20-year-old Walter Johnson late in the season pitched three shutouts against the Highlanders in four days! On Friday, September 4, he blanked New York on a six-hitter. The following day brought another Johnson shutout, this one on four hits. After an off day because of the ban on Sunday baseball, Johnson again took the mound on Monday and not only beat the Highlanders but once more denied them a single run and permitted only two hits. For the New Yorkers, it was a weekend of embarrassment.

It was also the beginning of a great rivalry the Yankees were to have with the memorable Johnson. It was not a bad rivalry for Johnson, who over his career had 60 wins over the Yankees. The next most successful pitchers against New York fell 25 games short of that mark. Lefty Grove and Eddie Cicotte are tied for second place with 35 victories apiece versus the Yanks.

The Highlanders led the AL in stolen bases (230) but had the worst pitching staff (3.16 ERA). In fact, this was the sixth year in a row, an AL record, that the Highlanders paced the circuit in the dubious category of fewest complete games. Coupled with the poor pitching was the worst defense in the AL (.947). The great Jack Chesbro was fading (14-20) at the age of 34 and Hal Chase (.257), the club's best player, jumped the team for a spell.

Establishing club records for most games lost (103) and fewest runs scored (459), the 1908 edition endured the most dismal season in Highlander/Yankee history. One of the few highlights of the year came on October 1. Chesbro, the club's first great pitcher, won his last game as a Highlander. He hurled a five-hitter to beat Walter Johnson and the Senators, 2-1.

1909

The Highlanders moved up to fifth place in the AL under new Manager George Stallings, later to gain the nickname of "The Miracle Man." But Stallings worked no miracles this year, although the Highlanders enjoyed their best attendance in Hilltop Park history (501,000).

Joe Lake (14-11, 1.88 ERA) was the ace of a staff of 15 pitchers, eight of whom started more than 10 games. These eight hurlers, averaging only 26 years of age, were Lake, 27; Jack Warhop, 24 (13-15); Rube Manning, 26 (7-11); Lew Brockett, 28 (10-8); Slow Joe Doyle, 27 (8-6); Jack Quinn, 25 (9-5); Tom Hughes, 25 (7-8); and Pete Wilson, 23 (6-5). It was a promising young mound corps, one that might have been more productive except for the illness that plagued Quinn, the rookie from Pennsylvania, who would continue to pitch ML baseball until 1933.

It was a young starting lineup, too. Willie Keeler (.264), playing his last Highlander season, was the only regular over the age of 30. But the torch had long since been passed to Hal Chase (.283), the team's number-one star. Before the season, Chase paid a $200 fine for having played in an outlaw league on the West Coast and was reinstated to organized baseball by the National Commission. He signed a $4,500 New York contract, one of the richest in the game, but was delayed from reporting until May 3 because of a bout with smallpox. The fans came to see Hal's wizardry around first base as much as his batting, but there were rumors that "Prince Hal" was not always giving his best effort. He did, in fact, lead AL first basemen in errors (28).

Also leading the league in errors were outfielder Ray Demmitt (21) and catcher Ed Sweeney (20), and for the third consecutive season, the Highlanders finished a league last in fielding (.948).

The mediocre Highlander offensive attack again relied on speed, stealing 187 bases. The three biggest base thieves were third baseman Jimmy Austin (30), Chase (25) and Kid Elberfeld (23), who was reduced to a part-time role at shortstop and third base. But the Highlanders had only two regulars—second baseman Frank LaPorte (.298) and Chase—who hit better than .280.

1910

New York's AL baseball club, formally still called the Highlanders but now widely known as the Yankees, were a pleasant surprise. Although a distant 14½ games behind the Philadelphia Athletics, the club finished in second place for the first time since 1906 and for the third time in its eight-season history.

And though New York's home attendance of 355,857 was a drop of about 150,000 from the previous year, it was a profitable season for the club; the Highlanders made $80,000, the biggest profit in Highlander/Yankee history until 1920, the year of Babe Ruth's New York arrival.

Manager George Stallings and star first baseman Hal Chase were at odds with each other for most of the year. Stallings was convinced that Chase was involved in baseball gambling, and after a mid-season game in St. Louis the two nearly came to blows when Stallings accused Chase of throwing games. Deep in his manager's doghouse, Chase played on and off; the newspapers wrote of Hal's "unavoidable absence" whenever he was not in the lineup. But Chase had allies in AL President Ban Johnson and Yankee President Frank Farrell.

Following a loss to Cleveland on September 23, Stallings resigned as Highlander manager. Front office interference (or lack of support) had, in effect, forced the resignation of the man who had molded a bunch of losers into a 79-61 team. The bizarre episode was topped off by Chase's becoming Highlander manager for the 11 games remaining in 1910. (New York was 9-2 under Chase.)

The late-season events eclipsed the astounding accomplishments of Canadian-born pitcher Russ Ford (26-6, 1.65 ERA). The single-season figures for wins (26), strikeouts (209), shutouts (eight) and ERA (1.65) for the rookie rank among the best for those categories in Yankee history. The 27-year-old Ford almost single-handedly turned the club's fortunes around.

But he was helped by strong, 22-year-old Jack Quinn (18-12); 25-year-old Jack Warhop (14-14) and a promising 22-year-old southpaw, Hippo Vaughn (13-11, 1.83 ERA). The mound corps produced the season's highlight with Tom Hughes (7-9) on August 6 pitching the first nine innings of no-hit baseball in Yankee history. Hughes gave up a hit in the 10th and was rocked in the 11th as Cleveland won, 5-0.

The Highlanders ran the bases with utter abandon, leading the AL in stolen bases and establishing the club record (288). Bert Daniels stole 41 bases, Chase 40 and Harry Wolter 39.

The batting was improved. Shortstop Jack Knight (.312), Chase (.290) and leftfielder Birdie Cree (.287) paced the attack. Chase and Cree each knocked in 73 runs and second baseman Frank LaPorte had 67 RBIs. The Highlanders also improved defensively, ranking fourth in the AL (.956).

1911

Two years of steady progress were reversed as the Highlanders slipped to sixth place with a 76-76 record. (Washington was 64-90 and St. Louis 45-107 as the seventh- and eighth-place teams while Philadelphia was champion with a 101-50 record. It was an unbalanced league.)

Hal Chase at the helm for New York was a curious choice for manager since he was a rogue, a known gambler, and a player suspected of throwing games. (Years later he would be unofficially banned from organized baseball.)

The season started on a high note with the Highlanders scoring 10 runs before making a single out in the Opening Day game with St. Louis. But this year's mound corps was weak, although Russ Ford (22-11, 2.27 ERA) once more was brilliant. Aside from Ray Caldwell (14-14), the rest of the Yankee pitching staff was shaky.

The club also had poor team defense, finishing in a tie for sixth in the league in fielding (.949). In a typically loosely played doubleheader on September 20, the Yanks made 12 errors, a club record.

As a team, the Yanks hit a respectable .272, led by Chase (.315) and Birdie Cree (.348) who enjoyed an outstanding season. Cree led the club in six major offensive categories: runs (90), hits (181), triples (22), homers (4), batting (.348) and slugging (.513). His 22 triples have been surpassed only once in Yankee history. Third baseman Roy Hartzell (.296) made his hits count, tallying 91 RBIs to lead the team.

The Yanks stole 270 bases, second most in the AL, and on September 28 the Yanks set a league record by stealing 15 bases in a 16-12 defeat of the St. Louis Browns.

The Yanks also did a good deed this year. When an April fire ravaged the Giants' home park, the Polo Grounds, Yankee owner Frank Farrell graciously offered the Giants the use of Hilltop Park for the rest of the season, and the Giants quickly accepted. Farrell's gesture seemed to bring to an end a period of animosity between the two clubs that began with the Yankees' 1903 "invasion" of New York.

1912

The Yankees under rookie Manager Harry Wolverton finished the season in the cellar with a miserable 50-102 record. This edition of the Yankees set a club record for the lowest winning percentage (.329). The pitching was inept.

Even Russ Ford (13-21) had a bad year, losing more games than any other AL pitcher; Jack Warhop accounted for another 19 losses—and Ford and Warhop were the cream of the Yankee staff!

Hal Chase and Bert Daniels led the regulars on a weak hitting team, each batting .274.

This team set such dubious Yankee club fielding records as most errors (386), lowest fielding average (.939), and fewest double plays (81).

There were memorable moments, however. The Yanks helped the Red Sox open Boston's spanking new Fenway Park on April 20, politely losing, 7-6, although being so rude as to take the game into extra innings. Another notable event was the benefit game with the Giants—played for the survivors of the Titanic. The lone highlight of the season came on August 15 when outfielder Guy Zinn (.262), the team home-run leader (six), stole home twice in one game. In fact, the Yanks established a major-league record for steals of home, pulling the theft 18 times. With this club, gambles were a necessity.

Even the fans took a beating this season, one Claude Lueker (Lucas in some accounts) in particular. Lueker, a taunter of the Tigers' Ty Cobb, went after Cobb with particular relish on May 15. The terrible tempered Cobb went to the stands and became embroiled in a swearing argument with Lueker.

Then he entered the stands and attacked Lueker with fists and feet flying. Yankee fans went to the aid of their comrade, and Detroit players entered the melee to rescue Cobb. The police finally restored order. The result of the disturbance: a badly beaten Lueker, a suspension and fine for Cobb and the beginning of the use of ushers and tighter security at baseball games.

All in all, when the Yanks played their final game ever in Hilltop Park on October 5, beating Washington, 8-6 (Hal Chase hit a three-run homer), no one much cared. The Yankees finished 55 games behind Boston!

1913

Now officially known as the Yankees (the name by which they were commonly known since 1903), New York's American Leaguers abandoned Hilltop Park and moved into the Polo Grounds as tenants of the Giants.

The Yankees this season had a "first" even before the season started. They trained in Bermuda, and thus became the first ML team in history to hold spring training outside the United States.

They were a new-look team, having lured future Hall of Famer Frank Chance to become their manager, and they hoped to take a big step up in class. But they could do no better than seventh place in the AL standings, leaving the Giants of John J. McGraw the clear and secure favorites of New York's baseball fans. (The Giants were more than favorites—they were the darlings of New York.) Chance, the man who had won four NL pennants with the Chicago Cubs and a legend in his own time, found only frustration with his new club.

This unhappy season brought with it a 13-game losing streak, longest in Yankee history. So, too, did it bring a couple of key personnel changes. Hal Chase, the splendid first baseman who began the season in a prolonged batting slump, was dealt to the White Sox. Chance believed Chase was purposely letting the team down, and a story in a New York newspaper lent refrain to the theory. Chase went to the White Sox (where he was soon to make four errors in one game) for a pair of mediocre players.

While the Yankees were primarily unloading in the Chase deal, they did pick up in an astute trade with the Indians a 22-year-old shortstop, Roger Peckinpaugh (.268), the foundation on which the Yanks would build their first great team.

But it was Birdie Cree who was the club's best player this year. The Pennsylvanian led the Yanks in batting (.272) and RBIs (63), and he led AL outfielders in fielding (.988). Offensively, the Yankees hit a lowly .237, ranking near the bottom of the AL. Those of Cree and Peckinpaugh aside, Yankee batting averages were anemic: second baseman Roy Hartzell hit .259; centerfielder Harry Wolter, .254; first baseman John Knight, .236; rightfielder Bert Daniels, .216; and third baseman Ezra Midkiff, .197.

Catcher Ed Sweeney (.265) led AL catchers in assists (180), but defensively Yankee catchers permitted 32 passed balls, a club record. Russ Ford (12-18) and Ray Fisher (12-16) were the best of a pitching corps that lacked just about everything.

Perhaps the year's most memorable day was Opening Day in Washington. President Wilson threw out the first ball and Walter Johnson, after allowing an unearned run in the first inning, shut the door on the New Yorkers as the Senators triumphed, 2-1.

In the "ouch" department: in the second game of a June 20 doubleheader, SIX Yankee batters were hit by pitches thrown by Washington pitchers, a ML record, and over both games, Yankee Bert Daniels was plunked three times. The Yankees swept the twin-bill by identical 9-3 scores to take much of the sting out of the day.

1914

The Yankees finished in a tie for sixth place with the White Sox, ending another disappointing season.

Ray Caldwell (17-9, 1.94 ERA) led a pitching staff that sorely missed Russ Ford who had deserted the club to play for Buffalo in the newly formed Federal League. Ray Fisher had a fine 2.28 ERA, but he was a hard luck 10-12, and King Cole (11-9) was the only other Yankee pitcher to win more than eight games.

Third baseman Fritz Maisel (.239) stole 74 bases to lead the AL, thereby setting a club stolen-base record until Rickey Henderson broke it with 80 in 1985. The speedy Yanks once again led the AL in stolen bases (251) but the club was next to last in home runs (12). Cree (.309), the Yanks' most consistent hitter, was the only Yankee to top the .300 mark, while Peckinpaugh (.223) drove in a club-leading 51 runs, a measly total for a club leader. This team produced the lowest slugging average (.287) in Yankee history, besides losing more shutout games (27) than any other Yankee club before or since. Thus, it is easy to believe that the Yanks were the weakest hitting club (.229) in all three major-leagues, including the Federal League.

There was one sterling moment, however. In a game played on August 3, Yankee catcher Les Nunamaker in a single inning cut down three runners attempting to steal. That is a major-league record that Nunamaker alone holds. Defensively, this was a good club, finishing second (.963) in the AL. The infield was especially solid, although Maisel led AL third basemen in errors (35).

But with such a pitifully weak attack, the Yankees were doomed to failure. Good pitching and solid defense cannot help a team that loses nine 1-0 games, as the Yanks did, setting an AL record for a 154-game schedule. Jack Warhop (8-15) was the hard-luck losing pitcher in five of those 1-0 Yankee defeats, a ML record.

1915

The Yankees' first dozen seasons having been less than spectacular, co-owners Frank Farrell and Bill Devery unloaded the club in disgust. Ownership was transferred in January to New Yorker Jacob Ruppert and Ohioan Til Huston.

What had cost Farrell and Devery $18,000 cost Ruppert and Huston $460,000. Eager for a winning team, the new owners hired 38-year-old Wild Bill Donovan to manage the club. Donovan had been a great pitcher and the previous year managed at Providence in the International League (where one of his charges was a kid named Babe Ruth). The Yanks improved somewhat under Donovan, climbing one position to fifth place in the AL.

Leading the pitchers were Ray Caldwell (19-16) and Ray Fisher (18-11), but the real pitching story in retrospect was a 24-year-old obtained during the season from Connie Mack's Athletics—Bob Shawkey. With a record of only 6-6 with the A's and 4-7 as a Yankee, Shawkey nonetheless was destined to become the first important pitcher of the Yankee dynasty that was just a few years around the corner. The only Yankee pitchers besides Caldwell and Fisher to make at least 20 appearances were Jack Warhop (7-9) and Cy Pieh (4-5); 17 pitchers participated in Yankee games.

The Yankees started 22-year-old Wally Pipp at first base. Pipp led AL first sackers in fielding (.992), putouts (1396), assists (85) and double plays (85). "Pipp the Pickler" (.246) also showed some promise at the plate. He and Roy Hartzell, now used primarily in the outfield, shared the club RBI leadership, each driving in a paltry 60 runs. Third baseman Fritz Maisel (.281), the "Flash" from Catonsville, Md., stirred up excitement with his 51 stolen bases, and outfielders Hartzell (.251), Doc Cook (.271), and Hugh High (.258) were respectable hitters.

But the hitting from middle infielders Roger Peckinpaugh (.220) and Luke Boone (.204) and from catchers Les Nunamaker (.225) and Ed Sweeney (.190) was poor. The Yanks' .233 team batting average was the lowest in the AL. But the Yankees were beginning to hit for power and led the AL in HRs with 31. It was the first of 34 years they would lead the league in HRs. Tying for the club HR title were Peckinpaugh and Boone; each hit five. Pitcher Caldwell pinch-hit HRs in consecutive games (still a major-league record for pitchers) on June 10 and 11 and on June 12 he pitched and beat the Browns in a game in which he hit still another homer!

Caldwell during the season scored 27 runs, second most by a pitcher in ML history. He also led the AL in pinch-hit at-bats (33). Besides his hitting ability (.243), he was a fine baserunner and led all AL pitchers in fielding (.988). The Yankees for the first time led the AL in fielding (.966). But those who bore witness to this defensive skill at the Polo Grounds numbered only 256,035, worst attendance in the club's 10-year (1913-22) stay in the Giants' ballpark.

Seasonal note: on May 6 at the Polo Grounds, Red Sox pitcher Babe Ruth cracked the first of his 714 career HRs. Ruth lost, 4-3, in 13 innings but gained headlines for the blast, off Jack Warhop, which ended in the second tier of the right field grandstand. A few weeks later, Ruth again connected off Warhop and drove the ball even deeper into the Polo Grounds' second deck.

1916

On February 15, co-owners Ruppert and Huston gave indication of their determination to make the Yankees a winning team. Frank "Home Run" Baker, the best third baseman in the game, was purchased from Connie Mack's Philadelphia A's.

Baker became a factor in the Yankees' continuing upward movement in the AL. The 1916 team finished in fourth place with an 80-74 record. Bob Shawkey was largely responsible for the Yankee progress, winning 24 games and leading the AL in saves (eight). But Nick Cullop (13-6) and Ray Fisher (11-8) were the only other Yankee pitchers to win more than seven games.

Young Wally Pipp (93 RBIs), an outstanding defensive first baseman and the league's home-run leader (12), emerged as a genuine star. Baker (.269), who had sat out the entire 1915 season, popped 10 homers (second best in the AL behind Pipp) and provided stability in the infield. Although the Yankees did not have a single .300 hitter, they were obviously becoming more power oriented (35 HRs to lead the AL) and less speed conscious. Pipp, Peckinpaugh, and Baker were the mainstays of a fine defensive infield.

1917

The Yankees dropped to sixth place in a disheartening season and the last under Wild Bill Donovan. Bob Shawkey (13-15) and Ray Caldwell (13-16) were the only Yankee pitchers to win more than nine games.

One of Caldwell's great efforts came on July 10 when he pitched nine and two-third innings of no-hit relief to beat the St. Louis Browns, 7-5, in 17 innings.

Another great mound stint was turned in by lefty George Mogridge (9-11) who on April 24 hurled a no-hitter against the Boston Red Sox. Three features attach to the Mogridge achievement: It was the first no-hitter in which the Yankees won, it was the first no-hitter ever pitched by a Yankee lefthander, and it was pitched in Fenway Park where a convenient left field wall makes life miserable for lefties. Mogridge also fielded 77 chances during the season without an error, establishing a Yankee fielding record for pitchers (since tied).

For the second straight season Wally Pipp (.244) led the league in home runs (nine) and Frank Baker led the team in batting (.282) and led the club in RBIs (71). The infield of Pipp, Maisel, Peckinpaugh and Baker was steady, but the outfielders and catchers were poor defensively and lacked offensive power. The Yanks had the league's lowest team batting average (.239), which did not help matters.

1918

The Yankees finished fourth in this World War I-shortened season (31 Yankee games were cancelled and a good deal of sentiment would have had the entire season called off), but the big story of 1918 was the little guy the Yankees got as manager, Miller Huggins. The feisty little (5'6", 140 lbs.) Huggins—"The Mighty Mite"—left his job as manager of the St. Louis Cardinals before the season opened to join the Yankees.

He was destined to become a Hall of Famer and the first great manager in Yankee history.

With Bob Shawkey in the military, George Mogridge (16-13, 2.27 ERA) was Huggins' pitching ace. It was one of Mogridge's finest seasons, and one of his busiest; he led AL pitchers in games pitched (45), a good many of them in relief. (He was 4-7 in relief with seven saves.) Slim Love (13-12) was a second important mound contributor, but the Yankees once again were hurt by a lack of pitching depth. Mogridge and Love were the only two pitchers to win more than 10 games. Spitballer Ray Caldwell (9-8) had a mediocre season as the Yanks' No. 2 starter. No. 4 starter Allan Russell was 8-11. The Yanks lost seven roster pitchers to military service, including veteran Ray Fisher, besides Shawkey. The patchwork staff remaining was the league's sixth best (3.03 ERA).

Top hitters on the club were Home Run Baker (.306) and Wally Pipp (.304). Rightfielder Frank Gilhooley (.276) and second baseman Del Pratt (.275) also were productive. But catchers Truck Hannah (.220) and Roxy Walters (.199) were weak at the plate. As usual, the outfield was a problem. Eight players were in 15 or more games as outfielders, including pitcher Caldwell. Perhaps the most interesting outfielder was leftfielder Ping Bodie (.256), the witty Italian, who was born with a last name of Pezzolo. Military duty plucked several fielders. Pipp and outfielder "Good Time" Bill Lamar (.227), a native of Rockville, Md., played only partial seasons, and Sammy Vick, Muddy Ruel and Aaron Ward barely got out of the blocks. Howie Camp missed the entire season.

The Yankees were a good fielding team, especially in the infield, with a league-leading 137 double plays. The middle infielders were outstanding: Pratt led AL second basemen in putouts (340) and double plays (82) and shortstop Roger Peckinpaugh led the league in assists (439) and double plays (75). Baker led third basemen in fielding (.972). For the third straight year, the Yankees turned a triple play, tying an AL record for most consecutive years having at least one triple play.

The Yankees and Indians on May 24 played a 19-inning game notable as the longest game ever played at the Polo Grounds notwithstanding the Giants' many decades of Polo Grounds occupancy. The Yankees finished at 60-63.

1919

Miller Huggins' Yankees moved up a notch to third place, finishing only 7½ games behind the pennant-winning White Sox (Black Sox). Because the owners had taken severe financial losses in the war-shortened 1918, the AL played only a 140-game schedule with the season not opening until May 1. (The Yanks' record in 139 official games was 80-59.)

Also, the owners cut the player roster from 25 to 21 and conspired to limit payrolls—namely, player salaries. Yankee co-owner Til Huston said, "The players can sign at the salaries offered or not at all." Attendance around the league was outstanding as America rediscovered the national pastime after grueling World War I, and the owners' lack of faith in the game cost them a bundle of money. The Yankees themselves drew 619,164 home customers, or 100,000 better than their previous high draw.

The Yankees put a good product on the field, including a fine pitching staff. Bob Shawkey (20-11, 2.72 ERA) returned to his excellent pre-war form, and 35-year-old Jack Quinn (15-14, 2.63 ERA), returning to the Yanks for his second tour of duty, was consistent and effective. Both Shawkey and Quinn turned in heroic performances during the season. On September 27, Shawkey tallied 15 strikeouts against the A's in a nine-inning game, setting the Yankee club record which stood until Ron Guidry broke it in 1978. On May 11, Quinn and the Senators' great Walter Johnson fought to a 0-0 tie in a game that was called after 12 innings because of darkness.

Johnson set down 28 Yankee batters in a row in the contest, an AL record for an extra-inning game. A former Yankee pitcher, Ray Caldwell, also silenced Yankee bats on another occasion. Pitching for Cleveland on September 10, Caldwell pitched a no-hitter against the Yanks.

Hank Thormahlen (12-10) and George Mogridge (10-7) rounded out a fine corps of pitchers. In fact, Yankee pitching for the first time led the league with a 2.78 ERA.

The Yankee infield was terrific with Pipp at first, Del Pratt at second, Peckinpaugh at shortstop, and Baker at third. Each led the league at his position in at least one fielding category.

Peckinpaugh (.305) led the club in batting and Baker (10 HRs, 83 RBIs, .293) had his best offensive season as a Yankee. The club led the league in home runs (45) for the fourth time in five years. So established was the Yanks' power game, that they were tabbed "Murderers' Row" in a cartoon. Sportswriter Bob Ripley, who came up with the name that was to stick, made particular reference to Baker, Pratt, Peckinpaugh, Pipp, Lewis and Bodie. Duffy Lewis (89 RBIs, .272), one of the greatest defensive outfielders of all time, was acquired to patrol the Polo Grounds' vast outfield, and pitching ace, Carl Mays, who had jumped the Boston Red Sox, was bought by the Yanks late in the campaign. It proved to be a wise purchase.

However, the acquisition almost tore the AL apart. League President Ban Johnson wanted Mays back in Boston under payless suspension, but the Yankees took the matter to court and obtained an injunction protecting Mays through the 1919 season. Skirmishes were set off throughout the league with the Yankee ownership leading the fight against Johnson and his extensive powers. At the same time, the Yankees had to deal with the Tigers, whom the Yankees beat out of third place by a half game. Detroit argued that Mays' wins should not count since he was under suspension. The National Commission withheld the Yanks' World Series shares (third-place teams share in Series proceeds). It was not until a historic league meeting in February that Mays was reinstated cleanly and the Yanks' third-place finish was upheld. Johnson was stripped of most of his powers and the stage was set for Judge Kenesaw Mountain Landis to become baseball's first commissioner.

Trivia note: This was the last season as a regular for the Yankees' rightfielder, Sammy Vick, and the first season of Sunday baseball for the Yankees, and both would have much to do with attendance. Vick (two HRs, 27 RBIs, .248) became expendable with the winter acquisition of George Herman Ruth who would soon be drawing fans in droves. (Vick was the real predecessor of Ruth although pro football Hall of Famer George Halas did play in right field in six games for New York, going two for 22.)

1920

In the winter before the 1920 season, the Yankees made a move that was to set the course of baseball history. Specifically, it was on January 3—third day of the decade to be known as the Roaring Twenties—that the club announced the acquisition of Babe Ruth, the man who would dominate the energetic decade in sports that lay ahead.

Ruth was obtained in a complicated deal that took weeks to work out but which Yankee owners Ruppert and Huston, who wanted Ruth badly, steadfastly pursued. In the end, the cash-short owner of the Red Sox, Harry Frazee, sold his star slugger for $125,000 and other considerations. The Babe was an immediate hit in New York, and he responded with a bat that boomed like none before. Ruth (54 HRs, 137 RBIs, .376) broke his own home-run record by 25, hitting more homers than any AL *team*

could claim and establishing a record for the highest slugging average (.847) that only he was to challenge—next season, actually, with a .846 slugging mark. Besides leading the league in homers and RBIs, Ruth was tops in runs (158) and walks (148).

It was simply the greatest personal exhibition baseball had ever seen. Ruth undoubtedly was helped by the end of the "dead ball era." Baseball in 1920 introduced a livelier sphere in happy response to the long-ball excitement the Babe was generating, and Ruth made the most of it.

The Yankees played good ball (95-59), finishing in third place but only three games behind the league champion Indians. They had a great shot at winning the pennant until late September when pennant hopes were crushed as the Yanks dropped a three-game set in Chicago. The Yankee second baseman, Del Pratt (97 RBIs, .314) had a sensational year, while Bob Meusel (11 HRs, 83 RBIs, .328) had a great rookie season. The Yanks easily led the league in home runs with 115 (the St. Louis Browns were second with 50) and slugging (.426).

In a July 6 game with the Washington Senators, the Yanks in one inning exploded for 14 runs, a single-inning Yankee record.

New York for the first time in 14 years had two 20-game winners. Submariner Carl Mays (26-11) had a season strewn with accomplishments and one tragic event. On August 16, Mays beaned the Indians' Ray Chapman. Chapman fell into a coma and died the next day—the only fatality as the result of an accident on a major-league baseball field. Bob Shawkey (20-13) led the AL in ERA (2.45), and old Jack Quinn (18-10) was a great third starter. The rest of the staff was balanced enough to enable the Yanks to once again post the lowest team ERA (3.31) in the circuit. This fine club was just one year away from greatness.

Perhaps more importantly, the Yankees finally overcame their second-class status in New York. The Yanks by far outdrew the Giants in the Polo Grounds, setting a then-major-league attendance record (1,289,422) and breaking the former record by nearly 380,000 fans. Ruth's presence, of course, had much to do with the Yanks' attractiveness, and the club was an exciting, developing and appealing team. But there was a third factor in the attendance surge.

Thanks to New York politicians Jimmy Walker (soon to become mayor of New York City) and Governor Al Smith, Sunday baseball, heretofore illegal, became legal in New York State. The Yankees reaped the rewards of an obviously wider market, beginning in 1920, and thus recorded the best attendance figure they ever had at the Polo Grounds. After the season, the envious Giants told the Yankees to look elsewhere for a place to play.

Actually, the Yankees could easily have rewarded their growing legions of fans with a pennant except for a couple of poor trades in previous years. Former Yankee hurlers Ray Caldwell, pitching for Cleveland, and Urban Shocker, pitching for the St. Louis Browns, each posted identical 20-10 records in 1920. With both these men, or possibly with either one, the Yankees would have gone to their first World Series.

Off the field, on October 28, Ed Barrow left the Red Sox and joined the Yankees as the club's business manager (general manager). Barrow would mold many of the great Yankee teams of the future.

1921

Behind brilliant Manager Miller Huggins, the Yankees won their first AL pennant, posting a 98-55 record and finishing 4½ games ahead of second-place Cleveland.

The Indians came to the Polo Grounds September 26 trailing the Yankees by half a game, and the season's big series was set up. The two clubs split a doubleheader, the Yanks winning the first game, 4-2, behind the clutch pitching of Waite Hoyt, and the Tribe taking the second in a rout, 9-0. The next day the largest crowd ever to witness a Yankee game at the Polo Grounds—more than 40,000 fans—saw the Yankees pummel the defending world champions, 21-7. Then the Yankees, behind Babe Ruth's two HRs, took the fourth game, giving them a 2½-game lead over the Indians and virtually giving them the pennant.

The flag was clinched October 1, the Yanks beating the Athletics, 5-3, in the first of two games. After winning that first game, the Yanks evened their all-time win-loss mark at 1412-1412. The club then moved over the .500 mark to stay *for all-time* by notching the second game. How fitting it was to pass this milestone on their very first pennant-clinching date! Over the decades, the Yankees have won so many more games than they have lost that on August 30, 1999, the Bronx Bombers achieved a franchise milestone that took them 78 years to attain: being *2,000* games over .500. *[For more about that achievement, see the 1999 season summary.]* Ruth, who won the nightcap pitching in relief, was phenomenal over the season. He hit .378 and blasted 59 HRs to break his own single-season HR record for the third straight year. He set ML records for total bases (457) and extra-base hits (119). He scored 177 runs, more than any 20th century player. He led the AL in RBIs (171), walks (144) and slugging (.846). No other Yankee player ever has hit more HRs at home than the 32 roundtrippers Ruth hit at the Polo Grounds in 1921. His hot streaks were white-hot. "The Bambino" hit seven HRs in four consecutive games (June 10-14) and made at least one extra-base hit in nine straight games (August 28—September 5).

Although the Babe's 1927 season has been more publicized, 1921 was probably his best all-round campaign. His 1921 may have been the greatest individual hitting season in ML history. He even found time to be a starting pitcher, beating the Tigers and striking out his archrival, Ty Cobb. The exploits of Ruth tend to eclipse the achievements of his teammates, and these were significant.

The Yanks' pitching staff was easily the best in the league and led the AL in ERA (3.79), complete games (92) and strikeouts (481). Controversial Yankee ace Carl Mays (27-9) had his submarine delivery working to perfection and enjoyed the greatest of his five 20-win seasons. Mays led AL pitchers in wins, winning percentage (.750), games pitched (49), innings pitched (337) and saves (seven). No Yankee pitcher since has pitched as many as 337 innings. And Carl also hit .343 (49 for 143), banging out the third highest number of hits by a pitcher in ML history. The Brooklyn-born Hoyt (19-13, 3.09 ERA),

Babe Ruth is shown in 1924 with kids in New York, passing on his love for the game of baseball. (AP/WIDE WORLD PHOTOS, The National Baseball Library, Cooperstown, N.Y.)

another Yankee acquisition from the Red Sox who enjoyed singing, writing and painting, pitched maturely at the age of 21. Rounding out the "big three," veteran Bob Shawkey (18-12) pitched well in spite of a leg injury. Rip Collins (11-5), Jack Quinn (8-7), Bill Piercy (5-4), Harry Harper (4-3), Alex Ferguson (3-1), Ruth (2-0), Tom Sheehan (1-0) and Tom Rogers (0-1) all contributed to the Yankees' first pennant.

The Yankees hit a resounding .300, with Ruth, Bob Meusel (.318), Wally Schang (.316) and Aaron Ward (.306) elevating the team average. RBIs were supplied mainly by Ruth, Meusel (135) and Wally Pipp (97). Old favorites Frank Baker (.294) and Roger Peckinpaugh (.288)—two players who were instrumental in establishing the Yanks' winning attitude—also hit well. The bench was both strong and deep, and included infielder Mike McNally (.260 in 215 at-bats), outfielders Chick Fewster (.280 in 207 at-bats), Braggo Roth (.283 in 152 at-bats) and Chicken Hawks (.288 in 73 at-bats).

This was a solid defensive club with fine jobs turned in by Schang behind the plate, Pipp at first, Ward at second, Baker at third, and Peckinpaugh at shortstop. In the outfield were Ruth, who at this point in his career was in excellent shape and was a fine fielder, Elmer Miller (.298) and the young Californian, Meusel, who possessed one of the best throwing arms in baseball history. "Long Bob" led AL outfielders in assists (28), thus setting the Yankee club record in that department. He also tied Ken Williams of the Browns for the second most HRs in the AL (24). Next to Ruth, Meusel may well have been the league's best all-round player. Yankee outfielders combined to make five assists, an AL record, in a September 5 game with the Red Sox.

It was a great Yankee team. And as this season was taking its illustrious direction, the New York Yankees baseball club in May bought land in the Bronx for the purpose of building a stadium.

1922

The Yankees won the AL pennant for the second year in a row but not without a season-long dogfight put up by the tough St. Louis Browns who boasted a lineup of four 100-RBI batters (Ken Williams, Marty McManus, George Sisler and Baby Doll Jacobson), a batting champ (Sisler at .420) and a 24-game winner (Urban Shocker). It was probably the greatest team in the history of the Browns.

The Browns were tenacious. They pulled one game out of the fire after being down to the Yankees by seven runs with just one out to go. The Yankees' pennant victory was by no means a foregone conclusion—they nosed out the Browns by a mere one game. The fact was that the Browns were a more powerful hitting club than the Yanks who failed to produce a single 100-RBI slugger.

The reason the Yanks lacked their usual firepower: Babe Ruth and Bob Meusel did not play until late in May. Commissioner Landis had suspended both for barnstorming after the 1921 World Series, a violation of major-league rules. Ruth and Meusel were properly warned the previous fall of the severity of the consequences were they to proceed with their barnstorming disobedience. The commissioner announced, "This case resolves itself into a question of who is the biggest man in baseball, the Commissioner or the player who makes the most home runs." Landis was under great pressure to go easy on Ruth for the good of the game (and the financial prospects of AL owners), but said Landis of the Babe: "In this office he's just another player."

Altogether, it was a difficult year for Ruth, who was suspended on several occasions for a variety of infractions. The Babe's hitting was affected. In a 7-1 Yankee loss on June 12, Ruth was fanned three straight times by St. Louis pitcher Hub Pruett. But "The Sultan of Swat" still managed to hit .315 and to pop 35 HRs in only 406 official at-bats, although for the first time since 1917 he was not the HR king of the AL, the honor going to the Browns' Williams who belted 39. (Tilly Walker of the A's was second with 37, followed by Ruth.)

Meusel (16 HRs, 84 RBIs, .319), Pipp (90 RBIs, .329) and Schang (.319) helped Babe with the offense—and with the fighting and bickering. This Yankee team was a fighting bunch and their fights were usually with one another. On one western road trip in the depth of July, the Yankee dugout staged the following bouts: Ruth vs. Pipp, Aaron Ward vs. Braggo Roth, Al DeVormer vs. Carl Mays and DeVormer vs. Bootnose Hofmann. There were still others—the team was on edge the entire season. But these Yankees caught the fancy of New York City.

This was an exciting team, and for a third consecutive season more than a million fans trekked to the Polo Grounds to see the Yanks, an attendance level unheard of at the time. On September 10 the largest crowd in Polo Grounds' history (up to that time) watched the Yanks sweep a doubleheader. Obviously, the New York Giants of John McGraw were comforted by the knowledge that this would be the Yanks' final year in the Polo Grounds.

Before the season, the team picked up from the Red Sox two more fine pitchers, Bullet Joe Bush and Sad Sam Jones. Bush compiled a spectacular record (26-7) and tied the club fielding record for pitchers, handling 77 chances without an error. Shawkey (20-12), Hoyt (19-12), Jones (13-13) and Mays (12-14) rounded out the starting pitchers who completed 98 games, the highest total in the AL.

Boston fans, already angry over the fact that four of the top five Yankee pitchers formerly were with the Red Sox, looked on in dismay as New York acquired still another Boston player, shortstop Everett Scott. Obtained before the season's start, Scott (.269) had a great year defensively, leading AL shortstops in fielding (.964). In still another Red Sox deal, New York during the season obtained the fine third sacker, Joe Dugan (.286). That deal, made late in July, caused uproar and indignation in St. Louis. With the Yankee acquisition of Dugan, Frank "Home Run" Baker (.278) closed out his memorable career as a part-time player and, with a salary of $16,000, the second highest paid Yankee behind Ruth who pocketed an incredible $52,000.

The Yanks established a club record for sacrifices (bunts and fly balls), a figure indicative of the sound fundamental baseball the team played. They were sound defensively, too, ranking second in the AL in fielding (.975). The team traveled to St. Louis in late September with a half-game lead over the Browns and the AL pennant on the line in a three-game series in Sportsman's Park. Centerfielder Whitey Witt (.297) in the first game was hit by a bottle thrown from inside a hostile crowd and had to be carried from the field amid the jeers of the throng. New York won that game but lost the second game. In the third game Witt, his head bandaged, courageously returned to knock in the Yankees' winning runs. New York left St. Louis with a 1½-game lead and the pennant safely tucked away.

On September 30 the Yankees made it official as Hoyt and Bush led the club to a 3-1 pennant-clinching victory over the Red Sox. With the season over and the World Series on tap, the Yankees were about to say good-bye to the Polo Grounds and to Coogan's Bluff as they looked beyond the Harlem River to the Bronx where their own stadium was in the process of construction.

1923

The Yankees won a third consecutive AL pennant. Merely winning the pennant was not enough for this Yankee edition—the margin over the second-place Detroit Tigers was 16 games.

The 1923 Yankees began the season as stylishly as they ended it, opening on April 18 in Yankee Stadium, destined to become the most famous stadium in America, and beating the Red Sox, 4-1, behind the pitching of Bob Shawkey. It was only natural that on that day, Babe would hit the first home run ever belted in the Bronx's beautiful new palace, a home run at least 25,000 fans—those who were turned away at the gate when the Stadium reached capacity—never got to see.

Ruth (41 HRs, 131 RBIs) had a great comeback season as he set two major-league records, walking 170 times and reaching base 379 times. The Babe led the AL in homers, RBIs, walks, runs (151), and slugging (.764), besides establishing the New York club batting record (.393). For his mighty achievements, Ruth was given the League Award, the 1920s version of the MVP Award.

Witt (.314), Meusel (.313) and Pipp (.304) along with Ruth made four .300 hitters in the Yankee lineup. Again, the Yanks led the league in home runs (105) and slugging (.422), an indication of the power-hitting philosophy the Yankees made so successful.

However, fielding excellence carried the team this season as New York led the AL in team defense (.977). Four Yankees (Ward, Dugan, Scott, Witt) led the league in fielding at their positions.

Still another deal with the Red Sox brought pitcher Herb Pennock to New York. He compiled a 19-6 record. But Sad Sam Jones (21-8) was the ace, capping a splendid season on September 4 with a no-hitter against the Philadelphia A's. With Bush (19-15), who went 15 innings to beat the Senators, 2-1, on July 3 (Ruth's 15th-inning home run won the game), Hoyt (17-9) and Shawkey (16-11), the Yanks had five top-drawer starters. These five started all but nine Yankee games in the 1923 season, and together with Carl Mays (5-2), who was basically ignored by Manager Huggins, made up the group of Yankee pitchers known as "The Six Star Final."

The pitching was great, the fielding was great, and the hitting was great—especially great in Boston on September 28 when the team set the then AL record for hits in a single game, cracking 30 hits off Red Sox pitching. The Yanks won the game, 24-4, and the highlight was an 11-run Yankee sixth inning in which 16 batters stepped to the plate to feast on Boston pitching. And then there was the kid who hit his first big-league home run earlier in that same Fenway Park series, a kid named Lou Gehrig.

1924

A grueling pennant race ended with the Yankees coming in second best, two games behind the surprising Washington Senators.

Pitchers Herb Pennock (21-9) and Waite Hoyt (18-13) had good years, but subpar performances from Bullet Joe Bush (17-16) and Sad Sam Jones (9-6) put a dent in the Yankee mound corps. Bush and Jones won 14 fewer games than their 1923 total. In Cincinnati, meanwhile, Carl Mays, the temperamental pitching star whose contract was sold to the Reds, was winning 20 games for the NL club.

Babe Ruth won two-thirds of the Triple Crown, snatching the AL titles for home runs (46) and batting average (.378). It was the Babe's only batting championship of his career. He also led the league in runs (143), walks (142) and slugging (.739). On this power-packed club, RBIs were supplied by Ruth (121), Meusel (120) and Pipp (113). These three and Jumpin' Joe Dugan (.302) provided most of the hitting. The Yankees finished only fifth in the AL in batting (.289), but they struck out only 420 times, the fewest whiffs in Yankee history.

And this was another fine Yankee team defensively, leading the league in fielding (.974) and with skill at every position.

Still, Miller Huggins' 1924 Yankees were a disappointment—they had been heavily favored to repeat as champions. The reason they did not, in the view of Babe Ruth, was the broken ankle sustained early in the season by the great rookie prospect Earle Combs, obtained in January from Louisville. Combs did well in the little playing time he got to see, going 14 for 35 trips to the plate (.400).

Certainly the Yanks' poor showing could not be attributed to any lack of fight. One memorable brawl was with the Tigers in Detroit on June 13. Bob Meusel, hit with a pitch, attacked the pitcher. Both teams swarmed onto the field, swinging. Ruth and Ty Cobb (the two never liked each other) squared off. After the fights were broken up, Tiger fans rioted on the field, and the Yanks were given the victory by forfeit. Later, Ruth and Meusel were each fined $100, and Meusel and the Tiger pitcher, Bert Cole, each received a ten-day suspension.

1925

The Yankees tumbled to seventh place and it hurt. The pitching staff fell apart. Only Herb Pennock (16-17, 2.96 ERA) pitched well, as his sparkling ERA attests. Sad Sam Jones (15-21) led the AL in losses, and Waite Hoyt (11-14) and Bob Shawkey (6-14) also endured off-years.

Because of his excessive indulgences during spring training, Babe Ruth (.290) had a serious stomach illness early in the season, played in only 98 games and hit just 25 home runs with 66 RBIs. It was the Babe's worst Yankee season. Things were going so badly for Ruth that on August 9 Bobby Veach pinch-hit for him and flied out in a 4-3 Yankee loss. (It was the only time Ruth was ever pinch-hit for as a Yankee.) Late in the season, Miller Huggins suspended Ruth for insubordination and fined him $5,000. With his assertion of authority, Huggins finally proved to Ruth that it was he, Huggins, who ran the team, and their stormy relationship entered a more mutually respectful phase.

Bob Meusel led the AL in home runs (33) and RBIs (138), but his stats were hardly enough to offset a general team impotence. The inglorious season was accented June 17 when Detroit dealt New York its worst loss ever at Yankee Stadium, 19-1. But the dismal season was not without hopeful developments.

Rookie Earle Combs (203 hits, .342) was impressive, using his good speed to patrol the Stadium's vast center field. Wally Pipp was unable to play in an early-season game because of a headache, and 22-year-old Lou Gehrig, who spent 1924 at Hartford, was told to handle first base. Gehrig (20 HRs, .295) remained in the lineup for a miraculous consecutive-game total of 2,130 games, a major-league record which seemed unbreakable until Cal Ripken Jr. of the Orioles started his streak on May 30, 1982. Coincidentally, it was in the spring of Gehrig's emergence that the Yanks' Everett Scott (soon to go to Washington) played the final game of his 1,307-game playing streak, the major-league record for shortstops, and, at the time, the endurance record for major-league players, irrespective of position.

Pee Wee Wanninger added another coincidence. He replaced Scott at shortstop on May 6 to end the Scott streak and was pinch-hit for on June 1 by Gehrig, the beginning of Lou's streak. (It was the following day that Lou replaced Pipp at first base.)

One of the season's highlights occurred on September 22 when reserve outfielder Ben Paschal (.360 and 12 HRs, 56 RBIs in only 247 at-bats) hit two inside-the-park HRs at Yankee Stadium.

A pair of traumatic losses early in the season symbolized the Yanks' rapid decline. In Washington on April 23, Hall of Fame pitcher Walter Johnson came to bat as a pinch-hitter in the bottom of the ninth with two on and Pennock nursing a 1-0 Yankee lead. "The Big Train" promptly doubled in the tying and winning runs, and the Yankees were left with a defeat that was disappointing but not as heartbreaking as their loss in Cleveland on May 20. The Indians, behind 9-4 when they came to bat in the ninth, scored six runs to win the game. Tris Speaker scored the winning run, coming from first base on a single.

Still this season had its bright aspects. Huggins was given an opportunity to see what youngsters such as Gehrig and Combs were made of. And while the Yanks' pitching and hitting declined for the third straight year, their fielding (.974) was the best in the AL.

1926

It was a great comeback season. The Yankees rallied from the disaster of 1925 by winning another AL pennant, finishing three games up on the second-place Indians.

Only Babe Ruth and sportswriter Fred Lieb had the courage to pick the Yankees in the preseason to capture the flag; they were ridiculed by most experts for their foolhardiness.

The Yankees got off to a good start, beating the Red Sox at Fenway Park in a wild Opening Day game, 12-11, and stayed hot until mid-August when they led the AL by 10 games. Then they stumbled, finishing with a 91-63 record. And as the Yanks were falling closer to the pack in September, the Indians were playing great baseball.

Late in September, the Yankees, nursing a four-game lead, traveled to Cleveland for a crucial six-game series. The Indians won the first two games, a twin bill, and the city of Cleveland went berserk with anticipation. But New York rebounded to win the final four games of the set and was never caught. Typical Yankee heroes in the 8-3 New York victory over Cleveland on September 19 were Lou Gehrig, who hit three doubles, a four-bagger and collected five RBIs, and Babe Ruth, who drilled a single and a homer and scored three runs.

For the season, the Yanks' pitching ace was the peerless veteran southpaw, Herb Pennock (23-11, 3.62 ERA), backed by 35-year-old Urban Shocker (19-11) and Waite Hoyt (16-12). These three had a combined 58-34 record; the combined record of the other Yankee pitchers was only 33-29.

In the previous year, the Yankees had purchased the contracts of two minor-league stars, Tony Lazzeri from Salt Lake City (Pacific Coast League) and Mark Koenig from St. Paul (American Association). Now the two rookies formed the double-play combo (Lazzeri at second, Koenig at short) providing good defense up the middle, and, along with Gehrig and Joe Dugan, gave the Yankees a defensively sound infield. However, New York was only the seventh best fielding team (.966) in the AL, a statistic that might be more reflective of a lack of experience at key positions than of the team's defensive stature overall.

All the regulars hit well. Catcher Benny Bengough began by hitting .381 in 36 games, but was lost for the rest of the season when a pitch by George Uhle of Cleveland injured his throwing arm. Pat Collins (.286) replaced Benny behind the plate and did a first-rate job. First baseman Gehrig (16 HRs, 107 RBIs, .313) emerged as a legitimate batting star. The youngsters, Lazzeri (18 HRs, 114 RBIs) and Koenig (.271), had little trouble adjusting to AL pitching, and third-sacker Dugan hit consistently as always at .288. It was the outfield of rightfielder Ruth (47 HRs, 145 RBIs, .372), centerfielder Earle Combs (113 runs, .299) and leftfielder Bob Meusel (81 RBIs, .315) that made up the brunt of the Yankee attack.

Paced by Meusel's three sacrifice flies on September 15, this team tied the Yankee club record for most sacrifices (flies and hits) in a season (218). This was a powerful offensive machine, these Yankees of 1926, leading the AL in five major offensive categories (runs, HRs, RBIs, walks, slugging). And it was a clutch-hitting team, too. Often the Yankee bats were silent until the late innings, only to explode against a tired pitcher.

A 5 p.m. factory whistle heard in Yankee Stadium, often when the team was on a late-inning rampage, inspired Combs to coin the phrase "Five O'clock Lightning" for the late afternoon uprisings. Sportswriter Frank Graham used it often, and the phrase became popular.

But occasional fielding lapses, the lack of pitching depth, and an absence of bench strength prevented the Yankees from running away with the pennant. Only Ben Paschal (.287) made a significant contribution coming off the Yanks' bench.

The Yankees and St. Louis Browns capped this unpredictable baseball season with a September 26 doubleheader that lasted only two hours and seven minutes (still a major-league record). The second game, which went the entire nine innings, lasted only 55 minutes, setting the AL record for game brevity. The day before, the Yankees had clinched the AL pennant by sweeping the Browns, 10-2 and 10-4, in another doubleheader.

Two players instrumental in helping the Yankees win their first row of pennants (1921-23), pitcher Sad Sam Jones (9-8 in 39 games) and infielder Aaron Ward (.323 in 22 games), were traded over the winter and were not aboard to play on a magical baseball team—the 1927 Yankees.

1927

They were, in the picturesque language of the time, the "Window Breakers" to the mild-mannered and "Murderers' Row" to the sanguinary types. They were Ruth, Gehrig, Meusel, Lazzeri, Combs, Dugan and Koenig—big swingers all. They gave the Yankees tremendous power, which with consistent hitting, clutch hitting, exceptional pitching (starting and relief) and solid defense, produced a remarkably successful season.

The 1927 edition played .714 ball (110-44), a then-American League record until broken by the Cleveland Indians (111-43, .721) in 1954 and later by the 1998 Yankee club (114-48, .704). In 1998, the Yankees eclipsed both prior American League records for wins in a season with 114. The 1927 Yankees finished 19 games in front of the second-place Philadelphia Athletics, a margin that then set another AL record that was broken by the 1936 Yankees, who finished 19 1/2 games ahead of the Detroit Tigers. In 1998, the Yanks broke that '36 team record by finishing 22 games ahead of the Boston Red Sox, who had finished with a very respectable record of 92-70 (.568). Prior to 1998, no Yankee team had won more games than the '27 edition, until Manager Joe Torre led his '98 club to 114 wins. The 1927 Yankees, however, still possess the best club winning percentage ever (.714), the '98 club falling a little short with a .704 mark. That there never was a pennant race in 1927 is sheer understatement. As John Kieran wrote in *The New York Times* on July 6, "It isn't a race in the American League, it's a landslide."

Nearly 100,000 people flocked to Yankee Stadium to see the Yankees play the A's on Opening Day. An unofficially reported throng of 73,206 was allowed through the turnstiles to see Waite Hoyt out-duel Lefty Grove and the Yanks win 8-3. The win put the Yankees in first place where they remained for 174 days—the entire season. By the end of May, the Yankees boasted a 23-10 record, and on Independence Day, after sweeping a doubleheader from Washington, 12-1 and 18-1, the Yanks led the AL by 11 1/2 games. Behind Hoyt's 20th victory and Babe Ruth's 51st and 52nd homers, on September 13 Yankees wrapped up the AL pennant against Cleveland.

One team that felt the full force of the New York steamroller was St. Louis. The Browns lost their first 21 games to the Yankees before beating them, 1-0, in the year's final meeting between the clubs. (Wilcy Moore took the loss in spite of a neat seven-hitter.)

In retrospect, it is hard to believe that this great Yankee team was not anticipated. But most of the experts were focused on the fact that the Yanks limped to an unexpected pennant title in 1926 and then lost in the World Series. In fact, in a preseason poll of 42 experts, only nine picked the Yankees to repeat as league champs. Yankee Manager Miller Huggins would only say that he expected "a closer race this time" and that "six clubs, with almost equal chance" would be in the thick of the 1927 race. Club owner Jacob Ruppert astutely and boldly predicted another Yankee pennant.

The chief competition was expected from Cleveland, Philadelphia and Washington, the second, third and fourth place finishers in 1926. The Indians were to have a miserable year and finish sixth. The Senators fielded a strong club and came in third with a respectable 85-69 record. The A's were terrific.

The A's hit .303 (compared to the Yanks' league-leading mark of .307), had seven future Hall of Famers (Lefty Grove, Al Simmons, Ty Cobb, Mickey Cochrane, Eddie Collins, Zack Wheat and Jimmie Foxx), had the AL's third best pitching staff (behind New York and Chicago), and finished with the same 91-63 record that won the pennant for the Yankees in 1926! Some of the A's batting averages: Simmons, .392; 40-year-old Cobb, .357; Cochrane, .338; Jimmy Dykes, .324; Sammy Hale, .313; Joe Boley, .311; Walt French, .304; 40-year-old Collins, .338; 41-year-old Wheat, .324; and 19-year-old Foxx, .323. Grove was 20-13. Yet, with all of this, the A's still couldn't make a race of it!

The Yankee pitching staff was superb. The ace was Hoyt (22-7) who led AL pitchers in wins and winning percentage (.759) and who claimed the ERA championship (2.63). Herb Pennock (19-8), Urban Shocker (18-6), Dutch Ruether (13-6), and George Pipgras (10-3) were all standouts. With any of these pitchers taking the mound, the Yanks were virtually assured of a well-pitched game.

Shocker was particularly gutsy; he was already afflicted with weak spells from the heart condition that was to claim his life the following year. Still, Urban gave the team a tremendous effort in spite of the pain, and, reportedly, a knowledge of his impending fate.

Wilcy Moore (19-7), a 30-year-old Oklahoma farmer whom General Manager Ed Barrow had discovered in the low minors, established himself as the first great Yankee relief pitcher. He tied for the AL lead in saves (13) and had an ERA of 2.28 but, unlike Hoyt, failed to meet the technical requirements for the official league ERA title. Bob Shawkey, now 36, was in the final season of a brilliant 13-year Yankee career and went 2-3. Myles Thomas chipped in with a 7-4 record.

This remarkable staff led the AL in ERA (3.20) and shutouts (11). The White Sox, the club with the second lowest ERA, trailed the Yanks' staff by 0.71. Hoyt, Shocker, Moore and Pennock had the four highest winning percentages in the AL among pitchers who hurled at least 200 innings (21 pitchers). Moore, Hoyt and Shocker also had the three lowest ERA's among the league's most active pitchers.

But the meat and potatoes of the 1927 Yankees was its power hitting, and the most exciting aspect of this power was the combination of Babe Ruth (60 HRs) and Lou Gehrig (47 HRs). All season long the baseball world and the public marveled at the Ruth-Gehrig HR race. Gehrig was the first real challenger to Babe's HR throne since Ruth changed the nature of the game in 1918. From April through mid-August Gehrig kept pace with "The Bambino", and as late as August 15 "Larrupin' Lou" actually held the lead, 38-36. Gehrig hit only nine HRs the rest of the way while Ruth in his final 42 games blasted 24! It was a torrid stretch run by Babe, a pace that would have given him 87.8 HRs over a 154-game schedule! With 17 games remaining, Babe needed 10 HRs to break his record of 59, and with four games left he needed four. In Game No. 152 (there were 155 official games) he hit No. 57 off Lefty Grove, a grand slammer. He hit HR No. 58, a solo shot, and No. 59, another grand slam homer, in Game No. 153 off the Senators at the Stadium. (Thus, in consecutive games on September 27 and 29,

Ruth hit grand slam HRs, setting an AL record later tied by several players.) He also just missed two other HRs in Game No. 153, hitting a triple off the fence and flying out deep.

The next day at the Stadium, Game No. 154, Ruth dramatically hit HR No. 60 off the Senators' Tom Zachary. Zachary maintained that the ball was foul, but it was fair by at least 10 feet, and for the fourth time, Ruth set a new HR standard.

Ruth was justifiably proud of his new HR record. In the clubhouse after the game he yelled: "Sixty, count 'em, sixty! Let's see some other son of a bitch match that!" He was phenomenal in September, belting a ML-record 17 HRs in that month; a mark that stood through 1999. For the entire season, "The Sultan of Swat" hit 28 HRs at Yankee Stadium and 32 on the road, the latter figure another ML record.

Gehrig's late-season decline may have cost him countless records, but there were at least two good reasons why he cooled off. As Ruth said in his autobiography, *The Babe Ruth Story,* "Pitchers began pitching to me, because if they passed me, they still had Lou to contend with." Ruth batted third, Gehrig fourth. Ruth may have seen good pitches, but not Gehrig. And then there was the state of Lou's mother's health. Mom Gehrig required a serious operation in September and was not taken off the critical list until the late stages of the World Series. Meanwhile, Lou was so worried about Mrs. Gehrig that he couldn't concentrate on baseball. He would rush to the hospital immediately after afternoon home games and remain there until Mrs. Gehrig was asleep. Had this situation not intervened, Lou might well have approached 200 RBIs; most of his league-leading 175 RBI total was rolled up by mid-September.

And dwell on this: Gehrig's 175 RBIs came in a season in which Ruth cleared the bases at least 60 times! Lou deservedly won the League Award honoring the AL's best player. (Babe, who won the award in 1923, was ineligible for the honor because of a rule preventing repeat winners.) There is no doubt that in this year Ruth and Gehrig formed the most feared batting duo in baseball history.

Together, they blasted 107 HRs while the entire remainder of the AL hit 176. (Babe personally out-homered EVERY AL team and Lou out-homered four of the seven rival clubs.) Adding Ruth's 164 RBIs to Gehrig's 175, the pair of thumpers knocked in 339 Yankees.

In all, the Yankees had four 100-RBI batsmen: Gehrig, Ruth, Bob Meusel (103) and Tony Lazzeri (102). The batting averages were just as impressive starting with Gehrig (.373) and followed by Ruth (.356), Earle Combs (.356), Meusel (.337), Lazzeri (.309) and Mark Koenig (.285). In fact, the Yanks' team batting average of .307 remains the highest of any AL pennant winner. The club's lefthanded power was Ruth-Gehrig, the right-handed power was Lazzeri-Meusel whose combined total of 26 HRs bested any other pair of righty teammates in the AL. Combs was the best lead-off man in the league.

A Yankee player won every offensive title in the AL except batting (claimed by Detroit's Harry Heilman) and stolen bases (won by St. Louis' George Sisler). Gehrig finished third in batting and Meusel was second in stolen bases (24). Ruth, of course, led the AL in HRs, followed by Gehrig and Lazzeri (18). Ruth led the AL in walks (138) and Gehrig was second (109). Ruth led the AL in slugging (.772) and Gehrig was runner-up (.765). Gehrig and Ruth were 1-2 in RBIs. Gehrig led the AL with 447 total bases, the third highest total in ML history, and Ruth had the runner-up's total of 417, the 11th highest in history. Combs was third with 331. "The Iron Horse" led the AL in doubles (52), until Don Mattingly broke it in 1986 with 53. Combs not only led the AL in hits (231), triples (23) and at-bats (648) but established a Yankee record for triples. Gehrig was second in the AL in both hits (218) and triples (18).

The awesome New Yorkers led AL teams in eight major offensive categories (every one but doubles and stolen bases), including a slugging mark (.489) that remains the ML record. The Yankees were not shutout until an early September game when Lefty Grove blanked them, 1-0.

Needless to say, the offensive highlights were many. On May 7, Gehrig hit a grand slam off Ted Lyons, the first HR to be hit into the new right field pavilion of enlarged Comiskey Park. In a 12-11 extra-inning Yankee win against the White Sox on June 8, Lazzeri hit three HRs, including a two-run shot that tied the game in the ninth. A few weeks later on June 23, Lou belted three HRs in an 11-4 Yankee romp at Fenway Park. Babe on August 26 hit the first HR clear out of the enlarged Comiskey. Combs had three triples September 22 in leading New York to an 8-7 win over the Tigers. Lazzeri, an especially popular member of the cast, was treated September 9 to a "Tony Lazzeri Day" at the Stadium.

Defensively, this was a sound club. The outfield of Meusel-Combs-Ruth had no peer defensively (or offensively). No one in baseball had Meusel's arm. Fleet centerfielder Combs roamed far and wide to lead AL outfielders in putouts (411), an indication of his great range. Ruth could still make all the plays in right: in fact, he was a superior fielder with an excellent arm.

Gehrig and Lazzeri were steady and dependable (although unspectacular) on the right side of the infield. The left side was sensational with Joe Dugan acting like a vacuum cleaner at third and Koenig, though making 47 errors to lead the AL, ranging into the holes to make great plays at shortstop. Dugan started slowly, hitting .220 for much of the first half, but turned red-hot in July and finished at .269. But Joe was having trouble with a knee and played in only 112 games. When Dugan did not play, generally Mike Gazella (.278) manned the hot corner. Second baseman Ray Morehart (.256) and outfielder Cedric Durst (.248) were also capable reserves. Ben Paschal hit .317 in 82 at-bats.

Most experts feel that if this team had a weakness it was in the catching. Still, the catching corps was excellent, and none of the three catchers, Pat Collins (.275), Johnny Grabowski (.277) or Benny Bengough (.247) was an easy out. Actually, Manager Huggins manipulated his injury-prone catchers superbly. Bengough was expected to be the first-string backstop, but he was slow in recovering from an arm injury of the previous year and got into just 31 games. As luck would have it, Collins also hurt his throwing arm and played in little more than half the Yanks' games. Grabowski, who was obtained from the White Sox prior to the season, caught in 70 games. With his speed and good arm, Grabowski played well.

Many baseball experts believe this powerful club to be the greatest in the history of the game. While the 1927 dollar admittedly was worth more than today's, the payroll for this dynamic club is worth noting. The average salary was about $11,000, and Ruth's $70,000 boosted this average considerably. A few of the other Yankee salaries included Hall of Famer Pennock's $17,500; Meusel's $13,000; Dugan's $12,000; Hall of Famer Hoyt's $12,000; Hall of Famer Combs' $10,000; Hall of Famer and MVP Gehrig's $8,000; Lazzeri's $8,000; and Koenig's

$7,000. Rookie sensation Wilcy Moore, for all his mound heroics, drew $2,500. And the players earned their salaries. On almost every open date, the team played exhibitions, and in little towns and cities people flocked to see the wondrous Yankees.

Were the 1927 Yankees truly the game's greatest team? The standard by which teams were judged were the NL's great Baltimore Oriole clubs of the 1890s. Uncle Wilbert Robinson, one of the stars of those clubs and the manager of the Brooklyn Dodgers in 1927, was asked during the Yanks' World Series romp how this team would have fared against his old Orioles. "They would have beat our brains out," Robinson candidly replied.

Then and now most people still believe the 1927 Yankees could beat any team's brains out. Their aura has departed the legendary and entered the mystical. In 1963 an academy of 100 sportswriters was asked to name baseball's greatest team. The result: the Yankees of 1927. The 1927 Yanks made the ballots of 84 percent of the academy, followed by the 1929 A's who were listed on 74 percent of the ballots. The Baseball Writers of America in 1969 voted the 1927 Yankees baseball's greatest team ever. Interestingly, the general manager of the 1927 Yankees, Ed Barrow, who along with Jake Ruppert, Huggins, and Paul Krichell built the team, steadfastly refused to name this club the all-time best.

The question of supremacy across time can never be answered with finality, of course, but the record speaks convincingly: 154 games played and 110 of them wins!

1928

The Yankees won their third straight AL pennant, the sixth and last for skipper Miller Huggins, finishing only 2½ games ahead of the improving Philadelphia A's. Early in the season, the Yankees looked like they would walk away with the pennant, but the A's played great ball over the summer.

On July 4, the Yanks held a 12-game lead, the biggest lead on Independence Day by a pennant-winner in AL history. But by September 8 the A's, largely on the strength of a 25-8 record in July, moved into first place, and on September 9, the streaking A's came to Yankee Stadium for a doubleheader. Before an unofficially reported crowd of 85,264, the Yankees swept both ends to retake the lead. The next day behind winning pitcher Hank Johnson and Babe Ruth's eighth-inning two-run HR, the Yanks beat Philadelphia ace Lefty Grove, 5-3, and that ended the pennant race.

Johnson (14-9) came through this season with five important victories against the A's. In fact, the Yankees defeated the A's 16 times in 22 contests, a most important factor in determining the year's AL champion.

It was not until September 28 that the Yanks clinched the flag by beating the Tigers, 11-6, with George Pipgras as the winning pitcher. Pipgras (24-13) was the top Yankee hurler, leading the AL in wins, games started (38) and innings pitched (301). Steady Waite Hoyt (23-7) had another truly spectacular season. The combined record of Hoyt's 1927-28 seasons was a tremendous 45-14! Thirty-four-year-old Herb Pennock (17-6) was ailing late in the season but had a great first half, enjoying his last great Yankee campaign. Johnson, a 22-year-old youngster, rounded out the "big four."

As usual, the club's offensive attack was thunderous as the Yanks led the AL in batting, homers, RBIs, runs, hits, walks and

Left to right: Leo Durocher, Lou Gehrig, Tony Lazzeri, Joe Dugan, Mike Gazella, Gene Robertson, and Mark Koenig, covered the infield for the New York Yankees during the World Series against the St. Louis Cardinals October 1, 1928. (AP/WIDE WORLD PHOTOS)

slugging. It was the sixth consecutive season that the Yanks led the league in home runs. Ruth (.323) was again potent, winning the AL home run title (54) and tying Gehrig (.374) for the AL RBI championship (142). Behind Ruth and Gehrig, the Yanks enjoyed the solid batting of Lazzeri (.332), Koenig (.319) and Combs (.310). Third baseman Joe Dugan (.276), Ruth's great pal, played his last season as a Yankee. Meusel (.297) tallied 113 RBIs and played excellent defense despite an ankle injury.

The Yanks were sixth in the AL in fielding (.968). However, one of the few bright spots in a sagging infield was the able work of utility man Leo Durocher.

This team had strong pitching, resiliency and an explosive offense that could be contained for only so long. Examples of all of these qualities were evident in a July 26 game in Detroit. The Tigers and Yankees were locked in a 1-1 extra-inning pitching duel until the Yankee bats erupted to produce 11 runs in the top of the 12th inning.

One tragic event marred this otherwise happy campaign. Yankee pitcher Urban Shocker, after courageously battling a heart ailment that felled him in the spring, died on September 9. Urban had been ill for some time, but his 18-6 record the previous season tended to shroud the state of his health. Most of the Yankee players were unaware of the seriousness of his physical condition. The team was stunned and deeply saddened by the death of the popular Urban Shocker.

1929

Manager Miller Huggins, suddenly taken ill, died Septebmer 25 at the age of 50. Babe Ruth and the other Yankee players cried when they learned of the death of The Mighty Mite. Huggins' death was the third on the Yankee scene this season. A sudden rainstorm at the Stadium May 19 set off a stampede for the exits. The right field exit jammed; two persons were killed and 62 injured in the crunch.

On the playing field things went badly—the Yankees finished a distant second to Connie Mack's A's—from the season's start to that late-season game in which the Yanks lost to a Cleveland team that scored nine runs after two were out in the ninth. New York's pitching was mediocre.

Only George Pipgras (18-12) and Tom Zachary, who won all 12 of his decisions, could be counted on. Seldom did the Yankees have an easy win (with the exception of a 17-3 victory September 5 over a prisoners' team at Sing Sing). The still-powerful offense led the AL in the home-run category (142) but also led in strikeouts (518), indicating a live-by-the-long-ball, die-by-the-long-ball attitude. Again Ruth (46 HRs, 154 RBIs, .345) was the heart of the lineup. On August 6 and 7, he duplicated a previous feat by cracking grand slams in consecutive games, and on August 11 the Babe hit his 500th major-league homer off Cleveland's Willis Hudlin. Gehrig (35 HRs 126 RBIs), Lazzeri (106 RBIs, .354) and Combs (.345, 202 hits) all

The Yankees put numbers on their uniforms this season, becoming the first big-league club to permanently wear them. Ruth's number "3" and Gehrig's "4" instantly became famous. (Regulars took numbers in accordance with their spot in the batting order.) But the one number that ruled this campaign was 18—the 18 games by which the Yanks trailed Mr. Mack's great A's at the close of the 1929 season.

1930

The Yankees slipped a notch to third place under freshman manager and former Yankee pitching great, Bob Shawkey.

Although the Yanks acquired talented young Red Ruffing (15-5) from the Red Sox, their team ERA was a staggering 4.88, ranking sixth in the AL. In fact, Yankee pitchers allowed 898 runs for the season, the most scored against the Yanks in the club's history. But Yankee hurlers were not alone in their sudden ineffectiveness. Pitchers across the majors were being victimized by a juiced-up baseball. The entire AL hit for a lofty .288! (The rabbit ball was born of the Depression—to keep turnstiles turning, the powers that be decided that baseball had to have more excitement.)

Of the six regular Yankee starters, George Pipgras' 4.11 ERA was the best. Ace Waite Hoyt (2-2), along with shortstop Mark Koenig, went to Detroit early in the season. Lefty Gomez (2-5) made his major-league debut at the age of 21 and showed much promise.

Yankee batters certainly could not be blamed for the Yanks' 86-68 record. This team set Yankee club records for most hits (1683), most triples (110) and highest batting average (.309). Nine Yanks batted over .300, the most in Yankee history, and the team scored more runs (591) on the road than any team in the majors since 1900.

Babe Ruth (153 RBIs, .359) led the AL in homers (49) as usual. He had a torrid June, belting 15 homers to establish a major-league home-run record for that month (Sammy Sosa holds the current record since hitting 20 in 1998). The Babe's season was not without its Ruthian touches. After hitting three homers in a row lefthanded, something he had never before done, Ruth in a May 22 game lightheartedly and unaccountably (and to the crowd's amazement) decided to swing from the right side and struck out! He had a complete game on the mound this season, too, beating the Red Sox on September 28, 9-3.

Lou Gehrig (41 HRs, .379), now in his prime, led the AL in RBIs (174). In one stretch of 10 games Gehrig got at least one RBI per game; 27 RBIs were credited to "Larrupin' Lou" during the spree. Tony Lazzeri (121 RBIs, .303) also produced plenty of punch. In fact, the Yanks led the AL in every major offensive statistic except doubles and stolen bases. The defending World Champion Philadelphia A's felt the full force of Yankee explosiveness in consecutive doubleheaders in June, losing to the New Yorkers by scores of 10-1, 20-13, 10-6, and 11-1. In one of those doubleheaders Ruth and Gehrig each had three home runs on the day, June 22.

But in fielding the team finished sixth in the league. Poor defensive play, especially on the left side, combined with mediocre pitching to prevent the Yanks from challenging the A's for the pennant.

1931

A new Yankee era dawned in 1931 with the hiring of 44-year-old Joe McCarthy as manager. During the previous autumn, the Yankees released unsuspecting Bob Shawkey and replaced him with McCarthy, himself the victim of a Chicago Cubs dismissal a few weeks earlier.

"Marse Joe," a native of the Philadelphia area, was one of the few ML managers who never played ML baseball. But he had gained tremendous respect as a minor-league skipper and a five-year manager in Chicago where he won the 1929 NL pennant. Under McCarthy, New York moved up to second place but once again failed to overtake Philadelphia. The Yanks were not even close, finishing 13½ games behind the powerful Athletics.

The improved Yankee pitching staff finished third in the AL in ERA (4.20, a figure bloated by the still juicy ball that was used). But second-year man Lefty Gomez (21-9, 2.63), "The Gay Castillion," had little trouble with AL hitters, with or without a rabbit ball. He proved to be one of baseball's top pitchers, one of the game's worst hitters (.133) and one of its most lovable people. Lefty and the formidable Red Ruffing (16-14), who was a marvelous hitting pitcher (.330), formed a duo that was destined to dominate the AL throughout the 1930s. The 205-pound Ruffing, who lost several toes in a mining accident, had a humming fastball and a solid bat that could be counted on by McCarthy. Hank Johnson (13-8) and Herb Pennock (11-6) also were big winners.

Lou Gehrig, voted the league MVP by *The Sporting News*, finally caught Babe Ruth in HRs; they tied for the AL lead in that category with 46 apiece. Lou would have had sole possession of the HR crown but for an unusual play at Washington's Griffith Stadium on April 26. Gehrig knocked one into the center field stands with Lyn Lary aboard. As Lary turned second base, he thought he saw the ball being caught (he actually saw the Senator centerfielder catching the ball on the rebound from the seats) and crossed third and went straight for the Yankee dugout. Gehrig, a ground gazer in his HR trot, failed to notice Lary's error, circled the bases and was called out for passing another base runner. As a result, Lou was credited with a triple for his base-running error. Gehrig (211 hits, 163 runs, .341) set the AL single-season RBI record of 184 in a remarkable personal season. From August 28 to September 1, "The Iron Horse" hit homers in six consecutive games. He was particularly deadly in St. Louis, where in 11 games he had nine HRs.

Babe Ruth (163 RBIs, .373) was a HR champion for the sixth year in a row, and at the age of 36 years and 231 days, set the AL record for being the oldest HR leader. It was his final HR title. In one of his classic streaks, the Babe got one or more RBIs in 11 consecutive games.

Six Yankee regulars batted over .300. Hitting stars included shortstop Lyn Lary (.280), who set a Yankee RBI record for shortstops with 107; Earle Combs (.318, 120 runs scored); and Bill Dickey (.327). Two new Yankees played important roles. Future Hall of Famer Joe Sewell (.302), who came to the Yankees after 11 years with Cleveland, scored 102 runs, struck out only eight times and anchored third base. Sewell brought much needed stability to the Yankee infield. The other newcomer was 22-year-old Ben Chapman. Actually, 1931 was Ben's sophomore ML season, but it was the year he emerged as a true

Bill Dickey, Yankee catcher, left, and Tony Lazzeri, second baseman, right, were all set to swing lustily at the Giants' pitcher's offerings when this photo was taken just before the start of the third game of the World Series at Yankee Stadium on October 6, 1936. (AP/WIDE WORLD PHOTOS)

outfield star. Chapman (17 HRs, 122 RBIs, .315) led both leagues in stolen bases with 61—most in the ML's for the period spanning Cobb's 96 in 1915 and Wills' 104 in 1962.

The powerful pinstriped Yankee machine established AL records for most runs scored (1067) and most players (six) scoring 100 or more runs—Gehrig, Ruth, Combs, Chapman, Sewell, and Lary. On August 2, Boston's Wilcy Moore, a former Yankee favorite, shutout the New Yorkers, 1-0. The Yanks would not be blanked for the next 308 games. The Yanks' 1,157 singles established a club record that stood until 1988.

Defensively, Dickey was tops at catcher, playing the entire season (125 games behind the plate) without allowing a passed ball. The Yankee catching corps (Dickey, Art Jorgens and Cy Perkins) was without a single passed ball, a ML record. Dickey also led AL catchers in fielding (.996) and putouts (670).

1932

The Yankees captured their seventh pennant and McCarthy's first, winning 107 games and finishing 13 games ahead of the second-place A's. On Opening Day, the Yankees immediately sent a clear message to the defending AL champion A's when the New Yorkers blasted five home runs against the Philadelphians: the Yanks were planning to take charge. (The five homers set an AL record for Opening Day.) In fact, the Yankees hit a four-bagger in each of their first eight contests (20 HRs were hit over that span), an AL record.

Ruth (41 HRs, 137 RBIs, .341) and Gehrig (34 HRs, 151 RBIs, .349) led the long-ball club that had six players with at least 10 homers (Ruth; Gehrig; Dickey-15; Lazzeri-15; Sewell-11; Chapman-10). In another assault against Philadelphia pitching, on June 3 Gehrig hit four consecutive homers in one game, a feat that only twice has been duplicated in the AL. A month later, on July 9, Chapman hit a pair of inside-the-park homers in one game (at Yankee Stadium) to establish himself as one of only two players to accomplish that rarity. Ironically, the Yankees lost the home-run championship for the first time in 10 years; the A's hit 172 homers, beating the Yanks by 12. Gehrig, Ruth, steady Lazzeri (113 RBIs) and the exciting Chapman (107 RBIs) accounted for 508 RBIs. That was plenty of power.

Combs (.321), Dickey (.310) and Sewell (.272) got on base enough times to keep Yankees forever circling the diamond. Sewell, a handy man with the bat, struck out only three times in 503 at-bats, setting a modern major-league record for fewest strikeouts per at-bat (.010). A major factor in Yankee success was rookie shortstop Frank Crosetti who gave the infield a big boost with solid defensive play. He and Sewell gave New York a strong left side in the infield, a problem area earlier.

This Yankee club led the AL in runs (1002), RBIs (955) and bases on balls (766). In fact, the 766 free passes established a club record. The Yankees never slumped at the plate, playing 155 games without once being shutout, another major-league record. They were especially tough when playing at Yankee Stadium, compiling an incredible 62-15 record at home. They were no pushovers on the road either (45-32).

The tremendous pitching staff made significant contributions to Yankee success. Gomez (24-7) and Ruffing (18-7) between them posted a gleaming 42-14 record. Ruffing led AL pitchers in strikeouts (190) and authored one of the spectacu-

lar individual efforts in baseball history. On August 13, he hit a 10th-inning home run to win his own game, 1-0! Johnny Allen (17-4), a 27-year-old rookie out of North Carolina, and George Pipgras (16-9) rounded out the best pitching staff in the AL (3.98 ERA), while 38-year-old Herb Pennock (9-5) chipped in as a capable fifth starter. In mid-season the Yanks obtained Danny MacFayden from the last-place Red Sox and MacFayden, who was 1-10 for Boston, finished the year with a 7-5 Yankee record.

Although the Yankees were no better than tied for third in the AL in fielding (.969), a good case could be made for the contention that this was the best team ever assembled. No fewer than nine of its members were to be inducted into the Baseball Hall of Fame (Gehrig, Ruth, Combs, Dickey, Sewell, Gomez, Ruffing, Pennock and Lazzeri). At least three others, while not in the Hall, are in the outskirts of Cooperstown (Chapman, Allen and Pipgras). And there never was a more solid and competitive player than Crosetti, the glue of the infield. It was a tough team, too.

After a hard play at the plate on July 6, the usually mild-mannered Bill Dickey took a punch at the Senators' Carl Reynolds, breaking Reynolds' jaw. Dickey drew a severe penalty—a 30-day suspension and a $1,000 fine. In another game with the Senators at Washington's Griffith Stadium, Ben Chapman slid hard at second base, and he and Buddy Myer got into a fight that almost precipitated a riot. As it was, fans poured onto the field swinging at anyone in sight, although their preference was a Yankee player. Uncharacteristically, Ruth sat this one out with Gehrig.

On a more pleasant note, on Memorial Day, the Yankees unveiled the first of their famous monuments in center field, this in memory of Miller Huggins.

1933

The Yankees dropped to second place, finishing seven games behind the Washington Senators. Poor pitching was again the cause of the Yankee demise.

Lefty Gomez (16-10), who this season started and won the first All-Star Game ever played, and Johnny Allen (15-7) were steady, but Red Ruffing had a poor year (9-14), and the other pitchers couldn't make up the difference. Rookie Russ Van Atta (12-4) was a surprise. In his major-league debut on April 25, Van Atta became one of the few players to get four hits in his first big-league game. The season also saw 39-year-old Yankee great, Herb Pennock (7-4) pitch his last Yankee game. The Yankees' best pitched game was hurled by Johnny Allen. On June 4, the A's got a hit off Allen in the first inning, then Johnny held the Mackmen hitless for the remainder of the game, as the Yanks won, 6-0.

Lou Gehrig (32 HRs, 139 RBIs, .334), Tony Lazzeri (18 HRs, 104 RBIs, .294) and Bill Dickey (14 HRs, 97 RBIs, .318) had their normal, productive years, but Babe Ruth was beginning to feel his 38 years. The Babe sagged in all major offensive statistics and lost much of his defensive agility. He was, however, anything but washed up (34 HRs, 103 RBIs, .301) and pitchers preferred to walk him a league-leading 114 times rather than risk a long ball. Babe did hit the first home run in All-Star Game history, but he was clearly not the great player he once was.

Others were getting old, too. Both Joe Sewell and Earle Combs were 34. It was Sewell's last season as a player and

The New York Yankees' Lou Gehrig, left, gets a rare smile from rookie sensation Joe DiMaggio during spring training in St. Petersburg, Fla., March 8, 1936. DiMaggio, called up from the San Francisco Seals, earned a reputation in training camp for very rarely smiling. (AP/WIDE WORLD PHOTOS)

Combs' last season as a regular. The Yankees were still a great hitting team, leading the league in six major offensive statistics, although their streak of 308 consecutive games without being shutout ended on August 3.

It was a team that achieved comebacks such as that of May 27. The White Sox led 11-3 when a 12-run Yankee explosion in the eighth, capped by Bill Dickey's grand slammer, gave New York the win, 15-11.

Yankee fielding was mediocre, finishing third in team defense (.972). One bright spot was Ben Chapman's leading AL outfielders in assists (24). A game played on September 23 demonstrated the Yanks' strengths (hitting) and weaknesses (defense, pitching). The Yankees beat the Red Sox, 16-12, but made seven errors.

Yankee fans were treated to the season's final highlight on October 1, when Ruth took the mound and defeated the Red Sox, 6-5. Naturally, he hit a game-winning homer!

1934

Joe McCarthy's Yankees again finished seven games back in second place, this time behind the Detroit Tigers. The Bronx Bombers were beginning to get the uncomplimentary reputation of being a "great second-place team." All the same, the 1934 edition was one of the more balanced Yankee clubs.

The pitching staff led the AL in ERA (3.75), and the team's fielding average (.973) was the league's third best. The Yanks indeed made fewer errors (157) than any other AL club. Once more the hitting was powerful, but the Yankees led the league in only one offensive category, walks (700). This team set a club record by leaving 1,239 runners on base. Clutch hitting was lacking.

One Yankee who had no responsibility for the inadequacy was Lou Gehrig, winner of *The Sporting News* MVP Award and the first Yankee ever to win the Triple Crown (49 HRs, 165 RBIs, .363). Gehrig hit four grand slams and 30 homers at Yankee Stadium, both club records. For the third time in his career, Lou drove in at least one run in 10 consecutive games. He copped 22 RBIs during that streak.

Although Bill Dickey (.322) and Ben Chapman (.308) hit well, the lineup lacked its usual top to bottom strength. A serious injury sidelined Earle Combs. On July 24, Earle suffered a fractured skull and other injuries when he ran into the centerfield wall in St. Louis while chasing a fly ball. (He never really recovered from this mishap.) Tony Lazzeri had an unusually poor season. Third baseman Jack Saltzgaver, a fine utility player, and Myril Hoag, notwithstanding his 6-for-6 game on June 6, contributed little punch.

Babe Ruth (22 HRs, 84 RBIs, .288) was in his final season, it being apparent that the Yankees' biggest superstar was near the end of the line. One of his last great moments came on July 13 when the Babe hit his 700th home run in Detroit. The next day's headline in *The New York Times:* "Ruth's Record of 700 Home Runs Likely to Stand for All Time in major-leagues."

Ruth and Gehrig played together for 10 years (1925-34) and over the decade combined for 771 home runs, averaging 77 homers per year. They hit homers in the same game on 72 occasions, and they hit back-to-back four-baggers 16 times. Together the Babe and Lou drove in 2,742 runs for a yearly RBI average of 274, these figures, again, for the 10-year period. But the decline in the Ruth side of the duo was obvious; the Yankees badly needed another power hitter to complement Gehrig.

The pitching was great. Yankee hurlers threw four one-hitters (a 154-game AL record). Lefty Gomez had one of the best years (26-5) in Yankee history, leading the AL in wins, winning percentage (.839), innings pitched (282), strikeouts (158), complete games (25), shutouts (6) and ERA (2.33). He was simply remarkable and for the second straight year was picked to start the All-Star Game. Red Ruffing (19-11) pitched well, and rookie Johnny Murphy (14-10, 4 saves) came through as both a starter and a relief pitcher.

The season ended rather sadly on September 24 with Ruth playing his final game at the Stadium. The Babe walked in the first inning and was replaced by a pinch-runner. He played his final game as a Yankee on September 30 and went 0 for 3 with a walk. A great era had come to an end.

1935

Once again the Yankees finished second best in the AL, although they came within three games of the champion Tigers. This team was still a year away from another pennant.

Although Gomez (12-15) fell off dramatically from his form of the previous four seasons, the Yanks still had the best pitching in the league. The New York staff led the AL in both ERA (3.60) and strikeouts (594). Ruffing was the top Yankee winner (16-11) for the first time in five years, followed by Johnny Broaca (15-7), a solid 25-year-old pitcher. Allen (13-6), Murphy (10-5) and Vito Tamulis (10-5) were other consistent winners.

Before the season, the Yanks released Babe Ruth. Ruth, who never cared for Joe McCarthy, had asked Yankee owner Jake Ruppert if he, Ruth, could manage the team. Ruppert steadfastly refused, and Ruth then asked to be set free. The Yanks worked out a deal with the Boston Braves in which Ruth would join the Braves in many capacities. So when the Babe left the Yanks, it was more or less on amicable terms. His departure rendered the club, now Ruthless for the first time since 1919, short on color; home attendance sank to a paltry 657,508, second lowest in Yankee Stadium history.

Gehrig (30 HRs, 119 RBIs, .329) was the only legitimate Yankee power hitter. He led the league in runs scored (125) and walks (132). That was the highest walk total of Gehrig's career—pitchers tended to work around Lou. Earle Combs, known as both "The Kentucky Colonel" and "The Mail Carrier," wrapped up his great career. George Selkirk (11 HRs, 94 RBIs, .312) played Ruth's old rightfield position and performed splendidly. Another youngster, Red Rolfe, became the third baseman and hit .300. This Yankee edition still had power, setting a major-league record for the most solo home runs in a single game—six. This was in a June 1 game with Boston (Dickey hit two, Crosetti one, Chapman one, Selkirk one, and Rolfe one).

This young Yankee club showed real promise. But the team appeared to very much need another slugger to aid Gehrig and also to relieve some of the emotional emptiness that the team and the City of New York felt in Ruth's absence.

1936

Joe DiMaggio, 21, had arrived, and New York's power was now such as to leave the rest of the league floundering in the Yankee wake. The Yanks won the AL pennant by a then-league record 19½ games! In 1998, the Bombers eclipsed their games-ahead mark by finishing 22 games in front of second-place Boston, who had won 92 games.

DiMaggio was exactly the slugger the Yanks needed to become a great team again. Obtained from the San Francisco Seals of the Pacific Coast League, "Joltin' Joe" (29 HRs, 125 RBIs, .323) not only hit the cover off the ball but roamed the huge Stadium outfield like a seasoned pro. Joe's first season started ominously. He badly burned a foot while taking heat treatment in spring training and missed the first 16 games of the season.

Manager Joe McCarthy eased some of the pressure on the heralded youngster by starting him in left field. Six weeks into the season, the Yankees traded Ben Chapman and Joe was shifted to center where he turned in a brilliant rookie performance. Joe showed offensive ability, too. In his very first big-league game he cracked three hits including a triple. For the season, the youngster set AL rookie records for most runs scored (132) and triples (15) in addition to setting the Yankee rookie home run record. In the fifth inning of a June 24 game, Joe came to bat twice and twice cracked home runs.

With another big bat in the lineup, Gehrig's productivity went up sharply (49 HRs, 152 RBIs, .354). Besides leading the AL in slugging (.696), runs (167) and walks (130), "Larrupin' Lou" was the undisputed home run king and was voted the league's MVP by *The Sporting News* and the Baseball Writers. The Cleveland Indians must have dreaded seeing Gehrig. He hit 14 homers off the Indians alone, a major-league record. Gehrig was spectacular, but he was characterized principally by a steadiness both at-bat and on the field.

Reliable second baseman Tony Lazzeri had his best season in three years (14 HRs, 109 RBIs) and George Selkirk (107 RBIs, .308) Rec Rolfe (116 runs, .319), Fran Crosetti (137 runs, 15 HRs) and Bill Dickey (22 HRs, 107 RBIs) all figured big in the attack. Dickey's .362 batting average is the best ever by an ML catcher playing a season minimum of 100 games behind the plate. Even the pitchers hit on this club. Red Ruffing (five HRs, 22 RBIs, .291) on June 17 set a league batting record for pitchers by getting 10 total bases, including two homers.

This Yankee team is the only team in baseball history to have five players who broke the sacred 100 RBI barrier (Gehrig, DiMaggio, Lazzeri, Selkirk, Dickey). The team set major-league records for most total bases (2,703) and most RBIs (995), besides establishing an AL record for most runs scored by a pennant winner (1,065). Also, a Yankee club record for doubles (315) was set. It was eventually broken by the 1997 club that had 325 two-baggers. In one game, the Yankees clobbered the Philadelphia A's, 25-2, scoring the most runs in their history. Chapman reached base safely seven times and Lazzeri hit two grand slam home runs. This May 24 game capped a Lazzeri streak of seven homers in four consecutive games. What a great hitting team!

The Yankees at the same time had the leading pitching staff in the league (4.17 ERA) featuring Ruffing (20-12), Monte Pearson (19-7), acquired from the Indians, and Bump Hadley (14-4). Gomez (13-7) was a winner, and Pat Malone (12-4)

came out of the bullpen to save nine games. Yankee pitchers went the whole season without a balk, an indication of their savvy. Backing these heady pitchers was a strong fielding team that ranked second in the league (.973).

No question, this was one of the greatest baseball teams of all time.

1937

The Yankees captured another AL pennant handily, finishing 13 games ahead of the Tigers. The club's ninth championship was McCarthy's third, but baseball people credited Yankee GM Ed Barrow with being behind much of the New York success. *The Sporting News* voted Barrow baseball's Executive of the Year.

The depth Barrow developed in the Yankee organization was indicated by the way their top farm club, the Newark Bears, won the International League title—by a convincing 25 games! The Bears' record was 109-43, and many felt Newark could finish in the first division of the AL. Barrow had created a wealth of talent (16 of this Newark team's players later toiled in the majors), but his prime concern, the Yankees, were hardly starving for talent. There was, therefore, a logjam of talent.

The Yankees had the AL's best pitching staff (3.65 ERA), which once more was led by Lefty Gomez. Having his best season since 1934, Lefty (21-11) led league pitchers in four categories—wins, strikeouts (194), shutouts (6) and ERA (2.33). He started in the All-Star Game for the fourth time in five years, winning his third Summer Classic without a loss. Red Ruffing (20-7) was an outstanding clutch pitcher and the best right-hander in the league. He and Gomez were the league's only 20-game winners. Johnny Murphy (13-4, 10 saves) was the ace out of the Yankee bullpen. While Yankee starters led the AL in complete games (82), the bullpen led the league in saves (21). And for the fourth year in a row, the Yankee pitching staff led AL teams in fewest hits allowed, an AL record.

"Joltin' Joe" DiMaggio (167 RBIs, .346), now an established American sports hero, led the league in runs scored (151), slugging (.673) and home runs (46)—highest single-season home run total for a right-handed Yankee ever then. He set the then big-league record for the most homers hit in the month of July (15). In 1998, Albert Belle surpassed Joe's total by one to set the new AL standard. Lou Gehrig (37 HRs, 159 RBIs) and Bill Dickey (29 HRs, 133 RBIs) also helped make the Yankees the cream of the league in all power categories. Dickey's 133 RBIs, the AL record for catchers, was helped by consecutive-game grand slams (August 3 and 4). Gehrig, DiMaggio and Dickey formed the most devastating threesome in baseball, knocking in 459 runs. George Selkirk (18 HRs, .328) also produced well, but missed much of the season because of an injury.

The Yankees had the ability to launch late-inning strikes as they showed in a September 8 doubleheader at the Stadium. The Yanks trailed Boston in the second game, 6-1, and with only one out remaining in the ninth, quickly scored five runs to tie, a prelude to Gehrig's three-run homer to hand the Yanks a startling 9-6 victory. And this after the Yankees won the opener on a ninth-inning single by Myril Hoag!

The defense, although a league third (.972), was splendid, especially in the infield with Gehrig at first, Tony Lazzeri at second, Red Rolfe at third and the dependable Frank Crosetti at shortstop. Hoag, Jake Powell and Selkirk played next to

DiMaggio, who was the best centerfielder in the game. The league's leading catcher in putouts (692) and assists (80), Bill Dickey again gave New York an excellent year behind the plate.

On a sad note, Yankee pitcher Bump Hadley beaned the Tigers' great Mickey Cochrane at the Stadium on May 25. The injury nearly killed Cochrane and brought a premature end to his career.

1938

Coasting to their third straight AL pennant, the Yankees finished 9½ games ahead of the archrival Boston Red Sox. Actually, the Yanks nailed down the pennant in August.

Faced with a murderous schedule of 36 games in 31 days, New York produced a 28-8 record for the month. The 28 wins is the AL record for most victories in one month.

The great pitching duo of Red Ruffing (21-7) and Lefty Gomez (18-12) combined for 39 Yankee victories. Ruffing led the circuit in wins. A 20-game winner for the third consecutive year, Ruffing at 34 seemed to get better with age. He had a no-hitter in an August 7 game until the ninth inning when Cleveland's Roy Weatherly doubled with one out. Red won, 7-0. Gomez allowed only three home runs in 239 innings of pitching, fewest homers allowed in AL history for a pitcher with at least 200 innings worked. Ruffing-Gomez anchored the staff, but Monte Pearson (16-7)—he beat Cleveland with a no-hitter on August 27—and Spud Chandler (14-5) were also reliable starters. "Grandma" Murphy (8-2) was the league's best relief pitcher with his rocking-chair style, saving a league-leading 11 contests. This staff led the AL in most of the major pitching statistics, including ERA (3.91), for the fifth consecutive season.

Five Yankees (Joe DiMaggio, Lou Gehrig, Bill Dickey, Joe Gordon, Tommy Henrich) each hit between 22 and 32 home runs. For the 13th consecutive season, Gehrig's runs scored and RBI totals went over 100—AL records. Gehrig (29 HRs, 114 RBIs, .295), DiMaggio (32 HRs, 140 RBIs, .324) and Dickey (27 HRs, 115 RBIs, .313) again led the attack, but the distribution of power was more balanced than the previous season.

Young Henrich (22 HRs, 91 RBIs) played right field and rookie Gordon (25 HRs, 97 RBIs) became the second baseman. Besides adding might to the Yankee attack, Henrich and Gordon were fine defensive players. Third baseman Red Rolfe (.311) would get on base a lot and the sluggers would drive him in. He scored 132 runs to lead the team. Shortstop Frank Crosetti (113 runs) added another dimension to the offense, leading the AL in stolen bases (27). He also established the Yankee record for being hit by pitched balls (15).

It was an exciting team, and on May 30, 81,841 people, officially the largest baseball crowd in Yankee Stadium history, saw New York sweep a doubleheader from the Red Sox. The crowd also saw a brawl erupt between the Yanks' Jake Powell and Red Sox Manager Joe Cronin—a fight for which each combatant was fined and suspended for 10 days.

This Yankee club is another that merits attention in best-team-ever discussions. It was the best team he had ever managed in his long career, said Joe McCarthy. It was the best team he had ever seen in his long association with baseball, said Connie Mack who began as a player in 1886 and managed until 1950. A team with a second baseman (Gordon) belting 25 homers and hitting primarily in the eighth spot had to be something special. If the season had a sad feature, it was the absence of the popular Tony Lazzeri who went to the Cubs before the campaign got underway to make room for Gordon at second base.

New York Yankees' Lou Gehrig, the "Iron horse," wipes away a tear during a sold-out tribute at Yankee Stadium July 4, 1939. Gehrigs' record-breaking career was cut short by neuromuscular disease. (AP/WIDE WORLD PHOTOS, Murray Becker)

1939

Joe McCarthy's Yankees ran away from the field, beating the second-place Red Sox by 17 games, to win a record-breaking fourth straight AL pennant. (The Yankees of 1949-53 would later break the record set by the 1939 club.) This was also a milestone year in the communication community of New York City, being the first season that Yankee home games were regularly broadcast on the radio. In fact, in this season all three New York teams (Yankees, Giants and Dodgers) became the final big-league franchises to broadcast their games. The famous announcer Arch McDonald and his young assistant, Mel Allen, brought Yankee play-by-play over the air waves.

This was a tremendous Yankee team, especially on the road. Away from the Stadium, New York posted the inconceivable record of 54-20 and won all 11 games with the Browns in St. Louis. At the Stadium, the Bronx Bombers were 52-25.

In July the Red Sox came to the Stadium and dramatically swept a five-game series. Following that humbling experience, the Yanks lost to the Tigers for their sixth straight loss. But shortly thereafter, the Yanks won eight games in a row to put the club back on the road to an easy pennant victory.

It was a sad year, however. The Yankee owner of 24 years, Jacob Ruppert, died January 13, and in the spring it was learned that Lou Gehrig, "The Iron Horse," was afflicted with a fatal disease. On May 2 Gehrig took himself out of the Yankee lineup because he felt his lack of hitting was hurting the team (4 for 28, .143), thus ending his playing streak at 2130 consecutive games. Lou never played another baseball game. A few weeks later his fatal illness was diagnosed at the Mayo Clinic.

Yankee Stadium was packed with 61,808 Gehrig fans on July 4 for "Lou Gehrig Appreciation Day" and the crowd heard Lou give a famous, emotional speech, telling the choked-up crowd, "I may have been given a bad break, but I have an awful lot to live for. With all this, I consider myself the luckiest man on the face of the earth." The Stadium crowd chanted, "We love you, Lou." Actually, "Gehrig Day" was the first event now known as "Old Timers' Day."

Returning to salute Lou were teammates from the great 1927 Yankees, including Babe Ruth, Waite Hoyt, Herb Pennock, Earle Combs, Bob Meusel, Bob Shawkey, Tony Lazzeri, Joe Dugan, Mark Koenig, George Pipgras, Benny Bengough and Art Fletcher, a Yankee coach in 1939. Other former Yankees present were Everett Scott, whose consecutive-game playing record was broken by Lou; Wally Pipp, whom Lou replaced at first base; and Wally Schang, the former Yankee catcher. Such notables as New York City Mayor LaGuardia, former mayor Jimmy Walker, politician Jim Farley and sportswriter Dan Daniel all gave short speeches at the "Gehrig Day" ceremonies. And, of course, Mom and Pop Gehrig and Lou's wife Eleanor were faithfully in attendance. Gehrig, the ultimate team player, remained in the Yankee dugout and traveled with the club for the rest of the season.

Even without Gehrig in the lineup, this was a powerful team. On June 28 the Yanks blasted eight homers and made 53 total bases, both Yankee records, against the Philadelphia A's in the first game of a doubleheader, winning 23-2. Lefty Gomez, supported by five more home runs and 16 hits, pitched a shutout in the second game to win, 10-0. For the day, the Yankees had 13 homers, 33 runs and 43 hits! The A's once again were to take abuse from the Yanks on August 13 when New York won 21-0! And on July 26 against the Browns, with Bill Dickey

hitting three consecutive home runs, the Yanks scored in EVERY INNING for a 14-1 rout. This Yankee team was an offensive machine.

Joe DiMaggio (30 HRs, 126 RBIs) won the AL batting championship (.381) and was voted the MVP of the league by both the Baseball Writers and *The Sporting News*. The latter also picked Joe as the major-league Player of the Year. All the Yankee starters had superb seasons. Red Rolfe (.329) led the league in runs (139), hits (213) and doubles (46). From August 9-25, Red reached home plate at least once in 18 consecutive games, scoring 30 runs in all. A remarkable record! A 22-year-old rookie named Charlie Keller (11 HRs, 83 RBIs, .334) cracked the lineup with his great bat. Joe Gordon (28 HRs, 111 RBIs), Bill Dickey (24 HRs, 105 RBIs) and George Selkirk (21 HRs, 101 RBIs) supplied amazing punch. Babe Dahlgren (87 RBIs) played a capable first base, but the shoes of Lou Gehrig were impossible to fill.

Red Ruffing was 21-7 for the second straight season, making him a 20-game winner for the fourth year in a row. Ruffing was consistently sensational. Lefty Gomez (12-8) was bothered by a bad arm that limited his action, but many others picked up the slack. This staff was deep. Bump Hadley (12-6) and Monte Pearson (12-5) were both dependable starters, while Johnny Murphy (3-6) again led the AL in saves (19). A 28-year-old rookie from the deep south, Atley Donald (13-3), set an AL rookie record by winning 12 consecutive games between May 9, June 25. The Yankees' seventh starter, Steve Sundra (11-1) posted the second-best club winning percentage (.917) ever for pitchers with at least 10 decisions. The mound staff had great fielding support.

Dickey (.989), Crosetti (.968) and Selkirk (.989) all were the AL fielding leaders at their positions. In fact, the Yankee team led the league in fielding (.978) and made the fewest errors (126).

In summary, this great team led the league in fielding, pitching (3.31 ERA) and such batting categories as home runs (166) and RBIs (903). The Yankees led the AL in five major batting categories (HRs, RBIs, slugging avg., walks and runs scored) and six important pitching statistics (ERA, wins, winning percentage, saves, complete games and shutouts). It was the fourth year in succession that the Yankees led the league in runs scored and the eighth time in the decade! And it was the sixth straight year that Yankee pitchers led the circuit in ERA, an AL record, and the seventh year in a row that New York hurlers paced the league in fewest hit batsmen, another AL record.

The 1939 season simply climaxed a decade of total Yankee dominance. The lowly Browns finished an AL record 64½ games behind the Yankees this season.

There were also a few "firsts" during the season. The Yanks played a night game at Shibe Park against the Philadelphia A's—their first under the lights. Yankee Stadium hosted its first All-Star Game before 62,892 fans who saw the AL win, 3-1. Ruffing started the game, and the crowd thrilled to a DiMaggio home run.

One of the weirdest games of the season was played at Boston's Fenway Park on September 3. It was the second game of a doubleheader, and the Yanks took the lead late in the game with the 6:30 Sunday curfew rapidly approaching. The Yanks tried to make outs; the Red Sox stalled. Finally, Sox Manager Joe Cronin charged the field and protested that the Yankees were making deliberate outs. When umpire Cal Hubbard ruled that the Yanks were within the rules of baseball, Red Sox fans decorated the playing field with garbage. It was clear that the game could not continue, and New York was awarded the win by forfeit.

A footnote to this incredible season: On April 20, a slim youngster named Ted Williams, playing for Boston, fanned twice facing Yankee ace Ruffing. In his third trip to the plate, Williams cracked a long double to the furthest reaches of Yankee Stadium's right-center field. It was the kid's first big-league hit.

1940

The Yankees' four-year AL reign ended. New York finished in third place, yet only two games behind the pennant-winning Detroit Tigers.

Although the Yankee pitching staff remained creditable, it was only the third best staff (3.89 ERA) in the league. The season marked the first since 1933 that Yankee pitching did not lead the league in ERA, a slip in quality that damaged New York's pennant hopes. Only Red Ruffing (15-12) and 22-year-old Marius Russo (14-8) won more than nine games. Pitching star Lefty Gomez (3-3) was inactive most of the season, pitching in only nine games because of a sore arm. What really hurt the team was the fact that Ruffing and Gomez, the two pitching aces, together won 15 fewer games than they had the previous season. Ernie Bonham (9-3, 1.90 ERA) proved a promising 26-year-old rookie, however.

Most of the hitting was provided by Joe DiMaggio (31 HRs, 133 RBIs), Joe Gordon (30 HRs, 103 RBIs), and Charlie Keller (21 HRs, 93 RBIs), the three sluggers who finished 1-2-3 on the team in homers and RBIs. DiMaggio (.352), who knocked in nine runs in a doubleheader sweep of the Browns on July 13, won his second consecutive AL batting championship and bossed center field with his customary greatness. But most of the other starters experienced off-years.

The team batting average fell to .259 from a mark of .287 in 1939. The only batting category in which the Yanks led the AL was homers (155). In fielding, the club finished a league second (.975).

The Yanks got off to a miserable start and spent two weeks of May in last place. As late as early August, the Yanks were merely a .500 team. But then New York won 16 of 19 games and crept close to Detroit. When the Bronx Bombers won the first game of a doubleheader at Cleveland on September 11, they momentarily moved into first place. But they lost the second game and fell back in the standings.

The Yankees continued to feast on the St. Louis Browns. On June 15, the Yanks won their 13th consecutive game at St. Louis, an AL road record. Philadelphia's pitcher, Johnny Babich, however, feasted on the Yanks to the tune of five victories, and probably single-handedly deprived the Yanks of the pennant.

Many felt the pennant still could have been won if Bonham had been recalled from the Kansas City farm club earlier than he was (in early August). Meanwhile, the health of Lou Gehrig, who was unable to be a member of the club this year, continued to worsen.

1941

Reestablishing their league preeminence, the Yankees breezed to their 12th pennant, the sixth under Manager Joe McCarthy, finishing 17 games in front of the Red Sox. Thanks in part to a 14-game winning streak (June 28—July 13), the Yanks clinched the pennant on September 4, earliest date in major-league history (before the leagues were split into divisions). At that point, the Yanks had a phenomenal record (91-45, .669) and finished 10-8 in meaningless games. New York played .862 ball (25-4) in July, the highest winning percentage for one month in league history.

Yankee GM Ed Barrow's deeds were rewarded by *The Sporting News* which named him major-league Executive of the Year. It was Barrow who built this memorable club. But the 1941 season will forever be remembered as the year Joe DiMaggio (30 HRs, 125 RBIs, .357) hit safely in 56 consecutive games.

The fantastic streak began on May 15 on a day the Yanks dropped their eighth game in ten contests, losing 13-1. The headline in the *New York Journal-American* said, "Yank Attack Weakest in Years." But during Joe's hitting streak, the Yankees were revived. His success meant Yankee success. The streak lasted until the Indians snapped it on July 17 in Cleveland, and it took two great plays by third baseman Ken Keltner to do it.

For six weeks the streak had created tremendous national attention, and basically because of the accomplishment and what it meant to the Yanks, DiMaggio was named MVP by both the Baseball Writers (edging out Ted Williams who had hit .406) and *The Sporting News*. The Associated Press Male Athlete of the Year Award also went to Joe. His incredible streak, and the unbelievable national publicity that resulted, created no jealousies on the Yankee team. In fact, Joe's Yankee teammates reveled in the excitement, cheered for Joe, and in a few instances helped keep the streak going. Late in the summer, Bill Dickey suggested to George Selkirk, Johnny Murphy, and Tom Henrich that the team do something special for Joe. The entire team pitched in and bought DiMaggio a sterling silver cigar humidor with an inscription that read, "Presented to Joe DiMaggio by his fellow players on the New York Yankees to express their admiration for his consecutive-game hitting record, 1941." Beneath the inscription were engraved the autographs of the Yankee team.

The Yanks gave the present to Joe at a surprise party (even Lefty Gomez kept the secret) at the Shoreham Hotel while the club was in Washington. It was a party that warmed DiMaggio and brought the team even closer together.

Supplying most of the Yankee power this season along with DiMaggio were Keller (33 HRs, 122 RBIs), Henrich (31 HRs, 85 RBIs) and Gordon (24 HRs, 87 RBIs). The Yankees set a club record by hitting at least one homer in 25 consecutive games, 40 homers in all. Rookie Phil Rizzuto (.307) became the Yankee shortstop at the age of 23 and did an excellent job, while Johnny Sturm, in his only major-league season, played first base. Bill Dickey (71 RBIs, .284), as always, excelled behind the plate, leading AL catchers in fielding (.994) for the fourth time in his career. Establishing a major-league record, Dickey caught at least 100 games (104) for the 13th straight season.

This was an excellent fielding club notwithstanding the fact it ranked only third in the AL (.973). New York led the league in turning double plays (196), and during one stretch the

NEW YORK YANKEES
1941
WORLD CHAMPIONS

Edw. G. Barrow
Pres.

Geo. E. Ruppert
Vice-Pres.

Top row (left to right)—Joe Gordon; Red Ruffing; Joe Di Maggio; Ken Silvestri; Lefty Gomez; Paul Schrieber; Twink Selkirk; Charlie Stanceau; Steve Peek; Red Rolfe.
Center row (left to right)—Marius Russo; Charlie Keller; Buddy Rosar; Tom Henrich; Bill Dickey; Johnny Murphy; Red Branch; John Sturm; Jerry Priddy; Frank Crosetti; Doc Painter.
Front Row (left to right)—Frenchy Bordergary; Phil Rizzuto; Spud Chandler; John Schulte; Art Fletcher; Manager Joe McCarthy; Earl Combs; Atley Donald; Marvin Breuer; Tiny Bonham; Mascot Tim Sullivan (center)

'41 champions

team made at least one double play in each of 18 straight games. Rizzuto and Gordon were a fine team around second base.

The Yankee pitching staff recorded the second best ERA (3.53) in the AL, and the staff was once again led by the duo of Gomez (15-5) and Ruffing (15-6). Ruffing, besides being a clutch performer, was an excellent hitter with a .303 average. He also led AL pitchers in fielding (1.000), proving that he was a great all-round athlete. A healthy Gomez was an important factor in the Yankee resurrection and, as always, contributed a memorable moment that was more than just a little odd; on August 1, Lefty managed to shutout the St. Louis Browns although he walked 11 batters, a ML record. Solid lefthander Marius Russo (14-10), right-hander Spud Chandler (10-4) and reliever Johnny Murphy (8-3) all pitched well. Russo on June 26 pitched a one-hitter against the Browns, allowing only a seventh-inning home run to George McQuinn, and won the game, 4-1. Murphy led the league in saves (15), again proving his immense value to the team. Johnny was the best known and most respected relief pitcher of his time.

It was a successful year—and a year of great loss. On June 2, amyotrophic lateral sclerosis claimed the life of Lou Gehrig. McCarthy and Dickey left the Yankee team in Detroit and returned to New York for Gehrig's funeral.

1942

The Yankees captured their 13th pennant in a suspense-lacking campaign, finishing nine games in front of the second place Red Sox. An established cast of Yankee heroes again excelled.

The mound corps led the AL in most pitching categories including ERA (2.91). The pitching ranked among the best in Yankee history. Ernie "Tiny" Bonham (21-5) had an ERA of 2.27; of the top six starters, Ruffing had the highest ERA with 3.21! Agreeable won-loss records were posted by Spud Chandler (16-5), Hank Borowy (15-4), Red Ruffing (14-7), and Atley Donald (11-3). That's some pitching!

Unhappily, it was the last season for the famed, classy, righty-lefty combination of Ruffing and Lefty Gomez. Ruffing had a big year in his last full season before joining the military (he would appear again in 1945 and 1946 in a total of 19 games) but 1942 was a sunset season for Gomez (6-4) who started in only 13 games. (Gomez in 1943 pitched one game for Washington.) Johnny Murphy led the AL in saves (11) for the fourth time in five seasons.

The Yanks' star this season was second baseman Joe Gordon (18 HRs, 103 RBIs, .322) who was voted the league's MVP by both the Baseball Writers and *The Sporting News*. Joe DiMaggio (21 HRs, 114 RBIs) and Charlie Keller (26 HRs, 108 RBIs) added power, and although New York hit 43 fewer home runs than in the previous season, the team still led the AL in homers (108), runs (801) and RBIs (744). Tommy Henrich (13 HRs), Phil Rizzuto (.284) and Bill Dickey (.295) all contributed to the

Yankee cause. Buddy Hassett (.284), in his only full Yankee season, gave Manager Joe McCarthy a fine performance at first base, while Frank Crosetti (.242) and Red Rolfe (.219) shared the duties at third base. This was the last season as a player for Rolfe, an all-time Yankee great.

The outstanding Yankee defense led the AL in fielding (.976), double plays (190), and had the fewest errors (142). Against the Philadelphia A's on August 14, the Yankees turned seven double plays, an AL record. If a baseball team's heart is supposed to be judged by its personnel up the middle—and those personnel are Dickey, Joe Gordon, Phil Rizzuto and DiMaggio—then the Yankees had a heart of gold.

This was the first season of baseball during America's involvement in World War II, and Yankee personnel were already affected. Before the season, Johnny Sturm joined the Air Corps and in the last month of the season, Henrich joined the Coast Guard. There was some debate whether the season would be played in the first place. A little more than a month after the Japanese attack on Pearl Harbor, President Roosevelt stated on January 15, 1942, "I honestly feel it would be best for the country to keep baseball going. These players are a definite recreational asset to their fellow citizens—and that, in my judgment, is thoroughly worthwhile."

1943

After a spring training stint in Asbury Park, N.J. (to conserve rail transport for the war effort), the Yankees went on to win their 14th AL pennant, Joe McCarthy's eighth and the club's seventh in eight seasons, pulling away from Washington in late summer to finish 13½ games ahead of the Senators.

New York won without Joe DiMaggio, Phil Rizzuto, Tommy Henrich, Buddy Hassett and Red Ruffing, all of whom were in the military. Setting a league record for a 154-game season, the Yankees won 38 games by one run (while losing 23 games by the same margin). The club may have lost some of its stars but not its ability to win close games. Perhaps it was merely the fact that the Yanks KNEW how to win that sustained them.

Spud Chandler (20-4) led the AL in five pitching categories and compiled the lowest ERA (1.64) in Yankee history. He became the first Yankee pitcher to be named the league's MVP, winning both *The Sporting News'* and the Baseball Writers' MVP Awards. *The Sporting News* also voted Chandler the major-league Player of the Year. Ernie Bonham (15-8), Hank Borowy (14-9), Butch Wensloff (13-11) and Johnny Murphy (12-4, 8 saves) all helped the club lead the league in ERA (2.93).

Behind this outstanding pitching staff was a solid defensive club (.974) notwithstanding its ranking fourth in the league in fielding.

The hitting was weakened by the loss of key players to the war effort, a circumstance shared throughout the league. Charlie Keller (31 HRs, 86 RBIs), Joe Gordon (17 HRs) and Nick Etten (14 HRs), new first baseman and club leader in RBIs (107), supplied the power. Veteran Frank Crosetti (.233) returned to his old shortstop position in Rizzuto's absence, although "The Crow" was suspended for the first 30 days of the season (along with being fined $250) for pushing umpire Bill Summers in Game 3 of the 1942 World Series. Bud Metheny (.261) and Johnny Lindell (.245) patrolled the outfield along with Keller. Rookie third baseman Billy Johnson (94 RBIs)

played in every Yankee game, making valuable contributions at the plate and in the field. The great Bill Dickey, now 36, played his last season as a regular and hit a blistering .351! Although the Yankees dropped off from the previous season in almost all batting categories, they still managed to lead the talent-starved AL in six categories: runs, triples, home runs, RBIs, bases on balls, and slugging average. Because of blackout restrictions, the Yanks played no night games on the road (there were no lights at the Stadium). The Yankees drew a record-low season attendance at Yankee Stadium in its then 20-year history, attracting but 645,006 fans.

1944

With many of the Yankees in the military, and after a disconcerting spring training camp at Atlantic City, N.J., the Yanks dropped to third place, finishing six games behind the champion St. Louis Browns. The Yankees did have a say in who was the AL pennant winner.

In the final series of the year, the Browns capped the season by sweeping four in a row from the Yankees. The Browns and Tigers were tied going into the final day of the season, October 1, and the Browns beat the Yanks at Sportsman's Park behind Sig Jakucki (his last ML victory) while the Tigers lost. The Browns had won their only pennant—ever.

All in all, it was a season that seemed something of a shadow of a normal campaign, so preoccupied was the public with the war effort. And the Yanks were hit hard by military service, playing the season without such stars as Joe DiMaggio, Tommy Henrich, George Selkirk, Charlie Keller, Bill Dickey, Joe Gordon, Phil Rizzuto, Billy Johnson, Red Ruffing, Spud Chandler, Marius Russo, and many others.

The war-curtailed offense was led by Nick Etten (22 HRs—tops in the league, 91 RBIs, .293). Outfielder Johnny Lindell (18 HRs, 103 RBIs, .300), a converted pitcher, became an excellent hitter. In an August 17 game, Lindell cracked four consecutive doubles. The only other long-ball threat was outfielder Bud Metheny (14 HRs, 67 RBIs). A third outfielder, 35-year-old Hersh Martin, a journeyman with a good stroke, batted .302. Exciting and popular Snuffy Stirnweiss (.319) led the AL in steals (55), hits (205), triples (16) and runs (125), besides being the league's top defensive second baseman (.982).

Yankee pitching was only fourth best in the AL (3.39 ERA), and its decline contributed to the so-so New York record (83-71). Hank Borowy (17-12), Atley Donald (13-10), Monk Dubiel (13-13) and Ernie Bonham (12-9) were first-rate starters but behind them was little depth. The retirement of Johnny Murphy weakened the bullpen, the Yanks having a total of only 13 saves. Defensively, the team was still spectacular, leading the AL in fielding (.974) and making the fewest errors (156).

1945

With the war still raging, Larry MacPhail, Dan Topping and Del Webb, who on January 26 bought the Yankees from the heirs of Jacob Ruppert, were already preparing for the progressive postwar era. For the present, the Yankee team was only a skeleton of its former self, its best personnel wearing khaki rather than pinstripes.

The fourth-place finish was the worst for the Yankees since 1925.

Bill Bevens (13-9) led a pitching staff that ranked fifth in the league (3.45 ERA). Yankee games were won by no less than 11 other pitchers, including Monk Dubiel (10-9) and Hank Borowy (10-5). Unwisely dealt to the Cubs in mid-season, Borowy was to go 11-2 the rest of the year, helping Chicago win the NL pennant. Pitcher Jim Turner (3-4) led the AL in saves (10) at the age of 41. The pitchers did not receive much support in the field, the Yanks ranking only a league sixth in defense (.971).

Nick Etten (18 HRs, .285) led the AL in RBIs (111) but the only other Yankee to do much with the bat was Snuffy Stirnweiss. In fact, the exciting Stirnweiss led the league in seven offensive categories: at-bats (632), runs (107), hits (195), triples (22), stolen bases (33), batting (.309), and slugging (.476). He was the league's best all-round offensive threat. In spite of a power shortage (compared with previous seasons), the 1945 Yankees still managed to lead the AL in homers (93), slugging (.373), runs (676), RBIs (639) and walks (618). Manager Joe McCarthy, upset all year over his club's performance, was occasionally ill during the season and was unable to manage for a short period of time, turning the reins over to his trusted aide and coach, Art Fletcher. The Yankees spent another unsettling spring training camp at Atlantic City where neither the weather nor the facilities were as accommodating as conditions and circumstances in Florida.

1946

Even with their regulars back from the Armed Forces, the Yankees could do no better than a third-place finish, ending up 17 games behind the pennant-winning Red Sox.

After 15 seasons in which he won eight AL pennants and seven World Championships, the managerial tenure of Joe McCarthy came to an abrupt end on May 24.

Proud and increasingly despondent over Yankee failures, McCarthy suffered a mild breakdown and went home to rest. First Bill Dickey and then Johnny Neun took over as manager.

The Yankees on May 28 played their first night game at Yankee Stadium, losing to the Washington Senators, 2-1. The newly installed Stadium lights were a big plus factor in the Yanks' home attendance of 2,265,512 for the season. It was the first time the Yankees drew over one million fans since 1930, the excitement beginning on April 19, Opening Day, when 54,826 people set a Yankee Stadium Opening Day record. When some 66,000 turned out for a doubleheader with Cleveland, the Yanks topped the one-million attendance mark at the earliest date in the majors up to that time—June 9.

Spud Chandler (20-8) returned from the military to post a 2.10 ERA. That this 38-year-old pitcher could be so effective after nearly three years absence was remarkable. Before 69,107 fans at the Stadium on July 1, Chandler had a no-hitter going until Bobby Doerr singled for the Red Sox with one out in the ninth. Chandler won, 2-1. Bill Bevens (16-13) and Randy Gumpert (11-3) were the only other Yankee pitchers to win more than nine games. The Yankees used 22 pitchers and 46 players overall during the season, the latter a then-Yankee record. The Yankee record currently for players used during a

season is 50 in 1989. Johnny "Grandma" Murphy (4-2) came out of retirement at the age of 37 to save seven games.

Joe DiMaggio (25 HRs, 95 RBIs), Charlie Keller (30 HRs, 101 RBIs), and Tommy Henrich (19 HRs, 83 RBIs) all returned to their familiar outfield positions, combining for 74 homers and 279 RBIs. Nick Etten remained at first base, Joe Gordon came back to second, and Phil Rizzuto resumed play at shortstop. Snuffy Stirnweiss and Billy Johnson shared the third base job. None of the infielders hit up to his potential.

The defense was much improved, however, especially in the infield where the Yanks turned 174 double plays, tops in the AL. As a team, New York tied for second in fielding (.975). Aaron Robinson was competent behind the plate and knocked the cover off the ball (16 HRs, .297), while Bill Dickey, Gus Niarhos, Ken Silvestri and 21-year-old Yogi Berra also caught during the season.

Although the Yankees led the AL in homers (136), the returning veterans appeared to be rusty. They compiled a team batting average of only .248, second worst in the league. Evidence of the poor hitting surfaced early in the season. On April 30, Bob Feller of the Indians hurled a no-hitter against the Yankees, the first no-hitter pitched against New York since 1919.

This was a season of two Yankee firsts, both happening in May. Besides playing the first Yankee Stadium game under the lights, the Yanks also in May made their first road trip by air. In fact, the Yanks were the first team in baseball to travel exclusively by air. Several Yankee players, however, preferred different modes of transportation and were permitted to travel by surface means.

1947

The Yankees under Bucky Harris won their first pennant in four years, finishing 12 games ahead of Detroit. After moving into first place on June 19, the Yanks were never threatened.

The Yanks continued to draw huge crowds at home, setting a club record May 26 when 74,747 fans packed into the Stadium for a night game. For the season, 2,178,937 fans passed through the Stadium turnstiles, including 60,000 who came to cheer Babe Ruth on "Babe Ruth Day" in April. Larry MacPhail arranged for the final game of the season to be a benefit for the Babe Ruth Foundation Inc., and the Yanks and A's of Connie Mack turned all proceeds over to the Foundation. Many great old players were in attendance, and the Babe was moved by the gesture. Also this year, the first official Yankee Stadium Old Timers' Day was held. The Yankees flew in a four-engine C-54 transport this season and had several near-tragic accidents, convincing the majority of Yankee players that flying was for the birds. In fact, the Yanks had more difficulty getting to games than actually playing them.

The Yankees probably assured themselves of the pennant with a 19-game winning streak (an AL record) that began June 29. Thirteen of the wins came on the road. The Tigers' Fred Hutchinson shutout the Yanks, 2-0, to end the streak on July 18.

In an important deal before the season's start, Joe Gordon (and Eddie Bockman) went to Cleveland for pitcher Allie Reynolds. As a Yankee Reynolds (19-8) led the AL in winning percentage (.704). He was the star of a pitching staff that led the league with an ERA of 3.39. Rookie Spec Shea (14-5) was consistent and Spud Chandler (9-5) had the league's best ERA (2.46). However, both Shea and Chandler were disabled during the campaign with arm trouble.

But in July, veteran traveler Bobo Newsom was acquired from the Senators and helped the Yanks in the season's second half with a 7-5 record and 2.79 ERA. Also helpful was Vic Raschi (7-2) who was recalled from the minors. Joe Page (14-8), the bullpen successor to Johnny Murphy, led the AL in saves (17).

Joe DiMaggio, now 32, had another fine season both with the bat (20 HRs, 97 RBIs, .315) and the glove (.997), leading AL outfielders in fielding. In spite of Ted Williams' winning of the Triple Crown, DiMaggio was voted the AL's MVP and *Sport* magazine picked Joe for the first "Champion of the Year" Award. Helping DiMaggio with the run production were Tommy Henrich (16 HRs, 98 RBIs), Billy Johnson (95 RBIs, .285), Johnny Lindell (11 HRs, 67 RBIs), Yogi Berra (11 HRs, .280) and George McQuinn (80 RBIs, .304). Signed before the season as a free agent, the 38-year-old McQuinn was a valuable addition to the team and an able first baseman. Charlie Keller, out with a back injury most of the season, hit 13 home runs in only 151 at-bats. New York led the AL in batting (.271), slugging (.407), RBIs (746), runs (794), hits (1439), triples (72) and home runs (115). It was the 12th consecutive season that the Yankees led the league in homers.

And this was a tremendous defensive club, finishing second in the AL in fielding (.981). The infield of McQuinn, Snuffy Stirnweiss, Phil Rizzuto, and Johnson was a fine one. DiMaggio and Henrich were excellent outfielders, while Aaron Robinson and Berra handled the catching chores. Berra was

improving rapidly as a backstop. New York committed only 109 errors, then the fewest in Yankee history. The current club record for fewest errors in a campaign is 91 by the 1996 World Champion Bombers.

A footnote: this was the year in which the crosstown Yankee-Dodger rivalry, already heated up by the 1941 World Series, really intensified. Respected Dodger coach Charlie Dressen was lured to the Yankees by Larry MacPhail, who used to run the Dodgers. This embittered the Dodgers' Branch Rickey and Leo Durocher who accused MacPhail of entertaining gamblers at a March Dodger-Yankee exhibition game in Havana. Durocher and his ghostwriter, Harold Parrott, used Durocher's column in the *Brooklyn Eagle* for anti-Yankee propaganda. MacPhail denied having gambling connections and filed a libel action against Durocher.

Commissioner Chandler was forced to intervene and suspended Durocher for the season "for conduct detrimental to baseball." Parrott was fined $5,000 and Dressen was suspended for 30 days for "violating a verbal agreement to coach with Brooklyn." Both the Dodgers and Yankees were fined $2,000 for "engaging in public feuding." The dispute lay just below the surface of the titanic field struggles ahead for the Yankees and Brooklyn Dodgers in the World Series of this year, 1949, 1952, 1953, 1955 and 1956.

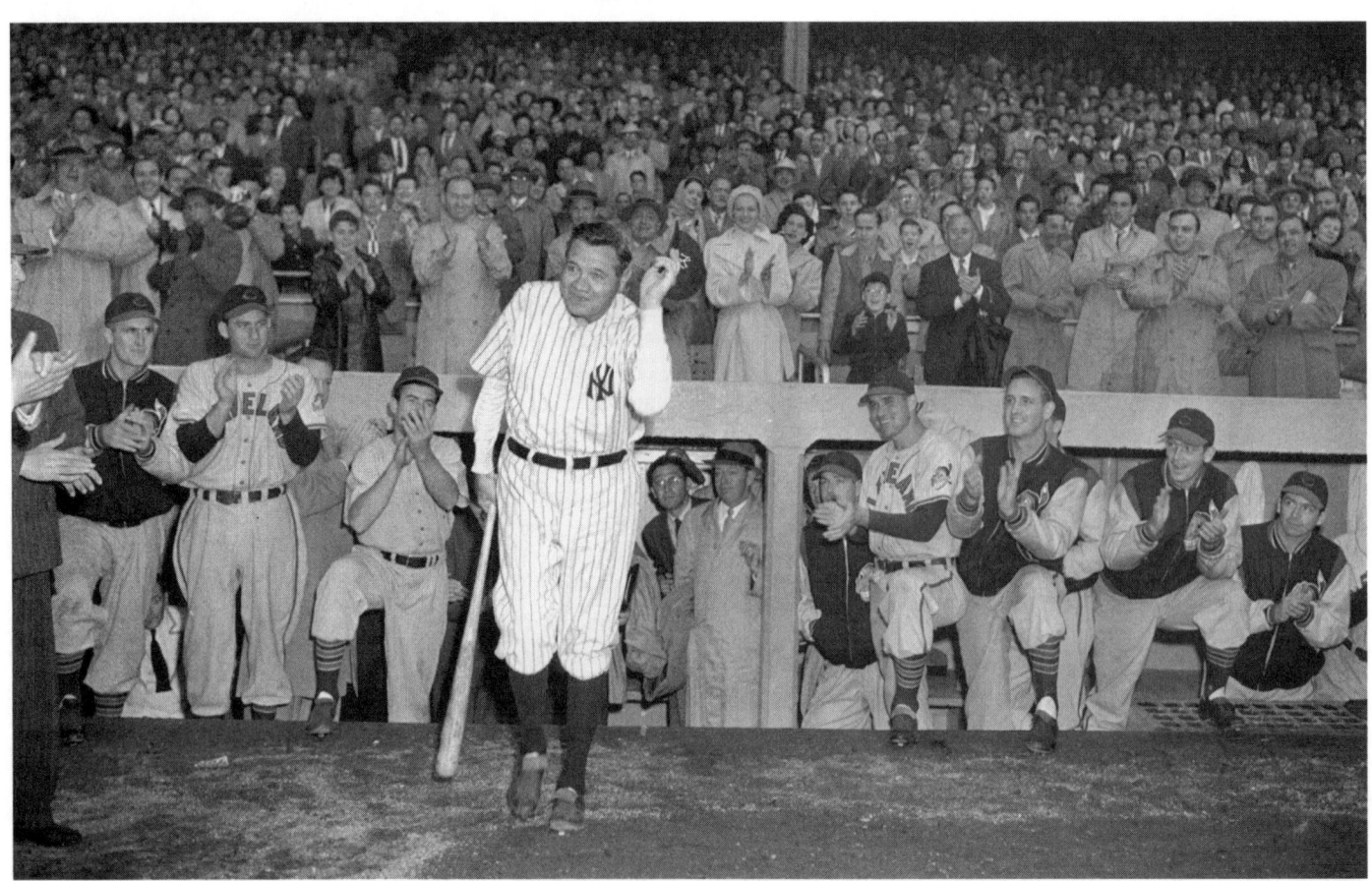

Babe Ruth, wearing his famous No. 3 Yankee uniform, doffs his cap as he comes out of the Cleveland Indians' dugout at Yankee Stadium, New York, June 13, 1948 to participate in ceremonies marking the 25th anniversary of the opening of Yankee Stadium and the retirement of Ruth's No. 3 for all time. Fans stand in the background applauding and cheering. (AP/WIDE WORLD PHOTOS)

1948

When the Yankees lost to the Red Sox on the next-to-last day of the season, they were eliminated from the pennant race. Boston then put themselves into a playoff game with Cleveland by defeating the Yanks on the season's final day. Thus, the Yanks finished third, but only 2½ games behind the pennant winners, the Cleveland Indians who beat the Red Sox in the playoff for the AL pennant.

Yankee Stadium hosted 2,373,901 baseball-hungry spectators this season, establishing a Yankee home attendance record that was not broken until 1979.

The Yanks had another great pitching staff, although it came up second best to the Indians. Vic Raschi (19-8), Ed Lopat (17-11), obtained from the White Sox before the season started, and Allie Reynolds (16-7) formed the "big three." Bullpen stopper Joe Page (7-8) saved 16 games and led the AL in game appearances (55).

On defense, however, the Yankees were only fourth best in the league (.979) and had the fewest assists (1493) in Yankee history. But second baseman Snuffy Stirnweiss turned in the all-time highest club fielding average (.993) at his position.

Club leader Joe DiMaggio (.320) was both the AL home-run king (39) and the league's RBI champ (155), although Joltin' Joe played most of the season with a painful heel injury. "Old Reliable" Tommy Henrich (25 HRs, 100 RBIs, .308) had another outstanding season, hitting four grand-slam home runs, tying a club record, on a team that belted seven grand slammers, also a club record. Catcher-outfielder Yogi Berra (14 HRs, 98 RBIs, .305) emerged as one of the best hitters in the league, and Billy Johnson (.294) and Johnny Lindell (.317) also figured importantly in the Yankee offense. Despite another disabling injury, this time to his hand (the previous season he slipped a disk), Charlie Keller (83 games) managed to hit consecutive pinch-hit homers on September 12 and 14.

New York had several promising young prospects on the club who were edging up to the kind of attention Berra was winning. They were Bobby Brown, 23; Hank Bauer and Joe Collins, both 25; and Cliff Mapes, 26.

Sadly, it was the final year of Babe Ruth's life. On June 13, the Yanks gave a gravely ill Ruth another "day" at the Stadium, and the Babe spoke his "farewell speech" before 49,641 fans who saw the Yankees retire Babe's No. 3 uniform. Ruth died of throat cancer on August 16. More than 100,000 people paid their respects to Babe as he lay in state at Yankee Stadium. And 6,500 people jammed into St. Patrick's Cathedral in Manhattan for Babe Ruth's funeral service.

Second-year Manager Bucky Harris, who had trouble getting along with Yankee GM George Weiss, was fired after the season ended, and on October 12 Casey Stengel was named as his surprise replacement.

1949

The Yankees began a new era under first-year field boss Casey Stengel by taking the pennant in a race that went down to the wire. The hiring of Stengel appeared to be a gamble; Casey was colorful, to be sure, but was he able? Casey, who turned 59 in July, proved the doubters wrong by managing superbly.

Behind Boston by one game when the Red Sox came to the Stadium for the last two games of the season, New York needed a sweep and succeeded by scores of 5-4 and 5-3 in thrilling struggles. In the first contest, reliever Joe Page walked in two runs with the bases loaded in the third inning, allowing Boston to take a 4-0 lead. However, Page settled down, and over the last 6⅔ innings, Page allowed just one single as no Red Sox player reached second base. Meanwhile, the Yanks fought back

Actually, the Yankees spent only four days out of first place all season, but those days were in the final week of the season. Jumping to a substantial early-season lead, the Yanks led the Red Sox by 8½ games when June ended. On the next-to-last weekend, however, Boston swept three Fenway Park games from New York to surge into the lead. But then the Yanks won the final two games at the Stadium to decide the matter.

Vic Raschi (21-10, 3.34 ERA), who pitched a complete game in the final victory, was the ace of the league's second best pitching staff (3.70 ERA). Teamed with Raschi in an almost strictly four-man rotation were Allie Reynolds (17-6), Tommy Byrne (15-7) and Ed Lopat (15-10). These four started all but 27 Yankee games. The only drawback to this wonderful staff was its wildness. Yankee pitchers walked a club-record 812 batters, as Byrne and Raschi were 1-2 in the AL and Reynolds was eighth. (The tables were turned in the third inning on September 11 when Washington pitchers walked 11 Yankees.) Perhaps the most indispensable member of the team was relief ace Joe Page (13-8, 2.59 ERA), league leader in games pitched (60) and saves (27). Thus Page had a hand in 40 of the 97 Yankee victories!

Tommy Henrich (24 HRs, 85 RBIs) and Yogi Berra (20 HRs, 91 RBIs) supplied most of the power on a club that was riddled with injuries all year. Henrich broke a bone in his back, Berra broke a thumb, and Johnny Mize (.261), obtained from the Giants during the season, had a torn shoulder. In fact, the Yanks were hobbled with more than 70 various disabilities, the most serious being bone spurs in the right heel of Joe DiMaggio.

"The Yankee Clipper" missed almost the entire first half of the season before playing in the Mayor's Trophy Game against the Giants. Afterwards, Joe left for Boston, and on June 28 he played his first regular-season game of the year at Fenway Park. In what was possibly DiMaggio's most dramatic feat ever, he blasted four homers and knocked in nine runs in the three-game series sweep of the Red Sox. DiMaggio (14 HRs, 67 RBIs, .346) was a powerful force in the second half of the season and an inspiration to the entire team. In September Joe was brought down again, this time by pneumonia, but he was in the Yankee lineup for the final two Red Sox games and played his heart out.

Four Yankee youngsters saw plenty of action, including outfielders Hank Bauer (10 HRs, .272), Cliff Mapes (7 HRs, .247) and Gene Woodling (5 HRs, .270) who all had some 300 at-bats each. Young Bobby Brown (.283) and veteran Billy Johnson (.249) were platooned at third base. The Yanks relied on platooning, hustle and dedication to offset an attack that failed to dominate the league in a single offensive category.

Casey used no less than seven first basemen: Henrich, Dick Kryhoski, Johnson, Jack Phillips, Fenton Mole, Joe Collins and Mize. Although the Yankees ranked a league fourth in fielding (.977), the team was strong up the middle. Rookie second baseman Jerry Coleman (.981) and veteran shortstop Phil Rizzuto (.971) each led the AL in fielding at their positions and

formed an excellent double-play duo. The Phil Rizzuto-Coleman combination, in fact, was the strength of the Yankee defense. Rizzuto was the solid guy of the team and its backbone. From his hospital bed during the season, Henrich said, "We have nothing to worry about as long as Rizzuto remains healthy. He's the team's sparkplug."

Catcher Berra, working hard to become the best defensive backstop in baseball, led AL catchers in double plays with 18. Whenever DiMaggio was in center field, New York had the best in the business.

This was an exciting, scrappy Yankee club, and 2,281,676 fans paid to see them at the Stadium. An interesting mixture of reliable veterans and aspiring youngsters was the 1949 edition, led by a colorful—and astute—manager.

1950

Casey Stengel's Yankees won their second consecutive AL pennant, the 17th in the club's history, finishing three games ahead of the Detroit Tigers. It was another surprise pennant victory for the Yanks because as usual the baseball writers and most of the other experts had picked Boston to win in the preseason. The Yankees' cause was helped by their refusal to lose both ends of a doubleheader all season.

One of the slugging highlights came on June 23 at Briggs Stadium (now Tiger Stadium). The Yanks and Tigers combined for 11 home runs in a game won by Detroit, 10-9.

Clearly the star of the Yanks was 32-year-old shortstop Phil Rizzuto (.324). Always known as a great defensive player, "The Scooter" really put the wood to the ball in 1950. He stroked 200 hits, scored 125 runs, knocked in 66 runs, cracked 36 doubles and stole 12 bases. He was the sparkplug of the Yankee attack and a graceful and often spectacular master at his position, leading AL shortstops in fielding (.982) once again. Throughout his career, Phil (5'6", 150 lbs.) was a reminder that physical size is not all-important. Deservedly, Rizzuto won the AL MVP Award, and *The Sporting News* named him the major-league Player of the Year.

Joe DiMaggio (32 HRs, 122 RBIs, .301) had the final great season of his career, hitting especially well down the stretch. On June 20, "The Yankee Clipper" stroked his 2,000th hit, an RBI single off Cleveland's Marino Pieretti in an 8-2 Yankee victory. Two weeks later, on July 3, Joe was asked to play first base for the first time. It was a controversial and unsuccessful experiment. Joe felt uncomfortable at the position, was moved back to the outfield late in the game, and never played first base again.

Yogi Berra (28 HRs, 124 RBIs, .322) also had an outstanding season, while Johnny Mize (.277), the former Cardinal and Giant great, hit 25 home runs in only 274 at-bats. On September 15, "The Big Cat" cracked three homers in one game. Hank Bauer (13 HRs, 70 RBIs, .320), Cliff Mapes (12 HRs, 61 RBIs),

Jerry Coleman (.287) and Gene Woodling (.283) all swung potent sticks, and in the eighth inning of his first major-league game, a 22-year-old utility infielder, Billy Martin, got two hits.

Although New York finished third in the league in fielding (.980), the Yankee regulars included fine defensive players and the bench depth was gratifying.

The pitching staff was occasionally brilliant and always dependable, although its ERA ballooned to 4.15 (ERAs around the league were considerably higher in general). There was one unusual pitching problem: Yankee hurlers balked 14 times to set a 154-game AL record.

Fireballing Vic Raschi (21-8) was in the prime of his career and repeated as the Yanks' top pitcher. Ed Lopat (18-8), Allie Reynolds (16-12) and Tommy Byrne (15-9) all were starters the team could count on in the pinch. After a string of sensational years, the Irishman from Pennsylvania, Joe Page (3-7, 5.07 ERA), experienced a disappointing year but still came through with 13 saves. An important and newly acquired complement to Page was relief pitcher Tom Ferrick who during the season came over from the St. Louis Browns. Ferrick compiled an 8-4 record with nine saves in 30 games, all in relief. The savior, however, was a 21-year-old lefty named Whitey Ford who was called up from the minors in June and responded with a 9-1 record, a 2.81 ERA and two shutouts. *The Sporting News* gave the cool and confident Ford its major-league Rookie Award.

The Sporting News also named Yankee GM George Weiss the major-league Executive of the Year, recognizing his contribution in building this club. Fans in the number of 2,081,380 came to the Stadium to see Weiss' creation; it was the fifth consecutive year that more than two million fans paid their way into Yankee Stadium. The Yanks became the first major-league team in history to draw two million for five years in a row.

1951

In what was a tight pennant race up to the final two weeks of the season, the Yankees won a third straight AL pennant, finishing five games ahead of Cleveland. A key factor in the Yankees' success was their 24 shutouts, a club record.

Ed Lopat (21-9) and Vic Raschi (21-10—21 wins for the third straight season) led the mound corps with their markedly dissimilar pitching styles. Raschi possessed an intimidating demeanor and a blazing fastball that gave him the AL strikeout title (164), while Lopat used off-speed pitches and a keen knowledge of the hitters to keep them off stride. But the most remarkable pitching came from Allie Reynolds (17-8 and 7 saves; Reynolds, used as a reliever as well as a starter, led the team in saves).

After a no-hitter against Cleveland on July 12, Reynolds kept Boston hitless on September 28, winning 8-0 and getting Ted Williams "twice" for the final out (Berra dropped one foul pop-up but caught the next one). No other Yankee has ever had two no-hitters in one season.

The season marked the end and the beginning of two Yankee eras. The great Joe DiMaggio (12 HRs, 71 RBIs) played his final season, while switch-hitter Mickey Mantle (13 HRs, 65 RBIs) played 96 games, 86 in right field and at the age of 19 showed much promise. Mantle hit his first major-league home run early in the season off the White Sox' Randy Gumpert at

Here is the Home Run King, Babe Ruth, wearing his famous No. 3 uniform for the last time, bowing as he acknowledges the cheers of thousands of fans who saw the No. 3 retired permanently by the Yankees during the June 13, 1948 observance of the 25th anniversary of Yankee Stadium in New York. (AP/WIDE WORLD PHOTOS)

Comiskey Park. It was what was to become a typical Mantle clout, traveling 450 feet.

Yogi Berra (27 HRs, 88 RBIs, .294) was not only outstanding with the bat but was the glue of the club behind the plate, leading AL catchers in double plays (25) and winning the league's MVP award. Gil McDougald (14 HRs, 63 RBIs, .306) at 23 was the Yanks' first AL Rookie of the Year winner, playing at third and second. Jerry Coleman (.249) and Phil Rizzuto (.274) provided excellent defense on either side of second base. Bobby Brown (.268) anchored third base in partnership with McDougald. Johnny Mize (.259) and Joe Collins (.286) split the work at first base while Hank Bauer (10 HRs, .296) and Gene Woodling (15 HRs, .281) shared the outfield duties with Mantle and DiMaggio. This was a good defensive club, but it ranked only fourth in the AL in fielding (.975).

Besides Mantle and McDougald, other young new faces—Jackie Jensen, Bob Cerv and Tom Morgan, to name three—dotted the team. The man most responsible for the wealth of fresh Yankee talent, GM George Weiss, was named-by *The Sporting News* as the major-league Executive of the Year. A brainchild of Weiss and Manager Casey Stengel was the "instructional school" camp held for the second straight year in Phoenix, Ariz., for young minor-league prospects. Conducted prior to spring training, the camp offered intensified training by Stengel and his best instructors, and it was through this program that Mantle, McDougald and Morgan were able to learn and impress enough to be invited to the big camp

The most important victory in the tough pennant race came on September 17 when New York defeated Cleveland, 2-1, moving into first place ahead of the Indians. Rizzuto's suicide squeeze bunt in the bottom of the ninth scored DiMaggio with the winning run. New York held onto first place and clinched the title in a September 28 doubleheader. Raschi beat the Red Sox, 11-3, in the second game, following Reynolds' no-hitter in the opener.

Realizing that he no longer was able to perform up to his heroic standards, Joe DiMaggio officially announced his retirement on December 11.

Philadelphia A's with clutch pitching efforts turned in by Lopat and Johnny Sain.

For the season, the Yankees won the season series over every AL club, including having a 12-10 edge over Cleveland, which provided the two-game margin between the two top clubs.

Reynolds (20-8, six saves) led the league's best pitching staff (3.14 ERA). Allie, known as "Superchief" because of his Indian blood, led the AL in strikeouts (160), shutouts (six) and ERA (2.06). Raschi (16-6), Sain (11-6, seven saves), the once-great Boston Brave who was used as a starter and reliever, and Lopat (10-5) were the other big Yankee winners. All four—averaging 34½ years of age—drew upon a wealth of mound savvy.

Once again Berra paced the Yankee power hitters and his total of 30 homers (98 RBIs) established the AL round-trip record for catchers. For the fourth straight year, Berra also led AL catchers in double plays (10) and for the third straight year, he led the league's catchers in both putouts (700) and assists (73). Mantle (23 HRs, 87 RBIs, .311), who had the dubious privilege of filling the retired DiMaggio's shoes in center field, blossomed into a star himself. Outfielders Bauer (.293) and Woodling (.309) combined for 29 homers and 137 RBIs. Woodling, underrated on defense, led AL outfielders in fielding (.996).

The Yanks as a whole were outstanding defensively, ranking second in the AL in fielding (.979) and leading the league in double plays (199). Though not necessarily meaningful, it is interesting to note that on July 17 against Cleveland, 14 Yankees made at least one putout, a ML record. Rizzuto (.254) and McDougald (.263) capably worked the left side of the infield while Billy Martin (.267), Casey's favorite player, did a fine job at second base. Martin accepted 24 chances during a September 24 doubleheader, setting an AL record.

Another big bat was supplied by first baseman Joe Collins (18 HRs, .280) who helped the Yanks lead the league in batting (.267) for the first time since 1947. GM Weiss was again named the major-league Executive of the Year by *The Sporting News*, the third consecutive year he was so honored.

1952

New York won its fourth consecutive AL flag behind Manager Stengel, its 19th pennant in all, nosing out Cleveland by two games.

Injuries and the calling up of key players into the military (Bobby Brown, Jerry Coleman and Tom Morgan) because of the Korean War made a tough race all the more grueling. By May's end, the Yankees stood only 18-17. During the early summer, the Yanks played fine ball and by July 19 had gained a 12-game lead in the AL. That was the biggest Yankee lead over the entire campaign. By Labor Day, the Yanks' lead on the Indians was cut to 2½ games. Most of the Yanks' September games were on the road, however, and their lead slimmed to a half game on September 14. And an important game was scheduled with Cleveland on this date.

The Indians pitched Mike Garcia who on the year was 4-0 against the Yankees. But New York's reliable "Steady Eddie" Lopat prevailed, winning 7-1. The Yankees clinched the pennant on September 26, winning an 11-inning game against the

1953

For the Yankees it was a record-breaking fifth consecutive AL pennant in a cakewalk, 8½ games better than second-place Cleveland. Casey Stengel, "The Old Perfessor," had won his fifth pennant in as many years! That remarkable achievement earned Manager Stengel *Sport* magazine's "Man of the Year" Award.

New York officially clinched the pennant on September 14, beating the Indians, 8-5, with Billy Martin driving in four runs. This was a hitting club. New York led the AL in five major offensive categories, including batting (.273) and slugging (.417) with every Yankee starter except Phil Rizzuto hitting at least 10 homers.

The two big offensive threats, Yogi Berra (27 HRs, 108 RBIs, .296) and Mickey Mantle (21 HRs, 92 RBIs, .295), proved a powerful duo in their second full season together. Mantle hit some tremendous home runs. On April 17, he blasted a home run over the left-field wall at Griffith Stadium off Washington's Chuck Stobbs, the first ball ever sent over that wall. The homer was measured at 565 feet and, as the first ever measured, it ushered in the age of tape for monumental clouts. Unbelievably, Mantle was upset with himself when he first let go of the bat—he felt he had not hit the ball well. His teammates just watched in awe as the ball kept climbing.

Joe Collins (17 HRs, .269), Billy Martin (15 HRs, 75 RBIs), Phil Rizzuto (.271), Gil McDougald (83 RBIs, .285), Hank Bauer (10 HRs, .304) and Gene Woodling (10 HRs, .306) all hit solidly. Johnny Mize, one of baseball's greatest sluggers, playing the final season of his illustrious career, was used mostly as a pinch-hitter and he led the AL in pinch-hits (19 for 61, .311). In June he cracked the 2,000th hit of his career.

Defensively, this team finished tied for second in the AL (.979) and once again it was sensational up the middle (Berra, Martin, Rizzuto, Mantle). Woodling led all AL outfielders in fielding (.996) for the third consecutive season.

Whitey Ford (18-6), back from his two-year stint in the military, was the biggest winner on the league's best pitching staff (3.20 ERA). Other key members of the mound staff were Ed Lopat (16-4), the league's ERA champ with 2.42; Johnny Sain (14-7, 3.00 ERA); Vic Raschi (13-6, 3.33 ERA); and Allie Reynolds (13-7, 13 saves). They were getting old—Lopat and Sain were 35, Raschi 34, and Reynolds 38, but they were effective on the mound and sometimes at the plate. In beating the Tigers, 15-0, on August 4, Raschi led the attack by driving in seven runs!

The Yankees got off to an aggressive start, meeting the St. Louis Browns around second base in a late April game that had already seen several rough plays before "Scrap Iron" Courtney (a former Yankee) slid hard into Phil Rizzuto. The fighting that ensued brought fines to two Browns, including Courtney, and four Yanks, and a dislocated collarbone to umpire John Stevens.

The Yankees pretty much nailed down the pennant in May when they put together an 18-game winning streak. That 15 of those victories came on the road made the feat all the more astounding. Ironically, the Yanks' 18-game winning streak was ended by the Browns who by winning snapped their own 14-game losing streak. For all practical purposes, the pennant race was over until the Yanks inexplicably lost nine games in a row in late June to raise for the moment the hopes of their AL rivals. But a complete game by Raschi and a game-winning pinch-hit by Mize ended the slide on July 2 against Boston. Twice Cleveland swept three-game series from the Yanks, but in the end the Yanks prevailed. It was the first time in the five consecutive pennants that the Yankees had been the pre-season favorites.

On December 15, former Yankee General Manager Ed Barrow, the man most responsible for building the Yankee dynasty, died at the age of 85.

1954

The Yankees won 103 games, more games than a Casey Stengel-managed club ever won, yet finished in second place, eight games behind a Cleveland Indian steamroller that won an AL record 111 games. The Yankees, who had a 13-game winning streak and a record of 103-51, had the highest winning percentage (.669) for a second-place team in league history.

Cleveland held a slim 2½-game lead over New York on August 20, but the Yankees went to Boston and lost three in a row. Stengel felt that was the turning point of the campaign.

The Yanks' last chance to catch the Tribe was wasted before the largest crowd in AL history. A Municipal Stadium crowd of 86,563 (84,587 paid), a ML record for a regular-season game, saw Cleveland sweep the Yanks, 4-1 and 3-2, on September 12 and for all intents and purposes clinch the flag.

New York's pitching staff, while compiling a fine 3.26 ERA, could not match the Indians' remarkable 2.78 team ERA. Bob Grim (20-6), the year's best surprise, was named AL Rookie of the Year by the Baseball Writers and won *The Sporting News'* AL Rookie Award. Whitey Ford (16-8, 2.82 ERA), Ed Lopat (12-4), and Tom Morgan (11-5) were all consistent starters. Yankee great Allie Reynolds (13-4, 7 saves) ended his career at the age of 39, starting 18 games and relieving in 18 games. Out of the Yankee bullpen came Johnny Sain (6-6) to lead the league in saves with 22.

Offensively, the Yanks once more led the league in batting (.268) and slugging (.408), and the biggest stick again belonged to catcher Yogi Berra (22 HRs, 125 RBIs, .307) who won his second MVP Award. It became apparent that 22-year-old centerfielder Mickey Mantle (27 HRs, 102 RBIs, .300) was already one of baseball's best players. Mickey led the AL in runs scored (129). Aside from the 1-2 punch of Mantle and Berra, however, the Yanks came up short on power, hitting 23 fewer home runs than the Indians. But outfielder Irv Noren (.319), 22-year-old third baseman Andy Carey (.302), Hank Bauer (.294) and Joe Collins (.271) all hit well for average.

The brightest newcomer of the season besides Grim was rookie Bill Skowron. Skowron, 23, hit .340 in 215 at-bats and played 61 games at first base.

The Yanks played their usual excellent defense. The team finished second in fielding (.979) and led the league in double plays (198). The latter statistic was a tribute to the infield of Collins, McDougald, Rizzuto and Carey. Mantle led AL outfielders in assists (20).

The end of the Yankees' five-year reign could not be credited to poor play on the New Yorkers' part; it was simply a matter of the Indians playing even better ball.

1955

The Yankees climbed back to the top of the AL, outdistancing Cleveland by three games to win the 21st pennant in Yankee history in a wild season-long race. On Labor Day Cleveland led New York by a half-game, Chicago by 1½ games and Boston by three games.

The key game of the year was played on September 16 with the Yankees a half game behind the Indians in the standings. The Red Sox were leading at Yankee Stadium, 4-3, when in the bottom of the ninth Hank Bauer and Yogi Berra homered to pull out the victory. Cleveland lost on that day, and the Yankees went into first place to stay. An eight-game winning streak solidified the Yankee position. It was snapped on the afternoon of September 23 at Boston, but in the night game of the twin-bill, Don Larsen beat the Red Sox, 3-2, clinching another Yankee pennant.

Cleveland won 13 games from the Yanks during the season, becoming the first team to win a season series from a Stengel managed Yankee team.

It was a total team effort and victory for the Yanks in 1955. No pitcher won more than 18 games or saved more than 11, and

Mickey Mantle, Yogi Berra and Gil McDougald were the only regulars to play in at least 140 games.

A great Yankee pitching staff led the AL in ERA (3.23) and allowed only 1,163 hits, the fewest in ML history for a 154-game season. Sixteen pitchers made contributions to the Yankee cause with eight of them winning at least seven games (Ford, Turley, Byrne, Larsen, Kucks, Konstanty, Morgan and Grim). Whitey Ford (2.63 ERA) was the league's best in wins (18-7) and complete games (18). He was the starter and winner of Yankee Stadium Opening Day against the Washington Senators on April 13, assisted by booming Yankee bats in a 19-1 victory. Among Ford's other wins were consecutive one-hitters on September 2 and 7. Whitey was selected the league's Pitcher of the Year by *The Sporting News*.

Turley, a 24-year-old fireballer who came from Baltimore in an off-season trade, pitched well (17-13, 3.06 ERA), and Byrne (16-5, 3.15 ERA) had a great comeback year at the age of 35, leading the AL in winning percentage (.762). Bullpen chores were handled by Konstanty (7-2, 11 saves) and Morgan (7-3, 10 saves). Ed Lopat (4-8), the great clutch pitcher, was traded to Baltimore during his final season as an active pitcher.

Defensively, the Yankees finished third in the AL in fielding (.987), but led in double plays (180). Another fine defensive year was turned in by Berra, who was durable enough to catch in 145 games. Berra also hit well (27 HRs, 108 RBIs, .272) and for the third time was voted the league's MVP. Mickey Mantle (99 RBIs, .306) not only was the circuit's home-run champ (37) and slugging champ (.611), but was an excellent centerfielder, tracking down fly balls with his tremendous speed and topping all AL outfielders in fielding (.995). Bauer (20 HRs) and Irv Noren (.253) flanked Mantle in the outfield and played consistently well. Billy Hunter (.227) and Phil Rizzuto (.259), now 37 years old, split the work at shortstop, while Andy Carey (.257) was solid at third base. First baseman Bill Skowron (.319) and Gil McDougald (.285), best among AL second basemen in fielding (.985), were sensational on the infield's right side.

A dynamite Yankee bench included Joe Collins (13 HRs), Eddie Robinson (16 HRs) and Elston Howard (ten HRs, .290), the first black player on the Yankees. In the ninth inning of a July 23 game, Yankee pinch-hitters hit two home runs.

For the first time since 1951, New York led the AL in homers (175). This team also set a club record for being hit by pitched balls; 46 Yankees were struck, an indication that the rest of the league did not take kindly to New York's return to the top of the circuit. In 1998, Yankee batters were hit by pitchers on 57 occasions to set a new club record.

After a World Series loss to the Brooklyn Dodgers, the Yanks went on a tour of the Far East, playing exhibitions in Hawaii, Wake Island, the Philippines, Guam and Japan. Crowds of 60,000 fans or more turned out for each exhibition game. Stengel played the games to win, and win the Yanks did. Their record against the best of the Far East was 23-0-1.

1956

The Yankees breezed to their 22nd AL pennant, finishing a full nine games in front of the Indians. Assuming first place on May 16, the Yanks had clear sailing thereafter. One pitcher who understood Yankee dominance was Washington's Camilo Pasqual who posted an 0-7 record against New York—tying a ML record for the most losses against one club in a season.

This was also the season of Mickey Mantle's emergence as the best player in the game. Mantle (52 HRs, 130 RBIs, .353) became the second Yankee to win the Triple Crown and he also led the AL in slugging (.705) and runs scored (132). For his awesome year, Mantle was bestowed many honors, among them the league's MVP by the Baseball Writers, the major-league Player of the Year by *The Sporting News*, "Sport's Man of the Year," and the Male Athlete of the Year by the Associated Press.

He blasted 16 home runs in May (later tied by Mark McGuire in his 1998 70-homer season), a record number for that month, including a May 30 clout off Washington's Pedro Ramos that reached the facade on the right field roof at Yankee Stadium. It was the closest a ball ever came to going out of the Stadium to that date. Mantle's 50th home run on September 17 beat the White Sox, 3-2, in extra innings and clinched the AL pennant for the Yankees. Mantle, however, had plenty of help from his teammates.

New York led the AL in homers (190), runs (857), RBIs (788) and slugging (.434). Berra (105 RBIs, .298) tied his own AL record for homers hit by a catcher (30). Bill Skowron (23 HRs, 90 RBIs, .308), Hank Bauer (26 HRs, 84 RBIs) and Gil McDougald (13 HRs, .311) all had outstanding seasons. In 22 games with the Kansas City A's, the Yanks cracked 48 homers, a major-league record. On September 21, the Bronx Bombers set a big-league record by stranding 20 men on base against the Red Sox—that takes ability!

The defense was sound, ranking second in the AL (.977). Sadly, 38-year-old shortstop, Phil Rizzuto, one of the most valuable Yankees during the 1940s and 1950s, ended his great Yankee career when he was released on Old Timers' Day. Billy Martin returned from his two-year military stint to take back his second-base job, and the versatile McDougald switched to shortstop. Martin and McDougald, along with first baseman Skowron and third baseman Andy Carey turned most of the Yankees' 214 double plays that led the league and established a club double-play record that still stands through 1999.

The Indians' pitching staff (3.32 ERA) had the edge on New York's hurlers (3.63 ERA) but the Yanks had their share of pitching heroes. Whitey Ford (19-6) was once again the ace, posting the league's lowest ERA (2.47) and highest winning percentage (.760). On July 20, he struck out six Kansas City A's in a row (Ginsberg, DeMaestri, C. Boyer, McMahon, H. Lopez, Pilarcik), tying an AL record. Ford should have had a 20-win season, but Baltimore's rookie pitcher Charlie Beamon threw a four-hitter to beat the Yanks and Whitey, 1-0, on the final day of the season. (It was one of three lifetime ML wins for Beamon.)

The other four Yankee starters in the five-man rotation were 22-year-old Johnny Kucks (18-9), Tom Sturdivant (16-8), Don Larsen (11-5), and Bob Turley (8-4). Larsen finished the season as the hottest Yankee pitcher, winning each of his four September starts on four-hitters, after experimenting with a no-windup delivery. (In October, of course, Larsen hurled his perfect game.) Tom Morgan (6-7, 11 saves) was the top pitcher out of the bullpen. Although Cleveland had a slightly better pitching staff, the Indians were out-hit by the Yankees (.270 to .244) and out-homered (190 to 153).

Some young heroes were on the way up through the Yankee farm system. When the 10 starters (two pitchers) were announced for the AAA American Association's All-Star team that played against the International League All-Stars, it was a shocking revelation that eight of the starters were Yankee farmhands from Ralph Houk's Denver club! (Among the Denver stars were Ralph Terry, Bobby Richardson, Tony Kubek, Johnny Blanchard, and Marv Throneberry.) Casey Stengel, enjoying his seventh pennant, could look to a future that bore signs of being equally prosperous.

1957

The Yankees were pennant winners for the 23rd time, the Chicago White Sox being the unlucky bridesmaids this season, coming in eight games behind New York. Chicago got off to a great start and on June 8 led the Yankees by six games.

But things turned around quickly, and on June 30 the Yanks culminated a seven-game winning streak by moving into first place for good. On August 27, New York, visiting Chicago's Comiskey Park holding a 12-game lead, swept the three-game series, and the pennant race was virtually put to rest.

The Yanks had the league's best pitching staff (3.00 ERA). And it was a balanced staff. Winning at least 10 games were Tom Sturdivant (16-6, 2.54 ERA); Bob Turley (13-6, 2.71 ERA); Bob Grim (12-8, 2.63 ERA) who led the AL with 19 saves; Bobby Shantz (11-5) who was the AL ERA champ at 2.45; Whitey Ford (11-5, 2.57 ERA); and Don Larsen (10-4, 3.74 ERA). Pitching star Ford was troubled much of the season with a sore shoulder, but Grim had an outstanding year out of the bullpen to pick up some of the slack. Shantz, acquired before the season from Kansas City, was a welcome addition. Besides being a fine pitcher, Shantz won the first Gold Glove Award as the major-league's best fielding pitcher.

Mantle (34 HRs, 94 RBIs, .365) had another illustrious year and won his second straight MVP Award. Mickey was a devastating combination of raw power and speed (16 stolen bases) and an excellent centerfielder. Berra (24 HRs, 82 RBIs), Bauer (18 HRs, 65 RBIs), Skowron (17 HRs, 88 RBIs, .304), who in April became only the third person in history to hit a home run out of Fenway Park via center field, and McDougald (13 HRs, 62 RBIs, .289) all had typically productive seasons.

But two rookies also were most impressive. Tony Kubek (.297) proved his value to the team and his versatility, playing shortstop, third, and the outfield. He was selected as the AL Rookie of the Year by the Baseball Writers and won *The Sporting News'* AL Rookie Award. The other promising rookie, Bobby Richardson (.256), was poised and frequently brilliant at second base in the 97 games in which he appeared.

This Yankee team was deep, and the bench was used extensively; 15 Yankees batted at least 100 times. The club led the AL in five major offensive categories, including batting (.268) and slugging (.409).

For the fourth consecutive season, New York led the league in double plays (183), a tribute to the infield of Skowron (Joe Collins), Richardson (Jerry Coleman), McDougald (Kubek) and Andy Carey (Kubek). Manager Stengel regularly changed his infield, but always got the same successful results.

On July 28, Berra began a phenomenal 148-game errorless streak behind the plate that extended over three seasons. He also led AL catchers in putouts (704) for the fourth straight season.

The season was marred by an accident that took some of the enjoyment out of the Yankees' success. On May 7, McDougald hit a wicked line drive that struck the Indians' Herb Score, a young pitcher with unlimited potential, in the eye. Score's season was over and the compassionate McDougald, one of the game's nice guys, was so distraught by the accident that he came close to quitting baseball.

The season was marked by another event. In June the Yankees and White Sox tangled in a brawl at Comiskey Park that went a long way toward invalidating the lore that baseball fights are picnics. Yankee pitcher Art Ditmar had thrown a dangerous high-inside pitch to Larry Doby, who in response punched Ditmar. While Skowron attempted to hold back Doby, the White Sox' Walt Dropo jumped on Skowron. Forty-one-year-old Enos Slaughter went to Skowron's aid, and when Dropo was beginning to get the best of Slaughter, Whitey Ford jumped in. Casey Stengel, helping Ford, got into an argument with Chicago's Jungle Jim Rivera. It took the Chicago police 30 minutes to bring order to the field. Two results of the melee: Skowron's pants were all but torn off, and Slaughter's shirt was in tatters.

Now enter Billy Martin. Doby, Billy was told, had threatened Ditmar, so Martin decided to attack Doby. This fight was quickly broken up, however, and peace was permanently restored. It was Billy's last big effort as a Yankee player—two days later he was gone in a trade that had nothing to do with this particular fight. Actually, Billy's involvement in the May Copacabana incident sealed his fate, giving GM George Weiss his long-sought excuse to trade Martin.

Also gone when 1957 ended were the New York Giants and Brooklyn Dodgers, both teams deserting New York City for the greener pastures of California. Fans of both teams were obviously brokenhearted and bitter. Initially, the Yankees thought they would gain the allegiance of the forsaken Giant and Dodgers fans, but that was not in the cards. The tense rivalries among the three baseball clubs would not permit any easy transfer of loyalties.

Many fans fell into a disgust—for the Giants and Dodgers and then for baseball in general. It would take years before some of these abandoned fans would join the Yankee camp, and indeed many never did, maintaining their National League loyalties for the subsequent arrival of the Mets. But some did become Yankee rooters, and many of the children of the Giant and Dodger legions in New York, not having the baseball orientation of their parents, would in the future become diehard pinstripers.

1958

The Yankees won a fourth consecutive AL pennant although the club slipped to only 92 victories (92-62). Still, the Yankees were good enough to finish 10 games ahead of the White Sox, basically because of the club's reliable combination of outstanding starting pitching, clutch relief pitching, tight defense up the middle and power hitting.

The Yanks went into first place on the season's fourth day and remained there, once owning a 17-game margin over Chicago. But the Yanks played mediocre baseball during the season's final two months. A remarkable road record of 48-29 helped the Yankee cause, while the team was 44-33 at Yankee Stadium.

Yankee fans in the New York area were treated to the heaviest television schedule in baseball as the Yanks telecast 77 of their home games and 63 road games. The Yankees received $850,000 in the sale of TV rights, the largest TV income in baseball. The rest of the league whined about the rich getting richer. But baseball's not a business, is it?

The Yanks were rich in pitching. And it was smart pitching; pitching that refused to beat itself. For the third straight year, Yankee pitchers led the AL in fewest sacrifice hits allowed and fewest intentional walks, both records for consecutive years leading the AL in those categories. Not only were Yankee pitchers tough to hit, but enemy teams had difficulty in moving up runners. And seldom did a free pass help their rallies. (Or perhaps Yankee hurlers did not often find the occasion to give a free pass.)

"Bullet Bob" Turley (21-7, 2.97 ERA) had his best year, leading the AL in wins, winning percentage (.750) and complete games (19). Turley became the first Yankee pitcher to win the Cy Young Award, and *The Sporting News* named Bob the major-league Player of the Year. On April 18, Whitey Ford beat the Orioles, 3-1, extending his home-opener winning streak to four.

Almost unbelievably, Ford (14-7), the league's ERA leader (2.01), was the only other Yankee pitcher to win more than nine games. In fact, Manager Casey Stengel had eight pitchers who started at least 10 games, including Don Larsen (9-6), Art Ditmar (9-8) and Johnny Kucks (8-8). A 29-year-old relief ace, fireballing Ryne Duren (64), led the AL in saves (20) and won *The Sporting News'* AL Rookie Pitcher Award. Besides his tremendous speed, Duren wore thick glasses and was occasionally wild, making batters wary of him. This unusual pitching staff was still the best in the AL (3.22 ERA), also leading the league in saves (33) and shutouts (21).

Mickey Mantle (97 RBIs, .304) was the league's home-run king (42) and once again led the Yankees in all three key batting categories. Mantle, who stole 18 bases, also led the league in runs scored (127) and walks (129). His sidekick, Yogi Berra (22 HRs, 90 RBIs), had another fine year, as did Bill Skowron (14 HRs, 73 RBIs). New York got plenty of production from outfielders Hank Bauer (12 HRs, 50 RBIs) and 24-year-old Norm Siebern (14 HRs, .300). Valuable catcher-outfielder Elston Howard (11 HRs, 66 RBIs, .314) hit consistently, and Andy Carey (12 HRs) and Gil McDougald (14 HRs) hit for occasional power.

The bench was deep, led by 42-year-old Enos Slaughter (.304). The Yanks led the AL in no less than seven positive batting categories, including homers (164) and batting (.268). Also, for the sixth straight year, New York led the league in slugging (.416). Only one pitcher seemed to find the Yankee batting order an easy mark. The Tigers' Frank Lary, the famed "Yankee Killer," beat New York seven times; no other pitcher had beaten the Yankees that often since 1916, the days of Eddie Cicotte and Walter Johnson.

Although the Yanks dropped to sixth in the AL in fielding (.978), they were not without lustre. For the fifth year in a row, setting an AL record, the Yankees paced the league in turning double plays (182). Skowron led the league's first basemen in fielding (.993), Bobby Shantz was selected as the Gold Glove

winner for AL pitchers, and Berra went the entire season without an error behind the plate.

The highlight of the year came on August 9 when 67,916 fans packed Yankee Stadium for Old Timers' Day. It was the biggest Old Timers' Day crowd in Yankee history, proving that Yankee fans love to see their old heroes.

A humbling event occurred on September 21 when Baltimore's Hoyt Wilhelm threw the last no-hitter pitched against the Yanks, dazzling the Bombers with his tricky knuckleball. Entering 2000, the Yanks have not been hitless in 6,489 games, the longest such streak in ML baseball, encompassing 41 seasons.

1959

It was a dismal year; the Bronx Bombers became instant Bomb-outs, finishing in third place 15 games behind the AL champion White Sox.

The Yankees won only four games more than they lost (79-75). So badly were things going early in the season that on May 20 New York fell into the AL cellar for the first time since May 8, 1940. Whitey Ford (16-10, 3.04 ERA), Duke Maas (14-8, 4.43 ERA) and Art Ditmar (13-9, 2.90 ERA) were the only big mound winners. The Yankee staff was the league's third best (3.60 ERA), the rest of the regular pitchers having poor seasons, with the exception of Ryne Duren (3-6, 1.88 ERA, 14 saves).

The team's fielding was basically dependable, the Yanks tying for second in the AL in fielding (.978). Yogi Berra, whose 148-game errorless streak ended May 10, led AL catchers in fielding (.997). Mickey Mantle topped the league's outfielders in fielding (.995) and nimble Bobby Shantz won another Gold Glove for his fielding at the pitching position. The Yankee hitting fell off badly.

The club led the league in a single batting category, hits (1397). Mantle (31 HRs, 21 stolen bases) still hit for power and ran well, but his batting average (.285) and RBIs (75) were down. Berra, Norm Siebern and 36-year-old Hank Bauer all experienced drop-offs in power production also. Second baseman Bobby Richardson (.301), 23, and shortstop Tony Kubek (.279), 22, both hit consistently and fielded well, but they combined for only eight homers. Bill Skowron (.298) was playing well when he suffered a serious injury on July 25. Bill reached for a bad throw at first base and the runner, Coot Veal, ran into Skowron, breaking his arm in two places and ending his season. Elston Howard (18 HRs, 73 RBIs) hit for power and was again very versatile, while Hector Lopez, obtained from the A's early in the season, was a pleasant surprise (16 HRs, 69 RBIs, .283).

But the 1959 Yankees lacked real power, and the pitching, instead of offsetting the power loss, joined in the decline. In fairness, the pitching staff was plagued by an unusually high number of sore arms.

Indeed, all of the team's key players were bedeviled by injuries and the Asian flu, the latter knocking out most of the players for short periods of time.

Oddly, the highlight of the season was an exhibition game played on May 7 at the Los Angeles Coliseum. The largest crowd in baseball history, 93,103, saw the Yanks beat the Dodgers, 6-2, in the benefit game for the crippled Dodger great, Roy Campanella.

1960

The Yankees bounced back from their poor 1959 showing to take the AL title, their 10th in 12 seasons under Casey Stengel. It turned out to be Stengel's final season as manager.

Posting a fine 97-57 record, the Yankees finished eight games ahead of the Baltimore Orioles. They started slow, fought for the lead with the White Sox and Orioles throughout the summer, then put on a strong finish. On October 2, the final day of the season, New York beat Washington, 8-7, to wind up the season with a 15-game winning streak.

A key preseason trade with the Kansas City A's brought rightfielder Roger Maris (39 HRs, .283) to bolster the Yankee lineup. Maris generated real power, leading the AL in RBIs (112) and slugging (.581). On top of this, he won a Gold Glove for his fielding excellence. His all-round play earned him the league's MVP.

Mickey Mantle (94 RBIs, .275), the league's home-run leader (40) for the fourth time, also led the circuit in runs scored (119). Mantle and Maris were the most productive power-hitting duo since Babe Ruth and Lou Gehrig, but they hardly were the whole offense. Bill Skowron (26 HRs, 91 RBIs, .309) had a sterling year, and 35-year-old Yogi Berra (15 HRs, 62 RBIs, .276), catching part-time and playing in the outfield, continued to shine. Hector Lopez (.284) also played in the outfield, and 23-year-old Clete Boyer (14 HRs) played 99 games at third base. Shortstop Tony Kubek (14 HRs, .273) contributed occasional power.

The defense was excellent, although ranking only third in the AL (.979). Elston Howard became the regular catcher and handled the pitchers superbly. It was the first season of the splendid infield of Bill Skowron, Bobby Richardson, Kubek and Clete Boyer. Gil McDougald, 32, playing his last season before retiring while still in his prime, worked at second and third and turned in his usual first-rate job. Berra, teamed with the greats, Maris and Mantle, did a fine job in the outfield as a converted catcher. The bench was strong as was in evidence in an 11-inning game on August 26 when four Yankee pinch-hitters delivered hits, tying an AL record.

The league's best pitching staff (3.52 ERA) was led by Art Ditmar (15-9), Jim Coates (13-3), Whitey Ford (12-9) and Ralph Terry. Ford blanked the Orioles, 5-0, at the Stadium on April 22, as the Yanks won their seventh home opener in a row. Ten pitchers recorded saves on a staff that led the AL in saves (42). The bullpen was a crucial factor in Yankee success since Stengel made 263 pitching changes this year, the most ever in a 154-game AL season. Bobby Shantz (5-4, 11 saves) was the Yanks' top reliever and helped his own cause with good fielding, winning his fourth consecutive Gold Glove.

The year's second All-Star Game was played at Yankee Stadium on July 13 and only 38,362 fans came to watch the NL win, 6-0, yet the Yankees this season drew 1,627,349 spectators to the Stadium, their best attendance since 1952.

For the fourth time, Yankee GM George Weiss was selected as the major-league Executive of the Year by *The Sporting News*. Their successes notwithstanding, Weiss and Stengel were to be let go by the Yankee owners; on October 15 Stengel was officially retired, and on November 2 the axe fell on Weiss, too.

1961

The Yanks behind rookie Manager Ralph Houk rolled to 109 victories (109-53, .673), setting major-league records for most wins and highest winning percentage for a 162-game season (begun in 1961), and captured their 26th AL pennant.

In doing so, the Bronx Bombers finished eight games ahead of the surprising and frustrated Detroit Tigers, who won 101 games and yet were eclipsed by the Yankee steamroller. (This may have been the greatest Tiger team of all time. It was led by Norm Cash, who won the batting title with a .361 mark and hit 41 HRs with 132 RBIs; Rocky Colavito hit 45 HRs with 140 RBIs; Al Kaline hit .324; Jake Wood stole 30 bases and led the AL with 14 triples; Billy Bruton hit 17 HRs; Dick Brown hit 16 HRs; and the starting staff of Frank Lary, Jim Bunning, Don Mossi, Paul Foytack and Phil Regan was outstanding.)

But the Yankees had one of the greatest teams of all time, especially when playing at Yankee Stadium; the Yankees won more games at home (65-16, .802) than any team in history. New York had one stretch of 13 consecutive wins, 12 of them coming at the Stadium. The Bombers lost only two extra-inning games all year, the fewest in the history of the 162-game AL season.

However, there was excitement; this was the year that involved Roger Maris and Mickey Mantle in a season-long chase of Babe Ruth's single-season home run record. Dramatically, on October 1, the last day of the season, and at Yankee Stadium, Maris hit No. 61 off Boston's Tracy Stallard. Maris (142 RBIs, .269) not only led the AL in home runs and RBIs but in runs (132) as well.

He began his home-run barrage in June when he belted 15 to tie Ruth's major-league record for homers in that month. He hit four homers in a July 25 doubleheader and seven in a six-game stretch, August 11-16. The 30 homers he hit at Yankee Stadium tied the Stadium single-season record set in 1934 by Lou Gehrig. The White Sox took a disproportionate share of the assault; in 18 games with the Yankees they saw 13 Maris four-baggers. Roger's 59th home run on September 20 led the Yankees to a 4-2 pennant-clinching win over Baltimore. Six days later he was to hit No. 60 off the Orioles' Jack Fisher.

Among the many honors bestowed on Maris were the AL MVP Award, *Sport Magazine's* "Man of the Year," *The Sporting News'* major-league Player of the Year, the Associated Press' Male Athlete of the Year, and *Sports Illustrated's* Sportsman of the Year. Roger is the only Yankee to win the latter award.

Mantle had just as spectacular a season. Mickey (54 HRs, 128 RBIs, .317) chased Ruth until foiled by a late-season injury. Still, he had the most homers ever hit by a switch-hitter and established a ML record for the most ever hit by a runner-up, until eclipsed in 1998 by Sammy Sosa, who was four behind Mark McGwire's total of 70 dingers. Mantle shared with Maris the league leadership for most runs scored (132) and led the league in walks (126) and slugging (.687). Only twice all season did Mantle ground into a double play, a club record. Together, Maris and Mantle hit 115 homers to break the Babe Ruth-Lou Gehrig major-league standard of 107 set in 1927.

Other 1961 edition Yankees were pounding the ball, too; as a team they hit 240 homers, more than any club in history up to that point. Several teams in the 90s would surpass the Bombers. Bill Skowron (28 HRs), Yogi Berra (22 HRs), Elston Howard (21 HRs) and Johnny Blanchard (21 HRs) gave New York, along with the "M & M boys," six players each having

NEW YORK YANKEES
1961 WORLD CHAMPIONS

First Row, Left to Right: WHITEY FORD, BILL SKOWRON, HAL RENIFF, JIM HEGAN, FRANK CROSETTI, RALPH HOUK, JOHN SAIN, WALLY MOSES, EARL TORGESON, CLETIS BOYER, YOGI BERRA, MICKEY MANTLE.
Second Row, Left to Right: GUS MAUCH (TRAINER), BILLY GARDNER, BOB HALE, JOE DE MAESTRI, TONY KUBEK, TEX CLEVENGER, RALPH TERRY, HECTOR LOPEZ, BOB CERV, ELSTON HOWARD, ROGER MARIS, BOB TURLEY, JOE SOARES (TRAINER).
Third Row, Left to Right: BOBBY RICHARDSON, AL DOWNING, LUIS ARROYO, JOHN BLANCHARD, BILL STAFFORD, ROLAND SHELDON, JIM COATES, SPUD MURRAY (BATTING PRACTICE PITCHER), BUD DALEY, BRUCE HENRY (TRAVELING SECRETARY).

Seated on Ground in Front: Batboys FRANK PRUDENTI, FRED BENGIS.

'61 Champions

more than 20 home runs to his credit, another AL record until Baltimore had seven 20-homer players in 1996. Blanchard hit his 21 homers in only 243 at-bats, a fantastic ratio. Blanchard, over three games in July hit four consecutive home runs, two of them pinch-hit blasts.

In all, the Yankees enjoyed ten pinch-hit homers on the season, a then-AL record (until Baltimore blasted 11 in 1982), and a tribute to the bench (Blanchard, Lopez, Cerv, among others). The Yanks also hit 128 home runs on the road, a major-league record. Howard hit .348, Skowron had 89 RBIs, and Clete Boyer hit 11 home runs.

Defensively, New York ranked first in the AL in fielding (.980), led the league in double plays (180), and made fewer errors (124) than any team in the league. The Skowron Richardson-Kubek-Boyer infield was the best in the game. Bobby Richardson won the AL Gold Glove at second base, played in all 162 games, and worked beautifully with shortstop Kubek, who possessed great range.

Although the Yankee pitching staff was only a league second best, it was accomplished. Whitey Ford (25-4, 3.21 ERA) did it all, winning the Cy Young Award and *The Sporting News'* AL Pitcher of the Year honor. He led the league in victories, winning percentage (.862), games started (39) and innings pitched (283). During one stretch, he won 14 straight games, tying a club record first set by Jack Chesbro in 1904. Ralph Terry (16-3), Bill Stafford (14-9), Jim Coates (11-5), and Rollie Sheldon (11-5) also were big

winners, and in the bullpen there was Luis Arroyo (15-5, 2.19 ERA) who led the AL in saves (29, many of them Ford-started games) and games pitched (65). Arroyo dazzled hitters all season long with his screwball. From July 1—September 9, Arroyo won 12 straight games in relief, a league record, and *The Sporting News* named Luis the AL Fireman of the Year.

All in all, this year's Yankees were awesome—a team that could, and did, beat its opponents in any number of ways.

1962

Waltzing to a third straight pennant and their 27th overall, the Yankees finished five full games in front of the young Minnesota Twins.

They had the second best pitching staff (3.70 ERA) in the league, led by Ralph Terry (23-12, 3.19 ERA). Terry topped the AL in wins, games started (39) and innings pitched (299); he was the league's premier pitcher. Whitey Ford (17-8, 2.90 ERA) and Bill Stafford (14-9, 3.67 ERA) were the only other Yankees to win more than eight games. Terry, Ford and Stafford, in fact, started 109 of the season's 162 games. Marshall Bridges (8-4, 3.14 ERA), rejected by Cincinnati, was a big help coming out of the bullpen (18 saves).

Mickey Mantle, notwithstanding the injuries that forced him to miss many games and to play hurt in many others gave a gritty, inspirational performance (30 HRs, 89 RBIs, .321), winning his third MVP Award and AL Player of the Year honors of *The Sporting News.* He also won a Gold Glove for his excellence in centerfield, and he again led the AL in walks (122) and slugging (.605), still an AL record.

Roger Maris (33 HRs, 100 RBIs, .256) had another splendid year even with pitchers refusing to give him good pitches to hit. In a 12-inning game on May 22, Maris was intentionally walked four times; Bill Skowron (23 HRs, 80 RBIs), Elston Howard (21 HRs, 91 RBIs) and Tom Tresh (20 HRs, 93 RBIs, .286), the AL Rookie of the Year and winner of *The Sporting News'* AL Rookie Award, also provided power.

Tresh, filling in at shortstop while Tony Kubek was in the military, did an amazing defensive job in addition to his great hitting. When Kubek returned in August, Tresh moved to left field and was equally skillful at the new position. Second baseman Bobby Richardson (eight HRs, 59 RBIs, .302) had an outstanding season leading the AL in hits (209) and at-bats (692), the latter establishing an AL record, since surpassed by Kansas City's Willie Wilson (705) in 1980. Clete Boyer improved at the plate (18 HRs, .272) and Hector Lopez (.275) was a steady performer. On May 23, twenty-one-year-old Joe Pepitone hit two home runs in one inning to join a handful of players who have accomplished that feat.

The Yanks pounded out 199 homers but failed to lead the league (the Tigers slugging 209). But the Bronx Bombers did lead the league in six batting categories, including slugging (.426). It was the 28th time—and the last time until 1986—that the Yankees led the AL in slugging.

Defensively, the club tied for fourth in the AL (.979), but Mantle and Bobby Richardson won Gold Gloves and Howard led AL catchers in fielding (.995). Again, the Yankees were solid up the middle, and Kubek and Boyer ate up everything on the left side of the infield.

A game of note this season was a 22-inning, seven-hour struggle with the Detroit Tigers on June 24, a game that the Yankees won, 9-7, on reserve outfielder Jack Reed's only big-league career home run. Richardson batted 11 times in this contest, which at the time was the longest game by time (seven hours exactly) in AL history. Through 1999, the longest game time-wise in ML history remains eight hours and six minutes in a 25-inning marathon, won by Chicago 7-6 over Milwaukee, begun on May 8, 1984 and concluded the following day.

The Bronx Bombers once again were one of baseball's best drawing cards, playing to 2,216,159 spectators on the road for one of the best road attendance figures in AL history.

1963

The Yankees breezed to their fourth consecutive AL pennant, the third under Manager Ralph Houk, ending the season 104-57 and 10½ games ahead of the second-place White Sox.

Whitey Ford had his greatest year (24-7, 2.74 ERA), leading the league in wins, winning percentage (.774), games started (37) and innings pitched (269). He was chosen by *The Sporting News* as the league's Pitcher of the Year, and chosen by the Yanks in the course of the season as their pitcher for key games. Jim Bouton (21-7, 2.53 ERA) was an outstanding 24-year-old, pitching six shutouts and constantly losing his cap while working to the delight of fans. Ralph Terry (17-15) and another fine young star, Al Downing (13-5), were also big winners.

Twenty-four-year-old Hal Reniff (4-3) led the club in saves (18) on a staff whose ERA (3.07) was second only to the White Sox.

The Yanks, however, out-homered Chicago 188 to 114. League MVP honors went to deserving Elston Howard (28 HRs, 85 RBIs, .287) who hit the ball consistently and was the glue that held the team together. He was the best catcher in the game, winning a Gold Glove and working beautifully with his pitchers. Houk had to call on the Yankee bench frequently because of injuries. The broken foot Mickey Mantle suffered when he ran into Baltimore's chain-link fence confined his play to only 65 games.

Mantle (15 HRs, .314), who had appeared to be on his way to another great year, again came close to hitting a fair ball out of Yankee Stadium. Against Kansas City's Bill Fischer on May 22, Mantle hit a blast that was still rising when it struck the Stadium facade beyond right field. It might have been his most awesome home run.

The strong Yankee bench included Hector Lopez (14 HRs, 52 RBIs), John Blanchard (16 HRs, 45 RBIs), young Phil Linz (.269) and 38-year-old Yogi Berra (8 HRs, .293). The clutch-hitting Berra in this final season of his great career served as a player–coach, catching 35 games and pinch-hitting for the 14th Yankee pennant winner of his career.

Joe Pepitone (27 HRs, 89 RBIs) who replaced the traded Bill Skowron at first base, Tom Tresh (25 HRs) and an injury-hampered Roger Maris (23 HRs) joined Howard in supplying the power. Bobby Richardson (.265), Tony Kubek (.257) and Clete Boyer (12 HRs, .251) got on base often enough to give the power hitters runners to drive in.

New York finished a league second in fielding (.982), but this was one of baseball's best defensive teams ever. Howard and Richardson won Gold Gloves, and Boyer was a most gifted third baseman. Even today there are those who will argue that he was the greatest at his position in the history of the game. Kubek handled his important shortstop chores with skill, and Pepitone was agile and able around first base, and around the mound to which he traveled one August game at the Stadium to challenge Cleveland's Gary Bell after some close pitches, thus precipitating a bench-emptying melee.

The key to this team was its refusal to beat itself; the Yanks grounded into only 91 double plays, fewest in club history.

For the season, the Yankees used only 30 players, the fewest in AL history for a 162-game season.

1964

The Yankees won their 29th pennant behind rookie Manager Yogi Berra. It was a fifth straight AL title, tying a Yankee record set in 1949-53, and it culminated a season-long three-team struggle.

A spectacularly successful September (22-6) enabled New York to finish one game ahead of Chicago and two games in front of Baltimore. The Yankees clinched the pennant on the eve of the season's closing day with an 8-3 win over the Indians.

These Yankees were a great fielding club. Over the season they made only 109 errors, tying a then-club record set in 1947. In 1996, the Yanks set a new club mark with the fewest errors (91) in a season until surpassed by Baltimore who had 104 error-free contests in 1998. Though only second best in the AL in 1964, their fielding mark of .983 was the best in Yankee history, until the 1995 club (.986) eclipsed that standard. They made more putouts (4520) than any team in league history. Bobby Richardson won still another Gold Glove for his play at second, and Tony Kubek and Clete Boyer ably worked the left side of the infield.

Elston Howard, another Gold Glove winner, led all AL catchers in fielding for the third straight season, and his .998 mark established the Yankee record for catchers. Tom Tresh led all AL outfielders in fielding with .996.

On the mound, New York got consistent pitching from Jim Bouton (18-13, 3.02 ERA), Whitey Ford (17-6, 2.13 ERA), and Al Downing (13-8, 3.47 ERA). Pete Mikkelsen (7-4), winner of the J. P. Dawson Award as the best Yankee rookie in spring training, came out of the bullpen to save 12 games. Two late-season additions helped the pitching markedly. In August, 22-year-old Mel Stottlemyre came up from the minors to pitch exceptionally well (9-3, 2.06 ERA), including a two-hitter against Washington September 26 in which he helped his own cause with five hits and won, 7-0. In September Pedro Ramos came from Cleveland to save eight critical games down the stretch.

Mickey Mantle, in his last truly great season (35 HRs, 111 RBIs, .303), was the team leader at-bat, in the field, dugout, and locker room. On August 12, when the Yankees sorely needed a win over the White Sox to stay in the pennant race, Mantle delivered two homers. The one off Ray Herbert went 500 feet into Yankee Stadium's center-field bleachers—the longest homer ever measured at the Stadium.

Joe Pepitone (28 HRs, 100 RBIs), Roger Maris (26 HRs, 71 RBIs), Ellie Howard (15 HRs, 84 RBIs, .313) and Tom Tresh (16 HRs, 73 RBIs) also supplied ample power. Richardson led the AL in at-bats (679) and Tresh set a major-league record for the most stolen bases in a season (13) without being nailed. This record stood until 1988.

In retrospect, Manager Berra did a great job in guiding this club to a pennant victory. The Yankees no longer could hope that the opposition would beat itself; most of their games were dogfights. In fact, the Yanks played in 26 extra-inning games, an AL 162-game season record. During the summer, the Yankees sputtered and played uninspired ball. The Yankee front office was dissatisfied with Berra's performance and gave him little support.

Yet, Yogi remained optimistic, even after an August argument aboard the team bus with utility infielder Phil Linz (.250). When Linz refused to stop practicing his harmonica playing, Manager Berra asserted his authority and a well-publicized quarrel ensued—one that delighted Yankee-haters around the nation. However, after the incident, the Yankees regrouped and staged the final successful drive that Berra had promised.

Only the additions of Stottlemyre and Ramos, the heroics of Mantle, and the managing of Berra saved the pennant. The Yankees had little depth, either on the bench or in the mound corps.

Off the field, in August the baseball world was startled to learn that the Columbia Broadcasting Company had bought the Yankees from Dan Topping and Del Webb. For CBS, it turned out to be a bad investment.

1965

It was the year of the Yankees' collapse. Under new Manager Johnny Keane, they finished sixth with a 77-85 record. It was the first season since 1925 that the Yanks failed to finish in the upper half of the AL standings. The once-great pitching staff declined. Mel Stottlemyre (20-9, 2.63 ERA), Whitey Ford (16-13, 3.24 ERA), and Pedro Ramos (19 saves, 2.92 ERA) performed well, but the fine young arms—Jim Bouton, Bill Stafford, Al Downing, Hal Reniff, Pete Mikkelsen—were ineffective.

Other key players were victimized by injuries and age. Elston Howard was 36, Roger Maris 30 and hurting, Art Lopez 32, and the great Mantle 33, and hounded by painful injuries. Their best baseball lay behind them. While Tom Tresh (26 HRs, 74 RBIs, .279), who hit three consecutive home runs against Chicago in a June game, and Joe Pepitone (18 HRs, 62 RBIs) were fine young players, too few of their kind were coming up through the Yankee farm system. In fact, the Yankee minors were dry.

Matters were not helped any when in June the first annual amateur free-agent draft was held, ending the Yanks' seeming monopoly on the signing of top high school and college prospects. The Yankees and Dodgers, with their array of wise scouts and attractive organizations, and the Mets' George Weiss, whose genius was constricted by a draft, were all anti-draft. The draft was chiefly an attempt to break up the Yankees.

The Yankee bench, once so reliable, contributed little save for rare bright spots such as Ray Barker's consecutive pinch-hit home runs on June 20 and 22. To add to problems, steady shortstop Tony Kubek, though only 28, retired as the season ended.

The Yankees dropped to sixth in the AL defensively (.978) yet led the league in double plays (166). Pepitone, Tresh, and Bobby Richardson all won Gold Gloves for their play at first base, left field, and second base. It was Richardson's fifth consecutive Gold Glove. Bobby also led the league's second basemen in turning double plays (121) for the fourth time in five years. Pepitone set the club fielding record for first basemen (.997) and Clete Boyer, who possessed amazing reflexes, a sure glove and a great arm, led AL third basemen in assists (354) for the third time. Pepitone's .997 fielding mark was later eclipsed by Yankee Captain Don Mattingly, who had a .998 mark in both 1994 and 1995, the latter season his final one.

Mostly because of the Yankees' poor season, Yankee Stadium attendance (1,213,552) was the lowest since 1945. Meanwhile, Casey Stengel's New York Mets, in their fourth season, were drawing crowds at Shea Stadium. For the Yankee legions, 1965 was anything but a happy year. For the Yankee kingpins, there was the acknowledgment that the brand of winning baseball the Yankees formerly played—the kind of baseball that brought fans to the Stadium—could no longer be counted on. The Yankee management was reduced to holding promotional days as did the other clubs. Bat Day, soon to be followed by every other conceivable giveaway, became the pattern in Yankeeland.

There was one bright moment, and it was on October 3, the final day of the season, when Ford beat the Red Sox at Fenway Park to become the all-time win leader among Yankee pitchers. This day, Whitey notched his 232nd win to surpass Red Ruffing's total of 231, which had stood since 1946.

1966

The Yankees dropped to last place in the ten-team AL, their once-proud dynasty now shattered. It would take years of rebuilding to get back to the league's higher elevations.

This was the first year the Yankees finished in the basement since 1912 (then an eight-club league) and naturally the season is a blight on Yankee history. Yet, the team was not as bad as one might think; the Yankee winning percentage of .440 (70-89) is the highest for a last-place team in AL history. Whitey Ford learned the day of the Yanks' home opener that this club lacked hitting, when he lost a tough 2-1 decision to Detroit. The Yanks hit a mere .235 as a team but hit 162 home runs, the third highest total in the AL.

A disastrous early season saw the end of Johnny Keane's reign. He was relieved as manager early in the season, the Yanks' record 4-16 at the time. Ralph Houk came down from the front office to fill the vacancy, but Houk's old magic was not enough to make this club a winner.

The pitching staff was fifth best in the AL (3.42 ERA). Rookie Fritz Peterson (12-11, 3.31 ERA), Mel Stottlemyre (12-20, 3.80 ERA) and Al Downing (10-11, 3.56 ERA) were all first-rate starters, and Pedro Ramos (13 saves) was the bullpen standout. New York tied for a league fifth in fielding (.977), its defense led by Joe Pepitone who won another Gold Glove for his first base play.

Playing in only 108 games, Mickey Mantle had a fine year (23 HRs, .288), while Pepitone (31 HRs, 83 RBIs) and Tom Tresh (27 HRs, 68 RBIs) provided through-the-season power. Roy White, 22, who won the J.P. Dawson Award as the top rookie in spring training, played 82 games in the outfield, led the club in stolen bases (14), and showed some power (seven HRs). With the season's merciful close, Bobby Richardson and Hector Lopez, two outstanding Yankees, retired, and Roger Maris, once one of baseball's most feared hitters, was traded to St. Louis for Charley Smith.

The Yankee home attendance dipped again (to 1,124,648), indication that fans were becoming disenchanted. This was the season of the smallest crowd in Yankee history—only 413 fans were at the Stadium September 25 to watch Chicago beat the once proud New Yorkers, 4-1.

1967

The Yankees climbed out of the cellar under Manager Ralph Houk, but only barely. Yankee fans were forewarned of another disastrous season immediately, in the home opener, when Bill Rohr, rookie Red Sox pitcher, came within one out of a no-hitter. Elston Howard singled with two outs in the ninth inning to end the no-hit bid and Rohr settled for a 3-0 shutout. His lifetime record was 3-3, but the Yanks made Bill Rohr look like a Hall of Famer.

Again the Yankee pitching staff (3.24 ERA), fourth best in the league, was better than the team's sorry ninth-place position in the league. Mel Stottlemyre (15-15, 2.96 ERA) and Al Downing (14-10, 2.63 ERA) were outstanding. Downing, who on August 11 struck out the side in one inning on NINE pitches to become one of only nine AL pitchers ever to achieve that feat, could throw as hard as anyone in baseball. Young Dooley Womack (18 saves, 2.41 ERA) was sparkling in relief, but sadly, pitching great Whitey Ford (2-4, 1.64 ERA) was

forced by arm miseries to retire at the age of 38. Ford left the team early in the season as the winningest pitcher in Yankee history.

The 1967 Yankees gave their pitchers little support, finishing last in the league in fielding (.976). Second baseman Horace Clarke was the most solid defensive player (.990), leading the AL at his position. Mickey Mantle was moved to first base in an effort to spare his troubled legs, and he played the position well while providing punch (22 HRs, 55 RBIs).

Aside from Mickey, there was little offense; only Washington had a lower team batting average than the Yanks' miserable .225. Moreover, the Yanks set a club record for strikeouts with 1,043 (later eclipsed by the 1997 club with 1,165 whiffs) and scored the fewest runs in the AL (522). Clarke hit best among the Yankees for average (.272) while Mantle, Tom Tresh (14 HRs), Joe Pepitone (13 HRs) and Steve Whitaker (11 HRs) were the long-ballers.

New York was involved in an unusually high number of extra-inning games at the Stadium. Two 18-inning games already had been played at the Stadium before the August 29 struggle with the Red Sox that took 20 innings to complete. The Yankees won this longest game in Yankee Stadium history, 4-3.

The highlight of the season came on May 13 when Mantle hit his 500th career home run off Baltimore's Stu Miller at the Stadium. True to his nature as a team player, Mickey was as happy that his homer won the game as he was about reaching the milestone.

1968

The Yankees pulled themselves up to fifth place in the AL, compiling a winning record (83-79) for the first time in four years.

Manager Houk's pitching staff, the league's fifth best (2.79 ERA), was led by three fine young hurlers, Mel Stottlemyre (21-12, 2.45 ERA), Fritz Peterson (12-11, 2.63 ERA), and Stan Bahnsen (17-12, 2.05 ERA), who won the league's Rookie of the Year designation and *The Sporting News'* AL Rookie Pitcher Award. Two veterans, Steve Hamilton (11 saves, 2.13 ERA) and Lindy McDaniel (10 saves, 1.75 ERA), gave excellent bullpen service. This good pitching staff won six 1-0 games over the season, tying a club record that had stood for 60 years. And for the third year in a row, tying an AL record, the Yankee staff led the AL in fewest wild pitches uncorked.

The New Yorkers were not a bad defensive club, tying for third in the AL (.979), but they were impotent at the plate. They had only 1,137 hits, the second fewest in Yankee history (in 1903, the Highlanders had 1,136 safeties), and hit only .214, lowest in Yankee history. The great Mickey Mantle (18 HRs, 54 RBIs) played the final season of his fabulous career. The last talented player of the Yankee dynasty had pushed his damaged body to the final limits.

Probably no other player in Yankee history was as appreciated by Yankee fans as was Mantle; he was as admired for his courage as he was for his marvelous play. On September 20, Mantle hit his 535th career home run off Detroit's Denny McLain (who easily won his 31st game of the season), the blast putting Mickey ahead of Jimmie Foxx on the all-time homer list. It seemed that McLain, who admitted that Mantle was his idol, threw a groove pitch to the Mick. Naturally, a controversy ensued.

But as sportswriter Red Smith wrote in his column several days later, quoting Madison Square Garden boxing director Harry Markson, "When a guy has bought 534 drinks in the same saloon, he's entitled to one on the house."

Roy White (17 HRs, 20 stolen bases), a very impressive 24-year-old outfielder, emerged as a player with power and speed.

Although the season gave Yankee fans reason to hope for a better future, their attendance at the Stadium was only 1,125,124. Across town, meanwhile, the Mets continued to prosper.

1969

On March 1 in Fort Lauderdale, Fla., the site of the Yanks' spring training camp, superstar Mickey Mantle publicly announced his retirement. Thus, the season began on a subdued note.

For the first time in baseball history, both the NL and AL were split into East and West divisions. The Yanks, placed in the AL East along with Baltimore, Detroit, Boston, Washington, and Cleveland, finished fifth, a whopping 28½ games behind the division-winning Orioles as Manager Ralph Houk's crew logged a mediocre 80-81 record.

The Yankee pitching staff, amazingly the second best in the entire league (3.23 ERA), was again led by Mel Stottlemyre (20-14, 2.82 ERA) and Fritz Peterson (17-16, 2.55 ERA), both of whom were truly sensational. But not another Yankee pitcher won more than nine games. Relief specialist Jack Aker (8-4, 2.06 ERA), acquired from the Seattle Pilots early in the season, led the Yanks in games saved (11). Yankee pitchers as a group did not commit a balk all season, only the second time in club history that the hurlers were so alert.

Defensively, the Yanks were tight, tying for third in the entire AL in fielding (.979). The best defensive player was Joe Pepitone (.995), best among the league's first basemen in fielding.

Unfortunately, New York had only two power hitters, Pepitone (27 HRs, 70 RBIs) and 23-year-old Bobby Murcer (26 HRs, 82 RBIs), who returned to the Yankee outfield after two years in the military. Pepitone and Murcer hit 53 of the Yanks' 94 home runs, second lowest total in the league. In a rare power display on August 10, Murcer, Thurman Munson (a young catcher just called up from the minors) and Gene Michael hit consecutive home runs in a Yankee victory. (The homer by Munson was his first in the majors.)

Horace Clarke (.285, 33 stolen bases) and Roy White (.290, 18 stolen bases) helped the running game as New York led the AL East in stolen bases (119). However, the club was in the division cellar in runs (562), RBIs (521), home runs (94) and batting (.235). The league's pitchers held little respect for Yankee batsmen, deigning to hit them only 14 times—the lowest total of hit batsmen in Yankee history.

The highlight of this season was easily "Mickey Mantle Day" on June 8. The Stadium was packed with 60,096 fans who came to hear Mickey's eloquent speech and to see his famous number "7" officially retired. Whatever Mantle did or said that day was lustily cheered!

1970

Somehow the Yankees managed a second-place finish in the AL East, although they ended up 15 games behind the powerful Orioles. The Yankees were never in a pennant race but their 93-69 record made it a most successful season.

The "big three" of the pitching staff, Fritz Peterson (20-11, 2.91 ERA), Mel Stottlemyre (15-13, 3.09 ERA) and Stan Bahnsen (14-11, 3.32 ERA), were splendid. However, the club had trouble finding reliable fourth and fifth starters. An excellent Yankee bullpen produced the most saves (49) in the AL East and the heart of the relief brigade was the duo of Lindy McDaniel (9-5, 29 saves) and Jack Aker (4-2, 16 saves).

Once more New York's attack was less than thundering. Roy White (22 HRs, 94 RBIs, .296), who played in 162 games to tie a club single-season record for games played, and Bobby Murcer (23 HRs, 78 RBIs) supplied the power. Murcer emerged as one of baseball's stars when he homered on each of four straight official at-bats during a June 24 doubleheader. Thurman Munson (.302) was selected as AL Rookie of the Year. Munson, 23, was proving to be not only a fine hitter but an excellent catcher. Danny Cater (.301) and Horace Clarke (23 stolen bases) also contributed to the attack.

Defensively, the Yankees were strong up the middle with Munson, Horace Clarke, Gene Michael and Murcer. They were improved in most offensive areas over the previous season, and, with an already strong pitching staff in place, the club had high hopes for the future. For the moment, though, they had regained respectability, thanks largely to what may have been Ralph Houk's most brilliant managing job with the club.

1971

Having a so-so 82-80 season, the Yankees fell back to fourth place in the AL East.

Five pitchers started 158 of the season's 162 games. The busy five were Mel Stottlemyre (16-12, 2.87 ERA), Fritz Peterson (15-13, 3.05 ERA), Stan Bahnsen (14-12, 3.35 ERA), Steve Kline (12-13, 2.96 ERA) and Mike Kekich (10-9, 4.08 ERA), an excellent starting rotation that got little support from the bullpen. Yankee relievers had an AL low of only 12 saves. Lindy McDaniel (5-10) and Jack Aker (4-4) tallied only four saves each after combining for 45 saves the previous season. Defensively, the 1971 Yankees were more than respectable, tying for second in the entire AL in fielding (.981).

Bobby Murcer (25 HRs, 94 RBIs, .331) had a great season at the plate, played a solid center field, and was entrenched as the darling of Yankee fans. Leftfielder Roy White (19 HRs, 84 RBIs, .292) hit for power and average. White set an AL season record with 17 sacrifice flies and was flawless in the field (1.000). His 145 games without an error set a club record for outfielders.

Thurman Munson (10 HRs, .251) was still getting used to major-league pitching but was already the best defensive catcher in the league. He led AL catchers in fielding (.998) and tied the Yankee fielding record for catchers set in 1964 by Elston Howard. Munson made only one error all season.

With shortstop Gene Michael (.224), second baseman Horace Clarke (.250), Munson and Murcer, the Yanks were in great shape up the middle, but the rest of the infield was unsteady, and stronger arms were needed in the outfield.

The season ended strangely when the Yanks were awarded a forfeit at Washington on September 30. It was the final home game ever for the Senators (they moved to Texas the next year) who were leading when fans swarmed onto the RFK Stadium playing field, making further play impossible. The Senators' Frank Howard hit a homer (Munson let him know the pitch) but the game went into the books as a 9-0 Yankee victory, the homer not counting because of the forfeit.

1972

The Yankees' record (79-76—a players' strike shortened the front end of the season by seven games) and finishing position, fourth in the AL East, were not all that impressive, but it was a good, interesting season; the Yankees were in the pennant race until mid-September and ended up only 6½ games behind division-winning Detroit. The Tigers, Boston, Baltimore and the Yankees scrapped for the lead the season through.

The Yanks were in contention largely because of relief pitcher Sparky Lyle (9-5, 35 saves), obtained in the preseason from the Red Sox. Lyle was nothing short of spectacular. He led the league in saves, established what was then a club record for saves, and was named AL Fireman of the Year by *The Sporting News*.

Fritz Peterson (17-15) and Steve Kline (16-9) paced the starting pitchers. In the course of the season, Mel Stottlemyre (14-18) pitched four consecutive shutouts against one club (the Angels), a league record.

Bobby Murcer had another outstanding year (33 HRs, 96 RBIs, .292) and led the league in runs scored (102). However, Murcer had little help from his teammates. What help there was came mainly from Thurman Munson (.280), first baseman Ron Blomberg (14 HRs, .268) and consistent Roy White (10 HRs, 23 stolen bases, .270), the latter the league leader in walks (99). Defensively, the Yanks were tied for seventh in the AL (.978).

Oddly though, the Yanks made more double plays (179) than any other club in the league, a tribute to the fine fielding of shortstop Gene Michael and Horace Clarke. Clarke, in fact, led league second basemen in assists (399) for the sixth consecutive season. Murcer, on top of his fine hitting, won a Gold Glove for his center field play.

One of the highlights of the season occurred April 18 when New York for the first time opened the season under the Yankee Stadium lights; the Yankees nipped the Brewers, 2-0.

Unfortunately, the home attendance slipped this season to 966,328. It was the first time the Yankees drew fewer than a million since 1945. With this grim gate picture in the background, CBS in December was in serious negotiations to sell the franchise to a group headed by George Steinbrenner, negotiations that would culminate January 3 with a price tag in the neighborhood of $10 million. Also noteworthy was the fact that the Yankees signed a 30-year lease to play in a renovated, city-owned Yankee Stadium. The contract was agreed upon in August, the 30-year period scheduled to begin in 1976.

1973

The Yankees remained lodged in fourth place in the AL East for the third straight season, Ralph Houk's last as Yankee manager.

Yankee hurlers, solid as always, composed the third best staff in the entire AL (3.33 ERA) and were again led by Mel Stottlemyre (16-16, 3.07 ERA). Rookie star Doc Medich (14-9, 2.91 ERA) and relief specialists Sparky Lyle (5-9, 2.51 ERA, 27 saves) and Lindy McDaniel (12-6, 2.81 ERA, 10 saves) were also outstanding. New York finished as only the ninth best fielding club in the league (.976), but there were many fine defensive players on the team.

Thurman Munson won his first Gold Glove for his skill behind the plate, and third baseman Graig Nettles, acquired from Cleveland in a preseason trade, gave the Yanks the best defense at the hot corner since the days of Clete Boyer. Nettles led the league's third basemen in assists (410), an indication of his great range. It was the second highest total for third basemen in baseball history. Munson led AL catchers in assists (80) and Bobby Murcer led all league outfielders in assists (14). Shortstop Gene Michael covered a lot of real estate up the middle.

Offensively, the Yanks improved from the previous year in all categories, hitting more home runs (131) than the team had hit since 1966. The Yanks' team batting average (.261) was the club's best since 1962, although the higher average was due partly to a new wrinkle, the designated hitter. (Ron Blomberg became the first DH in baseball history on April 6 at Fenway Park, going 1-for-3 with a walk.) However, New York hit into 142 double plays, the most in Yankee history until the 1982 team. Murcer (22 HRs, 95 RBIs, .304), who on July 13 hit three homers off Gene Garber of the Royals, had his third tremendous season in a row, and Munson (20 HRs, 74 RBIs, .301) became a great hitter and complement to Murcer.

In an August game at Fenway, Thurman crashed into Boston's Carlton Fisk in a play at the plate. The fight that followed initiated the tremendous rivalry between the two best catchers in the AL, a rivalry to coincide with the renewed intense competition between the Yanks and the Sox.

Nettles (22 HRs, 81 RBIs) added much-needed power, while young Blomberg (.329) gave every indication of being on the verge of stardom. Leading the AL in at-bats (639) and playing in all 162 Yankee games, Roy White (18 HRs, 60 RBIs) did the job in his customary quiet and dignified manner. September was a month of memories. Fred Stanley hit the final grand slam at the "old" Yankee Stadium on September 8.

On September 30, the Yankees played the final game at the "old" Yankee Stadium soon to undergo renovation—to be renewed in time for the 1976 season. The Tigers defeated the Yanks, 8-5, as McDaniel absorbed the loss, and Duke Sims hit the final Yankee homer at the "old" Stadium. Many in the crowd left with souvenirs and momentos of American's greatest and most famous stadium.

At the conclusion of the World Series, Dick Williams, manager of the World Champion Oakland A's, resigned. Since it had been decided that 1973 would be Houk's final season with the Yanks, New York was in the market for a manager and signed Williams. However, A's owner Charlie Finley objected, maintaining that Williams was still bound to the A's. Joe

Cronin, AL president, in December ruled in Finley's favor and the Yankees were left managerless.

1974

Finishing in second place in the AL East, only two games behind the champion Baltimore Orioles, the Yankees came as close to finishing first as they had in a decade. The Red Sox held the division lead for most of the season before fading in the second half to finish at 84-78, seven games behind the Orioles.

September was a dramatic month as the Yanks and Birds battled for the lead. Behind first-year manager Bill Virdon, New York actually held the lead in September, but the Orioles swept a three-game set at New York to grab the lead and never let go. It was a classic stretch run by the Orioles who won 28 of their last 34 games, 15 of which were one-run victories.

On the final weekend of the season, with the Yankees right on the tail of the Orioles, an incident took place that just about ended any chances the Yanks entertained. In a Milwaukee hotel, reserves Rick Dempsey and Bill Sudakis began to fight. Superstar Bobby Murcer, attempting to break up the brawl, suffered a damaged thumb. Unable to play, Murcer watched a ball drop in right field, a ball *he* might have caught but which was instead the hit that beat the Yankees, eliminating them from the pennant race.

The Yanks had an impressive 89-73 ledger, but their having to play in Shea Stadium during Yankee Stadium's renovation might have cost New York the division title; it was obvious that some Yankees had trouble hitting at Shea.

The club drew 1,273,075 fans to Shea, the best home attendance since 1964. The fans were finding the team attractive, and Yankee President Gabe Paul, in recognition of his success in building this surprise club, was named major-league Executive of the Year by *The Sporting News.*

Pat Dobson and Doc Medich (both 19-15) were the biggest winners on the AL's third best pitching staff (3.31 ERA). Because of a shoulder injury suffered in mid-season, 32-year-old Mel Stottlemyre (6-7) was forced to retire prematurely after a great career. On June 11, Mel's 272nd consecutive start established a league record. Dick Tidrow (11-9), who in an April trade was acquired from Cleveland along with first baseman Chris Chambliss, did a fine job as the Yanks' third starter, and for the third straight year, Sparky Lyle (9-3, 15 saves) was the bullpen ace.

In truth, the Yanks were not a very powerful hitting club, yet they finished third in the AL in RBIs (637), knocking in the exact number of runs as did the World Champion Oakland A's. Bobby Murcer (88 RBIs, .274) had trouble hitting home runs in Shea, belting only 10 all season. Graig Nettles (22 HRs, 75 RBIs) got off to a great start, hitting 11 home runs in April to set an AL homer record for that month. Nettles hit four homers during an April 14 doubleheader. Thurman Munson (13 HRs, 60 RBIs), who won another Gold Glove for his catching; first-year Yankee Lou Piniella (70 RBIs, .305); Ron Blomberg (.311); Elliott Maddox (.303); and Roy White (.275) all contributed much to the Yankee attack. The Yanks hit 72 sacrifice flies to tie a league record.

This was also a decent defensive club, tying for third in the AL in fielding (.977). Being involved in a tight pennant race was a novel exhilaration; so was the realization that the club was just a player or two away from the top. In fact, had Stottlemyre remained healthy, the Yanks would have won the division title this year.

When the A's star pitcher, Catfish Hunter, was declared a free agent after the World Series, New York sought his services. On New Year's Eve, Catfish signed a five-year contract to pitch for New York, and Yankee fans looked forward to a happy new year.

1975

The Yankees slipped to third place, 12 games behind the AL East Champion Red Sox. The season started dramatically enough, but Opening Day was a happy experience in Cleveland, not New York. Frank Robinson hit a home run in his first at-bat as baseball's first black manager, leading the Indians to a 5-3 win over the Yankees before a roaring Municipal Stadium crowd.

On August 2, Bill Virdon was fired as manager of the Yanks and was replaced by a former Yankee player, the scrappy Billy Martin. Under Virdon the Yanks were 53-51; behind Martin they were 30-26. Although two superstars, Catfish Hunter and Bobby Bonds, were added to the club, it was a disappointing season after hopes were raised by the fact that many experts picked the Yankees to win the pennant.

Hunter (23-14, 2.58 ERA) was spectacular, leading AL pitchers in wins, complete games (30) and innings pitched (328)—most innings for a Yankee since Carl Mays pitched 337 innings in 1921. Catfish led a pitching staff that again was the third best in the league, topped only by Baltimore's and Oakland's. Doc Medich (16-16), Rudy May (14-12) and Pat Dobson (11-14) all started at least 30 games and made a dependable front line, but the bullpen was unusually weak. Tippy Martinez (1-2) was the club saves leader with eight while Sparky Lyle (5-7, six saves) had an off-year.

Offensively, Bobby Bonds (32 HRs, 85 RBIs, 30 stolen bases) led the attack and became the only Yankee player to hit 30 homers and steal 30 bases in a season. He was a fine rightfielder and played much of the season hurt. Thurman Munson (12 HRs, 102 RBIs, .318) was proving a great clutch hitter and had become perhaps the best player in the league. His 102 RBIs were the most by a Yankee since Mantle drove in 111 runs in 1964, and his Gold Glove was his third in a row. Graig Nettles (21 HRs, 91 RBIs), Chris Chambliss (72 RBIs, .304) and Roy White (12 HRs, .290) helped Bonds and Munson with the run production, which was not helped by the fact that the Yanks hit into 142 double plays, tying the then-club record.

Defensively, New York tied for second in the AL (.978) and boasted an especially strong infield. Second baseman Sandy Alomar and shortstop Fred Stanley provided stability up the middle, and Nettles had become the best third baseman in baseball.

This was the Yankees' final season at Shea Stadium; the club would next season return to Yankee Stadium with the makings of a solid team.

1976

The Yankees celebrated their return to refurbished Yankee Stadium by winning their first pennant in 12 years.

Manager Billy Martin's men produced a 97-62 record and finished 10½ games ahead of Baltimore in the AL East. New York made important acquisitions in brilliant deals both before and during the season. The new Yankees: Ed Figueroa, Dock Ellis, Ken Holtzman, Doyle Alexander, Willie Randolph, Mickey Rivers, Oscar Gamble and Carlos May. The Stadium reopened with the home opener April 15 amid tremendous fan anticipation. The huge crowd was treated to an old-fashioned Yankee romp, the Yanks thrashing Minnesota, 11-4.

Fans poured into the Stadium throughout the season, pushing Yankee attendance over the two-million mark (2,012,434) for the first time since 1950.

The best pitching staff in the entire AL (3.19 ERA) was led by Figueroa (19-10, 3.02 ERA), while Catfish Hunter (17-15, 3.53 ERA) and Ellis (17-8, 3.19 ERA) were also outstanding. Alexander (10-5) and Holtzman (9-7), both obtained from Baltimore at the June 15 trading deadline, helped the team during the second half of the campaign. Sparky Lyle (7-8) returned to form, leading the AL in saves (23), and Dick Tidrow (4-5, 10 saves) helped Sparky with the relief work. Yankee pitchers intentionally walked only 16 batters, fewest in AL 162-game history.

Behind this excellent pitching staff was superb fielding, the Yanks finishing a league second in defense (.980). The outfield was weak-armed but quick; Rivers covered the Stadium's center-field pastures better than anyone since Mantle. Rookie second baseman Randolph showed spectacular range, and his double play partner Fred Stanley led AL shortstops in fielding (.983), a mark that set the club fielding record for shortstops. For the third time in his four seasons with the Yanks, Craig Nettles led AL third basemen in assists (383), further indication that he covered more ground at third than anyone in the league.

But the heart of the defense—the heart of everything about this team, for that matter—was Munson. He handled pitchers beautifully. He exuded leadership and was named the first Yankee captain since Gehrig. And he swung a potent bat (17 HRs, 105 RBIs, .302). Munson won the AL MVP Award and *The Sporting News* named him the AL Player of the Year.

Nettles (93 RBIs, .254) was the AL home run king (32), and Chris Chambliss (17 HRs, 96 RBIs, .293), Gamble (17 HRs), Roy White (14 HRs), Rivers (.312), and Lou Piniella (.281) provided added offense. But this club, often called the Bronx Bandits, was known for its speed. Rivers (43 SBs), Randolph (37 SBs), and White (31 SBs) led the Yanks to a division-leading 163 stolen bases. Thus, the Yanks combined speed, occasional power, and a .269 batting average with great pitching and fine defense to capture the AL East title.

The old Yankee-Red Sox rivalry, which had been heating up again since the early 1970s after a period of dormancy, turned red hot in a May game at the Stadium. Piniella's crashing slide into Boston's Carlton Fisk in a play at the plate precipitated a fight between the two that soon involved both squads which met at home plate with fists flying. Red Sox pitcher Bill Lee severely damaged his shoulder in the fight and was rendered virtually useless for the remainder of the season. Whether or not the incident may have sparked the Yankees is conjectural; however, it is a fact that New York played great baseball for the rest of the season. And it appeared that the hostile passions the Yanks and Sox held for each other were back to stay.

1977

The Yankees during the off-season signed free agents Reggie Jackson and Don Gullett as pennant insurance. And win the AL East title for the second year in a row the Yankees did, nosing out both Boston and Baltimore by 2½ games.

Because New York had signed Jackson and Gullett (for large sums) in the first annual free-agent reentry draft, the rest of the league seemed resentful and the Yankees were subjected to harassment and fan violence in every AL park, especially those parks in Baltimore, Boston and Kansas City. Internal problems also beset the club. On June 18 in Boston's Fenway Park, Manager Billy Martin and Jackson nearly exchanged nationally televised punches. The June 17-19 Fenway Park series was definitely the low point of the year, as the Red Sox set a ML record by hitting 16 HRs in their three-game sweep of the Yanks.

Yet, the Yanks would be strong enough to survive the pressures and inability to achieve sustained success, the club hovering just above the .500 mark until mid-season. In early August, New York began a string of 40 victories in 50 games, overtaking the Red Sox and Orioles. One of the big wins came September 14 at the Stadium when Reggie Jackson's ninth-inning, two-run homer beat Boston, 2-0, and pushed the Red Sox 3½ games behind the Yanks. The seven-hit shutout by Ed Figueroa left the Red Sox lifeless.

The rebuilt Yankees and the AL excitement drew 2,103,092 fans to the rebuilt Stadium while the Mets were fast losing customers—the baseball worm had turned in the Big Apple.

One of the season's noteworthy events occurred July 19 when a crowd of 56,683 saw the NL beat the AL, 7-5, in the third All-Star Game ever played at the Stadium. One of its painful events came on September 10 when lowly Toronto, an expansion team, beat the Yankees, 19-3, in one of the worst defeats the pinstripers ever absorbed at the Stadium.

Usually it was the Yanks who were doing the big scoring; the team was second in the AL in batting (.281), third in home runs (184) and fourth in runs (831). Jackson (32 HRs, 110 RBIs, .286), Graig Nettles (37 HRs, 107 RBIs, .255), Thurman Munson (18 HRs, 100 RBIs, .308) and Chris Chambliss (17 HRs, 90 RBIs, .287) were the heart of the offense, combining for 407 RBIs.

Consistently getting key hits were Lou Piniella (12 HRs, .330), Mickey Rivers (12 HRs, .326) and Roy White (14 HRs, .268). White's two-run homer in the bottom of the ninth inning with two outs tied a game with the Red Sox on June 24. What a clutch hit! The Yanks went on to win the game, sweep the series, and cut Boston's AL lead from four games to one. Because of Rivers' great speed, he hit into only two double plays all season, tying a Yankee record set by Mickey Mantle in 1961. Big Cliff Johnson was obtained in mid-season from Houston and provided valuable help (12 HRs, .296) down the stretch. Johnson hit two home runs in the eighth inning of a June 30 game against Toronto, making a total of three for the game.

Sparky Lyle (13-5, 2.17 ERA, 26 saves) had his greatest season and won the Cy Young Award, the first relief pitcher in AL history to take that honor. Lyle set a Yankee club record for game appearances (72) and finished more games (60) than any other pitcher in Yankee history. Through 1999, the Yankee record for games pitched is 77 by Jeff Nelson in 1997 and for games finished is 68 by Dave Righetti in 1986. On August 29, 30 and 31, Lyle in relief won three straight Yankee games, tying a league record. The pitching, weak early in the season, was given a boost when Ron Guidry (16-7, 2.82 ERA) was inserted into the rotation. Ed Figueroa (16-11), Don Gullett (14-4), Mike Torrez (14-12), Dick Tidrow (11-4) and Catfish Hunter (9-9) all were key members of the Yankee staff.

Although the Yankees were only tied for third in the AL in fielding (.979), the infield was the best in baseball. Bucky Dent and Willie Randolph were excellent up the middle, Chambliss was much improved at first base, and Nettles won the Gold Glove for his tremendous play at third. This edition of the Yankees played ten consecutive errorless games, a club record, later tied in 1993 and 1995.

This was a balanced club; it had hitting, speed, pitching and defense; and its record for the season, 100-62, was a natural consequence of its well-distributed strength.

1978

The Yankees captured their third consecutive AL East flag in one of the most exciting races in baseball history.

They got off to a good start (29-15), but injuries and internal problems were to catch up with them. In a July 17 extra-inning loss to the Royals, Reggie Jackson continued attempting a sacrifice bunt after Yankee Manager Billy Martin ordered the slugger to hit away. Jackson received a five-day suspension from the club. Worse, the loss to the Royals dropped the Yanks 14 games behind the Red Sox, a sorry position in which the Yanks would be mired for three long days. While New York was struggling in the early summer, Boston was playing the best baseball the game had seen in years. The Red Sox simply appeared awesome and uncatchable.

With Jackson suspended, the Yanks went on a five-game winning streak, and on July 23 the Yanks had cut the Red Sox lead to 10 games. But that day in Chicago's O'Hare Airport, Martin, seething again at Jackson now that Reggie had rejoined the team, made an uncomplimentary comment about Jackson and Yankee owner George Steinbrenner. These remarks were printed. On July 24, Martin, facing a sure firing, resigned as Yankee manager and was replaced by Bob Lemon. (Dramatically, on Old Timers' Day only five days later, Martin was renamed Yankee manager, his next term at the helm to begin in 1980.)

Under Lemon, the Yankees climbed to within 7½ games of Boston on July 31, but New York was still lodged in third place. After scoring five runs in the bottom of the ninth to pull out an 8-7 victory against the Brewers on August 9, the Yanks were still 7½ games behind the Red Sox but in second place. On September 1, the Yankees were seven games behind, and creeping up on the Red Sox by dint of their own efforts and a seemingly inexorable Boston decline that was now fully in motion. This disastrous Boston losing spell actually began in late August and lasted into mid-September.

Joe DiMaggio, the famed "Yankee Clipper" tips his hat to the fans as other former Yanks applaud. They are, from left, Mickey Mantle, Whitey Ford, Billy Martin, Phil Rizzuto, Eddie Lopat, Clete Boyer and Tommy Tresh. All were introduced before the beginning of the annual Old Timer's Day Game at Yankee Stadium, Saturday, August 13, 1977. (AP/WIDE WORLD PHOTOS)

By September 7, the Yankees trailed the Red Sox by only four games as the key series of the season opened in Beantown between the Yanks and Red Sox. In the so-called "Boston Massacre" at Fenway Park, the Yankees swept the four-game set (September 7-10) to tie Boston for the AL East lead. Boston was reeling! That the slaughter was complete is written plainly in the fact that the Bronx Bombers outscored the Red Sox, 42-9. (The Yankee wins—15-3, 13-2, 7-0, 7-4.) When the Yanks beat Boston September 16 at Yankee Stadium on a Thurman Munson sacrifice fly scoring Mickey Rivers in the bottom of the ninth, they increased their lead over Boston to 3½ games, and the Red Sox appeared dead. (New York had beaten Boston six times without a loss in 10 days.) But the next day Dennis Eckersley beat the Yanks, 7-3, and kept the Red Sox alive. (More than 165,000 fans saw the three-game series at the Stadium. In the first game, Ron Guidry pitched his second straight two-hitter over Boston to win, 4-0.)

Somehow the Red Sox righted themselves to win 12 of their last 14 games, including the final eight in a row. On the last day of the season, the Yankees lost to the Indians, 9-2, while the Red Sox won to tie the Yanks for first place. Thus, a one-game playoff was forced. The Fenway Park playoff was won by the Yanks, 5-4, in a thrilling game. Thus was capped the most amazing comeback in baseball history.

It was a great year at the box office, too, the Yankees drawing 2,335,871 fans. Only in 1948 and in eight seasons that would follow 1978 did the Yankees enjoy better home attendance.

The hero of this memorable season was pitcher Ron Guidry (25-3, 1.74 ERA). With the possible exception of Jack Chesbro's 1904 season, Guidry had the greatest pitcher's year in New York Yankee history. The slender lefty won his first 13 decisions, pitched nine shutouts, and recorded 248 strikeouts—all club records. In a June 17 game with California, he struck out 18 Angels, another club record. Ron's shutout total was the most for an AL lefty since Babe Ruth pitched nine for Boston in 1916. "Louisiana Lightning's" winning percentage (.893) was the best ever for a 20-game winner in the majors. Ron Guidry won all the honors—the AL Cy Young Award, the Associated Press Male Athlete of the Year Award, *Sport Magazine's* "Performer of the Year" Award, and *The Sporting News'* ML Player of the Year and Man of the Year Awards.

Of all his impressive statistics, what was particularly enthralling was his ability to win games, which immediately followed Yankee losses. He did that 14 times. He was THE stopper.

Ed Figueroa (20-9) and Catfish Hunter (12-6) also did great mound work, especially in the second half of the season. Rich Gossage (10-11) led AL pitchers in saves (27). *The Sporting News* named him the league's Fireman of the Year. The "Goose," finished more games (55) than any other right-hander in Yankee history until surpassed by Mariano Rivera who had 63 in 1999. Goose had a blazing fastball that made him almost unhittable. Sparky Lyle (9-3) also was a factor in what was the league's best pitching staff (3.18 ERA). Lyle's nine saves along with Gossage's 27 gave the team a league-leading 36.

Defensive standouts on this, the league's second best fielding team (.982), were Chris Chambliss and Graig Nettles, both winners of Gold Gloves. Chambliss (.997) tied the Yankee fielding record for first basemen and Nettles (.975) established the club record at third base.

Although the power production dropped off from 1977, Reggie Jackson (27 HRs, 97 RBIs, .274) and Nettles (27 HRs, 93 RBIs, .276) sent the ball long distances. Chambliss (12 HRs, 90 RBIs, .274), who played in all 162 Yankee games; Lou Piniella (.314); and Thurman Munson (.297) all had good years at the plate, while Willie Randolph (.279), Bucky Dent (.243) and Roy White (.269) came up with clutch hits in key games.

1979

It was a disheartening and emotionally draining season. Yankee captain and star catcher Thurman Munson was killed August 2 in a fiery crash while in Ohio practicing takeoffs and landings in his new twin-engine jet.

Thurman's Cessna Citation hit the ground several hundred feet from an Akron-Canton Airport runway, not far from his home. The days following were laden with sadness. Yankee Stadium filled August 3 with 51,151 fans who, amid banners everywhere eulogizing Thurman, heard Terence Cardinal Cooke characterize their catcher as "a good family man" who was "blessed...with skill and talent." The giant telescreen bore Thurman's image and this message: "Our captain and leader has not left us. Today, tomorrow, this year, and next our endeavors will reflect our love and admiration for him." The Stadium throng stood, applauded and cried for nearly 10 minutes. Finally the catcher's box, empty when the Yankees took the field, was filled by rookie catcher Jerry Narron, and the game began.

The entire Yankee team attended Munson's funeral August 6 along with what seemed to be the entire populace of Canton, Thurman's hometown. They heard messages of sympathy read from telegrams from Muhammad Ali, Mrs. Eleanor Gehrig, and others, and moving eulogies by teammates Lou Piniella and Bobby Murcer.

That night back at the Stadium, Murcer's two-run ninth-inning single won it for New York, 5-4. Murcer, without benefit of sleep and in mourning over the death of his best friend, knocked in all five Yankee runs in a stalwart performance to beat Baltimore, the team that dislodged the Yanks from the top of the AL East.

New York, in fact, finished fourth, although the team's 89-71 record was good enough to have won the AL West. Sparky Lyle, Paul Linblad, Gary Thomasson, and Mike Heath were dealt away before the season started; with the season in progress, Paul Blair was released and Dick Tidrow, Cliff Johnson, Jay Johnstone, and Mickey Rivers were traded. In fact, many of the stars of the 1978 World Champions were gone by the time 1979 became 1980. Catfish Hunter retired with the season's close, Roy White entered the reentry draft and Chris Chambliss and Jim Beattie were traded.

And then there was the managerial shake-up that occurred on June 19 when Bob Lemon (34-31) was replaced by Billy Martin (55-40). Martin was warmly greeted by the fans on his first appearance at Yankee Stadium, but not even his magic could ignite the Yankees.

The Orioles, a team enjoying a tremendous season, finished 13½ games ahead of New York. The Yanks played fine ball at home (51-30), but their road record (38-41) spelled doom. Consistency was not their hallmark. They never put together a winning skein of any consequence until the final week of the

New York Yankees manager Billy Martin kicks dirt on rookie home plate umpire Dallas Parks in the eighth inning of August 19, 1979 night game lost to the Minnesota Twins at Yankee Stadium. Martin was upset with Parks' calls during the evening. When Parks tossed him out of the game, Martin responded by kicking dirt on Parks several times. Parks was one of the umpires who worked during the umpires' strike. (AP/WIDE WORLD PHOTOS, Ray Stubblebine)

season when they won their final eight games. They lacked right-handed hitting, and opposing clubs constantly threw lefthanded pitchers at them. The result: the Yanks were 55-34 against righthanders and 34-37 against lefties.

But the hitting overall was not up to Yankee standards. Failing to lead the league in a single offensive statistic, New York ranked near the middle in most categories including slugging (.406). And there was little team speed. Yet, some Yankees had a good year at the plate.

Reggie Jackson (29 HRs, 89 RBIs, .297), despite missing 29 games because of injuries, led or tied for club leadership in all three Triple Crown categories, and his slugging average of .544 was the league's fifth highest. Jackson in 1979 passed Yankee greats Yogi Berra, Johnny Mize and Joe DiMaggio on baseball's all-time home run list and finished the year in 25th place with 369. It was the 12th straight year in which he hit more than 20 homers. Willie Randolph (.270) probably had his best season, leading the Yankees in games played (153), at-bats (573), runs (98), hits (155-tie), triples (13), walks (95) and stolen bases (33). Willie's great skills were better showcased and exploited by his new lead-off position in the batting order.

Lou Piniella had his usual outstanding season at-bat (11 HRs, 69 RBIs, .297), just missing another .300 year. Perhaps Jim Spencer (.288) had the best year of all with 23 home runs in only 295 at-bats! Oscar Gamble, returning to New York August 1 in the trade that sent Rivers to Texas, was not far behind. He hit .389 for the Yanks (44 for 113, 11 of them homers). Another returnee, Bobby Murcer (.273) hit eight homers in the final two months of the season. Like Martin, Bobby following his June 26 trade was received at the Stadium with the adulation reserved for an old hero who somehow, for four and a half seasons, became separated from his people. And Graig Nettles (.253, 73 RBIs) hit 20 homers to reach that mark for his seventh consecutive season as a Yankee.

Defensively, the Yankees led the AL in fielding (.981) for the first time since 1961. An especially impressive infield turned 183 double plays, the most by a Yankee club since 1957. Chris Chambliss (.995), Randolph (.985), Bucky Dent (.977) and Nettles (.966) all fielded near the top of the league at their respective positions. Randolph led all AL second basemen in putouts (355), assists (478) and double plays (128). But the Thurman Munson loss left the catching position with inexperienced personnel, and center field was a problem position all season.

The pitching staff suffered a damaging loss in April when bullpen stopper "Goose" Gossage damaged the thumb of his pitching hand in a clubhouse scuffle with Cliff Johnson. Gossage was on the disabled list from April 21 to July 9 and during that time the Yankee bullpen was woeful. Ron Davis, the rookie called up from Columbus early in the year, was the only effective reliever. Davis (14-2, 9 saves, 2.86 ERA) set a league record for most wins in relief by a rookie (14), but he could not carry the relief load by himself. The Goose returned in July and had a great second half (5-3, 18 saves, 2.64 ERA), but by then the Yankees were out of the pennant race.

Tommy John, signed as a free agent before the season opened, had a tremendous year (21-9), finessing hitters with his sinkerball and control. He led Yankee pitchers in wins, games started (36), complete games (17) and innings pitched (276), and his 2.97 ERA was the league's second best. Tommy also finished second in the Cy Young Award voting.

Ron Guidry (18-8) finished strong and had another great season, winning his second consecutive American League ERA championship with 2.78. Ron, who was third in the Cy Young balloting, demonstrated unselfishness early in the year when he voluntarily went to the bullpen for a couple weeks in the Yankees' time of need. His 201 strikeouts marked only the eighth time a Yankee pitcher collected more than 200 whiffs and distinguished Guidry as the first to do it twice.

Luis Tiant (13-8, 3.90 ERA) was a fine third starter, but the Yanks could not find a consistent fourth or fifth starter. Catfish Hunter (2-9, 5.31 ERA) closed out his marvelous career with a disappointing season. (Hunter departed with customary class, the Yankee Stadium crowd sending him off with "Catfish Hunter Day," a fittingly dignified occasion in September.) Ed Figueroa (4-6) was shelved in mid-season because of bone chips in his pitching elbow, and no one stepped forward to fill the void. The Figueroa injury was possibly the most damaging to the New York cause. The Guidry-Figueroa-Hunter threesome won 33 fewer games in 1979 than in 1978, and on top of this, Don Gullett spent the entire season on the disabled list.

But the Yankees continued to draw fans. The Yankee Stadium attendance of 2,537,765 easily broke the old home record set in 1948 (to be broken again in 1980, 1988, 1998 and 1999, the latter being the first three-million season). The Yankees drew 2,224,382 on the road, another club record (to be broken again in 1980). Home and away the Yankees played before 4,762,147 fans. It was a season of gate success, field mediocrity and emotional disquiet. Yankee fans were not happy to see Roy White (.215), one of the most popular and consistent players in Yankee history, play out his contract to end his 15-year Yankee career. (Roy played in Japan in 1980.)

The cloud of gloom lingered even with the season's close. On November 16, Jack Butterfield, the Yankee vice-president in charge of scouting and player development, was killed in an automobile accident. All in all, it was not a season to fondly remember.

1980

It was a successful comeback season, the Yankees bouncing back from their fourth-place finish in 1979 to win their fourth AL East title in five years.

Rookie Manager Dick Howser registered the most wins (103) of any first-year ML manager except for Ralph Houk who piled up 109 with the 1961 Yanks . It was baseball's best 1980 record, the most victories by an AL club since the Orioles' 108 in 1970 and the most by a Yankee team since the 1963 edition's 104 victories. The Yankees began slowly, but rallied to finish 9-9 in April, then manhandled the opposition in May (19-7) and June (19-9). By July 17 they had their largest lead of the season, a 9½-game bulge over Milwaukee.

But the next day the Yanks were gripped by a mediocrity that held through August 26. They were 18-21 for this period, their worst stretch of the year, which began against the Royals when the Yanks allowed Kansas City 34 runs and dropped two of three in their July 18-20 weekend series. Meanwhile, the resilient defenders of the AL championship, the Orioles, were getting hot.

A division race there would be, the Orioles seemed to assert in sweeping three at the Stadium August 8-10. In a five-game series at Baltimore August 14-18, the Yankees managed only two wins. The Orioles won six of eight August games with New York and cut the lead to 2½ games. All of Baltimore was now convinced of the inevitability of an Oriole division title. The Yankees reached their nadir on August 22, losing badly at California while Baltimore won a thriller to climb within a half game. That is how the standings stood for one dramatic week,

until August 28 when the Yanks returned home and began a string of wins.

They won 10 of 11 on the homestand, 21 of 28 in September and 28 of 37 from August 28 until the season's end. Some believe the Yanks won the division title by playing 23-4 ball between August 28 and September 24, but it may have been their performance in late July and August; however disappointing that performance, the Yanks still managed to play close to .500 ball. Baltimore's post-June 15 record was the best in baseball—it was the Orioles' horrendous start that proved their ruination. The Yankees went into first place to stay on May 14, Howser's birthday, and had the best record in baseball at the All-Star break, 51-27. Their 52-32 record after the All-Star Game was the best second-half record, too. The Yanks boasted the AL's finest home record, 53-28, AND road record, 50-31. Incredibly, the longest Yankee losing streak of the campaign was only three games (there were three such streaks).

Yankee pitching returned to form in 1980. The 3.59 team ERA was the second best in the AL, and the mound corps' 15 shutouts led the league. Tommy John (22-9) was the staff's ace, leading Yankee pitchers in wins, games started (36), complete games (16), innings pitched (265) and shutouts (6). He won his 200th game on June 6. Although he spent time in the bullpen working on his slider, Ron Guidry still had a fine year (17-10) and was among league leaders in strikeouts (166). Ron won his final four decisions under pressure conditions.

The acquisition of Rudy May (15-5, 3 saves) turned out to be the Yankee salvation. Rudy worked without complaint as a short reliever, long reliever and starter at different points in the season and showed himself a true professional. His 2.46 ERA led the AL. Competent Tom Underwood (13-9) rounded out the Yankee big four, all southpaws. (Yankee lefties won 68 games.) Luis Tiant (8-9) was the top right-handed starter.

The bullpen was sensational, setting a Yankee club record for saves (50) and leading the AL. Through 1999, the Yankee record for saves in a season is 58 in 1986. Rich Gossage (6-2, 2.27 ERA) who tied for the AL lead in saves (33), and fell just two shy of the Yankee record, led the relief staff. In 18 games between August 9 – September 21, Goose refused to allow a run. He retired 28 consecutive batters over one seven-game stretch and posted 17 saves after August 15. Ron Davis (9-3, 2.95 ERA, seven saves) and Doug Bird (3-0, 2.66 ERA) were both excellent in long relief, as were May, Underwood, and Guidry when they functioned in that underrated role. A tribute to the bullpen lies in this incredible stat: the Yanks were 77-2 in games in which they took a lead into the seventh inning!

Offensively, the Yankees were powerful, finishing second in the AL in runs scored (820) and home runs (189), the most Yankee homers since 1962. In fact, they tied a ML record by having nine players with at least 10 homers (Reggie Jackson, Craig Nettles, Bobby Brown, Rick Cerone, Oscar Gamble, Bobby Murcer, Jim Spencer, Bob Watson, Eric Soderholm). The record would have fallen had Ruppert Jones (.223, 9 HRs, 42 RBIs) not been sidelined in the spring by stomach surgery, returning only to suffer a serious shoulder injury and concussion when he hit the center field wall in Oakland on August 25. Rookie Joe Lefebvre (.227) had eight homers.

But the hitting star was Jackson (.300) who enjoyed his finest Yankee season. Reggie shared the AL home run crown with Ben Oglivie (41), the most four-baggers by a Yankee since

Hall of Famer Reggie Jackson demonstrates the powerful swing that enabled him to blast 563 homers in his career which spanned 21 seasons, 5 of which were with the Yankees.

1981

Roger Maris' 61 in 1961. Reggie's 111 RBIs were the most by a Yankee since Mickey Mantle's 111 in 1964. Jackson's bat carried the club through early summer. He hit 10 homers in July when he was AL Co-Player of the Month with George Brett. Reggie's 400th home run August 11 was a ceremonious affair, and he hit safely in the season's final 13 games, his three-run homer against Detroit October 4 clinching the division title for the Yankees.

But Jackson's hitting tailed off slightly after power-partner Nettles (16 HRs, 45 RBIs) contracted hepatitis in late July and was sidelined until the final weekend of the season. On July 21 Graig hit his 267th homer as an AL third baseman, breaking Brooks Robinson's record. The Yanks had an 8½-game lead when Nettles became ill and the team missed his bat and irreplaceable glove.

Cerone (.277, 14 HRs, 85 RBIs), who came to the Bronx Bombers with Underwood from Toronto in a great Yankee trade, provided timely power hitting. His 30 doubles led the club and were the most by a Yankee catcher since Yogi Berra's 30 in 1950. Perhaps baseball's best lead-off man in 1980 was Willie Randolph (.294, seven HRs, 46 RBIs) who had the league's second best on-base percentage (behind Brett). Willie used his incomparable batting eye to lead the AL in walks (119), walking in each of his final 15 contests. Willie's 1980 walk total is the most ever by a Yankee right-handed batter in history. Bucky Dent (.262, five HRs, 52 RBIs) had his best Yankee season. Watson (.307, 13 HRs, 68 RBIs) and Spencer (13 HRs, 43 RBIs) ably shared the first base job. Murcer (.269, 13 HRs, 57 RBIs) produced key hits, and fellow outfielders Lou Piniella (.287), Gamble (.278, 14 HRs, 50 RBIs) and Brown (.260, 14 HRs, 47 RBIs) all hit consistently.

A hallmark of the 1980 Yanks was a great bench. The Yanks had stomach, too, winning 20 games in their final at-bats. While they stole only 85 bases, they were successful in 70 percent of their attempts. Randolph (30 steals), Brown (27 steals), and Jones (18 steals) were the key base-stealing threats.

Defensively, the team, as usual, was brilliant up the middle. Cerone was as good as any receiver in baseball. He threw out 47 of 99 potential base-stealers, handled a new-to-him pitching staff with skill, blocked the plate bravely and generally did a magnificent job. Randolph and Dent had no equals in either circuit as a double-play combination. Jones, when healthy, made some of the year's greatest plays in center field, and Brown played satisfactorily in Jones' absence. Occasionally, the Yanks had outfield misplays, but by and large the defense was sound. Even with Nettles sidelined, Aurelio Rodriguez, obtained to plug the hole, provided fine glovework at third.

The Yanks set the AL afire as a drawing card. Establishing a new AL home attendance record (2,627,417, breaking Cleveland's 1948 mark), the Yanks also set a ML record by increasing home attendance for the eighth straight year. They set a ML road attendance record (2,461,240), thus becoming the first AL team to top the five-million mark in combined home and road attendance (5,088,657).

The Yankee past was remembered on Old Timers' Day, which was graced by the presence of Mrs. Thurman Munson. On September 20 a plaque in "Memorial Park" was dedicated to the great Munson.

The Yankees gained postseason play in this tormented year for the fifth time in six seasons. The season was split into halves—known as a First Season and a Second Season—because of a two-month players' strike, the second longest strike in the national pastime's history. Play was halted June 12, and day after day the nation looked on as three men—Marvin Miller, the players' representative; Ray Grebey, the owners' representative; and Ken Moffett, the federal mediator—sought to reach a settlement.

The owners, bolstered by lucrative strike insurance protection, were resolute in their desire to regain authority over the game. They wanted what they regarded as meaningful compensation for teams that lost players through free agency. The players were unwilling to give back the free movement of ballplayers in the baseball marketplace. Team compensation would dampen their ability to negotiate good contracts, they felt. Result: impasse.

Even the most ardent baseball fans shook their heads in disgust and disbelief. (But some of the truly intense fans found that summer without baseball can bring peace of mind.) Finally, as the seasonal clock was winding down and it looked like all was lost, a settlement was reached. The season—that is, the Second Season—picked up on August 10, following an All-Star Game that heralded the resumption of major-league play.

The Yankees made the playoffs as the First Season champions. They were in first place when the bell sounded for the First Season on June 12, thanks to their winning 11 out of 12 games between May 29 and June 9. With 34 wins and 22 losses, New York finished two games ahead of Baltimore and three games ahead of Milwaukee, notwithstanding a melancholy May when they went 14-14. The Yanks owed much to the Tigers and Royals—they were a combined 11-0 against these two clubs. Otherwise they were just a .500 team . They were 27-12 at night and 7-10 in day games.

The Yanks' strongest suit in the First Season was a bullpen led by Goose Gossage (17 saves, 2-1, 0.56 ERA). Ron Davis (4 saves, 2-2, 1.86 ERA) and Dave LaRoche (3-0, 0.63 ERA) were effective and Doug Bird (5-1, 2.70 ERA) performed ably as both a reliever and spot starter. This deep corps of relievers tallied 21 saves in only 56 Yankee games.

The starting pitchers were less spectacular but solid all the same. The included Ron Guidry (5-3, 3.74 ERA) and Tommy John (5-4, 3.19 ERA). Rudy May (4-5, 5.17 ERA) faltered after a strong start, but two youngsters—Gene Nelson (3-1, 5.00 ERA) and Dave Righetti (3-0, 1.50 ERA)—were outstanding. Nelson was great in spring training and made the big club as the youngest player in the ML's at 20. The flamethrowing Righetti, after going 5-0 at Columbus, was called up to the Yankees in mid-May .

The Yankees' First Season run production was unimpressive. They led the AL in HRs, out-homering opponents 57-38 but had poor totals in all other offensive categories. Their problems stemmed in part from injuries. Both Rick Cerone (.261 in 92 ABs) and Bob Watson (.182 in 44 ABs) were incapacitated for long periods of time. The team's sparkplug, Willie Randolph (.235), did not have the usual snap in his bat, although his 34 walks led the club. And Reggie Jackson (.199, six HRs, 24 RBIs) slumped through the entire First Season.

The First Season's most productive Yankees were former Padres, Jerry Mumphrey (.322) and millionaire free-agent addition Dave Winfield (.324, seven HRs, 40 RBIs). Winfield also was awesome on the base paths. Graig Nettles (.249, seven HRs, 23 RBIs) as usual delivered clutch hits, and Bucky Dent (.241, 6 HRs, 23 RBIs) displayed unexpected power. The club was strong at designated hitter with Oscar Gamble (.287, seven HRs) and Lou Piniella (.283) forming the left-right combination. Fan favorite Bobby Murcer (.276) chipped in clutch hits as a pinch hitter and part-time DH.

The defense was strong, with especially fine fielding turned in by Nettles and Winfield. Nettles made his well-known assortment of classic plays at third. Winfield gave the Yankees a new dimension in left field, showing a first-rate throwing arm, an immense range and an incredible ability to send his 6'6" frame skyward for would-be home runs. Up the middle the Yanks' defense was solid with Cerone (backed up by Barry Foote), Randolph, Dent, and Mumphrey.

The First Season's most splendid moment may have been Opening Day. A crowd of 55,123, the then-largest official Opening Day crowd in renovated Yankee Stadium history, saw Tommy John, aided by Dent's three-run HR and Murcer's dramatic pinch-hit grand slammer, overpower the Texas Rangers, 10-3. The Yankees were 11-6 in April, but in early May experienced a 5-6 West Coast trip. New York did sweep a doubleheader in Oakland on May 3, and the next night Davis struck out eight Angels in a row. But it was not until May 19 that the Yankees made a comeback to win a game that looked out of reach early. Trailing 5-0 to the Royals, the Yanks rallied for a 6-5 victory.

In the first important series of the year, the Yankees journeyed to Baltimore, and, with a warning from owner George Steinbrenner not to disappoint, lost three straight by scores of 10-1, 6-4 and 6-5 on May 25, 26 and 27. Again, May was not a prosperous month. The Birds were nesting in first place, as 124,464 paid to see the series, then the largest attendance for a weeknight series in Baltimore history.

After winning three of four games in Cleveland, the Yanks returned home to take three from the Orioles, winning the first two games on 11th-inning HRs, one by Dave Revering who was acquired from Oakland in May, and the other by Nettles. The third game of the vital series became a 12-3 Yankee laughter. Then the Yanks won three in a row from the White Sox and two in Kansas City (for nine straight wins) and, without being aware of it, clinched an automatic place in the playoffs as First Season champions. They dropped two in Chicago before the players' strike began, but these were meaningless to the standings.

As they were for the start of the First Season, the Yankees and Rangers on August 10 were again paired at the Stadium for the start of the Second Season. It was Tommy John on the mound for the Yankees as he was on Opening Day in April, and John allowed just two hits over seven innings to win, 2-0. Two Opening Days against Texas, and the Yankees didn't even play their first game against Boston until September 11.

The Yankees generally played poorly in the Second Season. They lost 10 of their first 17 games and played .529 ball for the remainder of the season. The under-motivated Yankees did not sweep a single series in the entire Second Season. Their only good stretch began with a Guidry win on August 28, starting a run of 10 Yankee victories in 12 games. This allowed the Yankees to remain in the Second Season race until mid-September, when they lost four of six games in Milwaukee and Boston.

The biggest Yankee news of the Second Season centered on Gene Michael, Steinbrenner's hand-picked choice for manager—the man who was, in fact, carefully groomed for the job. Gene informed the press on August 28 that he was tired of being threatened with firing. Steinbrenner could fire him if George wanted, and he told this to Steinbrenner, Michael said. And so on September 6 it happened. Michael was replaced by former Yankee skipper Bob Lemon.

The Yankees suffered from inconsistent hitting all season. They hit 100 homers, second only to Oakland in the AL, but as a team hit only .252, the ninth best batting average in the AL. And the Yanks ranked a lowly 11th in runs scored with 421.

Jackson was one player whose bat came alive in the Second Season. He played without emotion in the First season, but after being ordered to take a physical examination in August, Reggie came back with renewed determination, and his play was more inspired. Jackson (.237, 15 HRs, 54 RBIs) tied Nettles for club home-run honors. Reggie even seemed to enjoy mixing it up at the Stadium on September 23 following a couple of knock-down pitches thrown by Cleveland's John Denny.

Mumphry's .307 batting average led the Yankees, and Winfield (13 HRs, 68 RBIs, .294) was the club's RBI leader. Like Jackson, Nettles (15 HRs, 46 RBIs, .244) may have produced normal numbers in a full season. After Dent fractured his right hand in late August, Larry Milbourne stepped in and hit .313. But the Yankees got little offensive production from first base or catcher, and Randolph (.232) experienced his worst year at the plate.

Travis John, the son of Tommy John, in mid-August was critically injured in a fall from a window. Fortunately, the youngster made a great recovery after several weeks of agonizing concern. Understandably distracted, Tommy John finished the full season at 9-8. He posted a splendid 2.63 ERA, however.

Guidry (11-5, 2.76 ERA) had his fastball and slider working sharply, and he added a new pitch—a changeup—that made him even more artistic. Rudy May (6-11, 4.14 ERA) and Rick Reuschel (4-4), obtained between halves from the Cubs, added depth to the starting rotation. But it was Righetti (8-4) who made the headlines. He had only one bad outing all year, and if he had pitched another $1\frac{1}{3}$ innings on the year he would have won the ERA title with his 2.05 ERA. Righetti's fastball and curveball were reminiscent of a young Sandy Koufax.

The Yanks' bullpen cooled off some in the Second Season. Gossage, whose activities were limited by injuries, had only three Second Season saves, giving him 20 for the year to go with a 3-2 record. Davis (4-5, 2.71 ERA) and LaRoche (4-1, 2.49 ERA), while still strong, were not as consistent. George Frazier (three saves) was called up from the minors and contributed well. For the season, the Yankees were 53-3 when taking a lead into the seventh inning, but were 0-39 when trailing entering the seventh. (In 1980-81 combined, the Yankees were 130-5 when leading going into the seventh!)

The season ended with the Yankees the First Season champions and Milwaukee the champions of the Second Season. For the first time in history, a third playoff tier was added. The Yankees and Brewers would meet to determine the AL East champion.

1982

A season of distress for the Yankees ended with a losing record (79-83) and a fifth-place standing, 16 games out of first place and only one game ahead of last place. The Yankees for only the second time in their history used three managers—Bob Lemon (6-8), Gene Michael (44-42) and Clyde King (29-33)—and they also used five different pitching coaches.

The team began falling apart in the winter before the 1982 season, starting with the decision not to try to re-sign Reggie Jackson. Reggie as a free agent signed with the Angels. The Yankees did a lot of grandstanding in picking up Ken Griffey and Dave Collins; their speed was supposed to make the Yankees a running club.

What actually happened was not so good for the Yankees. On April 27, Jackson returned with the Angels to Yankee Stadium and hit a home run, igniting great cheering and the crowd to chant an obscenity directed at George Steinbrenner. Reggie would hit five homers on the season against New York, lead the league with 39 homers and help the Angels win the AL West.

Meanwhile, Griffey and Collins didn't work out. Griffey hit .277 with 12 homers and 10 stolen bases—not enough of either to offset the loss of Jackson—and Collins was one of three Yankees assigned to first base and had difficulty even getting playing time. The Yankees stole 69 bases for the year; not much more than their 47 stolen bases the previous season.

On February 9, spring training opened two weeks ahead of schedule for the Yankees. The early camp, with its emphasis on fundamentals, physical conditioning, and base running, was supposed to be voluntary, but the players weren't buying it. They resented being expected to report early, and it felt very much like punishment for losing the World Series the previous fall.

Just before the season opened, the Yankees obtained reliever Shane Rawley, who, ironically, eventually would find his best role in the starting rotation, but whose acquisition allowed the Yankees 10 days later to trade Ron Davis to Minnesota for Roy Smalley. Smalley hit 20 homers, including a new Yankee record 16 as a shortstop (Derek Jeter currently holds the Yankee shortstop mark with 24 roundtrippers in 1999), but the Yankees paid a big price for a few more homers. The bullpen, the strength of the 1981 club, was weakened without Davis. Defensively, Smalley wasn't as good as the man he replaced at shortstop, Bucky Dent. And Dent's unhappiness contributed to the overall poor morale of the team.

The scheduled April 6 Yankee Stadium opener was wiped out by a blizzard, blanketing New York City with a foot of snow. It took a tremendous effort by the groundcrew to have the Stadium ready to open five days later. And so the season opened with an Easter Sunday doubleheader, with Chicago sweeping both games from the Yankees. It was the only time in Yankee history that the season opened with a twinbill.

The Yankees finally won their first home game on April 25, but afterwards, Bob Lemon was replaced as manager by Gene Michael. The Yankees grumbled through May and had their worst month in June, going 9-16. When the Yanks lost both ends of an August 3 doubleheader at Yankee Stadium, which lasted late into the night, fans were offered free tickets as an amends from management, and with their record 50-50, the

Yanks replaced Michael with Clyde King. In September, the Yankees lost nine consecutive games.

Dent and Tommy John were traded in midseason. John (10-10, 3.66 ERA), unhappy with a demotion to the bullpen, demanded a trade but only to certain teams of his choice. His frustration boiled over on July 31 when he nearly had a clubhouse fistfight with Yankee executive Bill Bergesch.

Dave Righetti (11-10, 3.79 ERA), it was whispered, had the sophomore jinx. He was 5-5 and having control problems—with too many different coaches telling him what to do—when he was sent to Columbus on June 26 to get straightened out. Ron Guidry (14-8, Gold Glove) was the club's ace, Shane Rawley (11-10) the most pleasant surprise once he became a starter, and Goose Gossage saved 30 games, but perhaps the season's most entertaining pitcher was reliever Dave LaRoche, who occasionally threw a blooper pitch he called his "LaLob." On August 6, LaRoche finished a 6-0 win over Texas by striking out Lamar Johnson on a tantalizing LaLob. Johnson swung and missed, screwed himself into the ground and was counted out by the home-plate umpire.

The star of the season was Dave Winfield, whose 37 homers were the most by a Yankee right-handed batter other than Joe DiMaggio. Winfield also had 106 RBIs, finished second in the league with a .560 slugging average and won a Gold Glove. Other contributors included 39-year-old Lou Piniella, who hit .307 and had seven consecutive hits at one point; Jerry Mumphrey, who hit exactly .300; Oscar Gamble, who had 18 homers and 57 RBIs in only 316 at-bats; and Willie Randolph, who hit .280 and scored 85 runs.

But New York finished in the league's lower half in batting, as it did in pitching and fielding, too. The Yankees got poor production from left field, catcher, first base and third base, as the new Yankee captain, Graig Nettles (.232, 18 HRs, 55 RBIs) slipped from his normal production.

The Yankees on September 7 called up four youngsters, including 21-year-old Don Mattingly, who had hit .315 at Columbus. The next day Mattingly made his major-league debut when he replaced Winfield in left field. He got his first major-league hit on October 1, an 11th-inning single off Boston's Sammy Stewart.

King would have liked to remain the manager, but Billy Martin in October was fired by Oakland, and rumors swirled that Billy would be returning to the Yankees. These rumors were confirmed in January 1983 with Martin's appointment as Yankee manager.

1983

Returning to the familiar Billy Martin, and a Martin-type team, the Yankees were vastly improved, posting a record of 91-71. It was a wild season, featuring a no-hitter, the famous Pine Tar Game, a dead seagull, and a car accident that nearly killed the shortstop.

In the previous off-season, the Yankees seeking take-charge power hitters, signed free agents Don Baylor and Steve Kemp. Baylor's addition, plus better seasons from Ron Guidry and Graig Nettles, most helped the Yankees become contenders again. The Yankees were an excellent home team (51-30), but their difficulties on the road (40-41) contributed to the club eventually settling for third place.

Once again the club's biggest star was Dave Winfield. He walloped 32 homers, had 116 RBIs—third best in the league—and set a new Yankee record with 21 game-winning RBIs, later tied by Mattingly in 1985. Baylor (21 HRs, 85 RBIs) and Nettles (20 HRs, 75 RBIs) backed up Winfield in run production. Roy Smalley hit 18 homers and Ken Griffey batted .306, but Kemp was disappointing (.241, 12 homers).

Don Mattingly, who in spring training won the Dawson Award as the club's most outstanding rookie, signaled he was ready for a bigger role. In 91 games with the Yankees, Mattingly displayed a sweet stroke, hit a solid .283 and was impressive moving around first base.

Guidry proved that 1978 was no fluke. His record was 21-9, and he led the league with 21 complete games. Guidry and Winfield both won Gold Gloves and both were selected for the All-Star Game.

But Dave Righetti (14-8) turned in the year's most sensational pitching effort. At Yankee Stadium against Boston on the 4th of July, Righetti pitched the first no-hitter by a Yankee since Don Larsen's perfect game in the 1956 World Series. It was, in fact, the first no-hitter ever thrown by a southpaw at Yankee Stadium. And Rags dramatically struck out baseball's best hitter, Wade Boggs, for the final out, setting off an emotional holiday celebration.

Rounding out the key moundsmen were Shane Rawley (14-14, 3.78 ERA) and Goose Gossage (13-5, 22 saves). Ray Fontenot (8-2), a Louisiana Cajun like Guidry, impressed in his 15 starts, but free-agent pickup Bob Shirley (5-8) had a poor 5.08 ERA.

At Yankee Stadium on July 24, the Yankees and Royals met in the Pine Tar Game. The Yankees were leading, 4-3, in the ninth inning, when George Brett rocketed a two-run homer off Goose. However, Martin was able to successfully convince the umpires that Brett's bat had been illegally doctored; pine tar was applied above the point of the bat permitted by the rules. The homer was canceled, sending Brett into a rage, and the game would end with the Yankees 4-3 winners.

The Royals appealed the decision to American League President Lee MacPhail, who four days later overruled his umpires. MacPhail said there had been no intent to cheat by Brett and declared the game suspended with the score, 5-4, in favor of Kansas City. The game's last four outs were completed on August 18, and Martin treated it as a joke; he had Guidry playing center and Mattingly second base. The Yankees batted in the ninth without scoring. "We felt we had a game taken away from us," complained Martin. The Yankees never really recovered.

Also on August 18, the Yanks' Andre Robertson suffered a broken neck in an auto accident that demolished his car. The graceful and talented shortstop was lucky to be alive, but his promising major-league career was ended.

On August 4 in Toronto, a seagull's life was ended by Winfield, who was charged with cruelty to animals. Winny was finishing a between-innings warm-up with a ball boy when, thinking he would get the seagull off the field, he attempted bouncing the ball near the bird. But his throw was off target a little, conking the bird in the head and killing it. The crowd reacted with angry boos—and the authorities made the charge. Winfield didn't get off the hook until someone wisely decided Dave had no criminal intent and dropped the charge.

Martin and George Steinbrenner didn't get along any better than in the past. Martin in June agreed to Steinbrenner's request for an off-day workout, but he made it voluntary, and George was angry when he later learned of the workout's informality. Steinbrenner in July got even by firing pitching coach Art Fowler, which, naturally, angered Billy. Martin would be replaced by Yogi Berra after the season.

The Yankees were still in contention when the first-place Orioles came into Yankee Stadium for four games beginning September 9. The Yankees won the opener, closing to within four games of Baltimore. The next day, however, before a crowd of 55,605, the Yankees lost both ends of an ugly doubleheader. When the Yankees lost the series finale, too, they trailed by seven games, the final margin between the Yanks and Oriole's. Although Detroit moved ahead of New York, and the Yankees finished third, the Yanks had the fourth best record in the majors.

1984

Manager Yogi Berra was barely welcomed aboard when he looked up and saw he had no chance of contending for a division championship. Detroit sprinted to a 35-5 start, wrapping up the race before Memorial Day. The Yankees were eight games under .500 entering July, but put together monthly records of 17-11 in July, 21-10 in August and 16-13 in September, and had baseball's best record after the All-Star Game. Once again the Yankees were much better at home (51-30) than on the road (36-45). When it was over, the Yankees stood in third place, 17 games out of first.

Despite their winning ways at home, Yankee Stadium attendance dipped below two million for the first non-strike season since the renovated Stadium opened in 1976. Meanwhile, the Mets, sleepwalking for years, won 90 games in 1984. The Mets had a popular new manager, Davey Johnson, and a pitching phenom, Dwight Gooden, and they were beginning to surpass the Yankees as the city's showcase team.

The Yankees too had a phenom—Don Mattingly. In his first full season as a regular, Mattingly was suddenly the game's best first baseman. He had a quick and powerful bat—23 homers and 110 RBIs—turned the 3-6-3 double play as well as is humanly possible, led league first basemen with a .996 fielding average, and worked tirelessly at his game. He led the league in doubles (44), hits (207) and batting (.343).

Mattingly and Dave Winfield waged an exciting summer race for the batting crown. As September opened, Mattingly led Winfield .352 to .351. They seesawed back and forth all month. Going into the season's final game, against Detroit at Yankee Stadium, Winfield was ahead, .3410 to .3394. But Don went 4 for 5, finishing at .343, surpassing Dave, who went 1 for 4 and finished at .340. In their last at-bats in the eighth inning, Mattingly singled to right field and Winfield grounded out. If Mattingly had not gotten the hit, he would have hit .34163; and if Winfield had gotten a final-at-bat hit, he would have hit .34215 and won.

The crowd seemed to be pulling for Mattingly, which didn't bother Winfield as much as some of the boos he heard that day. He continued feuding with George Steinbrenner, but despite the distractions, he had a great year. He had a 20-game hitting streak, notched another 100-RBI season and won a third consecutive Gold Glove. "Winfield was my most valuable player," declared Berra.

Gone from the Yankees were Goose Gossage and Graig Nettles. Before the season, Goose signed with the Padres and Nettles was traded to the Padres, and they helped San Diego win the NL Pennant. The Yankees really missed Nettles because his third-base replacement, Toby Harrah, hit only .217 with one homer. Mike Pagliarulo was called up from the minors and did better (.239, 7 HRs).

Another unsettled position was shortstop. Bobby Meacham in June was recalled from Columbus, and hit .253, but he often made errors at critical times. Other players who were disappointments were light-hitting centerfielder Omar Moreno; Steve Kemp, who didn't reach double figures in homers; and Ken Griffey, whose batting average dropped to .273.

The most dependable bat other than Mattingly and Winfield belonged to Don Baylor, who led the club in homers with 27. He also had 89 RBIs and was hit by pitched balls 23 times, setting a new club record, which he broke the following season by one. Willie Randolph played consistently at second and hit .287.

The Yankee pitching staff's ERA of 3.78 was the league's third best. Dave Righetti, in a controversial shift, replaced Gossage as the bullpen closer, and in his first season in that role, he tallied 31 saves, fourth most in the league. Jay Howell (9-4, 7 saves) did an excellent job as the setup man for Righetti. Ron Guidry had an injury-plagued year (10-11, 4.51 ERA), but 45-year-old knuckleballer Phil Niekro (16-8, 3.09), signed after Atlanta released him, picked up the slack. The Yankees inexplicably traded Shane Rawley to the Phillies for Marty Bystrom; under normal conditions, it wasn't a good trade, but Bystrom got hurt and barely pitched.

A couple of young pitchers made their debuts. Jose Rijo, the 19-year-old Dawson Award winner in spring training, had only a 2-8 record, but his great potential was obvious to everyone. Jim Deshaies got rocked in his two starts, but he was another bright prospect.

The season included an Old Timers Day tribute to the late Elston Howard and Roger Maris, who had cancer and would die in 1985. Their respective uniform numbers, 32 and 9, were retired, and plaques in their honor were added to Monument Park. The inscription on the Maris plaque acknowledged that the Yankees were giving Maris belated recognition.

In a historic moment, Yankee rookie pitcher, Jim DeShaies, became the 1,000th Yankee to appear in a game, when he debuted on August 7.

1985

New York City, which hadn't had a Subway Series since 1956, came very close to one this season. The Yankees, battling Toronto in a two-team race, finished second but only two games behind the Blue Jays. The Mets barely got beaten in the NL East by St. Louis. The Yankees were 97-64; the Mets 98-64.

The trademark of Manager Yogi Berra's club was its togetherness. Yogi protected his players from the owner, and his players thought the world of him. But when the Yankees started the year with a 6-10 record, Berra was out, and Billy Martin strode in as manager for the fourth time. The players grieved for Berra, but Martin shrugged it off, and remained cool and calm long enough to get the club rolling in the right direction.

Actually, the Yankees were still only three games above .500 as June ended. Then the Yanks went 18-10 in July, 20-8 in August, 18-10 in September and 4-2 in October. The Yankees owned a home record of 58-22—a fantastic .725 winning percentage—including a 7-0 mark against Baltimore. Overall, the Yankees were 12-1 against the Orioles.

Four Yankees—Don Mattingly, Rickey Henderson, Dave Winfield and Ron Guidry—had absolutely tremendous years. Mattingly, rising to the position as the game's number-one star, won the American League MVP Award. He led the majors with 145 RBIs and 48 doubles, and he led the league with 370 total bases, 86 extra-base hits and 21 game-winning RBIs. He hit for power (35 homers) and high average (.324), and he led league first basemen in fielding (.995) and won a Gold Glove.

Mattingly missed the first 18 spring-training games following knee surgery, and then he homered in his first spring-training at-bat. He started the season slowly, however, and didn't hit his first homer until May 5. He soon warmed up and was sizzling with a 20-game hitting streak that started June 22. He added a 19-game hitting streak in August. His 211 hits were the most by a Yankee since Red Rolfe made 213 in 1939. Mattingly's ability to get hits, coupled with Rickey Henderson's ability to get into scoring position, were the significant factors in Don's winning the RBI title.

Centerfielder Rickey Henderson, obtained from Oakland the previous December, gave the Yankees their most exciting lead-off man ever. He led the league with 146 runs scored, the most in the majors since Ted Williams scored 150 in 1949. Rickey also led the league with 80 stolen bases, a new Yankee club record, which he would break in 1986 (87 steals) and then again in 1988 (93 thefts). The longstanding (since 1914) Yankee steals record mark was 74 by third baseman Fritz Maisel. Rickey was 4th in the league in both batting (.314) and walks (99). As an unexpected bonus, and completing the package as perhaps the game's best all-round player, Henderson hit 24 homers and had 72 RBIs.

Winfield continued to feud with George Steinbrenner about payments due the Winfield Foundation. In his most stinging critical statement about Winfield to date, in September, the Yankee owner called Winfield, "Mr. May"—an obviously negative comparison to "Mr. October," Reggie Jackson. However, Winfield won a Gold Glove, hit 26 home runs and had a second straight 100-RBI/100-run season (114 RBIs, 105 runs).

Led by this trio of everyday all-stars, the Yankees led the league in runs (839), RBIs (793) and stolen bases (155). And the team's home attendance jumped from 1.8 million in 1984 to 2.2 million this year.

Guidry was the primary reason the Yankees had the league's third best pitching staff (3.69 ERA). Enjoying his third 20-win season, Louisiana Lightning led the league in both wins and winning percentage (22-6, .786). His ERA was 3.27, and he won a Gold Glove. The staff thinned out after Guidry. Other big winners were Phil Niekro (16-12, 4.09), Joe Cowley (12-6, 3.95) and Ed Whitson (10-8, 4.88), all of whom were helped by the Yanks' potent scoring.

The Yankee bullpen led the league with 49 saves. Again, the closer was Dave Righetti (12-7, 29 saves), who set a Yankee record with 74 games pitched. Brian Fisher (4-4, 14 saves) was a revelation backing up Righetti.

Designated hitter Don Baylor smacked 23 homers with 91 RBIs and broke his own Yankee record by getting hit 24 times by pitched balls. Mike Pagliarulo emerged as a fine defensive third baseman and hit 19 homers. Willie Randolph was still an excellent second baseman, and he hit .276. The reserves were strong, led by Ron Hassey and Dan Pasqua; they combined for 22 homers. Catcher and shortstop were still weaknesses.

One of the great days of the year was Phil Rizzuto Day on August 4. Rizzuto was celebrating his 50th season with the Yankees; he broke into the Yankee farm system as a player in 1936. The Scooter's number 10 uniform was retired, and a plaque in his honor added to Monument Park.

The Yankees won 11 games in a row starting August 31. The streak was snapped with a 4-3 loss in Milwaukee on September 11, the Yankees falling two games behind first-place Toronto. The next night the Blue Jays invaded Yankee Stadium for a critical four-game series that would draw 214,510 fans. The Yankees won the opener but lost the final three games, and Toronto left town with a 4½-game cushion.

Worse, the Yankees extended their losing streak to eight games, dropping 6½ games behind. The Yankees finally won on September 21 in Baltimore. The Yankees won the next night, too, but later that night Ed Whitson (who had been stewing all year) and Martin got into a knock-down-drag-out brawl that started in the bar of the Cross Keys Inn (where the Yankees stayed in Baltimore) and ended in the parking lot. Martin sustained a broken arm, and three weeks after the season ended, he would be replaced as manager by Lou Piniella, largely because of the ugly brawl.

Somehow, when the Yankees journeyed to Toronto for the season's final three games, they weren't without hope, although they needed to sweep the series to tie Toronto and force a playoff. The Yankees tied the opener in dramatic fashion on Butch Wynegar's ninth-inning homer off Tom Henke, and the Yankees went on to win. But in the second game, the Yankees were handcuffed by Doyle Alexander, who as recently as 1982 and 1983 had pitched for the Yanks—though at times he more resembled a batting-practice pitcher—and the Blue Jays clinched the division championship. The only unfinished business was completed in the finale when Phil Niekro earned his 300th major-league victory on October 6, becoming the oldest pitcher ever, at 46, to toss a shutout, an 8-0 job over the Jays.

1986

Lou Piniella in his first season as Yankee manager somehow coaxed a 90-72 record from a Yankee team that for the first time in 36 years had a pitching staff giving up more than four runs per game (4.11 ERA). Another odd statistical fact keeping the Yankees from reaching first place—they finished second, five games behind Boston—was the Yankees played poorly at home (41-39); this included eight consecutive home losses in June. By comparison, their road record (49-33) was excellent; their .598 road winning percentage was the best in the league. The Yankees, who said good-bye for good to first place on May 14, stayed in the pennant race until early September.

Don Mattingly had another great year, hitting .352 with 31 homers and 113 RBIs. He led the league in slugging (.573), total bases (388), hits (238) and doubles (53), and he set Yankee records for hits and doubles, eclipsing the records held by Earle

Combs and Lou Gehrig, a pair of Hall of Famers who both established the previous club records in the great 1927 season. Mattingly, who also won a Gold Glove, hit safely in 24 consecutive games and finished only five points behind Wade Boggs in the race for the batting crown.

Dave Winfield battled adversity. While he was sidelined with a hamstring injury, his replacement, Dan Pasqua (.293, 16 HRs, 45 RBIs), did so well that when Winfield returned, Pasqua stayed in the lineup and often batted fourth and Winfield fifth or sixth. Sometimes Winfield didn't play at all against righthanders. Frustrated, Winfield finally bellowed his disapproval to the media. He still managed 24 homers and 104 RBIs, and after his last at-bat of the year at Yankee Stadium, the fans gave him a standing ovation.

The Yankees led the league with a .430 slugging average. Rickey Henderson hit 28 homers with 74 RBIs and led the league in runs (130) and stolen bases (87), breaking his own club record in stolen bases. Mike Pagliarulo hit 28 homers, Mike Easler hit .302, and Willie Randolph, named co-captain along with Ron Guidry in March, hit .276.

Shortstop and catcher continued being problem positions. Bobby Meacham, losing confidence, was returned to the minors, and Wayne Tolleson was a pop-gun hitter. Catcher Butch Wynegar (.206) grew increasingly unhappy and aloof and finally left the Yankees on July 31. He said he hadn't been happy playing for two high-strung managers, Billy Martin and Piniella, and he returned home to Florida; he didn't return. The Yankees unwisely had already traded Wynegar's backup, Ron Hassey.

Ken Griffey was unhappy about his situation, too. He purposely missed a game and was traded shortly thereafter.

Piniella had only two reliable pitchers, Dave Righetti and Dennis Rasmussen. Going into the final day of the season—a doubleheader played in Boston—Righetti was one save behind the major-league record of 45, held by Dan Quisenberry and Bruce Sutter. Rags saved both ends of the doubleheader for 46 saves—and a new big-league record. Through 1999, the saves leader is Bobby Thigpen, who had 57 in 1990 with the White Sox. Rasmussen (18-6, 3.88 ERA), while not as spectacular as Righetti, was the only double-figure winner on the staff.

Guidry and Joe Niekro had disappointing seasons, and Ed Whitson was traded in July for reliever Tim Stoddard. Guidry had the league's best control, but his record was 9-12. Joe Niekro was upset in spring training when brother Phil was cut, and he pitched like he never got over it, going 9-10 with a bloated 4.87 ERA. A couple of young pitchers, Bob Tewksbury (9-5) and Doug Drabek (7-8), broke into the rotation and showed promise.

Billy Martin Day was celebrated at Yankee Stadium on August 10, and Billy's #1 uniform was retired. This season Martin, always the manager in waiting, was a Yankee broadcaster.

Watching the World Series was a nightmare for many Yankee fans who didn't know which hated rival to most root against, the Mets or the Red Sox. The Mets won, and they were the undisputed darlings of New York City.

1987

The Yankees seemed untouchable in the season's first half. They won ten consecutive games in April, dramatically resumed first place in June, and built a 55-34 record and a three-game lead at the All-Star Break. After the break, however, the Yankees were 34-39, and they finished fourth, nine games behind first-place Detroit. New York broke down because of bad pitching, injuries and poor trading.

The Yankees in Toronto on June 29 seemed very much in command, as Don Mattingly and Dave Winfield each belted grand slams, and the Yanks came from behind to win, 15-14, and vault ahead of the Blue Jays into first place. The Yankees went on to sweep the three-game series.

But the bubble burst in August, with the Yankees going 11-17 in the month. Pitching was the biggest problem; the Yankees' ERA in August was 5.02. An early August 2-8 road trip, which included Detroit beating the Yankees, 15-4, on August 9 and knocking the Yanks permanently out of first place, was especially disheartening.

Problems between Manager Lou Piniella and George Steinbrenner surfaced during the 2-8 road trip. It started when Piniella missed a call from the owner. Both became irritable, and a feeling of tension gripped the club. Steinbrenner became openly critical of Piniella and suggested what Lou really needed, and hadn't been given, was experience managing in the minors. Piniella, in turn, turned on Rickey Henderson, questioning the severity of Henderson's hamstring injury that kept him out of the lineup periodically for 55 games over the summer.

The Yankees set a club record using 48 players this season, later broken by two in 1989. They used 15 starting pitchers—to no avail. The team ERA was an horrendous 4.36. Ron Guidry (5-8), often hurt, on July 11 did revert to his famous form when he struck out 14 White Sox. The top three starters were Tommy John (13-6, 4.03 ERA), Rick Rhoden (16-10, 3.86) and Charles Hudson (11-7, 3.61). But the impatient Yankees sent Hudson to Columbus for two weeks when he ran into a slump.

The Yankees in July made a disastrous trade, sending Bob Tewksbury (1-4), an occasional starter, to the Cubs for Steve Trout. Tewksbury was destined to become one of the National League's best pitchers. Trout (0-4) couldn't find the plate, issuing 37 walks and nine wild pitches in 46 innings pitched.

In a July 19 game at Texas, the Rangers became only the second team in Yankee history to score 20-plus runs against them in a game, a 20-3 rout. Yankee newcomer Trout took the loss in the debacle. The only previous instance of this occurred at Cleveland on July 29, 1928, when the Indians pounded the Yanks 24-6—the Yanks missed an extra point!

New York's bullpen was much better than the starters, leading the league with 47 saves. Dave Righetti (31 saves), Tim Stoddard (eight saves) and Pat Clements (seven saves) did their jobs well.

The Yankees were an excellent fielding club. They set club records for the fewest errors (102) and highest fielding average (.983), both eclipsed by the 1996 club with 91 errors and a .985 fielding mark. Don Mattingly and Dave Winfield won Gold Gloves.

One of the factors in the second-half decline was the dropoff in production from Winfield and Gary Ward, whose bat slowed considerably. Before the All-Star Break, Winfield had 20 homers and 68 RBIs; after the Break, he had only seven homers and 29 RBIs. Ward had 10 homers and 61 RBIs before the Break; after the Break he had only six homers and 17 RBIs.

Mattingly missed 18 games in June with two injured disks in his lower back. But on July 8 he homered, and he continued hitting a home run in each game until the streak reached eight consecutive games; thus, he tied the major-league record held by Dale Long.

Mattingly (.327, 30 HRs, 115 RBIs) also set a new major-league record with six grand slams in one season. He hit his sixth on September 29 at Yankee Stadium against Boston's Bruce Hurst, breaking the record set in 1955 by Ernie Banks and tied in 1961 by Jim Gentile. As a team, the Yankees hit 10 grand slams this year, which tied the big-league record set by the 1938 Tigers. The current slam mark is 12 by the 1996 Atlanta Braves.

Other big hitters included Mike Pagliarulo (87 RBIs), who led the Yankees with 32 homers. Willie Randolph hit .305, but he was sidelined in mid-season with torn knee cartilage. Claudell Washington, the centerfielder, hit .279. Outfielder Dan Pasqua blasted 17 homers, but he struck out 99 times in only 318 at-bats.

Shortstop and catcher were still bothersome. Shortstop Wayne Tolleson hit .221. Three catchers—Joel Skinner, Rick Cerone and Mark Salas—combined to hit only .206.

A few weeks after the season ended, the Yankees shook things up again. Piniella was kicked upstairs, becoming general manager, and Billy Martin was named manager for the fifth time.

1988

Billy Martin lasted only 2½ months in his final season as Yankee manager. Under Martin, the Yankees eased into first place on May 3, ended May with a 33-16 record, and were 40-28 and only two games removed from first place when Martin was fired on June 23.

Martin's problems began prior to the Yankees playing poorly in June (12-15). In early May in Texas, Billy got thrown out of a game and ended up in a sleazy strip bar frequented by an unsavory crowd. One thing led to another, and a bunch of tough guys beat up Martin so badly he needed 80 stitches to close his wounds.

On May 30 in Oakland, Billy and Umpire Dale Scott were arguing a call when Billy began kicking dirt on Scott. Suddenly, Billy scooped up a pile of dirt and threw it on the umpire. Martin was fined $1,000 and suspended three games. The umpires felt Martin got off too easy, and Billy escalated the war of words. The feud continued.

Clyde King, in his role as advisor to George Steinbrenner, traveled with the Yankees in June. King didn't like Martin's behavior on June 19, when Billy allowed reliever Tim Stoddard, whom Billy didn't want on the team to absorb a pounding from the Indians. King advised Steinbrenner to dump Martin.

The next stop was Detroit and three heart-wrenching Yankee losses. The first, won by the Tigers in 10 innings, 2-1, sent the Tigers past the Yankees into first place. Then the Yankees in the ninth inning blew a 6-1 lead and lost, 7-6, on Alan Trammell's grand slam. The following night, Detroit won in the 10th inning, 3-2.

The next day Lou Piniella replaced Martin as Yankee manager. Piniella led the Yankees back into first place for three days in late July, but the Yankees swooned in August, going 9-20 for the month and tying a 1917 club record for the most August defeats. The major culprit was a pitching staff whose ERA for August was 6.64.

The Yankees had one last chance in mid-September when they trailed the first-place Red Sox by 4½ games and went to Boston for four games. After winning the opener, the Yankees lost the next three games and left Boston 6½ games out. The fifth-place Yankees (85-76) finished five games out; their 4-9 record against Boston was a fatal factor. However, staying in the pennant race helped the Yankees set a new home attendance record of 2,633,701, breaking the previous mark set in 1980.

The Yankees were busy in the previous off-season putting this team together. Jack Clark was signed as a free agent, and in putting Clark into a lineup with Rickey Henderson, Don Mattingly, Dave Winfield and Mike Pagliarulo, the idea was for the Yankees to blast their way to the top.

The Yankees also obtained catcher Don Slaught and short-stop Rafael Santana for the positions with the most glaring weaknesses. New pitchers Richard Dotson and John Candelaria were supposed to help the beleaguered pitching staff.

The awesome offense never materialized, however, as New York ranked only a league fourth in batting (.263) and homers (148). Among the five players counted on for the most offensive production, only Dave Winfield achieved his expected numbers. Winfield, who was the American League Player of the Month in April when he set a league record with 29 RBIs, hit .322 with 25 homers and 107 RBIs.

Clark hit 27 homers with 93 RBIs, but he also set a Yankee record with 141 strikeouts and was prone to complaining. Don Mattingly hit a crisp .311, but his power numbers were down (18 HRs, 88 RBIs). Same for Henderson (six HRs, 50 RBIs), who hit .305 and led the league in stolen bases (93), breaking his own Yankee record. Pagliarulo (.216, 15 HRs, 67 RBIs) had a poor season altogether. Claudell Washington helped the cause, hitting .308. Claudell, in fact, hit the 10,000th homer by the Yanks in April 20.

Defensively, Slaught, and Santana didn't help much. In fact, the Yankees were worse in overall defense, finishing next to last in the league with a .978 fielding percentage. Mattingly, however, won a Gold Glove.

But pitching was the biggest problem. Only Baltimore and California owned higher ERAs than New York's 4.26. It would have been worse without Candelaria (13-7, 3.38 ERA), but the Candy Man was shelved at times with a knee injury. Dotson (12-9) wasn't as good as his record; he had a sky-high 5.00 ERA. Rick Rhoden (12-12, 4.29) and Tommy John (9-8, 4.49) also gave up too many runs.

Injuries impaired the effectiveness of Ron Guidry (shoulder and leg), Charles Hudson (shoulder), Neil Allen (side) and Al Leiter (finger). On May 31 in Oakland, Carney Lansford hit Leiter's first pitch off Al's left hand, forcing him out of the game. Neil Allen recorded all 27 outs, allowing only three hits and no runs. But according to the rules, Allen didn't get credit for the shutout.

Southpaw Leiter (4-4, 3.92 ERA), the Dawson Award winner, was given a big buildup as the star of the future, but he ran into bad luck. He went on the Disabled List on June 22 with a blister on his left middle finger and wasn't reactivated until July 26. Three days later he was sent down to Columbus and wasn't recalled until August 31.

Dave Righetti recorded 25 saves and became the Yankees' all-time saves leader, passing Goose Gossage. Cecilio Guante (5-6, 11 saves, 2.88) on the whole did a good job setting up Righetti, but in August he was traded to Texas for Dale Mohorcic in a puzzling deal.

The Yankee made a July trade that was even more baffling. For the sake of increased lefthanded power, the Yankees got Ken Phelps from Seattle for Jay Buhner. Phelps hit 10 homers, but he was a one-dimensional player—nothing more than a DH against right-handed pitching. Buhner was a complete player who had his best years ahead of him.

Another young player, Hal Morris, spent a lot of time on the Columbus shuttle. Morris never got a legitimate chance to show the Yankees what he could do, and he later became a batting star with Cincinnati.

The Yankees said good-bye to Willie Randolph, their solidly professional second sacker since 1976. Willie hit an uncharacteristic .230 in an injury-plagued season. The Yankees in November would sign free-agent second baseman Steve Sax, and Randolph would sign with Sax's old club, the Dodgers.

Piniella was gone, too. On October 7, the Yankees named Dallas Green the new manager. Tough-guy Green was supposed to come in and crack the whip.

1989

Manager Dallas Green lasted only until August when he was replaced by Bucky Dent. But the Yankees played poorly for Green (56-65) and Dent (18-22), struggling to an overall 74-87 record and a fifth-place finish. The Yankees used 50 players, the most by any team since the expansion Seattle Pilots in 1969.

The best players the Yankees once had were evaporating. Jack Clark the previous October was practically given away in a trade. Dave Winfield underwent surgery for a herniated disk and missed the entire season. Rickey Henderson wanted a new contract, playing without much interest, and the Yankees in June traded him to Oakland without receiving equal value; Henderson turned it on for the A's. Green platooned Mike Pagliarulo (.197, 4 HRs, 16 RBIs), who pressed, slumped and was finally traded, leaving a big hole at third base; the Yankees used seven third basemen in 1989.

The pitching was even worse than in recent years. Detroit (4.53 ERA) was the only team in the league with a worse ERA than New York's 4.50, and Yankee pitching gave up the most hits in the league. The previous December the Yankees signed free agents Andy Hawkins and Dave LaPoint. Hawkins (15-15, 4.80) was the club's big winner, but a staff ace he was not. LaPoint (6-9, 5.62) was hurt or ineffective most of the year. Rick Rhoden in January was traded for virtually nothing. Tommy John was released. Ron Guidry aborted a comeback attempt and retired. John Candelaria pitched in only 10 games due to a knee injury. Richard Dotson was traded. The Yankees in July got Walt Terrell for Pagliarulo, but Terrell wasn't any help (6-5, 5.20).

The most controversial trade was made in April when the Yankees, desperate to replace the injured Winfield, dealt Al Leiter, their celebrated pitching prospect, to Toronto for Jesse

Barfield. Leiter was injury riddled and never developed as advertised, but he could easily have developed into another star who got away for the sake of a quick-fix patch job. Through 1999, Al Leiter continued to pitch in the majors, while Jesse Barfield played his last season in 1992.

The Yankees needed three players to replace Winfield. In the outfield they used Mel Hall and Barfield, who led league outfielders with 20 assists and hit 18 homers. Steve Balboni was supposed to replace the right-handed power. Hall and Balboni each hit 17 homers.

Don Mattingly started slowly, but finished with his sixth straight .300 season (.303), and he hit .339 with runners in scoring position. "Donnie Baseball" hit 23 home runs and was second in the league with 113 RBIs.

Steve Sax, the new second baseman, played with an infectious enthusiasm, and he hit .315 with 205 hits and 43 stolen bases. He became the lead-off man after Henderson's departure. Shortstop Alvaro Espinoza (.282) was a revelation, and centerfielder Roberto Kelly hit .302 and stole 35 bases. Bob Geren in May was recalled from Columbus, and in August he took over the catching and hit .288.

The Yankee bullpen was capable. Dave Righetti saved 25 games, and his backup, Lee Guetterman, saved 13. Guetterman began the season with 30 scoreless innings pitched; then he gave up 20 runs over his next 30 innings. Goose Gossage returned to the Yankees briefly, but he was no longer the dominating Goose of old.

Dallas Green and George Steinbrenner bickered through the press for weeks before Steinbrenner replaced Green. Under Dent, the Yankees won nine games in a row in early September, their best month (15-10).

The Yankees continued displaying a willingness to trade their future for washed-up name players. In December, the Yankees traded Hal Morris to Cincinnati for pitcher Tim Leary.

1990

The Yankees hit rock bottom this year in more ways than one. They finished dead last with a miserable 67-95 record. In the history of the Yankees, only two teams lost more games—the 1908 Yankees (103) and the 1912 Yankees (102). Bucky Dent (18-31) was fired in May, and the new manager, Stump Merrill (49-64), inherited a team that couldn't hit or pitch; the Yankees finished with the league's worst batting average (.241) and the third worst ERA (4.21).

In a decision announced on July 30, Commissioner Fay Vincent banned George Steinbrenner permanently from the day-to-day operations of the Yankees, although Steinbrenner remained the principal owner. Vincent determined that the owner's "undisclosed working relationship" with admitted gambler Howard Spira—which Vincent decided led to Steinbrenner getting damaging information from Spira on Dave Winfield for $40,000—was the punishable offense. He wanted to suspend Steinbrenner only two years, but George wanted an agreement rather than a suspension so as not to jeopardize his relationship with the U.S. Olympic Committee. Vincent agreed but made the "agreement" permanent.

Amid a barrage of lawsuits directed at Vincent, Steinbrenner stepped down as managing general partner on August 20, and a period of confusion gripped the Yankee hierarchy. George's

son, Hank, turned down the job as managing general partner, and Leonard Kleinman, the chief operating officer, wasn't acceptable to Vincent, since the commissioner was planning an investigation of Kleinman's role in the Spira case. Finally in September, a limited partner in the ownership, Robert E. Nederlander, became managing general partner.

More importantly, in his last move before leaving the club, Steinbrenner named Gene Michael general manager. This turned out to be a blessing in putting the Yankees back on the right track.

Winfield in May was traded to California for pitcher Mike Witt (5-6, 4.47 ERA), who suffered an elbow injury and didn't help much. The top four starters were Tim Leary (9-19, 4.11), who led the league in losses; Dave LaPoint (7-10, 4.11), unsuccessful in achieving a winning form after shoulder surgery; Andy Hawkins (5-12, 5.37), who on July 1 in Chicago pitched a no-hitter and lost, 4-0; and Chuck Cary (6-12, 4.19), who had an elbow injury.

The starting pitching was so poor that Lee Guetterman, who pitched in 64 games without making a start, led the Yankees in wins with 11. Dave Righetti managed to record 36 saves in a limited number of opportunities.

The infield was dismal. Suffering from back pain, first baseman Don Mattingly played in only 102 games and had his least productive season (.256, 5 HRs, 42 RBIs). Steve Sax (.260), and Alvaro Espinoza (.224) both fell off significantly from 1989. The Yankees tried five third basemen but looked mostly at Randy Velarde, Jim Leyritz and Mike Blowers. Velarde and Leyritz weren't adequate defensively, and Velarde hit only .210 as well. Blowers hit .339 at Columbus but only .188 with the Yankees.

There wasn't much production from the outfield either. The best two outfielders were Jesse Barfield, who smoked 25 homers and led league outfielders with 16 assists (but who also set a then-Yankee record with 150 strikeouts, surpassed by Danny Tartabull who had 156 whiffs in 1993), and Roberto Kelly (.285, 15 HRs). Extroverted Deion Sanders, the famous football player, playing in 57 games for the Yankees, hit only .158. But he displayed power and speed (three HRs, eight SBs) and provided some much needed excitement until he left the Yankees to join the Atlanta Falcons before the baseball season ended.

Catcher Bob Geren hit only .213, and in June, the Yankees obtained catcher Matt Nokes (.238, eight HRs), who didn't hit up to his capability. DH Steve Balboni hit 17 four-baggers but batted an anemic .192. The most pleasant offensive news came from Kevin Maas, who wasn't even with the Yankees until getting called up from Columbus in late June. Maas hit 21 homers in only 254 at-bats and was runner-up in the AL Rookie of the Year voting.

Otherwise, Yankee fans had little to cheer about. Unless they cared to track the achievements of former Yankees, which were many. In the National League, Doug Drabek won the Cy Young Award, and Willie McGee, whom the Yankees traded in 1981 for pitcher Bob Sykes, was the batting champion. The World Series MVP and winning manager were, respectively, Jose Rijo and Lou Piniella. 'Nuff said!

1991

Unrealistic hope was temporarily sparked when the Yankees reached .500 shortly after the All-Star Break, but these hopes were cruelly dashed as the Yankees crashed, and the team finished fifth, 20 games out of first place, with a 71-91 record. Some of the Yankee players, blaming their manager, Stump Merrill, complained about Merrill to the press, and in some cases used anonymous-source quotes to undermine Merrill, who was fired shortly after the season ended.

The pitching was woeful except for Scott Sanderson (16-10, 3.81 ERA), whose contract the Yankees had bought from Oakland the previous December. He had great control, painting the corners and allowing only 1.25 walks per nine innings. He started 8-3 and was the Yanks' lone representative at the All-Star Game. Greg Cadaret (8-6, 3.62) also pitched decently. But the rest of the veteran starters had poor years. The Yankees dumped Andy Hawkins (0-2, 9.95). Tim Leary (4-10) struggled with an ERA of 6.49. Among the injured were Pascual Perez (2-4), shoulder; Dave Eiland (2-5), foot; and Mike Witt (0-1), elbow.

Merrill and General Manager Gene Michael gave young pitchers their chances. In June, the Yankees called up from Columbus three starters—Jeff Johnson (6-11, 5.95), Wade Taylor (7-12, 6.27) and Scott Kamieniecki (4-4, 3.90). Johnson, the team's number-two starter, needed to become more consistent. Taylor, the number-three starter, won his debut, but stumbled thereafter. Kamieniecki was the most consistent, but he was disabled with an upper-back injury from August 3 through the rest of the season.

The bullpen was without Dave Righetti, who signed as a free agent with the Giants the previous December. The Yankees signed free-agent Steve Farr (5-5, 23 saves), and Farr performed admirably as the new closer. Steve Howe (3-1, 3 saves), released by Salinas (Class A, California League) in October 1990 and signed by the Yankees in February, was impressive until developing an elbow injury.

Don Mattingly (.288, nine HRs, Gold Glove), hampered by his chronically sore back, was not always happy. He became Yankee captain in February but was humiliated by Merrill and Michael in August when he was benched for not getting a haircut. It was one of the few times Mattingly had ever been in the light of controversy—and he didn't like the glare.

The rest of the players were either veterans hanging on or players being considered for future plans. Among the veterans with no future in the club's plans were second baseman Steve Sax (.304), slow-footed shortstop Alvaro Espinoza (.256), and outfielders Jesse Barfield (17 homers) and Mel Hall (.285, 19 HRs, 80 RBIs). Barfield suffered from an ankle injury.

Roberto Kelly appeared to be the best of the up-and-coming players. He roamed center field beautifully, hit 20 homers and stole 32 bases. He also missed six weeks over the summer with an injury.

The Yankees expected more improvement than was made by the club's new M & M Boys, Kevin Maas and Hensley Meulens. Maas delivered 23 homers, but he hit only .220 and struck out 128 times. Meulens (.222, 6 HRs, 29 RBIs), the Dawson Award winner in spring training, arrived as the much heralded Bam Bam, but he couldn't keep his left-field job. He didn't deliver power or high average, and he fanned 97 times in 288 at-bats; Hall replaced him in left field.

Pat Kelly and Bernie Williams seemed to offer more. Kelly, an outstanding-fielding second baseman, was called up from Columbus in May, and deferring to Sax, shifted to third base (one of eight third basemen used by the Yankees). Kelly played third without complaint and would have hit better than .242 except for enduring a 0-for-25 slump. When Roberto Kelly was hurt in July, the fleet and graceful Williams was called up from Columbus. Williams (.238) was up and down offensively but finished the year with a five-hit game.

The Yankees weren't a good offensive team, and at one point in May, they went 32 innings without scoring a run, their worst scoreless-inning streak in 22 years. Other than catcher Matt Nokes (24 HRs, 77 RBIs), Maas and Hall, the Yankees didn't have enough lefthanded power to fully take advantage of Yankee Stadium.

After canning Merrill in October, Gene Michael began his search for a new manager. He wanted a manager with big-league managing experience, but in a meeting on October 18, the ownership partners encouraged him to hire Buck Showalter, a coach who had been fired along with Merrill. Michael wisely reconsidered, and on October 29 he introduced Showalter as the new manager.

1992

Superficially, the Yankees had another dreary season, finishing tied with Cleveland for fourth place and 20 games behind first-place Toronto. But, beyond the tangible five-game improvement over the previous season's record, there was a growing feeling that Manager Buck Showalter was sorting things out and putting the Yankees on the right track. For the first time since 1983, the Yankees (76-86) had a better record than the Mets (72-90).

Offensively, the Yankees were back, leading the league in home runs (182) and RBIs (791). But only Seattle (799) gave up more runs than the Yankees (794).

Don Mattingly (.288, 14 HRs, 86 RBIs), playing an uninterrupted season, no longer had his old power, but he hit 40 doubles, third best in the league, and led the Yankees with 89 runs scored. He also led league first basemen with a .997 fielding average.

The Yankees in January signed free-agent slugger Danny Tartabull, formerly of the Royals, to a five-year $25.5 million contract. He played right field and walloped 25 homers with 85 RBIs, and he had a nine-RBI game in Baltimore on September 8. Danny's RBI total of nine in one game has been surpassed by only one player in Yankee history—Tony Lazzeri, who had 11 RBI on May 24, 1936 in a game at Philadelphia, won by the Yanks 25-2!

Another free agent signed in January, infielder Mike Gallego (.254), played in only 53 games because of foot and wrist injuries. This allowed Pat Kelly (.226) a chance to play second base and Andy Stankiewicz (.268) shortstop. Charlie Hayes (18 HRs, 66 RBIs) was obtained to stabilize the third-base situation, and he led league third basemen in turning 29 double plays. Randy Velarde (.272) was an adequate utility man.

The outfield featured Tartabull and centerfielder Roberto Kelly, who hit .272, stole 28 bases, scored 81 runs and doubled in the All-Star Game. Leftfielder Mel Hall (15 HRs, 81 RBIs), fourth outfielder Bernie Williams (.280) and Dion James (.262) rounded out the outfield. James made quite a comeback, having been out of baseball in 1991.

The catching situation was improving. Matt Nokes wasn't much of a receiver, but he nailed 22 homers. Mike Stanley, a career backup catcher with Texas, signed a Columbus contract in January. He made the Yankees because he was a better receiver than Nokes, and Stanley hit eight homers in 173 at-bats. Jim Leyritz, the third catcher, hit .257.

Kevin Maas continued sliding backwards, hitting only .248 with 11 homers in 286 at-bats. He couldn't wrest first base away from Mattingly, leaving him without a position except designated hitter, and he wasn't productive enough to be a full-time DH.

The ace of the pitching staff was Melido Perez (13-16, 2.87 ERA), whom the Yankees in January "stole" from the White Sox, along with pitchers Bob Wickman and Domingo Jean, for an over-the-hill Steve Sax. Melido should have had a better record, but he suffered from a peculiar lack of run support. He pitched 248 innings and was second in the league with 218 strikeouts. His brother, Pascual, would have been a teammate, but Pascual was suspended for the season for violating baseball's drug policy. Steve Howe (3-0, 6 saves, 2.45), pitching well, was disqualified for the season on June 8, receiving his seventh suspension for drug abuse.

After Melido Perez, the rest of the rotation was Scott Sanderson (12-11, 4.93), who slipped from 1991; Scott Kamieniecki (6-14, 4.36), who pitched better in the second half; and Tim Leary (5-6, 5.57), whom the Yankees in August unloaded to Seattle. Greg Cadaret (4-8, 4.25) was the swingman, starting occasionally and relieving. Anchoring a good bullpen was Steve Farr (30 saves, 1.56), who pitched in 50 games, and John Habyan (seven saves, 3.84), who pitched in 56 games.

The developing pitchers were sorting themselves out. The Yankees were perhaps highest on Sam Militello (3-3, 3.45, nine starts). Bob Wickman (6-1, 4.11, eight starts) usually received good run support whenever he pitched. Jeff Johnson (2-3, 6.66) wasn't cutting it.

On July 24, Commissioner Fay Vincent, reducing the punishment he had given George Steinbrenner in 1990, announced that Steinbrenner could return to the Yankees on March 1, 1993. A few weeks later, Vincent was pushed out of office by the owners. The reasons were many, but probably a major reason was because the owners didn't want a real commissioner in their way as they prepared for war against the Players Association.

The Yankees in the final two months of 1992 made a series of transactions that would bolt them into serious contention in 1993. In November, the Yankees got outfielder Paul O'Neill from Cincinnati for Roberto Kelly, and in December, the Yankees obtained pitcher Jim Abbott from California, primarily for prospect J.T. Snow. The Yankees also signed three free agents—pitcher Jimmy Key, third baseman Wade Boggs and shortstop Spike Owen.

1993

Through the summer, the Yankees were locked in an exciting five-team division race with Toronto, Boston, Baltimore and Detroit. The Blue Jays never relinquished first place after July 20, although they were often tied. During the season, the Yankees owned a share of first place on 18 different days, but they weren't able to pass the Blue Jays. New York's best chance came when Toronto was losing six games in a row between September 3 and 9. On September 4, Jim Abbott provided an emotional lift in pitching a no-hitter, and the next day the Yankees beat Cleveland again, achieving a tie with Toronto. But then the Yankees were swept in a three-game series in Texas, and the door slammed shut.

Surging Toronto won 17 of their final 21 games, while the Yankees posted a September record of 11-15, their only losing month of the season. The Yankees finished second, seven games behind the Blue Jays, but with their first winning record (88-74) since 1988.

Manager Buck Showalter, who created a harmonious team, finished second to Gene Lamont of the White Sox in the league's Manager of the Year voting by the Baseball Writers. Showalter was blessed with a club that led the league in batting (.279) and home runs (178).

The club's offensive production was very well distributed. Eight players reached double figures in home runs, and a ninth, Kevin Maas, hit nine homers. For the first time since 1937, the Yankees boasted six .300-plus hitters!

Don Mattingly (17 HRs, 86 RBIs, .291) wasn't a .300 hitter, but he was close, and he found playing baseball fun again. He set a Yankee fielding record for first basemen with a .998 fielding average, and he won a Gold Glove. He hit .368 with runners in scoring position, and he hit .362 in July to raise his season average to .312. He fought through back pain, but tendinitis in his right wrist finally caught up with him in September, a month in which he hit .250. He had wrist surgery in November.

Mattingly and Wade Boggs, who started the All-Star Game at third base, inspired the younger players with their dedication, work habits and intensity. Boggs, who hit .259 with Boston in 1992, rebounded with a .302 mark and won the Silver Bat for third basemen. Boggs also led league third sackers in fielding (.970), assists (311) and double plays (29).

Showalter certainly made the right decision at catcher. Buck went with his best defensive receiver, Mike Stanley, who not only led league catchers in fielding (.996), but as a bonus Stanley was the best-hitting Yankee catcher since the prime of Thurman Munson. He hit .305 with 26 homers and 84 RBIs, becoming only the tenth catcher in big-league history ever to combine a .300 batting average with at least 25 homers. On July 20, Stanley hit his third grand slam in 21 days, and thus he became the first American League catcher to ever hit three grand slams in a season. Nudged into the backup role, Matt Nokes added 10 homers.

With Stanley leading the way, the Yankees were strong up the middle. Second baseman Pat Kelly improved his average to .273, led the Yankees with 14 stolen bases and was an excellent fielder. Shortstop Spike Owen (.234) didn't work out, but Mike Gallego (.283, 10 HRs) took over the position, and not only provided offensive punch, but he was incredible defensively—the glue of the infield. Centerfielder Bernie Williams (.268, 12 HRs, 68 RBIs), still developing and improving offensively, already was an accomplished fielder.

Flanking Williams were Paul O'Neill (.311, 20 HRs, 75 RBIs) and either Danny Tartabull (31 HRs, 102 RBIs) or Dion James (.332). O'Neill fit in nicely and also possessed a great arm. Tartabull was often a DH and he struck out a team record 156 times. He struggled with a right shoulder injury in September. James was a revelation and earned his playing time. After the season, he would leave the Yankees to play in Japan. Two other valuable sticks belonged to Jim Leyritz (.309, 14 HRs), who played first base, outfield, designated hitter and catcher; and Randy Velarde (.301), who played outfield, shortstop and third base.

The Yankees ranked a poor ninth in the league in pitching (4.35 ERA) but only slightly below Toronto (4.21). The Blue Jays missed new Yankee ace Jimmy Key (18-6), who finished fourth in the Cy Young voting and led the league in winning percentage (.750), and led or tied the Yankees in wins, ERA (3.00), complete games (four), shutouts (two), innings pitched (237) and strikeouts (173). Key was also 11-3 in games following a Yankee defeat. But after Key, there was a steep dropoff.

Overall, Abbott (11-14, 4.37) had a disappointing season. His two previous ERAs had been 2.77 and 2.89, so this year he gave up about 1½ more runs than he had in the recent past. One of his problems was losing about two m.p.h. from his fastball. His September no-hitter at Yankee Stadium was especially rejoiced because it came in the thick of the division race, it came against the hard-hitting Indians, and it was a tremendous accomplishment for a pitcher born without a right hand.

The third starter, Melido Perez (6-14), suffered with shoulder miseries, and his ERA ballooned from 2.87 in 1992 to 5.19 this season. Scott Kamieniecki (10-7, 4.08) was much better at Yankee Stadium than on the road; his 12-game home winning streak was broken in September. Inexperienced pitchers—Domingo Jean, Sterling Hitchcock, Mark Hutton and Sam Militello—combined for 18 starts, but not one of them was able to establish himself as the fifth starter. Bob Wickman was a lucky 14-4, considering his 4.63 ERA, and he eventually went to the bullpen and helped as a setup man.

The bullpen was weak. The Yankees were a league 13th in ERA in relief (4.62). Steve Farr saved 25 games, but his ERA was 4.21. Steve Howe (3-5, four saves) missed a month after spraining his right ankle walking down steps, and his ERA was 4.97. Young Bobby Munoz (3-3, 5.32) threw hard but hadn't yet harnessed his heat. Veteran Lee Smith (three saves) was obtained too late. Lee still holds the all-time saves mark through 1999 with 478 in 18 seasons.

The Yankees this season were sometimes accused of being too bland. "I think the media thinks we're boring," said Tartabull. "And that's because we don't fight, bitch or moan. We're just a bunch of old boys who play baseball."

Even George Steinbrenner, who returned to the Yankees on March 1 amid much hoopla, stayed mostly quiet and in the background. He did generate publicity about the future of Yankee Stadium, however, complaining about Yankee Stadium receipts and claiming home attendance was being hurt by inadequate parking and the public's perception of the Bronx as an unsafe place. He proclaimed "a test week" and wasn't happy with the attendance results.

Steinbrenner finally made his public peace with Reggie Jackson, who this year was inducted into the Baseball Hall of Fame. Reggie chose to wear a Yankee cap on his Hall of Fame plaque, and he joined the Yankee front office as a special advisor. And the season's big day at Yankee Stadium was "Reggie Jackson Day," with the official retirement of Reggie's #44 uniform.

1994

The Yankees returned to the top of the AL East, but their chances for championships and postseason glory were denied by the players' strike that ended the season on August 12. The Yankees finished the abbreviated campaign with an outstanding 70-43 record that was the best mark in the AL and led their division by 6½ games.

Events leading to the strike had been building for some time. The owners, observing the salary control that owners in other sports had gathered, insisted the baseball players fall in line and accept a salary-cap system, too, which the owners threatened to impose unilaterally in December. The players wanted no part of a salary cap and saw no other choice but to strike to force negotiations. But the owners weren't in a bargaining mood, and the season shut down instead. Over the next several months, the negotiations took many turns, but no agreement was in sight as spring training opened in 1995 with scab players.

Awards and honors in 1994 seemed less meaningful, but nevertheless, Buck Showalter deserved his award as Manager of the Year. "I see him as a guy who can manage here awhile," said Don Mattingly in the spring. "We're going in a positive way with our people, and I don't see that changing." Showalter worked hard, and his players were hard working, too. There was very little controversy, and if any did arise, Showalter and General Manager Gene Michael quickly defused it. Luis Polonia, who signed as a free agent with the Yankees in the off-season, stated how much more of a team the Yankees were in 1994 than the Yankee teams Polonia was on in 1989-90.

The Yankees changed very little from 1993. Polonia took over left field, with Danny Tartabull mostly a designated hitter. The Yankees also traded good prospects to Houston for bullpen closer Xavier Hernandez and to Philadelphia for starting pitcher Terry Mulholland.

Boston in May came into Yankee Stadium owning baseball's best record (20-7) and a seven-game winning streak. The Yankees promptly swept the three-game series—their first sweep of Boston at Yankee Stadium since 1985—and assumed command of the division.

The Yankees had a veteran and solid infield. First baseman Don Mattingly hit .304. Third baseman Wade Boggs hit .342 with 11 homers and started the All-Star Game. Shortstop Mike Gallego (.239) and second baseman Pat Kelly (.280) were an excellent double-play combination. Randy Velarde (.279, 9 HRs) was a valuable reserve.

Catcher Mike Stanley (.300, 17 HRs, 57 RBIs) continued his amazing hitting. Matt Nokes (.291) was swept into the background, but Jim Leyritz (17 HRs, 58 RBIs) was given a large role and was a productive all-purpose player.

The outfield of Polonia (.311, 20 SBs), Bernie Williams (.289, 12 HRs) and All-Star Paul O'Neill (21 HRs, 83 RBIs) was extremely potent. O'Neill led the league in batting with a .359 mark, and he hit .380 against righthanders and .409 at Yankee Stadium. Williams seemed on the verge of developing into an exceptional offensive player, too. Tartabull (19 HRs, 67 RBIs) hit .339 against lefthanders. Generally, it was a smart, patient, offensive club, drawing a lot of walks and making pitchers throw strikes.

Jimmy Key, the All-Star Game starting pitcher, was once again the ace of the pitching staff. Key (3.27 ERA) led the league in both wins and winning percentage (17-4, .810), and he was 10-0 on the road. Backing up Key were Jim Abbott (9-8, 4.55), Melido Perez (9-4, 4.10) and Scott Kamieniecki (8-6, 3.76), who reversed his recent pattern and went 3-4 at home and 5-2 on the road. Terry Mulholland (6-7, 6.49) didn't have it; opponents hit .303 against him.

Xavier Hernandez didn't work out either, leaving the bullpen without a legitimate closer. But Steve Howe, Bob Wickman and Sterling Hitchcock did good jobs. Opponents hit only .194 against Howe (15 saves, 1.80). Wickman (5-4, six saves, 3.09) led the league in games pitched (53). He went to Florida in the previous off-season and developed a changeup, and opponents hit only .213 against him. Hitchcock (4-1, two saves, 4.20) wasn't very consistent, but the young southpaw could be awfully tough against lefthanded batters.

The Yankees probably would have held on to win the division unless their pitching completely fell apart, especially since Toronto, the defending champions, had major pitching problems of their own. But everything shut down on August 12, and there would be no postseason championship for the first time since 1904 when John McGraw and the Giants refused to play the American League in the World Series.

1995

It was —in the end—a good season. Having started poorly, the Yankees fought back to gain the postseason opportunity cruelly denied them in 1994 by the strike. They finished 79-65, and though this record left them seven games behind first-place Boston, it represented the best record among all the teams that didn't win AL divisions. Thus, in an expanded playoff format, the Yankees made the playoffs as the wildcard.

Otherwise, it was a downer of a year. Mickey Mantle died, and the cloud that was cast across the entire nation was at its darkest over New York.

It was a season in which the warfare between the owners and players was suspended after a court ruling forced the club owners to reinstate elements of the old collective bargaining agreement, leading the players to end their strike on April 2. The 144-game season began on April 24, but the dispute was hardly resolved. The 144-games scheduled in '95 was the first time since 1919 that a season was *not* for either 154 or 162 games! In 1919, the ML schedule was set at 140 games for one season only. The two sides didn't meet between March 30 and November 15, and labor peace was left unassured to fans who hadn't taken the baseball stoppage all that well. Average attendance at Yankee Stadium was down around 24,000, well under the nearly 30,000 of the last normal season of 1993.

And then there was the speculation about the Yankees leaving Yankee Stadium. However one viewed the prospect of a new ballpark, there was something disquieting about leaving the old one. And the possibility that 1995 would be the end of Yankee pinstripes for Don Mattingly—that was discomforting. And Phil Rizzuto sounding like he might not return to the mike in 1996—that was disappointing.

Shattered in the course of the season was a record thought unassailable—the consecutive game-playing streak of Yankee great Lou Gehrig, brought down in Baltimore by Cal Ripken Jr. Doubtless many a Yankee fan would have preferred the Gehrig record to stand.

The death of Mantle was a real blow, especially after hope was raised by his successful liver transplant. But there was cancer, and it spread, and on August 13 the #7 went on the sleeves of the Yankees: The legendary Mick was gone, and grown men cried in the Stadium that day.

As for the team—the league's best team in 1994—what happened? The biggest factor in the club's decline was the injury to Jimmy Key, the team's ace in 1993 and 1994; Key was lost for most of the season after undergoing rotator-cuff surgery. Not only was Key shelved, but gone or hurt were all the top four starting pitchers of 1994. Jim Abbott was traded away, and Melido Perez (5-5, 5.58 ERA) and Scott Kamieniecki (7-6, 4.01) were disabled for considerable periods. Sterling Hitchcock (11-10, 4.70) was the only holdover from the 1994 rotation to pitch without interruption.

The bullpen was disappointing. John Wetteland (1-5. 2.93 ERA), the new closer, was sixth in the AL with 31 saves, but he was less consistent than advertised. Moreover, his primary setup men, Steve Howe (6-3, 4.96) and Bob Wickman (2-4, 4.05), never got untracked.

The preseason additions of Wetteland from the Expos and Jack McDowell from the White Sox supposedly made the favored Yankees unbeatable. But the pitching staff disintegrated. McDowell (15-10, 3.93) struggled early and was so frustrated in midsummer that he made an unmistakable gesture with his middle finger to a Yankee Stadium gathering as he departed a game. But Black Jack got it together and finished with four wins in a row.

The Yankees bolstered their staff during the season. David Cone (overall 18-8) was obtained from Toronto and won nine of 11 decisions with New York. And coming up from the minors to help tremendously was Andy Pettitte (12-9, 4.17), a smooth-delivering southpaw who finished with five wins in his final six decisions.

Another reason for New York's decline was an almost across-the-board drop from 1994 in offensive production (after factoring the longer 1995 season). The less productive included both catchers, Mike Stanley (.268, 18 HRs, 83 RBIs) and Jim Leyritz (.269, 7 HRs); first basemen Mattingly (.288, 7 HRs, 49 RBIs); second baseman Pat Kelly (.237), who was hurt much of the year; Tony Fernandez (.245), who was an acrobatic shortstop but wasn't as tough an out as Mike Gallego, the man he replaced; outfielder Paul O'Neill (22 HRs, 96 RBIs, .300), whose batting average was 59 points lower than his 1994 average; and outfielders Danny Tartabull and Luis Polonia.

Tartabull was a problem. He couldn't run, field, or throw, and all of a sudden in 1995 he couldn't hit for power, either. George Steinbrenner was determined to unload him. General Manager Gene Michael and Manager Buck Showalter, seeking to protect Tartabull's trade value, were less vocal about Tartabull's deficiencies than the principal owner—to the latter's distress. In time, Tartabull, who very much wanted out of New York, was traded to Oakland for Ruben Sierra, and Sierra was helpful as a DH.

Steinbrenner also signed Darryl Strawberry, who spent an extended time in the minors getting ready. When Strawberry reached the Yankees—he would get only 87 at-bats—the Yankees dumped Polonia, disgruntled with platooning but the club's only legitimate lead-off hitter. The Yankees finished the year with the unproductive left-field platoon of Dion James and

Gerald Williams, who combined for eight home runs and 54 RBIs.

The only two hitters matching previous production levels were Wade Boggs and Bernie Williams. Boggs hit a Boggs-like .324. Williams, hitting only .194 in mid-June, was a terror thereafter, he ended up batting .307 with 29 doubles, nine triples, and 18 homers.

The Yankees experienced road woes with a 33-39 away record. Particularly jarring were West Coast trips in May and August. They continued limping after the May swing and dropped into last place in mid-June, but Showalter's industriousness seemed to infuse the Yankees with a work ethic that kept them banging away. Beginning late in August, the Yankees were unrelenting in their pursuit of the wildcard. Their September record was 22-6, and on the very last day of the season they captured the wildcard.

The fans had been pulling especially for Mattingly, who all through his career had never seen a postseason pitch. Finally, following 1,785 games, he was going to the playoffs. During the year, he experienced injuries, an eye ailment and difficulties with Steinbrenner, but he never lost the adulation of Yankee fans who appreciated his overall excellence and commitment in 13 seasons in New York.

In the final home game of the season, the fans, afraid it was Mattingly's last game in the Bronx as a Yankee, gave "Donnie Baseball" multiple standing ovations. This kind of two-way loyalty made it, in the end, a rewarding season. The Yankees looked with great optimism to next season, and their wait would indeed be rewarded with their first appearance in the World Series since 1981.

1996

After an encouraging season in '95, the Bronx Bombers were tempered with hopeful aspirations for the 1996 campaign. Gone from the New York Yankees that in March 1996 gathered at their new baseball complex in Tampa, Fla., were Gene Michael and Buck Showalter, the former general manager and manager. Now running the show were GM Bob Watson and Manager Joe Torre. Also conspicuously absent were two former Yankees stars—Don Mattingly, the club's marquee player for over a decade, and catcher Mike Stanley. Mattingly had not officially retired, but he was sitting out the season. Stanley, the popular and hard-hitting catcher, had signed as a free agent with Boston.

Replacing Mattingly and Stanley were first baseman Tino Martinez and catcher Joe Girardi. Martinez pressed early, but Girardi settled into his new job quickly and comfortably. He would hit only two home runs during the regular season, but in every other way he made the fans forget Stanley. He would hit .294, lead the Yankees with 11 sacrifice bunts, adeptly handle the bat on the hit-and-run play, and set a club record for catchers with 13 stolen bases. He took charge behind the plate, too. Dwight Gooden said Girardi was the best catcher he ever worked with, and Gooden had pitched to Gary Carter with the Mets.

Torre had a couple of spring-training problems in the middle of his infield, but he somehow squeezed out the best possible outcomes. Second baseman Pat Kelly in March went on the Disabled List with an inflammation of his right shoulder.

Kelly would spend most of the year either disabled or playing his way into shape in the minors; he got into only 13 games with the Yankees. Torre turned to veteran Mariano Duncan, a lifetime .262 hitter, who had been signed in the off-season as a backup infielder. Duncan would not be the steadiest of fielders, but in 1996 he would hit an amazing .340 in 109 games.

Torre was willing to turn shortstop over to rookie Derek Jeter, although, frankly, Jeter wasn't very impressive in spring training. Yet Torre told Jeter he *was* the shortstop, and when the season was over and Jeter had unanimously won the AL Rookie of the Year Award, Jeter passed credit Torre's way for boosting his confidence. Jeter's statistics for the season: .314 BA, 10 HRs, six triples, 25 doubles, 104 runs and 78 RBIs. He was the first regular Yankee shortstop to hit over .300 since Gil McDougald hit .311 in 1956. His 78 RBIs were the most by a Yankee shortstop since Frank Crosetti had 78 in 1936. Jeter's 17-game hitting streak in September was the longest by a Yankee rookie since Joe DiMaggio's 18-game streak in 1936. And although Jeter made too many errors (22), he otherwise was spectacular defensively.

Torre inherited Boggs at third base and Bernie Williams and Paul O'Neill in the outfield. Gerald Willams and newcomer Tim Raines were being counted on in the outfield—Raines would miss much of the season with a hamstring injury—and Ruben Sierra was the DH. David Cone and Andy Pettitte, the top starting pitchers, were joined by free-agent signee Kenny Rogers and three pitchers trying to resurrect their careers—Jimmy Key, Gooden and Scott Kamieniecki. Melido Perez would miss the entire season with a bone spur in his right elbow. The bullpen included John Wetteland, Mariano Rivera, Jeff Nelson, Bob Wickman and Steve Howe.

The Yankees opened the season in Cleveland, winning, 7-1, with Cone pitching seven shutout innings, Jeter hitting his first big-league homer and Bernie Williams hitting a three-run homer. The next day, behind Pettitte, the Yankees beat the defending AL champions again, 5-1. There were developing reasons for concern, however. Gooden lost his first three starts and was hit hard in each outing. Nevertheless, Torre and Mel Stottlemyre, the pitching coach, stuck with him. Key and Kamieniecki were also struggling.

On the last day of April the Yankees opened a two-game series in Baltimore. The first-place Orioles, the pre-season favorites to win the division, had started 11-2. Now the Orioles were 14-11; the second-place Yankees were 12-10. The series opener lasted four hours and 21 minutes, setting a major-league record for length of a nine-inning game. (Ironically, in a game in 1997 on September 5, the Yankees and Orioles would break this mark by *one minute* (four hours and 22 minutes) in the 13-9 Baltimore win.) New York, overcoming a 9-4 deficit, took the lead on Martinez's seventh-inning three-run homer, winning, 13-10, and climbing over the Orioles into first place. The next night's 15-inning game, won by the Yankees, 11-6, lasted five hours and 34 minutes. Pettitte, who lasted only one inning the previous evening, notched the win with three shutout innings of relief. Gerald Williams had six hits, tying the club record set way back in June 1934 by Myril Hoag, but the big blow, a grand slam, was delivered by Martinez.

Tino Martinez, obtained from Seattle in a December 1995 trade, had the unenviable task of replacing the beloved Mattingly. Tino struggled over the first few weeks, but now he was reaching his stride—he would have 21 RBIs in May—and quietly and confidently assuming the role as the club's number-one run producer. He would lead the Yankees with 117 RBIs, hit 25 home runs and bat a respectable .292. He was a solid player.

The first-place Yankees left Baltimore riding high. Meanwhile, the Red Sox, the defending AL East champs, were losing 19 of their first 25 games and digging themselves a hole from which they would never recover. The Yankees had concerns of their own. After missing a start, on May 2 Cone threw a five-hitter and improved his record to 4-1. But the next day he went on the Disabled List, and on May 10, he underwent surgery to remove an aneurysm in his right shoulder. Although many observers didn't think Cone would return in 1996, over the next several months he worked diligently on a program designed to meet his stated goal of pitching again this season.

There were many who thought the Yankees couldn't stay on top without Cone. Certainly someone would need to fill the void. Up stepped Cone's old Mets teammate, Gooden. The one-time superstar, who had been banned from baseball for the final six weeks of 1994 and all of 1995 after testing positive for cocaine, had been signed in October 1995 by George Steinbrenner, who made Gooden his personal reclamation project. Now Doc was shaking off the cobwebs and rounding into form. After a pair of good starts (both no decisions), on May 8 "Doc" allowed only two hits over eight innings and beat Detroit for his first major-league win since June 19, 1994. Gooden was heating up for a great effort on May 14 at Yankee Stadium, when he captured the hearts of all baseball fans with a thrilling no-hitter against Seattle, a game he won, 2-0.

The crowd was standing during the ninth inning as Gooden faced the best hitters in the AL. Alex Rodriguez, leading off, walked. Ken Griffey Jr. hit a slow roller to Martinez, who dove to the bag just ahead of Griffey. Edgar Martinez walked. Gooden was laboring, and after a wild pitch, Stottlemyre went to the mound and momentarily broke the tension. Gooden, reaching back for a little more, struck out Jay Buhner. When Paul Sorrento popped to Jeter, Gooden pumped both arms in triumph and was carried off the field by his teammates. Then he returned to the field and saluted the fans who had been cheering him on. The most amazing aspect of Gooden's no-hitter was that he pitched it while focused on the status of his father's health; the next day his father would undergo heart surgery in Florida.

Opposing batters in May hit only .130 against Gooden. He continued his dominating pitching, winning six consecutive decisions from early June through mid-July, until his arm deadened in August. He struggled over the final two months and wasn't on the postseason roster, but his 11-7 record was a lifesaver.

While Gooden blossomed in May, Key and Kamieniecki continued to struggle. Key, owning a miserable 7.71 ERA, on May 15, went on the Disabled List with a stiff left shoulder. Kamieniecki (1-2, 11.12 ERA), unable to successfully rebound from off-season elbow surgery, went down to Columbus in late May; he did not return to the Yankees. Ramiro Mendoza won his first start, but thereafter he struggled; he would make 11 starts and go 4-5 with a 6.79 ERA. The Yankees were always in search of a fifth starter and often a dependable fourth starter.

Baltimore tied the Yankees for first place on May 28, and for three days the two clubs remained tied. On May 31, the Yankees assumed undisputed possession of first place, which they would hold for the rest of the campaign. It was no coincidence that on the day the Yankees assumed control of first place, Key returned from the DL and won in Oakland with six solid innings.

The Yankees were 17-10 in June. They were rolling now, although Rogers was inconsistent, Key returned to the Disabled List (strained left calf muscle), Brian Boehringer failed as a starter, and Mendoza seemed overmatched. The Yankees were thriving with two hot starting pitchers, Pettitte (5-1 in June) and Gooden (4-0 in June), an outstanding bullpen led by Wetteland, who had 15 saves in June, and an aggressive NL-type running game. Torre loved the hit and run and stealing bases. In a game on June 2 in Oakland, the Yankees stole eight bases. The Yankees also featured three streaking June hitters—Bernie Williams (.362, eight HRs), Martinez (.314, 26 RBIs) and Boggs (.340).

Cleveland was shocked late in June when the Yankees, scoring 34 runs, swept a four-game series at Jacobs Field. Closing the curtain on June, the Orioles and Yankees split a four-game series at Yankee Stadium, as the Yankees preserved a four -game lead over Baltimore. The lead stretched to six games going into the All-Star break.

The Yankees were adding bench strength. Outfielder Mike Aldrete, obtained in June from the Angels, hit an important home run against Boston's Roger Clemens on July 1. Three days later Steinbrenner acquired Darryl Strawberry from the St. Paul Saints of the Northern League.

Key, finding a groove, pitched 20 consecutive scoreless innings from late June through mid-July. He was New York's best starting pitcher in July (5-2, 3.02 ERA) and twice beat Clemens. The season's second half started with the Yankees in Baltimore for a crucial four-game series, and in the opener, Key and Mike Mussina were locked in a 2-2 struggle when in the eighth inning Mussina threw a high fastball on an 0-2 pitch to Jeter, who would hit .350 after the All-Star break. Jeter deposited Mussina's mistake in the seats for a two-run homer. Rivera worked the eighth, Wetteland the ninth, and the Yankees were 4-2 winners.

After a day of rain, the Yankees swept a doubleheader, winning 3-2 on the strength of a ninth-inning rally, and, 7-5, behind Strawberry's two homers and four RBIs. The next day Pettitte, with help from Wetteland who earned his fourth save of the series, completed the sweep with a 4-1 victory. Thus, the Yankees not only opened up a ten-game lead but finished the season 6-0 at Camden Yards. In no previous season had the Yankees won all their games in Baltimore. But what seemed to bother Orioles owner Peter Angelos more was the large number of fans on hand rooting for the Yankees. In the middle of the finale, one of Angelos' underlings assembled the press and issued a plea to season ticket holders—please, please, stop giving or selling your tickets to those damn Yankees fans.

The Yankees were ripe for a letdown, and over the next six to seven weeks, the Yankees indeed played poor-to-mediocre ball. The Yankees never fell apart, however, and, luckily, the Orioles didn't start applying pressure until August. In late July, Strawberry's 300th career home-run, a two-run shot in the bottom of the ninth to beat Kansas City, 3-2, gave the Yankees a 12-game lead, their largest lead of the year. Shortly thereafter, Strawberry hit five home runs in one Yankee Stadium series against Chicago, including a three-homer game on August 6.

In 1996, after the Yankees bought out his option following the 1995 season, Strawberry rediscovered the joy of playing baseball. When he joined the Yankees, he practiced hard, played hard, and didn't gripe when he didn't play. Torre seemed more comfortable with him than had been Showalter. In 63 games with New York, Strawberry produced 11 homers and 36 RBIs.

As July ended, the Yankees traded the disappointing Sierra (11 HRs and 52 RBIs in 96 games) and pitching prospect Matt Drews to Detroit for Cecil Fielder, the incomparable Big Daddy, the slugger of more home runs in the 1990s than any major-leaguer. He would be the new DH. The Yankees also obtained pitcher David Weathers from Florida.

Although stronger, the Yankees suffered through a dreary 13-17 August, and as the month closed, the Yankees (76-59) were leading the revitalized Orioles (72-63) by only four games. Keeping New York afloat with excellent August performances were Pettitte (4-1), Martinez (.343, 7 HRs, 24 RBIs), Jim Leyritz (.382), Duncan (.333) and Jeter (.325).

In August, Pettitte personally snapped Yankees' losing streaks of two, three and five games. Over the entire season, Pettitte was 13-3 in games that followed a Yankees' defeat. He would finish first in the AL in wins (21-8), third in winning percentage (.724) and eighth in ERA (3.87). He was a complete pitcher, possessing an assortment of effective pitches, fielding his position well and leading all major-league pitchers with 11 pick-offs. Much of the season he pitched with a painful left elbow. He had class, too. When he finished second to Toronto's Pat Hentgen in a close vote for the Cy Young Award, Pettitte said he had told his wife when the season ended that he thought Hentgen deserved the award.

The Yankees' strongest department, relief pitching, slipped slightly in August. A couple games were blown, and in mid-month Wetteland went on the Disabled List with a strained right groin muscle. Looking to add the quality lefthanded reliever the Yankees were lacking, on August 23 GM Watson boldly sent outfielder Gerald Williams (.270, 5 HRs, 30 RBIs, 99 games) and pitcher Bob Wickman (4-1, 4.67 ERA) to the Brewers for lefthanded reliever Graeme Lloyd and outfielder Pat Listach. Unfortunately, Listach had a broken foot and Lloyd an ailing elbow. Lloyd endured a miserable time the rest of the season with New York; his ERA was 17.47 in 13 games, and he heard terrible booing in Yankee Stadium. Unhappy over the deal, Steinbrenner put Watson's job on the line.

Watson, however, in late August steadfastly remained focused on improving the team. He picked up Luis Sojo, who would hit .275 and provide late-inning defensive help in the infield, and third baseman Charlie Hayes, who would hit .284. Boehringer was recalled from Columbus and was effective as a middle-to-long relief man. But at Yankee Stadium on August 25, the day the Yankees unveiled a new monument in tribute to the late Mickey Mantle, the Yankees lost, beginning a five-game losing streak, their longest of the season.

What Cone managed to do in Oakland on September 2 provided the Yankees a much-needed and powerful lift. Returning to the mound for his first Yankees' start since May 2, Cone did not allow a hit for seven innings. Torre, sticking to the game plan, wouldn't let Cone come out for the eighth, but nevertheless, the Yankees won, 5-0. With Mariano Rivera pitching the final two innings, the Yankees got a one-hitter from Cone and Rivera! Amazing! Two days later Pettitte

notched his 20th win, becoming the first Yankee to win 20 games since Ron Guidry in 1985. Things were beginning to look up.

The Yankees in mid-September won six of seven games on a critical road trip to Detroit and Toronto. Ruben Rivera saved a game with a diving catch in right field. Bernie Williams in one game had two homers and eight RBIs, and in another game, Tim Raines had two homers and six RBIs. Raines was a vital force in September, hitting .298 with seven homers for the month. Watson and Torre had put the pieces together for the stretch run.

The stage was set for another Yankees-Orioles showdown, and on September 17, the red-hot Orioles, trailing the Yankees by three games, invaded the Bronx for a three-game series. The series opener didn't last an inning before it was rained out, but Cone and Mussina each threw enough pitches to be unable to start the following night when, instead, Pettitte and Scott Erickson dueled. Baltimore took a 2-1 lead into the ninth, and Manager Davey Johnson brought in his closer, Randy Myers, who promptly walked O'Neill and Fielder. After Martinez popped out, Johnson replaced Myers with Alan Mills, which Myers later complained about. Bernie's run-scoring single tied the game, 2-2, setting up extra innings. In the tenth, with two outs and Jeter on third, Ruben Rivera poked a tough 2-2 pitch into right field for the game-winning single. The next night in a doubleheader the Orioles had to sweep, the teams split, and the Orioles (83-69) left town four games behind the Yankees (87-65).

With both teams having only ten games remaining, the race was practically over, and the Orioles, in fact, turned their attention to winning the wild card. It was now quite evident that the Yankees were much more together as a team than the feuding Orioles. Baltimore GM Pat Gillick, angry at owner Peter Angelos for nixing trades he wanted to make in August, wasn't even at Yankee Stadium for the showdown series.

On September 25 the Yankees clinched their first division title since 1981, beating Milwaukee in the first game of a doubleheader, 19-2. The 19 runs were the most in a game by the Yankees since scoring 21 runs on August 19, 1962. The Yankees very quickly eliminated the suspense by scoring four runs in the first inning and ten more runs in the second; the 14 runs represented the most productive first two innings in the team's 94-year history. The fans were in a playoff mood as early as the second inning, chanting "We want Texas! We want Texas!"

Having regrouped with a September record of 16-11, the Yankees (92-70) finished four games ahead of Baltimore (88-74), who made the playoffs as the wild-card team. When it was all said and done, no major-league team could match the Yankees' bullpen, led by Mariano Rivera and Wetteland. New York was 86-1 when leading after seven innings! Torre's formula for success was simple: Get the lead and give the ball to Rivera in the seventh and eighth innings and then to Wetteland in the ninth. The Yankees won 29 of the 31 games in which Rivera and Wetteland both appeared.

Wetteland (2-3, 2.83 ERA) led the AL with 43 saves. Opposing batters hit only .224 against him. He was a little flaky, psyching himself up in the bullpen playing the air guitar and wearing the same old, grungy, sweat-stained cap night after night, but, with his sizzling fastball and wicked breaking ball, on the mound he was supremely in command.

As the set-up man, Rivera (8-3, 2.09 ERA, five saves) didn't have the opportunity to earn glamorous statistics, yet he was so impressive that he finished third in the Cy Young Award

Reggie Jackson (left), Phil Rizzuto, Whitey Ford and Joe DiMaggio during the National Anthem at Yankee Stadium.

voting. What made the Panamanian so dominant was a blazing fastball that was released from a silky-smooth, seemingly effortless, delivery. Rivera faced 386 batters and allowed only one home run (to Baltimore's Rafael Palmeiro). Combined, all the first batters he faced hit a feeble .089 (five for 56, four walks, one hit by pitch). His 130 strikeouts set a new club record for relievers. He pitched 26 $\frac{2}{3}$ consecutive scoreless innings between mid-April and late May.

Also making contributions out of the bullpen were, among others, Jeff Nelson (4-4, 4.36 ERA, 2 saves), Jim Mecir (1-1, 5.13 ERA, 26 games) and Dave Pavlas (2.35 ERA, one save, 16 games). Nelson, who started the season slowly, came on strong and tied for fifth in the AL with 73 games pitched.

All season Torre and Watson were transforming a bullpen that had been deteriorating. Two fixtures, Steve Howe (6.35 ERA) and Bob Wickman (opponents' BA of .299), were discarded. Wetteland and Rivera were given clearly defined roles, and Torre patiently waited for Nelson to come around. Torre, understanding the need for a lefthanded reliever in the postseason, was showing similar patience with Lloyd. Late in the season Torre created relief roles for Boehringer and Weathers, too.

In 1996 the Yankees led the AL in saves (52), fewest home runs allowed (143), fewest hits allowed (1469) and lowest opponents' batting average (.265), and tied Cleveland for most shutouts (9). Yankees pitchers were supported by the league's second-best fielding team (.985), which finished just behind Texas (.986). The Yankees made only 91 errors, the fewest made in Yankee history.

The Yankees' corps of starting pitchers were led by Pettitte, Cone, Key, Gooden and Rogers. Pettitte was the star. Cone (7-2, 2.88 ERA), the leader, allowed opponents to bat only .198 against him. Gooden and Key (12-11 after a 1-5 start) were at their best when needed the most. Rogers (12-8, 4.68 ERA), however, endured a disquieting season. After signing with the Yankees as a high-dollar free agent, Rogers wasn't even in the early-season rotation, which understandably confused him. He would have flashes of brilliance but then pitch poorly, and late in the season Steinbrenner complained that Rogers wasn't giving him his money's worth.

The Yankees had the second-best hitting club in the AL (.288) but finished ninth in runs scored (871). There were two reasons for the lack of run production: The Yankees led the AL in leaving runners on base (1258) and finished only 12th in home runs (162). In a home-run happy season when three teams broke the 1961 Yankees' record of 240 homers—Baltimore (257), Seattle (245) and Oakland (243)—the Yankees cushioned their relative weakness by not allowing many homers.

The big gun was Bernie Williams, who hit .305 (.378 righthanded), with 29 homers, 108 runs, 102 RBIs and 17 stolen bases. He also played a sensational center field and made numerous catches to take away potential home runs. O'Neill (.302, 19 HRs, 91 RBIs), who started the year hitting .400 in April, didn't have his best season and often seemed frustrated with himself. However, he was among the league leaders in walks (102) and on-base percentage (.411) and was an outstanding defensive outfielder. Fielder produced 13 homers and 37 RBIs for the Yankees, finishing the year with a total of 39 homers and 117 RBIs. Boggs hit .311 and anchored third base.

The Yankees had a deep bench. Besides the already mentioned contributions by Strawberry, Aldrete, Hayes, Sojo and Raines, important reserve roles were filled by Leyritz, who was Pettitte's personal catcher; Andy Fox, a good backup infielder and pinch runner; and Ruben Rivera (.284 in 46 games), who offered a glimpse of the future stardom that awaits him—(but not in pinstripes as he was traded to the Padres in 1997 as part of the deal that brought pitcher Hideki Irabu to the Yankees.)

The Yankees were 25-16 in one-run games, a tribute to the bullpen, the depth and Torre's moves. The Yankees were weak against lefthanded pitching, especially at Yankee Stadium, where the Yanks were 10-14 against lefthanded starters, compared to 39-17 against righthanders. Incredibly, the Yankees were a combined 12-0 playing in Cleveland and Baltimore. The Yankees had 1-5 records in three road parks—Milwaukee, Seattle and Texas—which didn't bode well because the Yankees would be opening the AL playoffs against the Rangers (90-72), the AL West champions, and Texas would have the home-field advantage.

1997

In their quest to defend their 1996 World Series Championship, the Yankees had high hopes of duplicating that success in 1997. There were many new faces in the Yankee fold and many players from the '96 squad were gone. The Yankees would have to regroup in '97 and learn to feel comfortable being a team that everyone wanted to beat.

On opening-day 1997, only 15 Yanks remained from the '96 roster. They were: outfielders, Paul O'Neill, Bernie Williams and Tim Raines; infielders, Wade Boggs, Mariano Duncan, Derek Jeter, Pat Kelly and Tino Martinez; catcher Joe Girardi and pitchers, David Cone, Dwight Gooden, Jeff Nelson, Andy Pettitte, Mariano Rivera and Kenny Rogers. Fourteen were gone from the 1996 opening-day roster: outfielders, Gerald Williams, Matt Luke and Ruben Sierra; infielders, Robert Eenhoorn, Tony Fernandez and Andy Fox; catcher Jim Leyritz; and pitchers, Steve Howe, Mark Hutton, Scott Kamieniecki, Jimmy Key, Melido Perez, Bob Wickman and 1996 World Series MVP, John Wetteland. There were 11 new faces who were not on the opening-day roster from a year ago: catcher Jorge Posada; designated hitter Cecil Fielder; outfielders, Darryl Strawberry and Mark Whiten; pitchers, Brian Boehringer, Graeme Lloyd, Mike Stanton, David Weathers and David Wells; and infielders Luis Sojo and Charlie Hayes.

The 1997 Yankee season began with a 4-2 loss at Seattle on April 1, the earliest opener in club history. Their all-time record on opening day now stood at 55-39 (.585), with one tie way back in 1910 versus Boston. David Cone took the loss for New York, who as now 0-2 in West Coast-openers (their prior loss was a 5-4 decision at Seattle on April 5, 1983).

The second game of the season at Seattle, April 2, saw the Yankees destroying the Mariners, 16-2, Pettitte getting the victory. In the game, Tino Martinez hit three homers, a feat accomplished by 16 Yankee batters (some 22 times) in regular-season play. Four Yanks hit three homers in a game more than once: Joe DiMaggio and Lou Gehrig (three times) and Tony

Lazzeri and Bobby Murcer (twice). The last Yankee to hit three was Darryl Strawberry on August 6, 1996 versus Chicago at Yankee Stadium. In addition to regular-season play, two Yankees have hit three home runs in a game in postseason action: Babe Ruth did it twice (connecting in both the 1926 and 1928 World Series) and Reggie Jackson blasted three roundtrippers in the 1977 World Series. (It should be noted that Gehrig is the only Yankee to hit FOUR homers in a game, Lou achieving this on June 3, 1932 in a 20-13 New York win at Philadelphia.) Tino's three-homer game was the earliest (April 2) in Yankee history (Lou Gehrig hit three on May 4, 1929, for the second earliest date), and was the first to occur on the road since Cliff Johnson turned the trick at Toronto on June 30, 1977. Tino, along with his three homers, drove in a career-high seven runs and concluded the month of April with 34 RBI, the most in that month by any player in major-league history.

When they returned to New York after their first road trip, their record stood even at 4-4. On April 11, the home opener was played against the Oakland Athletics before a packed house of 56,710 at Yankee Stadium, the Bronx Bombers taking it on the chin, 3-1, in a 12-inning affair. The '97 home-opener saw a "new" Yankee Stadium record in attendance (the remodeled Stadium opened its doors in 1976), breaking the old mark set in 1994, by four (!) patrons. The Yanks finished April in second place, with a 14-13 record, four games behind Baltimore.

On May 2, in a 13-5 victory at Kansas City, the Yankees were to clinch second place for the remainder of the season. While in second place, the Yanks' largest deficit (that is, games behind) was on September 6, when they were nine games behind front-running Baltimore. In May, the Yanks were 15-12, winding up that month at 29-25 (.537), now 8½ games behind the Orioles. In June, the club fared much better with a 17-8 ledger to finish at 46-33 (.582), gaining some ground (three games) on Baltimore, who was now in the AL East lead by 51/2 games at the end of June.

At the All-Star break in July, the Yanks had a record of 48-37 (.565) and were in second place, seven games behind Baltimore. Five Yankees were named to the American League All-Star squad, the most since 1987, when the same number were named. Pitcher, David Cone, was named to his fourth and first as a Yankee; outfielder, Paul O'Neill, was in his fourth, second as a Yankee; first baseman, Tino Martinez, his second and first as a Yank; and pitcher, Mariano Rivera, and outfielder, Bernie Williams, were both named for their first time. All five Yankees played in the July 8 game at Cleveland, the Americans winning under Yankee Manager Joe Torre, 3-1. In the game, Yankee representatives were 0 for 4, collectively, with one run scored by Bernie Williams. Tino Martinez had 10 putouts at first and Mariano Rivera picked up a save. The Yanks would finish July with a ledger of 61-44 (.581), six games behind the Orioles and were 15-11 for the month.

The turning point of the season occurred in a August 17 victory versus Texas. In that game, pitcher David Cone was taken out in the second inning, after the Yanks had a comfortable 8-0 lead, complaining of pain in his right shoulder. Ramiro Mendoza would finish (and win) the game in high fashion, preserving the Yankee shutout, allowing only two Texas hits in six innings of work. Cone was placed on the Disabled List and made only two more starts, those being in the latter part of September, getting a no-decision in both games. In addition to Cone, other Yankee players experienced significant injuries: outfielder Darryl Strawberry was able to play in only 11 games due to a knee injury; designated hitter Cecil Fielder missed over two months with a thumb injury; outfielder Bernie Williams was on the DL twice with hamstring problems; outfielder Tim Raines missed half of the season, also with a hamstring injury; and second baseman Pat Kelly was on the DL twice, missing two months, with a leg injury. At the end of August, the Yankees were at 79-55 (.590), having gone 18-11 for the month. The club, still in second place, were trailing the Orioles by 6 1/2 games.

In September, the Yanks clinched a postseason berth for the third straight year, capturing the "wild card" slot for the second time in their history. In 1995, they entered the playoffs also, as the wild-card winner. In a home game versus Toronto on September 20, the Yanks clinched a playoff appearance with a 11-inning victory, 4-3. By the end of the 1997 season, the Yankees finished with a whopping 12-game lead over runner-up Anaheim in the wild card hunt. In a game at Baltimore on September 5, the Yankees and the Orioles played the longest (by time) nine-inning game, four hours and 22 minutes, the Oriole's beating the New Yorkers, 13-9 in a slugfest. The Yanks and Orioles had broken their mark set the previous season by one minute! The Yankees, who were down to the Orioles by 9 1/2 games on September 6, pulled to within two games of front-running Baltimore on September 26. By virtue of their 17-11 record in September (Baltimore was 13-16, their only losing month of the season), the Yanks had created excitement in the final days of the A.L. East Division race. With their two-game lead intact, Baltimore won their final two games of the year to clinch their eighth A.L. East title and their first since 1983. With their victory, the Orioles became only the third club in American League history (and sixth team overall) to be in first place every day for the entire season. The great 1927 Yankee club was the first AL club to do it, followed by the 1984 Detroit team that started the year with a record of 35-5.

For the season, 41 players participated in at least one game for the Yankees, including 18 pitchers. Among those pitchers was Wade Boggs, who made his major-league debut on August 19 at Anaheim, finishing a 12-4 Yankee loss in a relief effort. Wade pitched one full inning of scoreless ball, walking one and striking out one. Wade received no decision.

Of the 1,200+ players in Yankee history, the club never, prior to this season, had a player whose last name began with the letter "I". As fate would have it, two "I" players would become Yankees in 1997: Japanese-born pitcher Hideki Irabu became the first on July 10; later in the season Pete Incaviglia would become the second.

The statistical club leaders for 1997: Bernie Williams led the '97 Yanks in: batting average (.328) and on-base percent-age (.408); Derek Jeter led in at bats (654), runs (116), hits (190), triples (7) and stolen bases (23). Tino Martinez led the club in: total bases (343), home runs (44), RBI (141) and slugging percentage (.577); and finally, Paul O'Neill led with 42 doubles. In pitching stats, the club leaders included: David Cone in ERA (2.82) and strikeouts with 222; Andy Pettitte led with 18 wins and 240 1/3 innings pitched; David Wells was tops with five complete games and two shutouts; and lastly, Mariano Rivera paced the Yankees with his 43 saves.

Offensively as a team, the Yankees led the American League in: walks (676), men left on base (1276), sacrifice flies (70) and on-base percentage (.362). They were second in the following areas: batting average (.287), runs scored (891), hits (1636), runs batted in (846), and doubles (325). The 325 doubles were the most ever by a Yankee club in a season, surpassing the 315 two-baggers hit by the 1936 team. No other Yankee club had 300 or more doubles in a season. The Yanks finished in eighth place in team homers (161) and were fifth in slugging percentage (.436). The New Yorkers were tied with Milwaukee, who would eventually move to the National League beginning in 1998, for the best record at home (47-33, .588). On the road, only the AL Champion Baltimore Orioles had a better record (52-29, .642) than the Yankee ledger of 49-33 (.598). Defensively, the Yanks placed sixth in the league, with a .983 fielding percentage.

Individually, only two Yankees led the league in any statistical category. Shortstop Jeter led the AL in singles with 142 (tying for the first spot with Garret Anderson of Anaheim). The second Yankee leading the league was Tino Martinez, who was tops in sacrifice flies with 13 and had the most RBI on the road (78).

The Yankee pitching corps, a total of 18 for the 1997 season, were the best in the league in: staff ERA (3.84), innings pitched (1467 2/3), fewest earned runs allowed (626) and fewest home runs allowed (144). They were second in: shutouts (10-tied with Baltimore), fewest runs allowed (688) and strikeouts (1165). Their 51 saves were third in the Junior Circuit.

Yankee pitchers who finished at the top in their respective categories were: Andy Pettitte with 35 games started (tied with three others), Jeff Nelson with 12 intentional walks, David Cone 14 wild pitches (tied with three others) and Hideki Irabu with three balks (tied with three others).

Statistical highlights of selected Yankee batters:

Bernie Williams was fourth in the American League in batting with .328, seventh in on-base percentage (.408), eighth in runs scored (107) and 10th in slugging (.544). Bernie won his first Rawlings Gold Glove Award for his efforts in the Yankee outfield.

Tino Martinez was first with 13 sacrifice flies. He placed second in both home runs (44) and RBI (141). Tino's home run total was the most by a Yankee first baseman since Lou Gehrig hit 49 in 1936 and the most by any Yankee batter since Roger Maris' 61-homer season in 1961. Tino was third with 343 total bases and 77 extra-base hits (that is, doubles, triples and homers). His .577 slugging percentage was sixth overall. For his spectacular season, Tino finished second in voting for the Most Valuable Player award to Seattle's Ken Griffey, Jr. Also, Martinez was the only Yankee to be voted to The Sporting News major-league All-Star Team as its first baseman.

Derek Jeter was third in: at bats (654), hits (190) and multi-hit games (57), tying with Manny Ramirez of Cleveland. Derek was also fourth in runs scored (116) and fifth with five triples, tying with four other players.

Paul O'Neill was sixth with a .324 batting average, seventh in both RBI with 117 and doubles (42), tying with two others in the latter category. Paul was also ninth with a .399 on-base percentage and ninth with 179 hits, tying with Edgar Martinez of Seattle.

Statistical highlights of selected Yankee pitchers:

Andy Pettitte was first in games started in the American League (35), tying with three others and was third with 240 1/3 innings pitched. Andy place fourth in: ERA (2.88), wins

(18) and winning percentage (.720), a 18-7 record. He was also eighth in strikeouts with 166.

David Wells was tied for second with five other pitchers for shutouts (two). David was second in complete games (five), tying with two others and placed fifth overall with 16 victories, tying with four others.

Jeff Nelon was tied for third with Toronto's Paul Quantrill for the most games pitched (77).

Mariano Rivera placed second in saves (43) behind Randy Myers of Baltimore, who had 45.

David Cone was third in three different categories: ERA (3.82), opponent batting average (.218) and strikeouts (222). David's whiff total was the third most in Yankee history with only Ron Guidry (248 in 1978) and Jack Chesbro (239 in 1904) having more than David did in 1997!

In 1997, Yankee home attendance was 2,580,325 in 78 dates, for an average of 33,081 per game. That total was the third highest in franchise history, only being surpassed in 1980 and 1988.

The Yankees had made a great run at Baltimore's lead, winning their final 17 of 22, nine of their last 10, and ended the year with a five-game winning streak. Although the Yankees did improve their record (96-66, .593) over the 1996 World Championship team (92-70, .568), they would not share the winning ways of the '96 club, as they would be eliminated by Cleveland in the first round of the playoffs.

BEST SEASON OF THE CENTURY:
THE 1998 NEW YORK YANKEES

After being eliminated in five games by the Cleveland Indians in the 1997 American League Division Series, the Yankees hoped to regroup in '98 and reclaim their World Series crown that was last theirs in 1996. No Hollywood director or compelling novelist could have created the scenario of events that were to unfold for the Bronx Bombers in their 1998 season! This narrative can only hope to encapsulate a most memorable season that was experienced by THE sports franchise of the 20th Century—The New York Yankees!

During the off-season, several key transactions occurred. Say goodbye to pitchers Kenny Rogers and Brian Boehringer and third sacker Charlie Hayes. Say hello to new Yankees who were brought into the fold: third baseman Scott Brosius was obtained from Oakland and designated hitter Chili Davis, who spent most of the season on the disabled list, was signed as a free agent. Also, second baseman Chuck Knoblauch was signed from Minnesota. Most of the other players who would greatly contribute to the incredible success that would become the 1998 Yankees were signed: outfielders Bernie Williams, Tim Raines, and Darryl Strawberry; catcher Jorge Posada; shortstop Derek Jeter; infielder Luis Sojo; and pitchers, Graeme Lloyd, Mariano Rivera, Jeff Nelson, Andy Pettitte, and Orlando "El Duque" Hernandez, the latter having defected from Cuba on December 27, 1997. Of the 25 players on the '98 opening-day roster, 16 remained from the 1997 roster, plus one on the disabled list; thus, 10 Yankees that were on the opening-day roster in 1997 were no longer with the team. The Yankees of 1998 were now complete. On February 3, General Manager Bob Watson, who had greatly succeeded in building a club in the fine Yankee tradition, resigned with 31-year-old Assistant GM Brian Cashman

assuming Watson's duties. Both Watson and Cashman had been instrumental in obtaining new key players and re-signing those without whom 1998 may not have been so productive. Thank you, Bob and Brian, for a job well done!

The Yankees began the season versus the Angels in Anaheim on April 1, their earliest opener ever, duplicating the date of the 1997 inaugural. The game was a battle of lefties with Andy Pettitte of the Yanks being pitted against the Angels' Chuck Finley. The Angels scored all of their runs in the fourth inning, coming out on the better half of a 4-1 game. The loss by the Yankees moved their all-time opening-day record to 55-40 (with one tie) for a winning percentage of .578 and added to their winless record in West Coast openers, now standing at 0-3. The Joe Torre-led bunch would go on to lose another two games before getting their first win on April 5 at Oakland. In that game, a 10-inning affair won by the Yanks, 9-7, catcher Jorge Posada hit New York's first homer (the club would hit 206 more) of the season and Jeff Nelson picked up the win in a relief effort.

Celebrating their 75th Anniversary at Yankee Stadium, the Yankees opened their home campaign in the Bronx on April 10 with a wild one indeed! Playing before a home-opening record-breaking crowd of 56,717 (seven more than the home record established a year earlier), it was fitting that "The House That Ruth Built" would play host to a game with a football-like score of 17-13, the Bronx Bombers emerging victorious in the slugfest. The total of 30 runs by both clubs in the game were the most scored at The Stadium since June 3, 1933, when the Yankees defeated the then-Philadelphia Athletics, 17-11. Also, the combined run total of 30 was the most ever in a Yankee home opener, the prior mark being 21 with the New Yorkers beating the Washington Senators, 14-7, on April 21, 1950. The Yanks did fall two runs short of the most runs scored by a single team in an inaugural game at Yankee Stadium—on April 13, 1955, the Bombers blasted the Senators, 19-1! Back to the '98 home-opener, Tino Martinez would lead the Yanks, going 3-for-4, with four runs scored, a double and homer, and five runs batted in. In addition, Joe Girardi aided the Yankee cause, going 4-for-5 with two RBIs and Scott Brosius went 2-for-4 with four RBIs. The 17-13 Yankee win was quite a way of spending a nice afternoon in the Bronx and these hallowed grounds of Yankee Stadium, now 75 years young, were to host many more memorable events before the 1998 season was to come to a close!

One of those moments occurred on April 13 when a 500-pound beam fell from beneath the upper deck of Yankee Stadium. Fortunately, this occurred before the start of a scheduled night game with Anaheim and thus spared any physical injury to anyone who may have been in attendance. The incident reopened the discussion, led by Yankee owner George Steinbrenner, regarding the Yankees needing a new ballpark, located somewhere other than the Bronx (heaven forbid!!). In order to insure the structural integrity of The Stadium, a full-scale physical inspection was conducted, necessitating postponement of the April 13 and 14 games versus Anaheim. Also, the April 15 home game versus Anaheim was moved to Shea Stadium and thus, the Yankees would play their first "home" game at Shea since September 28, 1975. (In 1974 and 1975, the Yanks and Mets shared games at Shea Stadium while Yankee Stadium was getting a facelift.) The date of April 15 would prove "taxing" to Shea Stadium for it would witness two historic games that day. In the first game, an afternoon encounter, the Yankees would defeat the Anaheim club, 6-3, behind the fine pitching of David Wells. In the second contest, a night affair, the Mets would defeat Sammy Sosa and his Cubs, 2-1. The historic element of these two games was that it was the first time this century that four different teams played a regular season game in the same ballpark on the same day! Quite a day at Shea!

The beam-falling incident also required other changes in the Yankee home schedule. Three weekend home games scheduled against the Tigers for April 17, 18 and 19 were moved to Detroit and their scheduled meetings in Detroit, the following weekend, April 24, 25 and 26, were moved to New York, for a second re-opening of sorts at Yankee Stadium (got that!?) In that April 24 "re-opener" at Yankee Stadium, a Friday night crowd of 26,173, some 30,544 fewer than the "first" home opener on April 10, were entertained by a Yankee victory. In the game, Darryl Strawberry blasted a towering 432-foot two-run homer in the first inning, leading the Bronx Bombers in a 8-4 win. David Cone would pick up the win and Scott Brosius would contribute going 3-for-4 with two RBIs. Three days earlier, April 21, the Yankees clinched first place and they would remain atop the American League East until the end of the 1998 season, some 159 consecutive days in first place. It is noteworthy to point out that the Yankees did not hold the first- place position in the AL East for even one day during the entire 1997 season! At the end of April, the Yanks had a mark of 17-6 and were playing .739 ball up to that point in the season.

By mid-May, the Yankees continued their mastery of their successful ways by continuing to play at better than a .700 clip. When Minnesota rolled into New York, the stage was set for a remarkable individual performance by Yankee lefty, David Wells. On May 17, Mr. Wells, who was reportedly having difficulty concentrating fully for a whole game, proved his detractors wrong by doing the unthinkable—pitching a perfect game, 27 batters faced and 27 batters retired…27 up…27 down. Playing before 49,820 Beanie Baby giveaway attendees, David Wells orchestrated a masterful 120-pitch performance, shutting down the Twins utterly in a 4-0 win. **(For a pitch-by-pitch account of David's gem, see the special narrative "PERFECT GAME" found on page 263).** The perfect game by Wells was the 14th overall in major-league baseball history since the National League was founded in 1876 and the eighth in American League history, dating back to 1901. Although David's was the first "regular season" perfect game in Yankee history, righty Don Larsen tossed a 97-pitch 2-0 perfecto, this one coming in the fifth game of the World Series versus Brooklyn at Yankee Stadium on October 8, 1956 (a pitch-by-pitch account of Larsen's masterpiece may be found under Don's entry in the "Player Biographies" section). The 27th and final out of David's incredible game was recorded at 4:15 p.m. Eastern Time, when rightfielder Paul O'Neill squeezed a fly ball hit by Pat Meares. When the last out was made, teammates mobbed Wells, Bernie Williams and Darryl Strawberry lifting David on their shoulders to acclaim his masterful effort. Curiously, David Wells had often acknowledged his reverence for Yankee baseball history and now was a living and breathing continuance of that history! After his perfect game, Wells told reporters: "Nobody can take this away from me. Ever. I'm honored and couldn't be happier. I just wish a few other people

were here to see it." Wells went on to say: "It's easy to dedicate a game when something goes good, but I dedicate every game to my mom. My family is always with me in heart, mind and soul." David's mother had died over a year ago and he has a tattoo of her on his arm. David had, indeed, proved himself as a pitcher who could not only fully concentrate and excel at his craft but, who would himself become a vital part of the Yankee lore that he so cherishes.

As the season progressed, the Yankees continued to win more than 70% of their games. By the end of May, the Yanks had gained seven full games on the second-place (and hated…boo, hiss!!) Boston Red Sox and had won 37 of their first 50 games, a .740 clip! The Yankees continued their inexorable march to the AL East flag, finishing the month of June with a ledger of 56-20 (.737) and gained an additional three games on the BoSox, who were now 10 full games behind New York. At the halfway point of the season in July (81 games, which also coincided with the All-Star break), the New Yorkers were 61-20 (.753), 11 games up on the Red Sox, and concluded the month with a record of 76-27 (.738), moving 15 games ahead of Boston. As in 1997, five Yankees made the All-Star squad: Paul O'Neill (his fifth overall and third as a Yankee), Bernie Williams (his second straight, but could not play due to an injury), David Wells (his second overall and first as a Yankee), and Scott Brosius and Derek Jeter, both making their first All-Star Game. Yankee David Wells, starting for the American League, pitched for the first two innings. Four Yankees played in the game, going a collective 1-for-6, Scott Brosius getting the only Yankee hit, a single in the ninth inning, having a stolen base to boot. In the game, the Americans blasted the Nationals, 13-8. The Yankees had their best month of the season as far as wins with 22 in August, losing ten. In that month, they hit more home runs (54) than any other team in history had hit in that month. At the end of August, the Yankees were two wins shy of the century mark at 98-37 (.726) and were now 18 full games ahead of the Red Sox.

On September 4, the Yankees, in a 11-6 victory at Chicago, won their 100th game, establishing two records. First, the Yanks broke the American League record for the fewest number of games (138) to reach 100 wins, the prior mark being 140 by the 1954 Cleveland Indians. The second standard eclipsed by their 100th win was to set the major-league record for the earliest calendar date (September 4) to break the century mark. The previous mark was held jointly by the 1906 Chicago Cubs and the 1954 Cleveland Indians, who both won their 100th games on September 9. The Bombers clinched their seventh American League East championship on September 9 with a 7-5 win at Boston and this represented the second fastest clinching in club history. Only the 1941 Yankees were faster, clinching their 12th American League pennant on September 4 at Boston by a score of 6-3.

On a sad note, the oldest living Yankee died on September 17. Chester "Chet" Hoff had made his debut for the Highlanders (the team nickname in the early years of this century) on September 6, 1911. Also known as "Red," Chet was born in 1891 and was 107 years old when he died. Red, a left-handed pitcher, played four seasons in the Majors, three of those with New York. In his days with New York (1911-1913), he was 0-2 in 12 games. He ended his playing days with the 1915 St. Louis Browns, going 2-2, and finished his career with an overall record of 2-4. When Chet passed, there were to be no other living players from any Yankee teams in the teens or the '20s. Only members of clubs from the '30s (and on) remain. So long, Chet!

In a game at Camden Yards in Baltimore on September 20, only one thing was missing from the game—Cal Ripken Jr.'s name on the lineup card! Mr. Ripken chose to sit this one out, ending his fabulous streak at 2,632 consecutive games played! Cal's streak began on May 30, 1982, lasting over 16 seasons! The Yankees came away with a win, 5-4, their 107th, and Ryan Minor, batting sixth, became a trivia answer, replacing Ripken at third base; thus, Ryan began his own streak of sorts!

The last part of September saw the Yankees break even more records, seemingly in every game! On September 24 at Yankee Stadium versus the expansion Tampa Devil Rays, the Bombers faced their final opponent for the 1998 campaign with a 4-game series, September 24, 25, 26 and 27. (This writer had the privilege of witnessing all four of these historic games from the press box—what a treat, indeed, for a lifelong Yankee fan and historian!). In that first game on September 24, the Yankees won, 5-2, and surpassed the team-record win total (110) of the 1927 Yankees with their 111th victory of the season. In this game, rookie phenom Shane Spencer blasted his second grand slam of the month.

The following day at the Stadium, September 25, another record was shattered as the Yanks won their 112th game, 6-1, breaking the American League mark of 111 set by the Cleveland Indians in 1954. By collecting his 200th hit in this game, Derek Jeter, who would wind up with a total of 203 hits, became only the second Yankee shortstop to get as many hits in a season. Hall of Famer Phil Rizzuto (boy, does that ring true or what?! YES!!) finished with exactly 200 safeties in 1950, the Scooter's MVP season.

On September 26, the Yanks beat Tampa for the third day in a row, 3-1, David Cone notching his 20th win and breaking the major-league record for the longest stretch (10 years) between 20-win seasons. David had last won 20 while a member of that other New York club (commonly referred to as the Mets), winning 20 (and losing but three) in 1988. Also in this game, Mr. Spencer was at it again, hitting his seventh homer of the month and breaking the Yankee record (previously six by Ben Paschal in 1925 and Joe Gordon in 1938) for roundtrippers by a rookie in September. (This was getting weird, as some sort of record, whether they be team or individual, was being set in each of the final four games of the year versus Tampa).

In the final game of the regular season, September 27, the Yanks beat the 'Rays again, 8-3, for a four-game sweep. Prior to the start of this game, Yankee great, Joe DiMaggio, was honored in a special ceremony. In this final game of '98, the American League batting title was still up for grabs with Bernie Williams of the Yankees and Boston's Mo Vaughn running neck and neck for the title. The race wasn't settled until the latter innings of the game, with announcements coming periodically in the press box after every Mo Vaughn at bat. Finally, it was learned that Bernie had, indeed, won the batting title and a loud ovation was heard as longtime Yankee Stadium public address announcer, Bob Sheppard, informed the crowd of 49,608 of Bernie's accomplishment. Bernie became the eighth Yankee player to lead the American League in batting (Joe DiMaggio did it twice), finishing with a .339 mark (Mo Vaughn ended with .337). Williams also became only the second Yankee switch-hitter to lead the AL in batting, the only other player being the great Mickey Mantle, who led the Junior Circuit with

a .353 average. In addition, the Mick led the league in homers (52) and 130 RBI, to complete his triple crown and MVP sweep in 1956. With their final mark at 114-48, the Yanks tied yet another franchise record by equaling the 1927 Yankees' (not bad company, huh?) mark of 66 games over the .500 mark. The 1927 club, recognized by many baseball historians to be the greatest team in the history of the game, finished with 110 wins, 44 losses and a tie. (This writer believes that the '98 club would give the one from '27 a real run for their money!) Not to be outdone, rookie sensation Shane Spencer hit yet another homer, his eighth, for the month of September (extending his own record set only the day before). Shane's homer, in this final game of the season, came with the bases jammed with team-mates, his third grand slam of the month (tying a major-league record) and second of the week! What's amazing is that it took Spencer only one month to duplicate what other Yankees—six of them—had required an entire season to do—hitting three or more grand slammers in a year! Joining some elite company, Michael "Shane" Spencer shared the spotlight with the likes of Donald "Don" Arthur Mattingly, Thomas David "Tommy" Henrich, Henry Louis "Lou" Gehrig, Joseph "Joe D" Paul DiMaggio, George Herman "Babe" Ruth and lastly, Robert Michael "Mike" Stanley, each of whom hit three or more grand slams in a single season.

Speaking of grand slams, Darryl Strawberry became the very first American League player to belt two pinch-hit grand slammers in the same season. Two National Leaguers accomplished this feat: Dave Johnson of Philadelphia and Mike Ivie of San Francisco, both hitting the 'slams in 1978. Darryl blasted his first in the ninth inning of a May 2 win (12-6) at Kansas City and this rarity was witnessed in person from the press box by this writer—boy, what a blast!! Straw's second bases-loaded pinch-homer occurred in the second game of a doubleheader at Oakland, August 4, also occurring in the ninth inning. The Yanks had gone into the ninth inning trailing 5-1, when the Bombers unloaded nine runs against Athletic pitchers, the Yanks winning going away, 10-5. At the start of the Yankee postseason in early October, Darryl was diagnosed with colon cancer and endured a three-hour operation on October 3, finally being discharged from the hospital on October 16. Darryl's teammates rallied to his side when learning of his condition and dedicated themselves "to win it all for Darryl!" So as in 1996, when Joe Torre's brother, Frank, had heart surgery during the World Series, the Yankees had another intangible (Darryl's illness) that probably worked to their psychological benefit. However, such so-called "intangibles" cannot be measured by any statistical means and can only be relegated "to playing from the heart."

Several key injuries to Yankee players occurred in 1998. Infielder Luis Sojo missed one month; designated hitter Chili Davis missed four months and returned to the club in mid-August; outfielder Bernie Williams was out for five weeks in June and July; shortstop Derek Jeter missed two weeks in June; and pitchers Jeff Nelson (two months) and Mariano Rivera (18 days) missed some playing time as well. The results of these injuries did not, however, seem to impact the Yankees in their quest for a record-breaking season.

As this season was a true team effort, that team was led by a very experienced coaching staff under the guidance of Manager Joe Torre, who has done an outstanding job in piloting the Yankees since accepting his post in 1996. After three seasons, Joe has guided the Yanks to two World Series Championships. In 1998, Joe managed the Yankees to a record 125 wins (114 in the regular season, plus 11 in the postseason), breaking the major-league record (118) of the 1906 Chicago Cubs. That year, the Cubs who won 116 (still the all-time mark for wins in any major-league season) in the 1906 regular season and two in the World Series. Torre deservedly won several awards at the end of the '98 campaign, including the *Sporting News* Manager of the Year, the Baseball Writers' Association of America's American-League Manager of the Year Award and his second Associated Press Manager of the Year Award (also won with Atlanta in 1982). Brooklyn Joe has guided his club to the postseason his first three years, with only Casey Stengel (1949-1953) and Ralph Houk (1961-1964) accomplishing this. With 302 wins as manager of the Yankees, Torre placed second in franchise history for the most victories in his first three seasons, with only Ralph Houk having more (309) from 1961-1963.

A total of 38 players, including 19 pitchers, appeared in at least one game for the Yankees in 1998. Several notable individual performances highlighted this Yankee season and will be presented now.

Scott Brosius (third base)—Obtained from Oakland in 1997, he solidified the Yankee infield and led all American League third basemen in homers (17) and RBI (98). He led his team in games played (152), tying Paul O'Neill. Brosius had a career year with the Yanks, batting .300 (Scott had a lowly .203 average with the Athletics in '97), scoring 86 runs and leading the American League with a .372 mark with runners in scoring position. Brosius accomplished all of this batting from either the seventh, eighth or ninth positions in the lineup! Scott was named to the major-league All-Star Team as the third baseman for the American League.

Derek Jeter (shortstop)—Beginning his fourth season in pinstripes, Derek was among A.L. leaders in: batting (fifth, .324), runs (1st, 127), hits (third, 203), triples (tied fourth, eight), multi-hit games (tied second), and at bats (sixth, 626). Derek set career high for homers (19), RBIs (84), hits (203), triples (eight), stolen bases (30), and batting average (.324). Derek led his club in at bats, runs, hits, and triples. He finished third in the American League in Most Valuable Player voting. Jeter broke the Yankee single-season home-run mark for shortstops with 19, beating Roy Smalley's total of 16 in 1982. With 203 hits, Derek became the second Yankee shortstop with 200+ hits in a campaign, joining Phil Rizzuto, who had 200 safeties in his MVP 1950 season. Jeter also broke the major-league record for the most runs scored by a shortstop in his first three full seasons with 352, previously held by Donie Bush of Detroit, who had 343 tallies beginning in 1909! Also, Jeter joined Frankie Crosetti as the only Yankee shortstops to score 100+ runs in three consecutive seasons, with Frankie doing it four straight years beginning in 1936...and Derek is only in his mid-20s!

Chuck Knoblauch (second base)—Obtained from Minnesota in the off-season, he stabilized the Yankee infield and provided speed in the lead-off position. Chuck, whose Germanic last name translates into the word "garlic," led the club with 76 walks and 31 stolen bases. His 17 homers were a career high and were the most by a Yankee second sacker since Joe "Flash" Gordon hit the same total in 1943. On the down side, Chuck's .265 batting average was his career low, since breaking into the majors in 1991. Chuck had come to Yankees with a career average of .304 in 1,013 games. He was hit by a pitched ball the most in the American League (18). Only one Yankee, Don Baylor, has been hit more times in a year than Knoblauch. Don was hit 23 times in 1984 and 24 times in 1985. Along with shortstop Jeter, Derek and Chuck become the first middle-infield teammates in American League history to each steal 30+ bases in a single year, Jeter swiping 30 and Chuck 31.

Tino Martinez (first base)—Starting his third season in New York, Tino had yet another solid season, leading the Yanks with 29 homers and 123 RBIs, the latter being sixth in the American League. Tino has now hit 25+ homers and driven in 100+ for the fourth consecutive season. He is only the fourth Yankee player (Babe Ruth, Lou Gehrig and Joe DiMaggio are the others) in team history to have 120+ RBIs in two straight seasons. Tino, also in '98, became the first Yankee with 100+ RBIs in three consecutive seasons since Don Mattingly did it in four straight, beginning in 1984.

Paul O'Neill (right field)—Starting his sixth season with the Yanks, Paul continued to exemplify his consistent play throughout 1998, leading the club with 152 games played (tying with Scott Brosius) and 40 doubles. Paul finished with a .317 average, 24 homers and 116 RBI. He was among AL leaders in hits (tied seventh), multi-hit games (tied fifth), RBIs (tenth) and sacrifice flies (tied third). Paul has hit .300 or better in every season since joining New York in 1993 and finished the season fifth on the all-time Yankee batting list with .317—only Ruth (.349), Gehrig (.340), Combs (.325) and DiMaggio (.325) having better averages than O'Neill's.

Shane Spencer (outfielder)—In his first season in the Majors, Shane made his debut with the Yanks on April 10, being called up from the Triple-A Columbus Yankee farm club to replace Chili Davis, who was on the disabled list. He was recalled several times from Columbus during the course of the season, and 1998 was fairly uneventful for Shane until his final recall in September...and boy what a month he had! He would play 14 games in that final month, going 16 for 38 (.421), scoring 11 runs, 21 RBI, while striking out eight times. Shane blasted eight homers, three of which were grand slams, in September, and collected 42 total bases for a 1.105 slugging percentage!! His eight homers in September set a new Yankee rookie record for homers in that month, eclipsing the six hit by Ben Paschal in 1925 and Joe Gordon in 1938. Shane's three 'slams in a month tied the major-league record shared by six others players. Also, Spencer became only the seventh Yankee player to hit at least three slammers in the same year, the remaining six players requiring an entire season to blast three or more!! Quite a year for the 26-year-old Spencer, who had spent seven prior seasons in the minors!

Darryl Strawberry (outfield)—Playing in his fourth season as a Yankee, Straw belted 24 homers and established an American League record with two pinch-hit grand slams in the same season.

Bernie Williams (center field)—Beginning his eighth season with the Bronx Bombers, Bernie would become the first player in the history of the game to win a batting title, Gold Glove Award and World Series Championship in the same year! He won his first batting title (.339) on the final day of the '98 season, beating Boston's Mo Vaughn, who finished at .337. Thus, Bernie became the eighth Yankee to lead the AL in batting and only the second Yankee switch-hitter to accomplish this feat, Mickey Mantle doing it with his .353 mark in 1956. Williams finished second in the AL in on-base percentage (.422) and 10th in slugging (.575). He joined with Paul O'Neill (.317) as the first pair of Yankee outfielders since Babe Ruth and Earle Combs (1927-1933) to bat .300 or better in four consecutive seasons. At Yankee Stadium on August 16, the 50th anniversary of Babe Ruth's death, Bernie went 4-for-5, belting a game-winning solo home run in the bottom of the ninth, to defeat Texas 6-5! Bernie finished seventh in American League MVP voting.

David Cone (starting pitcher)—In his fourth year with the Yanks, Coney led the American League with 20 wins, tying with future Yankee Roger Clemens (Toronto) and Rick Helling of Texas. David was among league leaders in other categories: winning percentage (tied fourth, .741), ERA (eighth, 3.55), strikeouts (fifth, 209) and opponents batting average (fourth, .237). He led the club with 20 wins and 209 whiffs, the latter total being the ninth best ever by a Yankee pitcher. As a batter, Cone became the first Yankee pitcher to get an RBI since the designated hitter rule was implemented in 1973, a run-scoring fielder's choice in the fourth inning at Atlanta on June 24. David was also fourth in voting for the Cy Young Award.

Orlando Hernandez (starting pitcher)—In his first season with the Yanks, Orlando, or "El Duque" as he is known in his native Cuba, made an immediate impact upon the Yankee pitching corps. He led the club with a 3.13 ERA and won 12 games, while losing but four; his win total was the most by a Yankee rookie righthander since reliever Ron Davis won 14 in 1979. In terms of righty rookie starters, it was the most games won since Doc Medich won 14 in 1973. Orlando's personal story is one related to a triumph of spirit, as he was banned from the Cuban National Team (with whom he won 129 while losing but 47 for a .733 winning percentage) in October 1996 for allegedly planning to defect. El Duque DID eventually defect from Cuba with seven others the day after Christmas, 1997 and was picked up by the U. S. Coast Guard three days later. He established residence in Costa Rica and was granted free agency in mid-January 1998, signing a multi-year deal with the Yankees on March 7, 1998. Hernandez placed fourth in Rookie of the Year voting.

Andy Pettitte (starting pitcher)—Starting his fourth year with the Yankees, the lefty was the only pitcher to lose 10+ games (he lost 11) on a staff of 19 and led the club with 32 starts and 216 innings pitched. Andy tied for fifth place in the A.L. with 16 wins and his 55 victories over the last three seasons are the most by any pitcher in the American League.

Mariano Rivera (relief pitcher)—In four seasons with the Yanks, Mariano has a total of 86 saves, with 79 of those coming over the past two seasons, 43 in 1997 and 36 in 1998, the latter total tying for the fourth spot (with Righetti's 36 in 1990) in Yankee history. He prevented 20 of 23 (87%) inherited runners from scoring, posted an ERA of 1.91 and continues to be a very valuable asset to the Yankee club as its dependable closer.

Mike Stanton (middle relief pitcher)—In his second season as a Yankee, Mike pitched in the eighth most games (67) in Yankee history, all in relief.

David Wells (starting pitcher)—Beginning his second year with the Yanks, David had a phenomenal season in 1998. He led the American League with an .818 winning percentage (18-4) and his five shutouts were tops in the AL as well. David established an American League record by retiring 38 consecutive batters over three starts. The previous record was 33 and shared by Kansas City's Steve Busby in 1974 and Seattle's John Montagne in 1977. David's moment of glory, of course, was his perfect game versus Minnesota at Yankee Stadium on May 17. This was the first such "regular-season" pitching performance

in Yankee history, Don Larsen's perfecto coming in the World Series of 1956. David placed third in voting for the coveted Cy Young Award and was voted on the major-league All-Star Team as the starting left-handed pitcher for the American League in 1998.

Volumes have already been written in an attempt to explain, elucidate, and expound upon the whys and wherefores for the extraordinary success of the Yankees over the course of their incredible 1998 season. Suffice it to say that this club had phenomenal bench strength and a formidable combination of offense, defense and pitching that set numerous individual as well as team records. For more detailed information about the many team records set by the Yankees, see the special entry entitled "1998 YANKEE RECORD BREAKERS" found on the following page.

As a team, the Yankees batted .288, finishing a close second to Texas' .289. They scored more runs than any other team (AL or NL) with 965 tallies (six per game), the most they had scored since 1939, when they had 967. In RBIs, they were also tops in the majors, with 905, the most since 1938, when the Bombers drove in 917. The Yankees ranked among league leaders in other offensive categories: second in hits (1625), third in total bases (2,598), first with nine grand slams (second highest total in team history, ten being the record in 1987), tied for second in sacrifice flies (59), first in walks (653), second in steals (153), first in players left on base (1203) and second in both on-base (.460) and slugging (.364) percentages. They blasted 207 homers, the second most ever in their history. The Bombers used to hold the major-league mark with 240 in 1961 until recently, when the likes of Seattle, Baltimore and Oakland (all AL teams) surpassed the Yankees' 1961 total (no National League through 1999 has hit over 239 homers). Yankee designated hitters, as a group, placed eighth with a .276 average and their pinch-hitters were ninth in the AL with a paltry .203. In fielding, they were third in the league with .984. Only one Yankee, outfielder Bernie Williams, earned a Gold Glove Award for his fielding prowess in 1998. This was Bernie's second such award, winning in 1997 as well. Statistically, the pitching corps fared well, leading the AL with a 3.82 ERA and in other categories as well: complete games (22), shutouts (16), fewest relief appearances (334), fewest hits allowed (1357), fewest homers allowed (156), fewest walks (466), lowest opponent batting average (.247) and fewest runs allowed (656). In terms of run differential (those scored—965, minus those allowed—656), the 1998 Yankees finished on the plus side of 309 runs, the most since 1939. In '39, the differential was a whopping 411 runs (the club record), scoring 967 while allowing but 556.

1998 NEW YORK YANKEE
MISCELLANEOUS STANDINGS

At home	62-19 (.765)	Best in AL
On the road	52-29 (.642)	Best in AL
vs. East Division	33-15 (.688)	Best in AL
vs. Central Division	39-15 (.722)	Best in AL
vs. West Division	29-15 (.659)	Best in AL
vs. National League	13-3 (.813)	Best in AL
On grass fields	97-39 (.713)	Best in AL
On artificial surfaces	17-9 (.654)	2nd in AL
In day games	37-13 (.740)	Best in AL
In night games	77-35 (.688)	Best in AL
vs. left-hand starters	33-11 (.750)	Best in AL
vs. right-hand starters	81-37 (.686)	Best in AL
In shutouts	16-5 (.762)	2nd in AL
In one-run games	21-10 (.677)	Best in AL
In extra-inning games	9-2 (.818)	Best in AL
In doubleheaders	W-1, L-0, Split-1	2nd in AL
When led after 8 inn.	102-1 (.990)	Best in AL

The Yankees, as a team, had a 62-19 (.765) home record and were 52-29 (.642) on the road. The 62 wins at home equaled the total of the 1932 Yankees (who lost but 15) and is the second highest number of home wins in franchise history, the most being 65 (losing 16) by the 1961 team. Playing 18 different clubs (13 in the American League and five in the National) during 1998, the Yanks won 16 of those series, tying one (6-6, versus Toronto) and losing but one (5-6, versus Anaheim). Both at home and on the road, the Yankees played 16 different teams (13 in the AL and three in the NL): at home, the New Yorkers won 12, tied three and lost but one, 2-4 against Toronto; on the road, the Yanks won 11 series, tied three and lost two, being 2-3 against both Minnesota and Anaheim. The Yanks posted three separate streaks of at least nine wins in a row for the first time in franchise history, dating back to 1903. They also lost the fewest one-run games (10) in their history, the prior mark being 11 in 1903, when they were known as the Highlanders. The Yankees were fourth in the AL in attendance, setting a club record with 2,951,467 patrons attending games at Yankee Stadium, an average of 36,893.

This club, led by field general Joe Torre, made a shambles of the American League East race, winning by 22 games over the runner-up Boston Red Sox, who themselves had a very respectable season with a 92-70 (.568) mark. To put Boston's season in perspective, the Red Sox would have won two American League Divisions this season (the Central and West) with their record! The American League East month-by-month standings for 1998:

1998 AMERICAN LEAGUE EAST STANDINGS
(THE YANKEES IN FIRST PLACE)

Through:	W-L**	WIN%	GA*	2nd Place	HR
April 30	17-6	.739	+.5	Boston	21
May 31	37-13	.740	+7.5	Boston	33
June 30	56-20	.737	+10	Boston	30
July 31	76-27	.738	+15	Boston	37
August 31	98-37	.726	+18	Boston	54
September 27	114-48	.704	+22	Boston	32

**cumulative totals   *Yankee games ahead of second club

The Yankees in 1998 had the following monthly records: April (17-6, .739), May (20-7, .741), June (19-7, .731), July (20-7, .741), August (22-10, .688) and September (16-11, .593). The Yankees finished 22 games ahead of the Boston Red Sox and this was the widest margin of victory of any Yankee team in history, breaking the old mark of 19½ by the great 1936 club. Also, that 22-game victory over the Red Sox was the widest margin in American League history over a team with the league's second best record (Boston was 92-70, .568). Note: in August, the Bronx Bombers blasted 54 homers, the most in the month of August by any team in major-league history. That month total of 54 is surpassed in any month by only three different clubs: Baltimore-58 in May, 1987; Minnesota-55 in May, 1964; and by the National League New York Giants total of 55 in May, 1947.

The phenomenal season had by the Yankees in 1998 was sometimes seemingly minimized by the media and was overshadowed by the great home run race between Mark McGwire (70 homers) of the St. Louis Cardinals and Sammy Sosa (66 homers) of the Chicago Cubs. The mind boggles when speculating about the publicity that the Yankees would have garnered had McGwire become a Yankee, as had been rumored in seasons past! As Casey would've said: "That would be just amazin'! 'Nuff said!"

After claiming their unprecedented 35th American League pennant since clinching their first way back in 1921, the Bronx Bombers steamrolled into the playoffs. First, they swept the Texas Rangers in three games in the Division Series, allowing but one lone-star Ranger run. That one Texas run allowed by the Yankee pitching corps was the fewest runs allowed in the first three games of any postseason series, dating back to 1903, the year of the first World Series. Then, the Yankees won the American League Championship Series, in six games, defeating the high-powered Cleveland Indians, who had eliminated the Yanks in last year's Division Series. Finally, in the World Series, the Yankees swept future Hall of Famer Tony Gwynn and his San Diego Padres in four games, their seventh four-game sweep since 1927 when they first swept Pittsburgh, and their last since beating the "Whiz Kids" of Philadelphia in the 1950 Fall Classic. Winning their 24th World Series in 35 appearances was

1998 YANKEE RECORD BREAKERS

**With 114 wins, the Yankees finished second on the all-time, single-season win list...the all-time single-season records for wins:

116 - 1906 Chicago Cubs (lost 36, .763)	**109 - 1961 Yankees (lost 53, .673)**
114 - 1998 Yankees (lost 48, .704)	**109** - 1969 Baltimore Orioles (lost 53, .673)
111 - 1954 Cleveland Indians (lost 43, .721)	**108** - 1970 Baltimore Orioles (lost 54, .667)
110 - 1909 Pittsburgh Pirates (lost 42, .724)	**108** - 1975 Cincinnati Reds (lost 54, .667)
110 - 1927 Yankees (lost 44, .714)	**108** - 1986 New York Mets (lost 54, .667)

At 114-48, the Yankees established an American League record for **most wins in a single season, breaking the mark of 111 by the 1954 Cleveland Indians.

Finished the season **66 games over .500, equaling the franchise record set by the 1927 club, who were 110-54...prior to 1998, the last team to be as many as 66 games over .500 was the 1954 Cleveland Indians, who were 68 games over at 111-43.

At 114-48, the Yankees established the major-league record for **most wins in a 162-game schedule, surpassing the **1961 Yankees** and the 1969 Baltimore Orioles (both were 109-53).

Won 62 home games (lost 19, .765) in 1998, equaling the second highest total in franchise history with the 1932 club (62-15, ..805)...only the 1961 club (65-16, .803) won more **home** games than the '98 club.

Held a lead in 48 consecutive games, a major-league record...the streak started on 6/28 in a 2-1 loss to the Mets at Shea Stadium and was snapped on 8/20 in a 9-4 loss at Minnesota...the Yankees were 37-11 (.771) in those 48 games...the previous mark of 40 consecutive games with a lead was held by the **1932 Yankees.**

Were **61-20 (.753) in their first 81 games, breaking the 162-game schedule record of the 1970 Cincinnati Reds (58-23, .716)...major-league baseball went to the 162-game schedule in 1961.

Reached their **100th win on September 4, breaking the major-league record for the earliest calendar date to reach the century mark... the previous record was held by the 1906 Chicago Cubs and the 1954 Cleveland Indians, who both won their 100th games on September 9.

The Yankees' total of **207 home runs is the second highest in franchise history behind only the 1961 club's 240...their total of 207 is the highest in baseball history for a team without a single player with 30 or more homers, surpassing the 1996 Detroit Tigers' total of 204.

Finished **22 games ahead of the Boston Red Sox, the widest margin of victory in franchise history...the previous high was 19 ½ over Detroit in 1936.

With **24 straight series without a loss, the Yankees tied the major-league record of the 1912 Boston Red Sox and the 1970 Cincinnati Reds, who also went 24 straight series without a loss within one season...the record streak began with a two-game split at Oakland (April 4-5) and ended with the Yanks losing two of three at Baltimore (June 15-17)...prior to the series at Baltimore, the Yankees did not lose a series since they were swept in two games at Anaheim to open the '98 season (were 20-0-4 since).

Tied the major-league record of the 1991 Cincinnati Reds for the **most players in double figures in home runs and stolen bases with six (Brosius—19/11, Curtis—10/21, Jeter—19/30, Knoblauch—17/30, O'Neill—24/15 and Bernie Williams—26/15).

Had **eight players with 15 or more home runs in 1998 (Martinez—28, Williams—26, O'Neill—24, Strawberry—24, Brosius—19, Jeter—19, Knoblauch—17 and Posada—17) tying the major-league record of the 1991 Texas Rangers...the Yankees tied the major-league record with the 1998 Baltimore Orioles with **10 players hitting ten or more homers.**

Were the first team this century to play **.700 baseball in four consecutive months of any single season...in the first four months of '98, the Yanks were 17-6 in April (.739), 20-7 in May (.741), 19-7 in June (.731), and 20-7 in July (.741) before finishing the month of August 22-10 (.688).

Reached **100 wins in their 138th game, breaking the American League record for the fewest amount of games to reach the century mark (previous record was 140 games by the 1954 Cleveland Indians)...the 1906 Chicago Cubs hold the major-league record for the fewest games to reach 100 victories (132 games).

Reached **90 wins in their 120th game, tying the major-league record of the 1944 St. Louis Cardinals.

Became only the sixth team (and the first American League club) this century—and the **first since 1909—to win their 100th game of the season with fewer than 40 losses...only the 1906 Chicago Cubs (100-32), 1902 Pittsburgh Pirates (100-34), 1909 Pittsburgh Pirates (100-36), 1904 New York Giants (100-37), and 1907 Chicago Cubs (100-39) had accomplished this feat since 1900.

Clinched their seventh American League Eastern Division Championship on **September 9 at Boston...was the fastest clinching by a Yankee team since division play began in 1969, and the second fastest in the Majors since 1969 (the 1975 Cincinnati Reds—who clinched on September 7—are the only team to clinch earlier)...the clinching was also the Yankees' second fastest in club history (the 1941 Yankees clinched the AL flag on September 4).

At the conclusion of the 1998 World Series, the Yankees had amassed a total 114 wins in the regular season and 11 in the playoffs, for; a combined total of **125 wins in 175 games, a .714 winning clip (which was the same exact winning percentage of the great 1927 club!).

an appropriate ending to a storybook year for the Yanks, made especially sweet since Yankee Stadium was celebrating its 75th season of play since opening its doors in the Bronx in 1923, the year of their very first World Series Championship against the Giants, then of New York.

In a spectacular season that included a perfect game, an unprecedented 125 wins, and a World Series sweep of the San Diego Pardes, one wondered what would be in store for the 1999 club! The numerous memories created by the '98 edition of the New York Yankees, a team that can only be described as "A TEAM" with little ego, minimal controversy and an incredible desire and persistence to excel, will be indelibly etched into the collective consciousness of Yankee fans for all ages—they were truly a team that had THE BEST SEASON OF THE CENTURY!!

1999

The 1999 edition of the New York Yankees began its 97th season in the Big Apple and was ready to defend its World Championship title won the previous year. The new season would be met with high expectations by many, and it seemed that nothing short of winning yet another World Series title would make for a successful campaign. This is especially true when considering their unprecendetedly spectacular year of 1998. However, before 1999 would begin, the Yankee family would be hit hard by two different events, the first involving Joe DiMaggio and the second involving Yankee manager Joe Torre.

On March 8, just two days prior to Torre's announcement that he had prostate cancer, it was learned that Yankee great Joe DiMaggio had passed away after a lengthy illness. Joe D, who was 84, had a very well-attended funeral at St. Patrick's Cathedral in New York City and was laid to rest in San Francisco, his hometown. When Joe was still hospitalized, George Steinbrenner had approached DiMaggio to toss out the first pitch of the April 9 home opener and Joe seemed interested. When Joe was eventually released from the hospital in January, DiMaggio came home to find a note on his bed: "April 9 Yankee Stadium or Bust". But Joe's passing opened the way for George to ask Yogi Berra about paying a visit to Yankee Stadium (Yogi had not been there for 14 years due to a feud with Steinbrenner) to toss out the ceremonial first pitch—which eventually did come to fruition. The baseball world shared the grief that surrounded the loss of this great American icon, and on April 25, the Yankees fittingly honored the Yankee Clipper with all sorts of special ceremonies. Details regarding Joe D's new monument will be given later in this narration.

In the early part of spring training in Tampa, skipper Torre left the team on March 10, announcing that he had prostate cancer. Joe eventually would have successful surgery performed by Dr. Catalona at Barnes-Jewish Hospital in St. Louis on March 18, missing the club's first 36 games. In his absence, veteran manager Don Zimmer, the Yankees' bench coach, assumed Joe's managerial reins, the team going 21-15 under his tutelage. Regarding his thoughts on returning as manager, Torre said: "...I want to make sure when I come back, I'm strong enough to stay back." When Joe regained his duties at Boston (losing 6-3) on May 18, he was met by a warm ovation by Fenway fans. Nice touch! But now we must backtrack for a moment to an event that occurred in February.

In a blockbuster trade in February, the Yankees obtained future Hall of Famer and five-time Cy Young Award winner, Roger Clemens, in exchange for lefty David Wells, reliever Graeme Lloyd and infielder, Homer Bush. Outfielder Bernie Williams was kept in the Yankee fold signing a very hefty contract that runs through the year 2005. The '98 Yankee lineup remained essentially intact, with Tino Martinez at first, Chuck Knoblauch at second, Derek Jeter at short with Bernie Williams and Paul O'Neill, in center and right, respectively. The catching again was ably shared by Joe Girardi and Jorge Posada. There would be a change in left field with Tim Raines gone (granted free agency in October, 1998). Left would be a platoon job between Darryl Strawberry, '98 phenom Shane Spencer, and Ricky Ledee, who batted a hefty .600 (6 for 10 with four RBI) in the '98 World Series sweep versus the San Diego Padres. Chili Davis and Strawberry would share the DH spot. The pitching corps, with the addition of Clemens, had a four-man rotation with Roger, playoff ace Orlando Hernandez, Ramiro Mendoza and David Cone. Middle relievers included Mike Stanton, Jeff Nelson, and of course, closer par excellence, Mariano Rivera. Andy Pettitte was out of the starting equation initially, being placed on the 15-day DL with a strained elbow. Andy would have to wait until May 5 to make his first start of the '99 season.

On a sad note regarding Tim Raines, he would play 58 games with Oakland before being placed on the disabled list on July 19. At that time, it was discovered that Tim had lupus, a connective-tissue disease with no known cure. At the end of August, Tim visited the Yankee clubhouse where there was a tremendous outpouring of love and affection from his ex-mates. Tim's presence had been mostly responsible for keeping the clubhouse loose, eliciting fun and laughter during those especially difficult times in 1998. Now it was Tim's turn to get his spirits lifted... and lifted they were, indeed! The '99 club would be beset by other personal tragedies and losses...more later regarding those issues.

The 1999 Yankee season, their 97th, began, as usual, with a West Coast swing, this time a three-game set in Oakland. On April 5, newcomer Roger Clemens made his Yankee debut, ending with a no-decision after 6 $\frac{1}{3}$ innings, allowing three runs and striking out eight. The eight-inning rain-shortened loss (5-3) was their third straight loss in openers, setting their mark at 55-41 (.573) with one tie versus Boston in 1910, when the Yanks were known as the Highlanders. After winning the opening series with the A's two games to one, the Bombers headed for the friendly confines of Yankee Stadium to open versus Detroit on April 9.

Shunning all activities at Yankee Stadium for 14 long years due to a bitter disagreement between himself and Yankee Principal Owner, George Steinbrenner, Yogi Berra was willing to put the past behind him when asked to throw out the first pitch of the April 9 game. In a truly emotional moment, Yogi and George shared many embraces and, indeed, Berra's physical presence on the Yankee mound put closure to a situation that could finally be healed, thus promoting an even greater closeness within the Yankee family. Yankee starter David Cone held the Tigers hitless through five, until allowing a hit in the sixth frame. The contest, witnessed by a sellout crowd of 56,583, was eventually called after 6 $\frac{1}{2}$ innings due to rain, but the weather surely could not dampen the feelings that were evident between Berra and Steinbrenner.

On April 25 at the Stadium versus Toronto, the Yankees unveiled a new monument in honor of Joe DiMaggio prior to the game. It is the fifth such monument dedicated, the others honoring Miller Huggins, Lou Gehrig, Babe Ruth and Mickey Mantle. This monument has a beautiful inscription which reads:

JOSEPH PAUL DiMAGGIO
"THE YANKEE CLIPPER"
1914-1999

RECOGNIZED AS BASEBALL'S
"GREATEST LIVING PLAYER"

LIFETIME BATTING AVERAGE	.325
WON MVP AWARD	1939, 1941, 1947
SELECTED TO ALL-STAR GAME	13 TIMES
AMERICAN LEAGUE BATTING TITLE	1939,1940
ELECTED TO HALL OF FAME	1955

SET ONE OF BASEBALL'S MOST ENDURING RECORDS,
56-GAME HITTING STREAK
MAY 15 TO JULY 16, 1941

LED THE YANKEES TO AN INCREDIBLE NINE WORLD
CHAMPIONSHIPS IN HIS 13-YEAR CAREER

A BASEBALL LEGEND AND
AN AMERICAN ICON

"HE HAS PASSED, BUT HE WILL NEVER LEAVE US"

DEDICATED BY
THE NEW YORK YANKEES
APRIL 25, 1999

Singer Paul Simon (of Simon and Garfunkel fame) was even on hand to sing "Mrs. Robinson," getting a thunderous ovation when he uttered: "Where have you gone, Joe DiMaggio? A nation turns its lonely eyes to you. What's that you say, Mrs. Robinson? Joltin' Joe has left and gone away." For the remainder of 1999, Yankee players would wear Joe D's #5 on their left uniform sleeves, a great tribute for a great man. The Yanks won the game in 11, 4-3, with reliever Jason Grimsley picking up his first win in pinstripes. From the runway connecting the Yankee clubhouse with the field dugout, a sign was placed well in view for all to read on their way to the playing field—it read:

"I want to thank the Good Lord for making me a Yankee"
—Joe DiMaggio

On their first homestand of the year, the Yanks would win five of the six games played, and by the end of April the Bombers were 14-7, spending half of the 26 days either in first place or tied for that position. Don Zimmer had his troops playing very well in Joe Torre's absence. Like Torre, Zim was facing his own healing challenges, involving intense pain caused by a surgically repaired knee. In April, Jeter was ranked

among the leaders in many AL categories and batted .378 with 15 RBIs; DH Chili Davis was hitting a lofty .356 with 20 RBIs. On the hill, David Cone asserted himself with a 3-0 record for the month, with a 1.04 ERA in four starts. Ramiro Mendoza in the initial month had a pitching mark of 3-1, a 2.40 ERA and four saves in five attempts.

There was a difficult situation for Darryl Strawberry in mid-April in Tampa. It seems that Darryl was charged with drug and solicitation charges, which led to his 90-day suspension from baseball for violating his aftercare program. Straw, who would be allowed to return to the Yanks on September 1, did admit the renewal of his drinking, explaining that it was due to a depression related to his chemotherapy. Let's not forget that Darryl had undergone surgery for colon cancer in the midst of postseason play the previous season. Regardless, Darryl got himself into trouble and made amends for that later in the '99 campaign. Good for you, Darryl!

In a major-league first versus Seattle on May 7 at the Stadium, two Japanese starting pitchers were to face off against each other: Mac Suzuki for the M's versus Hideki Irabu of the Yanks. In the game, Irabu scattered four hits over seven innings to get the Yankee win, 10-1. Suzuki was charged with the defeat in this game of historic import. In yet another oddity two days later, again versus Seattle, Zimmer made Mike Stanton his starter, a move that Zim hoped would shake things up within the Bomber pitching corps. What's unusual about this is that Mike had gone for the most number of games (552) by a pitcher without ever starting a game, a major-league record. The prior record was 443 games by Gary Lavelle of San Francisco in 1981. Stanton, whose pitching days began with the Atlanta Braves in 1989, tossed four shutout frames, receiving a no-decision for his effort. For the month of May, the Yanks were in first place until supplanted by the BoSox on May 18, the date that Manager Joe Torre returned to the club. The Bostons remained atop the AL East until June 9, when the Yanks got it back for themselves alone for keeps, excepting for one day (June 21) when they were deadlocked with the Red Sox. For the month, the Yanks had a mediocre-at-best 15-13 record and were down 1½ games to front-running Boston. Jeter continued his torrid pace (.367), and Bernie Williams banged out the same average to share the club lead in that category. On the hill, Roger Clemens would go 2-0 in May, and along the way, he picked up his 18th consecutive pitching victory on May 22, establishing a new AL record. Clemens had broken the long-standing ties between Johnny Allen (Cleveland: 1936-37) and Dave McNally (Baltimore: 1968-69), who had each won 17 straight games. Carl Hubbell of the National League Giants was still well in front of Clemens with the major-league mark of 24 straight wins over the 1936 and 1937 seasons. On May 27, "Rocket" faced his ex-club, the Red Sox, for the first time at Yankee Stadium, notching his 19th consecutive win, 4-1. For all of his efforts, Rocket only continues to solidify his presence in the Hall of Fame upon his eligibility.

On June 1 versus Cleveland, Clemens extended his own AL record by defeating the Tribe, 11-5, now having his 20th straight victory. He now shared the 20+ consecutive-win club with only three other pitchers in all of baseball history, all National Leaguers: Carl Hubbell (24), Elroy Face (22) and Rube Marquard (20). Roger would see his streak at 20 come to a blinding halt versus the Mets at the Stadium, the rivals defeating Clemens, 7-2. In the game, Roger only lasted $2^2/_3$ innings, allowing seven runs in his shortest stint since his Boston days in 1995. As they say, all good things must come to an end! Thanks, Roger, for a gallant effort for the month the Yankees were 17-9 and had but a two-game edge over second-place Boston. After the 1998 domination in every situation, the Yankees found themselves in an unusual situation: they were in a pennant race! They did put together their longest win streak of the year (seven) in the latter days of June. Jeter, Williams and O'Neill all batted above .344 for the month. In fact, Derek had been on base in every Yankee game since the start of the season when his string of 53 games was snapped on June 6 versus the Mets. No researcher is really certain which Yankee holds the all-time club record from the beginning of a season, but Jeter does hold it for the post-expansion era, that is, from 1961 on. Pitchers Orlando Hernandez, Mariano Rivera and Hedeki Irabu continued to shine for New York. Through the first 67 games (a club record), the Yanks did not have a complete game and then, Orlando "El Duque" Hernandez tossed the first for the staff on June 22 (game 68) at Tampa Bay, a three-hit, 7-0, shutout of the 'Rays. The first round of interleague play ran from June 4-13, the Yanks going 5-4 versus the Mets, Phillies and Marlins. In the midst of their National League sojourn, the Yankees were honored for a day at the White House on June 10 to celebrate their fabulous 1998 season. The players and coaching staff got to meet the president, and for one day rubbed shoulders with the big boys!

The second and final set of interleague games was set for July 9-20, pitting the Yanks against the Mets, Braves and Expos. All in all, the Mets-Yankees series continued to draw tremendous crowds, having an average in mid-50s at both Shea and Yankee Stadiums. This annual rivalry adds an incredible energy and excitement to this city. In the six games, the Yanks and Mets were deadlocked with three wins each, each home club taking the series at their park.

At the All-Star break on July 12-14, the Yanks were up four full games on Boston. Played at Fenway Park, Torre would again get to lead his players versus the National Leaguers. Four Yanks made the squad and three played: Derek Jeter (0 for 1), Bernie Williams (0 for 1) and David Cone (two IP, four H, one ER, three SO); the fourth, Mariano Rivera declined the invitation to handle some personal business in his native Panama. With the American Leaguers coming out on top, 4-1, Torre now had a winning record (2-1) for the first time as All-Star Game manager.

On Sunday, July 18, in the Bronx versus the Montreal Expos of the NL, the crowd of 41,930 was really in for a treat. Not only was it Joe Torre's 59th birthday, but also the Yanks were honoring Yogi Berra and former perfect-game pitcher, Don Larsen, who was to toss out the ceremonial first pitch. After Larsen tossed the ball to Yogi, his catcher in the 1956 World Series perfect game versus Brooklyn, Larsen left the mound and found time to wish David Cone luck for the day. Well, as fate would have it, David would toss a perfecto at the Expos—27 up, 27 down. A pitch-by-pitch account of Cone's gem may be found in his biography section of this work. David required 88 pitches to complete the job, an amazing 68 of them (77%) were for strikes. There seemed to be no truly difficult fielding chances during the game, and when pinch-hitter Orlando Cabrera fouled to third baseman Scott Brosius for the 27th and final out, bedlam ensued on the field. Cone dropped

to his knees and was immediately surrounded by his jubilant teammates. In the third inning, there was a 33-minute rain delay, but the Yanks had already done their damage, scoring five of their six in the second frame. Both Ricky Ledee and Derek Jeter hit two-run shots to give Coney all the run support he needed for the afternoon. Some facts of the perfect game: Cone did not go to a three-ball count all day; in the sweltering 98-degree heat, Cone had four groundouts, 13 flyouts and 10 strikeouts (eight swinging, two called); there were nine outfield putouts; there were 15 first-pitch strikes, seven first-pitch balls and five first-pitch outs; the most pitches in an inning was 15 (seventh) and the fewest was five (sixth); the most balls in any inning were four (fifth) and the most strikes were 12 (seventh); in every inning from the sixth on, Cone sought refuge in Torre's office (with Joe's blessings, of course) while the Yankees were at bat; it was the first occurrence in major-league history of pitchers from the same team throwing a perfect game in consecutive seasons; Cone was now 34-9 (.791) at Yankee Stadium after his victory; there was a photo that went out on the wires that showed David Cone and Don Larsen embracing after the game. Thank yous go out to two pairs of great batterymates: to pitcher David Cone and catcher Joe Girardi and to Don Larsen and Yogi Berra! What a GREAT day! For his win, Torre's record as manager improved to 6-8 on his birthday.

On July 22, the Yankees would achieve a club milestone by playing in their 15,000th game since 1903. With the 5-4 win versus Tampa Bay, their record now stood at 8,451 wins with 6,463 losses with 83 ties and three games that were ordered replayed, a winning percentage of .5666. If the Yanks continue to play a 162-game schedule, they should be playing game #20,000 sometime in the year 2030. Two days later versus Cleveland at the Stadium, the Bronx Bombers returned with a vengeance, blasting the Indians 21-1 and did eventually sweep the three-game series. It was the 20th time that the Yanks had scored 20+ runs in a game and the first time since a 21-7 win against the Kansas City Athletics on August 19, 1962. The 21-run total was also the most scored by New York at Yankee Stadium since a 22-5 drubbing of the Chicago White Sox on July 26, 1931. (That 22-total in the 1931 game represents the most ever scored by the Yanks in a home game). The 20-run margin was the greatest since a 22-1 win at Washington on August 12, 1953. Every Yankee got at least one hit in the game except Paul O'Neill, and Chili Davis went 5-for-6 with three runs scored and six RBI! The Yanks conclude the month of July with a 16-11 record and widened their lead to six over Toronto and $6^1/_2$ over Boston. Leading the way for the Yanks for the month were: Derek Jeter (.339, 21 RBI), Scott Brosius (.347, 16 RBI), and Chuck Knoblauch (.330, 15 RBI); on the hill, Hideki Irabu was the American League Pitcher of the Month with a 4-0 record, a 2.64 ERA in six games started. Irabu would also conclude a personal-best eight-game winning streak that would come to a close on August 15. As the July 31 trading deadline fast approached, it was a foregone conclusion that Andy Pettitte would be gone come August 1. However, Joe Torre and GM Brian Cashman went to bat for Andy with Steinbrenner. The final outcome: Andy remained a Yankee. The Yanks did pick up ex-mate Jim Leyritz in a trade for minor-league pitcher Geraldo Padua with the San Diego Padres.

On August 2 versus Toronto, in a battle of lefties, almost-traded Andy Pettitte outdueled ex-Yankee David Wells, 3-1.

Andy went eight strong innings, allowing six hits, while walking none, to even his record at 8-8. Derek Jeter hit a game-winning two-run shot in the eighth, becoming the first Yankee shortstop ever to hit 20 homers in a season—and Derek is just 25 years old. Jeter would finish the season with 24 roundtrippers. These events occurred on August 2, 20 years after Yankee catcher Thurman Munson died tragically in a plane crash at the age of 32. Pettitte, went 4-1 in the next five games with a sparkling 0.92 ERA. Andy's strong competitive edge had returned. At Texas on August 23, the Yanks pummeled the Rangers, 21-3. It had not been since 1949, the year of this writer's birth, that the Yanks were to score 20+ runs in a game twice in one season, the last time being on July 24. They have now accomplished the feat of scoring 20+ runs twice in a season four times: 1931, 1939, 1949 and now, 1999. However, in 1939, they scored 20 or more runs in a game three times for the only time in their history. For the game, the Bombers pounded out a season-high 23 hits, the most since August 25, 1984 at Seattle when the Yanks also made 23 hits. Catcher Joe Girardi truly had a game for the ages, going four for six with a career-high seven RBIs. Scott Brosius added to the Yankee cause with a career-high six RBIs.

In the latter days of August, a Yankee milestone was approaching, and so that it would not go unnoticed, this writer contributed the following news for immediate release to the Associated Press:

A NEW YORK YANKEE MILESTONE IN THE MAKING SINCE 1921

With the year 2000 looming nearer every day, the New York Yankees are on the threshold of a milestone that is truly incredible! In their illustrious past, the Yankees have been synonymous with winning, and because of that consistency over the decades, the Bronx Bombers are about to go **2,000 games over the .500 mark**—when they go 32 games over .500 in 1999, they will achieve a milestone that no other baseball club even closely approaches. The Yankees have been over the .500 mark as a team since October 1, 1921, not coincidentally, the date that they clinched their first-ever American League pennant.

~Filed August 29, 1999 by Walter LeConte, editor of The Bronx Bomber Bulletin

Well, that historic day finally occurred on August 30 versus Oakland at the Stadium. With a record of 81-49 (32 games over .500), the Yankees' all-time mark was now at 8,475-6,475, or 2,000 games above .500. To put in perspective the incredible nature of this accomplishment: the Yankees could now hypothetically lose every game of a 162-game season for 12 consecutive years and then lose the next 56 for part of that 13th season—after doing that, the Yanks would be back exactly to the .500 mark again.

The Yanks went on to post their best month of the season (19-10) greatly assisted by: Bernie Williams (.384, 34 RBIs), Ricky Ledee (.371, 14 RBI) and Chuck Knoblauch (.317,19 RBIs); closer Mariano Rivera was voted American League Pitcher of the Month (Irabu had won the same award the prior month) with a 1-0 record, 11 saves in 13 games and an ERA of 0.00! Pettitte also posted masterful numbers for the month (5-1 record, 1.76 ERA in six games).

Coming off his suspension, Darryl Strawberry played in his first game of 1999 with the Yankees on September 2, going 0-for-2 with two strikeouts. He would return with a vengeance: Darryl appeared in 24 games, batted .327, scored 10 runs, drove in six, walked 17 times and had an on-base percentage of .500. His assistance could not have come at a more opportune moment in this season.

During an off day on September 9, the Yankee family was devastated by the news of the death of Jim "Catfish" Hunter. Hunter, who was 52, had been diagnosed with ALS, commonly known as Lou Gehrig's Disease, in November of the previous year. His condition had been deteriorating over the past several weeks. Catfish, a nickname given him for his Southern heritage by Athletics owner, Charles O. Finley, spent 15 years in the majors, the last five with the Yankees. Having 224 career victories, Jim posted 63 of those in the Yankee win column. He was elected on the first ballot to the Baseball Hall of Fame in Cooperstown, New York in 1987, along with the Cubs' Billy Williams. Hunter never pitched in the minors and became the first pitcher to toss a perfect game since 1922, when he defeated the Minnesota Twins on May 8, 1968. Catfish won 20+ games in five consecutive seasons beginning in 1971. His streak came to an end after his 23-14 mark in 1975, his first year as a Yankee, when he tossed 308 innings and completed a league-high 23 games. Hunter became the first multimillionaire player ever when declared a free agent on a technicality after the 1974 season. He eventually agreed to terms with the Yankees, signing a five-year deal worth $3.75 million. This contract was announced on New Year's Eve 1974 for tax reasons, and he put into motion the concept of full-scale free agency, which began after the 1976 season. Jim's funeral was held on September 13 in his hometown of Hertford, N.C. It was attended by many people, including ex-Yankees Reggie Jackson and Lou Piniella. Jim was laid to rest in a cemetery that was behind the field where he played baseball for his high school. As a tribute to Hunter, the Yankees added a black circle on their field jersey, just below the number 5, honoring Joe DiMaggio. Also, Scott Brosius had to leave for Oregon to attend the funeral of his father, Maury, who had died of colon cancer, September 12. The members of this club extended themselves in so many loving ways during these personal tragedies, having to do it two more times when Luis Sojo and Paul O'Neill each lost their fathers in the midst of the postseason play.

The Red Sox came to the Bronx on September 10 and brought with them their incredible pitcher, Pedro Martinez. Pedro would hold the Yanks to one hit, a solo home run by Chili Davis in the second inning, and strike out a record 17 Yankee batters. Many writers, including this one, felt that Pedro, with his phenomenal 1999 season, should have won the Cy Young Award and the MVP Award for his efforts (Pedro eventually won only the former). The Red Sox would sweep the three games at Yankee Stadium to move within 3 ½ games of the Yanks. In the game versus the BoSox on September 12, the Yanks would go over the three-million mark for the first time in their history with a sellout crowd of 56,028. For the year, the Yankees would draw 3,293,659, an average of 40,662 per game. In 1998, they had fallen short of the magic number by a total of 50,266. The Yanks would lose again the following night at Toronto, but no ground was lost as Boston also lost.

The Yanks would go on to win their next four in a row, beginning with the game at Toronto on September 14. In that game, the New Yorkers were down 6-1 in the eighth and seemed destined for their fifth loss in a row. But wait a minute...Williams hit his seventh career grand slam in that eighth inning...in the ninth, Paul O'Neill hit his fourth career grand slam...Yanks win 10-6! The Bronx Bombers had blasted grand slams in consecutive innings for the ONLY TIME in their history. For only the third time, they had hit two 'slams in the same game. In 1936, both were hit by Tony Lazzeri—second and fifth innings in his 11-RBI game, which is still the American League record for one game; and in 1987 by Don Mattingly—second inning—and Dave Winfield—eighth inning. Remember that 1987 was the year that Donnie blasted a major-league record six grand slams, which was still the standard through the 1999 season. In a four-game series at Cleveland, the Yanks managed to win three of the games, but their lead was still a mere three over the BoSox.

In late September, the Yanks returned to the Bronx for their final homestand of the season, and on September 24 versus Tampa Bay, the Yanks clinched their fifth consecutive playoff berth with an exciting 4-3 win in 11-innings. At Baltimore on September 28, the Yanks won, 9-5. In the game, Martinez had four RBI, making him the fourth Yankee to go over the 100 RBI plateau. Joining Tino (105 in 1999) was Bernie Williams (115), Paul O'Neill (110) and Derek Jeter (102). This was the first time that a Yankee club had four 100+ RBI players since 1939 when it was accomplished by Joe DiMaggio (126), Joe Gordon (111), Bill Dickey (105) and George Selkirk (101). In the second game of a doubleheader at Baltimore on September 30, the Yankees clinched their eighth American League East title in a stirring 12-5 win, highlighted by a six-run eighth inning, Orlando Hernandez picking up his 17th win of '99. Also in this game, Bernie Williams got his 200th hit, joining Derek Jeter, who had amassed #200 earlier in the month. They became the first Yankee teammates to have 200+ hits in the same season since Joe DiMaggio (215 hits) paired with Lou Gehrig (200) back in 1937. For September, Paul O'Neill would drive in 33 runs, tying his career-high of RBI in a month set in May of the previous year. Derek would hit .362 and Bernie .317 for the month of September. On the hill, Rivera was 1-0, 0.00 ERA and had seven saves in 13 games. Hernandez would go 3-2 with a 4.12 ERA in six games started. In September, they were 15-13 overall and posted a 2-1 mark in October. The Yankees closed out the 1999 campaign with an October 3 game at Tampa Bay, finishing with a record of 98-64, four games ahead of the Red Sox, the AL wild card representative for this season.

In terms of team statistics, the Yanks ranked fourth overall in the American League in batting (.282), third in runs scored (900), eighth in homers (193), third in walks (718), and were second with a .366 on-base percentage. They excelled in pitching numbers: second in ERA (4.13), second in runs allowed (731), second in shutouts (10), first in saves (50-tied with Boston), second in hits allowed (1402), second in innings pitched (1439 $^2/_3$), allowed the fewest home runs (158), were third with 1,111 strikeouts and finished second with a .255 opponents batting average. The Yankees ranked seventh in fielding in the AL and were tied with Boston for the fewest double plays made (132).

Individually, the Yanks had the American League's second and third ranked players in batting average, Derek Jeter (.349) and Bernie Williams (.342), respectively. In on-base percentage, Derek was third (.438) and Bernie was fourth (.435). In runs scored, Jeter was second (134, tied with Shawn Green of Toronto), Knoblauch was sixth (120) and Bernie was eighth with 116, tied with Ivan Rodriguez of Texas. Jeter was tied for

second in triples (nine) with two Kansas City Royal players (Carlos Febles and Johnny Damon). In the hit parade, Jeter was first with 219 safeties, while Bernie Williams was third with 202. Bernie Williams would place fifth in both walks (100) and multi-hit games (58). Jeter would finish first with 67 multi-hit games and fourth with 346 total bases, tied with Manny Ramirez of Cleveland. No Yankee players would finish anywhere near the top in such categories as home runs and slugging percentage. And, surprisingly, no Yanks were in the RBIs top 10, especially when they had four such players that hit the century mark or better! As far as ranked pitchers, the Yankees had several represented in various categories. In ERA, Cone was second (3.44) and Hernandez tenth (4.12); Mariano Rivera was first with his 45 saves and third with 63 games finished, the most ever by a Yankee right-handed pitcher. Orlando Hernandez placed fifth (tied with Garcia of Seattle, Nagy of Cleveland and Wells of Toronto) in wins with 17, sixth in winning percentage (.654, 17-9) and seventh with 214 $^1/_3$ innings pitched. Cone was fourth overall with his 177 strikeouts and Roger Clemens was tenth with 163. In terms of the lowest opponents batting average, Cone was second (.229), Hernandez third (.233) and Clemens ninth (.261). During the course of the '99 campaign, 39 different players appeared in at least one game for the Yankees, 18 of them pitchers. Exciting young prospects such as D'Angelo Jiminez (shortstop, 21 years old), Alfonso Soriano (shortstop, 21) and Ed Yarnall (lefty pitcher, 23) made their Yankee debuts during the season. Yarnall has a pretty good shot, this writer believes, of breaking into the Yankee starting rotation sometime during the 2000 season. The Yanks have incredible prospects on their way up through their excellent minor-league system, and the future looks very promising indeed!

The Yankees ended their last regular season of the 20th Century with a 98-64 record, closing out their ledger at 8,492 wins, 6,490 losses, 83 tied and three replayed games, totaling 15,068 games. Since 1903 (97 seasons), the Yanks have won an average of 87.5 games per year. In terms of their signature, the home run, the Yanks finished the century with a total of 11,880 homers and should surpass the 12,000 plateau easily in the year 2000. Their homer total averages over 97 years to 122.5 per season and computes to exactly 810 miles (or from New York City to Chicago) of traveling around the basepaths (for one home run, a player must run 360 feet around the bases to score).

As preparation began for the postseason, a very exciting possibility, especially for the citizens of New York, presented itself for the first time ever. It was the potential for the first subway series since 1956. After all, this was the first season ever that both the Yankees and the Mets were in the postseason in the same year! The American League postseason field was now complete, with the Yankees, Indians, Rangers, and Red Sox preparing to do battle. The Yankees would be paired with the Texas Rangers in the Division Series for the third time since 1996, Texas managing but one win in the two series. The New York Yankees were set to begin their sixth Division Series, the most by any club in either league. Also, they were about to play in their 48th postseason series, which includes 35 World Series, five Division Series, and seven League Championship Series! Amazing! The Yankees' march to their next World Series title was about to begin...

2000

When a major league team wins the World Series, the also-rans have plenty of time during the off-season to lick their wounds and gear up for another shot at the champs. "Wait till next year!" is the perennial cry of these losers. Even when the team they're constantly chasing is the seemingly unbeatable New York Yankees, who are widely recognized as the best team of the 20th century, that refrain represents more than wishful thinking. It is intended as a clear warning that the next year's Yankee squad had better adjust its rearview mirror—and check it often.

At the outset of the 2000 season, the Bronx Bombers knew they weren't going to have to wait till August to feel the heat. After having won their second straight World Series, the Yankees were seeking not only their third title in a row, but also their fourth in five years. Except for the 1972–74 Oakland A's, no big-league team had dominated the sport as handily as the old Yankee teams of 1936–39 and 1949–53. This was a franchise that owned more championships than any team in the history of sports—all sports.

Although some observers believed that the Yankees were due for a fall, primarily because many of their premium players were simply getting old, most experts figured they'd get the job done, regardless. It just seemed to work out that way. After all, winning—like losing—becomes a habit.

A perfect example of the cracks that were showing in the lineup was David Cone. After pitching a perfect game against the Montreal Expos on Yogi Berra Day at the Stadium on July 18, 1999, Cone began losing it. His deterioration continued into spring training 2000, when he could muster only a 1-1 record and an ERA of 6.16. Once the regular season began, it took him until April 28 to notch his first win. He would win only three more games the rest of the way, finishing at 4-14. His ERA, meanwhile, ballooned to 6.91.

Another mainstay, Paul O'Neill, was getting old, and his body was no longer able to bounce back quickly from the injuries that accompany the aging process. Still, he would gut it out and finish with a .283 batting average, 18 homers, and 100 RBIs.

Beginning the season on the road, the Yankees improved their all-time opening-day record to 56-41-1. In the process, they snapped a three-year losing streak in season openers and hiked their record to 16-9 in season openers following a World Series title. Although they started off a bit slowly, splitting their first six games of the year, the Yankees recovered once they returned home to the Bronx. After winning their home opener, the Yankees reeled off eight straight wins to take over first place in the AL East, where they remained until the middle of May.

Through it all, the Yankees continued to make their mark in the record books. Earlier, on April 23, catcher Jorge Posada and center fielder Bernie Williams each hit two homers in a 10-7 victory at Toronto's SkyDome. What made their accomplishments even more noteworthy was that both switch-hitters homered from both sides of the plate. It was the sixth time Williams had turned the trick, the third time Posada had done it. It also marked the first time in major league history that two players had performed the feat in the same game, period—let alone two players on the same team.

The switch-hitting Jorge Posada (above) and Bernie Williams made history in Toronto when they each homered from both sides of the plate in the same game. (Jim Mone, AP/Wide World Photos)

Throughout the month of June, the Yankees bounced back and forth between first and second place. They appeared vulnerable. When invaluable middle reliever and part-time starter Ramiro Mendoza went down with an injury on June 28 and was lost for the season, the Yankees were thrown for a loop. But they were hardly down for the count, as they used a bevy of arms to make up for Mendoza's absence.

In what would become a season filled with twists and turns, an interesting bit of history was made on July 8. The Yankees and the Mets had been rained out of an interleague game on June 11. (Ironically, Cone, the former Met, had started that game and was shutting out his ex-mates when the game was called in the third inning.) Due to the tight schedule, neither team could find time to reschedule the game. So representatives from the two clubs met with the players' union and came up with the following solution: baseball's first-ever split-admission doubleheader played in two different stadiums. An afternoon game would be played at Shea, and then the teams would travel to the Bronx for the nightcap at Yankee Stadium. In the day game, Dwight Gooden returned to the site of his glory days and allowed only two runs in five innings. With Tino Martinez homering and knocking in three runs, the Yankees took the opener of the historic home-and-home, day-night doubleheader, 4-2. For his part, Gooden no longer possessed the blazing fastball that had earned him the nickname "Dr. K," but his adrenalin was flowing, nonetheless. He was efficient with his pitches, allowing six hits, walking only one, and throwing 77 pitches in his five-inning stint. In the nightcap, teammate Roger Clemens tossed 7 1/3 strong innings in his second straight effective outing. He allowed only two runs on seven hits, walked one, and struck out four, improving to 2-4 overall against the Mets. The Yankee Stadium crowd of 55,821 greeted the Rocket with a standing ovation as skipper Joe Torre removed him in favor of reliever Mike Stanton.

Before he hit the showers, Clemens did manage to add fuel to the Met-Yankee rivalry by beaning Mets catcher Mike Piazza. It was a good-news, bad-news scenario. Clemens's triumph was the 253rd of his career, tying him for 37th place on the all-time win list with Carl Hubbell. But his head-hunting of Piazza turned off many observers. To be fair, Piazza shouldn't have been surprised. After all, he had belted three homers off Clemens in their previous seven confrontations. But there he lay, motionless, for several minutes, suffering from a concussion.

Meanwhile, as the season progressed, the throwing problems worsened for second baseman Chuck Knoblauch—a former Gold Glover. The Yankees had anticipated having the services of minor leaguer D'Angelo Jimenez, who would be used as a utility infielder. The potential they saw in Jimenez was one of the reasons they had let reserve Luis Sojo leave via the free-agent route. But Jimenez was injured in an auto accident before the season began, and the Yankees had to make do with 10-year minor league veteran Clay Bellinger. Although Bellinger filled in admirably, in both the infield and the outfield, GM Brian Cashman was still seeking a more established major league role player. He found him in Jose Vizcaino, who was picked up from the Dodgers (with cash considerations) in a trade for Jim Leyritz on June 20. Vizcaino played second, third, and short and batted .276 in 73 games. Eight days after signing Vizcaino, Cashman acquired slugging outfielder David Justice in a trade with the Cleveland Indians. Justice, a left-handed hitter, had a swing that was tailor-made for Yankee Stadium, and he went on to hit .305 with 20 home runs and 60 RBIs with the Yankees.

A few weeks later, on July 12, Cashman traded for the Yankees' much-needed fifth starter, Denny Neagle. The Yanks gave up a lot for Neagle—pitchers Ed Yarnall and Brian Reith and third baseman Drew Henson (who was slated to start at quarterback in the fall for the University of Michigan) and outfielder Jackson Melian. Although he started out well, Neagle faded in the stretch and finished at 7-7 with a 5.81 ERA for the Yankees. Along with Cone, he fell out of favor with Manager Joe Torre.

Four players represented the Yankees at the All-Star Game in 2000: Bernie Williams was selected for the fourth year in a row, and he was joined by Derek Jeter, Mariano Rivera, and Jorge Posada. It was the first appearance for Posada, the third each for Jeter and Rivera. Jeter, who had finished second to Seattle's Alex Rodriguez in the fan balloting, was tabbed by Torre to replace A-Rod, who was injured and couldn't play. As fate would have it, Jeter went 3-for-3, scored a run, and drove in another to lead the American League to a 6-3 triumph and earn the game's MVP award. It was the first time a Yankee had ever received that honor. (Not until 1962 did Major League Baseball begin naming All-Star Game MVPs.)

Even though the AL wound up winning the game, all did not sit well with Joe Torre's All-Star selections. Despite Posada's banner year, in which he finished with a .287 batting average, 28 homers, and 86 RBIs, many observers—opposing players and media alike—thought Torre should have added Baltimore's Charles Johnson to the squad instead. Even the Yankees' own Jeff Nelson felt slighted. He was having a fine year, and he let it be known that he was miffed that Torre had overlooked him. Nelson was so upset, in fact, that he let his anger affect his performance in the second half of the season. It wasn't until late August, when "the Boss"—New York's principal owner, George Steinbrenner—told Nelson to put up or shut up, that the reliever got back on track.

On July 15, the Yankees' game against the Florida Marlins was postponed due to rain. Ironically, the Yankees took over sole possession of first place in the AL East that day, as the Toronto Blue Jays lost an interleague game to the Philadelphia Phillies. From that point on, the Yankees would remain in first place. Although they once built their lead to nine games, they won the division by only 2 1/2 games over Boston.

Despite some spotty pitching, the Yankees' staff ended up allowing the fourth-fewest runs in the American League. A major factor in the staff's success was the performance of Andy Pettitte, spurred on by some sage advice from Roger Clemens. By bonding with and tutoring Pettitte, Clemens was instrumental in building Pettitte's confidence and helping him put up a 19-9 record. Pettitte's 4.35 ERA was on the high side, but it wasn't bad, considering the recent offensive explosion in the majors. In addition to helping Pettitte's game, Clemens worked with longtime pitching coach Billy Connors and regained his old form, which had helped him to win five Cy Young awards. Connors's advice? Just don't hold back.

One more trade engineered by Cashman helped the Yankees down the stretch. For a couple of minor leaguers, Cashman obtained slugger Glenallen Hill—a much-traveled outfielder/DH—from the Chicago Cubs. In only 40 games with New York, Hill batted .333, belted 16 homers, and drove in 29 runs. His impact was immediate. After hitting 10 dingers in his first 51 at-bats and batting .411 for the Yankees, Hill was named AL Player of the Month for August.

Also in August, the Yankees' front office used some sound strategy and ended up acquiring a famous slugger. When the Tampa Bay Devil Rays placed Jose Canseco on waivers, the Yankees put in a claim on him to prevent him from signing with one of their division rivals. Normally, Tampa Bay would have pulled Canseco back after a claim like that. But it didn't, and Canseco became a part-time outfielder and DH for the Yankees, batting .252 with 15 homers and 49 RBIs.

August also saw the front office bring back reserve infielder Luis Sojo, long a favorite of Torre's, who had left via free agency before the start of the season. The trade for Sojo from Pittsburgh helped salve the nightmarish throwing woes of Chuck Knoblauch and provided some added punch in the batter's box. With Knoblauch shelved for a time, Sojo batted .288 and contributed a number of timely hits.

Overall in 2000, the Yankees went 28-15-8 (wins-losses-splits) in their season series. They were 15-5-6 at home and 13-10-2 on the road. They won the AL East with a record of 87-74; but they lost 15 of their last 18 games, leaving their postseason foes a glimmer of hope.

2001

The Yankees started out the 2001 season on April 2, but the 55,814 fans had to check names on their scorecard when they looked around on Opening Day. There were only 12 players on the roster who were on the team when the 2000 season started. Some of those gone that had worn the pinstripes for a while included David Cone, Ricky Ledee, Jim Leyritz, and Jeff Nelson. Newcomers on the Opening Day roster included Mike Mussina, David Justice, Joe Oliver, and Alfonso Soriano.

The Yankees defeated the Kansas City Royals, 7-3, in the first season opener at Yankee Stadium since 1995. Roger Clemens got the victory, and this gave the Yankees a 57-41-1 record opening the season with the home portion of that record improving to 30-14.

While the Yankees faltered at the end of the 2000 regular season, they ran off several impressive winning streaks in 2001. The best streak was nine games from June 27 through July 6. Consecutive wins of eight and six games were also part of the season, with the largest losing streak being at four games (twice). The Yankees also improved their home record by seven games with a record of 51-28.

Besides Toronto, after the Opening Day contests, only the Yankees and the Red Sox shared the top spot in the AL East. A 4-3 victory over Baltimore on July 4 put the Yankees into sole possession of first place in the AL East, where they remained until the end of the season. At the All-Star break the Bronx Bombers were 52-34 and leading Boston by 1.5 games.

The 2001 Yankees had seven players named to the AL All-Star squad. Although Mariano Rivera could not make the trip to Seattle's Safeco Field due to a problem with his right ankle, Roger Clemens, Jorge Posada, Derek Jeter, Bernie Williams, Andy Pettitte, and Mike Stanton represented the team. Clemens was selected to be the AL starter, and Jeter hit the first All-Star Game home run by a Yankee player since Yogi Berra connected in one of the 1959 games.

The Yankees lost seven of 11 after the All-Star break, but the Red Sox failed to use this mini-slump to their advantage. An eight-game win streak was completed with a three-game sweep of the Blue Jays at the Skydome on July 27 through the 29. The series attendance at Toronto totaled 120,920 as part of the 2,817,798 the Yankees drew on the road in 2001.

The season was in cruise control the rest of the way, and the Yankees' first-place lead grew to 11 games when Orlando "El Duque" Hernandez bettered Pedro Martinez and the Red Sox, 3-2, before a Yankee Stadium crowd of 55, 524 on September 7. Not much was thought about when a September 10 rainout occurred with the Yankees having a record of 86-57 and a 13-game lead. However, there would no game with the Chicago White Sox the next evening and not again until September 18 in the aftermath of the September 11 attack and tragedy involving the destruction of the World Trade Center twin towers by a terrorist attack. The New York professional sports teams were all deeply affected and saddened by the loss of so many innocent people simply doing their jobs. The 10-9-1 record for the remainder of the season showed that the Yankees had more on their minds than baseball, but they clinched another AL East title. Their final record of 95-65 was just the third best in the AL, with Seattle topping the charts by establishing a new league record by winning 116 games. The Oakland Athletics won 102 games, but that was only good

enough for the AL West Wild Card and a divisional playoff date coming up with the Yankees.

The Yankees had only Mariano Rivera and Roger Clemens at the top of the league leaderboards. Rivera had 50 saves, and Clemens topped the winning percentage with .870 (20-3). Mike Mussina was second in ERA with a 3.15 mark in his first season with the Yankees. Both Alfonso Soriano and Chuck Knoblauch finished in the top five in stolen bases. The team hit 203 home runs to finish fourth in the AL while they batted .267 as a team to end up 5th in the league. A weak spot in the batting order was the DH position, where a paltry average of .218 was fashioned by 20 different players. Pinch hitting was even worse, with a .217 mark displayed there. However, the DH position did net 23 home runs to go with 81 RBIs. Tino Martinez led the Yankees with 34 home runs while Derek Jeter (.311) and Bernie Williams (.307) led the team in batting average. Clemens, Mussina, and Andy Pettitte all won at least 15 games. The 2001 team scored 4.99 runs per game while allowing 4.43.

2002

The Yankees once again went the route of retooling their offense and defense as they welcomed Rondell White, Robin Ventura, and Jason Giambi to the starting lineup. Gone were Chuck Knoblauch, Scott Brosius (retired), and Tino Martinez from those who regularly took the field in 2001. Free agent David Wells returned to the mound corps after an injury-plagued season with the Chicago White Sox. Another free agent signed was right-handed relief pitcher Steve Karsay. The mainstays of the 2001 starting lineup included Derek Jeter, Alfonso Soriano, Jorge Posada, and Bernie Williams. The designated hitter too was applied to 24-year old Nick Johnson, who would also spend time at first base.

All was in place as the Yankees traveled to Baltimore's Camden Yards with Roger Clemens assigned as the Opening Day starter. The Orioles were ready, though, and they jumped all over Clemens to defeat the Yankees, 10-3. This brought the Yanks' Opening Day record to 57-42-1 and was certainly not the beginning Joe Torre and his coaching staff had hoped for.

David Wells came back two days later to shut out Baltimore, 1-0, with Mariano Rivera picking up his first save. That win started the Yankees to a seven-game winning streak, which included a 16-3 pasting of the Toronto Blue Jays on April 8 at the Skydome. The Yankee Stadium home opener on April 5 showed a 4-0 whitewash of the Tampa Bay Devil Rays with Andy Pettitte picking up his first win.

Just as the offense seemed to be picking up, the Yankees lost six of seven, which included three one-run losses to the Red Sox. Boston was playing well under another new manager, and the Yankees could not afford to let the Red Sox build a big lead in the standings. Aside from being swept at home in early May during a three-game weekend series with the Mariners, the losing did not continue for the Yankees in 2002. On May 7, the Yankees' record stood at 18-14 as Mike Mussina took the mound at Tampa Bay. Mussina improved to 4-2 and with Rivera picking up his ninth save, the Yankees won 5-2 to begin another winning streak. By taking the next 12 of 13 games against Minnesota, Tampa Bay, and Toronto the Yankees appeared to have their sights set on the Red Sox once again. The Yanks even caused joy for the office 13-run pool contests when they scored back-to-back wins of 13-0 (Toronto) and 13-12 (Minnesota) on

May 16-17. The latter game finished past midnight in a driving rainstorm and included a dramatic walk-off grand slam by Jason Giambi.

A three-game losing streak on May 22-24 was the longest for the rest of the season. Another 13 runs scored came on June 4 (13-5) versus the Orioles. The "Baker's Dozen" mark was even surpassed as Yankee bats pounded opponent pitching by the likes of 14-7, 14-5 (twice), 16-3, and 20-10. The Yanks' offense was shut out only three times while they produced nine or more runs (during victories) a total of 30 times.

By the All-Star break their record stood at 55-32 with the Red Sox beginning to fade. Although the All-Star Game ended in a controversial extra-inning tie when Joe Torre and Arizona's Bob Brenly ran out of players, the Yankees were well represented in the Mid summer Classic. The July 9 game at Miller Park in Milwaukee had Jorge Posada, Jason Giambi, and Alfonso Soriano in the starting lineup for the AL. Also making appearances were Derek Jeter, Robin Ventura, and Mariano Rivera. An All-Star record of 60 players were used by the managers, who went to commissioner Bud Selig for permission to halt the game due to their roster status. Soriano hit a home run for the AL, while Giambi had a single and scored a run.

The Yankees started the second half a little slow by losing three of five, but then went 20-9, to be at 77-44 after defeating Seattle, 8-3, on August 17. The Red Sox hung around, but the Yankees' final record of 103-58 had them winning the AL Eastern Division flag by 10.5 games. The Yankees lost one less game than the Oakland Athletics to have the best winning percentage going into the playoffs. The Yankees topped the AL with 897 runs scored that averaged out to 5.57 runs per game. The team batting average of .275 led the AL, and they also slugged 223 home runs, which was the most by the Yankees since 1961. Team home run leaders were Jason Giambi (41), Alfonso Soriano (39), and Robin Ventura (27). Soriano was a big individual league-batting leader with tops in runs scored (128), hits (209), and stolen bases (41). Bernie Williams, Derek Jeter, and Jason Giambi also placed in the top five in several offensive categories. Giambi and Williams topped the league by being on base 300 and 290 times, respectively. The Yankee starting pitchers showed four with at least 13 wins. They were David Wells (19), Mike Mussina (18), Roger Clemens (13), and Andy Pettitte (13). Mike Stanton (79) and Steve Karsay (78) led the team in appearances. Karsay even picked up 12 saves with Mariano Rivera going on the disabled list three times in 2002. The team pitching ERA improved from 2001 (4.02) to 3.87, which was fourth in the league.

YANKEE ALL-TIME BATTING LEADERS
100 SEASONS (1903 THROUGH 2002)

SEASONS
18 Yogi Berra
18 Mickey Mantle
17 Frankie Crosetti
17 Bill Dickey
17 Lou Gehrig
16 Whitey Ford
15 Red Ruffing
15 Babe Ruth
15 Roy White

GAMES
2401 Mickey Mantle
2164 Lou Gehrig
2116 Yogi Berra
2084 Babe Ruth
1881 Roy White
1789 Bill Dickey
1785 Don Mattingly
1736 Joe DiMaggio
1694 Willie Randolph
1682 Frankie Crosetti

AT BATS
8102 Mickey Mantle
8001 Lou Gehrig
7546 Yogi Berra
7217 Babe Ruth
7003 Don Mattingly
6821 Joe DiMaggio
6650 Roy White
6303 Willie Randolph
6300 Bill Dickey
6277 Frankie Crosetti

RUNS
1959 Babe Ruth
1888 Lou Gehrig
1677 Mickey Mantle
1390 Joe DiMaggio
1186 Earle Combs
1174 Yogi Berra
1066 Bernie Williams
1027 Willie Randolph
1007 Don Mattingly
1006 Frankie Crosetti

HITS
2721 Lou Gehrig
2518 Babe Ruth
2415 Mickey Mantle
2214 Joe DiMaggio
2153 Don Mattingly
2148 Yogi Berra
1969 Bill Dickey
1866 Earle Combs
1833 Bernie Williams
1803 Roy White

HOME RUNS
659 Babe Ruth
536 Mickey Mantle
493 Lou Gehrig
361 Joe DiMaggio
358 Yogi Berra
250 Graig Nettles
226 Bernie Williams
222 Don Mattingly
205 Dave Winfield
203 Roger Maris

TOTAL BASES
5131 Babe Ruth
5060 Lou Gehrig
4511 Mickey Mantle
3948 Joe DiMaggio
3641 Yogi Berra
3301 Don Mattingly
3062 Bill Dickey
2968 Bernie Williams
2848 Tony Lazzeri
2685 Roy White

RUNS BATTED IN
1991 Lou Gehrig
1970 Babe Ruth
1537 Joe DiMaggio
1509 Mickey Mantle
1430 Yogi Berra
1209 Bill Dickey
1154 Tony Lazzeri
1099 Don Mattingly
1005 Bob Meusel
 998 Bernie Williams

WALKS
1847 Babe Ruth
1733 Mickey Mantle
1508 Lou Gehrig
1005 Willie Randolph
934 Roy White
831 Tony Lazzeri
827 Bernie Williams
792 Frank Crosetti
790 Joe DiMaggio
760 Charlie Keller

EXTRA BASE HITS
(2B + 3B + HR)
1190 Lou Gehrig
1189 Babe Ruth
 952 Mickey Mantle
 881 Joe DiMaggio
 728 Yogi Berra
 684 Don Mattingly
 631 Bernie Williams
 617 Bill Dickey
 611 Tony Lazzeri
 571 Bob Meusel

BATTING AVG.
(500+ Games)
.349 Babe Ruth
.340 Lou Gehrig
.325 Earle Combs
.325 Joe DiMaggio
.317 Derek Jeter
.313 Wade Boggs
.313 Bill Dickey
.311 Bob Meusel
.308 Bernie Williams
.307 Don Mattingly

SLUGGING PCT.
(500+ Games)
.711 Babe Ruth
.632 Lou Gehrig
.579 Joe DiMaggio
.557 Mickey Mantle
.526 Reggie Jackson
.518 Charlie Keller
.515 Roger Maris
.500 Bob Meusel
.498 Bernie Williams
.491 Tommy Henrich

YANKEE ALL-TIME PITCHING LEADERS
100 SEASONS (1903 THROUGH 2002)

SEASONS PITCHED	GAMES PITCHED	GAMES STARTED	COMPLETE GAMES
16 Whitey Ford	522 Dave Righetti	438 Whitey Ford	261 Red Ruffing
15 Red Ruffing	498 Whitey Ford	391 Red Ruffing	173 Lefty Gomez
14 Ron Guidry	448 Mariano Rivera	356 Mel Stottlemyre	168 Jack Chesbro
13 Lefty Gomez	428 Mike Stanton	323 Ron Guidry	164 Herb Pennock
13 Bob Shawkey	426 Red Ruffing	319 Lefty Gomez	161 Bob Shawkey
12 Johnny Murphy	420 Sparky Lyle	275 Waite Hoyt	156 Whitey Ford
11 Tommy Byrne	415 Bob Shawkey	274 Bob Shawkey	156 Waite Hoyt
11 Spud Chandler	383 Johnny Murphy	268 Herb Pennock	152 Mel Stottlemyre
11 Herb Pennock	368 Ron Guidry	265 Fritz Peterson	150 Ray Caldwell
11 Dave Righetti	367 Lefty Gomez	243 Andy Pettitte	109 Spud Chandler
11 Mel Stottlemyre			

INNINGS PITCHED	SHUTOUTS	WINS	SAVES
3170.1 Whitey Ford	45 Whitey Ford	236 Whitey Ford	243 Mariano Rivera
3168.2 Red Ruffing	40 Red Ruffing	231 Red Ruffing	224 Dave Righetti
2661.1 Mel Stottlemyre	40 Mel Stottlemyre	189 Lefty Gomez	224 Dave Righetti
2498.1 Lefty Gomez	28 Lefty Gomez	170 Ron Guidry	141 Sparky Lyle
2488.2 Bob Shawkey	27 Allie Reynolds	168 Bob Shawkey	104 Johnny Murphy
2392.0 Ron Guidry	26 Spud Chandler	164 Mel Stottlemyre	78 Steve Farr
2272.1 Waite Hoyt	26 Ron Guidry	162 Herb Pennock	76 Joe Page
2189.2 Herb Pennock	26 Bob Shawkey	157 Waite Hoyt	74 John Wetteland
1952.0 Jack Chesbro	24 Vic Raschi	131 Allie Reynolds	58 Lindy McDaniel
1857.1 Fritz Peterson	21 Bob Turley	128 Jack Chesbro	43 Luis Arroyo
		128 Andy Pettitte	43 Ryne Duren

WALKS	STRIKEOUTS	WINNING PCT. (100+ Decisions)	ERA (1000+ Innings)
1090 Lefty Gomez	1956 Whitey Ford	.717 Spud Chandler	2.54 Russ Ford
1086 Whitey Ford	1778 Ron Guidry	.706 Vic Raschi	2.58 Jack Chesbro
1066 Red Ruffing	1526 Red Ruffing	.690 Whitey Ford	2.72 Al Orth
855 Bob Shawkey	1468 Lefty Gomez	.686 Allie Reynolds	2.73 Tiny Bonham
819 Allie Reynolds	1257 Mel Stottlemyre	.669 Carl Mays	2.75 Whitey Ford
809 Mel Stottlemyre	1163 Bob Shawkey	.657 Ed Lopat	2.84 Spud Chandler
763 Tommy Bryne	1095 Andy Pettitte	.652 Lefty Gomez	2.91 Ray Fisher
761 Bob Turley	1028 Al Downing	.651 Ron Guidry	2.97 Mel Stottlemyre
633 Ron Guidry	967 Allie Reynolds	.651 Red Ruffing	3.00 Ray Caldwell
631 Waite Hoyt	940 Dave Righetti	.646 Andy Pettitte	3.10 Fritz Peterson
		.643 Tommy Byrne	
		.643 Herb Pennock	

YANKEE POSITION LEADERS IN GAMES PLAYED
(INCLUDING DESIGNATED HITTERS AND PINCH-HITTERS)
100 SEASONS (1903 THROUGH 2002)

PITCHERS	GAMES	CATCHER	GAMES	FIRST BASE	GAMES
Dave Righetti	522	Bill Dickey	1708	Lou Gehrig	2137
Whitey Ford	498	Yogi Berra	1697	Don Mattingly	1634
Mariano Rivera	448	Thurman Munson	1278	Wally Pipp	1468
Mike Stanton	428	Elston Howard	1029	Hal Chase	1016
Red Ruffing	426	Jeff Sweeney	598	Bill Skowron	986
Sparky Lyle	420	Rick Cerone	567	Tino Martinez	904
Bob Shawkey	415	Wally Schang	498	Chris Chambliss	854
Johnny Murphy	383	Red Kleinow	497	Joe Collins	715
Ron Guidry	368	Jake Gibbs	459	Joe Pepitone	698
Lefty Gomez	367	Butch Wynegar	434	Nick Etten	544

SECOND BASE	GAMES	THIRD BASE	GAMES	SHORTSTOP	GAMES
Willie Randolph	1688	Graig Nettles	1509	Phil Rizzuto	1647
Tony Lazzeri	1441	Red Rolfe	1084	Frankie Crosetti	1516
Bobby Richardson	1339	Clete Boyer	909	Roger Peckinpaugh	1214
Horace Clarke	1081	Joe Dugan	774	Derek Jeter	1091
Joe Gordon	970	Mike Pagliarulo	684	Tony Kubek	882
Snuffy Stirnweiss	700	Billy Johnson	673	Gene Michael	709
Jimmy Williams	685	Andy Carey	656	Bucky Dent	694
Aaron Ward	569	Home Run Baker	652	Kid Elberfeld	614
Gil McDougald	599	Wade Boggs	543	Mark Koenig	496
Jerry Coleman	572	Gil McDougald	508	Everett Scott	477

OUTFIELD	GAMES	DESIGNATED HITTER	GAMES	PINCH-HITTER	GAMES
Babe Ruth	2045	Don Baylor	403	Red Ruffing	181
Mickey Mantle	2019	Danny Tartabull	258	Yogi Berra	176
Joe DiMaggio	1721	Lou Piniella	222	Enos Slaughter	171
Roy White	1625	Kevin Maas	220	Johnny Mize	150
Bernie Williams	1511	Oscar Gamble	183	Elston Howard	149
Earle Combs	1387	Chili Davis	166	Hector Lopez	148
Hank Bauer	1347	Steve Balboni	164	Johnny Blanchard	147
Paul O'Neill	1221	Mike Easler	161	Bob Cerv	147
Bob Meusel	1192	Darryl Strawberry	143	Lou Piniella	138
Dave Winfield	1123	Reggie Jackson	135	Ray Caldwell	137

1997 New York Yankees

Back Row (L to R) — DARRYL STRAWBERRY, HIDEKI IRABU, ANDY PETTITTE, PAUL O'NEILL, GRAEME LLOYD, JEFF NELSON, DWIGHT GOODEN, DAVID WELLS, TINO MARTINEZ.
Third Row — MIKE STANLEY, KENNY ROGERS, JOE GIRARDI, BERNIE WILLIAMS, DEREK JETER, BRIAN BOEHRINGER, MARIANO RIVERA, WADE BOGGS, CHAD CURTIS, MIKE SILVERWISE (Massage Therapist).
Second Row — DR. STUART HERSHON (Team Physician), GARY TUCK (Bullpen Catcher), CHARLIE HAYES, HOMER BUSH, MIKE STANTON, DAVID CONE, TIM RAINES, REY SANCHEZ, RAMIRO MENDOZA, JORGE POSADA, ROB CUCUZZA (Assistant Equipment Manager), STEVE DONOHUE (Trainer), DAVID SZEN (Traveling Secretary).
First Row — GENE MONAHAN (Head Trainer), PAUL MASTROPASQUA (Strength and Conditioning Coach), TONY CLONINGER (Coach), CHRIS CHAMBLISS (Coach), JOSE CARDENAL (Coach), DON ZIMMER (Coach), JOE TORRE (Manager), MEL STOTTLEMYRE (Coach), WILLIE RANDOLPH (Coach), CHARLIE WONSOWICZ (Batting Practice Pitcher), MIKE BORZELLO (Batting Practice Pitcher), CARL TAYLOR (Video Coordinator).
Seated — (Batboys) JOE LEE, DAVID ROBERTS, DAVID POWELL.

1997 New York Yankees

1999 New York Yankees

Row 4, L/R: Scott Brosius, Jason Grimsley, Roger Clemens, Andy Pettitte, Bernie Williams, Paul O'Neill, Jeff Nelson, Chili Davis, Hideki Irabu, Ramiro Mendoza, Derek Jeter.

Row 3, L/R: Ricky Ledee, Allen Watson, Shane Spencer, Joe Girardi, Tino Martinez, Mariano Rivera, David Cone, Mike Borzello (Batting Practice Pitcher), Orlando Hernandez, Jorge Posada, Jeff Mangold (Strength & Conditioning Coach).

Row 2, L/R: Dr. Stuart Hershon (Team Physician), Gene Monahan (Head Trainer), Rob Cucuzza (Equipment Manager), Chad Curtis, Luis Sojo, Chuck Knoblauch, Mike Stanton, Jim Leyritz, Charlie Wonsowicz (Batting Practice Pitcher), Nick Testa (Batting Practice Pitcher), Lou Cucuzza Jr. (Visiting Clubhouse Manager), Steve Donahue (Trainer), David Szen (Traveling Secretary).

Row 1, L/R: Gary Tuck (Coach), Mel Stottlemyre (Coach), Tony Cloninger (Coach), Don Zimmer (Coach), Joe Torre (Manager), Chris Chambliss (Coach), Willie Randolph (Coach), Jose Cardenal (Coach), Rohan Baichu (Massage Therapist).

Photography By: Steve Crandall
Artwork & Digital Imaging By: Michael Alberse

Front Seated (Batboys) - George Brown, Mike Roth, Joe Lee, Craig Postolowski, Luigi Castillo.

The 1999 World Champions New York Yankees.

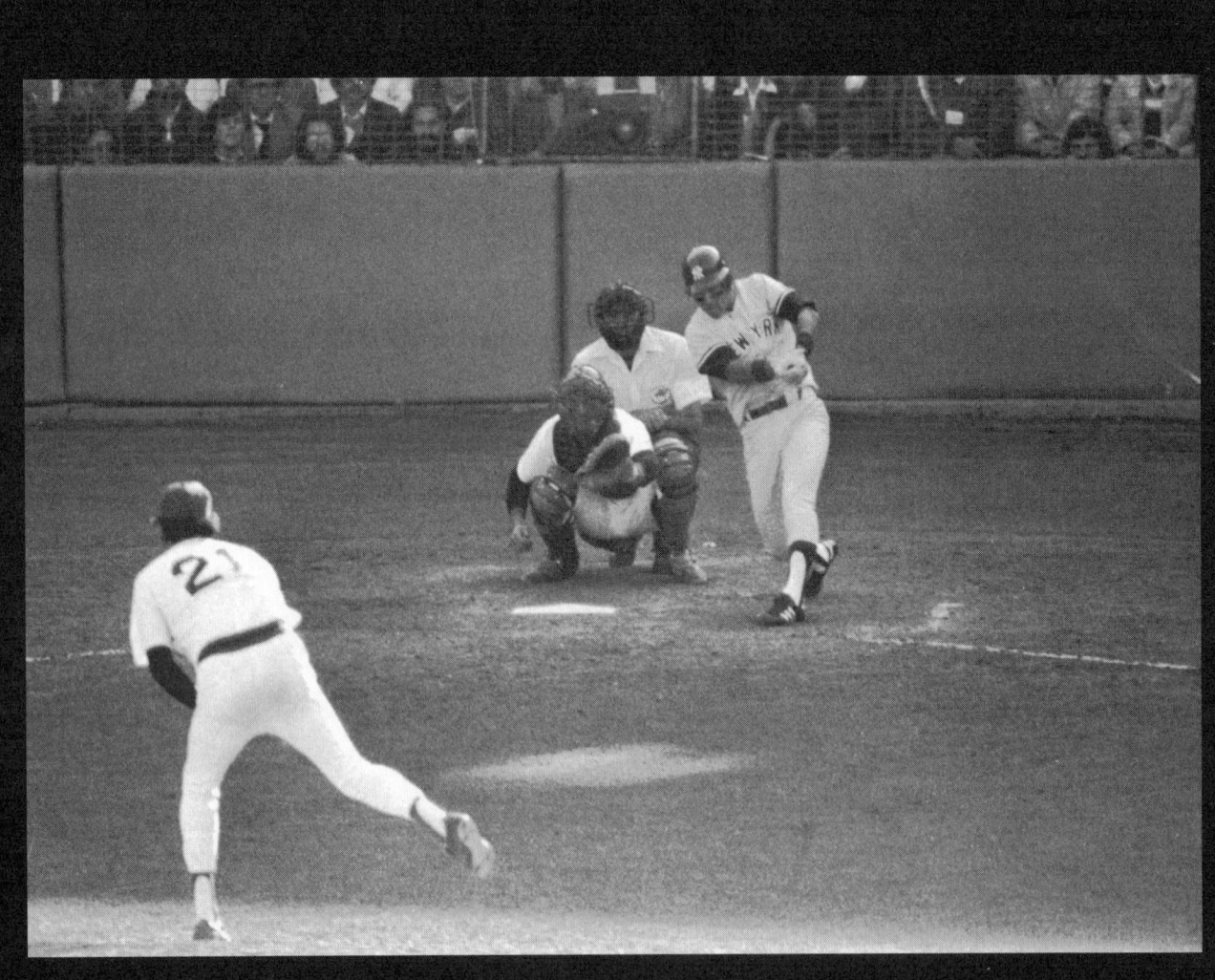

AMERICAN LEAGUE PLAYOFFS

New York Yankee Bucky Dent hits a homerun off a pitch from Boston Red Sox Mike Torrez in the seventh inning of the October 2, 1978 American League Playoff game at Fenway Park. Boston catcher is Carlton Fisk, and the umpire is Don Denkinger. (AP/WIDE WORLD PHOTOS)

In the expansion season of 1969, each of the two leagues were split into two divisions, East and West. In 1994, there was a third division (Central) added to each league. The reason for adding divisions was to increase the number of teams qualifying for the postseason playoffs.

Joined with each league's three division winners was a wildcard team, the team with the best record among the rest of the league's teams, making a total of eight teams going to the playoffs. The expanded playoff format, then, which was supposed to begin in 1994 but didn't actually start until 1995 because of the 1994 strike, begins with four teams in each league playing a first round, known as the Division Series, and the winners qualifying for the League Championship Series. The winners of the latter in each league then face one another in the World Series.

This chapter covers the Yankees' participation in intra-league postseason competition. It also includes the 1978 AL East playoff with Boston, made necessary by the teams finishing the season with identical records, and the 1981 Division Series with Milwaukee, made necessary by the strike-caused split season.

1976

CHAMPIONSHIP SERIES

It was the Yankees' first appearance in postseason play since 1964. The American League Championship would go to either them or the Kansas City Royals, winners of the AL West Division, the issue to be settled in five games.

In Game 1 at Kansas City, Catfish Hunter pitched a brilliant five-hitter to beat the Royals, 4-1. The Yanks scored twice in the first inning with the help of a couple of errors by third baseman George Brett, and the remainder of the game was a Hunter showcase.

The two teams then went even with one game to go, the Royals winning Game 2 and Game 4 and the Yanks taking Game 3 behind the clutch hurling of Dock Ellis, the winner, and Sparky Lyle, save-credited reliever. In Game 3, a two-run home run by Chris Chambliss helped erase an early 3-0 Yankee deficit.

The Yankees were leading, 6-3, in the deciding Game 5 at Yankee Stadium when Brett tied it up with a three-run homer in the eighth inning. Chambliss led off the bottom of the ninth by sending a Mark Littell pitch over the right field wall. The dramatic pennant-winning blast caused the Stadium to erupt; fans streamed from the stands to swarm Chambliss as he rounded the bases.

Chambliss was the hitting star, setting five-game Championship Series records for most RBIs (eight); most total bases (20); most hits (11); highest batting average (.524); and highest slugging average (.952). He was supported by Thurman Munson (.435) and Mickey Rivers (.348) in leading a strong Yankee attack throughout the Series.

The Yankees set such five-game Championship Series batting records for a team as most hits (55); most singles (36); most doubles (13); most extra-base hits (19); most total bases (84); highest batting average (.316); and highest slugging average (.483). The Kansas City pitching staff simply could not handle the Yanks.

It was a seesaw Series, not only in the back-and-forth trading of wins but in the fact that the team trailing early in three of the games came on to win. On the basis of the two clubs' regular-season records (Yankees: 97-62; Royals: 90-72), it appeared going into the Series that New York was the superior team. The outcome, which gave the Yankees their 30th pennant, confirmed pre-Series appraisals.

```
Game 1 at Royals Stadium, KC, October 9
NY      2 0 0   0 0 0   0 0 2  -  4  12  0
KC      0 0 0   0 0 0   0 1 0  -  1   5  2
W—Hunter; L—Gura.                A.—41,077

Game 2 at Royals Stadium, KC, October 10
NY      0 1 2   0 0 0   0 0 0  -  3  12  5
KC      2 0 0   0 0 2   0 3 X  -  7   9  0
W—Splittorff; L—Figueroa.        A.—41,091

Game 3 at Yankee Stadium, NY, October 12
KC      3 0 0   0 0 0   0 0 0  -  3   6  0
NY      0 0 0   2 0 3   0 0 X  -  5   9  0
W—Ellis; L—Hassler; HR—Chambliss (NY).   A.—56,808

Game 4 at Yankee Stadium, NY, October 13
KC      0 3 0   2 0 1   0 1 0  -  7   9  1
NY      0 2 0   0 0 0   1 0 1  -  4  11  0
W—Bird; L—Hunter; HR—Nettles (NY) 2.     A.—56,355

Game 5 at Yankee Stadium, NY, October 14
KC      2 1 0   0 0 0   0 3 0  -  6  11  1
NY      2 0 2   0 0 2   0 0 1  -  7  11  1
W—Tidrow; L—Littell; HR—Mayberry (KC), Brett (KC), Chambliss (NY).
                                 A.—56,821
```

BRING ON CINCINNATI—Chris Chambliss won the 1976 AL pennant for the Yankees with one swing of his bat. Leading off the bottom of the ninth inning in a tied Game 5 of the playoffs against Kansas City, Chambliss blasted a home run off Mark Littell, enabling the Yankees to journey to Cincinnati to begin the World Series. (New York Yankees Archives)

1977

CHAMPIONSHIP SERIES

Again it was the Kansas City Royals standing between the Yankees and the American League pennant.

The Royals walloped three home runs and bombed the Yanks, 7-2, in Game 1. In Game 2, the Yankees were trailing, 1-0, in the fifth inning when big Cliff Johnson boomed a tremendous home run to tie the game and seemingly bring the Yankees to life. Behind Ron Guidry's three-hitter, New York ultimately prevailed, 6-2.

In the sixth, Hal McRae crushed Yankee second baseman Willie Randolph with a cross body block that allowed a run to score, and that set the tone for the remainder of the Series. Both teams were very physical.

The Royals won Game 3, but the Yankees fought back to win Game 4, 6-4, largely on account of the outstanding relief pitching of Sparky Lyle. He gave up only two hits and no runs in the final 5 1/3 innings.

Game 5 was a classic. The Royals scored two runs in the first. When George Brett slid hard into Graig Nettles, the two third basemen came up fighting and both benches emptied. It was some time before order was restored. In the eighth, with the Royals leading, 3-1, Reggie Jackson delivered a pinch-hit single that produced a run and narrowed the Royals' lead to 3-2. In the ninth, Paul Blair singled and Roy White walked. Mickey Rivers singled to tie the score. Randolph's sacrifice fly gave the Yanks the lead, and Brett's throwing error made it 5-3. Lyle retired the Royals in the ninth to record his second consecutive victory, although it was Mike Torrez who had done an outstanding job in long relief.

Yankee batting stars for the Series were Cliff Johnson (.400), Mickey Rivers (.391), and Lou Piniella (.333), and the pitching hero was Sparky Lyle (2-0) who recorded a 0.96 ERA

in 9 1/3 innings, appearing in four of the five games. Ron Guidry and Mike Torrez also stopped Kansas City at crucial times.

Perhaps most important to the Yankees' success was their tight, aggressive baseball. The team made only two errors and fielded .989, both five-game Championship Series records. After the McRae incident in Game 2, the Yanks played with intensity and heart. (Graig Nettles made a crunching pay-back block at second base, a play symbolic of the Yankee verve.) It was a gritty Yankee team that captured the club's 31st AL pennant.

Game 1 at Yankee Stadium, NY, Oct 5												
KC	2	2	2	0	0	0	0	1	0	-	7	9	0
NY	0	0	2	0	0	0	0	0	0	-	2	9	0

W—Splittorff; L—Gullett; HR—McRae (KC), Mayberry (KC), Munson (NY), Cowens (KC).   A.—54,930

Game 2 at Yankee Stadium, NY, October 6												
KC	0	0	1	0	0	1	0	0	0	-	2	3	1
NY	0	0	0	0	2	3	0	1	X	-	6	10	1

W—Guidry; L—Hassler; HR—Johnson (NY).   A.—56,230

Game 3 at Royals Stadium, KC, October 7												
NY	0	0	0	0	1	0	0	0	1	-	2	4	1
KC	0	1	1	0	1	2	1	0	X	-	6	12	1

W—Leonard; L—Torrez.   A.—41,285

Game 4 at Royals Stadium, KC, October 8												
NY	1	2	1	1	0	0	0	0	1	-	6	13	0
KC	0	0	2	2	0	0	0	0	0	-	4	8	2

W—Lyle; L—Gura.   A.—41,135

Game 5 at Royals Stadium, KC, October 9												
NY	0	0	1	0	0	0	0	1	3	-	5	10	0
KC	2	0	1	0	0	0	0	0	0	-	3	10	1

W—Lyle; L—Leonard.   A.—41,133

1978

DIVISIONAL PLAYOFF

The Yankees and Boston Red Sox finished the regular season with identical 99-63 records. Thus, a one-game playoff was required to determine the American League East Division champion. The game is considered a regular-season game in the record book but was indeed a playoff game and will be treated as such here.

October 2, 1978—The Yankee-Red Sox playoff game at Fenway Park was one of the most exciting games in baseball history. Ron Guidry pitched against Boston's Mike Torrez.

In the second inning, Carl Yastrzemski lined a home run into the right-field seats; in the sixth, Jim Rice singled home a run and Boston led, 2-0. In the Yankee seventh, Chris Chambliss and Roy White singled, and with two out, Bucky Dent lofted a three-run homer just over the "Green Monster" in left field to give the Yanks a 3-2 lead. Mickey Rivers followed with a walk and stole second, and with reliever Bob Stanley now pitching, Thurman Munson crashed a double to score Rivers. In the eighth, Reggie Jackson slammed a mighty homer off Stanley that easily cleared the center-field fence to put New York up 5-2.

But the Red Sox rallied for a pair of runs in their half of the eighth off Rich Gossage to narrow the margin to 5-4. The bottom of the ninth was loaded with tension. After Rick Burleson drew a one-out walk, Jerry Remy lined a shot to right. Lou Piniella, who had made a great catch earlier, lost the ball in the sun but kept his composure and did not let Burleson know his problem. Luckily, Lou recovered to field the ball on one hop and kept Burleson at second base. It was a great play because Rice then flied to Lou on a ball Burleson could have scored on if he had been on third.

With two outs and the game on the line, Gossage coaxed Yastrzemski into popping to Graig Nettles in foul territory to end a thrilling game and send the Yankees into the AL Championship Series for the third straight year.

YANKEE-RED SOX BOX SCORE

New York	AB	R	H	RBI	Boston	AB	R	H	RBI
Rivers, cf	2	1	1	0	Burleson, ss	4	1	1	0
Blair, cf	1	0	1	0	Remy, 2b	4	1	2	0
Munson, c	5	0	1	1	Rice, rf	5	0	1	1
Piniella, rf	4	0	1	0	Yastrzemski, lf	5	1	2	2
Jackson, dh	4	1	1	1	Fisk, c	3	1	1	0
Nettles, 3b	4	0	0	0	Lynn, cf	4	0	1	1
Chambliss, 1b	4	1	1	0	Hobson, dh	4	0	1	0
White, lf	3	1	1	0	Scott, 1b	4	0	2	0
Doyle, 2b	2	0	0	0	Brohamer, 3b	1	0	0	0
Spencer, ph	1	0	0	0	Bailey, ph	1	0	0	0
Stanley, 2b	1	0	0	0	Duffy, 3b	0	0	0	0
Dent, ss	4	1	1	3	Evans, ph	1	0	0	0
	35	5	8	5		36	4	11	4

LOB—New York 6, Boston 9. 2b—Rivers, Munson, Scott, Burleson, Remy. HR—Dent (5), Yastrzemski (17), Jackson (27). SB—Rivers 2. S—Brohamer, Remy

Yankees Pitching	IP	H	R	ER	BB	SO	Red Sox Pitching	IP	H	R	ER	BB	SO
Guidry	6⅓	6	2	2	1	5	Torrez	6⅔	5	4	4	3	4
W 25-3							L 16-13						
Gossage	2⅔	5	2	2	1	2	Stanley	⅓	2	1	1	0	0
							Hassler	1⅔	1	0	0	0	2
							Drago	⅓	0	0	0	0	0

Save—Gossage (27). PB—Munson. T—2:52. A.—32,925

NY	0	0	0	0	0	0	4	1	0	-	5	8	0
BOS.	0	1	0	0	0	1	0	2	0	-	4	11	0

LEGENDARY MOMENT—A dramatic moment in a fantastic baseball game—the 1978 AL East playoff between the Yankees and Red Sox, played at Fenway Park. Bucky Dent leaps ecstatically on home plate after having lofted a three-run homer over the "Green Monster." Dent is congratulated by Roy White (6) and Chris Chambliss (10). (New York Yankees Archives)

CHAMPIONSHIP SERIES

The Yankees, meeting the Kansas City Royals for the third straight year to decide the league championship, in Game 1 cracked 16 hits to smash the Royals, 7-1. Jim Beattie pitched well for 5 1/3 innings, ran into control problems, and was relieved by Ken Clay, who pitched 3 2/3 innings of no-hit ball to record a save. Reggie Jackson paced the attack with a home run, a double, and three RBIs; he reached base safely five times, a single-game record for an AL Championship Series.

The Royals bounced back to win Game 2, 10-4. The Yankees salvaged an exciting Game 3 at the Stadium in spite of George Brett's three solo homers. Though Reggie Jackson hit another homer and drove in three runs, Thurman Munson was the real hero. With the Yankees down 5-4 in the eighth inning and Roy White on base, a tired and injured Munson blasted a 440-foot homer as the fans in Yankee Stadium went berserk. Rich Gossage held Kansas City in the ninth to preserve the 6-5 victory.

Ron Guidry allowed a first-inning run in Game 4 and then shut the door on the Royals. Graig Nettles and Roy White each hit home runs to give Guidry the 2-1 lead he took into the ninth. After Amos Otis led off with a double, Gossage came in to get the final three outs; the Yankees had captured their 32nd AL pennant.

Jackson (two HRs, six RBIs, .462) led the team in hitting and set four-game AL Championship Series records for most RBIs and highest batting average. But Mickey Rivers (.455),

Chris Chambliss (.400), Nettles (.333), White (.313), and Munson (.278) all hit the ball solidly themselves.

In fact, the Yanks set four-game AL Championship Series batting records for most runs (19); most hits (42); most singles (33); most home runs (five); most RBIs (18); most total bases (62); and highest batting average (.300). Defensively, New York was just as skillful, making only one error and fielding .993, both four-game Championship Series records.

```
Game 1 at Royals Stadium, KC, October 3
NY    0   1   1    0   2   0    0   3   0  -  7  16  0
KC    0   0   0    0   0   1    0   0   0  -  1   2  2
W—Beattie; L—Leonard; HR—Jackson (NY).        A.—41,143

Game 2 at Royals Stadium, KC, October 4
NY    0   0   0    0   0   0    2   2   0  -  4  12  1
KC    1   4   0    0   0   0    3   2   X  - 10  16  1
W—Gura; L—Figueroa; HR—Patek (KC).            A.—41,158

Game 3 at Yankee Stadium, NY, October 6
KC    1   0   1    0   1   0    0   2   0  -  5  10  1
NY    0   1   0    2   0   1    0   2   X  -  6  10  0
W—Gossage; L—Bird; HR—Brett (KC) 3, Jackson (NY), Munson (NY).
                                              A.—55,535

Game 4 at Yankee Stadium, NY, October 7
KC    1   0   0    0   0   0    0   0   0  -  1   7  0
NY    0   1   0    0   0   1    0   0   X  -  2   4  0
W—Guidry; L—Leonard; HR—Nettles (NY), White (NY).   A.—56,356
```

1980

CHAMPIONSHIP SERIES

For the fourth time in five years, the Yankees and Kansas City Royals met to decide the AL championship. The question: Which Yankee team would show up? The Yanks who won 103 games (the most in the AL since 1970) or the team that in this same season lost eight of 12 games to the Royals, some by lopsided scores?

More questions: Could the Royals forget their playoff conquests by the Yanks in 1976, 1977 and 1978? Would the Royals' easy ride to the playoffs help them, or would the momentum the Yanks had to have to win their pressure-packed division race carry them to victory?

The answers came all too quickly with Kansas City sweeping New York in three games.

Willie Randolph began Game 1 with a double and was stranded at third—a bad omen. In the second inning, Rick Cerone and Lou Piniella creamed back-to-back homers and Aurelio Rodriguez doubled. Royal starter Larry Gura was on the ropes, but the Yanks could not knock him out, and Gura settled down to pitch a fine game. Result: an easy 7-2 Kansas City win.

Rudy May in Game 2 pitched brilliantly for all but the third inning when he allowed three runs. The Yankees scored twice in the fourth, one run coming on Graig Nettles' courageous inside-the-park homer. (Graig returned for the playoffs after his serious bout with hepatitis.) But the game's key play came in the eighth with two out and Randolph on first. Bob Watson

smashed a double to left field that bounced back perfectly to Willie Wilson who overthrew his cutoff man. Baserunner Randolph, who on the pitch had thoughts of stealing, got a slow start when he slipped on the dirt. Now burning around third, Willie was waved home by coach Mike Ferraro. George Brett, who positioned himself behind the cutoff man, accepted Wilson's overthrow and made a perfect relay to get Randolph at the plate.

Ferraro took some heat, but considering, in retrospect, the Yanks' weak Series attack, all gambles were justified. Wilson was blessed with a lucky rebound, Brett was in the right place at the right time, and his throw was perfect. A ninth-inning New York rally fizzled, and the Yanks lost a heartbreaker, 3-2.

The teams moved to Yankee Stadium for Game 3, and New York scored twice in the sixth inning to take a 2-1 lead with the big hits delivered by Reggie Jackson and Cerone. But in the seventh, Wilson hit a gentle, two-out double that barely fell fair. Tommy John was replaced by Goose Gossage, and U.L. Washington chopped an infield hit off Goose. Up came Brett, and he blasted a Gossage fastball for a titanic home run.

The Yankees had a chance to overcome the Royals' 4-2 lead in the eighth when Watson smoked a leadoff triple and reliever Dan Quisenberry, intimidated by the crowd's thunderous roar, walked Jackson and Oscar Gamble to load the bases with none out. But Cerone lined a bullet to shortstop Washington who doubled Jackson off second base, and Jim Spencer followed with the third out. The Yanks came away empty. There was no Yankee rally in the ninth, and the Royals were suddenly the AL champs.

For the Yankees, it was a case of much too little scoring (though Watson hit .500), bad pitches at the wrong times, and an inability to make the big play when most needed. At the same time, the deserving Royals played sound baseball. Still, it was a disappointing finish for the losing team whose regular-season record was the best in baseball in 1980.

Game 1 at Royals Stadium, KC, October 8

NY	0	2	0	0	0	0	0	0	0	-	2	10	1
KC	0	2	2	0	0	0	1	2	X	-	7	10	0

W—Gura; L—Guidry; HR—Cerone (NY), Piniella (NY), Brett (KC).

A.—42,598

Game 2 at Royals Stadium, KC, October 9

NY	0	0	0	0	2	0	0	0	0	-	2	8	0
KC	0	0	3	0	0	0	0	0	X	-	3	6	0

W—Leonard; L—May; HR—Nettles (NY).

A.—42,633

Game 3 at Yankee Stadium, NY, October 10

KC	0	0	0	0	1	0	3	0	0	-	4	12	1
NY	0	0	0	0	0	2	0	0	0	-	2	8	0

W—Quisenberry; L—Gossage; HR—White (NY), Brett (KC).

A.—56,588

1981

A baseball strike split the season into halves, a First Season and a Second Season. The winners of the two seasons were required to battle for the division title in a quarter-final round, so to speak. In the AL East, the First-Season-winning Yankees (34-22) and the Second-Season-winning Milwaukee Brewers (31-22) met in a best-of-five Series to determine the AL East season champion. The two-season arrangement was fault-rich and controversial; it was, indeed, a makeshift response to a sorry situation imposed by the players/owners impasse.

DIVISION SERIES

The Yankees won their fifth AL East title in six seasons, earning a spot in the Championship Series by beating Milwaukee. New York won two road games, lost two at home, and won the fifth and deciding game at home in a tension-packed Series.

The keys to the three Yankee victories were, respectively, Graig Nettles' glove, Goose Gossage's arm, and Reggie Jackson's bat.

In Game 1, the Brewers had Ron Guidry on the ropes, leading 2-0 in the third inning with one out and runners on first and second. Ted Simmons creamed a liner down the third base line that looked like a sure double, but Nettles made a spectacular diving snare, and the rally was halted. Later, Oscar Gamble's two-run HR and Rick Cerone's two-run double put the Yanks ahead, 4-2. Then the Yankee bullpen took over. After Milwaukee scored a run in the fifth, Ron Davis entered and retired eight Brewers in a row. Gossage pitched a scoreless eighth and ninth, and the Yankees won, 5-3.

Game 2 was a pitching duel between the Yanks' Dave Righetti and Mike Caldwell. Righetti hurled six shutout innings, fanning 10, and got one run when Lou Piniella lined a fourth-inning HR. Davis loaded the bases with one out in the seventh, and Gossage was summoned to protect the slim 1-0 lead. After inducing Robin Yount to pop up, Gossage had to face the dangerous Cecil Cooper. In the game's essential moment, Goose struck out Cooper with a mean, exploding fastball that tailed away. Reggie Jackson's long two-run HR in the ninth made the final score, 3-0. Shifting to Yankee Stadium, the Brewers put on a gutsy performance, winning Games 3 and 4.

In Game 3, the Brew Crew broke a runless streak of 19 innings by scoring three runs in the seventh inning, the key hit being Simmons' two-run HR. Paul Molitor's HR later broke a 3-3 tie.

Game 4 was a battle between the Yanks' Rick Reuschel and the flu-stricken Pete Vuckovich. Reuschel pitched six strong innings, but a few seeing-eye hits led to a two-run Brewer fourth. The Yankees wasted numerous late-inning opportunities because of bad base running and lost, 2-1, sending owner George Steinbrenner into a locker-room tirade.

In the winner-takes-all finale, the Brewers took an early 2-0 lead and the Yankees appeared flat. Then Reggie blasted a two-run fourth-inning HR into the right-field upper deck, an amazing line-drive wallop that woke up both the crowd and the Yankees. Gamble followed with another long HR, Nettles singled, Bob Watson singled, and Cerone's groundout gave New York a 4-2 lead. Righetti pitched the fifth, sixth and seventh, permitting just one run, a run Cerone recovered with a towering HR. Later, Jackson's third hit helped the Yankees add a pair of runs. Gossage pitched the final two frames to nail down the 7-3 Yankee triumph.

For the Series, Yankee pitching was fantastic, especially in Milwaukee where Guidry, Davis, Gossage and Righetti struck out 26 Brewers in two games! Gossage saved all three Yankee wins, two of them won by Righetti. Great catches were made by Jackson in right and Cerone behind the plate (one beauty ended Game 2).

Big bats were wielded by Gamble (.556, 5-for-9), Watson (.438, 7-for-16), Dave Winfield (.350, 7-for-20), Cerone (.333, 6-for-18), Larry Milbourne (.316, 6-for-19) and Jackson (.300, 6-for-20). Cerone led the Yankees with five RBIs.

```
Game 1 at County Stadium, Mil., October 7
NY    0  0  0    4  0  0    0  0  1  -  5  13  1
MIL   0  1  1    0  1  0    0  0  0  -  3   8  3
W—Davis; L—Haas; HR—Gamble (NY).          A.—35,064

Game 2 at County Stadium, Mil., October 8
N.Y   0  0  0    1  0  0    0  0  2  -  3   7  0
MIL   0  0  0    0  0  0    0  0  0  -  0   7  0
W—Righetti; L—Caldwell; HR—Piniella (NY), Jackson (NY). A.—26,395

Game 3 at Yankee Stadium, NY, October 9
MIL   0  0  0    0  0  0    3  2  0  -  5   9  0
N.Y   0  0  0    1  0  0    2  0  0  -  3   8  2
W—Fingers; L—John; HR—Simmons (MIL), Molitor (MIL).  A.—54,171

Game 4 at Yankee Stadium, NY, October 10
MIL   0  0  0    2  0  0    0  0  0  -  2   4  2
NY    0  0  0    0  0  1    0  0  0  -  1   5  0
W—Vuckovich; L—Reuschel.                  A.—52,077

Game 5 at Yankee Stadium, NY, October 11
MIL   0  1  1    0  0  0    1  0  0  -  3   8  0
NY    0  0  0    4  0  0    1  2  X  -  7  13  0
W—Righetti; L—Haas; HR—Thomas (MIL), Jackson (NY), Gamble (NY),
Cerone (NY).                              A.—47,505
```

CHAMPIONSHIP SERIES

The Yankees in capturing their 33rd AL pennant swept three games from Oakland—their first postseason sweep since beating the Phillies in four straight in the 1950 World Series.

Amid much ballyhoo, Manager Billy Martin returned to New York to lead his young A's against his former team. It was Billyball vs. the Bronx Bombers (or Bobbyball, as Yankee Manager Bob Lemon joked). But the Yanks' 25-man squad proved too deep and outscored the A's 20-4 in the Series. The hitting leader was Graig Nettles (.500), whose nine RBIs set a Championship Series record for both the AL and NL, irrespective of Series length. He had one three-run hit in each game and was the Series' MVP.

In the first inning of Game 1, Graig's bases-loaded three-run double provided all the runs needed by Tommy John who allowed just one run in six innings. Reliever Ron Davis was coasting, but with one on and one out in the eighth, Davis was given a dose of Billyball as batter Cliff Johnson stalled excessively at the plate. Upset, Davis walked Johnson. But Goose Gossage's smoke settled both the issue and the game, which the Yankees won, 3-1.

Stalling tactics were not necessary in Game 2 as the Yankee Stadium faithful thrilled to 13 runs and 19 hits by the Yankees, both Championship Series records. Reggie Jackson knocked in the first Yankee run, but left the game soon afterwards because of a leg injury. (He did not return to the Series.) A tremendous leaping catch by Dave Winfield robbed Tony Armas of a homer in the second, but the A's tied it at 1–1 in the third. In the fourth, the A's began stinging the ball off starter Rudy May and George Frazier relieved. With two runs in and the bases loaded, Frazier induced speedy Ricky Henderson to tap into a 1-2-3 double play. Without allowing a run, Frazier finished the game, pitching 5 2/3 outstanding innings.

New York had a seven-run fourth inning, setting or tying several Championship Series records as they bombed Oakland's Steve McCatty and Dave Beard. The biggest hits were supplied by Winfield (two-run double) and Lou Piniella (three-run homer). Nettles' two singles made him the first player in either League Championship Series to get two hits in one inning. In the eighth, Nettles' three-run homer finished the 13-3 Yankee rout.

Game 3 in Oakland was more typical of playoff competition as both struggling starters, the Yanks' Dave Righetti and Oakland's Matt Keough, kept the game scoreless through five innings. Then Willie Randolph's long sixth-inning home run and Nettles' ninth-inning three-run double broke the game open. Davis and Gossage nailed the A's coffin shut for the last three frames for the 4-0 win.

Besides Nettles, Yankee hitting stars included the swift table setters, Jerry Mumphrey (.500), Larry Milbourne (.462), and Randolph (.333). Piniella was 3 for 5 (.600).

New York played nearly flawless defense, making only one error in the Series. And all those who pitched (John, Davis, Gossage, May, Frazier, and Righetti) did first-rate jobs, holding the A's scoreless over the final 14 innings. An altercation between Jackson and Nettles during a victory party following the game was the only blemish on an otherwise pleasant evening.

```
Game 1 at Yankee Stadium. NY October 13
OAK.  0  0  0    0  1  0    0  0  0  -  1  6  1
NY    3  0  0    0  0  0    0  0  X  -  3  7  0
W—John; L—Norris.                    A.—55,740

Game 2 at Yankee Stadium, NY, October 14
OAK.  0  0  1    2  0  0    0  0  0  -  3  11  1
NY    1  0  0    7  0  1    4  0  X  - 13  19  0
W—Frazier; L—McCatty; HR—Piniella (NY), Nettles (NY).  A.—48,497

Game 3 at Oakland-Alameda County Coliseum, Oak., October 15
NY    0  0  0    0  0  1    0  0  3  -  4  10  0
OAK.  0  0  0    0  0  0    0  0  0  -  0   5  2
W—Righetti; L—Keough.                A.—47,302
```

1995

The playoff format expanded in 1995 to include eight teams, four in each league. Qualifying for the AL playoffs were the champions of the three divisions—Boston, Cleveland, and Seattle—and the wildcard entry was earned by the Yankees. By winning 11 of their final 12 games, the Yankees reached the playoffs for the first time since 1981. Their first-round opponent, the Seattle Mariners, had charged out of the pack in the AL West to draw even with California and then beat the Angels in a one-game playoff. It was the first time Seattle ever qualified for postseason competition.

DIVISION SERIES

The Yankees-Mariners series was easily the best of the four Division Series, although many television fans missed it because the national pastime was regionalized. All four first-round games were played at the same time, and TV viewers saw one regional contest with frequent cutaways to the other games. Lots of highlights; no continuity.

It was a poor way to deliver exciting baseball, especially the Yankees-Mariners showcase series that opened in New York with the Yankees desperately needing to win both games at Yankee Stadium. Their record in Seattle was 1-6 during the regular season—and awesome Randy Johnson would be pitching Game 3.

Yankee Stadium was electric for Game 1, with Joe DiMaggio throwing out the first ball and a record-breaking crowd of 57,178 howling through the night. Surviving a pair of homers by Ken Griffey Jr., the Yankees hung on for a 9-6 victory. David Cone gave a gritty 135-pitch, eight-inning effort, and the key blows were two-run homers struck by Wade Boggs and Ruben Sierra. The crowd loved it. "Such a passion and energy here tonight," mused Yankees Manager Buck Showalter when it was over.

Game 2, a classic, was won by at the Yankees, 7-5. It was the longest AL playoff game ever, both in time elapsed (5:13) and innings (15), concluding in the rain at 1:22 a.m. with a Jim Leyritz home run.

The Yankees had overcome four deficits, and were led by Don Mattingly, who had three hits, including a homer, and picked off two Mariner baserunners with trick timing plays at first base. Ruben Sierra and Paul O'Neill also homered, and Mariano Rivera blanked Seattle over the final 3⅓ innings.

Seattle's Andy Benes cruised into the sixth inning nursing a 2-1 lead. But Sierra walloped a homer into the right field bleachers, and two pitches later, Mattingly gave the Yanks a 3-2 lead with a blast into the same bleachers. Describing the scene, Thomas Boswell in *The Washington Post* wrote: "You'd have thought a method had been discovered to ensure world peace for the entire millennium. Yankee fans threw everything on the field except their heads."

Mariner Manager Lou Piniella skillfully used the debris throwing as reason to pull his team off the field and halt the Yankees' momentum. The Mariners in the seventh went back ahead, 4-3. In the bottom half, O'Neill's homer tied it.

Showalter allowed his bullpen ace, John Wetteland, to pitch 3⅓ innings, his longest outing of the year, and Wetteland in the 12th surrendered a Griffey solo homer, which traveled far into the Bronx night. In the bottom of the 12th, with two on and two out, Sierra cracked a double off the left field wall. The tying run scored, but Bernie Williams, carrying what would have been the winning run, was nailed at the plate.

The rain set in about 1 a.m., but about 50,000 people remained. Many were standing. Leyritz in the 15th sent them home happy with his opposite-field two-run homer off Tim Belcher. The Yankees, winners of 13 of their last 14 games, were heading to Seattle with a two-games-to-none lead. "We're down but not out," insisted Piniella, "down but not out."

Game 3 was a matchup between the Yanks' Jack McDowell, pitching for the first time since hurting his back two weeks earlier, and Randy Johnson, on the heels of his three-hitter against California in the playoff game. Inspired by the deafening Kingdome crowd, Johnson delivered eight strong innings and won, 7-4.

The Yankees in pivotal Game 4 jumped out to a 5-0 lead, but starter Scott Kamieniecki couldn't hold it. Much of the substantial lead was wiped out in the third inning on a three-run homer by Edgar Martinez. But Kamieniecki wasn't the only ineffective pitcher in this contest. In not a single inning could Yankee pitching retire the side in order; Seattle's pitching matched suit.

The score was tied in the eighth when Edgar Martinez hit another home run, a grand slam off Wetteland, putting Seattle ahead, 10-6. The Mariners held on to win, 11-8, with Martinez setting a postseason record with seven RBIs in one game.

Decisive Game 5 seemed headed for a climax in the sixth inning with the score tied, 2-2. The Yankees loaded the bases for Mattingly, who lined an opposite-field two-run double that put the Yanks ahead, 4-2. However, the ball skipped into the stands for a ground rule double, denying the Yankees a third run that might have scored had the ball stayed in play.

Starter David Cone was in command. He protected the 4-2 lead, but in the eighth he suddenly ran out of gas. First, he allowed Griffey a solo homer, Junior's fifth of the Series. Then Cone couldn't find the plate, and Seattle loaded the bases. Showalter, having lost faith in his bullpen, didn't have anyone warming up; Buck was hoping to milk Cone for every possible pitch. With two outs and a full-count to Doug Strange, the laboring Cone walked in the tying run. Exhausted, he had thrown 147 pitches, and Showalter brought in McDowell who got the final out.

In the ninth, when Tony Fernandez doubled off the wall, just missing a homer, and Randy Velarde walked, Piniella pulled his trump card, bringing in Johnson to the roaring approval of the Kingdome crowd. Only 48 hours after his previous start, Johnson nonetheless was firing the ball. He fanned Boggs and induced two meek pop-ups. He struck out the side in the 10th, but in the 11th the Yankees scratched out a run on Velarde's run-scoring single.

McDowell took the 5-4 lead into the bottom of the 11th. Joey Cora beat out a bunt and Griffey singled. When McDowell hung a splitter, Edgar Martinez ripped it into the left field corner. Cora scored the tying run, and Griffey, never breaking stride, easily scored the winning run.

The fireworks that burst over the scene punctuated for the stunned Yankees the suddenness of their Series defeat. Yet, they had helped to provide a great Series, giving major-league baseball a sorely needed shot in the arm.

But the Yankees were left to reflect on two glaring factors in losing the Series. First was their exasperating inability in 1995 to win in Seattle; the three-game sweep left them with nine losses in their 10 games at the Kingdome. Second, the pitching staff wasn't up to the standards of championship baseball. The bullpen, especially Wetteland (14.55 ERA), took the brunt of the heat, but the starters weren't much better. Seattle hit an amazing .315 in the Series.

Facing a lineup that didn't have top-to-bottom strength, the Yankees needed to neutralize the Mariners' big hitters in the middle—the Martinezes, Griffey Jr., and Jay Buhner. Instead, Seattle got maximum production from their big hitters. Edgar Martinez (.571, 10 RBIs), Griffey Jr. (.391, five HRs), Buhner (.458), and Tino Martinez (.409) simply rocked Yankee pitching.

Mattingly (.417) was sensational, as were Bernie Williams (.429), who in Game 3 became the first player in postseason history to homer from both sides of the plate in the same game, and O'Neill (three HRs, six RBIs). Amid much speculation that the playoffs would be Mattingly's swan song with the Yankees, the crowds at Yankee Stadium were unrestrained in cheering him. One of the enduring memories of this Series will be those crowd chants: "Donnie Baseball! Donnie Baseball! Donnie Baseball!"

Game 1 at Yankee Stadium, NY, October 3

SEA.	0 0 0	1 0 1	2 0 2	-	6	9	0
NY	0 0 2	0 0 2	4 1 x	-	9	13	0

W—Cone; L—Nelson; HR—Boggs (NY), Sierra (NY), Griffey (SEA)
2.A.—57,178

Game 2 at Yankee Stadium, NY, October 4

SEA.	0 0 1	0 0 1	2 0 0	0 0 1	0 0 0	-	5	16	2
NY	0 0 0	0 1 2	1 0 0	0 0 1	0 0 2	-	7	11	0

W—M. Rivera; L—Belcher; HR—O'Neill (NY), Sierra (NY), Mattingly (NY), Leyritz (NY), Coleman (SEA), Griffey (SEA).
A.—57,126

Game 3 at Kingdome, SEA, October 6

NY	0 0 0	1 0 0	1 2 0	-	4	6	2
SEA.	0 0 0	0 2 4	1 0 x	-	7	7	0

W—Johnson; L—McDowell; HR—T. Martinez (SEA), B. Williams (NY) 2, Stanley (NY).
A.—57,944

Game 4 at Kingdome, SEA, October 7

NY	3 0 2	0 0 0	0 1 2	-	8	14	1
SEA.	0 0 4	0 1 1	0 5 x	-	11	16	0

W—Charlton; L—Wetteland; HR—Griffey (SEA), E. Martinez (SEA) 2, Buhner (SEA), O'Neill (NY).
A.—57,180

Game 5 at Kingdome, SEA, October 8

NY	0 0 0	2 0 2	0 0 0	0 1	-	5	6	0
SEA.	0 0 1	1 0 0	0 2 0	0 2	-	6	15	0

W—Johnson; L—McDowell; HR—Cora (SEA), Griffey (SEA), O'Neill (NY).
A.—57,411

1996

DIVISION SERIES

When the Yankees and Rangers opened their Division Series at Yankee Stadium, the Yankees for most of the first two games seemed intent on sleepwalking their way right out of the playoffs. Texas breezed to a 6-2 win in Game 1 and led Game 2, 4-3, going into the bottom of the eighth. Bernie Williams singled, tagged up and went to second on a fly ball and scored the tying run on a single by Cecil Fielder, who earlier had homered. The 4-4 drama moved through extra innings. Finally, in the bottom of the 12th, as a steady rain made the ball slippery, Texas third baseman Dean Palmer committed a throwing error, allowing the winning run to score, and the series was even.

The Yankees still needed to win two games in Texas, a tall order, and it didn't seem like they would pick up one of the necessary wins in Game 3. Although Jimmy Key and Jeff Nelson pitched well, Darren Oliver was better and took a 2-1 lead into the ninth. But Oliver got into trouble and his relief put gas on the fire; the Yankees scored twice on a sacrifice fly by Williams, who in the first inning had homered and then robbed Rusty Greer of a homer, and a run-scoring single by John Duncan.

Wetteland did what the Texas bullpen couldn't do—he blanked Texas in the bottom of the ninth—and the Yankees were 3-2 winners.

The next afternoon, Texas had a 4-0 lead until Bobby Witt ran into trouble in the fourth. Bernie Williams led off with a single, brazenly stole second, took third on a wild pitch/ball four to Tino Martinez and scored on Fielder's single. Two more runs followed, with the key hits being delivered by Joe Girardi, a bunt single, and Mariano Duncan.

Texas threatened in the bottom of the fourth, and Juan Gonzalez came up with two on and no outs. Gonzalez already had five homers, tying a postseason series record held by Reggie Jackson and Ken Griffey Jr., and he had driven in or scored nine of the Rangers' 16 runs in the series. Torre called in David Weathers, who had initially struggled after coming to the Yankees. On a full-count pitch, Weathers delivered a nasty low-and-away slider, and Gonzalez, chasing it, went down swinging. Will Clark grounded into an inning-ending double play, and Weathers went on to pitch three scoreless innings.

Torre used his formula to protect the lead. MarianoRivera, pitching the seventh and eighth, and Wetteland, working the ninth, combined for three hitless innings, and the Yankees won the game, 6-4, and the Division Series, three games to one. Remarkably, in 19 2/3 innings pitched, the Yankees' bullpen allowed only one earned run. Those who were unscored upon included Weathers (5 IP), Rivera (4 2/3 IP), Wetteland (4 IP), Nelson (3 2/3 IP) and Graema Lloyd (1 IP). Brian Boehringer allowed the only earned run among the relief brigade, but he was a hero in the Game 2 victory when he came in and got the final out with the bases loaded in the 12th inning. In the entire series, Texas did not score after the sixth inning. "If you don't score on that team early," said Ivan Rodriguez, the Texas catcher, "you can pretty much forget it."

As a striking contrast, the Texas bullpen blew three leads. The Rangers got their only win in Game 1 when Manager Johnny Oates allowed John Burkett to pitch a complete game. Also, as great as Gonzalez was, he had very little offensive help from his teammates. His Mickey Mantle League teammate when they were teenagers in Puerto Rico, Bernie Williams, was almost as great as Gonzalez, hitting .467, with three homers, five runs and five RBIs. And Bernie received more support from the likes of Derek Jeter (.412), Fielder (.364, four RBIs) and MarianoDuncan (.313, three RBIs).

```
Game 1 at Yankee Stadium, NY, October 1
TEX.      0  0  0   5  0  1   0  0  0  -  6   8   0
NY        1  0  0   1  0  0   0  0  0  -  2  10   0
W—Burkett; L—Cone; HR—Gonzalez (TEX), Palmer (TEX).
A.—57,205

Game 2 at Yankee Stadium, NY, October 2 (12 innings)
SEA.      0  1  3   0  0  0   0  0  0   0  0  0  -  4   8   1
NY        0  1  0   1  0  0   1  1  0   0  0  1  -  5   8   0
W—Boehringer; L—stanton; HR—Gonzalez 2 (TEX), Fielder (NY).
A.—57,156

Game 3 at The Ballpark in Arlington, Texas, October 4
NY.       1  0  0   0  0  0   0  0  2  -  3   7   1
TEX.      0  0  0   1  1  0   0  0  0  -  2   6   1
W—Nelson; L—Oliver; HR—Williams (NY), Gonzalez (TEX).
A.—50,860

Game 4 at The Ballpark in Arlington, Texas, October 5
NY.       0  0  0   3  1  0   1  0  1  -  6  12   1
TEX.      0  2  2   0  0  0   0  0  0  -  4   9   0
W—Weathers; L—Pavlik; HR—Williams 2 (NY), Gonzalez (TEX).
A.—50,066
```

CHAMPIONSHIP SERIES

Now the Yankees turned their attention to Baltimore, a team that, after upsetting Cleveland in the other Division Series, was going to get what seemed to be its third "last chance" against the Yankees. The Orioles were not without favorable matchups. The Game 1 starter, Scott Erickson, had a 1.92 ERA against New York in three games this year, and the Game 2 starter, David Wells, was 9-1 lifetime at Yankee Stadium. They would be pitching to a Paul O'Neill who was greatly handicapped at the plate with a deep hamstring pull. On the other side of the coin, the Orioles hit David Cone and Mariano Rivera well. No one could predict how Orioles' second baseman Roberto Alomar would react in the ALCS to his new role as baseball's villain. Late in the season, he had spit in the

face of Umpire John Hirschbeck during an argument, and Alomar had been booed and taunted in Cleveland.

After the scheduled opener was rained out, the ALCS opened October 9 at Yankee Stadium. The Orioles rode the home runs of Brady Anderson and Rafael Palmeiro to a 4-2 lead. The Yankees made it 4-3 in the seventh inning when Armando Benitez walked pinch-hitter Darrell Strawberry with the bases loaded.

Benitez was still on the mound in the bottom of the eighth. With one out, Derek Jeter lifted a high fly ball to right field, driving rightfielder Tony Tarasco flush against the wall. Suddenly, a fan, 12-year-old Jeff Maier of Old Tappan, N.J., wearing his glove, reached out over the wall and seemed to scoop the ball into the stands. Right-field Umpire Rich Garcia immediately signaled home run, and Tarasco began screaming at him. Soon several Orioles and Manager Davey Johnson were in right field arguing that fan interference was in order—they wanted Jeter called out. Johnson departed only after being ejected. The 4-4 tie stood.

Out in the right-field stands, reporters and TV crews quickly descended on Maier, who hadn't come up with the ball. "I wanted to get a ball real bad," Jeff explained, "but I hope I didn't do anything wrong."

Back on the field, the tense game moved into extra innings. In the 11th, Randy Myers hung a slider and Williams whacked it deep into the left-field seats, and the Yankees won, 5-4.

Afterward, the focus was still on Jeter's disputed home run. Garcia, after watching replays, admitted he had blown the call, but he maintained that the ball "probably would have hit the wall" and that he should have given Jeter a double. If he had done that, of course, he would have made everyone angry. Tarasco insisted he would have made a routine catch. Johnson was upset that "they were interviewing the kid like he was a hero." Johnson had no room to talk; he was playing Alomar, giving him a chance to be a hero, when most of the civilized world was wondering why Alomar wasn't suspended.

After the Orioles got revenge in Game 2, winning, 5-3, the ALCS moved to Camden Yards. Jimmy Key and Mike Mussina were in control. After allowing Todd Zeile's two-run homer in the first inning, Key settled down and retired 23 of the next 25 batters. But Mussina, working on a four-hitter, had a 2-1 lead with two outs and no one on base in the eighth. The Orioles' ace had retired 10 consecutive batters and was rolling. It fell apart for him in a span of only seven pitches.

First, Jeter doubled into the right-field corner. Next, Williams ripped a line-drive single, scoring Jeter with the tying run. Then Tino Martinez doubled into the left-field corner, where B.J. Surhoff retrieved the ball and fired to third baseman Zeile, as Bernie dove into third and Tino pulled into second. Zeile, faking a throw to second, pumped, and the ball, slipping from his hand, went straight into the ground and began rolling on the dirt. Bernie, never hesitating, broke for home, beating Cal Ripken's throw, and giving the Yankees a 3-2 lead. Cecil Fielder followed with a two-run homer into the left-field stands, and it was 5-2. Mussina departed, and as he walked down the runway leading to the locker room he angrily slammed a chair.

The deflated Orioles managed only three hits off Key and John Wetteland, who retired the side in order in the ninth. "I'm enjoying every minute of this," said Key, who had wondered if his career might not be over after rotator-cuff surgery in July 1995.

After notching each of their first five postseason wins through comebacks, the Yankees in Game 4 took an early lead and won in more routine fashion. Three homers off rookie Rocky Coppinger—a two-run homer by Williams, a solo homer by Strawberry and a two-run homer by O'Neill—staked Kenny Rogers to a 5-2 lead. But, still struggling, Rogers was knocked out in the fourth, as the Orioles narrowed the lead to 5-4. At this point, however, the Yankees' overpowering bullpen took over; David Weathers, Graeme Lloyd, Rivera and Wetteland pitched shutout ball over the final six innings. Strawberry added his second homer in the eighth, and the Yankees won, 8-4.

In the third inning of Game 5, the Yankees erupted for six runs against Erickson, although only one run was earned. Jim Leyritz led off with an opposite-field homer. One out later, Jeter singled. Wade Boggs hit a dribbler that Erickson couldn't handle. Williams hit a tailor-made double-play grounder right to Alomar, who lifted his glove too soon and allowed the ball to roll into rightfield, as Jeter scored and Boggs took third. Alomar did field Martinez's grounder and nailed Boggs at the plate. But Fielder followed with a three-run home run, and Strawberry walloped a 448-foot shot into the Yankees' left-centerfield bullpen, and it was 6-0. Erickson later said Alomar's error, the key to the big inning, hadn't bothered him. "It's happened all year," he explained.

Coasting, Andy Pettitte made exactly 100 pitches and turned over a 6-2 lead to Wetteland in the ninth. After Bobby Bonilla broke his 0-for-19 collar with a two-out two-run homer, Cal Ripken hit a grounder into the shortstop hole. Jeter fielded the ball and bounced his throw, but Martinez scooped it out, nipping the diving Ripken on a close play. Garcia made the call.

As the Yankees mobbed Wetteland, celebrating the club's 34th AL pennant, but its first since 1981, Torre, who had waited 37 years and 4,272 games as a player and manager to get into his first World Series, stood in the dugout and wept joyfully. He hugged his coaches and each of his players as they came off the field.

The Yankees in 1996 were 14-4 overall against the Orioles and, incredibly, 9-0 at Camden Yards. Johnson called his team's offense "one-dimensional," meaning his sluggers could convert mistake pitches into home runs but against quality pitchers Baltimore wasn't able to manufacture runs. In the ALCS, the Orioles didn't steal a base, seldom advanced runners and stranded numerous runners in scoring position. The Orioles as a team hit only .222. Worse, their third, fourth, fifth and sixth hitters—

Alomar, Rafael Palmeiro, Bobby Bonilla and Cal Ripken—hit a combined .188.

The Yankees not only manufactured runs but outhomered the Orioles, ten to nine. The big bats belonged to Williams (.474, two HRs, six runs, six RBIs), Jeter (.417, one HR, five runs) and Strawberry (.417, three HRs, five RBIs). The bullpen was once again wonderful, but solid starts were also turned in by Pettitte, Key and Cone.

Bernie Williams, whom Johnson called "a special player," was the Most Valuable Player. Baltimore didn't retire Bernie in more than two consecutive plate appearances. Throughout the postseason, Williams played with tremendous concentration and intensity. Perhaps it was because he was a late bloomer, or maybe it had more to do with his low profile, but it was only now that Williams was finally receiving some recognition.

There were those, including teammates, who once thought Bernie was too soft and more concerned with playing his guitar than center field. Trained as a classical musician, Williams would go off alone before games and practice his guitar. Although Bernie in 1996 remained quiet, modest and painfully shy, he was no longer afraid of being aggressive on the field. And no longer was his gentleness mistaken for softness either.

Game 1 at Yankee Stadium, NY, October 9 (11 innings)

														-			
BAL.	0	1	1	1	0	1	0	0	0		0	0	-	4	11	1
NY	1	1	0	0	0	0	1	1	0		0	1	-	5	11	0

W—Rivera; L—Meyers; HR—Anderson (BAL), Palmeiro (BAL), Jeter (NY), Williams (NY).
A.—56,495

Game 2 at Yankee Stadium, NY, October 10

BAL.	0	0	2	0	0	0	2	1	0	-	5	10	0
NY.	2	0	0	0	0	0	1	0	0	-	3	11	1

W—Wells; L—Nelson; HR—Zeile (BAL), Palmeiro (BAL).
A.—56,432

Game 3 at Oriole Park at Camden Yards, MD, October 11

NY.	0	0	0	0	0	0	0	4	0	-	5	8	0
BAL.	2	0	0	0	0	0	0	0	0	-	2	3	2

W—Key; L—Mussina; HR—Fielder (NY), Zeile (BAL).
A.—48,635

Game 4 at Oriole Park at Camden Yards, MD, October 12

NY.	2	1	0	2	0	0	0	3	0	-	8	9	0
BAL.	1	0	1	2	0	0	0	0	0	-	4	11	0

W—Weathers; L—Coppinger; HR—Williams (NY), Strawberry 2 (NY), O'Neill (NY), Hoiles (BAL).
A.—48,974

Game 5 at Oriole Park at Camden Yards, MD, October 13

NY.	0	0	6	0	0	0	0	0	0	-	6	11	0
BAL.	0	0	0	0	0	1	0	1	2	-	4	4	1

W—Pettitte; L—Erickson; HR—Leyritz (NY), Fielder (NY), Strawberry (NY), Zeile (BAL), Murray (BAL), Bonilla (BAL).
A.—48,718

David Cone

Andy Pettitte

1997

DIVISION SERIES

After claiming their third consecutive postseason berth, the Yankees began their World Series title defense against the powerful Cleveland Indians. The Indians were division winners for the third season in a row, all under the reins of Manager Mike Hargrove. The Yankees, under the watchful eye of Manager Joe Torre, on the other hand, were coming into the postseason as the wild-card team for their second time, the first coming in 1995, when they were defeated by Seattle in the Division Series. The Yankees were making their fourth appearance in the Division Series: 1981 (won), 1995 (lost), and 1996 (won); Cleveland was making their third: 1995 (won) and 1996 (lost).

Cleveland's Central Division standings fluctuated from first place to fourth in the first two months of 1997. Then, after a 5-4 11-inning win versus Chicago on June 5, the Indians clinched first place to stay, taking a ½-game lead over the Milwaukee Brewers. Their record after that June victory was only two games over .500 at 28-26, a paltry .519 winning percentage. Their greatest lead in the Central Division was on September 18, when they took an eight-game lead over the White Sox and Brewers (who were tied for second place), defeating the Twins in a game at Minnesota, 4-1. Cleveland's record of 86-75 (.534) was the worst of all four American League clubs appearing in the postseason, and their season-win total was ten fewer than the Yanks, who had a record of 96-66 (.593). The 1997 Yanks had four more wins than their World Champion club of '96. With a league-leading and club-record 220 homers in 1997 (no other American League club had 200 or more), the Indians became the first AL club in history to have three consecutive 200+ homer-seasons. Jim Thome led the Cleveland club with 40 roundtrippers. The Yankees blasted 59 fewer homers (161) than the Indians, while Tino Martinez, who had a career-season, led his Yankee club with a total of 44 dingers. Tino was the MVP for the Yankees in '98!

The first two games of the 1997 Division Series opened in New York, September 30 and October 2. Playing before the largest crowd (57,398) in the 22-year history of "remodeled" Yankee Stadium in the first game, the Yankees came out on top in the contest, 8-6. The opening-game pitching duel saw Cleveland's Orel Hershiser, 14-6 in 1997, pitted against 12-6 David Cone of the Yankees. Orel came into the game with a 8-1 record and an impressive 1.83 ERA in postseason play. The game did not begin on a promising note, Cleveland taking the lead in their first at bat with five runs. The Yanks put their first mark on the board with a single run in the third. Each team added one run in the fourth, the Yankees adding another in the fifth, Cleveland having the lead, 6-3. David Cone lasted into the fourth, when he was relieved by Ramiro Mendoza, the eventual winner of the game. Cone was ineffective in his stint against the Indians, allowing six runs, all earned. Hershiser pitched into the fifth, being replaced by Alvin Morman, who retired no Yankee batters, walking one. The next two Cleveland pitchers, Eric Plunk and Paul Assenmacher, ex-Yankees all, would allow a total of five runs when the Yankee sixth inning came to a close. Eric Plunk, the soon-to-be loser of the game, who had wore the pinstripes in three seasons (1989-1991), had relieved Morman in the fifth. After a scoreless Cleveland sixth, the Yankees came to bat to do their thing. The Bronx Bombers, holders of a very vast array of postseason batting records, added another to their stable in this inning. Mr. Plunk proceeded to give up two successive home runs, sending him to the showers. Paul Assenmacher, another ex-Yankee (one season, 1993), replaced Plunk. Assenmacher then promptly served up another home-run ball—and the Yankees had entered the record books again with three consecutive homers, the first time ever by any club in postseason play! Designated hitter Tim Raines began the onslaught with a three-run homer off Plunk, followed by solo shots from Derek Jeter (off Plunk) and Paul O'Neill (off Assenmacher), giving the Yankees the lead, 8-6. The game was scoreless after that, the Yankees winning by two, to take a one-game jump in the series. The Yankees, originally down by five runs in the first inning, had staged one of the greatest comebacks ever in postseason play. The Yankees had out-homered the powerful Indians, four to one. Personal firsts were recorded by Yankee pitchers in the game: Mendoza had picked up his first postseason win, while Mariano Rivera had earned his first save in postseason play.

Game two, also at Yankee Stadium, October 2, had Cleveland's 21-year-old rookie, Jaret Wright, 8-3 in '97, going against Andy Pettitte, with a fine 18-7 ledger. Wright was the first rookie to start for the Cleveland Indians in a postseason game since Gene Bearden did it versus the Boston Braves in the 1948 World Series. The Yankees wasted no time, taking a 3-0 lead after the first inning. New York could not hold the lead as the Indians put up five runs in the fourth, going up by a score of 5-3. In that fourth frame, Matt Williams hit a two-run homer off Pettitte. The Clevelanders added two more runs in the fifth, and Andy was history. Pettitte, who was to be tagged with the defeat, had allowed seven runs, all earned, in five total innings. Rookie Wright, the soon-to-be game's winning pitcher, was removed after six innings. The game was scoreless until the Yanks scored solo runs in the eighth and ninth innings. Derek Jeter hit a solo homer in the ninth off Jose Mesa, moving the Yanks to within two of Cleveland, 7-5. It was Jeter's second homer of the series. The Yanks could do no further damage, the Indians taking the game, 7-5, and tying the series at one game.

The series moved to Jacobs Field, where the Yankees had a record of 15-5, for the next three contests, October 4, 5 and 6. Yankee lefty David Wells was sent to the mound for New York versus righty Charles Nagy for Game 3. Each team traded solo runs for the first three frames, the Yanks in the lead, 2-1, after three. Then came the big blow in the Yankee fourth. With two down and the bases full of Yankees, Nagy was relieved by Chad Ogea, who promptly gave up a grand slam to Paul O'Neill. The runs were charged to starter Nagy, who was the eventual loser of the game. The Yanks were now up, 6-1, and Wells would not allow another Indian run. David would pitch a five-hit complete game, to win a Division Series game for the third straight year for three different clubs. He had one a game for Cincinnati in 1995, one for Baltimore in 1996, and now one with the Yankees in '97. Paul O'Neill's five-RBI game were the most for a Yankee player in a playoff game since Thurman Munson had five ribbies in Game 5 of the 1978 World Series against the Dodgers. It would turn out that the Cleveland bullpen would not allow the Yankees another run in the series!

In Game 4 on October 5, Dwight "Doc" Gooden, making his first postseason start since 1988, was pitted against Orel Hershiser, who started Game 1. Gooden was last on the hill in a starting role as a member of the New York Mets in the fourth game of the National League Championship Series, October 4, 1988. In that game, Doc, who pitched 8 $\frac{1}{3}$ innings and struck out nine Los Angeles batters, got a no-decision for his effort. It should be noted that Gooden did pitch in relief in the seventh and final game of that same series, October 12. In that final game, Orel Hershiser tossed a complete game 6-0 shutout, clinching the NL pennant for his Dodger club. It is interesting to note that Gooden and Hershiser were the starting pitchers—neither picking up a decision—in the first game of that 1988 series and now, nine years later, would be facing each other again. The Yankees got on the board first with two runs in the first inning, while Cleveland made its mark in the second with a lone run, a solo shot by David Justice. At that point, the Yankees had a narrow 2-1 lead, which remained until the Indian eighth. Up to this point, Yankee relievers had not allowed a Cleveland run in this series, but that would soon change. Since Gooden's departure in the sixth, three New York relievers would make way for Mariano Rivera to pitch in the eighth. With one out in the eighth, Mariano served up a home run, an opposite-field solo shot from Sandy Alomar, to tie the game at two. The Yanks were scoreless in the top of the ninth, presenting the Indians with an opportunity to win the game in their half of the inning...and they did just that! On the mound for New York now was Ramiro Mendoza, replacing Rivera, who had pitched through the eighth inning. Cleveland's Marquis Grissom started the ninth with a single to right, Bip Roberts then moved Grissom to second with a sacrifice. With one out, Omar Vizquel hit a grounder that glanced off Mendoza's glove, rolling past Derek Jeter into left field, scoring Grissom from second with the winning run, tying the series at two games. The Cleveland club and Indian fans were jubilant! For the game, Hershiser had pitched seven full innings before yielding to two Indian relievers, Paul Assenmacher and Mike Jackson, the latter picking up the win. Ramiro Mendoza suffered the loss for the Yankees, who used six pitchers in the game. With the defeat, the Yankees' nine-game postseason road winning streak had come to an end. Their prior road loss was in the fifth and final game of the 1995 Division Series, a 6-5 defeat at the hands of the Seattle Mariners on October 8. It was a one-game series now, with the winner moving on and the loser taking a vacation till spring.

The fifth and final game was played at Cleveland on October 6, and would see a repeat of the pitching duel of Game 2, the Yankees' Andy Pettitte facing the Indians' Jaret Wright. The contest was without a score till Cleveland scored three in their third. Manny Ramirez put his club ahead in the third with a two-run double and later scored on a single by Matt Williams, putting the Indians up, 3-0. In the fourth inning, a crucial play occurred when Jim Thome was able to bunt Sandy Alomar to third base. Then, the next batter, ex-Yankee Tony Fernandez, lifted a sacrifice fly, scoring Alomar and Cleveland's fourth run. The Yankees got on the scoreboard with two runs in the top of the fifth and a solo tally in the sixth, the game still in Cleveland's favor, 4-3. Wright, the soon-to-be winner of the game, was done for the Indians in the sixth, and Pettitte, the eventual loser, pitched into the seventh for the Yanks, being relieved by Jeff Nelson. What's curious is Yankee Manager Joe Torre's decision to not go with either Ramiro Mendoza or Mariano Rivera for the remainder of the game. Cleveland's next three relievers, Mike Jackson, Paul

Assenmacher and Jose Mesa, the latter on his way to a save, allowed New York four hits and pitched shutout ball the rest of the way. In the New York ninth, Paul O'Neill hit a two-out double, but was stranded on base when Bernie Williams flied out to left, ending the Yankees' season. Cleveland's fine relief efforts had paid off, with the Indians clinching victory in the series, three games to two. For the series, Omar Vizquel would lead all players, batting an even .500 on a series-high nine hits. For New York, Paul O'Neill would lead the club with a .421 mark, going 8-for-19, with a series-leading seven RBIs. Alomar was tops for the Indians, driving in five. Two Indians, Sandy Alomar and Matt Williams, led their team with four runs apiece and Derek Jeter would be the series leader, crossing the plate six times. Bernie Williams would have a disappointing series, making only one hit in 17 at bats, a paltry .118 average, playing in all five games.

Statistically, the Yanks outscored the Indians, 24 to 21 and outhomered them as well, six to four. Both teams has 43 hits, and the Yankees doubled the Indian total of walks with 20. Cleveland rookie hurler Jaret Wright won two games while losing none and struck out a series-leading 10 batters. David Cone, pitching in one game, had an uncharacteristic 16.20 ERA, and Andy Pettitte, starter (and loser) of two games, allowed 11 earned runs, finishing with an inflated ERA of 8.49. David Wells would fare the best for the Yankee staff with an ERA of exactly 1.00, with his 6-1 complete game win in the third game. For the most part, team pitching stats for the series were relatively even, except, of course, in the win column! The Indians won, in part, due to rookie Wright's fine pitching and Cleveland's bullpen shutting down the Yankee lineup, especially in the final two games. The Yankee relief corps, especially Mariano Rivera, were not as effective as Cleveland's bullpen in Games 4 and 5.

The Indians would go on to defeat the Baltimore club in the ALCS, later to be defeated by the upstart Florida Marlins in the 1997 World Series. Back in New York, Yankee hopes for a championship repeat would be squashed in '97. No one in their wildest dreams could envision the kind of season that was on the horizon for the Yankees in 1998... it would be a season for the ages!

Game 1 at Yankee Stadium, NY, September 30

```
CLE    5 0 0   1 0 0   0 0 0  -  6  11  0
NY     0 1 0   1 1 5   0 0 X  -  8  11  0
```
W—Mendoza; L—Plunk; HR—Alomar (CLE), Martinez (NY),Raines (NY), Jeter (NY), O'Neill (NY).
A.—57,398

Game 2 at Yankee Stadium, NY, October 2

```
CLE    0 0 0   5 2 0   0 0 0  -  7  11  1
NY     3 0 0   0 0 0   0 1 1  -  5   7  2
```
W—Wright; L—Pettitte; HR—MWilliams (CLE), Jeter (NY).
A.—57,360

Game 3 at Jacobs Field, OH, October 4

```
NY     1 0 1   4 0 0   0 0 0  -  6  4  1
CLE    0 1 0   0 0 0   0 0 0  -  1  5  1
```
W—Wells; L—Nagy; HR—None.
A.—45,274

Game 4 at Jacobs Field, OH, October 5

```
NY     2 0 0   0 0 0   0 0 0  -  2  9  1
CLE    0 1 0   0 0 0   0 1 1  -  3  9  0
```
W—Jackson; L—Mendoza; HR—Justice (CLE), Alomar (CLE).
A.—45,231

Game 5 at Jacobs Field, OH, October 6

```
NY     0 0 0   0 2 1   0 0 0  -  3  12  0
CLE    0 0 3   1 0 0   0 0 X  -  4   7  2
```
W—Wright; L—Pettitte; HR—None.
A.—45,203

1998

In mid-January, 1998, the Executive Council approved a new postseason format (later ratified by both the owners and the Players Association), replacing the rotational system for determining home-field advantage in the Division Series and Championship Series. The system that allows alternating the first games of the World Series between the two rival leagues (the American and the National) from season to season would remain unchanged. Here's how the new format works:

For the Division Series (best of five), matchups are based on won-loss records with the division champion having the best record meeting the playoff qualifier with the worst record, unless they are in the same division. Also, the teams with the home-field advantage in the Division Series are given Games 1, 2 and 5 at home. Similarly, of the two teams advancing to the Championship Series (best of seven), the club with the better record would play Games 1, 2, 6 and 7 at home.

DIVISION SERIES

After completing a spectacularly successful regular season, the Yankees (114-48, .704!) would face the Rangers in the Division Series, the fifth appearance for New York and the second for Texas. In a rematch of 1996 Division Series opponents, Texas, 88-74 (.543), came into the postseason as winners of the AL West for the second time in three seasons. The Rangers clinched their postseason berth by defeating the second-place Anaheim Angels (the only club to have a winning record (6-5) versus the '98 Yanks) in all five games during a one-week stretch in late September. Beating Anaheim in those five games certainly helped Texas in winning the AL West by three games over the Angels. Despite being a heavy underdog in the series, Texas had handily beaten a club, Anaheim, that gave the Yankees fits in '98. Prior to the series opener, so-called critics were quick to judge the Yankees' ability to shutdown the high-powered offense of the Rangers, led by outfielder Juan Gonzalez (who was later named AL MVP for 1998). Could Texas do the unthinkable and defeat the Yanks, just coming off a storybook season?

Using the new postseason format explained elsewhere, the five-game series opened in New York for the first two games, September 29 and 30. David Wells, who did not fare well in two of his three games versus Texas in '98, was matched against Todd Stottlemyre, son of the current Yankee pitching coach and ex-Yankee great. The Yankees won Game 1 with speed, scoring the only two runs that were needed to preserve the 2-0 victory. David Wells, the eventual winning pitcher of the game, tossed eight innings of shutout ball on 135 pitches and made way for Mariano Rivera's save in the ninth. With his eight-inning performance, Wells extended his postseason scoreless streak to 15 over his past two starts, improving his record to 5-1. Stottlemyre fired a complete game, allowing six Yankee hits in a losing cause, his club now down one in the series.

In Game 2 at Yankee Stadium, September 30, the pitching matchups were 20-game winner Rick Helling of Texas against Yankee lefty Andy Pettitte. Retiring the first 12 Rangers he faced, Pettitte picked up the win and went on to strike out eight Texas batters, allowing them one run in seven innings. Rivera came in to pick up his second consecutive save in two attempts. As it turned out, that would be the only run Texas would score in the

soon-to-be three-game sweep. In taking a 2-0 lead in the series, the Bronx Bombers won the game, 3-1, using that old Yankee trademark—the home run. Rookie sensation, Shane Spencer, Mr. September, continued to show off his power, blasting a solo homer in the third in his first postseason at bat! Scott Brosius hit a two-run shot in the fourth inning for his first postseason homer. Trying for a sweep, the Yankees moved on to Texas for Game 3. In this October 2 contest, 20-game winner David Cone was on the hill for New York, and Aaron Sele would do the tossing for the Rangers. The Yankees scored all four of their runs in the sixth frame on a solo homer by Paul O'Neill and a three-run blast by that guy again, Shane Spencer, his second homer in as many days. Shane's homer in this game was his ninth in his last 33 at bats, counting the regular season. Cone and the Yankees picked up the win, 4-0, in allowing Texas but three hits. Jeff Nelson and Mariano Rivera closed it for the winners.

In sweeping the Rangers in three straight, the Yankee pitching corps did not allow any homers by Texas, holding the Rangers in check with a .133 average for the brief three-game series. The Yanks outscored the Rangers 9-1 in the three-game sweep and out-homered them four to zip. The Yankees (who else?!) established a major-league record for the fewest runs (one) allowed in the first three games of any postseason series. Yankee pitchers allowed only one run in 27 innings for an ERA of 0.33 for the three-game series, giving up only 13 hits, while striking out 27 Texas Rangers. The bottom three slots of the Yankee batting order were a collective 12 for 28 (.429), while the first six positions went 11 for 63 (.175). Chad Curtis was 2-for-3 in the series, and Spencer had four RBIs with three runs scored, going 3-for-6. Commenting on Spencer's performance after the game, Texas Manager Johnny Oates said: "He doesn't get cheated. He uses that piece of wood—and not to clean off his shoes." In winning, the Yanks improved their record in Division Series play to 3-2, while the Rangers continued winless at 0-2. Not coincidentally, the Yankees, who dominate most all-time World Series records in many categories, also reign supreme with records for the Division Series. They have appeared in more series (five) than any other team in baseball, playing a record 22 games (13-9, .591). So much for the critics with their view of the '98 Yankees not being able to win in the postseason! With their victory, the Yankees moved on to the American League Championship Series to face the Cleveland Indians, their nemesis from the year before.

```
Game 1 at Yankee Stadium, NY, September 29
TEX   0 0 0   0 0 0   0 0 0   -  0    5  0
NY    0 2 0   0 0 0   0 0 0   -  2    6  0
W—Wells; L—Stottlemyre; HR—None.
A.—57,362

Game 2 at Yankee Stadium, NY, September 30
TEX   0 0 0   0 1 0   0 0 0 -  1   5  0
NY    0 1 0   2 0 0   0 0 X -  3   8  0
W—Pettitte; L—Helling; HR—Spencer (NY), Brosius (NY).
A.—57,360

Game 3 at The Ballpark in Arlington, Texas, Oct. 2
NY    0 0 0   0 0 4   0 0 0 -  4   9  1
TEX   0 0 0   0 0 0   0 0 0 -  0   3  1
W—Cone; L—Sele; HR—O'Neill (NY), Spencer (NY).
A.—49,450
```

CHAMPIONSHIP SERIES

After sweeping Texas three games to none in the Division Series, the Yankees turned their attention to the defending American League champs, the Cleveland Indians (89-73, .549), who had defeated the Red Sox three games to one in their series. Seeking revenge for being eliminated by Cleveland last season in the Division Series, the Yankees would face the Indians, who were the seventh club in history to lead their league or division from wire to wire. Manager Mike Hargrove's Cleveland club, making their third ALCS appearance (the Yankees their seventh), had now won four straight division titles dating back to 1995.

The series opened in New York for the first two games, October 6 and 7. Game 1 pitted Cleveland starter, rookie Jaret Wright, who had shutdown the Yanks in the 1997 Division Series, against David Wells, coming off a great series versus Texas. The Yankees wasted no time, scoring an ALCS-record five runs on six singles and a walk in the bottom of the first inning, taking a 5-0 lead, and knocking out Wright after just $^2/_3$ of an inning. In that first inning, the Yanks had batted around for the 37th time in 1998. The Indians did not score until the top of the ninth, when they tallied on a two-run homer by Manny Ramirez against David Wells. That ended David's streak of 23 consecutive scoreless innings in postseason play. With eight scoreless innings to begin Game 1, the Yankees established a club record of 21 straight scoreless innings in postseason play, the previous mark being 20 by the 1921 team. The Yankees had beaten Wright, the loser for Cleveland, and David Wells picked up a well-deserved victory, the New Yorkers winning, 7-2. Yankee catcher Jorge Posada blasted his first postseason homer, a solo shot in the sixth inning off Chad Ogea.

Up by one game over Cleveland, the Yankees, again playing at home, sent 20-game winner David Cone against Charles Nagy, a winner of 15 for the Indians. The contest was scoreless until the top of the third when Cleveland scored a lone run, on a solo homer by David Justice. The Yankees eventually tied the game, 1-1, with their own mark in the bottom of the seventh. Indeed, this was one of those old-fashioned pitching duels, with the game still being tied after nine innings. Neither club would score in the 10th and 11th frames, but then came the 12th, which would give the game to the Indians. After a leadoff single by Jim Thome in the 12th, Enrique Wilson was sent in as a pinch-runner for Thome. Travis Fryman then laid down a bunt that first baseman Tino Martinez fielded, and fired to first where Chuck Knoblauch was covering. On the Martinez throw, Fryman was hit in the back, the ball caroming about 20 feet away. Knoblauch, instead of fielding the ball, which was still in play, began a dialogue with first-base umpire, Ted Hendry. Chuck was insisting that Fryman had been running illegally inside the baseline and should have been called out for interference. While Knoblauch was jawing with umpire Hendry, Chuck eventually threw the ball home, but by that time pinch-runner Wilson had scored all the way from first, the Indians taking a 2-1 lead. Fans in attendance in Yankee Stadium booed Knoblauch when he came off the field. Later commenting on the controversial play in the 12th, Chuck said: "I don't feel like I didn't play the ball out. It's not that I was trying to be an umpire. I thought it was a no-doubter." Kenny Lofton added a two-run single after that, giving the Indians four runs in the frame. The Yankees could not score in the bottom of the 12th,

the Indians coming on top of a 4-1 game, the series now tied 1-all.

Games 3, 4 and 5 shifted to Jacobs Field in Cleveland, October 9, 10 and 11. The third game of the ALCS, October 9, saw lefty Andy Pettitte facing 23-year-old Bartolo Colon of Cleveland. The game was a close one, the Indians ahead, 2-1, until the bottom of the fifth rolled around. Andy Pettitte came unraveled after two outs in the fifth, giving up three Cleveland homers. Manny Ramirez began the onslaught with a solo shot, Jim Thome then hit a two-run job, his second of the game, and later ex-Yankee Mark Whiten blasted a Pettitte pitch 416 feet to left for a solo homer. The homers were not consecutive. When the dust had settled, the Indians scored four times to take a commanding 6-1 lead in the game, and Andy Pettitte, the eventual loser in the game, was ready to take a shower. All in all, in the fifth inning, Andy had allowed three homers and four scores on only 13 pitches. After the Yankees scored a lone run in the first inning, Cleveland hurler Colon shut them down for the remainder of the game, tossing a four-hitter and a complete-game victory, putting his club up two games to one. It was the first complete game in postseason play for the Cleveland club since the opening game of the 1954 World Series. The Yankees, who had been down many times before in the 1998 season, would regroup in Game 4...and beyond.

Again playing at "The Jake" in Cleveland on October 10, Game 4 of the series had Yankee rookie, Orlando "El Duque" Hernandez, making his first postseason appearance, versus ex-Yankee, Dwight "Doc" Gooden. The Yanks scored with a single run in the first stanza, a solo shot by Paul O'Neill. The Bombers added two more runs in the top of the fourth to take a 3-0 lead. A deciding factor in the eventual Yankee victory took place when Cleveland came to bat in the sixth inning. El Duque had retired nine Indians in a row before allowing a single to Omar Vizquel. With only one out and two runners on base, Vizquel and Justice, Hernandez faced the meat of the Cleveland lineup, Manny Ramirez and Jim Thome. Orlando put out the Indian uprising, striking out both power-hitters, Ramirez and Thome, to preserve the Yankee 3-0 lead. After pitching to one batter in the eighth, El Duque, who had utterly shutdown the powerful Indian lineup on three hits in a masterful way, made way for Mike Stanton. Stanton, who had pitched in the eighth most games (67) in Yankee history in '98, had to work out of a jam, like Hernandez did in the Cleveland sixth. In the eighth inning, Stanton, with the help of a double play, helped the Yankees keep the Indians without a run, setting the table for Mariano Rivera to pitch in the ninth. In that final inning, Rivera was flawless, striking out one and preserving the Yankee victory, 4-0, and more importantly tying the series at two games apiece. Doc Gooden took the loss for the Indians, establishing a record for the most postseason starts (nine) without a win. El Duque, in his first ever postseason game, earned a well-deserved victory. With the Yankee win, the club established a major-league record for the most wins (119) in a season (including postseason play), breaking the old standard (118) set by the 1906 Chicago Cubs.

The fifth game of the ALCS and the third straight at Cleveland's Jacob Field, saw David "Mr. Perfect" Wells, winner of Game 1, take the mound against ex-LSU star, Chad Ogea. The

Yankees scored all of the runs they needed in the first two innings (three in the first and a lone run in the second), chasing Ogea to the showers, taking a 4-2 lead. Wells had allowed Cleveland two runs in the bottom of the first. The Yanks scored their fifth and final run of the game in the top of the fourth and the Clevelanders countered with a single tally of their own in the bottom of the sixth, cutting the New York lead to 5-3. Wells, who pitched 7 $\frac{1}{3}$ innings and struck out a postseason career-high 11 Indians, gave the ball to Dave Nelson, who faced but two batters in the eighth. Mariano Rivera, relieving Nelson, pitched the final 1 $\frac{2}{3}$ innings, holding Cleveland hitless to earn another save and clinch the Yankee win, 5-3. Designated hitter Chili Davis led the way for the Yankees, driving in three of the five New York runs with a two-run single and a solo homer. David Wells, continuing his storybook season, was credited with the win, becoming the first lefty ever to win two games in an American League Championship Series. David improved his postseason record to 7-1. In the third, Scott Brosius cracked a three-run homer off starter Nagy. In the fifth, the Indians scored five times off Cone, highlighted by a tremendous third-deck grand slam by Jim Thome, pulling Cleveland within one run, 6-5. David Cone was done after five innings, Ramiro Mendoza coming in to relieve him in the sixth. The Yankees won the game and the series in the bottom of the sixth. Cleveland rightfielder, Manny Ramirez, misjudged a fly hit by Derek Jeter that hit the base of the outfield wall, Derek being credited with a two-run triple. Jeter would score from third with an insurance run to put the Yankees up by four, 9-5. That was all the Yanks needed as Ramiro Mendoza and Mariano Rivera put an end to Cleveland's bid to repeat as American League Champions, holding the mighty Indians to one hit in the final four innings of the game. Starter Charles Nagy took the loss for Cleveland, and shortstop Omar Vizquel made a throwing error that ended his 46-game playoff errorless streak at 237 chances.

David Wells won the ALCS Most Valuable Player Award, winning half of the Yankees' four games, posting an ERA of 2.87 and striking out 18 Cleveland batters. David Cone struck out 13 Indian batters in 13 innings, bringing the Yankee club strikeout total to 51 in six games. The Indians outhomered the Yanks, 9 to 5, and the Yanks walked an ALCS-record 35 times. In an interesting stat, the Yankees scored almost half (12, 44%) of their 27 total runs in the ALCS in the first inning of the six games played. In the first nine postseason games of 1998, the Yankee bullpen had allowed but three earned runs in 33 $\frac{1}{3}$ innings pitched, a phenomenal ERA of 0.80, and extended their collective scoreless streak to 11 innings. The Yankees had won their unprecedented 35th American League pennant, since winning their first in 1921. The Yanks were now 6-1 in the ALCS, which began in 1969 with a division playoff system that is still in use today. The Indians dropped to 2-1 in the ALCS, and their 1998 season was over. The Bronx Bombers, on the other hand, were set to face the National League Champion San Diego Padres, a club that had won 16 games fewer than the Yankees, in the 1998 World Series.

Game 1 at Yankee Stadium, NY, October 6
```
CLE  0 0 0  0 0 0  0 0 2 - 2  5  0
NY   5 0 0  0 0 1  1 0 X - 7 11  0
```
W—Wells; L—Wright; HR—Posada (NY), Ramirez (CLE).
A.—57,138

Game 2 at Yankee Stadium, NY, October 7 (12 INNINGS)
```
CLE  0 0 0  1 0 0  0 0 0  0 0 3 - 4  8  1
NY   0 0 0  0 0 0  1 0 0  0 0 0 - 1  7  1
```
W—Burba; L—Nelson; HR—Justice (CLE).
A.—57,128

Game 3 at Jacobs Field, OH, October 9
```
NY   1 0 0  0 0 0  0 0 0 - 1  4  0
CLE  0 2 0  0 4 0  0 0 X - 6 12  0
```
W—Colon; L—Pettitte; HR—Thome 2 (CLE), Ramirez (CLE), Whiten (CLE).
A.—44,904

Game 4 at Jacobs Field, OH, October 10
```
NY   1 0 0  2 0 0  0 0 1 - 4  4  0
CLE  0 0 0  0 0 0  0 0 0 - 0  4  3
```
W—Gooden; L—Hernandez; HR—O'Neill (NY).
A.—44,981

Game 5 at Jacobs Field, OH, October 11
```
NY   3 1 0  1 0 0  0 0 0 - 5  6  0
CLE  2 0 0  0 0 1  0 0 0 - 3  8  0
```
W—Wells; L-Ogea; HR—Lofton (CLE), Davis (NY), Thome (CLE).
A.—44,966

Game 6 at Yankee Stadium, NY, October 13
```
CLE  0 0 0  0 5 0  0 0 0 - 5  8  3
NY   2 1 3  0 0 3  0 0 X - 9 11  1
```
W—Cone; L—Nagy; HR—Brosius (NY), Thome (CLE).
A.—57,142

1999

DIVISION SERIES

As Yogi Berra once said: "It's deja vú all over again." This statement seems to apply to the 1999 Yankee-Ranger postseason, especially since, for the second season in a row, and for the third time since 1996, New York and Texas were scheduled to meet again as foes in the American League Division Series. New York would be making its major-league-record sixth trip to the Division Series, while the Rangers would be making their third, all against the Yankees—and all with the series beginning at Yankee Stadium.

The Rangers were coming off a record-breaking campaign, getting their most wins ever (95) enroute to their fourth Western Division title since 1994 and their third under the watchful eye of manager and ex-Yankee Johnny Oates. Oates would guide the Rangers to a first-place finish with an eight-game margin over runner-up Oakland. Offensively, the Rangers led the majors with a .293 club batting average, a new club record. They also set club standards in runs scored (945), hits (1653), homers (230), RBIs (897) and slugging percentage (.479). However, if Texas was to have a vulnerability, it would be their pitching corps, which was ranked 11th (of 14 teams) with a 5.07 team ERA. By comparison, the Yanks' team ERA (4.13) allowed almost one whole run fewer per game than did Texas! During a grueling 162-game schedule, that one-point difference in ERA can translate to a lot of opponent runs! Would pitching be a tremendous factor in this series?—Texas would find out quickly in the very first game!

The first two games opened at Yankee Stadium, October 5 and 7, and this writer was in attendance. In Game 1, Aaron Sele, who led the Rangers with his 18 wins, would face Yankee Orlando "El Duque" Hernandez, who led the Yankees with his 17 victories. Orlando was coming into the game with a postseason record of 2-0 with an ERA of 0.64, having allowed but one earned in 14 innings. On the other hand, Sele was 0-1, allowing four runs against the Yankees in Game 3 of the Division Series in 1998. Hernandez truly came out to pitch this day, shutting out Texas and allowing them but two hits in eight full innings of work, walking six and striking out the same total. For his fine effort, El Duque lowered his postseason ERA to a microscopic 0.41 (one ER in 22 IP)! With Orlando on the hill doing his thing, Bernie Williams was in the Yankee lineup carrying on as a one-man Texas wrecking crew, feasting on Ranger pitching! Mr. Williams would go 3-for-5 with six RBIs. He would bang out a two-run double in the fifth inning and would put the icing on the cake in the next inning with a three-run homer to right. For good measure, he singled in Knoblauch in the eighth, for his sixth RBI of the game. Bernie's homer was his tenth in postseason play, and he has a Division Series-leading 17 RBI. Bernie would get no more RBIs in this series. In a very tense moment not related to the game on the field, Chuck Knoblauch drilled a foul ball into the Yankees dugout, striking coach Don Zimmer in the left temple area. The 68-year-old Zim fell to ground, and for a few minutes worried Joe Torre and his players. Soon, Zim was taken to the clubhouse where he was attended to for an abrasion. Zim returned later to the game

with an ice pack and even later came out wearing a green combat helmet with the "NY" insignia prominently displayed. Zim said later: "one hundred ten thousand ears in this ballpark, and he's got to hit my ear." The high-powered Rangers had now scored but one lone run in 42 innings against Yankee pitching, a phenomenal 0.21 ERA! The Yankees won the game 8-0, and perhaps the slumbering lumber of the mighty Texas batters might wake up in time for Game 2...

After a one-day break, the series resumed on October 7, when Texas' Rick Helling would face Yankee lefty Andy Pettitte in a rematch of the 1998 Game 2 pitchers. In the 1998 encounter, Pettitte pitched a masterful game, allowing Texas but one run over seven full innings. This season's contest was scoreless until the Texas fourth, when Yankee-nemesis Juan Gonzalez blasted a solo homer, ending a 25-inning postseason scoreless drought for the Rangers. The home run was the sixth that Gonzalez has hit in Division Series play, all coming against Yankee pitching! The Yankees would counter with a run of their own in the fifth on a double by Scott Brosius. No other scoring occurred until the Yanks took the lead with a solo run in the seventh on a double by Ricky Ledee and added an insurance run in the next inning on a bases loaded walk. Mariano Rivera came in to pitch the ninth with a two-run Yankee lead and proceeded to strike out two of the three Rangers that he faced to pick up his first save of the series. The Yankees won the game 3-1 and went up two games to zip with the series moving on to The Ballpark at Arlington.

The third game of the series was played at Texas on Friday, October 8 and would have Yankee Roger Clemens, who would be making his first postseason start since Game 7 of the 1986 ALCS, facing Esteban Loaiza of Texas. This game could be summed with one word: Darryl. Darryl Strawberry, who had overcome so much adversity this season and in 1998, hit Loaiza's second offering for a three-run homer, scoring Derek Jeter and Bernie Williams, the Yanks jumping off to a 3-0 lead in the very first inning. It would be the only runs that the Yanks would need. With Clemens' fastball popping leather, the Rangers had no chance. Roger would toss seven full innings of shutout ball, scatter three hits and strike out but two. Jeff Nelson came in to face one batter, Tom Goodwin, who promptly singled to center. Torre then signalled for his ultra-stopper, Mariano Rivera, who induced a double play by Mark McLemore and struck out Ivan Rodriguez to end any Ranger threat in the eighth. Mariano, after allowing a leadoff single to Ricky Greer in the Texas ninth, proceeded to set down the next three Texas batters, giving the Yankees a 3-0 win, and more importantly, another series sweep of the Rangers. The Yanks, in six Division Series, are now 4-2, while Texas sliped to 0-3, all of their losses being at the hands of the Yankees! Mariano picked up his second save and only two Texas runners got as far as second base! Roger Clemens picked up his first postseason win since 1986. For the series, the Yanks ere led by Jeter (5 for 11, .455) and Williams (4 for 11, .364). I;n 1998, versus the Yankees, Texas managed to hit only .141 and in 1999, could not fare much better, going 14 for 92 (.152). The really unusual stat is that the Rangers, for the second year in a row, could muster but one run in exactly 27 innings (0.33 ERA!) against Yankee pitching. From this vantage point, it sounds like it was, in fact, deja vu all over again! The Rangers' 1999 season was at an end and the Yankees would continue their title quest, incredibly (as Cleveland had been heavily favored to defeat Boston in their series) against their bitter rival, the Boston Red Sox. The Yankees would be making their eighth appearance in the American League Championship Series, while the Red Sox would be making their fifth trip to the ALCS and their first since 1990.

```
Game 1 at Yankee Stadium, NY, October  5
TEX      0 0 0   0 0 0   0 0 0 - 0   2   1
NY       0 1 0   0 2 4   0 1 x - 8  10   0
W—Hernandez; L—Sele; HR—BWilliams (NY).        A.—57,099

Game 2 at Yankee Stadium, NY, October  6
TEX      0 0 0   1 0 0   0 0 0 - 1   7   0
NY       0 0 0   0 1 0   1 1 x - 3   7   2
W—Pettitte; L—Helling; HR—Gonzalez (TEX).      A.—57,485

Game 3 at The Ballpark at Arlington, TX, October  8
NY       3 0 0   0 0 0   0 0 0 - 3   6   0
TEX      0 0 0   0 0 0   0 0 0 - 0   5   1
W—Clemens; L—Loaiza; HR—Strawberry (NY).       A.—50,269
```

CHAMPIONSHIP SERIES

There has been a resigned anticipation for many years among the fans of the Red Sox and Yankees relating to their respective clubs duking it out in some sort of playoff series. But now, in 1999, the culmination of many years of hoping finally came to fruition with the Yanks and Red Sox squaring off against each other, not in a one-game playoff, but in a best-of-seven venue—the League Championship Series.

The Yanks would be playing in their eighth LCS (6-1), with an American League-best winning percentage of .645 (20-11) in overall games played. Coming into their fifth LCS, the Red Sox had played in 18 LCS games, winning but seven. The BoSox had earned a trip to the postseason, clinching their wild-card berth on September 29. They finished the season with a respectable 94-68 record, four full games behind the Yankees. In their Division Series versus Cleveland, the Indians took a 2-0 lead against the Red Sox in the series, then Boston proceeded to win the next three, to clinch a shot at the Yankees in the LCS. In those last three Red Sox victories, they won by the scores of 9-3, 23-7 (!!) and 12-8, outscoring the Tribe 44-18! (Was this the own Red Sox updated version of the 1978 "Boston Massacre," when the Yankees came to Fenway to destroy Boston in a devastating three-game sweep—but now it was Boston's turn to do the massacring?!) In that Game 4 rout at Fenway on October 10, the Boston run total (23) shattered the previous postseason mark by a club set by (you guessed it!) the Yankees (18), in an October 2, 1936 World Series game versus the New York Giants. The Red Sox set seven additional team and individual marks for postseason play. With their offensive prowess now in evidence, they were primed to face their longtime rival, the New York Yankees. With this series now on the horizon, renewed stories of "The Curse of the Bambino" emerged anew. (A great book bearing this title is a must read;

it was penned by veteran sports columnist Dan Shaughnessy and is in its umpteenth printing!). There are some of us Yankee people who believe that this "curse," as the story goes, was placed on the Red Sox after they traded Babe Ruth to the Yankees in January 1920. Since that Ruth trade, the Red Sox have been in the World Series four times (1946, 1967, 1975 and 1986), losing all four; conversely, the Yankees have been in 35 World Series since 1921, winning 24 of them. Prior to the Ruth sale, the Bostons had won all five World Series in which they had participated, including the first ever way back in 1903, when they were known as the Pilgrims! Ruth's presence as a great left-handed pitcher was a force to be reckoned with in their World Series victories in 1916 and 1918. That year, 1918, was the year that the Red Sox last won a World Series! Curse or no curse, it sure is interesting to speculate about, isn't it?

The first two games of the LCS were played at Yankee Stadium, October 13 and 14. In the first encounter, Boston lefty, Kent Mercker, was pitted against Yankee postseason ace, Orlando "El Duque" Hernandez. The BoSox would jump out to a 3-0 lead after two innings. Scoring runs against Hernandez has been as scarce as hen's teeth. Boston's runs were scored on singles and a Derek Jeter throwing error. The Yankees would answer with two runs in the bottom of the second on a two-run homer by Scott Brosius, trimming Boston's lead to one at 3-2. Starter Mercker would leave the game after four, making way for other Boston pitchers. The contest would remain scoreless until the Yankee seventh, when the game would be tied, thanks to a Derek Jeter single. Hernandez pitched through the eighth, allowing two earned runs. Torre brought Mariano Rivera in to pitch the ninth, the game remaining a deadlock after nine full. In the Boston tenth, Rivera retired the side in order. There was a controversial play in the inning that probably victimized Boston. On the play, Jose Offerman was ruled out at second, even though Yankee second sacker Chuck Knoblauch clearly did not have control of the ball. The Yanks would escape the top of the tenth without the Red Sox scoring a run. For Boston, ill-fated Rod Beck came in to pitch the New York tenth, and after taking one strike, Bernie Williams launched a walk-off game-winning homer to center, his 11th roundtripper in the postseason! The Yanks won 4-3 in ten to go up in the series, 1-0. Mariano Rivera notched the victory for the Bombers, who had rallied from a 3-0 deficit to again come away a winner.

Game 2 of the LCS was played in the Bronx on October 14. David "Mr. Perfect" Cone, working on 12 days' rest, would pitch for the New Yorkers, while Ramon J. Martinez, brother of teammate Pedro, would be on the hill for Boston. It was a pitchers' duel, with neither club being able to muster a run, until the Yankees broke through with a solo run in their fourth inning on a solo homer to right by Tino Martinez. Boston would take the lead in the top of the fifth on a two-run home run by Nomar Garciaparra. The game remained in favor of the Red Sox till the seventh, when the Yankees took the lead at 3-2. The Yankee runs came on a Knoblauch double and a Paul O'Neill bloop single. Cone pitched seven full innings (eventually getting the win), striking out nine Red Sox along the way. Boston pitcher Ramon Martinez pitched into the seventh and was eventually charged with the defeat. The game was won in the Boston eighth as Torre used four different Yankee pitchers in succession in a masterful strategy that worked to perfection:

Mike Stanton (faced one batter), Jeff Nelson (two batters), Allen Watson (one batter) and Ramiro Mendoza (two batters). Those four pitchers would allow one hit and one walk and strike out one...but more importantly, they denied Boston any runs. The Boston ninth made way for you know who: Mariano Rivera. It got a little tense there as Mariano allowed two hits and with two outs and Garciaparra the tying run at third, Rivera struck out Damon Buford to win the game for the Yanks, 3-2. David Cone got the victory (and Ramon Martinez the loss), Mariano had yet another save, and for the second straight day, the Yanks had rallied from a deficit to win their game. The Red Sox stranded 13 men on base during the contest. The Yanks were up on the BoSox, 2-0 in the series, which then shifted to venerable Fenway Park for the middle three games. However, in the third game, they would be facing the best pitcher in all of baseball, Pedro Martinez.

Games 3, 4 and 5 were played at Fenway, October 16, 17 and 18. In Game 3, the great Pedro, who earlier this season at Yankee Stadium on September 10, had struck out a franchise-record 17 batters, would face Roger Clemens. Roger, obtained from Toronto in the offseason, was making his return to the revered ballpark where he pitched as a member of the Red Sox team for 13 seasons (1984 through 1996). This was a game that the Yankees figured they probably would not win—and they were right as the Boston club knocked out Clemens after two innings, scoring five runs (all earned) off of his pitching morsels. Pedro, on the other hand, was using the game as a pitching clinic, eventually allowing two hits and two walks, no runs, and striking out 12 Yankee batters in seven full innings of work! Wow and double WOW!! The Yankees were pummeled by the Red Sox, who had 21 total hits, winning in grand style, 13-1! Pedro Martinez picked up the well-deserved win, John Valentin went 3-for-6 with five RBIs, and Garciaparra contributed with a 4-for-5 day with three RBIs! The only run scored by the Yankees in the game was a solo homer to left by Scott Brosius in the eighth inning. The loss for the Yankees was their 100th in postseason play, dating back to 1921. Among those defeats are: 79 in the World Series, nine in the Division Series and now their 12th in League Championship Series play, for a total of 100! That is truly an amazing statistic—think about it, the Yankees have lost more postseason games than most teams have played postseason games! As it turned out, this loss would be their final one for the remainder of the postseason! Boy, hindsight sure is wonderful!

In Game 4 on October 17, Yankee lefty Andy Pettitte would face 15-year veteran Bret Saberhagen. Bret, who started pitching for the Royals in 1984, when they had a major-league team, last appeared in the LCS in 1985. He was the winning pitcher of Game 7 of the I-70 World Series versus the St. Louis Cardinals. For his two victories, Bret was named MVP for that Series. Back to Game 4, each club traded runs in the second frame, the Yankees scoring on a solo shot by Darryl Strawberry to right. The Red Sox took the lead in their half of the third, and the Yankees countered with two in the fourth, now having a 3-2 lead. Saberhagen (the loser to be) was done after six, allowing three runs, only one of which was earned—but, as they say, they all count! Pettitte (the winner to be) would pitch into the eighth, having allowed two runs, while striking out five. In the Red Sox eighth, another controversial call (the

second of the series) did not go Boston's way. On the play (or non-play), Jose Offerman, with one out, was ruled out at second by Tim Tschida, the second-base umpire. Replays showed ad nauseam that second baseman Chuck Knoblauch did not tag out Offerman, and Knoblauch threw on to first to complete the double play, thus ending any Boston threat. An instant-replay procedure would have reversed the umpire's erroneous call—but hey, who wants instant replay in baseball anyway? Red Sox Manager Jimy Williams was eventually ejected following another disputed play at first, and Fenway fans started venting their collective frustration by throwing objects onto the field. With the situation truly becoming ugly and Yankee players being placed in harm's way, plate umpire Al Clark ordered the Yankees off the field. When order was felt to be restored after an eight-minute delay, the game resumed. The story of the game and of the series is summed up by the six-run Yankee uprising in the top of the ninth. In a short period, Fenway Park had been transformed from a noisy ballpark to a morgue for the Red Sox! In that ninth frame, Ricky Ledee blasted a pinch-hit grand slam to center, scoring O'Neill, Williams and Martinez ahead of him. The other two runs were scored on an Offerman throwing error and a single by Williams. The Red Sox were demoralized by a truly great team that came away as a 9-2 victor and, more importantly, had taken a commanding 3-1 lead in the series. The Yankees were just one win shy of their 36th World Series appearance. It wasn't any bad calls that did in the Red Sox, (to paraphrase the last line of the great movie "King Kong") "it was Yankees that killed the Sox!"

On October 18, Game 5 of the LCS would again be played at Boston's Fenway Park. The ceremonial first pitch was thrown out by Julia Ruth Stevens, Babe Ruth's daughter. First-game starters, Orlando Hernandez for the Yanks and Boston's Kent Mercker, would again be matched. The Yanks drew first blood, scoring two in their first at bat on a two-run blast to center by Derek Jeter. Hernandez had his best stuff working, holding Boston without a run for his seven full innings pitched. El Duque allowed five hits, walked four and struck out nine Red Sox batters. For his efforts, Orlando was rewarded with not only the victory, but also, the ALCS MVP Award. Well, let's not get ahead of ourselves... The Red Sox scored their only run in the eighth, on a Jason Varitek home run. The Yanks added two each in the seventh and ninth stanzas. In the ninth, Jorge Posada added salt to the Red Sox wounds with a two-run homer to conclude the Yankee scoring. Leaders in the series included Jose Offerman (.458, 11 for 24) and Garciaparra (.400, 8 for 20) for Boston. Pedro Martinez of the Red Sox led his pitchers with 12 strikeouts. The Red Sox added much to their own downfall, by committing an LCS-record ten errors in the five games. For the Yankees, who won the series four games to one, Derek Jeter (.350, seven for 20) and Chuck Knoblauch (.333, 6 for 18) were two of several batting stars. For Yankee pitchers, Mariano Rivera shone brightly again with his two saves and a victory and LCS MVP, Orlando Hernandez, was masterful in two contests, winning one, striking out 13 and allowing three earned runs in 15 full innings, an ERA of 1.80!

The Yankees were American League Champions for the 36th time and prepared for yet another visit to the World Series. As for the Red Sox, well, a group of Yankee fans were spotted at Fenway holding up a sign that said "The Curse Gets

Worse." If one was, indeed, a loyal Red Sox fan, it must have been the ultimate slap in the face for those dreaded Yankees to come to Fenway and clinch their AL pennant there! As a loyal Yankee fan (through thick and thin) for most of my 50 years, this writer thought of the Yankee clinching at Fenway and was reminded of that beer slogan: "It doesn't get any better than this!" When this fifth game was finished, the Mets were still in the running for the World Series. But the Mets' dream season would come to a close on October 19, in Game 6 versus Atlanta, the Braves winning in 11 innings, 10-9. In the game, the Mets, at one point were down 5-0 but stormed back to tie the game at seven-all in their half of the seventh inning. They would take the lead, 8-7, with a solo run in the eighth, but the Braves tied the game at eight in their half of the eighth. The Mets lost on a bases-loaded walk in the 11th, Gerald Williams scoring the winning run! Although denied a subway series, New Yorkers were rewarded by the gutsy and resilient play of a Mets team that forced Atlanta into the seventh and final game of their League Championship Series! Congratulations are in order to the Mets for a spectacular season! Let's say for 2000: "Bring on the Mets!" The Yankees were now poised for the start of their 36th World Series and third in the last four seasons.

Game 1 at Yankee Stadium, NY, October 13 (10 INNINGS)
```
BOS     2  1  0   0  0  0   0  0  0   0  -  3   8   3
NY      0  2  0   0  0  0   1  0  0   1  -  4  10   1
```
W—Rivera; L—Beck; HR—Brosius (NY), BWilliams (NY).
A.—57,181

Game 2 at Yankee Stadium, NY, October 14
```
BOS     0  0  0   0  2  0   0  0  0   -  2  10   0
NY      0  0  0   1  0  0   2  0  x   -  3   7   0
```
W—Cone; L—RMartinez; HR—Garciaparra (BOS), TMartinez (NY).
A.—57,180

Game 3 at Fenway Park, MA, October 16
```
NY      0  0  0   0  0  0   0  1  0   -   1   3   3
BOS     2  2  2   0  2  1   4  0  x   -  13  21   1
```
W—PMartinez; L—Clemens; HR—Brosius (NY), Valentin(BOS), Daubach (BOS), Garciaparra (BOS).
A.—33,190

Game 4 at Fenway Park, MA, October 17
```
NY      0  1  0   2  0  0   0  0  6   -  9  11   0
BOS     0  1  1   0  0  0   0  0  0   -  2  10   4
```
W—Pettitte; L—Saberhagen; HR—Strawberry (NY),Ledee (NY).
A.—33,586

Game 5 at Fenway Park, MA, October 19
```
NY      2  0  0   0  0  0   2  0  2   -  6  11   1
BOS     0  0  0   0  0  0   0  1  0   -  1   5   2
```
W—Hernandez; L—Mercker; HR—Jeter (NY), Posada (NY),Valentin (BOS).
A.—33,589

2000

DIVISION SERIES

Despite ending the 2000 regular season on a seven-game losing bender, the aging—and apparently vulnerable—New York Yankees remained a force to be reckoned with. Waiting for them in the divisional playoffs was a young and feisty Oakland A's club that had surprised many observers, who hadn't expected them to be this good, this soon. But thanks to an incredible September in which he batted .400, walloped 13 homers, drove in 32 runs, and slugged .800, American League MVP Jason Giambi personally made sure that Oakland would get first crack at unseating the Big Apple's two-time defending world champions—before the Yankees could even get as far as the World Series.

Frankly, the Bronx Bombers didn't look the part anymore. Second baseman Chuck Knoblauch could still field grounders, but every time he threw the ball to first baseman Tino Martinez, the folks in the box seats along the first-base line were prepared to duck. Outfielder Paul O'Neill was a year older and wiser, but he was hurting, and his best days were behind him. Shane Spencer, who had been a playoff wonder the previous two years, was a nonfactor because of a gimpy knee.

During the regular season, the Yankees' pitching staff had been relatively mediocre: David Cone (4-14, 6.91 ERA) wasn't even a shadow of his former self; Andy Pettitte won 19 games, but his 4.35 ERA was nothing to shout about; Roger Clemens finished with the lowest ERA of all the starters on the staff (3.70), but he still suffered from occasional control problems and posted only 13 victories; and Orlando "El Duque" Hernandez went 12-13 with a 4.51 ERA. The mainstays and saviors on the

hill were setup man Jeff Nelson (8-4, 2.45) and closer Mariano Rivera (7-4, 2.85, 36 saves). Come playoff time, the Yanks' pitching staff hardly inspired confidence.

Offensively, Derek Jeter, Bernie Williams, Jorge Posada, and newcomers David Justice and Glenallen Hill supplied the bulk of the speed, defense, and pop—but not nearly as much as in years past.

Yet, here they were again; and again, there they went. Even though the Yankees—who finished the season with a so-so 87 wins (fifth best in the AL)—didn't look like a good bet to win their third consecutive world championship (a feat that hadn't been accomplished since 1972–74, when the Oakland A's

Reliever Mariano Rivera's remarkable streak of shutout innings in the postseason reached 33 1/3, breaking Whitey Ford's long-standing record of 33 consecutive scoreless innings. (Bill Kostroum, AP/Wide World Photos)

won three in a row), they managed once again to scrap their way to the top.

Their first obstacle, Oakland, held the home-field advantage in the first round of the playoffs and won the series opener, 5-3, beating Clemens. But Pettitte and Rivera combined to shut out the A's, 4-0, in Game 2, sending the series to New York knotted at 1-1. Perhaps the turning point of the entire postseason for the Yankees was a bloop single by Glenallen Hill that broke the scoreless tie in that contest. Not only did it give the Yanks a lead they never relinquished, but it also changed the momentum of a team that had just lost its eighth consecutive game the previous day. Luis Sojo followed with a two-run double, just to make sure.

Thanks to a strong outing by El Duque, who upped his postseason record to 6-0 (and lowered his postseason ERA to 1.24), the Yankees won Game 3, 4-2, back at Yankee Stadium. It was the Yankees' 10th consecutive postseason triumph at home. Mariano Rivera recorded his second save of the series while, at the same time, extending his postseason scoreless streak to 29 innings. Bernie Williams went 1-for-3 to improve his career divisional-series hit total to 27. Interestingly, the popular Sojo, whom the Yankees had reacquired Aug. 7 (this time via a trade with Pittsburgh), was the offensive hero in Game 3, doubling and driving home two runs.

Despite having Clemens on the mound in Game 4, the Yankees got shellacked, 11-1. Barry Zito earned the win for Oakland, which set a team record for the greatest margin of victory in a postseason game. Olmedo Saenz clubbed a three-run homer off Clemens in the first inning, and it was all downhill from there.

Although the fifth and deciding game was played in Oakland, the Yankees erupted for six runs in the top of the first—thanks in part to three RBIs by Tino Martinez off starter Gil Heredia—and cruised to a 7-5 triumph. Rivera earned the save and stretched his postseason scoreless streak to 31 2/3 innings.

```
Game 1 at Oakland Coliseum, OAK, October 3
NY      0  2  0   0  0  1   0  0  0  -   3   7  0
OAK     0  2  0   0  0  0   1  0  0  -   5  10  2
W—Heredia; L—Clemens.
A.—47,360

Game 2 at Oakland Coliseum, OAK, October 4
NY      0  0  0   0  0  3   0  0  1  -  4  8  1
OAK     0  0  0   0  0  0   2  0  0  -  0  6  1
W—Pettitte; L—Appier.
A.—47,860

Game 3 at Yankee Stadium, NY, October 6
OAK     0  1  0   0  1  1   0  0  0  -  2  4  2
NY      0  2  0   1  0  0   0  1  x  -  4  6  1
W—O. Hernandez; L—Hudson; HR—Long (OAK).
A.—56,606

Game 4 at Yankee Stadium, NY, October 7
OAK     3  0  0   0  0  3   0  1  4  -  11  11  0
NY      0  0  0   0  0  1   0  0  0  -   1   8  0
W—Zito; L—Clemens; HR—Saenz (OAK).
A.—56,915

Game 5 at Oakland Coliseum, OAK, October 8
NY      6  0  0   1  0  0   0  0  0  -  7  12  0
OAK     0  2  1   2  0  0   0  1  0  -  5  13  0
W—Stanton; L—Heredia; HR—Justice (NY).
A.—41,170
```

CHAMPIONSHIP SERIES

Now, with the A's out of the way, New York returned to Yankee Stadium to prepare for wild-card Seattle in the ALCS. This series represented the first time the two clubs had met in the postseason since 1995, when the Mariners knocked off the Yankees in five games. Not only did the Yankees have the Mariners in their sights, but they were also getting a whiff of a potential Subway Series with the National League's New York Mets. (The Mets had dispensed with San Francisco in their divisional playoff and were looking to knock off St. Louis in the NLCS.)

After getting shut out by Freddy Garcia in Game 1, 2-0, with an RBI single by Rickey Henderson and a solo homer by Alex Rodriguez providing the necessary ammo, the Yankees spotted the Mariners a one-run lead in Game 2. But sparked by a home run off the bat of Derek Jeter and a 3-for-5 performance by Martinez (raising his 2000 postseason batting average to .444), the Yankees exploded for seven runs in the bottom of the eighth to win, 7-1, and tie the series at one win apiece behind the pitching of Hernandez, who chalked up his second win of the playoffs. The victory also extended El Duque's overall postseason winning streak to seven games, as he went eight innings, gave up six hits, and fanned seven.

Game 3, at Safeco Field in Seattle, saw more of the same. The Yankees broke open a tight game with four runs in the top of the ninth and won, 8-2, to take a 2-1 series lead. Pettitte got the win, and Bernie Williams and Tino Martinez each went downtown. Mariano Rivera threw 1 2/3 innings of scoreless relief, raising his postseason total to 33 1/3 consecutive innings of shutout pitching, breaking former Yankee Whitey Ford's record of 33 scoreless innings from 1960 to 1962.

In Game 4, Clemens was simply overpowering, pitching a one-hitter and getting home run support from Jeter and David Justice in a 5-0 victory that put the Yankees one victory away from a third consecutive trip to the World Series. The fans in Seattle witnessed an eye-popping performance by Clemens, who set an ALCS record by striking out 15 batters in nine innings.

After succumbing to Seattle's Garcia again—this time 6-2 in Game 5—the Yankees returned home and rocked Seattle, 9-7, to claim the American League pennant. New York trailed, 4-3, after four innings, but David Justice homered and drove in three runs, and the Yankees tallied six times in the bottom of the seventh and withstood a late rally by the Mariners to nail down the triumph. Rivera's record postseason scoreless streak came to an end in the eighth inning, when he finally surrendered a run. Justice, who raised his postseason RBI total to nine, earned ALCS MVP honors.

Game 1 at Yankee Stadium, NY, October 10
```
SEA   0 0 0   0 1 1   0 0 0  - 2  5  0
NY    0 0 0   0 0 0   0 0 0  - 0  6  1
```
W—Garcia; L—Neagle; HR—A. Rodriguez (SEA).
A.—54,481

Game 2 at Yankee Stadium, NY, October 11
```
SEA   0 0 1   0 0 0   0 0 0  - 1  7  2
NY    0 0 0   0 0 0   0 7 x  - 7 14  0
```
W—O. Hernandez; L—Rhodes; HR—Jeter (NY).
A.—55,317

Game 3 at Safeco Field, SEA, October 13
```
NY    0 2 1   0 0 1   0 0 4  - 8 13  0
SEA   1 0 0   0 1 0   0 0 0  - 2 10  1
```
W—Pettitte; L—Sele; HR—B. Williams (NY).
A.—47,827

Game 4 at Safeco Field, SEA, October 14
```
NY    0 0 0   0 3 3   0 2 0  - 5  5  0
SEA   0 0 0   0 0 0   0 0 0  - 0  1  0
```
W—Clemens; L—Abbott; HR—Jeter (NY), Justice (NY).
A.—47,803

Game 5 at Safeco Field, SEA, October 15
```
NY    0 0 0   2 0 0   0 0 0  - 2  8  0
SEA   1 0 0   0 5 0   0 0 x  - 6  8  0
```
W—Garcia; L—Neagle; HR—E. Martinez (SEA), Olerud (SEA).
A.—47,802

Game 6 at Yankee Stadium, NY, October 17
```
SEA   2 0 0   2 0 0   0 3 0  - 7 10  0
NY    0 0 0   3 0 0   6 0 x  - 9 11  0
```
W—O. Hernandez; L—Paniagua; HR—Guillen (SEA), A. Rodriguez (SEA), Justice
(NY).
A.—56,598

2001

DIVISION SERIES

The Oakland Athletics were again the divisional series opponent for the Yankees in 2001. The A's had been pretty much out of the race most of the season until a late rush secured them the AL Wild Card spot. Oakland matched up quite well with the Yankees in the final AL team statistics by finishing just ahead of New York in both batting and pitching. Joe Torre had Mariano Rivera as his closer, and Art Howe would not hesitate to bring in Jason Isringhausen to finish a game.

In Game 1, Roger Clemens departed in the fifth inning due to a tight hamstring. Terrence Long ripped two long home runs, and Isringhausen came on to record a save as the A's prevailed, 5-3.

In a seemingly must win, the Yankees could not get the bats going in Game 2 and left Yankee Stadium reeling from a 2-0 loss. They would have to win the next two games in Oakland to get another game back in Yankee Stadium. Jorge Posada homered in the fifth inning of Game 3, and Derek Jeter made an amazing backhand relay flip to nail a surprised Jeremy Giambi at the plate as he tried to score the tying run in the seventh inning. Rivera picked up another postseason save as the Yankees held off elimination with a tense 1-0 victory.

No such drama in Game 4, but it did take four hours and 13 minutes for New York to rough up the A's for 11 hits in a 9-2 win. It was back across the nation to the Bronx for Game 5. After spotting Oakland a 2-0 lead, the Yankees completed their miraculous playoff comeback by winning, 5-3. The Yankees became the first team in Major League Baseball history to win a best of five series after losing the first two games at home.

Game 1 at Yankee Stadium, NY, October 10
```
OAK   1 0 0   1 0 0   1 2 0  - 5 10  1
NY    0 0 0   0 1 0   0 2 0  - 3 10  1
```
W—Mulder; L—Clemens; HR—Long 2 (OAK), J. Giambi (OAK),
T. Martinez (NY).
A.—56,697

Game 2 at Yankee Stadium, NY, October 11
```
OAK   0 0 0   1 0 0   0 0 1  - 2 10  0
NY    0 0 0   0 0 0   0 0 0  - 0  7  0
```
W—Hudson; L—Pettitte; HR—Gant (OAK).
A.—56,684

Game 3 at Oakland Coliseum, OAK, October 13
```
NY    0 0 0   0 1 0   0 0 0  - 1  2  0
OAK   0 0 0   0 0 0   0 1 0  - 0  6  1
```
W—Mussina; L—Zito; HR—Posada (NY).
A.—55,861

Game 4 at Oakland Coliseum, OAK, October 14
```
NY    0 2 2   3 0 0   0 0 2  - 9 11  1
OAK   0 0 2   0 0 0   0 0 0  - 2 11  1
```
W—O. Hernandez; L—Lidle.
A.—43,681

Game 5 at Yankee Stadium, NY, October 15
```
OAK   1 1 0   0 1 0   0 0 0  - 3  7  3
NY    0 2 1   1 0 1   0 0 x  - 5 10  0
```
W—Stanton; L—Mulder; HR—Justice (NY).
A.—56,642

CHAMPIONSHIP SERIES

When the Yankees won 114 regular-season games in 1998, it was said by baseball purists that their win record would last for a very long time. After all, it took the Yankees 44 years to best the victory mark set by the 1954 Cleveland Indians. No one bothered to explain this historical fact to the Seattle Mariners as they won 116 games in the 2001 regular season. With only 46 losses, Lou Piniella's squad had watched in past seasons as Randy Johnson, Ken Griffey, Jr., and Alex Rodriguez departed from the team either via a forced trade or free agency, and then they amazingly got stronger, especially with outstanding play on the road in 2001. The Mariners were at the top of the league in both hitting and pitching, but they appeared a bit shaky in their divisional series victory over Cleveland. But so did the Yankees against Oakland in the first two games of their ALDS.

Now it was off to Seattle's Safeco Field, where the Yankees had played so well in the 2000 ALCS. No change from that again as the Yankees took the first two games by 4-2 and 3-2 scores. Mariano Rivera saved Game 1 for Andy Pettitte and Game 2 for Muke Mussina. Maybe an ALCS sweep was in the works, but the Mariners blasted the Yankees, 14-3, in Game 3 at Yankee Stadium to put an end to that thought. Former Yankee Jay Buhner blasted a pinch-hit homer in Game 3 that carried into the center field "batters eye" section. It was the first postseason dinger to get to that area of Yankee Stadium since Reggie Jackson did it in the 1977 World Series. The Yankees did not want this ALCS to go back to Safeco Field–though, so they proceeded to knock off the Mariners in the next two games by scores of 3-1 and 12-3.

Game 4 was another thrilling postseason win for the Yankees! Bret Boone homered to give Seattle a 1-0 lead in the eighth inning, but Bernie Williams tied the score with a home run in the bottom of the eighth. In the bottom of the ninth,

Alfonso Soriano hit a two-run "walk-off" homer off Kazuhiro Sasaki to win the game. It was the sixth game-ending home run in ALCS history and the Yankees now have four of them. Game 5 was over early as the Yankees were ahead 9-0 after six innings in cruising to the 12-3 final score. The Mariners did win a total of 120 games in 2001, but they had little to show for it as the Yankees prepared for another World Series competition.

```
Game 1 at Safeco Field, SEA, October 17
NY    0 1 0   2 0 0   0 0 1 - 4 9 0
SEA   0 0 0   0 1 0   0 0 1 - 2 4 0
W—Pettitte; L—Sele; HR—O'Neill (NY).
A.—47,644

Game 2 at Safeco Field, SEA, October 18
NY    0 0 3   0 0 0   0 0 0 - 3 9 1
SEA   0 0 0   2 0 0   0 0 0 - 2 6 0
W—Mussina; L—Garcia; HR—Javier (SEA).
A.—47,791

Game 3 at Yankee Stadium, NY, October 20
SEA   0 0 0   0 2 7   2 1 2 - 14 15 0
NY    0 0 0   0 0 0   0 1 0 - 3 7 2
W—Moyer; L—O. Hernandez; HR—Olerud (SEA), Boone (SEA),
Buhner (SEA), B. Williams (NY).
A.—56,517

Game 4 at Yankee Stadium, NY, October 21
SEA   0 0 0   0 0 0   0 1 0 - 1 2 0
NY    0 0 0   0 0 0   0 1 2 - 3 4 0
W—Rivera; L—Sasaki; HR-Boone (SEA), B. Williams (NY), Soriano (NY).
A.—56,375

Game 5 at Yankee Stadium, NY, October 22
SEA   0 0 0   0 0 0   3 0 0 - 3 9 1
NY    0 0 4   1 0 4   0 3 x - 12 13 1
W—Pettitte; L—Sele; HR—B. Williams (NY, O'Neill (NY), T. Martinez (NY).
A.—56,370
```

2002

DIVISION SERIES

With 103 regular-season victories and so much playoff experience in the starting lineup, the Yankees felt that they could handle just about any team in the AL to begin a quest for another World Series title. Their 2002 division series opponents were the Anaheim Angels, and the last time the Angels had even talked about a playoff was in 1995. That season the Angels blew a big lead and then lost a one-game tie-breaking playoff game to Randy Johnson and the Mariners. Prior to that the Angels had appeared in the ALCS three times and each time they went back to sunny California a loser. But now they were in a divisional series for the first time since the late Gene Autry acquired the franchise back in 1960 to begin play in the AL in 1961. Former Dodger catcher Mike Scioscia had lit a fire under his team after an early-season slump, and they responded with 99 wins to edge out Seattle and Boston for the AL Wild Card spot.

The Angels were fourth in batting and second in pitching, so they were ready to give notice to baseball that it was time for the loser label to fall from their franchise. The Yankees eked

out Game 1, 8-5, in the bottom of the eighth inning as the Anaheim relief pitching failed and the Angels team seemed flustered by the raucous Yankee Stadium playoff atmosphere. But that was the last moment of playoff glory for the Yankees in 2002. The Angels blasted four home runs in Game 2 to win, 8-6 and headed back to Anaheim with the series tied at one game each.

The Yankees opened up a 6-1 lead in Game 3 by the top of the third inning when the Angels simply dug in and answered their fans' call for the "Rally Monkey" to appear. They came back to beat the Yankees, 9-6, and then eliminated New York the next night with an eight spot in the fifth inning, to win 9-5 and advance to the ALCS.

This time it was the Yankees heading home after a 100-plus victory season. The Angels batted .376 for the series and had 19 extra base hits in the four games. The Yankees' ERA for the four games was a staggering 8.21 with the Angels' staff not faring much better at 6.17. The good pitching that stops good hitting in the postseason simply did not materialize in this series, with the Angels having six players hit over .385 for the series.

Game 1 at Yankee Stadium, NY, October 1
```
ANA   0 0 1   0 2 1   0 1 0  - 5 12 0
NY    1 0 0   2 1 0   0 4 x  - 8  8 1
```
W—Karsay; L—Weber; HR—Glaus 2 (ANA), Jeter (NY), J. Giambi (NY), White (NY), B. Williams (NY).
A.—56,710

Game 2 at Yankee Stadium, NY, October 2
```
ANA   1 2 1   0 0 0   0 3 1  - 8 17 1
NY    0 0 1   2 0 2   0 0 1  - 6 12 1
```
W—Rodriguez; L—O. Hernandez; HR—Salmon (ANA), Spiezio (ANA), Anderson (ANA), Glaus (ANA), Jeter (NY), Soriano (NY).
A.—56,695

Game 3 at Edison Field, ANA, October 4
```
NY    3 0 3   0 1 0   0 0 0  - 6  6 0
ANA   0 1 2   1 0 1   1 3 x  - 9 12 0
```
W—Rodriguez; L—Stanton; HR—Kennedy (ANA), Salmon (ANA).
A.—45,072

Game 4 at Edison Field, ANA, October 5
```
NY    0 1 0   0 1 1   1 0 1  - 5 12 2
ANA   0 0 1   0 8 0   0 0 x  - 9 15 1
```
W—Washburn; L—Wells; HR—Wooten (ANA), Posada (NY).
A.—45,067

DIVISION SERIES
INDIVIDUAL RECORDS

Player records are for the American League Division Series (ALDS). All are major-league records unless noted by (AL), which limits record to the American League.

BATTING

Highest Batting Average, Series
    4-Game Series—.467, BERNIE WILLIAMS, 1996 (1 Other)

Most At-Bats, Series
    5-Game Series—24, DON MATTINGLY 24, 1995 (1 Other)

Most Runs, Career
    29-BERNIE WILLIAMS (8 Series, 33 Games)

Most Hits 2 Consecutive Series
    16-BERNIE WILLIAMS 1995 (9), 1996 (7)

Most Singles, Series
    4-Game Series—6 DEREK JETER, 1996 (1 Other)

Most Doubles, Series
    3-Game Series—2 PAUL O'NEILL, 1998
    TINO MARTINEZ, 1998, RICKY LEDEE, 1999 (1 Other)
    5-Game Series—4 DON MATTINGLY, 1995

Most Home Runs, Series
    3-Game Series—2 SHANE SPENCER, 1998

Most Home Runs, Game-2
    BERNIE WILLIAMS (Twice)
    October 6, 1995; October 5, 1996 (Many Others)

Most Grand Slams, Game-1
    PAUL O'NEILL, October 4, 1997, 4th Inning (Many Others)

Hitting Home Runs From Both Sides of Plate, Game
    BERNIE WILLIAMS, October 6, 1995
    BERNIE WILLIAMS, October 5, 1996
    (Bernie is the only player to do this in postseason play—and he did it twice!)

Hitting Home Run in First Division Series at-bat
    SHANE SPENCER, September 30, 1998, 2nd Inning (5 Others)

Total Bases, Career-68
    BERNIE WILLIAMS, 8 Series, 33 Games

Most Extra-Base Hits, Career-18
    BERNIE WILLIAMS (11 doubles, 7 homers)

Most Runs Batted In, Career-26
    BERNIE WILLIAMS

Most Runs Batted In, Series
    3-Game Series-6 BERNIE WILLIAMS, 1999

Most Runs Batted In, Inning-4
    PAUL O'NEILL, October 4, 1997, 4th Inning (Many Others)

Most Walks, Career-22 (AL)
    BERNIE WILLIAMS

Most Walks
    5-Game Series-7 BERNIE WILLIAMS, 1995 (2 Others)

PITCHING

Most Saves, Career—11
    Mariano Rivera

Most Hits Allowed, Career—68
    Andy Pettitte

Most Home Runs Allowed, Career—7
    David Cone

FIELDING

First Baseman
Most Putouts, Series
    3-Game Series—29 Tino Martinez 1999

Most Putouts, Nine-Inning Game—16
    Tino Martinez, October 4, 2000

Second Baseman

Most Putouts, Series
   5-Game Series—15 Rey Sanchez, 1997

Most Putouts, Nine-Inning Game—8
   Rey Sanchez, October 4, 1997

Most Putouts, Extra-Inning Game—6
   Randy Velarde, October 4, 1995 (15 Innings)

Most Chances Accepted (Putouts and Assists), Errorless Series—29
   Rey Sanchez, 1997 (5-Game Series)

Third Baseman

Most Assists, Series
   3-Game Series—6 Scott Brosius, 1998 (2 Others)(AL)

Most Assists, Nine-Inning Game—5 (AL)
   Scott Brosius, October 4, 2000

Shortstops

Most Putouts, Career—47
   Derek Jeter, (7 series, 28 games)

Most Putouts, Series
   4-Game Series-Derek Jeter, 1996
   5-Game Series-Derek Jeter, 1997

Most Putouts, Game-5 (AL)
   Tony Fernandez, October 11, 1995 (11 Innings)(4 Others)

Most Chances Accepted (Putouts and Assists), Errorless Series—27 (AL)
   Derek Jeter, 1997

Most Double Plays Started, Game—2
   Tony Fernandez, October 6, 1995 (ML)

Outfielders

Most Putouts, Career—91
   Bernie Williams (8 Series, 33 Games)

Most Putouts, Series
   3-Game Series—15 Bernie Williams, 1999
   5-Game Series—15 Jerry Mumphrey, 1981

Most Putouts, Game (All Outfield Positions)—7
   Bernie Williams, October 5, 1999 (3 Others)

Most Putouts, Inning—3
   Bernie Williams, October 5, 1999 (3rd Inning-Centerfield)

Most Consecutive Errorless Games, Career—33
   Bernie Williams, October 3, 1995 through October 8, 2002

Most Chances Accepted (Putouts and Assists), Errorless Series—16
   Jerry Mumphrey, 1981, 5-Game Series (3 Others)

Catchers

Most Putouts, Series
   5-Game Series—42 Rick Cerone 1981

Most Putouts, Nine-Inning Game—15
   Rick Cerone, October 8, 1981 (1 Other)

Fewest Putouts, Game—1
   Rick Cerone, October 9, 1981
   Joe Girardi, October 4, 1997

Pitchers

Most Assists, Career—14
   Andy Pettitte (8 Series, 10 Games)

Most Assists, Series
   5-Game Series—5 Andy Pettitte, 1997

Most Assists, Game—4
   Andy Pettitte, October 6, 1997 (6 Others)

Most Assists, Inning—2
   Tommy John, October 9, 1981, 7th Inning
   Roger Clemens, October 7, 2000, 4th Inning

Most Chances Accepted (Putouts and Assists)—
   4-Roger Clemens, 2000, 3-Game Series
   6-Andy Pettitte, 1997, 5-Game Series

DIVISION SERIES TEAM RECORDS

BATTING
Most Games Played, Total Series—39 (Won 23, Lost 16)

Most At-Bats, Total Series—1328 (9 Series, 39 Games)

Most Runs, Total Series—177

Most Hits, Total Series—341

Most Singles, Total Series—228

Most Doubles, Total Series—67

Most Home Runs, Total Series—44

Most Home Runs, Series of Any Length—11
  vs. Seattle, 1995 (5 Games)

Most Home Runs, Game—4 (twice)
  vs. Seattle October 4, 1995 (15-Inning Game)
  vs. Cleveland September 30, 1997 (8 Other Clubs)

Most Home Runs, Inning—3
  vs. Cleveland (Consecutive) September 30,
  1997, 6th Inning (This is the only instance in postseason play that
  three consecutive home runs were hit in an inning)

Most Total Bases, Total Series—544

Most Extra-Base Hits, Total Series—115
  (67 Doubles, 4 Triples, 44 Home Runs)

Most Runs Batted in, Total Series—168

Most Walks, Total Series—134

Most Strikeouts, Total Series—243

PITCHING
Most Shutouts Won, Total Series—7

Most Consecutive Innings Shutting Out Opponent, Total Series—25
  vs. Texas, September 30 (6th Inning) 1998 through October 7 (3rd
  Inning) 1999

Most Innings Pitched, Total Series—355 $\frac{1}{3}$

Most Home Runs Allowed, Total Series—40

Largest Score, Shutout Game
  8-0 vs. Texas, October 5, 1999

Most Hits Allowed, Total series—343

Most Walks, Total Series—118

Most Strikeouts, Total Series—236

Most Saves, Total Series—16

FIELDING
Highest Fielding Average, Series
  3-Game Series—.991, 1998

Most Putouts, Total Series—1063

Most Putouts, Series
  4-Game Series—117, 1996

Most Putouts By Outfield, Game—13
  vs. Texas, October 5, 1999

Most Assists, Total Series—378

Most Assists, Nine-Inning Game—18
  vs. Milwaukee, October 9, 1981

Most Assists, Extra-Inning Game—21
  vs. Seattle, October 4, 1995, 15 Innings

Fewest Assists, Game—4
  vs. Milwaukee, October 11, 1981

Longest Errorless Game—15 Innings
  vs Seattle, October 4, 1995

Most Double Plays, Total Series—33

Most Double Plays, Series
  3-Game Series-5, 1999
  4-Game Series-6, 1997
  5-Game Series-7, 2000

GENERAL
Most Series Played: 9 (ML)—1981, 1995, 1996, 1997, 1998, 1999, 2000,
  2001, 2002

Most Series Won: 6 (AL)—1981, 1996, 1998, 1999, 2000, 2001

Most Times Winning Series in Three Consecutive Games: 2 (AL)—1998, 1999

Most Games Won, Total Series:
  23

Most Games Lost, Total Series:
  16

Longest Game: 15 innings (ML)
  YANKEES won 7-5 over Seattle at New York; October 4, 1995

Most Extra-inning Games, Total Series:
  3 (AL)

Most Extra-inning Games Won, Series:
  2 (AL)

Most Extra-inning Games, Total Series:
  5-games Series—2 (ML) New York vs. Seattle, 1995

Longest Nine-inning Game (by time): 4 hours, 13 minutes (ML)
  New York wins 9-2 at Oakland; October 14, 2001

Longest Extra-inning Game (by time): 5 hours, 13 minutes
  New York wins 7-5 at New York; October 4, 1995

Earliest Date for Series Game:
  September 29, 1998 (ML tied); Texas at New York

Largest Attendance, Series:
  3-game Series—164,853 (ML) vs. Texas, 1999
  5-game Series—286,839 (ML) vs. Seattle, 1995

Most Division Series Winners Managed: 5 (AL)
  JOE TORRE—1996, 1998, 1999, 2000, 2001

YANKEE PLAYER DIVISION SERIES SPECIAL ACHIEVEMENTS

HOME RUNS (44)

Date	Game	Player	Stadium
October 7, 1981	1	OSCAR GAMBLE	County Stadium
October 8, 1981	2	REGGIE JACKSON	County Stadium
October 8, 1981	2	LOU PINIELLA	County Stadium
October 11, 1981	5	REGGIE JACKSON	Yankee Stadium
October 11, 1981	5	OSCAR GAMBLE	Yankee Stadium
October 11, 1981	5	RICK CERONE	Yankee Stadium
October 3, 1995	1	WADE BOGGS	Yankee Stadium
October 3, 1995	1	RUBEN SIERRA	Yankee Stadium
October 4, 1995	2	PAUL O'NEILL	Yankee Stadium
October 4, 1995	2	RUBEN SIERRA	Yankee Stadium
October 4, 1995	2	DON MATTINGLY	Yankee Stadium
October 4, 1995	2	JIM LEYRITZ	Yankee Stadium
October 6, 1995	3	BERNIE WILLIAMS	The Kingdome
October 6, 1995	3	MIKE STANLEY	The Kingdome
October 7, 1995	4	PAUL O'NEILL	The Kingdome
October 8, 1995	5	PAUL O'NEILL	The Kingdome
October 2, 1996	2	CECIL FIELDER	Yankee Stadium
October 4, 1996	3	BERNIE WILLIAMS	Ballpark at Arlington
October 5, 1996	4	BERNIE WILLIAMS	Ballpark at Arlington
September 30, 1997	1	TIM RAINES	Yankee Stadium
September 30, 1997	1	DEREK JETER	Yankee Stadium
September 30, 1997	1	PAUL O'NEILL	Yankee Stadium
September 30, 1997	1	TINO MARTINEZ	Yankee Stadium
October 2, 1997	2	DEREK JETER	Yankee Stadium
October 4, 1997	3	PAUL O'NEILL	Yankee Stadium
September 30, 1998	2	SHANE SPENCER	Yankee Stadium
September 30, 1998	2	SCOTT BROSIUS	Yankee Stadium
October 2, 1998	3	PAUL O'NEILL	Ballpark at Arlington
October 2, 1998	3	SHANE SPENCER	Ballpark at Arlington
October 5, 1999	1	BERNIE WILLIAMS	Ballpark at Arlington
October 5, 1999	3	DARRYL STRAWBERRY	Ballpark at Arlington
October 8, 2000	5	DAVID JUSTICE	Oakland Coliseum
October 10, 2001	1	TINO MARTINEZ	Yankee Stadium
October 13, 2001	3	JORGE POSADA	Oakland Coliseum
October 15, 2001	5	DAVID JUSTICE	Yankee Stadium
October 1, 2002	1	DEREK JETER	Yankee Stadium
October 1, 2002	1	JASON GIAMBI	Yankee Stadium
October 1, 2002	1	RONDELL WHITE	Yankee Stadium
October 1, 2002	1	BERNIE WILLIAMS	Yankee Stadium
October 2, 2002	2	DEREK JETER	Yankee Stadium
October 2, 2002	2	ALFONSO SORIANO	Yankee Stadium
October 5, 2002	4	JORGE POSADA	Anaheim Stadium

Notes: On October 6, 1995, Bernie Williams became the first player in postseason history to hit home runs from both sides of the plate in the same game! He duplicated this feat the following season on October 5. Through the 1999 postseason, Bernie remains the only player in baseball history to accommplish this—and he did it TWICE! Also, on September 30, 1997, the Bronx Bombers became the first club ever to hit three consecutive home runs in the same inning in postseason play! In the sixth inning of that game versus Cleveland at Yankee Stadium, Tim Raines, Derek Jeter, and Paul O'Neill all connected with homers.

ALCS INDIVIDUAL RECORDS

Player records are American League Championship Series (ALCS) records.

BATTING

Most At-Bats, Single Series: 4-game Series—18; THURMAN MUNSON—1978 (2 others)

Most At-Bats, Single Series: 5-game Series—24; DEREK JETER—1996 (2 others)

Most Extra-Base Hits, Single Series: 3-game Series—4; BOB WATSON, 1980

Most Hits, Single Series: 5-game Series—11; CHRIS CHAMBLISS, 1976 (2 others)

Most Singles, Single Series: 4-game Series—6; CHRIS CHAMBLISS, 1978 (2 others)

Most Doubles, Single Series: 3-game Series—3; BOB WATSON, 1980

Most Home Runs, Single Series: 5-game Series—3; DARRYL STRAWBERRY, 1996 (1 other) BERNIEW WILLIAMS, 2001

Most Runs Batted In, Single Series: 3-game Series—9; GRAIG NETTLES, 1981 4-game Series—6; REGGIE JACKSON, 1978 6-game Series—8; DAVID JUSTICE, 2000

Highest Slugging Average, Single Series (10 or more at-bats): 3-game Series—.917; BOB WATSON, 1980, GRAIG NETTLES, 1981 (2 others) 5-game Series—1.167; DARRYL STRAWBERRY, 1996

Most Total Bases, Single Series: 5-game Series—20; CHRIS CHAMBLISS, 1976

Most At-Bats by Player with No Hits, Extra-inning Game: CHUCK KNOBLAUCH (YANKEES) October 3, 1998; 12 innings (1 other)

Most Times Reached Base Safely, Game (batting 1.000): 5 REGGIE JACKSON October 3, 1978 (2 walks, 1 single, 1 double, 1 home run) CRAIG NETTLES October 14, 1981 (1 hit-by-pitch, 3 singles, 1 home run) (6 others)

Most Hits, inning: 2 CRAIG NETTLES October 14, 1981; 4th inning (2 singles) (1 other)

Most Singles, Game: 4 CHRIS CHAMBLISS October 4, 1978 (3 others)

Most Singles, Inning: 2 CRAIG NETTLES October 14, 1981; 4th-inning (1 other)

Most Grand Slams, Game: 1 RICKY LEDEE October 17, 1999; 9th-inning (3 others)

Most Inside-the-Park Home Runs, Career: 1 CRAIG NETTLES October 9, 1980; 5th-inning (1 other)

Most Home Runs by Pinch-Hitter, Game: 1 RICKY LEDEE October 17, 1999; 9th-inning (5 others)

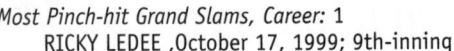

Most Pinch-hit Grand Slams, Career: 1
RICKY LEDEE ,October 17, 1999; 9th-inning

Hitting Home Runs in First Championship At-Bat:
RICK CERONE October 8, 1980; 1st-inning

Most Extra-Base Hits:
3-game Series—4; BOB WATSON 1980
(3 doubles, 1 home run)

Most Total Bases by Pinch-hitter: 4
RICKY LEDEE 1999 (5 others)

Most Runs Batted In by Pinch-hitter, Career: 4
(2 games, 2 series) RICKY LEDEE, 1998, 1999

Most Runs Batted In by Pinch-hitter, Single Series: 4
1-game; RICKY LEDEE 1999

Most Runs Battted In by Pinch-hitter, Game: 4
RICKY LEDEE October 17, 1999; 9th inning

Most Runs Batted In, Inning: 4
RICKY LEDEE October 17, 1999; 9th-inning (3 others)

Most Runs Batted In, Accounting for All Club's Runs, Game: 3
CRAIG NETTLES October 13, 1981 (1 other)

Most Consecutive Walks:
BERNIE WILLIAMS, October 10 (3), 11 (1), 1998

Most Hit-by-Pitch, Career: 3
TINO MARTINEZ 1996 (1), 1998 (1), 1999 (1) (5 others)

PITCHING

Most Games Finished, Single Series: 4
SPARKY LYLE, 1977 (many others)

Most Games Won As Relief Pitcher, Single Series:
5-game Series—2; SPARKY LYLE, 1977 (2 others)

Most Opening Games Won, Career: 2
MARIANO RIVERA 1996, 1999 (4 others)

Most Runs Allowed, Game: 8
HIDEKI IRABU October 16, 1999 (2 others)

Most Earned Runs Allowed, Game: 7
HIDEKI IRABU October 16, 1999 (3 others)

Most Doubles Allowed, Game: 4
HIDEKI IRABU October 16, 1999 (2 others)
ORLANDO HERNANDEZ, October 17, 2000

Most Triples Allowed, Game: 2
ED FIGUEROA October 8, 1977

Most Home Runs Allowed, Single Series: 4
5-game Series—ANDY PETTITTE, 1996
6-game Series—ANDY PETTITTE, 1998

Most Home Runs Allowed, Game: 4
ANDY PETTITTE October 9, 1998 (2 others)

Most Grand Slams Allowed, Game: 1
DAVID CONE October 13, 1998; 5th-inning (3 others)

Most Home Runs Allowed, Inning: 3
ANDY PETTITTE October 9, 1998; 5th-inning

Most Total Bases Allowed, Game: 23
HIDEKI IRABU October 16, 1999

FIELDING
Catchers—
Most Assists, Single Series:
3-game Series—4; RICK CERONE, 1980
5-game Series—6; THURMAN MUNSON, 1976

Most Runners Caught Stealing, Total Series: 12
THURMAN MUNSON—1976-78

Most Runners Caught Stealing, Single Series:
5-games Series—5; THURMAN MUNSON, 1976

Most Putouts:
3-game Series—23; RICK CERONE 1981

Most Assists, 14 Games, Career:
3-game Series—14; THURMAN MUNSON 1976, 1977,
1978

Most Errors, Game: 2
THURMAN MUNSON, October 10, 1976 (2 others)

First Baseman—
Most Consecutive Errorless Games, Career: 20
TINO MARTINEZ—October 9, 1998 through October 22, 2001

Most Putouts, Nine-inning Game: 15
CHRIS CHAMBLISS October 14, 1976 (1 other)

Most Assists:
3-game Series—5; BOB WATSON 1980 (1 other)

Most Unassisted Double Plays, Game: 1
TINO MARTINEZ October 11, 1996
TINO MARTINEZ October 22, 2001

Second Baseman—
Most Assists, Single Series:
3-game Series—12; WILLIE RANDOLPH, 1981

Most Putouts:
3-game Series—12; WILLIE RANDOLPH 1981

Third Baseman—
Most Assists, Nine-inning Game: 6
WADE BOGGS October 13, 1996 (3 others)

Shortstops—
Most Putouts, Game: 6
BUCKY DENT October 5, 1977 (3 others)

Outfielders—
Most Putouts by Left Fielder, Game: 7
ROY WHITE October 13, 1976

Most Consecutive Putouts by Right Fielder, Game: 4
OSCAR GAMBLE October 15, 1981
(3 in 6th-inning, 1 in 7th-inning)

Pitchers—
Most Putouts: 4
5-game Series—MARIANO RIVERA 2001

Most Putouts, Inning: 2
MIKE TORREZ October 2, 1977; 2nd-inning (3 others)
MARIANO RIVERA October 17, 2001; 9th-inning

YANKEE PLAYER ALCS SPECIAL ACHIEVEMENTS

HOME RUNS (52)

Date	Game	Player	Stadium
October 12, 1976	3	CHRIS CHAMBLISS	Yankee Stadium
October 13, 1976	4	GRAIG NETTLES (2)	Yankee Stadium
October 14, 1976	5	CHRIS CHAMBLISS	Yankee Stadium
October 5, 1977	1	THURMAN MUNSON	Yankee Stadium
October 6, 1977	2	CLIFF JOHNSON	Yankee Stadium
October 3, 1978	1	REGGIE JACKSON	Yankee Stadium
October 6, 1978	3	REGGIE JACKSON	Yankee Stadium
October 6, 1978	3	THURMAN MUNSON	Yankee Stadium
October 7, 1978	4	GRAIG NETTLES	Yankee Stadium
October 7, 1978	4	ROY WHITE	Yankee Stadium
October 8, 1980	1	RICK CERONE	Royals Stadium
October 8, 1980	1	LOU PINIELLA	Royals Stadium
October 9, 1980	2	GRAIG NETTLES	Royals Stadium
October 14, 1981	2	GRAIG NETTLES	Yankee Stadium
October 14, 1981	2	LOU PINIELLA	Yankee Stadium
October 15, 1981	3	WILLIE RANDOLPH	Oakland Coliseum
October 9, 1996	1	DEREK JETER	Yankee Stadium
October 9, 1996	1	BERNIE WILLIAMS	Yankee Stadium
October 11, 1996	3	CECIL FIELDER	Camden Yards
October 12, 1996	4	BERNIE WILLIAMS	Camden Yards
October 12, 1996	4	DARRYL STRAWBERRY	Camden Yards
October 12, 1996	4	PAUL O'NEILL	Camden Yards
October 12, 1996	4	DARRYL STRAWBERRY	Camden Yards
October 13, 1996	5	JIM LEYRITZ	Camden Yards
October 13, 1996	5	CECIL FIELDER	Camden Yards
October 13, 1996	5	DARRYL STRAWBERRY	Camden Yards
October 6, 1998	1	JORGE POSADA	Yankee Stadium
October 10, 1998	4	PAUL O'NEILL	Jacobs Field
October 11, 1998	5	CHILI DAVIS	Jacobs Field
October 13, 1998	6	SCOTT BROSIUS	Yankee Stadium
October 13, 1999	1	SCOTT BROSIUS	Yankee Stadium
October 13, 1999	1	BERNIE WILLIAMS	Yankee Stadium
October 14, 1999	2	TINO MARTINEZ	Yankee Stadium
October 16, 1999	3	SCOTT BROSIUS	Fenway Park
October 17, 1999	4	RICKY LEDEE	Fenway Park
October 17, 1999	4	DARRYL STRAWBERRY	Fenway Park
October 19, 1999	5	DEREK JETER	Fenway Park
October 19, 1999	5	JORGE POSADA	Fenway Park
October 11, 2000	2	DEREK JETER	Yankee Stadium
October 13, 2000	3	BERNIE WILLIAMS	Safeco Field
October 13, 2000	3	TINO MARTINEZ	Safeco Field
October 14, 2000	4	DEREK JETER	Safeco Field
October 14, 2000	4	DAVID JUSTICE	Safeco Field
October 17, 2000	6	DAVID JUSTICE	Yankee Stadium
October 17, 2001	1	PAUL O'NEILL	Safeco Field
October 20, 2001	3	BERNIE WILLIAMS	Yankee Stadium
October 21, 2001	4	BERNIE WILLIAMS	Yankee Stadium
October 21, 2001	4	ALFONSO SORIANO	Yankee Stadium
October 22, 2001	5	BERNIE WILLIAMS	Yankee Stadium
October 22, 2001	5	PAUL O'NEILL	Yankee Stadium
October 22, 2001	5	TINO MARTINEZ	Yankee Stadium

Notes: On October 8, 1980, Cerone and Piniella hit back-to-back homers, and for each of them it was their first ALCS homer; for Cerone, it came in his first ALCS at-bat. On October 9, 1980, Nettles' homer was hit inside the park.

.400 HITTERS (PLAYING IN ALL GAMES)

Player	G	AB	R	H	2B	3B	HR	TB	BA
LOU PINIELLA (1981)*	3	5	2	3	0	0	1	6	.600
CHRIS CHAMBLISS (1976)*	5	21	5	11	1	1	2	20	.524
BOB WATSON (1980)	3	12	0	6	3	1	0	11	.500
JERRY MUMPHREY (1981)	3	12	2	6	1	0	0	7	.500
GRAIG NETTLES (1981)	3	12	2	6	2	0	1	11	.500
BERNIE WILLIAMS (1996)*	5	19	6	9	3	0	2	18	.474
REGGIE JACKSON (1978)*	4	13	5	6	1	0	2	13	.462
LARRY MILBOURNE (1981)	3	13	4	6	0	0	0	6	.462
MICKEY RIVERS (1978)	4	11	0	5	0	0	0	5	.455
THURMAN MUNSON (1976)	5	23	3	10	2	0	0	12	.435
DEREK JETER (1996)	5	24	5	10	2	0	1	15	.417
PAUL O'NEILL (2001)*	5	12	2	5	0	0	2	11	.417
CLIFF JOHNSON (1977)	5	15	2	6	2	0	1	11	.400
CHRIS CHAMBLISS (1978)	4	15	1	6	0	0	0	6	.400
ALPHONSO SORIANO (2001)	5	15	5	6	0	0	1	9	.400

*Leading hitter of Series

YANKEE TEAM ALCS RECORDS

Team records are American League Championship Series (ALCS) records.

GENERAL
Most Series Won: 9
—1976, 1977, 1978, 1981, 1996, 1998, 1999, 2000, 2001

Most Consecutive Years Winning Series: 4

Fewest Players: 18
5-game Series—1977

Winning Series After Trailing 2 Games to 1:
5-game Series—vs. Kansas City, 1977
6-game Series—vs. Cleveland, 1998

Most Games Won, Total Series: 32
10 Series—47 Games

Largest Attendance, Single Series:
3-game Series—151,539; vs. Oakland 1981
6-game Series—306,828; vs Seattle (2000)

Longest Game: 12-innings
vs. Cleveland at New York, October 7, 1998
Cleveland won 4-1

Longest Game, 9-innings (by time): 4 hours, 14 minutes
vs. Seattle at Seattle
October 15, 2000 (Yankees won 6-2)

Latest Date for Series Start:
October 17, 2001; at Seattle

Latest Date for Series Finish:
October 22, 2001; Seattle at Yankee Stadium

BATTING
Most At-Bats, Single Series:
4-game Series—140; vs. Kansas City, 1978
5-game Series—184; vs. Boston, 1999

Most Hits, Single Series:
3-game Series—36; vs. Oakland, 1981 (1 other club)
4-game Series—42; vs. Kansas City, 1978
5-game Series—55; vs. Kansas City, 1976

Most Singles, Single Series:
3-game Series—29; vs. Oakland, 1981

Most Doubles, Single Series:
      5-game Series—13; vs. Kansas City, 1976 (2 others)

Most Home Runs, Single Series:
      5-game Series—10; vs. Baltimore, 1996

Most Total Bases, Single Series:
      5-game Series—91; vs. Baltimore, 1996

Highest Batting Average, Single Series:
      3-game Series—.336; vs. Oakland, 1981
      4-game Series—.300; vs. Kansas City, 1978
      5-game Series—.316; vs. Kansas City, 1976

Highest Slugging Average:
      5-game Series—.497; (1 other)

Most Strikeouts:
      5-game Series—44; vs. Boston 1999

Fewest Strikeouts, Single Series:
      3-game Series—10; vs. Oakland, 1981
      5-game Series—15; vs. Kansas City, 1976

Most Runs, Inning: 7 (4 others)
      vs. Oakland, October 14, 1981 4th Inning
      vs. Seattle, October 11, 2001; 8th Inning

Most Hits, Inning: 8
      vs. Seattle, October 11, 2000; 8th Inning

Most Singles, Game: 15
      vs. Oakland, October 14, 1981

Most Singles, Inning: 6
      vs. Cleveland, October 6, 1998; 1st-inning

Most Home runs, Game: 4
      vs. Baltimore, October 12, 1996

Most Home runs, Inning: 3
      vs. Baltimore, October 13, 1996; 3rd-inning (2 other clubs)
      JIM LEYRITZ, CECIL FIELDER, AND DARRYL STRAWBERRY
      (First 2 consecutive)

Most Runs Batted In, Game: 13
      vs. Oakland, October 14, 1981 (1 other club)

Most Runs Batted In, Inning: 7
      vs. Oakland, October 14, 1981; 4th-Inning
      vs. Seattle, October 11, 2001; 8th Inning

Most Walks:
      5-game Series—27; vs. Seattle 2000
      6-game Series—35; vs. Cleveland 1998

Most Walks, Game: 11
      vs. Cleveland, October 11, 1998 (1 other club)

Most Left on Base:
      3-game Series—30; vs. Oakland 1981

Most Runs, Total Series: 222
      10 Series—47 games

Most Hits, Total Series: 439
      10 Series—47 games

Most Singles, Total Series: 303
      10 Series—47 games

Most Doubles, Total Series: 77
      10 Series—47 games

Most Grand Slams, Total Series: 1 (3 other clubs)
      10 Series—47 games

Most Total Bases, Total Series: 666
      10 Series—47 games

Most Extra-Base Hits, Total Series: 136
      10 Series—47 games; (77 doubles, 7 triples, 52 home runs)

PITCHING
Fewest Pitchers, Single Series:
      3-game Series—4; vs. Kansas City, 1980
      (2 other clubs; Baltimore twice)

Most Saves:
      5-game Series—3; vs. Boston 1999

FIELDING
Highest Fielding Average, Single Series:
      4-game Series—.993; vs. Kansas City, 1978 (2 other clubs)
      5-game Series—.995; vs. Baltimore, 1996
      6-game Series—.995; vs. Seattle, 2000

Most Putouts:
      5-game Series—141; vs. Baltimore 1996

Fewest Putouts:
      3-game Series—75; vs. Kansas City 1980

Most Assists, Single Series:
      3-game Series—41; vs. Kansas City 1980
      5-game Series—60; vs. Kansas City 1976

Fewest Assists:
      5-game Series—38; vs. Boston 1999
      6-game Series—54; vs. Cleveland 1998
      6-game Series—54; vs. Seattle 2000

Most Errors, Game: 5
      vs. Kansas City, October 10, 1976

Fewest Errors, Single Series:
      4-game Series—1; vs. Kansas City 1978
      (2 other clubs)
      5-game Series—1; vs. Baltimore 1996
      6-game Series—1; vs. Seattle 2000

Most Double Plays, Single Series:
      3-game Series—6; vs. Oakland 1981
      5-game Series—7; vs. Boston 1999

Most Passed Balls, Total Series: 4 (2 other clubs)
      10 Series—47 games

YANKEE TEAM DIVISION SERIES STATS

OFFENSE

Year	G	AB	R	H	2B	3B	HR	RBI	BB	SB	BA	TB
1981	5	171	19	46	8	0	6	18	9	1	.269	72
1995	5	193	33	50	12	0	11	32	32	1	.259	95
1996	4	140	16	37	4	0	4	15	13	1	.264	53
1997	5	166	24	43	7	0	6	23	20	3	.259	68
1998	3	91	9	23	6	0	4	8	7	2	.253	41
1999	5	98	14	23	6	1	2	13	10	0	.235	37
2000	5	168	19	41	12	0	1	19	16	0	.244	56
2001	5	166	18	40	8	1	3	16	11	4	.241	59
2002	4	135	25	38	4	0	7	24	16	1	.281	63

PITCHING

Year	G	CG	IP	H	R	ER	BB	SO	W-L	SV	ERA
1981	5	0	45	36	13	13	13	39	3-2	3	2.60
1995	5	0	50	63	35	33	25	41	2-3	0	5.94
1996	4	0	39	31	16	15	20	30	3-1	2	3.46
1997	5	1	43⅓	43	21	21	10	22	2-3	1	4.36
1998	3	0	27	13	1	1	4	27	3-0	2	0.33
1999	3	0	27	14	1	1	9	17	3-0	2	0.33
2000	5	0	44	44	23	19	19	31	3-2	3	4.70
2001	5	0	45	43	12	11	11	31	3-2	2	2.20
2002	4	0	34	56	31	31	7	18	1-3	1	8.21

YANKEE DIVISION SERIES ATTENDANCE

Year	Series Length	Opponent	Attendance
1981	5 games	Milwaukee Brewers	215,212
1995	5 games	Seattle Mariners	286,839
1996	4 games	Texas Rangers	215,287
1997	5 games	Cleveland Indians	250,466
1998	3 games	Texas Rangers	164,672
1999	3 games	Texas Rangers	164,853
2000	5 games	Oakland Athletics	249,911
2001	5 games	Oakland Athletics	269,565
2002	4 games	Anaheim Angels	203,544

The 1995 attendance total set a 5-game ALDS record.

The 1999 attendance total set a 3-game ALDS record.

The largest Yankee Stadium ALDS game attendance was 57, 485 on October 9, 1999.

The smallest Yankee Stadium ALDS game attendance was 47,505 on October 11, 1981.

YANKEE TEAM ALCS STATS

OFFENSE

Year	G	AB	R	H	2B	3B	HR	RBI	BB	SB	BA	TB
1976	5	174	23	55	13	2	4	21	16	4	.316	84
1977	5	175	21	46	12	0	2	17	9	2	.263	64
1978	4	140	19	42	3	1	5	18	7	0	.300	62
1980	3	102	6	26	7	1	3	5	6	0	.255	44
1981	3	107	20	36	4	0	3	20	13	2	.336	49
1996	5	183	27	50	9	1	10	24	20	3	.273	91
1998	6	197	27	43	8	1	4	25	35	9	218	65
1999	5	176	23	42	4	1	8	21	18	3	239	72
2000	6	204	31	57	10	0	6	31	25	4	.279	85
2001	5	159	25	42	7	0	7	24	23	3	.264	70

PITCHING

Year	G	CG	IP	H	R	ER	BB	SO	W-L	SV	ERA
1976	5	1	44	40	24	23	11	18	3-2	1	4.70
1977	5	1	44	42	22	22	15	22	3-2	0	4.50
1978	4	0	35	35	17	15	14	21	3-1	2	3.86
1980	3	1	25	28	14	12	9	15	0-3	0	4.32
1981	3	0	27	22	4	4	6	23	3-0	1	1.33
1996	5	0	47	39	19	19	15	33	4-1	1	3.64
1998	6	0	56	45	20	20	16	51	4-2	1	3.21
1999	5	0	45	54	21	19	15	38	4-1	3	3.80
2000	6	1	53	41	18	18	21	48	4-2	1	3.06
2001	5	0	45	36	22	19	18	35	4-1	2	3.80

The Yankees made five of their six errors in the 1976 ALCS against Kansas City in a single game, October 10, setting a record; the Yankees lost, 7-3. The Yankees set a new ALCS five-game Series record in 1996 by making only one error.

The Yankees set a new ALCS six-game Series record in 2000 by making only one error. The 1978 Yankees share the ALCS four-game Series with two other clubs by making only one error.

YANKEE ALCS ATTENDANCE

Year	Series Length	Opponent	Attendance
1976	5 games	Kansas City Royals	252,152
1977	5 games	Kansas City Royals	234,713
1978	4 games	Kansas City Royals	194,192
1980	3 games	Kansas City Royals	141,819
1981	3 games	Oakland A's	151,539
1996	5 games	Baltimore Orioles	259,254
1998	6 games	Cleveland Indians	306,259
1999	5 games	Boston Red Sox	214,726
2000	6 games	Seattle Mariners	309,828
2001	5 games	Seattle Mariners	264,697

The 1981 attendance total set a three-game ALCS record.

The 2000 attendance total set a six-game ALCS record.

The largest Yankee Stadium ALCS game attendance was 57,181 on October 13, 1999.

The smallest Yankee Stadium ALCS game attendance was 48,497 on October 14, 1981.

YANKEE BATTING LEADERS IN AL DIVISION SERIES
EIGHT SERIES (1981 THROUGH 2002)

Note–*Several players listed on the BATTING LEADERS lists are pitchers. They have been removed from the lists.*

SERIES PLAYED
8 Bernie Williams
7 Derek Jeter
7 Paul O'Neill
7 Jorge Posada
6 Tino Martinez
4 Scott Brosius
4 Joe Girardi
4 Chuck Knoblauch

GAMES
34 Bernie Williams
29 Derek Jeter
29 Jorge Posada
27 Paul O'Neill
25 Tino Martinez
14 Chuck Knoblauch
13 Joe Girardi
11 Tim Raines
10 Many Tied

AT-BATS
128 Bernie Williams
111 Derek Jeter
110 Paul O'Neill
92 Tino Martinez
60 Jorge Posada
54 Chuck Knoblauch
54 Scott Brosius
39 Tim Raines
37 Joe Girardi
35 Alfonso Soriano

RUNS
29 Bernie Williams
20 Derek Jeter
18 Paul O'Neill
10 Tino Martinez
9 Jorge Posada
8 Tim Raines
5 Wade Boggs
5 Jason Giambi
4 Many Tied

HITS
40 Derek Jeter
36 Bernie Williams
27 Paul O'Neill
23 Tino Martinez
13 Jorge Posada
12 Chuck Knoblauch
10 Don Mattingly
9 Tim Raines
9 Scott Brosius
8 Wade Boggs
8 Mike Stanley

HOME RUNS
7 Bernie Williams
6 Paul O'Neill
4 Derek Jeter
2 Jorge Posada
2 Oscar Gamble
2 Reggie Jackson
2 Ruben Sierra
2 Shane Spencer
1 Many Tied

TOTAL BASES
68 Bernie Williams
58 Derek Jeter
51 Paul O'Neill
36 Tino Martinez
27 Jorge Posada
17 Don Mattingly
15 Wade Boggs
14 Scott Brosius
13 Chuck Knoblauch

RUNS BATTED IN
26 Bernie Williams
14 Paul O'Neill
10 Tino Martinez
9 Derek Jeter
6 Scott Brosius
6 Don Mattingly
6 Jorge Posada
5 Many Tied

WALKS
22 Bernie Williams
12 Paul O'Neill
12 Derek Jeter
9 Tino Martinez
7 Tim Raines
6 Randy Velarde
5 Joe Girardi
4 Chad Curtis
3 Graig Nettles
3 Wade Boggs

EXTRA-BASE HITS
(2B + 3B + HR)
18 Bernie Williams
12 Paul O'Neill
10 Tino Martinez
9 Derek Jeter
5 Jorge Posada
5 Don Mattingly
4 Wade Boggs
4 Ruben Sierra

BATTING AVG.
(20+ AT BATS)
.417 Don Mattingly
.400 Mike Stanley
.360 Derek Jeter
.350 Dave Winfield
.300 Paul O'Neill
.300 Charlie Hayes
.300 Reggie Jackson
.283 Jorge Posada
.281 Bernie Williams
.259 Scott Brosius

SLUGGING PCT.
(20+ AT BATS)
.708 Don Mattingly
.600 Reggie Jackson
.600 Mike Stanley
.531 Bernie Williams
.522 Derek Jeter
.500 Dave Winfield
.463 Paul O'Neill
.450 Jorge Posada
.395 Wade Boggs

YANKEE PITCHING LEADERS IN AL DIVISION SERIES
SIX SERIES (1981 THROUGH 2002)

SERIES PITCHED
8 Andy Pettitte
8 Mariano Rivera
5 Jeff Nelson
4 Roger Clemens
4 David Cone
4 Orlando Hernandez
4 Mike Stanton
3 *Many Tied*

GAMES PITCHED
19 Mariano Rivera
12 Jeff Nelson
10 Andy Pettitte
 9 Mike Stanton
 6 Roger Clemens
 6 John Wetteland
 5 *Many Tied*

GAMES STARTED
10 Andy Pettitte
 6 Roger Clemens
 5 David Cone
 5 Orlando Hernandez
 3 David Wells
 2 Ron Guidry
 2 Mike Mussina
 1 *Many Tied*

COMPLETE GAMES
Game 3 in 1997
1 David Wells

INNINGS PITCHED
60.0 Andy Pettitte
33.0 Roger Clemens
30.2 David Cone
29.1 Mariano Rivera
27.1 Orlando Hernandez

SHUTOUTS
Never accomplished
(seven combined - no
complete game shutouts)

WINS
3 Andy Pettitte
2 David Cone
2 Orlando Hernandez
2 Mike Stanton
2 David Wells
1 *Many Tied*

SAVES
11 Mariano Rivera
 3 Rich Gossage
 2 John Wetteland

HITS ALLOWED
68 Andy Pettitte
33 Roger Clemens
32 David Cone
20 Orlando Hernandez
20 David Wells
14 Mike Stanton
11 Mariano Rivera
10 Mike Mussina
10 John Wetteland

WALKS
17 Roger Clemens
15 Andy Pettitte
14 David Cone
13 Orlando Hernandez
 6 Jeff Nelson
 6 John Wetteland

STRIKEOUTS
33 Andy Pettitte
30 David Cone
23 Roger Clemens
21 Orlando Hernandez
17 Mariano Rivera
13 Dave Righetti
12 Jeff Nelson

YANKEES HITTING ONE OR MORE HOMERS IN AL DIVISION SERIES
(23 PLAYERS THROUGH 2002)

PLAYER	HR
Bernie Williams	7
Paul O'Neill	6
Derek Jeter	4
David Justice	2
Jorge Posada	2
Oscar Gamble	2
Reggie Jackson	2
Ruben Sierra	2
Shane Spencer	2
Tino Martinez	2
Alfonso Soriano	1
Rondell White	1
Jason Giambi	1
Wade Boggs	1
Scott Brosius	1
Rick Cerone	1
Cecil Fielder	1
Jim Leyritz	1
Don Mattingly	1
Lou Piniella	1
Tim Raines	1
Mike Stanley	1
Darryl Strawberry	1
DIVISION SERIES TOTALS:	**44**

PITCHERS WON-LOST RECORDS & SAVES IN AL DIVISION SERIES
(20 PITCHERS THROUGH 2002)

PITCHER	WON	LOST	SAVE
Andy Pettitte	3	3	0
Dave Righetti	2	0	0
Mike Stanton	2	1	0
David Wells	2	1	0
David Cone	2	1	0
Mariano Rivera	1	0	11
Brian Boehringer	1	0	0
Roger Clemens	1	3	0
Ron Davis	1	0	0
Orlando Hernandez	3	1	0
Steve Karsay	1	0	0
Mike Mussina	1	0	0
Jeff Nelson	1	0	0
David Weathers	1	0	0
Ramiro Mendoza	1	1	0
Rich Gossage	0	0	3
John Wetteland	0	1	2
Tommy John	0	1	0
Rick Reuschel	0	1	0
Jack McDowell	0	2	0
DIVISION SERIES TOTALS:	**23**	**16**	**16**

AMERICAN LEAGUE DIVISION SERIES ROSTER
97 YANKEE PLAYERS—NINE SERIES (1981 THROUGH 2002)

Bellinger, Clay	1999-2001	McDowell, Jack	1995
Boehringer, Brian	1996-97	Mendoza, Ramiro	1997, 2000-2002
Boggs, Wade	1995-97	Milbourne, Larry	1981
Brosius, Scott	1998-2001	Mondesi, Raul	2002
Brown, Rogers	1981	Mumphrey, Jerry	1981
Bush, Homer	1998	Murcer, Bobby	1981
Cerone, Rick	1981	Mussina, Mike	2001-2002
Choate, Randy	2000	Nelson, Jeff	1996-2000
Clemens, Roger	1999-2002	Nettles, Graig	1981
Cone, David	1995-98	O'Neill, Paul	1995-2001
Coomer, Ron	2002	Pettitte, Andy	1995-2002
Curtis, Chad	1997-99	Piniella, Lou	1981
Davis, Chili	1998-99	Polonia, Luis	2000
Davis, Ron	1981	Posada, Jorge	1995, 1997-2002
Davis, Russ	1995	Pose, Scott	1997
Duncan, Mariano	1996	Raines, Tim	1996-98
Fernandez, Tony	1995	Randolph, Willie	1981
Fielder, Cecil	1996-97	Reuschel, Rick	1981
Foote, Barry	1981	Revering, Dave	1981
Fox, Andy	1996-97	Righetti, Dave	1981
Gamble, Oscar	1981	Rivera, Juan	2002
Giambi, Jason	2002	Rivera, Mariano	1995-2002
Girardi, Joe	1996-99	Rivera, Ruben	1996
Gooden, Dwight	1997, 2000	Rogers, Kenny	1996
Gossage, Rich	1981	Sanchez, Rey	1997
Guidry, Ron	1981	Sierra, Ruben	1995
Hayes, Charlie	1996-97	Sojo, Luis	1996, 2000
Hernandez, Orlando	1999-2002	Soriano, Alfonso	2001-2002
Hill, Glenallen	2000	Spencer, Shane	1998, 2001-2002
Hitchcock, Sterling	1995, 2001	Stanley, Mike	1995, 1997
Howe, Steve	1995	Stanton, Mike	1997-2002
Jackson, Reggie	1981	Strawberry, Darryl	1995-96, 1999
James, Dion	1995	Vander Wal, John	2002
Jeter, Derek	1996-2002	Velarde, Randy	1995, 2001
John, Tommy	1981	Ventura, Robin	2002
Johnson, Nick	2002	Vizcaino, Jose	2000
Justice, David	2000-2001	Watson, Bob	1981
Kamieniecki, Scott	1995	Weathers, Dave	1996
Karsay, Steve	2002	Weaver, Jeff	2002
Kelly, Pat	1995	Wells, David	1997-98, 2002
Key, Jimmy	1996	Wetteland, John	1995-96
Knoblauch, Chuck	1998-2001	White, Rondell	2002
Ledee, Ricky	1999	Wickman, Bob	1995
Leyritz, Jim	1995-96, 1999	Williams, Bernie	1995-2002
Lloyd, Graeme	1996-98	Williams, Gerald	1995
Martinez, Tino	1996-2001	Wilson, Enrique	2002
Mattingly, Don	1995	Winfield, Dave	1981
May, Rudy	1981	Witasick, Jay	2001

YANKEE BATTING LEADERS IN AL CHAMPIONSHIP SERIES
TEN SERIES (1976 THROUGH 2001)

ALCS PLAYED
5 Derek Jeter
5 Tino Martinez
5 Graig Nettles
5 Lou Piniella
5 Paul O'Neill
5 Bernie Williams
4 *Many Tied*

GAMES
27 Bernie Williams
27 Derek Jeter
27 Tino Martinez
26 Paul O'Neill
22 Scott Brosius
22 Chuck Knoblauch
19 Jorge Posada
19 Graig Nettles
18 Lou Piniella

AT-BATS
108 Derek Jeter
105 Tino Martinez
100 Bernie Williams
89 Paul O'Neill
84 Chuck Knoblauch
72 Scott Brosius
70 Graig Nettles
62 Thurman Munson
60 Willie Randolph
59 Lou Piniella

RUNS
22 Bernie Williams
17 Derek Jeter
15 Tino Martinez
11 Paul O'Neill
11 Roy White
10 Mickey Rivers
9 Graig Nettles
8 Reggie Jackson
8 Thurman Munson
8 Jorge Posada

HITS
36 Bernie Williams
31 Derek Jeter
26 Paul O'Neill
24 Tino Martinez
22 Mickey Rivers
21 Thurman Munson
19 Graig Nettles
18 Chris Chambliss
18 Lou Piniella
16 Willie Randolph

HOME RUNS
7 Bernie Williams
5 Graig Nettles
4 Derek Jeter
4 Paul O'Neill
4 Darryl Strawberry
3 Scott Brosius
3 Tino Martinez

TOTAL BASES
63 Bernie Williams
49 Derek Jeter
40 Paul O'Neill
39 Tino Martinez
39 Graig Nettles
31 Scott Brosius
31 Thurman Munson
28 Mickey Rivers
22 Willie Randolph

RUNS BATTED IN
21 Bernie Williams
17 Graig Nettles
14 Paul O'Neill
13 Derek Jeter
11 Scott Brosius
10 Chris Chambliss
10 Thurman Munson
8 Cecil Fielder
8 Reggie Jackson
8 Tino Martinez

WALKS
21 Bernie Williams
16 Jorge Posada
12 Derek Jeter
12 Chuck Knoblauch
10 Tino Martinez
9 Paul O'Neill
7 Oscar Gamble
7 Reggie Jackson
7 Roy White

EXTRA-BASE HITS
(2B+3B+HR)
13 Bernie Williams
9 Derek Jeter
9 Tino Martinez
9 Graig Nettles
7 Scott Brosius
7 Roy White
6 Thurman Munson
6 Paul O'Neill
6 Lou Piniella

BATTING AVG.
(20+ AT BATS)
.386 Mickey Rivers
.375 Bob Watson
.360 Bernie Williams
.340 Chris Chambliss
.339 Thurman Munson
.316 Roy White
.305 Lou Piniella
.300 Fred Stanley
.292 Paul O'Neill
.287 Derek Jeter

SLUGGING PCT.
(20+ AT BATS)
.630 Bernie Williams
.583 Bob Watson
.557 Graig Nettles
.553 Roy White
.509 Chris Chambliss
.522 Ruben Sierra
.500 Thurman Munson
.475 Lou Piniella
.456 Mickey Rivers
.454 Derek Jeter

YANKEE PITCHING LEADERS IN AL CHAMPIONSHIP SERIES
TEN SERIES (1976 THROUGH 2001)

SERIES PITCHED
5 Andy Pettitte
5 Mariano Rivera
4 Orlando Hernandez
4 Jeff Nelson
3 *Many Tied*

GAMES PITCHED
16 Mariano Rivera
10 Jeff Nelson
 8 Mike Stanton
 7 Ramiro Mendoza
 7 Andy Pettitte
 6 Sparky Lyle
 6 Dick Tidrow

GAMES STARTED
7 Andy Pettitte
6 Orlando Hernandez
4 David Cone
4 Ed Figueroa
4 Ron Guidry
3 Catfish Hunter

COMPLETE GAMES
1 Roger Clemens
1 Ron Guidry
1 Catfish Hunter
1 Rudy May

INNINGS PITCHED
48.0 Andy Pettitte
42.0 Orlando Hernandez
26.0 David Cone
23.2 Mariano Rivera
22.1 Ron Guidry

SHUTOUTS
1 Roger Clemens

WINS
5 Andy Pettitte
4 Orlando Hernandez
3 Mariano Rivera
2 David Cone
2 Ron Guidry
2 Sparky Lyle
2 David Wells

SAVES
6 Mariano Rivera
2 Rich Gossage
1 Ken Clay
1 Sparky Lyle
1 Ramiro Mendoza
1 John Wetteland

HITS ALLOWED
46 Andy Pettitte
33 Orlando Hernandez
24 David Cone
24 Ed Figueroa
17 Catfish Hunter
17 Mariano Rivera
14 Tommy John
13 Hidecki Irabu

WALKS
21 Orlando Hernandez
14 David Cone
12 Andy Pettitte
 9 Dick Tidrow
 8 Ron Guidry

STRIKEOUTS
40 Orlando Hernandez
27 David Cone
24 Roger Clemens
23 Andy Pettitte
18 David Wells
17 Ron Guidry
17 Mariano Rivera
11 Jeff Nelson
10 Catfish Hunter

YANKEES HITTING ONE OR MORE HOMERS IN AL CHAMPIONSHIP SERIES
(22 PLAYERS THROUGH 2001)

PLAYER	HR
Bernie Williams	7
Graig Nettles	5
Darryl Strawberry	4
Derek Jeter	4
Paul O'Neill	4
Scott Brosius	3
Tino Martinez	3
Chris Chambliss	2
Cecil Fielder	2
Reggie Jackson	2
Thurman Munson	2
Lou Piniella	2
Jorge Posada	2
David Justice	2
Alfonso Soriano	1
Rick Cerone	1
Chili Davis	1
Cliff Johnson	1
Ricky Ledee	1
Jim Leyritz	1
Willie Randolph	1
Roy White	1
ALCS TOTALS:	**52**

PITCHERS WON-LOST RECORDS & SAVES IN AL CHAMPIONSHIP SERIES
(28 PITCHERS THROUGH 2001)

PITCHER	WON	LOST	SAVE
Mariano Rivera	3	0	6
Sparky Lyle	2	0	1
David Cone	2	0	0
Orlando Hernandez	4	1	0
David Wells	2	0	0
Ron Guidry	2	1	0
Andy Pettitte	5	1	0
Mike Mussina	1	0	0
Jim Beattie	1	0	0
Dock Ellis	1	0	0
George Frazier	1	0	0
Tommy John	1	0	0
Jimmy Key	1	0	0
Dave Righetti	1	0	0
Dick Tidrow	1	0	0
David Weathers	1	0	0
Rich Gossage	1	1	2
Catfish Hunter	1	1	0
Roger Clemens	1	1	0
Ken Clay	0	0	1
Ramiro Mendoza	0	0	1
John Wetteland	0	0	1
Don Gullett	0	1	0
Rudy May	0	1	0
Mike Torrez	0	1	0
Ed Figueroa	0	2	0
Denny Neagle	0	2	0
Jeff Nelson	0	2	0
ALCS TOTALS:	**32**	**15**	**12**

AMERICAN LEAGUE CHAMPIONSHIP SERIES ROSTER
108 YANKEE PLAYERS—TEN SERIES (1976 THROUGH 2001)

Aldrete, Mike	1996	Maddox, Elliott	1976
Alomar, Sandy	1976	Martinez, Tino	1996, 1998-2001
Beattie, Jim	1978	Mason, Jim	1976
Bellinger, Clay	1999-2001	May, Carlos	1976
Blair, Paul	1977-78	May, Rudy	1980-81
Boggs, Wade	1996	Mendoza, Ramiro	1998-2001
Brosius, Scott	1998-2001	Milbourne, Larry	1981
Brown, Rogers	1980-81	Mumphrey, Jerry	1981
Bush, Homer	1998	Munson, Thurman	1976-78
Cerone, Rick	1980-81	Murcer, Bobby	1980-81
Chambliss, Chris	1976-78	Mussina, Mike	2001
Choate, Randy	2000	Neagle, Denny	2000
Clay, Ken	1978	Nelson, Jeff	1996, 1998-2001
Clemens, Roger	1999-2001	Nettles, Graig	1976-78, 1980-81
Cone, David	1996, 1998-2001	O'Neill, Paul	1996, 1998-2001
Curtis, Chad	1998-99	Pettitte, Andy	1996, 1998-2001
Davis, Chili	1998-99	Piniella, Lou	1976-78, 1980-81
Davis, Ron	1980-81	Polonia, Luis	2000
Dent, Bucky	1977-78, 1980	Posada, Jorge	1998-2001
Doyle, Brian	1978	Raines, Tim	1996, 1998
Duncan, Mariano	1996	Randolph, Willie	1976-77, 1980-81
Ellis, Dock	1976	Revering, Dave	1981
Fielder, Cecil	1996	Righetti, Dave	1981
Figueroa, Ed	1976-78	Rivera, Mariano	1996, 1998-2001
Foote, Barry	1981	Rivers, Mickey	1976-78
Fox, Andy	1996	Robertson, Andre	1981
Frazier, George	1981	Rodriguez, Aurelio	1980-81
Gamble, Oscar	1976, 1980-81	Rogers, Kenny	1996
Girardi, Joe	1996, 1998-99	Soderholm, Eric	1980
Gooden, Dwight	2000	Sojo, Luis	1996, 1998-2001
Gossage, Rich	1978, 1980-81	Soriano, Alfonso	2001
Greene, Todd	2001	Spencer, Jim	1980
Grimsley, Jason	2000	Spencer, Shane	1998-2001
Guidry, Ron	1976-78, 1980	Stanley, Fred	1976-78
Gullett, Don	1977	Stanton, Mike	1998-2001
Hayes, Charlie	1996	Strawberry, Darryl	1996, 1999
Hendricks, Ellie	1976	Thomasson, Gary	1978
Hernandez, Orlando	1998-2001	Tidrow, Dick	1976-78
Hill, Glenallen	2000	Torrez, Mike	1977
Hunter, Catfish	1976, 1978	Underwood, Tom	1980
Irabu, Hideki	1999	Velarde, Randy	2001
Jackson, Grant	1976	Velez, Otto	1976
Jackson, Reggie	1977-78, 1980-81	Vizcaino, Jose	2000
Jeter, Derek	1996, 1998-2001	Watson, Allen	1999
John, Tommy	1980-81	Watson, Bob	1980-81
Johnson, Cliff	1977-78	Weathers, Dave	1996
Justice, David	2000-2001	Wells, David	1998
Key, Jimmy	1996	Wetteland, John	1996
Knoblauch, Chuck	1998-2001	White, Roy	1976-78
Ledee, Ricky	1998-99	Williams, Bernie	1996, 1998-2001
Lefebvre, Joe	1980	Wilson, Enrique	2001
Leyritz, Jim	1996	Winfield, Dave	1981
Lloyd, Graeme	1996, 1998	Witasick, Jay	2001
Lyle, Sparky	1976-78	Wohlers, Mark	2001

WORLD SERIES

Brooklyn shortstop Harold "Pee Wee" Reese, left, and his counterpart, Phil Rizzuto, right, on the New York Yankees "choose up" as they meet September 29 at Yankee Stadium, in preparation for the opening of the 1952 World Series at Ebbets Field, Brooklyn, N.Y. (AP Photo)

The 19th century witnessed several variations on the World Series theme, but the first "modern" World Series, between Boston of the American League and Pittsburgh of the National, was not played until 1903. And it was not until 1921 that the Yankees became part of the Fall Classic.

New York atoned for its late start by making more World Series appearances (36) and winning more times (25) than anyone else. Once in the gate, New York was a consistent part of the World Series scene—the Yankees took part in six World Series in the 1920s, five in the 1930s, five in the 1940s, eight in the 1950s, five in the 1960s, three in the 1970s, one in the 1980s, and three in the 1990s.

WHEN THE SUN HANGS LOW

1921

The Yankees' first World Series games were with their landlords, the New York Giants; thus all games were at the Polo Grounds.

The Yankees got off to a great start, taking Games 1 and 2 behind the consecutive shutout pitching of Carl Mays and Waite Hoyt. Hoyt also won Game 5, 3-1, but lost the finale, 1-0, a heartbreaker in which he was magnificent in defeat. In all, Hoyt pitched a total of 27 innings without allowing an earned run.

The critical game of this nine-game Series, however, was Game 3. The Yanks, up 2-0 in games, were threatening to blow the Series apart, scoring four runs in the third inning to take a 4-0 lead. But the Giants regrouped and pounded 20 hits off four Yankee pitchers to win, 13-5.

Game 4, played two days later, involved a little-known Yankee controversy. Carl Mays, having befuddled the Giant hitters through the first seven innings, took a 1-0 lead into the eighth. Then disaster struck; the Giants pummeled Mays. One of their key hits was a triple by Irish Meusel (Bob's brother), just prior to which Yankee Manager Miller Huggins ordered Mays to throw a fastball. A slow curve was delivered instead, and it was this pitch that Meusel crunched. George Burns doubled and soon the Giants scored three runs, going on to win, 4-2.

Huggins never forgave Mays for his insubordination. Sportswriter Fred Lieb reported years later in his book, *Baseball As I Have Known It,* that Commissioner Landis had Mays investigated after the Series because of an allegation made by a New York actor who believed Mays was paid to throw the Series game. One of the country's best detective agencies found nothing suspicious, and Landis cleared Mays. Yet, doubts linger.

Babe Ruth (.313), whose surprise bunt single triggered a winning two-run rally in Game 5, hit his first World Series home run in Game 4 off Paul Douglas. (It was also the first Yankee homer in Series history.) But sadly for the Yanks, Babe was unable to play after Game 5 when he hurt his knee, compounding an earlier injury. An abscess on his left elbow, which he developed before the Series, became infected during the Series and Babe was sidelined, except for an unsuccessful pinch-hit appearance in the ninth inning of Game 8. Babe took criticism from the press for not playing, but if possible Babe would have played. He wanted a Series victory badly.

Unfortunately, the other Yanks hit poorly, a lowly .207. The Yanks lost Game 8 ingloriously—and with it the Series, five games to three. Shortstop Roger Peckinpaugh made a first-inning error that allowed the game's only run to score. With one out in the Yankee ninth, Aaron Ward walked. Home Run Baker ripped a grounder through the right side but second baseman Johnny Rawlings made a great play on the ball and fired out Baker. Ward attempted to reach third in the meantime, and he, too, was gunned down. Thus, the Series ended on an unusual double play.

However, base running that was daring, unusual and sometimes foolish marked the Yankee performance throughout the Series. Ruth stole two bases in one inning, scored from first base on a single, but was thrown out stealing at a critical point. Mike McNally was 2-for-4 in steal attempts, including a steal of home in Game 1, but was thrown out at home on attempting to score from second on an infield grounder.

Bob Meusel stole home in Game 2, but a series of baserunning mistakes followed. He was once declared out for failing to touch first after tripling. He was out at home trying to score on an infield out and he was out trying to steal second base. In critical Game 5 Bob went daringly from first to third on a sacrifice bunt but was out at home when the ball got away from Frankie Frisch who recovered in time to get Meusel. But Bob scored from first base on a single in Game 6.

Wally Schang had an infield grounder hit to him for an automatic out and was once out at second trying to stretch a single. Wally Pipp stole second once, but was thrown out at third trying to advance from second on a roller to the left side. Chick Fewster singled but was thrown out trying for a double and Peckinpaugh was tossed out once attempting to steal. Daring base running to be sure, but not always wise.

This was the only time in Series history that a club (the Giants) lost the first two games by shutouts, only to rebound and win the Series.

```
Game 1 at the Polo Grounds, NY, October 5
NY (AL)    1  0  0    0  1  1    0  0  0  -  3   7  0
NY (NL)    0  0  0    0  0  0    0  0  0  -  0   5  0
W—Mays; L—Douglas.                    A.—30,202

Game 2 at the Polo Grounds, NY, October 6
NY (NL)    0  0  0    0  0  0    0  0  0  -  0   2  3
NY (AL)    0  0  0    1  0  0    0  2  X  -  3   3  0
W—Hoyt; L—Nehf.                       A.—34,939

Game 3 at the Polo Grounds, NY, October 7
NY (AL)    0  0  4    0  0  0    0  1  0  -  5   8  0
NY (NL)    0  0  4    0  0  0    8  1  X  - 13  20  0
W—Barnes; L—Quinn.                    A.—36,509

Game 4 at the Polo Grounds, NY, October 9
NY (NL)    0  0  0    0  0  0    0  3  1  -  4   9  1
NY (AL)    0  0  0    0  1  0    0  0  1  -  2   7  1
W—Douglas; L—Mays. HR—Ruth (AL).      A.—36,372

Game 5 at the Polo Grounds, NY, October 10
NY (AL)    0  0  1    2  0  0    0  0  0  -  3   6  1
NY (NL)    1  0  0    0  0  0    0  0  0  -  1  10  1
W—Hoyt; L—Nehf.                       A.—35,758

Game 6 at the Polo Grounds, NY, October 11
NY (NL)    0  3  0    4  0  1    0  0  0  -  8  13  0
NY (AL)    3  2  0    0  0  0    0  0  0  -  5   7  2
W—Barnes; L—Shawkey. HRs—E. Meusel (NL), Snyder (NL),
Fewster (AL).                         A.—34,283

Game 7 at the Polo Grounds, NY, October 12
NY (AL)    0  1  0    0  0  0    0  0  0  -  1   8  1
NY (NL)    0  0  0    1  0  0    1  0  X  -  2   6  0
W—Douglas; L—Mays.                    A.—36,503

Game 8 at the Polo Grounds, NY, October 13
NY (NL)    1  0  0    0  0  0    0  0  0  -  1   6  0
NY (AL)    0  0  0    0  0  0    0  0  0  -  0   4  1
W—Nehf; L—Hoyt.                       A.—25,410
```

1922

After a three-year experiment with a nine-game World Series, baseball reverted to a seven-game format. But it took the Yankees only five games to lose again to the New York Giants.

Actually, the Yankees failed to win a single game. Game 2 was a tie; after ten innings and with the score knotted, 3-3, umpires Bill Klem and George Hildebrand called the game because of darkness. It was a most controversial decision, because more than a half hour of daylight remained. The fans were furious and Commissioner Landis ordered game receipts ($120,000) turned over to military hospitals for disabled veterans. The Yanks, however, lost the four completed games.

Game 5 ended it all for the Yankees but not without another difference of opinion between Huggins and a Yankee

moundsman. Bullet Joe Bush took a 3-2 lead into the eighth inning but got himself into a jam. Manager Huggins directed Bush to intentionally walk a lefthanded batter so that he could face George Kelly, a right-handed hitter. Bullet Joe angrily cursed at Huggins in a voice so loud that many of the fans and press heard him spew his venom. After walking the batter, Bush threw a very hittable pitch which Kelly rapped for a single; the Giants went on to score three runs to win the game and Series. Obviously, neither Huggins nor the Yankees were happy with what had transpired in Game 5.

The Giants' Heinie Groh (.474) and Frankie Frisch (.471) terrorized Yankee pitching throughout the Series, while the Giants as a team hit an incredible .309. Although all the games were close, the Yankees produced a lowly .203 batting average. Babe Ruth (.118, 0 HRs) had the worst World Series of his career. In fact, Bob Meusel (.300) was the only Yankee to hit the ball at all consistently, and the only two Yankee home runs belonged to Aaron Ward.

This was a bitterly fought Series. The teams' managements were at each others' throats, 1922 being the last Yankee season at the Polo Grounds. And the players used plenty of brutal bench-jockeying. The play was rough and often dirty. Following one game, the Babe and Bob Meusel invaded the Giants' locker room looking for trouble. Babe wanted to fight Johnny Rawlings, a reserve Giant infielder, for insults he believed to be Rawlings' responsibility. Instead, Ruth and pitcher Jesse Barnes nearly exchanged punches. But before the brawl could begin, Giant Manager John McGraw entered the scene and booted Ruth and Meusel out of the locker room.

The fight on the playing field was clearly won by the Giants, and McGraw, who called every pitch his pitchers threw, enhanced his reputation as a genius.

This was the first Series to have play-by-play radio coverage (for all but the last two games). A direct line was set up between the Polo Grounds and WJZ in Newark. The signal was also picked up by WGY in Schenectady, NY, and WBZ in Springfield, Mass. The broadcasts, which created great interest, were handled by sportswriter Grantland Rice and Raymond F. Guy.

```
Game 1 at the Polo Grounds, NY, October 4
NY (AL)    0  0  0    0  0  1    1  0  0  -  2   7  0
NY (NL)    0  0  0    0  0  0    0  3  X  -  3  11  3
W—Ryan; L—Bush.                       A.—36,514

Game 2 at the Polo Grounds, NY, October 5
NY (NL)    3  0  0  0  0  0  0  0  0   0  -  3  8  1
NY (AL)    1  0  0  1  0  0  0  1  0   0  -  3  8  0
(Called after 10 innings because of darkness) Barnes vs. Shawkey.
HRs—E. Meusel (NL), Ward (AL).        A.—37,020

Game 3 at the Polo Grounds, NY, October 6
NY (AL)    0  0  0    0  0  0    0  0  0  -  0   4  1
NY (NL)    0  0  2    0  0  0    1  0  X  -  3  12  1
W—J. Scott; L—Hoyt.                   A.—37,620

Game 4 at the Polo Grounds, NY, October 7
NY (NL)    0  0  0    0  4  0    0  0  0  -  4   9  1
NY (AL)    2  0  0    0  0  0    1  0  0  -  3   8  0
W—McQuillan; L—Mays. HR—Ward (AL).    A.—36,242

Game 5 at the Polo Grounds, NY, October 8
NY (AL)    1  0  0    0  1  0    1  0  0  -  3   5  0
NY (NL)    0  2  0    0  0  0    0  3  X  -  5  10  0
W—Nehf; L—Bush.                       A—38,551
```

1923

The Yankees won their first World Championship by defeating the New York Giants in six games. It was the third straight year that these two teams played in the Fall Classic, but the first time a game was played at a place other than the Polo Grounds. Yankee Stadium, in its first year of existence, hosted three games to begin its glorious World Series history.

Early Series heroics and theatrics, however, belonged to Giant outfielder Casey Stengel. Casey's ninth-inning inside-the-park home run won Game 1, 5-4. Wrote Damon Runyon: "This is the way old Casey Stengel ran running his home run home when two were out in the ninth inning and the score was tied, and the ball still bounding inside the Yankee yard—his flanks heaving, his breath whistling, his head far back." Stengel's solo home run was the only run scored in Game 3. After that clout, Stengel wagged his fingers from his nose at the Yankee dugout, outraging Yankee owner Jake Ruppert who demanded that the Commissioner severely discipline Stengel (Landis fined Casey $50).

The Yankees were down two games to one until they rallied to win the Series behind the pitching of Herb Pennock who won two games and saved another in relief. Babe Ruth (.368, three HRs, one triple, one double), who was the Series batting star, was responsible for the Yankees' key victory in Game 2 by belting two home runs. It was an especially sweet day for the Babe who had a fierce rivalry in progress with Giant Manager John McGraw. McGraw enjoyed putting down Ruth's hitting abilities.

In fact, before Game 2, when asked about Ruth, McGraw disdainfully observed, "Why shouldn't we pitch to Ruth? I've said before and I'll say again, we pitch to better hitters than Ruth in the National League." But after Babe's great performance, sportswriter Heywood Broun opened his story in the *New York World* with a line that became famous: "The Ruth is mighty and shall prevail."

Too much importance cannot be put on the Yanks' Game 2 victory. It reestablished Yankee pride, breaking a string of eight consecutive losses to the Giants in Series play. One of Ruth's homers cleared the right-field roof of the Polo Grounds, and Aaron Ward homered into the left-field upper deck. Giants pitcher Jack Bentley retaliated during the two-run Yankee fourth inning by hitting Pennock in the back with a pitch. Herb was in great pain but he fought back, pitching a clever complete game with the help of some great defensive plays by third baseman Joe Dugan.

After Stengel re-stole the show in Game 3, pivotal Game 4 was won by the Yanks, 8-4. Six Yankee runs came in the second inning, which featured Everett Scott's three-run single and Bob Meusel's two-run triple. The next day Joe Dugan cracked four hits, including a three-run homer, leading the Yanks to an 8-1 slaughter.

Pennock won the finale, 6-4, as Ruth hit an important homer, and the Yanks sent five men across the plate in the eighth inning, helped by critical walks from Giant pitchers Art Nehf and Rosy Ryan. In that inning, bases-loaded walks to Joe Bush and Dugan forced in runs to cut the Giants lead to 4-3. With two out, Meusel cleared the bases with a single to center that gave the Yanks an advantage that stood at the conclusion, 6-4.

Pennock was the mound hero of the Series, and Ruth was the obvious batting star. But the Yanks had many heroes at the plate. Ward led both teams in batting (.417), Bob Meusel (two triples, one double) led everyone in RBIs (eight), and Dugan (one HR, one triple, two doubles, five RBIs), Everett Scott (.318) and Wally Schang (.318) also swung big bats. While McGraw spoke bravely of pitching to Ruth, his pitchers, who as in the 1922 Series did McGraw's bidding on every pitch, surrendered a Series-leading eight walks to the Babe. (Crowned a genius in the 1922 Series, McGraw in this Series received much of the blame for the Giants' defeat.)

After the final win, the Yankees held a tremendous victory party. In his speech to the happy throng, Ruppert said, "This is a wonderful occasion. I now have baseball's greatest park, baseball's greatest players and baseball's greatest team. We had a great Series and Babe 'Root,' Wardie, Meusel, Bush and Shawkey all had great Series. But let's give credit where credit is due and give most credit to little Hug."

All six games of this Series were broadcast as a result of the successful radio experiment with the 1922 Series. Stations in New York, South Dartmouth, Mass., and Washington, D.C., carried the games for which Graham McNamee provided play-by-play. The rich-voiced, well-spoken McNamee, hired by WEAF in New York and broadcasting from an open box, became something of a news item himself when forced to do his job in the rain.

Game 1 at Yankee Stadium, NY, October 10

												R	H	E
NY (NL)	0	0	4	0	0	0	0	0	1	-	5	8	0
NY (AL)	1	2	0	0	0	0	1	0	0	-	4	12	1

W—Ryan; L—Bush. HR—Stengel (NL).   A.—55,307

Game 2 at the Polo Grounds, NY, October 11

												R	H	E
NY (AL)	0	1	0	2	1	0	0	0	0	-	4	10	0
NY (NL)	0	1	0	0	0	1	0	0	0	-	2	9	2

W—Pennock, L—McQuillan. HR—Ward (AL), E. Meusel (NL), Ruth (AL) 2.   A.—40,402

Game 3 at Yankee Stadium, NY, October 12

												R	H	E
NY (NL)	0	0	0	0	0	0	1	0	0	-	1	4	0
NY (AL)	0	0	0	0	0	0	0	0	0	-	0	6	1

W—Nehf; L—Jones. HR—Stengel (NL).   A.—62,430

Game 4 at the Polo Grounds, NY, October 13

												R	H	E
NY (AL)	0	6	1	1	0	0	0	0	0	-	8	13	1
NY (NL)	0	0	0	0	0	0	0	3	1	-	4	13	1

W—Shawkey; L—J. Scott. HR—Youngs (NL).   A.—46,302

Game 5 at Yankee Stadium, NY, October 14

												R	H	E
NY (NL)	0	1	0	0	0	0	0	0	0	-	1	3	2
NY (AL)	3	4	0	1	0	0	0	0	X	-	8	14	0

W—Bush; L—Bentley. HR—Dugan (AL).   A.—62,817

Game 6 at the Polo Grounds, NY, October 15

												R	H	E
NY (AL)	1	0	0	0	0	0	0	5	0	-	6	5	0
NY (NL)	1	0	0	1	1	1	0	0	0	-	4	10	1

W—Pennock; L—Nehf. HR—Ruth (AL), Snyder (NL).   A.—34,172

1926

The Yankees lost the World Series in seven games in a Series made memorable by the superb pitching of the St. Louis Cardinals' Grover Cleveland Alexander.

Alexander, who had already won two games (including Game 6 the day before), was called in to pitch in relief in the seventh inning of Game 7 with two outs and the bases loaded. Protecting a one-run lead, he struck out Tony Lazzeri (not before Tony hit a long ball that was just foul) to end the inning, then retired the Yanks in the eighth and ninth innings to preserve the win for St. Louis. With two out in the ninth, Babe Ruth walked and was thrown out in an inexplicable attempt to steal second base.

Ruth was considered the World Series goat, an irony for a man who hit four home runs in the Series, including three in Game 4 in St. Louis to establish a Series record. Earle Combs (.357), Lou Gehrig (.348) and Joe Dugan (.333) also were batting stars, and Herb Pennock pitched two victories.

Yankee Series highlights included Gehrig's tie-breaking sixth-inning single scoring Ruth with the winning run in a 8-1 opening-game Yankee victory, as Pennock hurled a three-hitter; Game 4, which was a Yankee 10-5 rout, including Ruth's three Sportsman's Park home runs; and Pennock's nifty seven-hitter in Game 5 that beat St. Louis, 3-2, in 10 innings. Lazzeri's sacrifice fly scored Mark Koenig with the winning run.

But it was Alexander's clutch pitching and Ruth's steal attempt in Game 7 that for years have been the principal subjects of discussion. Later, referring to Lazzeri's near-miss home run and eventual strike-out, Alexander remarked, "Less than a foot made the difference between a hero and a bum." Also part of the legend, but never confirmed, is that Alexander, a tragic alcoholic, was nursing a severe hangover when he pitched those final innings of Game 7.

Alexander always denied that and resented it. After the game, a reporter asked how he felt and Alexander shot back: "How do I feel? Go ask Lazzeri how he feels." Oddly, Yankee Stadium was little more than half full (38,093) for that dramatic and historic Game 7. It was a cold, rainy day and rumors were afloat in late morning that Commissioner Landis had called off the game. But shortly after noon, Landis ordered the game to be played if possible. Unsure of the situation, thousands of New York fans missed the memorable event.

That the Babe would be considered a goat in the game did not seem possible in the early innings. He made a fantastic one-handed catch running into right-center field in the second inning, and he homered in the third for a 1-0 Yankee lead.

Yankee pitcher Waite Hoyt, bedeviled by such bad luck in the 1921 Series, was again victimized in the same manner, as the Cardinals scored all three of their runs in the fourth inning in unearned fashion. With one out and Jim Bottomley on first, Les Bell hit a potential double-play grounder to Yankee shortstop Mark Koenig who fumbled the ball. Then Chick Hafey hit a ball to left field, which Bob Meusel allowed to drop safely. With the bases loaded, Bob O'Farrell hit a fly to left-center. Preparing himself for the throw home, Meusel forgot to catch the fly, dropping it as one run scored and the bases remained loaded. Tommy Thevenow followed with a bloop hit to drive in the final two runs, the winning runs. Needless to say, Hoyt deserved a better fate.

The theatrics of Alexander, Lazzeri and Ruth have tended to obscure the above facts of St. Louis' rally. Thevenow, who led both teams in hitting (.417), was an unlikely hitting hero. He owns the lowest slugging average (.294) in NL history for players with at least 5,000 at-bats. He has the fewest home runs (two) in ML history for players with 4000 at-bats. Yet he had an inside-the-park homer in Game 2. His outstanding Series hitting average followed a .256 mark for the regular season.

The Cards' pitching strategy was simple—pitch around Ruth. Cardinal pitchers walked Babe 11 times and the ploy seemed reasonable after watching Babe's Game 3 exhibition. His first two homers cleared Sportsman's Park right-field bleacher roof (one of Ruth's blasts over the pavilion broke a display window in the Chevrolet dealership across from the park) and his third homer was a line drive deep in the center-field bleachers, one of the longest homers ever hit at Sportsman's Park. Following Ruth in the Yankee lineup were Meusel, then Gehrig who did not as yet have his awesome reputation, and between them only four extra-base hits were recorded. St. Louis did not mind walking the Babe.

Neither St. Louis (89-65) nor New York (91-63) was extremely powerful during the regular season. Both clubs were much stronger when they met in the World Series two years later.

This was the year NBC was founded, and the Series was carried by network with Graham McNamee and Phillips Carlin doing the play-by-play for 23 stations.

```
Game 1 at Yankee Stadium, NY, October 2
ST.L.     1  0  0   0  0  0   0  0  0  -  1   3  1
NY        1  0  0   0  0  1   0  0  X  -  2   6  0
W—Pennock; L—Sherdel.                A.—61,658

Game 2 at Yankee Stadium, NY, October 3
ST.L.     0  0  2   0  0  0   3  0  1  -  6  12  1
NY        0  2  0   0  0  0   0  0  0  -  2   4  0
W—Alexander; L—Shocker. HR—Southworth (ST. L.), Thevenow (ST. L.).
                                     A.—63,600

Game 3 at Sportsman's Park, St. Louis, October 5
NY        0  0  0   0  0  0   0  0  0  -  0   5  1
ST.L.     0  0  0   3  1  0   0  0  X  -  4   8  0
W—Haines; L—Ruether. HR—Haines (ST. L.).   A.—37,708

Game 4 at Sportsman's Park, St. Louis, October 6
NY        1  0  1   1  4  2   1  0  0  - 10  14  1
ST.L.     1  0  0   3  0  0   0  0  1  -  5  14  0
W—Hoyt; L—Reinhart. HR—Ruth (NY) 3.  A.—38,825

Game 5 at Sportsman's Park, St. Louis, October 7
NY        0  0  0   0  0  1   0  0  1  1  -  3  9  1
ST.L.     0  0  0   1  0  0   1  0  0  0  -  2  7  1
W—Pennock; L—Sherdel.                A.—39,552

Game 6 at Yankee Stadium, NY, October 9
ST.L.     3  0  0   0  1  0   5  0  1  - 10  13  2
NY        0  0  0   1  0  0   1  0  0  -  2   8  1
W—Alexander; L—Shawkey. HR—L. Bell (ST. L.).  A.—48,615

Game 7 at Yankee Stadium, NY, October 10
ST.L.     0  0  0   3  0  0   0  0  0  -  3  8  0
NY        0  0  1   0  0  1   0  0  0  -  2  8  3
W—Haines; L—Hoyt. HR—Ruth (NY).      A.—38,093
```

1927

The Yankees won their second World Championship by sweeping the Pittsburgh Pirates in four straight games, becoming the first American League team to sweep the representative from the senior circuit in Series play. Some think the Pirates were beaten before the first pitch was thrown.

In batting practice before the Series started, the Pirate players watched in awe as the Yanks sent every pitch screaming throughout immense Forbes Field. After putting four straight balls beyond the outfield wall, Babe Ruth pointed toward the bleachers and yelled at the numb, bewildered Pirate players, "O.K., sonnies, if any of you want my autograph, go out and collect those balls in the bleachers. I'll sign 'em for you."

When Pirate John Miljus wild-pitched home the winning run in the bottom of the ninth inning of Game 4, it was officially over. Ruth (.400) hit the only two home runs of the Series to lead the way, and defensive specialist Mark Koenig was 9-for-18 (.500) at the plate.

The Yankees swept the opening two games at Forbes Field behind the clutch pitching of Waite Hoyt, Wilcy Moore and George Pipgras. Lou Gehrig (.308), playing the Series with considerable concern for his mother who was undergoing an operation in New York, delivered important extra-base hits in each of the first two contests.

Game 3 was a Herb Pennock showcase. The classy, 33-year-old lefty from Pennsylvania set down the first 22 Pirate hitters (7 1/3 innings of perfect ball) before Pie Traynor singled in the eighth. Pennock finished with an easy three-hit 8-1 win.

The playing of Game 4 was a mere formality, but for the first time Yankee Stadium was the site of a World Series wrap-up. Yankee relief ace Wilcy Moore started the game and had the Yanks in a 3-3 tie as the Yanks came to bat in the home half of the ninth. Earle Combs led off with a walk and Koenig beat out a bunt. Both runners moved up a base on Miljus' wild pitch, and Ruth was walked intentionally. Courageously, Miljus fanned Gehrig and Bob Meusel, while being distracted by Combs who bluffed stealing home on every pitch. With one strike on Tony Lazzeri, Miljus threw another wild pitch, and the Series was over.

Joe Devine, later a Yankee scout, was associated with the Pirates in 1927. Years later he recalled the Series, stating, "If they had played 100 games, I honestly believe the Yankees would have won them all. That's how scared the Pittsburgh club was." And one must remember this was an outstanding Pirate club that started three future Hall of Famers (Traynor, Paul Waner and Lloyd Waner). It is also a fact that the Yanks won easily without ever getting their explosive offense in gear. Underrated Yankee pitching starred.

National radio broadcasts of the game allowed more than 20 million fans to hear the action and gave each fan the opportunity to decide whether the 1927 Yankees were indeed baseball's greatest team ever. This was the first World Series broadcast nationwide with NBC's Graham McNamee and Phillips Carlin and CBS' Andrew White doing the announcing.

Game 1 at Forbes Field, Pittsburgh, October 5

	1	2	3	4	5	6	7	8	9	-	R	H	E
NY	1	0	3	0	1	0	0	0	0	-	5	6	1
PITTS.	1	0	1	0	1	0	0	1	0	-	4	9	2

W—Hoyt; L—Kremer.   A.—41,567

Game 2 at Forbes Field, Pittsburgh, October 6

	1	2	3	4	5	6	7	8	9	-	R	H	E
NY	0	0	3	0	0	0	0	3	0	-	6	11	0
PITTS.	1	0	0	0	0	0	0	1	0	-	2	7	2

W—Pipgras; L—Aldridge.   A.—41,634

Game 3 at Yankee Stadium, NY, October 7

	1	2	3	4	5	6	7	8	9	-	R	H	E
PITTS.	0	0	0	0	0	0	0	1	0	-	1	3	1
NY	2	0	0	0	0	0	6	0	X	-	8	9	0

W—Pennock; L—Meadows. HR—Ruth (NY).   A.—60,695

Game 4 at Yankee Stadium, NY, October 8

	1	2	3	4	5	6	7	8	9	-	R	H	E
PITTS.	1	0	0	0	0	0	2	0	0	-	3	10	1
NY	1	0	0	0	2	0	0	0	1	-	4	12	2

W—Moore; L—Miljus. HR—Ruth (NY).   A.—57,909

1928

The Yankees were awesome, beating the St. Louis Cardinals in four games and running their winning streak of World Series games to eight. They won the four games of this Series easily and used only three pitchers to do it.

Waite Hoyt pitched complete game victories in Games 1 and 4. George Pipgras and Tom Zachary also pitched complete games in Games 2 and 3, respectively. And so Hoyt, Pipgras and Zachary were the Series' heroes. But Babe Ruth, ah, there was a performance!

Ruth hit for .625, highest average in Series history, icing his wonderful showing in the final game at Sportsman's Park with three home runs. Incredibly, Lou Gehrig was just a shade behind; he had a .545 average, walked six times, hit four home runs, and tallied nine RBIs.

That their pitching be superb and their two big sluggers excel were key requirements in the Yankee success plan, for a team effort could not be counted on—the Yanks were too saddled with injuries for that. Herb Pennock missed the Series because of a bad arm and Earle Combs, who had a broken finger and sprained wrist, made just one pinch-hit appearance. Tony Lazzeri played with a severe right shoulder injury and needed late-inning replacement. Joe Dugan, bothered by eye problems and an injured knee, played sparingly. "The Bambino" limped through the Series with a sprained ankle and a charley horse, and Mark Koenig hobbled about with a bruised heel.

Because of the Yankees' physical deterioration and the Cardinals' supposed pitching superiority, St. Louis, believe it or not, was favored. But the Yankees made winning look easy.

Bob Meusel's two-run home run was the big hit in Game 1, supporting Hoyt's sensational three-hit pitching. Game 2 and Game 3 belonged to Gehrig and his heroics, and Ruth was at center stage in Game 4. Of Babe's three homers in the latter, his seventh-inning blast was the most noteworthy. It appeared that Cardinal pitcher Bill Sherdel had struck out Ruth with a quick-pitch, except that before the Series the quick pitch had been declared illegal and the umpire correctly ruled "no pitch." The Cardinals furiously and futilely protested while Ruth and Sherdel exchanged unpleasantries, Ruth saying to Sherdel, "Put one in here again, and I'll knock it out of the park for you." And that is exactly what was to transpire!

Besides Ruth's three round-trippers were hit by reserve outfielder Cedric Durst and the streaking Gehrig to give Hoyt an easy 7-3 clinching win. St. Louis rallied in the ninth, but Ruth, playing left field, made a spectacular running catch in foul territory to end the game. Babe waved his glove in the air in a victory salute all the way to the Yankee dugout. The Babe later stated that this catch and victory dance were one of his greatest baseball thrills.

Certainly, Cardinal Manager Bill McKechnie must be thanked for the easy Yankee Series win. Contrary to the 1926 strategy of Hornsby, McKechnie in this Series allowed his moundsmen to pitch to Ruth. Ruth, who was walked only once, made the most of the strike-zone pitches, giving St. Louis something to remember.

On the train ride home from St. Louis, the Yanks had one of the most riotous rail parties of all time. At each train stop people flocked to the cars to get a glimpse of the storied champions.

```
Game 1 at Yankee Stadium, NY, October 4
ST.L.    0  0  0    0  0  0    1  0  0  -  1  3  1
NY       1  0  0    2  0  0    0  1  X  -  4  7  0
W—Hoyt; L—Sherdel. HR—Meusel (NY), Bottomley (ST. L.). A.—61,425

Game 2 at Yankee Stadium, NY, October 5
ST.L.    0  3  0    0  0  0    0  0  0  -  3  4  1
NY       3  1  4    0  0  0    1  0  X  -  9  8  2
W—Pipgras; L—Alexander. HR—Gehrig (NY).         A.— 60,714

Game 3 at Sportsman's Park, St. Louis, October 7
NY       0  1  0    2  0  3    1  0  0  -  7  7  2
ST.L.    2  0  0    0  1  0    0  0  0  -  3  9  3
W—Zachary; L—Haines. HR—Gehrig (NY) 2.        A.—39,602

Game 4 at Sportsman's Park, St. Louis, October 9
NY       0  0  0    1  0  0    4  2  0  -  7  15  2
ST.L.    0  0  1    1  0  0    0  0  1  -  3  11  0
W—Hoyt; L—Sherdel. HR—Ruth (NY) 3, Durst (NY), Gehrig (NY).
                                             A.—37,331
```

1932

The Yankees swept the Chicago Cubs in four games to run their World Series game winning streak to 12 (through the 1999 World Series, the Yankees have tied this mark having also won 12 consecutive games!) in a bitterly fought Series. There were several reasons, besides simple competitiveness, for the antagonism between the teams.

They included the natural rivalry between the nation's two largest cities (New York and Chicago), revenge, friendship and money matters. New York City and Chicago were always at odds, especially at this time, concerning the relative merits of their cities. The Yankee-Cub battle was an extension of the bitter Giant-Cub rivalry of the early 20th century.

Revenge was on the mind of Yankee Manager Joe McCarthy who had been fired by the Cubs two years earlier (after winning the NL pennant in 1929) allegedly because McCarthy lacked what it took to win a World Championship. Joe was single-minded in his determination to beat his old team, and his new players were anxious to give him a present.

In addition, Yankee players hung the cheap sign on the Cub players for voting a popular old Yankee teammate, Mark Koenig, only a partial share of their World Series earnings. Babe Ruth regarded stinginess as the most sinful of postures and

quite naturally led the Yanks in taunting Cub players who in turn used Ruth as the focal point for their bench jockeying. As the Series unfolded, the bantering grew ugly, the Cubs calling Ruth "Nigger," a name he had often heard in his early career. So a Series that began in a spirit of unfriendliness was soon awash in an outpouring of hostility.

The Yanks easily won Games 1 and 2 in Yankee Stadium behind Red Ruffing (ten strikeouts) and Lefty Gomez. Cub pitchers walked ten Yankee batters in the two games and nine of them scored in 12-6, 5-2 Yankee wins.

When the scene shifted to Wrigley Field, the Yanks were greeted with open and obscene hostility. Every possible form of verbal abuse was directed toward the Yankees, especially Ruth. Mrs. Ruth, in fact, was spat upon and taunted on the streets of Chicago, distressing the Babe terribly. But Ruth, once assured of his and his wife's physical safety, reveled in the highly competitive spirit of the Series.

It was in Game 3 at Wrigley Field that Ruth hit his famous "called shot" home run. He had hit a titanic three-run homer before his fabled blast, but the Cubs rallied to tie the score, 4-4. When strike one was called, the Babe raised one finger and declared: "It only takes one to hit it." It was the fifth inning and the bases were empty with one out, and somehow through the deafening cheers of the crowd, Ruth exchanged gibes with the Cub bench. He pointed toward the bleachers. Strike two. Again he pointed toward his target, or so the legend has it. What happened next, however, is fact. Ruth silenced the Cub crowd by depositing Charlie Root's next pitch deep into the center field bleachers—one of the longest homers ever seen at Wrigley! Legend has it that the ball landed exactly where the Babe had pointed! Ruth laughed and shouted at the Cubs as he happily jaunted around the bases.

Later Earle Combs told Babe how the Cubs reacted. Explained Earle, "There they were—all out on the top step and yelling their brains out—and then you connected and they watched it and then fell back as if they were being machine-gunned." Babe was pleased he had broken the hearts of Chicago. He later maintained the "called shot" was in retaliation for the poor treatment he and his wife received in the "Windy City." Following Ruth's blast, the forgotten man, Lou Gehrig, belted his second homer of the game, burying the Cubs.

The home run twins hit four homers between them in Game 3, and George Pipgras had a 7-5 win with ninth-inning relief help from 38-year-old Herb Pennock who recorded a save. Following Game 3, Joe McCarthy displayed his confidence by having a notice posted that the Yanks' departing train would leave Chicago for New York after Game 4.

The next day, the Yanks bombed Chicago, 13-6. Ruth was hit by a pitch on the right forearm and could not have played if Game 5 had been necessary. Tony Lazzeri hit a pair of two-run homers, and Pennock recorded his second consecutive save (Wilcy Moore was credited with the win in relief of Johnny Allen). After the clinching the Game 4 victory, Art Fletcher (coach) led the team in singing "The Sidewalks of New York." The Babe was great in his final World Series (.333, two HRs, six RBIs) and Gehrig was not to be stopped (.529, three HRs, nine runs scored, eight RBIs). Bill Dickey (.438), Earle Combs (.375), Joe Sewell (.333) and Ben Chapman (.294), whose two-run single was key to the Game 2 victory, all hit well. The Yanks aggregated a fantastic .313 batting average.

```
Game 1 at Yankee Stadium, NY, September 28
CHI.    2 0 0   0 0 0   2 2 0 -  6 10 1
NY      0 0 0   3 0 5   3 1 X - 12  8 2
W—Ruffing; L—Bush. HR—Gehrig (NY).        A.—41,459

Game 2 at Yankee Stadium, NY, September 29
CHI.    1 0 1   0 0 0   0 0 0 -  2  9 0
NY      2 0 2   0 1 0   0 0 X -  5 10 1
W—Gomez; L—Warneke.                       A.—50,709

Game 3 at Wrigley Field, Chicago, October 1
NY      3 0 1   0 2 0   0 0 1 -  7  8 1
CHI.    1 0 2   1 0 0   0 0 1 -  5  9 4
W—Pipgras; L—Root. HR—Ruth (NY) 2, Gehrig (NY) 2, Cuyler (CHI), Hartnett
(CHI).                                    A.—49,986

Game 4 at Wrigley Field, Chicago, October 2
NY      1 0 2   0 0 2   4 0 4 - 13 19 4
CHI.    4 0 0   0 0 1   0 0 1 -  6  9 1
W—Moore; L—May. HR—Demaree (CHI), Lazzeri (NY) 2, Combs (NY). A.—49,844
```

1936

The Yankees won their fifth World Championship by beating the New York Giants in the first "Subway Series" in 13 years. After the Giants snapped the Yankees' streak of 12 World Series game victories in a row, the American Leaguers bounced back to win four out of five, proving their anticipated predominance.

The Series began at the Polo Grounds and except for a long George Selkirk home run, the Giants' star pitcher King Carl Hubbell had his screwball working to perfection. King Carl pitched a seven-hit complete game and had the Yanks beating the ball into the ground to Giant infielders all day. There were 13 Yankee groundouts recorded in the game that was played in a steady drizzle.

The Yanks quickly gained revenge in Game 2, winning 18-4. The 18 Yankee runs established a record for most runs scored in a Series game, and every starter made at least one hit and scored at least one run. The highlight of the slaughter was Tony Lazzeri's grand-slam homer to the opposite field, the second grand slam in Series history.

The Yanks were lucky to win Game 3, although Bump Hadley pitched brilliantly and Pat Malone got a save. With the score tied in the bottom of the eighth, 1-1 (the Yankee run coming on a Lou Gehrig home run), George Selkirk led off with a single. Jake Powell walked and Tony Lazzeri sacrificed the runners to second and third. After Selkirk was thrown out at the plate on a ball tapped to "Fat Freddie" Fitzsimmons, the Giant pitcher, Frank Crosetti's grounder glanced off Fitzsimmons' glove for a hit, allowing the winning run to score and making a hard-luck loser of Fitzsimmons who allowed only four Yankee hits. Malone retired the Giants in scoreless fashion in the ninth to finish a critical 2-1 Yankee victory.

Gaining revenge off Hubbell in Game 4, the Yanks enjoyed a three-run third inning, highlighted by Gehrig's two-run home run, and went on to win, 5-2. With his win in Game 1 of the Series, Hubbell had a string of 17 consecutive victories. Thus the Yankees brought him back to earth in Game 4.

The Giants rallied to win Game 5, 5-4, in 10 innings at Yankee Stadium, but the Bronx Bombers ended the Series in Game 6 behind Lefty Gomez, Johnny Murphy, and an offense that generated 17 hits.

For the Series, Gomez won two games, Monte Pearson and Hadley each pitched one fine game in tight contests, and the Yankee offensive machine was led by Powell (.455), Red Rolfe

(.400), Joe DiMaggio (.346) and Selkirk (.333). Lazzeri and Gehrig led both clubs with seven RBIs each, but Lou for the first time in a Series hit below .300 (.292), although his two home runs came in the clutch. The powerful Yankees hit .302 as a team.

```
Game 1 at the Polo Grounds, NY, September 30
NY (AL)  0 0 1   0 0 0   0 0 0 -  1  7 2
NY (NL)  0 0 0   0 1 1   0 4 X -  6  9 1
W—Hubbell; L—Ruffing. HR—Bartell (NL), Selkirk (AL).     A.—39,419

Game 2 at the Polo Grounds, NY, October 2
NY (AL)  2 0 7   0 0 1   2 0 6 - 18 17 0
NY (NL)  0 1 0   3 0 0   0 0 0 -  4  6 1
W—Gomez; L—Schumacher. HR—Dickey (AL) Lazzeri (AL).      A.—43,543

Game 3 at Yankee Stadium, NY, October 3
NY (NL)  0 0 0   0 0 1   0 0 0 -  1 11 0
NY (AL)  0 1 0   0 0 0   0 1 X -  2  4 0
W—Hadley; L—Fitzsimmons. HR.—Gehrig (AL), Ripple (NL).   A.—64,842

Game 4 at Yankee Stadium, NY, October 4
NY (NL)  0 0 0   1 0 0   0 1 0 -  2  7 1
NY (AL)  0 1 3   0 0 0   0 1 X -  5 10 1
W—Pearson; L—Hubbell. HR—Gehrig (AL).                    A.—66,669

Game 5 at Yankee Stadium, NY, October 5
NY (NL)  3 0 0   0 0 1   0 0 1 -  5  8 3
NY (AL)  0 1 1   0 0 2   0 0 0 -  4 10 1
W—Schumacher; L—Malone. HR—Selkirk (AL).                 A.—50,024

Game 6 at the Polo Grounds, NY, October 6
NY (AL)  0 2 1   2 0 0   0 1 7 - 13 17 2
NY (NL)  2 0 0   0 1 0   1 1 0 -  5  9 1
W—Gomez; L—Fitzsimmons. HR—Moore (NL), Ott (NL), Powell (AL). A.—38,427
```

1937

The Yankees won their sixth World Championship by defeating the New York Giants in five games, as the National Leaguers managed to win only Game 4 behind Carl Hubbell to avert a Yankee sweep. The Yanks' control throughout the Series was so complete that it suffocated any budding excitement. Victory margins of 8-1, 8-1 and 5-1 in the first three games demonstrated Yankee excellence early, and the Game 5 victory gave the Yanks 20 wins in the club's last 23 Series games!

Yankee pitching was superb, posting an ERA of 2.45 for the Series. Lefty Gomez again won two games, both of which he completed. Tony Lazzeri (.400) was magnificent in this, his last World Series as a Yankee, capping his 12-year Yankee career by stroking at least one hit in every game. Myril Hoag (.300), Red Rolfe (.300) and George Selkirk (six RBIs) also were batting stars. Team captain and leader Lou Gehrig hit .294 but his so-so Series can be attributed to his feeling poorly. He complained of lumbago.

In Game 1, a pair of two-run bases-loaded singles, compliments of Joe DiMaggio and Selkirk, highlighted a seven-run sixth inning and knocked out Hubbell in the process. Contributing to the Giants' downfall were the two walks given Gomez, a terrible hitter, in the big inning. Lazzeri's home run later finished the Yankee rout.

Red Ruffing pitched a seven-hit complete game and drove in three runs himself in Game 2, and Monte Pearson was sensational in Game 3, hurling a five-hitter and helping to erase any sense of suspense early in the Series.

One of the humorous moments of Series history came in the final game. On the mound and in the midst of nailing down the Series clincher, Lefty Gomez became enthralled with an airplane passing high over the Polo Grounds. Both teams and the crowd were kept waiting under tension-ridden circumstances until the plane had flown from the airplane-loving Gomez' sight. Lefty also singled in the winning run in the fifth inning, held the Giants scoreless through the final six frames, and won, 4-2.

```
Game 1 at Yankee Stadium, NY, October 6
NY (NL)   0  0  0    0  1  0    0  0  0  -  1   6   2
NY (AL)   0  0  0    0  0  7    0  1  X  -  8   7   0
W-Gomez; L-Hubbell. HR-Lazzeri (AL).           A.-60,573

Game 2 at Yankee Stadium, NY, October 7
NY (NL)   1  0  0    0  0  0    0  0  0  -  1   7   0
NY (AL)   0  0  0    0  2  4    2  0  X  -  8  12   0
W-Ruffing; L-Melton.                           A.-57,675

Game 3 at the Polo Grounds, NY, October 8
NY (AL)   0  1  2    1  1  0    0  0  0  -  5   9   0
NY (NL)   0  0  0    0  0  0    1  0  0  -  1   5   4
W-Pearson; L-Schumacher.                       A.-37,385

Game 4 at the Polo Grounds, NY, October 9
NY (AL)   1  0  1    0  0  0    0  0  1  -  3   6   0
NY (NL)   0  6  0    0  0  0    1  0  X  -  7  12   3
W-Hubbell; L-Hadley. HR-Gehrig (AL).           A.-44,293

Game 5 at the Polo Grounds, NY, October 10
NY (AL)   0  1  1    0  2  0    0  0  0  -  4   8   0
NY (NL)   0  0  2    0  0  0    0  0  0  -  2  10   0
W-Gomez; L-Melton HR-DiMaggio (AL), Hoag (AL), Ott (NL).
                                               A.-38,216
```

1938

The Yankees became the first team in history to win three straight World Series as they swept the Chicago Cubs in four games.

Red Ruffing beat the Cubs, 3-1, in Game 1 and Lefty Gomez won Game 2, 6-3, beating a gutsy Dizzy Dean, now without his fastball. Gomez got some strange help! With runners on second and third, Joe Gordon hit an easy roller on which third baseman Stan Hack and shortstop Billy Jurges converged, cracking heads and allowing the ball to go through. The Yankees got two gift runs here. Later, after an apparent third strike was ruled a ball, Frank Crosetti hit a two-run homer to give Lefty a 4-3 lead. As "The Crow" circled the bases with what proved to be the winning run, Dizzy yelled to him, "I wish I could call back one year, Frank. You couldn't get a loud foul off me." To which Frank replied, "You're so right, Diz! You're so right!" Joe DiMaggio hit a two-run homer in the ninth inning for insurance.

Monte Pearson pitched a pretty five-hit complete game back at Yankee Stadium in Game 3 to win, 5-2, and Ruffing hurled his second complete game victory in Game 4. The Yanks won the clincher, 8-3, paced by Crosetti's four RBIs.

Yankee pitchers Ruffing, Gomez, Murphy and Pearson saved some of their best pitching of the season for the Series, posting a combined 1.75 ERA! Not once did Yankee Manager Joe McCarthy come to the mound to make a pitching change. His only pitching replacement was a pinch-hitter for Gomez in Game 2. Lefty got the win, and Johnny Murphy pitched two shutout innings to get credit for a save.

Bill Dickey, who rapped four singles in Game 1, and Joe Gordon, who homered and hit a two-run single in Game 3, each hit .400 for the Series to pace the Yankee attack and Frank

Crosetti, who stroked four extra-base hits, had six RBIs. Yankee great Lou Gehrig (.286) played in his final Series for his sixth World Championship Yankee club. The fact that Lou did not make a single extra-base hit was not overlooked by the joyous Yankees or their fans. The disease that was to take Lou's life would be diagnosed some eight months later.

```
Game 1 at Wrigley Field, Chicago, October 5
NY      0  2  0    0  0  0    1  0  0  -  3  12   1
CHI.    0  0  1    0  0  0    0  0  0  -  1   9   1
W-Ruffing; L-Lee.                              A.-43,642

Game 2 at Wrigley Field, Chicago, October 6
NY      0  2  0    0  0  0    0  2  2  -  6   7   2
CHI.    1  0  2    0  0  0    0  0  0  -  3  11   0
W-Gomez; L-Dean. HR-Crosetti (NY), DiMaggio (NY).  A.-42,108

Game 3 at Yankee Stadium, NY, October 8
CHI.    0  0  0    0  1  0    0  1  0  -  2   5   1
NY      0  0  0    0  2  2    0  1  X  -  5   7   2
W-Pearson; L-Bryant. HR-Dickey (NY) Gordon (NY), Marty (CHI). A.-55,236

Game 4 at Yankee Stadium, NY, October 9
CHI.    0  0  0    1  0  0    2  0  -  3   8   1
NY      0  3  0    0  0  1    0  4  X  -  8  11   1
NY 030001 04X- 8 11 1
W-Ruffing; L-Lee. HR-Henrich (NY), O'Dea (CHI).    A.-59,847
```

1939

The Yankees won the World Series a record-breaking fourth straight year. By sweeping the Cincinnati Reds in four games, they ran their World Series game-winning streak to nine. In addition, when the Yanks won Game 4, it was their 28th win in the club's last 31 games going back to the 1927 Series.

Red Ruffing led off the Series, making his third opening game start in four years, and this proved to be the Series' key game. Cincinnati nicked Red for a run in the fourth, but Joe Gordon singled and Babe Dahlgren doubled Gordon home in the Yankee fifth. Ruffing and Cincinnati ace Paul Derringer, who was 25-7 in the regular season, took their pitching duel into the bottom of the ninth, tied 1-1.

The Yankee Stadium crowd roared when rookie Charlie Keller tripled with one out. Instead of walking the bases loaded, Red Manager Bill McKechnie only had Joe DiMaggio walked, electing to have Derringer pitch to the dangerous Bill Dickey. (McKechnie said later he was afraid of on-deck hitter George Selkirk.) Dickey ended the game with a ground single to right-field, scoring Keller, and afterwards McKechnie, one of the game's greatest managers, was second-guessed. Ruffing was the winner with a splendid four-hitter.

The Game 2 pitching was even better. Monte Pearson, who retired the first 22 batters (7 1/3 innings) before Ernie Lombardi's clean single in the eighth, threw a two-hitter at the Reds, winning 4-0. The Yankees collected only five hits in Game 3 but four of them were home runs, two by Keller, one by DiMaggio, and the fourth off the bat of Dickey. The four shots brought in seven runs, making a winner of Bump Hadley, 7-3.

The final humiliation for the Reds came in Game 4. Until the ninth inning of Game 4, the Reds had played errorless ball and had reason to hold their heads high. The Reds even had a 4-2 lead as the Yanks came to bat in the top of the ninth at Crosley Field. Keller and DiMaggio each singled, before Dickey rapped a perfect double-play grounder to second baseman

Lonny Frey. However, shortstop Billy Myers dropped the relay, Keller scored, and everyone else was safe. After DiMaggio went to third on a fly, Gordon grounded to third baseman Bill Werber whose throw home failed to get "The Yankee Clipper."

The game went into extra-innings tied, 4-4. In the 10th, Frank Crosetti was on second with one out when Myers misplayed Keller's grounder for an error. Then came one of the weirdest plays in Series history. DiMaggio singled to right, scoring Crosetti, and when Ivan Goodman bobbled the ball, baserunner Keller attempted to score from first. He crashed cleanly into Reds' catcher Ernie Lombardi, knocking the ball loose and stunning Lombardi. As Lombardi lay dazed—"snoozing," some of the press put it—DiMaggio hustled home.

The Reds offered a mild threat in their half of the tenth, but the Yankees, with Johnny Murphy in relief, put this down to win the game and the Series. The Reds had made four costly errors in the final two innings of play, and Lombardi was unfairly branded the goat. There was enough blame to go around to others.

The Yankee hitting star of the Series was the sensational Keller (.438, three HRs, six RBIs). Other big bats belonged to DiMaggio (.313) and Dickey (two HRs, five RBIs), but the Yanks hit just .206 as a team. In fact, the Reds had as many hits as the Yanks (27), but the Yanks launched seven home runs to none for Cincinnati. For the third straight World Series, Yankee pitching was phenomenal, posting this year an unbelievable 1.22 ERA. With that kind of clout and pitching, the Yanks were riding high, and among those savoring the New York success was captain Lou Gehrig, no longer an active player but a lender of moral support.

```
Game 1 at Yankee Stadium, NY, October 4
CIN.      0  0  0    1  0  0    0  0  0  -  1   4   0
NY        0  0  0    0  1  0    0  0  1  -  2   6   0
W—Ruffing; L—Derringer.                A.—58,541

Game 2 at Yankee Stadium, NY, October 5
CIN.      0  0  0    0  0  0    0  0  0  -  0   2   0
NY        0  0  3    1  0  0    0  0  X  -  4   9   0
W—Pearson; L—Walters. HR—Dahlgren (NY). A.—59,791

Game 3 at Crosley Field, Cincinnati, October 7
NY        2  0  2    0  3  0    0  0  0  -  7   5   1
CIN.      1  2  0    0  0  0    0  0  0  -  3  10   0
W—Hadley; L—Thompson. HR—Keller (NY) 2, DiMaggio (NY), Dickey (NY).
                                       A.—32,723

Game 4 at Crosley Field, Cincinnati, October 8
NY        0  0  0    0  0  0    2  0  2  3  -  7   7  1
CIN.      0  0  0    0  0  0    3  1  0  0  -  4  11  4
W—Murphy; L—Walters. HR—Keller (NY), Dickey (NY).  A.—32,794
```

1941

The Yankees won their ninth World Championship by whipping the Brooklyn Dodgers in five games. It was the first Series meeting of the two teams, but it was not to be the last; they would face each other seven times in a span of 16 seasons.

Red Ruffing won Game 1, 3-2, pitching a complete game and enjoying his fourth success in a World Series opener. A big factor in Game 1 was a rare base-running mistake by Pee Wee Reese. Reese attempted to tag up and go from second to third on an infield pop foul, only to be thrown out to end a potential Brooklyn uprising.

The Yanks' ten-game World Series game-winning streak was snapped by Brooklyn in Game 2, and in Game 3 Yankee pitcher Marius Russo lined a shot off Dodger pitcher Freddie Fitzsimmons' knee in the seventh inning. Fitzsimmons was forced to leave the scoreless game and the Yanks, behind Russo's four-hitter, went on to win, 2-1.

The most bizarre play of the Series occurred in Game 4. The Dodgers desperately needed a win to tie the Series and were leading 4-3 with two out in the ninth at Ebbets Field. Hugh Casey struck out Tommy Henrich for the final out, but the ball (probably a wicked-breaking spitball) eluded Dodger catcher Mickey Owen, and Henrich alertly raced to first base. The Yankees took advantage of the incredible break by knocking across four runs to win the game, 7-4. (In sequence, DiMaggio singled sharply to left field, Keller doubled against the right-field fence to bring in the tying and go-ahead runs, Dickey walked, and Gordon doubled home two insurance runs.)

The shocked Dodgers caved in Game 5, managing only four hits off Yankee pitcher Ernie Bonham, to end the Series.

Joe Gordon (.500), Charlie Keller (.389) and Red Rolfe (.300) paced the Yankee hitters, but only Gordon and Henrich hit home runs. Seven Yankee pitchers posted an incredible team ERA of 1.80, holding Brooklyn to a .182 batting average. Only in Game 4 did the Dodgers make more than six hits, and the highest average of all Dodger regulars was Joe Medwick's .235.

Dodger diehards claimed for years that the Yankee victory was attributable to the Casey-Owen-Henrich play of Game 4, but the fact is the Dodgers were beaten because they could not hit Yankee pitching, even in the bandbox that was their home, Ebbets Field. The final game victory capped a sensational string of 32 Yankee victories in 36 World Series contests! It also was the eighth World Championship (beginning with 1927) in as many chances for the Yanks and the sixth for Manager Joe McCarthy.

```
Game 1 at Yankee Stadium, NY, October 1
BKN.      0  0  0    0  1  0    1  0  0  -  2   6   0
NY        0  1  0    1  0  1    0  0  X  -  3   6   1
W—Ruffing; L—Davis. HR—Gordon (NY).   A.—68,540

Game 2 at Yankee Stadium, NY, October 2
BKN.      0  0  0    0  2  1    0  0  0  -  3   6   2
NY        0  1  1    0  0  0    0  0  0  -  2   9   1
W—Wyatt; L—Chandler.                   A.—66,248

Game 3 at Ebbets Field, Brooklyn, October 4
NY        0  0  0    0  0  0    0  2  0  -  2   8   0
BKN.      0  0  0    0  0  0    0  1  0  -  1   4   0
W—Russo; L—Casey.                      A.—33,100

Game 4 at Ebbets Field, Brooklyn, October 5
NY        1  0  0    2  0  0    0  0  4  -  7  12   0
BKN.      0  0  0    2  2  0    0  0  0  -  4   9   1
W—Murphy; L—Casey. HR—Reiser (BKN).    A.—33,813

Game 5 at Ebbets Field, Brooklyn, October 6
NY        0  2  0    0  1  0    0  0  0  -  3   6   0
BKN.      0  0  1    0  0  0    0  0  0  -  1   4   1
W—Bonham; L—Wyatt. HR—Henrich (NY).    A.—34,072
```

1942

Red Ruffing won the World Series opener again—his fifth—and came close to pitching a no-hitter, and the Yankees, dominant in each of their last eight Series appearances, appeared headed for success once more. But the young St. Louis Cardinals weren't going along with the script.

St. Louis took the next four games and the Series. Cardinal heroes included pitcher Johnny Beazley, winner of Games 2 and 5; pitcher Ernie White, who in Game 3 shut the Yankees out; and the great outfield of Enos Slaughter, Terry Moore and Stan Musial, who all hit well and made spectacular catches (each made a great catch to help White in Game 3). Whitey Kurowski's two-run home run in the top of the ninth inning won the finale for St. Louis.

For the Yanks, Joe DiMaggio made great defensive plays and hit .333, while Phil Rizzuto (.381), Red Rolfe (.353) and Buddy Hassett (.333) also contributed.

There were two occasions in the Series when the Yankees appeared on the verge of regaining their customary control. They were Charlie Keller occasions. In the eighth inning of Game 2, Keller hit a two-run home run to tie the game at 3-3. However, a Musial single scored Slaughter in the bottom of the inning to regain the lead for the Cards, and a New York rally in the ninth was nipped when a Slaughter throw wiped out Tuck Stainback at third base. Another chance was allowed to slide away in Game 4. The Cardinals saw the 6-1 lead they had taken into the sixth inning dwindle as a packed Yankee Stadium thrilled to a five-run Yankee rally featuring a three-run Keller homer. But St. Louis met the challenge by scoring three more runs and going on to win by a final score of 9-6.

For the Yankees, the loss of the Series was their first defeat in the Fall Classic since St. Louis beat them in 1926. White's shutout of the Bronx Bombers in Game 2 was the first time the Yanks were blanked in World Series competition since 1926, a string of 42 games. The Cardinal upset shocked the public, ranking with some of the all-time World Series upsets. St. Louis fielded the major leagues' youngest team (Musial, Kurowski and Beazley were virtual rookies), and the New Yorkers were proven veterans of pressure play.

But what is often ignored is that the Cards were a great team, winning more games in 1942 than any team in the National League in 33 years. In all eight easy World Series triumphs between 1927-41, the Yankees recorded more regular season wins than their National League opponents, but this year St. Louis had 106 compared to New York's 103. Despite their youth, the Cards simply were not overawed by the Yankees' reputation; they played with confidence and aggressiveness.

Playing without Tommy Henrich, who entered the Coast Guard in the season's final month, and Buddy Hassett, who was hurt in his first Game 3 at-bat (Gerry Priddy finished the Series at first base), is an inadequate excuse for the Yanks' loss. The Yanks made half the number of errors committed by the Cards (five to ten), but these came at crucial points such as in the ninth inning of the finale when Joe Gordon was uncharacteristically picked off second base with two on and no outs, ruining the Yanks' last chance to stage a rally.

Cool were the St. Louis bats in the Series; they certainly did not bludgeon the Yanks, hitting .239 as a team. Jimmy Brown (.300) was the only Cardinal player to hit as high as .300.

Ruffing had a no-hitter going with two outs in the eighth inning of Game 1 when Moore singled. The Cardinals were obviously nervous, but a four-run Cardinal ninth drove Ruffing from the mound and though the rally fell short, it no doubt gave the young Cardinals confidence.

The significance of the great St. Louis plays of Game 3 cannot be minimized. Late in the game Moore robbed DiMaggio of a sure triple, Musial stole a home run from Gordon and Slaughter jumped high to take a potential four-bagger away from Keller. Meanwhile in that contest, Spud Chandler allowed only four Cardinal base runners in eight innings of superb pitching, yet was the loser of a 2-0 decision.

In previous World Series, the Yankees won such nail-biters when one of their pitchers gave such a gutsy performance. Not this year though, and for the first time since 1915 a team won four straight games after losing the opener.

Game 1 at Sportsman's Park, St. Louis, September 30													
NY	0	0	0	1	1	0	0	3	2	-	7	11	0
ST.L.	0	0	0	0	0	0	0	0	4	-	4	7	4

W—Ruffing; L—M. Cooper. A.—34,769

Game 2 at Sportsman's Park, St. Louis, October 1													
NY	0	0	0	0	0	0	0	3	0	-	3	10	2
ST. L.	2	0	0	0	0	0	1	1	0	-	4	6	0

W—Beazley; L—Bonham. HR—Keller (NY). A.—34,255

Game 3 at Yankee Stadium, NY, October 2													
ST.L.	0	0	1	0	0	0	0	0	1	-	2	5	1
NY	0	0	0	0	0	0	0	0	0	-	0	6	1

W—White; L—Chandler. A.—69,123

Game 4 at Yankee Stadium, NY, October 4													
ST.L.	0	0	0	6	0	0	2	0	1	-	9	12	1
NY	1	0	0	0	0	5	0	0	0	-	6	10	1

W—Lanier; L—Donald. HR—Keller (NY). A.—69,902

Game 5 at Yankee Stadium, NY, October 5													
ST.L.	0	0	0	1	0	1	0	0	2	-	4	9	4
NY	1	0	0	1	0	0	0	0	0	-	2	7	1

W—Beazley; L—Ruffing. HR—Rizzuto (NY), Slaughter (ST. L.), Kurowski (ST. L.). A.—69,052

1943

The Yankees avenged their defeat of the previous year at the hands of the St. Louis Cardinals by beating the Cardinals in five games.

Spud Chandler was the Yankee pitching ace in this World Series. He won Game 1, 4-2, then shut out the Cardinals for the championship in Game 5 (11 Cardinals were left stranded), both complete game victories.

The Yankees lost Game 2 and appeared headed for defeat in Game 3 when they broke out in the eighth inning with a five-run splurge that was helped along by two Cardinal errors. Johnny Lindell singled in leading off that fateful frame, taking second when Cardinal centerfielder Harry Walker fumbled the ball. Snuffy Stirnweiss bunted to first baseman Ray Sanders who fired to third base, the ball getting there ahead of Lindell, but Johnny crashed into Whitey Kurowski and knocked the ball loose. Then Tuck Stainback flied out, allowing Stirnweiss to tag to second and with first base open, the Cardinals intentionally walked Frank Crosetti.

The Series' biggest hit, Billy Johnson's bases-loaded triple, followed and was followed in turn by the scoring of two more Yankee runs. Receiving the win in the 6-2 Yankee victory was Hank Borowy with relief help from Johnny Murphy who made his final World Series appearance.

Marius Russo won Game 4, 2-1. Bill Dickey got the Yanks on the board in the fourth inning when he singled home Joe Gordon who had doubled with two outs. With the game knotted, 1-1, Russo led off the eighth with his second double of the game. He was sacrificed to third, and Frank Crosetti brought Russo home with a sacrifice fly. Russo's pitching was impressive, especially in the seventh, eighth and ninth innings when lionhearted Marius worked out of jams.

In Game 5, clutch-hitting Dickey blasted a two-run homer in the sixth inning, scoring the game's only runs and winning the finale for Chandler.

For the Cardinals in the Series, Mort and Walker Cooper, the winning battery of Game 2, deserve special recognition. The brothers played Game 2 following the death of their father that morning. St. Louis shortstop Marty Marion hit .357 to lead all batters.

For the Yankees, the most impressive hit was Gordon's 450-foot home run at Yankee Stadium in Game 1, but rookie third baseman Billy Johnson was the only Yankee regular to hit as high as .300. The next highest average turned in by a Yankee was the .278 marks recorded by reliable veterans Dickey and Crosetti who each laced key hits. But the Yanks did not need much hitting with the pitching staff aggregating a 1.40 ERA. (Chandler and Russo together permitted but one earned run in three complete-game wins.)

Because of World War II, both clubs played this World Series without many star players who were serving in the military. New York played without Joe DiMaggio, Tommy Henrich, Phil Rizzuto, George Selkirk, Red Ruffing and Buddy Hassett, while St. Louis lost Enos Slaughter, Terry Moore, Jimmy Brown, Johnny Beazley and Howie Pollet. General Dwight D. Eisenhower had this World Series broadcast to his troops, stating it helped morale. Yankee fans' morale was also boosted by the avenging of the 1942 loss to the Cardinals!

1947

The Yankees won their 11th World Championship by defeating the Brooklyn Dodgers in a World Series that was laced with some of the most outstanding plays and games in the history of the Fall Classic. But it took the Yanks all seven games to do it. It was only the second time that New York was forced to go to a climactic seventh game even though this was the Yanks' 15th World Series appearance. The Yanks were losers in the 1926 seven-game set, but this time the results were happier.

In Game 1, Ralph Branca retired the first 12 Yanks before New York exploded for five runs in the fifth. Johnny Lindell's bases-loaded double scored two runs, another run scored on pinch-hitter Bobby Brown's walk, and Tommy Henrich singled in two more. New York pitchers Spec Shea (win—five innings) and Joe Page (save—four innings) made the five runs stand, allowing only six hits in the 5-3 Yankee victory.

Allie Reynolds was the hero of Game 2, sprinkling nine hits and striking out six while his teammates made 15 hits to bomb the Dodgers, 10-3. Of the six Yankee extra-base hits, Lindell had a double and triple, and Henrich ripped a homer.

Brooklyn fought back to win Games 3 and 4 at their home field, Ebbets Field.

Game 3 found the Yanks continually trying to reduce big Dodger leads. The Yanks were down 6-0, 7-2, 9-4 and 9-7, before Yogi Berra's pinch-hit homer, the first in Series history, narrowed Brooklyn's lead to 9-8. (Joe DiMaggio also hit a two-run homer in the attempted comeback.) But veteran reliever Hugh Casey, who appeared in six games and collected two wins and a save, held the Yankees scoreless over the final two innings to preserve the 9-8 Dodger victory.

Game 4 had all the excitement a Yankee-Dodger meeting could produce. Yankee pitcher Bill Bevens, battling wildness, entered the ninth inning with a 2-1 lead and a no-hitter. (The Dodgers scored in the fifth on two walks, a sacrifice and an infield grounder.) Dodger Bruce Edwards led off the bottom of the ninth with a long fly to center that DiMaggio corralled. Carl Furillo walked, the ninth pass issued by Bevens. But Bevens induced Spider Jorgensen to foul out to first baseman George McQuinn.

One out away from immortality, Bevens faced pinch-hitter Pete Reiser, and Al Gionfriddo ran for Furillo. On a 2-1 pitch, Gionfriddo stole second, barely beating Berra's peg. Facing a 3-1 count on Reiser, Yankee Manager Bucky Harris ordered an intentional pass. That controversial move (putting the winning run on base) proved disastrous: Pinch-hitter Cookie Lavagetto stroked an opposite field double off the right-field wall to score Gionfriddo, the tying run, and pinch-runner Eddie Miksis, the winning run! It was Cookie's only hit to right-field all year and his last big league hit, but it gave Brooklyn a 3-2 victory. Yankee rightfielder Henrich later said, "I just knew that ball would hit the wall. Those were five seconds I could have lived without." Bill Bevens had pitched 8²/₃ innings of hitless ball and lost!

The Yankees, however, bounced back to win Game 5, 2-1, thanks to the four-hit pitching of Shea, who knocked in the first run with a single, and DiMaggio, whose home run was the

---

```
Game 1 at Yankee Stadium, NY, October 5
ST.L.    0  1  0    0  1  0    0  0  0  -  2  7  2
NY       0  0  0    2  0  2    0  0  X  -  4  8  2
W—Chandler; L—Lanier. HR—Gordon (NY).        A.—68,676

Game 2 at Yankee Stadium, NY, October 6
ST.L.    0  0  1    3  0  0    0  0  0  -  4  7  2
NY       0  0  0    1  0  0    0  0  2  -  3  6  0
W—M. Cooper; L—Bonham. HR—Marion (ST. L.), Sanders (ST. L.).
                                             A.—68,578

Game 3 at Yankee Stadium, NY, October 7
ST.L.    0  0  0    2  0  0    0  0  0  -  2  6  4
NY       0  0  0    0  0  1    0  5  X  -  6  8  0
W—Borowy; L—Brazle.                          A.—69,990

Game 4 at Sportsman's Park, St. Louis, October 10
NY       0  0  0    1  0  0    0  1  0  -  2  6  2
ST.L.    0  0  0    0  0  0    1  0  0  -  1  7  1
W—Russo; L—Brecheen.                         A.—36,196

Game 5 at Sportsman's Park, St. Louis, October 11
NY       0  0  0    0  0  2    0  0  0  -  2  7  1
ST.L.    0  0  0    0  0  0    0  0  0  -  0 10  1
W—Chandler; L—M. Cooper HR—Dickey (NY).      A.—33,872
```

game-winning hit. "The Yankee Clipper" also made two beautiful catches in center field, key plays in the game. Shea had the here-we-go-again criers in full gear when he kept Brooklyn hitless for four innings. In the bottom of the ninth, and with the tying run on second base, Spec fanned pinch-hitter Lavagetto to end the contest. What a difference a day makes! Following the game, the teams prepared to return to Yankee Stadium. Noted Henrich, "We said our farewell to Brooklyn yesterday. Now we'll give them something to remember in the Bronx."

But Game 6 went to the Dodgers. It is the game best remembered for Brooklyn outfielder Gionfriddo's tremendous catch of a screaming drive off DiMaggio's bat in the sixth inning, with two out and two on and the Yankees down, 8-5. Somehow Gionfriddo snared the ball at the base of Yankee Stadium's 415-foot barrier to save the game for Brooklyn. Many also remember DiMaggio's uncharacteristic reaction to the robbery—a swift kick of the dirt at second base. The game saw action by 38 players before the Dodgers prevailed, 8-6.

But the Yankees won Game 7 behind the clutch relief job of Page, who allowed only one hit over the final five frames. Phil Rizzuto's second-inning single drove in a run to cut an early Dodger lead to 2-1. In the fourth, two Yankee runs scored, one each on pinch-hitter Brown's double and Henrich's single. Rizzuto walked, stole second and scored on Allie Clark's single in the sixth. Aaron Robinson's sacrifice fly scored Billy Johnson who had tripled in the seventh to complete the scoring, giving the Yankees a 5-2 victory and sewing up a hard-fought Series.

The Yanks were loaded with heroes. Page was outstanding in four relief appearances (1-1, one save), and Shea won two games. Lindell hit .500 with seven RBIs, Brown was 3-for-3 as a pinch-hitter, Rizzuto hit .308, DiMaggio blasted a pair of homers, Johnson hit three triples and scored eight runs, and Henrich (.323) produced many clutch hits, including three game winners, to help the Yankees win this memorable Series.

For the first time, all seven Series games were shown on network television (NBC); the country seemed to pause for a week to watch the Yankees and Dodgers fight for the title. Television had turned thousands who never expected to see a World Series into Series ticket holders. Bars and department stores around New York City were jam-packed with fans enthralled with the drama of the interborough confrontation. And in the minds of the respective front offices, it was a bitter confrontation.

Larry MacPhail and Branch Rickey had been rivals for years, of course, but this was the year Leo Durocher was serving suspension as a direct result of that feud. During the Series, Yankee President MacPhail attempted to patch things up, but he was told by Rickey, "Never speak to me again." Apparently the two great Hall of Famers never conversed again. At the Yankee victory party following the final win, Larry was not in a celebrating mood. Beer in hand, MacPhail shouted, "My heart can't stand it any more. I'm through. I'm through." And he did retire, too.

A side note: The principal actors of the Game 4 drama, Bevens, Lavagetto and Gionfriddo, were through in the big leagues, also. None of them ever played another major-league game following the 1947 World Series.

```
Game 1 at Yankee Stadium, NY, Sept. 30
BKN.      1  0  0    0  0  1    1  0  0  -  3   6  0
NY        0  0  0    0  5  0    0  0  X  -  5   4  0
W—Shea; L—Branca.                          A.—73,365

Game 2 at Yankee Stadium, NY, October 1
BKN.      0  0  1    1  0  0    0  1  0  -  3   9  2
NY        1  0  1    1  2  1    4  0  X  - 10  15  1
W—Reynolds; L—Lombardi. HR—Walker (BKN), Henrich (NY).
                                           A.—69,865

Game 3 at Ebbets Field, Brooklyn, October 2
NY        0  0  2    2  2  1    1  0  0  -  8  13  0
BKN.      0  6  1    2  0  0    0  0  X  -  9  13  1
W—Casey; L—Newsom. HR—DiMaggio (NY), Berra (NY).  A.—33,098

Game 4 at Ebbets Field, Brooklyn, October 3
NY        1  0  0    1  0  0    0  0  0  -  2   8  1
BKN.      0  0  0    0  1  0    0  0  2  -  3   1  3
W—Casey; L—Bevens.                         A.—33,443

Game 5 at Ebbets Field, Brooklyn, October 4
NY        0  0  0    1  1  0    0  0  0  -  2   5  0
BKN.      0  0  0    0  0  1    0  0  0  -  1   4  1
W—Shea; L—Barney. HR—DiMaggio (NY).        A.—34,379

Game 6 at Yankee Stadium, NY, October 5
BKN.      2  0  2    0  0  4    0  0  0  -  8  12  1
NY        0  0  4    1  0  0    0  0  1  -  6  15  2
W—Branca; L—Page.                          A.—74,065

Game 7 at Yankee Stadium, NY, October 6
BKN.      0  2  0    0  0  0    0  0  0  -  2   7  0
NY        0  1  0    2  0  1    1  0  X  -  5   7  0
W—Page; L—Gregg.                           A.—71,548
```

1949

In their first World Series under Manager Casey Stengel, the Yankees won their 12th World Championship, stopping the Brooklyn Dodgers in five games. The teams appeared equal prior to the Series, posting identical 97-57 regular-season records.

New York City was abuzz with anticipation and excitement. Police officers stood guard at Yankee Stadium in the Bronx and Ebbets Field in Brooklyn, and rode the subways attempting to keep the peace between zealous fans of both sides. Hotel vacancies were hard to find around town.

For the first time in World Series history, a Series opened with back-to-back 1-0 games. Game 1 saw one of the greatest pitching duels in World Series history. The Yankees' Allie Reynolds and the Dodgers' Don Newcombe between them allowed only seven hits; Reynolds pitching a two-hitter and fanning nine batters. New York won in the bottom of the ninth inning when leadoff hitter Tommy Henrich hit a 2-0 pitch into the Stadium's lower right-field stands for the game's only score. Newcombe later described his pitch to Henrich as "a change of space."

After losing 1-0 to Preacher Roe in Game 2, the Yanks traveled to Ebbets Field where, behind the superb relief pitching of Joe Page, they won a hard-fought Game 3. The Yanks scored three times in the ninth to snap a 1-1 tie. With the bases loaded, Johnny Mize delivered a two-run pinch-hit single, and Jerry Coleman drove in another run with a single. In the bottom of the ninth, Luis Olmo and Roy Campanella homered to cut the Yankee lead to 4-3. But Page fanned pinch-hitter Bruce Edwards to end the game.

New York dominated Games 4 and 5 with Ed Lopat and Vic Raschi posting victories with saves recorded by Reynolds and Page respectively. The Yanks won Game 4 on the basis of a three-run fourth inning, the key hit being Cliff Mapes' two-run double, and a three-run fifth, the big blow being Bobby Brown's bases-loaded triple. Reynolds retired the final ten Dodgers. In Game 5, the Yanks built up a 10-1 lead and held on for a 10-6 final-game victory. It ended gloriously for relief ace Page who in the ninth permitted a double and walk, but also struck out dangerous Dodgers Duke Snider, Jackie Robinson, and Gil Hodges. Before the ninth inning began, Commissioner Chandler ordered the Ebbets Field lights turned on, and for the first time in history, a World Series game was completed under the lights.

As a team, the Yanks hit a modest .226 for the Series. Bobby Brown led with .500, all six of his important hits coming in the last three games, and he led both teams with five RBIs. Gene Woodling hit .400 in three games, but Henrich had the highest Yankee average (.263) for those who played in all five games. Dodger Pee Wee Reese's .316 was the highest in the Series for those playing in every game. It was solid Yankee pitching (2.80 ERA) that won this World Series.

```
Game 1 at Yankee Stadium, NY, October 5
BKN.   0  0  0    0  0  0    0  0  0  -  0   2  0
NY.    0  0  0    0  0  0    0  0  1  -  1   5  1
W—Reynolds; L—Newcombe. HR—Henrich (NY).     A.—66,230

Game 2 at Yankee Stadium, NY, October 6
BKN.   0  1  0    0  0  0    0  0  0  -  1   7  2
NY.    0  0  0    0  0  0    0  0  0  -  0   6  1
W—Roe; L—Raschi.                             A.—70,053

Game 3 at Ebbets Field, Brooklyn, October 7
NY.    0  0  1    0  0  0    0  0  3  -  4   5  0
BKN.   0  0  0    1  0  0    0  0  2  -  3   5  0
W—Page; L—Branca. HR—Reese (BKN), Olmo (BKN), Campanella (BKN).
                                             A.—32,788

Game 4 at Ebbets Field, Brooklyn, October 8
NY.    0  0  0    3  3  0    0  0  0  -  6  10  0
BKN.   0  0  0    0  0  4    0  0  0  -  4   9  1
W—Lopat; L—Newcombe.                         A.—33,934

Game 5 at Ebbets Field, Brooklyn, October 9
NY.    2  0  3    1  1  3    0  0  0  -  10 11  1
BKN.   0  0  1    0  0  1    4  0  0  -  6  11  2
W—Raschi; L—Barney. HR—DiMaggio (NY), Hodges (BKN). A.—33,711
```

1950

The Yankees swept the Philadelphia Phillies in four games to win their second consecutive World Series. It was the first World Series sweep since the Yankees abruptly disposed of the Reds in 1939. Philadelphia's "Whiz Kids" were simply no match for the veteran Yankee team, although the Yanks won each of the first three games by the slimmest of margins.

The Yanks hit only .222; they were carried by their pitching. Limiting the Phillies to three earned runs for the entire Series, Yankee pitchers Allie Reynolds, Vic Raschi, Whitey Ford, Ed Lopat and Tom Ferrick recorded an eye-popping 0.73 ERA! They were the real stars of the Series.

Gene Woodling (.429) tied the Phils' Granny Hamner for highest batting average (Hamner was the only Phillie to hit higher than .267), and Bobby Brown (.333), Joe DiMaggio (.308) and Jerry Coleman (two game-winning hits) were key figures in the measured Yankee attack.

When the Series prepared to open in Philadelphia, Phillie Manager Eddie Sawyer was in a dilemma. A brutal pennant race took its toll on overworked pitching ace Robin Roberts, and Sawyer's second best pitcher, Curt Simmons, had just been called into military service. Sawyer decided his relief ace, Jim Konstanty, who had appeared in 74 games without a start, would open for Philadelphia. Konstanty did a great job, but the Yanks' Raschi pitched a brilliant two-hit shutout to win Game 1, 1-0, the Yanks' ninth straight opening-game victory. The only run was scored in the fourth inning when Brown doubled and came home on long fly balls by Hank Bauer and Coleman. Reynolds won Game 2, 2-1. DiMaggio blasted a tremendous home run in the tenth inning at Shibe Park.

Trailing 2-1 in the eighth inning of Game 3 at Yankee Stadium, the Yanks tied the game on a gift run. Three consecutive walks and an error by shortstop Hamner allowed a run to score. In the ninth, Woodling and Phil Rizzuto were credited with hits on balls that second baseman Jimmy Bloodworth could have turned into outs. Coleman's two-out single scored Woodling, and the Yanks had a 3-2 victory.

Rookie pitcher Ford nailed down the championship in Game 4, winning 5-2, with the help of a Yogi Berra home run. Actually, Whitey should have had a shutout, but leftfielder Woodling lost the would-be-final-out fly ball in the bewildering autumn sunlight and haze at the Stadium. The ball hit Gene's leg, fell safely to the ground, and two unearned runs scored. It was a tough break for Woodling, normally a reliable fielder, but an even tougher break for young Ford. Reynolds was called into the fray and blew three fastballs by pinch-hitter Stan Lopata to eliminate the Phillies from further competition.

```
Game 1 at Shibe Park, Philadelphia, October 4
NY.    0  0  0    1  0  0    0  0  0  -  1  5  0
PHIL.  0  0  0    0  0  0    0  0  0  -  0  2  1
W—Raschi; L—Konstanty.                       A.—30,746

Game 2 at Shibe Park, Philadelphia, October 5
NY.    0  1  0    0  0  0    0  0  0  1  -  2 10  0
PHIL.  0  0  0    0  1  0    0  0  0  0  -  1  7  0
W—Reynolds; L—Roberts. HR—DiMaggio (NY).     A.—32,660

Game 3 at Yankee Stadium, NY, October 6
PHIL.  0  0  0    0  0  1    1  0  0  -  2 10  2
NY.    0  0  1    0  0  0    0  1  1  -  3  7  0
W—Ferrick; L—Meyer.                          A.—64, 505

Game 4 at Yankee Stadium, NY, October 7
PHIL.  0  0  0    0  0  0    0  0  2  -  2  7  1
NY.    2  0  0    0  0  3    0  0  X  -  5  8  2
W—Ford; L—Miller. HR—Berra (NY).             A.—68,098
```

1951

The Yankees defeated the New York Giants, who had won the National League pennant in a miracle finish (Miracle of Coogan's Bluff), to win their third straight World Championship. Twice the Yankees were forced to come from behind in the six-game Series.

The Giants grabbed Game 1, 5-1, behind the seven-hit pitching of Dave Koslo. The Yankees took Game 2, but the Giants with a five-run fifth inning claimed Game 3, 6-2. In that rally, feisty Eddie Stanky opened by drawing a one-out walk. Catcher Yogi Berra called for a pitch-out, guessing correctly that the hit-and-run was on. His throw had Stanky beaten, but Eddie kicked the ball out of Phil Rizzuto's glove. The big rally then unfolded, capped by Whitey Lockman's three-run home run.

Now down two games to one, a day of rain allowed Stengel to bring back Allie Reynolds for Game 4. As Casey said, "I put the whommy on the Giants. I needed the rain to bring my big pitcher back." Sure enough, the Yankees behind Reynolds tied the Series, winning 6-2, with the help of a two-run homer by Joe DiMaggio.

Steady Eddie Lopat pitched fantastic ball to win key games for the Yanks. Lopat had pitched a five-hitter to win Game 2, 3-1, then duplicated that feat in Game 5. But he need not have been so stingy in the latter: Led by Gil McDougald's grand-slam clout and Phil Rizzuto's two-run homer, the Yankees produced 13 runs.

The Yankees won Game 6, 4-3, the heroes being Hank Bauer, Bob Kuzava and Vic Raschi. The Yankee Stadium crowd was tense as the home team came to bat in the sixth inning of a 1-1 deadlock. With one out Berra, singled and continued to second when the hit was misplayed. DiMaggio was walked intentionally, and he and Berra moved up a base on Koslo's wild pitch. Johnny Mize drew a two-out walk, loading the bases for Bauer. The ex-Marine did not disappoint, driving a triple to deep left that cleared the sacks.

When Raschi, who had allowed only one unearned run, ran into trouble in the seventh, Johnny Sain came in to put out the fire. In the eighth, Sain pitched out of a bases-loaded mess and carried the Yanks into the ninth with their 4-1 lead intact. But in succession, Stanky singled, Al Dark beat out a bunt, and Whitey Lockman singled to load the bases with none out. Yankee Manager Casey Stengel threw away the book and brought in southpaw Kuzava to pitch to right-handed slugger Monte Irvin, the National League's RBI champ and the Series' most productive hitter.

Irvin touched off a drive to deep left, but Gene Woodling was there to make the catch as all three runners tagged up (Stanky scoring). Playoff hero Bobby Thomson also flied deep to left and Dark scored after Woodling's catch. Pinch-hitter Sal Yvars then sliced a low liner to right that looked like a game-tying hit. But Bauer made a fantastic diving catch, grabbing the shot just inches off the ground for the final out of the 4-3 Yankee win. The Yanks remained World Champs!

The Giants' Irvin (.458), whose steal of home in Game 1 was the first such feat in the World Series since 1928, and Dark (.417) were the offensive stars of the Series, but the only consistent threats the Giants posed. Leading the Yankees were Bobby Brown (.357), Rizzuto (.320), McDougald (seven RBIs to lead both teams) and DiMaggio (five RBIs). As always, "The

GRAND SLAM—The Yanks' Gil McDougald hits a grand-slam home run against the Giants at the Polo Grounds in the 1951 World Series.

Scooter" played a great all-round Series. After the final game, Giant coach Herman Franks said of Phil, "They never would have done it without that little pest."

And of course, Lopat's two beautifully pitched victories were instrumental in the Yankee success. The entire Yankee pitching staff compiled a 1.87 ERA.

This World Series also featured the battle of the two super rookies, Mickey Mantle and Willie Mays. Unfortunately, Mantle was seriously injured in Game 2 when he wrenched his knee in right-field after tripping over a protruding drainpipe. It was Mays who hit the fly that Mantle was chasing. The great DiMaggio finished his career as a champion. In his last major league at-bat in the eighth inning of Game 6, Joe doubled to right-field. When he was thrown out at third on McDougald's bunt attempt, the crowd rose to cheer Joe in this his final appearance as a player in Yankee Stadium. While the World Series had been televised on a network basis, the 1951 Series was the first televised coast-to-coast. Russ Hodges and Jim Britt were the announcers.

```
Game 1 at Yankee Stadium, NY, October 4
NY (NL)    2  0  0    0  0  3    0  0  0  -  5  10  1
NY (AL)    0  1  0    0  0  0    0  0  0  -  1   7  1
W—Koslo; L—Reynolds. HR—Dark (NL).        A.—65,673

Game 2 at Yankee Stadium, NY, October 5
NY (NL)    0  0  0    0  0  0    1  0  0  -  1   5  1
NY (AL)    1  1  0    0  0  0    0  1  X  -  3   6  0
W—Lopat; L—Jansen. HR—Collins (AL).       A.—66,018

Game 3 at the Polo Grounds, NY, October 6
NY (AL)    0  0  0    0  0  0    0  1  1  -  2   5  2
NY (NL)    0  1  0    0  5  0    0  0  X  -  6   7  2
W—Hearn; L—Raschi. HR—Lockman (NL), Woodling (AL). A.—52,035

Game 4 at the Polo Grounds, NY, October 8
NY (AL)    0  1  0    1  2  0    2  0  0  -  6  12  0
NY (NL)    1  0  0    0  0  0    0  0  1  -  2   8  2
W—Reynolds; L—Maglie. HR—DiMaggio (AL).   A.—49,010

Game 5 at the Polo Grounds, NY, October 9
NY (AL)    0  0  5    2  0  2    4  0  0  - 13  12  1
NY (NL)    1  0  0    0  0  0    0  0  0  -  1   5  3
W—Lopat; L—Jansen. HR—McDougald (AL) Rizzuto (AL). A.—47,530

Game 6 at Yankee Stadium, NY, October 10
NY (NL)    0  0  0    0  1  0    0  0  2  -  3  11  1
NY (AL)    1  0  0    0  0  3    0  0  X  -  4   7  0
W—Raschi; L—Koslo.                        A.—61,711
```

1952

The Yankees won the World Series for the fourth year in a row to tie their own World Series record (1936-39). The Series shaped up as another tough intra-city struggle with fans of both the Brooklyn Dodgers and New York Yankees confident of victory.

Each team's players were confident, too, except flaky Dodger hurler Billy Loes. Before the Series began, Dodger Manager Chuck Dressen angrily confronted Loes and demanded to know why the newspapers were saying Loes picked the Yanks to win in seven games. Flabbergasted, Loes answered, "I was misquoted. I picked them in six games!" Seven games proved to be right and the Dodgers made it a particularly tough seven-game Series; the Yanks in fact needed victories in the final two games to win the World Championship.

After losing Game 1, in which Dodger rookie Joe Black, primarily a relief pitcher, hurled a six-hitter to become the first black to win a World Series game, New York won Game 2, 7-1, on a Vic Raschi three-hitter. Raschi's support included Billy Martin's three-run homer, centerpiece of the Yanks' five-run sixth inning.

Game 3 delivered a disheartening Yankee loss. The Yanks entered the ninth inning down only 3-2, when Yogi Berra, who had homered earlier and who was probably the surest catcher in the league, allowed a passed ball on which Pee Wee Reese and Jackie Robinson scored. (The next batter, Andy Pafko, singled so the runs probably would have scored anyway.) The two runs proved to be the winning edge—the Yanks' Johnny Mize hit a pinch-hit solo home run in the bottom of the ninth.

Game 4, then, was a "must win" for the Yankees. Manager Stengel handed the ball to his old pro, 37-year-old Allie Reynolds. All Reynolds did was throw a complete-game four-hitter and strike out 10 Dodgers, including Robinson three times, to win 2-0. Another veteran great, the 39-year-old Mize, supplied the only run Reynolds needed, belting an opposite-field home run in the fourth inning. (Mickey Mantle also scored on one hit in the eighth, tripling to deep center and coming home on Reese's throw into the stands.) It was the game that moved sportswriter John Debringer—writing from the Dodger viewpoint—to note that the situation went from "Black to bleak."

But Brooklyn fought back to win thrilling Game 5 in 11 innings. Duke Snider knocked in four runs, including the tying and winning tallies; Pafko robbed Mize of a tenth-inning home run (Mize earlier had hit a three-run homer); and Carl Erskine retired the final 19 Yankees. The Dodgers left Yankee Stadium and, having won two of three games there, took to Ebbets Field a 3-2 lead in games and one of the biggest home-field advantages in baseball. But the Yankees bounced back to win Game 6, 3-2. Berra and Mantle hit clutch homers and another run scored when Raschi singled off Dodger pitcher Loes' knees. Loes later gave his famous "I lost it in the sun" explanation of the play.

In Game 7, Gene Woodling and Mantle hit middle-inning homers, and Mickey singled home another run in the seventh inning of the deciding game to give the Yanks a 4-2 lead. In the bottom of the seventh, the Series' most dramatic moment unfolded. It was set up when the Dodgers loaded the bases with

RIVAL MANAGERS—Prior to Game 1 of the 1952 World Series, Yankee Manager Casey Stengel (right) shakes hands with Dodger Manager Chuck Dressen. (New York Yankees Archives)

one out. Yankee Manager Casey Stengel brought in southpaw Bob Kuzava to pitch to the lefthanded Snider, and on a 3-2 pitch, the Duke popped out to third baseman Gil McDougald.

Certainly Stengel would now bring in a righthander since the next several hitters were dangerous righthanders, especially in bandbox Ebbets Field. But Casey confounded everyone by letting Kuzava pitch to Jackie Robinson. On another 3-2 count, Robinson hit a high pop-up between first base and the pitching mound for what appeared to be the last out of the inning. High drama gripped the scene when the Yankees seemed unable to bring the wind-molested ball into focus. The three Dodger runners were streaking homeward, and Yankee fans were panic stricken. All of a sudden second baseman Billy Martin raced in to make a lunging, shoestring catch to save three runs and probably the Series. Kuzava rewarded Stengel's faith in him by pitching hitless ball in his 2²/₃ inning stint.

Mantle (.345, two HRs, five runs), Mize (.400, three HRs, six RBIs) and Woodling (.348) were the Yankee batting stars. Raschi won two games as did Reynolds who also got a save. For Brooklyn, Snider was great (.345, four HRs, eight RBIs), but Gil Hodges went 0 for 21 at-bats.

```
Game 1 at Ebbets Field, Brooklyn, October 1
NY         0  1  0   0  0  0   0  1  0  -  2   6  2
BKN.       0  1  0   0  0  2   0  1  X  -  4   6  0
W—Black; L—Reynolds. HR—Robinson (BKN), Snider (BKN),
Reese (BKN), McDougald (NY).              A.—34,861

Game 2 at Ebbets Field, Brooklyn, October 2
NY         0  0  0   1  1  5   0  0  0  -  7  10  0
BKN.       0  0  1   0  0  0   0  0  0  -  1   3  1
W—Raschi; L—Erskine. HR—Martin (NY).     A.—33,792

Game 3 at Yankee Stadium, NY, October 3
BKN.       0  0  1   0  1  0   0  1  2  -  5  11  0
NY         0  1  0   0  0  0   0  1  1  -  3   6  2
W—Roe; L—Lopat. HR—Berra (NY), Mize (NY).  A.—66,698

Game 4 at Yankee Stadium, NY, October 4
BKN.       0  0  0   0  0  0   0  0  0  -  0   4  1
NY         0  0  0   1  0  0   0  1  X  -  2   4  1
W—Reynolds; L—Black. HR—Mize (NY).        A.—71,787

Game 5 at Yankee Stadium, NY, October 5
BKN.       0  1  0   0  3  0   1  0  0   0  1  - 6  10  0
NY         0  0  0   0  5  0   0  0  0   0  0  - 5   5  1
W—Erskine; L—Sain. HR—Snider (BKN), Mize (NY).  A.—70,536

Game 6 at Ebbets Field, Brooklyn, October 6
NY         0  0  0   0  0  0   2  1  0  -  3   9  0
BKN.       0  0  0   0  0  1   0  1  0  -  2   8  1
W—Raschi; L—Loes. HR—Snider (BKN) 2, Berra (NY), Mantle (NY).
                                          A.—30,037

Game 7 at Ebbets Field, Brooklyn, October 7
NY         0  0  0   1  1  1   1  0  0  -  4  10  4
BKN.       0  0  0   1  1  0   0  0  0  -  2   8  1
W—Reynolds; L—Black. HR—Woodling (NY), Mantle (NY).  A.—33,195
```

1953

The Yankees defeated the Brooklyn Dodgers in six games for the World Championship, their fifth in as many years. They broke their own record of four consecutive championships (1936-39) and gave Manager Casey Stengel five World Series triumphs in as many tries. It was the Yankees' 15th conquest

in their last 16 World Series appearances (they won in all of their last seven appearances.) The Yankee victory also marked the fifth time without a loss that the Bronx Bombers had defeated the Bums of Brooklyn. Dodger fans had an expression they used after each season—"Wait 'til next year"—but for them, the heartbreaking losses continued unabated.

This was the Golden Jubilee World Series, the 50th anniversary of the first Fall Classic of 1903. Surviving members of the initial Series were special guests, and 86-year-old Cy Young threw out the first ball. The customary Yankee-Dodger feud was expected, and before the Series opened, Commissioner Frick warned all players against umpire-abusing or fighting. After the Series, Frick fined Dodger Manager Dressen $100 for arguing with umpire Art Gore and Yankee Irv Noren $100 for waving a towel at the official scorer when Billy Martin was deprived of a hit on a scoring decision.

That was about the only time Billy was denied a hit. He put on one of the greatest one-man shows in World Series history. He was a terror at the plate (.500, 12 hits, two HRs, eight RBIs) and sensational in the field. It was his Series. Martin's bases-loaded triple got the Yanks rolling in the first inning of Game 1 at Yankee Stadium. Brooklyn fought back to a 5-5 tie, but New York went ahead to stay in the seventh inning on a Joe Collins home run. Reliever Johnny Sain was the winner, 9-5.

Game 2 also went to the Yanks. The strong pitching of Ed Lopat and home runs by Martin and Mickey Mantle (his two-run eighth-inning homer was the game-winner) gave the Yanks a 4-2 win. The scene shifted to Ebbets Field, and the Dodgers awoke. In Game 3, Dodger pitcher Carl Erskine dazzled Yankee batters with his curveball, setting a since-broken World Series strikeout record by fanning 14 Yankees. (Mantle and Collins each fanned four times.) Erskine won, 3-2, thanks to Roy Campanella's eighth-inning home run.

The Dodgers took Game 4 to tie the Series (Martin was the game's last out when he attempted to score in the 7-3 Yankee loss), but the Yankees roared back in Game 5 to out-produce their New York rivals, 11-7. Jim McDonald, the Yankee starter and winner, was supported grandly by Gene Woodling, Billy Martin, Gil McDougald and Mickey Mantle, all of whom hit home runs. Mantle's, off Russ Meyer, was a tremendous grand slammer that traveled into Ebbets Field's upper deck in left field.

Martin won Game 6 when he singled home the winning run in the bottom of the ninth. Hank Bauer had coaxed a leadoff walk, and the fleet Mantle beat out an infield hit to set things up for Martin's clutch stroke. When Bauer's foot touched the plate, the Yankees and their fans began the annual celebration.

Yankee pitching was not quite up to standard in this Series (4.50 ERA). Besides Martin, the principals in the Yankee offense were Berra (.429), Phil Rizzuto (.316), Woodling (.300), and Mantle (two HRs, seven RBIs). Defensively, the Yanks were sound, making only one error in the Series compared to seven by the Dodgers.

"Everyone contributed," said a jubilant Casey Stengel during the victory celebration, "but Billy was wonderful, really magnificent. We couldn't have won without him." Meanwhile, Dodger Manager Chuck Dressen lamented the fact that a soldiering Don Newcombe had missed the Series (indeed the season). A frustrated Dressen insisted, "If I had had Newcombe, I could've won this."

Game 1 at Yankee Stadium, NY, September 30

BKN.	0	0	0		0	1	3		1	0	0	- 5	12	2
NY	4	0	0		0	1	0		1	3	X	- 9	12	0

W—Sain; L—Labine. HR—Gilliam (BKN), Hodges (BKN), Shuba (BKN). Berra (NY), Collins (NY).   A.—69,374

Game 2 at Yankee Stadium, NY, October 1

BKN.	0	0	0		2	0	0		0	0	0	- 2	9	1
NY	1	0	0		0	0	0		1	2	X	- 4	5	0

W—Lopat; L—Roe. HR—Martin (NY), Mantle (NY).   A.—66,786

Game 3 at Ebbets Field, Brooklyn, October 2

NY	0	0	0		0	1	0		0	1	0	- 2	6	0
BKN.	0	0	0		0	1	1		0	1	X	- 3	9	0

W—Erskine; L—Raschi. HR—Campanella (BKN).   A.—35,270

Game 4 at Ebbets Field, Brooklyn, October 3

NY	0	0	0		0	2	0		0	0	1	- 3	9	0
BKN.	3	0	0		1	0	2		1	0	X	- 7	12	0

W—Loes; L—Ford. HR—McDougald (NY), Snider (BKN).   A.—36,775

Game 5 at Ebbets Field, Brooklyn, October 4

NY	1	0	5		0	0	0		3	1	1	- 11	11	1
BKN.	0	1	0		0	1	0		0	4	1	- 7	14	1

W—McDonald; L—Podres. HR— Woodling (NY), Mantle (NY), Martin (NY), McDougald (NY), Cox (BKN), Gilliam (BKN).   A.—36,775

Game 6 at Yankee Stadium, NY, October 5

BKN.	0	0	0		0	0	1		0	0	2	- 3	8	3
NY	2	1	0		0	0	0		0	0	1	- 4	13	0

W—Reynolds; L—Labine. HR—Furillo (BKN).   A.—62,370

1955

The Yankees lost a grueling seven-game World Series to the Brooklyn Dodgers, who after losing to the Bronx Bombers in five Series finally emerged the conquerors.

The Yankees jumped off to wins in Games 1 and 2 at the Stadium. Game 1's two-run homer by Elston Howard and two home runs by Joe Collins, good for three more runs, were the key hits in support of Whitey Ford, the winner, and Bob Grim, who pitched the ninth inning to record a save. Jackie Robinson stole home in the eighth inning to narrow the Yankee lead to 6-5, but the Yankees held on to win.

In Game 2, Tommy Byrne became the first lefty all season to pitch a complete game against the Dodgers. The Yankee victories were achieved without Mickey Mantle; the superstar, plagued with leg problems, was used sparingly in the remainder of the Series.

The Dodgers hit seven home runs and scored 21 runs in winning all three games played at Ebbets Field. The Yankees were forced to change pitchers eight times in the Ebbets Field games as Brooklyn racked up 34 hits. It was the four power hitters of the Dodgers, Duke Snider, Roy Campanella, Gil Hodges and Carl Furillo, who were particularly harsh toward Yankee pitching. They went 20 for 51 (.392) in Brooklyn's noted hitters' paradise.

But the Yanks rallied to win Game 6 at the Stadium with a three-run Bill Skowron homer and a four-hitter by Ford. Thus, in the first six games the home team invariably triumphed, a pattern that would be abused in Game 7—at the Stadium.

That game's sixth inning, which the Yankees entered down 2-0, was momentous. Billy Martin walked and Gil McDougald beat out a bunt. Yogi Berra then sliced a long fly to left field and Sandy Amoros, who had been shaded toward center, raced

toward the line, speared the ball with a one-handed catch, and fired into the infield to double up McDougald. Asked how he made the catch, Amoros, a Cuban, replied, "I run and run and run." That great hustling play saved the deciding game for the Dodgers and their 22-year-old lefty, Johnny Podres, who handled the Yanks with a good high fastball and a neat changeup for his second Series complete-game victory in as many efforts. Gil Hodges knocked in both Brooklyn runs in the 2-0 win, which made the Dodgers the first team in World Series history to win a seven-game Series after dropping the first two contests.

Needless to say, the Borough of Brooklyn went slightly berserk over the first and only World Championship in their history. On the front page of the New York Daily News the next day appeared the following headline: "THIS IS NEXT YEAR!" Podres, Amoros and Hodges were Brooklyn heroes for their Game 7 performances. Relief ace Clem Labine (one win, one save) and Duke Snider (.320, seven RBIs), who blasted four homers, were also toasted in Brooklyn.

For the Yankees, Hank Bauer (.429) who performed with a pulled muscle that limited his playing time, Berra (.417), Skowron (.333) and Martin (.320) all excelled. The injuries, the one to Bauer and especially the one to Mantle (two for 10, .200, one HR, one RBI), who played only in Games 3 and 4 and pinch-hit in Game 7, damaged the Yankee cause but failed to constitute an excuse.

The Dodgers won fair and square, making the clutch plays. It was a Series that saw plenty of power. Together the teams belted 17 home runs, setting a World Series record. This was the first Series to be televised in color, with Mel Allen and Vince Scully behind the mike.

Game 1 at Yankee Stadium, NY, September 28

BKN.	0	2	1		0	0	0		2	0		- 5	10	0
NY	0	2	1		1	0	2		0	0	X	- 6	9	1

W—Ford; L—Newcombe. HR—Furillo (BKN), Snider (BKN), Howard (NY), Collins (NY) 2.   A.—63,869

Game 2 at Yankee Stadium, NY, September 29

BKN.	0	0	0		1	1	0		0	0	0	- 2	5	2
NY	0	0	0		4	0	0		0	0	X	- 4	8	0

W—Byrne; L—Loes.   A.—64,707

Game 3 at Ebbets Field, Brooklyn, September 30

NY	0	2	0		0	0	0		1	0	0	- 3	7	0
BKN.	2	2	0		2	0	0		2	0	X	- 8	11	1

W—Podres; L—Turley. HR—Campanella (BKN), Mantle (NY). A.—34,209

Game 4 at Ebbets Field, Brooklyn, October 1

NY	1	1	0		1	0	2		0	0	0	- 5	9	0
BKN.	0	0	1		3	3	0		1	0	X	- 8	14	0

W—Labine; L—Larsen. HR—McDougald (NY), Campanella (BKN), Hodges (BKN), Snider (BKN).   A.—36,242

Game 5 at Ebbets Field, Brooklyn, October 2

NY	0	0	0		1	0	0		1	1	0	- 3	6	0
BKN.	0	2	1		0	1	0		0	1	X	- 5	9	2

W—Craig; L—Grim. HR—Cerv (NY), Berra (NY), Amoros (BKN), Snider (BKN) 2.   A.—36,796

Game 6 at Yankee Stadium, NY, October 3

BKN.	0	0	0		1	0	0		0	0	0	- 1	4	1
NY	5	0	0		0	0	0		0	0	X	- 5	8	0

W—Ford; L—Spooner. HR—Skowron (NY).   A.—64,022

Game 7 at Yankee Stadium, NY, October 4

BKN.	0	0	0		1	0	1		0	0	0	- 2	5	0
NY	0	0	0		0	0	0		0	0	0	- 0	8	1

W—Podres; L—Byrne.   A.—62,465

1956

The Yankees claimed their 17th World Championship and avenged the loss of the previous year by taking the Brooklyn Dodgers over the full, seven-game course and beating them. Since the Dodgers were soon to desert Brooklyn and settle in Los Angeles, this was the last World Series to have the added dimension of an intra-city rivalry.

Game 5 of this Series will always be prominent in memory, for it was in this game that the Yankees' Don Larsen pitched the only no-hitter in World Series history. Larsen indeed pitched a perfect game, retiring all 27 Dodgers. He was an unlikely candidate for immortality, although Don had enjoyed a tremendous September, experimenting with a no-windup delivery that allowed him to finish with a respectable 11-5 record.

But in Game 2, Don was wild and the Dodgers knocked him out in the second inning after the Yanks had staked Larsen to a 6-0 lead. After that awful experience, Larsen quipped, "That's the last time I'll ever get to bed early." After the Dodgers won that second game (at Ebbets Field) as they had the first, the Yankees rebounded to win the next two games at Yankee Stadium.

Larsen was then scheduled to pitch critical Game 5. The night before, Don had dinner in Manhattan, drank a few beers and took a cab back to his Bronx hotel. A noted night owl, Larsen did not foolishly stay out late and was asleep sometime after midnight. It wasn't an early beddy-bye that hurt him in Game 2. As Casey Stengel said, "He was just pushing the ball up to the plate in Brooklyn. Maybe he was scared of the fences. He can pitch better." And did he ever! Each inning of Game 5, three Dodgers came to the plate, and three Dodgers bit the dust. Mickey Mantle homered and saved Larsen's no-hitter in the fifth inning with a great catch of Gil Hodges' sinking line drive. Andy Carey also made two fine plays at third base (with help from shortstop Gil McDougald on one ricochet shot) to help preserve baseball's most thrilling mound achievement.

Late in the game, a thick haze hung over the Stadium and that worked in the weary Larsen's favor. With two outs in the ninth, umpire Babe Pinelli called pinch-hitter Dale Mitchell out

Yankee pitcher Don Larsen, one strike from a perfectly pitched game, stands with back to batter, head bowed, as he gets ready to throw a third strike past Dodger pinch-hitter Dale Mitchell. He touches his fingers to the resin bag only briefly, and then fires the third strike to become the first pitcher ever to hurl a perfect game in the World Series at New York's Yankee Stadium, October 8, 1956. (AP/WIDE WORLD PHOTOS)

on strikes on a 1-2 pitch, Larsen's 97th delivery. For Pinelli, it was his last game ever working behind the plate in a long and distinguished umpiring career. When the game ended, Babe was moved to tears. It was the first perfect game in The Bigs since an April 1922 regular-season game.

Not everyone saw the feat in its full magnitude, however; asked a reporter of Larsen in the locker room afterwards, "Is that the best game you ever pitched?" Also during the celebration Del Webb exclaimed, with pointed reference to the serious late-night car accident Larsen was involved in during spring training: "This will set spring training back forever."

The Larsen heroics capped the Yankees' emergence from serious trouble, gave them a three-game sweep of the Dodgers at the Stadium, and put the Dodgers one loss away from elimination. The most important Yankee win, however, was the Game 3 victory that Enos Slaughter won for Whitey Ford, who pitched a complete game, by stroking a three-run sixth-inning home run, probably the most important hit of the Series. Then, Tom Sturdivant six-hit Brooklyn in Game 4. Bob Turley lost a 10-inning, 1-0, heartbreaker in Game 6 to gutty Clem Labine. Turley gave up only four hits, one of them a run-producing single to Jackie Robinson in the bottom of the tenth to extend the Series to seven games.

For the second straight year of a Yankee-Dodger Series, the winning team of each of the first six games had been the home team. And the Series game winners were the exact reverse of the previous year when the Yanks won two, lost three, won one, and lost the finale.

In Game 7, the Yankees accomplished just what the Dodgers had done in 1955: they won the championship on the other fellow's home field. Yankee hurler Johnny Kucks, a native of northern New Jersey, pitched a cool three-hitter for the Yanks' fifth consecutive complete game by a starter. Kucks was supported by Bill Skowron's grand-slam homer, Yogi Berra's pair of two-run homers, and Elston Howard's solo blast. It was an easy Yankee victory and sweet revenge for 1955.

Berra (three HRs, .360), who hit a grand-slam homer in Game 2, swung a mighty stick, setting a then-World Series record with 10 RBIs. Slaughter (.350) and Mantle (three HRs) were other big contributors to the Yankee offense. A side note: President Eisenhower was at Ebbets Field to see Game 1.

Game 1 at Ebbets Field, Brooklyn, October 3

NY	2	0	0	1	0	0	0	0	0	-	3	9	1
BKN.	0	2	3	1	0	0	0	0	X	-	6	9	0

W—Maglie; L—Ford. HR—Mantle (NY), Robinson (BKN), Hodges (BKN), Martin (NY).   A.—34,479

Game 2 at Ebbets Field, Brooklyn, October 5

NY	1	5	0	1	0	0	0	0	1	-	8	12	2
BKN.	0	6	1	2	2	0	0	2	X	-	13	12	0

W—Bessent; L—Morgan. HR—Berra (NY), Snider (BKN).   A.—36,217

Game 3 at Yankee Stadium, NY, October 6

BKN.	0	1	0	0	0	1	1	0	0	-	3	8	1
NY	0	1	0	0	0	3	0	1	X	-	5	8	1

W—Ford; L—Craig. HR—Martin (NY), Slaughter (NY).   A.—73,977

Game 4 at Yankee Stadium, NY, October 7

BKN.	0	0	0	1	0	0	0	0	1	-	2	6	0
NY	1	0	0	2	0	1	2	0	X	-	6	7	2

W—Sturdivant; L—Erskine. HR—Mantle (NY), Bauer (NY).   A.—69,705

Game 5 at Yankee Stadium, NY, October 8

BKN.	0	0	0	0	0	0	0	0	0	-	0	0	0
NY	0	0	0	1	0	1	0	0	X	-	2	5	0

W—Larsen; L—Maglie. HR—Mantle (NY).   A.—64,519

Game 6 at Ebbets Field, Brooklyn, October 9

NY	0	0	0	0	0	0	0	0	0	0	-	0	7	0
BKN.	0	0	0	0	0	0	0	0	0	1	-	1	4	0

W—Labine; L—Turley.   A.—33,224

Game 7 at Ebbets Field, Brooklyn, October 10

NY	2	0	2	1	0	0	4	0	0	-	9	10	0
BKN.	0	0	0	0	0	0	0	0	0	-	0	3	1

W—Kucks; L—Newcombe. HR—Berra (NY) 2, Howard (NY), Skowron (NY).   A.—33,782

Larsen Top Hero of All World's Series

No-Windup Delivery Helps Don Achieve Perfect Game

Shakes Yogi Off Twice in 97-Pitch Gem

'Few Tosses They Hit Hard Were Sliders;' Aided by Several Sparkling Plays

By DAN DANIEL
NEW YORK, N. Y.

On October 1, 1903, the Red Sox and the Pirates started the first modern World's Series. On October 8, 1956, exactly 52 classics and 53 years later, Donald James Larsen of the Yankees pitched the first no-hitter in the history of the inter-league competition.

On April 30, 1922, Charley Robertson of the White Sox pitched a perfect game against the Tigers, winning by 2 to 0.

Thirty-four years later, Larsen hurled the only perfect contest seen in the major leagues since then, beating the Dodgers, 2 to 0, and giving the Yankees a three-to-two edge over the club which had routed that same Larsen in the second phase of the classic.

In short, Larsen made himself the most astonishing hero in World's Series history.

Nothing in the professional career of this 27-year-old native of Indiana, later transplanted to California, had hinted the extreme precocity which he demonstrated in that Series thriller.

• • •

64,519 Enthralled

Nothing in Don's pitching past had evidenced the potentialities which blossomed so dramatically that sunny Indian Summer afternoon before 64,519 enthralled

A Day to Remember . . . October 8, 1956

Adopted New Hurling Style in September

Big Righthander Suspected Bosox Coach Del Baker 'Was Stealing My Stuff'

the bench than any pilot ever had before," Stengel revealed. "The boys were helping me place the outfielders. It's a matter of thinking. It's a matter of sticking to business. He knows now how important that is if you want to make real money out of this game."

Within two hours after the contest had ended—it took only two hours and four minutes and was over at 3:04 EDT—Larsen had all sorts of offers making it possible for him to pick up several thousand dollars.

Pitched Without Windup

Larsen pitched that perfect game and routed the Dodgers at a very vital stage of the Series with a type of pitching that was some two weeks old with him. It was the no-windup delivery.

"How and why the no-windup?" Larsen, laughing, repeated the question. "I dug it up myself. On September 21 we opened our last series with the Red Sox in Boston. I had got the impression that Del Baker had been stealing my stuff and I decided to stop it. I made up my mind to go to the no-windup.

"Well, it has worked to perfection. How much more could I expect it to do for me? I feel the batters better. I have better control, I feel the Bakers. It's wonderful."

This man Larsen is a package of

The headlines of *The New York Times* say it all!

1957

The Yankees were the victims of a pitcher developed in their own farm system, Lew Burdette, and lost the World Series to the Milwaukee Braves in seven games.

Burdette won Games 2, 5, and 7. He pitched seven-hitters in all three games, and the final two were complete-game shutouts (1-0, 5-0.) The Yanks failed to score off Burdette in his final 24 innings on the mound; it was one of the greatest performances in World Series history. (The Yankees swore that Burdette's most unhittable pitch was the dreaded spitball, but the allegation was never proved.)

In Game 1 the Yankees enjoyed a masterful five-hitter by Whitey Ford to get them quickly out of the blocks. After Burdette's strong showing in Game 2, the Series traveled to Milwaukee for the first time in history.

Milwaukeean Tony Kubek, playing as a rookie before his friends and folks, cracked two homers to go with Mantle's two-run shot in the Yankees' 12-3 conquest of the Braves in Game 3. Six Brave pitchers walked 11 Yankees in the contest, but Yankee hurlers Bob Turley and Don Larsen walked a combined total of eight Braves themselves. Milwaukee stranded 14 base runners, and Larsen received credit for the win in a fine long-relief performance. Larsen retired the first seven Braves he faced to run his streak of consecutive batters retired in World Series play to 34.

Game 4 was an odd and exciting contest. With the Yanks trailing 4-1 in the top of the ninth inning, and with no one aboard and two outs, Yogi Berra and Gil McDougald each singled. Brave ace Warren Spahn ran the count full to Elston Howard before Ellie hit a three-run homer into the left-field stands to tie the game. When Hank Bauer's triple in the tenth scored Kubek to give New York a 5-4 lead, Howard and Bauer looked like surefire game heroes. But it was Milwaukee's turn to steal the drama.

Pinch-hitter Nippy Jones, leading off the bottom of the tenth, was allowed to take first base after Umpire Augie Donatelli ruled he had been hit by a pitched ball. Donatelli in making his decision was shown black shoe polish on the ball and decided that Jones, as he maintained, had been hit on the foot. Pinchrunner Felix Mantilla was sacrificed to second where he scored on a double by Johnny Logan to tie the game. Eddie Mathews followed with a two-run game-winning homer to knot the Series, 2-2.

The Braves then came on to win Games 5 and 7 behind the sensational Burdette. (Turley fashioned a neat four-hitter in between to win Game 6, supported by Berra's two-run homer and Bauer's solo shot off the left-field foul pole in a 3-2 Yankee win.) Ford lost a heartbreaker in Game 5. He had beaten the most famous pitcher in baseball in Game 1 (Warren Spahn), but in Game 5 Whitey ran into the hottest pitcher in the game (Burdette).

The only run of the game scored with two outs in the Brave sixth. Mathews bounced an infield hit to Jerry Coleman at second base. Hank Aaron blooped a single to shallow right, and Joe Adcock got the first legitimate single of the inning, a liner to right that scored Mathews. It was the only run Burdette needed.

Brave skipper Fred Haney was forced to hand the ball to Burdette to start Game 7 because Spahn was ill with the flu.

Pitching with only two days' rest, Burdette completed his mastery of the Yanks while his mates' four-run third inning iced

the game. The Yanks had the bases loaded in the bottom of the ninth, but third baseman Mathews turned Bill Skowron's hot smash down the line into a beautiful Series-ending force out.

For the losing Yanks, Coleman (.364), Berra (.320), Kubek (.286) and Bauer (two HRs, six RBIs) delivered key hits throughout the Series. Mickey Mantle played in pain, entering the Series troubled with a leg injury ("shin splints"). Then in the first inning of Game 3, Mickey severely damaged his shoulder diving back into second base on an attempted pick-off play and getting tangled with Brave second baseman Red Schoendienst. Aside from appearing as a pinch-runner, he was also out of the lineup in Games 5 and 6 and played in pain in other games. Also, Skowron played with a back that hurt terribly.

The Braves' Aaron (three HRs, seven RBIs) led both clubs in hitting (.393), but the obvious star of the Series was Burdette, who became the first pitcher in World Series competition to throw three complete-game victories since Stan Coveleski pulled the hat-trick in 1920. Ironically, Burdette had pitched only one shutout all season before his two Series shutouts, and the Yanks themselves were whitewashed just twice during the regular season. In the clubhouse following Game 7, Brave Manager Haney exclaimed, "If Lew could cook, I'd marry him!" The city of Milwaukee felt the same.

It was a bitter Series. Especially bad was the feeling in Milwaukee when the three games were played there. Casey Stengel grew angry and called the Milwaukee fans "bush," and the Braves' fans retaliated with choice insults. But the greatest affront of all was the seizing of the World Championship from New York City where it had resided since 1949.

Game 1 at Yankee Stadium, NY, October 2

	1	2	3		4	5	6		7	8	9		R	H	E
MIL.	0	0	0		0	0	0		1	0	0	-	1	5	0
NY	0	0	0		0	1	2		0	0	X	-	3	9	1

W—Ford; L—Spahn.   A.—69,476

Game 2 at Yankee Stadium, NY, October 3

	1	2	3		4	5	6		7	8	9		R	H	E
MIL.	0	1	1		2	0	0		0	0	0	-	4	8	0
NY	1	1	0		0	0	0		0	0	0	-	2	7	2

W—Burdette; L—Shantz. HR—Logan (MIL), Bauer (NY).   A.—65,202

Game 3 at County Stadium, Milwaukee, October 5

	1	2	3		4	5	6		7	8	9		R	H	E
NY	3	0	2		2	0	0		5	0	0	-	12	9	0
MIL.	0	1	0		0	2	0		0	0	0	-	3	8	1

W—Larsen; L—Buhl. HR—Kubek (NY) 2, Mantle (NY), Aaron (MIL).   A.—45,804

Game 4 at County Stadium, Milwaukee, October 6

	1	2	3		4	5	6		7	8	9	10		R	H	E
NY	1	0	0		0	0	0		0	0	3	1	-	5	11	0
MIL.	0	0	0		4	0	0		0	0	0	3	-	7	7	0

W—Spahn; L—Grim. HR—Aaron (MIL), Torre (MIL), Howard (NY), Mathews (MIL).   A.—45,804

Game 5 at County Stadium, Milwaukee, October 7

	1	2	3		4	5	6		7	8	9		R	H	E
NY	0	0	0		0	0	0		0	0	0	-	0	7	0
MIL.	0	0	0		0	0	1		0	0	X	-	1	6	1

W—Burdette; L—Ford.   A.—45,811

Game 6 at Yankee Stadium, NY, October 9

	1	2	3		4	5	6		7	8	9		R	H	E
MIL.	0	0	0		0	1	0		1	0	0	-	2	4	0
NY	0	0	2		0	0	0		1	0	X	-	3	7	0

W—Turley; L—Johnson. HR—Berra (NY), Torre (MIL), Aaron (MIL), Bauer (NY).   A.—61,408

Game 7 at Yankee Stadium, NY, October 10

	1	2	3		4	5	6		7	8	9		R	H	E
MIL.	0	0	4		0	0	0		0	1	0	-	5	9	1
NY	0	0	0		0	0	0		0	0	0	-	0	7	3

W—Burdette; L—Larsen. HR—Crandall (MIL).   A.—61,207

1958

With a great comeback, the Yankees won their 18th World Championship, defeating the Milwaukee Braves in a tense seven-game Series. The Braves held a 3-1 lead in games, but the courageous Yankees rallied when the chips were down to win the final three games and the Series. Only the World Champion Pirates of 1925 had ever rebounded from a 3-1 game disadvantage in Series play.

With this Series victory over the Braves, the Yanks now claimed victory in Series play over all eight original National League clubs of the 20th century (Braves, Dodgers, Giants, Phillies, Cardinals, Reds, Cubs and Pirates). Just as they had done to the Giants in 1923, the Cardinals in 1943 and the Dodgers in 1956, the Yanks this year avenged a Series loss to the same opponent the previous year.

Milwaukee and the club's fans got off to a flying start, however, at County Stadium. Warren Spahn and Lew Burdette pitched complete games in winning Games 1 and 2. Three Brave singles in the tenth inning of Game 1 (by Joe Adcock, Del Crandall and Bill Bruton) rendered earlier Yankee homers by Bill Skowron and Hank Bauer meaningless and gave Milwaukee's ace Spahn a 4-3 victory. The next day the Milwaukee crowd thrilled to a 13-5 humiliation of the Yanks. The Braves iced the game with a seven-run first inning, highlighted by Bruton's leadoff home run and Burdette's three-run homer. (Mickey Mantle's two long homers saved New York from total embarrassment.)

Perhaps the most discouraging aspect of the loss for New York was that Cy Young Award winner Bob Turley was driven from the mound after retiring only one Brave batter. That, following a Yankee loss with Whitey Ford pitching Game 1, left the Yankee pitching staff in terrible shape as the Series shifted to New York. Ford and Turley were the only Yankee pitchers to win more than nine games during the regular season, and Casey Stengel was forced to turn to 9-6 Don Larsen for Game 3 at the Stadium.

But Larsen (seven innings) and Ryne Duren (two innings) combined on a six-hit shutout, and the Yanks prevailed 4-0. Bauer knocked in all four Yankee runs with a two-run single and a two-run 400-foot homer, and—incredibly—hit in his 17th consecutive Series game, a streak that was halted the following day.

Yankee hopes sank after Spahn pitched a two-hit shutout to win Game 4, a game in which Norm Siebern was unfairly blamed for the loss. Siebern lost two flies in the terrible Stadium "sun field," left field, that led to Brave runs. But it is almost impossible to follow a fly ball out there on a clear October day, and after all, the Yanks failed to score anyway, falling 3-0 before Spahn's excellence. At this point, the Yankee situation appeared hopeless.

But Turley, leaving the memory of the Game 2 debacle behind him, halted the Brave momentum with a five-hit shutout in Game 5. The loser was Burdette, whose four-game Series winning streak over the Yanks was snapped with the help of a six-run, sixth-inning Yankee uprising. The key play of the Series, however, occurred in the top of the sixth when the Yanks held a slim 1-0 margin. A great diving catch by Elston Howard in left field robbed Red Schoendienst of a hit, and Howard fired to first to double-up Bruton. That play got Turley out of what could have become a serious jam, because Eddie Mathews followed with a single. However, Turley fanned Hank Aaron and escaped unscathed. Howard's hustle seemed to fire up the lethargic Yanks who finally jumped on Burdette in their next at-bat.

All three Yankee Stadium games were shutouts, and the suddenly interesting Series moved back to Milwaukee for the final two games. Game 6 was most dramatic with the starters Spahn and Ford. Four Brave errors were committed behind Spahn, but the Yanks had trouble capitalizing. Meanwhile, Whitey was knocked out early, but behind the brilliant relief pitching of Art Ditmar, Duren and Turley, the Yanks finally prevailed in 10 innings, 4-3.

Bauer put the Yanks on the board with a first-inning home run. However, the Braves scored once in both the first and second and missed an opportunity to break the game open in the second on another great play by Ellie Howard. With one run already in, one out and the bases loaded, Andy Pafko was waved home by third base coach Billy Herman on a fly to left field. Howard caught the fly and fired a perfect peg to catcher Berra to catch Pafko and end the inning. In the sixth, Mantle and Howard singled, and Berra's sacrifice fly scored Mantle to tie the score, 2-2. The tension mounted until the tenth inning, when Gil McDougald hit a leadoff homer. With two down, Howard, Berra and Skowron hit consecutive singles to give the Yanks a 4-2 lead. In the bottom of the inning, the Braves got one run and had the tying run on third and the winning run on first when Stengel summoned Turley from the bullpen. "Bullet Bob" induced pinch-hitter Frank Torre to line softly to second baseman McDougald for the game's final out.

In Game 7 the Braves scored once in the first inning, but had the bases loaded with only one out. The Yanks scored twice in the second without the benefit of a hit as Torre's two poor throws to first base were instrumental in the rally. The score was tied, 2-2, when Berra came to bat in the eighth with two out. Yogi doubled off the wall in right-field, and Howard singled him home. Andy Carey beat out an infield hit, and Skowron ended the suspense by walloping a three-run homer. With two outs in the ninth, Schoendienst flied to Mantle with runners on first and second, and the Series was over. The Yanks won the finale, 6-2, and Turley, the overworked star hurler who had relieved Don Larsen in the third inning and pitched so courageously, got the win that gave the Yanks possibly their greatest World Series triumph.

It was especially enjoyable because of the comeback and some uncomplimentary remarks the Braves made about the Yankees when it seemed Milwaukee had the Series wrapped up. Bauer (four HRs, eight RBIs, .323) and McDougald (two HRs, four RBIs, .321) were the most consistent hitters for the Yankees, who were out-hit .250 to .210, but who out-homered Milwaukee 10 to 3. Turley (two wins, one save) was the Yankee hero of this World Series.

But the comeback was the story. Stengel called it "a truly amazin' comeback." Johnny Logan had his own answer as to why the Yanks defeated his team. Said the Braves' shortstop, "Their determination beat us. Determination and Yankee Pride."

Game 1 at County Stadium, Milwaukee, October 1

NY	0	0	0	1	2	0	0	0	0	0	-	3	8	1
MIL.	0	0	0	2	0	0	0	1	0	1	-	4	10	0

W—Spahn; L—Duren. HR—Skowron (NY), Bauer (NY).   A.—46,367

Game 2 at County Stadium, Milwaukee, October 2

NY	1	0	0	1	0	0	0	0	3	-	5	7	0
MIL.	7	1	0	0	0	0	2	3	X	-	13	15	1

W—Burdette; L—Turley. HR—Bruton (MIL), Burdette (MIL), Mantle (NY) 2, Bauer (NY).   A.—46,367

Game 3 at Yankee Stadium, NY, October 4

MIL.	0	0	0	0	0	0	0	0	0	-	0	6	0
NY	0	0	0	0	2	0	2	0	X	-	4	4	0

W—Larsen; L—Rush. HR—Bauer (NY).   A.—71,599

Game 4 at Yankee Stadium, NY, October 5

MIL.	0	0	0	0	0	1	1	1	0	-	3	9	0
NY	0	0	0	0	0	0	0	0	0	-	0	2	0

W—Spahn; L—Ford.   A.—71,563

Game 5 at Yankee Stadium, NY, October 6

MIL.	0	0	0	0	0	0	0	0	0	-	0	5	0
NY	0	0	1	0	0	6	0	0	X	-	7	10	0

W—Turley; L—Burdette. HR—McDougald.   A.—65,279

Game 6 at County Stadium, Milwaukee, October 8

NY	1	0	0	0	0	1	0	0	0	2	-	4	10	1
MIL.	1	1	0	0	0	1	0	0	0	1	-	3	10	4

W—Duren; L—Spahn. HR—Bauer (NY), McDougald (NY).   A.—46,367

Game 7 at County Stadium, Milwaukee, October 9

NY	0	2	0	0	0	0	0	4	0	-	6	8	0
MIL.	1	0	0	0	0	1	0	0	0	-	2	5	2

W—Turley; L—Burdette. HR—Crandall (MIL), Skowron (NY). A.—46,367

1960

The Yankees, with Casey Stengel in charge for his final season lost the World Series to Pittsburgh when Bill Mazeroski won it all for the Pirates with a home run in the bottom of the ninth inning of Game 7. It was one of baseball history's most interesting Series.

The Yankees won Games 2, 3, and 6 by the overwhelming scores of 16-3, 10-0 and 12-0. They set these World Series batting records: highest batting average (.338), most runs (55), most RBIs (54), most total bases (142), most hits (91) and most extra-base hits (27). Mickey Mantle (three HRs, 11 RBIs, .400) and Bobby Richardson (12 RBIs—a Series record, .367) were exceptional, and it was almost impossible to be exceptional in this Yankee Series performance. A total of eight Yanks with at least 10 at-bats hit above .300! On the mound, too, the Yankees appeared superior. Yankee pitchers' combined ERA (3.54), helped by Whitey Ford's two shutouts, was less than half that posted by Pirate pitchers (7.11).

Yet Pittsburgh won the Series; when the Yankees won, they won big, but they could not win the tight games.

Stengel chose his biggest winner of the year, Art Ditmar (15-9), for Game 1, a move later criticized because of Ford's subsequent pair of shutouts. (The thinking was that Whitey could have started three games if he had opened.) In the first inning, Roger Maris became the seventh man in Series history to hit a home run in his first Series at-bat, booming one into Forbes Field's right-field upper deck. But the Pirates, helped by centerfielder Bill Virdon's circus catch that blunted what could have been a big Yankee fourth inning, went on to win, 6-4.

Jubilant Pittsburgh Pirates fans rush onto the field to congratulate second baseman Bill Mazeroski as he rounds third base after hitting his World Series-winning home run against the New York Yankees in the bottom of the ninth inning, ending the game 10-9 in Pittsburgh October 13, 1960. (AP Photo)

In Game 2 the Yankees came back to pound six Pittsburgh pitchers for 19 hits, routing the Pirates, 16-3. Mantle hit two tremendous home runs, one of them sailing more than 475 feet, and knocked in five runs.

Game 3 back at the Stadium saw Richardson hit a first-inning grand-slam homer and knock in six runs for a World Series single-game record. Ironically, Bobby hit his grand slammer into the lower left-field stands on a 3-2 pitch after having fouled a pitch off attempting a squeeze bunt. Instead of one run, he cleared the sacks. Mantle also contributed four hits, including a two-run homer that was another long, high drive, this time to left-center. The 16-hit Yankee attack supported Ford's four-hit pitching for an easy 10-0 Yankee rout. In two consecutive games, the Yanks had scored 26 runs and pounded out 35 hits!

In Game 4 the Pirates used a three-run fifth inning, highlighted by pitcher Vernon Law's run-scoring two-out double and Virdon's two-run single, to prevail 3-2. Another spectacular catch by Virdon on a drive to right-center by Bob Cerv halted a seventh-inning Yankee rally and was the biggest play of the game. Law and Harvey Haddix pitched creditable ball to win Games 4 and 5 for the Pirates, although Roy Face recorded brilliant saves, holding the Yanks hitless in 2⅔ innings of each game in relief. (Face had three saves for the Series and was probably the difference between the two clubs.)

Back in Pittsburgh for Game 6, the Yanks needed a win, which Ford's seven-hit shutout (Whitey's seventh lifetime World Series win but his first on the road) secured to even the Series and set up the drama of Game 7 at Forbes Field. New York was behind, 4-0, when Bill Skowron hit a solo home run in the fifth inning. The next inning, the Bronx Bombers exploded for four runs, thanks mainly to Yogi Berra's three-run homer, and then added two more in the eighth to take a 7-4 lead. Gino Cimoli led off the Pirate eighth with a single. Then came the biggest play of the Series. Virdon's potential double-play grounder struck a pebble (bad as the infield was, it might have been a rock), took a wicked hop, and struck shortstop Tony Kubek square in the throat. Kubek had to be hospitalized.

Dick Groat singled in a run, and Stengel lifted lefthanded Bobby Shantz, who since entering the game in the third inning baffled the Pirates and induced them into hitting infield grounders, in favor of righthanded Jim Coates. (This was another controversial move since the next two scheduled hitters were both lefties. Also, it was a sure bunting situation, and Shantz was the best fielding pitcher in baseball.) Stengel almost beat the percentages when Coates retired the first two Pirates (allowing a sacrifice bunt), but Roberto Clemente then beat out a weak chopper to score another run. When Hal Smith followed with a three-run homer, Forbes Field erupted with the Pirates on top, 9-7.

In the Yankee ninth, with one out and runners at the corners, Mantle singled in a run. Then Mantle made one of the smartest plays in Series history. Berra smashed a bouncer to first base, which Rocky Nelson fielded, stepping on first to retire Berra. Mantle, realizing that the force play was off at second base, dove back to first safely under Nelson's glove while the tying run scored. Unfortunately, Mickey's heady play was obliterated when Mazeroski led off the bottom of the ninth with the homer (on a 1-0 pitch) that gave Pittsburgh the game, 10-9, and the World Championship.

Thus, the Casey Stengel era ended dramatically and unhappily. Casey took the loss badly but refused to blame Ralph Terry who relieved Coates and off whom Mazeroski hit his Series winner. A few bad breaks, perhaps a few wrong managerial moves, and the inability of the Yankees to pull out close games conspired to deny Stengel his exit as a winner.

Game 1 at Forbes Field, Pittsburgh, October 5													
NY	1	0	0	1	0	0	0	0	2	-	4	13	2
PITTS.	3	0	0	2	0	1	0	0	X	-	6	8	0

W—Law; L—Ditmar. HR—Maris (NY), Mazeroski (PITTS), Howard (NY).

A.—36,676

Game 2 at Forbes Field, Pittsburgh, October 6													
NY	0	0	2	1	2	7	3	0	1	-	16	19	1
PITTS.	0	0	0	1	0	0	0	0	2	-	3	13	1

W—Turley; L—Friend. HR—Mantle (NY) 2.

A.—37,308

Game 3 at Yankee Stadium, NY, October 8													
PITTS.	0	0	0	0	0	0	0	0	0	-	0	4	0
NY	6	0	0	4	0	0	0	0	X	-	10	16	1

W—Ford; L—Mizell. HR—Richardson (NY), Mantle (NY).

A.—70,001

Game 4 at Yankee Stadium, NY, October 9													
PITTS.	0	0	0	0	3	0	0	0	0	-	3	7	0
NY	0	0	0	1	0	0	1	0	0	-	2	8	0

W—Law; L—Terry. HR—Skowron (NY).

A.—67,812

Game 5 at Yankee Stadium, NY, October 10													
PITTS.	0	3	1	0	0	0	0	0	1	-	5	10	2
NY	0	1	1	0	0	0	0	0	0	-	2	5	2

W—Haddix; L—Ditmar. HR—Maris (NY).

A.—62,753

Game 6 at Forbes Field, Pittsburgh, October 12													
NY	0	1	5	0	0	2	2	2	0	-	12	17	1
PITTS.	0	0	0	0	0	0	0	0	0	-	0	7	1

W—Ford; L—Friend.

A.—38,580

Game 7 at Forbes Field, Pittsburgh, October 13													
NY	0	0	0	0	1	4	0	2	2	-	9	13	0
PITTS.	2	2	0	0	0	0	0	5	1	-	10	11	0

W—Haddix; L—Terry. HR—Nelson (PITTS), Skowron (NY), Berra (NY); Smith (PITTS), Mazeroski (PITTS).

A.—36,683

1961

The Yankees won their 19th World Championship, easily defeating the Cincinnati Reds who managed to win only Game 2. The 1961 Yankees, the greatest home run-hitting team (240 regular-season homers) until the late 1990s , benefited from the long ball in the Series even though Mickey Mantle, their prime power hitter, was out of action for most of the Series.

Bothered by an abscess on his right hip, Mantle played in only Games 3 and 4 and then with a great deal of pain. But as it turned out, the Yanks succeeded without his services.

Whitey Ford pitched a two-hit shutout to win Game 1, 2-0 (Elston Howard and Bill Skowron each hit solo homers), and pitched five shutout innings in Game 4 before a foot injury forced his departure. With his two complete-game Series shutouts of the previous year, Ford broke the record Babe Ruth so cherished—29⅔ consecutive scoreless innings pitched in World Series play.

The Reds won Game 2 behind the four-hit pitching of Joey Jay and the daring running of Elio Chacon who in the fifth inning broke a 2-2 tie by scoring from third on a passed ball that barely eluded Elston Howard. (The ball squirted about 10 feet from Howard and Chacon slid in just ahead of Elston's tag.)

A potential upset was starting to brew in Game 3 when the Yankees came to bat trailing 2-1 in the eighth inning. With two out, pinch-hitter Johnny Blanchard hit a Bob Purkey pitch into Crosley Field's right-field bleachers to tie the score. Roger Maris hit a long home run in the ninth to win the game, 3-2, for reliever Luis Arroyo, who was pitted against his former team that had given up on him.

The Yanks won Games 4 and 5 easily, 7-0 and 13-5, pouring it on in the finale with substitutes Hector Lopez hitting a triple and a homer and knocking in five runs, and Blanchard hitting a double and homer and scoring three runs to lead a 15-hit Yankee attack against eight Reds pitchers, a Series record. Even with Mantle and Yogi Berra, who had a stiff shoulder, sitting out Game 5, and with Maris in the throes of a slump, the Yankee bench strength was able to end the Series in easy fashion.

The Yankee roster was replete with Series stars. Clete Boyer made some outstanding plays around third base, and Bobby Richardson (.391), Skowron (.353, five RBIs), Blanchard (.400, two HRs) and Lopez (.333, seven RBIs) spearheaded the New York attack. The Yankee pitching staff compiled an ERA of 1.60.

The Series lacked drama. After playing in five consecutive exciting seven-game Series (1955, '56, '57, '58, '60), the experts were correct in figuring an easy Yankee victory. The results substantiated the belief that this Yankee edition was one of the greatest teams in baseball history.

Yankee Manager Ralph Houk became only the third manager to win the World Championship in his rookie season.

```
Game 1 at Yankee Stadium, NY, October 4
CIN.    0  0  0    0  0  0    0  0  0  -  0   2  0
NY      0  0  0    1  0  1    0  0  X  -  2   6  0
W—Ford; L—O'Toole HR—Howard (NY), Skowron (NY).    A.—62,397

Game 2 at Yankee Stadium, NY, October 5
CIN.    0  0  0    2  1  1    0  2  0  -  6   9  0
NY      0  0  0    2  0  0    0  0  0  -  2   4  3
W—Jay; L—Terry HR—Coleman (CIN), Berra (NY).    A.—63,083

Game 3 at Crosley Field, Cincinnati, October 7
NY      0  0  0    0  0  0    1  1  1  -  3   6  1
CIN.    0  0  1    0  0  0    1  0  0  -  2   8  0
W—Arroyo; L—Purkey HR—Blanchard (NY), Maris (NY).    A.—32,589

Game 4 at Crosley Field, Cincinnati, October 8
NY      0  0  0    1  1  2    3  0  0  -  7  11  0
CIN.    0  0  0    0  0  0    0  0  0  -  0   5  1
W—Ford; L—O'Toole.    A.—32,589

Game 5 at Crosley Field, Cincinnati, October 9
NY      5  1  0    5  0  2    0  0  0  - 13  15  1
CIN.    0  0  3    0  2  0    0  0  0  -  5  11  3
W—Daley; L—Jay HR—Blanchard (NY), Robinson (CIN), Lopez (NY), Post (CIN).
                                       A.—32,589
```

1962

The Yankees claimed their 20th World Championship by defeating the San Francisco Giants in a seven-game World Series marred by rain-caused postponements. It was a fiercely fought seesaw Series. The Yanks won all odd-numbered games (1, 3, 5, 7), and the Giants were all the even-numbered (2, 4, 6).

Whitey Ford completed and won Game 1, 6-2, but his World Series consecutive-inning scoreless streak was snapped in the second inning at 33⅔ innings. Clete Boyer's seventh-inning home run broke a 2-2 tie, and the Yanks gave Ford three more runs before the day was done at Candlestick Park.

Jack Sanford three-hit the Yanks in Game 2, and the scene then shifted to Yankee Stadium where Yankee Bill Stafford and Giant Billy Pierce were locked in a Game 3 pitchers' duel. With the game scoreless, Tom Tresh, Mickey Mantle and Roger Maris hit consecutive seventh-inning singles. The last two hits were muffed in the Giant outfield, and Maris found himself on second with two runs in and no outs, then came around to score on a pair of outs. Ed Bailey's two-run ninth-inning homer made the final score, 3-2, the hit one of only four given up by Stafford.

Game 4 saw Chuck Hiller hit the first National League grand-slam homer in Series history. Giant Don Larsen won in relief, 7-3, six years to the day of his perfect game. The hero of Game 5, delayed a day because of rain, was Tom Tresh, whose three-run homer into the lower right-field stands broke an eighth-inning 2-2 tie. Ralph Terry went all the way to win, 5-3. The teams returned to San Francisco for Game 6, which was rained out three straight days. Finally, with idle time inducing a waning of interest, the skies cleared. Pierce three-hit the Yankees, pushing the Series to Game 7.

The deciding game was a beautiful pitching confrontation between Terry and Sanford, their third duel of the Series. The Yankees scored the only run of the game in the fifth inning when Tony Kubek grounded into a double play that scored Bill Skowron. Terry mowed down the first 17 Giants before Sanford singled with two out in the sixth. In the seventh, Tresh made a great one-handed catch in the left field corner to rob Willie Mays of a hit—just a moment before Willie McCovey was to triple. McCovey died at third.

The ninth inning was tension-filled, Terry struggling to hold his 1-0 lead. Matty Alou beat out a bunt to lead off, but with determined grittiness, Ralph struck out Felipe Alou and Chuck Hiller. Then Willie Mays stroked a liner down the right-field line. Maris hustled to his left, played the ball perfectly, and fired into the infield. Mays had his double, but Alou, the potential tying run, was held at third. With first base open and Orlando Cepeda on deck, Manager Ralph Houk and Terry decided to pitch carefully to McCovey. The strategy worked when McCovey hit a screaming line drive right at a perfectly positioned Bobby Richardson to end the game.

The Yanks had won another World Series, and Ralph Terry, with the Mazeroski homer two years behind him, was the undisputed hero (two wins, 1.80 ERA). The Yankees hit a feeble .199 for the Series, but this was no fault of Tom Tresh (.321) and Clete Boyer (.318). The Giants were not much better: they hit only .226.

The Series stretched over 13 days, tying the 1911 Series for the longest in history.

```
Game 1 at Candlestick Park, San Francisco, October 4
NY      2  0  0    0  0  0    1  2  1  -  6  11  0
S.F.    0  1  1    0  0  0    0  0  0  -  2  10  0
W—Ford; L—O'Dell. HR—Boyer (NY).           A.—43,852

Game 2 at Candlestick Park, San Francisco, October 5
NY      0  0  0    0  0  0    0  0  0  -  0   3  1
S.F.    1  0  0    0  0  0    1  0  X  -  2   6  1
W—Sanford; L—Terry. HR—McCovey (SF).       A.—43,910

Game 3 at Yankee Stadium, NY, October 7
S.F.    0  0  0    0  0  0    0  0  2  -  2   4  3
NY      0  0  0    0  0  0    3  0  X  -  3   5  1
W—Stafford; L—Pierce. HR—Bailey (SF).      A.—71,434

Game 4 at Yankee Stadium, NY, October 8
S.F.    0  2  0    0  0  0    4  0  1  -  7   9  1
NY      0  0  0    0  0  2    0  0  1  -  3   9  1
W—Larsen; L—Coates. HR—Haller (SF), Hiller (SF).  A.—66,607

Game 5 at Yankee Stadium, NY, October 10
S.F.    0  0  1    0  1  0    0  0  1  -  3   8  2
NY      0  0  0    1  0  1    0  3  X  -  5   6  0
W—Terry, L—Sanford. HR—Pagan (SF), Tresh (NY).    A.—63,165

Game 6 at Candlestick Park, San Francisco, October 15
NY      0  0  0    0  1  0    0  1  0  -  2   3  2
S.F.    0  0  0    3  2  0    0  0  X  -  5  10  1
W—Pierce; L—Ford. HR—Maris (NY).           A.—43,948

Game 7 at Candlestick Park, San Francisco, October 16
NY      0  0  0    0  1  0    0  0  0  -  1   7  0
S.F.    0  0  0    0  0  0    0  0  0  -  0   4  1
W—Terry; L—Sanford.                        A.—43,948
```

1963

The Los Angeles Dodgers humiliated the Yankees, denying the Yanks a single victory. It was only the second time that New York was swept in a World Series. (The 1922 Yanks managed to tie one game, however.)

The Yanks ran into some of the most remarkable pitching in Series history; a short series is often the product of fine pitching, and this was a classic example—the Dodger hurlers were unequaled. Dodger pitching chalked up an outstanding ERA (1.00), allowing the Yanks only four runs and 22 hits. New York's batting average was a paltry .171. The Yankee pitchers, in turn, were gallant in defeat (2.91 ERA), holding the Dodgers to a lowly .214 batting average.

In Game 1 Sandy Koufax set a World Series record (to be broken by Bob Gibson in 1968) by striking out 15 Yankees, including the first five batters. Former Yankee Bill Skowron knocked in one run, and Johnny Roseboro homered in three more in a second-inning rally, giving Koufax all the runs he needed. After Koufax's power pitching, veteran Johnny Podres finessed the Yankee hitters to win Game 2, 4-1, with ninth-inning relief help from Ron Perranoski. (Skowron hit a home run.)

The Yankees went to Los Angeles hoping for a change of fortune, and Jim Bouton responded with a great Game 3, but Don Drysdale was even better and won, 1-0. Whitey Ford outpitched Koufax in Game 4 but lost, 2-1, in a game Frank Howard and Mickey Mantle made graphic with gigantic home runs. The key play of the final game came in the seventh inning when third baseman Clete Boyer took a Jim Gilliam grounder in a play that would have been routine were it not for Gilliam's

speed. Joe Pepitone lost Boyer's throw in the white-shirted crowd, and Gilliam traveled to third base, from there to score on a sacrifice fly.

And so Los Angeles, scoring but 12 runs, won every game played to become the World Champions. It was a Series much like that of 1950 when the Yankees, on a grand total of 11 runs, swept the Philadelphia Phillies. Besides great pitching, the Dodgers enjoyed some good luck. Roseboro's three-run homer of Game 1, that contest's biggest hit, was a 300-foot fly ball that barely fell fair into the Stadium's right-field stands. In Game 2 Roger Maris damaged his left knee when he ran into the Stadium's right-field railing chasing a triple. After only five at-bats, Maris was unable to continue in the Series, and with Mantle able only to collect one bunt single and one homer in 15 at-bats, the Yanks' famed M & M power boys were rendered virtually useless.

The only run scored in Game 3 was a tainted Dodger tally in the first inning. Jim Gilliam drew a walk and with two outs, Bouton wild-pitched Gilliam to second where he scored on Tommy Davis' single, which kicked off the pitcher's mound and second baseman Bobby Richardson's shin. With two outs in the ninth, Pepitone flied deep to right, but Ron Fairly caught the ball in front of the fence to end the game. And of course, there was the unusual Boyer-to-Pepitone play in Game 4 caused by the white-shirted crowd. All these breaks helped the Dodgers, but they capitalized on every break and obviously deserved the victory.

```
Game 1 at Yankee Stadium, NY, October 2
L.A.    0  4  1    0  0  0    0  0  0  -  5   9  0
NY      0  0  0    0  0  0    0  2  0  -  2   6  0
W—Koufax; L—Ford. HR—Roseboro (LA), Tresh (NY).  A.—69,000

Game 2 at Yankee Stadium, NY, October 3
L.A.    2  0  0    1  0  0    0  1  0  -  4  10  1
NY      0  0  0    0  0  0    0  0  1  -  1   7  0
W—Podres; L—Downing. HR—Skowron (LA).      A.—66,455

Game 3 at Dodger Stadium, Los Angeles, October 5
NY      0  0  0    0  0  0    0  0  0  -  0   3  0
L.A.    1  0  0    0  0  0    0  0  X  -  1   4  1
W—Drysdale; L—Bouton.                      A.—55,912

Game 4 at Dodger Stadium, Los Angeles, October 6
NY      0  0  0    0  0  0    1  0  0  -  1   6  1
L.A.    0  0  0    0  1  0    1  0  X  -  2   2  1
W—Koufax; L—Ford. HR—F. Howard (LA), Mantle (NY).  A.—55,912
```

1964

The Yankees lost in seven games to the St. Louis Cardinals in what was to be the club's last World Series appearance until 1976. The Yanks were hurting going into the Series. Shortstop Tony Kubek did not play because of a sprained wrist, Mickey Mantle played with a bad leg, and Whitey Ford, after losing Game 1, was shelved for the rest of the Series with a very sore arm.

Yankee rookie Mel Stottlemyre bested the great Bob Gibson, 8-3, in Game 2, and Game 3 also went into the New York win column. In the minds of some Yankee followers, Game 3 was the most satisfying win ever. Starters Jim Bouton for the Yanks and Curt Simmons for the Cards pitched brilliantly, carrying the game to the ninth tied 1-1. A hurting Mickey Mantle stepped up to face knuckleballer Barney Schultz, just installed in relief of Simmons, to lead off the bottom of the ninth. Mantle caught one and sent it into the upper deck in right-field. The 2-1 New York sudden victory brought the Stadium to delirium.

It was a great Yankee win—and the momentum seemed to carry into Game 4 when in rapid succession Phil Linz doubled, Bobby Richardson doubled, Roger Maris singled, Mantle singled, and Elston Howard singled to produce three runs in all, but these first-inning runs were the only Yank scores for the day. In the sixth inning, Ken Boyer got the most important hit of the Series, a grand-slam homer that put the Cardinals ahead to stay, 4-3, thanks to the great relief pitching of Roger Craig and Ron Taylor. (The Yanks were held to just one hit after their first-inning barrage.)

Game 5 almost made Tom Tresh a hero of immense proportions. With New York down, 2-0, Tresh hit a two-out, two-run homer in the bottom of the ninth off legendary Bob Gibson, who recorded 13 strikeouts, to send the game into extra innings. It was a marvelous fielding play by Gibson that deprived Tresh of game-winning laurels. With Mantle on base and one out, Joe Pepitone smashed a wicked liner up the middle that Gibson's hip deflected toward the third-base line. In one motion, Gibson grabbed the ball, wheeled to first and nipped Pepitone. A moment later, Tresh's homer tied a game Tom would have won had Pepitone been aboard. Instead, Tim McCarver's three-run, tenth-inning home run won the game for St. Louis.

In St. Louis for Game 6, the Yanks beat the Cards, 8-3, behind back-to-back homers by Maris and Mantle and a Joe Pepitone grand slammer. Gibson and Stottlemyre faced each other in Game 7. St. Louis exploded for six runs in the middle innings before Mantle unloaded his final World Series home run to produce three runs and reduce the margin to 6-3. Gibson had enough left to finish the game, although Clete Boyer and Phil Linz hit solo homers in the ninth. But the Cardinals held on to take the game, 7-5, and with it the World Series.

Gibson set a World Series record with 31 strikeouts, a record he himself broke four years later. Stottlemyre faced the great Gibson on three occasions and certainly held his own, but pitching on only two days' rest for Game 7 did Mel in. It was a most discouraging Series failure for the Yankees, coming on the heels of the 1963 Series debacle.

Richardson was once again great in the Fall Classic (.406), setting a Series record by rapping out 13 hits, and so was Mantle (.333, three HRs, eight RBIs) in his final World Series. Mickey's three home runs set a new lifetime World Series home run standard of 18, breaking Babe Ruth's long-standing record of 15. Bouton won two games. St. Louis had many heroes, including Tim McCarver (.478) and Lou Brock (.300).

The Series saw a brotherly feud between the Cards' Ken Boyer (two HRs, six RBIs, .222) and the Yanks' Clete Boyer (one HR, three RBIs, .208), both outstanding third basemen. When each hit a home run in Game 7, it marked the first time in World Series history that brothers have cleared the fences in the same game.

Yankee Manager Yogi Berra in his first year at the helm returned to his home town of St. Louis for this Series, but unfortunately could not disappoint the locals with a Yankee victory. Instead, the champagne was poured on Card skipper Johnny Keane. Within days following the Series finale, the baseball world would be shocked to learn that Berra was fired unceremoniously and without justification by the Yanks, and in his place Keane was hired! Go figure!

Game 1 at Busch Stadium, St. Louis, October 7

NY	0	3	0	0	1	0	0	1	0	-	5	12	2
ST.L.	1	1	0	0	0	4	0	3	X	-	9	12	0

W—Sadecki; L—Ford. HR—Tresh (NY), Shannon (ST L.).   A.—30,805

Game 2 at Busch Stadium, St. Louis, October 8

NY	0	0	0	1	0	1	2	0	4	-	8	12	0
ST.L.	0	0	1	0	0	0	0	1	1	-	3	7	0

W—Stottlemyre; L—Gibson. HR—Linz (NY).   A.—30,805

Game 3 at Yankee Stadium, NY, October 10

ST.L.	0	0	0	0	1	0	0	0	0	-	1	6	0
NY	0	1	0	0	0	0	0	0	1	-	2	5	2

W—Bouton; L—Schultz. HR—Mantle (NY).   A.—67,101

Game 4 at Yankee Stadium, NY, October 11

ST.L.	0	0	0	0	0	4	0	0	0	-	4	6	1
NY	3	0	0	0	0	0	0	0	0	-	3	6	1

W—Craig; L—Downing. HR—K. Boyer (ST. L.).   A.—66,312

Game 5 at Yankee Stadium, NY, October 12

ST.L.	0	0	0	0	2	0	0	0	0	3	-	5	10	1
NY	0	0	0	0	0	0	0	2	0	-	2	6	2

W—Gibson; L—Mikkelsen. HR—Tresh (NY), McCarver (ST. L.).   A.—65,633

Game 6 at Busch Stadium, St. Louis, October 14

NY	0	0	0	0	1	2	0	5	0	-	8	10	0
ST.L.	1	0	0	0	0	0	0	1	1	-	3	10	1

W—Bouton; L—Simmons. HR—Maris (NY), Mantle (NY), Pepitone (NY).   A.—30,805

Game 7 at Busch Stadium, St. Louis, October 15

NY	0	0	0	0	0	3	0	0	2	-	5	9	2
ST.L.	0	0	0	3	3	0	1	0	X	-	7	10	1

W—Gibson; L—Stottlemyre. HR—Brock (ST. L.), Mantle (NY), K. Boyer (ST. L.), C. Boyer (NY), Linz (NY).   A.—30,346

1976

The Yankees were swept in their first World Series appearance in 12 years; the Cincinnati Reds were too powerful to permit a competitive Series. If it were possible to lose the Series in fewer than four games, the Yankees would have done so.

For the Reds had assembled one of the best teams in baseball history, combining good contact hitters (Pete Rose, Ken Griffey, Cesar Geronimo, Dave Concepcion), strong long-ball swingers (George Foster, Joe Morgan, Tony Perez, Johnny Bench), tremendous team speed (Morgan, Griffey, Geronimo, Concepcion, etc.), excellent defense up the middle (Bench, Morgan, Concepcion, Geronimo), a deep staff of starting pitchers (Don Gullett, Gary Nolan, Pat Zachry, Jack Billingham, Fred Norman, Santo Alcala) and formidable relief specialists (Eastwick, Pedro Borbon, Will McEnaney). The Reds were the defending World Champs and, having been in postseason play five of the last seven years, were seasoned to big-game pressure.

After destroying Philadelphia in three straight in the NL Championship Playoffs, the Reds had three days to relax before the World Series opened. The Yankees, on the other hand, were drained from five grueling playoff games with Kansas City. They had made rapid improvement during the 1970s and were now an excellent team. But they were young and short on big-game experience. Of the 25 Yanks eligible for the Series, only five (Catfish Hunter, Dock Ellis, Ken Holtzman, Grant Jackson and Elrod Hendricks) had a World Series in their past.

The team never seemed to reach an emotional peak for the Reds. The Reds were the better team, but not so superior as the relative ease with which they disposed of the Yanks would indicate. (The records of the two clubs over the next two years seem to bear out this assertion.)

Game 2 offered the Yanks their best chance to get into the Series. (Cincinnati had easily won Game 1, 5-1, behind Don Gullett.) Yankee ace Hunter surrendered three second-inning runs, then settled down, found his groove, and pitched fine ball the rest of the way. Thurman Munson, Chris Chambliss and Graig Nettles singled for a Yankee run in the fourth. In the seventh, Willie Randolph singled, Fred Stanley doubled, Roy White singled and Munson grounded out. Two more runs were in, and the score was 3-3.

But in the bottom of the ninth, Ken Griffey reached second base on a two-out, two-base error. Hunter intentionally walked Joe Morgan, but reliable Tony Perez singled to win it for the Reds, 4-3. The game was played on a cold, raw night at Riverfront Stadium. Yankee Manager Billy Martin bitterly remarked of the freezing weather, "It's ridiculous—football weather. Yogi had frostbite!" Indeed the first night game in Yankee World Series history did little to promote the concept of night games in October.

The Yanks never again threatened, the Reds easily winning Games 3 and 4 at the Stadium. The Reds' catcher and captain, Johnny Bench (.533), hit two big home runs in Game 4, and the Yankees' catcher and captain, Thurman Munson (.529), proved how great a player he was for the Yankees. He tied a World Series record with six consecutive hits. Yet, after playing his heart out and excelling in the field as well as offensively, Munson had to endure a downgrading by Cincinnati Manager Sparky Anderson, who compared his ability unfavorably with that of Bench. Lou Piniella (.333) and Chris Chambliss (.313) took their World Series baptisms well. Yankee Manager Billy Martin was not around for the finish. Late in Game 4 Billy was tossed out by the umpires.

```
Game 1 at Riverfront Stadium, Cincinnati, October 16
NY        0  1  0    0  0  0    0  0  0  -  1   5  1
CIN.      1  0  1    0  0  1    2  0  X  -  5  10  1
W—Gullett; L—Alexander. HR—Morgan (CIN).    A.—54,826

Game 2 at Riverfront Stadium, Cincinnati, October 17
NY        0  0  0    1  0  0    2  0  0  -  3   9  1
CIN.      0  3  0    0  0  0    0  0  1  -  4  10  0
W—Billingham; L—Hunter.                     A.—54,816

Game 3 at Yankee Stadium, NY, October 19
CIN.      0  3  0    1  0  0    0  2  0  -  6  13  2
NY        0  0  0    1  0  0    1  0  0  -  2   8  0
W—Zachary; L—Ellis. HR—Driessen (CIN), Mason (NY).   A.—56,667

Game 4 at Yankee Stadium, NY, October 21
CIN.      0  0  0    3  0  0    0  0  4  -  7   9  2
NY        1  0  0    0  1  0    0  0  0  -  2   8  0
W—Nolan; L—Figueroa. HR—Bench (CIN) 2.      A.—56,700
```

1977

Behind the home-run heroics of Reggie Jackson, the Yankees won their 21st World Championship, defeating the Los Angeles Dodgers in six games. It was only the second Yankee-Dodger matchup since 1957, the year the erstwhile crosstown rivals left Brooklyn and went cross-country to become the Los Angeles Dodgers. The Dodgers from LA met the Yankees in the 1963 Series and swept the New Yorkers in four.

For the 1977 Series, the experts considered the teams equal, and Game 1, at the Stadium, seemed to prove the thesis. Los Angeles jumped on Don Gullett for two first-inning runs, then Gullett settled down and shut out the Dodgers until the ninth. Meanwhile, the Yanks chipped away at Don Sutton.

First-inning singles by Thurman Munson, Reggie Jackson, and Chris Chambliss after two were out accounted for one run, and Willie Randolph's solo homer in the sixth tied the score, 2-2. In the eighth, Randolph walked and scored the go-ahead run on Munson's clutch double. But the Dodgers tied the score, 3-3, in the ninth, and extra innings were required. In the 12th Randolph doubled into the left-field corner. After Munson was intentionally walked, Paul Blair singled to bring Randolph home and win it for New York, 4-3. Sparky Lyle's $3^2/_3$ innings of strong relief pitching earned him the win.

The Dodgers blasted four home runs in winning Game 2, and with the Series shifting to the friendly confines of Dodger Stadium, the Yankees won Games 3 and 4 behind the outstanding pitching of Mike Torrez and Ron Guidry. In Game 4 the Yanks' Lou Piniella robbed Ron Cey of a home run, Reggie Jackson hit his first homer of the Series, and Guidry hurled a four-hitter.

The Dodgers won Game 5, 10-4, in spite of back-to-back homers by Munson and Jackson.

Back at Yankee Stadium, Game 6 was a Reggie Jackson showcase. Jackson took some pitches in the second inning to walk, but in his remaining at-bats he swung at the first pitch; he hit three consecutive home runs! Only the great Babe Ruth had ever hit three homers in a Series game. Indeed, the crowd was wild from the start of the game in anticipation of the club's first World Championship since 1962. But it was Los Angeles grabbing the early lead, scoring twice in the first inning off Mike Torrez. After Jackson's second-inning walk, Chris Chambliss tied the game with a home run, only to have the Dodgers regain the lead by virtue of Reggie Smith's solo homer in the third. But the Jackson hour was about to be ushered in.

With Munson aboard in the fourth, Reggie lined a home run to right-field, putting the Yanks in front, 4-3. (Another run scored that inning on Piniella's sacrifice fly.) In the fifth with Randolph aboard, Jackson lined another homer into the right-field stands, and in the eighth, Jackson sent a titanic home run to the center-field bleachers, the ball landing more than 450 feet from home plate! The Yankees behind Torrez won the game, 8-4, and with it the Series.

Following Reggie's incredible performance, Dodger first baseman Steve Garvey remarked, "I must admit, when Reggie hit his third homer and I was sure nobody was looking, I applauded in my glove." The Stadium fans cheered Reggie all night long, and the loud celebration continued throughout a ticker-tape parade through Manhattan for which millions of New Yorkers turned out to cheer their heroes. Jackson (.450, eight RBIs) set World Series records for most home runs (five), most runs scored (ten), and most total bases (25); in short, he put on one of the greatest individual performances in World Series history. Other important batsmen for New York were Munson (.320), Chambliss (four RBIs, .292) and Piniella (.273).

```
Game 1 at Yankee Stadium, NY, October 11
L.A.    2 0 0   0 0 0   0 0 1   0 0 0  -  3   6   0
NY      1 0 0   0 0 1   0 1 0   0 0 1  -  4  11   0
W—Lyle; L—Rhoden. HR—Randolph (NY).
                                          A.—56,668

Game 2 at Yankee Stadium, NY, October 12
L.A.    2 1 2   0 0 0   0 0 1  -  6   9   0
NY      0 0 0   1 0 0   0 0 0  -  1   5   0
W—Hooton; L—Hunter. HR—Cey (LA), Yeager (LA), Smith (LA), Garvey (LA).
                                          A.—56,691

Game 3 at Dodger Stadium, Los Angeles, October 14
NY      3 0 0   1 1 0   0 0 0  -  5  10   0
L.A.    0 0 3   0 0 0   0 0 0  -  3   7   1
W—Torrez; L—John. HR—Baker (LA).        A—55,992

Game 4 at Dodger Stadium, Los Angeles, October 15
NY      0 3 0   0 0 1   0 0 0  -  4   7   0
L.A.    0 0 2   0 0 0   0 0 0  -  2   4   0
W—Guidry; L—Rau. HR—Lopes (LA), Jackson (NY).
                                          A—55,995

Game 5 at Dodger Stadium, Los Angeles, October 16
NY      0 0 0   0 0 0   2 2 0  -  4   9   2
L.A.    1 0 0   4 3 2   0 0 X  - 10  13   0
W—Sutton; L—Gullett. HR—Yeager (LA), Smith (LA), Munson (NY), Jackson
(NY).                                     A—55,995

Game 6 at Yankee Stadium, NY, October 18
L.A.    2 0 1   0 0 0   0 0 1  -  4   9   0
NY      0 2 0   3 2 0   0 1 X  -  8   8   1
W—Torrez; L—Hooton. HR—Smith (LA), Chambliss (NY), Jackson (NY) 3.
                                          A.—56,407
```

1978

For the second straight year, the Yankees won the World Championship—their 22nd—by defeating the Los Angeles Dodgers in six World Series games. New York bowed in Games 1 and 2, then stormed back to win Games 3 through 6, becoming the first team in history to win a Series in six games after dropping the first two. This feat was later duplicated by the Yanks in the '96 World Series.

The Yanks were injury-plagued going into the Series and star-studded coming out. Among the hitting stars, surprisingly, were shortstop Bucky Dent (.417—10 hits, seven RBIs) and Brian Doyle (.438), who filled in spectacularly at second base for the injured Willie Randolph. (Mickey Rivers and Chris Chambliss also missed games because of injuries.) With the Yanks hurting and the first two games in the Dodgers' bank, Los Angeles appeared to have the Series wrapped up.

Game 1 was easy for the National Leaguers. They shelled four Yankee pitchers for 15 hits and three home runs (Davey Lopes hit two) for an 11-5 victory.

Game 2 contained a bit more tense drama. New York came to bat in the ninth trailing, 4-3. A single by Dent and a walk to Paul Blair put runners on first and second with one out. Rookie pitcher Bob Welch came in and retired Thurman Munson on a line drive to right-field. Welch and Reggie Jackson then entered a memorable confrontation; Welch running the count to 3 and 2 on Jackson and Reggie fouling off numerous pitches and finally swinging but not catching anything to end the

game before a delighted crowd in Los Angeles. The Yankees returned to the Stadium desperately needing a win to stay alive and Manager Bob Lemon handed the ball to pitching ace Ron Guidry.

Guidry pitched a complete game to win the crucial Game 3, 5-1, but it was Graig Nettles who saved the Yankees by making several wonderful plays at third base. All came in critical situations. His play in the third inning, two beauties in the fifth (one with the bases loaded) and his two-out bases- loaded play in the sixth kept Los Angeles from rallying.

The Yanks won Game 4 on Lou Piniella's tenth-inning single, 4-3. Munson's eighth-inning double tied the score, the Yanks having to battle back from a 3-0 deficit. The most critical and controversial play of the Series came in this game's sixth inning when Jackson was hit by Bill Russell's relay while standing in the base path between first and second.

The throw that was intended to complete a double play and end the inning glanced off Jackson's hip, allowing an alert Munson to score. Arguing loud and long, but to no avail, the Dodgers contended that Jackson intentionally deflected the ball. The disputed play placed New York within striking distance of the Dodgers, 3-2. Dick Tidrow and Rich Gossage (the winner) pitched brilliantly in relief, and with the key Munson and Piniella hits, New York went on to the 4-3 win and a 2-2 tie in Series games.

The stunned Dodgers were destroyed in Games 5 and 6, losing by scores of 12-2 and 7-2. The Yanks were clearly superior in every facet of the game, but most noticeably in the infield where New York made tough plays, and the Dodgers struggled with easy ones. As a team, the Yankees hit a remarkable .306; seven players hit over .300. Besides Dent and Doyle, they were Jackson (two HRs, eight RBIs, .391) who gained revenge off Welch by hitting a long two-run homer to ice Game 6, Munson (three doubles, seven RBIs, .320), Roy White (nine runs, .333), Rivers (.333), and Blair (.375).

Jim Beattie pitched a complete game in winning Game 5, and the great Catfish Hunter, fittingly enough, started and pitched seven innings of fine ball to win the final game with the help of another great relief stint by Gossage. It proved to be Hunter's final moment of glory as a major-league pitcher and one to be savored.

Yankee fans were delighted with the second consecutive World Championship, and they savored the moment by again treating the Yankees to a ticker-tape parade.

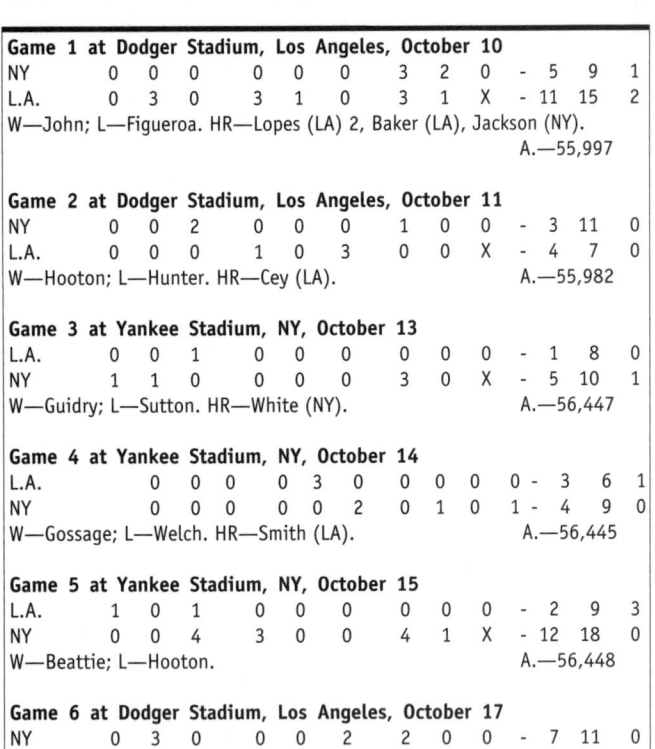

```
Game 1 at Dodger Stadium, Los Angeles, October 10
NY      0  0  0    0  0  0    3  2  0  -  5   9   1
L.A.    0  3  0    3  1  0    3  1  X  - 11  15   2
W—John; L—Figueroa. HR—Lopes (LA) 2, Baker (LA), Jackson (NY).
                                           A.—55,997

Game 2 at Dodger Stadium, Los Angeles, October 11
NY      0  0  2    0  0  0    1  0  0  -  3  11   0
L.A.    0  0  0    1  0  3    0  0  X  -  4   7   0
W—Hooton; L—Hunter. HR—Cey (LA).          A.—55,982

Game 3 at Yankee Stadium, NY, October 13
L.A.    0  0  1    0  0  0    0  0  0  -  1   8   0
NY      1  1  0    0  0  0    3  0  X  -  5  10   1
W—Guidry; L—Sutton. HR—White (NY).        A.—56,447

Game 4 at Yankee Stadium, NY, October 14
L.A.    0  0  0    0  3  0    0  0  0  0-  3   6   1
NY      0  0  0    0  0  2    0  1  0  1-  4   9   0
W—Gossage; L—Welch. HR—Smith (LA).        A.—56,445

Game 5 at Yankee Stadium, NY, October 15
L.A.    1  0  1    0  0  0    0  0  0  -  2   9   3
NY      0  0  4    3  0  0    4  1  X  - 12  18   0
W—Beattie; L—Hooton.                      A.—56,448

Game 6 at Dodger Stadium, Los Angeles, October 17
NY      0  3  0    0  0  2    2  0  0  -  7  11   0
L.A.    1  0  1    0  0  0    0  0  0  -  2   7   1
W—Hunter; L—Sutton HR—Lopes (LA), Jackson (NY).
                                           A.—55,985
```

1981

The Los Angeles Dodgers defeated the Yankees for the 1981 World Championship. They became the second team in World Series history to win four straight Series games after losing the first two, the Yanks doing it the previous year.

It was the spunky Dodgers' first world title since 1965 and their third triumph over the Yankees in 11 attempts. The loosely played Series displayed wild Dodger pitching, poor Yankee base running and absent Yankee clutch hitting. The Yankees left 55 men on base to establish a new record for a six-game Series. The Dodgers set records for most walks allowed in a six-game Series (33) and most errors made by a second baseman (six, Davey Lopes).

Yet, these Dodgers were more mature—and grittier—than the 1978 Dodgers from whom the Yankees won four straight games after losing the first two to be the first to do that trick. Examples: Though Davey Lopes was poor defensively, he was a terror as a baserunner, stealing four bases. Maturity. Though beaned by Goose Gossage in Game 5, Ron Cey was back in the lineup for Game 6. Grit.

Surprisingly, the Yankees lacked World Series experience. The four Yankee players with the most Series at-bats (Dave Winfield, Bob Watson, Rick Cerone and Larry Milbourne) were playing in their first Fall Classic—16 of the 24 players used by the Yankees, including six pitchers, were new to World Series competition.

New York easily captured the first two games at home behind the outstanding pitching of Ron Guidry, Tommy John and Gossage (two saves). Great Yankee defense marked the games in New York. Especially spectacular was a play by Graig Nettles late in Game 1. Soaring through the air, Nettles snagged Steve Garvey's wicked liner to snuff out a roaring Dodger rally and preserve a 5-3 lead for the Yanks. Watson's first-inning, three-run homer was the decisive clout of Game 1 and Milbourne's run-

scoring double in the fifth was the key hit of Game 2, won by the Yanks, 3-0. Yet the Yanks emitted bad vibes even in victory.

They managed only six hits in each win, for one thing. Reggie Jackson missed the New York games because of a calf strain. Nettles severely damaged his glove thumb in Game 2 and missed all three Los Angeles games. (Bucky Dent had been lost in August when an injury shelved him.) Jackson was benched in Game 3, and Jerry Mumphrey, who was not producing, sat out Games 4 and 5. (Thus, four key regulars were missing for all or much of the Series.)

Having just scored two great playoff comebacks and brimming with confidence, the Dodgers dramatically won three straight one-run games in Dodger Stadium. They used an assortment of timely home runs and numerous hits of the Baltimore chop variety off the hard Dodger infield.

On the morning of Game 3, Los Angeles experienced earthquakes; on the night of Game 3, the Dodgers shook things up themselves in a rare World Series match-up of rookie pitchers. The Yanks' Dave Righetti, having allowed a first-inning three-run homer to Cey, exited in the third. The Yanks took a 4-3 lead, fighting back on the strength of Rick Cerone's double and homer. But Dodger Manager Tom Lasorda's faith in Fernando Valenzuela paid off, as the Dodger rookie completed the game, allowing nine hits, seven walks and making 145 pitches, yet earning the win.

The Dodgers scored the winning runs in the fifth without hitting one ball hard. A couple of chopped hits over third baseman Aurelio Rodriguez, a couple of walks and a double play did the damage. (The double play hurt the Yanks not only by delivering the lead to the Dodgers, but by killing the rally and causing Lasorda to call back a pinch-hitter for Valenzuela who batted for himself—and stayed in the game.) With New York runners on first and second in the eighth, Manager Bob Lemon ordered Bobby Murcer to bunt for a hit (not sacrifice) and third baseman Cey, after making a great belly-flop catch of Murcer's bunted pop-up in foul territory, doubled up Milbourne at first. Lemon later admitted, "I got greedy."

Game 4 took three hours and 32 minutes to play and was the crucial game of the Series. It was an exciting but poorly played game—15 runs were scored and 22 runners were stranded—and the Yanks lost, 8-7. The Yankees squandered leads of 4-0 and 6-3. Jackson tied a record by getting on safely five times, but a key play was his failure to catch a fly ball he lost in the sun. Dodger Jay Johnstone's pinch-hit homer, good for two runs in the sixth, was perhaps the game's most important hit. The Dodgers scored the deciding runs in the seventh on a chopped infield hit, a bloop double misplayed by Bobby Brown, a sacrifice fly and another chopped infield hit. Bad Yankee base running hurt the cause in this contest.

Game 5 was a Guidry-Jerry Reuss pitching duel. After surviving several early-inning Yankee threats and allowing a second-inning run, Reuss junked his "curveball scouting report," threw fastballs, and pitched a courageous five-hitter. Guidry also was outstanding. Dusty Baker, leading off the seventh, became his ninth strikeout victim. But then "Louisiana Lightning" heard thunder—back-to-back homers by Pedro Guerrero and Steve Yeager—and the Dodgers won, 2-1.

Game 6, played in Yankee Stadium, was a disaster. Lemon made the Series' most controversial decision when, with the score 1-1 in the fourth, he had Murcer hit for John. On the one hand, John had allowed only one run in 13 innings, and on the other, Tommy did not appear to be at his sharpest. Murcer hit the ball hard but skied out, and the relief corps that followed John to the mound failed badly. Los Angeles romped, 9-2.

Several factors contributed to the Yanks' Series downfall. New York's 2-3-4 batters hit a combined .211 (15 for 71) with only five RBIs. Winfield hit .045 (one for 22) with one RBI. The best Yankee hitters were Lou Piniella (.438), Watson (.318, seven RBIs) and Willie Randolph who hit a pair of homers and walked nine times, getting a new six-game Series record for walks previously held by Babe Ruth.

But New York was outpitched, and the ineffectiveness of the bullpen, with the exception of Gossage, was as disappointing as it was surprising in the absence of a single completed game from the starting pitchers. Yankee relievers failed badly in Games 4 and 5. George Frazier became the first pitcher since Lefty Williams of the 1919 Black Sox to lose three Series games. Dodger relievers Tom Niedenfuer, Dave Stewart and Terry Forster did not allow an earned run in 8²/₃ combined innings, and Steve Howe recorded a win and save.

Lemon was constantly faced with pinch-hitting situations in the number-nine spot, decisions he did not normally make because of the AL's designated hitter. But there was no DH in this odd-year Series, and it hurt the Yankees. Yankee pitchers were a combined 0 for 14 and always seemed to bat in the middle of rallies.

In Game 3, Lasorda, who managed brilliantly, twice walked Milbourne with runners aboard and let the Yankee pitcher deflate the threat. And both times the pitcher was replaced the next inning! By the time he pinch-hit for John in Game 6, Lemon undoubtedly was frustrated.

Yankee owner George Steinbrenner may or may not have influenced Lemon, but even on the sidelines Steinbrenner's presence was felt, and his fight with detractors of the Big Apple in a Los Angeles hotel elevator made national headlines. When the Series ended, Steinbrenner apologized for the showing of his team to Yankee fans in New York and around the nation.

```
Game 1 at Yankee Stadium, NY, October 20
L.A.    0  0  0    0  1  0    0  2  0  -  3   5   0
NY      3  0  1    1  0  0    0  0  X  -  5   6   0
W—Guidry; L—Reuss. HR—Watson (NY), Yeager (LA).     A.—56,470

Game 2 at Yankee Stadium, NY, October 21
L.A.    0  0  0    0  0  0    0  0  0  -  0   4   2
NY      0  0  0    0  1  0    0  2  X  -  3   6   1
W—John; L—Hooton.                                   A.—56,505

Game 3 at Dodger Stadium, Los Angeles, October 23
NY      0  2  2    0  0  0    0  0  0  -  4   9   0
L.A.    3  0  0    0  2  0    0  0  X  -  5  11   1
W—Valenzuela; L—Frazier. HR—Cey (LA), Watson (NY), Cerone (NY). A.—56,236

Game 4 at Dodger Stadium, Los Angeles, October 24
NY      2  1  1    0  0  2    0  1  0  -  7  13   1
L.A.    0  0  2    0  1  3    2  0  X  -  8  14   2
W—Howe; L—Frazier. HR—Randolph (NY), Johnstone (LA), Jackson (NY).
                                                    A.—56,242

Game 5 at Dodger Stadium, Los Angeles, October 25
NY      0  1  0    0  0  0    0  0  0  -  1   5   0
L.A.    0  0  0    0  0  0    2  0  X  -  2   4   3
W—Reuss; L—Guidry. HR—Guerrero (LA), Yeager (LA).   A.—56,115

Game 6 at Yankee Stadium, NY, October 28
L.A.    0  0  0    1  3  4    0  1  0  -  9  13   1
NY      0  0  1    0  0  1    0  0  0  -  2   7   2
W—Hooton; L—Frazier. HR—Randolph (NY), Guerrero (LA). A.—56,513
```

1996

The Yankees had to wait several days for the World Series to begin, as Atlanta rebounded from a three-games-to-one hole and beat St. Louis in the NLCS. During the wait, the spotlight was on Joe Torre, not only for the genuine chemistry he had developed with the Yankees, but also for the human drama involving his family. It had been a difficult year for the Torres, as Joe's oldest brother Rocco, a New York City police officer, died in June of a heart attack. Now Joe's other brother, Frank, 64, who had had three heart attacks of his own, was awaiting a heart donor in Columbia Presbyterian Hospital. After Joe's parents had separated when Joe was in elementary school, he had been raised by Frank, who played on the Milwaukee Braves that won NL pennants in 1957 and 1958. Joe visited Frank in the hospital daily whenever the Yankees were in town, and Joe said he could tell when Frank was feeling well because Frank would second-guess his younger brother's managerial moves.

Frank was sitting in his hospital bed watching Game 2 of the AL Division Series when the monitor connected to his heart showed irregular activity. The doctor on duty paged Frank's cardiologist, who was at the game at Yankee Stadium. The cardiologist learned that Frank's vital signs were okay. "Well then," she told her colleague, "don't you dare make him turn off that game."

The Torre siblings had New York City covered. Joe was managing in the Bronx. Frank was in a Manhattan hospital. Sister Marguerite was running the Nativity of the Blessed Virgin Mary elementary school in Queens, and sister Rae was living in the same house in Brooklyn where they all had grown up. It seemed the whole country was now pulling for this tight-knit family.

The Yankees were idle five days, and then a sixth, when the scheduled World Series opener was rained out. Finally, the World Series opened at Yankee Stadium on October 20. The pre-game ceremonies were inspiring—Robert Merrill sang the National Anthem, and Joe DiMaggio threw out the first ball—but the Braves ruined the festivities by drubbing Andy Pettitte and the Yankees, 12-1. The hitting star was 19-year-old Andrew Jones, who hit two homers good for five runs, and he replaced Mantle as the youngest player to ever hit a home run in the World Series. Torre seemed unperturbed. "I didn't wait my whole life for this game," he said. "I waited for the *Series.*" But, if possible, Game 2 was even more dismal. Greg Maddux, in winning, 4-0, was masterful over eight innings, throwing only 82 pitches—62 for strikes. He recorded 19 outs by way of ground balls; five were weak tappers back to him. To say the least, he prevented the Yankees from getting good wood on his pitches.

The consensus now was that the World Series was over. Atlanta had won five-consecutive postseason games by a combined 48-2 score and seemed unbeatable. But while many were counting them out, the Yankees flew to Atlanta feeling embarrassed rather than discouraged. Torre knew his team's poor start was partly due to rust, and he knew the answer to digging out of the hole was in playing fundamentally sound baseball.

Once again Torre was setting a tone of calmness. Before Game 2, Steinbrenner had come into Torre's office talking about Game 2 being "a must win." Torre didn't fluster. He looked the Boss square in the eyes. "Hey, we'll probably lose tonight, too, George," he said. "But Atlanta's my town. We' ll sweep them there and win it back home."Torre *did* shake up the lineup for Game 3 at Atlanta-Fulton County Stadium. He played Cecil Fielder at first base, benching Tino Martinez, and Darryl Strawberry, who had a broken big toe, in right-field, benching Paul O'Neill. Torre also played Charlie Hayes over Wade Boggs at third base. The Yankees scored a run off Tom Glavine in the first inning when Bernie Williams, hitless thus far in the Series but batting righthanded for the first time, rifled a run-scoring single. The Yankees added an unearned run in the fourth.

Cone didn't have his best fastball, but he threw curveballs at the shins and splitters at the ankles—nibbling, teasing and battling. He protected the 2-0 lead until the sixth when, with one out, the Braves loaded the bases. Torre went to the mound; Cone convinced him he could get out of the jam. Fred McGriff popped out, but Cone walked Ryan Klesko, making it 2-1. The inning ended when Cone coaxed Javier Lopez to foul out to Joe Girardi. Thereafter, the Yankees' bullpen took over, the Yankees added three insurance runs against the Braves' bullpen. The Yankees won, 5-2.

However, seemingly regaining control in Game 4, Atlanta raced out to a 6-0 lead. But after the fifth inning, the Braves couldn't score against the Yankees' bullpen, and the Yankees rallied for three runs in the sixth. In the eighth, after Atlanta Manager Bobby Cox brought in his closer, Mark Wohlers, the Yankees put runners on the corners with one out. Up stepped Jim Leyritz, the one Yankee capable of catching up to Wohlers' 100 mph fastball. Wohlers delivered his best heat—and Leyritz fouled it back. Wohlers seemed worried. As the Yankees yelled encouragement from the dugout, Leyritz continued battling Wohlers and having good cuts. Wohlers decided to throw a slider, his third best pitch, which he hung, and Leyritz sent the ball over the left-field wall for a three-run homer and a 6-6 tie.

Torre still had Boggs available in the tenth when, with runners on first and second and two outs, Cox unconventionally ordered Steve Avery to walk Williams, loading the bases. Then Torre sent up Boggs, who took some close pitches but wound up

drawing a tie-breaking walk. Another run made it 8-6. In the bottom of the tenth, Graeme Lloyd came in and fanned Ryan Klesko, John Wetteland got the final two outs, and the Yankees had engineered the greatest World Series comeback since 1929 when the Philadelphia A's rallied from an 8-0 deficit to win, 10-8.

The next night, in the final game ever played at Atlanta-Fulton County Stadium, the Yankees won, 1-0. The only run off John Smoltz was unearned. Hayes led off the fourth inning with a fly to deep right-center field. Centerfielder Marquis Grissom was there, but rightfielder Jermaine Dye crossed in front of him. Momentarily distracted, Grissom dropped the ball, allowing Hayes to reach second base. Hayes scored on Fielder's double into the left-field corner.

Pettitte was artistic, mixing in more curves and changeups than he had thrown in Game 1. After Atlanta's first two batters reached in the sixth, Pettitte charged a good bunt, made a barehanded pick up, and, off balance, wheeled and fired to third for the force out. On the next pitch, he pounced on a comebacker and started a double play.

In the bottom of the ninth, Pettitte allowed a leadoff double to Chipper Jones, who went to third on a groundout. This was the critical moment for the Braves to recapture the momentum. The Chop Shop chanted and waved. Torre brought in the infield—and he brought in Wetteland, too. Lopez smoked a one-hop grounder right at Hayes, who threw to first for the second out as Jones held third. Torre had Wetteland intentionally walk Klesko. Pinch-hitter Luis Polonia smoked a drive into right center, but O'Neill, hobbling, finally reached it and made a last-instant backhanded catch to end the game. He pounded the wall in triumph.

The Yankees, now leading the Series three games to two, were a perfect 8-0 on the road in the post-season. And, in 1996, for the games the Yankees played in Baltimore, Cleveland and Atlanta, the Yankees' record was 18-0! The next day was an off day for the World Series, but a busy day for the Torres—Frank Torre had his heart transplant and was doing well.

Bobby Cox and Joe Torre shake hands prior to Game 1 of the 1996 Worlds Series at Yankee Stadium.

The Yankee Stadium crowd was even more frenzied than usual as the first pitch of Game 7 approached. Standing in the Yankees' way of winning the championship was the greatest pitcher of his generation, Greg Maddux, who promptly retired the first six Yankees in order. But, suddenly in the third, Maddux opened the door. O'Neill doubled and moved to third on a grounder by Duncan. Girardi ripped the first pitch over Grissom's head for a run-scoring triple. Jeter slapped a line-drive single, scoring Girardi. Jeter stole second, and after Boggs flied out, Jeter scored on Bernie's single to center. New York led, 3-0. Then Maddux shut the door again.

In the fourth inning, Key walked Jermaine Dye with the bases loaded, but on a 3-1 pitch Terry Pendleton hit a grounder right at Jeter for an easy inning-ending double play. In the fifth, Girardi threw out Grissom attempting to steal, setting off an argument in which Cox was ejected by Umpire Tim Welke, with whom he had been feuding most of the Series. In the sixth, with runners on the corners and two outs, Lloyd came in and retired Klesko and ended one of the Braves' best scoring opportunities. Lloyd appeared in eight postseason games and gave up no runs.

After Mariano Rivera pitched his two shutout innings, Wetteland took the mound for the ninth. The Braves, however, with three hits, made it 3-2. Finally, with two runners aboard, Wetteland induced Mark Lemke to lift a pop foul, which Hayes caught, and squeezed, ending the 3-2 victory and sewing up the Yankees' 23rd World Championship.

Hundreds of New York City police officers were lining the field as the Yankees swarmed Wetteland near the mound. O'Neill leaped and tumbled over the pile. On Torre's suggestion, the Yankees took a victory lap, circling the edge of the field and waving to the fans. The crowd cheered wildly but remained in the stands. Boggs jumped on the back of a police officer's horse and rode along the warning track. In the locker room Strawberry and Gooden shared a hug, but no champagne. Everyone in the city seemed to be celebrating.

The Yankees *must* have been a team of destiny. The Yanks hit only .216, and the three superstar Atlanta pitchers—Smoltz, Maddux and Tom Glavine—had a combined ERA of 1.19. The major difference was in the bullpens. Atlanta in the entire Series batted 19 times after the sixth inning—and scored two runs. Wetteland, who saved all four Yankees wins, was the Most Valuable Player, but right behind him in value were Rivera, Jeff Nelson, Lloyd, and David Weathers.

The Yankees exposed the two primary weaknesses of the Braves—a thin bullpen and a thinner bench. Braves General Manager John Schuerholz, sounding as if the Braves weren't also a wealthy team, complained that the difference between the Braves and Yankees was the extra $18 million the Yankees spent on its depth. Actually, Yankees GM Bob Watson simply did his job better than Schuerholz.

Torre outmanaged Cox, too. His sense of inner peace guided the Yankees through the rough times and helped the club do something never before accomplished; they won four consecutive games after losing the first two games at home. Cox, on the other hand, turning sour, wasn't able to regenerate his team after the Braves blew Game 4. After Atlanta led, 6-0, in the sixth inning of Game 4, the Braves scored only two runs over the final 23 innings of the Series.

All that remained was for the Yankees and their fans to enjoy the biggest ticker-tape parade in Manhattan since Charles Lindbergh came home in 1927. It was estimated that 3½ million exuberant New Yorkers lined the streets from Battery Park to City Hall. And it was a fitting tribute for a team. The story fittingly ends with such a proper salute for a team that was not only great but lovable, too.

Game 1 at Yankee Stadium, NY, Oct. 20

	1	2	3		4	5	6		7	8	9			R	H	E
ATL	0	2	6		0	1	3		0	0	0	-		12	13	0
NY	0	0	0		0	1	0		0	0	0	-		1	4	1

W—Smoltz; L—Pettitte; HR—AJones (ATL), McGriff (ATL).   A.—56,365

Game 2 at Yankee Stadium, NY, Oct. 21

	1	2	3		4	5	6		7	8	9			R	H	E
ATL	1	0	1		0	1	1		0	0	0	-		4	10	0
NY	0	0	0		0	0	0		0	0	0	-		0	7	1

W—Maddux; L—Key; HR—None.   A.—56,340

Game 3 at Fulton County Stadium, GA, Oct. 22

	1	2	3		4	5	6		7	8	9			R	H	E
NY	1	0	0		1	0	0		0	3	0	-		5	8	1
ATL	0	0	0		0	1	0		1	0	0	-		2	6	1

W—Cone; L—Glavine; HR—Williams (NY).   A.—51,843

Game 4 at Fulton County Stadium, GA, Oct. 23 (10 innings)

	1	2	3		4	5	6		7	8	9	10		R	H	E
NY	0	0	0		0	0	3		0	3	0	2 -		8	12	0
ATL	0	4	1		0	1	0		0	0	0	0 -		6	9	2

W—Lloyd; L—Avery; HR—Leyritz (NY), McGriff (ATL).   A.—51,881

Game 5 at Fulton County Stadium, GA, Oct. 24

	1	2	3		4	5	6		7	8	9			R	H	E
NY	0	0	0		1	0	0		0	0	0	-		1	4	1
ATL	0	0	0		0	0	0		0	0	0	-		0	5	1

W—Pettitte; L—Smoltz; HR—None.   A.—51,881

Game 6 at Yankee Stadium, NY, Oct. 26

	1	2	3		4	5	6		7	8	9			R	H	E
ATL	0	0	0		1	0	0		0	0	1	-		2	8	0
NY	0	0	3		0	0	0		0	0	x	-		3	8	1

W—Key; L—Maddux; HR—None.   A.—56,375

1998

After steamrolling over opposition in the regular season, the Division Series and the League Championship Series, only the National League San Diego Padres stood in the Yankees' way of yet another World Series title. The Yankees, appearing in their 35th Fall Classic, were pitted against the Padres, who had beaten the Houston Astros in four games in the Division Series and Atlanta in six in the National League Championship Series. The San Diego club, making their second trip to the World Series (in 1984, they lost in five to the record-breaking Detroit Tigers, who had won 35 of their first 40 games!), had clinched their second NL West title in three years. San Diego had now won three such titles, since entering the National League as an expansion club in 1969.

The Padres held the lead in the National League West race for most of 1998, not holding first-place for only six days in the entire season. After the Kevin Brown-led 2-1 win on June 10 versus Cincinnati, San Diego led the NL West for the remainder of the year, at one point having a 16-game lead over the second-place San Francisco Giants. The Padres, finishing with a record of 98-64 (.605), would end the season 9½ games ahead of the Giants. Their 1998 win total (98) was a new club record, eclipsing the old mark of 92, set in 1984, the year that they clinched their first NL West title. Led by Manager Bruce Bochy (who was second in Manager of the Year voting), the core of the San Diego club seemed to center around four players in '98: outfielders Tony Gwynn and Greg Vaughn and pitchers Trevor Hoffman and Kevin Brown.

Tony Gwynn—Outfielder, future hall of famer and 17-year veteran, Tony Gwynn led the club with a .321 average, his 16th consecutive .300+ season, a National League record. Tony, whose career average is .339, ended the '98 season with 2,928 hits, just 72 shy of 3,000 hits, which he would attain in 1999.

Greg Vaughn—Outfielder Greg Vaughn who finished fourth in National League MVP voting, hit a franchise-record 50 home runs (third in the NL behind McGwire's 70 and Sosa's 66) in addition to leading his club in: runs (112), hits (156), total bases (342), RBIs (119) and slugging percentage (.597). San Diego teammates often related that Greg carried the club offensively for the first three months of the 1998 campaign.

Trevor Hoffman—Reliever Trevor Hoffman, who was voted seventh in the MVP race and second for the Cy Young Award, converted a major-League-record 53 of 54 save situations (.981) and piled up 53 total saves, most in the majors for 1998 and the second most in baseball history (tying with Randy Myers of the Chicago Cubs, saving 53 in 1993). Only Bobby Thigpen of the 1990 Chicago White Sox finished with more saves (57).

Kevin Brown—Starter Kevin Brown ranked among league leaders in all major pitching categories: fifth in complete games (seven), third in shutouts (tied—three), second in innings pitched (257), second in strikeouts (257—a new team record), second in ERA (2.38), third in wins (tied—18) and fourth in winning percentage (.720, 18-7). Kevin also led his club in all of the categories just previously noted. For his effort, Kevin was voted third among candidates for the prestigious Cy Young Award.

1996 World Championship Trophy signifying the Yankees' 23rd World Championship Win.

The first two games of the 1998 World Series opened at Yankee Stadium October 17 and 18. In Game 1, San Diego's ace, Kevin Brown, was pitted against lefty David Wells. The Yankees were first to score with the aid of a two-run double by rookie Ricky Ledee, in the second inning, the New Yorkers with the lead at 2-0. San Diego countered with two runs of their own in the top of the third to tie the game. The highlight for the Padres in the third was a two-run homer by Greg Vaughn. San Diego took a 5-2 lead in the fifth, scoring three times on two home runs. The first roundtripper was a two-run shot by Tony Gwynn, who hit his first postseason homer; the other San Diego home run was a solo shot by Greg Vaughn, his second of the game. In the seventh, the Yankees broke the game wide open, scoring seven times to take a commanding 9-5 lead. In that inning, the Yanks scored with the aid of three walks, two singles and two long balls. With one out and Jorge Posada and Ricky Ledee on base, Chuck Knoblauch drilled a Donne Wall pitch for a three-run homer. It was Chuck's first postseason homer. Wall had come in to pitch for Kevin Brown, who had been taken out of the game after facing two batters in the seventh. With two outs and the bases crammed with Yankees, Tino Martinez blasted a full-count pitch from new San Diego hurler Mark Langston for a dramatic grand slam. Tino's slam was the Yankees' eighth grand slam overall in World Series play. It was their first 'slam since Joe Pepitone hit one on October 14, 1964 against the Cardinals. Joe's slammer occurred in the eighth inning against St. Louis reliever Gordie Richardson, and aided the 8-3 New York win. David Wells pitched seven full innings, being relieved by Jeff Nelson and later Mariano Rivera, who would close down the Padres with a save. San Diego scored their final run in the eighth, the Yankees winning the first game, 9-6. David Wells, although not as dominant as usual, won the game and now had started the first games of three different series in '98 (the Division Series, the League Championship Series and the World Series), winning all three!

At Yankee Stadium, on October 18, the second game of the Fall Classic was played, with Padre Andy Ashby, a 17-game winner, squaring off against Yankee rookie, Orlando "El Duque" Hernandez. It did not take the Yankees long to figure out Ashby, eventually tagging him for seven runs, four of which were earned. By the end of three innings, the Yanks held a 7-0 lead. The Bronx Bombers scored three in a first-inning salvo and a like number in the second. In that first frame, the Yanks scored three on a walk, a throwing error by third baseman Ken Caminiti, three singles and a stolen base. The second inning was highlighted by a two-run homer to right-center by Bernie Williams, scoring Derek Jeter. In the Padre first, rightfielder, Paul O'Neill, made a fine running catch of a drive hit by Wally Joiner. There were two San Diego runners on base when Paul probably saved two runs from scoring. The Padres were held scoreless by El Duque until scoring a lone run in the fifth frame on a Quilvio Veras double and then added two more in the eighth, closing out the Padre scoring for the game. After scoring a single run in the third, the Yanks scored two more in the fifth to take an eight-run lead, 9-1. In the fifth, catcher Jorge Posada tagged former Yankee Brian Boehringer for his first postseason homer, a two-run job. Hernandez pitched a masterful game, going seven full innings, allowing one earned run and six hits, while striking out seven Padres. Hernandez earned a well-deserved victory, the first Yankee rookie to win a World Series game since Jim Beattie's fifth-game complete-

Tino Martinez hit the eighth World Series Grand Slam by a Yankee in Game 1.

game 12-2 gem at New York against the Los Angeles Dodgers on October 15, 1978. Andy Ashby took the loss for the Padres, who were now down two games to none to the sweep-conscious Yankees.

The World Series shifted to San Diego's Qualcomm Stadium, October 20, for Game 3. David Cone went to the mound for the Yanks, and ex-Yankee Sterling Hitchcock (9-7 in '98) was on the hill for the Padres, who had set a club record with 54 wins at home in '98. The game was without a score until San Diego put a three-spot on the board in their half of the sixth. Pitcher Sterling Hitchcock started the rally with a single, the first hit off Cone in the game, and Veras followed with a base on balls. After Tony Gwynn singled to right, Paul O'Neill made a throwing error, scoring Hitchcock and Veras. Gwynn scored the final run of the inning on a sacrifice fly from Ken Caminiti. David Cone was taken out of the game after the sixth, as was Hitchcock. The seventh and eighth innings proved to be most productive for the Yankees and especially for Scott Brosius. In the seventh, the Bombers scored two, the first on a leadoff homer by Brosius and later Shane Spencer scored on a throwing error by Caminiti. After walks by O'Neill and Tino in the eighth, San Diego ace, Trevor Hoffman, soon to be charged with the loss, served up a home-run ball to Scott Brosius, scoring three Yankees runs and putting his club up by a count of 5-3. Brosius, prior to the World Series, had already collected nine RBI in the postseason with three in the Division Series and six in the League Championship Series. Scott's two homers, in this game, increased his postseason RBI total to 13 in 33 at bats! San Diego scored their final run in the eighth on a sacrifice fly by Greg Vaughn, the Yankee lead now one at 5-4. Ramiro Mendoza, who eventually was credited with the win and who relieved Graeme Lloyd, allowed that last Padre run. In that eighth inning, Yankee ace, Mariano Rivera, came in to protect New York's one-run lead and so he did,

picking up his second save in this series. Brosius finished Game 3 with four RBI and scored two of the five runs for the Yankees, already being the odds-on favorite to win the Series MVP Award, going into the fourth game. San Diego, now down three games to none, faced a challenge that not even the best Yankee clubs of the past could surmount—no team in history had come back from a 0-3 deficit to win the World Series...and the Padres wouldn't do it either!

Again playing in San Diego, October 21, Game 4 saw the Padres starting Kevin Brown against Yankee lefty Andy Pettitte, who had not pitched for ten days. In the San Diego second, the Padres loaded the bases on two walks and a single with two gone, but pitcher Kevin Brown was thrown out at first attempting to bunt by catcher Joe Girardi to squash the rally. The game was scoreless until the Yanks made a dent in the Padre armor with a single run in the sixth on a ground out by Bernie Williams. The game went to the Yankee eighth, when they put two more insurance runs up to take a 3-0 lead. In that inning, Brosius would get another postseason RBI (his 15th) on a single, and Ricky Ledee would drive the other in with a sac fly. Andy Pettitte, pitching into the San Diego eighth, allowed two runners on base with a walk and a single with one out. Pettitte had more than adequately done his job, holding powerful San Diego with nary a run and scattering five San Diego hits over 7 $\frac{1}{3}$ innings. Andy, who would extend his World Series scoreless-streak to 15 $\frac{2}{3}$ innings, would get the eventual series-clinching victory, while starter Kevin Brown, who pitched eight full innings, striking out eight Yankee batters, would take the loss. In relief of Pettitte, Jeff Nelson then came in to pitch to one batter, Greg Vaughn, who promptly struck out. Two outs. Still with runners on first and second and now two out, Mariano Rivera was hailed from the Yankee bullpen. Caminiti singled to right, loading the bases. Stepping to the plate was ex-Yankee Jim Leyritz, who was no stranger to performing heroics in a postseason game. Jim had hit that dramatic and most memorable (witnessed from the bleachers by yours truly) 15th-inning game-ending homer off Tim Belcher into the right-field stands in Game 2 of the 1995 Division Series. In this game at Yankee Stadium, October 4, the Bronx Bombers defeated the Seattle Mariners by a count of 7-5. That incredible victory, which put the Yanks up two games to none, was the longest postseason game in history at five hours and 13 minutes; also, it was the longest American League postseason game (by innings—15) since 1901, the year the AL came into being. Today, however, the result would be different for Mr. Leyritz, as he lined to Bernie Williams in center for the third out.

With the Yankees moving into the bottom of the ninth, with their 3-0 lead still intact, Mariano Rivera faced ex-teammate Ruben Rivera, who singled to center. Carlos Hernandez promptly grounded into a double play, shortstop Derek Jeter to second baseman Chuck Knoblauch to Tino Martinez at first. Two outs. Mark Sweeney, pinch-hitting for shortstop Chris Gomez, then grounded out, third baseman Scott Brosius to first sacker Tino Martinez. THE YANKEES WIN, TTTTHHHHEEEE YANKEES WIN! GAME OVER. SERIES OVER. SEASON OVER!! It was so fitting that Scott Brosius, named MVP in the World Series, was involved with the final out of the game. Scott ended with a .471 average (8-for-17) and six RBIs. For the entire '98 postseason, Scott, in 13 games, had 15 RBIs, and was 18 for 47 (.383)—an average that was not far from his 1998 AL-leading .372 with runners in scoring position! Yankee outfielder Ricky Ledee finished with a phenomenal series as well. Ricky was 6-for-10 (.600) in four games and would finish with the third-highest average in World Series history (Ricky had three games—the first, second and fourth—when he went 2-for-3)! Only Billy Hatcher (.750, 9-for-12) of Cincinnati in 1990 and Babe Ruth (.625, 10-for-16) with the 1928 New York Yankees have better averages. Ricky's .600 average was also the highest by any rookie in World Series history, dating back to 1903. Tony Gwynn would finish at .500 (8-for-16) to lead San Diego, and ex-Yankee, Jim Leyritz, would have a miserable series, going 0-for-10 (.000), with four strikeouts. Yankee outfielder Bernie Williams would have a disappointing series, going 1-for-16 (.063). The Yanks, as a team, batted .309, their highest since 1960 (.338) Their batting average in the 1960 World Series— which they lost to Pittsburgh and Bill Mazeroski in seven games—is the highest (.338) of any team in any postseason series. Not by coincidence, the Yankees have the second best average with a .336 in the 1981 League Championship Series, defeating Oakland, three games to none. The Yankees doubled San Diego's run total, 26 to 13, and their home-run total, six to three. Also, the Yanks ended the game with an eight-game winning streak in World Series play, dating back to the last four against Atlanta in 1996. Both clubs struck out 29 batters, but the Yanks fared better with a 2.75 staff ERA, compared to 5.82 for the Padres. Four Yankee pitchers (Wells, Hernandez, Mendoza and Pettitte) won a game apiece, and reliever Mariano Rivera notched each of the three Yankee saves. In addition, Mariano concluded his '98 postseason with 13 $\frac{1}{3}$ scoreless innings and converted all six save opportunities. His 0.51 ERA (two earned runs in 35 innings) is the lowest career postseason mark for any pitcher with 30-plus innings!

In defeating San Diego for their 24th World Series Championship in 35 visits (.686), the Yankees completed their seventh four-game sweep (they have lost three sweeps: 1922, 1963 and 1976), their last since defeating the "Whiz Kids" of Philadelphia in 1950. Other sweeps were by the Yankees of: 1927, 1928, 1932, 1938 and 1939—each a great team! In series other than the World Series, the Yanks were involved in three sweeps: a 3-0 win versus Texas in the 1998 Division Series; a 3-0 win versus Oakland in the 1981 League Championship Series; a 0-3 loss to the Kansas City Royals in the League Championship Series (Note: the League Championship Series expanded to seven games in 1985, a club needing four to clinch). The Bronx Bombers, who were 11-2 (.846) in the '98 postseason, also finished the year (regular season and postseason) with a mark of 125 wins and 50 losses, for a .714 winning percentage! Their 125 wins were seven better than the runner-up Chicago Cubs club of 1906, who had 118 victories. With yet another World Series victory, the Yankees continue to break their own all-time records with each game played, adding to their utter domination of all-time World Series records in virtually every category, such as batting, pitching, baserunning and fielding. Over the past three postseason, starting in 1996, the Yankees, on the road, have a record of 14-3 (.824) with a 24-9 (.727) mark overall.

Incredibly, the last game of the 1998 World Series was the 250th postseason game for the Yankees since being in their first against the then-New York Giants, in 1921. Of the 555 World Series games played through 1998, the Yankees have been in 197 (35.5%). If counting from the year of the very first Yankee World Series appearance in 1921, then the total number of Fall Classic games drops to 454 (101 games were played from 1903 through 1920), which means that the Yanks were in 43.4% (197 of 454) of all World Series games played since 1921!! All the rest of the American League clubs would appear in the remaining 257 games.

Shortly after the conclusion of the World Series, Yankee players gathered in a circle in the visitors' clubhouse and began chanting, "Strawman, Strawman!" repeatedly, the players feeling the presence of Darryl Strawberry, who had missed the Series, and was at home recovering from recent cancer surgery. The team had won it for Darryl, for themselves, for owner George Steinbrenner and for Yankee fans everywhere. When Manager Joe Torre was asked to assess the greatness of the 1998 New York Yankees, he said: "I have only about 40 years of history, but it's the best club I've ever been around. The '27 Yankees, they may be a better club—but we had the best record."

On a beautiful day in Manhattan in late October, the citizens of New York gathered en masse, as in 1996, to again celebrate their champions, this time the 1998 Yankees, with an enormous ticker-tape parade. At City Hall, Yankee players, coaches and other dignitaries spoke of the unprecedented accomplishments of this club. Throughout the gathering, spectators and players alike were chanting "Straw! Straw! Straw!" Owner George Steinbrenner, in a reference to himself, was asked: what about The Boss? George answered: "Me? All I did was sit there with a yellow legal pad. We won this one for Darryl and for Joe D. They are the guys in our hearts and prayers now."

When all is said and done, this 1998 New York Yankees team will undoubtedly go down in history as, this writer believes, the greatest single-season performance in baseball history! What a fitting way to end the season, which celebrated both the 75th anniversary of Yankee Stadium, The House That

Andy Pettitte won Game 4 of the 1998 World Series.

Ruth Built, as well as the 50th anniversary of the Babe's death. Thank you, Babe, for continuing to be in our midst and as long as baseball fans keep you alive in their hearts, you too, Babe, will remain alive! From the incredible 125 wins to the World Series sweep, the Yankees did have "the perfect season" with enough memories to capture the imagination of Yankee fans for the next millennium...and beyond.

```
Game 1 at Yankee Stadium, NY, October 17
SD       0 0 2  0 3 0  0 1 0 - 6  8  1
NY       0 2 0  0 0 0  7 0 X - 9  9  1
W—Wells; L—Wall; HR—Vaughn 2 (SD), Gwynn (SD), Knoblauch (NY).
                                        A.—56,172

Game 2 at Yankee Stadium, NY, October 18
SD       0 0 0  0 1 0  0 2 0 - 3  10  1
NY       3 3 1  0 2 0  0 0 X - 9  16  0
W—Hernandez; L—Ashby; HR—Williams (NY),Posada (NY).
                                        A.—56,692

Game 3 at Qualcomm Stadium, CA, October 20
NY       0 0 0  0 0 0  2 3 0 - 5  9  1
SD       0 0 0  0 0 3  0 1 0 - 4  7  1
W—Mendoza; L—Hoffman; HR—Brosius 2 (NY).
                                        A.—64,667

Game 4 at Qualcomm Stadium, CA, October 21
NY       0 0 0  0 0 1  0 2 0 - 3  9  0
SD       0 0 0  0 0 0  0 0 0 - 0  7  0
W—Pettitte; L—Brown; HR-None.
                                        A.—65,427
```

1999

The Yankees and Braves would be renewing their postseason rivalry, which began in the 1957 World Series, when the Braves were in Milwaukee. This would be the fourth meeting between the two clubs, the Yanks having a 2-1 lead. The Braves and

Scott Brosius hit two big home runs in Game 3 of the 1998 World Series.

Yankees had last met in the '96 World Series, won by the New Yorkers in six games.

For the Braves franchise, it would be their ninth trip to the Fall Classic: two visits (1-1) when they were in Boston, two (1-1) while in Milwaukee and now five (1-3) since moving to Atlanta in 1966. Overall, the Braves have won three World Series, while losing five. The Yankees would be making their 36th appearance, having won 24, while losing 11. Overall, it would be the Yankees' 50th postseason series, which includes six Division Series, eight League Championship Series and 36 World Series! Atlanta's road to the World Series was created by their defeat of the Houston Astros in the Division Series, three games to one, and by winning the NLCS versus the New York Mets, four games to two. The Yankees, on the other hand, earned their trip by defeating the Texas Rangers in three straight games of the Division Series and then beating the Boston Red Sox in the ALCS, four games to one.

The media created "the question" for this series: "which team would emerge as the team of the decade?" This writer had a strong sense from the start of what that answer might be— the New York Yankees! In terms of World Series titles in the '90s, the Yankees led Atlanta, two titles to one. The Braves had won the NL East title under manager ex-Yankee Bobby Cox, eight times since 1991. But with all of that winning, the Braves could win but one World Series title (1995) in four attempts. Any disputes would be settled on the field.

The first two games of the series were played at Turner Field in Atlanta on October 23 and 24. Yankee infielder Luis Sojo was not with the team for the first two games to attend the funeral of his father, Ambrosio, who had died just prior to Game 1. The first game pitted Orlando "El Duque" Hernandez versus Atlanta ace, Greg Maddux. The game was scoreless until Atlanta took the lead, scoring a lone run in their fourth inning on a solo homer by Chipper Jones. The Braves maintained their 1-0 lead through seven innings. Starter El Duque was removed after seven full innings, having allowed but one hit (the Chipper Jones homer), while striking out ten Atlanta batters— a truly masterful performance! Atlanta starter Greg Maddux took the 1-0 Braves lead into the eighth, facing four batters in that inning—all four eventually scoring. Derek Jeter had an RBI single, Paul O'Neill, who was playing with pain due to a rib injury, singled in two more, and then Jeter scored the Yankees' fourth run on a bases-loaded walk. Maddux, the eventual loser in the game, had allowed four runs, only two of which were earned. Relievers Jeff Nelson and Mike Stanton each tossed $\frac{1}{3}$ scoreless innings, until the great Mariano Rivera was brought into the game with two outs in the Atlanta eighth. Rivera faced six batters, allowing one single and a walk in the ninth. With runners on second and first and one out, Rivera faced the potential tying run at the plate twice. First, Brian Jordan struck out swinging, and then, Greg Myers, on the first Mariano offering, fouled to Scott Brosius for the final out of the game. Rivera had picked up another save, and although the Yankees won the game in ugly fashion, they did win, taking the series lead, 1-0.

Prior to the second game, living members of "The All-Century Team" were introduced in an emotionally stirring ceremony. Great ovations were given to Hank Aaron and Ted Williams, the latter requiring assistance due to severe physical challenges. However, the greatest ovation was given to Pete Rose, who was awarded temporary clemency by the Commissioner of Baseball, Allen "Bud" Selig, to attend the festivities. Such permission was necessitated due to the still-standing 10-year-old ban of Pete Rose from the game of baseball due to questions of gambling. Pete was visibly moved by the shower of applause that was focused on him, and after the inspiring ceremonies were completed, NBC reporter Jim Gray conducted a short interview of Pete Rose that would be seen by millions. In short, Gray bombarded Rose about the gambling issues of his past that have caused his ban from baseball. Rose did offer denials of any wrongdoing and did take offense to Gray's tenacity and timing of his questioning. Many people thought Gray was out of line, especially since Rose had just been basking in a joyful moment, only to have Gray ruin it with premeditated insensitivity that seems all too frequent in this day of the media circus. Rose came out looking like an innocent victim, while Gray came out looking unprofessional, callous and insensitive. In terms of "The All-Century Team" that was announced prior to Game two, two Yankees, Babe Ruth and Lou Gehrig, did make it to the starting lineup! Yankee pitcher Roger Clemens was also named a member of the team.

In Game 2, 36-year-old David Cone would face Atlanta's Kevin Millwood, a hard-throwing 24-year-oldster. The Yankees would jump out to a 3-0 lead to start the game, all three runs coming on singles by O'Neill, Tino Martinez and Brosius. Millwood would pitch into the third, the Yankees scoring two more times to take a commanding 5-0 lead. New York got on the board on a Ricky Ledee double (one RBI) and on an error by shortstop Ozzie Guillen. Millwood, who would be charged with the loss, would also be charged with all five New York runs. The Yanks added solo runs in the fourth (fielder's choice) and fifth innings (Chuck Knoblauch RBI single) to take a 7-0 lead. Cone made his work look effortless and came out of the game after seven innings, allowing but one hit! (Hernandez did the exact same thing in the first game—seven innings, no runs and one hit allowed!) David had pitched his heart out to earn a well-deserved victory. Atlanta did score two incidental runs in their ninth, making the final: 7-2 Yanks. With the victory, the Yankees went up 2-0 in the series and had now won ten World Series games in a row, the streak beginning with Game 3 in 1996 against these Braves. With the games now shifting to Yankee Stadium, that infernal "tomahawk chop" by Braves fans was now history. Richard Velky, chief of the Schaghticoke Tribal Nation, stated his belief that the Braves were "cursed" due to the persistent negativity of the chant that accompanies the dreaded chop! First, it was the "Curse of the Bambino" with the Red Sox and now the "Curse of the Tomahawk Chop and Chant" with the Braves! What next?!

On October 26 and 27, Games 3 and 4 were played in the Bronx—at Yankee Stadium, "The Cathedral of Baseball!" In Game 3, Andy Pettitte would get the nod for the Yankees, while Tom Glavine would take the hill for the Braves, in a battle of lefties. Both clubs got out of the box early, each scoring a solo run in their first at bats. The Braves would take the lead with a three-spot in the third and a solo tally in the fifth, taking a 5-1 lead. Pettitte was knocked out of the box, pitching 3 ⅔ innings, allowing ten hits and five runs, all earned. The Yankees continued to chip away at the Braves lead, scoring their second run in the fifth on a solo homer to right by light-hitting Chad Curtis. In the seventh, the Yankees closed the Braves' lead to 5-3, on a solo Tino Martinez shot to right. Atlanta starter Tom Glavine continued to pitch into the eighth

and served up a two-run game-tying homer by Chuck Knoblauch to right-field. It was now 5-5 going into the ninth. Mariano Rivera, who succeeded Jason Grimsley and Jeff Nelson, retired the Braves 1-2-3 in the ninth. Atlanta fireballer John Rocker, who had relieved Glavine in the eighth, retired the Yanks in order in the bottom of the ninth, the game going into extra innings. In Atlanta's tenth, Rivera, though allowing a pinch-hit single, did not permit a run. For the Braves, lefty Mike Remlinger came in to face right Chad Curtis, who had homered in the fifth inning. On a 1-1 count, Curtis launched Remlinger's serving into the left-field bullpen, the Yankees winning the game in dramatic fashion, 6-5. Chad, who had five homers in 96 games during the regular season, had blasted two homers in one World Series game! The infamous interviewer, Jim Gray, who had that pregame chat with Peter Rose prior to Game 2, asked Chad about his game-winning homer. Chad said to Gray that the players had agreed that they would not talk to him in light of his interview with Rose. For the game, Mariano got the win, while Remlinger got the loss, while facing but one batter—Mr. Curtis! This Game 3 was reminiscent of Game 4 of the 1996 World Series. In that game, the Braves had taken a 6-0 lead at Atlanta, only to have the Yankees win the game in ten, 8-6—the greatest comeback in World Series history! In both games, the Yankees had faced a deficit, but with resolve and a conviction to success, the Yanks could not be denied! This game for the Yankees was historic, as it was World Series game #200 for them! With the win, their Fall Classic record now stood at 120 wins, 79 losses and one tie (in 1922 versus the New York Giants)! The Yanks now had definite thoughts of yet another World Series sweep. It was easily within their grasp.

On the evening of October 27, Game 4 of the World Series was again played at Yankee Stadium. John Smoltz would take the hill for the Braves, while Roger Clemens would do the chucking for the Yankees. Prior to the game, it was learned that Paul O'Neill's father had passed away earlier that morning. Three Yankee players now had lost their fathers in about two months' time: Scott Brosius, Luis Sojo and now, Paul O'Neill. Paul, the trooper that he is, decided to play his right-field position in honor of his father, Charles. Grieving would come later.

The game was scoreless until the third, when the Yankees tallied three times. Tino would knock in two with a single, and Posada would have an RBI single. Both pitchers, Clemens and Smoltz, pitched well into the game, Smoltz taking the bench after seven full innings. John allowed six hits, three runs, and struck out 11 Yankee batters. Roger Clemens had pitched the game of his life, going 7 ⅔ innings, allowing but four hits, one run, had four strikeouts and, for good measure, was eventually awarded the victory! Replacing Roger was Jeff Nelson, who faced but one batter, Bret Boone. Boone promptly singled, driving in what would be Atlanta's only run of the game. With two outs and runners at the corners, Rivera came in to retire Chipper Jones, who promptly grounded out, ending the eighth inning. The Yankees were now three outs away from victory. Taking a 3-1 lead into their half of the eighth, Jim Leyritz, acquired by the Yanks on the day before the trading deadline of August 1, again did his thing—he hit a solo homer to left, boosting the Yankees' lead to 4-1. Amazingly, Leyritz seems to have an affinity for postseason homers: of his 13 total postseason hits with the Yanks, dating back to 1995, eight, count 'em eight, have been home runs! With his homer, Leyritz had canceled out the run that Atlanta had just scored in its eighth inning. Now to the ninth. Marino Rivera got his second save. In methodical, workmanlike fashion, Brian Jordan grounded out, Ryan Klesko popped to second, and Keith Lockhart hit a fly aptly to Chad Curtis, who had been the hero in Game 3. How fitting it was to end this century with the final out being made in the most fabled sports palace of them all—Yankee Stadium! Ruth and Gehrig and DiMaggio and Catfish and Thurman would have been so proud!

The Yankees were the World Series Champions for the 25th time in 36 attempts and for the second year in a row. Did the Braves ever show up for this series? With their win in the fourth game, the Yankees had now won a record-tying (1927, 1928 and 1932 Yankees) 12 World Series games in a row. The Bronx Bombers outscored Atlanta 21-9, and in the postseason, the Yanks outscored their foes, 58-31, in 11 games. It was their eighth sweep in the Fall Classic: 1927, 1928, 1932, 1936, 1939, 1950, 1998 and now, 1999. The Yankees had run roughshod over the best talent that could be thrown at them, and they simply overwhelmed all of the clubs that faced them. They posted an amazing 11-1 record in the 1999 postseason, the only loss coming at the hands of Red Sox pitcher Pedro Martinez. Combining their 1998 postseason results (11-2), the Yankees now were an astonishing 22-3 (.880) against the best of the best in the playoffs. For his efforts, Mariano Rivera, with one win and two saves, was voted MVP of the World Series. Other significant players: for the Braves, Bret Boone had one of the

highest averages ever (.538, 7-for-13); for the Yanks, Scott Brosius (.375, 6-for-16) and Derek Jeter (.353, 6-for-17) each excelled. Four different pitchers picked up a win each: Clemens, Cone, Hernandez and Rivera. Although the jubilation after the game was there, there was a restraint that was tempered by compassion and humility and an appreciation of what was really important in life. After all, three teammates had lost their fathers in the past two months. In 1999, this Yankee family-team had endured emotional pain and physical suffering. Because of their shared painful experiences, this Yankee club evolved into something that was much more than a collection of fine-tuned athletes. They were a group that had learned that simple love and compassion, combined with resolve and determination, could accomplish what seemed impossible. As in prior seasons, the winning Yankees were again honored with a super parade that could only fit in New York City. There was much emotion in open display from the coaches and players. But Darryl Strawberry, no longer holding back intense emotion, broke down, Joe Torre coming to his aid, like so many players did for one another throughout this magical 1999 season. In the midst of his emotion, Darryl said to Torre: "Thank you for caring for me." This sentiment embodied the feeling that was this Yankees club of 1999.

YANKEES IN THE POSTSEASON (1921 THROUGH 2002)									
	SERIES			**GAMES**					
SERIES NAME:	W	L	PCT	W	L	PCT	tot	home	road
Division (9)	6	3	.666	23	16	.590	39	20	19
Championship (10)	9	1	.900	32	15	.681	47	23	24
World (38)	26	12	.684	128	84	.604	213*	103	110
Postseason Totals	41	16	.719	183	115	.614	299*	146	153
*includes a tie at home in 1922									

Looking at the YANKEES IN THE POSTSEASON chart, note that they have played in three types of series (that is, Division Series (six times), Championship Series (eight times) and World Series (36 times) for a total of 50 series appearances, spanning 262 total games. Through 1999, the runner-up to the Yankees in the American League in total postseason games is the Athletics' franchise (Philadelphia-43 games, Kansas City-0— woe is them—and Oakland-77) with 120, which is 130 fewer than the Yanks! Next in line in the AL after the A's are the Boston Red Sox, with 85 postseason games. In terms of World Series games played, the second highest total to the Yankees (201) in the American League is the A's franchise with 75 games (Philadelphia with 43 and Oakland with 32). Regarding National League clubs, the most postseason appearances are by the Dodger franchise (Brooklyn-56 and Los Angeles-94) for a total of 150, exactly 100 fewer than the Yanks! In total World Series games, again, the Dodgers have the most played, 56 by Brooklyn and 49 by Los Angeles, for a total of 105, some 92 fewer than the Yankees.

Roger Clemens, winner of the final game of the '99 World Series.

```
Game 1 at Turner Field, GA, October 23
NY      0 0 0  0 0 0  0 4 0  - 4 6 0
ATL     0 0 0  1 0 0  0 0 0  - 1 2 2
W—Hernandez; L—Maddux; HR—CJones (ATL).    A.—51,342

Game 2 at Turner Field, GA, October 24
NY      3 0 2  1 1 0  0 0 0  - 7 14 1
ATL     0 0 0  0 0 0  0 0 2  - 2 5 1
W—Cone; L—Millwood; HR—None.               A.—51,226

Game 3 at Yankee Stadium, NY, October 26  (10 INNINGS)
ATL     1 0 3  1 0 0  0 0 0 0 - 5 14 1
NY      1 0 0  0 1 0  1 2 0 1 - 6 9 0
W—Rivera; L—Remlinger; HR—Curtis 2 (NY), TMartinez (NY), Knoblauch (NY).
                                           A.—56,794

Game 4 at Yankee Stadium, NY, October 27
ATL     0 0 0  0 0 0  0 1 0  - 1 5 0
NY      0 0 3  0 0 0  0 1 x  - 4 8 0
W—Clemens; L—Smoltz; HR—Leyritz (NY).      A.—56,752
```

Our hats go off to this great Yankee organization from the top on down. This club seems set for continued success for many years to come with many young prospects in the minors. Currently, there is an incredible passion for success, which starts with the positive attitude that flows from manager Joe Torre and filters down to his coaches and players. Torre has already won 400 regular seasons games since 1996, exactly 100 per year and, hopefully, many more are to come. Oh, that question earlier about "the team of the decade"—the answer is clear:

**THE NEW YORK YANKEES:
THE TEAM OF THE 1999 SEASON
THE TEAM OF THE DECADE
THE TEAM OF THE CENTURY!!**

2000

For the first time in 44 years, Major League Baseball fans were treated to a Subway Series. In years past, when New York boasted three major league teams—the AL's Yankees and the NL's Brooklyn Dodgers and New York Giants—the Subway Series was a fairly common occurrence come Fall Classic time. In the late '50s, though, the Dodgers and the Giants both moved to the west coast, leaving the Big Apple with only one big-league team, until the 1962 expansion Mets provided the National League with a fresh New York franchise.

In 2000, as the Yankees took care of Oakland and Seattle, the Mets upended San Francisco in the opening round of the NL playoffs and then dumped the St. Louis Cardinals in the NLCS to set up the newest version of the Subway Series.

The Yankees—the other New Yorkers—were ready and waiting. It was their 37th appearance in the World Series, 19 more than any other team. In Game 1 at Yankee Stadium, New York proved its worth right from the start. After falling behind the Mets, 3-2, on a Bubba Trammell pinch-hit single in the seventh, the Yankees tied the game, 3-3, in the bottom of the ninth when Chuck Knoblauch brought home Paul O'Neill with a sacrifice fly against Mets closer Armando Benitez. While relievers Mariano Rivera and Mike Stanton held the Mets at bay in extra innings, the opportunistic Yankees came through late. In the bottom of the 12th, reserve infielder Jose Vizcaino—a former Met—slapped a bases-loaded, opposite-field RBI single off Turk Wendell to give the Yankees the victory, 4-3. The marathon contest, which lasted four hours and 51 minutes, was the longest World Series game ever played. It was also the Yankees' 13th straight World Series victory, dating to 1996, when they beat the Atlanta Braves, four games to two.

Game 2 was plain weird. It was Roger Clemens against Mike Hampton, but it ended up being Roger Clemens against Mike Piazza. Or was it Roger Clemens against Roger Clemens? Nobody knows for sure. What baseball fans everywhere already knew was that earlier in the season, during an interleague game between the Yanks and the Mets, Clemens had beaned Piazza with a fastball. To say that their next meeting was widely anticipated would be a gross understatement. It was the pregame talk of the town. What actually happened in Piazza's first at-bat in Game 2 of the World Series is still up for debate. The flamethrowing Clemens started Piazza off with a fastball. Piazza swung, his bat splintered, and the barrel shot right at Clemens. As Piazza began running toward first (unaware that the ball had gone foul), Clemens picked up the barrel and hurled it in front of Piazza. Piazza, with the handle of his bat still in his hands, began walking toward Clemens to find out what the heck Clemens was thinking about. Both benches emptied, but no fisticuffs erupted. Clemens, who later gave reporters various reasons for his odd behavior—he thought the barrel of the bat was the baseball; he was "emotional"; he was helping out the batboy by throwing him the barrel of the bat—was not ejected from the game, but he was later fined $50,000 for his eccentric behavior. After the bizarre incident, a sense of normality returned, and Clemens worked eight innings, allowing only two hits. Although the Mets rallied for five runs in the top of the ninth (two coming on a home run by Piazza), they fell one run short in a 6-5 loss that gave the Yankees a 2-0 Series lead.

The Yankees, now on the verge of winning their third consecutive World Series, lost Game 3 at Shea Stadium, 4-2. Orlando Hernandez whiffed a dozen Mets in 7 1/3 innings, but Robin Ventura touched him up for a double and a homer and two RBIs. A pair of runs in the bottom of the eighth proved to be the margin of victory, as Benitez picked up the save, shutting down the Yankees in the top of the ninth. It was during this game that two Yankee records went by the boards. First, the Mets' victory marked the end of the Yankees' 14-game winning streak in World Series games. Second, despite a 12-strikeout performance (only the 11th time that feat had been accomplished in postseason play), El Duque's eight-game postseason winning streak came to an end.

Game 4 came down, once again, to good pitching and little hitting. The Yankees put up single runs in each of the first three innings—one on a home run by Jeter, leading off the game against Bobby J. Jones; the Mets countered with two in the bottom of the third on Piazza's homer with Timo Perez aboard; and that was that: 3-2, Yanks. Denny Neagle started for the Yankees, but lasted only 4 2/3 innings. Jeff Nelson picked up the win, while Rivera notched the save. Bobby J. Jones took the loss.

The fans at Shea held out slim hope in Game 5. The Mets took a 2-1 lead after two innings, but homers by Williams and Jeter proved too much. The Yankees tallied twice in the top of the ninth and held on to win the game, 4-2, and the World Series, 4-1.

Derek Jeter, who went 9-for-22 (.409) with two homers and 19 total bases and extended his World Series hitting streak to 14 games, was named Series MVP. He also scored at least one run in each game against the Mets.

As for Joe Torre, he improved his career World Series record to 4-0, tying longtime Dodgers manager Walt Alston for fourth place in that category.

So the cry of "Wait till next year" will again be the refrain of 29 other baseball teams who once more find themselves looking up at the reigning world champion New York Yankees.

```
Game 1 at Yankee Stadium, NY, October 21
NY (NL)    000  000  300  000  -  3 10 0
NY (AL)    000  002  001  001  -  4 12 0
W—Stanton; L—Wendell.
A.—55,913

Game 2 at Yankee Stadium, NY, October 22
NY (NL)    000  000  005  -  5  7 3
NY (AL)    210  010  11x  -  6 12 1
W—Clemens; L—Hampton; HR—Piazza (NYM), Payton (NYM), Brosius (NYY).
A.—56,059

Game 3 at Shea Stadium, NY, October 24
NY (AL)    001  100  000  -  2  8 0
NY (NL)    010  001  02x  -  4  9 0
W—Franco; L—O. Hernandez; HR—Ventura (NYM).
A.—55,299

Game 4 at Shea Stadium, NY, October 25
NY (AL)    111  000  000  -  3  8 0
NY (NL)    002  000  000  -  2  6 1
W—Nelson; L—B. J. Jones; HR—Jeter (NYY), Piazza (NYM).
A.—55,290

Game 5 at Shea Stadium, NY, October 26
NY (AL)    010  001  002  -  4  7 1
NY (NL)    020  000  000  -  2  8 1
W—Stanton; L—Leiter; HR—B. Williams (NYY), Jeter (NYY).
A.—55,292
```

2001

Lack of franchise postseason history notwithstanding, the Arizona Diamondbacks found themselves in the World Series in only their fourth season of existence. Owner Jerry Colangelo had pursued the free agent and shrewd trade route set before him by George Steinbrenner and had a roster full of experienced and hungry ballplayers. When the team faltered in 2000, he fired his manager (former Yankee skipper Buck Showalter) and hired former Giants catcher and coach Bob Brenly to bring a title to the Phoenix area.

The D-Backs squeaked by St. Louis in the divisional series and then knocked off the Atlanta Braves in the NLCS. Brenly packed his postseason hopes behind the twin threats of Curt Schilling and Randy Johnson to pitch his team to a championship. They did not disappoint, as Arizona took the first two games by 9-1 and 4-0 counts. Game 2 was the first shutout the Yankees had suffered in the World Series since 1963. President Bush threw out the first pitch in Game 3, and the Yankees applied the emotion of the opening ceremony to win, 2-1. Roger Clemens fired seven strong innings, with Mariano Rivera picking up his 24th postseason save.

The next two games topped the chart in the category of "Unvelievable." In Games 4 and 5 the Diamondbacks were one

out away from victory with their All-Star closer, Byung-Hyun Kim, on the mound firing "bullet-like" fastballs out of the late autumn night. But, in each game, a tying two-run home run was hit to send the Yankee Stadium crowds into pandemonium. After Tino Martinez knotted up Game 4 with his blast to the bleachers in right center, Derek Jeter sent a fly ball just over the right field wall to win the contest, 4-3. A sign in the crowd went up with "Mr. November" written on it as the clock was past midnight when the Yankees ran to the plate to greet Jeter.

The next night the first official November home run in major league baseball was hit by Scott Brosius to tie the game at 2. Alfonso Soriano delivered a single in the 12th inning to plate Chuck Knoblauch with the winning run. It was the seventh straight extra-inning World Series victory for the Yankees, and they now had the momentum as the Series shifted back to Arizona. The Diamondbacks regrouped in Game 5 and routed the Yankees by a 15-2 score to force a seventh game. It was the first seventh game for the Yankees since the 1964 Fall Classic against St. Louis. The Yankees tied the game in the seventh inning and went up 2-1 in the eighth on Soriano's solo home run. It was Rivera time in the ninth, and it first appeared that the Yankees would pick off another World Championship. It was not to be, though, as three hits, a walk, and an error plated two runs and the Diamondbacks had come back to win the game, 3-2, and Series. The Yankees only hit .183 in the series, but they showed a lot of heart in almost winning another world title.

```
Game 1 at Bank One Ballpark, AZ, October 27
NY    100  000  000  -  1  3 2
AZ    104  400  00x  -  0 10 0
W—Schilling; L—Mussina. HR—Counsell (AZ), Gonzalez (AZ).
A.—49,646

Game 2 at Bank One Ballpark, AZ, October 28
NY    000  000  000  -  0  3 0
AZ    010  000  30x  -  4  5 0
W—Johnson; L—Pettitte; HR—M. Williams (AZ).
A.—49,646

Game 3 at Yankee Stadium, NY, October 30
AZ    000  100  000  -  1  3 3
NY    010  001  00x  -  2  7 1
W—Clemens; L—Anderson; HR—Posada (NY).
A.—55,820

Game 4 at Yankee Stadium, NY, October 31
AZ    000  100  020  0  -  3  6 0
NY    001  000  002  1  -  4  7 0
W—Rivera; L—Kim; HR—Grace (AZ), Spencer (NY), T. Martinez (NY), Jeter (NY).
A.—55,863

Game 5 at Yankee Stadium, NY, November 1
AZ    000  020  000  000  -  2  8 0
NY    000  000  002  001  -  3  9 1
W—Hitchcock; L—Lopez; HR—Finley (AZ), Barajas (AZ), Brosius (NY).
A.—56,018

Game 6 at Bank One Ballpark, AZ, November 3
NY    000  002  000  -  2  7 1
AZ    138  300  00x  - 15 22 0
W—Johnson; L—Pettitte.
A.—49,707

Game 7 at Bank One Ballpark, AZ, November 4
NY    000  000  110  -  2  6 3
AZ    010  001  002  -  3 11 0
W—Johnson; L—Rivera; HR—Soriano (NY).
A.—49,589
```

YANKEE BATTING LEADERS IN THE WORLD SERIES
38 SERIES (1921 THROUGH 2001)

SERIES PLAYED
14 Yogi Berra
12 Mickey Mantle
11 Whitey Ford
10 Joe DiMaggio
9 Hank Bauer
9 Elston Howard
9 Phil Rizzuto
8 Bill Dickey
8 Gil McDougald
7 Seven tied

GAMES
75 Yogi Berra
65 Mickey Mantle
53 Hank Bauer
53 Gil McDougald
52 Phil Rizzuto
51 Joe DiMaggio
47 Elston Howard
39 Bill Skowron
38 Bill Dickey
36 Babe Ruth

AT-BATS
259 Yogi Berra
230 Mickey Mantle
199 Joe DiMaggio
190 Gil McDougald
188 Hank Bauer
183 Phil Rizzuto
153 Elston Howard
146 Tony Kubek
145 Bill Dickey
131 Bobby Richardson

RUNS
42 Mickey Mantle
41 Yogi Berra
37 Babe Ruth
30 Lou Gehrig
27 Joe DiMaggio
25 Elston Howard
23 Gil McDougald
22 Derek Jeter
21 Hank Bauer
21 Phil Rizzuto
21 Gene Woodling

HITS
71 Yogi Berra
59 Mickey Mantle
54 Joe DiMaggio
46 Hank Bauer
45 Gil McDougald
45 Phil Rizzuto
43 Lou Gehrig
41 Babe Ruth
40 Elston Howard
40 Bobby Richardson

HOME RUNS
18 Mickey Mantle
15 Babe Ruth
12 Yogi Berra
10 Lou Gehrig
8 Joe DiMaggio
8 Reggie Jackson
8 Bill Skowron
7 Hank Bauer
7 Gil McDougald
5 Many tied

TOTAL BASES
123 Mickey Mantle
117 Yogi Berra
93 Babe Ruth
87 Lou Gehrig
84 Joe DiMaggio
75 Hank Bauer
72 Gil McDougald
69 Bill Skowron
66 Elston Howard
55 Bill Dickey

RUNS BATTED IN
40 Mickey Mantle
39 Yogi Berra
35 Lou Gehrig
30 Babe Ruth
30 Joe DiMaggio
29 Bill Skowron
24 Hank Bauer
24 Bill Dickey
24 Gil McDougald

WALKS
43 Mickey Mantle
33 Babe Ruth
32 Yogi Berra
30 Phil Rizzuto
26 Lou Gehrig
20 Gil McDougald
19 Joe DiMaggio
19 Gene Woodling
15 Bill Dickey
14 Joe Collins
14 Frank Crosetti

EXTRA-BASE HITS
(2B + 3B + HR)
26 Mickey Mantle
22 Yogi Berra
21 Babe Ruth
21 Lou Gehrig
14 Joe DiMaggio
13 Elston Howard
13 Bill Skowron
12 Hank Bauer
12 Gil McDougald
11 Reggie Jackson

BATTING AVG.
(50+ AT BATS)
.400 Reggie Jackson
.373 Thurman Munson
.361 Lou Gehrig
.350 Earle Combs
.333 Billy Martin
.319 Lou Piniella
.318 Gene Woodling
.306 Charlie Keller
.305 Bobby Richardson
.291 Derek Jeter

SLUGGING PCT.
(50+ AT BATS)
.891 Reggie Jackson
.788 Babe Ruth
.731 Lou Gehrig
.611 Charlie Keller
.566 Billy Martin
.535 Mickey Mantle
.529 Gene Woodling
.508 Elston Howard
.508 Tom Tresh
.493 Thurman Munson

YANKEE PITCHING LEADERS IN THE WORLD SERIES
38 SERIES (1921 THROUGH 2001)

SERIES PITCHED
11 Whitey Ford
7 Red Ruffing
6 Waite Hoyt
6 Johnny Murphy
6 Vic Raschi
6 Allie Reynolds
5 Lefty Gomez
5 Ed Lopat
5 Ralph Terry
5 Bob Turley
5 Andy Pettitte

GAMES PITCHED
22 Whitey Ford
18 Mariano Rivera
15 Allie Reynolds
15 Bob Turley
11 Waite Hoyt
11 Vic Raschi
10 Red Ruffing
9 Herb Pennock
9 Ralph Terry
8 Andy Pettitte
8 Johnny Kucks
8 Johnny Murphy

GAMES STARTED
22 Whitey Ford
10 Waite Hoyt
10 Red Ruffing
9 Allie Reynolds
8 Vic Raschi
8 Bob Turley
8 Andy Pettitte
7 Lefty Gomez
7 Ed Lopat
6 Don Larsen
6 Ralph Terry

COMPLETE GAMES
8 Red Ruffing
7 Whitey Ford
6 Waite Hoyt
5 Allie Reynolds
4 Lefty Gomez
4 Herb Pennock
3 Ed Lopat
3 Carl Mays
3 Monte Pearson
3 Vic Raschi
3 Bob Turley

INNINGS PITCHED
146.0 Whitey Ford
85.2 Red Ruffing
77.2 Waite Hoyt
77.1 Allie Reynolds
60.1 Vic Raschi
53.2 Bob Turley
52.1 Herb Pennock
52.0 Ed Lopat
50.1 Lefty Gomez
46.0 Ralph Terry

SHUTOUTS
3 Whitey Ford
2 Waite Hoyt
2 Allie Reynolds
1 Spud Chandler
1 Johnny Kucks
1 Don Larsen
1 Carl Mays
1 Monte Pearson
1 Vic Raschi
1 Ralph Terry
1 Bob Turley

WINS
10 Whitey Ford
7 Allie Reynolds
7 Red Ruffing
6 Lefty Gomez
6 Waite Hoyt
5 Herb Pennock
5 Vic Raschi
4 Ed Lopat
4 Monte Pearson
4 Bob Turley

SAVES
8 Mariano Rivera
4 Johnny Murphy
4 Allie Reynolds
3 Herb Pennock
2 Rich Gossage
2 Bob Kuzava
2 Joe Page

HITS ALLOWED
132 Whitey Ford
74 Waite Hoyt
74 Red Ruffing
61 Allie Reynolds
54 Andy Pettitte
52 Vic Raschi
51 Lefty Gomez
51 Ed Lopat
43 Bob Turley
41 Bob Shawkey
41 Ralph Terry

WALKS
(20+ INNINGS)
34 Whitey Ford
32 Allie Reynolds
29 Bob Turley
27 Red Ruffing
25 Vic Raschi
22 Waite Hoyt
17 Don Larsen
15 Lefty Gomez
14 Ron Guidry
14 Bob Shawkey
14 Andy Pettitte
28 Andy Pettitte

STRIKEOUTS
(20+ INNINGS)
94 Whitey Ford
62 Allie Reynolds
61 Bob Turley
48 Red Ruffing
46 Vic Raschi
43 Waite Hoyt
40 Orlando Hernandez
32 Roger Clemens
31 Don Larsen
31 Lefty Gomez
28 Ron Guidry

ERA**
1.01 Monte Pearson
1.33 Mariano Rivera
1.48 Jim Bouton
1.62 Spud Chandler
1.62 Waite Hoyt
1.69 Ron Guidry
2.06 Herb Pennock
2.08 Bill Stafford
2.24 Vic Raschi
2.28 Orlando Hernandez

YANKEES HITTING ONE OR MORE HOMERS IN A WORLD SERIES
(59 PLAYERS THROUGH 2001)

PLAYER	HR	PLAYER	HR
Mickey Mantle	18	Tony Kubek	2
Babe Ruth	15	Jim Leyritz	2
Yogi Berra	12	Phil Linz	2
Lou Gehrig	10	Jorge Posada	2
Joe DiMaggio	8	Phil Rizzuto	2
Reggie Jackson	8	George Selkirk	2
Hank Bauer	7	Bob Watson	2
Gil McDougald	7	Alphonso Soriano	1
Bill Skowron	7	Rick Cerone	1
Bill Dickey	5	Bob Cerv	1
Elston Howard	5	Chris Chambliss	1
Charlie Keller	5	Earle Combs	1
Roger Maris	5	Frankie Crosetti	1
Billy Martin	5	Babe Dahlgren	1
Scott Brosius	4	Joe Dugan	1
Joe Collins	4	Cedric Durst	1
Tommy Henrich	4	Chick Fewster	1
Tony Lazzeri	4	Myril Hoag	1
Tom Tresh	4	Hector Lopez	1
Joe Gordon	3	Jim Mason	1
Johnny Mize	3	Bob Meusel	1
Willie Randolph	3	Thurman Munson	1
Aaron Ward	3	Joe Pepitone	1
Gene Woodling	3	Jake Powell	1
Tino Martinez	3	Bobby Richardson	1
Derek Jeter	3	Enos Slaughter	1
Bernie Williams	3	Roy White	1
Johnny Blanchard	2	Shane Spencer	1
Clete Boyer	2		
Chad Curtis	2		
Chuck Knoblauch	2		

WORLD SERIES TOTALS: 204

PITCHERS WON-LOST RECORDS & SAVES IN A WORLD SERIES
(80 PITCHERS THROUGH 2001)

PITCHER	WON	LOST	SAVE
Whitey Ford	10	8	0
Allie Reynolds	7	2	4
Red Ruffing	7	2	0
Lefty Gomez	6	0	0
Waite Hoyt	6	3	0
Herb Pennock	5	0	3
Vic Raschi	5	3	0
Monte Pearson	4	0	0
Ed Lopat	4	1	0
Bob Turley	4	3	1
George Pipgras	3	0	0
Roger Clemens	3	0	0
Ron Guidry	3	1	0
Don Larsen	3	2	0
Johnny Murphy	2	0	4
Wilcy Moore	2	0	1
David Cone	2	0	0

PITCHER	WON	LOST	SAVE
Marius Russo	2	0	0
Mike Stanton	2	0	0
Spec Shea	2	0	0
Mike Torrez	2	0	0
Joe Page	2	1	2
Orlando Hernandez	2	1	0
Jim Bouton	2	1	0
Bump Hadley	2	1	0
Mariano Rivera	2	1	8
Spud Chandler	2	2	1
Andy Pettitte	2	3	0
Ralph Terry	2	4	0
Rich Gossage	1	0	2
Sterling Hitchcock	1	0	0
Jeff Nelson	1	0	0
Luis Arroyo	1	0	0
Jim Beattie	1	0	0
Hank Borowy	1	0	0
Buddy Daley	1	0	0
Tom Ferrick	1	0	0
Tommy John	1	0	0
Johnny Kucks	1	0	0
Graeme Lloyd	1	0	0
Sparky Lyle	1	0	0
Jim McDonald	1	0	0
Ramiro Mendoza	1	0	0
Bill Stafford	1	0	0
Tom Sturdivant	1	0	0
David Wells	1	0	0
Tom Zachary	1	0	0
Ryne Duren	1	1	1
Tommy Byrne	1	1	0
Jimmy Key	1	1	0
Johnny Sain	1	1	0
Mel Stottlemyre	1	1	0
Tiny Bonham	1	2	0
Bob Shawkey	1	2	0
Joe Bush	1	3	0
Catfish Hunter	1	3	0
Carl Mays	1	3	0
John Wetteland	0	0	4
Bob Kuzava	0	0	2
Steve Hamilton	0	0	1
Jim Coates	0	1	1
Sam Jones	0	1	1
Pat Malone	0	1	1
Bobby Shantz	0	1	1
Mike Mussina	0	1	0
Doyle Alexander	0	1	0
Bill Bevens	0	1	0
Atley Donald	0	1	0
Dock Ellis	0	1	0
Don Gullett	0	1	0
Pete Mikkelsen	0	1	0
Tom Morgan	0	1	0
Bobo Newsom	0	1	0
Jack Quinn	0	1	0
Dutch Ruether	0	1	0
Urban Shocker	0	1	0
Bob Grim	0	2	1
Art Ditmar	0	2	0
Al Downing	0	2	0
Ed Figueroa	0	2	0
George Frazier	0	3	0
GRAND TOTALS:	**128**	**84**	**99**

YANKEE INDIVIDUAL WORLD SERIES RECORDS

SERVICE

Most World Series Played: 14
YOGI BERRA—1947, 1949-53, 1955-58, 1960-63

Most World Series An Active Player On Winning Club: 10
YOGI BERRA—1947, 1949-53, 1956, 1958, 1961-62

Most World Series Playing in All Games: 10
JOE DiMAGGIO—1936-39, 1941-42, 1947, 1949-51

Most World Series Eligible Without Playing: 6
CHARLIE SILVERA—1950-53, 1955-56 (He played in 1 game in 1949 World Series.)

Most Consecutive World Series Played: 5
HANK BAUER, YOGI BERRA, ED LOPAT, JOHN MIZE, VIC RASCHI, ALLIE REYNOLDS, PHIL RIZZUTO, and GENE WOODLING, all 1949-53; and JOHN BLANCHARD, CLETE BOYER, WHITEY FORD, ELSTON HOWARD, HECTOR LOPEZ, MICKEY MANTLE, ROGER MARIS, BOBBY RICHARDSON and RALPH TERRY, all 1960-64

BATTING

Most Consecutive Games Scoring At Least One Run: 9
BABE RUTH—1927 (last 2 games), 1928 (all 4 games), 1932 (first 3 games)

Most Runs, Single Series:
4-game Series—9; BABE RUTH, 1928
           LOU GEHRIG, 1932
6-game Series—10; REGGIE JACKSON, 1977
           (1 other)
7-game Series—8; BILLY JOHNSON, 1947
           MICKEY MANTLE, 1960
           BOBBY RICHARDSON, 1960
           MICKEY MANTLE, 1964
           (5 others)

Most Runs, Game: 4
BABE RUTH—October 6, 1926
EARLE COMBS—October 2, 1932
FRANK CROSETTI—October 2, 1936
REGGIE JACKSON—October 18, 1977
           (4 others)

Most Consecutive Games Making At Least One Hit: 17
HANK BAUER—1956 (7 games), 1957 (7 games), 1958 (first 3 games)

Most Hits, Single Series:
4-game Series—10; BABE RUTH, 1928
5-game Series— 9; BOBBY RICHARDSON, 1961
           DEREK JETER, 2000
           PAUL O'NEILL, 2000
           (8 others)
6-game Series—12; BILLY MARTIN, 1953
           (2 others)
7-game Series—13; BOBBY RICHARDSON, 1964
           (2 others)

Most Singles, Single Series:
4-game Series— 9; THURMAN MUNSON, 1976
5-game Series— 8; BOBBY RICHARDSON, 1961
           (6 others)

6-game Series—10; RED ROLFE, 1936
           (1 other)

Most Triples, Single Series:
4-game Series—2; LOU GEHRIG, 1927
           (2 others)
5-game Series—2; BOBBY BROWN, 1949
           PAUL O'NEIL, 2000
           (1 other)
6-game Series—2; BOB MEUSEL, 1923
           BILLY MARTIN, 1953
           (3 others)
7-game Series—3; BILLY JOHNSON, 1947 (1 other)

Most Consecutive Games Hitting At Least One Home Run: 4
LOU GEHRIG—1928 (last 3 games), 1932 (first game). Total—5 homers
REGGIE JACKSON—1977 (last 3 games), 1978 (first game). Total—6 homers

Most Home Runs, Single Series:
4-game Series—4; LOU GEHRIG, 1928
6-game Series—5; REGGIE JACKSON, 1977
7-game Series—4; BABE RUTH, 1926
           HANK BAUER, 1958
           (2 others; 3 other times)

Most Home Runs Hit By A Rookie, Single Series: 3
CHARLIE KELLER, 1939

Most Home Runs, Game: 3
BABE RUTH—October 6, 1926
BABE RUTH—October 9, 1928
REGGIE JACKSON—October 18, 1977 (consecutive; each hit on first pitch)

Most World Series Hitting At Least Two Home Runs: 6
MICKEY MANTLE—1952 (2), 1953 (2), 1956 (3), 1958 (2), 1960 (3), 1964 (3)

Most World Series Hitting At least Three Home Runs: 3
BABE RUTH—1923 (3), 1926 (4), 1928 (3)
MICKEY MANTLE—1956 (3), 1960 (3), 1964 (3)

Most Consecutive Games With At Least One Run Batted In: 8
LOU GEHRIG—1928 (4 games), 1932 (4 games). Total—17 RBIs
REGGIE JACKSON—1977 (last 4 games), 1978 (first 4 games). Total—14 RBIs

Most Runs Batted In, Single Series:
4-game Series— 9; LOU GEHRIG, 1928
7-game Series—12; BOBBY RICHARDSON, 1960

Most Runs Batted In, Game: 6
BOBBY RICHARDSON—October 8, 1960

Most Consecutive Walks In One World Series: 5
LOU GEHRIG—October 7, 1928 (2); October 9, 1928 (3)

Most Walks, Single Series:
5-game Series— 7; JOE GORDON, 1941
           (2 others)

6-game Series— 9; WILLIE RANDOLPH, 1981
7-game Series—11; BABE RUTH, 1926
      (1 other)

Most Walks, Game: 4
BABE RUTH—October 10, 1926
      (5 others)

Most World Series Batting .300 Or Better: 6
BABE RUTH—1921, 1923, 1926-28, 1932

Highest Batting Average, Single Series:
5-game Series—.500; JOE GORDON, 1941
      (1 other)
6-game Series—.500; BILLY MARTIN, 1953
      (2 others)
7-game Series—.500; JOHNNY LINDELL, 1947
      (2 others)

Highest Slugging Average, Single Series:
4-game Series—1.727; LOU GEHRIG, 1928
5-game Series—.929; JOE GORDON, 1941
6-game Series—1.250; REGGIE JACKSON, 1977

Most Total Bases, Single Series:
4-game Series—22; BABE RUTH, 1928
5-game Series—19; DEREK JETER, 2000
6-game Series—25; REGGIE JACKSON, 1977

Most Total Bases, Game: 12
BABE RUTH—October 6, 1926
BABE RUTH—October 9, 1928
REGGIE JACKSON—October 18, 1977

Most Extra-Base Hits, Total Series: 26
MICKEY MANTLE—1951-53, 1955-58, 1960-64

Most Extra-Base Hits, Single Series:
4-game Series—6; BABE RUTH, 1928
5-game Series—5; DEREK JETER, 2000
      (1 other)
6-game Series—6; REGGIE JACKSON, 1977
      (2 others)

PITCHING

Most Hits As A Pinch Hitter, Total Series: 3
BOBBY BROWN—1947 (3)
JOHN MIZE—1949 (2), 1952 (1)
BOB CERV—1955 (1), 1956 (1), 1960 (1)
JOHN BLANCHARD—1960 (1), 1961 (1), 1964 (1)
      (6 others)

Most World Series Pitched In: 11
WHITEY FORD—1950, 1953, 1955-58, 1960-64

Most Opening Games Started: 8
WHITEY FORD—1955-58, 1961-64 (4 wins, 3 losses, 1 no decision)

Most Opening Games Won: 5
RED RUFFING—1932, 1938-39, 1941-42 (4 complete games)

Most Consecutive Scoreless Innings Pitched, Total Series: $33^2/_3$
WHITEY FORD—1960 (18), 1961 (14), 1962 ($1^2/_3$)

Most Consecutive Perfect Innings Pitched (no batter reaching first base), Total Series: $11^1/_3$

DON LARSEN—October 8, 1956 (9); October 5, 1957 ($2^1/_3$)

Most Games Won Without A Defeat, Single Series:
4-game Series—2; WAITE HOYT, 1928 (both complete games)
RED RUFFING, 1938 (both complete games)
      (3 others)

Most Games Finished, Single Series:
4-game Series—3; HAL RENIFF, 1963 (3 innings)
4-game Series—3; MARIANO RIVERA, 1998 ($4^1/_3$ innings)
4-game Series—3; MARIANO RIVERA, 1999 ($4^2/_3$ innings)
6-game Series—5; JOHN WETTELAND, 1996 ($4^1/_3$ innings pitched)

Most Games Won By Relief Pitcher, Single Series: 2
MIKE STANTON, 2000 (6 others)

Most World Series Pitching In Relief: 6
JOHNNY MURPHY—1936-39, 1941, 1943

Most Saves, Single Series (since 1969):
6-game Series—4; JOHN WETTELAND, 1996

Most Innings Pitched, Single Series:
4-game Series—18; WAITE HOYT, 1928
              RED RUFFING, 1938
      (2 others)

Most Innings Pitched Without Allowing A Walk, Single Series: 26
CARL MAYS—1921

Most Earned Runs Allowed, 9-Inning Game: 8
JAY WITASICK, November 3, 2001

Lowest Earned Run Average (14 or more innings pitched), Single Series: 0.00
WAITE HOYT—1921 (27 innings)
WHITEY FORD—1960 (18 innings)
WHITEY FORD—1961 (14 innings)
      (5 others)

FIELDING
Catchers—
Most Games Played As Catcher, Total Series: 63
YOGI BERRA—1947, 1949-53, 1955-58, 1960, 1962

Most Consecutive Errorless Games, Total Series: 30
YOGI BERRA—October 4, 1952 through October 9, 1957

Highest Fielding Average (with most chances), Single Series:
8-game Series—1.000; WALLY SCHANG, 1921 (50 chances)

Most Putouts, Total Series: 421
YOGI BERRA—1947, 1949-53, 1955-58, 1960, 1962

Most Assists, Total Series: 36
YOGI BERRA—1947, 1949-53, 1955-58, 1960, 1962

Most Assists, Single Series:
4-game Series—7; THURMAN MUNSON, 1976

Most Double Plays, Total Series: 6
YOGI BERRA—1947, 1949-53, 1955-58, 1960, 1962
      (1 other)

Most Double Plays, Single Series:
8-game Series—3; WALLY SCHANG, 1921

Most Runners Caught Stealing, Single Series:
4-game Series—5; THURMAN MUNSON, 1976

First Basemen—
Highest Fielding Average (with most chances), Single Series:
8-game Series—1.000; WALLY PIPP, 1921 (93 chances)
(1 other)

Most Putouts, Single Series:
8-game Series—92; WALLY PIPP, 1921
Most Assists, Single Series:
4-game Series—6; JOE PEPITONE, 1963
(1 other)
5-game Series—5; BILL SKOWRON, 1961
(3 others)

Most Double Plays, Single Series:
4-game Series—7; JOE PEPITONE, 1963
5-game Series—7; WALLY PIPP, 1922

Second Basemen—
Most Consecutive Errorless Games, Total Series: 23
BILLY MARTIN—October 5, 1952 through October 10, 1956

Highest Fielding Average (with most chances), Single Series:
5-game Series—1.000; JOE GORDON, 1943 (43 chances)

Most Putouts, Single Series:
5-game Series—20, JOE GORDON, 1943

Most Assists, Single Series:
4-game Series—18; TONY LAZZERI, 1927
5-game Series—23; JOE GORDON, 1943
6-game Series—27; AARON WARD, 1923
8-game Series—34; AARON WARD, 1921

Third Basemen—
Most Games Played As Third Baseman, Total Series: 31
GIL MCDOUGALD—1951-53, 1955, 1960

Highest Fielding Average (with most chances), Single Series:
6-game Series—1.000; GRAIG NETTLES, 1978 (26 chances)

Most Putouts, Single Series:
6-game Series—14; RED ROLFE, 1936

Most Assists, Single Series:
6-game Series—20; GRAIG NETTLES, 1977

Most Double Plays, Single Series:
4-game Series—3; GRAIG NETTLES, 1976
6-game Series—3; GRAIG NETTLES, 1978

Shortstops—
Most Games Played As Shortstop, Total Series: 52
PHIL RIZZUTO—1941-42, 1947, 1949-53, 1955

Most Consecutive Errorless Games, Total Series: 21
PHIL RIZZUTO—October 3, 1942 through October 5, 1951

Highest Fielding Average (with most chances), Single Series:
5-game Series—1.000; EVERETT SCOTT, 1922 (29 chances)
8-game Series—1.000; ROGER PECKINPAUGH, 1921
(46 chances)

Most Putouts, Total Series: 107
PHIL RIZZUTO—1941-42, 1947, 1949-53, 1955

Most Putouts, Single Series:
4-game Series—16; FRANK CROSETTI, 1938
5-game Series—15; PHIL RIZZUTO, 1942
(1 other)
Most Assists, Total Series: 143
PHIL RIZZUTO—1941-42, 1947, 1949-53, 1955
Most Double Plays, Total Series: 32
PHIL RIZZUTO—1941-42, 1947, 1949-53, 1955

Most Double Plays, Single Series:
4-game Series—5; TONY KUBEK, 1963
(1 other)
5-game Series—6; EVERETT SCOTT, 1922
PHIL RIZZUTO, 1941
6-game Series—8; PHIL RIZZUTO, 1951

Outfielders—
Most Games Played As Outfielder, Total Series: 63
MICKEY MANTLE—1951-53, 1955-58, 1960-64

Most Consecutive Errorless Games, Total Series: 45
JOE DiMAGGIO—October 6, 1937 through October 10, 1951

Highest Fielding Average (with most chances), Single Series:
4-game Series—1.000; EARLE COMBS, 1927 (16 chances)
5-game Series—1.000; JOE DiMAGGIO, 1942 (20 chances)
6-game Series—1.000; MICKEY RIVERS, 1977 (25 chances)

Most Putouts, Total Series: 150
JOE DiMAGGIO—1936-39, 1941-42, 1947, 1949-51

Most Putouts, Single Series:
4-game Series—16; EARLE COMBS, 1927
5-game Series—20; JOE DiMAGGIO, 1942
6-game Series—24; MICKEY RIVERS, 1977

Most Double Plays, Single Series:
7-game Series—2; ELSTON HOWARD, 1958

Managers—
Most Years Managing In The World Series: 10
CASEY STENGEL—1949-53, 1955-58, 1960

Most World Series Winners Managed: 7
JOE McCARTHY—1932, 1936-39, 1941, 1943
CASEY STENGEL—1949-53, 1956, 1958

Most Consecutive World Series Winners Managed: 6
JOE McCARTHY—1932, 1936-39, 1941

Most Consecutive Years World Series Winners Managed: 5
CASEY STENGEL—1949-53

Coaches—
Most World Series As A Coach: 15
FRANK CROSETTI—1947, 1949-53, 1955-58, 1960-64

Most World Series Eligible As A Player Or Coach: 23
FRANK CROSETTI—1932, 1936-39, 1941-43 (player); 1947, 1949-53, 1955-58, 1960-64 (coach)

SPECIAL ACHIEVEMENTS BY YANKEE PLAYERS IN WORLD SERIES

SPECIAL WORLD SERIES PLAYER ACHIEVEMENTS

Hitting Home Run in First World Series At-bat
GEORGE SELKIRK—September 30, 1936
ELSTON HOWARD—September 28, 1955
ROGER MARIS—October 5, 1960
JIM MASON—October 19, 1976
BOB WATSON—October 20, 1981

Hitting Home Run as a Pinch Hitter
YOGI BERRA—October 2, 1947 (first ever)
JOHN MIZE—October 3, 1952
BOB CERV—October 2, 1955
ELSTON HOWARD—October 5, 1960
JOHN BLANCHARD—October 7, 1961
JIM LEYRITZ—October 27, 1999

Hitting Grand-Slam Home Run
TONY LAZZERI—October 2, 1936
GIL MCDOUGALD—October 9, 1951
MICKEY MANTLE—October 4, 1953
YOGI BERRA—October 5, 1956
BILL SKOWRON—October 10, 1956
BOBBY RICHARDSON—October 8, 1960
JOE PEPITONE—October 14, 1964
TINO MARTINEZ—October 17, 1998

Hitting Home Run Leading off a Game
PHIL RIZZUTO—October 5, 1942
GENE WOODLING—October 4, 1953
DEREK JETER—October 25, 2001

Hitting Two or More Home Runs in One Game
BABE RUTH, 2—October 11, 1923, at the Polo Grounds, New York
BABE RUTH, 3—October 6, 1926, at Sportsman's Park, St. Louis
LOU GEHRIG, 2—October 7, 1928, at Sportsman's Park, St. Louis
BABE RUTH, 3—October 9, 1928, at Sportsman's Park, St. Louis
BABE RUTH, 2—October 1, 1932, at Wrigley Field, Chicago
LOU GEHRIG, 2—October 1, 1932, at Wrigley Field, Chicago
TONY LAZZERI, 2—October 2, 1932, at Wrigley Field, Chicago
CHARLIE KELLER, 2 (rookie)—October 7, 1939, at Crosley Field, Cincinnati
JOE COLLINS, 2—September 28, 1955, at Yankee Stadium
YOGI BERRA, 2—October 10, 1956, at Ebbets Field, Brooklyn
TONY KUBEK, 2 (rookie)—October 5, 1957, at County Stadium, Milwaukee
MICKEY MANTLE, 2—October 2, 1958, at County Stadium, Milwaukee
MICKEY MANTLE, 2—October 6, 1960, at Forbes Field, Pittsburgh
REGGIE JACKSON, 3—October 18, 1977, at Yankee Stadium
SCOTT BROSIUS, 2—October 20, 1998, at Qualcomm Stadium, San Diego
CHAD CURTIS, 2—October 26, 1999, at Yankee Stadium (10 innings)

Making Four Hits in One Game
JOE DUGAN—October 14, 1923: 4 for 5; 3 singles, 1 homer
BILL DICKEY—October 5, 1938: 4 for 4; 4 singles
CHARLIE KELLER—October 5, 1941: 4 for 5; 2 singles, 2 doubles
MICKEY MANTLE—October 8, 1960: 4 for 5; 2 singles, 1 double, 1 homer
THURMAN MUNSON—October 21, 1976: 4 for 4; 4 singles

HITTING .400 OR BETTER IN A WORLD SERIES
(PLAYING ALL GAMES)

Player	G	AB	R	H	2B	3B	HR	TB	BA
BABE RUTH (1928)	4	16	9	10	3	0	3	22	.625
RICKY LEDEE (1998)	4	10	1	6	3	0	0	9	.600
LOU GEHRIG (1928)	4	11	5	6	1	0	4	19	.545
LOU GEHRIG (1932)	4	17	9	9	1	0	3	19	.529
THURMAN MUNSON (1976)	4	17	2	9	0	0	0	9	.529
MARK KOENIG (1927)	4	18	5	9	2	0	0	11	.500
JOE GORDON (1941)	5	14	2	7	1	1	1	13	.500
BILLY MARTIN (1953)	6	24	5	12	1	2	2	23	.500
PAUL O'NEILL (2000)	5	19	2	9	2	2	0	15	.474
SCOTT BROSIUS (1998)	4	17	3	8	0	0	2	14	.471
JAKE POWELL (1936)	4	22	8	10	1	0	1	14	.455
REGGIE JACKSON (1977)	6	20	10	9	1	0	5	25	.450
BILL DICKEY (1932)	4	16	2	7	0	0	0	7	.438
CHARLIE KELLER (1939)	4	16	8	7	1	1	3	19	.438
LOU PINIELLA (1981)	6	16	2	7	1	0	0	8	.438
BRIAN DOYLE (1977)	6	16	4	7	1	0	0	11	.438
GENE WOODLING (1950)	4	14	2	6	0	0	0	6	.429
YOGI BERRA (1953)	6	21	3	9	1	0	1	13	.429
AARON WARD (1923)	6	24	4	10	0	0	1	13	.417
YOGI BERRA (1955)	7	24	5	10	1	0	1	14	.417
BUCKY DENT (1978)	6	24	3	10	1	0	0	11	.417
DEREK JETER (2000)	5	22	6	9	2	1	2	19	.409
BOBBY RICHARDSON (1964)	7	32	3	13	2	0	0	15	.406
BABE RUTH (1927)	4	15	4	6	0	0	2	12	.400
RED ROLFE (1936)	6	25	5	10	0	0	0	10	.400
TONY LAZZERI (1937)	5	15	3	6	0	1	1	11	.400
JOE GORDON (1938)	4	15	3	6	2	0	1	11	.400
BILL DICKEY (1938)	4	15	2	6	0	0	1	9	.400
MICKEY MANTLE (1960)	7	25	8	10	1	0	3	20	.400

Pitching Perfect Game
DON LARSEN—October 8, 1956

Pitching One Hitter
BILL BEVENS—October 3, 1947 (lost no-hitter with two out in ninth inning)

Pitching Two Hitters
WAITE HOYT—October 6, 1921
MONTE PEARSON—October 5, 1939
ALLIE REYNOLDS—October 5, 1949
VIC RASCHI—October 4, 1950
WHITEY FORD—October 4, 1961

STRIKING OUT 10 OR MORE BATTERS IN ONE GAME

Pitcher	Date	Opponent	Strikeouts
RED RUFFING	September 8, 1932	Chicago Cubs	10
ALLIE REYNOLDS	October 4, 1952	Brooklyn Dodgers	10
BOB TURLEY	October 9, 1956	Brooklyn Dodgers	11
BOB TURLEY	October 6, 1958	Milwaukee Brewers	10
ORLANDO HERNANDEZ	October 23, 1999	Atlanta Braves	10
ORLANDO HERNANDEZ	October 24, 2000	New York Mets	12
MIKE MUSSINA	November 1, 2001	Arizona Diamondbacks	10
ROGER CLEMENS	November 3, 2001	Arizona Diamondbacks	10

PITCHING SHUTOUTS
(COMPLETE GAMES)

Pitcher	Date	Opponent
CARL MAYS	October 5, 1921	New York Giants
WAITE HOYT	October 6, 1921	New York Giants
MONTE PEARSON	October 5, 1939	Cincinnati Reds
SPUD CHANDLER	October 11, 1943	St. Louis Cardinals
ALLIE REYNOLDS	October 5, 1949	Brooklyn Dodgers
VIC RASCHI	October 4, 1950	Philadelphia Phillies
ALLIE REYNOLDS	October 4, 1952	Brooklyn Dodgers
DON LARSEN	October 8, 1956	Brooklyn Dodgers
JOHNNY KUCKS	October 10, 1956	Brooklyn Dodgers
WHITEY FORD	October 8, 1960	Pittsburgh Pirates
WHITEY FORD	October 12, 1960	Pittsburgh Pirates
WHITEY FORD	October 4, 1961	Cincinnati Reds
RALPH TERRY	October 16, 1962	San Francisco Giants

YANKEE TEAM WORLD SERIES RECORDS

The Yankees hold most of the total Series records in batting, pitching and fielding by virtue of having played in more World Series than any other team. No attempt is made to list all the total Series records. These records were compiled in 201 World Series games played.

GENERAL

Most World Series Played: 38
1921-23, 1926-28, 1932, 1936-39, 1941-43, 1947, 1949-53, 1955-58, 1960-64, 1976-78, 1981, 1996, 1998, 1999, 2000, 2001

Most World Series Won: 26
1923, 1927-28, 1932, 1936-39, 1941, 1943, 1947, 1949-53, 1956, 1958, 1961-62, 1977-78, 1996, 1998, 1999, 2000

Most Consecutive World Series Won: 8
1927-28, 1932, 1936-39, 1941

Most Consecutive Years Winning The World Series: 5
1949-53

Most Times Winning The World Series In Four Consecutive Games: 8
1927-28, 1932, 1938-39, 1950, 1998, 1999

Most World Series Games Played: 213
(38 World Series): Won—128; Lost—84; Tied—1
Yankees also own the records for most games won and lost.

Most Consecutive Games Won: 14
1996 (Last 4), 1998 (4), 1999 (4), 2000 (2)

Most Shutouts Won: 18
38 World Series

Largest Score Winning By Shutout: 12-0
12, Pittsburgh 0—October 12, 1960

Most Consecutive Games Without Being Shut Out, Total Series: 42
October 6, 1926 through October 1, 1942

Winning World Series After Losing The First Two Games:
1956 Beat Brooklyn (seven games)
1958 Beat Milwaukee (seven games)
1978 Beat Los Angeles (six games)
1996 Beat Atlanta (six games)
(5 other clubs)

Winning World Series After Winning One Game And Losing Three:
1958 Beat Milwaukee (seven games)
(4 other clubs)

Largest World Series Attendance, Single Series:
8-game Series—269,976; YANKEES vs. New York Giants, 1921

BATTING

Most At-Bats: 7,138

Most Runs: 936

Most Runs, Game: 18
(18) vs. Giants (4) October 2, 1936

Most Times Shutout: 15

Most Hits: 1,780

Most Singles: 1,271

Most Singles, Game: 16
vs. Los Angeles; October 15, 1978

Most Doubles: 254

Most Triples: 51

Most Home Runs: 204

Most Grand Slams: 8

Most Pinch-Hit Home Runs: 6

Most Home Runs, Game: 5
vs. St. Louis; October 9, 1928 (1 other club)

Most Total Bases: 2,748

Most Extra-Base Hits: 509
(254 doubles, 51 triples, 204 home runs)

Most Runs Batted In: 884

Most Runs Batted In, Game: 18
vs. New York Giants; October 2, 1936

Most Walks: 745

Most Walks, Game: 11
vs, Milwaukee; October 5, 1957 (2 other clubs)

Most Strikeouts: 1,192

Most Sacrifice Hits: 116

Most Sacrifice Flies: 18
(Since 1954)

Most Hit-by-Pitch: 46

Most Stolen Bases: 72

Most Left on Base: 1,471

Most Runs, Single Series:
4-game Series—37; 1932 vs. Chicago
7-game Series—55; 1960 vs. Pittsburgh

Most Hits, Single Series:
4-game Series—45; 1932 vs. Chicago (1 other club)
6-game Series—68; 1978 vs. Los Angeles
7-game Series—91; 1960 vs. Pittsburgh

Most Triples, Single Series:
  7-game Series—5; 1947 vs. Brooklyn
      (1 other club)

Most Home Runs, Single Series:
  4-game Series— 9; 1928 vs. St. Louis
      (1 other club)
  6-game Series— 9; 1953 vs. Brooklyn
      (1 other club)
  7-game Series—12; 1956 vs. Brooklyn
  8-game Series— 2; 1921 vs. New York Giants
      (2 other clubs)

Most Runs Batted In, Single Series:
  4-game Series—36; 1932 vs. Chicago
  7-game Series—54; 1960 vs. Pittsburgh

Most Walks, Single Series:
  4-game Series—23; 1932 vs. Chicago
  5-game Series—24; 1961 vs. Cincinnati
  8-game Series—27; 1921 vs. New York Giants

Highest Batting Average, Single Series:
  7-game Series—.338; 1960 vs. Pittsburgh

Highest Slugging Average, Single Series:
  7-game Series—.528; 1960 vs. Pittsburgh

Most Total Bases, Single Series:
  7-game Series—142; 1960 vs. Pittsburgh

Most Extra-Base Hits, Single Series:
  7-game Series—27; 1960 vs. Pittsburgh

Most Hits By Pinch Hitters, Single Series: 6
  1947 vs. Brooklyn (seven games)
  1960 vs. Pittsburgh (seven games)
      (2 other clubs)

PITCHING

Most Complete Games, Single Series:
  4-game Series—4; 1928 vs. St. Louis
  7-game Series—5; 1956 vs. Brooklyn
      (1 other club)

Fewest Pitchers Used, Single Series:
  4-game Series—3; 1928 vs. St. Louis
      (1 other club)

Most Innings Pitched: 1,899$^{1}/_{3}$

Most Complete Games: 79

Most Runs Allowed: 752

Most Earned Runs Allowed: 651

Most Shutouts Won: 17

Largest Score, Shutouts Game: 12-0
  vs. Pittsburgh; October 12, 1960

Most 1-0 Games Won: 4

Most Walks Allowed: 606

Most Strikeouts: 1,197

Most Home Runs Allowed: 135

Most Opponent At-Bats: 7,071

FIELDING

Most Consecutive Errorless Games, Single Series: 5
  1937 vs. New York Giants—October 6 through 10
  1955 vs. Brooklyn—September 29 through October 3 (1 other club)

Most Errorless Games, Single Series:
  5-game Series—5; 1937 vs. New York Giants
  6-game Series—5; 1953 vs. Brooklyn
      (3 other clubs)
  7-game Series—5; 1955 vs. Brooklyn
      (7 other clubs)

Most Double Plays, Single Series:
  4-game Series— 7; 1963 vs. Los Angeles
      (1 other club)
  5-game Series— 7; 1922 vs. New York Giants
              1941 vs. Brooklyn
      (1 other club)
  6-game Series—10; 1951 vs. New York Giants

Most Putouts: 5,698

Most Assists: 2,246

Most Errors: 158

Most Total Chances: 8,102
  (Putouts, Assists, and Errors)

Most Passed Balls: 14

Most Double Plays: 187

MISCELLANEOUS

Most One-Run Games: 67

Most One-Run Games Won: 36

Most One-Run Games Lost: 31

Longest Night Game: 12 innings
  (4) vs. Los Angeles (3) at New York; October 11, 1977
  (4) vs. New York Mets (3) at Yankee Stadium; October 21, 2000

Most Extra-inning Games: 18
  (Tied 1)

Most Extra-inning Games Won: 11

Most Extra-inning Games Lost: 6

Longest Extra-inning Night Game: 4 hours, 51 minutes, 12 innings
  (4) vs. New York Mets (3) at Yankee Stadium; October 21, 2000

Earliest Date for Series Final Game:
  4-game Series vs. Chicago Cubs; October 2, 1932

Latest date for series start:
  October 27, 2001—Yankees at Arizona

Latest date for series finish:
  November 4, 2001—Yankees at Arizona

YANKEE WORLD SERIES
ATTENDANCE/PLAYERS SHARE FIGURES

Year	Games	Outcome	Opponent	Attendance	Yankee Share	Year	Games	Outcome	Opponent	Attendance	Yankee Share
1921	8	Losers	New York Giants	269,976	$3,510.00	1953	6	Winners	Brooklyn Dodgers	307,350	8,280.68
1922	4	Losers	New York Giants	185,947	3,225.00	1955	7	Losers	Brooklyn Dodgers	362,310	5,598.00
1923	6	Winners	New York Giants	301,430	6,143.49	1956	7	Winners	Brooklyn Dodgers	345,903	8,714.76
1926	7	Losers	St. Louis Cardinals	328,051	3,417.75	1957	7	Losers	Milwaukee Braves	394,712	5,606.06
1927	4	Winners	Pittsburgh Pirates	201,705	5,592.17	1958	7	Winners	Milwaukee Braves	393,909	8,759.10
1928	4	Winners	St. Louis Cardinals	199,072	5,531.91	1960	7	Losers	Pittsburgh Pirates	349,813	5,214.64
1932	4	Winners	Chicago Cubs	191,998	5,231.77	1961	5	Winners	Cincinnati Reds	223,247	7,389.13
1936	6	Winners	New York Giants	302,924	6,430.55	1962	7	Winners	San Francisco Giants	376,864	9,882.74
1937	5	Winners	New York Giants	238,142	6,471.10	1963	4	Losers	Los Angeles Dodgers	247,279	7,874.32
1938	4	Winners	Chicago Cubs	200,833	5,782.76	1964	7	Losers	St. Louis Cardinals	321,807	5,309.29
1939	4	Winners	Cincinnati Reds	183,849	5,614.26	1976	4	Losers	Cincinnati Reds	223,009	19,935.48
1941	5	Winners	Brooklyn Dodgers	235,773	5,943.31	1977	6	Winners	Los Angeles Dodgers	337,708	27,758.04
1942	5	Losers	St. Louis Cardinals	277,101	3,018.77	1978	6	Winners	Los Angeles Dodgers	337,304	31,236.99
1943	5	Winners	St. Louis Cardinals	277,312	6,139.46	1981	6	Losers	Los Angeles Dodgers	338,081	39,609.00
1947	7	Winners	Brooklyn Dodgers	389,763	5,830.03	1996	6	Winners	Atlanta Braves	324,685	216,870.08
1949	5	Winners	Brooklyn Dodgers	236,716	5,665.54	1998	4	Winners	San Diego Padres	243,498	312,042.41
1950	4	Winners	Philadelphia Phillies	196,009	5,737.95	1999	4	Winners	Atlanta Braves	216,114	307,808.70
1951	6	Winners	New York Giants	341,977	6,446.09	2000	5	Winners	New York Mets	277,853	294,783.41
1952	7	Winners	Brooklyn Dodgers	340,706	5,982.65	2001	7	Losers	Arizona Diamondbacks	366,289	201,014.06

YANKEE TEAM WORLD SERIES STATISTICS

BATTING

Year	G	AB	R	H	2B	3B	HR	RBI	BB	SB	BA
1921	8	241	22	50	7	1	2	20	27	6	.207
1922	5	158	11	32	6	1	2	11	8	2	.203
1923	6	205	30	60	8	4	5	29	20	1	.293
1926	7	223	21	54	10	1	4	19	31	1	.242
1927	4	136	23	38	6	2	2	19	13	2	.279
1928	4	134	27	37	7	0	9	25	13	4	.276
1932	4	144	37	45	6	0	8	36	23	0	.313
1936	6	215	43	65	8	1	7	41	26	1	.302
1937	5	169	28	42	6	4	4	25	21	0	.249
1938	4	135	22	37	6	1	5	21	11	3	.274
1939	4	131	20	27	4	1	7	18	9	0	.206
1941	5	166	17	41	5	1	2	16	23	2	.247
1942	5	178	18	44	6	0	3	14	8	3	.247
1943	5	159	17	35	5	2	2	14	12	2	.220
1947	7	238	38	67	11	5	4	36	38	2	.282
1949	5	164	21	37	10	2	2	20	18	2	.226
1950	4	135	11	30	3	1	2	10	13	1	.222
1951	6	199	29	49	7	2	5	25	26	0	.246
1952	7	232	26	50	5	2	10	24	31	1	.216
1953	6	201	33	56	6	4	9	32	25	2	.279
1955	7	222	26	55	4	2	8	25	22	3	.248
1956	7	229	33	58	6	0	12	33	21	2	.253
1957	7	230	25	57	7	1	7	25	22	1	.248
1958	7	233	29	49	5	1	10	29	21	1	.210
1960	7	269	55	91	13	4	10	54	18	0	.338
1961	5	165	27	42	8	1	7	26	24	1	.255
1962	7	221	20	44	6	1	3	17	21	4	.199
1963	4	129	4	22	3	0	2	4	5	0	.171
1964	7	239	33	60	11	0	10	33	25	2	.251
1976	4	135	8	30	3	1	1	8	12	1	.222
1977	6	205	26	50	10	0	8	25	11	1	.244
1978	6	222	36	68	8	0	3	34	16	5	.306
1981	6	193	22	46	8	1	6	22	33	4	.238
1996	6	199	18	43	6	1	2	16	26	4	.216
1998	4	139	26	43	5	0	6	25	20	1	.309
1999	4	137	21	37	5	0	5	20	1	5	.270
2000	5	179	19	47	8	3	4	18	25	1	.263
2001	7	229	14	42	6	0	6	14	16	1	.183

FIELDING

Year	G	PO	A	E	DP	PB	FA
1921	8	210	106	6	8	0	.981
1922	5	129	62	1	7	1	.995
1923	6	162	77	3	6	0	.988
1926	7	189	82	7	3	1	.975
1927	4	108	44	3	4	0	.981
1928	4	108	28	6	3	0	.958
1932	4	108	41	8	1	0	.949
1936	6	162	57	6	2	0	.973
1937	5	132	47	0	2	0	1.000
1938	4	108	39	6	4	0	.961
1939	4	111	50	2	5	0	.988
1941	5	135	55	2	7	0	.990
1942	5	132	45	5	2	0	.973
1943	5	135	63	5	3	0	.975
1947	7	185	70	4	4	2	.985
1949	5	135	44	3	5	0	.984
1950	4	111	41	2	4	0	.987
1951	6	159	67	4	10	1	.982

Year	G	PO	A	E	DP	PB	FA
1952	7	192	66	10	7	1	.963
1953	6	156	60	1	5	0	.995
1955	7	180	72	2	7	0	.992
1956	7	185	66	6	7	0	.977
1957	7	187	72	3	5	0	.977
1958	7	191	65	3	5	1	.988
1960	7	183	93	8	9	0	.972
1961	5	135	50	5	1	1	.974
1962	7	183	67	5	5	0	.980
1963	4	102	49	1	7	0	.993
1964	7	186	82	9	6	3	.968
1976	4	104	41	2	6	0	.986
1977	6	168	68	3	2	1	.987
1978	6	159	54	2	9	1	.991
1981	6	153	55	4	2	1	.981
1996	6	165	64	5	7	0	.979
1998	4	108	36	2	4	0	.986
1999	4	111	48	1	5	0	.994
2000	5	141	46	2	1	1	.989
2001	7	190	75	8	7	0	.971

PITCHING

Year	G	CG	IP	H	R	ER	BB	SO	W-L	SV	ERA
1921	8	6	70	71	29	24	22	38	3-5	0	3.09
1922	5	2	43	50	18	16	12	15	0-4	0	3.35
1923	6	2	54	47	17	17	12	18	4-2	2	2.83
1926	7	3	63	65	31	22	11	28	3-4	0	3.14
1927	4	3	36	29	10	8	4	7	4-0	1	2.00
1928	4	4	36	27	10	9	11	29	4-0	1	2.25
1932	4	2	36	37	19	13	11	24	4-0	2	3.25
1936	6	2	54	50	23	20	21	33	4-2	2	3.33
1937	5	3	44	40	12	12	11	21	4-1	1	2.45
1938	4	3	36	33	9	7	6	26	4-0	1	1.75
1939	4	2	37	27	8	5	6	22	4-0	0	1.22
1941	5	3	45	29	11	9	14	21	4-1	0	1.80
1942	5	2	44	39	23	22	17	19	1-4	1	4.50
1943	5	3	45	37	9	7	11	26	4-1	1	1.40
1947	7	3	61 2/3	52	29	28	30	32	4-3	1	4.09
1949	5	1	45	34	14	14	15	38	4-1	2	2.80
1950	4	2	37	26	5	3	7	24	4-0	1	0.73
1951	6	3	53	46	18	11	25	22	4-2	1	1.87
1952	7	2	64	50	20	20	24	49	4-3	2	2.81
1953	6	2	52	64	27	26	15	30	4-2	1	4.50
1955	7	2	60	58	31	28	33	38	3-4	1	4.20
1956	7	5	61 2/3	42	25	17	32	47	4-3	0	2.48
1957	7	2	62 1/3	47	23	20	22	40	3-4	0	2.89
1958	7	1	63 2/3	60	25	24	27	56	4-3	2	3.39
1960	7	2	61	60	27	24	12	26	3-4	1	3.54
1961	5	1	45	35	13	8	8	27	4-1	1	1.60
1962	7	4	61	51	21	20	12	39	4-3	0	2.95
1963	4	0	34	25	12	11	11	25	0-4	0	2.91
1964	7	2	62	61	32	26	18	39	3-4	1	3.77
1976	4	0	34 2/3	42	22	21	12	16	0-4	0	5.45
1977	6	3	56	48	28	25	16	36	4-2	0	4.02
1978	6	2	53	52	23	22	20	31	4-2	1	3.74
1981	6	0	51	51	27	24	20	44	2-4	2	4.24
1996	6	0	55	51	26	24	23	38	4-2	4	3.93
1998	4	0	36	32	13	11	12	29	4-0	3	2.75
1999	4	0	37	26	9	9	15	26	4-0	2	2.19
2000	5	0	47	40	16	14	11	48	4-1	2	2.68
2001	7	0	63 1/3	65	37	31	17	70	3-4	1	4.41

YANKEE WORLD SERIES ROSTER
311 YANKEE PLAYERS—38 SERIES (1921 THROUGH 2001)

Adams, Spencer	1926	Collins, Rip	1921
Aldrete, Mike	1996	Combs, Earle	1926-28, 1932
Alexander, Doyle	1976	Cone, David	1996, 1998-2000
Allen, Johnny	1932	Crosetti, Frankie	1932, 1936-39, 1942-43
Andrews, Ivy	1937	Cullenbine, Roy	1942
Arroyo, Luis	1960-61	Curtis, Chad	1999
Baker, Frank	1921-22	Dahlgren, Babe	1939
Bauer, Hank	1949-53, 1955-58	Daley, Bud	1961-62
Beattie, Jim	1978	Davis, Chili	1998-99
Bellinger, Clay	2000-01	Davis, Ron	1981
Bengough, Benny	1927-28	DeMaestri, Joe	1960
Berra, Yogi	1947, 49-53, 55-58, 60-63	Dent, Bucky	1977-78
Bevens, Bill	1947	DeVormer, Al	1921
Blackwell, Ewell	1952	Dickey, Bill	1932, 1936-39, 1941-43
Blair, Paul	1977-78	Dickson, Murry	1958
Blanchard, Johnny	1960-64	DiMaggio, Joe	1936-39, 41-42, 1947, 49-51
Boehringer, Brian	1996	Ditmar, Art	1957-58, 1960
Boggs, Wade	1996	Donald, Atley	1941-42
Bollweg, Don	1953	Downing, Al	1963-64
Bonham, Ernie	1941-43	Doyle, Brian	1978
Bordagaray, Frenchy	1941	Drews, Carl	1947
Borowy, Hank	1942-43	Dugan, Joe	1922-23, 1926-28
Bouton, Jim	1963-64	Duncan, Mariano	1996
Boyer, Clete	1960-64	Duren, Ryne	1958, 1960
Breuer, Marv	1941-42	Durocher, Leo	1928
Bridges, Marshall	1962	Durst, Cedric	1927-28
Bright, Harry	1963	Ellis, Dock	1976
Brosius, Scott	1998-2001	Etten, Nick	1943
Brown, Bobby	1947, 1949-51	Ferrick, Tom	1950
Brown, Rogers	1981	Fewster, Chick	1921
Bush, Homer	1998	Fielder, Cecil	1996
Bush, Joe	1922-23	Figueroa, Ed	1976, 1978
Byrd, Sammy	1932	Foote, Barry	1981
Byrne, Tommy	1949, 1955-57	Ford, Whitey	1950, 1953, 55-58, 60-64
Canseco, Jose	2000	Fox, Andy	1996
Carey, Andy	1955-58	Frazier, George	1981
Carroll, Tommy	1955	Frey, Lonny	1947
Cerone, Rick	1981	Gamble, Oscar	1976, 1981
Cerv, Bob	1955-56, 1960	Gardner, Billy	1961
Chambliss, Chris	1976-78	Garlick, Stephen	1958, 1960-63
Chandler, Spud	1941-43, 1947	Gazella, Mike	1926
Chapman, Ben	1932	Gehrig, Lou	1926-28, 1932, 1936-38
Choate, Randy	2001	Girardi, Joe	1996, 1998-99
Clark, Allie	1947	Gomez, Lefty	1932, 1936-39
Clay, Ken	1977-78	Gonzalez, Pedro	1964
Clemens, Roger	1999-2001	Gordon, Joe	1938-39, 1941-43
Coates, Jim	1960-62	Gorman, Tom	1952-53
Coleman, Jerry	1949-51, 1955-57	Gossage, Goose	1978, 1981
Coleman, Rip	1955	Grabowski, Johnny	1927
Collins, Joe	1950-53, 1955-57	Grba, Eli	1960
Collins, Pat	1926-28	Greene, Todd	2001

Grim, Bob	1955, 1957	Lollar, Sherm	1947
Grimsley, Jason	1999	Long, Dale	1960, 1962
Guidry, Ron	1977-78, 1981	Lopat, Ed	1949-53
Gullett, Don	1977	Lopez, Hector	1960-64
Hadley, Bump	1936-37, 1939	Lumpe, Jerry	1957-58
Haines, Hinkey	1923	Lyle, Sparky	1976-77
Hamilton, Steve	1963-64	Maas, Duke	1958, 1960
Harper, Harry	1921	Maddox, Elliott	1976
Hassett, Buddy	1942	Malone, Pat	1936
Hayes, Charlie	1996	Mantle, Mickey	1951-53, 1955-58, 1960-64
Heath, Mike	1978	Mapes, Cliff	1949-50
Hegan, Mike	1964	Maris, Roger	1960-64
Hendrick, Harvey	1923	Martin, Billy	1951-53, 1955-56
Hendricks, Ellie	1976	Martinez, Tino	1996, 1998-2001
Henrich, Tommy	1938, 1941, 1947, 1949	Mason, Jim	1976
Hernandez, Orlando	1998-2001	May, Carlos	1976
Hildebrand, Oral	1939	May, Rudy	1981
Hill, Glenallen	2000	Mays, Carl	1921-22
Hitchcock, Sterling	2001	McDermott, Mickey	1956
Hoag, Myril	1932, 1937-38	McDonald, Jim	1953
Hofmann, Fred	1923	McDougald, Gil	1951-53, 1955-58, 1960
Hogue, Bobby	1951	McMillan, Norm	1922
Hopp, Johnny	1950-51	McNally, Mike	1921-22
Houk, Ralph	1947, 1952	McQuinn, George	1947
Howard, Elston	1955-58, 1960-64	Mendoza, Ramiro	1998-99
Hoyt, Waite	1921-23, 1926-28	Metheny, Bud	1943
Hunter, Catfish	1976-78	Meusel, Bob	1921-23, 1926-28
Jackson, Grant	1976	Mikkelsen, Pete	1964
Jackson, Reggie	1977-78, 1981	Milbourne, Larry	1981
Jensen, Jackie	1950	Miller, Elmer	1921
Jeter, Derek	1996, 1998-2001	Mize, Johnny	1949-53
John, Tommy	1981	Monroe, Zack	1958
Johnson, Billy	1943, 1947, 1949-50	Moore, Wilcy	1927, 1932
Johnson, Cliff	1977-78	Morgan, Tom	1951, 1955-56
Johnson, Ernie	1923	Mumphrey, Jerry	1981
Johnson, Roy	1936	Munson, Thurman	1976-78
Johnstone, Jay	1978	Murcer, Bobby	1981
Jones, Sam	1922-23, 1926	Murphy, Johnny	1936-39, 1941, 1943
Justice, David	2000-2001	Mussina, Mike	2001
Keller, Charlie	1939, 1941-43	Neagle, Denny	2000
Key, Jimmy	1996	Nelson, Jeff	1996, 1998-2000
Knoblauch, Chuck	1998-2001	Nettles, Graig	1976-78, 1981
Koenig, Mark	1926-28	Newsom, Bobo	1947
Kubek, Tony	1957-58, 1960-63	Niarhos, Gus	1949
Kucks, Johnny	1955-58	Noren, Irv	1952-53, 1955
Kuzava, Bob	1951-53	O'Neill, Paul	1996, 1998-2001
LaRoche, Dave	1981	Ostrowski, Joe	1951
Larsen, Don	1955-58	Page, Joe	1947, 1949
Lazzeri, Tony	1926-28, 1932, 1936-37	Paschal, Ben	1926, 1928
Ledee, Ricky	1998-99	Pearson, Monte	1936-39
Leyritz, Jim	1996, 1999	Peckinpaugh, Roger	1921
Lindblad, Paul	1978	Pennock, Herb	1923, 1926-27, 1932
Lindell, Johnny	1943, 1947, 1949	Pepitone, Joe	1963-64
Linz, Phil	1963-64	Pettitte, Andy	1996, 1998-2001
Lloyd, Graeme	1996, 1998	Phillips, Jack	1947

Piercy, Bill	1921	Spencer, Jim	1978
Piniella, Lou	1976-78, 1981	Spencer, Shane	1998, 2001
Pipgras, George	1927-28, 1932	Stafford, Bill	1960-62
Pipp, Wally	1921-23	Stainback, Tuck	1942-43
Polonia, Luis	2000	Stanley, Fred	1976-78
Posada, Jorge	1998-2001	Stanton, Mike	1998-2001
Powell, Jake	1936-38	Stirnweiss, Snuffy	1943, 1947, 1949
Priddy, Gerry	1942	Stottlemyre, Mel	1964
Quinn, Jack	1921	Strawberry, Darryl	1996, 1999
Raines, Tim	1996	Sturdivant, Tom	1955-57
Randolph, Willie	1976-77, 1981	Sturm, Johnny	1941
Raschi, Vic	1947, 1949-53	Sundra, Steve	1939
Reed, Jack	1961	Terry, Ralph	1960-64
Reniff, Hal	1963-64	Thomas, Myles	1926
Reuschel, Rick	1981	Thomasson, Gary	1978
Reynolds, Allie	1947, 1949-53	Throneberry, Marv	1958
Richardson, Bobby	1957-58, 1960-64	Tidrow, Dick	1976-78
Righetti, Dave	1981	Torrez, Mike	1977
Rivera, Mariano	1996, 1998-2001	Tresh, Tom	1962-64
Rivers, Mickey	1976-78	Turley, Bob	1955-58, 1960
Rizzuto, Phil	1941-42, 1947, 49-53, 1955	Turner, Jim	1942
Robertson, Andre	1981	Velarde, Randy	2001
Robertson, Gene	1928	Velez, Otto	1976
Robinson, Aaron	1947	Vizcaino, Jose	2000
Robinson, Eddie	1955	Ward, Aaron	1921-23
Rodriguez, Aurelio	1981	Watson, Bob	1981
Rogers, Kenny	1996	Weatherly, Roy	1943
Rogers, Tom	1921	Weathers, David	1996
Rolfe, Red	1936-39, 1941-42	Wells, David	1998
Rosar, Buddy	1941-42	Wensloff, Butch	1947
Ruether, Dutch	1926	Wetteland, John	1996
Ruffing, Red	1932, 1936-39, 1941-42	White, Roy	1976-78
Russo, Marius	1941, 1943	Wicker, Kemp	1937
Ruth, Babe	1921-23, 1926-28, 1932	Williams, Bernie	1996, 1998-2001
Sain, Johnny	1951-53	Williams, Stan	1963
Scarborough, Ray	1952	Wilson, Enrique	2001
Schallock, Art	1953	Wilson, George	1956
Schang, Wally	1921-23	Winfield, Dave	1981
Scott, Everett	1922-23	Witasick, Jay	2001
Seeds, Bob	1936	Witt, Whitey	1922-23
Selkirk, George	1936-39, 1941-42	Wohlers, Mark	2001
Severeid, Hank	1926	Woodling, Gene	1949-53
Sewell, Joe	1932	Zachary, Tom	1928
Shantz, Bobby	1957, 1960	Zeber, George	1977
Shawkey, Bob	1921-23, 1926		
Shea, Spec	1947		
Sheldon, Rollie	1964		
Shocker, Urban	1926		
Siebern, Norm	1956, 1958		
Silvera, Charlie	1949		
Simpson, Harry	1957		
Skowron, Bill	1955-58, 1960-62		
Slaughter, Enos	1956-58		
Smith, Elmer	1922		
Sojo, Luis	1996, 1998-2001		
Soriano, Alfonso	2001		

George Herman "Babe" Ruth, center, addresses the crowd at the baseball park and the nation over a radio network at the ceremony marking Babe Ruth Day, before the Yankees - Senators baseball game at Yankee Stadium, New York, April 27, 1947. In background are, left to right: Ford Frick, president of the National League; a radio technician; Mel Allen, radio announcer; Francis Cardinal Spellman, Archbishop of New York; and A.B. Chandler, baseball's high commissioner.

Through their history, the Yankees have had four home ballparks—Hilltop Park, the Polo Grounds, Yankee Stadium, and Shea Stadium. The latter, however, was less a permanent home than a welcome place to play while new life was being breathed into Yankee Stadium. Actually, there was another home park, but it was for only one game. On Sunday, July 17, 1904, the New Yorkers played a game (Sunday ball was illegal in New York City) at Wiedenmeyer Park in Newark, NJ. The Highlanders defeated the Detroits, 3-1. The stadium burned down and another was built in its place—it was called Ruppert Stadium, after Yankee owner Jacob Ruppert.

The home of the Yankees since 1923, except for those renovating seasons of 1974-75, has been the great Yankee Stadium, "The House That Ruth Built." In 1998, the Yankees had to play one "home" game versus Anaheim at Shea Stadium on April 15. Repairs were being done at Yankee Stadium, requiring the one-game shift to Shea. No ballpark—if ballpark is the right word for America's best-known and most richly storied stadium—has an aura approaching Yankee Stadium's. Still, baseball was great sports theater at Hilltop and the Polo Grounds, too...

BEFORE THERE WAS A YANKEE STADIUM

Hilltop Park was its christened name, but the first home of New York's American League baseball team was also known as Highlanders' Park, American League Park, and Hilltopper Park. The ballpark was built on the old Hill Top in Washington Heights, highest elevation on the Island of Manhattan and the inspiration for its name. What was most noteworthy about the new ballpark was its association with an American League new to New York; thus it was often called American League Park. When Highlanders play in Hilltop Park, Highlanders understandably come up in conversation as Hilltoppers, with the consequence that Hilltop Park then tends to be called Hilltopper Park. And again, because the Highlanders played there, the natural tendency was to call Hilltop Park Highlanders' Park.

The team was not only known as both the Highlanders and Hilltoppers, but still a third nickname was bandied about by the press. The press preferred the "Yankees."

The park was located between 165th and 168th Streets and Broadway and Fort Washington Avenue. The exact location is uncertain, but it was close to where the Columbia Presbyterian Medical Center stands today. In any case, Hilltop Park commanded so outstanding a view of the Hudson that the river and its traffic competed vigorously for the attention of fans who to begin with were not disposed to take the Highlanders all that seriously.

The park was the product of fast-moving events. In January of 1903, Frank Farrell and Bill Devery purchased Baltimore's American League franchise. In March, they won American League approval to transfer it to New York, and in little more than a month—by the April 30 home opener—they succeeded in having the ballpark built and ready for play.

Hilltop Park was a typical, wooden, turn-of-the-century ballpark, the kind that evokes "Casey at the Bat" images. It consisted of a covered grandstand that centered itself on home plate and reached to first and third bases, where the right-and left-field bleachers began their run to the foul poles. The park seated some 15,000 fans, but because of a liberal standing-room policy, along with a popular ticket that allowed fans to bring their own lawn chairs and sit between the foul lines and the stands, crowds sometimes topped 20,000. Nearly 28,000 jammed into the park on the final day of the 1904 season to see a pennant-deciding doubleheader between New York and Boston.

Hilltop Park and its team, the Highlanders (or Yankees), attracted a small following of hard-core fans. But there was no mistake about it; the club played in the shadow of the great New York Giants, the prestigious occupants of the Polo Grounds only a few blocks away. Many of the Hilltop Park customers came to enjoy a picnic-like atmosphere, to have a nice outing, and perhaps to satisfy their curiosity about the new team in town. The cost of a prime box seat never exceeded 50 cents in the 10 years the Yankees played at Hilltop. But the real baseball fan, the fan whose dish was an exciting, winning team, spent his afternoons at the Polo Grounds.

The Polo Grounds in April of 1911 was seriously damaged by fire, and the Giants accepted an offer to play that year's games at Hilltop Park. The accommodation put the two New York baseball clubs on cordial terms, and when the Yankees were invited by the Giants to move up in class for the 1913 season by moving into a rebuilt Polo Grounds as paying tenants of the Giants, they accepted. The Yankees were tenants, to be sure—the "other guys" at the Polo Grounds.

The Polo Grounds that the Yankees knew ran along Eighth Avenue between 155th and 158th Streets and seated about 35,000. By selling standing room and packing fans in the bleachers, however, 40,000 fans could be accommodated. A double-decked, concrete structure embraced not only the diamond but extended to both foul poles. Wooden bleachers stood beyond the outfield and they too stretched from foul pole to foul pole.

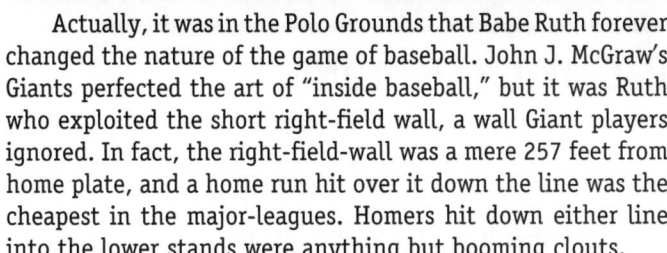

Actually, it was in the Polo Grounds that Babe Ruth forever changed the nature of the game of baseball. John J. McGraw's Giants perfected the art of "inside baseball," but it was Ruth who exploited the short right-field wall, a wall Giant players ignored. In fact, the right-field-wall was a mere 257 feet from home plate, and a home run hit over it down the line was the cheapest in the major-leagues. Homers hit down either line into the lower stands were anything but booming clouts.

As a member of the Boston Red Sox, Babe hit his first big-league homer on May 6, 1915, and he hit it against the Yankees at the Polo Grounds. After knocking out a record 29 homers in 1919, Ruth came to the Yankees and his meeting with destiny. He hit his first homer as a Yankee on May 1, 1920, and it went clear out of the stadium, coming to rest in the middle of an amateur baseball game! It was the first of three blasts by Ruth to take leave of the Polo Grounds; the only other person up to that time to hit a ball out of the Polo Grounds was Shoeless Joe Jackson. During May of 1920, Babe's first complete month in New York, he hit 11 Polo Grounds' fourbaggers and all were major-league homers—two went completely out of the stadium and four landed in the upper deck. Late in the month, the maintenance crew painted white foul lines vertically in right-field so as to better judge whether a blast was fair or foul. The baseball world was abuzz.

In 1921, Ruth walloped 32 home runs at the Polo Grounds, the most Yankee homers hit at home in a season in history. And in three Yankee seasons at the Polo Grounds (1920-22), Babe hit 148 total homers: 69 at home and 79 on the road. Obviously, Babe did not need the friendly confines of the Polo Grounds to hit the long ball. Grand home runs matched the Babe's style. But after the Yanks moved into Yankee Stadium, Babe appeared to miss the Polo Grounds, believing it an easier homering park for him than the Stadium. While practicing at the Polo Grounds during the 1923 World Series, Babe boasted, "I'd have hit 80 homers easily here this season." (He hit 41 playing at the Stadium.)

The Yankees played at the Polo Grounds for 10 seasons (1913-22). Their home attendance in 1920—the year Ruth joined the club—was 1,289,422. At Hilltop Park they never drew more than 501,000 customers who came to see them in 1909 (their average attendance over the 10 Hilltop years was 345,154). But no longer were they the forgotten little brother—their 1920 attendance bettered the Giants' draw by 350,000. In fact, the Yankees of 1920 established a then-major-league attendance record; certainly they beat their own best home attendance figure (619,164 in 1919). Giant Manager McGraw and owner Charley Stoneham were not entertained by this Yankee success. They were jealous of Yankee attendance, fan support, and press attention even before Babe Ruth joined the club. Yankee co-owner Jake Ruppert offered Stoneham a proposal in 1919: Together the Yankees and Giants would split the value of the Polo Grounds, abandon it, and build an all-sports stadium that would seat close to 100,000 and would be used by both teams. But Stoneham rejected the plan and toughened his stand in regard to his own ballpark. The Yankee Colonels, Ruppert and Huston, believed they had terms that gave them permanent use of the Polo Grounds, but Stoneham offered only a one-year lease in 1919 at $100,000.

At the time the Yankee owners were faced with another headache. They were quarreling with American League President Ban Johnson over the acquisition of Carl Mays from Boston. Johnson wanted the Yanks evicted from the Polo Grounds so he could reclaim the franchise on the grounds that Ruppert-Huston had no ballpark. (Johnson planned on finding more obedient owners for the Yankees.) Wisely, however, Ruppert had a vacant square block on hand in case of an emergency where he could erect a ballpark with the mandatory minimum 15,000 seating capacity.

In 1920, legend has it, Stoneham asked the Yankees to move out of the Polo Grounds at the Yanks' earliest convenience. The fiery McGraw told Stoneham, "Chase the Yankees out of the Polo Grounds and make them build their own park in the Bronx, because once they go up there, they will be forgotten." And against his better judgment, Stoneham took McGraw's advice and handed the Yankees their walking papers. The Giants were polite enough to allow the Yanks time to make moving plans.

Accordingly, Ruppert and Huston prepared to build Yankee Stadium. But first there were to be two bitter "Subway Series" between the Yanks and Giants, the World Series of 1921 and 1922, with all games at the Polo Grounds. On only one other occasion in Series history (1944) was the Fall Classic played in a single ballpark (St. Louis' Sportsman's Park). The Giants beat the Yankees in both World Series and smugly watched the vanquished upstarts depart their rented home.

YANKEE STADIUM—HOME OF CHAMPIONS

"Yankee Stadium was a mistake," Col. Jacob Ruppert once said, "not mine, but the Giants'." Envious of Yankee gate success, the Giants, following the 1920 campaign, asked their poor little brother—now a bona fide market rival—to prepare to leave the Polo Grounds.

Yankee co-owners Ruppert and Til Huston, who had dreamed of building their own stadium since buying the Yankees in 1915, thereupon set out to fulfill their dream. They were able to undertake such an ambitious and expensive project mostly because:
1) Babe Ruth was the biggest drawing card in baseball, and
2) Sunday baseball in New York, legalized in 1919, greatly widened the baseball market.

In May of 1921, Ruppert and a less-than-enthusiastic Huston paid $600,000 to the Astor Estate (the land had been owned by William Waldorf Astor) for 11.6 Bronx acres just across the Harlem River from the Polo Grounds, where the American League club would stay on as unwelcome tenants until 1923. Construction of the as-yet-unnamed stadium, designed by the Osborne Engineering Company of Cleveland and built by White Construction Company of New York, was begun in May of the following year. The construction area had been beautiful farmland where New Yorkers came to buy fresh milk and vegetables. Fill operations (Crowell's Creek was completely filled in) and grading involved 45,000 cubic yards of earth. Another 25,000 cubic yards had to be excavated for the Stadium foundation.

Col. Huston, an engineer himself, oversaw the building of America's first triple-decked stadium. However important Huston's experience and expertise may have been to the construction, Ruppert maintained an open dispute with him, and Huston was on the verge of selling out to Ruppert. But finally he agreed to remain until the great new sports palace was completed. Yankee Stadium is an achievement for which Huston deserves much credit; especially for the efficiency with which it was erected.

The Stadium was completed in April of 1923, only 284 working days from the start of construction. Approximately 500 men worked at the site. The cost: a mere $2.3-2.5 million—somewhat over the $2 million budgeted but still not a bad price for what was to become America's most famous stadium. The construction progress was followed closely by New Yorkers. A month before completion, some 10,000 of them turned out one day to see workmen begin the finishing touches. The Stadium was, after all, only 16 minutes by subway from 42nd Street.

The building of the Stadium took place amid a debate over what to call it. Most fans wanted it named after Babe Ruth, the man they felt was responsible for it. But Jake Ruppert insisted it be known simply as "Yankee Stadium." Ruppert's death in 1939 led to speculation that the Stadium would be renamed in his honor. But Yankee GM Ed Barrow reminded public and press alike of the Colonel's wish that Yankee Stadium be forever known as Yankee Stadium.

That other name for Yankee Stadium, "The House that Ruth Built," was coined in the spring of 1923 by the famous sportswriter, Fred Lieb, who used the phrase in the *New York Evening Telegram*. The right-field bleachers into which the Babe deposited many of his home runs were known as "Ruthville." Ruth had enjoyed enormous success in reaching the Polo Grounds' short right-field stands, and Yankee Stadium was designed to be approximately as accommodating of his lefthanded swats.

Since at the time all games were played in the daytime, natural lighting was an especially important subject of concern. Early architectural drawings show three decks of grandstand surrounding the playing field. This would have made for poor natural lighting and the wraparound plan was scrapped: the grandstand was carried only to the foul poles. More daylight was thus admitted to the playing field. In 1924 Ed Barrow repositioned the playing field by moving home plate 10 feet closer to center-field and swinging the foul lines slightly to the catcher's right. This improved the lighting, especially for autumn games, giving the fans a better view of the action.

The playing field at Yankee Stadium has always been asymmetrical, bulging out in center and left center. The dimensions in 1923: 281 feet down the leftfield line, a monstrous 490 feet to dead center, and 295 feet down the right-field line. The Stadium was a paradise for pull-hitters and a nightmare for hitters with power to center-field. A key dimension was the distance to straightaway right-field, an easily reachable target at about 350 feet. Ruth worked the fence from that point to the right-field foul line. Not that he needed the help of short fences; he could knock the ball out at any point of any ballpark.

But the famous right-field porch would shape the course of things to come. The Yankees would continually stack lineups with left-handed power hitters. Left-handed pitchers also were favored; they would let right-handed batters hit away in "Death Valley," the big belly of left-center-field that turns admirable drives into long outs. Since most teams are built around right-handed hitting and pitching, the Yankees over the years enjoyed an obvious advantage at the Stadium. (Boston's Fenway Park is another example of a stadium-team relationship, Fenway dictating a right-handed lineup. But any visiting right-hander can clear Boston's short left-field wall—and the Yanks always had righties to do the job. How many BoSox hitters have beaten "Death Valley"?)

The Yankees have always tailored their clubs to the unique dimensions of Yankee Stadium. Yankee teams have still done well on the road—they have paid no penalty for shaping themselves according to the shape of their ballpark. Meanwhile, left-handed Yankee hitters through the years have peppered the right-field porch with a barrage that began on April 18, 1923, when Babe Ruth hit the first home run in the first game ever played at the Stadium. Ruth showed the way and Ruth was the inspiration for the right-field configuring. In a real sense, Ruth shaped the Stadium, and the Stadium has since shaped Yankee teams.

Another unique aspect of Yankee Stadium is its "sun field"—left-field. Left-field play is especially tricky during the pennant stretch of September and the post-season games of October when a low-hanging sun's glare co-mingles with long shadows and the smoky haze of autumn. Teams try to get to the opposing pitcher early, before the shadows extend beyond home plate and they are forced to pick up a pitch that begins in sunlight and ends in shadow—a terrible presentation for a hitter.

Yankee Stadium's triple-decked grandstand ended at each foul pole in 1923. Stretching from foul pole to foul pole beyond the outfield fences were wooden bleachers (40,000 square feet of bleachers) and standing-room. So many people could be packed into the bleacher area that the Stadium's capacity was about 72,000 seated fans and 80,000 seated and standing. (Originally it was planned to build a stadium with 80,000 seats.)

The exact seating-standing capacity has been clouded since the Stadium's very first game, which according to Ed Barrow, drew 74,217 fans. But sportswriters later discovered that Opening Day attendance may have been as much as 10,000 below Barrow's figure. Attendance figures have since been taken with a grain of salt. Because of such factors as changes in fire regulations, standing room policies, the addition and reduction of seats, and the kinds of seats used, the Stadium's actual capacity has fluctuated over time. This, coupled with suspect reporting practices, has yielded an attendance chronicle that can be baffling.

In 1928 the three tiers of the grandstand were extended to curve around the left-field foul pole. The distance to dead center was reduced by 15 feet—to a mere 475 feet. In 1937 a more pronounced extension took the three tiers around the right-field foul pole. The Stadium configuration that we know today is the result of the two extensions.

The grandstand extensions presented predictable consequences in that they entailed predictable objectives—to extend linearly to the extent possible and to bring the fans close to the action. And so in the 1928 extension, the left-field foul line was lengthened from 281 to 301 feet. The grandstand in 1937 was extended linearly as far as possible and when the corner was turned, the three decks were brought in toward the action. The right-field foul line grew by one foot to 296 feet, while straightaway right shrank somewhat, to 344 feet. The right-center distance was 407 feet and what was to be a long-familiar center-field distance—a reachable 461 feet—was established. The capacity of the Stadium following the grandstand extensions was around 67,000 although, with standees, 75,000 to 80,000 fans could be squeezed in. On May 30, 1938, 81,841 people jammed into the Stadium to set a home attendance record (while others looked on from an elevated train platform and buildings along 161st Street).

The area surrounding Yankee Stadium has on occasion contributed to Stadium lore. The Yankees of Earle Combs' day (1924-35) were a power-oriented team known for late-inning rallies against tiring pitchers. At 5 p.m. daily, a nearby factory whistle blew while the Yanks, or so it seemed, were pulling off another come-from-behind-win. Combs called it "5 O'clock Lightning," a phrase often used by sportswriter Frank Graham, and the factory whistle associated with the late-afternoon surge became famous.

The 1928 and 1937 grandstand enlargements produced a comfortable place to watch baseball, a kind of baseball in which home runs sail without protest into the right-field porch while gargantuan shots are run down in "Death Valley." When the Cardinals' Curt Flood was introduced to the latter during the 1964 World Series and was alerted to the room out there, he quipped in reference to the commodious space: "That's no room. That's a penthouse." Center-field was so roomy it accommodated monuments, the first erected in 1932 in memory of Miller Huggins. The monuments became a unique feature of the Stadium. But what was most unique and identifying was the Stadium's Gothic facade (scalloped ornamental frieze) that hung from the roof inside the Stadium. It was 16 feet from top to bottom and a surefire way to identify Yankee Stadium in photos or films.

Larry MacPhail, who in 1945 became one-third owner and president of the Yankees, guided both the club and the Stadium into a progressive postwar era. In its 22-year life, the Stadium had acquired a rich sense of place as the home of the Yankees and the site of countless historic events, and MacPhail set out to accentuate the aura and excitement of it all, to make Yankee Stadium a landmark of the City of New York, the equal of the Statue of Liberty and the Empire State Building. MacPhail wanted to attract to the Stadium people other than the hard-core baseball fan whose attendance was assured regardless of the absence of atmosphere or level of accommodation. He sought to lure people who were as interested in the glamor of the crowd and the place as they were in the Yanks' won-lost record.

The top of the Stadium acquired lights in May of 1946, and the Yankees entered the era of night baseball. MacPhail imported Irish turf for greener grass and had the Stadium painted in esthetically pleasing blues and greens. Private boxes were established for season-ticket holders, a comfort gain that meant a sacrifice of some 1,000 seats. A private club was built inside the Stadium for the dining and drinking pleasures of Stadium boxholders. For years the Stadium Club had the largest bar in the State of New York. The players got a new clubhouse that was ready for the 1946 season (when the team switched dugouts moving to the first base side). All of the improvements were made under Larry MacPhail's leadership (1945-1947), and the effect MacPhail sought was subsequently realized with Stadium customers coming from all strata of society. Attendance between 1946 and 1950 (over two million each season) was the highest in Yankee history until the 1976-80 period. The 1948 attendance record of 2,373,901 stood as the all-time Yankee home record until 1979.

The Yankees sold Yankee Stadium and its grounds in 1953 to Earl and Arnold Johnson, the latter a wealthy Chicago industrialist-businessman who was a longtime friend of Dan Topping and George Weiss. Arnold Johnson, planning to buy the A's of Philadelphia and move them to Kansas City, needed to establish territorial rights in Kansas City, and the Yanks accommodated him by also selling him their Kansas City Blues franchise and Blues Stadium. Succeeding in his plan, Johnson in his ownership of Yankee Stadium was saddled with a conflict of interest that he resolved by selling the Stadium to Chicago banker John William Cox for $6.5 million, or for what he had paid for the two stadiums. He had sold Blues Stadium to the City of Kansas City for $650,000. (Johnson had still another stadium to dispose of, Connie Mack Stadium in Philadelphia, which he

Interior, original Yankee Stadium (1923 - 1973)

Exterior, original Yankee Stadium (1923 - 1973)

acquired with the A's; he sold it to the Phillies.) The Knights of Columbus bought the Yankee Stadium grounds from Cox for $2.5 million, and ownership of the Stadium itself fell to Rice University in 1962 when Cox donated much of the stock of his corporation, the Stadium's technical owner, to Rice. The 25-year $11.5 million lease the Yankees signed originally with Johnson, and that passed to Cox, was now in the hands of Rice. Thus Yankee Stadium, as vital a piece of New York as the Statue of Liberty or Grant's Tomb, was merely rented by New York's most famous sports organization, and the landlord was a Texas institution.

Yankee Stadium evolved over the years, not only in a fundamental sense, but through many improvements which, while not form-altering, represented significant upgradings. A new scoreboard was installed in 1950, and in 1959 a huge, $300,000 scoreboard, with the first changeable message area on a major-league scoreboard, was built beyond the right center-field bleachers. By the 1960s, however, Yankee Stadium was in desperate need of repair. Time had taken its toll on the historic ballpark. In the winter of 1966-67 the Stadium was given a $1.5 million facelift, the most complete since its construction in 1923. Ninety tons of paint were splashed on the structure (white on the outside, blue on the inside) and the wood bleacher benches became fiberglass benches. The changes cut into the Stadium's capacity, reducing it to about 65,000; moreover, fire laws now limited standing-room crowds so that not many more than 65,000 could be admitted.

These improvements notwithstanding, rumors circulated that the Yankees would build a new stadium in New Jersey. After all, the New York Giants of pro football fame were preparing to move to New Jersey, and authorities in the Garden State were making it inviting for the Yanks to cross the Hudson as well. There was much for the Yankees to go *to* and much to go *from* as well, and the latter included not only a down-at-the-heels ballpark but an urban environment that was in social and physical decline.

The once-proud neighborhoods surrounding the Stadium had deteriorated. Many fans outside the city were afraid to enter the area. And those who felt no fear were made to feel frustration by an impossible parking situation. New York's suburbs had burgeoned, but suburbanites faced a stressful task in attempting to park an automobile. Under these negative circumstances, New York Mayor John Lindsay led the effort to keep the Yankees in New York.

And to his credit, Yankee President Michael Burke resisted attempts to lure the Yankees across the Hudson. Burke understood that Yankee roots were dug deeply in New York City and Yankee Stadium. By contrast, the Mara family in the 1970s moved the New York Football Giants to the New Jersey Meadowlands, where the Giants nestled in a beautiful 75,000-seat stadium. But what is missing is that special feeling that stirred when the Giants played in Yankee Stadium (1956-73), the old girl rocking to the exhortations of that monolithic Giant gathering and reverberating to the chants of *Dee-fense, Dee-fense*...

New York City didn't want to lose the Yankees. A plan was developed in which the City in 1972 became the owner of Yankee Stadium with the Yankees signing a 30-year lease to remain in Yankee Stadium through the year 2002. And the House that Ruth Built became the House that the City Rebuilt.

Renovation began immediately after the 1973 baseball season. Workmen occupied Yankee Stadium for more than two years, as this historical sports palace, where 80 million people had attended a range of events in the previous 50 years, was renewed piece by piece. While the work proceeded, the Yankees played their home games in 1974 and 1975 in Shea Stadium, sharing that city-owned ballpark with the regular tenants, the Mets.

Architect Perry Green produced a beautiful "new" Yankee Stadium. A sellout crowd gathered April 15, 1976, for the grand opening, and, although there were still kinks to iron out—the $3 million-plus scoreboard wasn't working for one thing—the overall reviews were favorable. Some were unhappy that the Gothic facade was no longer hanging from the roof. Instead, the old copper facade was replicated in concrete atop what seemed to be a never-ending scoreboard.

The place was bright, clean, handsome and—best of all—freed by cantilever from the obstructing uprights that supported the "old" Stadium's mezzanine and upper deck. Those columns had been a source of continuing complaint ever since the Stadium opened in 1923. A new lighting system was neatly placed along the roofline, creating a luminous ribbon. Other improvements were made in restaurants, concession stands, rest rooms, luxury boxes, a modernized press box, and three new escalator towers.

The once-too-narrow wooden seats were replaced by wider plastic seats. Aisles were widened, a smaller bleacher area was improved, and areas were set aside for the handicapped. Thus, overall seating capacity was reduced to about 55,000.

Inside the Stadium, eyes are drawn to the wondrous scoreboard—560 feet long and 24 feet high. Various improvements have been made to the scoreboard since 1976, and it has a telescreen showing instant replays, but the one drawback is that fans aren't able to follow the developments of all the other games simultaneously. Instead, an area of the scoreboard flashes, in a revolving pattern, the scores of the other major-league games being played.

Outside Yankee Stadium, two new triple-decked parking lots and several smaller lots allowed parking for about 10,000 cars, and accessibility to the Stadium from the Major Deegan Expressway was made somewhat easier. However, parking and access were still problems.

The playing field was still the turf on which the game was meant to be played—natural grass—and the irregular field dimensions were still present. Just as in Ruth's day, there was a short right-field porch—the distance was 353 feet to straight-away right-field—and although the distances from straight-away left-field to right center were shortened—the fence in center was brought in to 417 feet from 461—there was the familiar bulge that was once Death Valley. It was still a mighty blast of 430 feet to reach the left-center-field fence.

Thus, Yankee Stadium remained a lefthanded home-run hitter's paradise and a curse to righthanded power hitters. But in the 1980s, further tinkering with the dimensions eased the burden on right-handed hitters. In 1985, the left-field fence was shortened from 387 to 379 feet; the left-center-field fence from 430 to 411 feet; and center-field from 417 to 410 feet. In 1988, the left-center-field fence was brought in further—to 399 feet.

The 1985 and 1988 changes were made so Monument Park would be more accessible and roomier for the fans. Monument

Interior, renovated Yankee Stadium (1976 - present)

Renovated Yankee stadium

Park was the 1976 renovation's answer to the problem about what to do with the famous monuments and plaques, which were removed from center-field and stored in Monument Park—beyond the left-center-field fence and between the two bullpens. This arrangement had proved unsatisfactory because Monument Park was off limits to the fans.

The charms of the pre-renovated Stadium included the three monuments in straightaway center-field, located about 10 feet in front of the fence. There was a tradition allowing the fans to exit through the center-field gates, and the fans would walk past the monuments, in memory of Miller Huggins, Lou Gehrig and Babe Ruth, and the plaques on the wall, honoring Jacob Ruppert, Ed Barrow, Joe DiMaggio and Mickey Mantle, and read the inscriptions.

For nine years after the renovation, the fans could only see Monument Park from the stands. This changed in 1985, and it soon became a popular pre-game pilgrimage to visit Monument Park and soak in the history.

Starting in 1976 with the addition of plaques honoring Joe McCarthy and Casey Stengel, Monument Park was soon bursting with new plaques honoring Thurman Munson, Elston Howard, Roger Maris, Phil Rizzuto, Billy Martin, Whitey Ford, Lefty Gomez, Bill Dickey, Yogi Berra and Allie Reynolds. Including the two plaques commemorating the visits of two popes, there are now 18 plaques and the three original monuments housed in Monument Park. The Yankees also opened up a special walk honoring those Yankees who have had their uniform numbers retired.

The 1976 renovation of Yankee Stadium was undertaken amid continuing debate. In the beginning, the work was estimated at $24 million, but at completion it was closer to $100 million—and at a time when the City of New York was in pitiful financial condition. The price escalated the social argument: Did it make sense to renovate a sports palace when even in the very shadow of the Stadium could be found hope-drained neighborhoods? Many felt the money could have been better spent in the community. Schemes to upgrade the neighborhood in the original renovation plans never materialized.

The other side of the argument, recognizing the Yankees as the most attractive business in the South Bronx, made a connection between fans coming to Yankee Stadium and increased business in the community. Simply put, Yankee Stadium brings money to the South Bronx. And the City of New York makes money on the city-owned parking lots, exacts taxes from concession sales, takes a small percentage of admission income and receives a small rental for the use of the Stadium.

In 1976, the Yankees settled into their second era at Yankee Stadium, but over the years concerns were raised occasionally about the long-range commitment of the Yankees to Yankee Stadium. The issue seemed resolved in October 1987 when the Yankees signed a 30-year lease extension with New York City and the State of New York, keeping the Yankees in Yankee Stadium through the year 2032. As part of the agreement, the city and state would make several upgrades in and around Yankee Stadium, including the building of a new parking garage, better access roads, a new railroad station, and new exterior lights and luxury boxes.

The Yankees, however, didn't seem happy with the follow through delivered by the city and state. Yankee owner George Steinbrenner in 1993 complained that his gate receipts weren't acceptable and that fans weren't coming to Yankee Stadium because of inadequate parking and the perception of the Bronx

as unsafe. Most observers agreed there was a need for better parking, and a train station as well. Mayor David Dinkins said it was important to keep the Yankees in New York City, and Gov. Mario Cuomo offered to build a new stadium for no more than $1 billion on Manhattan's lower West Side.

The prospect of the Yankees going to New Jersey seemed real again. Steinbrenner in 1993 declared a "test week" for Yankee fans, and the Boss wasn't pleased with a Friday night crowd of under 26,000.

The Yankees averaged about 24,000 in 1995 as Steinbrenner continued to complain. One thing might have been feeding into another; the more the principal owner growled, the more turned off the fans might have become. Also, light attendance in the majors was a general rule in 1995 because of the bad taste left by the strike. Still, some clubs did well, and in smaller markets, to boot. The Orioles in Baltimore averaged 43,000 and the Indians in Cleveland 40,000.

Doubtless two things about the foregoing impress the Yankees. One is that both Baltimore and Cleveland have new stadiums. (Incidentally, the stadiums are integrated with their cities' skylines; there is no hint of New York's famous skyline from any seat in Yankee Stadium.) And the other is the newer stadiums' luxury boxes, clearly a major ingredient in the mix apart from sheer attendance numbers. The appetite among bigtime sports owners for the luxury box crowd, with its high revenue potential and prestige, is voracious.

Dinkins and Cuomo were swept out of office in November 1994. An aide to the new mayor (Rudolph Giuliani) in January 1995 reportedly said taxpayers could be asked to shell out at least $600 million to keep the Yankees in the Bronx. He said that plans for a bridge across the Harlem River directly into a Yankee Stadium parking lot and the upgrading of Yankee Stadium with 100 luxury boxes and wider concourses would add nearly $250 million to a previous estimate. "Make no small plans," a great landscape architect once cautioned, and a big town like New York undoubtedly has yet to see the last of the big ideas for the Stadium and its environs, or for a stadium. The thinking so far has produced a concept for a "Yankeeland" theme park for the South Bronx. Yankee officials have a plan, too. At the start of the 2000 season, it looks like the Bombers will stay in the Bronx indefinitely until a decision is made regarding their future.

The fate of Yankee Stadium hangs in the balance. Without the Yankees, the Stadium probably couldn't survive. Not that the Stadium hasn't hosted a great variety of events other than Yankee baseball, going back to the original opening in 1923. "The day the Yankee Stadium opened [in 1923] it seemed the Palace of Baseball," recalled pitcher Waite Hoyt in 1979. It had grass like a golf green, only to be ruined that summer when the Yanks leased the park to a rodeo. Besides the rodeo, and later the circus, 29 championship boxing matches were held at the Stadium between 1923 and 1957, and a 30th, the Ali-Norton fight, was held on September 28, 1976. The once-great Notre Dame-Army football rivalry was renewed annually 22 times at the Stadium, and on November 12, 1928, Notre Dame Coach Knute Rockne made his famous "win one for the Gipper" speech, which inspired the Fighting Irish to beat a superior Army team. Fordham, NYU and Grambling also have football traditions of playing at the Stadium. In the 1960s, the popular New York Cosmos soccer team, featuring Pele, played at the Stadium.

The football Giants were a popular attraction at the Stadium from 1956 through 1973, and the Yankee and Giant organizations got along well. Most dedicated Giant fans can name at least 10 legendary Giant games played at the Stadium, but they would be sure to include the ultimate game in professional football, when the Giants and Baltimore Colts, playing "the greatest game ever played," as it has been often called, struggled for the 1958 NFL championship. It was the first sudden-death game in pro football history, and it generated a surge of interest in the sport that in turn spurred its phenomenal growth.

A variety of religious events have taken place at the Stadium, the most famous being Pope Paul's delivery of the Papal Mass in 1965 and Pope John Paul's visit in 1979. Rev. Billy Graham in 1957 addressed his followers at the Stadium. Concerts catering to a wide range of musical tastes have been held at the Stadium, including Billy Joel and U2 in the 1990s.

The Stadium's lore and mystique draw not only from what it has seen but from what it has not seen. No man has ever hit a baseball out of Yankee Stadium in fair territory. Mickey Mantle has come the closest, twice hitting the top of the old facade hanging from the grandstand roof in right-field. With a slight wind behind him, Mantle in 1956 hit a towering drive that struck the copper facade about a foot below the edge of the roof. He hit an even more awesome shot in 1963, the ball hitting the facade very near where his blow seven years earlier had kissed it but with one important difference: this time the ball was still rising! It was scientifically estimated that if the ball had cleared that obstacle and completed its natural trajectory, it would have traveled 620 feet. In 1964, Mickey blasted a homer well over the 461-foot screen in dead center that was measured at 502 feet, the longest major-league homer ever hit in Yankee Stadium. One of Babe Ruth's long shots hit the original scoreboard behind the right-field bleachers.

Josh Gibson, the great star of the Negro Leagues, nearly conquered the Stadium. At 19 years of age in 1931, Gibson hit one that Homestead Grays' shortstop Paul "Pee Wee" Stevens described this way: "It went up over the roof of the third deck in left-field and came down just to the right of where the grandstand ends, and it hit the back of the left-field bullpen. It was the highest, longest ball I've ever seen hit. If he had pulled it just a shade, it would have gone out."

Strangely enough, Babe Ruth, for whom the Stadium was tailored, is not the holder of its single-season home-run record. That distinction is jointly held by Lou Gehrig and Roger Maris. Gehrig hit 30 of his 49 homers in 1934 out of Yankee Stadium, and Maris matched that in his remarkable 1961 season. Although the Stadium is a paradise for left-handed power hitters, it is interesting to note that Maris hit 31 homers on the road in 1961 and that 32 of Ruth's 60 homers in 1927 were hit on the road. Incredibly, the 1961 Yankees in setting the then-major-league home-run record hit 16 more on the road than they did at home in rolling up their total of 240. The six 1961 Yankees who hit more than 20 homers—not just in a favoring Yankee Stadium but in ballparks throughout the league—were made up of three lefties (Maris, Yogi Berra and John Blanchard), two righties (Bill Skowron and Elston Howard) and one switch-hitter (Mantle).

Only once has a Yankee righthanded hitter had more than 40 homers in a season. Joe DiMaggio cracked 46 in 1937. While it is possible to quarrel with the thesis that the Stadium goes out of its way to favor left-handed hitters, its treatment of righthanders is unequivocal: "Death Valley" consumes them.

Yankee Stadium is marinated in great baseball memories. One wonders what the Stadium's considerable pigeon population has observed through the years in swooping the cavernous space or in perch at vantage points where they can be seen becoming visibly excited with the roar of the crowd. And the crowd has roared in appreciation of many great events, that in the pre-renovation Yankee Stadium (1923-73) include the following:

• The day the Stadium opened in 1923, with Bob Shawkey beating the Red Sox, 4-1, on a three-hitter, and Babe Ruth and Shawkey homering. Among the dignitaries at the opener: Commissioner Kenesaw Mountain Landis, New York Governor Al Smith (who threw out the first ball) and New York City Mayor Hylan. John Phillip Sousa led the Seventh Regiment Band in a two-hour pregame musical program.

• Game 1 of the 1923 World Series when an aging outfielder named Casey Stengel hit an inside-the-park home run to lead the Giants to a 5-4 victory over the Yanks.

• Game 7 of the 1926 World Series when with the bases loaded in the seventh inning, Grover Cleveland Alexander struck out Tony Lazzeri and preserved a Series victory for the Cardinals.

• The next-to-last day of the 1927 season when Babe Ruth set a new home-run record with his 60th four-bagger.

• Game 3 of the 1927 World Series when Herb Pennock retired the first 22 Pirates in order.

• The bottom of the ninth inning of the final game of the 1927 World Series when Earle Combs scored on a wild pitch to complete a four-game Yankee sweep.

• The September 8, 1928 doubleheader when the Yanks swept the A's before a packed house to regain first place and stay there.

• Memorial Day of 1932 when the Yankees dedicated a monument in center-field in memory of Miller Huggins.

• The May 4, 1936 major-league debut of Joe DiMaggio when Joe got a triple and two singles and scored three runs in a lopsided Yankee win over the Browns.

• The August game in 1938 when Monte Pearson pitched the first Stadium no-hitter.

• The final game of the 1938 World Series when Red Ruffing, supported by Frank Crosetti's two-run triple and Tommy Henrich's homer, beat the Cubs, 8-3, to bring the New Yorkers their third consecutive World Championship.

• "Lou Gehrig Day" on July 4, 1939, when a dying Gehrig told a tearful crowd he was the "luckiest man on the face of the earth" and was embraced by a Babe Ruth who was bigger than the rift that years earlier developed in the Gehrig-Ruth friendship.

• The thrill the Stadium crowd got from Joe DiMaggio's homer in the 1939 All-Star Game.

• Game 2 of the 1939 World Series when Monte Pearson flirted with immortality by carrying a no-hitter into the eighth inning against the Reds.

• The July 2, 1941 game with the Red Sox in which DiMaggio homered to extend his consecutive-game hitting streak to 45 games, breaking the old record of Willie Keeler.

• July 6, 1941, when DiMaggio hit safely in both games of a doubleheader against the A's, extending his streak to 48 games (where the record stood as the Yanks embarked on a long road trip).

• The ninth inning of the 1942 World Series' Game 5 when Whitey Kurowski's two-run home run beat the Yanks, 4-2, to give the Cardinals the World Championship and snap a Yankee success record of eight straight Series victories.

• Indian great Bob Feller's no-hitter against the Yankees in April of 1946.

• The first Stadium night game played on May 28, 1946, when the Yankees lost to the Washington Senators, 2-1.

• "Babe Ruth Day," April 27, 1947—proclaimed throughout the majors, when Ruth told a Stadium crowd "the only real game in the world...is baseball."

• Game 6 of the 1947 World Series when Al Gionfriddo made an amazing catch in deep left center to rob Joe DiMaggio of an extra-base hit, thus killing a Yankee rally and enabling the Dodgers to win, 8-6.

• Game 7 of the 1947 Series in which Tommy Henrich's two-run single and Joe Page's superb relief pitching spearheaded a 5-2 win and clinched the World Championship for the Yankees.

• The 25th anniversary of the Stadium ceremonies, honoring the great 1923 team and held on June 13,1948, the final Stadium appearance of the great Ruth.

• The days following the Babe's August 16, 1948 death and the thousands of mourners paying their respects in the Stadium's lobby where his body lay in state.

• The next-to-last day of the 1949 season when Johnny Lindell's eighth-inning homer beat the Red Sox, 5-4, enabling the Yanks to tie Boston for first place.

• The last day of the 1949 season when the Yanks beat the Red Sox, 5-3, and captured the pennant, behind the pitching of Vic Raschi, the hitting of Phil Rizzuto and Jerry Coleman, and the leadership of Joe DiMaggio who played though sick with pneumonia.

• Game 1 of the 1949 World Series when Tommy Henrich homered in the bottom of the ninth inning to give Allie Reynolds a 1-0 win over the Dodgers.

• Game 3 of the 1950 World Series when Yankee Jerry Coleman singled home the winning run in the ninth inning.

• Game 4 of the 1950 Series when Whitey Ford, helped by a Yogi Berra homer, won his Series debut against the Phillies, 5-2.

• Phil Rizzuto's perfect suicide squeeze bunt in the ninth inning of a September 17,1951 game with the Indians—it won the game and installed the Yanks in first place.

• The September 28,1951 game in which Allie Reynolds pitched his second no-hitter of the season, getting Red Sox slugger Ted Williams out twice for the final out after catcher Yogi Berra uncharacteristically dropped a foul pop, then made good on a second such pop.

• Game 2 of the 1951 Series when Mickey Mantle, only 19, stumbled in right-field, falling as if shot, severely damaging a knee.

• The last appearance of DiMaggio as a player in the final game of the 1951 Series and the tremendous ovation he received when he trotted off the field after being forced at third base following a double in his final major-league at-bat. Also, Bob Kuzava's clutch ninth-inning relief pitching and Hank Bauer's game-saving catch to end the game and notch another World Championship.

• Billy Martin's game-saving catch of a windblown infield pop-up, preserving the Yanks' victory over the Dodgers in Game 7 of the 1952 World Series.

• The final game of the 1953 World Series and the ninth-inning single by Martin to clinch the Yanks' fifth straight World Championship, a record.

• Johnny Podres' shutout of the Yanks in Game 7 of the 1955 World Series, leading the Dodgers to their only World Championship in Brooklyn.

• Mickey Mantle's May 30, 1956 blast that struck the Stadium facade in right-field.

• Don Larsen's perfect game, hurled against the Dodgers in Game 5 of the 1956 World Series.

• The September 20, 1958 game when the Orioles' Hoyt Wilhelm pitched the last no-hitter thrown at the Yanks.

• Game 3 of the 1960 World Series in which Bobby Richardson hit a grand-slam homer and knocked in six runs in all, while Whitey Ford shut out the Pirates, 10-0.

• Roger Maris' 61st home run of the 1961 season, coming on October 1 and breaking Babe Ruth's home-run record.

• Whitey Ford's shutout of the Reds in Game 1 of the 1961 World Series, extending his consecutive-inning scoreless streak to 27.

• Mickey Mantle's tremendous home run on May 22, 1963, the ball striking the right-field facade while still on the rise.

• That August 4, 1963 day when Mickey Mantle, who had missed 61 games because of a broken foot, was announced as a pinch-hitter and given a tremendous standing ovation before homering to tie the Orioles in a game that the Yanks eventually won in extra innings.

• The August 1964 homer by Mantle that was measured at 502 feet. It was the longest ever hit at the Stadium, and it helped Mel Stottlemyre win his major-league debut and turn the Yanks' season around.

• Game 3 of the 1964 World Series when Mantle led off the bottom of the ninth inning with a prodigious homer that beat the Cardinals, 2-1, and gave Mantle 16 lifetime Series homers, breaking Babe Ruth's Series home-run record.

• Game 5 of the 1964 Series when with two outs in the bottom of the ninth, Tom Tresh's two-run homer tied the game that the Yanks eventually lost.

• The game on May 13, 1967, when Mickey Mantle walloped his 500th home run off Baltimore's Stu Miller.

• The "longest day" on August 29, 1967, when the Yankees needed 20 innings to down the Red Sox, 4-3, in the second game of a doubleheader. Total innings: 29.

• "Mickey Mantle Day" on June 8, 1969, and the outstanding ovation Mickey received—Mantle and Joe DiMaggio exchanged plaques that were later placed on the center-field wall.

• The heavy nostalgia and momento-taking at the final game of the 1973 season—the last ever played at the "old" Stadium.

Since Yankee Stadium reopened in 1976, a new wave of memorable moments have unfolded. Who will ever forget:

• The 1976 home opener, the first baseball game in the renovated Stadium, with the Yankees rolling to an emphatic 11-4 win over the Twins.

• Chris Chambliss' ninth-inning home run in the deciding game of the 1976 American League Championship Series

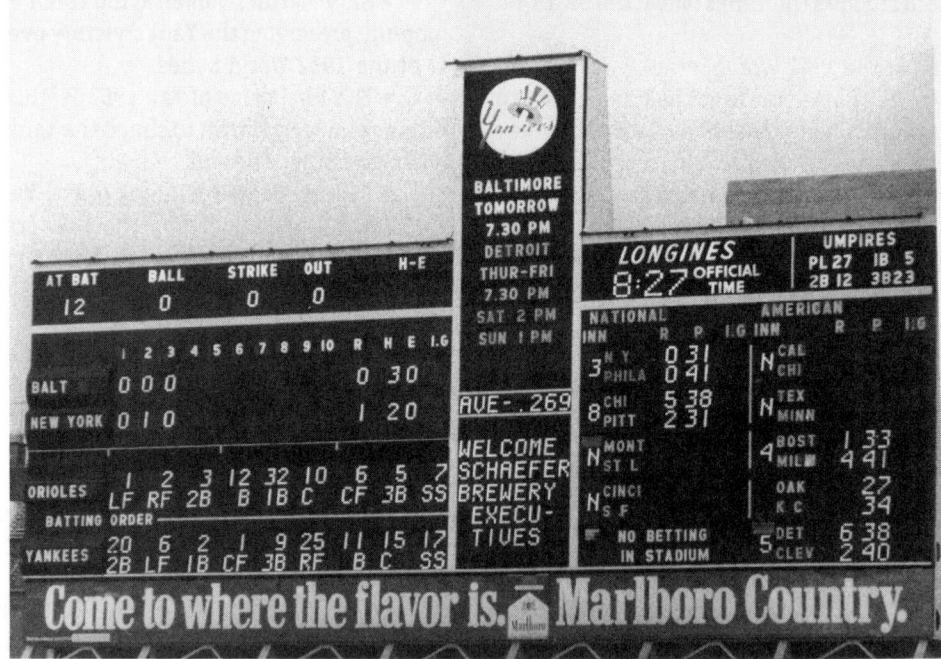

In 1959, this huge scoreboard made its appearance beyond the right centerfield bleachers at Yankee Stadium—it had the first ever changeable message area in the major leagues.

against the Royals, giving the Yankees the club's first pennant in 12 years.

• The two 1976 World Series losses to the Reds and Thurman Munson's outstanding hitting.

• The 1977 All-Star Game that the National League won, 7-5.

• Roy White's two-out, two-run home run in the bottom of the ninth inning that tied the Red Sox in a summer game that the Yanks eventually won and needed badly to stay in the 1977 pennant race with the Red Sox and Orioles.

• Game 1 of the 1977 World Series, which the Yanks won in extra innings when Paul Blair singled home the winning run.

• Reggie Jackson's remarkable power display in Game 6 of the 1977 Series when he hit three consecutive homers to lead the Yanks to the World Championship over the Dodgers.

• The home opener of 1978 when Mickey Mantle and Roger Maris raised the World Championship flag and Reggie Jackson was bombarded during the game with "Reggie Bars" after hitting a home run.

• June 17, 1978, when Ron Guidry struck out 18 Angels in a tremendous effort.

• Old Timers' Day, 1978, when Billy Martin was introduced to an adoring, cheering crowd a week after his resignation, and it was announced that he would later return as manager.

• Thurman Munson's eighth-inning two-run homer that beat the Royals in the third game of the 1978 Championship Series.

• The final game of the 1978 Championship Series when Graig Nettles and Roy White homered and Ron Guidry and Rich Gossage checked the Royals as the Yanks won, 2-1, to capture a third straight AL pennant.

• Game 3 of the 1978 World Series when Nettles made many unbelievable defensive plays to help Ron Guidry stop the Dodgers and turn the Series around.

• Game 4 of the 1978 Series when Reggie Jackson was hit on his hip by a relay throw, setting off a rhubarb and keeping a key Yankee rally going.

• Game 5 of the 1978 Series when the Yanks drilled the Dodgers, 12-2, and many Dodger players complained about the Stadium fans.

• The emotional events at the Stadium following the tragic August 1979 death of Yankee great, Thurman Munson.

• "Catfish Hunter Day" in September 1979 when the Stadium crowd gave a fond farewell to the great, classy pitcher on his retirement.

• The 1980 Old Timers' Day when Billy Martin, on hand with his Oakland club, donned his Yankee uniform to the delight of the crowd, and Mrs. Thurman Munson was saluted by the Stadium faithful.

• October 4, 1980, when Reggie Jackson creamed a three-run homer, his 41st of the year, to lead the Yankees to a division clinching 5-2 victory over Detroit.

• Game 3 of the 1980 Championship Series, won for the Royals by George Brett's three-run homer into the upper deck in right-field, enabling Kansas City to win its first AL pennant.

• Opening Day 1981, when a record crowd of 55,123 watched the Yankees thrash Texas, 10-3, in a game highlighted by Bobby Murcer's pinch-hit grand-slam homer.

• Game 5 of the 1981 Division Series when the Yankees downed Milwaukee, 7-3, as homers by Reggie Jackson, Oscar Gamble and Rick Cerone led the way.

• The Yanks' 13-3 slaughter of Oakland in Game 2 of the 1981 Championship Series, giving the Yankees a safe two games-to-none lead in New York's drive for the AL pennant.

• Game 1 of the 1981 World Series when Nettles made a sensational catch to halt a Dodger rally and save a Yankee victory.

• Reggie Jackson's first game back at the Stadium as an Angel in April 1982, and his home run that was met with a spontaneous celebration by the fans.

• Dave Righetti's July 4 no-hitter against Boston in 1983.

• The Pine Tar Game against the Royals on July 24, 1983, when George Brett's go-ahead ninth-inning homer was disquali-

RENEWED—On its reopening in 1976, a Yankee Stadium thoroughly renovated but still in its original configuration.

fied by the umpires after Manager Billy Martin successfully argued that Brett's bat had pine tar applied beyond the legal limit.

• The August 18, 1983 conclusion of the Pine Tar Game, won by the Royals, 5-4.

• Don Mattingly and Dave Winfield battling for the batting championship in the final game of the 1984 season, with Mattingly going 4-for-5 and beating Winfield, .343 to .340.

• Phil Rizzuto Day and the retiring of the Scooter's number 10 uniform on August 4, 1985.

• The September game against Boston in which Mattingly hit his sixth grand-slam homer of the 1987 season, setting a major-league single-season grand-slam record.

• The July 1993 game in which Mike Stanley hit his third grand-slam in 21 days.

• Reggie Jackson Day and the retiring of Jackson's number 44 uniform in 1993.

• Jim Abbott's September 4, 1993, no-hitter against Cleveland that nudged the Yankees within one game of first-place Toronto.

• Sweeping Boston in a pivotal three-game series in May 1994 and taking command of the division race.

• The dramatic 15-inning Yankees-Mariners 1995 playoff game, won by the Yankees, 7-5, on Jim Leyritz's homer at 1:22 a.m.

• Dwight "Doc" Gooden tossed a no-hitter versus the Seattle Mariners on May 14, 1996. The Yankees won, 2-0.

• The Yankees clinched their 23rd World Series Championship, defeating Atlanta 3-2 in the sixth game on October 26.

• Don Mattingly, Yankee Captain, officially announced his retirement at a media conference at Yankee Stadium on January 22, 1997.

• On May 17, 1998 Lefty David Wells, tossed the first regular-season perfect game for the Yankees. Minnesota is defeated, 4-0.

• On September 25, 1998, the Yankees established an American-League record with their 112th win of the season, a 6-1 win versus Tampa Bay. They would go on to establish a new record of 114 wins by seasons end.

• On July 18, 1999, Yankee pitcher David Cone pitched the second regular-season perfect game for the Yankees in as many seasons. Montreal is defeated, 6-0.

• On July 22, 1999 versus Tampa Bay, the Yankees played their 15,000th regular season game. Their record through that game stood at 8,451-6,463 with 86 ties.

• On October 27, 1999, the Yanks won their 25th World Series, defeating Atlanta 4-1 to complete their eighth four-game sweep in the World Series. It was be the last game at Yankee Stadium in the 20th century.

• On October 22, 2000, the Yankees defeated the Mets, 6-5, in Game two of the World Series. This marked their 14th consecutive World Series game victory and stands as a MLB Fall Classic record.

• On October 31, 2001, Tino Martinez smacked a two-out ninth inning two-run home run off Arizona's closer, Byung-Hyan Kim, to tie Game four of the World Series at 3-3. In the 10th inning, Derek Jeter also victimized Kim with a walk-off home run for a 4-3 Yankee win over the Diamondbacks.

• On November 1, 2001, another two-out ninth inning two-run home run was served up by Byung-Hyun Kim. This one was slugged by Scott Brosius to tie Game five of the World Series at 2-2. In the 12th inning, a single by Alfonso Soriano plated Chuck Knoblauch with the winning run in a heart-pounding 3-2 victory over Arizona. This was the first time in World Series history that a team won two games in the same series when entering the ninth inning losing by two runs.

YANKEE STADIUM FACTS AND FIGURES

THE BUILDING OF THE STADIUM—1922-1923

Location: 161st Street and River Avenue, Bronx, New York City

Stadium Land Purchased: May 1921. From: Astor Estate

Price of Land: $600,000

Stadium Designed By: Osborne Engineering Company of Cleveland, Ohio.

Stadium Built By: White Construction Company of New York.

Stadium Construction Begun: May 1922.

Completed: April 1923.

Number of Men on Job: 500 men.

Time Required to Construct Stadium: 284 working days.

Fill Soil Required: 45,000 cubic yards to fill site that contained Crowell's Creek.

Soil Excavated for Foundations: 25,000 cubic yards.

Stadium Materials: 2,500 tons of structural steel; 20,000 cubic yards of concrete; four miles of piping, 500 tons of iron; 1,000 tons of reinforcing steel.

Seating: Grandstand seating fabricated on site from 135,000 steel castings, 400,000 pieces of maple and one million brass screws; bleacher seating made from fir brought by ship from Pacific Coast through the Panama Canal; two million board feet of lumber used in construction.

Unique Stadium: First triple-decked in country.

Distinguishing Feature: Copper facade, 16 feet from top to bottom, suspended from roof.

Area of Stadium and Surrounding Grounds: 11.6 acres.

Area of Stadium Playing Field: 3.5 acres.

Sodding: 116,000 square feet of Long Island sod in infield and outfield.

Cost of Stadium: $2.3-2.5 million

MAJOR IMPROVEMENTS

1928—Three tiers of left-field grandstand extended around the left-field foul pole.

1937—Three tiers of right-field grandstand extended around the right-field foul pole well beyond straightaway right-field.

1946—Lights installed on roof.

1950—New scoreboard built.

1959—New $300,000 scoreboard built in right center-field with first changeable message area at a major-league park.

1966-67—During winter $1.5 million improvement project carried out, including 90-ton paint job and bleacher repairs.

THE REBUILDING OF THE STADIUM—1973-1976

Location, Site Dimensions and Basic Configuration: Unchanged.

Architect: Perry Green

Seating: Larger plastic seats and fewer of them.

Unique Feature: Main scoreboard runs 560 feet and stands 24 feet high.

Continuity Feature: Gothic facade (in copper) that hung from the original Stadium. Roof is replicated (in concrete) atop the main scoreboard.

Key Virtue of New Stadium Over Old: The renovated Stadium is entirely cantilevered and thus is free of the view-obstructing support posts that marred old Stadium sightlines.

Notable Additions: Three escalator towers and a tree-graced Lou Gehrig Plaza.

Lighting System: Some 800 multi-vapor and incandescent lamps.

Cost of Renovation: $100 million (including parking facilities).

MONUMENT PARK

Honoree	Monument/Plaque	Dedication Date
Miller Huggins	Monument	May 30, 1932
Jacob Ruppert	Plaque	April 23, 1940
Lou Gehrig	Monument	July 4, 1941
Babe Ruth	Monument	April 19, 1949
Edward Barrow	Plaque	April 15, 1954
Joe DiMaggio	Plaque	June 8, 1969
Mickey Mantle	Plaque	June 8, 1969
Joe McCarthy	Plaque	April 21, 1976
Casey Stengel	Plaque	July 30, 1976
Thurman Munson	Plaque	September 20, 1980
Elston Howard	Plaque	July 21, 1984
Roger Maris	Plaque	July 21, 1984
Phil Rizzuto	Plaque	August 4, 1985
Billy Martin	Plaque	August 10, 1986
Whitey Ford	Plaque	August 2, 1987
Lefty Gomez	Plaque	August 2, 1987
Bill Dickey	Plaque	August 21, 1988
Yogi Berra	Plaque	August 21, 1988
Allie Reynolds	Plaque	August 26, 1989
Mickey Mantle	Monument	August 25, 1996
Joe DiMaggio	Monument	April 25, 1999

There are also plaques commemorating Pope Paul's 1965 visit and Pope John Paul's 1979 visit.

CHANGING FIELD DIMENSIONS

1923	Feet
Left-field Foul Line	281
Dead Center field	490
Right-field Foul Line	295

1928 Changes:

Left-field Foul Line	301
Straightaway Left field	385
Dead Center field	475

1937 Changes:

Dead Center field	461
Straightaway Right field	344
Right-field Foul Line	296

Pre-Renovation Distances:

Left-field Foul Line	301
Straightaway Left field	402
Left Center field	457
Dead Center field	461
Right Center field	407
Straightaway Right field	344
Right-field Foul Line	296

Post-Renovation Distances (1976-84):

Left-field Foul Line	312
Straightaway Left field	387
Left Center field	430

Dead Center field 417
Right Center field 385
Straightaway Right field 353
Right-field Foul Line 310

1985 Changes:
Straightaway Left field 379
Left Center-field 408
Dead Center field 410

1988 Changes:
Left-field Foul Line 318
Left Center field 399
Dead Center field 408
Right-field Foul Line 314

STADIUM HOME RUN RECORDS

Most Home Runs Hit in a Season (including opponents): 171
    1961 (112 hit by Yankees; 59 hit by visitors)

Most Home Runs Hit by a Player in One Season: 30
    Lou Gehrig—1934
    Roger Maris—1961

Longest Home Run Measured in Stadium: 502 Feet
    Mickey Mantle—August 12, 1964 (Hit off Chicago's Ray
    Herbert)

Closest a Fair Ball Has Come to Being Hit Out of Stadium:
    May 30, 1956—Mickey Mantle hit a ball that struck the right-
    field facade about a foot below the roof (hit off Washington's
    Pedro Ramos)

    May 22, 1963—Mickey Mantle hit a ball that struck the right-
    field facade while still rising (hit off Kansas City A's Bill
    Fischer)

Babe Ruth's 60th Home Run Hit:
    September 30, 1927 (hit off Washington's Tom Zachary).

Roger Maris' 61st Home Run Hit:
    October 1, 1961 (hit off Boston's Tracy Stallard)

PLAYER "FIRSTS" AT THE STADIUM

First Player to Bat:
    The Red Sox' Chick Fewster—April 18, 1923

First Yankee to Bat:
    Whitey Witt—April 18, 1923

First Home Run Hit By:
    Babe Ruth—April 18, 1923

First Winning Pitcher:
    Bob Shawkey—April 18, 1923

First World Series Home Run Hit By:
    Casey Stengel (Giants)—October 10, 1923
    (inside-the-park home run)

First Yankee World Series Home Run Hit By:
    Joe Dugan—October 14, 1923

First Yankee World Series Winning Pitcher:
    Joe Bush—October 14, 1923

First Home Run Hit at Renovated Stadium By:
    Dan Ford (Twins)—April 15, 1976

First Yankee Winning Pitcher at Renovated Stadium:
    Dick Tidrow—April 15, 1976

First Yankee Home Run at Renovated Stadium:
    Thurman Munson—April 17, 1976

YANKEE HOME ATTENDANCE FIGURES
(1903-2002)

Year	Home Park	Attendance	AL Standing
1903	Hilltop Park	211,808	4th
1904	Hilltop Park	438,919	2nd
1905	Hilltop Park	309,100	6th
1906	Hilltop Park	434,700	2nd
1907	Hilltop Park	350,020	5th
1908	Hilltop Park	305,500	8th
1909	Hilltop Park	501,000	5th
1910	Hilltop Park	355,857	2nd
1911	Hilltop Park	302,444	6th
1912	Hilltop Park	242,194	8th
1913	Polo Grounds	357,551	7th
1914	Polo Grounds	359,477	6th
1915	Polo Grounds	256,035	5th
1916	Polo Grounds	469,211	4th
1917	Polo Grounds	330,294	6th
1918	Polo Grounds	282,047	4th
1919	Polo Grounds	619,164	3rd
1920	Polp Grounds	1,289,422	3rd
1921	Polo Grounds	1,230,696	1st
1922	Polo Grounds	1,026,134	1st
1923	Yankee Stadium	1,007,066	1st
1924	Yankee Stadium	1,053,533	2nd
1925	Yankee Stadium	697,267	7th
1926	Yankee Stadium	1,027,095	1st
1927	Yankee Stadium	1,164,015	1st
1928	Yankee Stadium	1,072,132	1st
1929	Yankee Stadium	960,148	2nd
1930	Yankee Stadium	1,169,230	3rd
1931	Yankee Stadium	912,437	2nd
1932	Yankee Stadium	962,320	1st
1933	Yankee Stadium	728,014	2nd
1934	Yankee Stadium	854,682	2nd
1935	Yankee Stadium	657,508	2nd
1936	Yankee Stadium	976,913	1st
1937	Yankee Stadium	998,148	1st
1938	Yankee Stadium	970,916	1st
1939	Yankee Stadium	859,785	1st
1940	Yankee Stadium	988,975	3rd
1941	Yankee Stadium	964,731	1st
1942	Yankee Stadium	988,251	1st
1943	Yankee Stadium	645,006	1st
1944	Yankee Stadium	822,864	3rd
1945	Yankee Stadium	881,846	4th
1946	Yankee Stadium	2,265,512	3rd
1947	Yankee Stadium	2,178,937	1st
1948	Yankee Stadium	2,373,901	3rd
1949	Yankee Stadium	2,281,676	1st
1950	Yankee Stadium	2,081,380	1st
1951	Yankee Stadium	1,950,107	1st

*Includes one home game at Wiedenmeyer Park in Newark, New Jersey
on July 17, due to Sunday Ball being illegal in New York City.

1952	Yankee Stadium	1,629,655	1st
1953	Yankee Stadium	1,537,811	1st
1954	Yankee Stadium	1,475,171	2nd
1955	Yankee Stadium	1,490,138	1st
1956	Yankee Stadium	1,491,784	1st
1957	Yankee Stadium	1,497,134	1st
1958	Yankee Stadium	1,428,438	1st
1959	Yankee Stadium	1,552,030	3rd
1960	Yankee Stadium	1,627,349	1st
1961	Yankee Stadium	1,747,736	1st
1962	Yankee Stadium	1,493,574	1st
1963	Yankee Stadium	1,308,920	1st
1964	Yankee Stadium	1,305,638	1st
1965	Yankee Stadium	1,213,552	6th
1966	Yankee Stadium	1,124,648	10th
1967	Yankee Stadium	1,141,714	9th
1968	Yankee Stadium	1,125,124	5th
1969	Yankee Stadium	1,067,996	5th (East)
1970	Yankee Stadium	1,136,879	2nd (East)
1971	Yankee Stadium	1,070,771	4th (East)
1972	Yankee Stadium	966,328	4th (East)
1973	Yankee Stadium	1,262,077	4th (East)
1974	Shea Stadium	1,273,075	2nd (East)
1975	Shea Stadium	1,288,048	3rd (East)
1976	Yankee Stadium	2,012,434	1st (East)
1977	Yankee Stadium	2,103,092	1st (East)
1978	Yankee Stadium	2,335,871	1st (East)
1979	Yankee Stadium	2,537,765	4th (East)
1980	Yankee Stadium	2,627,417	1st (East)
1981	Yankee Stadium	1,614,533	1st (East)
1982	Yankee Stadium	2,041,219	5th (East)
1983	Yankee Stadium	2,257,976	3rd (East)
1984	Yankee Stadium	1,821,815	3rd (East)
1985	Yankee Stadium	2,214,587	2nd (East)
1986	Yankee Stadium	2,268,116	2nd (East)
1987	Yankee Stadium	2,427,672	4th (East)
1988	Yankee Stadium	2,633,701	5th (East)
1989	Yankee Stadium	2,170,485	5th (East)
1990	Yankee Stadium	2,006,436	7th (East)
1991	Yankee Stadium	1,863,731	5th (East)
1992	Yankee Stadium	1,748,737	4th (East)
1993	Yankee Stadium	2,416,942	2nd (East)
1994	Yankee Stadium	1,675,557	1st (East)
1995	Yankee Stadium	1,705,257	2nd (East)
1996	Yankee Stadium	2,250,839	1st (East)
1997	Yankee Stadium	2,580,325	2nd (East)
1998**	Yankee Stadium	2,951,467	1st (East)
1999*	Yankee Stadium	3,292,736	1st (East)
2000	Yankee Stadium	3,227,657	1st (East)
2001	Yankee Stadium	3,264,777	1st (East)
2002	Yankee Stadium	3,465,807	1st (East)

*Includes one home game at Wiedenmeyer Park in Newark, New Jersey on July 17 due to Sunday Ball being illegal in New York City.

** Includes one home game at Shea Stadium on April 15 due to Yankee Stadium repairs—Attendance 40,743.

ALL-STAR GAMES AT YANKEE STADIUM

July 11, 1939

NL	0	0	1	0	0	0	0	0	0	-	1	7	1
AL	0	0	0	2	1	0	0	0	X	-	3	6	1

W—Bridges (Tigers); L—Lee (Cubs).
HR—DiMaggio (YANKEES).
A.—62,892

July 13, 1960 (Second game)

NL	0	2	1	0	0	0	1	0	2	-	6	10	0
AL	0	0	0	0	0	0	0	0	0	-	0	8	0

W—Law (Pirates); L—Ford (YANKEES).
HRs—Mathews (Braves), Mays (Giants), Musial (Cardinals).
Boyer (Cardinals).
A.—38,362

July 19, 1977

NL	4	0	1	0	0	0	0	2	0	-	7	9	1
AL	0	0	0	0	0	2	1	0	2	-	5	8	0

W—Sutton (Dodgers); L—Palmer (Orioles).
HRs—Morgan (Reds). Luzinski (Phillies), Garvey (Dodgers),
Scott (Brewers).
A.—56,683.

YANKEE STADIUM ATTENDANCE RECORDS

Highest Home Attendance, Season: 3,465,807—2002

Highest Home Attendance, Four-Day Series: 214,510
    YANKEES vs. Toronto—September 12, 13, 14, 15, 1985

Highest Home Attendance, Three-Day Series: 186,151
    YANKEES vs. Cleveland—June 11, 12, 13, 1948

Smallest Yankee Stadium Paid Crowd, Game: 413
    YANKEES vs. Chicago—September 25, 1966

Single Date Records:

Single Day Game	69,755	September 26, 1948 vs. Boston*
Single Night Game	74,747	May 26, 1947 vs. Boston
Doubleheader	81,841	May 30, 1938 vs. Boston**
Twi-Night Doubleheader	55,605	September 10, 1983 vs. Baltimore
Opening Day	56,717	April 10, 1998 vs. Oakland
Old-Timers' Day	67,916	August 9, 1958 vs. Boston
Division Series Game	57,485	October 6, 1999 vs. Texas
Championship Series Game	57,181	October 13, 1999 vs. Boston
World Series Game	74,065	October 5, 1947 vs. Brooklyn
All-Star Game	62,892	July 11, 1939
Largest Pro Football Crowd	71,163	November 9, 1958 New York Giants vs. Baltimore Colts
Largest Fight Crowd	79,222	June 12, 1930 Max Schmelling vs. Jack Sharkey for World Heavyweight Championship

Highest Yankee Road Attendance, Season:
    2,939,976 2002

*Unofficial crowd of 73,205 reported at April 19, 1931 day game.
**Unofficial crowd of 85,264 reported at September 9, 1928 doubleheader.

TOTAL YANKEE POSTSEASON HOME ATTENDANCE FIGURES

World Series Games at the Polo Grounds (13)
Total Attendance 455,923
Average Attendance Per Game 35,071

All-Star Games at Yankee Stadium (3):
Total Attendance 157,937
Average Attendance Per Game 52,646

AL Division Series Games at Yankee Stadium (20):
Total Attendance 1,123,431
Average Attendance Per Game 56,172

AL Championship Series Games at Yankee Stadium (23):
Total Attendance 1,288,214
Average Attendance Per Game 56,009

World Series Games at Yankee Stadium (97):
Total Attendance 5,998,987
Average Attendance Per Game 61,845

TOTAL POST-SEASON ATTENDANCE
AT YANKEE STADIUM (140) 8,410,632
Average Attendance Per Game 60,076

"FIRST" GAMES PLAYED BY YANKEES—HOME AND AWAY

First Yankee Game Ever Played: April 22, 1903
At Washington (Washington Senators—3; YANKEES—1)

First Yankee Home Game Ever Played: April 30, 1903
At Hilltop Park (YANKEES—6; Washington Senators—2)

First Yankee Sunday Home Game: June 17, 1917
At the Polo Grounds (St. Louis Browns—2; YANKEES—1)

First Yankee World Series Game: October 5, 1921
At the Polo Grounds (YANKEES—3; New York Giants—0)

First Yankee Game Played at Yankee Stadium: April 18, 1923
(YANKEES—4; Boston Red Sox—1)

First World Series Game Played at Yankee Stadium: October 10, 1923
(New York Giants—5; YANKEES—4)

First Yankee Game Played at Night: June 26, 1939
At Philadelphia (Philadelphia A's—3; YANKEES—2)

First Night Game Ever Played at Yankee Stadium: May 28, 1946
(Washington Senators—2; YANKEES—1)

First Yankee Day Game Completed with Lights: August 29, 1950
At Yankee Stadium (YANKEES—6; Cleveland Indians—5)

First Yankee Opening Game Night Game Played at Yankee Stadium:
April 18, 1972 (YANKEES—2; Milwaukee Brewers—0)

First Yankee Game Played at Shea Stadium: April 6, 1974
(YANKEES—6; Cleveland Indians—1)

First Yankee Game Played at Renovated Yankee Stadium:
April 15, 1976 (YANKEES—11; Minnesota Twins—4)

First Yankee Championship Series Game: October 9, 1976
At Kansas City (YANKEES—4; Kansas City Royals—1)

First Championship Series Game Played at Yankee Stadium:
October 12, 1976 (YANKEES—5; Kansas City Royals—3)

First Yankee World Series Game Played at Night: October 17, 1976
At Cincinnati (Cincinnati Reds—4; YANKEES—3)

First World Series Night Game Played at Yankee Stadium:
October 19, 1976 (Cincinnati Reds—6; YANKEES—2)

WORLD SERIES ATTENDANCE FOR GAMES AT YANKEE STADIUM

Date—(Game Number)	Att.	Opponent	Winner	Score
October 10, 1923 (1)	55,307	N.Y. Giants	Giants	5-4
October 12, 1923 (3)	62,430	N.Y. Giants	Giants	1-0
October 14, 1923 (5)	62,817	N.Y. Giants	YANKEES	8-1
October 2, 1926 (1)	61,658	St. L. Cardinals	YANKEES	2-1
October 3, 1926 (2)	63,600	St. L. Cardinals	Cardinals	6-2
October 9, 1926 (6)	48,615	St. L. Cardinals	Cardinals	10-2
October 10, 1926 (7)	38,093	St. L. Cardinals	Cardinals	3-2
October 7, 1927 (3)	60,695	Pitts. Pirates	YANKEES	8-1
October 8, 1927 (4)	57,909	Pitts. Pirates	YANKEES	4-3
October 4, 1928 (1)	61,425	St. L. Cardinals	YANKEES	4-1
October 5, 1928 (2)	60,714	St. L. Cardinals	YANKEES	9-3
September 28, 1932 (1)	41,459	Chicago Cubs	YANKEES	12-6
September 29, 1932 (2)	50,709	Chicago Cubs	YANKEES	5-2
October 3, 1936 (3)	64,842	N.Y. Giants	YANKEES	2-1
October 4, 1936 (4)	66,669	N.Y. Giants	YANKEES	5-2
October 5, 1936 (5)	50,024	N.Y. Giants	Giants	5-4
October 6, 1937 (1)	60,573	N.Y. Giants	YANKEES	8-1
October 7, 1937 (2)	57,675	N.Y. Giants	YANKEES	8-1
October 8, 1938 (3)	55,236	Chicago Cubs	YANKEES	5-2
October 9, 1938 (4)	59,847	Chicago Cubs	YANKEES	8-3
October 4, 1939 (1)	58,541	Cincinnati Reds	YANKEES	2-1
October 5, 1939 (2)	59,791	Cincinnati Reds	YANKEES	4-0
October 1, 1941 (1)	68,540	Bkn. Dodgers	YANKEES	3-2
October 2, 1941 (2)	66,248	Bkn. Dodgers	Dodgers	3-2
October 3, 1942 (1)	69,123	St. L. Cardinals	Cardinals	4-3
October 4, 1942 (4)	69,902	St. L. Cardinals	Cardinals	9-6
October 5, 1942 (5)	69,052	St. L. Cardinals	Cardinals	4-2
October 5, 1943 (1)	68,676	St. L. Cardinals	YANKEES	4-2
October 6, 1943 (2)	68,578	St. L. Cardinals	Cardinals	4-3
October 7, 1943 (3)	69,990	St. L. Cardinals	YANKEES	6-2
September 30, 1947 (1)	73,365	Bkn. Dodgers	YANKEES	5-3
October 1, 1947 (2)	69,865	Bkn. Dodgers	YANKEES	10-3
October 5, 1947 (6)	74,065	Bkn. Dodgers	Dodgers	8-6
October 6, 1947 (7)	71,548	Bkn. Dodgers	YANKEES	5-2
October 5, 1949 (1)	66,224	Bkn. Dodgers	YANKEES	1-0
October 6, 1949 (2)	70,053	Bkn. Dodgers	Dodgers	1-0
October 6, 1950 (3)	64,505	Phil. Phillies	YANKEES	3-2
October 7, 1950 (4)	68,098	Phil. Phillies	YANKEES	5-2
October 4, 1951 (1)	65,673	N.Y. Giants	Giants	5-1
October 5, 1951 (2)	66,018	N.Y. Giants	YANKEES	3-1
October 10, 1951 (6)	61,711	N.Y. Giants	YANKEES	4-3
October 3, 1952 (3)	66,698	Bkn. Dodgers	Dodgers	5-3
October 4, 1952 (4)	71,787	Bkn. Dodgers	YANKEES	2-0
October 5, 1952 (5)	70,536	Bkn. Dodgers	Dodgers	6-5
September 30, 1953 (1)	69,374	Bkn. Dodgers	YANKEES	9-5
October 1, 1953 (2)	66,786	Bkn. Dodgers	YANKEES	4-2
October 5, 1953 (6)	62,370	Bkn. Dodgers	YANKEES	4-3
September 28, 1955 (1)	63,869	Bkn. Dodgers	YANKEES	6-5
September 29, 1955 (2)	64,707	Bkn. Dodgers	YANKEES	4-2
October 3, 1955 (6)	64,022	Bkn. Dodgers	YANKEES	5-1
October 4, 1955 (7)	62,465	Bkn. Dodgers	Dodgers	2-0
October 6, 1956 (3)	73,977	Bkn. Dodgers	YANKEES	5-3
October 7, 1956 (4)	69,705	Bkn. Dodgers	YANKEES	6-2
October 8, 1956 (5)	64,519	Bkn. Dodgers	YANKEES	2-0
October 2, 1957 (1)	69,476	Mil. Braves	YANKEES	3-1
October 3, 1957 (2)	65,202	Mil. Braves	Braves	4-2
October 9, 1957 (6)	61,408	Mil. Braves	YANKEES	3-2
October 10, 1957 (7)	61,207	Mil. Braves	Braves	5-0
October 4, 1958 (3)	71,599	Mil. Braves	YANKEES	4-0

October 5, 1958 (4)	71,563	Mil. Braves	Braves	3-0
October 6, 1958 (5)	65,279	Mil. Braves	YANKEES	7-0
October 8, 1960 (3)	70,001	Pitts. Pirates	YANKEES	10-0
October 9, 1960 (4)	67,812	Pitts. Pirates	Pirates	3-2
October 10, 1960 (5)	62,753	Pitts. Pirates	Pirates	5-2
October 4, 1961 (1)	62,397	Cincinnati Reds	YANKEES	2-0
October 5, 1961 (2)	63,083	Cincinnati Reds	Reds	6-2
October 7, 1962 (3)	71,434	S.F. Giants	YANKEES	3-2
October 8, 1962 (4)	66,607	S.F. Giants	Giants	7-3
October 10, 1962 (5)	63,165	S.F. Giants	YANKEES	5-3
October 2, 1963 (1)	69,000	L.A. Dodgers	Dodgers	5-2
October 3, 1963 (2)	66,455	L.A. Dodgers	Dodgers	4-1
October 10, 1964 (3)	67,101	St. L. Cardinals	YANKEES	2-1
October 11, 1964 (4)	66,312	St. L. Cardinals	Cardinals	4-3
October 12, 1964 (5)	65,633	St. L. Cardinals	Cardinals	5-2
October 19, 1976 (3)	56,667	Cincinnati Reds	Reds	6-2
October 21, 1976 (4)	56,700	Cincinnati Reds	Reds	7-2
October 11, 1977 (1)	56,668	L.A. Dodgers	YANKEES	4-3
October 12, 1977 (2)	56,691	L.A. Dodgers	Dodgers	6-1
October 18, 1977 (6)	56,407	L.A. Dodgers	YANKEES	8-4
October 13, 1978 (3)	56,447	L.A. Dodgers	YANKEES	5-1
October 14, 1978 (4)	56,445	L.A. Dodgers	YANKEES	4-3
October 15, 1978 (5)	56,448	L.A. Dodgers	YANKEES	12-2
October 20, 1981 (1)	56,470	L.A. Dodgers	YANKEES	5-3
October 21, 1981 (2)	56,505	L.A. Dodgers	YANKEES	3-0
October 28, 1981 (6)	56,513	L.A. Dodgers	Dodgers	9-2
October 20, 1996 (1)	56,365	Atlanta Braves	Braves	12-1
October 21, 1996 (2)	56,340	Atlanta Braves	Braves	4-0
October 26, 1996 (6)	56,375	Atlanta Braves	YANKEES	3-2
October 17, 1998 (1)	56,712	San Diego Padres	YANKEES	9-6
October 18, 1998 (2)	56,692	San Diego Padres	YANKEES	9-3
October 26, 1999 (3)	56,794	Atlanta Braves	YANKEES	6-5
October 27, 1999 (4)	56,752	Atlanta Braves	YANKEES	4-1
October 21, 2000 (1)	55,913	New York Mets	YANKEES	4-3
October 22, 2000 (2)	56,059	New York Mets	YANKEES	6-5
October 30, 2001 (3)	55,820	Arizona Diamondbacks	YANKEES	2-1
October 31, 2001 (4)	55,863	Arizona Diamondbacks	YANKEES	4-3
November 1, 2001 (5)	56,018	Arizona Diamondbacks	YANKEES	3-2

OVERALL YANKEE WORLD SERIES RECORD BY GAMES AT YANKEE STADIUM:

Total Games: 97
Yankee Record: 63-34 (.649)
Game 1: 17-4
Game 2: 11-9
Game 3: 13-4
Game 4: 9-6
Game 5: 6-5
Game 6: 6-3
Game 7: 1-3

## CHAPTER 11

HONORS, AWARDS, AND LEAGUE LEADERS

Babe Ruth, right, immortal New York Yankee baseball player, comforts Lou Gehrig, who was almost too moved to speak to the vast throng that honored him at Yankee Stadium July 4, 1939, when the Yankees met the Washington Senators in a doubleheader. Gehrig, famed iron man of the Yankees, was honored by players and fans. The World Championship flag that the Yankees won in 1927 with a team hailed as one of baseball's greatest was unfurled at the stadium. (AP/Wide World Photos)

The honors and awards that through the years have been bestowed on Yankee players, managers, and executives are many. No other team in baseball approaches the number of Yankees—33—in the Baseball Hall of Fame. This chapter displays the Hall plaque inscriptions and includes other major Yankee awards, league leaders in offense, pitching, and defense, and All-Star Game participations.

HALL OF FAME MEMBERS AND OTHER ACHIEVERS

YANKEE PLAYERS AND MANAGERS ENSHRINED IN THE BASEBALL HALL OF FAME AT COOPERSTOWN (1936-2002)

1936— Babe Ruth (charter member)
1939— Willie Keeler
       Lou Gehrig
1946— Frank Chance
       Jack Chesbro
       Clark Griffith
1948— Herb Pennock
1954— Bill Dickey
1955— Joe DiMaggio
       Frank Baker
1957— Joe McCarthy
1964— Miller Huggins
1966— Casey Stengel
1967— Red Ruffing
1969— Waite Hoyt
1970— Earle Combs
1972— Yogi Berra
       Lefty Gomez
1974— Mickey Mantle
       Whitey Ford
1975— Bucky Harris
1976— Bob Lemon
1977— Joe Sewell
1981— Johnny Mize
1985— Enos Slaughter
1987— Catfish Hunter
1991— Tony Lazzeri
1993— Reggie Jackson
1994— Phil Rizzuto
2001— Dave Winfield

Also enshrined in the Hall for "meritorious service" are these Yankee executives:
1953— Ed Barrow
1971— George Weiss
1978— Larry MacPhail

Such Hall of Famers as Burleigh Grimes, Clark Griffith, Paul Waner, Dazzy Vance, Joe Sewell, Bill McKechnie, Branch Rickey, Leo Durocher, Frank "Home Run" Baker, Gaylord Perry, Phil Niekro, and Stan Coveleski played briefly in a Yankee uniform, but their principal contributions were overwhelmingly made elsewhere. One Yankee player, George Halas, is enshrined in the *Football* Hall of Fame in Canton, Ohio.

Two Yankee broadcasters, Mel Allen—the Voice of the Yankees— and Red Barber, in 1978 became the first broadcasters inducted into the Hall. Russ Hodges, who also did some broadcasting for the Yankees, was inducted in 1980.

Ten of the eleven living members of Baseball's Hall of Fame are shown June 12, 1939, as they met at Cooperstown, NY to celebrate the 100th anniversary of the invention of the game at that town. Back row, left to right, Honus Wagner, Grover Cleveland Alexander, Tris Speaker, Napoleon Lajoie, George Sisler, and Walter Johnson; and front row, left to right, Eddie Collins, Babe Ruth, Connie Mack, and Cy Young. (AP Photo).

AL MVP AWARDS

Begun in 1922, the Most Valuable Player Award (called the **League Award**, 1922-29) initially prohibited a player, such as Babe Ruth, from winning the honor more than once. The award all but vanished around 1930, but was brought back to life in 1931 when the responsibility of selecting the annual awardee was handed to the Baseball Writers Association of America (BBWAA). This group has run the program ever since.

The Baseball Writers Association of America's MVP Award (1931-2002)

1923—Babe Ruth	1954—Yogi Berra
1927—Lou Gehrig	1955—Yogi Berra
1936—Lou Gehrig	1956—Mickey Mantle
1939—Joe DiMaggio	1957—Mickey Mantle
1941—Joe DiMaggio	1960—Roger Maris
1942—Joe Gordon	1961—Roger Maris
1943—Spud Chandler	1962—Mickey Mantle
1947—Joe DiMaggio	1963—Elston Howard
1950—Phil Rizzuto	1976—Thurman Munson
1951—Yogi Berra	1985—Don Mattingly

AL CHAMPIONSHIP SERIES MVP AWARD (1980-2002)

1981— Graig Nettles
1996— Bernie Williams
1998— David Wells
1999— Orlando Hernandez
2000— David Justice
2001— Andy Pettitte

WORLD SERIES MVP AWARD

Babe Ruth Award selected by BBWAA (1949-2002)

1949— Joe Page
1950— Jerry Coleman
1951— Phil Rizzuto
1952— Johnny Mize
1953— Billy Martin
1956— Don Larsen
1958— Elston Howard
1961— Whitey Ford
1962— Ralph Terry
1977— Reggie Jackson
1978— Bucky Dent
1996— John Wetteland
1998— Scott Brosius
1999— Mariano Rivera
2000— Derek Jeter

Sport Magazine's MVP Award (1955-2002)

1956— Don Larsen
1958— Bob Turley
1960— Bobby Richardson
1961— Whitey Ford
1962— Ralph Terry
1977— Reggie Jackson
1978— Bucky Dent (given jointly with Major League baseball)

AL ROOKIE OF THE YEAR AWARD (1947-2002) SELECTED BY BBWAA

1951— Gil McDougald
1954— Bob Grim
1957— Tony Kubek
1962— Tom Tresh
1968— Stan Bahnsen
1970— Thurman Munson
1981— Dave Righetti
1996— Derek Jeter

JAMES P. DAWSON AWARD (1956-1998)

Given to an outstanding Yankee spring training rookie.

1956— Norm Siebern (OF)
1957— Tony Kubek (SS)
1958— John Blanchard (C)
1959— Gordon Windhorn (OF)
1960— Johnny James (P)
1961— Roland Sheldon (P)

1962— Tom Tresh (SS)
1963— Pedro Gonzalez (2B)
1964— Pete Mikkelsen (P)
1965— Arturo Lopez (OF)
1966— Roy White (OF)
1967— Bill Robinson (OF)
1968— Mike Ferraro (3B)
1969— Jerry Kenney (OF)
        Bill Burbach (P)
1970— John Ellis (1B, C)
1971— (none selected)
1972— Rusty Torres (OF)
1973— Otto Velez (OF)
1974— Tom Buskey (P)
1975— Tippy Martinez (P)
1976— Willie Randolph (2B)
1977— George Zeber (2B)
1978—Jim Beattie (P)
1979—Paul Mirabella (P)
1980— Mike Griffin (P)
1981— Gene Nelson (P)
1982— Andre Robertson (SS)
1983— Don Mattingly (1B, OF)
1984—Jose Rijo (P)
1985— Scott Bradley (C)
1986— Bob Tewksbury (P)
1987— Keith Hughes (OF)
1988— Al Leiter (P)
1989— (none selected)
1990— Alan Mills (P)
1991— Hensley Meulens (OF)
1992— Gerald Williams (OF)
1993— Mike Humphreys (OF)
1994— Sterling Hitchcock (P)
1995— (none selected)
1996— Mark Hutton (P)
1997—Jorge Posada (C)
1998—Homer Bush (2B)

YANKEE TRIPLE CROWN WINNERS (1903-2002)

1934— Lou Gehrig (.363, 49 HRs, 165 RBIs)
1956— Mickey Mantle (.353, 52 HRs, 130 RBIs)

BEST-OF-THE-YEAR AWARDS

These awards are made by the publication *The Sporting News*.

Major League Player of the Year (1936-2002)

1939— Joe DiMaggio
1943— Spud Chandler
1950— Phil Rizzuto
1956— Mickey Mantle
1958— Bob Turley
1961— Roger Maris
1978— Ron Guidry
1985— Don Mattingly

American League Player of the Year (1948-1991)

1950— Phil Rizzuto
1956— Mickey Mantle
1960— Roger Maris
1961— Roger Maris
1962— Mickey Mantle
1976— Thurman Munson
1984— Don Mattingly
1985— Don Mattingly
1986— Don Mattingly

American League Pitcher of the Year (1948-2002)

1955— Whitey Ford
1958— Bob Turley
1961— Whitey Ford
1963— Whitey Ford
1978— Ron Guidry
1994— Jimmy Key
2001— Roger Clemens

American League Fireman/Reliever of the Year (1960-2002)

1961— Luis Arroyo
1972— Sparky Lyle
1978— Rich Gossage
1986— Dave Righetti
1987— Dave Righetti
1996— John Wetteland
1997— Mariano Rivera
1999— Mariano Rivera
2001— Mariano Rivera

Major League Rookie of the Year (1946-1948, 1950)

1950— Whitey Ford

American League Rookie of the Year (1949, 1951-2002)

1954— Bob Grim
1957— Tony Kubek
1962— Tom Tresh
1996— Derek Jeter

American League Rookie Pitcher of the Year (1958-2002)

1958— Ryne Duren
1968— Stan Bahnsen
1981— Dave Righetti

Major League Executive of the Year (1936-2002)

1937— Ed Barrow
1941— Ed Barrow
1950— George Weiss
1951— George Weiss
1952— George Weiss
1960— George Weiss
1961— Dan Topping
1974— Gabe Paul

Major League Manager of the Year (1936-2002)

1936— Joe McCarthy
1938— Joe McCarthy
1943— Joe McCarthy
1947— Bucky Harris
1949— Casey Stengel
1953— Casey Stengel
1958— Casey Stengel
1961— Ralph Houk
1974— Bill Virdon

American League Manager of the Year (1986-2002)

1994— Buck Showalter
1996— Joe Torre (Tied with Johnny Oates of Texas)
1998— Joe Torre

GOLD GLOVE AWARD (1957-2002)

Given to best defensive player at each position in each league. *The Sporting News* makes the selections and the Rawlings Sporting Goods Company gives the award.

1957— Bobby Shantz (P)
       (Only year award given to best in majors.)
1958— Bobby Shantz (P)
       Norm Siebern (OF)
1959— Bobby Shantz (P)
1960— Bobby Shantz (P)
       Roger Maris (RF)
1961— Bobby Richardson (2B)
1962— Bobby Richardson (2B)
       Mickey Mantle (CF)
1963— Elston Howard (C)
       Bobby Richardson (2B)
1964— Elston Howard (C)
       Bobby Richardson (2B)
1965— Joe Pepitone (1B)
       Bobby Richardson (2B)
       Tom Tresh (LF)
1966— Joe Pepitone (1B)
1969— Joe Pepitone (1B)
1972— Bobby Murcer (CF)
1973— Thurman Munson (C)
1974— Thurman Munson (C)
1975— Thurman Munson (C)
1977— Graig Nettles (3B)
1978— Chris Chambliss (1B)
       Graig Nettles (3B)
1982— Ron Guidry (P)
       Dave Winfield (OF)
1983— Ron Guidry (P)
       Dave Winfield (OF)
1985— Ron Guidry (P)
       Don Mattingly (1B)
       Dave Winfield (OF)
1986— Ron Guidry (P)
       Don Mattingly (1B)
1987— Don Mattingly (1B)
       Dave Winfield (OF)
1988— Don Mattingly (1B)
1989— Don Mattingly (1B)
1991— Don Mattingly (1B)
1992— Don Mattingly (1B)
1993— Don Mattingly (1B)
1994— Don Mattingly (1B)
       Wade Boggs (3B)
1995— Wade Boggs (3B)
1997— Bernie Williams (OF)
1998— Bernie Williams (OF)
1999— Bernie Williams (OF)
       Scott Brosius (3B)
2000— Bernie Williams (OF)
2001— Mike Mussina (P)

SILVER SLUGGER AWARD (1980-2002)

Given by *The Sporting News* and Hillerich and Bradsby to the best offensive player at each position in the AL.

1980— Willie Randolph (2B)
         Reggie Jackson (DH)
1981— Dave Winfield (OF)
1982— Dave Winfield (OF)
1983— Dave Winfield (OF)
         Don Baylor (DH)
1984— Dave Winfield (OF)
1985— Don Mattingly (1B)
         Rickey Henderson (OF)
         Dave Winfield (OF)
         Don Baylor (DH)
1986— Don Mattingly (1B)
1987— Don Mattingly (1B)
1993— Mike Stanley (C)
         Wade Boggs (3B)
1994— Wade Boggs (3B)
1997— Tino Martinez (1B)
2000— Jorge Posada (C)
2001— Jorge Posada (C)
2002— Jason Giambi (1B)
         Alfonso Soriano (2B)
         Bernie Williams (OF)
         Jorge Posada (C)

BASEBALL'S CENTENNIAL AWARDS OF 1969

Selected in balloting conducted by ML Baseball.

"Greatest Player Ever"—Babe Ruth
"Greatest Living Player"—Joe DiMaggio
"Greatest Players Ever" by position—
                 1B—Lou Gehrig
                 OF—Babe Ruth
                 OF—Joe DiMaggio
"Greatest Living Players" by position—
                 C—Bill Dickey
                 CF—Joe DiMaggio
                 Casey Stengel, Manager

NATION'S BICENTENNIAL HONORS OF 1976

Selected through a nationwide poll celebrating the Bicentennial Year of America's independence, 1976

"Baseball's Most Memorable Personality"—Babe Ruth
"Most Memorable Moment in World Series/All-Star Game"—
         Don Larsen's perfect game in 1956 World Series.
"Most Memorable Moment in American League"—
         Joe DiMaggio's 56-game hitting streak in 1941.

ALL-CENTURY TEAM

Prior to the start of the 70th All-Star Game at Boston's Fenway Park, July 13, 1999, the All-Century Team was announced. Fans selected this stellar team which inluded: nine pitchers, two catchers, two first baseman, two second baseman, three shortstops, two third baseman, and ten outfielders, totalling 30 players. Of those 30, six were Yankees: Roger Clemens (pitcher), Yogi Berra (catcher), Lou Gehrig (first baseman), and outfielders Joe DiMaggio, Mickey Mantle, and Babe Ruth. Fans also selected the starting line-ups with two Yankees making the cut: Lou Gehrig at first and Babe Ruth in right.

RETIRED YANKEE UNIFORM NUMBERS

# 1	Billy Martin
# 3	Babe Ruth
# 4	Lou Gehrig
# 5	Joe DiMaggio
# 7	Mickey Mantle
# 8	Bill Dickey/Yogi Berra
# 9	Roger Maris
#10	Phil Rizzuto
#15	Thurman Munson
#16	Whitey Ford
#23	Don Mattingly
#32	Elston Howard
#37	Casey Stengel
#44	Reggie Jackson

CY YOUNG AWARD (1956-2002)

Selected by the BBWAA, the Cy Young Award honors the outstanding pitcher of each league. Prior to 1967, there was only one award made each year to baseball's best pitcher.

1958— Bob Turley
1961— Whitey Ford
1977— Sparky Lyle
1978— Ron Guidry
2001—Roger Clemens

THE STADIUM MONUMENTS

Five men—Miller Huggins, Lou Gehrig, Babe Ruth, Mickey Mantle, and Joe DiMaggio—are remembered with monuments in Yankee Stadium's Monument Park inscribed as follows:

MILLER JAMES HUGGINS
MANAGER OF THE NEW YORK YANKEES, 1918-1929
PENNANT WINNERS 1921-22-23-26-27-28
WORLD CHAMPIONS 1923, 1927 AND 1928
AS A TRIBUTE TO A SPLENDID CHARACTER WHO MADE
PRICELESS CONTRIBUTIONS TO BASEBALL AND ON THIS FIELD
BROUGHT GLORY TO THE NEW YORK CLUB
OF THE AMERICAN LEAGUE.
THIS MEMORIAL ERECTED BY COL. JACOB RUPPERT AND
BASEBALL WRITERS OF NEW YORK
MAY 30, 1932

HENRY LOUIS GEHRIG
JUNE 19TH, 1902-JUNE 2ND, 1941
A MAN, A GENTLEMAN AND A GREAT BALL PLAYER
WHOSE AMAZING RECORD OF 2,130 CONSECUTIVE GAMES
SHOULD STAND FOR ALL TIME.
THIS MEMORIAL IS A TRIBUTE FROM THE
YANKEE PLAYERS TO THEIR BELOVED
CAPTAIN AND TEAMMATE.
JULY THE FOURTH 1941

GEORGE HERMAN "BABE" RUTH
1895-1948
A GREAT BALL PLAYER
A GREAT MAN
A GREAT AMERICAN
ERECTED BY THE YANKEES AND
THE NEW YORK BASEBALL WRITERS
APRIL 19, 1949

MICKEY MANTLE
"A GREAT TEAMMATE"
1931-1995
536 HOME RUNS
WINNER OF TRIPLE CROWN, 1956
MOST WORLD SERIES HOMERS, 18
SELECTED TO ALL STAR GAME, 20 TIMES
WON MVP AWARD, 1956, 1957 & 1962
ELECTED TO HALL OF FAME, 1974
A MAGNIFICENT YANKEE
WHO LEFT A LEGACY OF
UNEQUALED COURAGE
DEDICATED BY
THE NEW YORK YANKEES
AUGUST 25, 1996

JOSEPH PAUL DIMAGGIO
"THE YANKEE CLIPPER"
1914-1999

RECOGNIZED AS BASEBALL'S
"GREATEST LIVING PLAYER"

LIFETIME BATTING AVERAGE	.325
WON MVP AWARD	1939, 1941, 1947
SELECTED TO ALL-STAR GAME	13 TIMES
AMERICAN LEAGUE BATTING TITLE	1939,1940
ELECTED TO HALL OF FAME	1955

SET ONE OF BASEBALL'S MOST ENDURING RECORDS,
56-GAME HITTING STREAK
MAY 15 TO JULY 16, 1941

LED THE YANKEES TO AN INCREDIBLE NINE WORLD CHAMPI-
ONSHIPS IN HIS 13-YEAR CAREER

A BASEBALL LEGEND AND
AN AMERICAN ICON

"HE HAS PASSED, BUT HE WILL NEVER LEAVE US"

DEDICATED BY
THE NEW YORK YANKEES
APRIL 25, 1999

1953 50TH YANKEE ANNIVERSARY ALL-TIME YANKEE TEAM

Selected by a poll of 48 veteran sportswriters, baseball officials and other experts.

Catcher—	Bill Dickey (unanimous)
First Base—	Lou Gehrig (46 votes)
	Hal Chase (2 votes)
Second Base—	Tony Lazzeri (36 votes)
	Joe Gordon (12 votes)
Third Base—	Red Rolfe (38 votes)
	Joe Dugan (10 votes)
Shortstop—	Phil Rizzuto (42 votes)
	Frank Crosetti (3 votes)
	Roger Peckinpaugh (1 vote)
	Everett Scott (1 vote)
	Tony Lazzeri (1 vote)
Utility Infielder—	Frank Crosetti (23 votes)
	Joe Gordon (11 votes)
	Tony Lazzeri (3 votes)
	Joe Dugan (2 votes)
	(Each receiving 1 vote: J. Saltzgaver, E. Johnson, M. Gazella, D. Heffner, A. Ward, L. Lary, G. McDougald, B. Johnson, P. Rizzuto
Outfield—	Babe Ruth (unanimous)
	Joe DiMaggio (unanimous)
	Bob Meusel (24 votes)
	Earle Combs (14 votes)
	Tommy Henrich (8 votes)
	Willie Keeler (2 votes)
RH Pitcher—	Red Ruffing (28 votes)
	Waite Hoyt (11 votes)
	Jack Chesbro (4 votes)
	Vic Raschi (2 votes)
	Bob Shawkey (2 votes)
	Spud Chandler (1 vote)
LH Pitcher—	Lefty Gomez (24 votes)
	Herb Pennock (24 votes)
Relief Pitcher—	Johnny Murphy (25 votes)
	Wilcy Moore (11 votes)
	Joe Page (10 votes)
	Waite Hoyt (1 vote)
	Lefty Gomez (1 vote)

CAPTAINS

Hal Chase,   ? -1912
Roger Peckinpaugh, 1914-1921
Babe Ruth, 5/20/22 - 5/25/22
Everett Scott, 1922-25
Lou Gehrig, 4/21/35 until he died 6/2/41
Thurman Munson, 4/17/76 until he died 8/2/79
Graig Nettles, 1/29/82 until traded 3/30/84
Ron Guidry, 3/14/86 until retirement 7/12/89
Willie Randolph, 3/4/86 until signing with the
    Dodgers 10/2/89
Don Mattingly, 2/28/91- 10/08/95, last game as a Yankee

ML ALL-STAR TEAMS (1926-1960)

The Sporting News, after each season would pick a Major League All-Star Team of two or three pitchers, three outfielders, and one player at each of the other positions.

1926— Babe Ruth (OF)
Herb Pennock (P)
1927— Lou Gehrig (1B)
Babe Ruth (OF)
1928— Lou Gehrig (1B)
Babe Ruth (OF)
Waite Hoyt (P)
1929— Babe Ruth (OF)
1930— Babe Ruth (OF)
1931— Lou Gehrig (1B)
Babe Ruth (OF)
1932— Tony Lazzeri (2B)
Bill Dickey (C)
1933— Bill Dickey (C)
1934— Lou Gehrig (1B)
Lefty Gomez (P)
1936— Lou Gehrig (1B)
Bill Dickey (C)
1937— Lou Gehrig (1B)
Red Rolfe (3B)
Joe DiMaggio (OF)
Red Ruffing (P)

1938— Red Rolfe (3B)
Joe DiMaggio (OF)
Bill Dickey (C)
Red Ruffing (P)
Lefty Gomez (P)
1939— Joe Gordon (2B)
Red Rolfe (3B)
Joe DiMaggio (OF)
Bill Dickey (C)
Red Ruffing (P)
1940— Joe Gordon (2B)
Joe DiMaggio (OF)
1941— Joe Gordon (2B)
Joe DiMaggio (OF)
Bill Dickey (C)
1942— Joe Gordon (2B)
Joe DiMaggio (OF)
Ernie Bonham (P)
1943— Billy Johnson (3B)
Spud Chandler (P)
1945— Snuffy Stirnweiss (2B)
1946— Aaron Robinson (C)
1947— Joe DiMaggio (OF)
1948— Joe DiMaggio (OF)

1949— Tommy Henrich (1B)
Phil Rizzuto (SS)
Joe Page (P)
1950— Phil Rizzuto (SS)
Yogi Berra (C)
Vic Raschi (P)
1951— Phil Rizzuto (SS)
Allie Reynolds (P)
1952— Phil Rizzuto (SS)
Mickey Mantle (OF)
Yogi Berra (C)
Allie Reynolds (P)
1954— Yogi Berra (C)
1955— Whitey Ford (P)
1956— Mickey Mantle (OF)
Yogi Berra (C)
Whitey Ford (P)
1957— Gil McDougald (SS)
Mickey Mantle (OF)
Yogi Berra (C)
1958— Bob Turley (P)
1960— Bill Skowron (1B)
Roger Maris (OF)

AL ALL-STAR TEAMS (1961-2002)

The Sporting News after each season picks an American League (as well as a National League) All-Star Team of two pitchers, one designated hitter (since 1974), three outfielders, and one player for each of the remaining positions.

1961— Bobby Richardson (2B)
Tony Kubek (SS)
Mickey Mantle (OF)
Roger Maris (OF)
Elston Howard (C)
Whitey Ford (P)
1962— Bobby Richardson (2B)
Tom Tresh (SS)
Mickey Mantle (OF)
Ralph Terry (P)
1963— Joe Pepitone (1B)
Bobby Richardson (2B)
Elston Howard (C)
Whitey Ford (P)
1964— Bobby Richardson (2B)
Mickey Mantle (OF)
Elston Howard (C)
1965— Bobby Richardson (2B)
Mel Stottlemyre (P)
1966— Bobby Richardson (2B)
1971— Bobby Murcer (CF)
1972— Bobby Murcer (CF)
1973— Bobby Murcer (RF)

Thurman Munson (C)
1974— Thurman Munson (C)
1975— Graig Nettles (3B)
Thurman Munson (C)
1976— Chris Chambliss (1B)
Mickey Rivers (CF)
Thurman Munson (C)
1977— Willie Randolph (2B)
Graig Nettles (3B)
1978— Graig Nettles (3B)
Ron Guidry (LHP)
1980— Willie Randolph (2B)
Reggie Jackson (RF)
Rick Cerone (C)
Reggie Jackson (DH)
Tommy John (LHP)
1981— Ron Guidry (LHP)
1982— Dave Winfield (OF)
1983— Dave Winfield (OF)
Ron Guidry (LHP)
1984— Don Mattingly (1B)
Dave Winfield (OF)
1985— Don Mattingly (1B)

Rickey Henderson (OF)
Don Baylor (DH)
Ron Guidry (LHP)
1986— Don Mattingly (1B)
1987— Don Mattingly (1B)
Willie Randolph (2B)
1993— Mike Stanley (C)
Jimmy Key (LHP)
1994— Wade Boggs (3B)
Jimmy Key (LHP)
1996— Andy Pettitte (LHP)
1997— Tino Martinez (1B)
1998— Scott Brosuis (3B)
David Wells (LHP)
2000— Bernie Williams (OF)
Jorge Posada (C)
2001— Roger Clemsn (RHP)
Jorge Posada (C)
2002— Jason Giambi (1B)
Alfonso Soriano (2B)
Bernie Williams (OF)
Jorge Posada (C)

ALL-STAR GAME SELECTIONS (1933-2002)

In the seasons 1959-62 two All-Star Games were played, and no game was played in 1945 due to wartime travel restrictions. The players are currently selected by fan ballot. Since 1933, 98 Yankees (totaling 312 yearly selectees) have been named to All-Star squads. Of those 98, 57 were chosen as batters (non-pitchers), while the remaining 41 were pitchers. Yankees named to the All-Star squad through 1999:

1933— Bill Dickey (C)
Lou Gehrig (lB)
Tony Lazzeri (2B)
Ben Chapman (OF)
Babe Ruth (OF)
Lefty Gomez (P)
1934— Lefty Gomez (P)
Red Ruffing (P)
Bill Dickey (C)
Lou Gehrig (lB)
Ben Chapman (OF)
Babe Ruth (OF)
1935— Lefty Gomez (P)
Lou Gehrig (lB)
Ben Chapman (OF)
1936— Lefty Gomez (P)
Monte Pearson (P)
Bill Dickey (C)
Lou Gehrig (1B)
Frank Crosetti (SS)
Joe DiMaggio (OF)
George Selkirk (OF)
1937— Lefty Gomez (P)
Johnny Murphy (P)
Bill Dickey (C)
Lou Gehrig (1B)
Red Rolfe (3B)
Joe DiMaggio (OF)
1938— Lefty Gomez (P)
Red Ruffing (P)
Bill Dickey (C)
Lou Gehrig (1B)
Red Rolfe (3B)
Joe DiMaggio (OF)
1939— Lefty Gomez (P)
Johnny Murphy (P)
Red Ruffing (P)
Bill Dickey (C)
Joe Gordon (2B)
Frank Crosetti (SS)
Red Rolfe (3B)
Joe DiMaggio (OF)
George Selkirk (OF)
1940— Monte Pearson (P)
Red Ruffing (P)
Bill Dickey (C)
Joe Gordon (2B)
Red Rolfe (3B)
Joe DiMaggio (OF)
Charlie Keller (OF)
1941— Red Ruffing (P)
Marius Russo (P)
Bill Dickey (C)
Joe Gordon (2B)
Joe DiMaggio (OF)
Charlie Keller (OF)
1942— Ernie Bonham (P)
Spud Chandler (P)

Red Ruffing (P)
Bill Dickey (C)
Buddy Rosar (C)
Joe Gordon (2B)
Phil Rizzuto (SS)
Joe DiMaggio (OF)
Tommy Henrich (OF)
1943— Ernie Bonham (P)
Spud Chandler (P)
Bill Dickey (C)
Joe Gordon (2B)
Charlie Keller (OF)
Johnny Lindell (OF)
1944— Hank Borowy (P)
Joe Page (P)
Rollie Hemsley (C)
1945— (no game)
1946— Spud Chandler (P)
Bill Dickey (C)
Joe Gordon (2B)
Snuffy Stirnweiss (3B)
Joe DiMaggio (OF)
Charlie Keller (OF)
1947— Spud Chandler (P)
Joe Page (P)
Spec Shea (P)
Aaron Robinson (C)
George McQuinn (1B)
Billy Johnson (3B)
Joe DiMaggio (OF)
Tommy Henrich (OF)
Charlie Keller (OF)
1948— Joe Page (P)
Vic Raschi (P)
Yogi Berra (C)
George McQuinn (lB)
Joe DiMaggio (OF)
Tommy Henrich (OF)
1949— Vic Raschi (P)
Allie Reynolds (P)
Yogi Berra (C)
Joe DiMaggio (OF)
Tommy Henrich (OF)
1950— Tommy Byrne (P)
Vic Raschi (P)
Allie Reynolds (P)
Yogi Berra (C)
Tommy Henrich (lB)
Jerry Coleman (2B)
Phil Rizzuto (SS)
Joe DiMaggio (OF)
1951— Ed Lopat (P)
Yogi Berra (C)
Phil Rizzuto (SS)
Joe DiMaggio (OF)
1952— Vic Raschi (P)
Allie Reynolds (P)
Yogi Berra (C)

Gil McDougald (2B)
Phil Rizzuto (SS)
Hank Bauer (OF)
Mickey Mantle (OF)
1953— Allie Reynolds (P)
Johnny Sain (P)
Yogi Berra (C)
Johnny Mize (lB)
Phil Rizzuto (SS)
Hank Bauer (OF)
Mickey Mantle (OF)
1954— Whitey Ford (P)
Allie Reynolds (P)
Yogi Berra (C)
Hank Bauer (OF)
Mickey Mantle (OF)
Irv Noren (OF)
1955— Whitey Ford (P)
Bob Turley (P)
Yogi Berra (C)
Mickey Mantle (OF)
1956— Whitey Ford (P)
Johnny Kucks (P)
Yogi Berra (C)
Billy Martin (2B)
Gil McDougald (SS)
Mickey Mantle (OF)
1957— Bob Grim (P)
Bobby Shantz (P)
Yogi Berra (C)
Elston Howard (C)
Bill Skowron (lB)
Bobby Richardson (2B)
Gil McDougald (SS)
Mickey Mantle (OF)
1958— Ryne Duren (P)
Whitey Ford (P)
Bob Turley (P)
Yogi Berra (C)
Elston Howard (C)
Bill Skowron (lB)
Gil McDougald (2B)
Tony Kubek (Inf.)
Mickey Mantle (OF)
1959— Ryne Duren (P)
Whitey Ford (P)
Yogi Berra (C)
Elston Howard (C)
Bill Skowron (1B)
Bobby Richardson (2B)
Tony Kubek (SS)
Gil McDougald (SS)
Mickey Mantle (OF)
1960— Jim Coates (P)
Whitey Ford (P)
Yogi Berra (C)
Elston Howard (C)
Bill Skowron (lB)

Mickey Mantle (OF)
Roger Maris (OF)
1961— Luis Arroyo (P)
Whitey Ford (P)
Elston Howard (C)
Bill Skowron (1B)
Tony Kubek (SS)
Yogi Berra (OF)
Mickey Mantle (OF)
Roger Maris (OF)
1962— Ralph Terry (P)
Yogi Berra (C)
Elston Howard (C)
Bobby Richardson (2B)
Tom Tresh (SS)
Mickey Mantle (OF)
Roger Maris (OF)
1963— Jim Bouton (P)
Elston Howard (C)
Joe Pepitone (1B)
Bobby Richardson (2B)
Mickey Mantle (OF)
Tom Tresh (OF)
1964— Whitey Ford (P)
Elston Howard (C)
Joe Pepitone (1B)
Bobby Richardson (2B)
Mickey Mantle (OF)
1965— Mel Stottlemyre (P)
Elston Howard (C)
Joe Pepitone (1B)
Bobby Richardson (2B)
Mickey Mantle (OF)
1966— Mel Stottlemyre (P)
Bobby Richardson (2B)
1967— Al Downing (P)
Mickey Mantle (1B)
1968— Mel Stottlemyre (P)
Mickey Mantle (1B)
1969— Mel Stottlemyre (P)
Roy White (OF)
1970— Fritz Peterson (P)
Mel Stottlemyre (P)
Roy White (OF)
1971— Thurman Munson (C)
Bobby Murcer (OF)
1972— Bobby Murcer (OF)
1973— Sparky Lyle (P)
Thurman Munson (C)
Bobby Murcer (OF)
1974— Thurman Munson (C)
Bobby Murcer (OF)

1975— Catfish Hunter (P)
Thurman Munson (C)
Graig Nettles (3B)
Bobby Bonds (OF)
1976— Catfish Hunter (P)
Sparky Lyle (P)
Thurman Munson (C)
Chris Chambliss (1B)
Willie Randolph (2B)
Mickey Rivers (OF)
1977 —Sparky Lyle (P)
Thurman Munson (C)
Willie Randolph (2B)
Graig Nettles (3B)
Reggie Jackson (OF)
1978— Ron Guidry (P)
Rich Gossage (P)
Thurman Munson (C)
Graig Nettles (3B)
Reggie Jackson (OF)
1979— Ron Guidry (P)
Tommy John (P)
Graig Nettles (3B)
Reggie Jackson (OF)
1980— Tommy John (P)
Rich Gossage (P)
Willie Randolph (2B)
Graig Nettles (3B)
Bucky Dent (SS)
Reggie Jackson (OF)
1981— Rich Gossage (P)
Ron Davis (P)
Willie Randolph (2B)
Bucky Dent (SS)
Dave Winfield (OF)
Reggie Jackson (OF)
1982— Ron Guidry (P)
Rich Gossage (P)
Dave Winfield (OF)
1983— Ron Guidry (P)
Dave Winfield (OF)
1984— Phil Niekro (P)
Don Mattingly (1B)
Dave Winfield (OF)
1985— Don Mattingly (1B)
Rickey Henderson (OF)
Dave Winfield (OF)
1986— Dave Righetti (P)
Don Mattingly (1B)
Rickey Henderson (OF)
Dave Winfield (OF)

1987— Dave Righetti (P)
Don Mattingly (1B)
Willie Randolph (2B)
Rickey Henderson (OF)
Dave Winfield (OF)
1988— Don Mattingly (1B)
Rickey Henderson (OF)
Dave Winfield (OF)
1989— Don Mattingly (1B)
Steve Sax (2B)
1990— Steve Sax (2B)
1991— Scott Sanderson (P)
1992— Roberto Kelly (OF)
1993— Jimmy Key (P)
Wade Boggs (3B)
1994— Jimmy Key (P)
Wade Boggs (3B)
Paul O'Neill (OF)
1995— Wade Boggs (3B)
Paul O'Neill (OF)
Mike Stanley (C)
1996— Wade Boggs (3B)
Andy Pettitte (P)
John Wetteland (P)
1997— David Cone (P)
Mariano Rivera (P)
Tino Martinez (1B)
Paul O'Neill (OF)
Bernie Williams (OF)
1998— David Wells (P)
Derek Jeter (SS)
Scott Brosius (3B)
Paul O'Neill (OF)
Bernie Williams (OF)
1999— David Cone (P)
Derek Jeter (SS)
Mariano Rivera (P)
Bernie Williams (OF)
2000— Derek Jeter (SS)
Jorge Posada (C)
Mariano Rivera (P)
Bernie Williams (OF)
2001— Roger Clemens (P)
Derek Jeter (SS)
Andy Pettitte (P)
Jorge Posada (C)
Mike Stanton (P)
Bernie Williams (OF)
2002— Jason Giambi (1B)
Alfonso Soriano (2B)
Derek Jeter (SS)
Robin Ventura (3B)
Jorge Posada (C)
Mariano Rivera (P)

ALL-STAR GAME STATS FOR BATTERS
(1933-2002)

Composite batting statistics of Yankee players (excluding pitchers) and including only those years in which the player wore the Yankee uniform. Fifty-seven Yankee players (non-pitchers) have played in an All-Star Game, totalling 214 appearances through 2002. Mickey Mantle represented the Yankees in 16 All-Star Games, the most by any Yankee player.

Player	Yrs. and Position	G	AB	R	H	2B	3B	HR	RBI	BA
Bauer, Hank	1952-54; OF	3	7	0	2	0	0	0	0	.286
Berra, Yogi	1949-62; C, PH	15	41	5	8	0	0	1	3	.195
Boggs, Wade	1993-96; 3B	4	9	1	2	0	0	0	0	.222
Bonds, Bobby	1975; OF	1	3	0	0	0	0	0	0	.000
Brosius, Scott	1998; 3B	1	2	1	1	0	0	0	0	.500
Chambliss, Chris	1976; PH	1	1	0	0	0	0	0	0	.000
Chapman, Ben	1933-35: OF	3	7	0	2	0	1	0	0	.286
Coleman, Jerry	1950: 2B	1	2	0	0	0	0	0	0	.000
Crosetti, Frank	1936: PH	1	1	0	0	0	0	0	0	.000
Dent, Bucky	1980-81: SS	2	4	0	3	1	0	0	0	.750
Dickey, Bill	1934,36-41,46:C, PH	8	19	3	5	2	0	0	1	.263
DiMaggio, Joe	1936-42,47-50: OF, PH	11	40	7	9	2	0	1	6	.225
Gehrig, Lou	1933-38: IB	6	18	4	4	1	0	2	5	.222
Giambi, Jason	2002; 1B	1	2	1	1	0	0	0	0	.500
Gordon, Joe	1939-42,46: 2B	5	14	1	2	1	0	0	2	.143
Hemsley, Rollie	1944: C	1	2	0	0	0	0	0	0	.000
Henderson, Rickey	1985-88; OF	4	11	1	3	0	0	0	0	.273
Henrich, Tommy	1942,47-48,50; OF, PH	4	9	1	1	1	0	0	0	.111
Howard, Elston	1960-64; C	6	9	1	0	0	0	0	0	.000
Jackson, Reggie	1977,79-81; OF	4	6	0	2	0	0	0	0	.333
Jeter, Derek	1998-2002; SS, PH	5	7	2	4	1	0	1	3	.571
Johnson, Billy	1947; 3B	1	0	0	0	0	0	0	0	.000
Keller, Charlie	1940-41,46; OF	3	7	2	1	0	0	1	2	.143
Kelly, Roberto	1992; OF	1	2	0	1	1	0	0	2	.500
Kubek, Tony	1959,61; PH, SS	2	5	1	0	0	0	0	0	.000
Mantle, Mickey	1953-62,64,67-68;OF, PH	16	43	5	10	0	0	2	4	.233
Maris, Roger	1960-62; OF, PH	6	17	2	2	1	0	0	2	.118
Martin, Billy	1956: PH	1	1	0	0	0	0	0	0	.000
Martinez, Tino	1997; 1B	1	2	0	0	0	0	0	0	.000
Mattingly, Don	1984-89; 1B, PH	6	8	0	1	1	0	0	0	.125
McDougald, Gil	1952,57-59; PH, SS, PR	4	4	1	1	0	0	0	1	.250
McQuinn, George	1947-48 1B	2	8	1	2	0	0	0	0	.000
Mize, Johnny	1953: PH	1	1	0	1	0	0	0	0	1.000
Munson, Thurman	l971, 73-77; PH, C	6	10	1	2	1	0	0	0	.200
Murcer, Bobby	1971-74; OF	4	11	0	1	0	0	0	0	.091
Nettles, Graig	1975,77-80; 3B	5	9	0	2	0	0	0	0	.222
Noren, Irv	1954; OF	1	0	0	0	0	0	0	0	.000
O'Neill, Paul	1994-95, 1997-98; OF, PH	4	6	0	0	0	0	0	0	.000
Pepitone, Joe	1963-65; 1B, PR, PH	3	5	0	0	0	0	0	0	.000
Posada, Jorge	2000-2002; C	3	6	0	1	1	0	0	0	.167
Randolph, Willie	1977, 80-81; 87; 2B	4	13	0	4	0	0	0	1	.308
Richardson, Bob	1959, 62-66; 2B, PR, PH	6	11	1	1	0	0	0	0	.091
Rivers, Mickey	1976; PH, OF	1	2	0	1	0	0	0	0	.500
Rizzuto, Phil	1950-53; SS	4	9	0	2	0	0	0	0	.222
Rolfe, Red	1937, 39; 3B	3	8	2	3	0	1	0	2	.375
Ruth, Babe	1933-34: OF	2	6	2	2	0	0	1	2	.333
Sax, Steve	1989-90; 2B	2	2	0	0	0	0	0	0	.000
Selkirk, George	1936, 39; OF, PH	2	2	0	1	0	0	0	1	.500
Skowron, Bill	1957-60; 1B	5	14	1	6	1	0	0	0	.429
Soriano, Alfonso	2002; 2B	1	2	1	1	0	0	1	1	.500
Stanley, Mike	1995; C	1	1	0	0	0	0	0	0	.000
Stirnweiss, Snuffy	1946; 2B	1	3	1	1	0	0	0	0	.333
Tresh, Tom	1962-63; SS, OF	2	2	0	1	1	0	0	1	.500
Ventura, Robin	2002;3B	1	1	0	0	0	0	0	0	.000
White, Roy	1969; PH	1	1	0	0	0	0	0	0	.000
Williams, Bernie	1997,1999-2001; OF	4	5	1	0	0	0	0	0	.000
Winfield, Dave	1981-88; OF, PH	8	25	4	9	5	0	0	1	.360

Yankee home runs in All-Star Games:

Date	Player	Pitcher	Stadium
July 6, 1933	Babe Ruth	B. Hallahan	Comiskey Park, Chicago
July 7, 1936	Lou Gehrig	C. Davis	Braves Field, Boston
July 7, 1937	Lou Gehrig	D. Dean	Griffith Stadium, Washington
July 11, 1939	Joe DiMaggio	B. Lee	Yankee Stadium, New York
July 9, 1946	Charlie Keller	C. Passeau	Fenway Park, Boston
July 12, 1955	Mickey Mantle	R. Roberts	County Stadium, Milwaukee
July 10, 1956	Mickey Mantle	W. Spahn	Griffith Stadium, Washington
August 3, 1959	Yogi Berra	D. Drysdale	Memorial Coliseum, Los Angeles
July 10, 2001	Derek Jeter	J. Lieber	Safeco Field, Seattle
July 9, 2002	Alfonso Soriano	E. Gagne	Miller Park, Milwaukee

ALL-STAR GAME STATS FOR PITCHERS
(1933-2002)

Composite pitching statistics of Yankee pitchers including only those years in which the pitcher wore the Yankee uniform. Thirty-two Yankees have pitched in an All-Star Game, totalling 99 appearances through 2002. Yankee starters are 5-4 overall, while the Yankee pitcher records are 6-10 in All-Star play. Whitey Ford has represented the Yankees on six occasions, the most by a Yankee hurler.

Pitcher	Yrs	G	IP	H	R	BB	SO	W-L	PCT.
Borowy, Hank	1944	1	3	3	0	1	0	0-0	.000
Bouton, Jim	1963	1	1	0	0	0	0	0-0	.000
Chandler, Spud	1942	1	4	2	0	0	2	1-0	1.000
Clemens, Roger	2001	1	2	0	0	0	1	0-0	.000
Coates, Jim	1960	1	2	2	0	0	0	0-0	.000
Cone, David	1997	2	3	4	1	3	3	0-0	.000
Davis, Ron	1981	1	1	1	1	0	1	0-0	.000
Downing, Al	1967	1	2	2	0	0	2	0-0	.000
Duren, Ryne	1959	1	3	1	0	1	4	0-0	.000
Ford, Whitey	1954-56,59-61	6	12	19	13	3	5	0-2	.000
Gomez, Lefty	1933-35, 37-38	5	18	11	6	3	9	3-1	.750
Gossage, Rich	1978, 1980	2	2	5	4	1	1	0-1	.000
Grim, Bob	1957	1	1/3	0	0	0	0	0-0	.000
Guidry, Ron	1978-79	2	2/3	1	0	1	0	0-0	.000
Hunter, Catfish	1975-76	2	4	7	4	0	5	0-1	.000
John, Tommy	1980	1	2 1/3	4	3	0	1	0-1	.000
Key, Jimmy	1993-94	2	3	3	2	0	2	0-0	.000
Lopat, Ed	1951	1	1	3	3	0	0	0-1	.000
Lyle, Sparky	1973, 1977	2	3	4	2	0	2	0-0	.000
Page, Joe	1947	1	1 1/3	1	0	1	0	0-0	.000
Peterson, Fritz	1970	1	0	1	0	0	0	0-0	.000
Pettitte, Andy	2001	1	1	1	0	0	1	0-0	.000
Raschi, Vic	1948-50-1952	4	11	7	3	4	8	1-0	1.000
Reynolds, Allie	1950, 1953	2	5	3	2	2	2	0-1	.000
Righetti, Dave	1986-87	2	1	3	0	0	0	0-0	.000
Rivera, Mariano	1997, 2000, 02	3	3	3	1	0	1	0-0	.000
Ruffing, Red	1934,39-40	3	7	13	7	2	6	0-1	.000
Shea, Spec	1947	1	3	3	1	2	2	1-0	1.000
Stanton, Mike	2001	1	2/3	0	0	0	0	0-0	.000
Stottlemyre, Mel	1966,68-70	4	6	5	3	1	4	0-1	.000
Turley, Bob	1958	1	1 2/3	3	3	2	0	0-0	.000
Wells, David	1998	1	2	0	0	1	1	0-0	.000

Yankee winning pitchers in All-Star Games:

Date	Pitcher	Stadium
July 6, 1933	Lefty Gomez	Comiskey Park, Chicago
July 8, 1935	Lefty Gomez	Municipal Stadium, Cleveland
July 7, 1937	Lefty Gomez	Griffith Stadium, Washington
July 6, 1942	Spud Chandler	Polo Grounds, New York
July 8, 1947	Spec Shea	Wrigley Field, Chicago
July 13, 1948	Vic Raschi	Sportsman's Park, St. Louis

Yankee starting pitchers in All-Star Games:

Date		(Decision)	Stadium
July 6, 1933	Lefty Gomez	(W)	Comiskey Park, Chicago
July 10, 1934	Lefty Gomez	(W)	Polo Grounds, New York
July 8, 1935	Lefty Gomez	(W)	Municipal Stadium, Cleveland
July 7, 1937	Lefty Gomez	(W)	Griffith Stadium Washington
July 6, 1938	Lefty Gomez	(L)	Crosley Field, Cincinnati
July 11,1939	Red Ruffing		Yankee Stadium, New York
July 9, 1940	Red Ruffing	(L)	Sportman's Park, St. Louis
July 6, 1942	Spud Chandler	(W)	Polo Grounds, New York
July 11, 1944	Hank Borowy		Forbes Field Pittsburgh
July 11, 1950	Vic Raschi		Comiskey Park, Chicago
July 8, 1952	Vic Raschi		Shibe Park, Philadelphia
July 13, 1954	Whitey Ford		Municipal Stadium, Cleveland
July 8, 1958	Bob Turley		Memorial Stadium, Baltimore
July 13, 1960	Whitey Ford	(L)	Yankee Stadium, New York
July 11, 1961	Whitey Ford		Candlestick Park, San Francisco
July 23, 1969	Mel Stottlemyre	(L)	RFK Stadium, Washington
July 12, 1994	Jimmy Key		Three Rivers Stadium, Pittsburgh
July 7, 1998	David Wells		Coors Field, Denver
July 10, 2001	Roger Clemens		Safeco Field, Seattle

Offense (1903-2002)

YANKEE AMERICAN LEAGUE LEADERS BY SEASON

At-Bats
1923— Joe Dugan 644
1927— Earle Combs 648
1939— Frank Crosetti 656
1945— Snuffy Stirnweiss 632
1962— Bobby Richardson 692
1963— Bobby Richardson 630
1964— Bobby Richardson 679
1965— Bobby Richardson 664
1969— Horace Clarke 641
1970— Horace Clarke 686
1973— Roy White 639
1989— Steve Sax 651
2002— Alfonso Soriano 696

Runs
1920— Babe Ruth 158
1921— Babe Ruth 177
1923— Babe Ruth 151
1924— Babe Ruth 143
1926— Babe Ruth 139
1927— Babe Ruth 158
1928— Babe Ruth 163
1931— Lou Gehrig 163
1933— Lou Gehrig 138
1935— Lou Gehrig 125
1936— Lou Gehrig 167
1937— Joe DiMaggio 151
1939— Red Rolfe 139
1944— Snuffy Stirnweiss 125
1945— Snuffy Stirnweiss 107
1948— Tommy Henrich 138
1954— Mickey Mantle 129
1956— Mickey Mantle 132
1957— Mickey Mantle 121
1958— Mickey Mantle 127
1960— Mickey Mantle 119
1961— Mickey Mantle 132
       Roger Maris 132
1972— Bobby Murcer 102
1976— Roy White 104
1985— Rickey Henderson 146
1986— Rickey Henderson 130
1998— Derek Jeter 127
2002— Alfonso Soriano 128

Hits
1927— Lou Gehrig 231
1931— Lou Gehrig 211
1939— Red Rolfe 213
1944— Snuffy Stirnweiss 205
1945— Snuffy Stirnweiss 195
1962— Bobby Richardson 209
1984— Don Mattingly 207
1986— Don Mattingly 238
1999— Derek Jeter 219
2002— Alfonso Soriano 209

Doubles
1927— Earle Combs 52
1928— Lou Gehrig 47
1939— Red Rolfe 46
1984— Don Mattingly 44
1985— Don Mattingly 48
1986— Don Mattingly. 53

Triples
1924— Wally Pipp 19
1926— Lou Gehrig 20
1927— Earle Combs 23

1928— Earle Combs 21
1930— Earle Combs 22
1934— Ben Chapman 13
1936— Joe DiMaggio 15
       Red Rolfe 15
1943— Johnny Lindell......................... 12
1944— Johnny Lindell......................... 16
       Snuffy Stirnweiss 16
1945— Snuffy Stirnweiss 22
1947— Tommy Henrich 13
1948— Tommy Henrich 14
1955— Andy Carey 11
       Mickey Mantle 11
1957— Hank Bauer 9
       Gil McDougald 9

Home Runs
1916— Wally Pipp 12
1917— Wally Pipp 9
1920— Babe Ruth 54
1921— Babe Ruth 59
1923— Babe Ruth 41
1924— Babe Ruth 46
1925— Bob Meusel 33
1926— Babe Ruth 47
1927— Babe Ruth 60
1928— Babe Ruth 54
1929— Babe Ruth 46
1930— Babe Ruth 49
1931— Babe Ruth 46
       Lou Gehrig 46
1934— Lou Gehrig 49
1936— Lou Gehrig 49
1937— Joe DiMaggio 46
1944— Nick Etten 22
1948— Joe DiMaggio 39
1955— Mickey Mantle 37
1956— Mickey Mantle 52
1958— Mickey Mantle 42
1960— Mickey Mantle 40
1961— Roger Maris 61
1976— Graig Nettles 32
1980— Reggie Jackson 41

RBIs
1920— Babe Ruth 137
1921— Babe Ruth 171
1923— Babe Ruth 131
1925— Bob Meusel 138
1926— Babe Ruth 145
1927— Lou Gehrig 175
1928— Lou Gehrig 142
       Babe Ruth 142
1930— Lou Gehrig 174
1931— Lou Gehrig 184
1934— Lou Gehrig 165
1941— Joe DiMaggio 125
1945— Nick Etten 111
1948— Joe DiMaggio 155
1956— Mickey Mantle 130
1960— Roger Maris 112
1961— Roger Maris 142
1985— Don Mattingly 145

Bases on Balls
1920— Babe Ruth 148
1921— Babe Ruth 144
1922— Whitey Witt 89
1923— Babe Ruth 170
1924— Babe Ruth 142
1926— Babe Ruth 144

1927— Babe Ruth 138
1928— Babe Ruth 135
1930— Babe Ruth 136
1931— Babe Ruth 128
1932— Babe Ruth 130
1933— Babe Ruth 114
1935— Lou Gehrig 132
1936— Lou Gehrig 130
1937— Lou Gehrig 127
1940— Charlie Keller 106
1943— Charlie Keller 106
1944— Nick Etten 97
1955— Mickey Mantle 113
1957— Mickey Mantle 146
1958— Mickey Mantle 129
1961— Mickey Mantle 126
1962— Mickey Mantle 122
1972— Roy White 99
1980— Willie Randolph 119

Stolen Bases
1914— Fritz Maisel 74
1931— Ben Chapman 61
1932— Ben Chapman 38
1933— Ben Chapman 27
1938— Frank Crosetti 27
1944— Snuffy Stirnweiss 55
1945— Snuffy Stirnweiss 33
1985— Rickey Henderson 80
1986— Rickey Henderson 87
1988— Rickey Henderson 93
2002— Alfonso Soriano 41

Batting Average
1924— Babe Ruth .... .378
1934— Lou Gehrig .... .363
1939— Joe DiMaggio .... .381
1940— Joe DiMaggio .... .352
1945— Snuffy Stirnweiss .... .309
1956— Mickey Mantle .... .353
1984— Don Mattingly .... .343
1994— Paul O'Neill .... .359
1998— Bernie Williams .... .339

Slugging Average
1920— Babe Ruth .... .847
1921— Babe Ruth .... .846
1922— Babe Ruth .... .672
1923— Babe Ruth .... .764
1924— Babe Ruth .... .739
1926— Babe Ruth .... .737
1927— Babe Ruth .... .772
1928— Babe Ruth .... .709
1929— Babe Ruth . ... .697
1930— Babe Ruth .... .732
1931— Babe Ruth .... .700
1934— Lou Gehrig .... .706
1936— Lou Gehrig .... .696
1937— Joe DiMaggio .... .673
1945— Snuffy Stirnweiss .... .476
1955— Mickey Mantle .... .611
1956— Mickey Mantle .... .705
1960— Roger Maris .... .581
1961— Mickey Mantle .... .687
1962— Mickey Mantle .... .605
1986— Don Mattingly .... .573

Pitching (1903-2002)

Wins
1904— Jack Chesbro 41
1906— Al Orth 27

1921— Carl Mays 27
1927— Waite Hoyt 22
1928— George Pipgras 24
1934— Lefty Gomez 26
1937— Lefty Gomez 21
1938— Red Ruffing 21
1943— Spud Chandler 20
1955— Whitey Ford 18
1958— Bob Turley 21
1961— Whitey Ford 25
1962— Ralph Terry 23
1963— Whitey Ford 24
1975— Catfish Hunter 23
1978— Ron Guidry 25
1985— Ron Guidry 22
1994— Jimmy Key 17
1996— Andy Pettitte 21
1998— David Cone 20

Win Percentage
1904— Jack Chesbro .... .774(41-12)
1921— Carl Mays .... .750 (27-9)
1922— Bullet Joe Bush .... .788 (26-7)
1923— Herb Pennock .... .760 (19-6)
1927— Waite Hoyt .... .759 (22-7)
1934— Lefty Gomez .... .839 (26-5)
1941— Lefty Gomez .... .750 (15-5)
1942— Ernie Bonham. .... .808 (21-5)
1943— Spud Chandler .... .833 (20-4)
1953— Ed Lopat .... .800 (16-4)
1956— Whitey Ford .... .760 (19-6)
1957— Tom Sturdivant .... .727 (16-6)
1958— Bob Turley .... .750 (21-7)
1961— Whitey Ford .... .862 (25-4)
1963— Whitey Ford .... .774 (24-7)
1978— Ron Guidry .... .893 (25-3)
1985— Ron Guidry .... .786 (22-6)
1993— Jimmy Key .... .750 (18-6)
1994— Jimmy Key .... .810 (17-4)
1998— David Wells .... .818 (18-4)
2001— Roger Clemens .... .870 (20-3)

Saves
1916— Bob Shawkey 9
1918— George Mogridge 6
1921— Carl Mays 7
1922— Sad Sam Jones 8
1927— Wilcy Moore 13
1928— Waite Hoyt 8
1936— Pat Malone 9
1938— Johnny Murphy 11
1939— Johnny Murphy 19
1941— Johnny Murphy 15
1942— Johnny Murphy 11
1945— Jim Turner 10
1947— Joe Page 17
1949— Joe Page 27
1954— Johnny Sain 22
1957— Bob Grim 19
1958— Ryne Duren 20
1961— Luis Arroyo 29
1972— Sparky Lyle 35
1976— Sparky Lyle 23
1978— Rich Gossage 27
1980— Rich Gossage 33
1986— Dave Righetti 46
1996— John Wetteland 43
1999— Mariano Rivera 45
2001— Mariano Rivera 50

Games Pitched
1904— Jack Chesbro 55
1906— Jack Chesbro 49
1918— George Mogridge 45
1921— Carl Mays 49
1948— Joe Page 55

1949— Joe Page 60
1961— Luis Arroyo 65
1977— Sparky Lyle 72
1986— Dave Righetti.............................. 74
1994— Bob Wickman.............................. 53

Games Started
1904— Jack Chesbro 51
1906— Jack Chesbro 42
1928— George Pipgras 38
1949— Vic Raschi 37
1951— Vic Raschi 34
1961— Whitey Ford 39
1962— Ralph Terry 39
1963— Whitey Ford 37
         Ralph Terry 37
1994— Jimmy Key 25
1997— Andy Pettitte 35

Complete Games
1904— Jack Chesbro 48
1906— Al Orth 36
1934— Lefty Gomez 25
1942— Ernie Bonham 22
1943— Spud Chandler 20
1955— Whitey Ford 18
1958— Bob Turley 19
1963— Ralph Terry 18
1965— Mel Stottlemyre 18
1969— Mel Stottlemyre 24
1975— Catfish Hunter 30
1983— Ron Guidry 21
1995— Jack McDowell 8

Innings Pitched
1904— Jack Chesbro 455
1906— Al Orth 339
1921— Carl Mays 337
1925— Herb Pennock 277
1928— George Pipgras 301
1934— Lefty Gomez 282
1961— Whitey Ford 283
1962— Ralph Terry 299
1963— Whitey Ford 269
1965— Mel Stottlemyre 291
1975— Catfish Hunter 328
1976— Catfish Hunter 299

Strikeouts
1932— Red Ruffing 190
1933— Lefty Gomez 163
1934— Lefty Gomez 158
1937— Lefty Gomez 194
1951— Vic Raschi 164
1952— Allie Reynolds........................... 160
1964— Al Downing 217

Shutouts
1920— Carl Mays 6
1928— Herb Pennock 5
1930— George Pipgras 3
1934— Lefty Gomez 6
1937— Lefty Gomez 6
1938— Lefty Gomez 3
         Red Ruffing 3
1939— Red Ruffing 4
1942— Ernie Bonham 6
1943— Spud Chandler 5
1951— Allie Reynolds 7
1952— Allie Reynolds 6
1958— Whitey Ford 7
1960— Whitey Ford 4
1978— Ron Guidry 9
1980— Tommy John 6
1998— David Wells 5

ERA
1920— Bob Shawkey 2.45
1927— Wilcy Moore 2.28
1934— Lefty Gomez 2.33
1937— Lefty Gomez 2.33
1942— Ernie Bonham 2.27
1943— Spud Chandler 1.64
1947— Spud Chandler 2.46
1952— Allie Reynolds 2.06
1953— Ed Lopat 2.42
1956— Whitey Ford 2.47
1957— Bobby Shantz 2.45
1958— Whitey Ford 2.01
1978— Ron Guidry 1.74
1979— Ron Guidry 2.78
1980— Rudy May 2.46

Fielding (1903-2002)
By position as well as season.
Fielding Average*
1903— 1B, John Ganzel 988
1913— OF, Birdie Cree 988
1915— 1B, Wally Pipp 992
1918— 3B, Frank Baker 972
1922— SS, Everett Scott 964
1923— 2B, Aaron Ward 980
         3B, Joe Dugan 974
         SS, Everett Scott 961
         OF, Whitey Witt 979
1924— 1B, Wally Pipp 994
1925— C, Benny Bengough 993
         3B, Joe Dugan 970
1931— C, Bill Dickey 996
1934— OF, Sammy Byrd 988
1935— C, Bill Dickey 995
         3B, Red Rolfe 964
1936— 3B, Red Rolfe 957
1939— C, Bill Dickey 989
         SS, Frank Crosetti 968
         OF, George Selkirk 989
1941— C, Bill Dickey 994
1944— 2B, Snuffy Stirnweiss 982
1947— OF, Joe DiMaggio 997
1948— 2B, Snuffy Stirnweiss 993
1949— 2B, Jerry Coleman 981
         SS, Phil Rizzuto 971
1950— SS, Phil Rizzuto 982
1952— OF, Gene Woodling 996
1953— OF, Gene Woodling 996
1955— 2B, Gil McDougald 985
         OF, Mickey Mantle 995
1958— 1B, Bill Skowron 993
1959— C, Yogi Berra 997
         OF, Mickey Mantle 995
1962— C, Elston Howard 995
1963— C, Elston Howard 994
1964— C, Elston Howard 998
         OF, Tom Tresh 996
1965— 1B, Joe Pepitone 997
1966— 1B, Joe Pepitone 995
1967— 2B, Horace Clarke 990
1969— 1B, Joe Pepitone 995
1971— C, Thurman Munson 998
         OF, Roy White 1.000
1975— 2B, Sandy Alomar 985
1976— SS, Fred Stanley 983
1978— 1B, Chris Chambliss 997
1980— SS, Bucky Dent 982
1984— 1B, Don Mattingly 996
1985— 1B, Don Mattingly 995
1986— 1B, Don Mattingly 996
1987— C, Rick Cerone 998
         1B, Don Mattingly 996
1989— 2B, Steve Sax 987
1992— 1B, Don Mattingly 997

1993— C, Mike Stanley .... .996
1B, Don Mattingly .... .998
3B, Wade Boggs .... .970
1994— 1B, Don Mattingly .... .998
1996— 1B, Tino Martinez .... .996
OF, Paul O'Neill 1.000
2000— OF, Bernie Williams 1.000
2002— OF, Rondell White 1.000

Putouts
1911— 1B, Hal Chase 1255
1912— C, Ed Sweeney 548
1915— 1B, Wally Pipp 1396
1917— 3B, Frank Baker 202
1918— 2B, Del Pratt 304
3B, Frank Baker 175
1919— 1B, Wally Pipp 1488
3B, Frank Baker 176
1920— 1B, Wally Pipp 1649
1922— 1B, Wally Pipp 1667
1927— 1B, Lou Gehrig 1662
OF, Earle Combs 411
1928— 1B, Lou Gehrig 1488
OF, Earle Combs 424
1931— C, Bill Dickey 670
1933— C, Bill Dickey 721
1935— C, Bill Dickey 536
1937— C, Bill Dickey 692
OF, Joe DiMaggio 413
1938— C, Bill Dickey 518
SS, Frank Crosetti 352
1939— C, Bill Dickey 571
2B, Joe Gordon 370
SS, Frank Crosetti 323
1940— 1B, Babe Dahlgren 1488
1942— SS, Phil Rizzuto 324
1943— 3B, Billy Johnson 183
1944— 2B, Snuffy Stirnweiss 433
OF, Johnny Lindell 468
1945— 2B, Snuffy Stirnweiss 432
1950— C, Yogi Berra 777
SS, Phil Rizzuto 301
1951— C, Yogi Berra 693
1952— C, Yogi Berra 700
1954— C, Yogi Berra 717
1955— C, Yogi Berra 721
3B, Andy Carey 154
1956— C, Yogi Berra 732
1957— C, Yogi Berra 704
1959— C, Yogi Berra 698
1960— 1B, Bill Skowron 1202
1961— 2B, Bobby Richardson 413
1962— 3B, Clete Boyer 187
1964— C, Elston Howard 939
1B, Joe Pepitone 1333
2B, Bobby Richardson 400
1968— 2B, Horace Clarke 357
1969— 1B, Joe Pepitone 1254
2B, Horace Clarke 373
1970— 2B, Horace Clarke 379
1971— 2B, Horace Clarke 386
1972— OF, Bobby Murcer 382
1974— 3B, Graig Nettles 147
1979— 2B, Willie Randolph 355
1986— 1B, Don Mattingly 1377
1995— OF, Bernie Williams 432
2001— C, Jorge Posada 996
2002— C, Jorge Posada 965
2B, Alfonso Soriano 300

Assists
1903— 2B, Jimmy Williams 438
1904— 2B, Jimmy Williams 465
1913— C, Ed Sweeney 180
1915— 1B, Wally Pipp 85
1916— SS, Roger Peckinpaugh 468

1917— 1B, Wally Pipp 109
3B, Frank Baker 317
1918— SS, Roger Peckinpaugh 439
1919— 2B, Del Pratt 491
SS, Roger Peckinpaugh 434
1920— 2B, Del Pratt 515
1921— OF, Bob Meusel 28
1922— 2B, Aaron Ward 489
SS, Everett Scott 538
OF, Bob Meusel 24
1923— 2B, Aaron Ward 493
1929— C, Bill Dickey 95
1930— 1B, Lou Gehrig 89
1933— OF, Ben Chapman 24
1935— OF, Ben Chapman 25
1936— OF, Joe DiMaggio 22
1937— C, Bill Dickey 80
1938— C, Bill Dickey 94
SS, Frank Crosetti 506
1939— 2B, Joe Gordon 461
1940— 2B, Joe Gordon 505
1943— 2B, Joe Gordon 490
3B, Billy Johnson 490
1944— 2B, Snuffy Stirnweiss 326
1950— C, Yogi Berra 64
1951— C, Yogi Berra 82
1952— C, Yogi Berra 73
SS, Phil Rizzuto 458
1954— OF, Mickey Mantle 20
1955— 3B, Andy Carey 301
1956— 1B, Bill Skowron 80
1961— 3B, Clete Boyer 353
1962— 3B, Clete Boyer 396
1964— 1B, Joe Pepitone 121
1965— 3B, Clete Boyer 354
1967— 2B, Horace Clarke 410
1968— 2B, Horace Clarke 444
1969— 2B, Horace Clarke 429
1970— C, Thurman Munson 80
2B, Horace Clarke 478
1971— 2B, Horace Clarke 455
1972— 2B, Horace Clarke 399
1973— C, Thurman Munson 80
3B, Graig Nettles 410
OF, Bobby Murcer 14
1974— C, Thurman Munson 75
OF, Bobby Murcer 21
1975— 3B, Graig Nettles 379
1976— 3B, Graig Nettles 383
1979— 2B, Willie Randolph 478
1982— OF, Dave Winfield 17
1990— OF, Jesse Barfield 16
1993— 3B, Wade Boggs 311
1997— SS, Derek Jeter 457
1999— 1B, Tino Martinez 706

Double Plays
1904— 2B, Jimmy Williams 52
1905— 2B, Jimmy Williams 51
1906— C, Red Kleinow 8
1909— 3B, Jimmy Austin 19
1911— 1B, Hal Chase 62
1915— 1B, Wally Pipp 85
1916— 1B, Wally Pipp 89
1917— 1B, Wally Pipp 97
SS, Roger Peckinpaugh 84
1918— C, Truck Hannah 16
2B, Del Pratt 86
SS, Roger Peckinpaugh 75
OF, Frank Gilhooley 8
1919— 3B, Frank Baker 28
1920— 1B, Wally Pipp 101
2B, Del Pratt 77
1926— C, Pat Collins 14

1929— C, Bill Dickey 13
2B, Tony Lazzeri 101
1935— OF, Ben Chapman 7
1938— 1B, Lou Gehrig 157
SS, Frank Crosetti 120
1939— 1B, Babe Dahlgren 140
2B, Joe Gordon 116
SS, Frank Crosetti 118
1940— OF, George Selkirk 6
1941— 2B, Joe Gordon 109
SS, Phil Rizzuto 109
OF, Joe DiMaggio 5
1942— 2B, Joe Gordon 121
SS, Phil Rizzuto 114
1943— 3B, Billy Johnson 32
1945— 1B, Nick Etten 149
2B, Snuffy Stirnweiss 119
3B, Oscar Grimes 35
OF, Tuck Stainback 6
1949— C, Yogi Berra 18
1950— C, Yogi Berra 16
1951— C, Yogi Berra 25
1952— C, Yogi Berra 10
SS, Phil Rizzuto 116
3B, Gil McDougald 38
OF, Mickey Mantle 5
1953— 2B, Billy Martin 121
1954— C, Yogi Berra 14
1955— 2B, Gil McDougald 119
3B, Andy Carey 37
1956— C, Yogi Berra 15
1B, Bill Skowron 138
1957— SS, Gil McDougald 104
1961— 1B, Bill Skowron 146
2B, Bobby Richardson 136
1962— 2B, Bobby Richardson 116
3B, Clete Boyer 41
1963— 2B, Bobby Richardson 105
1964— 1B, Joe Pepitone 128
1965— 2B, Bobby Richardson 121
3B, Clete Boyer 46
1967— OF, Steve Whitaker 6
1969— 2B, Horace Clarke 112
1972— 2B, Horace Clarke 104
1973— C, Thurman Munson 11
1975— C, Thurman Munson 14
1976— 3B, Graig Nettles 30
1977— OF, Roy White 4
1978— 3B, Graig Nettles 30
1979— 2B, Willie Randolph 128
1984— 2B, Willie Randolph 112
1985— 1B, Don Mattingly 154
1988— OF, Rickey Henderson 5
1989— 2B, Steve Sax 117
1991— 1B, Don Mattingly 135
1992— 3B, Charlie Hayes 29
1993— 3B, Wade Boggs 29

*Various methods have been used to determine the winner at each position for fielding average. 1903-1919: INFIELDERS, OUTFIELDERS must have played at the position in 60% of their team's games; CATCHERS in 50% of the games. 1920-1956: INFIELDERS, OUTFIELDERS must have played at the position in 100 games; CATCHERS in 90 games. 1957-2002: INFIELDERS, OUTFIELDERS must have played at the position in two-thirds of their team's games; CATCHERS in one-half of the games.

These genial guys smile sweetly now, but when Lou Gehrig, Joe DiMaggio, and Bill Dickey, (left to right), got out on the field with the Boston Red Sox, they had a different expression. A four-game series between the Yanks and Sox opened August 10, 1937, in Boston where the three Yanks are shown as they arrived.

## CHAPTER 12

REGULAR SEASON STATISTICS AND RECORDS— PLAYER AND TEAM

Mrs. Babe Ruth, widow of former New York Yankee star Babe Ruth poses with two current stars, Roger Maris, left, and Mickey Mantle on Babe Ruth League Day at Yankee Stadium August 16, 1961. This is the anniversary of Ruth's death. Both Maris and Mantle are well on their way to eclipsing Ruth's record of 60 homers in a season, set in 1927. Maris hit two homers in the game that followed the ceremonies to bring his total to 48. Mantle has 45. (AP Photo)

Roger Marls had 61 homers and the Babe Ruth belted 60. Joe hit in 56 straight games and Whitey chalked up 236 wins. Yankee statistics—some vastly more important than others, but all of them defining.

They are not just numbers; they stand for leadership (club, American League, and Major League). They stand for offensive, pitching, and defensive excellence on the part of individual players. And when they pertain to the team, they stand for collective excellence—the whole that can be even greater than its great parts.

OFFENSIVE LEADERS

Most Years on Club, Except Pitchers: 18
  YOGI BERRA (1946-63)
  MICKEY MANTLE (1951-68)

Most Games Played, Season: 162
  BOBBY RICHARDSON—1961
  ROY WHITE—1970, 1973
  CHRIS CHAMBLISS—1978
  DON MATTINGLY—1986
  ROBERTO KELLY—1990

Most Games Played, With Club: 2401
  MICKEY MANTLE (1951-68)

Most At-Bats, Season: 696
  ALFONSO SORIANO—2002

Most At-Bats, With Club: 8102
  MICKEY MANTLE (1951-68)

Most Runs Scored, Season: 177
  BABE RUTH—1921

Most Runs Scored, With Club: 1959
  BABE RUTH (1920-34)

Most Hits, Season: 238
  DON MATTINGLY—1986

Most Hits, With Club: 2721
  LOU GEHRIG (1923-39)

Most Singles, Season: 171
  STEVE SAX—1989

Most Singles, With Club: 1531
  LOU GEHRIG (1923-39)

Most Doubles, Season: 53
  DON MATTINGLY—1986

Most Doubles, With Club: 535
  LOU GEHRIG (1923-39)

Most Triples, Season: 23
  EARLE COMBS—1927

Most Triples, With Club: 162
  LOU GEHRIG (1923-39)

Most Home Runs, Right-handed Batter, Season: 46
  JOE DiMAGGIO—1937

Most Home Runs, Left-handed Batter, Season: 61
  ROGER MARIS—1961

Most Home Runs, Switch-Hitter, Season: 54
  MICKEY MANTLE—1961

Most Home Runs, Rookie Season: 29
  JOE DiMAGGIO—1936

Most Home Runs, Season, At Home: 32
  BABE RUTH—1921 (at the Polo Grounds)

Most Home Runs, Season, At Yankee Stadium: 30
  LOU GEHRIG—1934
  ROGER MARIS—1961

Most Home Runs, Season, On Road: 32
  BABE RUTH—1927

Most Home Runs, One Month, Right-handed Batter: 15
  JOE DiMAGGIO—July, 1937

Most Home Runs, One Month, Left-handed Batter: 17
  BABE RUTH—September, 1927

Most Home Runs, One Month, Switch-Hitter: 16
  MICKEY MANTLE—May, 1956

Most Home Runs, With Club, Right-handed Batter: 361
  JOE DiMAGGIO (1936-51)

Most Home Runs, With Club, Left-handed Batter: 659
  BABE RUTH (1920-34)

Most Home Runs, With Club, Switch-Hitter: 536
  MICKEY MANTLE (1951-68)

Most Grand Slam Home Runs, Season: 6
  DON MATTINGLY—1987

Most Grand Slam Home Runs, With Club: 23
  LOU GEHRIG (1923-39)

Most Total Bases, Season: 457
  BABE RUTH—1921

Most Total Bases, With Club: 5131
  BABE RUTH (1920-34)

Most Extra-Base Hits, Season: 119
  BABE RUTH—1921

Most Extra-Base Hits, With Club: 1190
  LOU GEHRIG (1923-39)

Most Sacrifice Hits, Season: 42
  WILLIE KEELER—1905

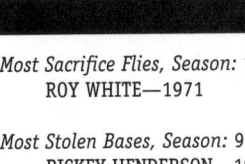

Most Sacrifice Flies, Season: 17
    ROY WHITE—1971

Most Stolen Bases, Season: 93
    RICKEY HENDERSON—1988

Most Caught Stealing, Season: 23
    BEN CHAPMAN—1931

Most Times Stealing Home, With Club: 14
    LOU GEHRIG (1923-39)

Most Stolen Bases, With Club: 326
    RICKEY HENDERSON—(1985-89)

Most Bases on Balls, Season: 170
    BABE RUTH—1923

Most Bases on Balls, With Club: 1847
    BABE RUTH (1920-34)

Most Strikeouts, Season: 157
    ALFONSO SORIANO—2002

Fewest Strikeouts, Season: 3
    JOE SEWELL—1932 (124 games)

Most Strikeouts, With Club: 1710
MICKEY MANTLE (1951-68)

Most Times Hit by a Pitched Ball, Season: 24
    DON BAYLOR—1985

Most Runs Batted In, Season: 184
    LOU GEHRIG—1931

Most Runs Batted In, With Club: 1995
    LOU GEHRIG (1923-39)

Most Consecutive Games With One or More RBIs, Season:
    11—BABE RUTH—1931 (Total—18)
    10—LOU GEHRIG—1930 (Total—27)
    10—LOU GEHRIG—1931 (Total—27)
    10—LOU GEHRIG—1934 (Total—22)
    10—GRAIG NETTLES—1974 (Total—18)
    10—REGGIE JACKSON—1979(Total—20)

Highest Batting Average, Season: .393
    BABE RUTH—1923

Highest Batting Average, With Club: .349
    BABE RUTH (1920-34)

Highest Slugging Average, Season: .847
    BABE RUTH—1920

Highest Slugging Average, With Club: .711
    BABE RUTH (1920-34)

Most Consecutive Games Batted Safely In, Season: 56
    JOE DiMAGGIO—1941

Most Times Grounded Into Double Play, Season: 30
    DAVE WINFIELD—1983

Fewest Times Grounded Into Double Play, Season: 2
    MICKEY MANTLE—1961
    MICKEY RIVERS—1977

Most Times Reaching Base on Catcher's Interference, Season: 8
    ROBERTO KELLY—1992

YANKEE CAREER LEADERS BY POSITION (1903-2002)

(At least 75 percent of the games played by the player must be at the position shown.)

Catchers

Games	Bill Dickey	1708
At-Bats	Yogi Berra	7546
Runs	Yogi Berra	1174
Hits	Yogi Berra	2148
Doubles	Bill Dickey	343
Triples	Bill Dickey	72
Home Runs	Yogi Berra	358
Runs Batted In	Yogi Berra	1430
Bases on Balls	Yogi Berra	704
Stolen Bases	Jeff Sweeney	62
BA (1500 at-bats)	Bill Dickey	.313

First Basemen

Games	Lou Gehrig	2137
At-Bats	Lou Gehrig	8001
Runs	Lou Gehrig	1888
Hits	Lou Gehrig	2721
Doubles	Lou Gehrig	535
Triples	Lou Gehrig	162
Home Runs	Lou Gehrig	493
Runs Batted In	Lou Gehrig	1991
Bases on Balls	Lou Gehrig	1508
Stolen Bases	Hal Chase	248
BA (1500 at-bats)	Lou Gehrig	.340

Second Basemen

Games	Willie Randolph	1688
At-Bats	Willie Randolph	6303
Runs	Willie Randolph	1027
Hits	Tony Lazzeri	1784
Doubles	Tony Lazzeri	327
Triples	Tony Lazzeri	115
Home Runs	Tony Lazzeri	169
Runs Batted In	Tony Lazzeri	1154
Bases on Balls	Willie Randolph	1055
Stolen Bases	Willie Randolph	251
BA (1500 at-bats)	Tony Lazzeri	.293

Third Basemen

Games	Graig Nettles	1509
At-Bats	Graig Nettles	5519
Runs	Red Rolfe	942
Hits	Graig Nettles	1396
Doubles	Red Rolfe	257
Triples	Red Rolfe	67
Home Runs	Graig Nettles	250
Runs Batted In	Graig Nettles	834
Bases on Balls	Graig Nettles	627
Stolen Bases	Fritz Maisel	183
BA (1500 at-bats)	Red Rolfe	.289

Shortstops

Games	Frank Crosetti	1647
At-Bats	Frank Crosetti	6277
Runs	Frank Crosetti	1006
Hits	Phil Rizzuto	1588
Doubles	Frank Crosetti	260
Triples	Frank Crosetti	65
Home Runs	Derek Jeter	117
Runs Batted In	Frank Crosetti	649
Bases on Balls	Frank Crosetti	792
Stolen Bases	Derek Jeter	167
BA (1500 at-bats)	Derek Jeter	.317

Outfielders

Games	Babe Ruth	2045
At-Bats	Mickey Mantle	8102
Runs	Babe Ruth	1959
Hits	Babe Ruth	2518
Doubles	Babe Ruth	424
Triples	Earle Combs	154
Home Runs	Babe Ruth	659
Runs Batted In	Babe Ruth	1970
Bases on Balls	Babe Ruth	1847
Stolen Bases	Rickey Henderson	326
BA (1500 at-bats)	Babe Ruth	.349

CLUB LEADERS YEAR BY YEAR (1903-2002)

Games Played—The first number represents the player's total; the second, in parentheses, is season's total for team.

1903	Willie Keeler	132 (136)
	Jimmy Williams	132 (136)
1904	Jimmy Williams	146 (155)
1905	Willie Keeler	149 (152)
1906	Willie Keeler	152 (155)
1907	Wid Conroy	140 (152)
1908	Charlie Hemphill	142 (155)
1909	Jimmy Austin	136 (153)
1910	Harry Wolter	135 (156)
1911	Roy Hartzell	144 (153)
1912	Bert Daniels	133 (153)
1913	Birdie Cree	145 (153)
1914	Roger Peckinpaugh	157 (157)
1915	Roger Peckinpaugh	142 (154)
1916	Wally Pipp	151 (156)
1917	Wally Pipp	155 (155)
1918	Del Pratt	126 (126)
	Frank Baker	126 (126)
1919	Frank Baker	141 (141)
	Duffy Lewis	141 (141)
1920	Del Pratt	154 (154)
1921	Wally Pipp	153 (153)
	Aaron Ward	153 (153)
1922	Everett Scott	154 (154)
	Aaron Ward	154 (154)
1923	Babe Ruth	152 (152)
	Everett Scott	152 (152)
	Aaron Ward	152 (152)
1924	Wally Pipp	153 (153)
	Babe Ruth	153 (153)
	Everett Scott	153 (153)
1925	Bob Meusel	156 (156)
1926	Lou Gehrig	155 (155)
	Tony Lazzeri	155 (155)
1927	Lou Gehrig	155 (155)
1928	Lou Gehrig	154 (154)
	Babe Ruth	154 (154)
1929	Lou Gehrig	154 (154)
1930	Lou Gehrig	154 (154)
1931	Lou Gehrig	155 (155)
	Lyn Lary	155 (155)
1932	Lou Gehrig	155 (155)
1933	Lou Gehrig	152 (152)
1934	Lou Gehrig	154 (154)
1935	Lou Gehrig	149 (149)
	Red Rolfe	149 (149)
1936	Lou Gehrig	155 (155)
1937	Lou Gehrig	157 (157)
1938	Frank Crosetti	157 (157)
	Lou Gehrig	157 (157)
1939	Frank Crosetti	152 (152)
	Red Rolfe	152 (152)
1940	Babe Dahlgren	155 (155)
	Joe Gordon	155 (155)
1941	Joe Gordon	156 (156)
1942	Joe DiMaggio	154 (154)
1943	Billy Johnson	155 (155)
1944	Nick Etten	154 (154)
	Snuffy Stirnweiss	154 (154)
1945	Nick Etten	152 (152)
	Snuffy Stirnweiss	152 (152)
1946	Tommy Henrich	150 (154)
	Charlie Keller	150 (154)
1947	Phil Rizzuto	153 (155)
1948	Joe DiMaggio	153 (154)
1949	Phil Rizzuto	153 (155)
1950	Phil Rizzuto	155 (155)
1951	Phil Rizzuto	144 (154)

Year	Player	Games
1952	Gil McDougald	152 (154)
	Phil Rizzuto	152 (154)
1953	Billy Martin	149 (151)
1954	Yogi Berra	151 (155)
1955	Yogi Berra	147 (154)
	Mickey Mantle	147 (154)
1956	Mickey Mantle	150 (154)
1957	Mickey Mantle	144 (154)
1958	Mickey Mantle	150 (155)
1959	Mickey Mantle	144 (155)
1960	Mickey Mantle	153 (155)
1961	Bobby Richardson	162 (163)
1962	Bobby Richardson	161 (162)
1963	Joe Pepitone	157 (161)
1964	Joe Pepitone	160 (164)
1965	Bobby Richardson	160 (162)
1966	Joe Pepitone	152 (160)
1967	Mickey Mantle	144 (163)
1968	Roy White	159 (164)
1969	Horace Clarke	156 (162)
1970	Roy White	162 (163)
1971	Horace Clarke	159 (162)
1972	Roy White	155 (155)
1973	Roy White	162 (162)
1974	Bobby Murcer	156 (162)
1975	Thurman Munson	157 (160)
	Graig Nettles	157 (160)
1976	Graig Nettles	158 (159)
1977	Bucky Dent	158 (162)
	Graig Nettles	158 (162)
1978	Chris Chambliss	162 (163)
1979	Willie Randolph	153 (160)
1980	Rick Cerone	147 (162)
1981	Dave Winfield	105 (107)
1982	Willie Randolph	144 (162)
1983	Dave Winfield	152 (162)
1984	Don Mattingly	153 (162)
1985	Don Mattingly	159 (161)
1986	Don Mattingly	162 (162)
1987	Dave Winfield	156 (162)
1988	Jack Clark	150 (161)
1989	Don Mattingly	158 (161)
	Steve Sax	158 (161)
1990	Roberto Kelly	162 (162)
1991	Steve Sax	158 (162)
1992	Don Mattingly	157 (162)
1993	Wade Boggs	143 (162)
1994	Bernie Williams	108 (113)
1995	Bernie Williams	144 (145)
1996	Derek Jeter	157 (162)
1997	Derek Jeter	159 (162)
1998	Scott Brosius	152 (162)
	Paul O'Neill	152 (162)
1999	Tino Martinez	159 (162)
2000	Tino Martinez	155 (161)
2001	Alfonso Soriano	158 (160)
2002	Derek Jeter	157 (161)

At-Bats

Year	Player	AB
1903	Willie Keeler	515
1904	Jimmy Williams	559
1905	Willie Keeler	560
1906	Hal Chase	597
1907	Wid Conroy	530
1908	Wid Conroy	531
1909	Clyde Engle	492
1910	Hal Chase	524
1911	Hal Chase	527
	Roy Hartzell	527
1912	Hal Chase	522
1913	Birdie Cree	534
1914	Roger Peckinpaugh	570
1915	Roger Peckinpaugh	540
1916	Roger Peckinpaugh	552
1917	Wally Pipp	587

*AL leader

Year	Player	AB
1918	Frank Baker	504
1919	Frank Baker	567
1920	Wally Pipp	610
1921	Bob Meusel	598
1922	Wally Pipp	577
1923	Joe Dugan	644*
1924	Joe Dugan	610
1925	Bob Meusel	624
1926	Mark Koenig	617
1927	Earle Combs	648*
1928	Earle Combs	626
1929	Earle Combs	586
1930	Lou Gehrig	581
1931	Lou Gehrig	619
1932	Lou Gehrig	596
1933	Lou Gehrig	593
1934	Ben Chapman	588
1935	Red Rolfe	639
1936	Joe DiMaggio	637
1937	Red Rolfe	648
1938	Frank Crosetti	631
	Red Rolfe	631
1939	Frank Crosetti	656*
1940	Joe Gordon	616
1941	Joe Gordon	588
1942	Joe DiMaggio	610
1943	Billy Johnson	592
1944	Snuffy Stirnweiss	643
1945	Snuffy Stirnweiss	632*
1946	Tommy Henrich	565
1947	Snuffy Stirnweiss	571
1948	Joe DiMaggio	594
1949	Phil Rizzuto	614
1950	Phil Rizzuto	617
1951	Yogi Berra	547
1952	Phil Rizzuto	578
1953	Billy Martin	587
1954	Yogi Berra	584
1955	Yogi Berra	541
1956	Hank Bauer	539
1957	Gil McDougald	539
1958	Tony Kubek	559
1959	Mickey Mantle	541
1960	Tony Kubek	568
1961	Bobby Richardson	662
1962	Bobby Richardson	692*
1963	Bobby Richardson	630*
1964	Bobby Richardson	679*
1965	Bobby Richardson	664
1966	Bobby Richardson	610
1967	Horace Clarke	588
1968	Horace Clarke	579
1969	Horace Clarke	641*
1970	Horace Clarke	686*
1971	Horace Clarke	625
1972	Bobby Murcer	585
1973	Roy White	639*
1974	Bobby Murcer	606
1975	Thurman Munson	597
1976	Chris Chambliss	641
1977	Chris Chambliss	600
1978	Chris Chambliss	625
1979	Willie Randolph	574
1980	Rick Cerone	519
1981	Dave Winfield	388
1982	Willie Randolph	553
1983	Dave Winfield	598
1984	Don Mattingly	603
1985	Don Mattingly	652
1986	Don Mattingly	677
1987	Dave Winfield	575
1988	Don Mattingly	599
1989	Steve Sax	651*
1990	Roberto Kelly	641
1991	Steve Sax	652
1992	Don Mattingly	640
1993	Bernie Williams	567

Year	Player	AB
1994	Bernie Williams	408
1995	Bernie Williams	563
1996	Tino Martinez	595
1997	Derek Jeter	654
1998	Derek Jeter	626
1999	Derek Jeter	627
2000	Derek Jeter	593
2001	Derek Jeter	614
2002	Alfonso Soriano	696*

Runs Scored

Year	Player	R
1903	Willie Keeler	95
1904	Patsy Dougherty	80
1905	Willie Keeler	81
1906	Willie Keeler	96
1907	Danny Hoffman	81
1908	Charlie Hemphill	62
1909	Ray Demmitt	68
1910	Bert Daniels	68
1911	Birdie Cree	90
1912	Bert Daniels	72
1913	Roy Hartzell	60
1914	Fritz Maisel	78
1915	Fritz Maisel	77
1916	Wally Pipp	70
1917	Wally Pipp	82
1918	Frank Baker	65
	Del Pratt	65
1919	Roger Peckinpaugh	89
1920	Babe Ruth	158*
1921	Babe Ruth	177*
1922	Whitey Witt	98
1923	Babe Ruth	151*
1924	Babe Ruth	143*
1925	Earle Combs	117
1926	Babe Ruth	139*
1927	Babe Ruth	158*
1928	Babe Ruth	163*
1929	Lou Gehrig	127
1930	Babe Ruth	150
1931	Lou Gehrig	163*
1932	Earle Combs	143
1933	Lou Gehrig	138*
1934	Lou Gehrig	128
1935	Lou Gehrig	125*
1936	Lou Gehrig	167*
1937	Joe DiMaggio	151*
1938	Red Rolfe	132
1939	Red Rolfe	139*
1940	Joe Gordon	112
1941	Joe DiMaggio	122
1942	Joe DiMaggio	123
1943	Charlie Keller	97
1944	Snuffy Stirnweiss	125*
1945	Snuffy Stirnweiss	107*
1946	Charlie Keller	98
1947	Tommy Henrich	109
1948	Tommy Henrich	138*
1949	Phil Rizzuto	110
1950	Phil Rizzuto	125
1951	Yogi Berra	92
1952	Yogi Berra	97
1953	Mickey Mantle	105
1954	Mickey Mantle	129*
1955	Mickey Mantle	121
1956	Mickey Mantle	132*
1957	Mickey Mantle	121*
1958	Mickey Mantle	127*
1959	Mickey Mantle	104
1960	Mickey Mantle	119*
1961	Mickey Mantle	132*
	Roger Maris	132*
1962	Bobby Richardson	99
1963	Tom Tresh	91
1964	Mickey Mantle	92
1965	Tom Tresh	94
1966	Joe Pepitone	85

Year	Player	
1967	Horace Clarke	74
1968	Roy White	89
1969	Horace Clarke	82
	Bobby Murcer	82
1970	Roy White	109
1971	Bobby Murcer	94
1972	Bobby Murcer	102*
1973	Roy White	88
1974	Elliott Maddox	75
1975	Bobby Bonds	93
1976	Roy White	104*
1977	Graig Nettles	99
1978	Willie Randolph	87
1979	Willie Randolph	98
1980	Willie Randolph	99
1981	Willie Randolph	59
1982	Willie Randolph	85
1983	Dave Winfield	99
1984	Dave Winfield	106
1985	Rickey Henderson	146*
1986	Rickey Henderson	130*
1987	Willie Randolph	96
1988	Rickey Henderson	118
1989	Steve Sax	88
1990	Roberto Kelly	85
1991	Steve Sax	85
1992	Don Mattingly	86
1993	Danny Tartabull	87
1994	Bernie Williams	80
1995	Bernie Williams	93
1996	Bernie Williams	108
1997	Derek Jeter	116
1998	Derek Jeter	127
1999	Derek Jeter	134*
2000	Derek Jeter	119
2001	Derek Jeter	110
2002	Alfonso Soriano	128*

Hits

Year	Player	
1903	Willie Keeler	164
1904	Willie Keeler	186
1905	Willie Keeler	169
1906	Hal Chase	193
1907	Hal Chase	143
1908	Charlie Hemphill	150
1909	Clyde Engle	137
1910	Hal Chase	152
1911	Birdie Cree	181
1912	Hal Chase	143
1913	Birdie Cree	145
1914	Doc Cook	133
1915	Fritz Maisel	149
1916	Wally Pipp	143
1917	Frank Baker	156
1918	Frank Baker	154
1919	Frank Baker	166
1920	Del Pratt	180
1921	Babe Ruth	204
1922	Wally Pipp	190
1923	Babe Ruth	205
1924	Babe Ruth	200
1925	Earle Combs	203
1926	Babe Ruth	184
1927	Earle Combs	231*
1928	Lou Gehrig	210
1929	Earle Combs	202
1930	Lou Gehrig	220
1931	Lou Gehrig	211*
1932	Lou Gehrig	208
1933	Lou Gehrig	198
1934	Lou Gehrig	210
1935	Red Rolfe	192
1936	Joe DiMaggio	206
1937	Joe DiMaggio	215
1938	Red Rolfe	196
1939	Red Rolfe	213*
1940	Joe DiMaggio	179
1941	Joe DiMaggio	193
1942	Joe DiMaggio	186
1943	Billy Johnson	166
1944	Snuffy Stirnweiss	205*
1945	Snuffy Stirnweiss	195*
1946	Charlie Keller	148
1947	Joe DiMaggio	168
1948	Joe DiMaggio	190
1949	Phil Rizzuto	169
1950	Phil Rizzuto	200
1951	Yogi Berra	161
1952	Mickey Mantle	171
1953	Gil McDougald	154
1954	Yogi Berra	179
1955	Mickey Mantle	158
1956	Mickey Mantle	188
1957	Mickey Mantle	173
1958	Mickey Mantle	158
1959	Mickey Mantle	154
1960	Bill Skowron	166
1961	Bobby Richardson	173
1962	Bobby Richardson	209*
1963	Bobby Richardson	167
1964	Bobby Richardson	181
1965	Tom Tresh	168
1966	Bobby Richardson	153
1967	Horace Clarke	160
1968	Roy White	154
1969	Horace Clarke	183
1970	Roy White	180
1971	Bobby Murcer	175
1972	Bobby Murcer	171
1973	Bobby Murcer	187
1974	Bobby Murcer	166
1975	Thurman Munson	190
1976	Chris Chambliss	188
1977	Mickey Rivers	184
1978	Thurman Munson	183
1979	Chris Chambliss	155
	Willie Randolph	155
1980	Reggie Jackson	154
1981	Dave Winfield	114
1982	Willie Randolph	155
1983	Dave Winfield	169
1984	Don Mattingly	207*
1985	Don Mattingly	211
1986	Don Mattingly	238*
1987	Don Mattingly	186
1988	Don Mattingly	186
1989	Steve Sax	205
1990	Roberto Kelly	183
1991	Steve Sax	198
1992	Don Mattingly	184
1993	Wade Boggs	169
1994	Paul O'Neill	132
1995	Bernie Williams	173
1996	Derek Jeter	183
1997	Derek Jeter	190
1998	Derek Jeter	203
1999	Derek Jeter	219*
2000	Derek Jeter	201
2001	Derek Jeter	191
2002	Alfonso Soriano	209*

Doubles

Year	Player	
1903	Jimmy Williams	30
1904	Jimmy Williams	31
1905	Jimmy Williams	20
1906	Jimmy Williams	25
1907	Hal Chase	23
1908	Wid Conroy	22
1909	Clyde Engle	20
1910	Jack Knight	25
1911	Hal Chase	32
1912	Bert Daniels	25
1913	Birdie Cree	25
1914	Fritz Maisel	23
1915	Wally Pipp	20
1916	Frank Baker	23
1917	Wally Pipp	29
1918	Frank Baker	24
1919	Ping Bodie	27
	Del Pratt	27
1920	Bob Meusel	40
1921	Babe Ruth	44
1922	Wally Pipp	32
1923	Babe Ruth	45
1924	Bob Meusel	40
1925	Earle Combs	36
1926	Lou Gehrig	47
1927	Lou Gehrig	52*
1928	Lou Gehrig	47*
1929	Tony Lazzeri	37
1930	Lou Gehrig	42
1931	Lyn Lary	35
1932	Lou Gehrig	42
1933	Lou Gehrig	41
1934	Lou Gehrig	40
1935	Ben Chapman	38
1936	Joe DiMaggio	44
1937	Lou Gehrig	37
1938	Red Rolfe	36
1939	Red Rolfe	46*
1940	Joe Gordon	32
1941	Joe DiMaggio	43
1942	Tommy Henrich	30
1943	Nick Etten	35
1944	Snuffy Stirnweiss	35
1945	Snuffy Stirnweiss	32
1946	Charlie Keller	29
1947	Tommy Henrich	35
1948	Tommy Henrich	42
1949	Phil Rizzuto	22
1950	Phil Rizzuto	36
1951	Gil McDougald	23
1952	Mickey Mantle	37
1953	Gil McDougald	27
1954	Yogi Berra	28
1955	Mickey Mantle	25
1956	Yogi Berra	29
1957	Mickey Mantle	28
1958	Hank Bauer	22
	Bill Skowron	22
1959	Yogi Berra	25
	Tony Kubek	25
1960	Bill Skowron	34
1961	Tony Kubek	38
1962	Bobby Richardson	38
1963	Tom Tresh	28
1964	Elston Howard	27
1965	Tom Tresh	29
1966	Clete Boyer	22
1967	Tom Tresh	23
1968	Roy White	20
1969	Roy White	30
1970	Roy White	30
1971	Bobby Murcer	25
1972	Bobby Murcer	30
1973	Thurman Munson	29
	Bobby Murcer	29
1974	Elliott Maddox	26
	Lou Piniella	26
1975	Chris Chambliss	38
1976	Chris Chambliss	32
1977	Reggie Jackson	39
1978	Lou Piniella	34
1979	Chris Chambliss	27
1980	Rick Cerone	30
1981	Dave Winfield	25
1982	Jerry Mumphrey	24
	Dave Winfield	24
1983	Don Baylor	33

*AL leader

Year	Player	
1984	Don Mattingly	44*
1985	Don Mattingly	48*
1986	Don Mattingly	53*
1987	Don Mattingly	38
1988	Dave Winfield	37
1989	Don Mattingly	37
1990	Roberto Kelly	32
1991	Steve Sax	38
1992	Don Mattingly	40
1993	Paul O'Neill	34
1994	Bernie Williams	29
1995	Don Mattingly	32
1996	Paul O'Neill	35
1997	Paul O'Neill	42
1998	Paul O'Neill	40
1999	Paul O'Neill	39
2000	Tino Martinez	37
	Bernie Williams	37
2001	Bernie Williams	38
2002	Alfonso Soriano	51

Triples

Year	Player	
1903	Wid Conroy	12
	Jimmy Williams	12
1904	John Anderson	12
	Wid Conroy	12
1905	Wid Conroy	11
1906	Hal Chase	10
	Wid Conroy	10
1907	Wid Conroy	11
	Frank LaPorte	11
	Jimmy Williams	11
1908	Charlie Hemphill	9
1909	Ray Demmitt	12
1910	Birdie Cree	16
1911	Birdie Cree	22
1912	Bert Daniels	11
	Roy Hartzell	11
1913	Roger Peckinpaugh	7
1914	Roy Hartzell	9
	Fritz Maisel	9
1915	Wally Pipp	13
1916	Wally Pipp	14
1917	Wally Pipp	12
1918	Wally Pipp	9
1919	Wally Pipp	10
1920	Wally Pipp	14
1921	Bob Meusel	16
	Babe Ruth	16
1922	Bob Meusel	11
1923	Babe Ruth	13
1924	Wally Pipp	19*
1925	Earle Combs	13
1926	Lou Gehrig	20*
1927	Earle Combs	23*
1928	Earle Combs	21*
1929	Earle Combs	15
1930	Earle Combs	22*
1931	Lou Gehrig	15
1932	Tony Lazzeri	16
1933	Earle Combs	16
1934	Ben Chapman	13*
1935	George Selkirk	12
1936	Joe DiMaggio	15*
	Red Rolfe	15*
1937	Joe DiMaggio	15
1938	Joe DiMaggio	13
1939	Red Rolfe	10
1940	Charlie Keller	15
1941	Joe DiMaggio	11
1942	Joe DiMaggio	13
1943	Johnny Lindell	12*
1944	Johnny Lindell	16*
	Snuffy Stirnweiss	16*
1945	Snuffy Stirnweiss	22*

*AL leader

Year	Player	
1946	Charlie Keller	10
1947	Tommy Henrich	13*
1948	Tommy Henrich	14*
1949	Phil Rizzuto	7
	Gene Woodling	7
1950	Joe DiMaggio	10
	Gene Woodling	10
1951	Gene Woodling	8
1952	Phil Rizzuto	10
1953	Gil McDougald	7
1954	Mickey Mantle	12
1955	Andy Carey	11*
	Mickey Mantle	11*
1956	Hank Bauer	7
1957	Hank Bauer	9*
	Gil McDougald	9*
1958	Hank Bauer	6
1959	Gil McDougald	8
1960	Roger Maris	7
1961	Tony Kubek	6
	Mickey Mantle	6
1962	Bill Skowron	6
1963	Elston Howard	6
	Bobby Richardson	6
1964	Clete Boyer	5
	Tom Tresh	5
1965	Clete Boyer	6
	Tom Tresh	6
1966	Clete Boyer	4
	Horace Clarke	4
	Joe Pepitone	4
	Tom Tresh	4
1967	Joe Pepitone	3
	Charley Smith	3
	Tom Tresh	3
	Steve Whitaker	3
1968	Bill Robinson	7
	Roy White	7
1969	Horace Clarke	7
1970	Jerry Kenney	7
1971	Horace Clarke	7
	Roy White	7
1972	Bobby Murcer	7
1973	Thurman Munson	4
1974	Roy White	8
1975	Roy White	5
1976	Mickey Rivers	8
1977	Willie Randolph	11
1978	Mickey Rivers	8
1979	Willie Randolph	13
1980	Willie Randolph	7
1981	Jerry Mumphrey	5
1982	Jerry Mumphrey	10
1983	Dave Winfield	8
1984	Omar Moreno	6
1985	Dave Winfield	6
1986	Rickey Henderson	5
	Dave Winfield	5
1987	Rickey Henderson	3
	Mike Pagliarulo	3
1988	Claudell Washington	3
1989	Roberto Kelly	3
	Steve Sax	3
	Don Slaught	3
1990	Roberto Kelly	4
1991	Pat Kelly	4
	Bernie Williams	4
1992	Mel Hall	3
1993	Bernie Williams	4
1994	Luis Polonia	6
1995	Bernie Williams	9
1996	Bernie Williams	7
1997	Derek Jeter	7
1998	Derek Jeter	8
1999	Derek Jeter	9
2000	Bernie Williams	6

Year	Player	
2001	Derek Jeter	3
	Chuck Knoblauch	3
	Alfonso Soriano	3
2002	Alfonso Soriano	2
	Shane Spencer	2
	Bernie Williams	2
	Enrique Wilson	2

Home Runs

Year	Player	
1903	Herm McFarland	5
1904	John Ganzel	6
1905	Jimmy Williams	6
1906	Wid Conroy	4
1907	Danny Hoffman	4
1908	Harry Niles	4
1909	Hal Chase	4
	Ray Demmitt	4
1910	Birdie Cree	4
	Harry Wolter	4
1911	Birdie Cree	4
	Harry Wolter	4
1912	Guy Zinn	6
1913	Jeff Sweeney	2
	Harry Wolter	2
1914	Roger Peckinpaugh	3
1915	Luke Boone	5
	Roger Peckinpaugh	5
1916	Wally Pipp	12*
1917	Wally Pipp	9*
1918	Frank Baker	6
1919	Frank Baker	10
1920	Babe Ruth	54*
1921	Babe Ruth	59*
1922	Babe Ruth	35
1923	Babe Ruth	41*
1924	Babe Ruth	46*
1925	Bob Meusel	33*
1926	Babe Ruth	47*
1927	Babe Ruth	60*
1928	Babe Ruth	54*
1929	Babe Ruth	46*
1930	Babe Ruth	49*
1931	Lou Gehrig	46*
	Babe Ruth	46*
1932	Babe Ruth	41
1933	Babe Ruth	34
1934	Lou Gehrig	49*
1935	Lou Gehrig	30
1936	Lou Gehrig	49*
1937	Joe DiMaggio	46*
1938	Joe DiMaggio	32
1939	Joe DiMaggio	30
1940	Joe DiMaggio	31
1941	Charlie Keller	33
1942	Charlie Keller	26
1943	Charlie Keller	31
1944	Nick Etten	22*
1945	Nick Etten	18
1946	Charlie Keller	30
1947	Joe DiMaggio	20
1948	Joe DiMaggio	39*
1949	Tommy Henrich	24
1950	Joe DiMaggio	32
1951	Yogi Berra	27
1952	Yogi Berra	30
1953	Yogi Berra	27
1954	Mickey Mantle	27
1955	Mickey Mantle	37*
1956	Mickey Mantle	52*
1957	Mickey Mantle	34
1958	Mickey Mantle	42*
1959	Mickey Mantle	31
1960	Mickey Mantle	40*
1961	Roger Maris	61*
1962	Roger Maris	33
1963	Elston Howard	28
1964	Mickey Mantle	35

Year	Player	
1965	Tom Tresh	26
1966	Joe Pepitone	31
1967	Mickey Mantle	22
1968	Mickey Mantle	18
1969	Joe Pepitone	27
1970	Bobby Murcer	23
1971	Bobby Murcer	25
1972	Bobby Murcer	33
1973	Bobby Murcer	22
	Graig Nettles	22
1974	Graig Nettles	22
1975	Bobby Bonds	32
1976	Graig Nettles	32*
1977	Graig Nettles	37
1978	Reggie Jackson	27
	Graig Nettles	27
1979	Reggie Jackson	29
1980	Reggie Jackson	41*
1981	Reggie Jackson	15
	Graig Nettles	15
1982	Dave Winfield	37
1983	Dave Winfield	32
1984	Don Baylor	27
1985	Don Mattingly	35
1986	Don Mattingly	31
1987	Mike Pagliarulo	32
1988	Jack Clark	27
1989	Don Mattingly	23
1990	Jesse Barfield	25
1991	Matt Nokes	24
1992	Danny Tartabull	25
1993	Danny Tartabull	31
1994	Paul O'Neill	21
1995	Paul O'Neill	22
1996	Bernie Williams	29
1997	Tino Martinez	44
1998	Tino Martinez	28
1999	Tino Martinez	28
2000	Bernie Williams	30
2001	Tino Martinez	34
2002	Jason Giambi	41

Runs Batted In

Year	Player	
1903	Jimmy Williams	82
1904	John Anderson	82
1905	Jimmy Williams	60
1906	Jimmy Williams	77
1907	Hal Chase	68
1908	Charlie Hemphill	44
1909	Clyde Engle	71
1910	Hal Chase	73
	Birdie Cree	73
1911	Roy Hartzell	91
1912	Hal Chase	58
1913	Birdie Cree	63
1914	Roger Peckinpaugh	51
1915	Roy Hartzell	60
	Wally Pipp	60
1916	Wally Pipp	93
1917	Frank Baker	71
1918	Frank Baker	68
1919	Duffy Lewis	89
1920	Babe Ruth	137*
1921	Babe Ruth	171*
1922	Babe Ruth	99
1923	Babe Ruth	131*
1924	Babe Ruth	121
1925	Bob Meusel	138*
1926	Babe Ruth	145*
1927	Lou Gehrig	175*
1928	Lou Gehrig	142*
	Babe Ruth	142*
1929	Babe Ruth	154
1930	Lou Gehrig	174*
1931	Lou Gehrig	184*

*AL leader

Year	Player	
1932	Lou Gehrig	151
1933	Lou Gehrig	139
1934	Lou Gehrig	165*
1935	Lou Gehrig	119
1936	Lou Gehrig	152
1937	Joe DiMaggio	167
1938	Joe DiMaggio	140
1939	Joe DiMaggio	126
1940	Joe DiMaggio	133
1941	Joe DiMaggio	125*
1942	Joe DiMaggio	114
1943	Nick Etten	107
1944	Johnny Lindell	103
1945	Nick Etten	111*
1946	Charlie Keller	101
1947	Tommy Henrich	98
1948	Joe DiMaggio	155*
1949	Yogi Berra	91
1950	Yogi Berra	124
1951	Yogi Berra	88
1952	Yogi Berra	98
1953	Yogi Berra	108
1954	Yogi Berra	125
1955	Yogi Berra	108
1956	Mickey Mantle	130*
1957	Mickey Mantle	94
1958	Mickey Mantle	97
1959	Mickey Mantle	75
1960	Roger Maris	112*
1961	Roger Maris	142*
1962	Roger Maris	100
1963	Joe Pepitone	89
1964	Mickey Mantle	111
1965	Tom Tresh	74
1966	Joe Pepitone	83
1967	Joe Pepitone	64
1968	Roy White	62
1969	Bobby Murcer	82
1970	Roy White	94
1971	Bobby Murcer	94
1972	Bobby Murcer	96
1973	Bobby Murcer	95
1974	Bobby Murcer	88
1975	Thurman Munson	102
1976	Thurman Munson	105
1977	Reggie Jackson	110
1978	Reggie Jackson	97
1979	Reggie Jackson	89
1980	Reggie Jackson	111
1981	Dave Winfield	68
1982	Dave Winfield	106
1983	Dave Winfield	116
1984	Don Mattingly	110
1985	Don Mattingly	145*
1986	Don Mattingly	113
1987	Don Mattingly	115
1988	Dave Winfield	107
1989	Don Mattingly	113
1990	Jesse Barfield	78
1991	Mel Hall	80
1992	Don Mattingly	86
1993	Danny Tartabull	102
1994	Paul O'Neill	83
1995	Paul O'Neill	96
1996	Tino Martinez	117
1997	Tino Martinez	141
1998	Tino Martinez	123
1999	Bernie Williams	115
2000	Bernie Williams	121
2001	Tino Martinez	113
2002	Jason Giambi	122

Bases on Balls

Year	Player	
1903	Herm McFarland	46
1904	Wid Conroy	43
1905	Jimmy Williams	50
1906	Wid Conroy	47
1907	Danny Hoffman	42
1908	Charlie Hemphill	59
1909	Ray Demmitt	55
1910	Harry Wolter	66
1911	Roy Hartzell	63
1912	Roy Hartzell	64
1913	Harry Wolter	80
1914	Fritz Maisel	76
1915	Wally Pipp	66
1916	Roger Peckinpaugh	62
1917	Roger Peckinpaugh	64
1918	Frank Gilhooley	53
1919	Roger Peckinpaugh	59
1920	Babe Ruth	148*
1921	Babe Ruth	144*
1922	Whitey Witt	89*
1923	Babe Ruth	170*
1924	Babe Ruth	142*
1925	Earle Combs	65
1926	Babe Ruth	144*
1927	Babe Ruth	138*
1928	Babe Ruth	135*
1929	Lou Gehrig	122
1930	Babe Ruth	136*
1931	Babe Ruth	128*
1932	Babe Ruth	130*
1933	Babe Ruth	114*
1934	Lou Gehrig	109
1935	Lou Gehrig	132*
1936	Lou Gehrig	130*
1937	Lou Gehrig	127*
1938	Lou Gehrig	107
1939	George Selkirk	103
1940	Charlie Keller	106*
1941	Charlie Keller	102
1942	Charlie Keller	114
1943	Charlie Keller	106*
1944	Nick Etten	97*
1945	Oscar Grimes	97
1946	Charlie Keller	113
1947	Snuffy Stirnweiss	89
1948	Snuffy Stirnweiss	86
1949	Tommy Henrich	86
1950	Phil Rizzuto	91
1951	Gene Woodling	62
1952	Mickey Mantle	75
1953	Gene Woodling	82
1954	Mickey Mantle	102
1955	Mickey Mantle	113*
1956	Mickey Mantle	112
1957	Mickey Mantle	146*
1958	Mickey Mantle	129*
1959	Mickey Mantle	94
1960	Mickey Mantle	111
1961	Mickey Mantle	126*
1962	Mickey Mantle	122*
1963	Tom Tresh	83
1964	Mickey Mantle	99
1965	Mickey Mantle	73
1966	Tom Tresh	86
1967	Mickey Mantle	107
1968	Mickey Mantle	106
1969	Roy White	81
1970	Roy White	95
1971	Bobby Murcer	91
1972	Roy White	99*
1973	Graig Nettles	78
	Roy White	78
1974	Elliott Maddox	69
1975	Bobby Bonds	89
1976	Roy White	83
1977	Roy White	75
1978	Willie Randolph	82
1979	Willie Randolph	95
1980	Willie Randolph	119*
1981	Willie Randolph	57
1982	Willie Randolph	75

1983	Roy Smalley	58
	Dave Winfield	58
1984	Willie Randolph	86
1985	Rickey Henderson	99
1986	Willie Randolph	94
1987	Willie Randolph	82
1988	Jack Clark	113
1989	Jesse Barfield	82
1990	Jesse Barfield	82
1991	Kevin Maas	83
1992	Danny Tartabull	103
1993	Danny Tartabull	92
1994	Paul O'Neill	72
1995	Bernie Williams	75
1996	Paul O'Neill	102
1997	Tino Martinez	75
	Paul O'Neill	75
1998	Chuck Noblauch	76
1999	Bernie Williams	100
2000	Jorge Posada	107
2001	Bernie Williams	78
2002	Jason Giambi	109

Stolen Bases

1903	Wid Conroy	33
1904	Wid Conroy	30
1905	Dave Fultz	44
1906	Danny Hoffman	32
1907	Wid Conroy	41
1908	Charlie Hemphill	42
1909	Jimmy Austin	30
1910	Bert Daniels	41
1911	Birdie Cree	48
1912	Bert Daniels	37
1913	Bert Daniels	27
1914	Fritz Maisel	74*
1915	Fritz Maisel	51
1916	Lee Magee	29
1917	Fritz Maisel	29
1918	Roger Peckinpaugh	12
	Del Pratt	12
1919	Del Pratt	22
1920	Babe Ruth	14
1921	Bob Meusel	17
	Wally Pipp	17
	Babe Ruth	17
1922	Bob Meusel	13
1923	Babe Ruth	17
1924	Bob Meusel	26
1925	Ben Paschal	14
1926	Tony Lazzeri	16
	Bob Meusel	16
1927	Bob Meusel	24
1928	Tony Lazzeri	15
1929	Earle Combs	11
1930	Earle Combs	16*
1931	Ben Chapman	61*
1932	Ben Chapman	38*
1933	Ben Chapman	27*
1934	Ben Chapman	26
1935	Ben Chapman	17
1936	Frank Crosetti	18
1937	Frank Crosetti	13
1938	Frank Crosetti	27*
1939	George Selkirk	12
1940	Joe Gordon	18
1941	Phil Rizzuto	14
1942	Phil Rizzuto	22
1943	Snuffy Stirnweiss	11
1944	Snuffy Stirnweiss	55*
1945	Snuffy Stirnweiss	33*
1946	Snuffy Stirnweiss	18
1947	Phil Rizzuto	11
1948	Phil Rizzuto	6
1949	Phil Rizzuto	18

1950	Phil Rizzuto	12
1951	Phil Rizzuto	18
1952	Phil Rizzuto	17
1953	Mickey Mantle	8
1954	Andy Carey	5
	Mickey Mantle	5
1955	Billy Hunter	9
1956	Mickey Mantle	10
1957	Mickey Mantle	16
1958	Mickey Mantle	18
1959	Mickey Mantle	21
1960	Mickey Mantle	14
1961	Mickey Mantle	12
1962	Bobby Richardson	11
1963	Bobby Richardson	15
1964	Tom Tresh	13
1965	Bobby Richardson	7
1966	Roy White	14
1967	Horace Clarke	21
1968	Horace Clarke	20
	Roy White	20
1969	Horace Clarke	33
1970	Roy White	24
1971	Horace Clarke	17
1972	Roy White	23
1973	Roy White	16
1974	Roy White	15
1975	Bobby Bonds	30
1976	Mickey Rivers	43
1977	Mickey Rivers	22
1978	Willie Randolph	36
1979	Willie Randolph	33
1980	Willie Randolph	30
1981	Willie Randolph	14
1982	Willie Randolph	16
1983	Don Baylor	17
1984	Omar Moreno	20
1985	Rickey Henderson	80*
1986	Rickey Henderson	87*
1987	Rickey Henderson	41
1988	Rickey Henderson	93*
1989	Steve Sax	43
1990	Steve Sax	43
1991	Roberto Kelly	32
1992	Roberto Kelly	28
1993	Pat Kelly	14
1994	Luis Polonia	20
1995	Luis Polonia	10
1996	Bernie Williams	17
1997	Derek Jeter	23
1998	Chuck Knoblauch	31
1999	Chuck knoblauch	28
2000	Derek Jeter	22
2001	Alfonso Soriano	43
2002	Alfonso Soriano	41*

Batting Average (at least 350 at-bats)

1903	Willie Keeler	.318
1904	Willie Keeler	.343
1905	Willie Keeler	.302
1906	Hal Chase	.323
1907	Hal Chase	.287
1908	Charlie Hemphill	.297
1909	Hal Chase	.283
1910	Jack Knight	.312
1911	Birdie Cree	.348
1912	Hal Chase	.274
	Bert Daniels	.274
1913	Birdie Cree	.272
1914	Doc Cook	.283
1915	Fritz Maisel	.281
1916	Frank Baker	.269
1917	Frank Baker	.282
1918	Frank Baker	.306

1919	Roger Peckinpaugh	.305
1920	Babe Ruth	.376
1921	Babe Ruth	.378
1922	Wally Pipp	.329
1923	Babe Ruth	.393
1924	Babe Ruth	.378*
1925	Earle Combs	.342
1926	Babe Ruth	.372
1927	Lou Gehrig	.373
1928	Lou Gehrig	.374
1929	Tony Lazzeri	.354
1930	Lou Gehrig	.379
1931	Babe Ruth	.373
1932	Lou Gehrig	.349
1933	Lou Gehrig	.334
1934	Lou Gehrig	.363*
1935	Lou Gehrig	.329
1936	Bill Dickey	.362
1937	Lou Gehrig	.351
1938	Joe DiMaggio	.324
1939	Joe DiMaggio	.381*
1940	Joe DiMaggio	.352*
1941	Joe DiMaggio	.357
1942	Joe Gordon	.322
1943	Billy Johnson	.280
1944	Snuffy Stirnweiss	.319
1945	Snuffy Stirnweiss	.309*
1946	Joe DiMaggio	.290
1947	Joe DiMaggio	.315
1948	Joe DiMaggio	.320
1949	Tommy Henrich	.287
1950	Phil Rizzuto	.324
1951	Gil McDougald	.306
1952	Mickey Mantle	.311
1953	Gene Woodling	.306
1954	Irv Noren	.319
1955	Mickey Mantle	.306
1956	Mickey Mantle	.353*
1957	Mickey Mantle	.365
1958	Elston Howard	.314
1959	Bobby Richardson	.301
1960	Bill Skowron	.309
1961	Elston Howard	.348
1962	Mickey Mantle	.321
1963	Elston Howard	.287
1964	Elston Howard	.313
1965	Tom Tresh	.279
1966	Elston Howard	.256
1967	Horace Clarke	.272
1968	Roy White	.267
1969	Roy White	.290
1970	Thurman Munson	.302
1971	Bobby Murcer	.331
1972	Bobby Murcer	.292
1973	Bobby Murcer	.304
1974	Lou Piniella	.305
1975	Thurman Munson	.318
1976	Mickey Rivers	.312
1977	Mickey Rivers	.326
1978	Lou Piniella	.314
1979	Reggie Jackson	.297
	Lou Piniella	.297
1980	Bob Watson	.307
1981	Jerry Mumphrey (319 at-bats)	.307
1982	Jerry Mumphrey	.300
1983	Don Baylor	.303
1984	Don Mattingly	.343*
1985	Don Mattingly	.324
1986	Don Mattingly	.352
1987	Don Mattingly	.327
1988	Dave Winfield	.322
1989	Steve Sax	.315
1990	Roberto Kelly	.285
1991	Steve Sax	.304
1992	Don Mattingly	.288

*AL leader

1993	Paul O'Neill	.311
1994	Paul O'Neill	.359*
1995	Wade Boggs	.324
1996	Mariano Duncan	.340
1997	Paul O'Neill	.324
1998	Bernie Williams	.339*
1999	Derek Jeter	.349
2000	Derek Jeter	.339
2001	Derek Jeter	.311
2002	Bernie Williams	.333

CLUB SINGLE-SEASON LEADERS
(1903-2002)
(BY CATEGORY)

At-Bats
1.	Alfonso Soriano	696 (2002)
2.	Bobby Richardson	692 (1962)
3.	Horace Clarke	686 (1970)
4.	Bobby Richardson	679 (1964)
5.	Don Mattingly	677 (1986)

Runs Scored
1.	Babe Ruth	177 (1921)**
2.	Lou Gehrig	167 (1936)
3.	Babe Ruth	163 (1928)
	Lou Gehrig	163 (1931)
5.	Babe Ruth	158 (1920)
	Babe Ruth	158 (1927)

Hits
1.	Don Mattingly	238 (1986)
2.	Earle Combs	231 (1927)
3.	Lou Gehrig	220 (1930)
4.	Derek Jeter	219 (1999)
5.	Lou Gehrig	218 (1927)

Doubles
1.	Don Mattingly	53 (1986)
2.	Lou Gehrig	52 (1927)
3.	Don Mattingly	48 (1985)
4.	Lou Gehrig	47 (1926)
	Bob Meusel	47 (1927)
	Lou Gehrig	47 (1928)

Triples
1.	Earle Combs	23 (1927)
2.	Birdie Cree	22 (1911)
	Earle Combs	22 (1930)
	Snuffy Stirnweiss	22 (1945)
5.	Earle Combs	21 (1928)

Home Runs
1.	Roger Maris	61 (1961)*
2.	Babe Ruth	60 (1927)
3.	Babe Ruth	59 (1921)
4.	Babe Ruth	54 (1920)
	Babe Ruth	54 (1928)
	Mickey Mantle	54 (1961)

Runs Batted In
1.	Lou Gehrig	184 (1931)*
2.	Lou Gehrig	175 (1927)
3.	Lou Gehrig	174 (1930)
4.	Babe Ruth	171 (1921)
5.	Joe DiMaggio	167 (1937)

Bases on Balls
1.	Babe Ruth	170 (1923)**
2.	Babe Ruth	148 (1920)
3.	Mickey Mantle	146 (1957)
4.	Babe Ruth	144 (1921)
	Babe Ruth	144 (1926)

Stolen Bases
1.	Rickey Henderson	93 (1988)
2.	Rickey Henderson	87 (1986)
3.	Rickey Henderson	80 (1985)
4.	Fritz Maisel	74 (1914)
5.	Ben Chapman	61 (1931)

Batting Average (at least 350 at-bats)
1.	Babe Ruth	.393 (1923)
2.	Joe DiMaggio	.381 (1939)
3.	Lou Gehrig	.379 (1930)
4.	Babe Ruth	.378 (1921)
	Babe Ruth	.378 (1924)

Total Bases
1.	Babe Ruth	457 (1921)
2.	Lou Gehrig	447 (1927)
3.	Lou Gehrig	419 (1931)
4.	Joe DiMaggio	418 (1937)
5.	Babe Ruth	417 (1927)

*AL record
**ML record

BASEBALL RECORDS-OFFENSE

Records are major-league records except when otherwise indicated; (AL) stands for American League record.

Runs Scored
Most Years Scoring 150 More Runs: 6 (AL)
  Babe Ruth—1920-21, 1923, 1927-28, 1930

Most Years Scoring 100 or More Runs: 13 (AL)
  Lou Gehrig—1926-38

Most Runs Scored, Season: 177 (AL)
  Babe Ruth—1921
Most Runs Scored In Rookie Season: 132 (AL)
  Joe DiMaggio—1936

Most Consecutive Games Scoring One Or More Runs, Season: 18 (AL)
  Red Rolfe—August 9-25, 1939 (30 runs scored)

Runs Batted In
Most Years With 150 Or More Runs Batted In: 7
  Lou Gehrig—1927, 1930-32, 1934, 1936-37

Most Years With 100 Or More Runs Batted In: 13
  Lou Gehrig—1926-38
  (1 other)

Most Runs Batted In, Season: 184 (AL)
  Lou Gehrig—1931

Most Runs Batted In By A Catcher, Season: 133 (AL)
  Bill Dickey—1937

Most Runs Batted In, Game: 11 (AL)
  Tony Lazzeri—May 24, 1936

Most Runs Batted In, Inning (since 1920): 6 (AL)
  Gil McDougald—May 3, 1951 (ninth inning)
  (10 others)

Extra-Base Hits
Most Extra-Base Hits, Season: 119
  Babe Ruth—1921 (44 doubles, 16 triples, 59 homers)

Hits
Most Consecutive Games Getting At Least One Hit, Season: 56
  Joe DiMaggio—May 15 through July 16, 1941

Most Times Hitting For The Cycle—Single, Double, Triple, Homer—In A Game: 3
   Bob Meusel—1921, 1922, 1928

Home Runs
Most Career Home Runs By A First Baseman: 493 (AL)
   Lou Gehrig—1923-39

Most Consecutive Years Leading The League In Home Runs: 6 (AL)
   Babe Ruth—1926-31

Most Years Hitting 50 Or More Home Runs: 4 (AL)
   Babe Ruth—1920-21, 1927-28

Most Years Hitting 40 Or More Home Runs: 11
   Babe Ruth—1920-21, 1923-24, 1926-32

Most Years Hitting 30 Or More Home Runs: 13 (AL)
   Babe Ruth—1920-24, 1926-33

Most Games Hitting Home Runs From Both Sides Of The Plate In One Game: 10 (AL)
   Mickey Mantle—1951-68

Most Home Runs, Season: 61 (AL)
   Roger Maris—1961

Most Home Runs For League Runner-Up In Home Runs, Season: 54 (AL)
   Mickey Mantle—1961

Most Home Runs Hit On The Road, Season: 32
   Babe Ruth—1927

Most Home Runs Hit In May, Season: 16 (AL)
   Mickey Mantle—1956

Most Home Runs Hit In June, Season: 15 (AL)
   Babe Ruth—1930
   Roger Maris—1961
   (1 other)

Most Home Runs Hit In September, Season: 17
   Babe Ruth—1927
   (1 other)

Most Consecutive Home Runs Hit In One Game: 4
   Lou Gehrig—June 3, 1932
   (3 others)

Most Consecutive Home Runs (official at-bats) Hit Over Two Games: 4
   Mickey Mantle—July 4,6; 2 in game 2 (July 4) and 2 on July 6, 1962
   Bobby Murcer—June 24, 1970 (doubleheader); 1 in Game 1 and 3 in Game 2
   (many others)

Most Consecutive Home Runs Hit Over Three Games: 4
   John Blanchard—July 21, 22, and 26, 1961
   (1 other)

Most Consecutive Games Hitting At Least One Home Run In Each Game: 8
   Don Mattingly—July 8-18, 1987 (10 home runs)
   (2 others)

Most Home Runs Over Four Consecutive Games, Hitting At Least One Home Run In Each Game: 7 (AL)
   Tony Lazzeri—May 21, 23 (DH) and 24, 1936
   (2 others)

Most Home Runs, Inning: 2 (AL)
   Joe DiMaggio—June 24, 1936 (fifth inning)
   Joe Pepitone—May 23, 1962 (eighth inning)
   Cliff Johnson—June 30, 1977 (eighth inning)
   (10 others)

Grand Slams
Most Career Grand-Slam Home Runs: 23
   Lou Gehrig—1923-39

Most Grand Slams, Season: 6
   Don Mattingly—1987

Total Bases
Most Years Making 400 Or More Total Bases: 5
   Lou Gehrig—1927, 1930-31, 1934, 1936

Most Years Making 300 Or More Total Bases: 13 (AL)
   Lou Gehrig—1926-38

Most Total Bases, Season: 457
   Babe Ruth—1921

Most Total Bases, Nine-Inning Game: 16 (AL)
   Lou Gehrig—June 3, 1932 (4 homers)
   (5 others)

Most Total Bases Made By A Pitcher, Nine-Inning Game: 10 (AL)
   Red Ruffing—June 17, 1936 (2 singles, 2 homers)
   (3 others)

Bases on Balls
Most Years Leading The League In Bases On Balls: 11 (AL)
   Babe Ruth—1920-21, 1923-24, 1926-28, 1930-33

Most Bases On Balls, Season: 170 (AL)
   Babe Ruth—1923

Most Intentionally Given Bases On Balls, Game: 4 (AL)
   Roger Maris—May 22, 1962 (12 innings)
   (1 other)

Batting Average
Highest Batting Average For A Catcher, Season (100 or more games): .362
   Bill Dickey—1936

Slugging Average
Most Years With An .800 Or Better Slugging Average: 2
   Babe Ruth—1920-21 (only times ever accomplished)

Most Years With A .700 Or Better Slugging Average: 9
   Babe Ruth—1920-21, 1923-24, 1926-28, 1930-31

Highest Slugging Average, Season (100 or more games): .847 (AL)
   Babe Ruth—1920

Stolen Bases
Most Steals Of Home, Game: 2
   Guy Zinn—August 15, 1912
   (4 others)

Sacrifice Flies
Most Sacrifice Flies, Season (batting in a run): 17 (AL)
   Roy White—1971 (1 other)

Most Sacrifice Flies, Game (batting in a run): 3
   Bob Meusel—September 15, 1926
   Don Mattingly—May 3, 1986
   (7 others)

PITCHING LEADERS

Most Years on Club: 16
WHITEY FORD (1950, 1953-67)

Most Games Pitched, Righthander, Season: 78
STEVE KARSAY—2002

Most Games Pitched, Lefthander, Season: 79
MIKE STANTON—2002

Most Games Pitched, Righthander, With Club: 426
RED RUFFING (1930-42, 1945-46)

Most Games Pitched, Lefthander, With Club: 498
WHITEY FORD (1950, 1953-67)

Most Games Started, Righthander, Season: 51
JACK CHESBRO—1904

Most Games Started, Lefthander, Season: 39
WHITEY FORD—1961

Most Games Started, Lefthander, With Club: 438
WHITEY FORD (1950, 1953-67)

Most Games Started, Righthander, With Club: 391
RED RUFFING (1930-42, 1945-46)

Most Complete Games, Righthander, Season: 48
JACK CHESBRO—1904

Most Complete Games, Lefthander, Season: 25
HERB PENNOCK—1924
LEFTY GOMEZ—1934, 1937

Most Complete Games, Righthander, With Club: 261
RED RUFFING (1930-42, 1945-46)

Most Complete Games, Lefthander, With Club: 173
LEFTY GOMEZ (1930-42)

Most Games Finished, Righthander, Season: 63
MARIANO RIVERA—1999

Most Games Finished, Lefthander, Season: 68
DAVE RIGHETTI—1986

Most Innings Pitched, Righthander, Season: 454
JACK CHESBRO—1904

Most Innings Pitched, Lefthander, Season: 286
HERB PENNOCK—1924

Most Innings Pitched, Lefthander, With Club: 3170
WHITEY FORD (1950, 1953-67)

Most Innings Pitched, Righthander, With Club: 3169
RED RUFFING (1930-42, 1945-46)

Most Games Won, Righthander, Season: 41
JACK CHESBRO—1904

Most Games Won, Lefthander, Season: 26
LEFTY GOMEZ—1934

Most Games Won, Lefthander, With Club: 236
WHITEY FORD (1950, 1953-67)

Most Games Won, Righthander, With Club: 231
RED RUFFING (1930-42, 1945-46)

Most Years Winning 20 or More Games: 4
BOB SHAWKEY—1916, 1919, 1920, 1922
LEFTY GOMEZ—1931, 1932, 1934, 1937
RED RUFFING—1936, 1937, 1938, 1939

Highest Percentage Games Won (official AL stats), Season:. 893
RON GUIDRY—1978 (won 25, lost 3)

Most Consecutive Games Won, Season: 14
JACK CHESBRO—1904
WHITEY FORD—1961

Most Consecutive Games lost, Season: 11
GEORGE MOGRIDGE—1916

Most Consecutive Games Won, Start of Season: 13
RON GUIDRY—1978

Most Games Lost, Righthander, Season: 22
JOE LAKE—1908

Most Games Lost, Lefthander, Season: 17
HERB PENNOCK—1925

Most Games Lost, Righthander, With Club: 139
MEL STOTTLEMYRE (1964-74)

Most Games Lost, Lefthander, With Club: 106
WHITEY FORD (1950, 1953-67)

Most Consecutive Games Lost, Season: 11
GEORGE MOGRIDGE—1916

Most Saves, Lefthander, Season: 46
DAVE RIGHETTI—1986

Most Saves, Righthander, Season: 50
MARIANO RIVERA—2001

Most Saves, Lefthander, With Club: 224
DAVE RIGHETTI—(1979, 1981-90)

Most Saves, Righthander, With Club: 243
MARIANO RIVERA—(1996-2002)

Most Strikeouts, Lefthander, Season: 248
RON GUIDRY—1978

Most Strikeouts, Righthander, Season: 239
JACK CHESBRO—1904

Most Strikeouts, Lefthander, With Club: 1956
WHITEY FORD (1950, 1953-67)

Most Strikeouts, Righthander, With Club: 1526
RED RUFFING (1930 42, 1945-46)

Most Strikeouts, Nine-Inning Game: 18
RON GUIDRY—June 17, 1978

Most Bases on Balls, Lefthander, Season: 179
TOMMY BYRNE—1949

Most Bases on Balls, Righthander, Season: 177
BOB TURLEY—1955

Most Bases on Balls, Lefthander, With Club: 1090
LEFTY GOMEZ (1930-42)

Most Bases on Balls, Righthander, With Club: 1066
RED RUFFING (1930-42, 1945-46)

Most Shutouts, Lefthander, Season: 9
RON GUIDRY—1978

Most Shutouts, Righthander, Season: 8
RUSS FORD—1910

Most Shutouts, Lefthander, With Club: 45
WHITEY FORD (1950, 1953-67)

Most Shutouts, Righthander, With Club: 40
MEL STOTTLEMYRE (1964-74)

Most 1-0 Shutouts Won, With Club: 7
BOB SHAWKEY (1915-27)

Most Shutouts Lost, Season: 7
BILL ZUBER—1945

Most 1-0 Shutouts Lost, Season: 5
JACK WARHOP—1914

Lowest Earned Run Average, Righthander (official AL stats), Season: 1.64
SPUD CHANDLER—1943 (253 innings pitched)
Lowest Earned Run Average, Lefthander (official AL stats), Season: 1.74
RON GUIDRY—1978 (274 innings pitched)

Lowest Earned Run Average, Righthander (at least 800 innings), With Club: 2.54
RUSS FORD (1909-13)

Lowest Earned Run Average, Lefthander (at least 800 innings), With Club: 2.75
WHITEY FORD (1950, 1953-67)

Most Earned Runs Allowed, Season: 127
SAM JONES—1925

Most Batsmen Faced, Season: 1406
CARL MAYS—1921

Most Hits Given Up, Season: 337
JACK CHESBRO—1904

Most Home Runs Given Up, Season: 40
RALPH TERRY—1962

Most Hit Batsmen, Season: 26
JACK WARHOP—1909

Most Wild Pitches, Season: 23
TIM LEARY—1990

NO-HITTERS PITCHED BY YANKEES
(ELEVEN—1903 through 2002)

#	Date	Description
1.	April 24, 1917	George Mogridge (LHP) at Boston. Mogridge won 2-1.
2.	September 4, 1923	Sad Sam Jones (RHP) at Philadelphia. Jones won 2-0.
3.	August 27, 1938	Monte Pearson (RHP) vs. Cleveland (2nd game). Pearson won 13-0.
4.	July 12, 1951	Allie Reynolds (RHP) at Cleveland. Reynolds won 1-0.
5.	September 28, 1951	Allie Reynolds (RHP) vs. Boston (1st game). Reynolds won 8-0.
6.	October 8, 1956	**Don Larsen (RHP) vs. Brooklyn. Larsen won 2-0. (World Series)
7.	July 4, 1983	Dave Righetti (LHP) vs. Boston. Righetti won 4-0.
8.	September 4, 1993	Jim Abbott (LHP) vs. Cleveland. Abbott won 4-0.
9.	May 14, 1996	Dwight (Doc) Gooden (RHP) vs. Seattle. Gooden won 2-0.
10.	May 17, 1998	**David Wells (LHP) vs. Minnesota. Wells won 4-0.
11.	July 18, 1999	**David Cone (RHP) vs. Montreal. Cone won 6-0.

**Perfect game   (LHP) = Left-handed pitcher   (RHP) = Right-handed pitcher
Ten in regular season by nine pitchers plus one in postseason

CLUB LEADERS YEAR BY YEAR

Year		Wins	Year		Wins	Year		Wins
1903	Jack Chesbro	21	1920	Carl Mays	26	1940	Red Ruffing	15
1904	Jack Chesbro	41*	1921	Carl Mays	27*	1941	Lefty Gomez	15
1905	Jack Chesbro	19	1922	Bullet Joe Bush	26		Red Ruffing	15
1906	Al Orth	27*	1923	Sad Sam Jones	21	1942	Ernie Bonham	21
1907	Al Orth	14	1924	Herb Pennock	21	1943	Spud Chandler	20*
1908	Jack Chesbro	14	1925	Herb Pennock	16	1944	Hank Borowy	17
1909	Joe Lake	14	1926	Herb Pennock	23	1945	Bill Bevens	13
1910	Russ Ford	26	1927	Waite Hoyt	22*	1946	Spud Chandler	20
1911	Russ Ford	22	1928	George Pipgras	24*	1947	Allie Reynolds	19
1912	Russ Ford	13	1929	George Pipgras	18	1948	Vic Raschi	19
1913	Russ Ford	12	1930	George Pipgras	15	1949	Vic Raschi	21
	Ray Fisher	12		Red Ruffing	15	1950	Vic Raschi	21
1914	Ray Caldwell	17	1931	Lefty Gomez	21	1951	Ed Lopat	21
1915	Ray Caldwell	19	1932	Lefty Gomez	24		Vic Raschi	21
1916	Bob Shawkey	23	1933	Lefty Gomez	16	1952	Allie Reynolds	20
1917	Bob Shawkey	13	1934	Lefty Gomez	26*	1953	Whitey Ford	18
	Ray Caldwell	13	1935	Red Ruffing	16	1954	Bob Grim	20
1918	George Mogridge	16	1936	Red Ruffing	20	1955	Whitey Ford	18*
1919	Bob Shawkey	20	1937	Lefty Gomez	21*	1956	Whitey Ford	19
			1938	Red Ruffing	21*	1957	Tom Sturdivant	16
			1939	Red Ruffing	21	1958	Bob Turley	21*
						1959	Whitey Ford	16
						1960	Art Ditmar	15
						1961	Whitey Ford	25*
						1962	Ralph Terry	23*
						1963	Whitey Ford	24*
						1964	Jim Bouton	18
						1965	Mel Stottlemyre	20
						1966	Fritz Peterson	12
							Mel Stottlemyre	12
						1967	Mel Stottlemyre	15
						1968	Mel Stottlemyre	21
						1969	Mel Stottlemyre	20
						1970	Fritz Peterson	20
						1971	Mel Stottlemyre	16
						1972	Fritz Peterson	17
						1973	Mel Stottlemyre	16
						1974	Pat Dobson	19
							Doc Medich	19
						1975	Catfish Hunter	23*

*AL leader

Year	Pitcher	W
1976	Ed Figueroa	19
1977	Ed Figueroa	16
	Ron Guidry	16
1978	Ron Guidry	25*
1979	Tommy John	21
1980	Tommy John	22
1981	Ron Guidry	11
1982	Ron Guidry	14
1983	Ron Guidry	21
1984	Phil Niekro	16
1985	Ron Guidry	22*
1986	Dennis Rasmussen	18
1987	Rick Rhoden	16
1988	John Candelaria	13
1989	Andy Hawkins	15
1990	Lee Guetterman	11
1991	Scott Sanderson	16
1992	Melido Perez	13
1993	Jimmy Key	18
1994	Jimmy Key	17*
1995	Jack McDowell	15
1996	Andy Pettitte	21*
1997	Andy Pettitte	18
1998	David Cone	20*
1999	Orlando Hernandez	17
2000	Andy Pettitte	19
2001	Roger Clemens	20
2002	David Wells	19

Saves

Year	Pitcher	SV
1903	Doc Adkins	1
	Snake Wiltse	1
1904	Clark Griffith	1
1905	Clark Griffith	3
1906	Clark Griffith	2
1907	Bobby Keefe	3
1908	Jack Chesbro	3
1909	Jack Warhop	4
1910	Jack Warhop	2
1911	Jack Quinn	2
1912	Jack Warhop	3
1913	George McConnell	2
1914	Marty McHale	2
1915	King Cole	1
	Cy Pieh	1
1916	Bob Shawkey	9*
1917	Allan Russell	2
1918	George Mogridge	7*
1919	Bob Shawkey	4
1920	Jack Quinn	3
1921	Carl Mays	7*
1922	Sad Sam Jones	8*
1923	Sad Sam Jones	4
1924	Waite Hoyt	4
1925	Waite Hoyt	6
1926	Sad Sam Jones	5
1927	Wilcy Moore	13*
1928	Waite Hoyt	8*
1929	Wilcy Moore	8
1930	George Pipgras	4
	Roy Sherid	4
1931	Hank Johnson	4
1932	Johnny Allen	4
	Wilcy Moore	4
1933	Wilcy Moore	8
1934	Johnny Murphy	4
1935	Johnny Murphy	5
1936	Pat Malone	9*
1937	Johnny Murphy	10
1938	Johnny Murphy	11*
1939	Johnny Murphy	19*
1940	Johnny Murphy	9
1941	Johnny Murphy	15*
1942	Johnny Murphy	11*
1943	Johnny Murphy	8
1944	Jim Turner	7
1945	Jim Turner	10*
1946	Johnny Murphy	7
1947	Joe Page	17*
1948	Joe Page	16
1949	Joe Page	27*
1950	Joe Page	13
1951	Allie Reynolds	7
1952	Johnny Sain	7
1953	Allie Reynolds	13
1954	Johnny Sain	22*
1955	Jim Konstanty	11
1956	Tom Morgan	11
1957	Bob Grim	19*
1958	Ryne Duren	20*
1959	Ryne Duren	14
1960	Bobby Shantz	11
1961	Luis Arroyo	29*
1962	Marshall Bridges	18
1963	Hal Reniff	18
1964	Pete Mikkelsen	12
1965	Pedro Ramos	19
1966	Pedro Ramos	13
1967	Dooley Womack	18
1968	Steve Hamilton	11
1969	Jack Aker	11
1970	Lindy McDaniel	29
1971	Jack Aker	4
	Lindy McDaniel	4
1972	Sparky Lyle	35*
1973	Sparky Lyle	27
1974	Sparky Lyle	15
1975	Tippy Martinez	8
1976	Sparky Lyle	23*
1977	Sparky Lyle	26
1978	Rich Gossage	27*
1979	Rich Gossage	18
1980	Rich Gossage	33*
1981	Rich Gossage	20
1982	Rich Gossage	30
1983	Rich Gossage	22
1984	Dave Righetti	31
1985	Dave Righetti	29
1986	Dave Righetti	46*
1987	Dave Righetti	31
1988	Dave Righetti	25
1989	Dave Righetti	25
1990	Dave Righetti	36
1991	Steve Farr	23
1992	Steve Farr	30
1993	Steve Farr	25
1994	Steve Howe	15
1995	John Wetteland	31
1996	John Wetteland	43*
1997	Mariano Rivera	43
1998	Mariano Rivera	36
1999	Mariano Rivera	45*
2000	Mariano Rivera	36
2001	Mariano Rivera	50*
2002	Mariano Rivera	28

Games Pitched

Year	Pitcher	G
1903	Jack Chesbro	40
1904	Jack Chesbro	55*
1905	Jack Chesbro	41
1906	Jack Chesbro	49*
1907	Al Orth	36
1908	Jack Chesbro	45
1909	Jack Warhop	36
1910	Jack Warhop	37
1911	Ray Caldwell	41
1912	Jack Warhop	39
1913	Ray Fisher	43
1914	Jack Warhop	37
1915	Ray Caldwell	36
1916	Bob Shawkey	53
1917	Slim Love	33
1918	George Mogridge	45*
1919	Bob Shawkey	41
1920	Carl Mays	45
1921	Carl Mays	49*
1922	Sad Sam Jones	45
1923	Sad Sam Jones	39
1924	Waite Hoyt	46
1925	Herb Pennock	47
1926	Urban Shocker	41
1927	Wilcy Moore	50
1928	George Pipgras	46
1929	Wilcy Moore	41
1930	Hank Johnson	44
	George Pipgras	44
1931	Lefty Gomez	40
	Hank Johnson	40
1932	Lefty Gomez	37
1933	Lefty Gomez	35
	Red Ruffing	35
1934	Johnny Murphy	40
1935	Johnny Murphy	40
1936	Johnny Broaca	37
1937	Johnny Murphy	39
1938	Lefty Gomez	32
	Johnny Murphy	32
1939	Johnny Murphy	38
1940	Johnny Murphy	35
1941	Johnny Murphy	35
1942	Johnny Murphy	31
1943	Johnny Murphy	37
1944	Hank Borowy	35
	Jim Turner	35
1945	Jim Turner	30
1946	Spud Chandler	34
1947	Joe Page	56
1948	Joe Page	55*
1949	Joe Page	60*
1950	Joe Page	37
1951	Allie Reynolds	40
1952	Allie Reynolds	35
	Johnny Sain	35
1953	Allie Reynolds	41
1954	Johnny Sain	45
1955	Jim Konstanty	45
1956	Tom Morgan	41
1957	Art Ditmar	46
	Bob Grim	46
1958	Ryne Duren	44
1959	Ryne Duren	41
1960	Ryne Duren	42
	Bobby Shantz	42
1961	Luis Arroyo	65*
1962	Marshall Bridges	52
1963	Hal Reniff	48
1964	Pete Mikkelsen	50
1965	Pedro Ramos	65
1966	Hal Reniff	56
1967	Dooley Womack	65
1968	Dooley Womack	45
1969	Lindy McDaniel	51
1970	Lindy McDaniel	62
1971	Lindy McDaniel	44
1972	Sparky Lyle	59
1973	Sparky Lyle	51
1974	Sparky Lyle	66
1975	Sparky Lyle	49
1976	Sparky Lyle	64
1977	Sparky Lyle	72*
1978	Rich Gossage	63
1979	Ron Davis	44
1980	Rich Gossage	64
1981	Ron Davis	43
1982	George Frazier	63
1983	George Frazier	61
1984	Dave Righetti	64

*AL leader

Year	Player	
1985	Dave Righetti	74
1986	Dave Righetti	74*
1987	Dave Righetti	60
1988	Dave Righetti	60
1989	Lee Guetterman	70
1990	Lee Guetterman	64
1991	Greg Cadaret	68
1992	John Habyan	56
1993	Steve Howe	51
1994	Bob Wickman	53*
1995	Bob Wickman	63
1996	Jeff Nelson	73
1997	Jeff Nelson	77
1998	Mike Stanton	67
1999	Mike Stanton	73
2000	Jeff Nelson	73
2001	Mike Stanton	76
2002	Mike Stanton	79

Games Started

Year	Player	
1903	Jack Chesbro	36
1904	Jack Chesbro	51*
1905	Jack Chesbro	38
1906	Jack Chesbro	42*
1907	Al Orth	33
1908	Jack Chesbro	31
1909	Joe Lake	26
1910	Russ Ford	33
1911	Russ Ford	33
1912	Russ Ford	35
1913	Ray Fisher	31
1914	Ray Fisher	26
1915	Ray Caldwell	35
1916	Bob Shawkey	27
1917	Ray Caldwell	29
1918	Slim Love	29
1919	Jack Quinn	31
1920	Carl Mays	37
1921	Carl Mays	38
1922	Bob Shawkey	33
1923	Bob Shawkey	31
1924	Herb Pennock	34
1925	Sad Sam Jones	31
	Herb Pennock	31
1926	Herb Pennock	33
	Urban Shocker	33
1927	Waite Hoyt	32
1928	George Pipgras	38*
1929	George Pipgras	33
1930	George Pipgras	30
1931	Red Ruffing	30
1932	Lefty Gomez	31
1933	Lefty Gomez	30
1934	Lefty Gomez	33
1935	Lefty Gomez	30
1936	Red Ruffing	33
1937	Lefty Gomez	34
1938	Lefty Gomez	32
1939	Red Ruffing	28
1940	Red Ruffing	30
1941	Marius Russo	27
1942	Ernie Bonham	27
1943	Spud Chandler	30
1944	Hank Borowy	30
1945	Bill Bevens	25
1946	Spud Chandler	32
1947	Allie Reynolds	30
1948	Ed Lopat	31
	Vic Raschi	31
	Allie Reynolds	31
1949	Vic Raschi	37*
1950	Ed Lopat	32
	Vic Raschi	32
1951	Vic Raschi	34*
1952	Vic Raschi	31
1953	Whitey Ford	30
1954	Whitey Ford	28
1955	Bob Turley	34
1956	Johnny Kucks	31
1957	Tom Sturdivant	28
1958	Bob Turley	31
1959	Whitey Ford	29
1960	Whitey Ford	29
1961	Whitey Ford	39*
1962	Ralph Terry	39*
1963	Whitey Ford	37*
	Ralph Terry	37*
1964	Jim Bouton	37
1965	Mel Stottlemyre	37
1966	Mel Stottlemyre	35
1967	Mel Stottlemyre	36
1968	Mel Stottlemyre	36
1969	Mel Stottlemyre	39
1970	Fritz Peterson	37
	Mel Stottlemyre	37
1971	Fritz Peterson	35
	Mel Stottlemyre	35
1972	Mel Stottlemyre	36
1973	Mel Stottlemyre	38
1974	Pat Dobson	39
1975	Catfish Hunter	39
1976	Catfish Hunter	36
1977	Ed Figueroa	32
1978	Ed Figueroa	35
	Ron Guidry	35
1979	Tommy John	36
1980	Tommy John	36
1981	Rudy May	22
1982	Ron Guidry	33
1983	Shane Rawley	33
1984	Phil Niekro	31
1985	Ron Guidry	33
	Phil Niekro	33
1986	Dennis Rasmussen	31
1987	Tommy John	33
1988	Tommy John	32
1989	Andy Hawkins	34
1990	Tim Leary	31
1991	Scott Sanderson	34
1992	Melido Perez	33
	Scott Sanderson	33
1993	Jimmy Key	34
1994	Jimmy Key	25*
1995	Jack McDowell	30
1996	Andy Pettitte	34
1997	Andy Pettitte	35*
1998	Andy Pettitte	32
1999	Orlando Hernandez	33
2000	Roger Clemens	32
	Andy Pettitte	32
2001	Mike Mussina	34
2002	Mike Mussina	33

Complete Games

Year	Player	
1903	Jack Chesbro	33
1904	Jack Chesbro	48*
1905	Al Orth	26
1906	Al Orth	36*
1907	Al Orth	21
1908	Jack Chesbro	21
1909	Jack Warhop	21
1910	Russ Ford	29
1911	Russ Ford	26
1912	Russ Ford	32
1913	Russ Ford	16
1914	Ray Caldwell	22
1915	Ray Caldwell	31
1916	Bob Shawkey	21
1917	Ray Caldwell	21
1918	Ray Caldwell	14
1919	Bob Shawkey	22
1920	Carl Mays	26
1921	Carl Mays	30
1922	Sad Sam Jones	21
	Carl Mays	21
1923	Bullet Joe Bush	23
1924	Herb Pennock	25
1925	Herb Pennock	21
1926	Herb Pennock	19
	Urban Shocker	19
1927	Waite Hoyt	23
1928	George Pipgras	22
1929	George Pipgras	13
1930	George Pipgras	15
1931	Red Ruffing	19
1932	Red Ruffing	22
1933	Red Ruffing	18
1934	Lefty Gomez	25*
1935	Red Ruffing	19
1936	Red Ruffing	25
1937	Lefty Gomez	25
1938	Red Ruffing	22
1939	Red Ruffing	22
1940	Red Ruffing	20
1941	Marius Russo	17
1942	Ernie Bonham	22*
1943	Spud Chandler	20*
1944	Hank Borowy	19
	Monk Dubiel	19
1945	Bill Bevens	14
1946	Spud Chandler	20
1947	Allie Reynolds	17
1948	Vic Raschi	18
1949	Vic Raschi	21
1950	Vic Raschi	17
1951	Ed Lopat	20
1952	Allie Reynolds	24
1953	Whitey Ford	11
1954	Whitey Ford	11
1955	Whitey Ford	18*
1956	Whitey Ford	18
1957	Bobby Shantz	9
	Bob Turley	9
1958	Bob Turley	19*
1959	Whitey Ford	9
1960	Art Ditmar	8
	Whitey Ford	8
1961	Whitey Ford	11
1962	Ralph Terry	14
1963	Ralph Terry	18*
1964	Whitey Ford	12
1965	Mel Stottlemyre	18*
1966	Fritz Peterson	11
1967	Al Downing	10
	Mel Stottlemyre	10
1968	Mel Stottlemyre	19
1969	Mel Stottlemyre	24*
1970	Mel Stottlemyre	14
1971	Mel Stottlemyre	19
1972	Fritz Peterson	12
1973	Mel Stottlemyre	19
1974	Doc Medich	17
1975	Catfish Hunter	30*
1976	Catfish Hunter	21
1977	Mike Torrez	15
1978	Ron Guidry	16
1979	Tommy John	17
1980	Tommy John	16
1981	Tommy John	7
1982	Tommy John	9
1983	Ron Guidry	21*
1984	Ron Guidry	5
	Phil Niekro	5
1985	Ron Guidry	11
1986	Ron Guidry	5
1987	Charlie Hudson	6
1988	John Candelaria	6
1989	Andy Hawkins	5
1990	Tim Leary	6

*AL leader

1991	Scott Sanderson	2
1992	Melido Perez	10
1993	Jim Abbott	4
	Jimmy Key	4
1994	Jim Abbott	2
	Terry Mulholland	2
1995	Jack McDowell	8*
1996	Andy Pettitte	2
	Kenny Rogers	2
1997	David Wells	5
1998	David Wells	8
1999	Orlando Hernandez	2
	Hideki Irabu	2
2000	Orlando Hernandez	3
	Andy Pettitte	3
2001	Mike Mussina	4
2002	Andy Pettitte	3

Innings Pitched

1903	Jack Chesbro	325
1904	Jack Chesbro	455*
1905	Al Orth	305
1906	Al Orth	339*
1907	Al Orth	249
1908	Jack Chesbro	289
1909	Jack Warhop	243
1910	Russ Ford	300
1911	Russ Ford	281
1912	Russ Ford	292
1913	Ray Fisher	246
1914	Jack Warhop	217
1915	Ray Caldwell	305
1916	Bob Shawkey	277
1917	Ray Caldwell	236
	Bob Shawkey	236
1918	George Mogridge	230
1919	Jack Quinn	264
1920	Carl Mays	312
1921	Carl Mays	337*
1922	Bob Shawkey	300
1923	Bullet Joe Bush	276
1924	Herb Pennock	286
1925	Herb Pennock	277*
1926	Herb Pennock	266
1927	Waite Hoyt	256
1928	George Pipgras	301*
1929	George Pipgras	225
1930	George Pipgras	221
1931	Lefty Gomez	243
1932	Lefty Gomez	265
1933	Lefty Gomez	235
	Red Ruffing	235
1934	Lefty Gomez	282*
1935	Lefty Gomez	246
1936	Red Ruffing	271
1937	Lefty Gomez	278
1938	Red Ruffing	247
1939	Red Ruffing	233
1940	Red Ruffing	226
1941	Marius Russo	210
1942	Ernie Bonham	226
1943	Spud Chandler	253
1944	Hank Borowy	253
1945	Bill Bevens	184
1946	Spud Chandler	257
1947	Allie Reynolds	242
1948	Allie Reynolds	236
1949	Vic Raschi	275
1950	Vic Raschi	257
1951	Vic Raschi	258
1952	Allie Reynolds	244
1953	Whitey Ford	207
1954	Whitey Ford	211
1955	Whitey Ford	254
1956	Whitey Ford	226

1957	Tom Sturdivant	202
1958	Bob Turley	245
1959	Whitey Ford	204
1960	Art Ditmar	200
1961	Whitey Ford	283*
1962	Ralph Terry	299*
1963	Whitey Ford	269*
1964	Jim Bouton	271
1965	Mel Stottlemyre	291*
1966	Mel Stottlemyre	251
1967	Mel Stottlemyre	255
1968	Mel Stottlemyre	279
1969	Mel Stottlemyre	303
1970	Mel Stottlemyre	271
1971	Fritz Peterson	274
1972	Mel Stottlemyre	260
1973	Mel Stottlemyre	273
1974	Pat Dobson	281
1975	Catfish Hunter	328*
1976	Catfish Hunter	299*
1977	Ed Figueroa	239
1978	Ron Guidry	274
1979	Tommy John	276
1980	Tommy John	265
1981	Rudy May	148
1982	Ron Guidry	222
1983	Ron Guidry	250
1984	Phil Niekro	216
1985	Ron Guidry	259
1986	Dennis Rasmussen	202
1987	Tommy John	188
1988	Rick Rhoden	197
1989	Andy Hawkins	208
1990	Tim Leary	208
1991	Scott Sanderson	208
1992	Melido Perez	248
1993	Jimmy Key	237
1994	Jimmy Key	168
1995	Jack McDowell	218
1996	Andy Pettitte	221
1997	Andy Pettitte	240.1
1998	Andy Pettitte	216.1
1999	Orlando Hernandez	214.1
2000	Andy Pettitte	204.2
2001	Mike Mussina	228.2
2002	Mike Mussina	215.2

Strikeouts

1903	Jack Chesbro	147
1904	Jack Chesbro	239
1905	Jack Chesbro	156
1906	Jack Chesbro	152
1907	Slow Joe Doyle	94
1908	Jack Chesbro	124
1909	Joe Lake	117
1910	Russ Ford	209
1911	Russ Ford	158
1912	Russ Ford	112
1913	Ray Fisher	92
1914	Ray Keating	109
1915	Ray Caldwell	130
1916	Bob Shawkey	122
1917	Ray Caldwell	102
1918	Slim Love	95
1919	Bob Shawkey	122
1920	Bob Shawkey	126
1921	Bob Shawkey	126
1922	Bob Shawkey	130
1923	Bullet Joe Bush	125
	Bob Shawkey	125
1924	Bob Shawkey	114
1925	Sad Sam Jones	92
1926	Waite Hoyt	79
1927	Waite Hoyt	86
1928	George Pipgras	139
1929	George Pipgras	125

1930	Red Ruffing	117
1931	Lefty Gomez	150
1932	Red Ruffing	190*
1933	Lefty Gomez	163*
1934	Lefty Gomez	158*
1935	Lefty Gomez	138
1936	Monte Pearson	118
1937	Lefty Gomez	194*
1938	Lefty Gomez	129
1939	Lefty Gomez	102
1940	Red Ruffing	97
1941	Marius Russo	105
1942	Hank Borowy	85
1943	Spud Chandler	134
1944	Hank Borowy	107
1945	Bill Bevens	76
1946	Spud Chandler	138
1947	Allie Reynolds	129
1948	Vic Raschi	124
1949	Tommy Byrne	129
1950	Allie Reynolds	160
1951	Vic Raschi	164*
1952	Allie Reynolds	160*
1953	Whitey Ford	110
1954	Whitey Ford	125
1955	Bob Turley	210
1956	Whitey Ford	141
1957	Bob Turley	152
1958	Bob Turley	168
1959	Whitey Ford	114
1960	Ralph Terry	92
1961	Whitey Ford	209
1962	Ralph Terry	176
1963	Whitey Ford	189
1964	Al Downing	217*
1965	Al Downing	179
1966	Al Downing	152
1967	Al Downing	171
1968	Stan Bahnsen	162
1969	Fritz Peterson	150
1970	Fritz Peterson	127
1971	Fritz Peterson	139
1972	Mel Stottlemyre	110
1973	Doc Medich	145
1974	Pat Dobson	157
1975	Catfish Hunter	177
1976	Catfish Hunter	173
1977	Ron Guidry	176
1978	Ron Guidry	248
1979	Ron Guidry	201
1980	Ron Guidry	166
1981	Ron Guidry	104
1982	Dave Righetti	163
1983	Dave Righetti	169
1984	Phil Niekro	136
1985	Phil Niekro	149
1986	Ron Guidry	140
1987	Rick Rhoden	107
1988	John Candelaria	121
1989	Andy Hawkins	98
1990	Tim Leary	138
1991	Scott Sanderson	130
1992	Melido Perez	218
1993	Jimmy Key	173
1994	Melido Perez	109
1995	Jack McDowell	157
1996	Andy Pettitte	162
1997	David Cone	222
1998	David Cone	209
1999	David Cone	177
2000	Roger Clemens	188
2001	Mike Mussina	214
2002	Roger Clemens	192

Shutouts

1903	Clark Griffith	2

*AL leader

Year	Pitcher	No.
	Jesse Tannehill	2
1904	Jack Chesbro	6
1905	Al Orth	4
1906	Jack Chesbro	4
1907	Tacks Neuer	3
1908	Jack Chesbro	3
1909	Lew Brockett	3
	Slow Joe Doyle	3
	Joe Lake	3
1910	Russ Ford	8
1911	Ray Fisher	3
1912	Ray Caldwell	3
1913	Ray Caldwell	2
	Ray Keating	2
1914	King Cole	2
	Ray Fisher	2
1915	Ray Fisher	4
1916	Bob Shawkey	4
1917	Ray Fisher	3
1918	Hank Thormahlen	3
1919	Jack Quinn	4
1920	Carl Mays	6*
1921	Bob Shawkey	3
1922	Waite Hoyt	3
	Bob Shawkey	3
1923	Bullet Joe Bush	3
	Sad Sam Jones	3
1924	Herb Pennock	4
1925	Herb Pennock	2
	Urban Shocker	2
1926	Waite Hoyt	1
	Sad Sam Jones	1
	Herb Pennock	1
	Bob Shawkey	1
1927	Waite Hoyt	3
	Dutch Ruether	3
1928	Herb Pennock	5*
1929	Fred Heimach	3
	George Pipgras	3
	Ed Wells	3
1930	George Pipgras	3*
1931	Herb Pennock	1
	Red Ruffing	1
1932	Johnny Allen	3
	Red Ruffing	3
1933	Lefty Gomez	4
1934	Lefty Gomez	6*
1935	Vito Tamulis	3
1936	Red Ruffing	3
1937	Lefty Gomez	6*
1938	Lefty Gomez	4*
1939	Red Ruffing	5*
1940	Ernie Bonham	3
	Red Ruffing	3
1941	Spud Chandler	4
1942	Ernie Bonham	6*
1943	Spud Chandler	5*
1944	Hank Borowy	3
	Monk Dubiel	3
1945	Bill Bevens	2
	Atley Donald	2
1946	Spud Chandler	6
1947	Allie Reynolds	4
1948	Vic Raschi	6
1949	Ed Lopat	4
1950	Ed Lopat	3
1951	Allie Reynolds	7*
1952	Allie Reynolds	6*
1953	Vic Raschi	4
1954	Tom Morgan	4
	Allie Reynolds	4
1955	Bob Turley	6
1956	Johnny Kucks	3
1957	Bob Turley	4

*AL leader

Year	Pitcher	No.
1958	Whitey Ford	7*
1959	Bob Turley	3
1960	Whitey Ford	4*
1961	Whitey Ford	3
	Bill Stafford	3
1962	Ralph Terry	3
1963	Jim Bouton	6
1964	Whitey Ford	8
1965	Mel Stottlemyre	4
1966	Mel Stottlemyre	3
1967	Al Downing	4
	Mel Stottlemyre	4
1968	Mel Stottlemyre	6
1969	Fritz Peterson	4
1970	Stan Bahnsen	2
	Fritz Peterson	2
1971	Mel Stottlemyre	7
1972	Mel Stottlemyre	7
1973	Mel Stottlemyre	4
1974	Doc Medich	4
1975	Catfish Hunter	7
1976	Ed Figueroa	4
1977	Ron Guidry	5
1978	Ron Guidry	9*
1979	Tommy John	3
1980	Tommy John	6*
1981	13 combined shutouts were thrown, but not one Yankee went the route for shutout credit.	
1982	Tommy John	2
1983	Ron Guidry	3
1984	Joe Cowley	1
	Ron Guidry	1
	Phil Niekro	1
1985	Ron Guidry	2
	Ed Whitson	2
1986	Scott Nielson	2
1987	Charlie Hudson	3
1988	John Candelaria	2
1989	Andy Hawkins	2
1990	Andy Hawkins	1
	Tim Leary	1
	Mike Witt	1
1991	Scott Sanderson	2
1992	Greg Cadaret	1
	Shawn Hillegas	1
	Melido Perez	1
	Scott Sanderson	1
1993	Jimmy Key	2
1994	none by any one pitcher	
1995	Jack McDowell	2
1996	Doc Gooden	1
	Kenny Rogers	1
1997	David Wells	2
1998	David Wells	5*
1999	Roger Clemens	1
	David Cone	1
	Orlando Hernandez	1
	Hideki Irabu	1
2000	Ramiro Mendoza	1
	Andy Pettitte	1
2001	Mike Mussina	3
2002	Mike Mussina	2

Earned Run Average (at least 10 decisions and 100 innings pitched)

Year	Pitcher	ERA
1903	Clark Griffith	2.70
1904	Jack Chesbro	1.82
1905	Clark Griffith	1.67
1906	Walter Clarkson	2.32
1907	Jack Chesbro	2.53
1908	Jack Chesbro	2.93
1909	Joe Lake	1.88
1910	Russ Ford	1.65
1911	Russ Ford	2.27
1912	George McConnell	2.75
1913	Ray Caldwell	2.41
1914	Ray Caldwell	1.94
1915	Ray Fisher	2.11
1916	Nick Cullop	2.05
1917	Ray Fisher	2.19
1918	George Mogridge	2.27
1919	Carl Mays	1.65
1920	Bob Shawkey	2.45*
1921	Carl Mays	3.05
1922	Bob Shawkey	2.91
1923	Waite Hoyt	3.02
1924	Herb Pennock	2.83
1925	Herb Pennock	2.96
1926	Urban Shocker	3.38
1927	Wilcy Moore	2.28
1928	Herb Pennock	2.56
1929	Tom Zachary	2.48
1930	George Pipgras	4.11
1931	Lefty Gomez	2.63
1932	Red Ruffing	3.09
1933	Lefty Gomez	3.18
1934	Lefty Gomez	2.33*
1935	Red Ruffing	3.12
1936	Monte Pearson	3.71
1937	Lefty Gomez	2.33*
1938	Red Ruffing	3.31
1939	Marius Russo	2.41
1940	Atley Donald	3.03
1941	Ernie Bonham	2.98
1942	Ernie Bonham	2.27
1943	Spud Chandler	1.64*
1944	Hank Borowy	2.64
1945	Hank Borowy	3.13
1946	Spud Chandler	2.10
1947	Spud Chandler	2.46*
1948	Tommy Byrne	3.30
1949	Joe Page	2.59
1950	Whitey Ford	2.81
1951	Ed Lopat	2.91
1952	Allie Reynolds	2.06*
1953	Ed Lopat	2.42*
1954	Whitey Ford	2.82
1955	Whitey Ford	2.63
1956	Whitey Ford	2.47*
1957	Bobby Shantz	2.45*
1958	Whitey Ford	2.01*
1959	Art Ditmar	2.90
1960	Art Ditmar	3.06
1961	Luis Arroyo	2.19
1962	Whitey Ford	2.90
1963	Jim Bouton	2.53
1964	Whitey Ford	2.13
1965	Mel Stottlemyre	2.63
1966	Jim Bouton	2.69
1967	Bill Monbouquette	2.36
1968	Stan Bahnsen	2.05
1969	Fritz Peterson	2.55
1970	Lindy McDaniel	2.01
1971	Mel Stottlemyre	2.87
1972	Sparky Lyle	1.92
1973	Lindy McDaniel	2.86
1974	Sparky Lyle	1.66
1975	Catfish Hunter	2.58
1976	Sparky Lyle	2.26
1977	Sparky Lyle	2.17
1978	Ron Guidry	1.74*
1979	Ron Guidry	2.78*
1980	Rudy May	2.46*
1981	Dave Righetti	2.06
1982	Tommy John	3.66
1983	Ron Guidry	3.42
1984	Jay Howell	2.69
1985	Bob Shirley	2.64
1986	Dave Righetti	2.45
1987	Charlie Hudson	3.61
1988	John Candelaria	3.38

1989	Lee Guetterman	2.45
1990	Lee Guetterman	3.39
1991	Greg Cadaret	3.62
1992	Melido Perez	2.87
1993	Jimmy Key	3.00
1994	Jimmy Key	3.27
1995	Jack McDowell	3.93
1996	Mariano Rivera	2.09
1997	Andy Pettitte	2.88
1998	Orlando Hernandez	3.13
1999	David Cone	3.44
2000	Roger Clemens	3.70
2001	Mike Mussina	3.15
2002	David Wells	3.75

CLUB SINGLE-SEASON LEADERS

1903-2002 by pitching category

Wins
1. Jack Chesbro   41 (1904)**
2. Al Orth   27 (1906)
   Carl Mays   27 (1921)
4. Russ Ford   26 (1910)
   Carl Mays   26 (1920)
   Bullet Joe Bush   26 (1922)
   Lefty Gomez   26 (1934)

Saves
1. Mariano Rivera   50 (2001)
2. Dave Righetti   46 (1986)
3. Mariano Rivera   45 (1999)
4. Mariano Rivera   43 (1997)
   John Wetteland   43 (1996)

Games Pitched
1. Mike Stanton   79 (2002)
2. Steve Karsay   78 (2002)
3. Jeff Nelson   77 (1997)
4. Dave Righetti   74 (1985)
   Dave Righetti   74 (1986)

Games Started
1. Jack Chesbro   51 (1904)**
2. Jack Powell   45 (1904)
3. Jack Chesbro   42 (1906)
4. Al Orth   39 (1906)
   Whitey Ford   39 (1961)
   Ralph Terry   39 (1962)
   Mel Stottlemyre   39 (1969)
   Pat Dobson   39 (1974)
   Catfish Hunter   39 (1975)

Complete Games
1. Jack Chesbro   48 (1904)**
2. Jack Powell   38 (1904)
3. Al Orth   36 (1906)
4. Jack Chesbro   33 (1903)
5. Russ Ford   32 (1912)

Innings Pitched
1. Jack Chesbro   455 (1904)
2. Jack Powell   390 (1904)
3. Al Orth   339 (1906)
4. Carl Mays   337 (1921)
5. Catfish Hunter   328 (1975)

Strikeouts
1. Ron Guidry   248 (1978)
2. Jack Chesbro   239 (1904)
3. David Cone   222 (1997)
4. Melido Perez   218 (1992)
5. Al Downing   217 (1964)

---

*AL leader
**Modern ML record (since 1900)

Shutouts
1. Ron Guidry   9 (1978)
2. Russ Ford   8 (1910)
   Whitey Ford   8 (1964)
4. Allie Reynolds   7 (1951)
   Whitey Ford   7 (1958)
   Mel Stottlemyre   7 (1971)
   Mel Stottlemyre   7 (1972)
   Catfish Hunter   7 (1975)

Earned Run Average (starting pitchers)
1. Spud Chandler   1.64 (1943)
2. Russ Ford   1.65 (1910)
3. Ron Guidry   1.74 (1978)
4. Jack Chesbro   1.82 (1904)
5. Hippo Vaughn   1.83 (1910)

BASEBALL RECORDS— PITCHING

The following records are Major League records except when otherwise indicated; (AL) confines the record to the American League.

Games Won
Highest Winning Percentage With 200 Or More Decisions: .690
   WHITEY FORD—1950, 1953-67
   (236-106 record)

Highest Winning Percentage With 100 Or More Decisions: .717
   SPUD CHANDLER—1937-47

Highest Winning Percentage With 20 Or More Wins, Season: .893
   RON GUIDRY—1978 (25-3 record)

Most Games Won As A Rookie, Season: 26 (AL)
   RUSS FORD—1910

Most Consecutive Games Won As A Rookie, Season: 12 (Since 1900)
   ATLEY DONALD—May 9 - July 25, 1939
   RUSS FORD—Aug 9 - Oct 6, 1910

Games Started
Most Games Started, Season (since 1900): 51
   JACK CHESBRO—1904

Complete Games
Most Complete Games, Season (since 1900): 48
   JACK CHESBRO—1904

Strikeouts
Most Consecutive Strikeouts By A Relief Pitcher, Game: 8
   RON DAVIS—May 4, 1981
   2 in 7th inning, 3 in 8th inning,
   3 in 9th inning

Recording Three Strikeouts In One Inning Using Nine Pitches: (AL)
   AL DOWNING—August 11, 1967
   (second inning, first game)
   RON GUIDRY—August 7, 1984
   (ninth inning, second game)
   (many others)

Shutouts
Most Shutouts Won By A Lefthander, Season: 9 (AL)
   RON GUIDRY—1978
   (1 other—Babe Ruth when he was with the Red Sox, 1916)

Most Shutouts By A Rookie, Season: 8 (AL)
   RUSS FORD—1910
   (1 other)

Most Shutouts Won In First Two Major-League Games: 2
   SLOW JOE DOYLE—August 25 and 30, 1906—1st in AL to do this
   (7 others)

Low-Hit Games
Most No-Hitters, Season: 2
   ALLIE REYNOLDS—July 12 and September 28, 1951
   (4 others)

Most Consecutive One-Hitters Pitched: 2
   WHITEY FORD—September 2 and 7, 1955
   (6 others)

Allowing Home Runs
Fewest Home Runs Allowed (pitching at least 200 innings), Season: 3 (AL)
   LEFTY GOMEZ—1938
   (239 innings pitched)

Most Home Runs Allowed, inning 4:
   CATFISH HUNTER—June 17, 1977 (1st inning)
   SCOTT SANDERSON—May 2, 1992 (5th inning)

Most Home Runs Allowed by Opposing Pitcher, Game 6:
   AL THOMAS—June 27, 1946, St. Louis
   (1 other)

Wins in Relief
Most Career Games Won In The League As A Relief Pitcher: 87 (AL)
   SPARKY LYLE—1967-71 (Boston); 1972-78 (Yankees); 1979-80 (Texas)

Most Consecutive Games Won As A Relief Pitcher, Season: 12 (AL)
   LUIS ARROYO—July 1– September 9, 1961

Games in Relief
Most Career Games In The League As A Relief Pitcher: 807 (AL)
   SPARKY LYLE—1967-71 (Boston); 1972-78 (Yankees); 1979-80 (Texas), 1982 (Chicago)

Most Career Games Finished In The League: 599 (AL)
   SPARKY LYLE—1967-71 (Boston), 1972-78 (Yankees); 1979-80 (Texas); 1982 (Chicago)

DEFENSIVE MAINSTAYS

YEAR-BY-YEAR REGULARS BY POSITION

Catchers
1903— M. Beville
       J. O'Connor
1904— D. McGuire
       R. Kleinow
1905— R. Kleinow
       D. McGuire
1906— R. Kleinow
1907— R. Kleinow
1908— R. Kleinow
       W. Blair
1909— R. Kleinow
       E. Sweeney
1910— E. Sweeney
       F. Mitchell
1911— E. Sweeney
       W. Blair
1912— E. Sweeney
1913— E. Sweeney
1914— E. Sweeney
       L. Nunamaker
1915— L. Nunamaker
       E. Sweeney
1916— L. Nunamaker
       R. Walters
1917— L. Nunamaker
       R. Walters
1918— T. Hannah
       R. Walters
1919— M. Ruel
       T. Hannah
1920— M. Ruel
       T. Hannah
1921— W. Schang
1922— W. Schang
1923— W. Schang
       F. Hofmann
1924— W. Schang
1925— B. Bengough
       W. Schang
1926— P. Collins
1927— P. Collins
       J. Grabowski
1928— J. Grabowski
       B. Bengough
       P. Collins
1929— B. Dickey
1930— B. Dickey
1931— B. Dickey
1932— B. Dickey
1933— B. Dickey
1934— B. Dickey
1935— B. Dickey
1936— B. Dickey
1937— B. Dickey
1938— B. Dickey
1939— B. Dickey
1940— B. Dickey
       B. Rosar
1941— B. Dickey
       B. Rosar
1942— B. Dickey
       B. Rosar
1943— B. Dickey
       K. Sears
       R. Hemsley
1944— M. Garbark

R. Hemsley
1945— M. Garbark
       A. Robinson
       B. Drescher
1946— A. Robinson
1947— A. Robinson
       Y. Berra
1948— Y. Berra
       G. Niarhos
1949— Y. Berra
1950— Y. Berra
1951— Y. Berra
1952— Y. Berra
1953— Y. Berra
1954— Y Berra
1955— Y. Berra
1956— Y. Berra
1957— Y. Berra
1958— Y. Berra
       E. Howard
1959— Y. Berra
1960— E. Howard
       Y. Berra
1961— E. Howard
1962— E. Howard
1963— E. Howard
1964— E. Howard
1965— E. Howard
1966— E. Howard
1967— J. Gibbs
       E. Howard**
1968— J. Gibbs
1969— J. Gibbs
       F. Fernandez
1970— T. Munson
1971— T. Munson
1972— T. Munson
1973— T. Munson
1974— T. Munson
1975— T. Munson
1976— T. Munson
1977— T. Munson
1978— T. Munson
1979— T. Munson
       (J. Narron/B. Gulden)*
1980— R. Cerone
1981— R. Cerone
1982— R. Cerone/B. Wynegar
1983— B. Wynegar
1984— B. Wynegar
1985— B. Wynegar
1986— B. Wynegar***
       J. Skinner
       R. Hassey**
1987— R. Cerone
1988— D. Slaught
1989— D. Slaught
1990— B. Geren
1991— M. Nokes
1992— M. Nokes
1993— M. Stanley
1994— M. Stanley
1995— M. Stanley
1996— J. Girardi
1997— J. Girardi
1998— J. Posada
1999— J. Posada

2000— J. Posada
2001— J. Posada
2002— J. Posada

First Basemen
1903— J. Ganzel
1904— J. Ganzel
1905— H. Chase
1906— H. Chase
1907— H. Chase
1908— H. Chase
1909— H. Chase
1910— H. Chase
1911— H. Chase
1912— H. Chase
1913— J. Knight (3 others)
1914— C. Mullen
1915— W. Pipp
1916— W. Pipp
1917— W. Pipp
1918— W. Pipp
1919— W. Pipp
1920— W. Pipp
1921— W. Pipp
1922— W. Pipp
1923— W. Pipp
1924— W. Pipp
1925— L. Gehrig
1926— L. Gehrig
1927— L. Gehrig
1928— L. Gehrig
1929— L. Gehrig
1930— L. Gehrig
1931— L. Gehrig
1932— L. Gehrig
1933— L. Gehrig
1934— L. Gehrig
1935— L. Gehrig
1936— L. Gehrig
1937— L. Gehrig
1938— L. Gehrig
1939— B. Dahlgren
1940— B. Dahlgren
1941— J. Sturm
1942— B. Hassett
1943— N. Etten
1944— N. Etten
1945— N. Etten
1946— N. Etten
1947— G. McQuinn
1948— G. McQuinn
       T. Henrich
1949— T. Henrich
       D. Kryhoski
       (5 others)
1950— J. Mize
       J. Collins
       T. Henrich
1951— J. Mize
       J. Collins
1952— J. Collins
1953— J. Collins
1954— J. Collins
1955— B. Skowron
       J. Collins
1956— B. Skowron
1957— B. Skowron

1958— B. Skowron
1959— B. Skowron
       E. Howard
       M. Throneberry
1960— B. Skowron
1961— B. Skowron
1962— B. Skowron
1963— J. Pepitone
1964— J. Pepitone
1965— J. Pepitone
1966— J. Pepitone
1967— M. Mantle
1968— M. Mantle
1969— J. Pepitone
1970— D. Cater
1971— D. Cater
       J. Ellis
1972— R. Blomberg
       F. Alou
1973— R. Blomberg
       F. Alou
       M. Hegan
1974— C. Chambliss
1975— C. Chambliss
1976— C. Chambliss
1977— C. Chambliss
1978— C. Chambliss
1979— C. Chambliss
1980— B. Watson
       J. Spencer
1981— B. Watson
       D. Revering
1982— J. Mayberry
       D. Collins
1983— K. Griffey
1984— D. Mattingly
1985— D. Mattingly
1986— D. Mattingly
1987— D. Mattingly
1988— D. Mattingly
1989— D. Mattingly
1990— D. Mattingly
       K. Maas
1991— D. Mattingly
1992— D. Mattingly
1993— D. Mattingly
1994— D. Mattingly
1995— D. Mattingly
1996— T. Martinez
1997— T. Martinez
1998— T. Martinez
1999— T. Martinez
2000— T. Martinez
2001— T. Martinez
2002— J. Giambi

Second Basemen
1903— J. Williams
1904— J. Williams
1905— J. Williams
1906— J. Williams
1907— J. Williams
1908— H. Niles
1909— F. LaPorte
1910— F. LaPorte
       E. Gardner
1911— E. Gardner
1912— H. Simmons
1913— R. Hartzell

*Played position after Munson's death. **Traded during season. ***Jumped club in mid-season.

1914— L. Boone
1915— L. Boone
1916— J. Gedeon
1917— F. Maisel
1918— D. Pratt
1919— D. Pratt
1920— D. Pratt
1921— A. Ward
1922— A. Ward
1923— A. Ward
1924— A. Ward
1925— A. Ward
1926— T. Lazzeri
1927— T. Lazzeri
1928— T. Lazzeri
1929— T. Lazzeri
1930— T. Lazzeri
    B. Chapman
    J. Reese
1931— T. Lazzeri
    J. Reese
1932— T. Lazzeri
1933— T. Lazzeri
1934— T. Lazzeri
    D. Heffner
1935— T. Lazzeri
1936— T. Lazzeri
1937— T. Lazzeri
1938— J. Gordon
1939— J. Gordon
1940— J. Gordon
1941— J. Gordon
1942— J. Gordon
1943— J. Gordon
1944— S. Stirnweiss
1945— S. Stirnweiss
1946— J. Gordon
1947— S. Stirnweiss
1948— S. Stirnweiss
1949— J. Coleman
1950— J. Coleman
1951— J. Coleman
1952— B. Martin
1953— B. Martin
1954— G. McDougald
    J. Coleman
1955— G. McDougald
1956— B. Martin
1957— B. Richardson
1958— G. McDougald
1959— B. Richardson
1960— B. Richardson
1961— B. Richardson
1962— B. Richardson
1963— B. Richardson
1964— B. Richardson
1965— B. Richardson
1966— B. Richardson
1967— H. Clarke
1968— H. Clarke
1969— H. Clarke
1970— H. Clarke
1971— H. Clarke
1972— H. Clarke
1973— H. Clarke
1974— S. Alomar†
1975— S. Alomar
1976— W. Randolph
1977— W. Randolph
1978— W. Randolph
1979— W. Randolph
1980— W. Randolph
1981— W. Randolph
1982— W. Randolph

1983— W. Randolph
1984— W. Randolph
1985— W. Randolph
1986— W. Randolph
1987— W. Randolph
1988— W. Randolph
1989— S. Sax
1990— S. Sax
1991— S. Sax
1992— P. Kelly
1993— P. Kelly
1994— P. Kelly
1995— P. Kelly
    R. Velarde
1996— M. Duncan
1997— L. Sojo
1998— C. Knoblauch
1999— C. Knoblauch
2000— C. Knoblauch
2001— A. Soriano
2002— A. Soriano

Third Basemen
1903— W. Conroy
1904— W. Conroy
1905— J. Yeager
    W. Conroy
1906— F. LaPorte
1907— G. Moriarty
    F. LaPorte
1908— W. Conroy
1909— J. Austin
1910— J. Austin
1911— R. Hartzell
1912— R. Hartzell
    D. Paddock
1913— E. Midkiff
    F. Maisel
1914— F. Maisel
1915— F. Maisel
1916— F. Baker
1917— F. Baker
1918— F. Baker
1919— F. Baker
1920— A. Ward
1921— F. Baker
1922— J. Dugan
    F. Baker
1923— J. Dugan
1924— J. Dugan
1925— J. Dugan
1926— J. Dugan
1927— J. Dugan
1928— J. Dugan
    G. Robertson
1929— G. Robertson**
    L. Lary
1930— B. Chapman
    T. Lazzeri
1931— J. Sewell
1932— J. Sewell
1933— J. Sewell
1934— J. Saltzgaver
1935— R. Rolfe
1936— R. Rolfe
1937— R. Rolfe
1938— R. Rolfe
1939— R. Rolfe
1940— R. Rolfe
1941— R. Rolfe
1942— F. Crosetti
    R. Rolfe
1943— B. Johnson
1944— O. Grimes

    D. Savage
1945— O. Grimes
1946— S. Stirnweiss
    B. Johnson
1947— B. Johnson
1948— B. Johnson
1949— B. Brown
    B. Johnson
1950— B. Johnson
    B. Brown
1951— B. Brown
    G. McDougald
1952— G. McDougald
1953— G. McDougald
1954— A. Carey
1955— A. Carey
1956— A. Carey
1957— A. Carey
1958— A. Carey
    J. Lumpe
1959— H. Lopez
1960— C. Boyer
    G. McDougald
1961— C. Boyer
1962— C. Boyer
1963— C. Boyer
1964— C. Boyer
1965— C. Boyer
1966— C. Boyer
    T. Tresh
1967— C. Smith
1968— B. Cox
1969— J. Kenney
    B. Cox
1970— J. Kenney
1971— J. Kenney
1972— C. Sanchez
    B. Allen
1973— G. Nettles
1974— G. Nettles
1975— G. Nettles
1976— G. Nettles
1977— G. Nettles
1978— G. Nettles
1979— G. Nettles
1980— G. Nettles
1981— G. Nettles
1982— G. Nettles
1983— G. Nettles
1984— T. Harrah
    M. Pagliarulo
1985— M. Pagliarulo
1986— M. Pagliarulo
1987— M. Pagliarulo
1988— M. Pagliarulo
1989— M. Pagliarulo**
    T. Brookens
1990— R. Velarde
    J. Leyritz
    M. Blowers
1991— P. Kelly
    R. Velarde
1992— C. Hayes
1993— W. Boggs
1994— W. Boggs
1995— W. Boggs
1996— W. Boggs
1997— C. Hayes
1998— S. Brosius
1999— S. Brosius
2000— S. Brosius
2001— S. Brosius
2002— R. Ventura

Shortstops
1903— K. Elberfeld
1904— K. Elberfeld
1905— K. Elberfeld
1906— K. Elberfeld
1907— K. Elberfeld
1908— N. Ball
1909— J. Knight
    K. Elberfeld
1910— J. Knight
    R. Roach
1911— J. Knight
1912— J. Martin
1913— R. Peckinpaugh
1914— R. Peckinpaugh
1915— R. Peckinpaugh
1916— R. Peckinpaugh
1917— R. Peckinpaugh
1918— R. Peckinpaugh
1919— R. Peckinpaugh
1920— R. Peckinpaugh
1921— R. Peckinpaugh
1922— E. Scott
1923— E. Scott
1924— E. Scott
1925— P. W. Wanninger
1926— M. Koenig
1927— M. Koenig
1928— M. Koenig
1929— L. Durocher
    M. Koenig
1930— L. Lary
1931— L. Lary
1932— F. Crosetti
    L. Lary
1933— F. Crosetti
1934— F. Crosetti
1935— F. Crosetti
1936— F. Crosetti
1937— F. Crosetti
1938— F. Crosetti
1939— F. Crosetti
1940— F. Crosetti
1941— P. Rizzuto
1942— P. Rizzuto
1943— F. Crosetti
    S. Stirnweiss
1944— M. Milosevich
    F. Crosetti
1945— F. Crosetti
1946— P. Rizzuto
1947— P. Rizzuto
1948— P. Rizzuto
1949— P. Rizzuto
1950— P. Rizzuto
1951— P. Rizzuto
1952— P. Rizzuto
1953— P. Rizzuto
1954— P. Rizzuto
1955— B. Hunter
    P. Rizzuto
1956— G. McDougald
1957— G. McDougald
1958— T. Kubek
1959— T. Kubek
    G. McDougald
1960— T. Kubek
1961— T. Kubek
1962— T. Tresh
1963— T. Kubek
1964— T. Kubek
1965— T. Kubek
    P. Linz
1966— H. Clarke

---

*Acquired by trade during season. **Traded during season. †Many second basemen used until Alomar was traded to the Yankees on July 8

C. Boyer
1967— R. Amaro
1968— T. Tresh
1969— G. Michael
1970— G. Michael
1971— G. Michael
1972— G. Michael
1973— G. Michael
1974— J. Mason
1975— J. Mason
F. Stanley
1976— F. Stanley
J. Mason
1977— B. Dent
1978— B. Dent
1979— B. Dent
1980— B. Dent
1981— B. Dent
1982— R. Smalley*
B. Dent**
1983— A. Robertson***
R. Smalley
1984— B. Meacham
1985— B. Meacham
1986— B. Meacham
W. Tolleson
1987— W. Tolleson
1988— R. Santana
1989— A. Espinoza
1990— A. Espinoza
1991— A. Espinoza
1992— A. Stankiewicz
R. Velarde
1993— S. Owen
M. Gallego
1994— M. Gallego
1995— T. Fernandez
1996— D. Jeter
1997— D. Jeter
1998— D. Jeter
1999— D. Jeter
2000— D. Jeter
2001— D. Jeter
2002— D. Jeter

Leftfielders
1903— L. Davis
1904— P. Dougherty
1905— P. Dougherty
1906— F. Delahanty
1907— W. Conroy
1908— J. Stahl
1909— C. Engle
1910— B. Cree
1911— B. Cree
1912— B. Daniels
1913— B. Cree
1914— R. Hartzell
1915— R. Hartzell
1916— H. High
1917— H. High
1918— P. Bodie
1919— D. Lewis
1920— D. Lewis
1921— B. Ruth
1922— B. Ruth
1923— B. Meusel
1924— B. Meusel
1925— B. Meusel
1926— B. Meusel
1927— B. Meusel
1928— B. Meusel
1929— B. Meusel
1930— E. Combs
1931— B. Chapman

***Car accident ended season.

1932— B. Chapman
1933— B. Chapman
1934— M. Hoag
S. Byrd
1935— J. Hill
E. Combs
1936— J. Powell
J. DiMaggio
1937— J. Powell
G. Selkirk
1938— G. Selkirk
1939— G. Selkirk
1940— G. Selkirk
1941— C. Keller
1942— C. Keller
1943— C. Keller
1944— H. Martin
1945— H. Martin
1946— C. Keller
1947— J. Lindell
1948— J. Lindell
C. Keller
1949— G. Woodling
J. Lindell
1950— G. Woodling
1951— G. Woodling
1952— G. Woodling
I. Noren
1953— G. Woodling
I. Noren
1954— I. Noren
G. Woodling
1955— I. Noren
E. Howard
1956— E. Howard
N. Siebern
J. Collins
1957— E. Slaughter
E. Howard
T. Kubek
1958— N. Siebern
1959— N. Siebern
1960— H. Lopez
1961— Y. Berra
H. Lopez
1962— H. Lopez
J. Blanchard
T. Tresh
1963— H. Lopez
1964— T. Tresh
1965— M. Mantle
T. Tresh
1966— T. Tresh
R. White
1967— T. Tresh
1968— R. White
1969— R. White
1970— R. White
1971— R. White
1972— R. White
1973— R. White
1974— L. Piniella
1975— R. White
1976— R. White
1977— R. White
L. Piniella
1978— L. Piniella
R. White
1979— L. Piniella
1980— L. Piniella
B. Murcer
O. Gamble
J. Lefebvre
1981— D. Winfield
1982— D. Winfield
1983— D. Winfield

1984— S. Kemp
1985— K. Griffey
1986— D. Pasqua
K. Griffey
1987— G. Ward
D. Pasqua
1988— R. Henderson
1989— R. Henderson**
M. Hall
1990— O. Azocar
M. Hall
1991— M. Hall
1992— M. Hall
1993— D. James
R. Velarde
1994— L. Polonia
1995— L. Polonia**
D. James
1996— G. Williams**
T. Raines
1997— C. Curtis
1998— C. Curtis
1999— R. Ledee
2000— R. Ledee
D. Justice
2001— C. Knoblauch
2002— Rondell White

Centerfielders
1903— H. McFarland
D. Fultz
1904— D. Fultz
J. Anderson
1905— D. Fultz
1906— D. Hoffman
1907— D. Hoffman
1908— C. Hemphill
1909— R. Demmitt
1910— C. Hemphill
B. Daniels
1911— B. Daniels
1912— R. Hartzell
1913— H. Wolter
1914— B. Cree
T. Daley
1915— H. High
1916— L. Magee
1917— T. Hendryx
1918— E. Miller
1919— P. Bodie
1920— P. Bodie
1921— E. Miller
C. Fewster
1922— W. Witt
1923— W. Witt
1924— W. Witt
1925— E. Combs
1926— E. Combs
1927— E. Combs
1928— E. Combs
1929— E. Combs
1930— H. Rice
S. Byrd
E. Combs
1931— E. Combs
1932— E. Combs
1933— E. Combs
1934— B. Chapman
E. Combs
1935— B. Chapman
1936— J. DiMaggio
J. Powell
1937— J. DiMaggio
1938— J. DiMaggio
1939— J. DiMaggio
1940— J. DiMaggio

1941— J. DiMaggio
1942— J. DiMaggio
1943— J. Lindell
1944— J. Lindell
1945— T. Stainback
R. Derry
J. Lindell
1946— J. DiMaggio
1947— J. DiMaggio
1948— J. DiMaggio
1949— C. Mapes
J. DiMaggio
1950— J. DiMaggio
1951— J. DiMaggio
1952— M. Mantle
1953— M. Mantle
1954— M. Mantle
1955— M. Mantle
1956— M. Mantle
1957— M. Mantle
1958— M. Mantle
1959— M. Mantle
1960— M. Mantle
1961— M. Mantle
1962— M. Mantle
1963— T. Tresh
1964— M. Mantle
1965— T. Tresh
M. Mantle
1966— M. Mantle
1967— J. Pepitone
1968— J. Pepitone
1969— B. Robinson
J. Hall
1970— B. Murcer
1971— B. Murcer
1972— B. Murcer
1973— B. Murcer
1974— E. Maddox
1975— E. Maddox
W. Williams
R. Coggins
1976— M. Rivers
1977— M. Rivers
1978— M. Rivers
1979— M. Rivers**
B. Murcer*
1980— R. Jones
B. Brown
1981— J. Mumphrey
1982— J. Mumphrey
1983— J. Mumphrey
1984— O. Moreno
1985— R. Henderson
1986— R. Henderson
1987— R. Henderson
C. Washington
1988— C. Washington
1989— R. Kelly
1990— R. Kelly
1991— R. Kelly
B. Williams
1992— R. Kelly
1993— B. Williams
1994— B. Williams
1995— B. Williams
1996— B. Williams
1997— B. Williams
1998— B. Williams
1999— B. Williams
2000— B. Williams
2001— B. Williams
2002— B. Williams

Rightfielders
1903— W. Keeler

1904— W. Keeler	1952— H. Bauer
1905— W. Keeler	1953— H. Bauer
1906— W. Keeler	1954— H. Bauer
1907— W. Keeler	1955— H. Bauer
1908— W. Keeler	1956— H. Bauer
1909— W. Keeler	1957— H. Bauer
1910— H. Wolter	1958— H. Bauer
1911— H. Wolter	1959— H. Bauer
1912— G. Zinn	1960— R. Maris
1913— B. Daniels	1961— R. Maris
1914 - D. Cook	1962— R. Maris
1915— D. Cook	1963— R. Maris
1916— F. Gilhooley	J. Blanchard
R. Oldring	1964— R. Maris
1917— E. Miller	1965— H. Lopez
1918— F. Gilhooley	R. Repoz
1919— S. Vick	R. Maris
1920— B. Ruth	1966— R. Maris
1921— B. Meusel	1967— S. Whitaker
1922— B. Meusel	1968— R. Robinson
1923— B. Ruth	A. Kosco
1924— B. Ruth	1969— B. Murcer
1925— B. Ruth	1970— C. Blefary
B. Paschal	R. Woods
1926— B. Ruth	1971— F. Alou
1927— B. Ruth	R. Blomberg
1928— B. Ruth	1972— J. Callison
1929— B. Ruth	R. Torres
1930— B. Ruth	1973— M. Alou
1931— B. Ruth	1974— B. Murcer
1932— B. Ruth	1975— B. Bonds
1933— B. Ruth	1976— O. Gamble
1934— B. Ruth	L. Piniella
G. Selkirk	1977— R. Jackson
1935— G. Selkirk	1978— R. Jackson
1936— G. Selkirk	1979— R. Jackson
1937— M. Hoag	1980— R. Jackson
T. Henrich	1981— R. Jackson
1938— T. Henrich	1982— K. Griffey
M. Hoag	1983— S. Kemp
1939— C. Keller	1984— D. Winfield
T. Henrich	1985— D. Winfield
1940— C. Keller	1986— D. Winfield
T. Henrich	1987— D. Winfield
1941— T. Henrich	1988— D. Winfield
1942— T. Henrich	1989— J. Barfield
1943— B. Metheny	1990— J. Barfield
R. Weatherly	1991— J. Barfield
1944— B. Metheny	1992— D. Tartabull
1945— B. Metheny	1993— P. O'Neill
1946— T. Henrich	1994— P. O'Neill
1947— T. Henrich	1995— P. O'Neill
1948— T. Henrich	1996— P. O'Neill
1949— H. Bauer	1997— P. O'Neill
T. Henrich	1998— P. O'Neill
1950— H. Bauer	1999— P. O'Neill
C. Mapes	2000— P. O'Neill
1951— H. Bauer	2001— P. O'Neill
M. Mantle	2002— R. Mondesi

CLUB SINGLE-SEASON FIELDING LEADERS (1903-2002)

A minimum of 100 games played at each position is required to qualify for fielding average.

Catchers
Fielding Average—.998
    ELSTON HOWARD, 1964 (146 games)
    THURMAN MUNSON, 1971 (117 games)
Putouts—939
    ELSTON HOWARD, 1964
Assists—180
    JEFF SWEENEY, 1913

Double Plays—25
    YOGI BERRA, 1951

First Basemen
Fielding Average—.998
    DON MATTINGLY, 1993 (130 games)
Putouts—1667
    WALLY PIPP, 1922
Assists—124
    DON MATTINGLY, 1984
Double Plays—157
    LOU GEHRIG, 1938

Second Basemen
Fielding Average—.993
    SNUFFY STIRNWEISS, 1948 (141 games)
Putouts—433
    SNUFFY STIRNWEISS, 1944
Assists—515
    DEL PRATT, 1920
Double Plays—137
    JERRY COLEMAN, 1950
    GRAIG NETTLES, 1978 (159 games)
Putouts—206
    FRITZ MAISEL, 1914
Assists—410
    GRAIG NETTLES, 1973
Double Plays—46
    CLETE BOYER, 1965

Shortstops
Fielding Average—.983
    FRED STANLEY, 1976 (110 games)
Putouts—356
    ROGER PECKINPAUGH, 1914
Assists—538
    EVERETT SCOTT, 1922
Double Plays—123
    PHIL RIZZUTO, 1950

Outfielders
Fielding Average—1.000
    PAUL O'NEILL, 1996 (146 games)
    BERNIE WILLIAMS, 2000 (137 games)
    RONDELL WHITE, 2002 (113 games)
Putouts—468
    JOHNNY LINDELL, 1944
Assists—28
    BOB MEUSEL, 1921
Double Plays—8
    HARRY WOLTER, 1911
    FRANK GILHOOLEY, 1918
    BOB MEUSEL, 1921

BASEBALL RECORDS— DEFENSE

The following are Major League records except when otherwise indicated; (AL) confines the record to the American League.

Pitchers
Most Assists In Nine-Inning Game: 11
    AL ORTH—August 12, 1906
    GEORGE McCONNELL—September 2, 1912
    (3 others)

Catchers
Most Years Leading The League In Games Caught: 8
    YOGI BERRA—1950-57

Most Consecutive Years Catching 100 Or More Games: 13
    BILL DICKEY—1929-41 (AL)

Most Years Leading The League In Chances Accepted: 8
    YOGI BERRA—1950-52, 1954-57, 1959
    (2 others)

Most Consecutive Chances Accepted Without Making An Error: 950
 YOGI BERRA—July 28, 1957 through
 May 10, 1959 (148 games) (AL)

Most Consecutive Errorless Games: 159
 RICK CERONE—July 5, 1987 through
 May 8, 1989; Yankees and Boston
 (896 chances accepted) (AL)
Fewest Passed Balls With 100 Or More Games Caught, Season: 0
 BILL DICKEY—1931 (125 games)
 (4 others)

Most Runners Caught Stealing, Inning: 3
 LES NUNAMAKER—August 3, 1914 (second inning)

Most Years Leading The League In Double Plays: 6
 YOGI BERRA—1949-52, 1954, 1956 (1 other)

First Basemen
Most Consecutive Games Playing First Base: 885
 LOU GEHRIG—June 2, 1925 –
 September 27, 1930

Most Years Leading The League In Games Played At First Base: 7 (AL)
 LOU GEHRIG—1926-28, 1932, 1936-38

Most Years Leading The League In Chances Accepted: 4 (AL)
 WALLY PIPP—1915, 1919-20, 1922

Highest Career Fielding Average (1,000 or more games): .996
 DON MATTINGLY—1983-95
 (1634 games)
 (2 others)

Most Years Leading The League In Fielding Average (100 or more games): 6 (AL)
 DON MATTINGLY—1984-87, 1992-93
 (1 other)

Most Years Leading The League In Putouts: 4 (AL)
 WALLY PIPP—1915, 1919-20, 1922

Most Putouts In Nine-Inning Game: 22
 HAL CHASE—September 21, 1906 (Game 1)

DON MATTINGLY—July 20, 1987
 (4 others)

Most Years Leading The League In Double Plays: 4 (AL)
 WALLY PIPP—1915-17, 1920
 (2 others)

Most Double Plays, Game: 6 (AL)
 BOB OLIVER—April 29, 1975
 (7 others)

Second Basemen
Most Consecutive Years Leading The League In Assists: 6
 HORACE CLARKE—1967-72

Most Chances Accepted In Extra-Inning Game:
20 (AL)
 WILLIE RANDOLPH—August 25, 1976 (19 innings)

Most Assists In Extra-Inning Game: 13 (AL)
 WILLIE RANDOLPH—August 25, 1976 (19 innings)
 (1 other)

Third Basemen
Most Assists In Nine-Inning Game: 11
 MIKE FERRARO—September 14, 1968
 (5 others)

Most Unassisted Double Plays, Season: 4
 JOE DUGAN—1924

Most Double Plays, Game: 4
 ANDY CAREY—July 31, 1955 (second game)
 (5 others)

Outfielders
Most Consecutive Years Leading The League In Fielding Average: 3 (AL)
 GENE WOODLING—1951-53

Most Assists In Nine-Inning Game: 4
 LEE MAGEE—June 28, 1916
 BOB MEUSEL—Sept. 5, 1921 (second game)
 (6 others)

PERFORMANCE AS A TEAM

YANKEE TEAM RECORDS

The shortened seasons of 1918, 1981, and 1994 do not figure in club records, except for the entry "Fewest Games Played."

Most Players Used in a Season: 50—1989
Fewest Players Used in a Season: 25—1923, 1927
Most Games Played: 164—1964, 1968
Fewest Games Played: 107—1981
Most At-Bats: 5705—1964
Most Runs: 1067—1931*
Fewest Runs: 459—1908
Most Runs by Opponents: 898—1930
Most Hits: 1683—1930
Fewest Hits: 1137—1968
Most Singles: 1237—1988
Most Doubles: 325—1997
Most Triples: 110—1930
Most Home Runs: 240—1961
Most Home Runs by Pinch-Hitter: 10—1961
Most Grand Slam Home Runs: 10—1987
Most Extra-Base Hits: 580—1936
Most Total Bases: 2703—1936
Most Sacrifices (Hits and Flies): 218—1922, 1926
Most Sacrifice Hits: 178—1906
Most Sacrifice Flies: 72—1974
Most Stolen Bases: 289—1910
Most Caught Stealing: 82—1920
Most Bases on Balls: 766—1932
Most Strikeouts: 1043—1967

Fewest Strikeouts: 420—1924
Most Batters Hit By a Pitched Ball: 64—2001
Fewest Batters Hit By a Pitched Ball: 14—1969
Most Runs Batted In: 995—1936**
Highest Batting Average: .309—1930
Lowest Batting Average: .214—1968
Highest Slugging Average: .489—1927**
Lowest Slugging Average: .287—1914
Most Double Plays Grounded Into: 152—1982
Fewest Double Plays Grounded Into: 91—1963
Most Left on Bases: 1247—1993
Fewest Left on Bases: 1010—1920
Most .300 Hitters: 9—1930
Most Putouts: 4520—1964**
Fewest Putouts: 3993—1935
Most Assists: 2086—1904
Fewest Assists: 1487—2000
Most Chances Accepted: 6383—1980
Fewest Chances Accepted: 5551—1935
Most Errors: 386—1912
Fewest Errors: 102—1987
Most Errorless Games: 91—1964
Most Consecutive Errorless Games: 10—1977, 1993
Most Double Plays Made: 214—1956
Fewest Double Plays Made: 81—1912
Most Consecutive Games, One or More Double Plays Made: 19—1992
 (27 DPs in all)
Most Passed Balls: 32—1913
Fewest Passed Balls: 0—1931**
Highest Fielding Average: .986—1995

Lowest Fielding Average: .939—1912
Most Games Won: 110—1927
Most Games Lost: 103—1908
Highest Percentage Games Won: .714 —1927 (won 110, lost 44)
Lowest Percentage Games Won: .329—1912 (won 50, lost 102)
Most Shutouts Won: 24—1951
Most Shutouts Lost: 27—1914
Most 1-0 Games Won: 6—1908, 1968
Most 1-0 Games Lost: 9—1914
Most Consecutive Games Won: 19—1947
Most Consecutive Games Lost: 13—1913
Most Saves: 58—1986
Most Complete Games Pitched: 123—1904
Most Innings Pitched: 1506 ⅔—1964**
Most Strikeouts Recorded by Pitchers: 1139—1996
Lowest Earned Run Average: 2.57—1904
Most Runs Scored, Game: 25—May 24, 1936
  Yankees—25; Philadelphia A's—2
Most Runs Scored, Shutout Game: 21—August 13, 1939
  Yankees—21; Philadelphia A's—0 (8 innings)
Most Runs Scored, Inning: 14—July 6, 1920 vs. Washington (fifth inning)
Most Runs Scored, Game, by Opponent: 24—July 29, 1928
  Cleveland Indians—24; Yankees—6
Most Runs Scored, Shutout Game, by Opponent: 15 (twice)
  July 15, 1907—Chicago White Sox—15; Yankees—0
  May 4, 1950—Chicago White Sox—15; Yankees—0
Most Hits, Game: 30—September 28, 1923 vs. Boston
Most Home Runs, Game: 8—June 28, 1939 vs. Philadelphia
Most Consecutive Games, One or More Home Runs: 25—1941**
  (40 HRs in all) (1 other club)
Most Home Runs in Consecutive Games in Which Home Runs Were Hit: 40—1941
  (25 games)
Most Total Bases, Game: 53—June 28, 1939 vs. Philadelphia

---

* AL Record
** ML Record

LONGEST AND SHORTEST GAMES IN YANKEE HISTORY

Longest Extra-Inning Game, by Time: 7 hours, 0 minutes
  At Detroit—June 24, 1962 (Yankees—9; Detroit Tigers—7)

Longest Extra-Inning Game, by Innings: 22 innings
  At Detroit—June 24, 1962 (Yankees—9, Detroit Tigers—7)

Longest Extra-Inning Game Played at the Polo Grounds: 19 innings
  May 24, 1918 (Cleveland Indians—3; Yankees—2)

Longest Extra-Inning Game Played at Hilltop Park: 15 innings
  July 15, 1904 (Highlanders—3; Cleveland—2)
  May 21, 1910 (Highlanders—5; Cleveland—4)

Longest Extra-Inning Game Played at Yankee Stadium:
  20 innings—August 29, 1967 (Yankees—4; Boston Red Sox—3)

Longest Nine-Inning Game, by Time: 4 hours, 22 minutes
  At Yankee Stadium—September 5, 1997 (Orioles—13; Yankees—9)
  (set Major League record for nine-inning game, by time)

Shortest Nine-Inning Game, by Time: 55 minutes (AL Record)
  At. St. Louis—September 26, 1926
  (St. Louis Browns—6; Yankees—2. Second Game)

Shortest 18-Inning Doubleheader, by Time: 2 hours, 7 minutes
  At St. Louis—September 26, 1926

TEAM OFFENSIVE STATISTICS
Year-by-year 1903-2002

YEAR	G	AB	R	H	2B	3B	HR	RBI	BB	SB	BA	SA
1903	136	4565	579	1136	193	62	18	474	332	160	.249	.330
1904	155	5220	598	1354	195	91	27	499	312	163	.259	.347

YEAR	G	AB	R	H	2B	3B	HR	RBI	BB	SB	BA	SA
1905	152	4957	586	1228	163	61	23	480	360	200	.248	.319
1906	155	5095	644	1354	166	77	17	528	331	192	.266	.339
1907	152	5044	605	1258	150	67	15	497	304	206	.249	.315
1908	155	5046	459	1190	142	50	13	372	288	231	.236	.292
1909	153	4981	590	1234	143	61	16	473	407	187	.248	.311
1910	156	5051	626	1254	164	75	20	492	464	288	.248	.322
1911	153	5052	684	1374	190	96	25	577	493	269	.272	.362
1912	153	5092	630	1320	168	79	18	502	463	247	.259	.334
1913	153	4880	529	1157	155	45	8	430	534	203	.237	.292
1914	157	4992	537	1144	149	52	12	416	577	251	.229	.287
1915	154	4982	584	1162	167	50	31	459	570	198	.233	.305
1916	156	5198	577	1277	194	59	35	492	516	179	.246	.326
1917	155	5136	524	1226	172	52	27	445	496	136	.239	.308
1918	126	4224	491	1085	160	45	20	406	367	88	.257	.330
1919	141	4775	578	1275	193	49	45	499	386	101	.267	.356
1920	154	5176	838	1448	268	71	115	747	539	64	.280	.426
1921	153	5249	948	1576	285	87	134	861	588	89	.300	.464
1922	154	5245	758	1504	220	75	95	674	497	62	.287	.412
1923	152	5347	823	1554	231	79	105	770	521	69	.291	.422
1924	153	5240	798	1516	248	74	98	734	478	69	.289	.426
1925	156	5353	706	1471	247	74	110	638	470	67	.275	.410
1926	155	5221	847	1508	262	75	121	794	642	79	.289	.437
1927	155	5347	975	1644	291	103	158	908	635	90	.307	.489*
1928	154	5337	894	1578	269	79	133	817	562	51	.296	.450
1929	154	5379	899	1587	262	74	142	828	554	51	.295	.450
1930	154	5448	1062	1683	298	110	152	986	644	91	.309	.488
1931	155	5608	1067*	1667	277	78	155	990	748	138	.297	.457
1932	156	5477	1002	1564	279	82	160	955	766	77	.286	.454
1933	152	5274	927	1495	241	75	144	849	700	76	.283	.440
1934	154	5368	842	1494	226	61	135	791	700	71	.278	.419
1935	149	5214	818	1462	255	70	104	755	604	68	.280	.416
1936	155	5591	1065	1676	315	83	182	995*	700	76	.300	.483
1937	157	5487	979	1554	282	73	174	922	709	60	.283	.456
1938	157	5410	966	1480	283	63	174	917	749	91	.274	.446
1939	152	5300	967	1521	259	55	166	903	701	72	.287	.451
1940	155	5286	817	1371	243	66	155	757	648	59	.259	.418
1941	156	5444	830	1464	243	60	151	774	616	51	.269	.419
1942	154	5305	801	1429	223	57	108	744	591	69	.269	.394
1943	155	5282	669	1350	218	59	100	636	624	46	.256	.376
1944	154	5331	674	1410	216	74	96	631	523	91	.264	.387
1945	152	5176	676	1343	189	61	93	639	618	64	.259	.373
1946	154	5139	684	1275	208	50	136	649	627	48	.248	.387
1947	155	5308	794	1439	230	72	115	746	610	27	.271	.407
1948	154	5324	857	1480	251	75	139	806	623	24	.278	.432
1949	155	5196	829	1396	215	60	115	759	731	58	.269	.400
1950	154	5361	914	1511	234	70	159	863	687	41	.282	.441
1951	154	5194	798	1395	208	48	140	741	605	78	.269	.408
1952	154	5294	727	1411	221	56	129	672	566	52	.267	.403
1953	151	5194	801	1420	226	52	139	762	656	34	.273	.417
1954	155	5226	805	1400	215	59	133	747	650	34	.268	.408
1955	154	5161	762	1342	179	55	175	722	609	55	.260	.418
1956	154	5312	857	1433	193	55	190	788	615	51	.270	.434
1957	154	5271	723	1412	200	54	145	682	562	49	.268	.409
1958	155	5294	759	1418	212	39	164	715	537	48	.268	.416
1959	155	5379	687	1397	224	40	153	651	457	45	.260	.402
1960	155	5290	746	1377	215	40	193	699	537	37	.260	.426
1961	163	5559	827	1461	194	40	240	782	543	28	.263	.442
1962	162	5644	817	1509	240	29	199	791	584	42	.267	.426
1963	161	5506	714	1387	197	35	188	666	434	42	.252	.403
1964	164	5705	730	1442	208	35	162	688	520	54	.253	.387
1965	162	5470	611	1286	196	31	149	576	489	35	.235	.364
1966	160	5330	611	1254	182	36	162	569	485	49	.235	.374
1967	163	5443	522	1225	166	17	100	473	532	63	.225	.317
1968	164	5310	536	1137	154	34	109	501	566	90	.214	.318
1969	162	5308	562	1247	210	44	94	521	565	119	.235	.344
1970	163	5304	680	1381	208	41	111	627	588	105	.251	.365
1971	162	5413	648	1377	195	43	97	607	581	75	.254	.360
1972	155	5168	557	1288	201	24	103	526	491	71	.249	.357
1973	162	5492	641	1435	212	17	131	616	489	47	.261	.378
1974	162	5524	671	1451	220	30	101	637	515	53	.263	.368
1975	160	5415	681	1430	230	39	110	642	486	102	.264	.382

YEAR	G	AB	R	H	2B	3B	HR	RBI	BB	SB	BA	SA
1976	159	5555	730	1496	231	36	120	682	470	163	.269	.389
1977	162	5605	831	1576	267	47	184	784	533	93	.281	.444
1978	163	5583	735	1489	228	38	125	693	505	98	.267	.388
1979	160	5421	734	1443	226	40	150	694	509	65	.266	.406
1980	162	5553	820	1484	239	34	189	772	643	86	.267	.425
1981	107	3529	421	889	148	22	100	403	391	47	.252	.391
1982	162	5526	709	1417	225	37	161	666	590	69	.256	.398
1983	162	5631	770	1535	269	40	153	728	533	84	.273	.416
1984	162	5661	758	1560	**275**	32	130	725	534	62	.276	.404
1985	161	5458	**839**	1458	272	31	176	**793**	620	**155**	.267	.425
1986	162	5570	797	1512	275	23	188	745	645	139	.271	**.430**
1987	162	5511	788	1445	239	16	196	749	604	105	.262	.418
1988	161	5592	772	1469	272	12	148	713	588	146	.263	.395
1989	161	5458	698	1470	229	23	130	657	502	137	.269	.391
1990	162	5483	603	1322	208	19	147	561	427	119	.241	.366
1991	162	5541	674	1418	249	19	147	630	473	109	.256	.387
1992	162	5593	733	1462	281	18	163	703	536	78	.261	.406
1993	162	5615	821	**1568**	294	24	178	793	629	39	**.279**	.435
1994	113	3986	670	1155	238	16	139	632	**530**	55	**.290**	.462
1995	145	4947	749	1365	280	34	122	709	**625**	50	.276	.420
1996	162	5628	871	1621	293	28	162	830	632	96	.288	.436
1997	162	5710	891	1636	325	23	161	846	**676**	99	.287	.436
1998	162	5643	**965**	1625	290	31	207	**907**	653	153	.288	.460
1999	162	5568	900	1568	302	36	193	855	718	104	.282	.453
2000	161	5556	871	1541	294	25	205	833	631	99	.277	.450
2001	161	5577	804	1488	289	20	203	774	519	161	.267	.435
2002	161	5601	**897**	1540	314	12	223	**857**	640	100	.275	**.455**

Boldface Led AL
Boldface* ML Record

TEAM PITCHING STATISTICS
Year-by-year 1903-2002

YEAR	WON	LOST	PCT	SV	G	CG	IP	SO	SH	ERA
1903	72	62	.537	2	136	111	1201	463	7	3.08
1904	92	59	.609	1	155	123	1381	684	15	2.57
1905	71	78	.477	4	152	88	1354	642	16	2.93
1906	90	61	.596	5	155	99	1358	605	18	2.78
1907	70	78	.473	5	152	93	1334	511	10	3.03
1908	51	**103**	.331	3	155	90	1366	585	11	3.16
1909	74	77	.490	3	153	94	1366	597	18	2.65
1910	88	63	.583	**8**	156	110	1399	654	14	2.61
1911	76	76	.500	3	153	91	1361	667	5	3.54
1912	50	**102**	.329	3	153	105	1335	637	5	4.13
1913	57	94	.377	7	153	75	1344	530	8	3.27
1914	70	84	.455	5	157	**98**	1397	563	9	2.81
1915	69	83	.454	2	154	**101**	1383	559	12	3.06
1916	80	74	.519	**17**	156	84	1428	616	12	2.77
1917	71	82	.464	6	155	87	1411	571	10	2.66
1918	60	63	.488	**13**	126	59	1157	370	8	3.00
1919	80	59	.576	7	141	85	1287	500	14	**2.82**
1920	95	59	.617	11	154	88	1368	480	15	3.32
1921	98	55	**.641**	15	153	92	1364	481	8	**3.82**
1922	94	60	**.610**	14	154	100	1394	458	7	3.39
1923	98	54	**.645**	10	152	**101**	1381	506	9	**3.62**
1924	89	63	.586	13	153	76	1359	487	**13**	3.86
1925	69	85	.448	13	156	80	1388	492	8	4.33
1926	**91**	63	**.591**	20	155	63	1372	486	4	3.86
1927	110	44	.714	20	155	82	1390	431	11	3.20
1928	**101**	53	**.656**	**21**	154	82	1375	487	13	3.74
1929	88	66	.571	18	154	63	1367	484	12	4.19
1930	86	68	.558	15	154	65	1368	572	7	4.88
1931	94	59	.614	17	155	78	**1410**	686	4	4.20
1932	**107**	47	**.695**	15	**156**	95	1408	780	11	3.98
1933	91	59	.607	22	152	70	1355	**711**	8	4.36
1934	94	60	.610	10	154	**83**	1383	656	**13**	3.75
1935	89	60	.597	13	149	76	1331	**594**	12	**3.60**
1936	**102**	51	**.667**	**21**	155	77	**1400**	624	6	4.17
1937	**102**	52	**.662**	**21**	157	**82**	1396	652	**15**	3.65
1938	**99**	53	**.651**	13	157	**91**	1382	567	11	3.91
1939	**106**	45	**.702**	**26**	152	87	1349	565	**15**	3.31
1940	88	66	.571	14	155	76	1373	559	10	3.89
1941	**101**	53	**.656**	**26**	156	75	1396	589	13	3.53
1942	**103**	51	**.669**	**17**	154	**88**	1375	558	**18**	**2.91**
1943	**98**	56	**.636**	13	155	83	1415	653	14	**2.93**
1944	83	71	.539	13	154	78	1390	529	9	3.39
1945	81	71	.533	14	152	78	1355	474	9	3.39
1946	87	67	.565	17	154	68	1361	653	17	3.13
1947	**97**	57	**.630**	21	155	73	1374	**691**	14	**3.39**
1948	94	60	.610	24	154	62	1366	654	16	3.75
1949	**97**	57	**.630**	**36**	155	59	1371	**671**	12	3.69
1950	**98**	56	**.636**	31	155	66	1373	**712**	12	4.15
1951	**98**	56	**.636**	22	154	66	1367	**664**	24	3.56
1952	**95**	59	**.617**	27	154	72	1381	666	21	**3.14**
1953	**99**	52	**.656**	**39**	151	50	1358	604	18	3.20
1954	103	51	.669	37	155	51	1379	655	16	3.26
1955	**96**	58	**.623**	33	154	52	1372	732	19	**3.23**
1956	**97**	57	**.630**	35	154	50	1382	731	10	3.63
1957	**98**	56	**.636**	42	154	41	1395	**810**	13	**3.00**
1958	**92**	62	**.597**	33	155	53	1379	796	21	**3.22**
1959	79	75	.513	28	155	38	1399	**836**	15	3.60
1960	**97**	57	**.630**	42	155	38	1398	712	**16**	**3.52**
1961	**109**	53	**.673**	39	163	47	1451	866	14	3.46
1962	**96**	66	**.593**	42	162	33	**1470**	838	10	3.70
1963	**104**	57	**.646**	31	161	**59**	1449	965	19	3.07
1964	**99**	63	**.611**	45	**164**	46	**1507***	989	18	3.15
1965	77	85	.475	31	162	41	1460	1001	11	3.28
1966	70	89	.440	32	160	29	1416	842	7	3.41
1967	72	90	.444	27	163	37	1481	898	16	3.24
1968	83	79	.512	27	**164**	45	1467	831	14	2.79
1969	80	81	.497	20	162	53	1441	801	13	3.23
1970	93	69	.574	49	163	36	1472	777	6	3.24
1971	82	80	.506	12	162	67	1452	707	15	3.43
1972	79	76	.510	39	155	35	1373	625	19	3.05
1973	80	82	.494	39	162	47	1428	708	16	3.34
1974	89	73	.549	24	162	53	1455	829	13	3.31
1975	83	77	.519	20	160	**70**	1424	809	11	3.29
1976	**97**	62	**.610**	37	159	62	1455	674	15	**3.19**
1977	100	62	.617	34	162	52	1449	758	16	3.61
1978	**100**	63	**.613**	**36**	163	39	1461	817	16	**3.18**
1979	89	71	.556	37	160	43	1432	731	10	3.83
1980	**103**	59	**.636**	**50**	162	29	1464	845	**15**	3.58
1981	59	48	.551	30	107	16	948	**606**	**13**	**2.90**
1982	79	83	.488	39	162	24	1459	939	8	3.99
1983	91	71	.562	32	162	**47**	1457	892	12	3.86
1984	87	75	.537	43	162	15	1465	**992**	12	3.78
1985	**97**	64	**.602**	49	161	25	1440	907	9	3.69
1986	90	72	.556	**58**	162	13	1443	878	8	4.11
1987	89	73	.549	**47**	162	19	1446	900	10	4.36
1988	85	76	.528	43	161	16	1456	861	5	4.50
1989	74	87	.460	44	161	15	1415	787	9	4.50
1990	67	**95**	.414	41	162	15	1445	909	6	4.21
1991	71	91	.438	37	162	3	1444	936	11	4.42
1992	76	86	.469	44	162	20	1453	851	9	4.21
1993	88	74	.543	38	162	11	1438	899	**13**	4.35
1994	**70**	43	**.619**	31	113	8	1020	656	2	4.34
1995	79	65	.549	35	145	18	1285	908	5	4.56
1996	92	70	.568	**52**	162	6	1440	1139	9	4.65
1997	96	66	.593	51	162	11	**1468**	1165	10	**3.84**
1998	**114**	48	**.704**	48	162	**22**	1457	1080	**16**	3.82
1999	**98**	64	**.605**	50	162	6	1440	1111	10	4.13
2000	87	74	.540	40	161	9	1424	1040	11	4.76
2001	95	65	.594	57	161	7	1451	**1266**	9	4.02
2002	103	58	.640	53	161	9	1452	1135	11	3.87

Boldface Led AL
Boldface* ML record

TEAM DEFENSIVE STATISTICS
Year-by-year 1903-2002

Year	FIELDING AVERAGE	FIELDING RANK (AL)	ERRORS	DOUBLE PLAYS	Year	FIELDING AVERAGE	FIELDING RANK (AL)	ERRORS	DOUBLE PLAYS
1903	.953	4th (tie)	264	87	1971	.981	2nd (tie)	125	159
1904	.958	7th	275	90	1972	.978	7th (tie)	134	179*
1905	.952	7th	293	88	1973	.976	9th	156	172
1906	.957	4th	272	69	1974	.977	3rd (tie)	142	158
1907	.947	8th	334	79	1975	.978	2nd (tie)	135	148
1908	.947	8th	337	78	1976	.980	2nd (tie)	126	141
1909	.948	8th	329	94	1977	.979	3rd (tie)	132	151
1910	.956	4th (tie)	284	95	1978	**.982**	**2nd** (1st tie)	113	134
1911	.949	6th (tie)	328	99	1979	**.981***	**1st (tie)**	122	183
1912	.940	8th	382	77	1980	.978	6th (tie)	138	160
1913	.954	6th (tie)	293	94	1981	.982	4th (tie)	72	100
1914	.963	2nd (tie)	238	93	1982	.979	9th (tie)	128	158
1915	**.966***	**1st**	**217***	118	1983	.978	10th (tie)	139	157
1916	.967	4th	219	119	1984	.977	10th (tie)	142	177*
1917	.965	3rd	225	129	1985	.979	8th (tie)	126	172
1918	.970	2nd	161	**137***	1986	.979	8th (tie)	127	153
1919	.968	3rd	192	108	1987	.983	2nd	102	155
1920	.969	3rd	194	129	1988	.978	13th	134	161
1921	.965	4th	222	138	1989	.980	6th (tie)	122	183*
1922	**.975**	**2nd** (1st tie)	157	124	1990	.980	6th (tie)	126	164
1923	**.977***	**1st**	**144***	131	1991	.979	12th (tie)	133	181
1924	**.974***	**1st**	**156***	131	1992	.982	5th (tie)	114	165
1925	**.974***	**1st**	**160***	150	1993	.983	5th	105	166
1926	.966	7th	210	117	1994	.982	4th	80	122
1927	.969	3rd (tie)	195	123	1995	**.986**	**2nd** (1st tie)	74	121
1928	.968	6th	194	136	1996	.985	2nd	91	146
1929	.971	3rd	178	153	1997	.983	6th	104	156
1930	.965	6th	207	132	1998	.984	3rd	98	146
1931	.972	3rd	169	131	1999	.982	7th	111	132
1932	.969	3rd (tie)	188	124	2000	.981	7th	109	135
1933	.972	4th	165	122	2001	.982	4th (tie)	109	132
1934	.973	3rd	**157***	151	2002	.979	11th (tie)	127	100
1935	.974	3rd	151	114					
1936	.973	2nd (tie)	163	148					
1937	.972	3rd (tie)	170	134					
1938	.973	4th	169	177					
1939	**.978***	**1st**	**126***	159					
1940	.975	**2nd** (1st tie)	152	158					
1941	.973	3rd	165	**196***					
1942	**.976***	**1st**	**142***	**190***					
1943	.974	4th	160	166					
1944	**.974***	**1st**	**156***	170					
1945	.971	6th	175	170					
1946	.975	2nd (tie)	150	**174***					
1947	.981	2nd	109	151					
1948	.979	4th	120	161					
1949	.977	4th (tie)	138	195					
1950	.980	3rd	119	188					
1951	.975	4th (tie)	144	190					
1952	.979	2nd	127	**199***					
1953	.979	2nd (tie)	126	182					
1954	.979	2nd (tie)	126	**198***					
1955	.978	3rd	128	**180***					
1956	.977	3rd (tie)	136	**214***					
1957	.980	3rd (tie)	123	**183***					
1958	.978	6th	128	**182***					
1959	.978	2nd (tie)	131	160					
1960	.979	3rd (tie)	129	162					
1961	**.980***	1st	124*	**180***					
1962	.979	4th (tie)	131	151					
1963	.982	2nd (tie)	110	162					
1964	.983	2nd	109	158					
1965	.978	6th	137	**166***					
1966	.977	5th (tie)	142	142					
1967	.976	10th	154	144					
1968	.979	3rd (tie)	139	142					
1969	.979	3rd (tie)	131	158					
1970	.980	3rd (tie)	130	146					

Boldface* Led AL

YANKEE MAJOR LEAGUE RECORDS

The following are Major-League records except where otherwise indicated; (AL) confines the record to the American League.

Winning

Most Games Won By One Club In American League History: 8777
    1903-2002

Most League Championships Won by One Club: 38
    1921-23, 1926-28, 1932, 1936-39, 1941-43, 1947, 1949-53, 1955-58, 1960-64, 1976-78, 1981, 1996, 1998, 1999, 2000, 2001

Most Consecutive League Championships Won by One Club: 5
    1949, 1950, 1951, 1952, 1953

Most Consecutive World Series Appearances by One Club: 5
    twice 1949-53,1960-64

Most Consecutive Years Finishing In The First Division: 39
    1926-64

Most Years Winning 100 Or More Games: 16
    1927-28, 1932, 1936-37, 1939, 1941-42, 1954, 1961, 1963, 1977-78, 1980, 1998, 2002

Most Days In First Place, Season: 174 (AL)
    1927 (April 12 through October 2—154 game season)

Earliest Pennant-Clinching Date (through 1968 old league format): September 4
    1941 (136th game; record 91-45)

Most Games Won In One Month: 28 (AL)
August 1938 (record, 28-8)
(1 other club)

Most Consecutive Games Won, Season: 19 (AL)
1947, June 29 through July 17

Most Games Won At Home, Season:
162-game season—65; 1961 (record, 65-16)
154-game season—62; 1932 (record, 62-15)

Most Games Won On Road, Season:
154-game season—54 (AL); 1939 (record, 54-20)

Most Games Winning By One Run, Season:
154-game season—38 (AL); 1943

Most Won from One Club, Season: 21
1927–St. Louis (lost 1) (3 others)

Batting/Offense

Most Years Leading The League in Runs Scored: 25
1921, 1926-28, 1930-33, 1936-39, 1942-43, 1945, 1947,
1953-54, 1956-58, 1960, 1962, 1985, 2002

Most Runs Scored, Season: 1067 (AL)
1931

Most Runs Scored By League Pennant Winner, Season: 1065 (AL)
1936

Most Runs Scored On The Road, Season (since 1900): 591
1930

Most Players On One Club Scoring 100 or More Runs, Season: 6 (AL)
1931 (Gehrig, Ruth, Combs, Chapman, Sewell, Lary)

Most Consecutive Games Played Without Being Shut Out: 308
August 3, 1931 through August 2, 1933

Most Years Leading The League in Home Runs: 35
1915-17, 1919-21, 1923-31, 1933, 1936-47, 1951,
1955-56, 1958, 1960-61, 1993

Most Home Runs by One Club in AMERICAN LEAGUE History: 12,511

Most Consecutive Years Leading League (or tied) in Home Runs: 12
1936 through 1947

Most Years with 100 or more Home Runs: 77

Most Home Runs Against One Club, Season: 48
Kansas City vs. Athletics, 1956

Most Home Runs by Two Players, Season: 115
1961—Roger Maris (61)
Mickey Mantle (54)

Most Home Runs by Three Players, Season: 143
1961—Roger Maris (61)
Mickey Mantle (54)
Bill Skowron (28)

Most Consecutive Games With One Or More Home Runs: 25
1941, June 1, 2nd game, through June 29,
2nd game, (40 homers)

Most Players Hitting 30 or More Home Runs, Season: 3 (AL)
1941 (Keller, Henrich, DiMaggio)
(10 other clubs)

Most Players Hitting 40 Or More Home Runs, Season: 2 (AL)
1927, 1930, 1931 (Ruth, Gehrig)
1961 (Maris, Mantle)
(4 other clubs)

Most Players Hitting 50 Or More Home Runs, Season: 2 (AL)
1961 (Maris, Mantle)

Most Runs Batted In, Season: 995
1936

Most Players With 100 Or More RBIs, Season: 5
1936 (Gehrig, DiMaggio, Lazzeri, Selkirk, Dickey)

Most Times Stealing Home, Season: 18
1912 (245 Stolen Bases)

Most Times Stealing Home, Game: 3
April 17, 1915 vs. Philadelphia Athletics
(4 other clubs)

Most Stolen Bases, Game: 15 (AL)
September 28, 1911 vs. St. Louis Browns

Highest Batting Average By A League Pennant-Winner, Season: .307 (AL)
1927

Most Years Leading The League In Slugging Average: 30
1920-21, 1923-24, 1926-28, 1930-31, 1936-39, 1943-45,
1947-48, 1951, 1953-58, 1960-62, 1986, 2002

Highest Slugging Average, Season: .489
1927

Pitching

Most Years Leading The League In Shutouts: 20
1920, 1924, 1927, 1932, 1934, 1937-39, 1942, 1950-53,
1955, 1958-60, 1980-81, 1996 (tied)

Most Years Leading The League In Lowest ERA: 26
1919-21, 1923, 1927, 1932, 1934-39, 1942-43, 1947,
1952-53,1955, 1957-58, 1960, 1976, 1978, 1980-81

Most Innings Pitched, Season: 1506 $^2/_3$
1964

Fielding

Fewest Passed Balls, Season: 0
1931

Most Putouts, Season: 4520
1964

Most Outfield Assists, Game: 5
September 5, 1921 vs. Boston
(2 other clubs)

Most Years Leading The League in Making Double Plays: 15
1918, 1941-42, 1946, 1952, 1954-58, 1961, 1965,
1972, 1984, 1989

Most Double Plays Made, Game: 7
August 14, 1942 vs. Philadelphia Athletics

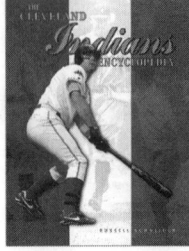